Contemporary Theatre, Film, and Television

ISSN 0749-064X

Contemporary Theatre, Film, and Television

A Biographical Guide Featuring Performers, Directors, Writers, Producers, Designers, Managers, Choreographers, Technicians, Composers, Executives, Dancers, and Critics in the United States and Great Britain

Emily J. McMurray
Owen O'Donnell
Editors

Volume 9

Includes Cumulative Index Containing References to
Who's Who in the Theatre and *Who Was Who in the Theatre*

 **Gale Research Inc.** • DETROIT • LONDON

STAFF

Emily J. McMurray and Owen O'Donnell, *Editors*

Marilyn K. Basel, Barbara Carlisle Bigelow, Kathleen J. Edgar, Sharon Gamboa,
Kevin S. Hile, Thomas Kozikowski, Sharon Malinowski, Neil R. Schlager,
Diane Telgen, Polly A. Vedder, and Thomas Wiloch, *Associate Editors*

Sonia Benson, Suzanne M. Bourgoin, Elizabeth A. Des Chenes, Katherine Huebl,
Denise E. Kasinec, Mary K. Ruby, Susan M. Reicha, and Edward Scheff,
Assistant Editors

Lillie Balinova, James R. Kirkland, Glenn Naftchi,
and Arlene True, *Sketchwriters*

Rahadyan T. Sastrowardoyo, *Contributing Editor*

Hal May, *Senior Editor*

Victoria B. Cariappa, *Research Manager*
Mary Rose Bonk, *Research Supervisor*
Jane A. Cousins, Andrew Guy Malonis, and Norma Sawaya, *Editorial Associates*
Mike Avolio, Patricia Bowen, Reginald A. Carlton, Dorothy Carter, Clare Collins,
Catherine A. Coulson, Theodore J. Dumbrigue, Shirley Gates, Yvette Jones, Sharon McGilvray,
and Tracey Head Turbett, *Editorial Assistants*

Mary Beth Trimper, *Production Manager*
Evi Seoud, *External Production Associate*
Mary Winterhalter, *External Production Assistant*

Arthur Chartow, *Art Director*
C. J. Jonik and Yolanda Y. Latham, *Keyliners*

Special acknowledgment is due to Kenneth R. Shepherd for his technical assistance in the preparation of this volume.

The paper used in this publication meets the minimum requirements
of the American National Standard for Information Sciences—
Permanence Paper for Printed Library Materials, ANSI Z39.48-1984. ∞™

Contents

Preface vii

Biographies 1

Cumulative Index
   (Including references to
   Who's Who in the Theatre and
   Who Was Who in the Theatre) 427

Preface

Provides Broad, Single-Source Coverage in the Entertainment Field

Contemporary Theatre, Film, and Television (*CTFT*) is a biographical reference series designed to provide students, educators, researchers, librarians, and general readers with information on a wide range of entertainment figures. Unlike single-volume reference works that focus on a limited number of artists or on a specific segment of the entertainment field, *CTFT* is an ongoing publication that includes entries on individuals active in the theatre, film, *and* television industries. Before the publication of *CTFT*, information-seekers had no choice but to consult several different sources in order to locate the in-depth biographical and credit data that makes *CTFT*'s one-stop coverage the most comprehensive available on the lives and work of performing arts professionals.

Scope

CTFT covers not only performers, directors, writers, and producers, but also behind-the-scenes specialists such as designers, managers, choreographers, technicians, composers, executives, dancers, and critics from the United States and Great Britain. With nearly 450 entries in *CTFT 9*, the series now provides biographies on more than 5500 people involved in all aspects of theatre, film, and television.

CTFT gives primary emphasis to people who are currently active. New entries are prepared on major stars as well as those who are just beginning to win acclaim for their work. *CTFT* also includes entries on personalities who have died but whose work commands lasting interest.

Compilation Methods

CTFT editors identify candidates for inclusion in the series by consulting biographical dictionaries, industry directories, entertainment annuals, trade and general interest periodicals, newspapers, and on-line databases. Entries are compiled from published biographical sources and then mailed to the listees or their agents for review and verification.

Revised Entries

To ensure *CTFT*'s timeliness and comprehensiveness, entries from previous volumes, as well as from Gale Research's *Who's Who in the Theatre*, are updated for individuals who have been active enough to require revision of their earlier biographies. Such individuals will merit revised entries as often as there is substantial new information to provide. Obituary notices for deceased entertainment personalities already listed in *CTFT* are also published.

Accessible Format Makes Data Easy to Locate

CTFT entries, modeled after those in Gale's highly regarded *Contemporary Authors* series, are written in a clear, readable style designed to help users focus quickly on specific facts. The following is a summary of the information sections found in *CTFT* sketches:

- *ENTRY HEADING:* the form of the name by which the listee is best known.

- *PERSONAL:* full or original name; dates and places of birth and death; family data; colleges attended, degrees earned, and professional training; political and religious affiliations when known; avocational interests.

- *ADDRESSES:* office, agent, publicist, and/or manager addresses.

- *CAREER:* tagline indicating principal areas of entertainment work; resume of career positions and other vocational achievements; military service.

- *MEMBER:* memberships and offices held in professional, union, civic, and social organizations.

- *AWARDS, HONORS:* theatre, film, and television awards and nominations; literary and civic awards; honorary degrees.

- *CREDITS:* comprehensive title-by-title listings of theatre, film, and television appearance and work credits, including roles and production data as well as debut and genre information.

- *RECORDINGS:* album, single song, video, and taped reading releases; recording labels and dates when available.

- *WRITINGS:* title-by-title listing of plays, screenplays, scripts, and musical compositions along with production information; books, including autobiographies, and other publications.

- *SIDELIGHTS:* favorite roles; portions of agent-prepared biographies or personal statements from the listee when available.

- *OTHER SOURCES:* books and periodicals where interviews, feature stories, or reviews can be found.

Access Thousands of Entries Using *CTFT*'s Cumulative Index

Each volume of *CTFT* contains a cumulative index to the entire series. As an added feature, this index also includes references to all seventeen editions of *Who's Who in the Theatre* and to the four-volume compilation *Who Was Who in the Theatre.*

Suggestions Are Welcome

Contemporary Theatre, Film, and Television is intended to serve as a useful reference tool for a wide audience, so comments about any aspect of this work are encouraged. Suggestions of entertainment professionals to include in future volumes are also welcome. Send comments and suggestions to: The Editor, *Contemporary Theatre, Film, and Television,* Gale Research Inc., 835 Penobscot Bldg., Detroit, MI 48226-4094; call toll-free at 1-800-347-GALE; or fax to 1-313-961-6815.

Contemporary
Theatre, Film,
and Television

Contemporary Theatre, Film, and Television

Indicates that a listing has been compiled from secondary sources believed to be reliable, but has not been personally verified for this edition by the listee.

ACKERMAN, Robert Allan 1945-

PERSONAL: Born in 1945.

CAREER: Director.

AWARDS, HONORS: Obie Award from the *Village Voice*, 1978, for *A Prayer for My Daughter;* Outer Critics Circle Award and Drama Desk Award nomination, both 1982, for *Extremities;* Outer Critics Circle Award, 1983, for *Slab Boys.*

CREDITS:

STAGE DIRECTOR

Ionescopade, Theatre Four, New York City, 1974.
Joe's Opera, Musical Theatre Lab, St. Clement's Church Theatre, New York City, 1975.
Memphis Is Gone, St. Clement's Church Theatre, 1977.
Fathers and Sons, New York Shakespeare Festival (NYSF), Public Theatre, New York City, 1978.
A Prayer for My Daughter, NYSF, Public Theatre, 1978.
Broadway, Wilbur Theatre, Boston, MA, 1978.
A Christmas Carol: Scrooge and Marley, Center Stage, Baltimore, MD, 1978.
Taken in Marriage, NYSF, Public Theatre, 1979.
Bent, New Apollo Theatre, New York City, 1979.
Salt Lake City Skyline, NYSF, Public Theatre, 1980.
Holiday, Center Theatre Group, Ahmanson Theatre, Los Angeles, 1981.
Family Devotions, NYSF, Public Theatre, 1981.
Extremities, Westside Arts Center, Cheryl Crawford Theatre, New York City, 1982, then Los Angeles Public Theatre, Los Angeles, 1983.
Slab Boys, Playhouse Theatre, New York City, 1983.
A Madhouse in Goa, Lyric Hammersmith Theatre, London, 1989.
Legs Diamond, Mark Hellinger Theatre, New York City, 1989.

Burn This, Lyric Theatre, London, 1990.
When She Danced, Globe Theatre, London, 1991.

Also directed at the Yale Repertory Theatre, New Haven, CT; Eugene O'Neill Playwrights Conference, Waterford, CT; Williamstown Theatre Festival, Williamstown, MA; Haifa Municipal Theatre, Haifa, Israel; directed productions of *Torch Song Trilogy, Flesh and Blood,* and *The Mystery of the Rose Bouquet,* all in London.*

*   *   *

ADDISON, John 1920-

PERSONAL: Born March 16, 1920, in Cobham, Surrey, England. *Education:* Attended Wellington College; received degree from Royal College of Music, London, c. 1948; studied with Gordon Jacob, Herbert Fryer, Leon Goossens, and Frederick Thurston.

ADDRESSES: Agent—Gorfaine-Schwartz Agency, 3815 West Olive Avenue, Suite 202, Burbank, CA 91505.

CAREER: Composer. Began film composing career in 1948; Royal College of Music, London, England, professor, beginning in 1961. *Military service:* British Armed Services, 1939-46.

AWARDS, HONORS: Academy Award, best score, and Grammy Award, best original score for motion picture or television, both 1963, for *Tom Jones;* Emmy Award nominations, best music direction of a variety, musical, or dramatic program and best music composition, 1971, for *Hallmark Hall of Fame* movie "Hamlet"; Academy Award nomination, best original dramatic score, 1972, for *Sleuth;* British Academy Award, 1977, for *A Bridge Too Far;* Emmy Award, outstanding achievement in music composition for a series, 1985, for *Murder, She Wrote.*

CREDITS:

FILM WORK; MUSIC DIRECTOR

That Lady, Twentieth Century-Fox, 1955.

Hell, Heaven or Hoboken (also known as *I Was Monty's Double*), National, 1958.

Look Back in Anger (also see below), Warner Brothers, 1959.

A Taste of Honey (also see below), Continental Distributing, 1962.

Tom Jones (also see below), Lopert, 1963.

Guns at Batasi (also see below), Twentieth Century-Fox, 1964.

The Girl with Green Eyes (also see below), Lopert, 1964.

The Model Murder Case (also known as *Girl in the Headlines;* also see below), Cinema V, 1964.

Start the Revolution without Me (also see below), Warner Brothers, 1970.

STAGE WORK

Musical adviser, *A Patriot for Me,* Royal Court Theatre, London, 1965.

TELEVISION WORK

Music conductor, *Phantom of the Opera* (also see below), NBC, 1990.

WRITINGS:

FILM SCORES

Seven Days to Noon, Mayer/Kingsley/Distinguished, 1950.

Pool of London, Universal, 1951.

High Treason, General Film Distributors/Pacemaker-Mayer-Kingsley, 1951.

Brandy for the Parson, Associated British Films, 1952.

The Hour of Thirteen, Metro-Goldwyn-Mayer (MGM), 1952.

The Man Between, United Artists, 1953.

Terror on a Train (also known as *Time Bomb*), MGM, 1953.

Time Gentlemen Please, Mayer-Kingsley, 1953.

The Black Night, Columbia, 1954.

The End of the Road, Group Three, 1954.

High and Dry (also known as *The Maggie*), Universal, 1954.

Make Me an Offer, British Lion, 1954.

Paratrooper (also known as *The Red Beret*), Columbia, 1954.

The Cockleshell Heroes, Columbia, 1955.

Josephine and Men, British Lion, 1955.

The Light Touch (also known as *Touch and Go*), Universal, 1955.

One Good Turn, General Film Distributors, 1955.

That Lady, Twentieth Century-Fox, 1955.

Privates Progress, Black Lion, 1956.

Lucky Jim, Kingsley International, 1957.

Reach for the Sky, Rank, 1957.

The Shiralee, MGM, 1957.

All at Sea (also known as *Barnacle Bill*), MGM, 1958.

Three Men in a Boat, Valiant, 1958.

Hell, Heaven or Hoboken (also known as *I Was Monty's Double*), National, 1958.

Look Back in Anger, Warner Brothers, 1959.

Man in a Cocked Hat (also known as *Carlton-Browne of the Foreign Office*), Show, 1960.

School for Scoundrels, Continental Distributing, 1960.

French Mistress, Black Lion, 1960.

His and Hers, Eros, 1961.

Go to Blazes, Pathe, 1962.

The Loneliness of the Long Distance Runner (also known as *Rebel With a Cause*), Continental Distributing, 1962.

A Taste of Honey, Continental Distributing, 1962.

Tom Jones, Lopert, 1963.

The Girl with Green Eyes, Lopert, 1964.

Guns at Batasi, Twentieth Century-Fox, 1964.

The Model Murder Case (also known as *Girl in the Headlines*), Cinema V, 1964.

The Amorous Adventures of Moll Flanders, Paramount, 1965.

The Loved One, MGM, 1965.

A Fine Madness, Warner Brothers, 1966.

Torn Curtain, Universal, 1966.

The Honey Pot (also known as *It Comes Up Murder, Anyone for Venice?,* and *Mr. Fox of Venice*), United Artists, 1967.

Smashing Time, Paramount, 1967.

Charge of the Light Brigade, United Artists, 1968.

Brotherly Love (also known as *Country Dance!*), MGM, 1970.

Start the Revolution without Me, Warner Brothers, 1970.

Cry of the Penguins (also known as *Mr. Forbush and The Penguins*), Black Lion, 1972.

Sleuth, Twentieth Century-Fox, 1972.

Luther, American Film Theatre, 1974.

The Entertainer, Seven Keys, 1975.

Ride a Wild Pony, Buena Vista, 1976.

Swashbuckler (also known as *The Scarlet Buccaneer*), Universal, 1976.

A Bridge Too Far, United Artists, 1977.

Joseph Andrews, Paramount, 1977.

The Seven-Per-Cent Solution, Universal, 1977.

The Pilot, Summit, 1979.

Strange Invaders, Orion, 1983.

High Point, New World, 1984.

The Ultimate Solution of Grace Quigley (also known as *Grace Quigley*), Metro-Goldwyn-Mayer/United Artists (MGM/UA), 1984.

Code Name: Emerald, MGM/UA, 1985.
To Die For, Skouras, 1989.

Also composer of film score for *Time Lost and Time Remembered* (also known as *I Was Happy Here*), 1966.

STAGE MUSIC

Cranks (revue), Bijou Theatre, New York City, 1956.
The Entertainer, Royal Court Theatre, 1957, then Studio Theatre, Washington, DC, 1986-87.
The Chairs, Phoenix Theatre, London, 1958.
The Lesson, Phoenix Theatre, 1958.
Luther, Royal Court Theatre, 1961, then St. James Theatre, New York City, 1963.
Saint Joan of the Stockyards, Queen's Theatre, London, 1964.
(With David Henecker), Music, *Popkiss,* Globe Theatre, London, 1972.
Antony and Cleopatra, Los Angeles Theatre Center, CA, 1987.

Also composer of music for productions of *A Midsummer Night's Dream, The Broken Heart, The Workhouse Donkey, Semi-Detached, The Seagull, Listen to the Mockingbird, I, Claudius, Twelfth Night,* and *Bloomsbury.*

TELEVISION MUSIC; MOVIES

"Hamlet," *Hallmark Hall of Fame,* NBC, 1970.
Death in Canaan, CBS, 1978.
The Power Within, ABC, 1979.
Love's Savage Fury, ABC, 1979.
Like Normal People, ABC, 1979.
Mistress of Paradise, ABC, 1981.
Charles and Diana: A Royal Love Story, ABC, 1982.
I Was a Mail Order Bride, CBS, 1982.
Eleanor, First Lady of the World, CBS, 1982.
Agatha Christie's "Thirteen at Dinner," CBS, 1985.
Something in Common, CBS, 1986.
Firefighter, CBS, 1986.
Agatha Christie's "Dead Man's Folly," CBS, 1986.
Phantom of the Opera, NBC, 1990.

Also composer of music for *Mr. Boogedy,* 1986; *Strange Voices,* 1987; and *Bride of Boogedy,* 1987.

TELEVISION MUSIC; SERIES

Theme, *Grady,* NBC, 1975-76.
(With John Cacavas) *The Eddie Capra Mysteries,* NBC, 1978.
Theme, *Nero Wolfe,* NBC, 1981.
The Devlin Connection, NBC, 1982.
(With David Bell) Theme, *Murder, She Wrote,* CBS, 1984.

TELEVISION MUSIC; MINI-SERIES

Pearl, ABC, 1978.
Black Beauty, NBC, 1978.

The Bastard, syndicated, 1979.
Centennial, NBC, 1979.
The French Atlantic Affair, ABC, 1979.
Ellis Island, CBS, 1984.
Beryl Markham: A Shadow on the Sun, CBS, 1988.

Also composed music for *I, Claudius,* 1972.

TELEVISION MUSIC; PILOTS

Fit for a King, NBC, 1982.

OTHER

Composer of orchestral music, including the ballets *Carte Blanche* and *Cat's Cradle,* a trumpet concerto, a divertimento for brass, a partita for strings and percussion, and the symphonic work *Wellington Suite.**

*   *   *

ADJANI, Isabelle   1955-

PERSONAL: Born June 27, 1955, in Paris, France; children: Barnabe Nuytten (with Bruno Nuytten, a director and cinematographer).

ADDRESSES: Office—c/o Secretariat de la Commission d'avances sur recettes, 11 rue Galilee, Paris 75116, France. *Agent*—Jeff Berg, International Creative Management, 8899 Beverly Blvd., Los Angeles, CA 90048; Marjorie Israel, 56 rue de Passy, Paris 75016, France.

CAREER: Actress and producer.

AWARDS, HONORS: Prix Suzanne Biandetti, 1974; New York Film Critics Award and Academy Award nomination, both for Best Actress, 1975, for *L'Histoire d' Adele H.;* Cannes Film Festival Award, Best Actress, 1981, for *Quartet* and *Possession;* Cesar Award, Best Actress, 1982, for *Possession;* Cesar Awards, Best Actress, 1984, for *L'Ete meurtrier,* and 1989, for *Camille Claudel;* nominated for Academy Award, Best Actress in a Leading Role, 1989, for *Camille Claudel.*

CREDITS:

FILM APPEARANCES

Camille, *Faustine et le bel ete* (also known as *Faustine and the Beautiful Summer*), CIC, 1971.
Isabelle, *La Gifle* (also known as *The Slap*), Gaumont International, 1974.
Adele Hugo, *L'Histoire d'Adele H.* (also known as *The Story of Adele H.*), Les Films du Carrosse/Artistes Associates/New World, 1975.
Laure, *Barocco,* Films la Boetie, 1976.
Stella, *Le Locataire* (also known as *The Tenant*), CIC/Paramount, 1976.
The Player, *The Driver,* Twentieth Century-Fox, 1978.

Emily Bronte, *Les Soeurs Bronte* (also known as *The Bronte Sisters*), Gaumont International/Roissy, 1979.

Lucy Harker, *Nosferatu, Phantom der Nacht* (also known as *Nosferatu, The Vampire* and *Nosferatu, The Vampyre*), Twentieth Century-Fox, 1979.

Anna and Helen, *Possession,* Oliane-Soma-Marianne/ Limelight International, 1981.

Marya Zelli, *Quartet,* Lyric International/New World, 1981.

Pauline Valance, *Tout feu, tout flamme* (also known as *All Fired Up*), Gaumont International, 1981.

Eliane/Elle, *L'Ete meurtrier* (also known as *One Deadly Summer*), Societe Nouvelle de Cinema/Universal, 1982.

Antonieta, Gaumont/Conacine/Nuevo Cinema, 1982.

Mortelle randonnee (also known as *Deadly Circuit*), GEF/ CCFC/Ofer-Omnifilms, 1982;

Helena, *Subway,* Gaumont/Films du Loup/TSF-TFI/ Island Alive, 1985.

Shirra Assel, *Ishtar,* Columbia, 1987.

Title role, *Camille Claudel,* Gaumont International/ Roissy/Orion Classics, 1989.

Henry and June, Universal, 1990.

Also appeared in *Le Petit Bougnat* (film debut), 1969. Appeared in *Violette et Francois,* 1977; *Clara et les chics types,* 1980; *L'Annee prochaine si tout va bien* (also known as *Next Year If All Goes Well*), 1981.

FILM WORK

Co-producer, *Camille Claudel,* Gaumont/Roissy/Orion Classics, 1989.

STAGE APPEARANCES

(Stage debut) *The House of Bernarda Alba,* Maison de la Culture, Reims, France, 1972.

Also appeared in title role, *Ondine,* France. Appeared in *L'Ecole des femmes,* Comedie Francaise, Paris. Appeared in productions for the Comedie Francaise, 1972-74.

TELEVISION APPEARANCES

Made television debut in *Le Secret des Flamands* (also known as *The Secret of the Flemish*), 1972. Appeared in *Le Petit Bougnat* (movie), 1969; *L'Ecole des femmes,* 1973; and *Top a Sacha Distel,* 1974.

OTHER SOURCES:

PERIODICALS

Interview, March, 1976.
New York Times, January 6, 1990.*

AIMEE, Anouk   1934(?)-

PERSONAL: Born Francoise Sorya Dreyfus, April 27, 1934 (one source says 1932), in Paris, France; daughter of Henri (an actor; professional name Murray) and Genevieve Sorya (Durand) Dreyfus; married Edouard Zimmermann, 1949 (divorced); married Nico Papatakis (a director), 1951 (divorced, 1954); married Pierre Barouh, 1966 (divorced); married Albert Finney (an actor), 1970 (divorced, 1978); children: (second marriage) Manuela. *Education:* Studied dance at Marseilles Opera; studied theatre in England, then at Cours Bauer-Therond.

ADDRESSES: Agent—Artmedia, 10 av. George-V, 75008 Paris, France.

CAREER: Actress.

AWARDS, HONORS: Academy Award nomination, best actress, 1966, British Academy of Film and Television Arts Award, best actress, 1967, and Golden Globe Award, best actress—drama, 1967, all for *Un Homme et une femme;* Cannes International Film Festival Award, best actress, 1980, for *Salto nel vuoto;* Studios International Circle of Achievement, 1985.

CREDITS:

FILM APPEARANCES

(Film debut) Anouk, *La Maison sous la mer,* 1946.

The Golden Salamander, General Films, 1949.

Georgia Maglia, *Les Amants de Verone* (also known as *The Lovers of Verona*), Souvaine Selective, 1951.

Jeanne, *La Bergere et le ramoneur* (also known as *The Paris Express* and *The Man Who Watched Trains Go By*), Raymond Stross/George Schaefer, 1953.

Forever My Heart (also known as *Happy Birthday*), British Lion, 1954.

Elena Vargas, *Contraband Spain,* British Pathe, 1955.

Carve Her Name With Pride, J. Arthur Rank, 1958.

Eva, *The Journey* (also known as *Some of Us May Die*), Metro-Goldwyn-Mayer (MGM), 1959.

Helene LaRouche, *Le Farceur* (also known as *The Joker*), Lopert, 1961.

Maddalena, *La Dolce Vita,* Astor/American International, 1961.

Title role, *Donna Di Vita* (also known as *Lola*), Rome Paris/Euro International/Films-Around-the-World, 1961.

Jeanne Hebuterne, *Modigliani of Montparnasse* (also known as *Montparnasse* and *The Lovers of Montparnasse*), Franco-London/Astra-Pallavicina/Continental Distributing, 1961.

Queen Bera, *Sodome et Gomorrhe* (also known as *Sodom and Gomorrah, Sodom e Gomorra,* and *The Last Days of Sodom and Gomorrah*), Titanus/Pathe Cinema/ S.G.C./Twentieth Century-Fox, 1962.

Luisa Anselmi, *Otto e mezzo* (also known as *8 1/2* and *Fellini's 8 1/2*), Embassy, 1963.

Liola (also known as *A Very Handy Man*), Federiz-Francinex-Cinecitta/ Rizzoli, 1963.

Anna, *Les Grands Chemins* (also known as *Of Flesh and Blood* and *Il Baro*), Copernic-Saphrene-Dear/Times, 1964.

Lorenza, *Le Sexe des Anges* (also known as *Le voci bianche, I castrati, Undercover Rouge,* and *White Voices*), Franca-Federiz-Francoriz/Rizzoli, 1965.

Luisa, *La Fuga,* Cine 3/International Classics (Fox), 1966.

Anne Gauthier, *Un Homme et une femme* (also known as *A Man and a Woman*), Les Films 13/Allied Artists, 1966.

Mita, *La stagione del nostro amore* (also known as *A Very Handy Man*), Federiz-Francinex-Cinecitta/Rizzoli, 1966.

Anne, *Un Soir, un train* (also known as *One Night . . . a Train*), Parc-Fox Europa Films du Siecle/Twentieth Century-Fox, 1968.

Carla, *The Appointment,* MGM, 1969.

Title role, *Justine,* Twentieth Century-Fox, 1969.

Lola, *The Model Shop,* Columbia, 1969.

Sarah, *Si c'etait a refaire* (also known as *Second Chance* and *If It Were To Do Over Again*), United Artists, 1976.

Mother, *Mon Premier Amour* (also known as *My First Love,*), 7 Films/Gaumont, 1978.

Marta Ponticelli, *Salto nel vuoto* (also known as *A Leap in the Dark* and *Leap Into the Void*), Summit, 1982.

Barbara, *Tragedia di un uomo ridiculo* (also known as *The Tragedy of a Ridiculous Man*), Warner Brothers, 1982.

Helene, *Qu-est-ce qui fait courir David?* (also known as *What Makes David Run?*), Columbia/EMI Warners/MK2-Diffusion, 1982.

Countess Betsy, *Le General de l'Armee Morte* (also known as *The General of the Dead Army*), WMF/Union Generale Cinematographique, 1983.

Monique de Fontaine, *Success Is the Best Revenge,* Gaumont, 1984.

Viva la Vie! (also known as *Long Live Life*), Union Generale Cinematographique, 1984.

Flagrant Desire, Hemdale, 1985.

Anne Gauthier, *Un Homme et une femme: Vingt ans deja* (also known as *A Man and a Woman: 20 Years Later*), Films 13/Warner Brothers, 1986.

Arrivederci e Grazie (also known as *Goodbye and Thank You*), Medusa Distribuzione, 1988.

Il y a des jours . . . et des lunes, JP2 Audiovisuel/AFMD-Roissy, 1990.

Also appeared in *La Fleur de l'age,* 1947; *Conquetes du froid,* 1951; *Noche de tormenta,* 1951; *Le Rideau cramoisi* (also known as *The Crimson Curtain*), 1951; *Ich suche dich,* 1955; *Les Mauvaises Rencontres,* 1955; *Nina,* 1956; *Stresemann,* 1956; *Tous peuvent me tuer* (also known as *Anyone Can Kill Me*), 1957; *Pot bouille* (also known as *The House of Lovers*), 1957; *La Tete contre les murs* (also known as *The Keepers*), 1958; *Les Dragueurs* (also known as *The Chasers* and *The Young Have No Morals*), 1959; *L'imprevisto,* 1961; *Quai Notre Dame,* 1961; *Il guidizio universale* (also known as *The Last Judgement*), 1961; *Il giorno piu corto* (also known as *The Shortest Day*), 1963; *Il terroista,* 1963; *Il successo,* 1963; *Il morbidone,* 1965; *Lo scandalo,* 1966.

STAGE APPEARANCES

Appeared in *Sud,* 1954.

TELEVISION APPEARANCES

Haute Couture: The Great Designers (special), PBS, 1987.

Also appeared in *Une Page d'amour* (movie), 1979.*

*   *   *

ALDREDGE, Thomas
  See ALDREDGE, Tom

*   *   *

ALDREDGE, Tom 1928-
  (Thomas Aldredge)

PERSONAL: Full name, Thomas Ernest Aldredge; born February 28, 1928, in Dayton, OH; son of W. J. (a colonel in the U.S. Air Force) and Lucienne Juliet (Marcillat) Aldredge; married Theoni Athanasiou Vachlioti (a costume designer), December 10, 1953. *Education:* Attended University of Dayton, 1947-49; Goodman Memorial School of Theatre, B.F.A., 1953; studied acting with Maurice Gnesin, Mary Agnes Doyle, and David Itkin. *Avocational interests:* Sailing, boat design.

ADDRESSES: Agent—William Morris Agency, 1350 Avenue of the Americas, New York, NY 10019.

CAREER: Actor, director, and television producer. *Military service:* U.S. Army, 1946-47; became first sergeant.

MEMBER: American Federation of Radio and Television Artists, Actors' Equity Association, Screen Actors Guild.

AWARDS, HONORS: Obie awards, distinguished performance, from *Village Voice,* both 1967, for *Measure for Measure* and *Stock Up on Pepper 'Cause Turkey's Going to War;* Drama Desk Award, best actor, 1972, for *Sticks and Bones;* Antoinette Perry Award nominations, best actor, 1972, for *Sticks and Bones,* best supporting actor in a musical, 1975, for *Where's Charley?,* and outstanding performance by featured actor in a play, 1981, for *The Little Foxes;* Emmy Award, 1978, for *Henry Winkler Meets William Shakespeare.*

CREDITS:

STAGE APPEARANCES

Messenger, *Hamlet,* Goodman Memorial Theatre, Chicago, IL, 1950.

Bud Norton, *Personal Appearance,* Crystal Palace Theatre, St. Louis, MO, 1950.

Jason, Tower Ranch Tenthouse Theatre, Rhinelander, WI, c. 1951.

The Corn Is Green, Tower Ranch Tenthouse Theatre, c. 1951.

Summer and Smoke, Tower Ranch Tenthouse Theatre, c. 1951.

The Play's the Thing, Tower Ranch Tenthouse Theatre, c. 1951.

Death of a Salesman, Tower Ranch Tenthouse Theatre, c. 1952.

The Hasty Heart, Tower Ranch Tenthouse Theatre, c. 1952.

Blood Wedding, Tower Ranch Tenthouse Theatre, c. 1952.

The Drunkard, Tower Ranch Tenthouse Theatre, c. 1952.

The Glass Menagerie, Tower Ranch Tenthouse Theatre, c. 1952.

Private Lives, Tower Ranch Tenthouse Theatre, c. 1952.

Tovarich, Tower Ranch Tenthouse Theatre, c. 1953.

Our Town, Tower Ranch Tenthouse Theatre, c. 1953.

The Little Foxes, Tower Ranch Tenthouse Theatre, c. 1953.

Laura, Tower Ranch Tenthouse Theatre, c. 1953.

Blithe Spirit, Tower Ranch Tenthouse Theatre, c. 1953.

Inherit the Wind, Tower Ranch Tenthouse Theatre, c. 1953.

Arms and the Man, Tower Ranch Tenthouse Theatre, 1954.

The Guardsman, Tower Ranch Tenthouse Theatre, 1954.

A Streetcar Named Desire, Tower Ranch Tenthouse Theatre, 1954.

The Heiress, Tower Ranch Tenthouse Theatre, 1954.

Shadow and Substance, Tower Ranch Tenthouse Theatre, 1954.

Here Today, Tower Ranch Tenthouse Theatre, 1954.

Saturday's Children, Tower Ranch Tenthouse Theatre, 1954.

The Rope, Tower Ranch Tenthouse Theatre, 1954.

I Am a Camera, Tower Ranch Tenthouse Theatre, 1954.

The Moon Is Blue, Tower Ranch Tenthouse Theatre, 1954.

The Immoralist, Tower Ranch Tenthouse Theatre, 1954.

The Lady's Not for Burning, Tower Ranch Tenthouse Theatre, 1954.

Sabrina Fair, Tower Ranch Tenthouse Theatre, 1954.

Mister Roberts, Tower Ranch Tenthouse Theatre, 1954.

The Rainmaker, Tower Ranch Tenthouse Theatre, 1955.

Cat on a Hot Tin Roof, Tower Ranch Tenthouse Theatre, 1955.

Will Success Spoil Rock Hunter, Tower Ranch Tenthouse Theatre, 1958.

Inherit the Wind, Tower Ranch Tenthouse Theatre, 1958.

No Time for Sergeants, Tower Ranch Tenthouse Theatre, 1958.

Teahouse of the August Moon, Tower Ranch Tenthouse Theatre, 1958.

A Member of the Wedding, Tower Ranch Tenthouse Theatre, 1958.

(Off-Broadway debut) Messenger, *Electra,* Jan Hus Playhouse, 1958.

Vladimir, *Waiting for Godot,* Crystal Palace Theatre, 1958.

Hamm, *Endgame,* Crystal Palace Theatre, 1958.

Danny, *The Nervous Set,* Crystal Palace Theatre, then Henry Miller's Theatre, New York City, both 1959.

Trinculo, *The Tempest,* East 74th Street Theatre, New York City, 1959.

David, *Between Two Thieves,* York Playhouse, New York City, 1960.

Dauphin, *Henry V,* New York Shakespeare Festival (NYSF), Delacorte Theatre, New York City, 1960.

(Under name Thomas Aldredge) *The Premise* (improvisational revue), Premise Theatre, 1960, then Shoreham Hotel, Washington, DC, and later London debut at Comedy Theatre, both 1962, then Ivar Theatre, Los Angeles, 1964.

Boyet, *Love's Labour's Lost,* NYSF, Delacorte Theatre, 1965.

Ulysses, *Troilus and Cressida,* NYSF, Delacorte Theatre, 1965.

Eugene Boyer, *UTBU (Unhealthy to Be Unpleasant),* Helen Hayes Theatre, New York City, 1966.

Angelo, *Measure for Measure,* NYSF, Delacorte Theatre, 1966.

Murderer and citizen, *Richard III,* NYSF, Delacorte Theatre, 1966.

Bernie, "The Mutilated," *Slapstick Tragedy,* Longacre Theatre, New York City, 1966.

Chorus, *Antigone,* American Shakespeare Festival, Stratford, CT, 1966.

Gratiano, *The Merchant of Venice,* American Shakespeare Festival, 1966.

Macduff, *Macbeth,* American Shakespeare Festival, 1966.

Jack McClure, *The Butter and Egg Man,* Cherry Lane Theatre, New York City, 1966.

Gilbert, *Everything in the Garden,* Plymouth Theatre, New York City, 1967.

McKeating, *Stock Up on Pepper 'Cause Turkey's Going to War,* Ellen Stewart Theatre, New York City, 1967.

Peter Quince, *A Midsummer Night's Dream,* American Shakespeare Festival, 1967.

Tybalt, *Romeo and Juliet* NYSF, Delacorte Theatre, 1968.

Sir Andrew Aguecheek, *Twelfth Night,* NYSF, Delacorte Theatre, 1968.

Wurz, *Ergo,* NYSF, Public Theatre, New York City, 1968.

Emory, *The Boys in the Band,* Wyndham's Theatre, London, 1969.

Senator Logan, *Indians,* Brooks Atkinson Theatre, New York City, 1969.

Victor Bard, *The Engagement Baby,* Helen Hayes Theatre, 1970.

William Detweiler, *How the Other Half Loves,* Royale Theatre, New York City, 1971.

Title role, *The Tale of Cymbeline,* NYSF, Delacorte Theatre, 1971.

Ozzie, *Sticks and Bones,* NYSF, Public Theatre, 1971, then John Golden Theatre, New York City, 1972.

Second grave digger, *Hamlet,* NYSF, Delacorte Theatre, 1972.

Fool, *King Lear,* NYSF, Delacorte Theatre, 1973.

James Cameron, *The Iceman Cometh,* Circle in the Square, New York City, 1973.

Calchas, *The Orphan,* NYSF, Public Theatre, 1973.

Mr. Spettigue, *Where's Charley?,* Circle in the Square, 1974.

Shaughnessy, *The Leaf People,* Booth Theatre, New York City, 1976.

Will Somers, *Rex,* Lunt-Fontanne Theatre, New York City, 1976.

Father, *Canadian Gothic/American Modern,* Phoenix Theatre, New York City, 1976.

Painter, *Vieux Carre,* St. James Theatre, New York City, 1977.

Archbishop of Rheims, *Saint Joan,* Circle in the Square, 1977.

Norman Thayer, *On Golden Pond,* Apollo Century Theatre, then John Golden Theatre, 1979.

Love's Labour's Lost, Folger Theatre Group, Washington, DC, 1980-81.

Horace, *The Little Foxes,* Martin Beck Theatre, New York City, 1981.

Puget, *The Black Angel,* Circle Repertory Theatre, New York City, 1982.

Harmon, *Actors and Actresses,* Hartman Theatre, Stamford, CT, 1983.

Old Man, *Fool for Love,* Circle Repertory Theatre, then Douglas Fairbanks Theatre, New York City, both 1983.

Sandy Castle, *Getting Along Famously,* Hudson Guild Theatre, New York City, 1984.

Marius, *The Road to Mecca,* Yale Repertory Theatre, New Haven, CT, 1984.

"Pa" Lester, *Tobacco Road,* Long Wharf Theatre, New Haven, CT, 1985.

Professor Henry Leeds, *Strange Interlude,* Nederlander Theatre, New York City, 1985.

John of Gaunt, *Richard II,* NYSF, Delacorte Theatre, 1987.

Narrator and mysterious man, *Into the Woods,* Martin Beck Theatre, 1987.

Also appeared in *The Imaginary Invalid,* Hartman Theatre, 1985-86; *Neon Psalms; Colette.*

STAGE WORK; DIRECTOR

The Fourposter, Tower Ranch Tenthouse Theatre, Rhinelander, WI, 1954.

Here Today, Tower Ranch Tenthouse Theatre, 1954.

Saturday's Children, Tower Ranch Tenthouse Theatre, 1954.

The Rope, Tower Ranch Tenthouse Theatre, 1954.

Arms and the Man, Tower Ranch Tenthouse Theatre, 1954.

The Guardsman, Tower Ranch Tenthouse Theatre, 1954.

A Streetcar Named Desire, Tower Ranch Tenthouse Theatre, 1954.

The Heiress, Tower Ranch Tenthouse Theatre, 1954.

Shadow and Substance, Tower Ranch Tenthouse Theatre, 1954.

Years Ago, Tower Ranch Tenthouse Theatre, 1954.

I Am a Camera, Tower Ranch Tenthouse Theatre, 1955.

The Happiness Cage, NYSF, Public Theatre, New York City, 1970.

FILM APPEARANCES

Wendover, *The Mouse on the Moon,* United Artists, 1962.

Jack Armstrong, *The Troublemaker,* Janus, 1964.

Who Killed Teddy Bear?, Phillips/Magna, 1965.

Mr. Alfred, *The Rain People,* Warner Brothers, 1969.

Medic, *The Happiness Cage* (also released as *The Mind Snatchers*), Cinerama, 1972.

Ben Amed, *Countdown at Kusini,* Columbia, 1976.

Sid, *Batteries Not Included,* Universal, 1987.

Mr. Guttman, *What About Bob?,* Buena Vista, 1991.

Also appeared in *Brenda Starr,* 1989; *See You in the Morning.*

TELEVISION APPEARANCES; SERIES

Host, *The Curious One,* Chicago Educational Television Association, 1956.

Matthew Pearse, *Ryan's Hope,* ABC, 1981-82.

Mr./Mrs. Tony Nargo, *Search for Tomorrow,* CBS, 1984.

Also appeared in episodes of *N.Y.P.D., Candid Camera,* and *Love of Life.*

TELEVISION APPEARANCES; SPECIALS

Sticks and Bones, CBS, 1972.

King Lear, PBS, 1973.

William Shakespeare, *Henry Winkler Meets William Shakespeare,* CBS, 1977.

Mazzini, *Heartbreak House,* Channel Four, 1989.

Older Edward, *Sensibility and Sense,* PBS, 1990.

Narrator, *Into the Woods,* PBS, 1991.

Also appeared as Washington Irving, *Robbers, Rooftops and Witches,* 1982; Joseph Miller and Joseph Hauptmann, *A Matter of Conscience,* 1989. Appeared in *Ten Blocks on the Camino Real,* PBS; *Seasons of Youth,* ABC; *The Threepenny Opera,* PBS.

TELEVISION APPEARANCES; MOVIES

Fred Eberhardt, *The Storyteller,* NBC, 1977.

Kelly O'Brien, *Nurse,* CBS, 1980.

Monsignor Nicholson, *The Gentleman Bandit,* CBS, 1981.

Glendon Lane, *Double Take,* CBS, 1985.

Also appeared as Jailer, *Full Moon High,* 1981; Rappaport, *Seize the Day,* 1986; Jefferson Davis, *A Special Friendship,* 1987. Appeared in "The Spy Who Returned from the Dead," *ABC Mystery Movie.*

OTHER TELEVISION APPEARANCES

The Adams Chronicles (miniseries), PBS, 1976.

TELEVISION WORK

Producer and director, Chicago Educational Television Association, 1955-56.*

*   *   *

ALEANDRO, Norma   1941-

PERSONAL: Born in 1941 in Argentina.

CAREER: Actress. As a child performed with parents in theater troupe.

AWARDS, HONORS: Obie Award from *Village Voice,* 1985, for *About Love and Other Stories;* Cannes Film Festival Award, best actress, 1986, for *The Official Story;* Academy Award nomination, best supporting actress, 1988, for *Gaby—A True Story.*

CREDITS:

STAGE APPEARANCES

Title role, *La Senorita de Tacna,* Festival Latino, Public Theatre, New York City, 1987.

About Love and Other Stories (one-woman show), La Mama Theatre, Argentina, later Public Theater, New York City, 1986.

MAJOR TOURS

Toured South America in *About Love and Other Stories.*

FILM APPEARANCES

Alicia, *La Historia Oficial (The Official Story;* also known as *The Official Version),* Almi Pictures, 1985.

Florencia Morales, *Gaby—A True Story,* Tri-Star, 1987.

Edie Costello, *Cousins,* Paramount, 1989.

Henrietta, *Vital Signs,* Twentieth Century-Fox, 1990.

Also appeared in *La Tregua,* 1974; in *Tobi,* 1978; and as Carmen Siri, *Cien Veces No Debo* (title means "A Hundred Times, No"), 1990.

TELEVISION APPEARANCES

Nidia Filartiga, "One Man's War," *HBO Showcase,* HBO, 1991.

Appeared in the movies *Isha* and *Dark Holiday,* and as a presenter at the 58th and 62nd *Annual Academy Awards.*

WRITINGS:

Poemas y cuentos de Atenazor (poems and short stories), Editorial Sudamericana, 1985.

Also author of a screenplay titled *Los Herederos.**

*   *   *

ALLEN, Dede   1924(?)-

PERSONAL: Full name, Dorothea Carothers Allen; born in 1924 (some sources say 1925) in Cincinnati, OH; married Stephen Fleischman (a director); children: one daughter, one son.

CAREER: Film editor and producer. Worked as messenger, sound lab worker, and assistant editor for Columbia Pictures and as a script clerk and editor of industrial films, documentary shorts, and television commercials.

AWARDS, HONORS: British Academy Award and Academy Award nomination, both for Best Film Editing, 1975, for *Dog Day Afternoon;* Academy Award nomination (with Craig McKay), Best Film Editing, 1981, for *Reds.*

CREDITS:

FILM EDITOR, EXCEPT WHERE INDICATED

Because of Eve, International, 1948.

Terror from the Year 5000 (also known as *Cage of Doom, Terror from 5000 A.D.,* and *The Girl from 5000 A.D.*), American International, 1958.

Odds against Tomorrow, United Artists, 1959.

The Hustler, Twentieth Century-Fox, 1961.

America, America (also known as *The Anatolian Smile*), Warner Brothers, 1963.

Bonnie and Clyde, Warner Brothers, 1967.

Rachel, Rachel, Warner Brothers, 1968.

Alice's Restaurant, United Artists, 1969.

Production assistant, *Story of a Woman,* Universal, 1970.

Little Big Man, National General, 1970.

Slaughterhouse Five, Universal, 1972.

Co-editor, *Visions of Eight,* Cinema V, 1973.

(With Richard Marks) *Serpico,* Paramount, 1973.

Dog Day Afternoon, Warner Brothers, 1975.

(With Jerry Greenberg and Stephen Rotter) *Night Moves,* Warner Brothers, 1975.

(With Greenberg and Rotter) *The Missouri Breaks,* United Artists, 1976.

Slap Shot, Universal, 1977.

The Wiz, Universal, 1978.

(With Craig McKay; also executive producer with Simon Relph) *Reds,* Paramount, 1981.

Harry and Son, Orion, 1984.

(With Jeff Gourson) *Mike's Murder,* Warner Brothers, 1984.

The Breakfast Club, Universal, 1985.

(With Angelo Corrao) *Off Beat,* Buena Vista, 1986.

(With Jim Miller) *The Milagro Beanfield War,* Universal, 1988.

(With Miller) *Let It Ride,* Paramount, 1989.

Also editor of the short films *Endowing Your Future,* 1957, and *It's Always Now,* 1965.*

*   *   *

ALLEN, Peter   1944-

PERSONAL: Full name, Peter Woolnough Allen; born February 10, 1944, in Tenterfield, Australia; married Liza Minnelli (a singer and actress), 1967 (divorced, 1972).

ADDRESSES: Agent—Burton Taylor, Agency for the Performing Arts (APA), 9000 Sunset Blvd., Suite 1200, Los Angeles, CA 90069. *Publicist*—Eliot Sekuler, Rogers & Cowan, Inc., 10000 Santa Monica Blvd., Los Angeles, CA 90067. *Manager*—Alan Margulies Organization, 3111 Bel Air Dr., Suite 20H, Las Vegas, NV 89109.

CAREER: Singer, composer, and actor.

AWARDS, HONORS: Grammy Award nomination, Song of the Year, 1974, for "I Honestly Love You"; Academy Award, Best Song, and Grammy Award nomination, Song of the Year, both 1981, both for "Arthur's Theme (The Best That You Can Do)," from *Arthur;* Order of Australia, 1990.

CREDITS:

STAGE APPEARANCES

(Broadway debut) Henry, *Soon,* Ritz Theatre, New York City, 1971.

Up in One—More Than a Concert, Biltmore Theatre, New York City, then Los Angeles, later Australia, all 1979.

Jack Diamond, *Legs Diamond,* Mark Hellinger Theatre, New York City, 1988.

FILM APPEARANCES

Sergeant Pepper's Lonely Hearts Club Band, Universal, 1978.

FILM WORK

Song performer, "Everything Old Is New Again," *All That Jazz,* Twentieth Century-Fox, 1979 (also see below).

Song performer, "One and Only," *Chanel Solitaire,* United Film Distribution, 1981.

Song performer, "But It's a Nice Day," *Kiss Me Goodbye,* Twentieth Century-Fox, 1982.

Song performer, "I Go to Rio," *Dominick and Eugene,* Orion, 1988.

TELEVISION APPEARANCES; SPECIALS

Loretta Lynn in the Big Apple, NBC, 1982.

Bob Hope's Tropical Comedy Special from Tahiti, NBC, 1987.

Maureen McGovern On Stage at Wolf Trap, PBS, 1988.

The Hollywood Game, CBS, 1991.

Also appeared in *Disneyland's 30th Anniversary Celebration,* 1985; *Born America: A March of Dimes Television Event,* 1986; *The Noel Edmonds Show,* 1986; *The National AIDS Awareness Test: What Do You Know about Acquired Immune Deficiency Syndrome?,* 1987; *A Star-Spangled Celebration,* 1987; *Stradivarius on Stage,* 1988; *Dionne Warwick in London,* 1988; *Macy's Thanksgiving Day Parade,* 1988; *Reno's Cabaret Reunion,* 1989; *The Australian Royal Bicentennial Concert,* 1989.

TELEVISION APPEARANCES; EPISODIC

Good Morning America, ABC, 1990.

Regis and Kathy Lee, CBS, 1990.

CBS Morning Show, CBS, 1990.

Also appeared on the *Joan Rivers Show* and *Rick Dees Show,* both 1990.

TELEVISION WORK

(With Carole Bayer Sager) Theme song performer, "Here We Go Again," *Here We Go Again* (series), ABC, 1973.

Song performer, "I Go to Rio," *Tales from the Crypt,* HBO, 1991.

RECORDINGS:

ALBUMS

Taught by Experts, A & M, 1977.
It's Time for Peter Allen, A & M, 1977.
Making Every Moment Count, RCA/BMG, 1990.

Also recorded *I Could Have Been a Sailor,* A & M; *Bi-Coastal,* A & M; *Continental American,* A & M; *Not the Boy Next Door,* Arista; and *Peter Allen—Captured Live at Carnegie Hall.*

WRITINGS:

STAGE

Song contributor, *The Madwoman of Central Park West,* 22 Steps Theatre, New York City, 1979.
Music and lyrics, *Legs Diamond,* Mark Hellinger Theatre, New York City, 1989.

FILM

(With Burt Bacharach, Carole Bayer Sager, and Christopher Cross) "Arthur's Theme (The Best That You Can Do)," *Arthur,* Warner Brothers, 1981.

SONGS

"Six-Thirty Sunday Morning," 1971.
(With Carole Bayer Sager) "Jennifer," 1971.
(With Jeff Barry) "I Honestly Love You," 1974.
"Tenterfield Saddler," 1974.
(With Bayer Sager) "Quiet Please, There's a Lady on Stage," 1975.
(With Adrienne Anderson) "I Go to Rio," 1976.
(With Bayer Sager) "I'd Rather Leave While I'm in Love," 1977.
(With Bayer Sager) "Don't Cry Out Loud," 1978.
"All I Wanted Was the Dream," 1988.
"The Music Went out of My Life," 1988.

Also composer of the songs "You and Me (We Wanted It All)," "Someone Waits for You," "Everything Old Is New Again," and "I Could Have Been a Sailor."

ALVIN, John 1917-

PERSONAL: Full name, John Alvin Hoffstadt; born October 24, 1917, in Chicago, IL. *Education:* Trained at the Pasadena Playhouse, Pasadena, CA.

CAREER: Actor. Worked in radio in Chicago, IL, and Detroit, MI.

CREDITS:

FILM APPEARANCES

Orderly, *Northern Pursuit,* Warner Brothers, 1943.
Sound man, *Destination Tokyo,* Warner Brothers, 1944.
Photographer, *Janie,* Warner Brothers, 1944.
Matt, *The Sullivans* (also known as *The Fighting Sullivans*), Twentieth Century-Fox, 1944.
Cal Wheeler, *The Very Thought of You,* Warner Brothers, 1944.
Hogan, *Objective, Burma,* Warner Brothers, 1945.
Lawton Meckall, *Roughly Speaking,* Warner Brothers, 1945.
Pony Smith, *San Antonio,* Warner Brothers, 1945.
Donald Arlington, *The Beast with Five Fingers,* First National, 1946.
Petey, *Night and Day,* Warner Brothers, 1946.
Announcer, *One More Tomorrow,* Warner Brothers, 1946.
Carl, *Shadow of a Woman,* Warner Brothers, 1946.
Janice Clerk, *Three Strangers,* Warner Brothers/First National, 1946.
Single Jack, *Cheyenne* (also known as *The Wyoming Kid*), Warner Brothers, 1947.
Convict, *Deep Valley,* Warner Brothers, 1947.
William, *Love and Learn,* Warner Brothers, 1947.
Jeff, *Under Colorado Skies,* Republic, 1947.
Don Post, *The Bold Frontiersman,* Republic, 1948.
Ralph, *Open Secret,* Eagle Lion, 1948.
Travel agent, *Romance on the High Seas* (also known as *It's Magic*), Warner Brothers, 1948.
Vic Armstrong, *The Shanghai Chest,* Monogram, 1948.
Nick, *Train to Alcatraz,* Republic, 1948.
Jim Crocker, *Two Guys from Texas* (also known as *Two Texas Knights*), Warner Brothers, 1948.
Rocky, Monogram, 1948.
Young intellectual, *The Fountainhead,* Warner Brothers, 1949.
Calder Taylor, *This Side of the Law,* Warner Brothers, 1950.
Haggard man, *Close to My Heart,* Warner Brothers, 1951.
Travis Ashbourne III, *Come Fill the Cup,* First National, 1951.
Jack White, *Goodbye, My Fancy,* Warner Brothers, 1951.
Eddie Ennis, *Missing Women,* Republic, 1951.
Photographer, *The Unknown Man,* Metro-Goldwyn-Mayer (MGM), 1951.
Stage manager, *Carrie,* Paramount, 1952.

Tracy, *April in Paris,* Warner Brothers, 1953.
Reporter, *Dream Wife,* MGM, 1953.
Professor, *Torpedo Alley,* Allied Artists, 1953.
Mr. Mulvaney, *Deep in My Heart,* MGM, 1954.
Mr. Warren, *The Shanghai Story,* Republic, 1954.
Percy, *A Bullet for Joey,* United Artists, 1955.
Kentucky Rifle, Howco, 1956.
Sloan, *The Couch,* Warner Brothers, 1962.
Customer, *Irma La Douce,* United Artists, 1963.
Arthur's father, *Somewhere in Time,* Universal, 1980.

Also appeared in *The Legend of Lylah Claire; Mr. Tibbs; Marnie; Inside Daisy Clover;* and *They Shoot Horses, Don't They?*

TELEVISION APPEARANCES; EPISODIC

All in The Family, CBS, 1975.

Also appeared in *Meet Millie, Burns and Allen, Death Valley Days, Asphalt Jungle, Climax, The Jack Benny Show, My Three Sons, The Texan, Adventures in Paradise, Rawhide, The Rifleman, Omnibus, Wells Fargo, Alfred Hitchcock, Mannix, I Spy, McDuff, Lineup, My Favorite Husband, Family Affair, The Incredible Hulk, The Lucy Show, Ironside, Nightstalker, M*A*S*H, Lou Grant, Hart to Hart, Yellow Rose, Murder She Wrote, Monster Squad, House of Evil, Aftermash, General Hospital, Starsky and Hutch, Policewoman, Amazing Stories, Capitol, The Quest, Visions/KCET,* and *The Swallows Came Back.*

OTHER TELEVISION APPEARANCES

Surgeon, *Sweet, Sweet Rachel* (movie), ABC, 1971.
Dr. Draper, *The Legend of Lizzie Borden* (movie), ABC, 1975.
Minister, *Passions* (movie), CBS, 1984.
E. Wilfred, *Return to Green Acres* (movie), CBS, 1990.

Also appeared in the pilot *Dennis the Menace.*

STAGE APPEARANCES

Appeared in productions of *Leaning on Letty,* and *Life of the Party,* New York City.*

*　　*　　*

AMSTERDAM, Morey 1908-

PERSONAL: Born December 14, 1908, in Chicago, IL; son of Max and Jenny (Finder) Amsterdam; married Catherine Amayia Patrick, December 17, 1941; children: Gregory, Cathy. *Education:* Attended University of California, Berkeley.

CAREER: Actor, comedian, composer, producer, singer, and writer. Performer with the Optimistic Doughnut Program, 1930, and the Rube Wolf Orchestra. Writer for the Al Pearce Gang, 1932, and Metro-Goldwyn-Mayer, 1937. Owner of The Playgoers Club; vice-president, American International Pictures. Writer for celebrities and politicians, including Will Rogers, Fanny Brice, Robert Taylor, Franklin Roosevelt, Lyndon Johnson, and Ronald Reagan.

CREDITS:

FILM APPEARANCES

It Came from Outer Space, Universal, 1953.
Fandango, *Machine Gun Kelly,* American International Pictures, 1958.
Walter Sage, *Murder Inc.,* Twentieth Century-Fox, 1960.
Gay Purree, Warner Brothers, 1962.
Cappy, *Beach Party,* American International Pictures, 1963.
Cappy, *Muscle Beach Party,* American International Pictures, 1964.
Charlie, *Don't Worry, We'll Think of a Title,* United Artists, 1966 (also see below).
Charlie Blake, *The Horse in the Gray Flannel Suit,* Buena Vista, 1968.
James Brandy, *Mr. Magoo's Holiday Festival,* Maron, 1970.
Custard pie star, *Won Ton Ton, The Dog Who Saved Hollywood,* Paramount, 1976.
Baby Bullets, *When Nature Calls,* Troma, 1985.

FILM WORK

Producer, *Don't Worry, We'll Think of a Title,* United Artists, 1966.

TELEVISION APPEARANCES; SERIES

Regular, *Stop Me If You've Heard This One,* NBC, 1948.
Regular, *Who Said That?,* NBC, 1949.
Host, *The Morey Amsterdam Show,* CBS, 1949-50.
Host, *Broadway Open House,* NBC, 1950.
Host, *Battle of the Ages,* CBS, 1952.
Regular, *Keep Talking,* CBS, 1958.
Buddy Sorrell, *The Dick Van Dyke Show,* CBS, 1961-66.
Regular, *Can You Top This?,* syndicated, 1970 (also see below).
Morey, *The Young and the Restless,* CBS, 1973.
Moe, *Mixed Nuts,* ABC, 1977.

Also appeared on *Hollywood Squares,* NBC.

TELEVISION APPEARANCES; EPISODIC

Guest emcee, *The Milton Berle Show,* NBC, 1948.
Guest, *Leave It to the Girls,* NBC, 1949.
The Love Boat, ABC, 1978.

Also appeared in episodes of more than fifty other shows, including *Guide Right,* 1952; *The John Gary Show,* 1966;

One Man Show, 1969; *The Danny Thomas Show; Oh, Susanna!, Gunsmoke, Fame,* and *Alice.*

OTHER TELEVISION APPEARANCES

Charlie, *Honeymoon Suite* (pilot), ABC, 1972.
Voice of One Million B.C., *Rudolph's Shiny New Year* (special), ABC, 1976.
Moe, *Mixed Nuts* (pilot), ABC, 1977.
Eddie Nova, *Sooner or Later* (movie), NBC, 1979.
Host, *Here It Is Burlesque* (special), HBO, 1980.
Moe, *Side by Side* (movie), CBS, 1988.

TELEVISION WORK; SERIES

Producer, *The Morey Amsterdam Show,* CBS, 1948-50 (also see below).
Executive producer, *Can You Top This?,* CBS, 1970.

RADIO APPEARANCES

Boy soprano, Radio KPO, San Francisco, CA, 1922.

WRITINGS:

SCREENPLAYS

Ghost and the Guest, Producers Releasing Corporation, 1943.
(With Gerald J. Schnitzer), *Kid Dynamite* (also known as *Queen of Broadway*), Monogram, 1943.
(With John Hart, George W. Schenck, and William Marks) *Don't Worry, We'll Think of a Title,* United Artists, 1966.

TELEVISION SERIES

(With Irving Mansfield and Lou Meltrer) *The Morey Amsterdam Show,* CBS, 1948-50.

Also wrote material for the series *Can You Top This?,* syndicated, 1970.

OTHER

Keep Laughing, Citadel, 1959.
Betty Cooker Crock Book for Drunks, Regnery, 1977.

Composer of songs, including "Why Oh Why Did I Ever Leave Wyoming?," "Yuk-A-Puk," and "Rum and Coca-Cola."

*　　*　　*

ANDERSON, John 1922-

PERSONAL: Born October 20, 1922, in Clayton, IL.

ADDRESSES: Agent—Paul Kohner, Inc., 9169 Sunset Blvd., Los Angeles, CA 90069; and Herb Tannen & Associates, 1800 North Vine St., Suite 120, Los Angeles, CA 90028.

CAREER: Actor.

CREDITS:

FILM APPEARANCES

Harry Sykes, *Treasure Island,* Metro-Goldwyn-Mayer (MGM), 1934.
Doc, *The True Story of Lynn Stuart,* Columbia, 1958.
California Charlie, *Psycho,* Paramount, 1960.
Burns, *Geronimo,* United Artists, 1962.
Elder Hammond, *Ride the High Country* (also released as *Guns in the Afternoon*), MGM, 1962.
Preacher, *Walk on the Wild Side,* Columbia, 1962.
Sergeant Buell, *The Hallelujah Trail,* United Artists, 1965.
Reagan, *The Satan Bug,* United Artists, 1965.
Dietrich, *A Covenant with Death,* Warner Brothers, 1966.
Joe Clausen, *Namu, the Killer Whale,* United Artists, 1966.
Ezra/Isaac Maple, *Welcome to Hard Times* (also known as *Killer on a Horse*), MGM, 1967.
Captain Addis, *Day of the Evil Gun,* MGM, 1968.
Marshal Dana, *Five Card Stud,* Paramount, 1968.
Kincaid, *The Great Bank Robbery,* Warner Brothers, 1969.
Asa Beck, *Heaven with a Gun,* MGM, 1969.
Capper, *A Man Called Gannon,* Universal, 1969.
Frank Boone, *Young Billy Young* (also known as *Who Rides with Kane?*), United Artists, 1969.
Bryce, *Cotton Comes to Harlem,* United Artists, 1970.
Colonel Iversion, *Soldier Blue,* Avco-Embassy, 1970.
Sheriff Allan Pierce, *The Animals,* XYZ, 1971.
Stretch, *Man and Boy,* Levitt Pickman, 1972.
Sheriff Parker, *Molly and Lawless John,* Producer Distributors Corporation, 1972.
Halliday, *Executive Action,* National General, 1973.
Mike Turk, *The Dove,* Paramount, 1974.
Pike, *The Specialist,* Crown, 1975.
Abraham Lincoln, *The Lincoln Conspiracy,* Sunn Classics, 1977.
Caiaphas, *In Search of Historic Jesus,* Sunn Classics, 1980.
Governor, *Smokey and the Bandit Part II* (also released as *Smokey and the Bandit Ride Again*), Universal, 1980.
Judge, *Zoot Suit,* Universal, 1981.
TV interviewer, *Out of the Blue,* Discovery, 1982.
Burnside, *Lone Wolf McQuade,* Orion, 1983.
Arliss, *Never Too Young to Die,* Paul Entertainment, 1986.
Neal G. Koch, *Scorpion,* Crown International, 1986.
Judge Kenesaw Mountain Landis, *Eight Men Out,* Orion, 1988.

Also appeared as Vito Albanese in *Il Consigliori,* 1973; in *The Stepmother,* 1973; *Amerasia,* 1986; and *Deadly Innocents,* 1989.

TELEVISION APPEARANCES; SERIES

Deputy Virgil Earp, *The Life and Legend of Wyatt Earp,* ABC, 1955.

Sergeant Bullock, *Boots and Saddles: The Story of the Fifth Cavalry,* syndicated, 1957.

Sam Gidds, *The Rifleman,* ABC, 1958.

Foster Hancock, *Ben Casey,* ABC, 1961.

Mr. Claymore, *Checking In,* CBS, 1981.

TELEVISION APPEARANCES; PILOTS

Heber Greshon, *Second Chance,* ABC, 1962.

Rankin, *Won't It Ever Be Morning,* NBC, 1965.

Standish, *Scalplock,* ABC, 1966.

Cruett, *Hitched,* NBC, 1973.

Edward McClure, *Call to Danger,* CBS, 1973.

Joe Cupis, *Brock's Last Case,* NBC, 1973.

J. R. King, *Egan,* ABC, 1973.

Eric Kort, *The Log of the Black Pearl,* NBC, 1975.

Captain Edwin O'Hare Lewis, *Death among Friends* (also known as *Mrs. R—Death among Friends*), NBC, 1975.

Jason Monroe, *Dead Man on the Run,* ABC, 1975.

TELEVISION APPEARANCES; EPISODIC

Ebonite Interrogator, "Nightmare," *The Outer Limits,* ABC, 1963.

"The Gray Flannel Shrink", *The Bob Newhart Show,* CBS, 1974.

"Say No More", *M*A*S*H,* CBS, 1983.

TELEVISION APPEARANCES; MOVIES

Henry Kealey, *Set This Town on Fire,* NBC, 1973.

Colonel John Lockport, *Smile Jenny, You're Dead,* ABC, 1974.

Aaron Denver, *Manhunter,* CBS, 1974.

Toler, *Heatwave!,* ABC, 1974.

George Varney, *Once an Eagle,* NBC, 1976.

Marshal, *The Quest,* NBC, 1976.

President Andrew Jackson, *Bridger,* ABC, 1976.

Moose Matlock, *Banjo Hackett: Roamin' Free,* NBC, 1976.

Stephen Hancock, *The Dark Side of Innocence,* NBC, 1976.

Amos Force, *The Last Hurrah,* NBC, 1977.

General George Marshall, *Tail Gunner Joe,* NBC, 1977.

Alexander Majors, *Peter Lundy and the Medicine Hat Stallion,* NBC, 1977.

Patrick Breen, *Donner Pass: The Road to Survival,* NBC, 1978.

Hutter, *The Deer Slayer,* NBC, 1978.

Franklin Delano Roosevelt, *Backstairs at the White House,* NBC, 1979.

Paul Cooper, *The First Time,* ABC, 1982.

Stanley Willard, *Missing Children: A Mother's Story,* CBS, 1982.

Reverend Donald Randolph, *Sins of the Past,* ABC, 1984.

William Hazard, *North and South,* ABC, 1985.

Brigadier General Brooke, *Dream West,* CBS, 1986.

Holbrook, *I-Man,* ABC, 1986.

Judge Meriweather, *American Harvest,* CBS, 1987.

Dutton, *Full Exposure: The Sex Tapes Scandal,* NBC, 1989.

Josh, *Follow Your Heart,* NBC, 1990.

OTHER TELEVISION APPEARANCES

Mr. Scott, *Rich Man, Poor Man—Book II* (mini-series), ABC, 1976.

President Franklin Delano Roosevelt, *Backstairs at the White House* (mini-series), NBC, 1979.

Himself, *Johnny Cash Cowboy Heroes* (special), CBS, 1982.

Also appeared as Curtis George in *Mayday! Mayday!,* 1981, and as Maxwell Eaton II in *Hardesty House,* 1986.

STAGE APPEARANCES

Gethsemane Springs, Mark Taper Forum, New Theatre For Now, Los Angeles, CA, 1977.

Also appeared as guest artist with the Arizona Theatre Company, Tucson, AZ, 1978-79.*

*   *   *

ANDERSON, Loni   1945(?)-

PERSONAL: Born August 5, 1945 (some sources say 1946 or 1950), in St. Paul, MN; daughter of Klaydon (a pharmaceutical executive) and Maxine (a model) Anderson; second husband, Ross Bickell (divorced, 1981); married third husband, Burt Reynolds (an actor), April 29, 1988; children: (first marriage) Deidre; (third marriage) Quinton Anderson (adopted). *Education:* Received B.A. in art and drama from the University of Minnesota.

ADDRESSES: Agent—Creative Artists Agency, 9830 Wilshire Boulevard, Beverly Hills, CA 90212; Nina Blanchard Enterprises Inc., 7060 Hollywood Boulevard, Suite 1010, Los Angeles, CA 90028. *Publicist*—Freeman and Sutton Public Relations, 8961 Sunset Boulevard, Suite 2-A, Los Angeles, CA 90069.

CAREER: Actress. Worked as a school teacher prior to acting career.

AWARDS, HONORS: Emmy nominations, best supporting actress in a comedy, variety, or music series, 1980 and 1981, for *WKRP in Cincinnati.*

CREDITS:

TELEVISION APPEARANCES; SERIES

Jennifer Marlowe, *WKRP in Cincinnati,* CBS, 1978-82.
Sydney Kovak, *Partners in Crime,* NBC, 1984.
L. K. McGuire, *Easy Street,* NBC, 1986-87.

TELEVISION APPEARANCES; MOVIES

Miss Davour, *The Magnificent Magical Magnet of Santa Mesa,* NBC, 1977.
Angela Ross, *Three on a Date,* ABC, 1978.
Title role, *The Jayne Mansfield Story,* CBS, 1980.
Julie Davis, *Sizzle,* ABC, 1981.
Mollie Dean Purcell, *Country Gold,* CBS, 1982.
Ellen Blake, *My Mother's Secret Life,* ABC, 1984.
Lora Mae Holloway, *A Letter to Three Wives,* NBC, 1985.
Stacy Tweed, *Stranded,* NBC, 1986.
Ellen Berent, *Too Good to Be True,* NBC, 1988.
Lauren LaSalle, *Necessity,* CBS, 1988.
Liz Bartlett, *A Whisper Kills,* ABC, 1988.
Madelyn Coltrane Stevenson, *Sorry, Wrong Number,* USA, 1989.
Title role, *White Hot: The Mysterious Murder of Thelma Todd,* NBC, 1991.

TELEVISION APPEARANCES; SPECIALS

Circus of the Stars, CBS, 1979.
Host, *Merry Christmas from the Grand Ole Opry,* ABC, 1979.
Host, *The Fantastic Funnies,* CBS, 1980.
Bob Hope's All-Star Look at TV's Prime Time Wars, NBC, 1980.
Siegfried and Roy, NBC, 1980.
Host, *The New and Spectacular Guinness Book of World Records,* ABC, 1980.
Bob Hope's All-Star Comedy Birthday Party, NBC, 1980.
The Bob Hope Christmas Special, NBC, 1980.
Bob Hope's Spring Fling of Comedy and Glamour, NBC, 1981.
Host, *The Candid Camera Special,* NBC, 1981.
Bob Hope's All-Star Comedy Look at the Fall Season: It's Still Free and Worth It!, NBC, 1981.
Magic with the Stars, NBC, 1982.
Bob Hope's Women I Love—Beautiful But Funny, NBC, 1982.
Bob Hope's Christmas Special, NBC, 1982.
Host, *Sunday Funnies,* NBC, 1983.
Bob Hope's Wicki-Wacky Special from Waikiki, NBC, 1984.
Dom DeLuise and Friends—Part IV, ABC, 1986.
Voice of Blondie, *Blondie and Dagwood* (animated), CBS, 1987.
Friday Night Surprise! (also known as *Surprise!*), 1988.

Voice of Blondie, *The Blondie and Dagwood Second Wedding Workout,* CBS, 1989.
Host, *New and Improved Kids* (documentary; also known as *Raising Good Kids in Bad Times*), syndicated, 1990.

TELEVISION APPEARANCES; PILOTS

Swenson, *Winner Take All,* CBS, 1977.
Tom Snyder's Celebrity Spotlight, NBC, 1980.

TELEVISION APPEARANCES; EPISODIC

The Bob Newhart Show, CBS, 1977.
Whodunnit?, NBC, 1979.
Lovely, *Amazing Stories,* NBC, 1985.
Win, Lose, or Draw, syndicated, 1987.
Dawn St. Clair, "Grand Theft Hotel," *B. L. Stryker,* ABC, 1990.

Also appeared on *Three's Company,* ABC; *The Love Boat,* ABC; *Barnaby Jones,* CBS; *Phyllis,* CBS; and as Lindsay, *Harry O,* ABC.

FILM APPEARANCES

Pembrook Feeney, *Stroker Ace,* Universal/Warner Brothers, 1983.
Voice of Flo, *All Dogs Go to Heaven* (animated), United Artists, 1989.

STAGE APPEARANCES

Appeared in regional and dinner theatre productions as Billie Dawn, *Born Yesterday,* Tzeitel, *Fiddler on the Roof,* and Sophie, *The Star Spangled Girl;* also appeared in productions of *Never Too Late, Can-Can, The Threepenny Opera, Any Wednesday, Send Me No Flowers,* and *The Secret Life of Walter Mitty.*

*   *   *

ANN-MARGRET   1941-

PERSONAL: Full name, Ann-Margret Olsson; born April 28, 1941, in Valsobyn, Sweden; daughter of Gustaav and Anna (Aronson) Olsson; married Roger Smith (an actor, director, and producer), 1967. *Education:* Attended Northwestern University.

ADDRESSES: Office—435 North Bedford Dr., Beverly Hills, CA 90210. *Agent*—Nicole David, Triad Agency, 10100 St. Monica—16th Floor, Los Angeles, CA 90067.

CAREER: Actress and entertainer. Early in her career, Ann-Margret performed on radio shows and toured with a band; performs at nightclubs such as Caesar's Palace in Las Vegas, and in Lake Tahoe; performed with George Burns at the Sahara Hotel, Las Vegas, 1960.

AWARDS, HONORS: Golden Globe Award, Most Promising Newcomer, 1962; Gold Medal Award, Most Popular Actress, *Photoplay* magazine, 1971 and 1972; Golden Globe Award, Best Supporting Actress, and Academy Award nomination, Best Supporting Actress, both 1972, for *Carnal Knowledge;* Golden Globe Award, Best Motion Picture Actress—Musical/Comedy, and Academy Award nomination, Best Actress, both 1975, for *Tommy;* Golden Apple Award, Star of the Year, Hollywood Women's Press Club, 1983; Golden Globe Award, Best Performance by an Actress in a Mini-Series or Motion Picture Made for Television, 1985, for *A Streetcar Named Desire;* Emmy Award nomination, Outstanding Lead Actress, 1987, for *The Two Mrs. Grenvilles;* Female Star of the Year Award, United Motion Pictures Association, three times; Outstanding Box-Office Star of the Year, Theatre Owners of America, twice; Citation for outstanding performances (tours of Vietnam and Far East) from president Lyndon B. Johnson; Royal Command Performance for Queen Elizabeth II of England; Italian Motion Picture Industry Award.

CREDITS:

FILM APPEARANCES

(Film debut) Louise, *Pocketful of Miracles,* United Artists, 1961.
Emily Porter, *State Fair,* Twentieth Century-Fox, 1962.
Kim McAfee, *Bye Bye Birdie,* Columbia, 1963.
Jody Dvorak, *Kitten with a Whip,* Universal, 1964.
Fran Hobson, *The Pleasure Seekers,* Twentieth Century-Fox, 1964.
Rusty Martin, *Viva Las Vegas,* (also known as *Love in Las Vegas*), Metro-Goldwyn-Mayer (MGM), 1964.
Laurel, *Bus Riley's Back in Town,* Universal, 1965.
Melba, *The Cincinnati Kid,* MGM, 1965.
Kristine Pedak, *Once a Thief,* MGM, 1965.
Maggie Scott, *Made in Paris,* MGM, 1966.
Suzie Solaris, *Murderer's Row,* Columbia, 1966.
Dallas, *Stagecoach,* Twentieth Century-Fox, 1966.
Kelly Ollson, *The Swinger,* Paramount, 1966.
Carolina, *The Tiger and the Pussycat,* Embassy, 1967.
Rhoda, *R.P.M.,* (also known as *R.P.M. [Revolutions Per Minute]*), Columbia, 1970.
Ann McCalley, *C. C. and Company,* Avco-Embassy, 1971.
Bobbie Templeton, *Carnal Knowledge,* Avco-Embassy, 1971.
Nancy, *The Outside Man,* United Artists, 1973.
Mrs. Lowe, *The Train Robbers,* Warner Brothers, 1973.
Nora Walker Hobbs, *Tommy,* Columbia, 1975.
Charley, *The Twist,* (also known as *Follies Bourgeoisie*), UGC/Parafrance, 1976.
Lady Booby, *Joseph Andrews,* Paramount, 1977.

Lady Flavia Geste, *The Last Remake of Beau Geste,* Universal, 1977.
Jezebel Dezire, *The Cheap Detective,* Columbia, 1978.
Peggy Ann Snow, *Magic,* Twentieth Century-Fox, 1978.
Charming Jones, *The Villain,* (also known as *Cactus Jack*), Columbia, 1979.
Sue Ann, *Middle Age Crazy,* Twentieth Century-Fox, 1980.
Stephanie, *I Ought to Be in Pictures,* Twentieth Century-Fox, 1982.
Patti Warner, *Lookin' to Get Out,* Paramount, 1982.
Jenny, *The Return of the Soldier,* Twentieth Century-Fox, 1983.
Audrey Minelli, *Twice in a Lifetime,* Yorkin, 1985.
Barbara Mitchell, *52 Pick-Up,* Cannon, 1986.
Rose, *A Tiger's Tale,* Atlantic Entertainment, 1988.
Jackie Giardino, *A New Life,* Paramount, 1988.

Also appeared in *Rebus,* 1969; *The Prophet,* 1976.

TELEVISION APPEARANCES; HOST

The Ann-Margret Show, CBS, 1968.
Ann-Margret: From Hollywood With Love, CBS, 1969.
Ann-Margret—When You're Smiling, NBC, 1973.
Ann-Margret Smith, NBC, 1975.
Ann-Margret Olsson, NBC, 1975.
Memories of Elvis, NBC, 1977.
Ann-Margret . . . Rhinestone Cowgirl, NBC, 1977.
Ann-Margret's Hollywood Movie Girls, ABC, 1980.

OTHER TELEVISION APPEARANCES

The Jack Benny Show, CBS, 1961.
The Andy Williams Special, NBC, 1962.
Jack Benny's Birthday Special, NBC, 1969.
The Bob Hope Show, NBC, 1969, 1970, 1973.
Swing Out, Sweet Land, NBC, 1971.
Perry Como in Las Vegas, NBC, 1975.
Las Vegas Entertainment Awards, NBC, 1977.
The George Burns One-Man Show, CBS, 1977.
Bob Hope's All-Star Comedy Spectacular from Lake Tahoe, NBC, 1977.
Happy Birthday, Bob, NBC, 1978.
Las Vegas Palace of Stars, CBS, 1979.
The Way They Were (syndicated), 1981.
George Burns' Early, Early, Early Christmas Show, NBC, 1981.
Bob Hope's 30th Anniversary TV Special, NBC, 1981.
Hollywood's Private Home Movies, ABC, 1983.
Lucille Fray, *Who Will Love My Children?* (movie), ABC, 1983.
Blanche DuBois, *A Streetcar Named Desire* (movie), ABC, 1984.
Perry Como's Christmas in England, ABC, 1984.
Ann Arden, *The Two Mrs. Grenvilles* (mini-series), NBC, 1987.

America's Tribute to Bob Hope, NBC, 1988.
George Burns' 95th Birthday, CBS, 1991.
Our Sons, ABC, 1991.

Made television debut as a contestant on *Ted Mack's Amateur Hour;* also appeared as Ruby, *Dames at Sea;* Ann-Margrock (voice only), *The Flintstones,* ABC. Appeared on *The Barbara Walter's Special,* ABC.

RECORDINGS:

ALBUMS

Bye, Bye Birdie, original soundtrack, Victor; *Ann-Margret,* Victor; *Vivacious One,* Victor; *Love Rush,* MCA.*

* * *

ARCENAS, Loy 1953(?)-

PERSONAL: Born c. 1953 in the Philippines; son of a doctor and a banker. *Education:* Attended the University of the Philippines; studied design at the English National Opera.

ADDRESSES: Contact—Jon Geidt, American Repertory Theatre, 64 Brattle St., Cambridge, MA 02138.

CAREER: Set designer. Worked as stage manager with the Manila Symphony, Manila, Philippines.

AWARDS, HONORS: Los Angeles Drama Critics Circle Award nomination, Best Scenic Design, 1988, for *Three Postcards;* Drama Desk Award nomination, Best Set Design, 1989, for *Reckless.*

CREDITS:

STAGE SET DESIGNER

(And costume designer) *Take Death to Lunch,* Impossible Ragtime Theatre, New York City, 1979.
The Barber of Seville, Soho Repertory Theatre, New York City, 1979.
When the War Was Over, Impossible Ragtime Theatre, 1980.
Vera, with Kate, Wonderhorse Theatre, New York City, 1980.
(And costume designer) *Murder in the Cathedral,* St. Malachy's Theatrespace, New York City, 1981.
Redback, New York Theatre Studio, American Musical and Drama Academy, Studio One, New York City, 1981.
Cubisticue, New York Theatre Studio, Actors and Directors Theatre, New York City, 1981.
Finding Donis Anne, Ark Theatre Company, New York City, 1982.
The Quilling of Prue, New York Theatre Studio, American Musical and Drama Academy, Studio One, 1983.

(With Kalina Ivanov) *Macbeth,* Ark Theatre Company, 1983.
Dementos, Production Company, Theatre Guinevere, New York City, 1983.
Second Lady, Production Company, Theatre Guinevere, New York City, 1983.
Blue Window, Production Company, Theatre Guinevere, then Long Wharf Theatre, New Haven, CT, both 1984.
The Man Who Could See Through Time, Ark Theatre Company, 1984.
Souvenirs, New York Theatre Workshop, Cubiculo Theatre, New York City, 1984.
Maneuvers, South Street Theatre, New York City, 1985.
Bosoms and Neglect, New York Theatre Workshop, Perry Street Theatre, New York City, 1986.
Dry Land, New Arts Theatre Company, Judith Anderson Theatre, New York City, 1986.
The Merchant of Venice, Classic Stage Company Repertory Theatre, New York City, 1986.
The Day Room, American Repertory Theatre, Cambridge, MA, 1986.
The Real Thing, Studio Arena Theatre, Buffalo, NY, 1986.
Three Postcards, Playwrights Horizons, New York City, then South Coast Repertory Theatre, Costa Mesa, CA, both 1987.
The Cannibal Masque/A Serpent's Egg, American Repertory Theatre, 1987.
Mrs. Sorken Presents, American Repertory Theatre, 1987.
The Birthday Party, Classic Stage Company Repertory Theatre, 1988.
The Debutante Ball, Manhattan Theatre Club, City Center, New York City, 1988.
Right Behind the Flag, Playwrights Horizons, 1988.
Butterfly, Goodspeed Opera House, Norma Terris Theatre, East Haddam, CT, 1988.
Benefactors, Studio Arena Theatre, 1988.
Gilette, American Repertory Theatre, Loeb Drama Center, Cambridge, MA, 1988.
Reckless, Circle Repertory Theatre Company, New York City, 1988.
Prelude to a Kiss, South Coast Repertory Theatre, 1988, then Circle Repertory Theatre Company, 1989.
The Glass Menagerie, Kreeger Theatre, Washington, DC, 1989.
Once on This Island, Playwrights Horizons, then Booth Theatre, New York City, 1990.
El Dorado, South Coast Repertory Theatre, 1991.

OTHER SOURCES:

PERIODICALS

New York Times, October 14, 1990.*

ASHER, William 1919-

PERSONAL: Born in 1919.

CAREER: Director, producer, and writer.

AWARDS, HONORS: Emmy Award, Outstanding Directorial Achievement in Comedy, 1965, for *Bewitched.*

CREDITS:

FILM WORK; DIRECTOR

(And producer with Richard Quine), *Leather Gloves* (also known as *Loser Take All*), Columbia, 1948.

Mobs Inc. (also known as *Mobs Incorporated*), Premier, 1956.

The Shadow on the Window, Columbia, 1957.

The 27th Day, Columbia, 1957.

Beach Party, American International Pictures, 1963.

(And producer) *Johnny Cool,* United Artists, 1963.

Bikini Beach, American International Pictures, 1964.

Muscle Beach Party, American International Pictures, 1964.

Beach Blanket Bingo, American International Pictures, 1965.

How to Stuff a Wild Bikini, American International Pictures, 1965.

Fireball 500, American International Pictures, 1966.

Butcher Baker (Nightmare Maker) (also known as *Night Warning; Nightmare Maker*), International Films, 1982.

(And producer with Charles Grodin, Richard Carrothers, and Dennis D. Hennessey) *Movers & Shakers,* United Artists, 1985.

TELEVISION WORK; SERIES

Director, *Willy,* CBS, 1954-55.

Producer and director, *Fibber McGee and Molly,* NBC, 1959-60.

Producer (with Robert Cosello), *The Patty Duke Show,* ABC, 1963-66.

Producer and director, *Bewitched,* ABC, 1964-72.

Director (with others), *Gidget,* ABC, 1965-66.

Producer and director, *Temperatures Rising,* ABC, 1972-73.

Producer and director, *The Paul Lynde Show,* ABC, 1972-73.

Director (with others), *Lucas Tanner,* NBC, 1974-75.

Director, *Alice,* CBS, 1976-85.

Director (With John Astin, Norman Abbott, Hollingsworth Morse, and Alan Bergmann), *Operation Petticoat,* ABC, 1977-78.

Director (with others), *The Bad News Bears,* CBS, 1979-80.

Director (with others), *The Dukes of Hazzard,* CBS, 1979-85.

Director (with Mel Ferber and Tony Mordente), *Flatbush,* CBS, 1979.

Director (with E. W. Swackhamer, Alan Myerson, and John Patterson), *Foul Play,* ABC, 1981.

Director (with others), *Harper Valley PTA,* NBC, 1981.

Director (with others), *Private Benjamin,* CBS, 1981-83.

TELEVISION WORK; PILOTS

Director, *Mr. Bevis,* ABC, 1949.

Director, *The Doctor Was a Lady,* NBC, 1958.

Director, *Mickey and the Contessa,* CBS, 1963.

Producer and director, *Tabitha,* ABC, 1976.

Director, *A Christmas for Boomer,* NBC, 1979.

Director (with Gary Nelson, Paul Crasna, Stuart Margolin, and Bob Sweeney), *Crazy Like a Fox,* CBS, 1984.

Executive producer, *Kay O'Brien,* CBS, 1986.

Also supervising producer, *Whattley By the Bay,* 1988.

TELEVISION WORK; EPISODIC

Director, *I Love Lucy,* CBS, 1951-57.

Director (with David Brown), *Short Story Theater* (syndicated), 1952.

Producer (with Henry Jaffe and Alvin Copperman), *Shirley Temple's Storybook,* NBC, 1958.

OTHER TELEVISION WORK

Director, *Charley's Aunt* (special), The Entertainment Channel, 1983.

Director, *I Dream of Jeannie . . . 15 Years Later* (movie), NBC, 1985.

Director, *Me and Mom* (special), ABC, 1985.

Director, *Return to Green Acres* (movie), CBS, 1990.

Also producer, *Jane Wyman Presents the Fireside Theater,* NBC.

WRITINGS:

MOVIE SCREENPLAYS

(With Leo Townsend and Robert Dillon) *Bikini Beach,* American International Pictures, 1964.

(With Dillon) *Muscle Beach Party,* American International Pictures, 1964.

(With Townsend) *How to Stuff a Wild Bikini,* American International Pictures, 1965.

(With Townsend) *Fireball 500,* American International Pictures, 1966.*

ASHMAN, Howard 1950-1991

OBITUARY NOTICE—See index for *CTFT* sketch: Full name, Howard Elliott Ashman; born May 17, 1950, in Baltimore, MD; died of complications from acquired immune deficiency syndrome (AIDS), March 14, 1991, in New York, NY. Administrator, producer, director, editor, librettist, lyricist, and playwright. Ashman will probably be best remembered as the award-winning author of dialogue and lyrics for *Little Shop of Horrors,* a highly successful musical about a man-eating plant. The show, which Ashman adapted from a cult film by Roger Corman, received a Tony nomination, became Off-Broadway's most lucrative musical, and garnered the London *Evening Standard* award for best musical of the 1983 to 1984 season. Ashman also won an Academy Award for best original song for "Under the Sea," from the film *The Little Mermaid.* Ashman began his career writing plays, including *'Cause Maggie's Afraid of the Dark* and *The Confirmation;* later, he collaborated on the musical adaptations *God Bless You, Mr. Rosewater* and *Smile.* Shortly before his death, he had finished contributions to the films *Beauty and the Beast* and *Aladdin.* Aside from writing, Ashman served as artistic director of the WPA Theatre, edited paperbacks for Grosset & Dunlap, directed several productions of his own plays, and helped to produce *The Little Mermaid.*

OBITUARIES AND OTHER SOURCES:

PERIODICALS

Los Angeles Times, March 15, 1991.
Newsweek, March 25, 1991.

* * *

AYR, Michael 1953-

PERSONAL: Born September 8, 1953, in Great Falls, MT. *Education:* Graduated from Southern Methodist University.

ADDRESSES: Agent—Karg/Weissenbach and Associates, 329 N. Wetherly Dr., Suite 101, Beverly Hills, CA 90211.

CAREER: Actor.

CREDITS:

STAGE APPEARANCES

(Off-Broadway debut) Peter Roome, Jr., *Mrs. Murray's Farm,* Circle Repertory Company, Circle Repertory Theatre, New York City, 1976.
Albert, *The Farm,* Circle Repertory Company, Circle Repertory Theatre, 1976.

Bruce Garrick, *Ulysses in Traction,* Circle Repertory Company, Circle Repertory Theatre, 1977-78.
Edward, *Stargazing,* Circle Repertory Company, Circle Repertory Theatre, 1978.
The Man, *Cabin 12,* Circle Repertory Company, Circle Repertory Theatre, 1978.
August, Escherich, Ferdinand, and inspector, *Lulu,* Circle Repertory Company, Circle Repertory Theatre, 1978.
Jake, *I'm Getting My Act Together and Taking It on the Road,* Circle in the Square, New York City, 1978.
The Soldier, *The Deserter,* Circle Repertory Theatre, 1979.
Laertes, *Hamlet,* Circle Repertory Theatre, 1979.
Mortimer, *Mary Stuart,* Circle Repertory Theatre, 1979.
(Broadway debut) Tony Crawford, *Hide and Seek,* Belasco Theatre, 1980.
Charles Malcolm, *Save Grand Central,* Phoenix Theatre, Marymount Manhattan Theatre, New York City, 1980.
Judge Wehrhahn, *The Beaver Coat,* Circle Repertory Company, Circle Repertory Theatre, 1981.
Little Louis, German soldier, Lucien, and dope pusher, *Piaf,* Plymouth Theatre, New York City, 1981.
Thomas Mowbray and Exton, *Richard II,* Circle Repertory Company, Entermedia Theatre, New York City, 1982.
Jed Kohler, *The Great Grandson of Jedediah Kohler,* Circle Repertory Company, Entermedia Theatre, 1982.
The Dining Room, Playwrights Horizons Theatre, then Astor Place Theatre, New York City, 1982-83.
Medvedenko, *The Seagull,* Circle Repertory Company, American Place Theatre, New York City, 1983.
Stephen Porter, *Domestic Issues,* Circle Repertory Company, Circle Repertory Theatre, 1983.
Berowne, *Love's Labor's Lost,* Circle Repertory Company, Circle Repertory Theatre, 1984.
Rodger Potter and Ramon, *Rum and Coke,* New York Shakespeare Company, Susan Stein Shiva Theatre, New York City, 1986.
Ken de la Maize, *The Musical Comedy Murders of 1940,* Circle Repertory Company, Circle Repertory Theatre, then Longacre Theatre, New York City, 1987.
Fuller, *El Salvador,* Circle Repertory Company, Circle Repertory Theatre, 1987.

FILM APPEARANCES

Peter, *Boardwalk,* Atlantic Releasing, 1979.
Scott, *Lisa* (also known as *Lisa's Mother*), Metro-Goldwyn-Mayer/United Artists, 1990.

TELEVISION APPEARANCES; MOVIES

Joel, *Classified Love,* CBS, 1986.
Blind Faith, NBC, 1990.

"Christine Cromwell: Only the Good Die Young," *ABC
    Saturday Night Mystery,* ABC, 1990.

TELEVISION APPEARANCES; EPISODIC

Harv, *Kate and Allie,* CBS, 1987.
Barry, *Murphy Brown,* CBS, 1989.
Joel Anderson, *Coach,* ABC, 1989.
Mr. Henderson, *Perfect Strangers,* ABC, 1990.

TELEVISION APPEARANCES; SPECIALS

Little Louis, *Piaf,* Entertainment Channel, 1982.*

B

BAGNERIS, Vernel 1949-

PERSONAL: Born July 31, 1949, in New Orleans, LA. *Education:* Graduated from Xavier University.

ADDRESSES: Agent—Barry Douglas, DGRW Agency, 1501 Broadway, New York, NY 10019.

CAREER: Actor, director, lyricist, and writer. Founder of New Experience Players, a multi-racial experimental theatre company. Directed workshops for Broadway musicals, including *Bojangles,* 1982, and *Rev. Jenkins,* 1988.

AWARDS, HONORS: Lawrence Olivier Award nomination, outstanding achievement in a musical, 1981, for *One Mo' Time;* Inducted into the Southwest Theatre Conference Hall of Fame, 1988.

CREDITS:

STAGE APPEARANCES

Papa Du, *One Mo' Time,* The Village Gate, New York City, 1979-81, Phoenix Theatre, London, 1981-82 (also see below).
Staggerlee, Second Avenue Theatre, New York City, 1987 (also see below).
Further Mo', The Village Gate, 1990 (also see below).

Also appeared in touring productions of *One Mo' Time;* in productions for New Experience Players; and in productions for regional theatres.

STAGE WORK; DIRECTOR

One Mo' Time, The Village Gate, New York City, 1979-82.
Staggerlee, Second Avenue Theatre, New York City, 1987.
Further Mo', The Village Gate, 1990.

Also directed productions for New Experience Players and for regional theatres.

FILM APPEARANCES

Jelly Roll Morton, *French Quarter,* Crown International, 1978.
Accordion man, *Pennies from Heaven,* Metro-Goldwyn-Mayer, 1981.
Preston, *Down by Law,* Island, 1986.

TELEVISION APPEARANCES; SPECIALS, EXCEPT WHERE NOTED

Papa Du, *One Mo' Time,* syndicated, 1986.
Joe Witherspoon, *The Gift of Amazing Grace,* ABC, 1986.
Jean Toomer, *The American Place,* PBS, 1991.
"A Marriage: Georgia O'Keefe and Alfred Stieglitz," *American Playhouse,* PBS, 1991.

Also appeared in *Friday Night Surprise,* NBC, and narrated the documentary *Purple Rose of Cairo,* PBS.

WRITINGS:

STAGE

One Mo' Time, produced in New York City at The Village Gate, October 22, 1979, produced in London at the Phoenix Theatre, 1981-82.
(And co-lyricist) *Staggerlee,* produced in New York City at Second Avenue Theatre, February 27, 1987.
Further Mo', produced in New York City at The Village Gate, 1990.

TELEVISION

(With others) *One Mo' Time,* syndicated, 1986.

BAILEY, Pearl 1918-1990

PERSONAL: Born Pearl May Bailey, March 29, 1918, in Newport News, VA; died after collapsing, August 17, 1990, in Philadelphia, PA; daughter of Joseph James (a minister) and Pearl Bailey; married John Randolph Pinkett, Jr., August 31, 1948 (divorced, March, 1952); married Louis Bellson, Jr. (a jazz drummer), November 19, 1952; children: (second marriage) Tony Bellson, DeeDee Bellson. *Education:* Georgetown University, B.A., 1985. *Avocational interests:* Cooking.

ADDRESSES: Agent—William Morris Agency, 1350 Avenue of the Americas, New York, NY 10019.

CAREER: Singer, stage performer, and author. Began as a singer at religious services led by her father, then in small clubs in Washington, DC, 1931; soon thereafter, became singer for vaudeville acts, then cabaret performer. Numerous concert appearances include shows at O'Keefe Center, Toronto, Canada, and Philharmonic Hall, Lincoln Center, New York City.

MEMBER: American Society of Composers, Authors, and Publishers, Screen Actors Guild, American Guild of Variety Artists, American Guild of Musical Artists, American Federation of Television and Radio Artists.

AWARDS, HONORS: Donaldson Award, 1946, for *St. Louis Woman;* Entertainer of the Year Award, *Cue* Magazine, 1967; Antoinette Perry Award, 1968, for *Hello, Dolly!;* March of Dimes Award, 1968; Woman of the Year Award, U.S.O., 1969; John V. Lindsay New York City Award; appointed by President Gerald R. Ford special advisor to the U.S. Mission of the United Nations General Assembly, 30th session, 1975; Coretta Scott King Book Award, American Library Association, 1976, for *Duey's Tale.*

CREDITS:

STAGE APPEARANCES

(Broadway debut) Butterfly, *St. Louis Woman,* Martin Beck Theatre, New York City, 1946.

Connecticut, *Arms and the Girl,* 46th Street Theatre, New York City, 1950.

Bless You All, Mark Hellinger Theatre, New York City, 1950.

Madame Fleur, *House of Flowers,* Alvin Theatre, New York City, 1954.

Sally Adams, *Call Me Madam,* Melodyland Theatre, Berkeley, CA, 1966.

Title role, *Hello, Dolly!,* St. James Theatre, New York City, 1967-69, later Minskoff Theatre, New York City, 1975.

Festival at Ford's, Circle in the Square at Ford's, Ford's Theatre, Washington, DC, 1970-71.

The Pearl Bailey Show, Starlight Theatre, Kansas City, MO, 1973.

Night of 100 Stars, Radio City Music Hall, New York City, 1982.

MAJOR TOURS

Title role, *Hello Dolly!,* U.S. cities, 1969-71 and U.S. and Canadian cities, 1975-76.

FILM APPEARANCES

Specialty, *Variety Girl,* Paramount, 1947.

Addie, *Isn't It Romantic,* Paramount, 1948.

Frankie, *Carmen Jones,* Twentieth Century-Fox, 1954.

Gussie, *That Certain Feeling,* Paramount, 1956.

Aunt Hagar, *St. Louis Blues,* Paramount, 1957.

Maria, *Porgy and Bess,* Columbia, 1959.

Ruby Jones, *All the Fine Young Cannibals,* Metro-Goldwyn-Mayer, 1960.

Marge, *The Landlord,* United Artists, 1970.

Beatrice Chambers, *Norman, Is That You?,* United Artists, 1976.

Voice of Big Mamma, *The Fox and the Hound,* Buena Vista, 1981.

Also appeared in *The Last Generation,* 1971.

TELEVISION APPEARANCES; SERIES

Host, *The Pearl Bailey Show,* ABC, 1971.

Mrs. Washington, *The Love Boat,* ABC, 1977.

Lulu Baker, *Silver Spoons,* NBC, 1982.

Life's Most Embarrassing Moments, syndicated, 1988.

Also appeared as guest on numerous shows, including *The Ed Wynn Show,* NBC, *The Nat "King" Cole Show,* NBC, *The Milton Berle Show,* NBC, *What's My Line?,* CBS, *The Perry Como Show,* NBC, *The Danny Kaye Show,* CBS, *The Johnny Carson Show,* NBC, *The Jack Paar Show,* NBC, and *The Mike Douglas Show,* CBS.

TELEVISION APPEARANCES; SPECIALS

The Big Party for Revlon (variety), CBS, 1959.

Carol Channing and Pearl Bailey on Broadway, ABC, 1966.

Something Special (variety), syndicated, 1966.

Mike and Pearl (variety), syndicated, 1968.

Johnny Mann's Stand Up and Cheer (variety), syndicated, 1971.

Bing Crosby and His Friends (variety), NBC, 1972, CBS, 1974.

One More Time (variety), CBS, 1974.

Bing! . . .A Fiftieth Anniversary Special (variety), CBS, 1977.

The 50th Presidential Inaugural Gala, ABC, 1985.

Martha Dermody, "Cindy Eller: A Modern Fairy Tale," *ABC Afterschool Special,* ABC, 1986.

Miss Ruby's Southern Holiday Dinner, PBS, 1988.
A Salute to Broadway: The Shows (also known as *In Performance at the White House*), PBS, 1988.
A Capital Fourth 1989 (concert), PBS, 1989.

Also appeared on Bob Hope specials, 1956, 1968, 1978, 1981, 1982.

OTHER TELEVISION APPEARANCES

As the World Turns (episodic), CBS, 1956.
Bernice, *Member of the Wedding* (movie), NBC, 1982.
Mother, *Peter Gunn* (movie), ABC, 1989.

RECORDINGS:

ALBUMS

Hello, Dolly!, RCA, 1968

WRITINGS:

TELEVISION

The Pearl Bailey Show, ABC, 1971.

BOOKS

The Raw Pearl (autobiography), Harcourt, 1968.
Talking to Myself (autobiography), Harcourt, 1971.
Pearl's Kitchen: An Extraordinary Cookbook, Harcourt, 1973.
Duey's Tale (juvenile), Harcourt, 1975.
Hurry Up, America, and Spit, Harcourt, 1976.
Between You and Me: A Heartfelt Memoir on Learning, Loving, and Living, Doubleday, 1989.

OBITUARIES AND OTHER SOURCES:

BOOKS

Bailey, Pearl, *The Raw Pearl,* Harcourt, 1968.
Bailey, *Talking to Myself,* Harcourt, 1971.
Bailey, *Between You and Me: A Heartfelt Memoir on Learning, Loving, and Living,* Doubleday, 1989.
Contemporary Authors, Volume 132, Gale, 1991.

PERIODICALS

Chicago Tribune, August 19, 1990.
Los Angeles Times, August 18, 1990.
New York Times, August 19, 1990.
Times (London), August 20, 1990.*

*   *   *

BALIN, Ina   1937-1990

PERSONAL: Born Ina Rosenberg, November 12, 1937, in Brooklyn, NY; died of complications from chronic lung disease, June 20, 1990, in New Haven, CT; children: Ba-

Nhi Mai, Kim Thuy, and Nguyet Baty (all adopted). *Education:* Attended New York University.

CAREER: Actress. Co-owner, Balin-Traube Art Gallery. Before acting, worked variously as a model, photographer, receptionist, and salesperson.

AWARDS, HONORS: Theatre World Award, 1959, for *A Majority of One;* Golden Globe Award, Most Promising Newcomer, 1961; Western Heritage Award from the National Cowboy Hall of Fame.

CREDITS:

FILM APPEARANCES

(Film debut) Mary Valente, *The Black Orchid,* Paramount, 1959.
Natalie, *From the Terrace,* Twentieth Century-Fox, 1960.
Pilar, *The Comancheros,* Twentieth Century-Fox, 1961.
Cathy Hunt, *The Young Doctors,* United Artists, 1961.
Ellen Betz, *The Patsy,* Paramount, 1964.
Martha of Bethany, *The Greatest Story Ever Told,* United Artists, 1965.
Mona Shannon, *Run Like a Thief* (also known as *Robo de diamantes*), Feature Film, 1968.
Tracy, *Charro,* National General, 1969.
The Girl, *The Projectionist,* Maron, 1970.
Nella, *The Don Is Dead* (also known as *Beautiful But Deadly*), 1973.
Julie Thomas, *The Come Back Trail,* Dynamite Entertainment/Rearguard, 1982.
Regine, *Vasectomy: A Delicate Matter,* Seymour Burde and Associates, 1986.

Also appeared as Sister Mary Enquirer, *That's Adequate,* 1989.

STAGE APPEARANCES

(Broadway debut) *Compulsion,* Ambassador Theatre, 1957.

Also appeared in *A Majority of One,* New York City, 1959, and *Face to Face,* an Off-Broadway production.

TELEVISION APPEARANCES; MOVIES

Karen Menardos, *The Lonely Profession,* NBC, 1969.
Otilla, *The Desperate Mission,* NBC, 1971.
Marla Hayes, *Call to Danger,* CBS, 1973.
Countess Hedy Maria Tovarese, *Panic on the 5:22,* ABC, 1974.
Marla Fears, *Danger in Paradise,* NBC, 1977.
Maria Cassala, *The Immigrants,* syndicated, 1978.
Herself, *The Children of An Lac,* CBS, 1980.
Jane, *Hostage Flight,* NBC, 1985.

OTHER TELEVISION APPEARANCES

The Dupont Show of the Week, NBC, 1961.

Martha LaFrita, *The Police Story* (pilot), NBC, 1973.
Marla Hayes, *Call to Danger* (pilot), CBS, 1973.

Also appeared as Marsha in *There Were Times, Dear,* 1987.

TELEVISION WORK

Story originator and executive producer, *The Children of An Lac* (movie), CBS, 1980.

OBITUARIES AND OTHER SOURCES:

PERIODICALS

New York Times, June 21, 1990.*

*   *   *

BANERJEE, Victor   1946-

PERSONAL: Born October 15, 1946, in Calcutta, India; married; wife's name, Maya; children: two daughters. *Education:* Received M.A. in comparative literature. *Avocational interests:* Tennis, swimming, hockey, soccer.

ADDRESSES: Agent—Scott Zimmerman, William Morris Agency, 151 El Camino Drive, Beverly Hills, CA 90212. *Publicist*—Rogers and Cowan Public Relations, 10000 Santa Monica Boulevard, Los Angeles, CA 90067.

CAREER: Actor. Founder and founding secretary of India's first Screen Extras Union.

AWARDS, HONORS: National Board of Review Award, Best Actor, National Association of Theatre Owners of Texas Award, International Star of the Year, and United Motion Picture Association Award, all 1985, for *A Passage to India;* National Critics Association Award, Best Actor, for *Pratidan;* National Debate Champion Award, India.

CREDITS:

FILM APPEARANCES

(Debut) Ali Naqi Khan—Prime Minister of Oudh, *Shatranj ke Khilari* (also known as *The Chess Players*), Connoisseur Films Ltd., 1977.
Georgie—Maharaja of Tasveer, *Hullabaloo Over Georgie and Bonnie's Pictures,* Contemporary Films Ltd./ New Yorker, 1979.
Dr. Aziz, *A Passage to India,* Columbia, 1984.
Nikhilesh Choudhury, *Ghare Baire* (also known as *The Home and the World*), European Classics, 1984.
Ram Das, *Foreign Body,* Orion, 1986.
Hard to Be a God (also known as *Es Ist Night Leicht Ein Gott Zu Zein* and *E'Difficile essere un dio es*), Union Generale Cinematographique/Jugendfilm Verleigh/ Titanus Distribuzione/Films du Volcan, 1989.

Also appeared in *Arohan* (also known as *The Ascent*), 1982, and in *Madhurban, Tanaya, Pratidan, Prarthana, Dui Prithri, Kalyug,* and *Jaipur Junction.*

STAGE APPEARANCES

Made stage debut in *Pirates of Penzance.* Also appeared in productions of *Desert Song* and *Godspell.*

STAGE WORK

Directed *An August Requiem,* 1981.

TELEVISION APPEARANCES

Karpal Singh, *Dadah Is Death* (movie), CBS, 1988.
"Subway Safari," *Travels* (documentary special), PBS, 1989.*

*   *   *

BARBER, Frances   1957-

PERSONAL: Born in 1957 in Wolverhampton, England. *Education:* Attended University of Wales, University College of North Wales, Bangor; graduate studies in theatre at University of Wales, University College, Cardiff.

ADDRESSES: Agent—James Sharkey Associates Ltd., Third Floor, 15 Golden Sq., London W1R 3AG, England.

CAREER: Actress. Member of the improvisational Hull Truck Theatre Company; member, Glasgow Citzens Theatre and Tricycle Theatre, Killburn.

CREDITS:

STAGE APPEARANCES

Woman, angel of despair, first love, treachery, *The Mission,* Soho Poly Theatre, London, 1982.
Viv, *Hard Feelings,* Oxford Playhouse Company, Bush Theatre, London, 1983.
Penny, *Turning Over,* Bush Theatre, 1983.
Marguerite Gautier, *Camille,* Royal Shakespeare Company (RSC), Comedy Theatre, London, 1985.
Hamlet, RSC, Barbican Theatre, London, 1985.
Dolores, *The Dead Monkey,* RSC, The Pit, London, 1986.
Miss Alma, *Summer and Smoke,* Haymarket Theatre, Leicester, England, 1987.
Viola, *Twelfth Night,* Renaissance Theatre Company, Riverside Studio Theatre, London, 1987-88.

FILM APPEARANCES

Mission girl, *The Missionary,* Columbia, 1982.
Jill, *Acceptable Levels,* Famous Players, 1983.
Woman, *Those Glory Glory Days,* Cinecom, 1983.
Venus de Milo, *A Zed and Two Noughts,* Skouras, 1985.
Sister Saint Winifred, *Castaway,* Cannon, 1986.

Leonie Orton, *Prick up Your Ears,* Samuel Goldwyn, 1987.

Rosie Hobbs, *Sammy and Rosie Get Laid,* Cinecom, 1987.

Megan, *We Think the World of You,* Cinecom, 1988.

Gert, *Chambre a part* (also known as *Separate Bedrooms*), Union Generale Cinematographic, 1989.

Duck, Film Four, 1989.

Also appeared as Ann, *Young Soul Rebels,* 1991. Appeared in *The Grasscutter.*

TELEVISION APPEARANCES; MINI-SERIES

Helga Bauer, *The Nightmare Years,* TNT, 1989.

Behaving Badly, Channel 4, 1989.

Also appeared in *Clem; Jackie's Story; Home Sweet Home; Flame to the Phoenix; Reilly, Ace of Spies;* and *Hard Feelings.*

RECORDINGS:

VIDEOS

White City, Vestron, 1985.*

*　　*　　*

BARNES, Priscilla   1955-

PERSONAL: Born December 7, 1955, in Fort Dix, NJ.

CAREER: Actress. Performer with the dance troupe "The Vivacious Vixens." Teenage beauty contest winner.

CREDITS:

FILM APPEARANCES

Beyond Reason, Allwyn, 1977.

The Seniors, Cinema Shares, 1978.

Texas Detour, Hikmet Aredis, 1978.

Karen, *Delta Fox,* Sebastian International, 1979.

Helena Dryden, *The Last Married Couple in America,* Universal, 1980.

Donna, *Sunday Lovers,* United Artists, 1980.

Mayor Alexandria Gray, *Traxx,* De Laurentiis Entertainment Group, 1988.

Claire, *Lords of the Deep,* Concorde, 1989.

Della Churchill, *License to Kill,* Metro-Goldwyn-Mayer/ United Artists, 1989.

TELEVISION APPEARANCES; MOVIES

Weena, *The Time Machine,* NBC, 1978.

Denise, *A Vacation in Hell,* NBC, 1979.

Maggie McCulloch, *The Wild Women of Chastity Gulch,* ABC, 1982.

Amy, *Perfect People,* ABC, 1988.

TELEVISION APPEARANCES; EPISODIC

Vicky Gallegos, *Murder, She Wrote,* CBS, 1985.

Maryanne Thompson, *Blacke's Magic,* NBC, 1986.

Donna Shepard, *Hotel,* ABC, 1987.

Tawny and Mary, *Highway to Heaven,* NBC, 1989.

OTHER TELEVISION APPEARANCES

Rebecca Tomkins, *The American Girls* (series), CBS, 1978.

Melanie Adams, *Scruples* (pilot), ABC, 1981.

Terri Alden, *Three's Company* (series), ABC, 1981-84.

Host, *The Funniest Joke I Ever Heard* (special), ABC, 1984.

STAGE APPEARANCES

Appeared in *Bus Stop,* Flint, MI, 1985.*

*　　*　　*

BARRY, Ray
See BARRY, Raymond J.

*　　*　　*

BARRY, Raymond
See BARRY, Raymond J.

*　　*　　*

BARRY, Raymond J.   1939-
(Raymond Barry, Ray Barry)

PERSONAL: Born March 14, 1939, in Hempstead, NY; son of Raymond (in sales) and Barbara (an actress; maiden name, Duffy) Barry; married Robyn Mundell (an actress); children: Oona. *Education:* Attended Yale University, School of Drama; Brown University, B.A.; studied acting with William Hickey and Kenneth MacMillan. *Religion:* Catholic.

ADDRESSES: Agent—Progressive Artists Agency, 400 South Beverly Dr., Suite 216, Beverly Hills, CA 90212.

CAREER: Actor, director, and writer. Actor with various theatrical companies, including Living Theatre, 1964, Joseph Chaikin's Open Theatre, 1967-73, Joseph Papp's Public Theatre, 1970-1982, Richard Forman's Ontological-Hysterical Theatre, 1980-82, Performance Garage, 1983. Director, Quena Company, 1973-83 and Street Theatre, 1975-80. Also director of Puerto Rican Writer's Workshop, 1974-76, and workshops at Grasslands and Sing Sing penitentiaries.

AWARDS, HONORS: Dramalogue Award, 1986, for performance in *Buried Child,* and 1989, for writing and ensemble performance, for *Once in Doubt;* Los Angeles Drama Critics Circle Award, 1990, for *Once in Doubt.*

CREDITS:

STAGE APPEARANCES

Prisoner #2, *The Brig,* Living Theatre, New York City, 1962.

(Off-Broadway debut) *Man is Man,* Masque Theatre, New York City, 1963.

The Amerind, *The Last Days of British Honduras,* New York Shakespeare Festival (NYSF), Public Theatre, New York City, 1974.

(Broadway debut) Gitaucho, *The Leaf People,* Booth Theatre, New York City, 1975.

Rory, *Fishing,* NYSF, Public Theatre, 1975.

Masked man, dope king, King of Providence, bank teller *Landscape of the Body,* NYSF, Public Theatre, 1977.

Johnny "Baby Face" Flint, *Happy End,* Martin Beck Theatre, New York City, 1978.

Slater, *Curse of the Starving Class,* NYSF, Public Theatre, 1978.

Sheriff, *Zoot Suit,* Martin Beck Theatre, 1979.

Volker, *Hunting Scenes From Lower Bavaria,* Manhattan Theatre Club, New York City, 1981.

Dangerous man, *Penguin Touquet,* NYSF, Public Theatre, 1981.

Messenger, *Antigone,* NYSF, Public Theatre, 1982.

Strong man #1, *Egyptology,* NYSF, Public Theatre, 1983.

(And author) *Once in Doubt,* La Mama Experimental Theatre Company, New York City, 1983.

Buried Child, South Coast Repertory Theatre, Costa Mesa, CA, 1986.

Once in Doubt, People's Light and Theatre Company, Philadelphia, 1989.

Once in Doubt, Cast Theatre, Los Angeles, 1989.

Also appeared as Woyzek, Buchner, grandmother, drum major, and Marlon Brando in *A Movie Star Has to Star in Black or White,* NYSF, 1975; *Hot Lunch Apostles,* La Mama Experimental Theatre Company; transvestite agent, *Tourists and Refugees,* La Mama Experimental Theatre Company, Winter Project; Mike, *Soft Targets,* La Mama Experimental Theatre Company; clown, *Night–walk;* man who hits himself, *Mutation Show;* executed man, *Terminal;* Cain, *The Serpent,* all Open Theatre, New York City.

MAJOR TOURS

Appeared with the Open Theatre in U.S., Canadian, European, and Far Eastern cities.

FILM APPEARANCES; UNDER NAME RAYMOND J. BARRY

Edward Thoreau, *An Unmarried Woman,* Twentieth Century-Fox, 1978.

Hurley, *Out of Bounds,* Columbia, 1986.

Senator Kitteridge, *Three for the Road,* New Century-Vista, 1987.

Daddy, *Daddy's Boys,* Concorde, 1988.

Fred Gaffney, *Cop,* Atlantic, 1988.

Mr. Kovic, *Born on the Fourth of July,* Universal, 1989.

FILM APPEARANCES; UNDER NAME RAYMOND BARRY

Mr. Hatcher, Chloe's father, *Playing for Keeps,* Universal, 1986.

Louis Bukowski, *Year of the Dragon,* Metro-Goldwyn-Mayer (MGM), 1985.

FILM APPEARANCES; UNDER NAME RAY BARRY

Shakespearean actor, *The GoodBye Girl,* MGM, 1978.

Herbert Fisk, conceptual artist, *Between the Lines,* Midwest Film, 1977.

OTHER FILM APPEARANCES

Nothing But Trouble, Warner Brothers, 1990.

K2, Majestic, 1990.

TELEVISION APPEARANCES; SERIES

Captain Ted Ronson, *Scarecrow and Mrs. King,* 1985.

Lieutenant Marco Zaga, *The Oldest Rookie,* CBS, 1987-88.

Also appeared as Jenks in *As The World Turns;* Sonny Lundstrom in *One Life to Live;* Stavros in *The Hamptons;* Sergeant Spinoli in *All My Children;* Sutar in *Texas;* and a gangster in *The Doctors.*

TELEVISION APPEARANCES; MOVIES

Tony, *Daddy, I Don't Like It Like This* (also known as *Daddy, I Don't Like It This Way Anymore*), CBS, 1978.

Sid, *The Face of Rage,* ABC, 1983.

Gerald McMurty, *Slow Burn,* Showtime, 1986.

Also appeared as Jack Lawn in *Drug Wars: The Camarena Story,* 1990.

TELEVISION APPEARANCES; SPECIALS

Appeared in *Cat in the Ghetto,* 1981; and *Works of the Open Theatre.*

*   *   *

BARTON, Peter

PERSONAL: Born July 19 in Valley Stream, NY.

CAREER: Actor.

CREDITS:

TELEVISION APPEARANCES; SERIES

Bill Miller, *Shirley,* NBC, 1979.
Matthew Star/Ehawk, *The Powers of Matthew Star,* NBC, 1982.
Scott Grainger, *The Young and the Restless,* CBS, 1988—.

TELEVISION APPEARANCES; EPISODIC

Simon Gordon, *The Fall Guy,* ABC, 1985.

Also appeared as Brady Laeden on *Rags to Riches,* 1987.

OTHER TELEVISION APPEARANCES

Ace, *Three Eyes* (pilot), NBC, 1982.
Murph, *Leadfoot* (special), syndicated, 1982.
Steve Kingsley, *The First Time* (movie), ABC, 1982.
NBC team member, *Battle of the Network Stars* (special), ABC, 1983.

FILM APPEARANCES

Jeff, *Hell Night,* Compass International, 1981.
Doug, *Friday the Thirteenth—The Final Chapter,* Paramount, 1984.

*   *   *

BATES, Ralph   1940-

PERSONAL: Born in 1940 in Bristol, England; father, a brain surgeon and psychiatrist; mother, a psychiatrist; married Joanna Van Gyseghem (an actress); married Virginia Wetherell (an actress). *Education:* Received an arts degree from Trinity College, Dublin, Ireland; studied drama at the Yale University School of Drama.

ADDRESSES: Contact—St. James Management, 22 Groom Place, London SW1X 7BA, England.

CAREER: Actor. Performed at Colchester and with the Citizen's Theatre, Glasgow, Scotland, UK.

CREDITS:

STAGE APPEARANCES

Ensemble, *Would Anyone Who Saw the Accident . . . ?* (revue), Theatre Royal, Stratford-on-Avon, England, 1962.
Harry and Simon Blake, *Mary Rose,* 69 Theatre Company, London, 1972.
Malcolm, *Instant Enlightenment Including Vat,* New Half Moon Theatre, London, 1981.
Jurgen Tesman, *Hedda Gabler,* Cambridge Theatre, London, 1982.

FILM APPEARANCES

(Film debut) Lord Courtley, *Taste the Blood of Dracula,* Hammer/Warner Brothers, 1970.
Victor Frankenstein, *The Horror of Frankenstein,* Hammer/EMI/American Continental, 1970.
Dr. Jekyll, *Dr. Jekyll and Sister Hyde,* Hammer/American International, 1971.
Giles Barton, *Lust for a Vampire* (also known as *To Love a Vampire*), Hammer/EMI/Levitt-Pickman, 1971.
Robert Heller, *Fear in the Night,* Hammer/International, 1972.
David Masters, *Persecution* (also known as *The Terror of Sheba* and *Sheba*), Fanfare, 1974.
Gino, *The Devil within Her* (also known as *I Don't Want to Be Born*), Hammer/American International, 1976.
Bernard, *Letters to an Unknown Lover* (also known as *Les Louves*), Channel 4, 1985.

TELEVISION APPEARANCES; MINI-SERIES

Caligula, *The Caesars,* Granada, 1968.
Thomas Culpepper, *The Six Wives of Henry VIII,* BBC, 1970, then CBS, 1971, later *Masterpiece Theatre,* PBS, 1972.
George Warleggan, *Poldark,* BBC, then *Masterpiece Theatre,* PBS, 1977.
George Warleggan, *Poldark II,* BBC, then *Masterpiece Theatre,* PBS, 1978.

OTHER TELEVISION APPEARANCES

Mike Spencer, *Murder Motel* (special), ATV, then ABC, 1975.
Laurance Castallack, *Penmarric* (series), Entertainment Channel, 1982.

Also appeared in the series *Broad and Narrow,* 1965; *Rain on the Leaves,* 1968; title role, *Dear John,* 1986. Appeared in the specials *Wicked Women, The Secret Army,* as Sanders in *Dangerous Knowledge,* and as Lebrun in *Moonbase 3.**

*   *   *

BAXTER, Meredith   1947-
(Meredith Baxter-Birney)

PERSONAL: Born June 21, 1947, in Los Angeles, CA; daughter of Tom (a radio announcer) and Whitney (an actress; professional name, Whitney Blake) Baxter; divorced; married second husband, David Birney (an actor), April 10, 1974 (divorced, 1989); children: (first marriage) Ted, Eva; (second marriage) Kate, Peter and Mollie (twins). *Education:* Studied acting at the Interlochen Arts Academy.

ADDRESSES: Agent—Triad Artists Inc., 10100 Santa Monica Blvd., 16th Floor, Los Angeles, CA 90067. *Publicist*—Jody Frisch, Jody Frisch Public Relations, 11693 Santa Monica Blvd., Suite 210, Los Angeles, CA 90049.

CAREER: Actress and producer.

MEMBER: American Diabetes Association (co-chairperson).

CREDITS:

STAGE APPEARANCES

Appeared as Eve, *The Diaries of Adam and Eve*, Los Angeles, 1988; Sally Talley, *Talley's Folly*; Joanne, *Vanities*; Melissa, *Love Letters*; appeared in productions of *Guys and Dolls, Butterflies Are Free*, and *The Country Wife*.

FILM APPEARANCES

Eve Garrison, *Ben*, Cinerama, 1972.
Tracy, *Stand Up and Be Counted*, Columbia, 1972.
Debbie Sloan, *All the President's Men*, Warner Bros., 1976.
(As Meredith Baxter-Birney) Patricia, *Bittersweet Love*, AVCO-Embassy, 1976.
(As Baxter-Birney) Amanda Faberson, *Jezebel's Kiss*, Shapiro Glickenhaus, 1990.

TELEVISION APPEARANCES; SERIES

The Interns, CBS, 1971.
The Young Lawyers, ABC, 1971.
Bridget Fitzgerald Steinberg, *Bridget Loves Bernie*, CBS, 1972-73.
(As Baxter-Birney) Nancy Lawrence Maitland, *Family*, ABC, 1976-80.
(As Baxter-Birney) Elyse Keaton, *Family Ties*, NBC, 1982-89.

Also appeared in *The Streets of San Francisco*, ABC; *Police Woman*, NBC; *Medical Story*, NBC; *McMillan and Wife*, NBC; *City of Angels*, NBC; *What Really Happened to the Class of '65?*, NBC.

TELEVISION APPEARANCES; MINI-SERIES

(As Baxter-Birney) Meg March, *Little Women*, NBC, 1978.

TELEVISION APPEARANCES; MOVIES

Rena Carter, *The Cat Creature*, ABC, 1973.
Joanne Denver, *The Stranger Who Looks Like Me*, ABC, 1974.
Linda Flayly, *Target Risk*, NBC, 1975.
Linda Davis, *The Night That Panicked America*, ABC, 1975.
Julie Watson, *The Imposter*, NBC, 1975.

(As Baxter-Birney) Mercedes Cole, *The Family Man*, CBS, 1979.
(As Baxter-Birney) Lauretta Pennington, *Beulah Land*, NBC, 1980.
(As Baxter-Birney) Title role, *The Two Lives of Carol Letner*, CBS, 1981.
(As Baxter-Birney) Carol Marriner, *Take Your Best Shot*, CBS, 1982.
(As Baxter-Birney) Barbara McKee, *The Rape of Richard Beck*, ABC, 1985.
(As Baxter-Birney) Elyse Keaton, *Family Ties Vacation*, NBC, 1985.
(As Baxter-Birney) Kate Stark, *Kate's Secret*, NBC, 1986.
(As Baxter-Birney) Maura Wells, *The Long Journey Home*, CBS, 1987.
(As Baxter-Birney) Title role, *Winnie*, NBC, 1988.
(As Baxter-Birney) Samantha White, *She Knows Too Much*, NBC, 1989.
Florence Tulane, *The Kissing Place*, USA, 1990.
Lynn Hollinger, *Burning Bridges*, ABC, 1990.
Red Tierney, *A Bump in the Night*, CBS, 1991.
Lilah Comminger, *A Mother's Justice*, NBC, 1991.

TELEVISION APPEARANCES; SPECIALS

(As Baxter-Birney) Joanne, *Vanities*, HBO, 1981.
(As Baxter-Birney) *Battle of the Network Stars*, ABC, 1983.
(As Baxter-Birney) *Night of 100 Stars II*, ABC, 1985.
(As Baxter-Birney) *Missing . . . Have You Seen This Person?*, NBC, 1985.
(As Baxter-Birney) *Inside "Family Ties": Behind the Scenes of a Hit*, PBS, 1988.
(As Baxter-Birney) *The Valvoline National Driving Test*, CBS, 1989.
Heart Attack: The Silent Killer, syndicated, 1991.

Also host, *Diabetes Update '86*, 1986.

TELEVISION WORK

Executive producer (with David Birney), *The Long Journey Home*, CBS, 1987.
Production executive, *The Diaries of Adam and Eve*, PBS, 1989.

*   *   *

BAXTER-BIRNEY, Meredith
   See BAXTER, Meredith

*   *   *

BECK, John   1943(?)-

PERSONAL: Born January 28, 1943 (some sources say 1944 or 1946), in Chicago, IL.

ADDRESSES: Agent—Artists Alliance Agency, Inc., 8457 Melrose Place Suite 200, Los Angeles, CA 90069.

CAREER: Actor.

CREDITS:

TELEVISION APPEARANCES; MOVIES

John Cole, *The Silent Gun,* ABC, 1969.
Gene Carey, *The Law,* NBC, 1974.
George Greg, *Attack on Terror: The F.B.I. Versus the Ku Klux Klan,* CBS, 1975.
John Thornton, *The Call of the Wild,* NBC, 1976.
Neil Perry, *The Time Machine,* NBC, 1978.
Buzz Gregory, *Gridlock* (also known as *The Great American Traffic Jam*), NBC, 1980.
Dorian Blake, *Peyton Place: The Next Generation,* NBC, 1985.
Doug Vickers, *Perry Mason: The Case of the Lady in the Lake,* NBC, 1988.
Captain Conners, *Fire and Rain,* USA, 1989.

Also appeared in *Greatest Heroes of the Bible, Time Express, Mind Over Murder,* and *Partners in Crime.*

TELEVISION APPEARANCES; PILOTS

Micah, *Lock, Stock, and Barrel,* NBC, 1971.
Luke, *Sidekicks,* CBS, 1974.
Colonel Frank "Buckshot" O'Conner, *The Buffalo Soldiers,* NBC, 1979.
Sam Curtis, *Flamingo Road,* NBC, 1980.

TELEVISION APPEARANCES; SERIES

Ketcham, *Nichols,* NBC, 1971-72.
Sam Curtis, *Flamingo Road,* NBC, 1981-82.
Mark Graison, *Dallas,* CBS, 1983-86.

TELEVISION APPEARANCES; EPISODIC

Brad Bingham, *Matlock,* NBC, 1986.
Carter Welles, *Hotel,* ABC, 1986.
Neil Jordan, *Hunter,* NBC, 1986.
Durant, *Magnum P.I.,* CBS, 1987.
Matthew Grady, *Paradise,* CBS, 1989.
Michael Hayworth, *Hunter,* NBC, 1990.
Hill, *Midnight Caller,* NBC, 1990.

Also appeared in *Bonanza,* NBC; *Mannix,* CBS; *Hawaii Five-O,* CBS; *Love American Style,* ABC; *Gunsmoke,* CBS; *Lancer,* CBS; *What Really Happened to the Class of '65?,* NBC.

OTHER TELEVISION APPEARANCES

Peter Flodehale, *Arthur Hailey's Wheels* (mini-series), NBC, 1978.
Battle of the Network Stars (special), ABC, 1980.
Battle of the Network Stars (special), ABC, 1983.

Also appeared as Dan Gatlin, *Crazy Dan,* 1986.

FILM APPEARANCES

CyBorg 2087, Features, 1966.
Jake, *Three in the Attic,* American International, 1968.
Jason Bronson, *Lawman,* United Artists, 1971.
Sergeant Lulash, *Mrs. Pollifax—Spy,* United Artists, 1971.
Pov, *Paperback Hero,* Rumson, 1973.
Poe, *Pat Garrett and Billy the Kid,* Metro-Goldwyn-Mayer (MGM), 1973.
Erno Windt, *Sleeper,* United Artists, 1973.
Lee, *Nightmare Honeymoon,* MGM, 1973.
Reverend Philip Norman, *Only God Knows,* Canart/Queensbury, 1974.
Moonpie, *Rollerball,* United Artists, 1975.
Shoulders O'Brien, *The Big Bus,* Paramount, 1976.
Ben Miller, *Sky Riders,* Twentieth Century-Fox, 1976.
Bill Templeton, *Audrey Rose,* United Artists, 1977.
Larry Douglas, *The Other Side of Midnight,* Twentieth Century-Fox, 1977.
Alex Burton, *Deadly Illusion,* Cinetel, 1987.

Also appeared in *From Father to Son.*

STAGE APPEARANCES

The Collected Works of Billy the Kid, Center Theatre Group, Mark Taper Forum, Los Angeles, 1973.

Also has performed in regional theatres.*

*   *   *

BECK, Kimberly   1956-

PERSONAL: Born January 9, 1956, in Glendale, California.

ADDRESSES: Agent—c/o Stone Manners Talent Agency, 9113 Sunset Blvd., Los Angeles, CA 90069.

CAREER: Actress.

CREDITS:

FILM APPEARANCES

Torpedo Run, Metro-Goldwyn-Mayer, 1958.
Janette, *Yours, Mine, and Ours,* United Artists, 1968.
Teresa, *Massacre at Central High,* Brian-Newline, 1976.
Lana, *Roller Boogie,* United Artists, 1979.
Trish, *Friday the Thirteenth—The Final Chapter,* Paramount, 1984.
Kim, *Maid to Order,* Vista, 1987.
Piety Beecham, *Messenger of Death,* Cannon, 1988.
Sally, *The Big Blue* (also known as *Le Grand Bleu*), Columbia, 1988.

Also appeared as Cheri Griffiths in *Nightmare at Noon,* 1988; and as Kim in *Private War,* 1989.

TELEVISION APPEARANCES; SERIES

Kim Schuster, *Peyton Place,* ABC, 1964.
Terry, *Lucas Tanner,* NBC, 1974.
Robin Andrews, *The Westwind,* NBC, 1975.
Nancy Bedford, *Eight Is Enough,* ABC, 1977.
Claire Prentice, *Dynasty,* ABC, 1986-87.

Also appeared as Julie Clegg on *Capitol,* CBS.

TELEVISION APPEARANCES; MOVIES

Bonnie Buehler, *Murder in Peyton Place,* NBC, 1977.
Cathy, *Zuma Beach,* NBC, 1978.
Sally Raynor, *Deadly Intentions,* ABC, 1985.

TELEVISION APPEARANCES; EPISODIC

Cindy, *Fantasy Island,* ABC, 1977.
Stella Moran, *Crazy Like a Fox,* CBS, 1986.
Lisa Burnett, *The New Mike Hammer,* CBS, 1986.
Phoebe Cabot, *The Law and Harry McGraw,* CBS, 1987.
Nancy Tritchler, *L.A. Law,* NBC, 1987.

OTHER TELEVISION APPEARANCES

Diane Porter, *Rich Man, Poor Man Book II* (mini-series), ABC, 1976.
Stephanie Harris, *Starting Fresh* (pilot), NBC, 1979.
Nurse Connie Primble, *Scalpels* (pilot), NBC, 1980.*

* * *

BECKEL, Graham

ADDRESSES: Agent—The Gersh Agency, 222 N. Canon Dr., Beverly Hills, CA 90210.

CAREER: Actor.

CREDITS:

STAGE APPEARANCES

Aide to the king, *Hamlet,* New York Shakespeare Festival (NYSF), Delacorte Theatre, New York City, 1975.
Ah, Wilderness!, Stage West Theatre, West Springfield, MA, 1975.
Time Trial, NYSF, Public Theatre, 1975.
Slick Jessup, *The Elusive Angel,* New Dramatists, Inc., New York City, 1976.
Skip Hampton, "Lu Ann Hampton Laverty Oberlander," and Skip Hampton, "The Last Meeting of the Knights of the White Magnolia," *A Texas Trilogy,* John F. Kennedy Center for the Performing Arts, Washington, DC, 1976, then Broadhurst Theatre, New York City, 1976.
Rain, Hartford Stage Company, Hartford, CT, 1977.

Slick Jessup, *The Elusive Angel,* Marymount Manhattan Theatre, New York City, 1977.
Garrison, *Fathers and Sons,* NYSF, Public Theatre, 1978.
Dancin' to Calliope, New Dramatists, Inc., 1978.
Amazing Grace, New Dramatists, Inc., 1978.
Macbeth, Long Wharf Theatre, New Haven, CT, 1978.
Harold, *Father's Day,* American Place Theatre, New York City, 1979.
Larry, "Stops Along the Way," and number five, "In Fireworks Lie Secret Codes," *The One Act Play Festival,* Lincoln Center Theatre Company, Mitzi E. Newhouse Theatre, New York City, 1981.
The Woods, Center Stage Theatre, Baltimore, MD, 1981.
Savages, Center Stage Theatre, 1982.
Last Looks, Center Stage Theatre, 1982.
Sammy, *Flirtations,* T.O.M.I. Terrace Theatre, New York City, 1983.
Ed, *The Vampires,* Astor Place Theatre, New York City, 1984.
Boo, *The Marriage of Bette and Boo,* NYSF, Public Theatre, 1985.
Dad, *the dreamer examines his pillow,* Forty-seventh Street Theatre, New York City, 1986.
Alfred Chamberlain, *Little Murders,* Second Stage Theatre, New York City, 1986.

FILM APPEARANCES

Eric, *Happy as the Grass Was Green* (also known as *Hazel's People*), Martin, 1973.
Ford, *The Paper Chase,* Twentieth Century-Fox, 1973.
Roland, *The Money,* Calliope, 1975.
Val, *C.H.U.D.,* New World, 1984.
Charlie Benson, *Marie,* Metro-Goldwyn-Mayer (MGM)/United Artists, 1985.
Richard Doolan, *Lost Angels,* Orion, 1989.
Sklaroff, *True Believer* (also known as *Coupable Ressemblance* and *Verdetto Finale*), Columbia, 1989.
Les, *Welcome Home, Roxy Carmichael,* Paramount, 1990.
Ricker, *Liebestraum,* MGM-Pathe, 1991.

TELEVISION APPEARANCES; MOVIES

Dan, *Class of '63,* ABC, 1973.
Detective Clever, *Seventh Avenue,* NBC, 1977.
Rich, *The Face of Rage,* ABC, 1983.
Vic Graham, *The Execution of Raymond Graham,* ABC, 1985.
Billy, *Rising Son,* TNT, 1990.
Jerry Whitworth, *Family of Spies* (also known as *Family of Spies: The Walker Spy Ring*), CBS, 1990.

TELEVISION APPEARANCES; EPISODIC

Kojak, CBS, 1976.
Jimmy, *Love, Sidney,* NBC, 1982.
Marty Cates, *Miami Vice,* NBC, 1986.

BECKETT *CONTEMPORARY THEATRE, FILM, AND TELEVISION* • Volume 9

Bill Davis, *Crime Story,* NBC, 1987.
George Hershey, *The Equalizer,* CBS, 1987.
Richard Cooper, *Moonlighting,* ABC, 1988.
Sully, *Spenser: For Hire,* ABC, 1988.
Kosar, *L.A. Law,* NBC, 1988.

TELEVISION APPEARANCES; MINI-SERIES

Clayton Cullen, *Amerika* (also known as *Topeka, Kansas . . . U.S.S.R.*), ABC, 1987.
Josiah Tulley, *Separate but Equal,* ABC, 1991.

OTHER SOURCES:

PERIODICALS

Hollywood Reporter, April 5, 1991.

* * *

BECKETT, Samuel 1906-1989

OBITUARY NOTICE—See index for *CTFT* sketch: Full name, Samuel Barclay Beckett; born April 13, 1906, in Foxrock, Dublin, Ireland; died of respiratory failure, December 22, 1989, in Paris, France. Educator, playwright, poet, novelist, and short story writer. Beckett was a pivotal figure in the development of modern drama. An assistant to and friend of Irish expatriate writer James Joyce during the 1930s, he served brief stints as a language instructor in both France and Dublin and then traveled widely before settling permanently in Paris in 1937. There, Beckett became an active fighter in the French Resistance during World War II. After the war, he devoted most of his time to literary endeavors, experiencing his most prolific and acclaimed phase of creativity during the 1950s. The author's dark and ponderous works, published in both French and English, explore the bleaker aspects of human existence. Largely remembered as the inspiration for absurdist theater, Beckett is probably best known for his classic 1952 drama *Waiting for Godot,* about two tramps who wait in vain for the arrival of a savior, and for his introspective, experimental trilogy of novels *Molloy, Malone Dies,* and *The Unnameable.* Other works by the pioneering dramatist include *Happy Days* and *Krapp's Last Tape.* Beckett earned the 1969 Nobel Prize for literature for his body of revolutionary plays, verses, novels, and short stories.

OBITUARIES AND OTHER SOURCES:

BOOKS

Bair, Deirdre, *Samuel Beckett: A Biography,* Harcourt, 1978.
Dictionary of Literary Biography, Gale, Volume 13: *British Dramatists since World War II, Second Series,* 1982, Volume 15: *British Novelists, 1930-1959,* 1983.

PERIODICALS

Chicago Tribune, December 27, 1989.
Los Angeles Times, December 27, 1989.
New York Times, December 27, 1989.

* * *

BELL, Tom 1932(?)-

PERSONAL: Born in 1932 (some sources say 1933) in Liverpool, England.

ADDRESSES: Contact—International Creative Management, 388-396 Oxford St., London W1, England.

CAREER: Actor.

CREDITS:

FILM APPEARANCES

Ben, *Echo of Barbara,* RFD Productions, 1961.
Paul, *The Kitchen,* Kingsley International, 1961.
Evans, *Damn the Defiant* (also known as *H.M.S. Defiant*), Columbia, 1962.
Toby, *The L-Shaped Room,* Davis-Royal-Columbia, 1962.
Blackie, *Payroll* (also known as *I Promised to Pay*), Allied Artists, 1962.
Fenner, *A Prize of Arms,* Black Lion, 1962.
Dan, *Rebels against the Light* (also known as *Sands of Beersheba*), David, 1964.
Steve Collins, *Blues for Lovers* (also known as *Ballad in Blue*), Twentieth Century-Fox, 1966.
Peter Rayston, *He Who Rides a Tiger,* Sigma III, 1966.
Captain Ian Peyton-Reid, *In Enemy Country,* Universal, 1968.
Tom, *The Long Day's Dying,* Paramount, 1968.
Shaftoe, *Lock Up Your Daughters,* Columbia, 1969.
Sean Rogan, *The Violent Enemy,* Monarch, 1969.
Colin, *Quest for Love,* Rank, 1971.
Len, *All the Right Noises,* Fox, 1973.
Jimmy Lindsay, *Straight On Till Morning,* International Co-Productions, 1974.
De Gautet, *Royal Flash,* Twentieth Century-Fox, 1975.
William Targett, *The Sailor's Return,* Osprey, 1978.
Alan, *Stronger Than the Sun,* BBC, 1980.
Mr. Dobson, *The Innocent,* TVS-Curzon, 1985.
Eric, *Wish You Were Here,* Atlantic, 1987.
Mr. Deakin, *Resurrected,* Hobo, 1989.
Jack "The Hat" McVitie, *The Krays,* Miramax, 1990.

Also appeared as Uncle Philip in *The Magic Toy Shop,* 1989.

TELEVISION APPEARANCES

Adolph Eichman, *Holocaust* (mini-series), NBC, 1978.

30

Made television debut in *Promenade.* Also appeared in the series *Sons and Lovers,* PBS, 1983; appeared in *Reilly: Ace of Spies,* 1984, *The Rainbow,* 1989, as Tulayev in *Red King, White Knight,* 1989, and in *No Trams to Lime Street, Love on the Dole, A Night Out, Cul de Sac, The Seekers, Long Distance Blue,* and *The Virginian.**

* * *

BEN-ARI, Neal 1952-

PERSONAL: Born Neal Klein, March 20, 1952, in Brooklyn, NY; son of Louis (a postal employee) and Rhea (a bookkeeper; maiden name, Hammerman) Klein. *Education:* Received B.A. from University of Pennsylvania.

CAREER: Actor.

CREDITS:

STAGE APPEARANCES

(Broadway debut) Swing, *The First,* Martin Beck Theatre, New York City, 1981.
Mr. Hamil/Yusef Kadir, *Roza,* Mark Taper Forum, Los Angeles, 1986-87, then Royale Theatre, New York City, 1987.
One Two Three Four Five, Manhattan Theatre Club, City Center Stage II, New York City, 1987.
Gregor Vassy, *Chess,* Imperial Theatre, New York City, 1988.
(Understudy) Shylock, *The Merchant of Venice,* Forty-Sixth Street Theatre, New York City, 1989-90.
Sweeney, *Sweeney Todd,* Anchorage Opera, 1991.

Also appeared as a waiter in *Scapino!,* Buffalo Studio Arena, Buffalo, NY, and in a production of *La Boheme* for the New York Shakespeare Festival.

MAJOR TOURS

Thenardier, *Les Miserables,* Forrest Theatre, Philadelphia, 1987-88.

Also toured as Sidney Cohn, *On Your Toes,* Miami and Dallas.

FILM APPEARANCES

Iranian bodyguard, *Sea of Love,* Universal, 1989.

TELEVISION APPEARANCES

Swami, *Mathnet,* Child Television Work, PBS, 1989.
Stan Plover, *H.E.L.P.,* ABC, 1990.
Law and Order, NBC, 1990.

BENING, Annette 1958-

PERSONAL: Born May 29, 1958, in Topeka, KS; father, an insurance salesman; married Steven White (a university administrator; separated). *Education:* Attended Mesa College; received a degree in theatre from San Francisco State University; also studied at American Conservatory Theatre. *Avocational interests:* Scuba diving.

ADDRESSES: Agent—Bob Gersh, Gersh Agency, 232 N. Canon Dr., Beverly Hills, CA 90210.

CAREER: Actress. Performed with Colorado Shakespeare Festival, 1980, American Conservatory Theatre, 1983-85, and Denver Center Theatre Company, 1985-86. Also worked as cook on a charter boat.

AWARDS, HONORS: Antoinette Perry Award nomination, 1986, Clarence Derwin Award, 1987, and *Theatre World* Award, 1987, all for *Coastal Disturbances;* Academy Award nomination, best supporting actress, 1990, for *The Grifters.*

CREDITS:

FILM APPEARANCES

Kate Craig, *The Great Outdoors,* Universal, 1988.
Marquise DeMerteuil, *Valmont,* Orion, 1989.
Myra Langtry, *The Grifters,* Miramax/Cineplex Odeon, 1990.
Evelyn Ames, *Postcards from the Edge,* Columbia, 1990.
Ruth Merrill, *Guilty by Suspicion,* Warner Brothers, 1991.
Sarah Turner, *Regarding Henry,* Paramount, 1991.

STAGE APPEARANCES

Holly Dancer, *Coastal Disturbances,* Second Stage, New York City, 1986, then (Broadway debut) Circle in the Square, New York City, 1987.
Zookeeper, *Spoils of War,* Second Stage, 1988.

Also appeared as Juliet, *Romeo and Juliet;* Lady Macbeth, *Macbeth,* American Conservatory Theatre, San Francisco, CA; Emily, *Our Town;* Eliza Doolittle, *Pygmalion;* Tatania, *A Midsummer Night's Dream;* showgirl, *The Sleeping Prince;* Helena, *All's Well;* Blanche, *King John;* Anya, *The Cherry Orchard;* and the Virgin Mary, *The Christmas Miracles.*

TELEVISION APPEARANCES; MOVIES

Ann Tillman, *Manhunt for Claude Dallas,* CBS, 1986.
Jill, *Hostage,* CBS, 1988.

TELEVISION APPEARANCES; EPISODIC

"Milos Forman: Portrait," *American Masters,* PBS, 1989.

Also appeared in *Miami Vice,* NBC.

OTHER TELEVISION APPEARANCES

The 41st Annual Tony Awards (special), CBS, 1987.

Appeared in the pilot *It Had to Be You,* ABC.

OTHER SOURCES:

PERIODICALS

Interview, November, 1989.
New York, January 14, 1991.
Premiere, July, 1991.
Rolling Stone, May 16, 1991.*

* * *

BENNETT, Hywel 1944-

PERSONAL: Born April 8, 1944, in Garnant, Wales; son of Gordon and Sarah Gwen (Lewis) Bennett; married Cathy McGowan (divorced). *Education:* Attended the National Youth Theatre; trained for the stage at the Royal Academy of Dramatic Art.

ADDRESSES: Office—33 Thornton Rd., Wimbledon, London SW19, England. *Agent*—James Sharkey Associates, 15 Golden Square, Third Floor Suite, London W1R 3AG, England. *Publicist*—Judy Tarlow Associates, 7 Floral St., London WC2E 9DH, England.

CAREER: Actor and director.

CREDITS:

STAGE APPEARANCES

(London debut) Ophelia, *Hamlet,* Youth Theatre, Queen's Theatre, 1959.
Scott of the Antarctic, *Terra Nova,* Chichester Festival Theatre, Chichester, England, 1965.
Wally, *The Gift,* Vanbrugh Theatre Club, London, 1965.
Lennie, *A Smashing Day,* New Arts Theatre, London, 1966.
Puck, *A Midsummer Night's Dream,* Edinburgh Festival, Edinburgh, Scotland, 1967.
Prince Hal, *Henry IV, Parts One and Two,* Mermaid Theatre, London, 1970.
Mark Antony, *Julius Caesar,* Young Vic Theatre, London, 1972.
Bakke, *Bakke's Night of Fame,* Dolphin Theatre Company, Shaw Theatre, London, 1972.
Stanley, *The Birthday Party,* Gardner Center, Brighton, England, 1973.
Jimmy Porter, *Look Back in Anger,* Belgrade Theatre, Coventry, England, 1974.
Danny, *Night Must Fall,* Sherman Theatre, Cardiff, Wales, 1974, then Shaw Theatre, 1975.
Toad, *Toad of Toad Hall,* Birmingham Repertory Theatre, Birmingham, England, 1975.

Simon, *Otherwise Engaged,* Comedy Theatre, London, 1977.
Andreas Capodistriou and Inspector Bowden, *The Case of the Oily Levantine,* Her Majesty's Theatre, London, 1979.
Tim, *Fly Away Home,* Lyric Studio Theatre, London, 1983.
Marlow, *She Stoops to Conquer,* National Theatre Company, Lyttelton Theatre, London, 1984.
Andrey Prozorov, *Three Sisters,* Albery Theatre, London, 1987.
Long John Silver, *Treasure Island,* Edinburgh Festival, 1990.

Also appeared in repertory productions in Salisbury, England, and Leatherhead, Surrey, England, 1965.

STAGE DIRECTOR

Director of *Gaslight,* Lincoln, England, 1971; *The Promise,* Sheffield, England, 1974; *A Lily in Little India,* Coventry, England, 1974; *I Have Been Here Before,* Cardiff, Wales, 1975; *Move Over Mrs. Markham,* Leatherhead, Surrey, England, 1975; *Rosencrantz and Guildenstern Are Dead,* Leatherhead, 1975; and *A Man for All Seasons,* Birmingham, England, 1976.

MAJOR TOURS

Wormwood, *Dear Wormwood,* U.K. cities, 1965.
Title role, *Hamlet,* South African cities, 1974.
Konstantin, *The Seagull,* U.K. cities, 1974.
Marlow, *She Stoops to Conquer,* National Theatre Company, U.K. cities, 1984.

FILM APPEARANCES

Arthur Fitton, *The Family Way,* Warner Brothers, 1966.
Leonardo, *Drop Dead, My Love* (also known as *Il Marito e mio e l'amazzo quando mi pare*), Clesi Cinematografica, 1968.
Martin Durnley, Georgie Clifford, *Twisted Nerve,* National General, 1969.
Private Brigg, *The Virgin Soldiers,* Columbia, 1970.
France, *The Buttercup Chain,* Columbia, 1971.
Dennis, *Loot,* Cinevision, 1971.
Edwin Anthony, *Percy,* Metro-Goldwyn-Mayer, 1971.
It's a 2 "6" Above the Ground World (also known as *The Love Ban*), British Lion, 1972.
Mike Jessop, *War Zone* (also known as *Deadline*), Skouras/CineTel, 1986.

Also appeared in *Alice in Wonderland.*

TELEVISION APPEARANCES

Pennies from Heaven (mini-series), BBC, then PBS, 1979.
Ricki Tarr, *Tinker, Tailor, Soldier, Spy* (mini-series), BBC, then *Great Performances,* PBS, 1980.

Dr. Edmund Bickleigh, *Malice Aforethought* (mini-series), BBC, then *Mystery!,* PBS, 1980.

Title role, *Shelley* (series), BBC, 1980-81.

Title role, *Return of Shelley* (series), BBC, 1981-82.

Also appeared in *The Idiot; Romeo and Juliet; A Month in the Country; The Critic; The Consultant; Absent Friends; Frankie and Johnnie; Where the Buffalo Roam; Death of a Teddy Bear;* and *Unman, Wittering, and Zigo.**

*   *   *

BENNETT, Joan   1910-1990

OBITUARY NOTICE—See index for *CTFT* sketch: Born February 27, 1910, in Palisades, NJ; died of a heart attack, December 7, 1990. Actress and writer. Bennett appeared in classic films and popular television shows during her long career. She made her debut on Broadway in 1928, appearing with her father in *Jarnegan.* The next year, she appeared in her first film, *Bulldog Drummond.* Skilled at portraying both virtuous women and dangerous seductresses, Bennett eventually appeared in more than seventy films, including classics such as *Little Women, Father of the Bride, We're No Angels, Moby Dick,* and *Desire in the Dust.* Her television credits include the series *Too Young to Go Steady* and *Dark Shadows* as well as movies such as *Suddenly Love* and *This House Possessed.* Among the stage productions she appeared in are *The Pirate, Fallen Angels, The Boy Friend,* and *Never Too Late.* Bennett also wrote two books, *How to Be Attractive* and *The Bennett Playbill,* which she authored with Lois Kibbee.

OBITUARIES AND OTHER SOURCES:

PERIODICALS

Hollywood Reporter, December 10, 1990.

*   *   *

BENNETT, Peter   1917-1990(?)

PERSONAL: Born September 17, 1917, London, U.K.; died c. 1990, in London, U.K.; son of R. H. E. and Dorothy (Lowe) Bennett; married Sheila Bramwell-Jones. *Education:* Attended Malvern College; studied for the stage at Royal Academy of Dramatic Art.

CAREER: Actor and director.

MEMBER: British Actors' Equity (council member, 1970-80), National Council for Drama Training, Green Room Club, Garrick Club.

CREDITS:

STAGE APPEARANCES

(Stage debut) Ma Ta, *Lady Precious Stream,* Pleasure Gardens Theatre, Folkestone, U.K., 1936.

(London debut) Possum and Ed Sweet, *Little Ol' Boy,* Arts Theatre, London, 1936.

Hui Ming, *The Western Chamber,* New Theatre, London, 1939.

Johann Breitstein, *Counsellor-at-Law,* Embassy Theatre, London, 1939.

General Wei, *Lady Precious Stream,* Kingsway Theatre, London, 1939.

Pandar, *Pericles,* Open Air Theatre, 1939, London, 1939.

Fabian, *Twelfth Night,* Open Air Theatre, 1939.

Kasim Baba, *Chu-Chin-Chow,* Palace Theatre, London, 1940-41.

Starkey, *Peter Pan,* Adelphi Theatre, London, 1941.

Gratiano, *The Merchant of Venice,* Westminster Theatre, London, 1942.

Vernon and Poins, *King Henry the Fourth (Part 1),* Westminster Theatre, 1942.

Poins and Davy, *King Henry the Fourth, (Part 2),* Westminster Theatre, 1942.

Quince, *A Midsummer Night's Dream,* Westminster Theatre, 1942.

De Beausset, *War and Peace,* Phoenix Theatre, London, 1943.

Starkey, *Peter Pan,* Cambridge Theatre, U.K., 1943.

Clown, *Winter's Tale,* Open Air Theatre, 1944.

Third Witch and Porter, *Macbeth,* Lyric, Hammersmith, 1944.

Arthur Clough, *The Spinster of South Street,* King's Theatre, Hammersmith, 1945.

Face, *The Alchemist,* King's Theatre, Hammersmith, 1945.

Ernie, *Zoo in Silesia,* Embassy Theatre, 1945.

Corporal Cramp, *Love Goes to Press,* Embassy Theatre, 1946.

John Dashwood, *Sense and Sensibility,* Embassy Theatre, 1946.

(New York debut) Corporal Cramp, *Love Goes to Press,* Biltmore Theatre, 1947.

Henry, *Symphony in Violence,* Embassy Theatre, 1948.

Mr. Calthorpe, *For Better, For Worse,* Q Theatre, 1948.

Gavin Bainbridge, *Burn, Witch, Burn,* Gateway Theatre, U.K., 1949.

Fag, *The Rivals,* Fortune Theatre, London, 1949.

Scrooge, *A Christmas Carol,* Theatre Royal, Stratford-upon-Avon, U.K., 1950.

Dr. Miseria, *To Live in Peace,* Royal Theatre, Bristol, U.K., 1951.

Caiaphas, *The Man Born to Be King,* Festival of Britain Church, U.K., 1951.

Motley, *The Castle Spectre,* Players' Theatre, U.K., 1952.

Prosser, *Portrait of a Gentleman,* New Torch Theatre, U.K., 1953.

Mr. Harrison Crockstead, *A Marriage Has Been Arranged,* New Torch Theatre, 1953.

Mr. Hughes, *Birds of Sadness,* Q Theatre, London, 1954.

Mr. Allnut, *The Name Is Smith,* Richmond Theatre, U.K., 1954.

Wedgewood, *Wild Goose Chase,* Embassy Theatre, 1954.

Councillor Hedges, *Let's Talk Turkey,* Royal Windsor Theatre, London, 1954.

Lon Dennison, *The Wooden Dish,* Guildford Theatre Company, 1955.

Carlos Gervanzoni, *The Strong Are Lonely,* Piccadilly Theatre, London, 1955.

Bernard Fell, *A For Angel, B For Bed,* New Lindsey Theatre, U.K., 1957.

James Walton, *The Waiting of Lester Abbs,* Royal Court Theatre, London, 1957.

Mr. Noah, *Noddy in Toyland,* Scala Theatre, London, 1962.

Scrooge, *A Christmas Carol,* New Theatre, Cardiff, 1964.

Scrooge, *A Christmas Carol,* Arts Theatre, Cambridge, 1966.

Mr. Sole, *The Old Boys,* Mermaid Theatre, London, 1971.

Hector, *Humulus the Muted Lover,* Act Inn, London, 1972.

Albert, *Heroes,* Theatre Upstairs, London, 1975.

Boswell, *The Trial of Dr. Johnson,* Chiltern Theatre Festival, 1977.

Also appeared at Playhouse Theatre, Amersham, U.K., and Theatre Royal, Stratford-upon-Avon, 1949-50.

MAJOR TOURS

Appeared as Perkins, *The Golden Fleece,* 1944; Scrooge, *A Christmas Carol,* 1967; and Mr. Sole, *The Old Boys,* 1971.

STAGE DIRECTOR

Avalanche in Speculum, Gateway Theatre, 1952.

Steambath, George Street Playhouse, New Brunswick, NJ, 1977.

The Passion of Dracula, Cherry Lane Theatre, New York City, 1977.

With Love and Laughter, Harold Clurman Theatre, New York City, 1982.

Fool For Love, Theatre by the Sea, Portsmouth, NH, 1985.

She Loves Me, Pittsburgh Public Theatre, Pittsburgh, PA, c. 1986.

Fool For Love, Missouri Repertory Theatre, Kansas City, MO, c. 1986.

Also director for Festival of British Theatre Ltd., 1975; and Theatre By The Sea, 1981-82.

FILM APPEARANCES

Butler, *Lady Chatterly's Lover,* Prodis, 1981.

Also appeared in *Tarka the Otter.*

TELEVISION APPEARANCES

Leonides, *Adventures of Sir Lancelot* (series), NBC, 1956-67, and ABC, 1957-58.

Also appeared in televised play *The Old Crowd.*

OBITUARIES AND OTHER SOURCES:

PERIODICALS

Variety, January 17, 1990.*

*   *   *

BENTON, Barbi 1950-

PERSONAL: Born Barbara Klein, January 28, 1950, in Sacramento, CA (some sources say New York City); married George Gradow. *Education:* Attended University of Barcelona, 1964, Sacramento State University, 1965-68, and University of California, Los Angeles, 1968-70.

ADDRESSES: Agent—Joshua Gray and Associates, 6736 Laurel Canyon Blvd., Suite 306, North Hollywood, CA 90212.

CAREER: Actress. Singer and model.

CREDITS:

FILM APPEARANCES

Susan Jeremy, *Hospital Massacre* (also known as *Ward Thirteen* and *Be My Valentine, or Else*), Cannon, 1982.

Codille, *Deathstalker* (also known as *El Cazador de la Muerte*), New World, 1984.

Made film debut in *What's a Nice Girl Like You Doing in a Place Like This?,* 1969.

TELEVISION APPEARANCES; MOVIES

Miss Iowa, *The Great American Beauty Contest,* ABC, 1973.

Melanie, *The Third Girl from the Left,* ABC, 1973.

As herself, *Murder at the Mardi Gras,* CBS, 1978.

Anita Carney, *For the Love of It,* ABC, 1980.

TELEVISION APPEARANCES; SERIES

Host, *Playboy after Dark,* syndicated, 1969.

Regular, *Hee Haw,* syndicated, 1971-76.

Maxx Douglas, *Sugar Time!,* ABC, 1977-78.

TELEVISION APPEARANCES; EPISODIC

Gina Potter, *Riptide,* NBC, 1986.

Sue Beth, *Murder, She Wrote*, CBS, 1986.

Also appeared on *Fantasy Island*, ABC; *Love Boat*, ABC; *Vegas*, ABC; *McCloud*, CBS; and *Charlie's Angels*, ABC.

TELEVISION APPEARANCES; SPECIALS

Barbi Benton Special: A Barbi Doll for Christmas, syndicated, 1978.
Celebrity Challenge of the Sexes, CBS, 1979.
A Country Christmas, CBS, 1979.
Circus of the Stars, CBS, 1979, 1980, and 1982.
Doug Henning's World of Magic III, NBC, 1980.
Men Who Rate a "10," NBC, 1980.
Dean Martin at the Wild Animal Park, NBC, 1982.
Magic with the Stars, NBC, 1982.
Celebrity Daredevils, ABC, 1983.

TELEVISION APPEARANCES; PILOTS

As herself, *Bowzer*, syndicated, 1981.
Interceptor, syndicated, 1989.

STAGE APPEARANCES

Made stage debut in *I Love My Wife*, 1982; also appeared in *Oklahoma!*, 1982; *Dames at Sea*, Detroit, MI, 1991.

RECORDINGS:

ALBUMS

Albums include *Barbi Doll, Barbie Benton, Something New*, and *Brass Buckles.**

*   *   *

BERENGER, Tom   1950-

PERSONAL: Born May 31, 1950, in Chicago, IL; first wife's name, Barbara (divorced); married present wife Lisa, July 29, 1986; children: (first marriage) Allison, Patrick; (second marriage) Chelsea, Chloe. *Education:* Attended University of Missouri; studied acting at H.B. Studios.

ADDRESSES: Agent—Paula Wagner, Creative Artists Agency, 9830 Wilshire Blvd., Beverly Hills, CA 90212.

CAREER: Actor.

AWARDS, HONORS: Academy Award nomination, best supporting actor, 1986, for *Platoon*.

CREDITS:

FILM APPEARANCES

(Film debut) Matthew Jackson, *Beyond the Door* (also known as *Oltre la Porta*), Premier Releasing/Gaumont, 1975.
Gary Cooper White, *Looking for Mr. Goodbar*, Paramount, 1977.

Man at end, *The Sentinel*, Universal, 1977.
Andras Vayda, *In Praise of Older Women*, AVCO-Embassy, 1978.
Butch Cassidy, *Butch and Sundance: The Early Days*, Twentieth Century-Fox, 1979.
Drew, *The Dogs of War*, United Artists, 1980.
Sam, *The Big Chill*, Columbia, 1983.
Frank Ridgeway, *Eddie and the Cruisers*, Embassy, 1983.
Matt Rossi, *Fear City*, Chevy Chase Distribution, 1984.
Rex O'Herlihan, *Rustler's Rhapsody*, Paramount, 1985.
Sergeant Barnes, *Platoon*, Orion, 1986.
Mike Keegan, *Someone to Watch over Me*, Columbia, 1987.
Jonathan Knox, *Shoot to Kill*, Buena Vista, 1988.
Gary Simmons, *Betrayed*, Metro-Goldwyn-Mayer (MGM)/United Artists, 1988.
Father Michael Pace, *Last Rites*, MGM/United Artists, 1988.
Jake Taylor, *Major League*, Paramount, 1989.
Recruiting sergeant, *Born on the Fourth of July*, Universal, 1989.
Harry Dobbs, *Love at Large* (also known as *L'Amour poursuite*), Orion, 1990.
American, *The Field*, Avenue Pictures, 1990.

STAGE APPEARANCES

Soldier, Tybalt, and a Montague, *Death Story*, Manhattan Theatre Club, New York City, 1975.
The Country Club, Playwrights Horizons, New York City, 1976.
Jack, *The Rose Tatoo*, Long Wharf Theatre, New Haven, CT, 1977.
Stanley Kowalski, *A Streetcar Named Desire*, Milwaukee Repertory Theatre, Milwaukee, WI, 1981.
National Anthems, Long Wharf Theatre, 1988.

Also appeared Jocko, *End as a Man*, Circle Repertory Theatre, New York City; as Orestes, *Electra;* and in *Who's Afraid of Virginia Woolf?* at the University of Missouri. Appeared as Stanley Kowalski in Japanese touring production of *A Streetcar Named Desire*.

TELEVISION APPEARANCES; EPISODIC

Tim Siegel, *One Life to Live*, ABC, 1975-76.

TELEVISION APPEARANCES; MOVIES

Billy Sutton, *Johnny, We Hardly Knew Ye*, NBC, 1977.
Bobby Fallon, *Flesh and Blood*, CBS, 1979.
Jeff Stevens, *If Tomorrow Comes*, CBS, 1986.

OTHER TELEVISION APPEARANCES

Narrator, *Dear America: Letters Home from Vietnam* (special), HBO, 1987.*

BESSELL, Ted   1942-

PERSONAL: Born May (one source says March) 20, 1942, in Flushing, NY.

ADDRESSES: Agent—International Creative Management, 8899 Beverly Blvd., Los Angeles, CA 90048.

CAREER: Actor, director, and producer.

AWARDS, HONORS: Emmy Award nomination, outstanding continued performance by an actor in a leading role in a comedy series, 1971, for *That Girl;* Emmy Award, outstanding variety, music, or comedy program (with Richard Sakai), and Emmy Award nomination, outstanding directing in a variety or music program, both 1989, for *The Tracey Ullman Show.*

CREDITS:

TELEVISION APPEARANCES; MOVIES

Preston Albright, *Two on a Bench,* ABC, 1971.
Dan Cramer, *Your Money or Your Wife,* CBS, 1972.
Jeffrey Elliot, *Scream Pretty Peggy,* ABC, 1973.
Paul Nesbitt, *What Are Best Friends For?,* ABC, 1973.
Pete McCann, *Breaking up Is Hard to Do,* ABC, 1979.
Jesse Hooten, *The Acorn People,* NBC, 1981.

TELEVISION APPEARANCES; SERIES

Tom-Tom DeWitt, *It's a Man's World,* NBC, 1962-63.
Frankie Lombardi, *Gomer Pyle, U.S.M.C.,* CBS, 1966.
Don Hollinger, *That Girl,* ABC, 1966-71 (also see below).
Harry Jenkins, *Good Time Harry,* NBC, 1980.
General Oliver Mansfield, *Hail to the Chief,* ABC, 1985.

TELEVISION APPEARANCES; EPISODIC

Joe Warner, *The Mary Tyler Moore Show,* CBS, 1975.

Also appeared in episodes of *Great Adventure,* CBS, and *The Greatest Show on Earth,* ABC.

OTHER TELEVISION APPEARANCES

Ted Harper, *The Ted Bessell Show* (pilot), CBS, 1973.
Bobby Parker, *Bobby Parker and Company* (pilot), CBS, 1974.
ABC Comedy Special, ABC, 1986.

Also appeared as Max Harrison, *The Arena* (special), 1986.

TELEVISION WORK

Episode director, *That Girl,* ABC, 1966-71.
Producer (with Richard Sakai) and episode director, *The Tracey Ullman Show* (series), Fox, 1987-90.

FILM APPEARANCES

Elevator operator, *Lover Come Back,* Universal, 1961.
Kid, *The Outsider,* Universal, 1962.

Carrozzo, *Captain Newman, M.D.,* Universal, 1963.
Bob Matthews, *Billie,* United Artists, 1965.
Lieutenant Wilbur Harkness, *McHale's Navy Joins the Air Force,* Universal, 1965.
Axel Magee, *Don't Drink the Water,* AVCO-Embassy, 1969.

STAGE APPEARANCES

George, *Same Time, Next Year,* Brooks Atkinson Theatre, New York City, 1976.

*   *   *

BETHUNE, Zina   1950(?)-

PERSONAL: Born February 17, 1950 (one source says 1946), in New York, NY; daughter of William Charles and Ivy (an actress; maiden name, Vigder) Bethune; married Sean Feeley, December 27, 1970.

ADDRESSES: Office—The Legend Company, 1831 S. Beverly Glen Blvd., Los Angeles, CA 90025. *Agent*—c/o Dade/Rosen/Schultz Agency, 15010 Ventura Blvd., Suite 219, Sherman Oaks, CA 91403.

CAREER: Actress, choreographer, dancer, and singer. Paradigm Films, New York City, associate producer and sound engineer, 1966-68; The Legend Company (film distribution and production), Hollywood, CA, joint owner, 1974—. Affiliated with the New York City Ballet, Zina Bethune and Company Dance Theatre, and Bethune Ballet Theatre Danse. Spokeswoman for various health and public service organizations, including Retarded Infant Services, Muscular Dystrophy Association, National Cystic Fibrosis Foundation.

MEMBER: American Federation of Television and Radio Artists, Academy of Television Arts and Sciences, Screen Actors Guild, Actors Equity Association.

AWARDS, HONORS: Citations from the City of New York, Army Nursing Corps., and Air Force Nursing Corps.

CREDITS:

STAGE APPEARANCES

Appeared in *Most Happy Fella,* New York City.

MAJOR TOURS

Appeared in touring productions of *Sweet Charity, Carnival, Oklahoma!, Damn Yankees, Member of the Wedding, The Owl and the Pussycat,* and *Nutcracker.*

FILM APPEARANCES

Anna Roosevelt, *Sunrise at Campobello,* Warner Brothers, 1960.

Young girl, *Who's That Knocking at My Door?* (also known as *I Call First* and *J.R.*), Joseph Brenner, 1968.

Dance teacher and choreographer, *The Boost,* Hemdale, 1988.

TELEVISION APPEARANCES; SERIES

Robin Holden, *The Guiding Light,* CBS, 1956-58.

Lisha Steele, *Young Dr. Malone,* NBC, 1959.

Gail Lucas, *The Nurses* (became *The Doctors and the Nurses*), ABC, 1965-67.

Barbara Latimer, *Love of Life,* CBS, 1965-1971.

OTHER TELEVISION APPEARANCES

Amy March, *Little Women* (special), CBS, 1958.

Also appeared as Leslie Wade in the special *The Gymnast,* 1980; as Paula in the movie *Nutcracker: Money, Madness and Murder,* 1987; as dance performer in the special *From the Heart . . . The First International Very Special Arts Festival;* and in the movie *Route 66;* also appeared in *Lancer, Cains Hundred, Naked City, Santa Barbara, Judy Garland Show, Jackie Gleason Show, Gunsmoke, Dr. Kildare, Emergency, Planet of the Apes, Police Story, Chips, Hardy Boys,* and *Heart Dancing.*

TELEVISION WORK

Served as choreographer for the movie *Nutcracker: Money, Madness and Murder,* 1987.*

*   *   *

BEYMER, Richard   1939-

PERSONAL: Full name, George Richard Beymer, Jr.; born February 21, 1939, in Avoca, IA. *Education:* Studied at the Actors Studio.

ADDRESSES: Agent—Century Artists Limited, 9744 Wilshire Boulevard, Suite 308, Beverly Hills, CA 90212.

CAREER: Actor, director, producer, and cinematographer.

AWARDS, HONORS: Golden Globe Award, Most Promising Newcomer-Male, 1962.

CREDITS:

FILM APPEARANCES

Roelf, age 12-16, *So Big,* Warner Brothers, 1953.

Paul, Mary's nephew, *Indiscretion of an American Wife* (also known as *Terminal Station Indiscretion*), Columbia, 1954.

Peter Van Daan, *The Diary of Anne Frank,* Twentieth Century-Fox, 1959.

Bob Bannerman, *High Time,* Twentieth Century-Fox, 1960.

Tony, *West Side Story,* United Artists, 1961.

Nick Adams, *Adventures of a Young Man* (also known as *Hemingway's Adventures of a Young Man*), Twentieth Century-Fox, 1962.

Mike, *Bachelor Flat,* Twentieth Century-Fox, 1962.

Philip Harrington, *Five Finger Exercise,* Columbia, 1962.

Schultz, *The Longest Day,* Twentieth Century-Fox, 1962.

Kenny Baird, *The Stripper* (also known as *Woman of Summer*), Twentieth Century-Fox, 1963.

Dean Free, *Grass* (also known as *Scream Free*), Hollywood Star Pictures, 1969.

Evan Bley, *Cross Country,* Metro-Goldwyn-Mayer/United Artists, 1983.

Dr. Newbury, *Silent Night, Deadly Night III: Better Watch Out,* Quiet Films, 1989.

Also appeared in *The Innerview* (also see below), Richard Beymer, 1974; and *Johnny Tremaine.*

FILM WORK

Producer, director, and cinematographer, *The Innerview* (also see below), Richard Beymer, 1974.

TELEVISION APPEARANCES

Ralph Belmonte, *Guilty or Not Guilty* (pilot), NBC, 1966.

David Fenton, *Paper Dolls* (series), ABC, 1984.

Allan Breed, *Generation* (movie), ABC, 1985.

Jeff Larkin, *Dallas* (episode), CBS, 1987.

Morgan McCormack, *Murder, She Wrote* (episode), CBS, 1987.

Sidney Jarvis, *Murder, She Wrote* (episode), CBS, 1987.

John Locke, *The Bronx Zoo* (episode), NBC, 1988.

Max Winitski, *Buck James* (episode), ABC, 1988.

Benjamin Horne, *Twin Peaks* (series), ABC, 1990–91.

Also appeared in *Playhouse 90,* CBS.

TELEVISION WORK

Photographer, *The Juggler of Notre Dame* (special), syndicated, 1982.

Photographer, *Leadfoot* (special), syndicated, 1982.

Also director, *Insight.*

STAGE APPEARANCES

Guest artist, Arena Stage Company, Washington, D.C., 1987-88.

WRITINGS:

The Innerview (film), Richard Beymer, 1974.*

BISHOP, Andre 1948-

PERSONAL: Born November 9, 1948, in New York, NY; son of Andre V. (an investment banker) and Felice H. (Francis) Smolianinoff. *Education:* Attended Harvard College, 1970.

ADDRESSES: Office—Playwrights Horizons, 416 West 42nd St., New York, NY 10036.

CAREER: Producer and director. Worked with the New York Shakespeare Festival, American Place Theatre, and as a production associate on *Ghost Dance* for The New Dramatists Incorporated, New York City, 1973; Playwrights Horizons, New York City, 1975-1991, began as literary manager, became artistic director; Lincoln Center Theatre, New York City, director, 1992—. New York University, Hunter College, instructor. Harvard University, Loeb Drama Center and Opera Musical Theatre, member of board of overseers; National Endowment for the Arts, member of theatre panel; CAPS Playwriting Program, consultant.

AWARDS, HONORS: Margo Jones Award, 1983; Lucille Lortel Award, 1989.

CREDITS:

STAGE WORK; ARTISTIC DIRECTOR; PLAYWRIGHTS HORIZONS, NEW YORK CITY

Living at Home, Mainstage Theatre, 1978.
Say Goodnight Gracie, 1978.
Sweet Main Street, 1979.
Don't Tell Me Everything, 1979.
The Songs of Jonathan Tunick, 1979.
Table Settings, 1979.
Breaking and Entering, 1979.
In Trousers, 1979.
The Terrorists, 1979.
The Vienna Notes, 1979.
Two Small Bodies, 1979.
Justice, Mainstage Theatre, 1979.
Fables for Friends, 1980.
Passione, 1980.
Survival Kitsch, 1980.
Coming Attractions, 1980.
March of the Falsettos, 1981.
Summer Friends, 1981.
The Actor's Nightmare and *Sister Mary Ignatius Explains It All for You* (double bill), 1981, then Westside Arts Theatre, 1982.
Herringbone, 1982.
Geniuses, 1982, then Douglas Fairbanks Theatre, 1982.
The Rise and Rise of Daniel Rocket, 1982.
The Dining Room, 1982, then Astor Place Theatre, 1982.
America Kicks Up Its Heels, 1983.
The Transfiguration of Benno Blimpie, 1982.

Christmas on Mars, 1983.
That's It Folks!, 1983.
Sunday in the Park with George, 1983.
Isn't It Romantic, 1984, then Lucille Lortel Theatre, 1984.
Baby with the Bathwater, 1984.
Romance Language, 1984.
Life and Limb, 1985.
Carmines Sings Whitman Sings Carmines, 1985.
The Young Playwrights Festival (series of one-acts), 1985.
Fighting International Fat, 1985.
Paradise!, 1985.
Raw Youth, 1985.
Anteroom, 1985.
Miami, 1986.
Little Footsteps, 1986.
The Perfect Party, 1986, then Astor Place Theatre, 1986.
The Nice and the Nasty, 1986.
Highest Standard of Living, 1986.
Fifth Annual Young Playwrights Festival (series of one-acts), 1986.
Coup d'Etat, 1986.
A Delicate Situation, 1986.
Remedial English, 1986.
Black Sea Follies, 1987.
The Maderati, 1987.
Driving Miss Daisy, 1987, then John Houseman Theatre, 1987.
Three Post Cards, 1987.
Tiny Mommy, 1987.
Sparks in the Park, 1987.
Ebony, 1987.
Laughing Wild, 1987.
Another Antigone, 1988.
Cold Sweat, 1988.
Lucky Stiff, 1988.
Gus and Al, 1988.
Right behind the Flag, 1988.
Yankee Dawg You Die, 1989.
The Heidi Chronicles, 1989, then Plymouth Theatre, 1989.
Miriam's Flowers, 1990.
Kate's Diary, 1990.
Hyde in Hollywood, 1990.
When She Danced, 1990.
Once on This Island, 1990, then Booth Theatre, 1990.
Falsettoland, 1990, then Lucille Lortel Theatre, 1990.
Subfertile, 1990.
Assassins, 1990.
The Substance of Fire, 1991.
The Old Boy, 1991.

STAGE APPEARANCES

Man with stag's head, *The Old Glory,* American Place Theatre, New York City, 1976.

BIXBY, Bill 1934-

PERSONAL: Born January 22, 1934, in San Francisco, CA; married Brenda Bennett (deceased); children: one (deceased). *Education:* Attended University of California at Berkeley.

ADDRESSES: Agent—Paul Brandon, Brandon & Associates, 200 North Robertson Blvd. Suite 223, Beverly Hills, CA 90211.

CAREER: Actor, director, and producer. Has done industrial films for General Motors and Chrysler Corporation; spokesman for Radio Shack.

AWARDS, HONORS: Emmy Award nominations, including one for *The Courtship of Eddie's Father.*

CREDITS:

TELEVISION APPEARANCES; SERIES

Charles Raymond, *The Joey Bishop Show,* NBC, 1962.
Tim O'Hara, *My Favorite Martian,* CBS, 1963-66.
Tom Corbett, *The Courtship of Eddie's Father,* ABC, 1969-72.
Anthony Blake, *The Magician,* NBC, 1973-74.
Panelist, *Masquerade Party,* syndicated, 1974-75.
Host, *Once Upon a Classic,* PBS, 1977-78.
Dr. David Bruce Banner, *The Incredible Hulk,* CBS, 1978-82.
Host, *The Book of Lists,* CBS, 1982.
Matt Cassidy, *Goodnight Beantown,* CBS, 1983-84.
Host, *True Confessions,* 1986.
Host, *Exploring Psychic Powers . . . Live,* syndicated, 1989.

TELEVISION APPEARANCES; PILOTS

Of Men of Women, ABC, 1972.
Anthony Dorian, *The Magician,* NBC, 1973.
William, *Rex Harrison Presents Short Stories,* NBC, 1974.
Philo McGrew, *Spencer's Pilots,* CBS, 1976.
Arnold Greenwood, *Fantasy Island,* ABC, 1977.
Dr. David Bruce Banner, *The Incredible Hulk,* CBS, 1977.
Dr. David Bruce Banner, *The Return of the Incredible Hulk,* CBS, 1977.
Dr. Bud Harrison, *The Natural Look,* NBC, 1977.
Whatever Became Of . . . ?, ABC, 1982.

TELEVISION APPEARANCES; MOVIES

Johnny Gaines, *Congratulations, It's a Boy!,* ABC, 1971.
Jeff Hamilton, *The Couple Takes a Wife,* ABC, 1972.
Teddy Bush, *Shirts/Skins,* ABC, 1973.
Philippe Despard, *The Barbary Coast,* ABC, 1975.
Reverend Arthur Ford, *The Great Houdini,* ABC, 1976.
Sam Lowell, *The Johnson County Invasion,* NBC, 1976.
Herbert Freemont, *Black Market Baby,* ABC, 1977.

Luke Williams, *Agatha Christie's "Murder Is Easy,"* CBS, 1982.
Harvey Jameson, *International Airport,* ABC, 1985.
David McGary, *Sin of Innocence,* CBS, 1986.
Dr. David Bruce Banner, *The Incredible Hulk Returns,* CBS, 1988.
Dr. David Bruce Banner, *The Trial of the Incredible Hulk,* CBS, 1989.
Dr. David Bruce Banner, *The Death of the Incredible Hulk,* CBS, 1990.

TELEVISION APPEARANCES; SPECIALS

Mitzi and a Hundred Guys, CBS, 1975.
Nashville Remembers Elvis on His Birthday, NBC, 1978.
Elvis Remembered: Nashville to Hollywood, NBC, 1980.
The Sensational, Shocking, Wonderful, Wacky 70's, NBC, 1980.
I've Had It Up to Here, NBC, 1981.

Also appeared as host, *Yabba Dabba Doo,* 1982; *The Chemical People,* 1983; host, *The Legend of King Arthur,* 1985.

OTHER TELEVISION APPEARANCES

Willie Abbott, *Rich Man, Poor Man—Book I* (miniseries), ABC, 1976.
Donald Iskin, *J.J. Starbuck* (episodic), NBC, 1987.

Also appeared in *Night Gallery,* NBC, 1971; *The Many Loves of Dobie Gillis; The Andy Griffith Show; The Danny Thomas Show.*

TELEVISION DIRECTOR; PILOTS

The Barbary Coast, ABC, 1975.
The Many Loves of Arthur, NBC, 1978.
The Best of Times, CBS, 1983.
*W*A*L*T*E*R,* CBS, 1984.

TELEVISION DIRECTOR; EPISODIC

Kate McShane, CBS, 1975.
Charlie's Angels, ABC, 1976.
Bart D'Angelo/Superstar, ABC, 1976.
Spencer's Pilots, CBS, 1976.
The Oregon Trail, NBC, 1977.
MacNamara's Band, ABC, 1977.
Herbie, the Love Bug, CBS, 1982.
Wizards and Warriors, CBS, 1983.
Dreams, CBS, 1984.
"Death of a Few Salesmen," *Sledge Hammer!,* ABC, 1987.
"Play It Again, Sledge," *Sledge Hammer!,* ABC, 1988.
"Ice Breaker," *Sledge Hammer!,* ABC, 1988.
"Hammer Hits the Rock," *Sledge Hammer!,* ABC, 1988.
"The Last of the Red Hot Vampires," *Sledge Hammer!,* ABC, 1988.

Also directed episodes of *Better Days,* 1986; *Spies,* CBS, 1987; *Murphy's Law,* ABC, 1988; *The Nutt House,* 1989; *The Courtship of Eddie's Father,* ABC; *Mannix,* CBS; *Mr. Merlin,* CBS; *Goodnight Beantown,* CBS; *The Barbary Coast,* ABC.

OTHER TELEVISION WORK

Director, *Rich Man, Poor Man—Book II* (mini-series), ABC, 1976.
Director, *Three on a Date* (movie), ABC, 1978.
Director, *I Had Three Wives,* CBS, 1985.
Executive producer, *The Incredible Hulk Returns* (movie), CBS, 1988.
Director and executive producer, *The Trial of the Incredible Hulk* (movie), CBS, 1989.
Executive producer, *The Death of the Incredible Hulk* (movie), CBS, 1990.

Also director of *Rockhopper,* 1985.

FILM APPEARANCES

Lonely Are the Brave, Universal, 1962.
Tattooed sailor, *Irma La Douce,* United Artists, 1963.
Boy, Track Team, *Under the Yum Yum Tree,* Columbia, 1963.
Johnsy Boy Hood, *Ride Beyond Vengeance* (also released as *Night of the Tiger*), Columbia, 1966.
James Jamison III, *Clambake,* United Artists, 1967.
Kenny Donford, *Speedway,* Metro-Goldwyn-Mayer (MGM), 1967.
Russell Donavan, *The Apple Dumpling Gang,* Buena Vista, 1975.
Dick Bender, *Doctor, You've Got to be Kidding,* MGM, 1977.
Himself, *Kentucky Fried Movie,* United Film, 1977.

Also appeared in *This Way Out Please.*

STAGE APPEARANCES

(Broadway debut) Charlie Rodgers, *The Paisley Convertible,* Henry Miller's Theatre, 1967.
Send Me No Flowers, Marriott's Lincolnshire Theatre, Lincolnshire, IL, 1977.

Also appeared in *Under the Yum Yum Tree;* major tour of U.S. cities with *The Fantasticks.**

*   *   *

BLAKE, Bobby
  See BLAKE, Robert

BLAKE, Robby
  See BLAKE, Robert

*   *   *

BLAKE, Robert 1933(?)-
  (Bobby Blake, Robby Blake)

PERSONAL: Born Michael Gubitosi, September 18, 1933 (some sources say 1934), in Nutley, NJ; married Sondra Kerry (an actress), divorced; children: two.

CAREER: Actor and producer. *Military service:* Served in the U.S. military.

AWARDS, HONORS: Emmy Award, Outstanding Lead Actor in a Drama Series, 1975, for *Baretta.*

CREDITS:

TELEVISION APPEARANCES; SERIES

Detective Tony Baretta, *Baretta,* ABC, 1975-78.
Father Noah "Hardstep" Rivers, *Hell Town,* NBC, 1985 (also see below).

TELEVISION APPEARANCES; EPISODIC

Fireside Theater, NBC, 1949.
"Gypsy," *One Step Beyond,* ABC, 1959.
The Richard Boone Show, NBC, 1963-64.

Also appeared on "He's Only a Boy," *The Rebel; Have Gun, Will Travel;* and *Bat Masterson.*

TELEVISION APPEARANCES; MOVIES

Joe Dancer, *The Big Black Pill,* NBC, 1981 (also see below).
Joe Dancer, *The Monkey Mission,* NBC, 1981 (also see below).
George Milton, *Of Mice and Men,* NBC, 1981 (also see below).
James Hoffa, *Blood Feud,* syndicated, 1983.
Joe Dancer, *Murder 1, Dancer 0,* NBC, 1983 (also see below).
Father Noah "Hardstep" Rivers, *Father of Hell Town,* NBC, 1985.
Lenny Mancini, *Heart of a Champion: The Ray Mancini Story,* CBS, 1985.

TELEVISION APPEARANCES; SPECIALS

An All-Star Tribute to Elizabeth Taylor, CBS, 1977.
The NBC All-Star Hour, NBC, 1985.

Also appeared on *The American Film Institute Salute to John Huston,* 1983.

TELEVISION WORK; MOVIES, EXCEPT WHERE NOTED

Creator and executive producer, *The Big Black Pill,* NBC, 1981.

Creator and executive producer, *The Monkey Mission,* NBC, 1981.

Executive producer, *Of Mice and Men,* NBC, 1981.

Executive producer, *Murder 1, Dancer 0,* NBC, 1983.

Executive producer, *Hell Town* (series), NBC, 1985.

FILM APPEARANCES; AS BOBBY BLAKE, EXCEPT WHERE NOTED

Littlejohn, Jr., *I Love You Again,* Metro-Goldwyn-Mayer (MGM), 1940.

Tooky, *Andy Hardy's Double Life,* MGM, 1942.

Chinese boy, *China Girl,* Twentieth Century-Fox, 1942.

Title role, *Mokey,* MGM, 1942.

Small boy, *Salute to the Marines,* MGM, 1943.

Boy on porch, *Slightly Dangerous,* MGM, 1943.

Egbert, *The Big Noise,* Twentieth Century-Fox, 1944.

Jerry, *Lost Angel,* MGM, 1944.

(As Robby Blake) Little Beaver, *Tucson Raiders,* Republic, 1944.

Little Beaver, *Marshal of Reno,* Republic, 1944.

Jimmy, age seven, *Meet the People,* MGM, 1944.

Little Beaver, *The San Antonio Kid,* Republic, 1944.

Little Beaver, *Vigilantes of Dodge City,* Republic, 1944.

Cheyenne Wildcat, Republic, 1944.

Colorado Pioneers, Republic, 1945.

Great Stage Coach Robbery, Republic, 1945.

Little boy, *Dakota,* Republic, 1945.

Junior, *The Horn Blows at Midnight,* Warner Brothers, 1945.

Little Beaver, *Lone Texas Ranger,* Republic, 1945.

Little Beaver, *Marshal of Laredo,* Republic, 1945.

Little Beaver, *Phantom of the Plains,* Republic, 1945.

Wilbur, *Pillow to Post,* Warner Brothers, 1945.

Dickie Wanley, *The Woman in the Window,* RKO Radio Pictures, 1945.

Santa Fe Uprising, Republic, 1946.

Sheriff of Redwood Valley, Republic, 1946.

Sun Valley Cyclone, Republic, 1946.

Little Beaver, *Conquest of Cheyenne,* Republic, 1946.

Alan Schroeder, *A Guy Could Change,* Republic, 1946.

Cub Garth, *Home on the Range,* Republic, 1946.

Paul Boray as a child, *Humoresque,* Warner Brothers, 1946.

Newsboy, *In Old Sacramento* (also known as *Flame of Sacramento*), Republic, 1946.

Danny McCoy, *Out California Way,* Republic, 1946.

Little Beaver, *Stagecoach to Denver,* Republic, 1946.

Homesteaders of Paradise Valley, Republic, 1947.

Mike, *The Last Round-Up,* Columbia, 1947.

Little Beaver, *The Marshal of Cripple Creek,* Republic, 1947.

Little Beaver, *Oregon Trail Scouts,* Republic, 1947.

Paul, refugee lad, *The Return of Rin Tin Tin,* Republic, 1947.

Little Beaver, *Rustlers of Devil's Canyon,* Republic, 1947.

Little Beaver, *Vigilantes of Boomtown,* Republic, 1947.

Mexican, *The Treasure of the Sierra Madre,* Warner Brothers, 1948.

Mahmoud, *The Black Rose,* Twentieth Century-Fox, 1950.

Luis, *Apache War Smoke,* MGM, 1952.

Stable boy, *Treasure of the Golden Condor,* Twentieth Century-Fox, 1953.

Beggar boy, *The Veils of Bagdad,* Universal, 1953.

Italian soldier, *The Rack,* MGM, 1956.

Hernandez, *Screaming Eagles,* Allied Artists, 1956.

Rafael, *Three Violent People,* Paramount, 1956.

Little Beaver, *Wagon Wheels Westward,* Republic, 1956.

Also appeared in *Sheriff of Las Vegas* (also known as *Billy the Kid, Sheriff of Sage Valley*), 1942, and *California Gold Rush,* 1946. As Mickey Gubitosi, appeared in the *Our Gang* series of movie shorts.

FILM APPEARANCES; AS ROBERT BLAKE

Blackout, Eros, 1950 (also see below).

Chuck, *Rumble on the Docks,* Columbia, 1956 (also see below).

Enrique Acosta Mesa, *The Tijuana Story,* Columbia, 1956 (also see below).

Karolyi, *The Beast of Budapest,* Allied Artists, 1958.

Rudy, *Revolt in the Big House,* Allied Artists, 1958.

Corporal Pacheco, *Battle Cry,* Allied Artists, 1959.

Velie, *Pork Chop Hill,* United Artists, 1959.

Honeyboy, *The Purple Gang,* Allied Artists, 1960.

Jim, *Town Without Pity* (also known as *Stadt Ohne Mitleid, Ville Sans Pitie,* and *Shocker*), United Artists, 1961.

Bucky Harris, *PT 109,* Warner Brothers, 1963.

Simon of Cyrene, *The Greatest Story Ever Told,* United Artists, 1965.

Sidney, *This Property Is Condemned,* Paramount, 1966.

Perry Smith, *In Cold Blood,* Columbia, 1967.

Willie Boy, *Tell Them Willie Boy Is Here,* Universal, 1969.

Ripped-Off, Alliance, 1971.

Title role, *Corky* (also known as *Lookin' Good*), MGM, 1972.

John Wintergreen, *Electra Glide in Blue,* United Artists, 1973.

Farrell, *Busting,* United Artists, 1974.

Charlie Callahan, *Coast to Coast,* Paramount, 1980.

Loyal, *Second-Hand Hearts* (also known as *Hamsters of Happiness*), Paramount, 1981.

Also appeared in *The Connection.*

FILM WORK

Producer (with Monty Berman), *Blackout,* Eros, 1950.
Stuntman, *Rumble on the Docks,* Columbia, 1956.
Stuntman, *The Tijuana Story,* Columbia, 1956.

STAGE APPEARANCES

Appeared in *Hatful of Rain,* Gallery Theatre.*

*   *   *

BOGARDE, Dirk   1921(?)-

PERSONAL: Born Dirk Jules Gaspard Ulric Niven Van den Bogarde, March 29 (some sources say March 28), 1921 (some sources say 1920), in Hampstead, London, England; son of Ulric Jules (an art editor) and Margaret (an actress; maiden name, Niven) Van den Bogarde. *Education:* Attended Allan Glens College, Glasgow, and University College, London. *Avocational interests:* Riding, talking, painting.

ADDRESSES: Agent— London Management, 235 Regent Street, London W1, England.

CAREER: Actor and writer. Formerly a scenic designer and commercial artist. *Military service:* British Army Service, 1940-46.

AWARDS, HONORS: British Academy Awards, British Academy of Film and Television Arts, Best Actor, 1963, for *The Servant,* and 1965, for *Darling.*

CREDITS:

STAGE APPEARANCES

When We Are Married, Queen's Theatre, London, 1939.
Diversion, Wyndham's Theatre, London, 1940.
Lawrence, *Cornelius,* Westminster Theatre, London, 1940.
Cliff, *Power without Glory,* New Lindsey Theatre, later Fortune Theatre, London, 1948.
Tony, *For Better, For Worse,* Queen's Theatre, London, 1948.
Dennis Paterson, *Foxhole in the Parlour,* New Lindsey Theatre, 1949.
Simon, *Sleep on My Shoulder,* Queen's Theatre, London, 1949.
Captain Molyneux, *The Shaughraun,* Bedford Theatre, London, 1950.
Orpheus, *Point of Departure,* Lyric Theatre, Hammersmith, later Duke of York's Theatre, London, 1950.
Nicky Lancaster, *The Vortex,* Lyric Theatre, 1952.
Alberto, *Summertime,* Apollo Theatre, London, 1955.
Marc, *Jezebel,* Oxford Playhouse, 1958.

FILM APPEARANCES

William Latch, *Esther Waters,* General Film Distributors, 1948.
Alfie Rawlins, *Boys in Brown,* General Film Distributors, 1949.
Charles Prohack, *Dear Mr. Prohack,* General Film Distributors, 1949.
George Bland, *Quartet,* Eagle Lion, 1949.
Tom Riley, *The Blue Lamp,* General Film Distributors, 1950.
Bob Baker, *Five Angels On Murder* (also known as *The Woman in Question*), General Film Distributors, 1950.
Stephen Mundy, *Blackmailed,* General Film Distributors, 1951.
Bill Fox, *Maniacs on Wheels* (also known as *Once a Jolly Swagman*), International Releasing, 1951.
George Hathaway, *So Long at the Fair,* Eagle Lion-Rank, 1951.
Matt Sullivan, *The Gentle Gunman,* General Film Distributors, 1952.
Chris Lloyd, *The Stranger in Between* (also known as *Hunted*), Universal, 1952.
Tim Mason, *Appointment in London,* Black Lion, 1953.
Simon Van Halder, *Desperate Moment,* General Film Distributors, 1953.
Tony Craig, *Penny Princess,* Universal, 1953.
Simon, *Doctor in the House,* General Film Distributors, 1954.
Tony Howard, *For Better for Worse* (also known as *Cocktails in the Kitchen*), Stratford, 1954.
Frank Clements, *The Sleeping Tiger,* Anglo Amalgamated, 1954.
Lieutenant Graham, *They Who Dare,* Black Lion, 1954.
Simon Sparrow, *Doctor at Sea,* Rank, 1955.
Flight Sergeant Mackay, *The Sea Shall Not Have Them,* United Artists, 1955.
Allan Howard, *Simba,* Lippert, 1955.
Bruce Campbell, *Campbell's Kingdom,* Rank, 1957.
Simon Sparrow, *Doctor at Large,* Rank, 1957.
Jose, *The Spanish Gardener,* Rank, 1957.
Edward Bare, *Cast a Dark Shadow,* Eros, 1958.
Louis Dubedat, *The Doctor's Dilemma,* Metro-Goldwyn-Mayer, 1958.
Major Paddy Leigh-Fernor, *Night Ambush* (also known as *Ill Met by Moonlight*), Rank, 1958.
Sydney Carton, *A Tale of Two Cities,* Rank, 1958.
Michael Quinn, *The Wind Cannot Read,* Fox, 1958.
Sir Mark Loodon/Frank Welney/Number Fifteen, *Libel,* Metro-Goldwyn-Mayer, 1959.
Arturo Carrera, *The Angel Wore Red,* Metro-Goldwyn-Mayer, 1960.
Franz Lizt, *Song Without End,* Columbia, 1960.

Anacleto, *The Singer Not the Song,* Warner Brothers, 1961.

Melville Farr, *Victim,* Pathe, 1961.

Lieutenant Scott-Padget, *Damn The Defiant* (also known as *H.M.S. Defiant*), Gulf Western Films, 1962.

Simon Sparrow, *We Joined the Navy* (also known as *We Are in the Navy Now*), Warner Brothers, 1962.

Simon Sparrow, *Doctor in Distress,* Rank, 1963.

David Donne, *I Could Go On Singing,* United Artists, 1963.

Dr. Henry Longman, *The Mind Benders,* American International Pictures, 1963.

Captain Hargreaves, *King and Country,* Allied Artists, 1964.

Hugo Barrett, *The Servant,* Landau, 1964.

Robert Gold, *Darling,* Embassy Pictures, 1965.

Nicholas Whistler, *Agent 8 3/4* (also known as *Enough For June*), Continental, 1965.

Major McGuire, *McGuire, Go Home!* (also known as *The High Bright Sun*), Continental Distributing, 1966.

Gabriel, *Modesty Blaise,* Twentieth Century-Fox, 1966.

Stephen, *Accident,* London Independent Producers, 1967.

Charlie Hook, *Our Mother's House,* Metro-Goldwyn-Mayer, 1967.

Bibikov, *The Fixer,* Metro-Goldwyn-Mayer, 1968.

Title Role, *Sebastian,* Paramount, 1968.

Pursewarden, *Justine,* Twentieth Century-Fox, 1969.

Gustav Von Aschenbach, *Death in Venice,* Warner Brothers, 1971.

Philip Boyle, *The Serpent* (also known as *Night Flight from Moscow*), Avco Embassy, 1973.

Max, *The Night Porter,* Avco Embassy, 1974.

Alan Curtis, *Permission to Kill,* Avco Embassy, 1975.

Claude Langham, *Providence,* Cinema 5, 1977.

Lieutenant General Browning, *A Bridge Too Far,* United Artists, 1977.

Hermann Hermann, *Despair,* Swan Diffusion, 1978.

Daddy, *Daddy Nostalgie* (also known as *These Foolish Things*), Ciga Productions, 1990.

Also appeared as Prince Charlie in *Upon This Rock,* 1970.

TELEVISION APPEARANCES

Kenneth Boyd, *Little Moon of Alban* (special), NBC, 1964.

Charles Condomine, *Blithe Spirit* (special), NBC, 1966.

Roald Dahl, *The Patricia Neal Story* (movie), CBS, 1981.

James Marriner, *The Vision* (movie), BBC, 1987.

WRITINGS:

A Postillion Struck by Lightning (memoir), Holt, 1977.

Snakes and Ladders (memoir), Holt, 1979.

A Gentle Occupation (novel), Knopf, 1980.

Voices in the Garden (novel), Knopf, 1981.

An Orderly Man (memoir), Knopf, 1983.

West of Sunset, Viking, 1984.

Also author of the memoir *Backcloth,* 1986.

SIDELIGHTS: Favorite roles: Cliff in *Power without Glory* and Orpheus in *Point of Departure.**

*   *   *

BOLOGNA, Joseph   1938-

PERSONAL: Born December 30, 1938, in Brooklyn, NY; married Renee Taylor (an actress and writer), 1965; children: Gabriel. *Education:* Attended Brown University.

ADDRESSES: Agent—c/o Rodney Sheldon, Artists Alliance, Los Angeles, CA.

CAREER: Actor and writer. Director and producer of television commercials for an advertising agency; collaborated with wife, Renee Taylor on *2,* a short film, shown at New York Film Festival, 1966. *Military service:* Served in the U.S. Marine Corps.

AWARDS, HONORS: Emmy Award (with wife, Renee Taylor), outstanding writing achievement in comedy, variety, or music special, 1973, for *Acts of Love and Other Comedies;* Screenwriters Guild nomination (with Taylor), best screenplay, 1972, for *Made for Each Other;* Emmy Award nomination, writing, 1975, for *Paradise.*

CREDITS:

STAGE APPEARANCES

Vito Pignoli, *It Had to Be You,* John Golden Theatre, New York City, 1981, and Marilyn Monroe Theatre.

Lovers and Other Strangers, Brooks Atkinson Theatre, New York City, 1968.

FILM APPEARANCES

Gig "Giggy" Pinimba, *Made for Each Other,* Twentieth Century-Fox, 1971.

Pete, *Mixed Company,* Lienroc/United Artists, 1974.

Dan Torrance, *The Big Bus,* Paramount, 1976.

Leo Schneider, *Chapter Two,* Columbia, 1979.

King Kaiser, *My Favorite Year,* Brooksfilms/Metro-Goldwyn-Mayer/United Artists, 1982.

Victor Lyons, *Blame It on Rio,* Twentieth Century-Fox, 1984.

Joe, *The Woman in Red,* Woman in Red Productions/Orion, 1984.

Dr. Malavaqua, *Transylvania 6-5000,* New World, 1985.

Also appeared as Vito Pignoli, *It Had to Be You,* 1989; Uncle Phil, *Coupe de Ville,* 1990.

FILM WORK

Also director (with others), *It Had to Be You,* 1989.

TELEVISION APPEARANCES; MOVIES

Salvatore "Bill" Bonnanno, *Honor Thy Father,* CBS, 1973.
Sam Rodino, *Woman of the Year,* CBS, 1976.
Ted Conti, *Torn between Two Lovers,* CBS, 1979.
Max Boone, *One Cooks, the Other Doesn't,* CBS, 1983.
Rico Castelli, *Copacabana,* CBS, 1985.
Chuck Hassan, *A Time to Triumph,* CBS, 1986.

Also appeared as Judge Manza, *Prime Target,* 1989.

TELEVISION APPEARANCES; SPECIALS

Acts of Love and Other Comedies, ABC, 1973.
David, Biff, Tony, and Nick, *Paradise,* CBS, 1974.
Peter, *A Lucille Ball Special: What Now Catherine Curtis?,* CBS, 1976.
Bill and David, *Bedrooms,* HBO, 1984.
The Joe Piscopo Special, HBO, 1984.

Also appeared in *The Barbour Report,* 1986.

OTHER TELEVISION APPEARANCES

Carlucci's Department (episodic), CBS, 1973.
Steve Bryant, *Sins* (mini-series), CBS, 1986.
Gordon Vogel, *Not Quite Human* (mini-series), 1987.
Nick Foley, *Rags to Riches* (series), NBC, 1987-88.

TELEVISION WORK

Producer (With Howard Gottfried, Elliot Shoerman, Rudy De Luca, and Taylor), *Carlucci's Department* (episodic), CBS, 1976.
Director and producer (With Richard S. Harwood), *Good Penny* (pilot), NBC, 1977.
Producer (With Taylor), *Lovers and Other Strangers* (pilot), ABC, 1983.
Director (With Taylor), *Bedrooms* (special), HBO, 1984.

WRITINGS:

PLAYS

(With Taylor) *Lovers and Other Strangers* (produced at Brooks Atkinson Theatre, 1968), Samuel French, 1968.
It Had to Be You, produced at John Golden Theatre, 1981.

SCREENPLAYS

(With Taylor and David Zelag Goodman) *Lovers and Other Strangers,* ABC/Cinerama, 1970.
(With Taylor) *Made for Each Other,* Twentieth Century-Fox, 1971.

Also author of *It Had to Be You,* 1989, and *The Witch of Naples.*

TELEVISION; WITH RENEE TAYLOR

Benny (special), PBS, 1971.

Acts of Love and Other Comedies (special), ABC, 1973.
A Lucille Ball Special Starring Lucille Ball and Jackie Gleason, CBS, 1975.
(And Bernard M. Kahn) *Woman of the Year* (movie), CBS, 1976.
Good Penny (pilot), NBC, 1977.
A Cry for Love (movie), NBC, 1980.
Lovers and Other Strangers (pilot), ABC, 1983.
Bedrooms (special), HBO, 1984.

OTHER

Honor Thy Father, CBS, 1973.
Paradise (special), CBS, 1974.
Carlucci's Department (episodic), CBS, 1976.

Contributor to *The Great American Dream Machine* (series), PBS. *

*   *   *

BOTTIN, Rob   1959(?)-

PERSONAL: Surname is pronounced "Bo-*teen*"; born in 1959 (some sources say 1958). *Education:* Studied special effects design with Rick Baker.

ADDRESSES: Agent—Gersh Agency, 232 N. Canon Dr., Beverly Hills, CA 90210.

CAREER: Special makeup effects and special effects designer. Designer with New World Pictures.

AWARDS, HONORS: Academy Award nomination (with Peter Robb-King), best makeup, 1986, for *Legend;* Academy Award (with others), special achievement award, 1990, for *Total Recall.*

CREDITS:

FILM APPEARANCES

Captain Blake, *The Fog,* AVCO-Embassy, 1980.

FILM WORK

Special makeup effects apprentice, *King Kong,* Paramount, 1976.
Special makeup effects apprentice, *Star Wars,* Twentieth Century-Fox, 1977.
Special makeup effects designer and special effects designer, *Piranha,* New World, 1978.
Giant mouse designer, *Rock 'n' Roll High School,* New World, 1979.
Special makeup effects design assistant, *Mistress of the Apes,* Cineworld, 1979.
Special makeup effects designer and special effects designer, *The Fog,* AVCO-Embassy, 1980.
Humanoids designer, *Humanoids from the Deep* (also known as *Monster*), New World, 1980.

Special makeup effects designer and associate producer, *The Howling,* AVCO-Embassy, 1981.

Special effects designer (with Rick Baker) and special makeup effects designer, *Tanya's Island,* International Film Exchange/Fred Baker, 1981.

Special makeup effects designer, *The Thing,* Universal, 1982.

Special makeup effects designer (with Craig Reardon and Michael McCracken), "It's a Good Life," *Twilight Zone—The Movie,* Warner Brothers, 1983.

Special makeup effects designer, *Explorers,* Paramount, 1985.

Special makeup effects designer (with Peter Robb-King), *Legend,* Universal, 1986.

Special makeup effects designer, *Innerspace,* Warner Brothers, 1987.

Special makeup effects designer and Robocop designer, *Robocop,* Orion, 1987.

Special makeup effects designer, *The Witches of Eastwick,* Warner Brothers, 1987.

Special makeup effects designer, *The Great Outdoors,* Universal, 1988.

Robocop designer and Robocop costume designer, *Robocop 2,* Orion, 1990.

Special makeup effects designer and character visual effects designer, *Total Recall,* Tri-Star, 1990.

TELEVISION WORK

Special effects designer for the special *Manbeast! Myth or Monster,* 1978.*

* * *

BOYLE, Peter 1933(?)-

PERSONAL: Born October 18, 1933 (one source says 1935), in Philadelphia, PA; married Lorraine Alterman, October, 1977. *Education:* Attended LaSalle College.

ADDRESSES: Agent—Andrea Eastman, International Creative Management, 8899 Beverly Blvd., Los Angeles, CA 90048.

CAREER: Actor. Member of the Second City Company, Chicago, IL. Monk in Christian Brothers Order until early 1960s.

AWARDS, HONORS: Emmy Award nomination, Outstanding Lead Actor in a Drama or Comedy Special, 1977, for *Tail Gunner Joe;* Emmy Award nomination, Outstanding Guest Actor in a Drama Series, 1989, for *Midnight Caller.*

CREDITS:

FILM APPEARANCES

General Heath, *The Virgin President,* New Line, 1968.

Gun clinic manager, *Medium Cool,* Paramount, 1969.

Man in group therapy session, *Diary of a Mad Housewife,* Universal, 1970.

Joe Curran, *Joe,* Cannon, 1970.

Jack Mitchell, *T.R. Baskin* (also known as *Date with a Lonely Girl*), Paramount, 1971.

Lucas, *The Candidate,* Warner Brothers, 1972.

Dillon, *The Friends of Eddie Coyle,* Paramount, 1973.

Preacher Bob, *Kid Blue,* Twentieth Century-Fox, 1973.

Barry Fenaka, *Slither,* Metro-Goldwyn-Mayer, 1973.

Eagle Throneberry, *Steelyard Blues* (also known as *The Final Crash*), Warner Brothers, 1973.

Title role, *Crazy Joe,* Columbia, 1974.

Monster, *Young Frankenstein,* Twentieth Century-Fox, 1974.

Lord Durant, *Swashbuckler* (also known as *The Scarlet Buccaneer*), Universal, 1976.

Wizard, *Taxi Driver,* Columbia, 1976.

Joe McGinnis, *The Brink's Job,* Universal, 1978.

Max Graham, *F.I.S.T.,* United Artists, 1978.

Frank Massetti, *Beyond the Poseidon Adventure,* Warner Brothers, 1979.

Andy Mast, *Hard Core* (also known as *Hard Core Life*), Columbia, 1979.

Dr. Sebastian Melmoth, *In God We Trust,* Universal, 1980.

Karl Lazlo, *Where the Buffalo Roam,* Universal, 1980.

Sheppard, *Outland,* Warner Brothers, 1981.

Jimmy Ryan, *Hammett,* Orion/Warner Brothers, 1982.

Moon, *Yellowbeard,* Orion, 1983.

Jocko Dundee, *Johnny Dangerously,* Twentieth Century-Fox, 1984.

Joe, *Joe II,* Cannon, 1984.

Detective Ryan, *Turk 182!,* Twentieth Century-Fox, 1985.

Jay Bass, *Surrender,* Warner Brothers, 1987.

Commodore Cornelius Vanderbilt, *Walker,* Universal, 1987.

The In Crowd, Orion, 1987.

Lou Donnelly, *Red Heat,* Tri-Star, 1988.

Chief Edsel, *Speed Zone,* Orion, 1989.

Actor, *Funny* (documentary), Original Cinema, 1989.

Jack McDermott, *The Dream Team,* Universal, 1989.

Also appeared as Ras Mohammed, *Ghost in the Noonday Sun,* 1974.

TELEVISION APPEARANCES; MOVIES

Charlie Datweiler, *The Man Who Could Talk to Kids,* ABC, 1973.

Joseph McCarthy, *Tail Gunner Joe,* NBC, 1977.

Detective Vannort, *Echoes in the Darkness,* CBS, 1987.

David Dellinger, *Conspiracy: The Trial of the Chicago Eight,* HBO, 1987.

General Sanger, *Disaster at Silo Seven,* ABC, 1988.

John Poindexter, *Guts and Glory: The Rise and Fall of Oliver North,* CBS, 1989.

Roger Boisjoly, *Challenger,* ABC, 1990.

TELEVISION APPEARANCES; SERIES

Regular, *Comedy Tonight,* CBS, 1970.

Sergeant Fatso Judson, *From Here to Eternity,* NBC, 1979.

Officer Joe Bash, *Joe Bash,* ABC, 1986.

TELEVISION APPEARANCES; EPISODIC

Phillip Greenlow, *Cagney and Lacey,* CBS, 1988.

J. J. Killian, *Midnight Caller,* NBC, 1989, 1990, and 1991.

TELEVISION APPEARANCES; SPECIALS

Superman's Fiftieth Anniversary: A Celebration of the Man of Steel, CBS, 1988.

National Basketball Players Association Awards, syndicated, 1989.

Jake, "Twenty-Seven Wagons Full of Cotton," *American Playwrights Theatre: The One Acts,* Arts and Entertainment, 1990.

OTHER TELEVISION APPEARANCES

Klein Time (pilot), CBS, 1977.

Sergeant Fatso Judson, *From Here to Eternity* (miniseries), NBC, 1979.

STAGE APPEARANCES

Mikoyan, *Shadow of Heroes,* York Playhouse, New York City, 1961.

Ensemble, *Paul Sills' Story Theatre* (revue), Ambassador Theatre, New York City, 1970.

Phil Alexander, *The Roast,* Winter Garden Theatre, New York City, 1980.

Lee, *True West,* New York Shakespeare Festival, Public Theatre, New York City, 1981.

Rocco, *Snow Orchid,* Circle Repertory Company, New York City, 1982.

MAJOR TOURS

Murray and understudy for Oscar, *The Odd Couple,* U.S. cities, 1965-67.*

*   *   *

BRANAGH, Kenneth   1960-

PERSONAL: Surname pronounced "*Bran*-och"; born December 10, 1960, in Belfast, Northern Ireland; father, a plumber; married Emma Thompson (an actress), August, 1989. *Education:* Royal Academy of Dramatic Art, graduate, 1981.

ADDRESSES: Agent—Clifford Stevens, STE Representation, 9301 Wilshire Blvd., Suite 312, Beverly Hills, CA 90210, and 888 Seventh Ave. Suite 201, New York, NY 10019.

CAREER: Actor, director, producer, and writer. Member of Royal Shakespeare Company for two years; Renaissance Theatre Company, London, founder, producer, and director, with David Parfitt, 1987—.

AWARDS, HONORS: Laurence Olivier Award, Most Promising Newcomer of the Year, 1982, for *Another Country;* Chicago Film Critics Award, Best Foreign Film, New York Film Critics Circle, Best New Director Award, Academy Award nominations, Best Actor and Best Director, and British Academy Award, Best Director, 1990, all for *Henry V;* Bancroft Gold Medal, Royal Academy of Dramatic Art, for *Hamlet.*

CREDITS:

STAGE APPEARANCES

(Stage debut) Judd, *Another Country,* London, 1982.

Laertes, *Hamlet,* Royal Shakespeare Company (RSC), Stratford-upon-Avon, then Barbican Theatre Center, London, 1985.

Title role, *Hamlet,* Tivoli Festival, Renaissance Theatre Company at Elsinore Castle, Denmark, 1988.

Edgar, *King Lear,* Renaissance Theatre Company, Mark Taper Forum, Los Angeles, 1990.

A rustic, *A Midsummer Night's Dream,* Renaissance Theatre Company, Mark Taper Forum, 1990.

Also appeared as St. Francis of Assisi, *St. Francis,* and in *Romeo and Juliet,* both London.

MAJOR TOURS

Toured as Laertes, *Hamlet,* UK cities; Benedict, *Much Ado About Nothing,* UK cities; Touchstone, *As You Like It,* UK cities.

STAGE WORK

Producer (With David Parfitt), *Hamlet,* Tivoli Festival, Renaissance Theatre Company at Elsinore Castle, Denmark, 1988.

Director, *Twelfth Night,* Renaissance Theatre Company, 1989.

Director, *A Midsummer Night's Dream,* Renaissance Theatre Company, Mark Taper Forum, 1990.

Director, *King Lear,* Renaissance Theatre Company, Mark Taper Forum, 1990.

Also director of *The Life of Napoleon,* Renaissance Theatre Company.

FILM APPEARANCES

(Film debut) Rick, *High Season,* Hemdale, 1987.

Charles Moon, *A Month in the Country,* Orion Classics, 1987.
Title role, *Henry V,* Samuel Goldwyn Company, 1989.
Mike Church/Roman Strauss, *Dead Again,* Paramount, 1991.

FILM WORK

Director and producer, *Henry V,* Samuel Goldwyn Company, 1989.
Director, *Dead Again,* Paramount, 1991.

TELEVISION APPEARANCES

Jack, *The Boy in the Bush* (series), PBS, 1988.
Guy Pringle, "The Fortunes of War" (mini-series), *Masterpiece Theatre,* PBS, 1988.
Gordon Evans as an adult, "Strange Interlude" (special), *American Playhouse,* PBS, 1988.

Also appeared as Charles Tansley, *To the Lighthouse* (special), 1984; in *Thompson* (episodic), 1990; *The Billy Trilogy* (series).

WRITINGS:

Tell Me Honestly (play), produced by Royal Shakespeare Company, 1985.
Public Enemy (play; produced in London, 1987), Faber, 1988.
(Adapter) *Henry V* (film), Samuel Goldwyn Company, 1989.
Beginning (autobiography), Chatto & Windus, 1989, Norton, 1990.

OTHER SOURCES:

PERIODICALS

Film Comment, November-December, 1989.
Hollywood Reporter, March 22, 1990.
Interview, October, 1989.
New Republic, December 4, 1989.
Newsweek, February 19, 1990.
New York Times, January 8, 1989; November 5, 1989; November 8, 1989; January 21, 1990.
People, February 12, 1990.
Publishers Weekly, March 23, 1990.
Rolling Stone, November 30, 1989; February 8, 1990.
Sunday Times (London), October 1, 1989; October 8, 1989.
Time, November 13, 1989; February 5, 1990.
Times (London), August 17, 1985; July 18, 1987.
Times Literary Supplement, October 20-26, 1989.
Tribune Books (Chicago), May 20, 1990.*

BRENNER, Dori

PERSONAL: Born December 16 in New York, NY. *Education:* Attended Sarah Lawrence College; received M.F.A. degree from the Yale University School of Drama.

ADDRESSES: Agent—Harris and Goldberg Talent Agency, 1999 Avenue of the Stars, Suite 2850, Los Angeles, CA 90067.

CAREER: Actress.

AWARDS, HONORS: Emmy Award nomination, 1977, for *Seventh Avenue.*

CREDITS:

STAGE APPEARANCES

(Broadway debut) Corporal Shulman, "Defender of the Faith," folk singer, "Epstein," and nurse, "Eli, the Fanatic," *Unlikely Heroes* (triple-bill), Plymouth Theatre, 1971.
The Trial of the Catonsville Nine, Studio Arena Theatre, Buffalo, NY, 1971.
The Charlatan, Center Theatre Group, Mark Taper Forum, Los Angeles, 1974.

Also appeared with the Guthrie Theatre, Minneapolis, MN, 1973-74.

FILM APPEARANCES

Scarecrow in a Garden of Cucumbers, New Line, 1972.
Anna, *Summer Wishes, Winter Dreams,* Columbia, 1973.
Connie, *Next Stop, Greenwich Village,* Twentieth Century-Fox, 1976.
Cookie, *The Other Side of the Mountain* (also known as *A Window to the Sky*), Twentieth Century-Fox, 1977.
Sylvia Rosenberg, *Altered States,* Warner Brothers, 1980.
Jill, *The Oasis,* Titan, 1984.
Park mom, *Baby Boom,* Metro-Goldwyn-Mayer/United Artists, 1987.
Loretta, *The Boys,* Twentieth Century-Fox, 1991.

TELEVISION APPEARANCES; MOVIES

Nicki, *All Together Now,* ABC, 1975.
Renee De Reda, *I Want to Keep My Baby!,* CBS, 1976.
Natalie, *Sex and the Single Parent,* CBS, 1979.
Dori Green, *I Dream of Jeannie . . . Fifteen Years Later,* NBC, 1985.
Carole Karasick, *Obsessed with a Married Woman,* ABC, 1985.
Amy Roberts, *The Operation,* CBS, 1990.

Also appeared in *Split Ticket,* 1990; *The Last to Go,* 1991.

TELEVISION APPEARANCES; SERIES

Meryl Foxx, *Cassie and Company,* NBC, 1982.
Sally Miller, *The Charmings,* ABC, 1987-88.

TELEVISION APPEARANCES; EPISODIC

Molly, *Dallas,* CBS, 1985.
Emily Johnson, *Cagney and Lacey,* CBS, 1985.
Wendy Wittener, *Who's the Boss?,* ABC, 1985, 1986, and 1987.
Penny Calloway, *Falcon Crest,* CBS, 1988.
Mancuso, FBI, NBC, 1989.

Also appeared as Luana Belker, *Hill Street Blues,* NBC. Appeared in *Equal Justice,* ABC; *Sons and Daughters,* CBS.

TELEVISION APPEARANCES; SPECIALS

Cindy Chalmers, "Journey to Survival," *CBS Afternoon Playhouse,* CBS, 1982.

Also appeared in "The Home," *American Playhouse,* PBS.

TELEVISION APPEARANCES; PILOTS

Sandy, *The Oath: The Sad and Lonely Sundays,* ABC, 1976.
Sheila Levine, *Sheila,* CBS, 1977.
Karen, *Sparrow,* CBS, 1978.
Leslie Frankel, *Friends,* CBS, 1978.
Sheri Radford, *Brothers,* CBS, 1980.

TELEVISION APPEARANCES; MINI-SERIES

Rhoda Gold Blackman, *Seventh Avenue,* NBC, 1977.*

* * *

BRICUSSE, Leslie 1931-

PERSONAL: Born 1931 in England; married Yvonne Romain (an actress); children: one son. *Education:* Attended Cambridge University.

ADDRESSES: Office—c/o Broadcast Music Incorporated, 320 West 57th St., New York, NY 10019.

CAREER: Composer, lyricist, actor, director, and writer.

AWARDS, HONORS: Ivor Novello Award, 1962, for song, "My Kind of Girl"; Ivor Novello Award (with Anthony Newley), 1962, Broadcast Music Award, Best Song of the Year, 1962, and Grammy Award, all for "What Kind of Fool Am I?" from *Stop the World—I Want To Get Off;* Whitbread Anglo-American Theatre Award (with Newley), 1965, for *The Roar of the Greasepaint—The Smell of the Crowd;* Grammy Award, 1967, for "Talk to the Animals," from *Dr. Doolittle;* inducted into Songwriter's Hall of Fame, 1989; Academy Award nomination, Best Original Song, 1990, for "Somewhere in My Memory," from *Home Alone.*

CREDITS:

STAGE APPEARANCES

An Evening with Beatrice Lillie, Globe Theatre, London, England, 1954.

STAGE WORK

Director, *Out of the Blue* (revue), Cambridge University Footlights, then Phoenix Theatre, London, 1954.

TELEVISION WORK

Theme performer, *It's a Living* (special), ABC, 1980.

Also performed song "In Trouble," *In Trouble* (special), 1981; performed songs "A New Life," and "Candy Man," *Songwriters Hall of Fame 20th Anniversary . . . The Magic of Music,* 1989.

WRITINGS:

STAGE

Book, music, and lyrics (with Anthony Newley), *Stop the World—I Want To Get Off,* Queen's Theatre, London, 1961, then Sam S. Shubert Theatre, New York City, 1962.
Lyrics, *Pickwick,* London, 1963, then San Francisco, CA, and 46th Street Theatre, New York City, 1965.
Book, music, and lyrics (with Newley), *The Roar of the Greasepaint—The Smell of the Crowd,* Sam S. Shubert Theatre, 1965.
The Good Old Bad Old Days, London, 1973.
Book, music, and lyrics, *Kings and Clowns,* London, 1978.
(With Newley) *The Travelling Music Show,* London, 1978.
Lyrics, *Over the Rainbow,* London, 1978.
Book, music, and lyrics, *Sherlock Holmes—The Musical,* Cambridge Theatre, London, 1989.
Book and lyrics, *Jekyll and Hyde,* Alley Theatre, Houston, TX, 1990.

Also composed music and lyrics, *Lady at the Wheel,* 1958.

FILM SCORES

(With John Cresswell) *Charley Moon,* British Lion, 1956.
(With Frederick Raphael) *Bachelor of Hearts,* Rank, 1958.
(With Vivian A. Cox) *The Swinging Maiden* (also known as *The Iron Maiden*), Gregory, Hake and Walker/Anglo Amalgamated/Columbia, 1963.
Music (with Talbot Rothwell and Eric Rogers), *Three Hats for Lisa,* Seven Hills/Warner Brothers/Pathe, 1965.
Music, lyrics (with Newley, David Donable, Al Ham, Marilyn Bergman, and Alan Bergman), *Stop the World—I Want To Get Off,* Warner Brothers, 1966.
Dr. Doolittle, Twentieth Century-Fox, 1967.

Music, lyrics, *Goodbye Mr. Chips,* Metro-Goldwyn-Mayer, 1969.

Book, music, *Scrooge,* Waterbury/National General, 1970.

Music, lyrics, *Willy Wonka and the Chocolate Factory,* Paramount, 1971.

Music, lyrics (with Newley), *Sammy Stops the World* (also known as *Stop the World—I Want To Get Off*), Ed Rood Sr./Special Events Entertainment, 1978.

Sunday Lovers, Viaduc-Medusa/United Artists, 1980.

Lyrics, *Victor/Victoria,* United Artists, 1982.

Also author of *The Very Edge,* 1963.

TELEVISION SERIES

Theme song, *Hart To Hart,* 1979.

Theme song (with Alision Tipton), *I'm a Big Girl Now,* ABC, 1980-81.

TELEVISION SPECIALS

Composed music and lyrics, *Babes in Toyland,* 1986.

OTHER

(With Newley) "Saint Jack" (title-song), *Goldfinger,* United Artists, 1964.

(With Jerry Goldsmith) *In Like Flint* (title-song), Twentieth Century-Fox, 1967.

Co-songwriter, *Gunn,* Paramount, 1967.

Lyrics (title song), *A Guide for the Married Man,* Twentieth Century-Fox, 1967.

"Can You Read My Mind" (song), *Superman: The Movie,* Warner Brothers, 1978.

"Move 'Em Out" (song), *Revenge of the Pink Panther,* United Artists, 1978.

"The Precious Moment" (song), *The Sea Wolves,* Paramount, 1980.

"Thank You Santa," "Every Christmas Eve," "Making Toys," and "Patch! Natch" (songs), *Santa Claus: The Movie,* Tri-Star, 1985.

Also composed lyrics, "Life in a Looking Glass," (song), *That's Life,* 1986; "My Kind of Girl," (song), 1962.*

*   *   *

BRIERS, Richard   1934-

PERSONAL: Born January 14, 1934, in Croydon, Surrey, England; son of Joseph Benjamin and Morna Phyllis (Richardson) Briers; married Ann Davies. *Education:* Trained for the stage at the Royal Academy of Dramatic Art; studied at the Liverpool Playhouse Repertory Company, 1956-57. *Avocational interests:* Reading, gardening, and going to the cinema and theatre.

ADDRESSES: Agent—International Creative Management Ltd., 388/396 Oxford St., London W1N 9HE, England.

CAREER: Actor. Actor in television commercials. Worked for a time as a clerk.

AWARDS, HONORS: Silver Medal from the Royal Academy of Dramatic Art.

CREDITS:

STAGE APPEARANCES

(London debut) Joseph Field, *Gilt and Gingerbread,* Duke of York's Theatre, 1959.

Bill, "Special Providence," *Double Yoke* (double-bill), St. Martin's Theatre, London, 1960.

Christian Martin, *It's in the Bag,* Duke of York's Theatre, London, 1960.

Bartholomeus II, *The Shepherd's Chameleon,* and detective, *Victims of Duty* (double bill), Arts Theatre, London, 1960.

James Whinby, "The Form," and the tramp, "A Slight Ache," *Three* (triple-bill), Arts Theatre, 1961, then Criterion Theatre, London, 1961.

David Madison, *Miss Pell Is Missing,* Criterion Theatre, 1962.

Lieutenant William Hargreaves, *Hamp,* Edinburgh Festival, Lyceum Theatre, Edinburgh, Scotland, 1964.

Roland Maule, *Present Laughter,* Queen's Theatre, London, 1965.

Mortimer Brewster, *Arsenic and Old Lace,* Vaudeville Theatre, London, 1966.

Greg, *Relatively Speaking,* Duke of York's Theatre, 1967.

William Falder, *Justice,* St. Martin's Theatre, 1968.

Moon, *The Real Inspector Hound,* Criterion Theatre, 1968.

Bois d'Enghien, *Cat Among the Pigeons,* Prince of Wales' Theatre, London, 1969.

Five roles, *The Two of Us,* Garrick Theatre, London, 1970.

Title role, *Butley,* Criterion Theatre, 1972.

Sidney Hopcroft, *Absurd Person Singular,* Criterion Theatre, 1973.

Colin, *Absent Friends,* Garrick Theatre, 1975.

Colin, *Middle-Age Spread,* Lyric Theatre, London, 1979.

Captain Bluntschli, *Arms and the Man,* Lyric Theatre, 1981.

John Smith, *Run for Your Wife,* Shaftesbury Theatre, London, 1983.

John Bailey, *Why Me?,* Strand Theatre, London, 1985.

Lord Foppington, *The Relapse,* Chichester Festival Theatre, Chichester, United Kingdom, 1986.

Malvolio, *Twelfth Night,* Renaissance Theatre Company, Riverside Studio Theatre, London, 1987-88.

Title role, *King Lear,* Renaissance Theatre Company, Mark Taper Forum, Los Angeles, 1990, then Dominion Theatre, London, 1990.

Bottom, *A Midsummer Night's Dream,* Renaissance Theatre Company, Mark Taper Forum, 1990, then Dominion Theatre, 1990.

Also appeared as the Dame, *Babes in the Wood;* appeared in repertory in Leatherhead, Surrey, United Kingdom, and at the Belgrade Theatre, Coventry, United Kingdom, both 1958.

MAJOR TOURS

Blisworth, *Something About a Sailor,* United Kingdom cities, 1957.

Joseph Field, *Gilt and Gingerbread,* United Kingdom cities, 1958.

Gerald Popkiss, *Rookery Nook,* United Kingdom cities, 1964.

Title role, *Richard III,* United Kingdom cities, 1972.

Title role, *King Lear,* Renaissance Theatre Company, international cities, 1990.

Bottom, *A Midsummer Night's Dream,* Renaissance Theatre Company, international cities, 1990.

FILM APPEARANCES

Colbourne, *Bottoms Up,* Associated British, 1960.

"Mrs. Binster," *Murder She Said* (also known as *Meet Miss Marple*), Metro-Goldwyn-Mayer (MGM), 1961.

Eustace Hignett, *The Girl on the Boat,* Knightsbridge, 1962.

Jamieson, *A Matter of Who,* MGM, 1962.

Meteorological official, *The V.I.P.s,* MGM, 1963.

Tomkins, *The Bargee,* Associated British/Warner-Pathe, 1964.

Timothy, *Fathom,* Twentieth Century-Fox, 1967.

Nigel Hadfield, *All the Way Up,* Granada/Anglo Amalgamated, 1970.

Voice of Fiver, *Watership Down* (animated), AVCO-Embassy, 1978.

Ted Washbrook, *A Chorus of Disapproval,* South Gate Entertainment, 1989.

Bardolph, *Henry V,* Samuel Goldwyn, 1989.

Also appeared in *Girls at Sea,* Associated British/Seven Arts, 1958, and *Rentadick,* Virgin, 1972.

TELEVISION APPEARANCES; SERIES

Tom Good, *The Good Life* (also known as *Good Neighbors*), BBC, 1975.

Tom Good, *The Good Life,* PBS, 1980.

Ever Decreasing Circles, BBC-1, 1989.

Mr. Bean, ITV, 1990.

Also appeared in *Brothers in Law; Marriage Lines;* and *The Other One.*

OTHER TELEVISION APPEARANCES

Reg, *The Norman Conquests* (special), Thames, 1978.

Reg, "The Norman Conquests," *Great Performances,* PBS, 1978.

Rector, *The Aerodrome* (movie), BBC, 1983.

RADIO APPEARANCES

Appeared on the series *Brothers in Law* and *Marriage Lines.*

SIDELIGHTS: Favorite roles: Sidney Hopcroft in *Absurd Person Singular,* the title role in *Butley.*

OTHER SOURCES:

PERIODICALS

Hollywood Reporter, January 23, 1990.
Sunday Times (London), July 29, 1990.*

*   *   *

BROOKS, Avery   1949-

PERSONAL: Born October 2, 1949, in Evansville, IN; son of Samuel (a tool and die worker and union official) and Eva Lydia (a musician and chorale conductor; maiden name, Crawford) Brooks; married Vicki Lenora; children: Ayana, Cabral, Asante. *Education:* Attended Indiana University; Oberlin College; received B.A. and M.F.A. from Rutgers University.

ADDRESSES: Agent—c/o Brian Riordan, Bloom & Associates, 233 Park Ave. S., New York, NY 10003.

CAREER: Actor, teacher, director and choreographer. Worked as a professor of theatre and drama at Rutgers, The State University, for thirteen years.

CREDITS:

STAGE APPEARANCES

Sean David, *A Photograph: A Study of Cruelty,* New York Shakespeare Festival (NYSF), Public Theatre, New York City, 1978.

Paul Robeson, *Are You Now or Have You Ever Been?,* Promenade Theatre, New York City, 1978.

Title role, *Paul Robeson* (one-man show), John Golden Theatre, New York City, 1988.

Also appeared in *Spell #7,* NYSF, Public Theatre, 1979.

STAGE WORK

Choreographer, *The Mighty Gents,* NYSF, Mobile Theatre, 1979.

Director, *Manfred* (staged reading), Music With Words Festival, New England Conservatory, 1986.

TELEVISION APPEARANCES

Solomon Northrup's Odyssey (special), PBS, 1984.
Dude on Bus, *Finnegan Begin Again* (movie), HBO, 1985.
Hawk, *Spenser: For Hire* (series), ABC, 1985-89.
Cletus Moyer, *Roots: The Gift* (mini-series), ABC, 1988.
Uncle Tom, *Uncle Tom's Cabin* (movie), 1987.
Title role, *A Man Called Hawk* (series), ABC, 1989.

Also appeared in the special *Gordon Parks: Moments without Proper Names,* 1988; served as the host of the episode, "Prisoners on the Street," *Trackdown,* 1988; played a role in *Trackdown,* 1988; and served as the host and narrator of *The Musical Legacy of Roland Hayes,* 1990.

OTHER SOURCES:

PERIODICALS

New York Post, August 10, 1988.*

*   *   *

BROTHERSON, Eric   1911-1989

PERSONAL: Born May 10, 1911, in Chicago, IL; died October 21, 1989, in New York, NY; son of John Henry and Ella Stankowitz Brotherson; married Helen Harsh (deceased). *Education:* Attended Illinois Wesleyan University; received B.A. from University of Wisconsin. *Avocational interests:* Swimming, bridge.

CAREER: Actor. Worked as a schoolmaster, in insurance, and as a puppeteer before beginning acting career. *Military service:* U.S. Navy, 1944-46.

CREDITS:

STAGE APPEARANCES

(Stage debut) Guest, *Between the Devil,* Shubert Theatre, New Haven, CT, then (Broadway debut) Imperial Theatre, 1937.
Chorus member, *Set to Music,* Music Box Theatre, New York City, 1939.
Russell Paxton, *Lady in the Dark,* Alvin Theatre, New York City, 1941-43.
Byron Burns, *My Dear Public,* 46th Street Theatre, New York City, 1943.
Falke, *Rosalinda,* Los Angeles Civic Light Opera, Los Angeles, CA, 1947.
Henry Spofford, *Gentlemen Prefer Blondes,* Ziegfeld Theatre, New York City, 1949.
Simon Jenkins, *Room Service,* Playhouse Theatre, New York City, 1953.
Ferelli, *The Fifth Season,* Cort Theatre, New York City, 1954.
Sir Edward Ramsey, *The King and I,* New York State Theatre, 1964.

Hartkopf, *The Great Waltz,* Music Center, Los Angeles, 1965.
(London debut) Hartkopf, *The Great Waltz,* Theatre Royal and Drury Lane Theatre, both 1970.
Van Corlandt, *Knickerbocker Holiday,* Curran Theatre, San Francisco, CA, 1971.
Max Detweiler, *The Sound of Music,* Los Angeles Civic Light Opera, 1972.
Sam Nash, *Jesse Kiplinger,* Cirque Theatre, Seattle, WA, 1975.
Roy Hubley, *Plaza Suite,* Cirque Theatre, 1975.
Ensemble, *A Musical Jubilee* (revue), St. James Theatre, New York City, 1975.
Colonel Pickering, *My Fair Lady,* St. James Theatre, 1976.
Colonel Pickering, *My Fair Lady,* Showboat Theatre, Tampa, FL, 1978.

Also appeared as guest artist with the Goodman Theatre, Chicago, IL, 1971-72 season.

MAJOR TOURS

Jamie, later Zottan Karpathy and Colonel Pickering, *My Fair Lady,* United States and Soviet Union, 1957-63.
Horace Vandergelder, *Hello Dolly!,* U.S. cities, 1967-68.

Also toured in *Make Mine Manhattan,* 1949, in *Gentlemen Prefer Blondes,* 1951-52, and as Radbury, *Pleasures and Palaces,* 1965.

FILM APPEARANCES

Real estate agent, *Blacula,* American International Pictures, 1972.
Larrabee's butler, *What's Up Doc?,* Warner Brothers, 1972.

Also appeared in *Star,* 1967, *Bedknobs and Broomsticks,* 1970, and as maitre d', in *The Black Bird,* 1975.

TELEVISION APPEARANCES

Porter, *The Hound of the Baskervilles* (pilot), ABC, 1972.
Mr. Hall, *Betrayal* (movie), ABC, 1974.

SIDELIGHTS: Favorite roles: Russell Paxton, *Lady in the Dark,* and Henry Spofford, *Gentlemen Prefer Blondes.*

OBITUARIES AND OTHER SOURCES:

PERIODICALS

Variety, November 1, 1989.*

*   *   *

BROWN, Georgia   1933-

PERSONAL: Born Lillian Claire Laizer Getel Klot, October 21, 1933, in London, England; daughter of Mark (a furrier) and Anne (Kirshenbaum) Klot; married Gareth Wigan, November 7, 1974. *Education:* Attended Central Foundation Grammar School for Girls, London, England, 1944-50; studied singing with Keith Davis and acting with Curt Conway.

CAREER: Actress, singer, and writer.

MEMBER: Actors' Equity Association, American Guild of Variety Artists, American Federation of Television and Radio Artists.

AWARDS, HONORS: Variety Critics Poll Award, London, 1961, for *Oliver!;* Antoinette Perry Award nomination, 1963, for *Oliver!;* British Academy Award nomination, for *Raging Moon;* Los Angeles Drama Critics Award and Drama-Logue Award, for *Roza.*

CREDITS:

STAGE APPEARANCES

(New York City debut) Lucy Brown, *The Threepenny Opera,* Theatre de Lys, New York City, 1955, then Royal Court Theatre, London, 1956.

Jeanie, *The Lily White Boys,* Royal Court Theatre, 1960.

Nancy, *Oliver!,* New Theatre, London, 1960, then Imperial Theatre, New York City, 1963.

Title role, *Maggie May,* Aldelphi Theatre, London, 1964.

Artists against Apartheid, Prince of Wales Theatre, London, 1965.

Widow Begbick, *Man Is Man,* Royal Court Theatre, 1971.

Ensemble, *Side by Side by Sondheim* (revue), Music Box Theatre, New York City, 1977.

The Al Chemist Show, Los Angeles Actors Theatre, Los Angeles, CA, 1979-80.

As herself, *Georgia Brown and Friends* (also see below), Curran Theatre, San Francisco, CA, 1982.

Greek, Actors Playhouse, New York City, 1983, then Wyndham's Theatre, London, 1988.

Madame Roza, *Roza,* Center Theatre Group, Mark Taper Forum, Los Angeles, CA, 1986-87, then Royale Theatre, New York City, 1987.

Mrs. Peachum, *The Threepenny Opera,* Lunt-Fontanne Theatre, New York City, 1989.

Made stage debut in girls club pageant, London, 1950. Also appeared in variety show, Empire Theatre, London, 1951; *Seven Deadly Sins,* Royal Ballet, England; *Carmelina,* New York City; *42nd Street.*

MAJOR TOURS

Nancy, *Oliver!,* U.S. cities, 1962.

Also appeared in Moss Empire Tour, England, 1954.

FILM APPEARANCES

Myra, *Murder Reported,* Fortress/Columbia, 1958.

Saloon singer, *A Study in Terror* (also known as *Sherlock Holmes Grosster Fall; Fog*), Compton-Tekli Sir Nigel-Planet/Columbia, 1966.

Marfa Golov, *The Fixer,* Metro-Goldwyn-Mayer, 1968.

Nell, *Lock Up Your Daughters,* Domino/Columbia, 1969.

Sarah Charles, *Long Ago, Tomorrow* (also known as *The Raging Moon*), EMI/Cinema 5, 1971.

Running Scared, Wigan-Hemmings-O'Toole/Paramount, 1972.

Fay Patterson, *Tales that Witness Madness,* Amicus-Hemmings/World Film Services, 1973.

Ballad Singers Wife, *Galileo,* American Film Theatre, 1975.

Joan Foster, *Nothing But the Night* (also known as *The Resurrection Syndicate*), Charlemagne/Cinema Systems, 1975.

Jenny Jones and Mrs. Waters, *The Bawdy Adventures of Tom Jones,* Universal, 1976.

Mrs. Freud, *The Seven-Per-Cent Solution,* Universal, 1977.

Widow Chastity, *Burnin' Love,* De Laurentiis Entertainment Group, 1987.

TELEVISION APPEARANCES; EPISODIC

Tophat, BBC, 1950.

Show Time, BBC, 1954.

Password, CBS, 1964.

Get the Message, ABC, 1964-65.

The Ed Sullivan Show, CBS, 1964-65.

Girl Talk, ABC, 1964-65.

Dorothy Westerfield, *Murder, She Wrote,* CBS, 1989.

Madame Lazora, *Cheers,* NBC, 1990.

Also appeared as Margaret Flowers, *Peaceable Kingdom,* 1989.

OTHER TELEVISION APPEARANCES

Yvette Pottier, *Mother Courage* (play), BBC, 1960.

Take a Sapphire (special), BBC, 1965.

The Heart of Showbusiness (special), ATV, 1967.

Annie Kenny, "Shoulder to Shoulder," *Masterpiece Theatre* (special), PBS, 1975.

Salche Weisenfreund, *Actor: The Life of Paul Muni* (special), PBS, 1978.

Singer, "An Evening With Alan Jay Lerner," *Great Performances* (special), PBS, 1989.

Appeared in specials, including *The Trini Lopez Show,* 1968; as Lola Montero, (also theme song performer), *The Roads to Freedom,* 1972; as Mrs. Peachum, *Rebel,* 1975; as Maggie, *The Emperor's New Clothes,* 1985; and as Widow Chastity, *Love at Stake,* 1987.

Producer, "Shoulder to Shoulder," *Masterpiece Theatre*, PBS, 1975.

RECORDINGS:

The Many Shades of Georgia Brown (album), Capitol, 1965.
Georgia Brown Sings Kurt Weill (album), Capitol, 1970.

WRITINGS:

Georgia Brown and Friends (stage production), Curran Theatre, 1982.*

*   *   *

BROWN, Graham   1924-

PERSONAL: Born October 24, 1924, in New York City. *Education:* Howard University, B.A., 1949; Columbia University, 1951; studied acting at American Theatre Wing, 1950.

CAREER: Actor. Appeared with the Minnesota Theatre Company, Tyrone Guthrie Theatre, Minneapolis, MN, 1965; Center Stage Theatre, Baltimore, MD, 1966-67; Arena Stage, Washington, DC, 1978-79; and Cleveland Playhouse, Cleveland, OH, 1982-83.

CREDITS:

STAGE APPEARANCES

Widower's Houses, Downtown Theatre, New York City, 1959.
Understudy for Archibald Wellington and governor, *The Blacks,* Negro Ensemble Company, St. Mark's Playhouse, New York City, 1961.
Hamlet, Tyrone Guthrie Repertory Theatre, Minneapolis, MN, c. 1963-65.
The Three Sisters, Tyrone Guthrie Repertory Theatre, c. 1963-65.
Henry V, Tyrone Guthrie Repertory Theatre, c. 1963-65.
Volpone, Tyrone Guthrie Repertory Theatre, c. 1963-65.
St. Joan, Tyrone Guthrie Repertory Theatre, c. 1963-65.
Richard III, Tyrone Guthrie Repertory Theatre, c. 1963-65.
The Way of the World, Tyrone Guthrie Repertory Theatre, c. 1963-65.
The Caucasian Chalk Circle, Tyrone Guthrie Repertory Theatre, c. 1963-65.
The Miser, Tyrone Guthrie Repertory Theatre, c. 1963-65.
Babu, *Benito Cereno,* Center Stage Repertory, Baltimore, MD, c. 1966-67.
The Balcony, Center Stage Repertory, c. 1966-67.
Noah, Center Stage Repertory, c. 1966-67.

Titus Andronicus, Center Stage Repertory, c. 1966-67.
A Penny for a Song, Center Stage Repertory, c. 1966-67.
(Broadway debut) Dr. Hampton, *Weekend,* Broadhurst Theatre, 1968.
Daddy Goodness, Negro Ensemble Company, 1968.
Sam, *The Man in the Glass Booth,* Royale Theatre, New York City, 1968.
Song of the Lusitania Bogey, Negro Ensemble Company, 1968.
Voice, *God Is a (Guess What?),* Negro Ensemble Company, St. Mark's Playhouse, 1968.
Charlemagne, "Malcochon," *An Evening of One Acts,* Negro Ensemble Company, St. Mark's Playhouse, 1969.
Man, *Neighbors,* American National Theatre and Academy Matinee Series, Theatre De Lys, New York City, 1969.
Portagee Joe, *Man Better Man,* Negro Ensemble Company, St. Mark's Theatre, 1969.
Chorus member, *Antigone,* Inner City Repertory Theatre, Los Angeles, CA, 1971.
Dr. Vanderkellan, *Behold! Cometh the Vanderkellans,* Theatre De Lys, 1971.
Carl Blanks, *Ride a Black Horse,* Negro Ensemble Company, St. Mark's Playhouse, 1971.
Dr. Dudley Stanton, *The River Niger,* Negro Ensemble Company, St. Mark's Playhouse, 1972, then Brooks Atkinson Theatre, New York City, 1973.
Wine, Old Grandad, Poppa, and Blood Leader, *The Great Macdaddy,* Negro Ensemble Company, St. Mark's Playhouse, 1974.
Helicanus and Pander, *Pericles,* New York Shakespeare Festival (NYSF), Delacorte Theatre, New York City, 1974.
Doc, *Waiting for Mongo,* Negro Ensemble Company, St. Mark's Playhouse, 1975.
Norman, *Black Picture Show,* NYSF, Vivian Beaumont Theatre, New York City, 1975.
Title role, *Gilbeau,* New Federal Theatre, New York City, 1976.
Joseph Barton, *Eden,* Negro Ensemble Company, St. Mark's Playhouse, 1976.
Tiresias, "Oedipus," *Kings,* Alvin Theatre, New York City, 1976.
The Brownsville Raid, Negro Ensemble Company, 1976.
Wine, Old Grandad, Soldier, Poppa, and Blood Leader, *The Great Macdaddy,* Negro Ensemble Company, Theatre De Lys, 1977.
Jared, *Nevis Mountain Dew,* Negro Ensemble Company, St. Mark's Playhouse, 1979.
A Season to Unravel, Negro Ensemble Company, St. Mark's Playhouse, 1979.
The Confession Stone, Theatre Off Park, New York City, 1979.

Pontiflax, *Lagrima del Diablo* (title means "The Devil's Tear"), Negro Ensemble Company, St. Mark's Playhouse, 1980.

Nevis Mountain Dew, Los Angeles Actors' Theatre, Los Angeles, 1981.

Culpepper, *Abercrombie Apocalypse,* Negro Ensemble Company, Westside Arts Center/Cheryl Crawford Theatre, New York City, 1982.

Fred T. Blachley and Johnny, *Sons and Fathers of Sons,* Negro Ensemble Company, Theatre Four, New York City, 1983.

Actor nine, *District Line,* Negro Ensemble Company, Theatre Four, 1984.

William Jenkins, *Ceremonies in Dark Old Men,* Negro Ensemble Company, Ford Theatre, Washington, DC, 1984, then Theatre Four, 1985.

Eyes of the American, Negro Ensemble Company, Theatre Four, 1985.

Bishop of Carlisle, *King Richard II,* NYSF, Delacorte Theatre, 1987.

Baptista and Minola, *The Taming of the Shrew,* Triplex Theatre, New York City, 1988.

Antigonus, *The Winter's Tale,* NYSF, Public Theatre, New York City, 1989.

Father and Sam Griggs, *The Talented Tenth,* Manhattan Theatre Club, Stage I, New York City, 1989.

Also appeared in *The Emperor's Clothes; Time of Storm; Major Barbara; A Land Beyond the River,* 1957; *Firebugs,* 1963; and *Behold Cometh the Vanderkellans,* 1972.

MAJOR TOURS

Sergeant Waters, *A Soldier's Play,* U.S. cities, 1983-84.

FILM APPEARANCES

Fan, *Rude Boy,* Tigon, 1980.

Mr. Wrightson, *The Muppets Take Manhattan,* Tri-Star, 1984.

Doc Frischer, *Bloodhounds of Broadway,* Columbia, 1989.

TELEVISION APPEARANCES; MOVIES

Minister, *Cindy,* ABC, 1978.

Jeremiah, *A Special Friendship,* CBS, 1987.

Mr. Munson, *The Littlest Victims* (also known as *Innocent Victims*), CBS, 1989.

Also appeared on episodes of *Matt Lincoln, The Storefront Lawyers, The Interns, N.Y.P.D., The Guiding Light, The Edge of Night, The Doctors, The Days of Our Lives, Ironside, Medical Center, Owen Marshall,* and *Sanford and Son.**

BROWN, Jim   1936-

PERSONAL: Full name, James Nathaniel Brown; born February 17, 1936, in St. Simons Island, GA; son of Swinton and Theresa Brown; married Sue Jones, 1958 (divorced); children: four. *Education:* Graduated from Syracuse University.

CAREER: Actor and producer. Professional football player with the Cleveland Browns, National Football League, 1957-65; founder of Black Economic Union, a small business administration fund.

AWARDS, HONORS: Named Marlboro National Football League Player of the Year by the *Sporting News,* 1957, 1958, and 1965; received the Hickok Belt as Professional Athlete of the Year from the Hickok Manufacturing Company, 1964; awarded the Jim Thorpe Trophy from the Newspaper Enterprise Association, 1965; inducted into the Football Hall of Fame, 1974.

CREDITS:

FILM APPEARANCES

Sergeant Ben Franklyn, *Rio Conchos,* Twentieth Century-Fox, 1964.

Robert Jefferson, *The Dirty Dozen,* Metro-Goldwyn-Mayer (MGM), 1967.

Ruffo, *Dark of the Sun* (also known as *The Mercenaries*), MGM, 1968.

Captain Leslie Anders, *Ice Station Zebra,* Filmways/MGM, 1968.

McClain, *The Split,* MGM, 1968.

Title role, *Kenner* (also known as *Year of the Cricket*), MGM, 1969.

Culley Briston, *Riot,* Paramount, 1969.

Lyedecker, *100 Rifles,* Twentieth Century-Fox, 1969.

Luke, *El Condor,* National General, 1970.

Tommy Marcott, *The Grasshopper,* National General, 1970.

As himself, *The Phynx,* Warner Brothers, 1970.

Jimmy Price, *. . .Tick. . .Tick. . .Tick. . .,* MGM, 1970.

Gunn, *Black Gunn,* Columbia, 1972.

Title role, *Slaughter,* American International, 1972.

Le Bras, *I Escaped from Devil's Island,* United Artists, 1973.

Curtis Hook, *The Slams,* MGM, 1973.

Title role, *Slaughter's Big Rip-Off,* American International, 1973.

Jimmy Lait, *Three the Hard Way,* Allied Artists, 1974.

Pike, *Take a Hard Ride,* Twentieth Century-Fox, 1975.

Trooper, *Whiffs,* Twentieth Century-Fox, 1975.

Isaac, *Kid Vengeance,* Cannon, 1977.

Deems, *Fingers,* Brut, 1978.

J, *One Down Two to Go,* Almi, 1982.

Clyde Preston, *Pacific Inferno,* VCL, 1985.
Fireball Stalker, *The Running Man,* Tri-Star, 1987.
Slammer, *I'm Gonna Git You Sucka,* MGM/United Artists, 1988.
Steadman, *Crack House* (also known as *Rock House*), Twenty-First Century Releasing, 1989.
Captain, *L.A. Heat,* Raedon Entertainment Group, 1989.
First gladiator, *Wildest Dreams,* Lightning, 1990.
Morris, *Twisted Justice,* Borde Releasing Corporation, 1990.

Also appeared in *Sam's Song* (also known as *The Swap*), Cannon, 1971; *Adios Amigo,* Atlas, 1975; *Mean Johnny Barrows,* Atlas, 1976; and *Abducted,* InterPictures Releasing/Modern Cinema Marketing, 1986.

FILM WORK

Executive producer, *Richard Pryor: Here and Now* (documentary), Columbia, 1983.
Executive producer, *Pacific Inferno,* VCL, 1985.

TELEVISION APPEARANCES; SERIES

Commentator, *NFL on CBS,* CBS, 1977.
As himself, *Dynamic Duos,* NBC, 1978.

OTHER TELEVISION APPEARANCES

Stoker, *Lady Blue* (movie), ABC, 1985.
Black Champions (special documentary), PBS, 1986.
The Record Breakers of the Sport (special), HBO, 1990.*

* * *

BROWN, Julie   1958-

PERSONAL: Born August 31, 1958, in Burbank, CA; daughter of Celia McCann (a secretary) and Leonard Brown (a technical expert); married Terence McNally, June 11, 1983 (divorced, August 3, 1989). *Education:* Received A.A. from San Fernando Valley College.

ADDRESSES: Agent—Sandi Dudek, International Creative Management, 8899 Beverly Blvd., Los Angeles, CA 90048.

CAREER: Actress, comedian, singer, and writer.

MEMBER: Writers Guild of America, American Federation of Television and Radio Artists, Screen Actors Guild.

AWARDS, HONORS: Annual Cable Excellence (ACE) Award nominations, 1990 and 1991.

CREDITS:

TELEVISION APPEARANCES

(Debut) Suzy, *Happy Days,* CBS (episode), 1980.
Regular, *TV Funnies* (pilot), NBC, 1982.
"Sam at Eleven," *Cheers* (episode), NBC, 1982.

Gidget, *Evening at the Improv,* syndicated, 1982-84.
Julie Brown: The Show (series), CBS, 1989.
Just Say Julie (talk show), MTV, 1989-90.

Also appeared in episodes of *Laverne and Shirley, The Jeffersons, Buffalo Bill,* and *Newhart.*

FILM APPEARANCES

Debbie, *Any Which Way You Can,* Warner Brothers, 1980.
Chloe, *Police Academy 2: Their First Assignment,* Warner Brothers, 1985.
Beverly Brody, *Bloody Birthday* (also known as *Creeps*), Judica, 1986.
Candy, *Earth Are Girls Easy,* Vestron, 1989 (also see below).
Judy, *Shakes the Clown,* Columbia, 1991.
Zoe, *Rules of the Game,* Miramax, 1991.
Nancy, *Nervous Ticks,* Columbia, 1991.

STAGE APPEARANCES

(Stage debut) Juliet, *Romeo and Juliet,* American Conservatory Theatre, San Francisco, 1978.
Ellen, *Ladies Room,* Tiffany Theatre, 1988-89.

WRITINGS:

(With others) *Olivia Newton John's Hollywood Nights* (television special), CBS, 1981.
(With Charlie Coffey and Terence McNally) *Earth Girls Are Easy* (screenplay), Vestron Films, 1989.

RECORDINGS:

Recorded *Goddess in Progress* (album) and *Homecoming Queen's Got a Gun* (single and video).

OTHER SOURCES:

PERIODICALS

Vogue, May, 1989.

* * *

BROWN, Kermit   1939(?)-

PERSONAL: Full name, Kermit E. Brown, Jr.; born February 3, 1939 (one source says 1937), in Asheville, NC; son of Kermit English (a doctor) and Rosalind (Read) Brown. *Education:* Studied at Christ School for Boys, Arden, NC; received B.A. from Duke University.

CAREER: Actor. Affiliated with Charles Playhouse, Boston, MA, 1968-69; Hartford Stage Company, Hartford, CT, 1970-71; Great Lakes Shakespeare Festival, Lakewood, OH, stage manager, 1973; Cleveland Playhouse, Cleveland, OH, guest artist, 1973-74; and Alabama Shakespeare Festival, Montgomery, AL, 1981, 1983, 1985-86, and 1987-88. *Military service:* U.S. Army.

MEMBER: Actors' Equity Association, Screen Actors Guild, American Federation of Television and Radio Artists.

CREDITS:

STAGE APPEARANCES

Radical, *Winterset,* The American Revival Company, Jan Hus Playhouse, New York City, 1966.

(New York debut) Bank Manager, *Pantagleize,* APA Phoenix Repertory Company, Lyceum Theatre, 1967.

John-Paul, *The Death of the Well-Loved Boy,* St. Mark's Playhouse, New York City, 1967.

Soldier, peasant, and servant, *War and Peace,* APA Phoenix Repertory Company, Lyceum Theatre, 1967.

Station Master, *The Cherry Orchard,* APA Phoenix Repertory Company, Lyceum Theatre, 1968.

Man, *The Millionairess,* Sheridan Square Playhouse, New York City, 1969.

Sebastian, *The Tempest,* Center Stage, Baltimore, MD, 1969-70.

Arthur Harris, "Things," *Four Americans,* Brooklyn Academy of Music, Chelsea Theater Center, New York City, 1971.

Mr. Gallogher, *The Shadow of a Gunman,* Sheridan Square Playhouse, 1972.

Orgon, *Tartuffe,* Great Lakes Shakespeare Festival, Lakewood, OH, 1973.

Randall Utterword, *Heartbreak House,* Equity Library Theatre, New York City, 1976.

Dr. Muncie, *The Laboratory,* The Cubiculo Theatre, New York City, 1977.

Gus, *Glad Tidings,* Equity Library Theatre, 1977.

Cecil, *Elizabeth the Queen,* Studio Arena Theatre, Buffalo, NY, 1977.

Jeremiah Sant, *Hadrian VII,* York Players Company, Church of the Heavenly Rest Theatre, New York City, 1980.

Praed, *Mrs. Warren's Profession,* Virginia Stage Company, Norfolk, VA, 1981.

Carr Gomm, *The Elephant Man,* Alaska Repertory Theatre, Anchorage, AK, 1981.

Godalming, *The Passion of Dracula,* GeVa Theatre, Rochester, NY, 1982.

Tony Greeves, *The Arcata Promise,* No Smoking Playhouse, New York City, 1982.

Mayor, *The Enchanted,* York Theatre Company, Church of the Heavenly Rest Theatre, 1982.

Peter Quince, *A Midsummer Night's Dream,* York Theatre Company, Church of the Heavenly Rest Theatre, 1983.

Harry, *Home,* York Theatre Company, Church of the Heavenly Rest Theatre, 1985.

Also appeared in *The Rivals,* Playwrights Horizons, New York City, 1976; *Facade,* York Players Company, Church of the Heavenly Rest Theatre, 1981; and *The Dining Room,* Plaza Theatre, Dallas, TX, 1984. Appeared as Mr. Ford, *The Merry Wives of Windsor;* Leonato, *Much Ado About Nothing;* Player King, *Hamlet;* Oswald, *King Lear;* Nicola, *Arms and the Man;* Nonancourt, *The Italian Straw Hat;* Hastings, *Richard III;* Sir Andrew Aguecheek, *Twelfth Night;* Father Tim, *Mass Appeal;* Tranio, *The Taming of the Shrew;* Casca, *Julius Caesar;* Roderigo, *Othello;* and Teleygin, *Uncle Vanya;* all at the Alabama Shakespeare Festival, Montgomery, AL, and at the Great Lakes Shakespeare Festival, Buffalo, NY. Appeared as Peter, *The Zoo Story;* Besinger, *The Front Page;* player, *Rosencrantz and Guildenstern Are Dead;* Peterbono, *Thieves Carnival;* George, *That Championship Season;* and Jimmy, *The Gingerbread Lady;* all at The Court Theatre. Appeared as Mr. Rogers, *The Show-Off,* and in *Man and Superman* and *Judith,* all APA Phoenix Repertory Company, Lyceum Theatre. Also appeared as Detmold, *Anyone Can Whistle,* and Cromwell, *A Man for All Seasons,* both York Theatre Company; appeared as Geoffrey Thornton, *The Dresser,* Cincinnati Playhouse in the Park, Cincinnati, OH; Charles, *Blithe Spirit,* Limestone Valley Dinner Theatre; Jacques, *Pajama Tops,* Beef 'n Boards, Dinner Theatre; Joshua, *Ring Round the Moon,* Hartford Stage Company; Harry Dalton, *Equus,* Buffalo Studio Arena Theatre, Buffalo, NY; Diamond Louis, *The Front Page;* and in *Lulu.*

MAJOR TOURS

Toured as Lawyer Craven in *Sly Fox,* Fred in *Present Laughter,* and Henderson in *You Can't Take It with You.*

FILM APPEARANCES

Appeared in *Without a Trace, Daniel,* and *Nighthawks.*

TELEVISION APPEARANCES; EPISODIC

Appeared on *The Edge of Night* and *Kojak.*

OTHER TELEVISION APPEARANCES

Appeared on *After the Fall* (play).*

*   *   *

BRUCE, Brenda   1922-

PERSONAL: Born in 1922 in Manchester, United Kingdom; daughter of George Alexander Findlay and Ellen Isabella (Vowles) Bruce; married Roy Rich (deceased); married Clement McCallin (deceased). *Education:* Studied ballet with Margaret Saul. *Avocational interests:* Painting and writing.

ADDRESSES: Agent—Duncan Heath Associates, Paramount House, 162/170 Wardour St., London W1V 3AT, England.

CAREER: Actress. Appeared at the Malvern Festivals as a member of the Birmingham Repertory Company, 1936-39; appeared at the Liverpool Playhouse, Liverpool, United Kingdom, 1939; with the Alexandra Theatre Company, Birmingham, United Kingdom, 1940; and at the Shaw Festival, Arts Theatre, 1951. Associate member of the Royal Shakespeare Company; radio performer.

AWARDS, HONORS: British Academy of Film and Television Arts Award, Best Television Actress, 1962.

CREDITS:

STAGE APPEARANCES

(Stage debut) *The Babes in the Wood* (ballet), Theatre Royal, Exeter, United Kingdom, 1934.

(London debut) Chorus, *1066 and All That,* Strand Theatre, 1935.

Lydia Languish, *The Rivals,* Birmingham Repertory Company, Birmingham, United Kingdom, c. 1936-39.

Toni Rakonitz, *The Matriarch,* Birmingham Repertory Company, c. 1936-39.

Anne, *The Brontes of Haworth Parsonage,* Birmingham Repertory Company, c. 1936-39.

Vivie Warren, *Mrs. Warren's Profession,* Q Theatre, London, 1943.

Mary, *Michael and Mary,* Q Theatre, London, 1943.

Kate Hardcastle, *She Stoops to Conquer,* Q Theatre, London, 1943.

Ensemble, *Sweet and Low* (revue), Ambassadors Theatre, London, 1943.

Mabel Crum, *While the Sun Shines,* Globe Theatre, London, 1943-46.

Marcella Prince, *No Footlights,* Repertory Players, New Theatre, London, 1946.

Polly Eccles, *Caste,* Hammersmith Lyric Theatre, Hammersmith, United Kingdom, 1946.

Pam, *Fools Rush In,* Fortune Theatre, London, 1946.

Eliza Doolittle, *Pygmalion,* Hammersmith Lyric Theatre, 1947.

Dolly Clandon, *You Never Can Tell,* Wyndham's Theatre, London, 1947.

Doris Mead, *The Gioconda Smile,* New Theatre, 1948.

Miss Hardcastle, *She Stoops to Conquer,* Arts Theatre, London, 1949.

Susan Lawn, *Love in Albania,* Hammersmith Lyric Theatre, 1949, then St. James's Theatre, London, 1949.

Vivie Warren, *Mrs. Warren's Profession,* Arts Theatre, 1950.

Leonora Yale, *The Green Bay Tree,* Playhouse Theatre, London, 1950.

Victoria, *Home and Beauty,* Arts Theatre, 1950, then St. Martin's Theatre, London, 1950.

Anne-Marie, *Figure of Fun,* Aldwych Theatre, London, 1951.

Francie Dosson, *Letter from Paris,* Aldwych Theatre, 1952.

Title role, *Peter Pan,* Scala Theatre, London, 1952.

(Broadway debut) Freda Jefferies, *Gently Does It,* Playhouse Theatre, 1953.

Margaret Ross, *Both Ends Meet,* Apollo Theatre, London, 1954.

Odette, *The Captain's Lamp,* Theatre Royal, Brighton, United Kingdom, 1955.

Mademoiselle de Sainte-Euverte, *The Waltz of the Toreadors,* Arts Theatre, 1956, then Criterion Theatre, London, 1956.

Z, *Village Wooing,* Edinburgh Festival, Edinburgh, Scotland, 1956.

Dora Delaney, *Fanny's First Play,* Edinburgh Festival, 1956.

Adelina Barbier, *No Laughing Matter,* Arts Theatre, 1957.

Lily Loudon, *What Shall We Tell Caroline?,* Hammersmith Lyric Theatre, 1958, then Garrick Theatre, London, 1958.

Louie, *This Year, Next Year,* Vaudeville Theatre, London, 1960.

Winnie, *Happy Days,* Royal Court Theatre, London, 1962.

Amy Preston, *Woman in a Dressing Gown,* New Theatre, Bromley, United Kingdom, 1963, then Vaudeville Theatre, 1964.

Emilie Paumelle, *Victor,* Mrs. Murray, *Eh?,* and Mistress Margaret Page, *The Merry Wives of Windsor,* all Royal Shakespeare Company (RSC), 1964.

Duchess, *The Revenger's Tragedy,* RSC, Stratford-on-Avon, United Kingdom, 1966-1967.

Marjorie Newquist, *Little Murders,* and Cuca, *The Criminals,* both RSC, Aldwych Theatre, 1967.

Mistress Margaret Page, *The Merry Wives of Windsor,* RSC, Stratford-on-Avon, 1969, then Aldwych Theatre, 1969.

Bawd and Dionyza, *Pericles,* RSC, Stratford-on-Avon, 1969.

Paulina, *The Winter's Tale,* RSC, Stratford-on-Avon, 1969.

Maria, *Twelfth Night,* RSC, Stratford-on-Avon, 1969.

Queen Gertrude, *Hamlet,* RSC, Stratford-on-Avon, 1970.

Queen Elizabeth, *Richard III,* RSC, Stratford-on-Avon, 1970.

Paulina, *Enemies,* Aldwych Theatre, 1971.

Irma, *The Balcony,* Aldwych Theatre, 1971.

Lady Capulet, *Romeo and Juliet,* RSC, Stratford-on-Avon, 1973.

Voice I, *Sylvia Plath,* RSC, the Place, London, 1973, then Brooklyn Academy of Music, Brooklyn, NY, 1974.

Mrs. Hall, *Comrades,* RSC, The Place, 1974.

Madame Poitier, *The Beast,* RSC, The Place, 1974.

Queen Margaret, *Richard III,* RSC, The Other Place, London, 1975.

Mistress Margaret Page, *The Merry Wives of Windsor,* RSC, Stratford-on-Avon, 1975, then Aldwych Theatre, 1976.

Mistress Quickly, *Henry V,* RSC, Brooklyn Academy of Music, 1976.

Margaret Devize, *The Lady's Not for Burning,* Prospect Theatre Company, Old Vic Theatre, London, 1978.

Babakina, *Ivanov,* Prospect Theatre Company, Old Vic Theatre, 1978.

Gertrude, *Hamlet,* Prospect Theatre Company, Old Vic Theatre, 1978.

Nurse, *Romeo and Juliet,* RSC, Stratford-on-Avon, 1980, then Aldwych Theatre, 1981.

Margery Eyre, *The Shoemaker's Holiday,* National Theatre, Olivier Theatre, London, 1981.

Witch, *Hansel and Gretel,* RSC, Warehouse Theatre, London, 1981.

Gwen, *Real Estate,* Tricycle Theatre, London, 1984.

Lil, *Ask for the Moon,* Hampstead Theatre, London, 1986.

Patient, *Mystery of the Rose Bouquet,* Donmar Warehouse Theatre, London, 1987.

Mabel Groomkirby, *One Way Pendulum,* Old Vic Theatre, 1988.

MAJOR TOURS

Carol Sands, *Goodness, How Sad!,* United Kingdom cities, 1939.

Joanna, *Yes and No,* and Sally, *The Two Mrs. Carrolls,* United Kingdom cities, 1941.

Ensemble, *More New Faces* (revue), United Kingdom cities, 1942.

Z, *Village Wooing,* and Dora Delaney, *Fanny's First Play,* United Kingdom, German and Dutch cities, 1956.

The Hollow Crown, United Kingdom cities, 1975.

Gertrude, *Hamlet,* Prospect Theatre Company, Chinese cities, 1979.

Also toured with the Entertainment National Service Association (ENSA), United Kingdom cities, 1941.

FILM APPEARANCES

(Film debut) *Millions Like Us,* General Films Distributors, 1943.

Woman on hillside, *They Came to a City,* Ealing, 1944.

Maudie Chapman, *Carnival,* General Films Distributors, 1946.

Lily Leggett, *Night Boat to Dublin,* Pathe, 1946.

Ruby Chapman, *When the Bough Breaks,* General Films Distributors, 1947.

Sally Benton, *Piccadilly Incident* (also known as *They Met at Midnight*), Associated British Films, 1948.

Miss Smith, *Don't Ever Leave Me,* General Films Distributors, 1949.

Brenda, *Marry Me!,* General Films Distributors, 1949.

Winnie Foreman, *My Brother's Keeper,* Eagle-Lion, 1949.

Mabel Crum, *While the Sun Shines,* Monogram/Stratford, 1950.

Janet, *School for Brides* (also known as *Two on the Tiles*), Hoffberg, 1952.

Cora, *The Final Test,* General Films Distributors, 1953.

Elizabeth Fallon, *Behind the Mask,* GW Films, 1958.

Mary Cooper, *Law and Disorder,* Continental Distributing, 1958.

Dora, *Peeping Tom* (also known as *Face of Fear*), Astor, 1960.

Mary, *Nightmare,* Universal, 1963.

Addie, *The Uncle,* Lenart, 1966.

Nursing sister, *The Virgin Soldiers,* Columbia, 1970.

Doreen, *That'll Be the Day,* EMI, 1974.

Miss Harbottle, *All Creatures Great and Small,* EMI, 1975.

Mrs. Dixon, *Swallows and Amazons,* LDS, 1977.

Title role, *Kathe Kollwitz* (short documentary), Concord, 1981.

Mrs. Casson, *Farmers Arms,* BBC, 1983.

Mrs. Meadows, *Steaming,* Columbia, 1985.

June Swift, *Time after Time,* BBC-TV/Arts & Entertainment/Australian Broadcasting, 1985.

Duchess, *Little Dorrit,* Cannon, 1988.

Martha, *December Bride,* Film Four International, 1990.

Also appeared in *A Yank in London* (also known as *I Live in Grosvenor Square*), Twentieth Century-Fox, 1946.

TELEVISION APPEARANCES; MOVIES

Anne of Austria, *The Man in the Iron Mask,* NBC, 1977.

Madame Mangeot, *The Tenth Man,* CBS, 1988.

Beatie, *Back Home,* Disney, 1990.

OTHER TELEVISION APPEARANCES

Miss Harbottle, "All Creatures Great and Small," *The Hallmark Hall of Fame* (special), NBC, 1975.

Mistress Quickly, *Henry IV, Part One* (special; also known as *The Shakespeare Plays*), PBS, 1980.

Great Aunt Betsy, "David Copperfield," *Masterpiece Theatre* (mini-series), PBS, 1988.

Also appeared in *Jeeves and Wooster,* LWT, 1990, then *Masterpiece Theatre,* PBS, 1990; *Bingo,* BBC-2, 1990; *An-*

tonia and Jane, BBC-2, 1990; *The Plantagenets; Nearer to Heaven; Wrong Side of the Park; The Lodger; The Monkey and the Mohawk; Love Story; A Piece of Resistance; Give the Clown His Supper; Knock on Any Door; The Browning Version; Death of a Teddy Bear; The Girl; Happy; Family at War; Budgie; Rich and Rich; Mary Britton; Girl in a Bird Cage; A Chance to Shine; Dr. Finlay's Casebook;* and *Softly, Softly.*

SIDELIGHTS: Favorite roles: Vivie Warren in *Mrs. Warren's Profession* and Z in *A Village Wooing.**

*   *   *

BRYGGMAN, Larry   1938-

PERSONAL: Born December 21, 1938, in Concord, CA. *Education:* Attended City College of San Francisco; trained for the stage at the American Theatre Wing.

ADDRESSES: Agent—Jeff Hunter, Triad Artists Inc., 888 Seventh Ave., Suite 1602, New York, NY 10106.

CAREER: Actor. Performed with Pittsburgh Playhouse, Pittsburgh, PA, 1966-67; with Theatre Company of Boston, Boston, MA, 1967-68, 1969-71, and 1972-73; with Long Wharf Theatre, New Haven, CT, 1968-69; and with Hartford Stage Company, Hartford, CT, 1971-72 and 1974-75.

AWARDS, HONORS: Emmy Award nominations, outstanding actor in a daytime drama series, 1980-81, 1981-82, and 1984-85, and Emmy Award, outstanding actor in a daytime drama series, 1983-84 and 1985-86, all for *As the World Turns.*

CREDITS:

TELEVISION APPEARANCES; SERIES

Dr. John Dixon, *As the World Turns,* CBS, 1969-   .

Also appeared on *Love Is A Many Splendored Thing,* CBS.

TELEVISION APPEARANCES; SPECIALS

Celebration for William Jennings Bryan, PBS, 1968.
Soap Opera Digest Awards, NBC, 1988.
The Fifteenth Annual Daytime Emmy Awards, CBS, 1988.

STAGE APPEARANCES

(Off-Broadway debut) Tallahassee, "A Summer Ghost," *Charlatans,* in *A Pair of Pairs,* Vandam Theatre, New York City, 1962.
Armstrong's Last Goodnight, Theatre Company of Boston, Boston, MA, 1966.
Live Like Pigs, Theatre Company of Boston, 1966.
Tiny Alice, Theatre Company of Boston, 1967.
The Duchess of Malfi, Long Wharf Theatre, New Haven, CT, 1968.

The Fun War, Theatre Company of Boston, 1968.
Jeff, *Mod Donna,* New York Shakespeare Festival (NYSF), Public Theatre, New York City, 1969.
Title role, "Terrible Jim Fitch," *Stop, You're Killing Me,* Stage 73 Theatre, New York City, 1969.
Pozzo, *Waiting for Godot,* Sheridan Square Playhouse, New York City, 1971.
Play Strindberg, Theatre Company of Boston, 1972.
Buck Mulligan, Watch, Dr. Mulligan, and Bishop of Erin, *Ulysses in Nighttown,* Winter Garden Theatre, New York City, 1974.
Christian, *Dearly Beloved,* Manhattan Theatre Club, New York City, 1976.
Dr. Sheldon Henning, *Checking Out,* Longacre Theatre, New York City, 1976.
Kress, *The Basic Training of Pavlo Hummel,* Theatre Company of Boston, Longacre Theatre, 1977.
Lieutenant Brann, *Two Small Bodies,* Playwrights Horizons Theatre, New York City, 1977.
The guard, *Museum,* NYSF, Public Theatre, 1978.
Earl of Derby, *Richard III,* Cort Theatre, New York City, 1979.
Fool, *The Winter Dancers,* Marymount Manhattan Theatre, New York City, 1979.
Sir, *A Life in the Theatre,* Westchester Regional Theatre, Harrison, NY, 1980.
Tramb, Major, and manager, *The Resurrection of Lady Lester,* Manhattan Theatre Club, 1981.
Arturo, *Modern Ladies of Guanabacoa,* Ensemble Studio Theatre, New York City, 1983.
Robert Ingersoll, *Royal Bob,* StageArts Theatre Company, Chernuchin Theatre, New York City, 1983.
Calvin Barkdull, *The Ballad of Soapy Smith,* NYSF, Public Theatre, 1984.
Hank, "Life Under Water," *Marathon '85,* Ensemble Studio Theatre, 1985.
Bijou Billins, *Walk the Dog, Willie,* The Production Company, Theatre Guinevere, New York City, 1985.
Tom Tanner and Larry Peters, *Rum and Coke,* NYSF, Susan Stein Shiva Theatre, New York City, 1986.
Blood Sports, New York Theatre Workshop, Perry Street Theatre, New York City, 1987.
Andrew, *Spoils of War,* Second Stage Theatre, New York City, 1988.
Bill, "Just Horrible," *Class 1 Acts,* Manhattan Class Company, Nat Horne Theatre, New York City, 1988.
Coriolanus, NYSF, 1989 and 1990.
Banquo, *Macbeth,* NYSF, Public Theatre, 1990.
Prelude to a Kiss, Helen Hayes Theatre, New York City, 1990.
Henry, *Henry IV Parts One and Two,* NYSF, 1990 and 1991.

Also appeared at National Home Theatre, New York City, 1990; as Biff in *Death of a Salesman* (stage debut),

San Francisco, CA; and in *Ballymurphy; Marco Polo Sings a Solo; The Cherry Orchard; The Lincoln Mask; Irma La Douce; More Stately Mansions; Who's Afraid of Virginia Woolf?;* and *Brecht on Brecht.*

FILM APPEARANCES

Warren Fresnell, *. . . And Justice for All,* Columbia, 1979.

Stacy, *Hanky-Panky,* Columbia, 1982.

* * *

BULLARD, Thomas 1944-

PERSONAL: Born Thomas Allan Bullard, November 14, 1944, in Oakland, CA; son of Allan Fleming (an attorney) and Carolyn Culver (Oliver) Bullard; married Susan V. Smyly (a sculptor), January 12, 1984. *Education:* Middlebury College, B.A. (cum laude), 1966; Yale University School of Drama, M.F.A., directing, 1969.

ADDRESSES: Office—P.O. Box 181, New York, NY 10038.

CAREER: Director. Penn Players, University of Pennsylvania, artistic director, 1969-70; Annenberg Center, Philadelphia, associate director, 1970-71; Lincoln Center Institute, teaching artist, 1972—; Manhattan Theatre Club, associate director, 1972-79, 1983-84, artistic associate, 1984-86; Brooklyn College, guest lecturer, 1977-79, adjunct professor, 1979-80, 1985, 1991; State University of New York at Stony Brook, adjunct professor, 1980-81.

MEMBER: Society of Stage Directors and Choreographers, Phi Beta Kappa.

AWARDS, HONORS: Audelco Award, Best Dramatic Production, 1977, for *The Last Street Play;* Village Voice Obie Award, Outstanding Directorial Achievement, 1978, for *Statements After an Arrest Under the Immorality Act.*

CREDITS:

STAGE DIRECTOR

Strings Snapping, Manhattan Theatre Club, New York City, 1972.
The Marriage, Manhattan Theatre Club, 1972.
Marouf, Manhattan Theatre Club, 1973.
Blessing, Manhattan Theatre Club, 1974.
Staircase, Manhattan Theatre Club, 1975.
The Blood Knot, Manhattan Theatre Club, 1976.
La Voix Humaine, Manhattan Theatre Club, 1976.
Boesman and Lena, Manhattan Theatre Club, 1977.
The Last Street Play, Manhattan Theatre Club, 1977.
Krapps Last Tape, Lincoln Center Institute, New York City, 1977.
Scenes from Soweto, Manhattan Theatre Club, 1978.

Statements After an Arrest Under the Immorality Act, Manhattan Theatre Club, 1978.
Unfinished Women, New York Shakespeare Festival, Public Theatre, New York City, and Joseph Papp's Public Theatre, 1978.
Sizwe Bansi Is Dead, GeVa Theatre, Rochester, NY, 1978.
The Blood Knot, Philadelphia Drama Guild, Philadelphia, PA, and Syracuse Stage, Syracuse, NY, 1979.
Willie Callendar, Philadelphia Drama Guild, 1979.
"Ice Farm," *New Voices* (one-act), Ensemble Studio Theatre, New York City, 1979.
Henry the Fourth, Part One, Dallas Shakespeare Festival, Dallas, TX, 1979.
One Wedding, Two Rooms, Three Friends, Manhattan Theatre Club, 1980.
The Last Few Days of Willie Callendar, Philadelphia Drama Guild, 1980.
One Tiger to a Hill, Manhattan Theatre Club, 1980.
Playboy of the Western World, University of Washington, 1981.
Miss Julie, Lincoln Center Institute, 1981.
Strange Snow, Manhattan Theatre Club, 1982.
A Lesson from Aloes, Cincinnati Playhouse, Cincinnati, OH, 1982.
Misalliance, Actors Theatre of Louisville, Louisville, KY, 1982-83.
Elba, Manhattan Theatre Club, 1983.
A Raisin in the Sun, Goodman Theatre, Chicago, IL, 1983.
The Dining Room, Actors Theatre of Louisville, 1984.
Astronauts, Actors Theatre of Louisville, 1986.
Rules of the Game, Actors Theatre of Louisville, 1986.
Death of a Salesman, Actors Theatre of Louisville, 1986-87.
Benefactors, Old Globe Theatre, San Diego, CA, 1987-88.
The Elephant Man, Tennessee Repertory Theatre, 1987.
Danger: Memory, Seattle Repertory Theatre, Seattle, WA, 1987.
The Foreigner, Pennsylvania Stage Company, Allentown, PA, 1987.
The Voice of the Prairie, Old Globe Theatre, San Diego, CA, 1987-88.
Merry Wives of Windsor-Texas, Red Clay Ramblers, Alley Theatre, 1988.
To Kill A Mockingbird, Tennessee Repertory Theatre, 1988
Wolf-Man, Manhattan Theatre Club, 1989.
Road to Mecca, Northlight Theatre, Chicago, IL, 1989.
You Can't Take It with You, Tennessee Repertory Theatre, 1989.
Betrayal, Cape Playhouse, Cape Cod, MA, 1989.
White Man Dancing, Old Globe Theatre, 1990.
2, Actors Theatre of Louisville, 1990.
Krapp's Last Tape, Lincoln Center Institute, 1990.

Fences, Alabama Shakespeare Festival, Montgomery, AL, 1991.

MAJOR TOURS

Extremities, Actors Theatre of Louisville, Japanese cities, 1984.

*   *   *

BURNS, George   1896-

PERSONAL: Full name George Nathan Birnbaum Burns; born January 20, 1896, in New York City; married Gracie Ethel Rosalie Allen, January 7, 1926 (died August 27, 1964); children: (adopted) Sandra Jean, Ronald John. *Education:* Attended public schools in New York City.

ADDRESSES: Office—c/o Irving Fine, 1100 Alta Loma Rd., Los Angeles, CA 90069. *Contact*—c/o Putnam Publishing Group, 200 Madison Ave., New York, NY 10016.

CAREER: Comedian, actor, singer, producer, and writer. Sang with "Peewee Quartet," on streets of New York; trick roller-skater, dancing teacher, and vaudeville comedian; spokesman for commercial products.

AWARDS, HONORS: Clio Award, 1967, for appearance in El Producto Cigars commercial; Academy Award, best performance by an actor in a supporting role, 1975, for *The Sunshine Boys;* Golden Apple Star of the Year Award, 1975; Louella Parsons Award, Hollywood Women's Press Club, 1980; honored at 1988 Kennedy Center Honors; H.H.D., University of Hartford, 1988; inducted into Television Academy Hall of Fame, 1989; Grammy Award, best spoken or non-musical recording, 1990, for *Gracie: A Love Story;* Emmy Award for outstanding individual achievement in informational programming, 1990, for *A Conversation with George Burns.*

CREDITS:

STAGE APPEARANCES

Burns and Allen, Keith and Orpheum Vaudeville Circuit, 1923.
Parade of Stars Playing the Palace, Palace Theatre, New York City, 1983.

Also performed as dancer, singer, and comedian in Kieth Vaudeville Circuit (stage debut), and in U.S. and European tour of *Burns and Allen.*

FILM APPEARANCES

George, *The Big Broadcast,* Paramount, 1932.
As himself, *College Humor,* Paramount, 1933.
Dr. Burns, *International House,* Paramount, 1933.
Burns, *Many Happy Returns,* Paramount, 1934.
George Edwards, *Six of a Kind,* Paramount, 1934.

George, *We're Not Dressing,* Paramount, 1934.
George, *The Big Broadcast of 1936,* Paramount, 1935.
As himself, *Here Comes Cookie,* Paramount, 1935.
George, *Love in Bloom,* Paramount, 1935.
Mr. Platt, *The Big Broadcast of 1937,* Paramount, 1936.
George Hymen, *College Holiday,* Paramount, 1936.
George, *A Damsel in Distress,* RKO, 1937.
George Jonas, *College Swing* (also known as *Swing, Teacher, Swing*), Paramount, 1938.
Joe Duffy, *Honolulu,* Metro-Goldwyn-Mayer, 1939.
Narrator, *The Solid Gold Cadillac,* Columbia, 1956.
Al Lewis, *The Sunshine Boys,* United Artists, 1975.
Title role, *Oh, God!,* Warner Brothers, 1977.
Mr. Kite, *Sergeant Pepper's Lonely Hearts Club Band,* Universal, 1978.
Joe, *Going in Style,* Warner Brothers, 1979.
Bill, *Just You and Me, Kid,* Columbia, 1979.
Title role, *Oh God!, Book II,* Warner Brothers, 1980.
Devil/God, *Oh God! You Devil,* Warner Brothers, 1984.
Jack Watson, *18 Again,* New World, 1988.

Also appeared in *Two Girls and a Sailor,* 1944.

TELEVISION APPEARANCES; SERIES

The George Burns and Gracie Allen Show, CBS, 1950-58.
The George Burns Show, NBC, 1958-59.
Wendy and Me (also see below), ABC, 1964-65.
Host, *The George Burns Comedy Week,* CBS, 1985.

TELEVISION APPEARANCES; SPECIALS

Host, *George Burns in the Big Time,* NBC, 1959.
Ensemble, *Startime* (musical revue), NBC, 1960.
The Perry Como Special, NBC, 1963.
An Evening with Carol Channing, CBS, 1966.
Host, *Tin Pan Alley Today,* NBC, 1967.
The Brass Are Coming, NBC, 1969.
Jack Benny's New Look, NBC, 1969.
The Bob Hope Show, NBC, 1969, 1970.
Everything You Always Wanted to Know about Jack Benny and Were Afraid to Ask, NBC, 1971.
The Osmond Brothers Show, CBS, 1971.
Ann-Margret—When You're Smiling, NBC, 1973.
The Many Faces of Comedy, NBC, ABC, 1973.
Jack Benny's Second Farewell Show, NBC, 1974.
One More Time, CBS, 1974.
The Rich Little Show, NBC, 1975.
Host, *The George Burns Special,* CBS, 1976.
The Second Annual Circus of the Stars, CBS, 1977.
The George Burns One-Man Show, CBS, 1977.
Co-host, *Marilyn Beck's Second Annual Hollywood Out-Takes,* NBC, 1977.
The Goldie Hawn Special, CBS, 1978.
Bob Hope's All-Star Tribute to the Palace Theatre, NBC, 1978.
The National Cheerleading Championships, CBS, 1978.

Co-host, *CBS: On the Air,* CBS, 1978.
Dean Martin Celebrity Roast: Frank Sinatra, NBC, 1978.
Guest of honor, *Dean Martin Celebrity Roast: George Burns,* NBC, 1978.
Dean Martin Celebrity Roast: Jimmy Stewart, NBC, 1978.
Host, *The Other Broadway,* syndicated, 1979.
Ann-Margret's Hollywood Movie Girls, ABC, 1980.
Host, *100 Years of America's Popular Music,* NBC, 1981.
Bob Hope's 30th Anniversary TV Special, NBC, 1981.
Host, *George Burns' Early, Early, Early, Christmas Show,* NBC, 1981.
Host, *A Love Letter to Jack Benny,* NBC, 1981.
Host, *Two of a Kind: George Burns and John Denver,* ABC, 1981.
Host, *George Burns' 100th Birthday Party,* NBC, 1982.
Bob Hope Laugh with the Movie Awards, NBC, 1982.
Host, *George Burns and Other Sex Symbols,* NBC, 1982.
Bob Hope's Road to Hollywood, NBC, 1983.
Happy Birthday Bob!, NBC, 1983.
Host, *George Burns Celebrates 80 Years in Show Business,* NBC, 1983.
Host, *The Kids from Fame,* NBC, 1983.
Parade of Stars, ABC, 1983.
Bob Hope in Who Makes the World Laugh, Part 2, NBC, 1984.
The Funniest Joke I Ever Heard, ABC, 1984.
Host, *George Burns' How to Live to Be 100,* NBC, 1984.
Comedy Tonight, syndicated, 1985.
Host, *Disney's Magic in the Magic Kingdom,* NBC, 1988.
America's Tribute to Bob Hope, NBC, 1988.
Happy Birthday, Bob—50 Stars Salute Your 50 Years with NBC, NBC, 1988.
George Burns' 95th Birthday Party, CBS, 1991.

Also hosted *George Burns in Nashville?,* 1981, and appeared in *A Conversation with George Burns,* 1990.

OTHER TELEVISION APPEARANCES

Monologue, *That's Life* (episode), ABC, 1969.
As himself, *The Comedy Company* (movie), CBS, 1978.
Ross "Boppy" Minor, *Two of a Kind* (movie), CBS, 1982.

Also appeared on *The Muppet Show* (episode), syndicated; *Wayne and Shuster Take an Affectionate Look* (episode), CBS; and *Grandpa, Will You Run with Me?* (movie).

TELEVISION WORK

Producer, *No Time for Sergeants* (series), ABC, 1964-65.
Producer, *Wendy and Me* (series), ABC, 1964-65.
Producer, *Meet Mona McCluskey* (series), NBC, 1965-66.
Producer, "McNab's Lab," *Summer Fun* (pilot), ABC, 1966.

RADIO APPEARANCES

The Burns and Allen Radio Show (series), CBS, 1932-50.

Appeared on episodes of *The Rudy Vallee Show* and *The Guy Lombardo Show.* Made his radio debut on BBC, 1932.

RECORDINGS:

I Wish I Was Eighteen Again, Mercury, 1980.

Also recorded *Gracie: A Love Story* (also see below); *George Burns in Nashville,* 1981; and *George Burns: His Wit and Wisdom* (video), 1989.

WRITINGS:

(With Cynthia Hobart Lindsay) *I Love Her, That's Why!,* Simon & Schuster, 1955.
Living It Up; or They Still Love Me in Altoona!, Putnam, 1976.
The Third Time Around: Confessions of a Happy Hoofer, Putnam, 1980.
How to Be One Hundred—Or More: The Ultimate Diet, Sex and Exercise Book, Putnam, 1983.
George Burns: An Hour of Jokes and Songs (television special), HBO, 1984.
Dear George: Advice and Answers from America's Leading Expert on Everything from A to B, Putnam, 1985.
Dr. Burn's Prescription for Happiness, Putnam, 1985.
Gracie: A Love Story, Putnam, 1988.
(With David Fisher) *All My Best Friends,* Putnam, 1989.*

* * *

BURR, Raymond   1917-

PERSONAL: Full name, Raymond William Stacey Burr; born May 21, 1917, in New Westminster, British Columbia, Canada. *Education:* Attended the University of California, Stanford University, Columbia University, and the University of Chungking.

ADDRESSES: Agent—David Shapira and Associates, 15301 Ventura Blvd., Suite 345, Sherman Oaks, CA 91403.

CAREER: Actor. Performed on stage throughout Canada and England during the 1930s and 1940s; radio actor during the 1940s and 1950s; founder, with Robert Benevides, Royal Blue Ltd. (a television production company), 1988. *Military service:* U.S. Navy, World War II.

AWARDS, HONORS: Emmy Award, Best Actor in a Continuing Lead Role in a Dramatic Series, 1959 and 1961, for *Perry Mason.*

CREDITS:

TELEVISION APPEARANCES; SERIES

Title role, *Perry Mason,* CBS, 1957-66.
Chief Robert T. Ironside, *Ironside,* NBC, 1967-75.
R. B. Kingston, *Kingston: Confidential,* NBC, 1977.

Host, *Trial by Jury,* syndicated, 1989-90.

TELEVISION APPEARANCES; MOVIES

Chief Robert T. Ironside, *Split Second to an Epitaph,* NBC, 1968.

Narrator, *The Bastard* (also known as *The Kent Chronicles*), syndicated, 1978.

Lyle Taggart, Sr., *Love's Savage Fury,* ABC, 1979.

Estes Hill, *Disaster on the Coastliner,* ABC, 1979.

Jonash Sabastian, *The Curse of King Tut's Tomb,* NBC, 1980.

Mayor, *The Night the City Screamed,* ABC, 1980.

Herod Agrippa I, *Peter and Paul,* CBS, 1981.

Title role, *Perry Mason Returns,* NBC, 1985.

Title role, *Perry Mason: The Case of the Notorious Nun,* NBC, 1986.

Title role, *Perry Mason: The Case of the Shooting Star,* NBC, 1986.

Title role, *Perry Mason: The Case of the Lost Love,* NBC, 1987.

Title role, *Perry Mason: The Case of the Murdered Madam,* NBC, 1987.

Title role, *Perry Mason: The Case of the Scandalous Scoundrel,* NBC, 1987.

Title role, *Perry Mason: The Case of the Sinister Spirit,* NBC, 1987.

Title role, *Perry Mason: The Case of the Avenging Ace,* NBC, 1988.

Title role, *Perry Mason: The Case of the Lady in the Lake,* NBC, 1988.

Title role, *Perry Mason: The Case of the All-Star Assassin,* NBC, 1989.

Title role, *Perry Mason: The Case of the Lethal Lesson,* NBC, 1989.

Title role, *Perry Mason: The Case of the Musical Murder,* NBC, 1989.

Title role, *Perry Mason: The Case of the Desperate Deception,* NBC, 1990.

Title role, *Perry Mason: The Case of the Poisoned Pen,* NBC, 1990.

Title role, *Perry Mason: The Case of the Silenced Singer,* NBC, 1990.

Title role, *Perry Mason: The Case of the Maligned Mobster,* NBC, 1991.

Title role, *Perry Mason: The Case of the Glass Coffin,* NBC, 1991.

TELEVISION APPEARANCES; MINI-SERIES

Armand Perfido, *Harold Robbins' "79 Park Avenue,"* NBC, 1977.

Herman Bockweiss, *Centennial,* NBC, 1978-79.

TELEVISION APPEARANCES; PILOTS

The Human Bomb (broadcast as an episode of *Chesterfield Sound Off Time*), NBC, 1951.

Chief Robert T. Ironside, *Ironside,* NBC, 1967.

Chief Robert T. Ironside, *The Priest Killer,* NBC, 1971.

R. B. Kingston, *Kingston: The Power Play,* NBC, 1976.

Daniel Mallory, *Mallory: Circumstantial Evidence,* NBC, 1976.

Frank Jordan, *The Jordan Chance,* CBS, 1978.

Also appeared as Ziggy Moline, *Command Performance* (never broadcast), ABC.

TELEVISION APPEARANCES; SPECIALS

Jack Benny with Guest Stars, CBS, 1959.

Host, *Keep U.S. Beautiful,* NBC, 1973.

Narrator, *Christmas Around the World,* PBS, 1977.

Narrator, "Haiti: Waters of Sorrow" and "Cape Horn: Waters of the Wind," *Cousteau's Rediscovery of the World,* TBS, 1986.

NBC's 60th Anniversary Celebration, NBC, 1986.

Host and narrator, *Unsolved Mysteries,* NBC, 1987.

55th Annual King Orange Jamboree Parade, NBC, 1988.

Perry Mason, *The Case of the Courtroom Legend* (documentary; also known as *Perry Mason: Case of the Courtroom Legend*), Showtime, 1989.

Night of 100 Stars III, NBC, 1990.

Super Bloopers and New Practical Jokes, NBC, 1990.

TELEVISION APPEARANCES; EPISODIC

Stars over Hollywood, NBC, 1951.

The Unexpected, syndicated, 1952.

"The Tiger," "Face Value," and "The Leather Coat," *Gruen Guild Playhouse,* DuMont, 1952.

"Pearls from Paris," *Mr. Lucky at Seven,* ABC, 1952.

"How Much Land Does a Man Need?," *Favorite Story,* syndicated, 1952.

"The Mask of Medusa," *Twilight Theatre,* ABC, 1953.

"The Fugitives," *Ford Theatre,* NBC, 1954.

"The Room," *Four Star Playhouse,* CBS, 1954.

"Ordeal of Dr. Sutton," *Schlitz Playhouse of Stars,* CBS, 1955.

"The Wreck," *Counterpoint,* syndicated, 1955.

"The Ox-Bow Incident," *Twentieth Century-Fox Hour,* CBS, 1955.

"The Web," *Lux Video Theatre* (also known as *The Lux Playhouse*), NBC, 1955.

"Man without a Fear," *Ford Theatre,* NBC, 1956.

"The Sound of Silence" and "The Shadow of Evil," *Climax!,* CBS, 1956.

"Flamingo Road," *Lux Video Theatre* (also known as *The Lux Playhouse*), NBC, 1956.

"Savage Portrait," *Climax!,* CBS, 1956.

"The Greer Case" and "The Lone Woman," *Playhouse 90,* CBS, 1957.

It Takes a Thief, ABC, 1968.

The Bold Ones, NBC, 1972.

Also appeared as narrator, *Actuality Specials,* NBC, and as Howard Knight, *Eischied,* NBC; also appeared on episodes of *Undercurrent,* CBS; *The Love Boat,* ABC; and *Tales of Tomorrow,* ABC.

FILM APPEARANCES

Paul Gill, *Without Reservation,* RKO, 1946.

Torrance, *San Quentin,* RKO, 1946.

Carter, *Code of the West,* RKO, 1947.

Walt Radak, *Desperate,* RKO, 1947.

Herb, *I Love Trouble,* Columbia, 1947.

Prosecuting attorney, *Fighting Father Dunne,* RKO, 1948.

Mack MacDonald, *Pitfall,* United Artists (UA), 1948.

Rick Coyle, *Raw Deal,* Eagle-Lion/Reliance, 1948.

Pete Vendig, *Ruthless,* Eagle-Lion, 1948.

Lieutenant Strake, *Sleep, My Love,* United Artists, 1948.

Mark Bristow, *Station West,* RKO, 1948.

Krebs, *Walk a Crooked Mile,* Columbia, 1948.

Kerric, *Abandoned* (also known as *Abandoned Woman*), Universal, 1949.

Captain Alvarez, *Adventures of Don Juan* (also known as *The New Adventures of Don Juan*), Warner Brothers, 1949.

Alexandre Dumas, Jr., *Black Magic,* UA, 1949.

Michelotto, *Bride of Vengeance,* Paramount, 1949.

Alphonse Zoto, *Love Happy,* UA, 1949.

Nick Cherney, *Red Light,* UA, 1949.

Criss Cross, Universal, 1949.

Pete Richie, *Borderline,* Universal, 1950.

Les Taggart, *Key to the City,* Metro-Goldwyn-Mayer (MGM), 1950.

Roger Lewis, *Unmasked,* Republic, 1950.

Barney Chavez, *Bride of the Gorilla,* Real Art, 1951.

Nick Ferraro, *His Kind of Woman,* RKO, 1951.

Pottsy, *M,* Columbia, 1951.

Boreg, *The Magic Carpet,* Columbia, 1951.

Private Anderson, *New Mexico,* UA, 1951.

Marlowe, *A Place in the Sun,* Paramount, 1951.

Steve Loomis, *The Whip Hand,* RKO, 1951.

Cord Hardin, *Horizons West,* Universal, 1952.

Brock Benedict, *Mara Maru,* Warner Brothers, 1952.

Nick Driscoll, *Meet Danny Wilson,* Universal, 1952.

Jonatto, *The Bandits of Corsica* (also known as *Return of the Corsican Brothers*), UA, 1953.

Harry Prebble, *The Blue Gardenia,* Warner Brothers, 1953.

Amir, *Fort Algiers,* UA, 1953.

Mark Anthony, *Serpent of the Nile,* Columbia, 1953.

Vargo, *Tarzan and the She-Devil,* RKO, 1953.

Bragadin, *Casanova's Big Night,* Paramount, 1954.

Cyrus Miller, *Gorilla at Large,* Twentieth Century-Fox, 1954.

Ahmed, *Khyber Patrol,* UA, 1954.

Captain Rodriquez, *Passion,* RKO, 1954.

Lars Thorwald, *Rear Window,* Paramount, 1954.

Thunder Pass, Lippert, 1954.

Yancey Hoggins, *Count Three and Pray,* Columbia, 1955.

Stanley, *A Man Alone,* Republic, 1955.

Coltos, *They Were So Young,* Lippert, 1955.

Noonan, *You're Never Too Young,* Paramount, 1955.

Tris Hatten, *The Brass Legend,* UA, 1956.

Loftus, *A Cry in the Night,* Warner Brothers, 1956.

Steve Martin, *Godzilla, King of the Monsters* (also known as *Gojira*), Toho, 1956.

Jumbo Means, *Great Day in the Morning,* RKO, 1956.

Craig Carlson, *Please Murder Me,* Distributors Corporation of America, 1956.

Ziggy Moline, *Ride the High Iron,* Columbia, 1956.

Cash Larsen, *Secret of Treasure Mountain,* Columbia, 1956.

Mallabee, *Affair in Havana,* Allied Artists, 1957.

Inspector Pope, *Crime of Passion,* UA, 1957.

Colonel Ben Marquand, *Desire in the Dust,* Twentieth Century-Fox, 1960.

William Orbison, *P.J.* (also known as *New Face in Hell*), Universal, 1968.

Burke, *Tomorrow Never Comes,* Rank, 1978.

Industrialist, *The Return,* Greydon Clark, 1980.

Judge, *Airplane II: The Sequel,* Paramount, 1982.

Brean, *Out of the Blue,* Discovery, 1982.

Steve Martin, *Godzilla,* New World, 1985.

Carter Hedison, *Delirious,* MGM-Pathe, 1991.

Also appeared in *The Alien's Return,* 1980.

STAGE APPEARANCES

Appeared in productions of *Night Must Fall, Mandarin, Crazy with the Heat,* and *Duke in Darkness.*

STAGE WORK

Director with the Pasadena Community Playhouse, Pasadena, CA, 1943.

OTHER SOURCES:

PERIODICALS

Hollywood Reporter, February 11, 1991.*

*   *   *

BURTON, Tim   1960-

PERSONAL: Born in 1960. *Education:* Attended California Institute of the Arts; studied film at Walt Disney Studios.

ADDRESSES: Agent—c/o William Morris Agency, 151 El Camino, Beverly Hills, CA 90212.

CAREER: Director, animator, and screenwriter. Cartoonist.

AWARDS, HONORS: NATO/ShoWest Award, Director of the Year, from National Association of Theatre Owners West, 1989, for *Batman;* Emmy Award (with others), Outstanding Animated Program, 1989-90, for *Beetlejuice.*

CREDITS:

FILM WORK; DIRECTOR

(Also animator) *Vincent* (animated short film), Buena Vista, 1982.
Pee Wee's Big Adventure, Warner Brothers, 1985.
Beetlejuice, Warner Brothers, 1988.
Batman, Warner Brothers, 1989.
(Also producer with Denise De Novi) *Edward Scissorhands* (also see below), Twentieth Century-Fox, 1990.

Also director and animator, *Frankenweenie* (animated), Buena Vista.

TELEVISION WORK; SERIES

Executive producer (with David Geffen) of animated series *Beetlejuice,* ABC.

TELEVISION WORK; EPISODIC

Director, *Alfred Hitchcock Presents,* NBC, 1986.
Director, "Aladdin and His Wonderful Lamp," *Faerie Tale Theatre,* Showtime, 1986.
Animation designer, *Amazing Stories,* NBC, 1987.

WRITINGS:

TELEVISION EPISODES

Alfred Hitchcock Presents, NBC, 1986.

FILM

(Story originator with Caroline Thompson) *Edward Scissorshands,* Twentieth Century-Fox, 1990.*

*   *   *

BUTTRAM, Pat   1917(?)-

PERSONAL: Born June 19, c. 1917, in Addison, AL; married Sheila Ryan (an actress), c. 1952 (died, 1975); children: Kathleen Kerry.

ADDRESSES: Contact— P.O. Box 710, Los Angeles, CA 90078.

CAREER: Actor. Toastmaster at testimonial dinners for entertainers.

CREDITS:

FILM APPEARANCES

Hank, *The Strawberry Roan,* Columbia, 1948.
Chuckwalla Jones, *Riders in the Sky,* Columbia, 1949.
Mike Rawley, *Beyond the Purple Hills,* Columbia, 1950.
Mike, *The Blazing Sun,* Columbia, 1950.
Shadrach Jones, *Indian Territory,* Columbia, 1950.
Smokey Argyle, *Mule Train,* Columbia, 1950.
Scat Russell, *Gene Autry and the Mounties,* Columbia, 1951.
Dusty Cosgrove, *Hills of Utah,* Columbia, 1951.
Cougar Claggett, *Silver Canyon,* Columbia, 1951.
Pecos Bates, *Texans Never Cry,* Columbia, 1951.
Breezie Larrabee, *Valley of Fire,* Columbia, 1951.
As himself, *Apache Country,* Columbia, 1952.
Buckeye Buttram, *Barbed Wire,* Columbia, 1952.
As himself, *Night Stage to Galveston,* Columbia, 1952.
Panhandle Gibbs, *The Old West,* Columbia, 1952.
As himself, *Wagon Team,* Columbia, 1952.
Cole Clinton, *Twilight of Honor* (also known as *The Charge Is Murder*), Metro-Goldwyn-Mayer, 1963.
Harry Carver, *Roustabout,* Paramount, 1964.
President, *Sergeant Deadhead* (also known as *Sergeant Deadhead the Astronut*), American International, 1965.
Texan, *The Sweet Ride,* Twentieth Century-Fox, 1968.
Pat, *I Sailed to Tahiti with an All Girl Crew,* World, 1969.
Voice of Napoleon, *The Aristocats* (animated), Buena Vista, 1970.
Tin Pot, *The Gatling Gun,* Ellman International, 1972.
Voice of Sheriff of Nottingham, *Robin Hood* (animated), Buena Vista, 1973.
Voice of Luke, *The Rescuers* (animated), Buena Vista, 1977.
Voice of Chief, *The Fox and the Hound* (animated), Buena Vista, 1981.
Pope, *Choices,* Oaktree, 1981.
Voice of first bullet, *Who Framed Roger Rabbit?* (animated), Buena Vista, 1988.
Saloon old timer, *Back to the Future, Part III,* Universal, 1990.

Also appeared in *National Barn Dance,* Paramount, 1944; *Blue Canadian Rockies,* Columbia, 1952; and *Angels Brigade,* Arista, 1980.

TELEVISION APPEARANCES; MOVIES

Otis Honeywell, *The Hanged Man,* NBC, 1964.
Tathill, *Louis L'Amour's "The Sacketts,"* NBC, 1979.
Mr. Haney, *Return to Green Acres,* CBS, 1990.

TELEVISION APPEARANCES; SERIES

As himself, *The Gene Autry Show,* CBS, 1950-56.
Mr. Haney, *Green Acres,* CBS, 1965-71.

TELEVISION APPEARANCES; EPISODIC

Buck, *Knight Rider,* NBC, 1986.

Also appeared on episodes of *The Mouse Factory,* syndicated, 1972; *Chico and the Man,* NBC, 1974; "Love and the Longest Night," "Love and the Country Girl," and "Love and the Competitors," *Love, American Style,* ABC; *The Munsters,* CBS; *Petticoat Junction,* CBS; and *The Real McCoys,* ABC.

TELEVISION APPEARANCES; SPECIALS

Arthur Godfrey in Hollywood, CBS, 1962.
Danny Thomas Goes Country and Western, NBC, 1966.
When the West Was Fun: A Western Reunion, ABC, 1979.
Voice of Washington Irving and voice of Ichabod's horse, *The New Misadventures of Ichabod Crane* (animated), syndicated, 1981.
Voice characterization, *Rick Moranis in Gravedale High* (animated; also known as *Gravedale High*), NBC, 1990.

TELEVISION APPEARANCES; PILOTS

Hardy Madison, *Down Home,* CBS, 1965.
Narrator, *Evil Roy Slade,* NBC, 1972.

Also appeared in *Howdy.*

RADIO APPEARANCES; SERIES

Appeared on *Gene Autry's Melody Ranch,* CBS, and *The National Barn Dance,* NBC.

WRITINGS:

TELEVISION

(With Milt Rosen) *Danny Thomas Goes Country and Western* (special), NBC, 1966.
(With others) *The Jerry Reed When You're Hot, You're Hot Hour* (series), CBS, 1972.*

C

CADELL, Simon 1950-

PERSONAL: Full name, Simon John Cadell; born July 19, 1950, in London, England; son of John (a theatrical agent) and Gillian (a drama school principal; maiden name, Howell) Cadell. *Education:* Trained for the stage at Bristol Old Vic Theatre School.

ADDRESSES: Agent—MLR, 200 Fulham Road, London SW10, England.

CAREER: Actor.

CREDITS:

STAGE APPEARANCES

The Betrothed, *Geneva,* Mermaid Theatre, London, 1971.

Simon Green, *Lloyd George Knew My Father,* Savoy Theatre, London, 1972.

Julian Underwood, *The Case in Question,* Haymarket Theatre, London, 1975.

Justin Jackson, *Lies,* Albery Theatre, London, 1975.

Dr. Harry Trench, *Widowers' Houses,* and William Featherstone, *How the Other Half Loves,* both Actors' Company, Wimbledon Theatre, London, 1976.

Andre, Count de Grival, *The Amazons,* Actors' Company, Wimbledon Theatre, 1977.

Ernest, *You Should See Us Now,* Greenwich Theatre, London, 1983.

Noel, *Noel and Gertie,* King's Head Theatre, London, 1983.

Jeffrey Fairbrother, *Hi-De-Hi,* Victoria Palace Theatre, London, 1983.

Archie, *Jumpers,* Aldwych Theatre, London, 1985.

Charles, *Blithe Spirit,* Vaudeville Theatre, London, 1986.

Aubrey Henry Maitland Allington, *Tons of Money,* National Theatre Company, Lyttelton Theatre, London, 1986.

Benedict Hough, *A Small Family Business,* National Theatre Company, Olivier Theatre, London, 1987.

Noel Coward, *Noel and Gertie,* Comedy Theatre, London, 1990.

Appeared as Oswald, *Ghosts,* and in title role, *Hamlet,* both Birmingham Repertory Theatre, Birmingham, United Kingdom; in title role, *Raffles,* Watford Palace Theatre, Watford, United Kingdom; in *A Close Shave, Antigone,* and *The Balcony,* all Nottingham Theatre, Nottingham, United Kingdom; and in *Zigger Zagger,* National Youth Theatre. Also appeared in *Major Barbara, Macbeth, School for Scandal, The Importance of Being Earnest,* and *Arms and the Man,* all Bristol Old Vic Theatre, Bristol, United Kingdom.

MAJOR TOURS

Performed as Elyot in British National Tour of *Private Lives,* United Kingdom cities.

TELEVISION APPEARANCES; MOVIES

Colin Wilson, *Pride and Extreme Prejudice,* USA, 1990.

Also appeared in *Two Sundays,* BBC; *Plaintiff and Defendant,* BBC; *The Dame of Sark,* Anglia Television; *The Promise,* Anglia Television; *The Trials of Oscar Slater,* BBC; and *Name for the Day,* BBC.

TELEVISION APPEARANCES; EPISODIC

Appeared on episodes of *Tales of the Unexpected,* Anglia Television, then syndicated; *The Glittering Prizes,* BBC; *When the Boat Comes In,* BBC; *Minder,* Euston Films; and *Bergerac,* BBC.

OTHER TELEVISION APPEARANCES

Dundridge, *Blott on the Landscape* (series), BBC, then Arts and Entertainment, 1986.

Also appeared as lead, *Hi De Hi* (mini-series), BBC; on *Enemy at the Door* (series), London Weekend Television; *Edward and Mrs. Simpson* (series), Thames; and *She Fell Among Thieves* (mini-series), BBC, then *Mystery!*, PBS.

FILM APPEARANCES

Voice characterization, *Watership Down*, AVCO-Embassy, 1978.*

* * *

CADY, Frank 1915-

PERSONAL: Born in 1915 in Susanville, CA.

ADDRESSES: Agent—Greenvine Agency, 110 East Ninth St., Suite C-1005, Los Angeles, CA 90079.

CAREER: Actor.

CREDITS:

TELEVISION APPEARANCES; SERIES

Doc Williams, *The Adventures of Ozzie and Harriet*, ABC, 1954-65.
Sam Drucker, *Petticoat Junction*, CBS, 1963-70.
Sam Drucker, *Green Acres*, CBS, 1965-71.
Voice of Homer, *These Are the Days* (animated), ABC, 1974-76.

TELEVISION APPEARANCES; EPISODIC

New Girl in His Life (broadcast as an episode of *The General Electric Theatre*), CBS, 1957.
Luke, *The Andy Griffith Show*, CBS, 1965.
Farley Upchurch, *The Andy Griffith Show*, CBS, 1966.

Appeared as Sam Drucker in *The Beverly Hillbillies*, CBS; also appeared in episodes of *December Bride*, CBS, and *Guestward Ho!*, ABC.

TELEVISION APPEARANCES; PILOTS

Will Hoople, *The Andy Griffith Show* (broadcast as an episode of *The Danny Thomas Show*), CBS, 1960.
Doc Medford, *Sutters Bay*, CBS, 1983.

OTHER TELEVISION APPEARANCES

Mr. Minney, "The Winged Colt," *ABC Children's Novel for Television* (special), ABC, 1977.
Mr. Sutter, *Soup and Me* (special), ABC, 1978.
Sam Drucker, *Return to Green Acres* (movie), CBS, 1990.

FILM APPEARANCES

Violence, Monogram, 1947.
Professor Edwards, *Sarge Goes to College*, Monogram, 1947.
Gus Barton, *Bungalow Thirteen*, Twentieth Century-Fox, 1948.

Suspect, *He Walked by Night*, Eagle-Lion, 1948.
Shirley's partner, *City Across the River*, Universal, 1949.
Mr. Crane, *The Lady Takes a Sailor*, Warner Brothers, 1949.
Clerk, *Sky Dragon*, Monogram, 1949.
Player, *Take One False Step*, Universal, 1949.
Prejudice, Motion Picture Sales, 1949.
Eddie, *Convicted* (also known as *One Way Out*), Columbia, 1950.
Mr. Hoff, *Emergency Wedding*, Columbia, 1950.
Max Henry, *Experiment Alcatraz*, RKO, 1950.
Timid guest, *Father of the Bride*, Metro-Goldwyn-Mayer (MGM), 1950.
Tax investigator, *The Great Rupert*, Eagle-Lion, 1950.
Geologist, *Perfect Strangers* (also known as *Too Dangerous to Love*), Warner Brothers, 1950.
Elevator operator, *Three Husbands*, United Artists (UA), 1950.
Hotel clerk, *Young Man with a Horn*, Warner Brothers, 1950.
Mr. Creavy, *Dear Brat*, Paramount, 1951.
Ferguson, *Let's Make It Legal*, Twentieth Century-Fox, 1951.
Bennie Amboy, *The Sellout*, MGM, 1951.
Mr. Federber, *The Big Carnival* (also known as *Ace in the Hole* and *The Human Interest Story*), Paramount, 1951.
Harold Ferris, *When Worlds Collide*, Paramount, 1951.
Weinberg, *The Atomic City*, Paramount, 1952.
Mr. Watts, *Half a Hero*, MGM, 1953.
Dr. Day, *Marry Me Again*, RKO, 1953.
Fire escape man, *Rear Window*, Paramount, 1954.
Trader Joe, *The Indian Fighter*, UA, 1955.
Canford, *Trial*, MGM, 1955.
Mr. Daigle, *The Bad Seed*, Warner Brothers, 1956.
Pop, *The Girl Most Likely*, Universal, 1957.
Abe Pickett, *The Tin Star*, Paramount, 1957.
Willie Poole, *The Missouri Traveler*, Buena Vista, 1958.
Milstead, *The Man Who Understood Women*, Twentieth Century-Fox, 1959.
Mayor James Sargent, *Seven Faces of Dr. Lao*, MGM, 1964.
Charlie Pettibone, *The Gnome-Mobile*, Buena Vista, 1967.
Assayer, *The $1,000,000 Duck*, Buena Vista, 1971.
Pa Allan, *Zandy's Bride*, Warner Brothers, 1974.
Pa Tater, *Hearts of the West* (also known as *Hollywood Cowboy*), MGM/UA, 1975.

Also appeared in *The Checkered Coat*.

STAGE APPEARANCES

Henry IV, Part I, Center Theatre Group, Mark Taper Forum, Los Angeles, 1971.
What Are You Doing After the War?, Center Theatre Group, New Theatre for Now, Los Angeles, 1972.*

CAESAR, Sid 1922-

PERSONAL: Born September 8, 1922, in Yonkers, NY; son of Max (a restaurant owner) and Ida (Raffel) Caesar; married Florence Levy, June 17, 1943; children: Michele, Richard, Karen. *Education:* Attended public schools in Yonkers, NY; studied the saxophone and clarinet.

ADDRESSES: Agent—c/o Tom Korman, Agency For the Performing Arts, 9000 Sunset Blvd., Suite 1200, Los Angeles, CA 90069.

CAREER: Comedian, actor, and writer. Has worked as a movie usher and doorman; played saxophone and clarinet in bands of Charlie Spivak, Shep Fields, and Claude Thornhill. *Wartime service:* United States Coast Guard Orchestra, 1942-44.

AWARDS, HONORS: Donaldson Award, best debut of an authentic clown, for *Make Mine Manhattan,* 1949; Best Comedian on Television Award, *Look* Magazine, 1951, 1956; Emmy Award, best actor, 1951; Emmy Award, best continuing performance by a comedian in a series, 1956; Sylvania Award, best comedy/variety show of 1958; Antoinette Perry Award nomination, best actor, 1963, for *Little Me;* inducted into United States Hall of Fame, 1967; inducted into Television Hall of Fame, 1985; Emmy Award, outstanding variety special, *The Sid Caesar, Imogene Coca, Carl Reiner, Howard Morris Special.*

CREDITS:

STAGE APPEARANCES

(Debut) Ensemble, *Tars and Spars* (revue), U.S. Coast Guard, then Strand Theatre, New York City, 1948.

Make Mine Manhattan, Broadhurst Theatre, New York City, 1948.

Little Me, Lunt-Fontanne Theatre, New York City, 1962.

Four on a Garden, Broadhurst Theatre, 1971.

Barney Cashman, *Last of the Red Hot Lovers,* Westport Country Playhouse, Westport, CT, 1972.

Mel Edison, *The Prisoner of Second Avenue,* Arlington Park Theatre, Arlington Heights, IL, 1974.

Double Take, Arlington Park Theatre, 1974.

Barney Cashman, *Last of the Red Hot Lovers,* Crystal Palace, Dallas, TX, 1975.

Night of 100 Stars, Radio City Music Hall, New York City, 1982.

Night of 100 Stars, Radio City Music Hall, New York City, 1985.

Frosch, *Die Fledermaus,* Metropolitan Opera, New York City, 1988.

An Evening with Sid Caesar . . . The Legendary Genius of Comedy (revue), Village Gate Theatre, New York City, 1989.

Sid Caesar & Company: Does Anybody Know What I'm Talking About? (revue), Village Gate Theatre, then John Golden Theatre, New York City, 1989.

As himself, *Together Again,* Michael's Pub, New York City, 1990.

Cabaret appearances include Caribe Hilton Hotel, San Juan, Puerto Rico, 1973, Rainbow Grill, New York City, 1974, and *The Legend of Comedy,* Rivera Hotel, Las Vegas, NV, 1988.

MAJOR TOURS

Cast member, *Little Me,* U.S. cities, 1964.
Cast member, *Moonface, Anything Goes,* U.S. cities, 1980.
Ensemble, *A Touch of Burlesque* (revue), U.S. cities, 1981.

FILM APPEARANCES

(Debut) Chuck Enders, *Tars and Spars,* Columbia, 1946.
Sammy Weaver, *The Guilt of Janet Ames,* Columbia, 1947.
Melville Crump, *It's a Mad, Mad, Mad, Mad, World,* Casey/United Artists, 1963.
A Guide for the Married Man, Twentieth Century-Fox, 1967.
George Norton, *The Busybody,* Paramount, 1967.
Ben Powell, *The Spirit Is Willing,* Paramount, 1967.
Talkative Passenger, *Airport '75,* Universal, 1974.
Studio Chief, *Silent Movie,* Twentieth Century-Fox, 1976.
Zabbar, *Fire Sale,* Twentieth Century-Fox, 1977.
Ezra Dezire, *The Cheap Detective,* Columbia, 1978.
Coach Calhoun, *Grease,* Paramount, 1978.
Joe Capone, *The Fiendish Plot of Dr. Fu Manchu,* Orion, 1980.
Chief Caveman, *History of the World, Part 1,* Brooksfilm/Fox, 1981.
Coach Calhoun, *Grease 2,* Paramount, 1982.
Fisherman, *Cannonball Run II,* Warner Brothers, 1984.
Uncle Benjamin, *Over the Brooklyn Bridge,* Metro-Goldwyn-Mayer/United Artists, 1984.
Dr. Dixyer Minder, *Stoogemania,* Tromas Coleman-Michael Rosenblatt/Atlantic, 1986.
Emperor, *The Emperor's New Clothes,* Golan-Globus/Cannon, 1987.

TELEVISION APPEARANCES; SERIES

Host, *Sid Caesar's Your Show of Shows* (also see below), NBC, 1950-54.
Bob Victor and Host, *Caesar's Hour,* NBC, 1954-57.
Host, *Sid Caesar Invites You,* ABC, 1958.
Host, *The Sid Caesar Show,* ABC, 1963-64.
Host, *The Hollywood Palace,* NBC, 1964-1970.

Also, *Cavalcade of Stars,* Dumont, 1949-52; *The Jack Carter Show,* 1950-51; *Love American Style,* 1969-1974; *That's Life,* ABC, 1968-69.

TELEVISION APPEARANCES; MOVIES

Lazlo Cozart, *Curse of the Black Widow*, ABC, 1977.
George Beam, *Flight to Holocaust*, NBC, 1977.
Dr. Dustin Diablo, *The Munsters' Revenge*, NBC, 1981.
Sam Green, *Found Money*, NBC, 1983.
Mr. Petrakis, *Love Is Never Silent*, NBC, 1985.
Max, *Freedom Fighter*, NBC, 1988.
Louis Hammerstein, *Side by Side*, CBS, 1988.
Dr. Diablo and Emil Hornshumler, *The Munsters' Revenge*, NBC, 1989.

Also *Nothing's Impossible*, 1988.

TELEVISION APPEARANCES; SPECIALS

The Bob Hope Show, NBC, 1951.
Dateline, NBC, 1954.
Host, *The Sid Caesar Show*, NBC, 1958.
Host, *The Sid Caesar Special*, CBS, 1959.
Host, *Marriage—Handle With Care*, CBS, 1959.
Host, *Variety! The World of Showbiz*, CBS, 1960.
Host, *Tip Toe Through TV*, CBS, 1960.
Host, *As Caesar Sees It*, NBC, 1962.
The Edie Adams Show (*Here's Edie*), NBC, 1963, 1964.
The Bob Hope Show, NBC, 1969.
A Salute to Television's 25th Anniversary, ABC, 1972.
Ann-Margret Smith, NBC, 1975.
Host, *Your Show of Shows* (also see below), NBC, 1976.
Perry Como's Christmas in Australia, NBC, 1976.
Gabriel Kaplan Presents the Small Event, ABC, 1977.
Voice of the Wizard of Oz, *Dorothy in the Land of Oz*, CBS, 1981.
NBC's 60th Anniversary Celebration, NBC, 1986.

Also appeared in *10 From Your Show of Shows*, 1973; *All Star Party for Lucille Ball*, 1984; Mr. Reginald Snyder, *Christmas Snow*, 1986; *The 38th Annual Emmy Awards*, 1986; *Comic Relief*, 1986; *The Television Academy Hall of Fame*, 1986; song performer, *The Princess Academy*, 1986; *Happy Birthday Hollywood*, 1987; *Improv Tonight*, 1988; *JFK—That Day in November*, 1988; *Neil Simon: Not Just For Laughs*, 1989; *Ooh-La-La—It's Bob Hope's Fun Birthday Spectacular from Paris' Bicentennial*, 1989; *30 Years of Comedy*, NBC; and *The Sid Caesar, Imogene Coca, Carl Reiner, Howard Morris Special*, CBS.

OTHER TELEVISION APPEARANCES

Voice of Max, the Computer, *America 2100* (pilot), ABC, 1979.
Pink Lady (episode), NBC, 1980.
It Only Hurts When You Laugh (pilot), NBC, 1983.
Lou Bundles, *Amazing Stories* (episode), NBC, 1985.
Gryphon, *Alice in Wonderland* (mini-series), CBS, 1985.

(Debut appearance) Host, *Admiral Broadway Revue*, 1949. Also appeared on *On Stage America* (episode), 1984;

Life's Most Embarrassing Moments (episode), 1986; and *The Big Show; The Misadventures of Sheriff Lobo* (episode).

WRITINGS:

Author of United States Coast Guard sketches for *Six On, Twelve Off* (stage revue), 1942-44; author of *Your Show of Shows* (television special), 1976; and author (with Bill Davidson) of *Where Have I Been?*, 1982.*

*   *   *

CAIN, William 1931-

PERSONAL: Born May 27, 1931, in Tuscaloosa, AL; son of John Calhoun (a machinist) and Minnie Lee (Smith) Cain; married Leta Anderson (an actress). *Education:* George Washington University, A.A., 1951; Catholic University, B.A., 1953.

CAREER: Actor and director. Appeared in repertory with Milwaukee Repertory Theatre Company, 1974-75; Actors Theatre of Louisville, 1975-76; Trinity Square Repertory Company, 1964-76; and Actors Theatre of Louisville, 1974-81. *Military service:* Served in the U.S. Army, 1953-55, became corporal.

AWARDS, HONORS: Nominated for Best New Actor on Broadway, 1969, for *Wilson and the Promised Land*.

CREDITS:

STAGE APPEARANCES

(Stage debut) Shand, *What Every Woman Knows*, Patchwork Players, Roanoke, VA, 1949.
(New York City debut) Ayamonn Braydon, *Red Roses For Me*, Greenwich Mews Theatre, 1959.
The Birthday Party, Trinity Square Repertory Company, 1966-67.
The Importance of Being Earnest, Trinity Square Repertory Company, 1967-68.
Brother to Dragons, Trinity Square Repertory Company, 1968-69.
Wilson in the Promise Land, Trinity Square Repertory Company, 1969-70.
The Taming of the Shrew, Trinity Square Repertory Company, 1970-71.
Woodrow Wilson, *Wilson in the Promised Land*, Trinity Square Repertory Company, American National Theatre and Academy (ANTA) Theatre, New York City, 1970.
Dobbs, *Child's Play*, and Walter, *The Price* (double bill), Trinity Square Repertory Theatre, Providence, RI, 1971-72.
Play Strindberg, Actors Theatre of Louisville, KY, 1973-74.

Relatively Speaking, Actors Theatre of Louisville, 1974-75.

The Gin Game, Actors Theatre of Louisville, 1976-77.

Philip, *Relatively Speaking,* York Players Company, Church of the Heavenly Rest, New York City, 1980.

Jacob Mercer, *Of the Fields, Lately,* Century Theatre, New York City, 1980.

Lloyd, *Young Bucks,* Tyson Studio, New York City, 1981.

Vikings, Royal Poinciana Playhouse, Palm Beach, FL, 1981.

Derelict, Studio Arena Theatre, Buffalo, NY, 1981-82.

Jeffrey, *Night and Day,* ACT: A Contemporary Theatre, Seattle, WA, 1981-82, then Huntington Theatre Company, Boston, MA, 1982-83.

Understudy, Martin, Kirby, and Paul, *You Can't Take It With You,* Plymouth Theatre, New York City, 1983.

Man, *After the Fall,* Hartford Stage Company, Playhouse 91, New York City, 1984.

You Never Can Tell, Center Stage Theatre, Baltimore, MD, 1983-84.

Rainsnakes, Long Wharf Theatre, New Haven, CT, 1984-85.

Painting Churches, Cincinnati Playhouse in the Park, OH, 1985-86.

Clay Baker, *Paducah,* American Place Theatre, New York City, 1985.

Peasant, *Wild Honey,* Virginia Theatre, New York City, 1986.

Prince Irakly Stratonych Dulyebov, *Artists and Admirers,* CSC Repertory Theatre, New York City, 1986.

Understudy, Henry, *The Boys in Autumn,* Circle in the Square Theatre, New York City, 1986.

Reverend Paul Raeder, *Copperhead,* WPA Theatre, New York City, 1987.

Dr. Mayberry, *I Never Sang for My Father,* John F. Kennedy Center for the Performing Arts, Washington, D.C., and Center Theatre Group, Ahmanson Theatre, Los Angeles, 1987-88.

Miller, *Ah, Wilderness!,* Yale Repertory Theatre, New Haven, CT, 1987-88.

David McComber, *Ah, Wilderness!,* Neil Simon Theatre, New York City, 1988.

Other appearances include Arthur Kir, *Nuts,* Birmingham, MI; President Harding, *The Gang's All Here,* Creon, *Antigone,* and Jim Crow, *Jericho Jim Crow,* all in New York City; Andrew, *Sleuth;* coach, *That Championship Season;* Franklin Delano Roosevelt, *Sunrise at Campobello;* Edward P. Dowd, *Harvey;* Stockman, *Enemy of the People;* Dysart, *Equus;* Marcus, *Another Part of the Forest;* Horace, *The Little Foxes;* Russell, *The Best Man;* Proctor, *The Crucible;* Jamie, *A Moon for the Misbegotten;* Hero, *The Rehearsal;* Scott, *Terra Nova;* Devil, *Don Juan in Hell.* Also appeared in *Henry V, I Married an Angel in Concert,* and *Buddha,* all in New York City.

MAJOR TOURS

Steve, *Broadway,* West Coast tour, 1964.

Dr. Seward, *Dracula,* East Coast tour, 1979.

Also performed in *Year of the Locusts,* Edinburgh Festival, Scotland, and *School for Wives,* Phoenix Festival.

STAGE WORK

Director, *The Private Ear/The Public Eye,* York Theatre Company, Church of the Heavenly Rest, 1981.

FILM APPEARANCES

(Debut) Butler, *The Betsy,* Allied Artists, 1978.

Poker player, *The Dogs of War,* United Artists, 1980.

George Quigley, *The Ultimate Solution of Grace Quigley,* (also known as *Grace Quigley*), Metro-Goldwyn-Mayer/United Artists/Cannon, 1984.

TELEVISION APPEARANCES

Hughes, *All My Children* (series), ABC, 1970.

Mr. Whitney, *Live Among the Lowly* (special), PBS, 1976.

Crying client, *Sessions* (movie), ABC, 1983.

H.T. Jillks, *Kane and Abel* (mini-series), CBS, 1985.

Weehawken Police Captain, *Double Take,* CBS, 1985.

Also appeared as Dr. Paul Romney, *The Littlest Victims* (movie), 1989.

*   *   *

CAIRNS, Tom 1952-

PERSONAL: Born November 1, 1952, in Dromara, Northern Ireland; son of Thomas James and Nora Lillian Cairns. *Education:* College of Art and Design, Belfast, Northern Ireland, B.A., c. 1976; studied theatre design at Riverside Studios under Margaret Harris.

ADDRESSES: Agent—Harriet Cruickshank, 97 Old South Lambeth Rd., London SW8, England.

CAREER: Set designer and director.

CREDITS:

STAGE WORK; SET DESIGNER, EXCEPT WHERE INDICATED

Hamlet, Crucible Theatre, Sheffield, England, 1983.

Don Giovanni, Crucible Theatre, 1986.

The Midsummer Marriage, Opera North, Leeds, England, 1986.

Edward the Second, Royal Exchange Theatre, Manchester, England, 1987.

The Trojans, Welsh National Opera, Cardiff, Wales, 1987.

Twelfth Night, Crucible Theatre, 1988.

The Winters Tale, Crucible Theatre, 1988.

The Park, Crucible Theatre, 1988.

(And director) *Uncle Vanya,* Crucible Theatre, 1988.

Billy Budd, English National Opera, London, England, 1988.

Samson & Dalila, Bregenz Festival, Bregenz, Austria, 1988.

(And director) *The Lady from the Sea,* Citizens Theatre, Glasgow, Scotland, 1988.

Beatrice & Benedict, English National Opera, 1989.

Sunday in the Park with George, National Theatre, London, 1990.

Director, *Miss Julie,* Greenwich Theatre, London, 1990.

Director, *King Priam,* Opera North, 1991.

Also designed sets for *Philistines,* Royal Shakespeare Company, 1986. Directed *La Boheme,* Stuttgart Opera, 1991.

*   *   *

CALHOUN, Rory   1922-

PERSONAL: Full name, Francis Timothy McCown; born August 8, 1922, in Los Angeles, CA. *Education:* Attended public schools in Santa Cruz, CA.

CAREER: Actor, director, producer, writer. Has also worked as a recording artist and cattle rancher. Arizona Valley Development Corporation, vice president.

CREDITS:

FILM APPEARANCES

James J. Corbett, *The Great John L.* (also known as *A Man Called Sullivan*), United Artists, 1945.

Jose, *Nob Hill,* Twentieth Century-Fox, 1945.

Mr. Herrick, *Adventure Island,* Paramount, 1947.

Teller, *The Red House,* United Artists, 1947.

Ken Freneau, *That Hagen Girl,* Warner Brothers, 1947.

Larry, *Miraculous Journey,* Film Classics, 1948.

Phil Acton, *Massacre,* Allied Artists/Monogram, 1949.

Peter Brennan, *County Fair,* Monogram, 1950.

Larrabee, *Return of the Frontiersman,* Warner Brothers, 1950.

Dakota Gunman, *Ticket to Tomahawk,* Twentieth Century-Fox, 1950.

Jack Stark, *I'd Climb the Highest Mountain,* Twentieth Century-Fox, 1951.

David Hemmingway, *Meet Me After the Show,* Twentieth Century-Fox, 1951.

Ownie Rogers, *Rogue River,* Eagle Lion, 1951.

Martin, *Way of a Gaucho,* Twentieth Century-Fox, 1952.

John Burns, *With a Song in My Heart,* Twentieth Century-Fox, 1952.

Eben, *How to Marry a Millionaire,* Twentieth Century-Fox, 1953.

Chino Bullock, *Powder River,* Twentieth Century-Fox, 1953.

Sheriff Tom Davisson, *The Silver Whip,* Twentieth Century-Fox, 1953.

Ed Stone, *A Bullet Is Waiting,* Columbia, 1954.

Brett Wade, *Dawn at Socorro,* Universal, 1954.

Ray Cully, *Four Guns to the Border,* Universal, 1954.

Harry Weston, *River of No Return,* Twentieth Century-Fox, 1954.

Adam, *The Yellow Tomahawk,* United Artists, 1954.

Kenneth Post, *Ain't Misbehavin',* Universal, 1955.

Jesse Hill, *The Looters,* Universal, 1955.

Alex McNamara, *The Spoilers,* Universal, 1955.

Tom Bryan, *The Treasure of Pancho Villa,* RKO Radio Pictures, 1955.

Tony Dumont, *Flight to Hong Kong,* United Artists, 1956.

Alec Longmire, *Red Sundown,* Universal, 1956.

Frank Harber, *The Big Caper,* United Artists, 1957.

Domino, *Domino Kid,* Columbia, 1957.

Gil McCord, *The Hired Gun,* Metro-Goldwyn-Mayer (MGM), 1957.

Tate, *Ride Out for Vengeance,* United Artists, 1957.

Utah Blaine, *Utah Blaine,* Columbia, 1957.

Logan Cates, *Apache Territory,* Columbia, 1958.

Hemp Calhoun, *The Saga of Hemp Brown,* Universal, 1958.

Mitch Cooper, *Thunder in Carolina,* Howco, 1960.

Dario, *The Colossus of Rhodes,* MGM, 1961.

Captain Adam Corbett, *The Secret of Monte Cristo* (also known as *The Treasure of Monte Cristo*), MGM, 1961.

Title role, *Marco Polo* (also known as *L'Avventura di un Italiano incina; Grand Khan*), American International Pictures, 1962.

Rand, *A Face in the Rain,* Embassy, 1963.

Blaine Madden, *The Gun Hawk,* Allied Artists, 1963.

Sergeant Ed Brent, *The Young and the Brave,* MGM, 1963.

Santee, *Black Spurs,* Paramount, 1965.

Larry Wintin, *Finger on the Trigger* (also known as *El Dedo en El Gatillo*), Allied Artists, 1965.

Clint McCoy, *Young Fury,* Paramount, 1965.

Jim Walker, *Apache Uprising,* Paramount, 1966.

Rory, *Operation Delilah* (also known as *Opercion Dalila*), Comet, 1966.

Mike Page, *Dayton's Devils,* Cue, 1968.

Sergeant Sean MacAfee, *Operation Cross Eagles* (also known as *Unakasna Vatra*), Continental, 1969.

Cole Hillman, *Night of the Lepus,* MGM, 1972.

Philip Hart, *Won Ton Ton: The Dog Who Saved Hollywood,* Paramount, 1976.

Len Thompson, *Love and Midnight Auto Supply,* Producers Capitol, 1978.

Fighter in the Kid's Camp, *The Main Event,* Warner Brothers, 1979.

Vincent Smith, *Motel Hell,* United Artists, 1980.

Kit Carson, *Angel,* New World, 1984.

Also, (debut) *Something for the Boys,* 1944; *Requiem for a Heavyweight,* Columbia, 1962; *Call Me Bwana,* 1963; *Our Man in Bagdad,* 1965; *Lady of the Nile,* 1966; *Low Price of Fame,* 1971; *Koo Lau,* 1973; *The West Is Still Wild,* 1975; *Kino, the Padre on Horseback,* 1977; *Mule Feathers,* 1977; *Now I Lay Me Down to Sleep,* 1977; *Bitter Heritage,* 1978; *Revenge of Bigfoot,* 1978; *Just Not the Same Without You,* 1978; Looney Tunes, *Hell Comes to Frogtown,* 1988; Sam Harper, *Bad Jim,* 1989.

FILM WORK

Producer, director, *Domino Kid,* Columbia, 1957.
Producer, director, *The Hired Gun,* MGM, 1957.
(With Victor M. Orsath) Producer, *Apache Territory,* Columbia, 1958.

Also director, *Koo Lau,* 1973.

STAGE APPEARANCES

Appeared in *Belle Star,* London, 1969-70.

TELEVISION APPEARANCES

Ford Television Theater, NBC, 1952.
Climax, CBS, 1954.
Screen Director's Playhouse, NBC, 1955.
Screen Director's Playhouse, ABC, 1956.
Ford Television Theater, ABC, 1956.
The Desilu Revue, CBS, 1959.
Zane Grey Theater, CBS, 1962.
Captain Voctor Kihlgren, *Luxury Liner* (pilot), NBC, 1963.
Host, *Western Star Theatre,* syndicated, 1963.
Circle of Fear, NBC, 1973.
Ed Davis—Engineer, *Flight to Holocaust* (movie), NBC, 1977.
Farner, *Flatbed Annie & Sweetiepie: Lady Truckers* (movie), CBS, 1979.
Breen, *The Rebels* (movie), syndicated, 1979.
Sundance Ewbanks, *Pottsville* (pilot), CBS, 1980.
General George Meade, *The Blue and Gray* (series), CBS, 1982.
Judson Tyler, *Capitol* (series), CBS, 1982.
General George Meade, *The Blue and the Gray* (movie), CBS, 1982.
Awards presenter, *The Wildest West Show of the Stars* (special), 1986.

Also appeared in episodes of *The Road Ahead,* 1950; *Death Valley Days,* 1952; *Day Is Done,* 1955; *Bet the Wild Queen,* 1955; *Chrysler Theater,* 1955; *U.S. Camera,* 1957; Bill Longley, *The Texan* (series), 1958; *Killer Instinct,* 1958; *Lands End,* 1959; *Ghost Story,* 1972.

WRITINGS:

(With Kenneth Garnet and Hal Biller), *Domino Kid* (screenplay), Columbia, 1957.

Also author of *Shotgun,* 1955; *The Texan,* (television series), 1957-60; and stage play, *The Man from Padera.*

*   *   *

CANONERO, Milena

PERSONAL: Born in Italy.

CAREER: Costume designer and producer.

AWARDS, HONORS: Academy Award (with Ulla-Britt Soderlund), Best Costume Design, 1975, for *Barry Lyndon;* Academy Award, Best Costume Design, 1981, and British Academy Award, Best Costume Design, 1982, both for *Chariots of Fire;* special Coty American Fashion Critics' Award, 1984; Academy Award nomination, Best Costume Design, 1985, and British Academy Award nomination, Best Costume Design, 1986, both for *Out of Africa;* Academy Award nomination, Best Costume Design, 1988, for *Tucker: The Man and His Dream;* Academy Award nomination, Best Costume Design, 1990, for *Dick Tracy.*

CREDITS:

FILM WORK; COSTUME DESIGNER, EXCEPT AS INDICATED

A Clockwork Orange, Warner Brothers, 1971.
(With Ulla-Britt Soderlund) *Barry Lyndon,* Warner Brothers, 1975.
Midnight Express, Columbia, 1978.
The Shining, Warner Brothers, 1980.
Chariots of Fire, Twentieth Century-Fox, 1981.
The Hunger, Metro-Goldwyn-Mayer/United Artists, 1983.
The Cotton Club, Orion, 1984.
Give My Regards to Broad Street, Twentieth Century-Fox, 1984.
Out of Africa, Universal, 1985.
(Also visual consultant) *Barfly,* Cannon, 1987.
Associate producer, *Good Morning Babylon,* Vestron, 1987.
Haunted Summer, Cannon, 1988.
Tucker: The Man and His Dream, Paramount, 1988.
Costume design consultant, *Lost Angels,* Orion, 1989.
Dick Tracy, Buena Vista, 1990.
Costume design consultant, *Reversal of Fortune,* Warner Brothers, 1990.
The Godfather, Part III, Paramount, 1990.

Also associate producer and costume design consultant, *Mamba,* 1988.*

CAPRA, Frank   1897-1991

PERSONAL: Born May 18, 1897, in Palermo, Italy; immigrated to United States, 1903; died in his sleep, September 3, 1991, in La Quinta, CA; son of Salvatore (a fruit grower) and Sarah (Nicolosi) Capra; married Helen Howell, 1924 (marriage ended); married Lucille Rayburn Warner, 1932; children: Frank Jr., John, Lulu, Thomas. *Education:* California Institute of Technology, B.S., 1918. *Avocational interests:* Hunting, fishing, music, lecturing at universities.

ADDRESSES: Contacts—P.O. Box 980, La Quinta, CA 92253; and c/o Academy of Motion Picture Arts and Sciences, 8949 Wilshire Boulevard, Beverly Hills, CA 90211.

CAREER: Director, producer, and writer. Worked as a lab assistant, prop man, film cutter, and editor in the early 1920s; writer of film titles, assistant director, and writer for Hal Roach and Mack Sennett, 1923-25; formed Frank Capra Productions with Robert Riskin, 1939; founder with Sam Briskin, William Wyler, and George Stevens, and president, Liberty Films, 1945-48; United States delegate to the International Film Festival in Bombay, India, 1952; U.S. State Department delegate to the Soviet Union, 1963. Member of board of directors of California Institute of Technology. *Military service:* U.S. Army, 1918-19; became first lieutenant; U.S. Army Signal Corps, 1942-45; became colonel; awarded Distinguished Service Medal, 1945; awarded Legion of Merit for the production of army films.

MEMBER: Academy of Motion Picture Arts and Sciences (president, 1935-39); Screen Directors' Guild (president, 1938-40).

AWARDS, HONORS: Academy Award nomination, best director, 1933, for *Lady for a Day;* Academy Awards, best director, 1934, for *It Happened One Night,* 1936, for *Mr. Deeds Goes to Town,* and 1938, for *You Can't Take It with You;* Academy Award nomination, best director, 1939, for *Mr. Smith Goes to Washington;* Belgian Film Award, 1941, for *Arsenic and Old Lace;* Academy Award, best documentary, 1942, for "Prelude to War," *Why We Fight;* New York Film Critics Circle, special award, 1943, for *Why We Fight;* Academy Award nomination, best director, 1946, and Golden Globe Award, best motion picture director, 1947, both for *It's a Wonderful Life;* D. W. Griffith Award from the Directors Guild of America, 1958; Society of Motion Picture and Television Engineers Award, 1973; American Film Institute Lifetime Achievement Award, 1982; National Medal of Arts from the National Endowment of the Arts, 1986; Order of the British Empire.

CREDITS:

FILM DIRECTOR

The Strong Man, First National, 1926.
For the Love of Mike, First National, 1927.
Long Pants, First National, 1927.
The Matinee Idol, Columbia, 1928.
The Power of the Press, Columbia, 1928.
Say It with Sables, Columbia, 1928.
So This Is Love, Columbia, 1928.
Submarine, Columbia, 1928.
That Certain Thing, Columbia, 1928.
The Way of the Strong, Columbia, 1928.
Flight, Columbia, 1929.
The Donovan Affair, Columbia, 1929.
Younger Generation, Columbia, 1929.
Ladies of Leisure, Columbia, 1930.
Rain or Shine, Columbia, 1930.
Dirigible, Columbia, 1931.
The Miracle Woman, Columbia, 1931.
Platinum Blonde, Columbia, 1931.
American Madness, Columbia, 1932.
Forbidden, Columbia, 1932.
The Bitter Tea of General Yen, Columbia, 1933.
Lady for a Day, Columbia, 1933.
Broadway Bill (also known as *Strictly Confidential*), Columbia, 1934.
It Happened One Night, Columbia, 1934.

Also director of *Fultah Fisher's Boarding House,* 1922; *The Swim Princess,* 1928; and *The Burglar* (also known as *Smith's Burglar*), 1928.

FILM DIRECTOR AND PRODUCER

Mr. Deeds Goes to Town, Columbia 1936.
Lost Horizon, Columbia, 1937.
You Can't Take It with You, Columbia, 1938.
Mr. Smith Goes to Washington, Columbia, 1939.
Meet John Doe, Warner Brothers, 1941.
Arsenic and Old Lace, Warner Brothers, 1944.
It's a Wonderful Life, Liberty/RKO Radio Pictures, 1946 (also see below).
State of the Union (also known as *The World and His Wife*), Metro-Goldwyn-Mayer, 1948.
Riding High, Paramount, 1950.
Here Comes the Groom, Paramount, 1951.
A Hole in the Head, United Artists, 1959.
Pocketful of Miracles, United Artists, 1961.

PRODUCER; FILM DOCUMENTARIES

Why We Fight, U.S. War Department, Part 1: (and director) "Prelude to War," 1942; Part 2: (and director with others) "The Nazis Strike," 1943; Part 3: (and director with others) "Divide and Conquer," 1943; Part 4: "The Battle of Britain," 1943; Part 5: "The

Battle of Russia," 1944; Part 6: (and director with others) "The Battle of China," 1944; Part 7: "War Comes to America," 1945.

(And director with others) *Tunisian Victory*, U.S. War Department, 1944.

Know Your Ally: Britain, U.S. War Department, 1944.

The Negro Soldier, U.S. Office of War Information, 1944.

Two Down, One to Go, U.S. War Department, 1945.

(And director with others) *Know Your Enemy: Japan*, U.S. War Department, 1945.

Know Your Enemy: Germany, U.S. War Department, 1945.

Our Mr. Sun, Bell System Science Series, 1956 (also see below).

Hemo the Magnificent, Bell System Science Series, 1957 (also see below).

The Strange Case of the Cosmic Rays, Bell System Science Series, 1957 (also see below).

The Unchained Goddess, Bell System Science Series, 1958 (also see below).

Also producer of *Attack! The Battle of New Britain*, 1944; producer and director of *Rendezvous in Space*, 1964.

FILM APPEARANCES

George Stevens: A Filmmaker's Journey (documentary), Castle Hill, 1985.

Arriva Frank Capra (documentary; also known as *Here Comes Frank Capra*) Electra, 1987.

TELEVISION APPEARANCES: SPECIALS

The American Film Institute Salute to Frank Capra, CBS, 1982.

The American Film Institute Salute to John Huston, CBS, 1983.

WRITINGS:

Frank Capra: The Name above the Title (autobiography), Macmillan, 1971.

SCREENPLAYS; EXCEPT WHERE NOTED

(With Arthur Ripley) *Lucky Stars* (short film), Warner Brothers, 1925.

(With Ripley) *Saturday Afternoon* (short film), Warner Brothers, 1925.

(With Tim Whelan, Hal Conklin, J. Frank Holliday, Gerald Duffy, and Murry Roth) *Tramp, Tramp, Tramp*, First National, 1926.

(With Ripley) *The Strong Man*, First National, 1926.

(With Ripley) *His First Flame*, Pathe Exchange, 1927.

(With Howard J. Green) *Flight*, Columbia, 1929.

(With Frances Goodrich, Albert Hackett, and Jo Swerling) *It's a Wonderful Life*, Liberty/RKO Radio Pictures, 1946.

Our Mr. Sun (documentary), Bell System Science Series, 1956.

Hemo the Magnificent (documentary), Bell System Science Series, 1957.

The Strange Case of the Cosmic Rays (documentary), Bell System Science Series, 1957.

The Unchained Goddess (documentary), Bell System Science Series, 1958.

Also author, with Arthur Ripley, of short films *Picking Peaches, Smile Please, Shanghaied Lovers, Flickering Youth, The Cat's Meow, His New Mama, The First 100 Years, The Luck 'o the Foolish, The Hansom Cabman, All Night Long*, and *Feet of Mud*, all 1924; *The Sea Squawk, Boobs in the Woods, His Marriage Wow, Plain Clothes, Remember When?, Horace Greeley, Jr., The White Wing's Bride*, and *There He Goes*, all 1925; and *Fiddlesticks* and *The Soldier Man*, both 1926.

OBITUARIES AND OTHER SOURCES:

PERIODICALS

Detroit Free Press, September 4, 1991.*

*   *   *

CAPUCINE   1935(?)-1990

PERSONAL: Born Germaine Lefebvre, January 6, 1935 (some sources say 1933), in Toulon, France; committed suicide, March 17, 1990, in Lausanne, Switzerland. *Education:* Attended schools in Saumur, France; received B.A.; studied acting during the late 1950s with Gregory Ratoff in Hollywood, CA.

CAREER: Actress. Worked for a time as a photographer's model in Paris, France.

CREDITS:

FILM APPEARANCES

Michelle "Angel," *North To Alaska*, Twentieth Century-Fox, 1960.

Princess Carolyne, *Song without End*, Columbia, 1960.

Christine, *The Lion*, Twentieth Century-Fox, 1962.

Hallie, *Walk on the Wild Side*, Columbia, 1962.

Simone Clouseau, *The Pink Panther*, United Artists (UA), 1964.

Dhana, *The Seventh Dawn*, UA, 1964.

Renee Lefebvre, *What's New Pussycat?* (also known as *Quoi de neuf, Pussycat?*), UA, 1965.

Princess Dominique, *The Honey Pot* (also known as *It Comes Up Murder, Anyone for Venice?*, and *Mr. Fox of Venice*), UA, 1967.

Marta, *The Queens* (also known as *Le Fate* and *Les Orgresses*) Royal, 1968.

Tryphaena, *Fellini's Satyricon* (also known as *Satyricon*), UA, 1969.

Dr. Saforet, *Fraulein Doktor* (also known as *Gospodjica Doktor-Spijunka Bezimena*), Paramount, 1969.

Pepita, *Red Sun* (also known as *Soleil Rouge*), National General, 1972.

Vahista, *Arabian Adventure,* Orion/Warner Brothers, 1979.

Nicole, *From Hell to Victory,* New Film Princess Films-Jose Frade, 1979.

Amalia Mazzorani, *Nest of Vipers* (also known as *Ri Tratto Di Borghesia In Nero*), Paramount, 1979.

Zina Vanacore, *Jaguar Lives!,* American International Pictures, 1979.

Helene, *Incorrigible,* EDP, 1980.

Belle, *The Con Artists* (also known as *The Con Man*), S. J. International Pictures, 1981.

Lady Litton, *The Trail of the Pink Panther,* UA, 1982.

Lady Litton, *Curse of the Pink Panther,* UA, 1983.

Massimiliano, Caracciolo's Mother, *I Miel Primi Quarant'Anni* (also known as *My First Forty Years*), Columbia, 1987.

Flora, *Le Foto di Gioia* (also known as *Gioia's Photograph*), Medusa Distribuzione, 1987.

Other appearances include teenager, *Rendez-Vous de Juillet* (film debut), 1949; Parker, *Las Crueles,* 1971; Mrs. Levine, *De l'enfer a la Victoire,* 1979; and Madam Teufminn, *Balles Perdues,* 1983. Also appeared in *Jackpot* (unfinished), 1974; *Per Amore,* 1976; *Da Dunkerque alla Vittoria,* 1979; *Aphrodite, Blackout,* and *Stray Bullets,* all 1982; *Blue Blood,* 1988; *Betrand Coeur de Lion; Frou-Frou; The Triumph of Michael Strogoff; I Don Giovanni della Costa Azzurra; Exquisite Cadaver; Ne pas de Ranger; Search; Story of a Woman; Martin Eden; Bluff; For Love; Scoop;* and *Neapolitan Thriller.*

TELEVISION APPEARANCES; MOVIES

Appeared as Odile, *Sins,* 1986, and in *Dying To Sing, Blue Blood, Honor Thy Father, Dead Heat, Quartier Negre, Gila and Rick, Delirium,* and *My First Forty Years.*

TELEVISION APPEARANCES; EPISODIC

Appeared on *Hart to Hart.*

OBITUARIES AND OTHER SOURCES:

PERIODICALS

Variety, March 28, 1990.*

*   *   *

CARTER, Thomas

PERSONAL: Born July 17 in Austin, TX. *Education:* Graduated from Southwest Texas State University.

ADDRESSES: Agent—Lee Gabler, Creative Artists Agency, 9830 Wilshire Blvd., Beverly Hills, CA 90212.

CAREER: Actor and director.

AWARDS, HONORS: Directors Guild of America Award, outstanding directorial achievement for television (dramatic shows/night), 1983, for "The Rise and Fall of the Wall," *Hill Street Blues;* Emmy Award nomination, outstanding directing in a drama series, 1989, for "Conversations with the Assassin," *Midnight Caller;* Emmy Award, outstanding directing in a drama series, 1989-90, for "Promises to Keep," *Equal Justice;* received other Emmy Award nominations.

CREDITS:

TELEVISION APPEARANCES; SERIES

Ray Gun, *Szysznyk,* CBS, 1977-78.

James Hayward, *The White Shadow,* CBS, 1978-80.

TELEVISION DIRECTOR; EPISODIC, EXCEPT WHERE INDICATED

The White Shadow, CBS, 1978.

Hill Street Blues, NBC, 1981.

Fame, NBC, 1982.

Remington Steele, NBC, 1982.

Alfred Hitchcock Presents (two episodes), NBC, 1985.

Amazing Stories (two episodes), NBC, 1986.

A Year in the Life, NBC, 1987.

Equal Justice, ABC, 1990-91.

TELEVISION DIRECTOR; PILOTS

St. Elsewhere, NBC, 1982.

Trauma Center, ABC, 1983.

Call to Glory, ABC, 1984.

Miami Vice, NBC, 1984.

Heart of the City, ABC, 1986.

A Year in the Life, NBC, 1986.

Midnight Caller, NBC, 1988.

Equal Justice (also see below), ABC, 1990.

OTHER TELEVISION WORK

Director, *Under the Influence* (movie), CBS, 1986.

Creator (with Christopher Knopf and David A. Simons) and executive producer, *Equal Justice* (series), ABC, 1990—.

FILM APPEARANCES

Dean Hampton, *Almost Summer,* Universal, 1978.

Orderly John, *Whose Life Is It Anyway,* Metro-Goldwyn-Mayer/United Artists, 1981.

CASSEL, Seymour 1937-

PERSONAL: Born January 22, 1937, in Detroit, MI; son of a burlesque performer. *Education:* Studied acting at American Theatre Wing and Actor's Studio.

ADDRESSES: Agent—Gersh Agency, 280 South Beverly Dr., Suite 400, Beverly Hills, CA 90212.

CAREER: Actor. Toured as a child with a troupe of burlesque performers; teacher and director in workshop with John Cassavetes.

CREDITS:

FILM APPEARANCES

Seymour, *Juke Box Racket,* Brenner, 1960.
Red, *Too Late Blues,* Paramount, 1962.
Vic, *The Webster Boy* (also known as *Middle of Nowhere*), Regal Films, 1962.
Young hood, *Coogan's Bluff,* Universal, 1968.
Chet, *Faces,* Continental Distributing, 1968.
Surfer/cyclist, *The Sweet Ride,* 20th Century-Fox, 1968.
Leonard, *The Revolutionary,* United Artists (UA), 1970.
Seymour Moskowitz, *Minnie and Moskowitz,* Universal, 1971.
Mort Weil, *The Killing of a Chinese Bookie,* Faces, 1976.
Homer, *Black Oak Conspiracy,* New World, 1977.
George Manning, *Death Game,* Levitt-Pickman Film, 1977.
Dr. Jaelki, *Scott Joplin,* Universal, 1977.
George Ullman, *Valentino,* UA, 1977.
Governor Haskins, *Convoy,* UA, 1978.
Duke, *California Dreaming,* American International, 1979.
Dobbs, *Sunburn,* Paramount, 1979.
Labont, *The Mountain Men,* Columbia, 1980.
Barry Tanner, *King of the Mountain,* Universal, 1981.
Double Exposure, Crown, 1982.
Jack Lawson, *Love Streams,* UA, 1984.
Sheriff, *Eye of the Tiger,* Scotti Brothers-International Video Entertainment, 1986.
Dave Forrest, *Survival Game,* Trans World Entertainment, 1987.
Cheese, *Tin Men,* Buena Vista, 1987.
Wallace Gibson, *Johnny Be Good,* Orion, 1988.
Ed, *Plain Clothes,* Paramount, 1988.
Sam Catchem, *Dick Tracy,* Touchstone, 1990.
Miner, *White Fang,* Walt Disney, 1991.

Also appeared as Nic Roeq, *Cold Haven,* 1990; Alex Rockwell, *In the Soup,* 1991; hit man, *Roy London,* 1991; appeared in *John Cassavetes—The Man and His Work* (documentary); *Murder, Inc.; Shadows; Opening Night; The Last Tycoon; I'm Almost Not Crazy; Track 29; Wicked Stepmother.*

TELEVISION APPEARANCES; MOVIES, EXCEPT AS NOTED

Bellboy, *The Hanged Man,* NBC, 1964.
Ralph, *Nightside* (pilot), ABC, 1973.
Dr. Jaelki, *Scott Joplin: King of Ragtime,* NBC, 1978.
Smiley Nitchell, *Angel on My Shoulder,* ABC, 1980.
Jack Santo, *I Want to Live,* ABC, 1983.
Tony, *Beverly Hills Madame,* NBC, 1986.
Kierdorff, *Blood Feud,* syndicated, 1989.
Sweet Bird of Youth, NBC, 1990.

Also appeared in movies *My Shadow,* 1991, and *The Killers.*

STAGE APPEARANCES

Appeared in *The World of Suzie Wong* and *The Disenchanted,* both New York City.

*   *   *

CAVANAUGH, Michael

PERSONAL: Born in New York, NY. *Education:* Attended San Francisco State College.

CAREER: Actor.

CREDITS:

STAGE APPEARANCES

(Broadway debut) *Oh! Calcutta!,* Eden Theatre, 1969.
Randle Patrick McMurphy, *One Flew Over the Cuckoo's Nest,* Charles Playhouse, Boston, MA, 1973.

Also appeared with the American Conservatory Theatre of San Francisco, CA, 1970-71.

FILM APPEARANCES

Lalo, *The Enforcer,* Warner Brothers, 1976.
Feyderspiel, *The Gauntlet,* Warner Brothers, 1977.
Peanuts, *Heroes,* Universal, 1977.
Rich, *Over-under Sideways-down,* Cine Manifest, 1978.
Partrick Scarfe, *Any Which Way You Can,* Warner Brothers, 1980.
Stan, *Forced Vengeance,* United Artists, 1982.
NHRA Boss, *A Heart Like a Wheel,* Twentieth Century-Fox, 1983.

Also appeared as an undercover cop in *The Lady in Red,* 1979; *Comeback,* 1981; and *Full Fathom Five,* 1990.

TELEVISION APPEARANCES; MOVIES

Steve Vector, *Portrait of a Stripper,* CBS, 1979.
Steve, *Eleventh Victim,* CBS, 1979.
Captain Lake, *A Rumor of War,* CBS, 1980.
Stocker, *Gideon's Trumpet,* CBS, 1980.
Jesse James, *Belle Starr,* CBS, 1980.
George, *Miracle on Ice,* ABC, 1981.

Gene Brooks, *Death In California,* ABC, 1985.
Garage attendant, *Final Jeopardy,* NBC, 1985.
Bill Orfman, *Hostage Flight,* NBC, 1985.
Gene Scott, *Second Serve,* CBS, 1986.
Lieutenant Marcus, *Street of Dreams,* CBS, 1988.
Detective, *Promised a Miracle,* CBS, 1988.

Also appeared as a U.S. Marshal in *Blood Feud,* 1983; as Dean Boyle in *Two to Tango,* 1989; and in *People Like Us,* 1990.

TELEVISION APPEARANCES; EPISODIC

Detective Roy Henderson, *Partners,* CBS, 1983.
John Lefferts, *Amazing Stories,* NBC, 1985.
Lieutenant Johnson, *Cagney & Lacey,* 1985.
Michael Donahue, Viking, *MacGyver,* ABC, 1986.
Richardson, *L.A. Law,* NBC, 1989.
Proctor, *Tour of Duty,* CBS, 1990.

Also appeared as Stoner in *Airwolf,* 1985; Mac Hoover in *Our House,* 1987; and Phillips in *Wolf,* 1989.

OTHER TELEVISION APPEARANCES

Whitey, *Doctor Scorpion* (pilot), ABC, 1978.
Bobby Joe Adams, *The Texas Rangers* (pilot), NBC, 1981.
Captain Lester Cain, *Hunter* (series), NBC, 1984.
George Fox, *Starman* (series), ABC, 1986.

Also appeared as Lieutenant Pendleton, *Joe Bash* (series), 1986, and in the 1990 television special, *To the Moon, Alice.**

* * *

CHAN, Jackie 1955(?)-

PERSONAL: Born Chan Kwong Sang, c. 1955 in Hong Kong; father and mother cooked and cleaned for the United States Consulate in Canberra, Australia. *Education:* Studied martial arts, acrobatics, and mime at the Chinese Opera Research Institute.

CAREER: Actor, director, and producer. Worked variously as a film extra, stand-in, stuntman, and martial arts coordinator.

CREDITS:

FILM APPEARANCES

Ai Long, *New Fist of Fury,* Lo Wei Motion Picture Company, 1976.
Drunken Money in the Tiger's Eye (also known as *Drunken Master*), Seasonal, 1978.
Spiritual Kung Fu, All Seasons, 1978.
The Fearless Hyena, Alpha, 1979.
The Young Master, Golden Harvest, 1979.
The Young Tiger, Fourseas, 1980.

Jerry, *The Big Brawl,* Warner Brothers (Warner), 1980.
Snake and Crane Arts of Shaolin, All Seasons, 1980.
The Dragon Fist, Alpha, 1980.
First Subaru Driver, *The Cannonball Run,* Twentieth Century-Fox, 1981.
Jackie, *Cannonball Run II,* Warner, 1983.
Project A, Alpha, 1984.
Wheels on Meals, Golden Harvest, 1984.
Heart of the Dragon, Golden Harvest, 1985.
To Kill with Intrigue, All Seasons, 1985.
Billy Wong, *The Protector,* Warner/Columbia/Cannon, 1985.
Ka Kui Chan/Kevin Chan, *Jingcha Gushi* (also known as *Police Story* and *Jackie Chan Police Story*), Cinema Group Entertainment/Golden Way/Palace, 1985.
Cheng Leng (Jackie—Hawk of Asia), *Long Xiong Hu Di* (also known as *The Armour of God*), Toho-Towa/Target International/Video Programme Distributors, 1986.
The Fearless Hyena, Part II, All Seasons, 1986.
A Jihua Xuji (also known as *A Gai Juk Jap* and *Project A, Part II*), Golden Harvest/Golden Way, 1987.
Ninja Thunderbolt, IFD Films and Arts Ltd., 1987.
Kuo Cheng-wah (Mr. Canton), *Oiji* (also known as *Mr. Canton and Rose, Mr. Canton and Lady Rose Oiji,* and *Miracles*), Golden Communications, 1989.

Also appeared in *Snake in the Eagle's Shadow,* Seasonal; *My Lucky Stars,* Golden Harvest; *Twinkle, Twinkle, Lucky Star,* Golden Harvest; *Fantasy Mission Force,* All Seasons; *In Eagle Shadow Fist,* All Seasons; *Magnificent Bodyguard; Dragon Lord; Half a Loaf of Kung Fu;* and *Shaolin Wooden Men.*

FILM WORK; DIRECTOR, EXCEPT WHERE INDICATED

Fists of Fury, National General, 1973.
(And stunt choreographer) *The Young Master,* Golden Harvest, 1979.
The Fearless Hyena, Alpha, 1979.
Executive producer (with Willie Chan and Raymond Chow), *Jingcha Gushi* (also known as *Police Story* and *Jackie Chan Police Story*), Cinema Group Entertainment/Golden Way/Palace, 1985.
The Fearless Hyena, Part II, All Seasons, 1986.
Long Xiong Hu Di (also known as *The Armour of God*), Toho-Towa/Target International/Video Programme Distributors, 1986.
A Jihua Xuji, Golden Harvest, 1987.
Executive producer (with Chan and Leonard Ho), *Inji kau* (also known as *Yanzhi Kov* and *The Legend of Flowers*), Golden Communications, 1988.

SIDELIGHTS: Number one box-office star in China and Japan.*

CHAPLIN, Geraldine   1944-

PERSONAL: Born July 31, 1944, in Santa Monica, CA; daughter of Charlie (an actor and director) and Oona (O'Neill) Chaplin; children: (with director Carlos Saura) Shane. *Education:* Studied at the Royal Ballet School, London, 1961.

ADDRESSES: Agent—William Morris Agency, 151 El Camino Dr., Beverly Hills, CA 90212.

CAREER: Actress.

CREDITS:

STAGE APPEARANCES

Dancer in chorus, *Cinderella,* London, 1963.
(Broadway debut) Alexandra Giddens, *The Little Foxes,* Vivian Beaumont Theatre, December 19, 1967.

FILM APPEARANCES

(Debut) Street urchin, *Limelight,* Chaplin/United Artists, 1951.
Tonya, *Doctor Zhivago,* Metro-Goldwyn-Mayer, 1965.
Angela Sawyer, *Cop-Out* (also known as *Stranger in the House*), Cinerama, 1967.
A Countess from Hong Kong, Chaplin/Rank/Universal, 1967.
Purity Hoxworth, *The Hawaiians* (also known as *Master of the Islands*), United Artists, 1970.
Sur un arbre perche (also known as *Perched on a Tree*), Societe Nouvelle de Cinema/Imperia, 1971.
La Casa sin fronteras (also known as *The House without Boundaries*), Amboto, 1971.
Carole McNeil, *Z.P.G.* (also known as *Zero Population Growth*), Paramount, 1972.
Miriam Loman, *Innocent Bystanders,* Paramount, 1973.
Marie des Anges, *Le Mariage a la mode,* Society Nouvelle de Cinema, 1973.
Anne of Austria, *The Three Musketeers* (also known as *The Queen's Diamonds*), Twentieth Century-Fox, 1974.
Queen Anne of Austria, *The Four Musketeers* (also known as *The Revenge of Milady*), Twentieth Century-Fox, 1975.
Opal, *Nashville,* Paramount, 1975.
Annie Oakley, *Buffalo Bill and the Indians; or, Sitting Bull's History Lesson,* United Artists, 1976.
Ana as an adult and Maria, *Cria cuervos* (also known as *Cria* and *Raise Ravens*), Interama/Gala Film Distributors/Colifilms, 1976.
Morag, *Noroit* (also known as *Northwest Wind, Scenes de la vie parallele; 3 Noroit; Une Vengeance;* and *Nor'west*), Sunchild, 1976.
Lise, *Une Page d'amour,* (also known as *A Page of Love*), Progres, 1977.

Elisa, vidi mia (also known as *Elisa My Love*), Interama/Colifirlms, 1977.
Karen Hood, *Welcome to L.A.,* Lion's Gate, 1977.
Marilyn, "The Hustle" episode, *Roseland,* Merchant-Ivory/Cinema Shares International, 1977.
Catherine, *L'Adoptin* (also known as *The Adoption*), Les Films Moliere, 1978.
Emily, *Remember My Name,* Columbia, 1978.
Rita Billingsley, *A Wedding,* Twentieth Century-Fox, 1978.
Emilia, *Los ojos vendados* (also known as *Blindfolded Eyes* and *Mit verbindenen Augen*), Elias Duerjeta Productin Company, 1978.
Anna, *Mama cumple 100 anos* (also known as *Mama Turns 100* and *Mom's 100 Years Old*), Interama, 1979.
Isabelle, *Mais ou et donc ornicar,* Mallia, 1979.
Lucie, *Le Voyage en douce* (also known as *Travels on the Sky*), Gaumont International/New Yorker, 1979.
Ella Zielinsky, *The Mirror Crack'd,* EMI/Associated Film Distribution, 1980.
Suzan/Sara Glenn, *Bolero* (also known as *Les Uns et les autres*), Double 13, 1982.
Nora Winkle, *Life Is a Bed of Roses* (also known as *La Vie est un roman*), Soprofilm-A2-Fideline-Ariane-Filmedis/Spectrafilm, 1984.
Charlotte, *Love on the Ground* (also known as *L'amour par terre*), La Cecilia-French Ministry of Culture/Spectrafilm, Cannon/Gakam 1984.
Buried Alive, Aquarius, 1984.
Nina, *White Mischief,* Goldcrest-Umbrella-Power Tower/Columbia, 1987.
Nathalie de Ville, *The Moderns,* Alive, 1988.
The Queen, *The Return of the Musketeers,* Universal, 1989.
Joyce Wheater, *The Children,* Film Four International, 1990.

Other appearances include Ana, *Ana y los Lobos* (also known as *Anna and the Wolves*), 1973; Paulina, *In Memorium,* 1977; and Terry Armstrong, *Je veux rentrer a la maison,* 1989, Also appeared in *Dernier soir,* 1964; *Para un beau matin d'ete,* 1964; *Andremo in citta,* 1966; *I Killed Rasputin* (also known as *J'ai tue Raspoutine*), 1967; *Peppermint Frappe,* 1967; *Stress es tres tres,* 1968; *La madriguera* (also known as *The Honeycomb*), 1969; *El jardin de las delicias,* 1970; *Y el projimo?,* 1973; *La Banda de Jaider* (also known as *Verflucht dies Amerika!*), 1974; *Sommerfuglene* (also known as *Summer of Silence*), 1974; *The Gentleman Tramp,* documentary, 1975; *Scrim,* 1976; *The Masked Bride,* 1978; *Tous est a nous,* 1979; *La viuda de Montiel,* 1980; and *Hidden Talent,* 1984.

TELEVISION APPEARANCES

Naomi Dunn, *The Word* (mini-series), CBS, 1978.

Rachel "My Cousin Rachel," *Mystery!* (series), BBC, 1985.

Madame da Franchi, *The Corsican Brothers* (movie), CBS, 1985.

Appeared in *La familia Colon* (series), Spain, 1966-67; and *Don Carlos* (movie), West Germany, 1971.

WRITINGS:

Author, with Carlos Saura and Rafael Azcona, of *La madriguera* (screenplay), 1969.*

*   *   *

CHASE, Chevy   1943-

PERSONAL: Born Cornelius Crane Chase, October 8, 1943, in New York, NY; son of Edward Tinsely (a publishing executive) and Cathalene (Crane) Chase; married Jacqueline Carlin, December 4, 1976 (divorced, 1980); married Jayni (a production coordinator), 1982; children: (second marriage) Cydney Cathalene, Caley Leigh. *Education:* Bard College, B.A. (English), 1967; Massachusetts Institute of Technology, M.A.; studied audio research at CCS Institute. *Politics:* Democrat.

ADDRESSES: Agent—Michael Ovitz or Rick Nicita, Creative Artists Agency Inc., 1888 Century Park East, Suite 1400, Los Angeles, CA 90067.

CAREER: Actor, producer, writer, and comedian. Worked as an artist for Metro-Goldwyn-Mayer Records, 1968, and *Mad* magazine, 1973.

MEMBER: Actors' Equity Association, Screen Actors Guild, American Federation of Television and Radio Artists, American Federation of Musicians.

AWARDS, HONORS: Emmy Awards, outstanding single or continuing performance by a supporting actor in variety or music, 1975-76, for *Saturday Night Live;* (with Anne Beatts, Tom Davis, Al Franken, Lorne Michaels, Marilyn Suzanne Miller, Michael O'Donoghue, Herb Sergent, Tom Schiller, Rosie Schuster, and Alan Zweibel), outstanding writing in a comedy-variety or music series (a single episode of a regular or limited series), 1975-76, for *Saturday Night Live;* (with Paul Simon, Lily Tomlin, Davis, Franken, Charles Grodin, Michaels, and Zweibel), outstanding writing in a comedy-variety or music special, 1977-78, for *The Paul Simon Special;* and Best Comedy Script Award, Writers Guild.

CREDITS:

STAGE APPEARANCES

Ensemble, *Lemmings* (revue; also see below), Off-Broadway, 1973.

Also appeared in *Channel One* (revue; also see below), Bard College.

STAGE WORK

Producer (with Kenny Shapiro and Lane Sarahnson), *Groove Tube,* New York City, 1973.

FILM APPEARANCES

(Debut) Four Leaf Clover, *The Groove Tube,* Levitt-Pickman, 1974.

Tony Carlson, *Foul Play,* Paramount, 1978.

Ty Webb, *Caddyshack,* Orion/Warner Brothers, 1980.

Nick Gardenia, *Seems Like Old Times,* Columbia, 1980.

Benjamin Browning, *Oh, Heavenly Dog!,* Twentieth Century-Fox, 1981.

Bruce Thorpe, *Under the Rainbow,* Orion/Warner Brothers, 1981.

Max, *Modern Problems,* Twentieth Century-Fox, 1981.

Eddie Muntz, *Deal of the Century,* Warner Brothers, 1983.

Clark W. Griswold, *National Lampoon's Vacation,* Warner Brothers, 1983.

Title role, *Fletch,* Universal, 1984.

Clark W. Griswold, *National Lampoon's European Vacation,* Warner Brothers, 1985.

Newscaster, *Sesame Street Presents: Follow that Bird,* Warner Brothers, 1985.

Emmett Fitz-Hume, *Spies Like Us,* Warner Brothers, 1985.

Dusty Bottoms, *The Three Amigos,* Orion, 1986.

Ty Webb, *Caddyshack II,* Orion/Warner Brothers, 1988.

Clark W. Griswold, *National Lampoon's Christmas Vacation,* Warner Brothers, 1989.

Title role, *Fletch Lives,* Universal, 1989.

Chris Thorne, *Nothing but Trouble,* Warner Brothers, 1991.

Also appeared in *Tunnelvision,* 1976; Andy, *Funny Farm,* 1988; and Condom Father, *The Couch Trip,* 1988.

TELEVISION APPEARANCES

Regular, *The Great American Dream Machine* (series), PBS, 1971-72.

Not Ready for Prime Time Player, *Saturday Night Live* (series; also see below), NBC, 1975-76.

Host, *The Chevy Chase Show* (special; also see below), NBC, 1977.

The Paul Simon Special (also see below), NBC, 1977.

Hollywood Foreign Press Association's 35th Annual Golden Globe Award (special), NBC, 1978.

Host, *The Chevy Chase National Humor Test* (special), NBC, 1979.

Guest, *Playboy's 25th Anniversary Celebration* (special), ABC, 1979.

Tom Snyder's Celebrity Spotlight (pilot), NBC, 1980.

Saturday Night Live 15th Anniversary, NBC, 1989.
The Dave Thomas Comedy Show (episodic), CBS, 1990.
The Barbara Walters Special, ABC, 1990.

Also appeared in *It's Gary Shandling's Show,* 1989. Appeared in numerous other specials, including *The Screen Actors Guild 50th Anniversary Celebration,* 1984; guest, *Bob Hope's Happy Birthday Homecoming,* 1985; *The Kennedy Center Honors: A Celebration of the Performing Arts,* 1985; *The American Music Awards,* 1986; *Bugs Bunny/Looney Tunes All-Star 50th Anniversary,* 1986; *Kraft Salutes the George Burns 90th Birthday Special,* 1986; host, *59th Annual Academy Awards Presentation,* 1987; host, *Will Rogers: Look Back in Laughter,* 1987; guest, *Humor and the Presidency,* 1987; host, *60th Annual Academy Awards Presentation,* 1988; *The American Comedy Awards,* 1988, 1989; *Coca-Cola Presents Live: The Hard Rock,* 1988; *MTV's 1989 Video Music Awards,* 1989; *Mike Tyson—A Portrait of the People's Champion,* 1989; presenter, *62nd Annual Academy Awards Presentation,* 1990; *Life of Python,* 1990; *Time Warner Presents the Earth Day Special,* 1990; host, *That's What Friends Are For,* 1990.

RADIO APPEARANCES

Appeared in *National Lampoon Radio Hour* series.

WRITINGS:

FOR TELEVISION

(With others) *The Smothers Brothers Show* (series), ABC, 1975.

(With Anne Beatts, Tom Davis, Al Franken, Lorne Michaels, Marilyn Suzanne Miller, Michael O'Donoghue, Herb Sergent, Tom Schiller, Rosie Schuster, and Alan Zweibel) *Saturday Night Live* (series), NBC, 1975-76.

(With Stuart Birnbaum, Brian Doyle-Murray, and Thomas Leopold) *The Chevy Chase Show* (special), NBC, 1977.

(With Paul Simon, Lily Tomlin, Davis, Franken, Grodin, Michaels, and Zweibel) *The Paul Simon Special,* NBC, 1977.

OTHER

(With others) *Lemmings* (stage revue), produced in New York City, 1973.

The Groove Tube (screenplay), Levitt-Pickman Films, 1974.

Also author of *Channel One* (stage revue), Bard College.*

CHER 1946-

PERSONAL: Full name, Cherilyn Sarkisian LaPiere; born May 20, 1946, in El Centro, CA; daughter of John Sarkisian and Georgia Holt (a model and actress); married Sonny Bono (a singer, restaurateur, and politician), October 27, 1964 (divorced, May, 1975); married Gregg Allman (a musician), June, 1975 (divorced); children: (first marriage) Chastity; (second marriage) Elijah Blue. *Education:* Trained for the stage with Jeff Corey.

ADDRESSES: Agent—Creative Artists Agency, 1888 Century Park East, Suite 1400, Los Angeles, CA 90069; Bill Sammeth Organization, 9200 Sunset Boulevard, Suite 1001, Los Angeles, CA 90069.

CAREER: Actress and singer. Began career as backup singer for the Crystals and Ronettes; appeared with Sonny Bono as Caesar and Cleo, then as Sonny and Cher, beginning in 1964; recorded and performed in duo Sonny and Cher, 1964-75 and 1977; member of rock band Black Rose, 1979-80; performer in night clubs in Las Vegas and Atlantic City. Head of independent film company, Isis Productions.

AWARDS, HONORS: Golden Globe Award, Best Actress in a Television Comedy or Musical, 1974, for *Sonny and Cher;* Academy Award nomination, Best Supporting Actress, and Golden Globe Award, Best Actress in a Supporting Role in a Motion Picture, both 1983, for *Silkwood;* Cannes Film Festival, Palm d'Or Award, Best Actress, 1985, for *Mask;* Hasty Pudding Woman of the Year Award, 1985; Academy Award, Best Actress, and Golden Globe Award, Best Actress in a Motion Picture Comedy or Musical, both 1987, for *Moonstruck.*

CREDITS:

FILM APPEARANCES

Herself, *Good Times,* Columbia, 1967.
Title role, *Chastity,* American International, 1969.
Sissy, *Come Back to the Five and Dime, Jimmy Dean, Jimmy Dean,* Viacom, 1982.
Dolly Pelliker, *Silkwood,* Twentieth Century-Fox, 1983.
Rusty Dennis, *Mask,* Universal, 1985.
Kathleen Riley, *Suspect,* Tri-Star, 1987.
Alexandra Medford, *The Witches of Eastwick,* Warner Brothers, 1987.
Loretta Castorini, *Moonstruck,* Metro-Goldwyn-Mayer/United Artists, 1987.
Rachel Flax, *Mermaids,* Orion, 1990.

TELEVISION APPEARANCES; SERIES

Host, *The Sonny and Cher Comedy Hour,* CBS, 1971-74.
Host, *Cher,* CBS, 1975-76.
Host, *The Sonny and Cher Show,* CBS, 1976-77.

TELEVISION APPEARANCES; EPISODIC

(With Sonny Bono) *Shindig,* ABC, 1964.

Also appeared with Sonny Bono on *Love, American Style,* ABC, and *Hullabaloo,* NBC.

TELEVISION APPEARANCES; SPECIALS

Where the Girls Are, NBC, 1968.
Third wife, *The First Nine Months Are the Hardest,* NBC, 1971.
How to Handle a Woman, NBC, 1972.
Host, *Cher,* CBS, 1975.
The Flip Wilson Special, NBC, 1975.
Cher . . . Special, ABC, 1978.
Host, *Cher and Other Fantasies,* NBC, 1979.
Tom Snyder's Celebrity Spotlight, NBC, 1980.
Host, *Cher—A Celebration at Caesar's Palace,* Showtime, 1983.
Superstars & Their Moms, ABC, 1987.
Cher . . . At the Mirage, CBS, 1991.

STAGE APPEARANCES

Come Back to the Five and Dime, Jimmy Dean, Jimmy Dean, Martin Beck Theatre, New York City, 1982.

RECORDINGS:

ALBUMS; WITH SONNY BONO, EXCEPT WHERE NOTED

Look at Us, Atco, 1965.
Wondrous World, Atco, 1966.
In Case You're in Love, Atlantic, 1967.
Good Times, Atlantic, 1967.
The Best of Sonny and Cher, Atlantic, 1968.
Sonny & Cher Live, Kapp, 1969, re-released, MCA, 1972.
All I Ever Need Is You, Kapp, 1971, re-released, MCA, 1975.
Live in Las Vegas, MCA, 1974.
Greatest Hits, MCA, 1975.
The Beat Goes On, Atco, 1975.
(With Black Rose) *Black Rose,* Casablanca, 1980.

Also recorded *Baby Don't Go,* Reprise. Singles with Sonny Bono include "I Got You Babe" and "You Better Sit Down Kids"; also recorded single "After All" (theme song from the film *Chances Are*), with Peter Cetera, 1989.

SOLO ALBUMS

All I Really Want to Do, Imperial, 1965.
Sonny Side of Cher, Imperial, 1966.
With Love, Imperial, 1966.
Cher, Imperial, 1967.
Backstage, Imperial, 1968.
3614 Jackson Highway, Atco, 1969.
Cher, Kapp, 1972.
Foxy Lady, MCA, 1972.

Hits of Cher, United Artists, 1972.
Bittersweet White Light, MCA, 1973.
Dark Lady, MCA, 1974.
Half Breed, MCA, 1974.
Stars, Warner Brothers, 1975.
Greatest Hits, MCA, 1975.
I'd Rather Believe in You, Warner Brothers, 1977.
Cherished, Warner Brothers, 1977.
Take Me Home, Casablanca, 1978.
Prisoner, Casablanca, 1979.
The Best of Cher, EMI America, 1987.
Cher, Geffen, 1988.
Heart of Stone, Geffen, 1989.

Also recorded *Golden Greats,* 1968; *This Is Cher,* Sunset; *Cher Sings the Hits,* Springboard; *Greatest Hits,* Springboard; *Live; The Two of Us;* and *Allman and Woman.* Singles include "Gypsies, Tramps and Thieves"; "Dark Lady"; "Take Me Home"; "Half Breed"; and "I Found Someone."

WRITINGS:

(With Robert Haas) *Forever Fit: The Lifetime Plan for Health, Beauty, and Fitness,* Bantam, 1991.

OTHER SOURCES:

PERIODICALS

New York Times, March 20, 1988.
People, January 21, 1991.
Premiere, February, 1988.

*   *   *

CHILES, Linden

PERSONAL: Born in St. Louis, MO.

ADDRESSES: Agent—Contemporary Artists, 132 Lasky Dr., Suite B, Beverly Hills, CA 90212.

CAREER: Actor.

CREDITS:

FILM APPEARANCES

Randy, *Sanctuary,* Twentieth Century-Fox, 1961.
Brock Caldwell, *A Rage to Live,* United Artists, 1965.
Dr. Hanneford, *Incident at Phantom Hill,* Universal, 1966.
Yellow Knife, *Texas Across the River,* Universal, 1966.
Long, *Counterpoint,* Universal, 1967.
Patrick Sullivan, *Sullivan's Empire,* Universal, 1967.
Bendetto, *Eye of the Cat,* Universal, 1969.
Second reporter, *Where the Buffalo Roam,* Universal, 1980.

Dr. Gordon Hauser, *Forbidden World* (also known as *Mutant*), Universal, 1982.

Airport security chief, *Cloak and Dagger,* Universal, 1984.

Bradley Anderson, *The Forbidden Dance* (also known as *Lambada! The Forbidden Dance* and *Lambada—El Baile Prohibido*), Columbia, 1990.

TELEVISION APPEARANCES; MOVIES

Tony Ebsen, *Panic on the 5:22,* ABC, 1974.

Ken Reardon, *Hitchhike!,* ABC, 1974.

Matthew Evans, *Adventures of the Queen,* CBS, 1975.

Dr. Tracy Putnam, *Death Be Not Proud,* ABC, 1975.

Dr. Walter Coppin, *Who Is the Black Dahlia?,* NBC, 1975.

J. Miller Leavy, *Helter Skelter,* CBS, 1976.

Lloyd, *Act of Violence,* CBS, 1979.

John Loring, *Scared Straight! Another Story,* CBS, 1980.

Colonel Collette, *Red Flag: The Ultimate Game,* CBS, 1981.

Senator John Warner, *To Heal a Nation,* NBC, 1988.

Larry DeRoche, *Things That Go Bump in the Night* (also known as *Christine Cromwell* and *Amanda Cromwell*), ABC, 1989.

TELEVISION APPEARANCES; SERIES

Chief Officer Steve Kirkland, *Convoy,* NBC, 1965.

Paul Britton, *The Secret Storm,* CBS, 1970.

Paul Hunter, *James at Fifteen,* NBC, 1977-78.

TELEVISION APPEARANCES; EPISODIC

Judge, *Alfred Hitchcock Presents,* NBC, 1985.

Alan Rollins, *Matlock,* NBC, 1986.

Kenton Peak, *Benson,* ABC, 1986.

Nolting, *The A-Team,* NBC, 1986.

Sanderson North, *Scarecrow and Mrs. King,* CBS, 1986.

Whitney Borgen, *Foley Square,* CBS, 1986.

Al, *Our House,* NBC, 1987.

Dr. Pointsman, *Werewolf,* Fox, 1987.

Buzz Brown, *Our House,* NBC, 1987.

Howard Dytman, *Simon and Simon,* CBS, 1988.

Serverino, *A Year in the Life,* NBC, 1988.

Lawyer, "Meet the Munceys," *The Disney Sunday Movie,* ABC, 1988.

Also appeared as Charles Hanson, *East Side/West Side,* CBS.

TELEVISION APPEARANCES; PILOTS

Dr. David Latham, *Come a Running,* CBS, 1963.

Dwight Wainwright, *Freeman,* ABC, 1976.

Alan Hunter, *James at Fifteen,* NBC, 1977.

TELEVISION APPEARANCES; MINI-SERIES

Jack Atherton, *Washington: Behind Closed Doors,* ABC, 1977.

Richard Armstrong, *Judith Krantz's "Till We Meet Again,"* CBS, 1989.*

*   *   *

CHRISTIE, Julie   1940(?)-

PERSONAL: Full name, Julie Frances Christie; born April 14, 1940 (some sources say 1941), in Chukua, Assam, India; daughter of Frank St. John (a tea planter) and Rosemary (Ramsden) Christie. *Education:* Attended Central School of Dramatic Arts and Brighton Technical College.

ADDRESSES: Agent—Ben Benjamin, International Creative Management, 8899 Beverly Blvd., Los Angeles, CA 90048; and 388-396 Oxford St., London W1, England.

CAREER: Actress.

AWARDS, HONORS: Academy Award, best actress, and New York Film Critics Circle Award, both 1965, for *Darling;* Donatello Award, 1965, for *Doctor Zhivago;* Laurel Award, best dramatic actress, and *Motion Picture Herald* Award, both 1967; Academy Award nomination, best actress, 1971, for *McCabe and Mrs. Miller.*

CREDITS:

FILM APPEARANCES

(Film debut) Babette, *Crooks Anonymous,* Janus, 1963.

Liz, *Billy Liar,* Warner/Pathe, 1963.

Claire Chingford, *The Fast Lady,* Rank, 1963.

Diana Scott, *Darling,* Embassy, 1965.

Lara, *Doctor Zhivago,* Metro-Goldwyn-Mayer (MGM), 1965.

Daisy Battles, *Young Cassidy,* MGM, 1965.

Linda and Clarisse, *Fahrenheit 451,* Universal, 1966.

Bathsheba, *Far From the Madding Crowd,* MGM, 1967.

Petulia Danner, *Petulia,* Warner Brothers, 1968.

Catherine Morelli, *In Search of Gregory* (also known as *Alla ricerca de Gregory*), Universal, 1970.

Marian Maudsley, *The Go-Between,* Columbia, 1971.

Constance Miller, *McCabe and Mrs. Miller,* Warner Brothers, 1971.

Laura Baxter, *Don't Look Now,* Paramount, 1973.

As herself, *Nashville,* Paramount, 1975.

Jackie Shawn, *Shampoo,* Columbia, 1975.

Dr. Susan Harris, *Demon Seed,* United Artists, 1977.

Betty Logan, *Heaven Can Wait,* Paramount, 1978.

"D," *Memoirs of a Survivor,* EMI, 1981.

Narrator, *The Animals Film* (documentary), Blue Dolphin Film Distributors, 1981.

Anne, *Heat and Dust,* Curzon/Universal, 1983.

Kitty Baldry, *The Return of the Soldier,* Twentieth Century-Fox, 1983.

Ruby, *The Gold Diggers,* British Film Institute, 1984.

Ellen Freeman, *Power,* Twentieth Century-Fox, 1985.
Miss Mary Mulligan, *Miss Mary,* New World, 1987.
Narrator, *Yilmaz Guney: His Life, His Films* (documentary), Jane Balfour Films, 1987.
Betty, *La Memoire tatouee* (also known as *Secret Obsession; Silent Memory; Champagne Amer;* and *Tattooed Memory*), Vidmark Entertainment, 1988.
Mrs. Quinton, *Fools of Fortune,* Film Four International, 1990.

Also appeared in *Gold,* 1980; *Les Quarantiemes Rugissants,* 1981; *Across the River and into the Trees.*

STAGE APPEARANCES

Luciana, *A Comedy of Errors,* Royal Shakespeare Company (RSC), 1964.
Yelena, *Uncle Vanya,* Circle in the Square, New York City, 1973.

Also appeared with the Birmingham Repertory Company, Birmingham, England, 1963.

MAJOR TOURS

Luciana, *A Comedy of Errors,* RSC, U.S. and European cities, 1964.

TELEVISION APPEARANCES; MOVIES

Barbara Barlow, *Dadah Is Death* (also known as *A Long Way Home; A Long Way From Home;* and *Deadly Decision*), CBS, 1988.
Charlotte Deutz, *Sins of the Fathers* (also known as *Fathers and Sons*), Showtime, 1988.

OTHER TELEVISION APPEARANCES

A Is for Andromeda (series), 1962.
Anne Shank and Sybil Railton-Bell, *Separate Tables* (special), HBO, 1983.

Also appeared in the mini-series *Mary, Mary,* 1986, and in the documentary *Taking on the Bomb.**

*   *   *

CHUNG, Connie 1946-

PERSONAL: Full name, Constance Yu-Hwa Chung; born August 20, 1946, in Washington, DC; daughter of William Ling (a financial manager and former diplomat) and Margaret (Ma) Chung; married Maury Povich (a journalist), December 2, 1984. *Education:* University of Maryland, B.A., journalism, 1969.

ADDRESSES: Office—CBS News, Columbia Broadcasting System, Inc., 51 West 52nd St., New York, NY 10019.

CAREER: Broadcast journalist and writer. WTTG-TV, Washington, DC, news reporter, 1969-71; Columbia

Broadcasting System (CBS-TV), CBS News, Washington, DC, radio and television news correspondent, 1971-76; KNXT-TV, Los Angeles, CA, news anchor and reporter, 1976-83; National Broadcasting Company (NBC-TV), New York City, news anchor and reporter, 1983-89, co-host of television news magazines, 1985-86; CBS News, New York City, news anchor, reporter, and host of television news magazines, 1989—.

AWARDS, HONORS: Certificate of Achievement, United States Humane Society, 1969, for series of broadcasts that enhanced public awareness of cruelty in seal hunting; Metro Area Mass Media Award, Association of American University Women, 1971; National Association of Media Women award, Atlanta Chapter, 1973; Outstanding Excellence in News Reporting and Public Service Award, Chinese-American Citizens Alliance, 1973; honorary doctorate in journalism, Norwich University, 1974; nominated Woman of the Year, *Ladies Home Journal,* 1975; Outstanding Young Woman of the Year, *Ladies Home Journal,* 1975; Outstanding Television Reporting, Los Angeles Press Club, 1977; Outstanding Television Broadcasting Award, Valley Press Club, 1977; Emmy Awards for individual achievement, 1978, 1980, and 1987, and award in 1987 for "Shot in Hollywood," *1986;* Women in Communications Award, California State University, Los Angeles, CA, 1979; George Foster Peabody Award, 1980, for *Terra Our World;* Newscaster of the Year Award, Temple Emanuel Brotherhood, 1981; Portraits of Excellence Award, B'nai B'rith, Pacific Southwest Region, 1981; First Amendment Award, Anti-Defamation League of B'nai B'rith, 1981; Mr. Blackwell's Fashion Independents, 1983; D.H.L., Brown University, 1987.

CREDITS:

TELEVISION APPEARANCES

Terra Our World, Maryland Center for Public Broadcasting, 1980.
Anchor and reporter, *NBC Nightly News,* NBC, 1983-89.
Anchor and reporter, *Today Show,* NBC, 1983-89.
Anchor and reporter, *News Digest,* NBC, 1983-89.
Anchor and reporter, *NBC News at Sunrise,* NBC, 1983-89.
Co-host, *American Almanac* (news magazine), NBC, 1985-86.
Co-host, *1986* (news magazine), NBC, 1985-86.
Correspondent, *NBC News Report on America: Life in the Fat Lane* (special), NBC, 1987.
Reporter, *NBC News Reports on America: Stressed to Kill* (special), NBC, 1988.
Anchor and reporter, *Presidential Inauguration* (special), NBC, 1989.
As herself, *Murphy Brown* (episodic), CBS, 1989.
Anchor and reporter, *CBS Evening News,* CBS, 1989—.

Host, *Saturday Night with Connie Chung* (series), CBS, 1989—.

Host, *Face to Face with Connie Chung,* CBS, 1989—.

Also appeared in *American Almanac,* 1985; anchor, "Shot in Hollywood," *1986,* 1986; *NBC's 60th Anniversary Celebration,* 1986; correspondent, *The Baby Business,* 1987; correspondent, *Scared Sexless,* 1987; *David Letterman's Old Fashioned Christmas,* 1987; *Men, Women, Sex and Aids,* 1987; anchor, *Summer Showcase,* 1988; correspondent, *Campaign Countdown: The California Battleground,* 1988; correspondent, *Campaign Countdown: The Great Lakes Battle,* 1988; correspondent, *Everybody's Doing It,* 1988; host, *"Sarafina!" Words of Freedom . . . Songs of Hope,* 1988; reporter (exit polls), *Decision '88,* 1988; *Campaign Countdown: Is This Any Way to Elect a President?,* 1988; anchor, *Guns, Guns, Guns,* 1988; *Shot in Hollywood,* 1987.

WRITINGS:

NBC News Report on America: Life in the Fat Lane (television special), NBC, 1987.

Also writer for television specials *Everybody's Doing It; Guns, Guns, Guns;* and *Summer Showcase,* all 1988.

OTHER SOURCES:

PERIODICALS

Asiam, December, 1988.
Detroit News, July 31, 1983.
Los Angeles Times, March 21, 1989; October 25, 1989.
Ms., December, 1984.
Newsweek, August 15, 1983.
New York, August 8, 1983.
New York Times, July 31, 1990.
Parade, May 29, 1988.
People, June 13, 1983; June 10, 1985; April 10, 1989; August 20, 1990.
Philadelphia Inquirer, July 31, 1983.
Savvy, April, 1988.
Time, April 3, 1989.
USA Today, October 8, 1985.
Washington Journalism Review, September, 1983; March, 1985.
Washington Post, September 23, 1989; September 25, 1989.*

*   *   *

CLOSE, Glenn 1947-

PERSONAL: Born March 19, 1947, in Greenwich, CT; daughter of William (a surgeon) and Bettine Close; married Cabot Wade (a guitarist), 1969 (divorced, 1972); married James Marlas (a venture capitalist), 1984 (divorced, 1987); children: Annie Maude Starke (with John Starke, a producer). *Education:* College of William and Mary, B.A., drama, 1974.

ADDRESSES: Agent—Fred Specktor, Creative Artists Agency, 9830 Wilshire Boulevard, Beverly Hills, CA 90212. *Publicist*—Heidi Schaeffer, PMK Public Relations Inc., 8436 W. Third Street, Suite 650, Los Angeles, CA 90048.

CAREER: Actress. Performed with Fingernails, a repertory group; lyric soprano; has sung the national anthem at Mets baseball games at Shea Stadium, New York City; singer with touring folk-singing groups and toured the United States and Europe with the singing group Up With People.

MEMBER: Actors' Equity Association, Screen Actors Guild, American Federation of Television and Radio Artists, American Society of Composers, Authors, and Publishers, Phi Beta Kappa.

AWARDS, HONORS: Antoinette Perry Award nomination, best featured actress in a musical, 1980, for *Barnum;* Obic Award from the *Village Voice,* 1982, for *The Singular Life of Albert Nobbs;* Academy Award nominations, best supporting actress, 1982, for *The World According to Garp,* 1983, for *The Big Chill,* and 1984, for *The Natural;* Antoinette Perry Award, best actress in a play, 1984, for *The Real Thing;* Emmy Award nomination, outstanding lead actress in a limited series or special, and Golden Globe Award nomination, both 1984, for *Something About Amelia;* Golden Globe nomination, 1985, for *Maxie;* Academy Award nomination, best actress, and Golden Globe Award nomination, best performance by an actress in a motion picture, both 1988, for *Fatal Attraction;* Academy Award nomination, best actress, 1989, for *Dangerous Liaisons;* New York Women in Film Award "for artistic excellence and continued support of women in the film and television industry," 1989; National Organization of Theatre Owners (NATO) Award, Star of the Year, 1989; Harvard University Hasty Pudding Woman of the Year, 1990; Grammy Award nomination for *The Legend of Sleepy Hollow.*

CREDITS:

STAGE APPEARANCES

Angelica, *Love for Love,* New Phoenix Repertory Company, Helen Hayes Theatre, New York City, 1974.
Neighbor, *The Rules of the Game,* New Phoenix Repertory Company, Helen Hayes Theatre, 1974.
Janice, *The Member of the Wedding,* New Phoenix Repertory Company, Helen Hayes Theatre, 1975.
King Lear, Milwaukee Repertory Theatre, Milwaukee, WI, 1975-76.

Princess Mary, *Rex,* Lunt-Fontanne Theatre, New York City, 1976.

Leilah, *Uncommon Women and Others,* Phoenix Theatre, Marymount Manhattan Theatre, New York City, 1977.

Irene St. Claire, *The Crucifer of Blood,* Studio Arena Theatre, Buffalo, NY, then Helen Hayes Theatre, both 1978.

Helen, *Wine Untouched,* Harold Clurman Theatre, New York City, 1979.

Kettle, *The Winter Dancers,* Phoenix Theatre, Marymount Manhattan Theatre, 1979.

Chairy Barnum, *Barnum,* St. James Theatre, New York City, 1980.

Uncle Vanya, Yale Repertory Theatre, New Haven, CT, 1981.

Title role, *The Singular Life of Albert Nobbs,* Manhattan Theatre Club, New York City, 1982.

Annie, *The Real Thing,* Plymouth Theatre, New York City, 1984.

Actress, *Childhood,* Harold Clurman Theatre, Samuel Beckett Theatre, 1985.

Title role, *Joan of Arc at the Stake,* York Theatre Company, Church of the Heavenly Rest Theatre, New York City, 1985.

Jane, *Benefactors,* Brooks Atkinson Theatre, New York City, 1985-86.

Also appeared in *The Rose Tattoo,* Long Wharf Theatre, New Haven, CT; *A Streetcar Named Desire,* McCarter Theatre, Princeton, NJ; and *The Crazy Locomotive,* New York City.

MAJOR TOURS

Chairy Barnum, *Barnum,* U.S. cities, 1981-82.

FILM APPEARANCES

(Debut) Jenny Fields, *The World According to Garp,* Warner Brothers, 1982.

Sarah, *The Big Chill,* Columbia, 1983.

Iris Gaines, *The Natural,* Tri-Star, 1984.

Ruth Hillerman, *The Stone Boy,* Twentieth Century-Fox, 1984.

Voice of Miss Jane Porter, *Greystoke: The Legend of Tarzan, Lord of the Apes,* Warner Brothers, 1984.

Teddy Barnes, *Jagged Edge,* Columbia, 1985.

Jan/Maxie, *Maxie,* Orion, 1985.

Alex Forrest, *Fatal Attraction,* Paramount, 1987.

Marquise de Merteuil, *Dangerous Liaisons,* Warner Brothers, 1988.

Voice of Queen Ambisextra, *Light Years* (animated), Miramax, 1988.

Linda Spector, *Immediate Family,* Columbia, 1989.

Sunny von Bulow, *Reversal of Fortune,* Warner Brothers, 1990.

Gertrude, *Hamlet,* Warner Brothers, 1990.

Birdie, *Brooklyn Laundry,* Columbia, 1991.

TELEVISION APPEARANCES; EPISODIC

Host and narrator, "The Emperor's Nightingale," *Children's Storybook Classics* (animated), Showtime, 1987.

Host, "The Elephant's Child," *Children's Storybook Classics* (animated), Showtime, 1987.

Narrator, "The Legend of Sleepy Hollow," *Children's Storybook Classics* (animated), Showtime, 1988.

Narrator, "Do You Mean There Are Still Real Cowboys?," *The American Experience* (also see below), PBS, 1988.

The Tracey Ullman Show, Fox, 1990.

TELEVISION APPEARANCES; MOVIES

Jessica, *Orphan Train,* CBS, 1979.

Rebecca Kuehn, *Too Far to Go,* NBC, 1979.

Gail Bennett, *Something About Amelia,* ABC, 1984.

Sara Everton, "Stones for Ibarra," *Hallmark Hall of Fame,* CBS, 1988.

Sarah Wheaton, "Sarah, Plain and Tall," *Hallmark Hall of Fame* (also see below), CBS, 1991.

TELEVISION APPEARANCES; SPECIALS

Kennedy Center Honors: A Celebration of the Performing Arts, CBS, 1986.

Host, "The Music Makers: An ASCAP Celebration of American Music at Wolf Trap," *Great Performances,* PBS, 1987.

The Barbara Walters Special, ABC, 1988.

60th Annual Academy Awards Presentation, ABC, 1988.

Narrator, *Hunger in America,* PBS, 1989.

The Third Annual Hollywood Insider Academy Awards Special, USA, 1989.

The 62nd Annual Academy Awards Presentation, ABC, 1990.

The Siskel and Ebert Special, CBS, 1990.

Host, *The Divine Garbo,* TNT, 1990.

Also appeared on *The 41st Annual Tony Awards,* 1988.

TELEVISION WORK; EPISODIC

Associate producer, "Do You Mean There Are Still Cowboys?," *The American Experience,* PBS, 1988.

TELEVISION WORK; MOVIES

Executive producer, "Sarah, Plain and Tall," *Hallmark Hall of Fame,* CBS, 1991.

RECORDINGS:

Barnum (original cast recording album), CBS Masterworks, 1980.

Also recorded *The Legend of Sleepy Hollow,* Windham Hill.

OTHER SOURCES:

BOOKS

Newsmakers 88, Gale, 1988.

PERIODICALS

Hollywood Reporter, January 30, 1989.*

*   *   *

COCA, Imogene 1908-

PERSONAL: Born November 18, 1908, in Philadelphia, PA; daughter of Joe Coca (an orchestra leader) and Sadie (an actress and dancer; maiden name, Brady) Coca; married Robert Burton, January 7, 1935 (died 1955); married King Donovan (an actor), 1960; stepchildren: two sons, one daughter. *Avocational interests:* Dogs and other animals.

CAREER: Actress.

AWARDS, HONORS: Award of Merit, Women's Division of the Federation of Jewish Philanthropies, 1950; Saturday Review Poll Award, 1951; Emmy Award, best actress, 1952; George Foster Peabody Broadcasting Award, 1953; Emmy Award, outstanding variety special, 1967, for *Sid Caesar, Imogene Coca, Carl Reiner, Howard Moss Special;* American Comedy Award, female lifetime achievement, 1988; Albert Schweitzer Medal for artistry in comedy, 1989.

CREDITS:

STAGE APPEARANCES

(New York debut) Chorus Girl, *When You Smile,* National Theatre, New York City, 1925.

Jan, *Bubbling Over* (also see below), Werba's, Brooklyn, NY, 1926.

Dancer, *Snow and Columbus,* Palace, NY, 1927.

Ensemble, *Garrick Gaities* (revue), Guild Theatre, New York City, 1930.

Ensemble, *Shoot The Works* (revue), George M. Cohan Theatre, New York City, 1931.

Ensemble, *Flying Colors* (revue), Imperial Theatre, New York City, 1932.

New Faces of 1934 (revue), Fulton Theatre, New York City, 1934.

Ensemble, *Fools Rush In* (revue), Playhouse Theatre, New York City, 1934.

Comique Star, *Up to the Stars,* Lydia Mendelssohn Theatre, Flint, MI, 1935.

Ensemble, *New Faces of 1936* (revue), Vanderbilt Theatre, New York City, 1936.

Spring Dance, Cape Playhouse, MA, 1936.

Priscilla Paine, *Calling All Men,* Cape Playhouse, 1937.

Ensemble, *Straw Hat Revue* (revue), Ambassador Theatre, New York City, 1939.

Tonight at 8:30, Community Playhouse, Spring Lake, NJ, 1940.

All in Fun, Majestic Theatre, New York City, 1940.

Ensemble, *Concert Varieties* (revue), Ziegfeld Theatre, New York City, 1945.

Addie, *Happy Birthday* (also see below), Music Hall, Clinton, NJ, 1948.

Ruth, *Wonderful Town,* State Fair Music Hall, Dallas, TX, 1954.

Jessica, *Janus,* Plymouth Theatre, New York City, 1956.

Mimsy, *The Girls in 509* (also see below), Belasco Theatre, New York City, 1958.

Agnes, *The Fourposter,* Playhouse at Deep Well, Palm Springs, CA, 1960.

The Queen, *Under the Sycamore Tree,* Pasadena Playhouse, Pasadena, CA, 1962.

Mr. Alden and Aunt Veronica, *Why I Went Crazy,* Westport Country Playhouse, Westport, CT, and Falmouth Summer Theatre, Falmouth, MA, 1969.

Penny Moore, *A Girl Could Get Lucky,* Playhouse on the Mall, Paramus, NJ, 1970.

Mrs. Malaprop, *The Rivals,* Philadelphia Drama Guild, Philadelphia, PA, 1972.

Agnes, *The Fourposter,* Showboat Dinner Theatre, St. Petersburg, FL, 1972.

Edna Edison, *The Prisoner of Second Avenue* (also see below), Arlington Park, Chicago, IL, 1973.

Letitia Primrose, *On the Twentieth Century,* St. James, NY, 1978.

Mrs. Midgit, *Outward Bound,* Apple Corps Theatre, 1984.

Heloise, *My Old Friends,* American Jewish Theatre, New York City, 1985.

Letitia Primrose, *On the Twentieth Century* (also see below), Coconut Grove Playhouse, 1986.

As herself, *Together Again,* Michael's Pub, New York City, 1990.

Made stage debut as a dancer in vaudeville. Also appeared as Essie Sebastian, in *The Sebastians;* in *Double Take,* Arlington Park; in *Send Me No Flowers;* in *The Solid Gold Cadillac;* and ensemble, *Hey Look Me Over* (revue), Avery Fisher Hall, New York City. Cabaret appearances in New York City include Silver Slipper, 1926; Rainbow Room, 1937; La Martinque, 1940, 1942; Le Ruban Blew, 1944, 1954; Cafe Society Uptown, 1945; Blue Angel, 1948; Fifth Avenue Club; New Yorker Club; and Jay C. Flippen Club. Also appeared at Sahara Hotel, Las Vegas, NV, 1955; Trump Plaza, 1990; Sands Hotel, Las Vegas, 1991; Boca Raton, 1991; Westwood Playhouse, 1991; Piccadilly Club, Philadelphia, PA; Palmer House, Chicago, IL; and Park Plaza, St. Louis, MO.

MAJOR TOURS

Jan, *Bubbling Over,* U.S. cities, 1926.

Jimmy, the office assistant, *Queen High,* Mayfair, NY, 1928.

Addie, *Happy Birthday,* U.S. cities, 1948.

Essie Sebastian, *The Great Sebastians,* U.S. cities, 1957.

Mimsy, *The Girls in 509,* U.S. cities, 1959.

Princess Winnifred, *Once Upon a Mattress,* U.S. cities, 1960-61.

A Thurber Carnival, U.S. cities, 1961-62.

(With Sid Caesar) *Caesar-Coca Revue,* U.S. cities, 1961-62.

Ella Peterson, *Bells Are Ringing,* U.S. cities, 1962.

Ellen Manville, *Luv,* U.S. cities, 1967.

Edna Edison, *The Prisoner of Second Avenue,* U.S. cities, 1973-74.

Letitia Primrose, *On the Twentieth Century,* U.S. cities, 1978, 1986-87.

Also toured with George Olsen's orchestra, 1938; *A Night at the Folies Bergere,* 1940; *You Know I Can't Hear You When The Water's Running,* 1968-69; cabaret tour with Sid Caesar, 1977.

FILM APPEARANCES

As herself, *Promises, Promises* (also known as *Promise Her Anything*), NTD, 1963.

Dorkus, *Under the Yum-Yum Tree,* Columbia, 1963.

Mademoiselle Marie, *Rabbit Test,* Avco Embassy, 1978.

Aunt Edna, *National Lampoon's Vacation,* Warner Brothers, 1983.

Daisy Schackman, *Nothing Lasts Forever,* Metro-Goldwyn Mayer/United Artists, 1984.

Also appeared in *Bashful Ballerina* (film debut), 1937; *Ten from Your Show of Shows,* Walter Reade, 1973; *Buy and Cell;* and *Papa Was a Preacher.*

TELEVISION APPEARANCES; SERIES

Regular, *Admiral Broadway Revue,* NBC, 1949.

Regular, *Your Show of Shows,* NBC, 1950-54.

Betty Crane, *The Imogene Coca Show,* NBC, 1954-55.

Regular, *Sid Caesar Invites You,* ABC, 1958.

Title role, *Grindl,* NBC, 1963-64.

Shad, *It's about Time,* CBS, 1966-67.

Host, *Hollywood Palace,* ABC, 1967.

Aunt Jenny, *The Brady Bunch,* ABC, 1974.

Also appeared as Gladys Mason, *One Life to Live.*

OTHER TELEVISION APPEARANCES

The Bob Hope Show (special), NBC, 1951, 1970, 1971.

Hostess, *Panorama,* NBC, 1956.

The Funny Heart (special), CBS, 1956.

Helpmate (special), NBC, 1956.

"Made In Heaven," *Playhouse 90* (special), CBS, 1956.

Effie Floud, *Ruggles of Red Gap* (special), NBC, 1957.

Fireside Theatre, NBC, 1957-58.

Fireside Theatre, ABC, 1963.

Sid Caesar, Imogene Coca, Carl Reiner, Howard Moss Special, CBS, 1967.

Jackie Gleason Show (episodic), CBS, 1968.

Carol Burnett Show (episodic), CBS, 1969.

Love, American Style, ABC, 1969.

The Bob Hope Show (special), NBC, 1970.

The Bob Hope Show (special), NBC, 1971.

Bewitched (episodic), ABC, 1971.

Night Gallery (episodic), NBC, 1971.

The Dick Cavett Show (episodic), CBS, 1975.

Emily, *Getting There* (pilot), CBS, 1980.

Granny's Maw, *Return of the Beverly Hillbillies* (movie), CBS, 1981.

Hollywood Stars' Screen Tests (special), NBC, 1984.

Cook, *Alice in Wonderland* (movie), CBS, 1985.

Made television debut as host of *Buzzy Wuzzy,* 1948. Also appeared on episodes of *Kup's Show; Moonlighting.* Also, *The American Comedy Awards; The 38th Annual Emmy Awards; Broadway Plays Washington! Kennedy Center Tonight; Bob Hope Special: Bob Hope's Women I Love—Beautiful But Funny.*

*　　　*　　　*

COHEN, Edward M. 1936-

PERSONAL: Full name, Edward Martin Cohen; born April 15, 1936, in New York, NY; son of Harry M. (an attorney) and Betty (Mendell) Cohen; married Sheila H. Miller, 1955 (divorced, 1959); married Susan Simon (a psychoanalyst), June 22, 1969; children: (first marriage) Noel Aram, Joy Alison. *Education:* Attended Queens College (now Queens College of the City University of New York), 1952-55.

ADDRESSES: Office—c/o KLR Agency, 853 Seventh Ave., New York, NY 10022. *Agent*—Candida Donadio & Associates, Inc., 111 West Fifty-seventh St., New York, NY 10019.

CAREER: Director and playwright. Westminster Records, New York City, production manager, 1955-58; Everest Records, New York City, operations manager, 1958-59; Interdisca, Inc., New York City, general manager, 1959-63; Dubbins Electronics Inc., New York City, director of artists and repertoire, 1963—; Playwrights Horizons, playwright in residence, 1975-76, script reader, 1977-80; Jewish Repertory Theatre, literary adviser and associate director, 1979—. National Foundation for Jewish Culture, consultant on play writing projects, 1980—.

Guest lecturer at Hebrew University College, Hunter College, New York University, Manhattan Marymount College, and Fairleigh Dickinson University. Hospital Audiences Inc., CETA panel review board member, 1979.

MEMBER: Society of Stage Directors and Choreographers, Dramatists Guild, Eugene O'Neill Playwrights Group (chairman, 1972).

AWARDS, HONORS: Playwright fellow, National Playwrights Conference, Eugene O'Neill Theatre Center, 1971; Edward Albee Foundation fellow, 1972-75; John Golden Award, 1976, for *Cakes with the Wine;* directing fellowship, National Endowment for the Arts, 1982-83.

CREDITS:

STAGE DIRECTOR, EXCEPT AS NOTED

Night Thoughts, Theatre at St. Clements, New York City, 1973.
Urlicht, Playwrights Horizons, New York City, 1974.
Typhoid Mary, Theatre Genesis, New York City, 1974.
Zero Sum, Cubiculo Theatre, New York City, 1975.
Apple Pie (workshop), New York Shakespeare Festival, Public Theatre, New York City, 1975.
Beethoven/Karl, Playwrights Horizons, 1975.
Once and for All, Cubiculo Theatre, 1976.
(And playwright) *Cakes with the Wine,* Playwrights Horizons, 1976.
Dances with Words, Cubiculo Theatre, 1976.
When Petulia Comes, Playwrights Horizons, 1976, then Theatre Genesis, New York City, 1978.
The Cold Wind and the Warm, Jewish Repertory Theatre, New York City, 1977.
Pop-a-Few, Playwrights Horizons, 1977.
Benny Leonard and the Brooklyn Bridge, Open Space Theatre, New York City, 1977.
The Hot L Baltimore, Sarah Lawrence College, Bronxville, NY, 1978.
Canzada and the Boys, Hudson Guild Theatre, New York City, 1978.
Unlikely Heroes, Jewish Repertory Theatre, 1979.
Liliom, Jewish Repertory Theatre, 1979.
Any Wednesday, Little Theatre of Winston-Salem, Winston-Salem, NC, 1979.
The Children's Hour, Sarah Lawrence College, 1980.
Home Bodies, Playwrights Horizons, 1980.
Me and Molly, Jewish Repertory Theatre, 1980.
The Loves of Shirley Abramowitz, Ensemble Studio Theatre, New York City, 1981, then International Festival of Jewish Theatre, Tel Aviv University, Tel Aviv, Israel, 1982, later Jewish Repertory Theatre, 1982.
Elephants, Jewish Repertory Theatre, 1981.
Taking Steam, Jewish Repertory Theatre, 1983, then Leah Posluns, Toronto, Ontario, Canada, 1983.
Shlemiel The First, Jewish Repertory Theatre, 1984.

"The Shy and Lonely" and "Sailor Off the Bremen," *I, Shaw* (double-bill), Jewish Repertory Theatre, 1986.
Roots, Jewish Repertory Theatre, 1986.
(Producer) *Our Own Family* (four plays), Jewish Repertory Theatre, 1987.
Yard Sale, Jewish Repertory Theatre, 1988.

Also directed *Beethoven/Karl,* Queens Festival Playhouse, 1975, and Green Gate Summer Theatre, 1977; *Cakes with the Wine,* Queens Festival Playhouse, 1976; *Candida,* 1977, and *Old Times,* 1978, both Green Gate Summer Theatre; *La Musica* and *The Square,* both White Barn Theatre, 1979.

WRITINGS:

PLAYS

Breeding Ground, produced in New York City, 1971.
Cakes with the Wine, produced in New York City, 1971, produced Off-Broadway, 1975.
The Complaint Department Closes at Five, produced at Eugene O'Neill Theatre Center's National Playwrights Conference, 1971, produced in New York City, 1972, produced Off-Broadway, 1973.
A Gorgeous Piece, produced in New York City, 1972.
Two Girls and a Sailor, produced Off-Broadway, 1973.
The Last Stage of Labor, produced Off-Broadway, 1978.

OTHER

Two Hundred and Fifty Thousand Dollars (novel), Putnam, 1967.
(Editor) *Plays of Jewish Interest,* Jewish Theatre Association, 1982.

Contributor of short stories to *Carleton Miscellany* and *Evergreen Review.**

*   *   *

COLE, George   1925-

PERSONAL: Born April 22, 1925, in London, England; son of George and Florence (Smith) Cole; married Penelope Morell. *Education:* Attended Morden Council School.

ADDRESSES: Agent—Joy Jameson Ltd., West Eaton Place Mews, London SW1X 8LY, England; and c/o Donnelly, Hewnham Hill Bottom, Nettlebed, Oxfordshire, England.

CAREER: Actor. *Military service:* Royal Air Force, 1943-47.

CREDITS:

STAGE APPEARANCES

(Stage debut) *White Horse Inn,* Grand Theatre, Blackpool, England, 1939.

(London debut) Ronald, *Cottage to Let,* Wyndham's Theatre, 1940.

Ronald, *Cottage to Let,* Prince of Wales Theatre, Birmingham, England, 1940.

Percy King, *Goodnight Children,* New Theatre, London, 1942.

Percy, *Flare Path,* Apollo Theatre, London, 1942.

Cohen, *Mr. Bolfry,* Playhouse, London, 1943.

Dr. Johnson, *Dr. Angelus,* Phoenix Theatre, London, 1947.

Walter Anderson, *The Anatomist,* Westminster Theatre, London, 1948.

Tom Donnelly, *Mr. Gillie,* Garrick Theatre, London, 1950.

Tegeus-Chromis, *A Phoenix Too Frequent,* and Hoel, *Thor, with Angels* (double bill), Lyric Theatre, Hammersmith, England, 1951.

Joe Mascara, *The Blaikie Charivari,* Citizens' Theatre, Glasgow, Scotland, 1952.

Adam, *Misery Me,* Duchess Theatre, London, 1955.

Cohen, *Mr. Bolfry,* Aldwych Theatre, London, 1956.

Phanocles, *The Brass Butterfly,* Strand Theatre, London, 1958.

Morgan, *The Bargain,* St. Martin's Theatre, London, 1961.

Leslie Edwards, *The Sponge Room,* and Stanley Mintey, *Squat Betty* (double bill), Royal Court Theatre, London, 1962.

George Tesman, *Hedda Gabler,* New Arts Theatre, London, then St. Martin's Theatre, London, 1964.

Mark, *A Public Mischief,* St. Martin's Theatre, 1965.

Sergeant Fielding, *Too True to Be Good,* Strand Theatre, 1965.

Toby Pilgrim, *The Waiting Game,* New Arts Theatre, 1966.

Andrey, *The Three Sisters,* Royal Court Theatre, 1967.

Ballad, "The Ghost," and Butler, "No Principals," *Doubtful Haunts* (double bill), Hampstead Theatre Club, London, 1968.

Mr. Mortymer and Mr. Pollard, *There Was an Old Woman,* Thorndike Theatre, Leatherhead, England, 1969.

Victor Cadwallader, *The Man Most Likely To . . . ,* New Theatre, Bromley, England, 1970.

Philip, *The Philanthropist,* May Fair Theatre, London, 1971.

Richard, *Country Life,* Hampstead Theatre, London, 1973.

Deja Revue, New Theatre, London, 1974.

Willoughby Pink, *Banana Ridge,* Savoy Theatre, London, 1976.

Andreas Capodistriou and Inspector Fathom, *The Case of the Oily Levantine,* Arnaud Theatre, London, 1978.

Mr. Bates, *Brimstone and Treacle,* Open Space Theatre, London, 1979.

Skinner, *Liberty Hall,* Greenwich Theatre, London, 1980.

Major-General Stanley, *The Pirates of Penzance,* Theatre Royal, London, 1982.

Cooper, *First Sunday in Every Month,* Nuffield Theatre, Southampton, England, 1985, retitled *A Month of Sundays,* Duchess Theatre, 1986.

Mr. Darling/Captain Hook, *Peter Pan,* Cambridge Theatre, London, 1987.

Ted Forest, *A Piece of My Mind,* Nuffield Theatre, then Apollo Theatre, 1987.

Also appeared in *Something's Afoot,* Hong Kong, 1978.

MAJOR TOURS

Appeared as Ronald, *Cottage to Let,* 1941; *Old Master,* 1942; Toby Pilgrim, *The Yes-Yes-Yes Man,* 1963; Dr. Peter Estriss, *The Passionate Husband,* 1969; Andrew Creed, *Motive,* Arnaud, Guildford, and tour, 1976; Philip, *The Philanthropist.*

STAGE WORK

Co-producer, *The Bargain,* St. Martin's Theatre, 1961.

FILM APPEARANCES

(Film debut) Ronald Mittsby, *Bombsight Stolen* (also known as *Cottage to Let*), General Films Distributors, 1941.

Charlie, *Those Kids From Town,* Anglo American, 1942.

Boy, *Henry V,* United Artists, 1946.

Journey Together, English Films, 1946.

Willie Stannard, *My Brother's Keeper,* Eagle-Lion, 1949.

Herbert Sunbury, "The Kite," *Quartet,* Eagle-Lion, 1949.

Scrooge as a young man, *A Christmas Carol,* United Artists, 1951.

John Hannah, *Flesh and Blood,* British Lion, 1951.

Herbert Russell, *Laughter in Paradise,* Associated British Films/Pathe, 1951.

E. R. A. Marks, *Operation Disaster* (also known as *Morning Departure*), Universal, 1951.

Cyril, *Mr. Lord Says No* (also known as *The Happy Family*), Souvaine, 1952.

Arthur Crisp, *The Passionate Sentry* (also known as *Who Goes There?*), Fine Arts, 1952.

Marc, *The Spider and the Fly,* General Films Distributors, 1952.

Albert, *The Wild Heart* (also known as *Gone to Earth* and *Gypsy Blood*), RKO/Selznick, 1952.

Gobo, *The Clue of the Missing Ape* (also known as *Gibraltar Adventure*), Continental Distributing, 1953.

Private, *Folly to Be Wise,* Fine Arts, 1953.

George Potts, *Mr. Potts Goes to Moscow* (also known as *Top Secret*), Stratford, 1953.

Flash Harry, *The Belles of St. Trinian's,* British Lion, 1954.

Terence, *Tonight's the Night* (also known as *Happy Ever After* and *O'Leary Night*), Pathe, 1954.

Jimmy Carroll, *The Adventures of Sadie* (also known as *Our Girl Friday*), Twentieth Century-Fox, 1955.

Luigi Sopranelli, *The Constant Husband,* British Lion, 1955.

John Summers, *The Intruder,* British Lion, 1955.

Johnny, *Lady Godiva Rides Again,* Carroll, 1955.

Sergeant Roger Morris, *A Prize of Gold,* Columbia, 1955.

Hayraddin, *Quentin Durward* (also known as *The Adventures of Quentin Durward*), Metro-Goldwyn-Mayer, 1955.

Fred Slater, *Where There's a Will,* Eros, 1955.

Henry Sterling, *Will Any Gentleman?,* Stratford, 1955.

Ken Miller, *It's a Wonderful World,* Renown, 1956.

William Blake, *The Green Man,* Distributors Corporation of America, 1957.

Joshua Henry, *The Weapon,* Republic, 1957.

Flash Harry, *Blue Murder at St. Trinian's,* British Lion, 1958.

Sergeant Bruce, *The Bridal Path,* British Lion, 1959.

Finch, *Don't Panic Chaps!,* Columbia, 1959.

Fingers, *Too Many Crooks,* Lopert, 1959.

Flash Harry, *The Pure Hell of St. Trinian's,* Continental Distributing, 1961.

The Anatomist, British International Pictures, 1961.

Flavius, *Cleopatra,* Twentieth Century-Fox, 1963.

Defense counsel and friend, *One Way Pendulum,* Lopert, 1965.

Flash Harry, *The Great St. Trinian's Train Robbery,* Braywild/British Lion, 1966.

Roger Morton, *The Vampire Lovers,* American International, 1970.

Jim, *Fright* (also known as *Night Legs*), Allied Artists, 1971.

Take Me High, EMI, 1973.

Gone in 60 Seconds, Halicki International, 1974.

Mr. Mipps, *Dr. Syn, Alias the Scarecrow,* Disney, 1975.

Dog, *The Blue Bird,* Twentieth Century-Fox, 1976.

George, *Double Nickels,* Smokey, 1977.

Also appeared in *The Legend of Young Dick Turpin; Murder on the Orient Express.*

TELEVISION APPEARANCES

Mipps, "The Scarecrow of Romney Marsh," *Walt Disney's Wonderful World of Color* (episode), NBC, 1964.

Also appeared as Trevor, *The Bounder* (series), 1984-85; Sir Giles, *Blott on the Landscape* (special), 1986. Appeared in *The Sex Game,* 1968; *Out of the Unknown,* 1968; *30 Minute Theatre,* 1968; *Half Hour Story,* 1968; *Murder,*

1969; *Root of All Evil,* 1969; *The God Robbers,* 1969; *The Comic,* 1969; *A Man of Our Times,* 1969; *U.F.O.,* 1970; *The Right Prospectus,* 1970; *Menace,* 1970; *The Ten Commandments,* 1970; *A Room in Town,* 1970; *Six Faces of a Man,* 1972; *Madigan* (episodic), 1972; *Away From it All,* 1973; *Dial M for Murder,* 1974; *Village Hall,* 1974; *Affair of the Heart,* 1974; *The Sweeney,* 1975; *Quiller,* 1975; *Lloyd George Knew My Father,* 1975; *Losing Her,* 1978; *The Good Life,* 1978; *Return of the Giant,* 1978; *Don't Forget to Write,* 1978; *Minder,* 1979-85; *Getting in On Concorde,* 1980; *Comrade Dad,* 1984; *Heggerty, Haggerty,* 1984; *Natural Causes,* ITV, 1988; *Life of Bliss.* *

* * *

COLLEY, Kenneth 1937-

PERSONAL: Born in 1937 in Manchester, England.

ADDRESSES: Office—64A Notting Hill Gate, London W11, England. *Agent*—Al Parker Ltd., 55 Park Lane, London W1, England.

CAREER: Actor.

CREDITS:

STAGE APPEARANCES

Wick, *Little Malcolm and His Struggle Against the Eunuchs,* Garrick Theatre, London, 1966.

Cleet, *Cromwell,* Royal Court Theatre, London, 1973.

Peter Alphon, *Hanratty in Hell,* Open Space Theatre, London, 1976.

Howard, *Golden Leaf Strut,* Bush Theatre, London, 1981.

Tom, *Seachange,* Riverside Studios, London, 1984.

FILM APPEARANCES

Replacement, *How I Won the War,* United Artists, 1967.

De Winter, *The Jokers,* Universal, 1967.

Tony Farrell, *Performance,* Warner Bros., 1970.

Modeste Tchaikovsky, *The Music Lovers,* United Artists, 1971.

Legrand, *The Devils,* Warner Bros., 1971.

Boldt, *Hitler: The Last Ten Days,* Paramount, 1973.

Detective Brown, *Juggernaut,* United Artists, 1974.

Krenek, *Mahler,* Visual Programme Systems, 1974.

Little Malcolm, Multicetera, 1974.

Flame, UPS/Goodtimes, 1974.

Triple Echo, Hemdale, 1975.

Edmund Baluka, *Three Days in Szczecin,* British Film Institute, 1975.

Lisztomania, Warner Bros., 1976.

Jabberwocky, Cinema V, 1977.

Jesus Christ, *Monty Python's Life of Brian,* Warner Bros./Orion, 1979.

Admiral Piett, *The Empire Strikes Back,* Twentieth Century-Fox, 1980.

Colonel Kontarsky, *Firefox,* Warner Bros., 1982.

Martin, *Giro City* (also known as *And Nothing But the Truth*), Cinegate, 1982.

Admiral Piett, *Return of the Jedi,* Twentieth Century-Fox, 1983.

Traveler, *Return to Waterloo,* New Line Cinema, 1985.

Bill Pickett, *The Whistle Blower,* Hemdale, 1987.

Jim, *A Summer Story,* Atlantic, 1988.

Mr. Brunt, *The Rainbow,* Vestron, 1989.

TELEVISION APPEARANCES; MOVIES

Police prefect, *Les Miserables,* CBS, 1978.

Theodotus, *Peter and Paul,* CBS, 1981.

Captain Hirsch, *The Scarlet and the Black,* CBS, 1983.

Colonel Adolf Eichmann, *Wallenberg: A Hero's Story,* NBC, 1985.

Le Duc, *Casanova,* ABC, 1987.

Keitel, *The Plot to Kill Hitler,* CBS, 1990.

TELEVISION APPEARANCES; EPISODIC

"Kremlin Farewell," *Screen Two,* BBC-2, 1990.

Title role, "Napoleon's Last Battle," *Timewatch,* BBC-2, 1990.

Also appeared in *Z Cars* and *The Avengers.*

TELEVISION APPEARANCES; SPECIALS

The Sweeney, syndicated, 1976.

Duke Vincentio, *Measure for Measure,* BBC, 1977, then PBS, 1979.

Also appeared in *Maupassant,* 1974; *The Baron; Family at War; Love School; Fall of Eagles;* and *The Eleventh Hour.*

TELEVISION APPEARANCES; MINI-SERIES

The Accordion Man, *Pennies from Heaven,* BBC, 1978, then PBS, 1979.

King Vittorio Emmanuele, *Mussolini: The Untold Story,* NBC, 1985.

S.S. Colonel Adolf Paul Blobel, *War and Remembrance,* ABC, 1988.*

*　　　*　　　*

COMENCINI, Luigi   1916-

PERSONAL: Born June 8, 1916, in Salo, Italy. *Education:* Studied architecture at Politecnico, Milan, 1934-39.

CAREER: Director and screenwriter. Has also worked as a documentary filmmaker and photographer. During the 1940s, was a correspondent for *Tempo,* film critic for *Cor-* rente, and worked as an assistant film director; editor for *Avanti!,* after World War II. Founder (with Alberto Lattuada and Mario Ferrari) of a private cinema club for viewing old films, 1930s; founder (with Lattuada), Cineteca Italiana film archives, 1949.

CREDITS:

FILM WORK; DIRECTOR, EXCEPT AS NOTED

Persiane chiuse (also known as *Behind Closed Shutters*), Lux, 1952.

Bread, Love, and Dreams (also see below), IFC, 1953.

Heidi, United Artists, 1954.

Pane amore e gelosia (also known as *Frisky* and *Bread, Love, and Jealousy*), DCA, 1955.

Il segno di Venere (also known as *The Sign of Venus;* also see below), Gala/Titanus, 1955.

Tutti a casa (also known as *La grande pagaille* and *Everybody Go Home!;* also see below), Davis Royal, 1962.

La ragazza di Bube (also known as *Bebo's Girl;* also see below), Lux/Uhra/Vides, 1964.

"Il trattato di eugenetica" (also known as "Treatise in Eugenics"), *Bambole!* (also known as *Le bambole* and *Four Kinds of Love: The Dolls*), Columbia, 1965.

Six Days a Week (also known as *Le partager de Catherine, Lu bugiarda,* and *La Mentirosa;* also see below), Atlantic, 1966.

Italian Secret Service (also see below), Cineriz, 1968.

"Fatebenefratelli," *Three Nights of Love* (also known as *Tre notti d'amore;* also see below), Magna, 1969.

Scientific Cardplayer (also known as *Lo scopone scientifico*), CIC, 1972.

Delitto d'amore (also known as *Somewhere Beyond Love;* also see below), Titanus, 1974.

La Donna della domenica (also known as *Sunday Woman*), Fox Europa, 1976.

"L'ascensore," *Quelle strane occasioni* (also known as *Strange Events*), Fox Europa, 1976.

(Two episodes) *Signore e signori, buonanotte* (also known as *Goodnight, Ladies and Gentlemen;* also see below), Titanus, 1977.

Il Gatto (also known as *The Cat*), United Artists, 1978.

Till Marriage Do Us Part (also known as *Mio Dio, come sono caduta in basso* and *How Low Can You Fall;* also see below), Franklin Media, 1979.

Le Grand embouteillage (also known as *L'Ingorgo, Bottleneck,* and *Traffic Jam;* also see below), CineTel/Titanus, 1979.

(Also art director and costume designer) *Eugenio* (also known as *Voltati Eugenio;* also see below), Intercontinental/Films du Losange, 1980.

Cercasi Gesu (also known as *Jesus Wanted*), Intercontinental, 1982.

La storia, Sacis/MK2/Diffusion, 1986.

Un ragazzo di calabria (also known as *A Boy from Calabria*), Sacis International, 1987.

(Also producer) *La Boheme* (also see below), Union Generale cinematographique/New Yorker/Electric, 1987.

Buon Natale, Buon Anno (also known a *Merry Christmas, Happy New Year, Joyeux Noel,* and *Bonne Annee;* also see below), Titanus/Belga/AFMD, 1989.

Also director of *La Novelletta* (short film), 1937; *Bambini in citta* (short film), 1946; *Il museo dei sogni* (short film), 1948; *L'ospedale del delitto* (short film), 1948; *Probita rubara,* 1948; *L'imperatore di Capri,* 1949; *La tratta della bianche* (also known as *Girls Marked for Danger;* also see below), 1952; *La bella di Roma* (also see below), 1955; *La finestra sul Luna Park* (also see below), 1956; *Mariti in citta* (also see below), 1957; *Mogli pericolose* (also see below), 1958; *Und das am Montagmorgen* (also see below), 1959; *A cavallo della tigre* (also see below), 1961; *Il commissario,* 1962; *Il compagno Don Camillo,* 1964; *Senza sapere niente di lei* (also see below), 1969; *Infanzia vocazione e prime esperienze di Giacomo Casanova veneziano* (also see below), 1969; *Le avventure di Pinocchio* (also see below), 1971; *Educazione civica* (short film), 1974; *La Goduria* (also see below), 1976; *Vasata che non i sappia in giro,* 1976; *L'ingorgo, una Tra moglie e marito,* 1977; "L'equivoco," *Storia impossibile* (also see below), 1979; and *Voltati Andrea,* 1979.

TELEVISION DIRECTOR

Il matrimonio di Caterina (also known as *Catherine's Wedding*), RAI-TV Channel 3, 1982.

Cuore (also known as *Heart;* also see below), RAI-TV Channel 2, 1984.

Also directed *I bambini e noi,* 1970, and *L'amore in Italia,* 1978.

WRITINGS:

SCREENPLAYS

Bread, Love, and Dreams, IFC, 1953.

(With Franca Valeri, Agenore Incrucci, Ennio Flaino, and Cesare Zavattini) *Il segno di Venere,* Gala/Titanus, 1955.

(With Marcello Fondato) *Tutti a casa,* Davis Royal, 1962.

(With Fondato) *La ragazza di Bube,* Lux/Uhra/Vides, 1964.

(With Fondato) *Six Days a Week,* Atlantic, 1966.

Italian Secret Service, Cineriz, 1968.

(With others) "Fatebenefratelli," *Tre notti d'amore,* Magna, 1969.

(With others) *Delitto d'amore,* Titanus, 1974.

(With Agel Scarpelli, Leo Benvenuti, Piero De Bernard, Nanni Loy, Ruggero Maccari, Luigi Magni, Mario

Monicelli, Ugo Pirro, and Ettore Scola) *Signore e signori, buonanotte,* Titanus, 1977.

(With Cristina Comencini, Rafaella Festa, and Paola Comencini) *Buon Natale, Buon Anno,* Titanus/BElga/AFMD, 1989.

Author of additional screenplays, including (with others) *Proibito rubare,* 1948; (with others) *L'imperatoare di Capri,* 1949; (with others) *La tratta della bianche,* 1952; (with others) *La valigia dei sogni,* 1953; (with others) *La bella di Roma,* 1955; (with others) *La finestra sul Luna Park,* 1956; (with others) *Mariti in citta,* 1957; (with others) *Mogli pericolose,* 1958; (with others) *Und das am Montagmorgen,* 1959; (with others) *La sorprese dell'amore,* 1959; (with others) *A cavallo della tigre,* 1961; (with others) *Incompreso,* 1967; (with others) *Senza sapere niente di lei,* 1969; (with others) *Infanzia, vocazione e prime espeienze di Giacomo Casanova veneziano,* 1969; (with others) *Le avventure di Pinocchio,* 1971; (with Ivo Perilli) *Mio Dio, come sono caduta in basso,* 1974; *La Goduria,* 1976; (with Maccari and Bernardino Zapponi) *L'Ingorgo,* 1979; (with others) *L'ingorgo, una storia impossibile,* 1979; *Eugenio,* 1980; (with Suso Cecchi D'Amico and Cristina Comencini) *Cuore,* 1984; (with D'Amico and Cristina Comencini) *La Storia,* 1986; and (with Pirro and Francesca Comencini) *Un Ragazzo di Calabria,* 1987. Adaptor of *La Boheme,* 1988.*

*   *   *

CONN, Didi   1951-

PERSONAL: Born July 13, 1951, in Brooklyn, NY.

CAREER: Actress.

CREDITS:

FILM APPEARANCES

Voice of Raggedy Ann, *Raggedy Ann and Andy,* Twentieth Century-Fox, 1977.

Laurie Robinson, *You Light Up My Life,* Columbia, 1977.

Donna DeVito, *Almost Summer,* Universal, 1978.

Frenchy, *Grease,* Paramount, 1978.

Frenchy, *Grease II,* Paramount, 1982.

Actress, "Mutual Orgasms," *Funny,* Original Cinema, 1988.

TELEVISION APPEARANCES; MOVIES

Television actress, *Genesis II,* CBS, 1973.

Julie Evans, *Murder at the Mardi Gras,* CBS, 1978.

Eve Harris, *Three on a Date,* ABC, 1978.

TELEVISION APPEARANCES; SERIES

Keep on Truckin', ABC, 1975.

Helen, *The Practice,* NBC, 1976.

Voice characterization, *The Scooby-Doo and Scrappy-Doo Show* (animated), ABC, 1980.
Voice of Cup Cake, *Fonz and the Happy Days Gang* (animated), ABC, 1980-82.
Denise Stevens Downey, *Benson,* ABC, 1981-85.
Voice characterization, *Bad Cat* (animated), ABC, 1984.
Voice characterizations, *The New Jetsons* (animated), syndicated, 1985.

TELEVISION APPEARANCES; EPISODIC

"Working," *American Playhouse,* PBS, 1982.
Dinah Roswell, *Cagney and Lacey,* CBS, 1987.
Highway to Heaven, NBC, 1987.

OTHER TELEVISION APPEARANCES

Nurse Jackie Morse, *Handle with Care* (pilot), CBS, 1977.
Circus of the Stars (special), CBS, 1982.
Stacy Jones, *Shining Time Station* (special), PBS, 1989.*

*   *   *

CONNORS, Michael
See CONNORS, Mike

*   *   *

CONNORS, Mike   1925-
(Michael Connors, Touch Connors)

PERSONAL: Name originally Krekor Ohanian; born August 15, 1925, in Fresno, CA. *Education:* Attended the University of California, Los Angeles.

ADDRESSES: Manager—Charter Management, 9000 Sunset Blvd., Suite 1112, Los Angeles, CA 90069. *Publicist*—Mike Mamakos, Mamakos and Associates, 14200 Ventura Blvd., Suite 106, Sherman Oaks, CA 91423.

CAREER: Actor and producer.

AWARDS, HONORS: Golden Globe Award, best television actor—drama, 1970, for *Mannix;* Emmy Award nominations, outstanding continued performance by an actor in a leading role in a dramatic series, 1969, 1970, 1971, and 1972, for *Mannix.*

CREDITS:

FILM APPEARANCES; AS TOUCH CONNORS

(Film debut) Junior Kearney, *Sudden Fear,* RKO Radio Pictures, 1952.
Lieutenant Hobson Lee, *Sky Commando,* Columbia, 1953.
Lieutenant Magrew, *The Forty-Ninth Man,* Columbia, 1953.
Gainer, *Island in the Sky,* Warner Brothers, 1953.

Andrew, *Day of Triumph,* Century Films, 1954.
Hale Clinton, *Five Guns West,* American Releasing, 1955.
Lou, *The Twinkle in God's Eye,* Republic, 1955.
Sheriff, *The Oklahoma Woman,* American Releasing, 1956.
Bob, *Swamp Women* (also known as *Swamp Diamonds* and *Cruel Swamp*), Favorite Films of California, 1956.
Tony, *The Day the World Ended,* American International, 1956.
Amalekite herder, *The Ten Commandments,* Paramount, 1956.
Stacy, *Flesh and the Spur,* American International, 1957.
Garry, *Shake, Rattle, and Rock!,* American International, 1957.
Ted Bronson, *Voodoo Woman,* American International, 1957.

FILM APPEARANCES; AS MICHAEL CONNORS

Rick, *Live Fast, Die Young,* Universal, 1958.
Major Matt McCormack, *Suicide Battalion,* American International, 1958.
Dalton That Got Away, Dalton Film Company, 1960.
Frank Pagano, *Panic Button,* Gorton, 1964.
Howard Ebbetts, *Good Neighbor Sam,* Columbia, 1964.
Luke Miller, *Where Love Has Gone,* Paramount, 1964.
Jack Harrison, *Harlow,* Paramount, 1965.
Lucky, *Situation Hopeless—But Not Serious,* Paramount, 1965.
Hatfield, *Stagecoach,* Twentieth Century-Fox, 1966.
Kelly, *Kiss the Girls and Make Them Die* (also known as *Se Tutte le donne del mondo* and *Operazione Paradiso*), Dino De Laurentiis/Columbia, 1967.

FILM APPEARANCES; AS MIKE CONNORS

Haller, *Avalanche Express,* Twentieth Century-Fox, 1979.
Lieutenant Dinardo, *Too Scared to Scream,* Movie Store, 1985.
Billy Vance, *Fist Fighter,* Taurus Entertainer, 1989.

Also appeared in *Seed of Violence,* 1964.

FILM WORK

Producer (with A. Kitman Ho), *Too Scared to Scream,* Movie Store, 1985.

TELEVISION APPEARANCES; SERIES

Nick, *Tightrope,* CBS, 1959-60.
Title role, *Mannix,* CBS, 1967-75.
Ben Slater, *Today's F.B.I.,* ABC, 1981-82.
Host, *Crimes of the Century,* syndicated, 1989.

TELEVISION APPEARANCES; MINI-SERIES

Colonel Harrison "Hack" Peters, *War and Remembrance,* ABC, 1988.

TELEVISION APPEARANCES; MOVIES

Captain Lou Mikalich, *High Midnight,* CBS, 1970.
Victor Cummings, *Beg, Borrow . . . Or Steal,* ABC, 1973.
Travis Green, *Revenge for a Rape,* ABC, 1976.
Vic Casella, *Long Journey Back,* ABC, 1978.
Sam Jackson, *The Death of Ocean View Park,* ABC, 1979.

TELEVISION APPEARANCES; PILOTS

The agent, *Getaway Car* (broadcast as an episode of *Studio '57*), syndicated, 1958.
Kirk Ohanian, *The Killer Who Wouldn't Die,* ABC, 1976.
Nick, *Casino,* ABC, 1980.
Captain Jim Adams, *The Earthlings,* ABC, 1984.

TELEVISION APPEARANCES; SPECIALS

Reporter, *ABC News Closeup—Arson: Fire for Hire,* ABC, 1970.
Super Comedy Bowl 2, CBS, 1972.
Mitzi . . . The First Time, CBS, 1973.
Joe Mannix, *Bob Hope in "Joys,"* NBC, 1976.
Charo, ABC, 1976.
Circus of the Stars, CBS, 1981.
The Funniest Joke I Ever Heard, ABC, 1984.
Screen Actors Guild 50th Anniversary Celebration, CBS, 1984.
The 37th Annual Prime Time Emmy Awards, ABC, 1985.
Happy Birthday Hollywood, ABC, 1987.
Host, *Crimes of the Century,* ABC, 1988.
Host, *The Secret Files of J. Edgar Hoover,* syndicated, 1989.
Christmas with the Stars—An International Earthquake Benefit, Discover Channel, 1989.
The Television Academy Hall of Fame, Fox, 1990.
The Tube Test, ABC, 1990.

OTHER TELEVISION APPEARANCES

Walter Murray, *Murder, She Wrote* (episode),CBS, 1989.

Also appeared in *Frontier,* NBC; *Schlitz Playhouse of Stars,* CBS; *Cheyenne,* ABC; and *Maverick,* ABC.*

*   *   *

CONNORS, Touch
    See CONNORS, Mike

*   *   *

CONVERSE, Frank   1938-

PERSONAL: Born May 22, 1938, in St. Louis, MO. *Education:* Attended Carnegie Mellon University; trained for stage in New York.

ADDRESSES: Agent—c/o Triad Artists, 10100 Santa Monica Blvd., 16th Floor, Los Angeles, CA 90067.

CAREER: Actor. Performed with the PAF Playhouse, Huntington Station, NY, 1972-73.

CREDITS:

STAGE APPEARANCES

(Broadway debut) David, *First One Asleep, Whistle,* Belasco Theatre, New York City, 1966.
The Night of the Iguana, Seattle Repertory Theatre, Seattle, WA, 1967.
Billy Einhorn, *The House of Blue Leaves,* Truck and Warehouse Theatre, New York City, 1971.
The Widowing of Mrs. Holroyd, Long Wharf Theatre, New Haven, CT, 1973.
The Seagull, McCarter Theatre, Princeton, NJ, 1973.
Afore Night Come, Long Wharf Theatre, 1975.
"On the Inside," *On the Outside,* and *On the Inside* (double-bill), Long Wharf Theatre, 1976.
Hobson's Choice, Long Wharf Theatre, c. 1977-78.
The Philadelphia Story, Long Wharf Theatre, c. 1977-78.
C. K. Dexter Haven, *The Philadelphia Story,* Lincoln Center Theatre Company, Vivian Beaumont Theatre, New York City, 1980.
Harry, *Brothers,* Music Box Theatre, New York City, 1983.
Otto, *Design for Living,* Circle in the Square, New York City, 1984.
Mr. Webb, *Our Town,* Long Wharf Theatre, 1987-88.
Harold Mitchell, *A Streetcar Named Desire,* Circle in the Square, 1988.

Also performed in *The Seagull, Death of a Salesman, The Night of the Iguana, A Man for All Seasons,* and *Arturo Ui,* all in the American Shakespeare Festival, Stratford, CT.

FILM APPEARANCES

Virgil Earp, *Hour of the Gun,* United Artists, 1967.
Reverend Clem DeLavery, *Hurry Sundown,* Paramount, 1967.
Andrew Scott, *The Rowdyman,* Crowley, 1973.
The Pilot, Summit, 1979.
Captain Hawk, *The Bushido Blade* (also released as *The Bloody Bushido Blade*), Trident, 1982.
Louis Corman, *Spring Fever,* Comworld, 1983.
Charlie Haggerty, *Everybody Wins,* Orion, 1990.

TELEVISION APPEARANCES; SERIES

Michael Alden, *Coronet Blue,* CBS, 1967.
Detective Johnny Corso, *N.Y.P.D.,* ABC, 1967-69.
Will Chandler, *Movin' On,* NBC, 1974-76.
Kevin Nichols, *The Family Tree,* NBC, 1983.
Harry O'Neill, *One Life to Live,* ABC, 1984-85.
Michael Larson, *Dolphin Cove,* CBS, 1989-90.

TELEVISION APPEARANCES; PILOTS

Dr. Sam Delaney, *D.H.O.,* ABC, 1973.
Dr. Ben Voorhees, *Stat!,* CBS, 1973.
Will Chandler, *In Tandem,* NBC, 1974.
Modge Modgelewsky, *Steeltown,* CBS, 1979.
Marion Walker, *Gabe and Walker,* ABC, 1981.
Tom Hackman, *Mama the Detective,* ABC, 1981.

TELEVISION APPEARANCES; EPISODIC

Blackmore, "The Widowing of Mrs. Holroyd," *Theatre in America,* PBS, 1974.
Circle of Fear, NBC, 1975.
Gutherie Browne, *The Equalizer,* CBS, 1985.
Sam Henderson, *Magnum, P.I.,* CBS, 1985.
John Dunson, *Hotel,* ABC, 1986.
Nils Anderson, "Home at Last," *Wonderworks,* PBS, 1988.

Also appeared in *The Mod Squad,* ABC; *Medical Center,* CBS; *The Bold Ones,* NBC; and *The Guest House.*

TELEVISION APPEARANCES; MOVIES

Jim Tennyson, *Dr. Cook's Garden,* ABC, 1971.
Steve Butler, *A Tattered Web,* CBS, 1971.
Dr. Paul Jeffries, *Killer on Board,* NBC, 1977.
Matt Lazarus, *Cruise into Terror,* ABC, 1978.
Captain Larsen Jaenicke, *Sergeant Matlovich versus the U.S. Air Force,* NBC, 1978.
Joe DiMaggio, *Marilyn: The Untold Story,* ABC, 1980.
Larry Miller, *The Miracle of Kathy Miller,* CBS, 1981.
Haley, *Uncle Tom's Cabin,* Showtime, 1987.
John Hamilton, *Alone in the Neon Jungle,* CBS, 1988.
Peter Morgan, *Voices within: The Lives of Truddi Chase,* ABC, 1990.

OTHER TELEVISION APPEARANCES

"You're a Poet and Don't Know It! . . . The Poetry Power Hour," *The CBS Festival of Lively Arts for Young People* (special), CBS, 1976.
Hal McKain, "A Movie Star's Daughter," *ABC Afterschool Special,* ABC, 1979.
Dan Alexander, "Mystery at Fire Island," *CBS Children's Mystery Theatre,* CBS, 1981.
Morgan Harris, *Anne of Avonlea: The Continuing Story of Anne of Green Gables* (mini-series), Disney Channel, 1987.

Also appeared in *Shadow of a Gunman.**

*   *   *

COOKSON, Peter   1913-1990

PERSONAL: Born May 8, 1913, in Milwaukee, OR; died of bone cancer, January 7, 1990, in Southfield, MA; son

of Gerald (a career British Army officer) and Helen (a nurse; maiden name, Willis), Cookson; married Maurine Gray, June, 1937 (divorced 1948); married Beatrice Straight (an actress), June, 1949; children: (first marriage) Peter Jr., Brooksie Jane, (second marriage) Gary, Anthony. *Education:* Attended public schools in California; studied acting at the Pasadena Playhouse School of Theatre.

CAREER: Actor, producer, and writer.

MEMBER: Actors' Equity Association, American Federation of Television and Radio Artists.

AWARDS, HONORS: Theatre World Award, 1946-47.

CREDITS:

STAGE APPEARANCES

(Debut) Laertes, *Hamlet,* Old Globe Shakespeare Theatre, San Diego, CA, 1935.
(Broadway debut) Robert Chalcot, *Message for Margaret,* Plymouth Theatre, 1947.
Morris Townsend, *The Heiress,* Biltmore Theatre, New York City, 1947.
Ellis, *The Little Blue Light,* ANTA Theatre, New York City, 1951.
Judge Aristide Forestier, *Can-Can,* Shubert Theatre, New York City, 1953.
Garrett Scott, *Four Winds,* Cort Theatre, New York City, 1957.
Robert Baker, *Wonderful Town,* City Center Theatre, New York City, 1958.

Also appeared in stock in Dallas, TX, 1936.

STAGE PRODUCER

(With Beatrice Straight) *The Innocents,* Playhouse, New York City, 1950.
(With Amy Lynn and Walter Schwimmer) *The Right Honourable Gentleman,* Billy Rose Theatre, New York City, 1965.
The Contrast, Eastside Playhouse, New York City, 1972.

Also producer of *The Heiress* and *The Turn of the Screw,* both produced in New York City.

FILM APPEARANCES

Sergeant Hanson, *A Guy Named Joe,* Metro-Goldwyn-Mayer, 1943.
Johnny, *Adventures of Kitty O'Day,* Monogram, 1944.
Soldier, *The Imposter* (also known as *Strange Confession*), Universal, 1944.
Jimmy, *Shadow of Suspicion,* Monogram, 1944.
Jonathan, *Swingtime Johnny,* Universal, 1944.
The Girl Who Dared, Republic, 1944.
Lance Marlow, *Behind City Lights,* Republic, 1945.

Bob, *G.I. Honeymoon,* Monogram, 1945.
Bob Randall, *Don't Gamble with Strangers,* Monogram, 1946.
Larry Crain, *Fear* (also known as *Suspense*), Monogram, 1946.
William Sommers, *Strange Conquest,* Universal, 1946.

TELEVISION APPEARANCES

Tony, *First Love,* NBC, 1954.

WRITINGS:

Henderson's Head (novel), Putnam, 1973.
Million Rosebuds (play), New Dramatists, New York City, 1978.

Also author of the plays *Pigeons, Stanley,* and *Grace at Table Six.**

*   *   *

CORBETT, Glenn   1929(?)-

PERSONAL: Born in 1929 (some sources say 1934), in El Monte, CA.

CAREER: Actor.

CREDITS:

FILM APPEARANCES

Mack Miller, *The Fireball,* Twentieth Century-Fox, 1950.
The Violent Years (also known as *Female*), Headliner Productions, 1956.
Detective Sergeant Charlie Bancroft, *The Crimson Kimono,* Columbia, 1959.
Wade, *All the Young Men,* Columbia, 1960.
Frank Sanford, *Man On a String* (also known as *Confessions of a Counterspy*), Columbia, 1960.
Collins, *The Mountain Road,* Columbia, 1960.
Karl, *Homicidal,* Columbia, 1961.
Henry, *The Pirates of Blood River,* Columbia, 1962.
Jacob Anderson, *Shenandoah,* Universal, 1965.
Tom Evens, *Guns in the Heather* (also known as *Spy Busters*), Buena Vista, 1968.
Chance, *This Savage Land* (also known as *The Road West*), Universal, 1969.
Pat Garrett, *Chisum,* Warner Bros., 1970.
O'Brien, *Big Jake,* National General, 1971.
Sandy, *Dead Pigeon on Beethoven Street,* Bavaria Atelier Gesellschaft, 1972.
Ride in a Pink Car, Ambassador, 1974.
Lieutenant Commander John Waldron, *Midway* (also known as *The Battle of Midway*), Universal, 1976.
Jeb, *New Girl In Town* (also known as *Nashville Girl Country Music Daughter*), New World, 1977.
Lamp operator, *Vibes,* Imagine/Columbia, 1988.

Also appeared in *Erotikus,* 1973.

TELEVISION APPEARANCE; SERIES

Wes Macauley, *It's a Man's World,* NBC, 1962-63.
Linc Case, *Route 66,* CBS, 1963-64.
Jason Aldrich, *The Doctors,* NBC, 1963.
Chance Reynolds, *The Road West,* NBC, 1966-67.
Paul Morgan, *Dallas,* CBS, 1983-84.

TELEVISION APPEARANCES; PILOTS

Detective Burke, *Egan,* ABC, 1973.
Neil Stryker, *The Stranger,* NBC, 1973.
Michael Devlin, *The Log of the Black Pearl,* NBC, 1975.
Andy Hill, *Law of the Land* (also known as *The Deputies*), NBC, 1976.
Dirk Macauley, *Stunts Unlimited,* ABC, 1980.

TELEVISION APPEARANCES; EPISODIC

Silver Theater, CBS, 1950.
Escape, NBC, 1973.*

*   *   *

CORBY, Ellen   1913-

PERSONAL: Original name, Ellen Hansen; born June 3, 1913, in Racine, WI.

CAREER: Actress. Worked as a script girl for twelve years prior to acting career.

AWARDS, HONORS: Emmy Award, Outstanding Performance by an Actress in a Supporting Role in a Drama, 1973, for *The Waltons;* Golden Globe Award, Best Supporting Television Actress, 1974, for *The Waltons;* Emmy Award, Outstanding Continuing Performance by a Supporting Actress in a Drama Series, 1975 and 1976, both for *The Waltons.*

CREDITS:

FILM APPEARANCES

French maid, *Cornered,* RKO, 1945.
Maid, *Crack-Up,* RKO, 1946.
Maid, *The Dark Corner,* Twentieth Century-Fox, 1946.
Mother, *From This Day Forward,* RKO, 1946.
Kitchen girl, *The Locket,* RKO, 1946.
Rita, *Lover Come Back* (also known as *When Lovers Meet*), Universal, 1946.
Nurse, *Sister Kenny,* RKO, 1946.
Neighbor, *The Spiral Staircase,* RKO, 1946.
Mrs. Sumpter, *Till the End of Time,* RKO, 1946.
In Old Sacramento (also known as *Flame of Sacramento*), Republic, 1946.
It's a Wonderful Life, RKO, 1946.
Screaming woman, *They Won't Believe Me,* RKO, 1947.

Marge, *Forever Amber,* Twentieth Century-Fox, 1947.
Agnes, *The Dark Past,* Columbia, 1948.
Colpeck's secretary, *Fighting Father Dunne,* RKO, 1948.
Aunt Trina, *I Remember Mama,* RKO, 1948.
Woman, *If You Knew Susie,* RKO, 1948.
Maid, *The Noose Hangs High,* Eagle-Lion, 1948.
Mrs. Harkins, *Strike It Rich,* Allied Artists, 1948.
Mighty Joe Young, RKO, 1949.
Miss Endicott, *Captain China,* Paramount, 1949.
Sophie, *Little Women,* Metro-Goldwyn-Mayer (MGM), 1949.
Felicite, *Madame Bovary,* MGM, 1949.
Miss Simmons, *Rusty Saves a Life,* Columbia, 1949.
Nurse, *A Woman's Secret,* RKO, 1949.
Emma, *Caged,* Warner Bros., 1950.
Mrs. Moore, *Edge of Doom* (also known as *Stronger Than Fear*), RKO, 1950.
Mrs. Devlin, *The Gunfighter,* Twentieth Century-Fox, 1950.
Lottie, *Harriet Craig,* Columbia, 1950.
Emily, *Ma and Pa Kettle Go to Town* (also known as *Going to Town*), Universal, 1950.
Mrs. Privet, *Peggy,* Universal, 1950.
Sister Veronica, *Angels in the Outfield* (also known as *Angels and the Pirates*), MGM, 1951.
Miss Della, *The Barefoot Mailman,* Columbia, 1951.
Miss Birdeshaw, *Goodbye My Fancy,* Warner Bros., 1951.
Mrs. McGonigle, *Here Comes the Groom,* Paramount, 1951.
Annie, *The Mating Season,* Paramount, 1951.
Miss Stevens, *On Moonlight Bay,* Warner Bros., 1951.
Mrs. Drinkwater, *The Sea Hornet,* Republic, 1951.
Mrs. Blackburn, *The Big Trees,* Warner Bros., 1952.
Mrs. Ardley, *Fearless Fagan,* MGM, 1952.
Singing woman, *A Lion Is in the Streets,* Warner Bros., 1953.
Katie, *Monsoon,* United Artists (UA), 1953.
Mrs. Torrey, *Shane,* Paramount, 1953.
Mrs. Barbour, *The Vanquished,* Paramount, 1953.
First woman, *The Woman They Almost Lynched,* Republic, 1953.
Mrs. Croffman, *About Mrs. Leslie,* Paramount, 1954.
Amelia, *The Bowery Boys Meet the Monsters,* Allied Artists, 1954.
Miss McCardle, *Sabrina* (also known as *Sabrina Fair*), Paramount, 1954.
Waitress, *Susan Slept Here,* RKO, 1954.
Mrs. Manny, *Untamed Heiress,* Republic, 1954.
Miss Hinkel, *Illegal,* Warner Bros., 1955.
Martha, *Slightly Scarlet,* RKO, 1956.
Sarah, *Stagecoach to Fury,* Twentieth Century-Fox, 1956.
Mrs. Raiden, *All Mine to Give* (also known as *The Day They Gave Babies Away*), Universal, 1957.

Mrs. Dalton, *God Is My Partner,* Twentieth Century Fox, 1957.
Mrs. Feeney, *Night Passage,* Universal, 1957.
Mrs. Wellington, *Rockabilly,* Twentieth Century-Fox, 1957.
Sister St. Joseph, *The Seventh Sin,* MGM, 1957.
Mettie McPherson, *As Young As We Are,* Paramount, 1958.
Miss Kushins, *Macabre,* Allied Artists, 1958.
Manageress, *Vertigo,* Paramount, 1958.
Mrs. Mayberry, *Visit to a Small Planet,* Paramount, 1960.
Soho Sal, *Pocketful of Miracles,* UA, 1961.
Mrs. McKenzie, *Saintly Sinners,* UA, 1962.
Four for Texas, Warner Bros., 1963.
Irene, *The Caretakers* (also known as *Borderlines*), UA, 1963.
Town gossip, *Hush. . . Hush, Sweet Charlotte,* Twentieth Century-Fox, 1964.
Mrs. Kroll, *The Strangler,* Allied Artists, 1964.
Plane passenger, *The Family Jewels,* Paramount, 1965.
Miss Tremaine, *The Ghost and Mr. Chicken,* Universal, 1966.
Anna Miller, *The Glass Bottom Boat,* MGM, 1966.
Hazel Squires, *The Night of the Grizzly,* Paramount, 1966.
Etta Pettibone, *The Gnome-Mobile,* Buena Vista, 1967.
Script girl, *The Legend of Lylah Clare,* MGM, 1968.
Older woman, *Angel in My Pocket,* Universal, 1969.
Mrs. Walker, *A Fine Pair* (also known as *Una Coppia Tranquilla* and *Ruba al Prossimo Tuo*), National General, 1969.
Abigail, *Support Your Local Gunfighter,* UA, 1971.
Gertrude, *Napoleon and Samantha,* Buena Vista, 1972.

TELEVISION APPEARANCES; SERIES

Martha O'Reilly, *Please Don't Eat the Daisies,* NBC, 1965-67.
Esther "Grandma" Walton, *The Waltons,* CBS, 1972-79.

TELEVISION APPEARANCES; PILOTS

Meet McGraw (broadcast as a segment of *Four Star Playhouse,* also known as *The Best in Mystery*), CBS, 1954.
Isabelle, *On Trial,* NBC, 1955.
Birdie Hackett, *Alias Mike Hercules,* ABC, 1956.
Minerva Comstock, *The Marriage Broker* (broadcast as a segment of *The Twentieth Century-Fox Hour*), CBS, 1957.
Mrs. Butterworth, *Safari* (broadcast as a segment of *The Dick Powell Show*), NBC, 1962.
Ma Jericho, *The Graduation Dress,* CBS, 1964.
Miss Purdy, *Holloway's Daughters* (broadcast as a segment of *The Bob Hope Chrysler Theatre*), NBC, 1966.
Esther "Grandma" Walton, *The Homecoming—A Christmas Story,* CBS, 1971.

TELEVISION APPEARANCES; MOVIES

Mrs. Simmons, *A Tattered Web,* CBS, 1971.
Ma Floyd, *The Story of Pretty Boy Floyd,* ABC, 1974.
Great grandmother, *All the Way Home,* NBC, 1981.
Esther "Grandma" Walton, *A Day for Thanks on Walton's Mountain,* NBC, 1982.
Esther "Grandma" Walton, *Mother's Day on Walton's Mountain,* NBC, 1982.
Esther "Grandma" Walton, *Wedding on Walton's Mountain,* NBC, 1982.

TELEVISION APPEARANCES; EPISODIC

I Love Lucy, CBS, 1956.
G.E. Summer Originals, ABC, 1956.
The Tab Hunter Show, NBC, 1961.
Myrt Lesh, *The Andy Griffith Show,* CBS, 1966.
Hal's mother, *Mr. Terrific,* CBS, 1967.
Pride of the Family, NBC, 1967.

Also appeared as mother Lurch, *The Addams Family,* ABC; as Mrs. Blackwell, *McKeever and the Colonel,* NBC; *The Bill Cosby Show,* NBC; *Dennis the Menace,* CBS; *The Donna Reed Show,* ABC; *Farmer's Daughter,* ABC; *Gomer Pyle,* CBS; *Hennesey,* CBS; *The Nanny and the Professor,* ABC; *The People's Choice,* NBC; *Stars over Hollywood,* NBC; *Your Jeweler's Showcase,* CBS; *Hazel; Get Smart.*

TELEVISION APPEARANCES; SPECIALS

CBS: On the Air, CBS, 1978.

WRITINGS:

(With J. Benton Cheney and Cecile Kramer) *Twilight on The Trail* (screenplay), Paramount, 1941.*

*   *   *

CORD, Alex 1933(?)-

PERSONAL: Name originally Alexander Viespi; born May 3, 1933 (some sources say August 3, 1931, or 1935), in Floral Park, NY; son of Alexander (in construction business) and Marie (Paladino) Viespi; married Joanna Pettet (an actress), 1968; children: Wayne, Toni, Damien. *Education:* Attended New York University; studied acting with Lee Strasberg, Walt Witcover, Herbert Berghof, Morris Cornovsky, at the American Shakespeare Festival and the Actors Studio. *Avocational interests:* Horse training and polo.

ADDRESSES: Agent—Gores-Fields Agency, 10100 Santa Monica Boulevard, Los Angeles, CA 90067.

CAREER: Actor and writer. Professional rodeo rider.

MEMBER: Screen Actors Guild; PIAGET (founding member).

AWARDS, HONORS: London Critics Award, Best Actor, for *Play with a Tiger.*

CREDITS:

STAGE APPEARANCES

Appeared as Laertes, *Hamlet,* American Shakespeare Festival, Stratford, CT. Also appeared in *Play with a Tiger,* London; *A Midsummer Night's Dream* and *The Umbrella,* both London; and with the Compass Players, Crystal Palace, St. Louis, MO.

FILM APPEARANCES

(Film debut) Zankie Albo, *Synanon* (also known as *Get Off My Back*), Columbia, 1965.
Ringo, *Stagecoach,* Twentieth Century-Fox, 1966.
Vince Ginetta, *The Brotherhood,* Paramount, 1968.
Clay McCord, *A Minute to Pray, A Second to Die* (also known as *Un minuto per pregare, un istante per morire* and *Dead or Alive*), Cinerama, 1968.
Count Cesare Cardinali, *Stiletto,* AVCO-Embassy, 1969.
Kip Thompson, *The Last Grenade,* Cinerama, 1970.
Jason, *The Dead Are Alive,* National General/Alexander Korda, 1972.
Steven Mayes, *Chosen Survivors,* Columbia, 1974.
Cal Kincaid, *Inn of the Dammed,* Terryrod/Roadshow, 1974.
Title role, *Grayeagle,* American International, 1977.
Packard Gentry, *Sidewinder One,* AVCO-Embassy, 1977.
Nicky, *Jungle Warriors,* Aquarius Releasing, 1984.
Walter Graham, *Uninvited,* Amazing Movies, 1988.
Street Asylum (also known as *Squad*), Manson International, 1990.
A Girl to Kill For, Epic Home Video/RCA/Columbia Pictures Home Video, 1990.

Also appeared in *The Prodigal Gun,* 1968.

TELEVISION APPEARANCES; SERIES

Jack Kiley, *W.E.B.,* NBC, 1978.
Mike Holland, *Cassie and Company,* NBC, 1982.
Michael Archangel, *Airwolf,* CBS, 1984-86.

TELEVISION APPEARANCES; MINI-SERIES

Evans Kinsella, *Beggarman, Thief,* NBC, 1979.
Dr. Sam Marlow, *Goliath Awaits,* NBC, 1981.

TELEVISION APPEARANCES; PILOTS

Dylan Hunt, *Genesis II,* ABC, 1973.
The Captain, *Hunter's Moon,* CBS, 1979.

TELEVISION APPEARANCES; EPISODIC

Branded, NBC, 1966.

"The Lady Is My Wife," *Bob Hope Presents the Chrysler Theatre*, NBC, 1967.

Room 222, ABC, 1969.

"Keep in Touch, We'll Think of Something," *Night Gallery* (also known as *Rod Serling's "Night Gallery"*), NBC, 1971.

Gunsmoke, CBS, 1972.

Mission: Impossible, CBS, 1972.

The F.B.I., ABC, 1973.

Police Story, NBC, 1973-76.

Matt Helm, ABC, 1975.

Joe Forrester, NBC, 1976.

The Quest, NBC, 1976.

Police Woman, NBC, 1976.

The Six Million Dollar Man, ABC, 1976.

Preston Bartholomew, *Murder, She Wrote*, CBS, 1986.

Alec Harris, *The Law and Harry McGraw*, CBS, 1987.

Roland Vincente, Harry Lubash, *Simon and Simon*, CBS, 1988.

Wallace Cogan, *Jake and the Fatman*, CBS, 1989.

Daniel Travers, *Mission: Impossible*, ABC, 1989.

Also appeared in *Playhouse 90*, CBS; *U.S. Steel Hour*; *Kraft Theatre*; *Naked City*; *Eastside-Westside*.

TELEVISION APPEARANCES; MOVIES

Joe Christopher, *The Scorpio Letters*, NBC, 1967.

Dr. Alex Wilson, *Fire!*, NBC, 1977.

Dravko Demchuk, *The Dirty Dozen: The Fatal Mission*, NBC, 1988.

Also appeared in *The Girl Who Saved America*.

TELEVISION APPEARANCES; SPECIALS

Dan Levine, *Have I Got a Christmas for You*, NBC, 1977.

Bill, *The Best of Friends*, syndicated, 1981.

The Wildest West Show of the Stars, CBS, 1986.

Also appeared in *The Joker*, ITV; *The Rose Tattoo*, BBC.

WRITINGS:

Author of the novels *Sandsong* and *The Harbinger*.*

*   *   *

CORMAN, Gene   1927-

PERSONAL: Full name, Eugene H. Corman; born September 24, 1927, in Detroit, MI; son of William (an engineer) and Anne (Hugh) Corman; married Nan Chandler Morris, September 4, 1955; children: Todd William, Craig Allan. *Education:* Graduated from Stanford University. *Politics:* Republican.

CAREER: Producer and screenwriter. Talent executive with MCA Agency, 1950-57; partner, with Roger Corman

(brother), Corman Company and New World Distributors (independent production company specializing in science fiction and youth-oriented features); Twentieth Century-Fox Television, vice-president, 1983-87; 21st Century Film Corporation, executive vice-president worldwide production. Board of directors, Academy of Motion Picture Arts and Sciences.

MEMBER: Academy of Television Arts and Sciences, Theta Delta Chi, Los Angeles County Museum, Beverly Hills Tennis Club.

AWARDS, HONORS: U.S. entry at Cannes Film Festival, and *Time* magazine ten best films, 1980, for *The Big Red One;* Emmy Award for outstanding drama special, 1981-82, and Christopher Award, 1983, both for *A Woman Called Golda.*

CREDITS:

FILM PRODUCER

Hot Car Girl, Allied Artists, 1958.

Night of the Blood Beast (also see below), American International Pictures, 1958.

Attack of the Giant Leeches (also known as *The Giant Leeches*), American International Pictures, 1959.

Blood and Steel, Twentieth Century-Fox, 1959.

(With Edward L. Alperson and Roger Corman) *I, Mobster*, Twentieth Century-Fox, 1959.

Beast from the Haunted Cave, Filmgroup, 1960.

The Secret of the Purple Reef (also see below), Twentieth Century-Fox, 1960.

Valley of the Redwoods (also see below), Twentieth Century-Fox, 1960.

The Cat Burglar, Harvard Film/United Artists (UA), 1961.

Tower of London, Admiral/UA, 1962.

The Secret Invasion, San Carlos/UA, 1964.

Ski Party, American International Pictures, 1965.

Tobruk, Gibraltar/Universal, 1966.

Von Richthofen and Brown (also known as *The Red Baron*), UA, 1970.

(With Harold Buck) *You Can't Win 'Em All*, Columbia, 1970.

Cool Breeze, Metro-Goldwyn-Mayer (MGM), 1972.

Hit Man, Penelope/MGM, 1972.

Private Parts, Penelope/MGM, 1972.

(With Roger Corman) *I Escaped from Devil's Island*, UA, 1973.

Vigilante Force, UA, 1976.

The Big Red One, UA, 1980.

Also producer of *The Slams*, 1973; *A Man Called Sarge*, 1990; *Avalanche Express*, Lorimar/Twentieth Century-Fox; *Not of This Earth*; and *The Intruder*.

OTHER FILM WORK

Executive producer, *F.I.S.T.,* UA, 1978.
Executive producer, *If You Could See What I Hear,* Jensen Farley, 1982.
Creative consultant, *Paradise,* Embassy, 1982.

TELEVISION PRODUCER

Mary and Joseph: A Story of Faith (movie), NBC, 1979.
Target: Harry (movie; also known as *How To Make It* and *What's In It For Harry?*), ABC, 1980.
A Woman Called Golda (movie), Operation Prime Time, 1982.

Also producer of *Emerald Point* (series), CBS/Twentieth Century-Fox Television.

WRITINGS:

SCREENPLAYS

(With Martin Varno) *Night of the Blood Beast,* American International Pictures, 1958.
(With Harold Yablonsky) *The Secret of the Purple Reef,* Twentieth Century-Fox, 1960.
(With Leo Gordon and Daniel Madison) *Valley of the Redwoods,* Twentieth Century-Fox, 1960.*

*   *   *

COSBY, Bill   1937-

PERSONAL: Full name, William Henry Cosby, Jr.; born July 12, 1937, in Philadelphia, PA; son of William (in the U.S. Navy) and Anna Cosby; married Camille Hanks, January 25, 1964; children: Erika Ranee, Erinn Chalene, Ensa Camille, Evin Harrah, Ennis William. *Education:* Temple University, 1961-62; University of Massachusetts, M.A., 1972, Ed.D., 1977. *Avocational interests:* Tennis.

ADDRESSES: Office—c/o The Brokaw Company, 9255 Sunset Blvd., Los Angeles, CA 90069; and c/o *The Cosby Show,* Kaufman/Astoria Studios, New York, NY.

CAREER: Comedian, actor, producer, and writer. Creator (with Ed Weinberger and Michael Zagor), executive producer, and director of episodes, *The Bill Cosby Show,* NBC, 1969-71; creator and executive producer, *Fat Albert and the Cosby Kids* (animated), CBS, 1972-79, and *The New Fat Albert Show,* CBS, 1979-84. Commercial spokesperson for Del Monte, Jell-O Pudding (General Mills, Inc.), Coca-Cola Co., Ford Motor Co., Texas Instruments, E. F. Hutton, and Kodak Film. Rhythm and Blues Hall of Fame, president, 1968—; member of Carnegie Commission for the Future of Public Broadcasting; member of board of directors for National Council on Crime and Delinquency, Mary Holmes College, and

Ebony Showcase Theatre; Sickle Cell Foundation, member of board of directors and national chairman; member of advisory board, Direction Sports; communications council member, Howard University; trustee, Temple University. *Military service:* U.S. Navy Medical Corps, 1956-60.

MEMBER: NAACP, PUSH.

AWARDS, HONORS: National Society of Recording Arts and Sciences, Grammy awards for best comedy album, 1964, for *Bill Cosby Is a Very Funny Fellow . . . Right!,* 1965, for *I Started Out as a Child,* 1966, for *Why Is There Air?,* 1967, for *Wonderfulness* and *Revenge,* and 1969, for *To Russell, My Brother, Whom I Slept With;* Emmy awards, best actor in a dramatic series, 1965-66, 1966-67, 1967-68, for *I Spy;* Most Promising New Male Star, *Fame* Magazine, 1966; Golden Apple Star of the Year Award, Hollywood Women's Press Club, 1966 and 1985; Emmy Award, 1969, for *The First Bill Cosby Special;* Hasty Pudding Man of the Year, Harvard University, 1969; Seal of Excellence, Children's Theatre Association, 1973; Ohio State University Award, 1975, for *Fat Albert and the Cosby Kids;* National Association for the Advancement of Colored People Image Award, 1976; Star Presenter, *Advertising Age* magazine, 1978; Gold Award for Outstanding Children's Program, International Film and Television Festival, 1981, for *Fat Albert and the Cosby Kids;* Golden Globe Award, best actor in a comedy or musical, Hollywood Foreign Press Association, 1985 and 1986, for *The Cosby Show;* National Association for the Advancement of Colored People Spingarn Medal, 1985; voted "Most Believable Celebrity Endorser" three times in surveys by Video Storyboard Tests Inc; recipient of seven Recording Industry Association of America Gold Records and five People's Choice awards; honorary degree, Brown University.

CREDITS:

TELEVISION APPEARANCES; SERIES

Alexander Scott, *I Spy,* NBC, 1965-68.
Chet Kincaid, *The Bill Cosby Show,* NBC, 1969-71.
Host, *The New Bill Cosby Show,* CBS, 1972-73.
Host and voices of Bill, Fat Albert, Mush Mouth, Dumb Donald, and Weird Harold, *Fat Albert and the Cosby Kids* (animated), CBS, 1972-79, then *The New Fat Albert Show,* CBS, 1979-84.
Regular, *Feeling Good,* PBS, 1974-75.
Host, *COS,* ABC, 1976.
Host of "Picture Page," *Captain Kangaroo's Wake Up,* CBS, 1981-82.
Dr. Heathcliff "Cliff" Huxtable, *The Cosby Show* (also see below), NBC, 1984—.

TELEVISION APPEARANCES; SPECIALS

Host, *The Comics,* NBC, 1965.
It's What's Happening, Baby!, CBS, 1965.
The Wonderful World of Burlesques II, NBC, 1966.
The Bill Cosby Special (also see below), NBC, 1968.
Host, *Bill Cosby Does His Own Thing,* NBC, 1969.
Host, *A Special Bill Cosby Special,* NBC, 1969.
Host, *A World of Love,* CBS, 1970.
Host, *The Bill Cosby Special, or ?,* NBC, 1971.
Diana, NBC, 1971.
Host, *Dick Van Dyke Meets Bill Cosby,* CBS, 1972.
Host, *The Bill Cosby Comedy Special,* CBS, 1975.
Host, *The World of Magic,* NBC, 1975.
Lola, ABC, 1976.
Host, *The Fat Albert Christmas Special,* CBS, 1977.
Celebrity Challenge of the Sexes, CBS, 1977, 1979.
The All-Star Salute to Women's Sports, ABC, 1978.
Playboy's 25th Annual Celebration, ABC, 1979.
Doug Henning's World of Magic III, NBC, 1980.
Host, *Hollywood's Private Home Movies,* ABC, 1983.
Steve Martin's The Winds of Whoopie, NBC, 1983.
S.O.S.—Secrets of Surviving, NBC, 1984.
It's Showtime at the Apollo, syndicated, 1987.
Host, *Sesame Street . . . Twenty and Still Counting,* NBC, 1989.

OTHER TELEVISION APPEARANCES

Milkman, Ken Kane, *The Electric Company* (episodic), PBS, 1971.
Blue, *To All My Friends on Shore* (movie; also see below), CBS, 1972.
People (episodic), CBS, 1978.
Aaron Strickland, *Top Secret* (pilot), NBC, 1978.
Dr. Heathcliff "Cliff" Huxtable, *A Different World* (episodic), NBC, 1987.
The Wil Shriner Show (episodic), syndicated, 1987.

Also appeared on *Children's Theatre* (episodic), NBC; *The Tonight Show* (episodic), NBC.

TELEVISION WORK; EXECUTIVE PRODUCER

The Bill Cosby Special, or ? (special; also see below), NBC, 1971.
To All My Friends on Shore (movie), CBS, 1972.
The Fat Albert Christmas Special (special), CBS, 1977.
(And story consultant) *The Cosby Show* (series), NBC, 1984—.

FILM APPEARANCES

(Debut) Caleb Revers, *Man and Boy,* Levitt-Pickman, 1972.
Al Hickey, *Hickey and Boggs,* United Artists, 1972.
Wardell Franklin, *Uptown Saturday Night,* Warner Brothers, 1974.

Billy Foster, *Lets Do It Again,* Warner Brothers, 1975.
Mother, *Mother, Juggs, and Speed,* Twentieth Century-Fox, 1976.
Dave Anderson, *A Piece of the Action,* Warner Brothers, 1977.
Dr. Willis Panama, *California Suite,* Columbia, 1978.
Barney Satin, *The Devil and Max Devlin,* Buena Vista, 1981.
Bill Cosby Himself, HBO Pictures, 1985.
Leonard, *Leonard, Part 6,* Columbia, 1987.
Ghost Dad, Universal, 1990.

Also provided voice for *Aesop's Fables* (animated), 1978.

FILM WORK

Producer, *Leonard, Part 6,* Columbia, 1987.

STAGE APPEARANCES

An Evening with Bill Cosby, Radio City Music Hall, New York City, 1986.

Made his stage debut as a comedian at "The Underground," in a room called "The Cellar," Philadelphia, PA; made Broadway debut in *Two Friends,* 1983; also appeared on stage at the Las Vegas Hilton, 1989.

RADIO APPEARANCES

Appeared on the series *The Bill Cosby Radio Program.*

RECORDINGS:

ALBUMS

Albums include *Bill Cosby Is a Very Funny Fellow . . . Right!,* 1964; *I Started Out as a Child,* 1965; *Why Is There Air?,* 1966; *Wonderfulness,* 1967; *Revenge,* 1967; *To Russell, My Brother, Whom I Slept With,* 1969; *Bill Cosby Is Not Himself These Days, Rat Own, Rat Own, Rat Own,* 1976; *My Father Confused Me . . . What Must I Do? What Must I Do?,* 1977; *Disco Bill,* 1977; *Bill's Best Friend,* 1978; *Cosby and the Kids,* 1986; *It's True, It's True; Bill Cosby Himself; 200 MPH; Silverthroat; Hooray for the Salvation Army Band; 8:15, 12:15; For Adults Only; Bill Cosby Talks to Kids About Drugs; Inside the Mind of Bill Cosby.*

VIDEO

Bill Cosby: 49 (children's pre-school cassette), produced by Walt Disney Studios.

WRITINGS:

TELEVISION

(With Bill Persky, and Sam Denoff) *The Bill Cosby Special* (special), NBC, 1968.
(With Michael Elias, Frank Shaw, Sid Green, Dave Hill, and Ray Jessel) *The Bill Cosby Special, or ?* (special), NBC, 1971.

Music, *To All My Friends on Shore* (movie), CBS, 1972.

OTHER

The Wit and Wisdom of Fat Albert, Windmill Books, 1973.

Bill Cosby's Personal Guide to Tennis Power; or Don't Lower the Lob, Raise the Net, Random House, 1975.

Contributor, *You Are Somebody Special,* McGraw-Hill, 1978.

Fatherhood, Doubleday, 1986.

Leonard, Part 6 (screenplay), Columbia, 1987.

Time Flies, Doubleday, 1987.*

*   *   *

COSTIGAN, Ken   1934-

PERSONAL: Born April 4, 1934, in New York, NY; son of Thomas Joseph (a doctor) and Kathleen (McCrann) Costigan; married Barbara Sue Ellenberger, July, 1972 (divorced, February, 1983); children: Kevin T. *Education:* Fordham University, B.S., 1956; Yale University, M.F.A. (directing), 1960.

ADDRESSES: Agent—c/o Phoenix Artists, 311 West 43rd St. #1401, New York, NY, 10036.

CAREER: Actor, director. Tyrone Guthrie Theatre, Minneapolis, MN, stage manager, 1965; Pittsburgh Playhouse, Pittsburgh, PA, artistic director, 1971-74; Indiana University Theatre, Bloomington, IN, director, 1990. Also worked as a director for McCarter Repertory Company, 1967-68, and Barter Theatre, 1973-74 and 1986-91. *Military service:* U.S. Army Reserve, Signal Corps, 1956-64; became first lieutenant.

MEMBER: International Alliance of Stage Employees and Moving Picture Machine Operators, Actors' Equity Association, Screen Actors Guild, American Federation of Television and Radio Artists, Society of Stage Directors and Choreographers.

CREDITS:

STAGE APPEARANCES

(Broadway debut) Purah, *Gideon,* Plymouth Theatre, 1962.

Joe Egg, Pittsburgh Playhouse, Pittsburgh, PA, 1969-70.

Lawyer, *The Runner Stumbles,* Manhattan Theatre Club, New York City, 1974.

Montgomery Hawkes, *Peg o' My Heart,* Theatre Four, New York City, and Lion Theatre Company, New York City, 1977.

Mr. Kraler, *The Diary of Anne Frank,* Theatre Four, 1978.

Mr. Rogers, *The Show-Off,* Roundabout Stage Two Theatre, New York City, 1978.

Peter Quince, *A Midsummer Night's Dream,* Equity Library Theatre, New York City, 1978.

Richard III, Virginia Museum Theatre, Richmond, VA, 1978.

Shamraev, *The Sea Gull,* New York Shakespeare Festival Public Theatre, New York City, 1980.

Shirley Basin, New Dramatists Inc., New York City, 1980-81.

Zellito, *Declassee,* Lion Theatre, New York City, 1981.

Arlen, *Big Apple Messenger,* WPA Theatre, New York City, 1981.

Manager, *When We Dead Awaken,* Open Space Theatre, New York City, 1982.

You Can't Take It with You, Barter Theatre, Abingdon, VA, 1982-83.

Alibius, *The Changeling,* Equity Library Theatre, 1983.

Artichoke, Barter Theatre, 1984-85.

Doctor, *A Streetcar Named Desire,* Circle in the Square, New York City, 1988.

Also appeared in *The Browning Version,* Roundabout Theatre. Appeared as W. O. Gant, *Look Homeward Angel;* Mayor Quinn, *Hogan's Goat;* Mayor Shinn, *The Music Man;* George, *Who's Afraid of Virginia Woolf?;* Harry Berlin, *Luv;* Hank, *The Boys in the Band;* Rossetti, *Boy Meets Girl;* Old Man Mahon, *The Playboy of the Western World.* Has also appeared with Clarence Brown Theatre Company, Knoxville, TN, 1975; McCarter Repertory Company, Princeton, NJ, 1966-68; and Asolo State Theatre, Sarasota, FL, 1975-77.

MAJOR TOURS

Appeared in *The Matchmaker,* Phoenix Theatre tour, U.S. cities, and *A Short Happy Life,* U.S. cities.

STAGE WORK

Stage manager, *The Hostage,* One Sheridan Square, New York City, 1961.

Director, *Shoemaker's Holiday,* Orpheum Theatre, New York City, 1967.

Stage manager, *Curley McDimple,* Bert Wheeler Theatre, New York City, 1967.

Director, *The Diary of Anne Frank,* New Jersey Shakespeare Festival, Madison, NJ, 1987-88.

FILM APPEARANCES

Father Quinn, *Hannah and Her Sisters,* Orion, 1986.

TELEVISION APPEARANCES

Debuted as Deacon Billson, *The Man That Corrupted Hadleyburg,* American Short Story Series, PBS; also appeared on episodes of *One Life to Live, Ryan's Hope, Love of Life, The Guiding Light, All My Children,* and *Search for Tomorrow;* and on specials *John Adams, Patrick Henry,* and *Decades of Decision.*

COSTNER, Kevin 1955-

PERSONAL: Born January 18, 1955, in Compton, CA; father, a telephone company employee; mother, a state welfare department employee; married Cindy Silva, 1975; children: Annie, Lily, Joe. *Education:* California State University, Fullerton, B.S., marketing, 1978; studied acting at South Coast Actors' Co-op.

ADDRESSES: Agent—Michael Ovitz, Creative Artists Agency, 9830 Wilshire Blvd., Beverly Hills, CA 90212.

CAREER: Actor, director, and producer. Prior to acting worked as a marketing representative. Stage manager at Raleigh Studios, Hollywood, CA, 1980-83. Head of own production company, TIG Productions, 1989—.

MEMBER: Delta Chi.

AWARDS, HONORS: "Star of Tomorrow" award, National Association of Theater Owners, 1987. Hasty Pudding Man of the Year, Harvard University, 1990. Academy Awards, best picture (with Jim Wilson) and best director; Academy Award nomination, best actor; Golden Globe Awards, best motion picture—drama (with Jim Wilson) and best director; Golden Globe Award nomination, best actor; and Directors Guild of America Award, best director for a feature film, all 1990, for *Dances with Wolves.*

CREDITS:

FILM APPEARANCES

First fraternity boy, *Night Shift,* Warner Bros., 1982.
Luther Adler, *Frances,* Universal, 1982.
Phil Pitkin, *Testament* (originally produced as a television movie; also see below), Paramount, 1983.
Will Bonner, *Stacy's Knights* (also known as *Double Down*), Crown, 1983.
Alex, *The Big Chill,* Columbia, 1983.
Newlywed husband, *Table for Five,* Warner Bros., 1983.
Gardner Barnes, *Fandango,* Warner Bros., 1985.
Jake, *Silverado,* Columbia, 1985.
Marcus Sommers, *American Flyers,* Warner Bros., 1985.
Eliot Ness, *The Untouchables,* Paramount, 1987.
Tom Farrell, *No Way Out,* Orion, 1987.
Crash Davis, *Bull Durham,* Orion, 1988.
Ray Kinsella, *Field of Dreams,* Universal, 1989.
Cochran, *Revenge,* Columbia, 1990 (also see below).
Lieutenant John J. Dunbar, *Dances with Wolves,* Orion, 1990 (also see below).
Title role, *Robin Hood: Prince of Thieves,* Warner Bros., 1991.

Also appeared in films released only on videocassette, including *Sizzle Beach, U.S.A.* (filmed, late 1970s), Troma, 1986; as Jimmy Scott, *Shadows Run Black* (filmed, 1981), Troma, 1986; *Chasing Dreams* (filmed, 1981), Nascent,

1989; and as Ted Beaubien, *The Gunrunner* (filmed, 1983), New World, 1989.

FILM WORK

Executive producer, *Revenge,* Columbia, 1990.
Producer (with Jim Wilson) and director, *Dances with Wolves,* Orion, 1990.

TELEVISION APPEARANCES; SPECIALS, EXCEPT WHERE NOTED

Phil Pitkin, *Testament* (movie), PBS, 1983.
60th Annual Academy Awards Presentation, ABC, 1988.
Face to Face with Connie Chung, CBS, 1990.
Robert Wuhl's World Tour, HBO, 1990.
Voices That Care, Fox, 1991.

Also appeared as the Captain in "The Mission," an episode of *Amazing Stories,* NBC, and on *Time Warner Presents the Earth Day,* 1990.

STAGE APPEARANCES

Made stage debut in *Invitation to March,* Costa Mesa Civic Playhouse. Also appeared in productions of *Waiting for Lefty* and *A View from the Bridge.*

OTHER SOURCES:

PERIODICALS

Elle, January, 1987.
Los Angeles Times, August 19, 1987; April 21, 1989; March 19, 1991.
New York Times, April 23, 1989.
People, December 26, 1988.
Premiere, October, 1990; June, 1991.
Rolling Stone, July 14, 1988.
Time, September 7, 1987; April 24, 1989.
Washington Post, August 14, 1987; June 15, 1988.*

*   *   *

COTTON, Oliver 1944-

PERSONAL: Born June 20, 1944, in London, England; son of Robert Norman and Ester Cotton; married Catherine Stevens (divorced). *Education:* Attended the Drama Centre, 1962-65. *Avocational interests:* Guitar playing and running.

ADDRESSES: Agent—Jeremy Conway Ltd., 18-21 Jermyn Street, London SW1Y 6HB, England.

CAREER: Actor and writer. National Theatre Company, London, member, 1966-68, 1975-79, and 1990-91; Cheltenham Repertory Company, Cheltenham, England, member, 1969; Watford Palace, Watford, England, pantomime performer, 1972; West End Theatre, member, 1978,

1982, and 1984; Royal Shakespeare Company, member, 1988-89. Joint Stock Company, England, founder, 1973.

CREDITS:

STAGE APPEARANCES; ROYAL COURT THEATRE, LONDON

Graham, *The Local Stigmatic,* 1966.
Mike, *It's My Criminal,* 1966.
A Provincial Life, 1966.
Lauffer, *The Tutor,* 1968.
Erogenous Zones 1969.
The Enoch Show, 1969.
Dean, *The Sport of My Mad Mother,* 1970.
Ferdinand, *The Duchess of Malfi,* 1971.
Polly Baker, *Man Is Man,* 1971.
Carpenter, *Lear,* 1971.
Fergy, *Captain Oates' Left Sock,* 1973.
Son, *Bingo,* 1974.

STAGE APPEARANCES; NATIONAL THEATRE COMPANY, OLD VIC THEATRE, LONDON

Diego, *The Royal Hunt of the Sun,* 1966.
Love for Love, 1966.
The Storm, 1966.
Borachio, *Much Ado about Nothing,* 1967.
First player, *Rosencrantz and Guildenstern Are Dead,* 1967.
Oliver Martext and Sylvius, *As You Like It,* 1967.
Volpone, 1968.
Oedipus, 1968.
Edward II, 1968.
In His Own Write, 1968.
Rosencrantz, *Hamlet,* 1975.

STAGE APPEARANCES; NATIONAL THEATRE, LONDON

Techelles, *Tamburlaine the Great,* 1976.
Clown, *Force of Habit,* 1977.
Von Hierlinger, *Tales from the Vienna Woods,* 1977.
Decius Brutus and Messala, *Julius Caesar,* 1977.
Judas, *The Passion,* 1977.
Major Hippisley Thomas, *The Madras House,* 1977.
Mike Clayton, *Half-Life,* 1977.
Title role, *The Man with a Flower in His Mouth,* 1977.
General Fairfax, *The World Turned Upside Down,* 1978.
Orrin, *Dispatches,* 1979.

OTHER STAGE APPEARANCES

Mark, *The Dwarfs,* Stage 73, New York City, 1965.
Kedge, *A Night Out,* Stage 73, 1965.
The Beggars Opera, Stage 73, 1965.
Mark, *The Dwarfs,* Traverse Theatre, Edinburgh, U.K., 1966.
Graham, *The Local Stigmatic,* Traverse Theatre, 1966.
Mercutio, *Romeo and Juliet,* Ludlow Festival, U.K., 1969.

Various roles, *Cato Street,* Young Vic Theatre, London, 1971.
Cortes, *Quetzalcoatl,* Round House Theatre, London, 1972.
John Abud, *The Marrying of Anne Leete,* Royal Shakespeare Company (RSC), Aldwych Theatre, London, 1975.
Teddy, *The Homecoming,* Garrick Theatre, London, 1978.
Kochetov, *Liberty Hall,* Greenwich Theatre, London, 1980.
Loveless, *The Relapse,* Lyric Theatre, Hammersmith, U.K., 1983.
David, *Benefactors,* Vaudeville Theatre, London, 1984.
Freeman, *The Plain Dealer,* RSC, Swan Theatre, Stratford-on-Avon, U.K., 1988.
Jack Cade, *Henry VI,* RSC, c. 1988-89.
Duke of Buckingham, *Richard III,* RSC, c. 1988-89.
Earl of Suffolk, *Henry VI,* RSC, c. 1988-89.
Philip Brown, *Some Americans Abroad,* RSC, Pit Theatre, London, 1989.
Reverend Parris, *The Crucible,* National Theatre Company, Olivier Theatre, London, 1990.

Also appeared in *Children of a Lesser God.*

MAJOR TOURS

Four Hundred Years of English Comedy, Piccolo Theatre, U.K. cities, 1966.
Axel Ney Hoch, *The Speakers,* Joint Stock Company, U.K. cities, 1973.

FILM APPEARANCES

(Film debut) Curtis, *Here We Go Round the Mulberry Bush,* United Artists, 1968.
Dmitri Priabin, *Firefox,* Warner Bros., 1982.
Katis, *Eleni,* Warner Bros., 1985.
Landis, *Hiding Out,* De Laurentiis Entertainment Group, 1987.
Commander Roccofino, *The Sicilian,* Twentieth Century-Fox, 1987.

TELEVISION APPEARANCES

Earl of Surrey, "Henry VIII," *The Shakespeare Plays* (special), BBC, then PBS, 1979.
John, *The Day Christ Died* (movie), CBS, 1980.
Monks, *Oliver Twist* (movie), CBS, 1982.
Cesare Borgia, *The Borgias* (series), BBC, then Arts and Entertainment, 1985.
Mr. Murdstone, "David Copperfield," *Masterpiece Theatre* (mini-series), PBS, 1988.
"The Bretts II," *Masterpiece Theatre,* PBS, 1989.

Also appeared in *Return to Treasure Island; Robin of Sherwood; The Peasants Revolt; The Year of the French;*

Sovereign's Company; Ross; Lovejoy; Thank You Miss Jones; Cat's Eyes; The Party; and *Redemption.*

WRITINGS:

Scrabble (play), National Theatre, Jeannetta Cochrane Theatre, London, 1969.

(With others) *The Enoch Show* (play), Royal Court Theatre, London, 1969.

Also author of the teleplay *The Intruder,* 1967.

SIDELIGHTS: *Favorite roles:* Axel Ney Hoch in *The Speakers,* John Abud in *The Marrying of Anne Leete,* and Jack Cade in *Henry VI.*

*   *   *

COUNTRYMAN, Michael 1955-

PERSONAL: Born September 15, 1955, in St. Paul, MN. *Education:* Graduated from Trinity College; trained for the stage at the American Academy of Dramatic Art.

ADDRESSES: *Agent*—Ambrosio/Mortimer and Associates, 165 W. 46th St., Suite 1109, New York, NY 10036.

CAREER: Actor.

CREDITS:

STAGE APPEARANCES

Robert, *Changing Palettes,* Richard Allen Center, New York City, 1983.

Fred Stevens, *June Moon,* Manhattan Punch Line, Lion Theatre, New York City, 1983-84.

Evans, *Terra Nova,* Playwrights Horizons, American Place Theatre, New York City, 1984.

Delmont, *The Miss Firecracker Contest,* Manhattan Theatre Club, New York City, then standby, Westside Arts Center/Cheryl Crawford Theatre, New York City, 1984-85.

Ralph Marvell, *The Custom of the Country,* Second Stage Theatre, New York City, 1985.

Bruce, "Want Ad," Butch, "Dandruff of the Gods," and Larry, "Separate Vacation/Grounds for Divorce/Sexual History," *Love As We Know It,* Manhattan Punch Line, INTAR Theatre, New York City, 1985.

Second man, Russel, Jeremy, Billy, Daddy, and Kid, *And They Dance Real Slow in Jackson,* Hudson Guild Theatre, New York City, 1985.

Doug McLean, *Bullie's House,* Long Wharf Theatre, 1985.

Martin Musgrove, *The Common Pursuit,* Long Wharf Theatre, New Haven, CT, 1985, then Promenade Theatre, New York City, 1986.

Wayne, "Mink on a Gold Hook," *Marathon '86,* Ensemble Studio Theatre, New York City, 1986.

Joe Jackson, *Out!,* Judith Anderson Theatre, New York City, 1986.

Poppy and David Quinn, *The Voice of the Prairie,* Hartford Stage Company, Hartford, CT, 1987.

Albertus, *Intermezzo,* Yale Repertory Theatre, New Haven, CT, 1988.

Tony, *Woman in Mind,* Manhattan Theatre Club, City Center Stage One Theatre, New York City, 1988.

Title role, *Amorphous George,* Philadelphia Festival for New Plays, Harold Prince Theatre-Annenberg Center, Philadelphia, PA, 1989.

Andrew May, *Pravda: A Fleet Street Comedy,* Tyrone Guthrie Theatre, Minneapolis, MN, 1989.

Trinculo, *The Tempest,* Roundabout Theatre, New York City, 1989.

Robert, *Making Movies,* Promenade Theatre, New York City, 1990.

Jerry, *Tales of the Lost Formicans,* Women's Project, New York City, 1990.

Sam Weinberg, *A Few Good Men,* Music Box Theatre, New York City, 1990-91.

Tom Pullet, *The Stick Wife,* Manhattan Theatre Club, City Center Theatre, 1991.

TELEVISION APPEARANCES; EPISODIC

Louis, *Kate and Allie,* CBS, 1986-87.
Nick Griffin, *Spenser: For Hire,* ABC, 1987.
Martin, *Friday the 13th: The Series,* Fox, 1988.

TELEVISION APPEARANCES; SPECIALS

Network vice president, "Late for Dinner," *Cinemax Comedy Experiment,* Cinemax, 1988.

*   *   *

COX, Brian 1946-

PERSONAL: Born June 1, 1946, in Dundee, Scotland; son of Charles (a weaver) and Mary Ann Guillerline (a spinner; maiden name, McCann) Cox; married Caroline Burt (an actress), c. 1967; children: one son (Alan) and one daughter. *Education:* Attended London Academy of Music and Dramatic Arts. *Avocational interests:* Gymwork, working with drama students.

ADDRESSES: *Agent*—Marion Rosenberg Office, 8428 Melrose Place, Suite C, Los Angeles, CA 90069; and Jeremy Conway Ltd., Eagle House, 109 Jermyn St., London SW1, England.

CAREER: Actor.

AWARDS, HONORS: Olivier Award, best actor, 1984, for *Rat in the Skull;* Olivier Award, best actor in a revival, 1988, for *Titus Andronicus.*

CREDITS:

STAGE APPEARANCES

Orlando, *As You Like It,* Birmingham Repertory, Birmingham, England, 1966, then (London debut) Vaudeville Theatre, London, 1967.

Title role, *Peer Gynt,* Birmingham Repertory, 1967.

Ulfhejm, *When We Dead Awaken,* Assembly Hall, Edinburgh, Scotland, 1968.

Steven, *In Celebration,* Royal Court Theatre, London, 1969.

Gregers Werle, *The Wild Duck,* Edinburgh Festival, Edinburgh, Scotland, 1969.

Alan, *The Big Romance,* Royal Court Theatre, 1970.

Norman, *Don't Start Without Me,* Garrick Theatre, London, 1971.

Knight of Riprafratta, *Mirandolina,* Gardner Centre Theatre, Brighton, England, 1971.

Brian Lowther, *Getting On,* Queen's Theatre, London, 1971.

Gustav, *The Creditors,* Open Space Theatre, London, 1972.

Eilert Lovborg, *Hedda Gabler,* Royal Court Theatre, London, 1972.

Berowne, *Love's Labour's Lost,* Playhouse, Nottingham, England, 1972.

Title role, *Brand,* Playhouse, 1972.

Sergeant Match, *What the Butler Saw,* Playhouse, 1972.

D'Artagnan, *The Three Musketeers,* Playhouse, 1972.

Proctor, *Cromwell,* Royal Court Theatre, London, 1973.

Sergius, *Arms and the Man,* Royal Exchange Theatre, Manchester, England, 1974.

Sir Henry Harcourt Reilly, *The Cocktail Party,* Royal Exchange Theatre, 1975.

Emigres, National Theatre Company, Young Vic Theatre, 1976.

Theridamas, *Tamburlaine the Great,* Olivier Theatre, London, 1976.

Brutus, *Julius Caesar,* Olivier Theatre, 1977.

De Flores, *The Changeling,* Riverside Studios, London, 1978.

Title role, *Herod,* National Theatre, London, 1978.

Ireton, *The Putney Debates,* National Theatre, 1978.

Mickey, *On Top,* Royal Court Theatre, London, 1979.

Vicomte Robert de Trivelin, *Have You Anything to Declare?,* Royal Exchange Theatre, then Round House Theatre, London, 1981.

Title role, *Danton's Death,* National Theatre Company, Olivier Theatre, 1982.

Edmund Darrell, *Strange Interlude,* Duke of York Theatre, London, 1984, then (Broadway debut) Nederlander Theatre, New York City, 1985.

D. I. Nelson, *Rat in the Skull,* Royal Court Theatre, London, 1984, then New York Shakespeare Festival, Public Theatre, New York City, 1985.

Paul Cash, *Fashion,* Royal Shakespeare Company, The Pit, London, 1988.

Johnny, *Frankie and Johnny in the Clair-de-Lune,* Comedy Theatre, London, 1989.

Also appeared in *Titus Andronicus,* London, 1988, and as Captain Ahab in *Moby Dick,* Manchester. Appeared with the Dundee Repertory Theatre, Dundee, Scotland, 1961.

MAJOR TOURS

Christian, *The Pilgrim's Progress,* Prospect Theatre Company, 1974.

Also toured in *Rogues and Vagabonds.*

STAGE WORK

Director, *The Man with a Flower in His Mouth,* Royal Exchange Theatre, Manchester, 1973.

Director, *The Stronger,* Royal Exchange Theatre, Manchester, 1973.

Director, *I Love My Love,* Orange Tree Theatre, Richmond, England, 1982.

FILM APPEARANCES

Trotsky, *Nicholas and Alexandra,* Columbia, 1971.

Steven Shaw, *In Celebration,* American Film Theatre, 1975.

Dr. Lektor, *Manhunter,* De Laurentiis Entertainment Group, 1986.

Duffy, *Shoot for the Sun,* BBC, 1986.

Also appeared as Peter Kerrigan in *Hidden Agenda,* 1990.

TELEVISION APPEARANCES

Laurent, "Therese Raquin," *Masterpiece Theatre,* (miniseries), PBS, 1981.

Father Gora, *Pope John Paul II* (movie), CBS, 1984.

Dr. McGrigor, *Florence Nightingale* (movie), NBC, 1985.

Alexander "Jock" Purves, *Beryl Markham: A Shadow on the Sun* (movie), CBS, 1988.

Colonel Fedorenko Voronov, *Murder by Moonlight* (movie), CBS, 1989.

Andrew Neil, *Secret Weapon* (movie), TNT, 1990.

Also appeared in *The Changeling, The Master Ballantrae, Shades of Green, Targets, The Devil's Crown, The Silent Scream, A Cotswold Death,* and *King Lear.*

SIDELIGHTS: Favorite roles: De Flores in *The Changeling* and Brand.*

CRONYN, Tandy 1945-

PERSONAL: Born November 26, 1945; daughter of Hume (an actor, writer, producer, and director) and Jessica Tandy (an actress) Cronyn. *Education:* Attended Central School of Speech and Drama, London, England, 1965-67.

CAREER: Actress. Colonnades Theatre Lab, New York City, trustee, 1974-77, assistant to the director, 1974-76; National Theatre of the Deaf, business manager, 1976-77.

CREDITS:

STAGE APPEARANCES

(Stage debut) Doreen, *The Private Ear,* Instant Theatre, Montreal, Quebec, Canada, 1965.

(British debut) Sibyl, *Private Lives,* Theatre Royal, Bury Saint Edmunds, England, 1967.

Regina, *Ghosts,* Theatre Royal, 1967.

Uncle Ted, *A Resounding Tinkle,* Theatre Royal, 1967.

(New York debut) Sally Bowles, *Cabaret,* Broadway Theatre, 1969.

Niece, *The Good Woman of Setzuan,* Lincoln Center Repertory, Vivian Beaumont Theatre, New York City, 1970.

Ismene, *Antigone,* Lincoln Center Repertory, Vivian Beaumont Theatre, 1971.

Honor Blake, *The Playboy of the Western World,* Lincoln Center Repertory, Vivian Beaumont Theatre, 1971.

Petra, *An Enemy of the People,* Lincoln Center Repertory, Vivian Beaumont Theatre, 1971.

Alva, *Heyday,* New Dramatists, New York City, 1972.

Jo Munson, *An Evening with the Poet-Senator,* Playhouse 2, New York City, 1973.

The Miser, Studio Arena Theatre, Buffalo, NY, 1973-74.

Catsplay, Studio Arena Theatre, 1978-79.

Poets from the Inside, Public Theatre/Other Stage, New York City, 1979.

Natella, *The Caucasian Chalk Circle,* Denver Center Theatre Company, Denver, CO, 1980.

Armande, *The Learned Ladies,* Denver Center Theatre Company, 1980.

Lady Capulet, *Romeo and Juliet,* Old Globe Theatre, San Diego, CA, 1980.

Silvia, *Two Gentlemen of Verona,* Old Globe Theatre, 1980.

Princess of France, *Love's Labour's Lost,* Old Globe Theatre, 1980.

Helen, *Bodies,* South Coast Repertory Theatre, Costa Mesa, CA, 1981-82.

Hypatia, *Misalliance,* Denver Center Theatre Company, 1981.

Lady Percy, *Henry IV, Part 1,* Denver Center Theatre Company, 1981.

Chorus, *Medea,* Denver Center Theatre Company, 1981.

Dear Liar, National Shakespeare Festival, San Diego, 1981.

American Mosaic, Aquarius Theatre, Los Angeles, CA, 1982.

Grace, *The Philanderer,* Yale Repertory Theatre, New Haven, CT, 1982.

Lina Szczepanowska, *Misalliance,* Old Globe Theatre, 1982.

Celimene, *The Misanthrope,* Hartford Stage Company, Hartford, CT, 1983.

Woman, "Winners," and She, "How He Lied to Her Husband," in *Winners/How He Lied to Her Husband* (double bill), Roundabout/Susan Bloch Theatre, New York City, 1983.

Alice "Childie" McNaught, *The Killing of Sister George,* Susan Bloch Theatre, 1983-84.

Rachel, *Season's Greetings,* Old Globe Theatre, 1984-85.

Much Ado about Nothing, Playmakers Repertory Company, Chapel Hill, NC, 1985-86.

Lucille, *The Impromptu of Outremont,* Lincoln Theatre, University of Hartford, Hartford, CT, 1986.

Waiting for Godot, Playmakers Repertory Company, 1987.

Mourning Becomes Electra, Playmakers Repertory Company, 1987-88.

Beatrice, *Much Ado about Nothing,* Stratford Festival, Stratford, Ontario, Canada, 1987.

Helen, *Troilus and Cressida,* Stratford Festival, 1987.

Lucia, *A Shayna Maidel,* Westside Arts Theatre, New York City, 1988.

H'Lynn, *Steel Magnolias,* Coconut Grove Playhouse, Coconut Grove, FL, 1990.

Appeared in a reading of *Memories of an Immortal Spirit: Tennessee Williams,* Parsons School May Auditorium, 1985; appeared at Eugene O'Neill Theatre Center, National Playwrights Conference, 1970, 1972, 1983, and 1986; appeared as Mrs. Patrick Campbell, *Dear Liar,* Old Globe Theatre.

MAJOR TOURS

Sally Bowles, *Cabaret,* U.S. cities, 1969-70.

Myrtle Mae Simmons, *Harvey,* U.S. cities, 1971.

Amy, *Company,* U.S. cities, 1972.

Nina, *The Cocktail Hour,* Florida cities, 1990.

FILM APPEARANCES

American girl, *Praise Marx and Pass the Ammunition,* Mithras, 1970.

Shuster's secretary, *All Night Long,* United Artists (UA), 1981.

Lana, *The January Man,* Metro-Goldwyn-Mayer/UA, 1989.

Tracy Loxton, *The Fear Is Spreading* (special; first broadcast in England as *The Crazy Kill*), ABC, 1975.

Lynn Hyatt, *The Guardian* (movie), HBO, 1984.

Tina, *Streets of Justice* (movie), NBC, 1985.

Beatrice, *Much Ado about Nothing* (special), CBC, 1988.

Julia, *Age-Old Friends* (movie), HBO, 1989.

Also appeared in "Seaway" (television debut), *A Medal for Mirko*, Canada, 1965; *Murder: An Even Chance*, 1968, *Star Quality*, 1968, and *Boy Meets Girl*, 1968, all in England.

*   *   *

CROWDEN, Graham   1922-

PERSONAL: Born November 30, 1922, in Edinburgh, Scotland; son of Harry Graham and Anne Margaret (Paterson) Crowden; married Phylida Hewat. *Education:* Attended Edinburgh Academy. *Avocational interests:* Music, walking, tennis.

CAREER: Actor.

MEMBER: Savile Club.

CREDITS:

STAGE APPEARANCES

(London debut) Charles Lomax, *Major Barbara*, Old Vic Theatre, 1956.

Bernard, *Quartet for Five*, Arts Theatre, London, England, 1959.

Prosecuting Counsel, *One Way Pendulum*, Royal Court Theatre, London, 1959, then Criterion Theatre, London, 1960.

Wing Commander Howard, *Nil Carborundum*, Arts Theatre, 1962.

Doctor, *Exit the King*, Royal Court Theatre, then Criterion Theatre, later Edinburgh Festival, Edinburgh, Scotland, all 1963.

Casca, *Julius Caesar*, Royal Court Theatre, then Criterion Theatre, later Edinburgh Festival, all 1964.

Augustus Colpous, *Trelawny of the Wells*, National Theatre Company (NTC), Old Vic Theatre, 1965.

Berlebeyo, *A Bond Honoured*, NTC, Old Vic Theatre, 1966.

Player, *Rosencrantz and Guildenstern are Dead*, NTC, Old Vic Theatre, 1967.

Foresight, *Love for Love*, NTC, Old Vic Theatre, 1967.

Augustin Feraillon, *A Flea in Her Ear*, NTC, Old Vic Theatre, 1967.

Sir Politik Would-be, *Volpone*, NTC, Old Vic Theatre, 1968.

Archbishop of Winchester, and Lightborn, *Edward the Second*, NTC, Old Vic Theatre, 1968.

Devil, *The Soldiers Tale*, Bath Festival, Bath, England, 1968.

Pantalone, *The Servant of Two Masters*, Queen's Theatre, London, 1968.

Title role, *Henry IV, Part One* and *Part Two*, Mermaid Theatre Shakespeare Festival (MTSF), Mermaid Theatre, London, 1970.

Prospero, *The Tempest*, MTSF, Mermaid Theatre, 1970.

Archie, *Jumpers*, NTC, Old Vic Theatre, 1972.

James, *The Freeway*, NTC, Old Vic Theatre, 1974.

Hector Hushabye, *Heartbreak House*, NTC, Old Vic Theatre, 1975.

Rogues and Vagabonds (recital), Edinburgh Festival, 1976.

Dead-Eyed Dicks, Dublin Festival, Dublin, Ireland, 1976.

Dr. Wangel, *The Lady from the Sea*, Royal Exchange Theatre, Manchester, England, 1978.

Menius Agrippa, *Coriolanus*, Royal Shakespeare Company (RSC), Aldwych Theatre, London, 1979.

Dr. Wangel, *The Lady from the Sea*, Roundhouse Theatre, London, 1979.

Red, Cottesloe Theatre, London, 1989.

Also appeared at Memorial Theatre, Stratford-upon-Avon, England, 1944; Open Air Theatre, Regents Park, England, 1952; Royal Court Theatre, 1957-65. Appeared as Duke of Gloucester, *Henry IV, Part One* and *Part Two*, Le Beau, *As You Like It*, 1978, and Filippo Stozzi, *The Lorenzaccio Story*, 1979, all RSC; Colonel Melkett, *Black Comedy*. Appeared at Statford Theatre, Nottingham Playhouse, Bristol Old Vic, and Citizens Theatre.

MAJOR TOURS

Dead-Eyed Dicks, U.K. cities, 1976.

Menius Agrippa, *Coriolanus*, U.K. cities, 1979.

FILM APPEARANCES

Murchie, *Dead Man's Chest*, Allied Artists, 1965.

Prosecuting Counsel, Caretaker, *One Way Pendulum*, Lopert, 1965.

Counsel, *Morgan* (also known as *A Suitable Case for Treatment*), Cinema V, 1966.

Smythe, *The File of the Golden Goose*, United Artists (UA), 1969.

Max, *Leo the Last*, UA, 1970.

Medical Officer, *The Virgin Soldiers*, Columbia, 1970.

Mr. Bolton, *The Night Digger* (also known as *The Road Builder*), Metro-Goldwyn-Mayer (MGM), 1971.

Up the Chastity Belt, Associated London-International Company Productions, 1971.

Truscott, *The Ruling Class*, AVCO/Embassy, 1972.

Lay Preacher, *Something to Hide*, Atlantic Releasing, 1972.

Dr. Millar, Professor Stewart, Meths Drinker, *O Lucky Man,* Warner Bros., 1973.

Cardinal Barberini, *The Abdication,* Warner Bros., 1974.

Voice of the General, *The Little Prince* (animated), Paramount, 1974.

Dr. Smiles, *The Last Days of Man on Earth* (also known as *The Final Programme*), New World Pictures, 1975.

Fanatics Leader, *Jabberwocky,* Cinema V, 1977.

First Sea Lord, *For Your Eyes Only,* UA, 1981.

Millar, *Brittania Hospital,* Universal, 1982.

Reverend Fitzbanks, *The Missionary,* Columbia, 1982.

Sir Geoffrey Macklin, *Code Name: Emerald,* MGM/UA, 1985.

Old Priest, *The Company of Wolves,* Cannon, 1985.

Lord Belfield, *Out of Africa,* Universal, 1985.

Also appeared as Bishop of Cowley, *The Rise and Rise of Michael Rimmer,* 1970; Judge Hate, *Didn't You Kill My Brother?,* 1987; Mr. Graceful, *A Handful of Dust,* 1988.

TELEVISION APPEARANCES

Recruiting Officer, *The Snow Goose* (special), NBC, 1971.

Bishop, "Monsignor Quixote," *Great Performances* (episodic), PBS, 1987.

Herbert, *All Passion Spent* (special), 1989.

Waiting for Godot (special), BBC-1, 1990.*

*   *   *

CRUISE, Tom   1962-

PERSONAL: Born Thomas Cruise Mapother IV, July 3, 1962, in Syracuse, NY; son of Thomas Cruise III (an electrical engineer) and Mary Lee (a special education teacher) Mapother; married Mimi Rogers (an actress), May 9, 1987 (marriage ended); married Nicole Kidman (an actress), December 24, 1990. *Education:* Attended high school in Glen Ridge, NJ.

ADDRESSES: Agent—Paula Wagner, Creative Artists Agency, 9830 Wilshire Blvd., Beverly Hills, CA 90212.

CAREER: Actor.

AWARDS, HONORS: Academy Award nomination, Best Actor, Golden Globe Award, Best Actor—Drama, and Chicago Film Festival Critics Award, Best Actor, all 1989, all for *Born on the Fourth of July.*

CREDITS:

FILM APPEARANCES

(Film debut) Billy, *Endless Love,* Universal, 1981.

David Shawn, *Taps,* Twentieth Century-Fox, 1981.

Woody, *Losin' It,* Embassy, 1983.

Steve Randle, *The Outsiders,* Warner Bros., 1983.

Joel Goodson, *Risky Business,* Warner Bros., 1983.

Stef Djordjevic, *All the Right Moves,* Twentieth Century-Fox, 1983.

Jack, *Legend,* Twentieth Century-Fox/Universal, 1985.

Lieutenant Pete Mitchell, *Top Gun,* Paramount, 1986.

Vincent Lauria, *The Color of Money,* Buena Vista, 1986.

Brian Flanagan, *Cocktail,* Buena Vista, 1988.

Charlie Babbitt, *Rain Man,* Metro-Goldwyn-Mayer/United Artists, 1988.

Ron Kovic, *Born on the Fourth of July,* Universal, 1989.

Cole Trickle, *Days of Thunder,* Paramount, 1990.

STAGE APPEARANCES

Appeared in a dinner theater production of *Godspell.*

TELEVISION APPEARANCES; EPISODIC

Appeared on *Amazing Stories,* NBC.

OTHER SOURCES:

PERIODICALS

Cosmopolitan, January, 1984.

Maclean's, August 15, 1983; November 7, 1983.

Mademoiselle, April, 1985.

Moviegoer, December, 1985.

National Review, October 14, 1983.

New Republic, September 19, 1983.

Newsweek, August 15, 1983; November 7, 1983.

New Yorker, September 5, 1983.

Parade, January 8, 1989.

People, September 5, 1983; March 5, 1984.

Premiere, July, 1988.

Rolling Stone, January 11, 1990.

Seventeen, February, 1984; April, 1985.

Sports Illustrated, November 14, 1983.

Teen, November, 1982; December, 1983.

Time, December 14, 1981; April 4, 1983; November 7, 1983.*

*   *   *

CURTIS, Tony   1925-

PERSONAL: Born Bernard Schwartz, June 1, 1925, in New York, NY; son of Manuel Mond (an actor) and Helen (Klein) Schwartz; married Janet Leigh (an actress), June 4, 1951 (divorced, 1963); married Christine Kaufman (an actress), February 8, 1963 (divorced, 1967); married Leslie Allen, 1968 (divorced, 1981); children: (first marriage) Kelly Lee, Jamie Leigh; (second marriage) Alexandra, Allegra; (third marriage) Nicholas, Benjamin. *Education:* Attended Seward Park High School and City College of New York; studied acting at New York Dramatic Workshop and New School for Social Research.

CREDITS:

FILM APPEARANCES

Hot rod driver, *The One False Step,* Universal, 1949.

Kit Dalton, *Kansas Raiders,* Universal, 1950.

Julna, *The Prince Who Was a Thief,* Universal, 1951.

Paul Callan, *Flesh and Fury,* Universal, 1952.

Man in nightclub, *Meet Danny Wilson,* Universal, 1952.

Alvah Morrell, *No Room for the Groom,* Universal, 1952.

Kashma Baba, *Son of Ali Baba,* Universal, 1952.

Nick Bonelli, *The All-American* (released in England as *The Winning Way*), Universal, 1953.

Eddie, *Forbidden,* Universal, 1953.

Title role, *Houdini,* Paramount, 1953.

Burke, *Beachhead,* United Artists (UA), 1954.

Myles Falworth, *The Black Shield of Falworth,* Universal, 1954.

Title role, *Johnny Dark,* Universal, 1954.

Joe Maxwell, *So This Is Paris,* Universal, 1954.

Rene, *The Purple Mask,* Universal, 1955.

Jerry Florea, *Six Bridges to Cross,* Universal, 1955.

Eddie Quaid/Packy Glennon, *The Square Jungle,* Universal, 1955.

Ben Mathews, *The Rawhide Years,* Universal, 1956.

Tino Orsini, *Trapeze,* Susan/UA, 1956.

Joe Martini, *The Midnight Story* (released in England as *Appointment with a Shadow*), Universal, 1957.

Cory, *Mister Cory,* Universal, 1957.

Sidney Falco, *Sweet Smell of Success,* Norma-Curtleigh/UA, 1957.

John "Joker" Jackson, *The Defiant Ones,* UA, 1958.

Sergeant Britt Harris, *Kings Go Forth,* Frank Ross-Eton/UA, 1958.

Corporal Paul Hodges, *The Perfect Furlough* (released in England as *Strictly for Pleasure*), Universal, 1958.

Eric, *The Vikings,* Bryna/UA, 1958.

Lieutenant Nick Holden, *Operation Petticoat,* Granarte/Universal, 1959.

Joa/Josephine, *Some Like It Hot,* Ashton-Mirish/UA, 1959.

Ferdinand Waldo Demara, Jr., *The Great Imposter,* Universal, 1960.

Unbilled guest appearance, *Pepe,* Columbia, 1960.

Peter Hammond, Jr., *Rat Race,* Paramount, 1960.

Antonius, *Spartacus,* Bryna/Universal, 1960.

David Wilson, *Who Was That Lady?,* Ansark-Sidney/Columbia, 1960.

Steve McCluskey, *Forty Pounds of Trouble,* Universal, 1962.

Ira Hamilton Hayes, *The Outsider,* Universal, 1962.

Andre Bulba, *Taras Bulba,* Hecht-Curtleigh/UA, 1962.

Corporal Jackson Laibowitz, *Captain Newman, M.D.,* Universal, 1963.

Italian, *The List of Adrian Messenger,* Universal, 1963.

George Tracy, *Goodbye Charlie,* Twentieth Century-Fox, 1964.

Second Policeman, *Paris When It Sizzles,* Quine-Charleston/Paramount, 1964.

Bob Weston, *Sex and the Single Girl,* Warner Bros., 1964.

Terry Williams, *Wild and Wonderful,* Universal, 1964.

Bernard Lawrence, *Boeing Boeing,* Paramount, 1965.

The Great Leslie, *The Great Race,* Warner Bros., 1965.

Nick Johnson, *Arrivederci, Baby!,* Paramount, 1966.

Mr. Julian, *Chamber of Horrors,* Warner Bros., 1966.

Tom Ferris, *Not with My Wife, You Don't,* Fernwood-Reynard/Warner Bros., 1966.

Carlo Cofield, *Don't Make Waves,* Filmways-Reynard/Metro-Goldwyn-Mayer, 1967.

Guerrando, *The Chastity Belt* (also known as *On My Way to the Crusades I Met a Girl Who . . .*), Titanus/Warner Bros./Seven Arts, 1968.

Voice of Donald Baumgart, *Rosemary's Baby,* Paramount, 1968.

Albert De Salvo, *The Boston Strangler,* Twentieth Century-Fox, 1968.

Chester Schofield, *Those Daring Young Men in Their Jaunty Jalopies* (released in England as *Monte Carlo or Bust*), Dino De Laurentiis—Marianne-Basil Keys/Paramount, 1969.

Sergeant Shannon Gambroni, *Suppose They Gave a War and Nobody Came?* (also known as *War Games*), ABC/Cinerama, 1970.

Adam Dyer, *You Can't Win 'Em All,* Columbia, 1970.

Louis "Ledke" Buchalter, *Ledke,* AmeriEuro/Warner Bros., 1975.

Mondego, *Count of Monte Cristo,* ITC, 1976.

Rodriguez, *The Last Tycoon,* Paramount, 1976.

Marvin Lazar, *The Bad News Bears Go to Japan,* Paramount, 1978.

Harry Erskine, *The Manitou,* Weist-Simon/Avco Embassy, 1978.

Alexei Karansky, *Sexette,* Crown International, 1978.

Some Like It Cool (also known as *Casanova and Co.*), Neue Delta-Pan-Panther-COFCI-TV 13/Pro International, 1979.

Blackie, *Little Miss Marker,* Universal, 1980.

Marty N. Fenn, *The Mirror Crack'd,* EMI/Associated Film Distribution, 1980.

Frank Renzetti, *Title Shot,* Regenthall/Cinepax, 1982.

Dr. Clavius, *Brainwaves,* Motion Picture Marketing, 1983.

The Senator, *Insignificance,* Zenith-Recorded Picture Co./Island Alive, 1985.

Ernie Stoddard, *Balboa,* Production Associates/Entertainment Artists-Vestron Video, 1986.

Charles Foster, *The Last of Philip Banter,* Tesauro-Banter, 1986.

Hector, *Club Life,* Tiger Productions-Cineworld Entertainment/Troma Team, 1987.

Also appeared as Parsifal Katzenellenbogen, *Where Is Parsifal?,* Terrence Young.

TELEVISION APPEARANCES; MOVIES

Joey Jordan, *The Third Girl from the Left,* ABC, 1973.
McCoy, *The Big Ripoff,* NBC, 1975.
Modego, *The Count of Monte-Cristo,* NBC, 1975.
Randy Brent, *The Users,* ABC, 1978.
David O. Selznick, *Moviola: The Scarlett O'Hara War,* NBC, 1980.
Flanagan, *Inmates: A Love Story,* ABC, 1981.
Chester Masterson, *The Million Dollar Face,* NBC, 1981.
Joey De Leon, *Portrait of a Showgirl,* CBS, 1982.
Charles Cartwright, *Agatha Christie's "Murder in Three Acts,"* CBS, 1986.
Sam Giancana, *Mafia Princess,* ABC, 1986.

Also appeared as Archimedes Porter, *Tarzan in Manhattan,* 1989; appeared in *Harry's Back,* 1987.

TELEVISION APPEARANCES; SPECIALS

The Red Skelton Revue, CBS, 1954.
The Bob Hope Show, NBC, 1970.
Super Comedy Bowl 2, CBS, 1972.
Annie and the Hoods, ABC, 1974.
Gunther Gebel-Williams: The Lord of the Ring, CBS, 1977.
Playboy's 25th Anniversary Celebration, ABC, 1979.

Also appeared in *Magic with the Stars,* 1982; *Circus of the Stars,* 1983; *American Film Institute Salute to Billy Wilder,* 1986.

TELEVISION APPEARANCES; SERIES

Danny Wilde, *The Persuaders,* ABC, 1971-72.
Title role, *McCoy,* NBC, 1975-76.
Philip Roth, *Vega$,* ABC, 1978-81.

Also appeared in episodes of *Schlitz Playhouse of the Stars,* CBS, 1951-59. Appeared in *Good Company,* ABC, 1967; and "The Stone," *General Electric Theatre,* CBS.

WRITINGS:

Kid Andrew Cody and Julie Sparrow, Doubleday, 1977.*

*   *   *

CYPHER, Jon 1932-

PERSONAL: Born January 13, 1932, in Brooklyn, New York. *Education:* Received degree in romance languages from University of Vermont.

ADDRESSES: Agent—Harry Gold & Associates, 12725 Ventura Blvd., Suite C, Studio City, CA 91604.

CAREER: Actor.

CREDITS:

STAGE APPEARANCES

Dr. Carrasco, *Man of La Mancha,* ANTA Washington Square Theatre, New York City, 1965.
Bert Jefferson, *Sherry!,* Alvin Theatre, New York City, 1967.
District Attorney Klossowski, *The Great White Hope,* Alvin Theatre, 1968-69.
Papa, *Coco,* Mark Hellinger Theatre, New York City, 1969-70.
Edward Rutledge, *1776,* 46th Street Theatre, New York City, 1969.
Ray Schaeffer, *Prettybelle,* Shubert Theatre, Boston, MA, 1971.
Julian Marsh, *Forty-Second Street,* Shubert Theatre, 1984.

Also appeared on Broadway in *The Disenchanted,* 1958, *The Wives,* and *The Great Western Union;* appeared in *Jennie* and *Night of the Iguana.*

MAJOR TOURS

Thomas Jefferson, *1776,* U.S. cities, 1970.
Bill Sykes, *Oliver,* U.S. cities, 1973.
Juan Peron, *Evita,* U.S. cities, 1980.

FILM APPEARANCES

Alan, *Believe in Me,* Metro-Goldwyn-Mayer, 1971.
Frank Tanner, *Valdez is Coming,* United Artists, 1971.
Peterson, *Blade,* Pintoff, 1973.
Eddy Stell, *Lady Ice,* National General Pictures, 1973.
Brad, *Memory of Us,* Cinema Financial of America, 1974.
Brian, *Food of the Gods,* American International Pictures, 1976.
Johnny, *The Kingfish Caper* (also known as *The Kingfisher Caper*), Cinema Shares International, 1976.
Off the Mark (also known as *Crazy Legs),* Fries Entertainment, 1987.
Man-at-arms, *Masters of the Universe,* Cannon, 1987.
Dr. Marsh, *Spontaneous Combustion,* Taurus Entertainment, 1989.

Also appeared in *Accidents* (1989) and *Kid and the Killers.*

TELEVISION APPEARANCES; SERIES

Dr. Alex Keith, *As the World Turns,* CBS, 1977-79.
Police Chief Fletcher P. Daniels, *Hill Street Blues,* NBC, 1981-87.
Jeff Munson, *Knots Landing,* CBS, 1982-83.
General Marcus Craig, *Major Dad,* CBS, 1989.

Also appeared as John Green, *Duet,* 1988-89, and as Dr. Arthur Donnelly, *Santa Barbara,* NBC.

TELEVISION APPEARANCES; MOVIES

Colonel Imbert, *Evita Peron,* NBC, 1981.

Dr. Harry "Docky" Martin, *Malice in Wonderland,* CBS, 1985.

Dr. Peter Lattimore, *Perry Mason: The Case of the Notorious Nun,* NBC, 1986.

Captain Paul Beaulieu, *Elvis and Me,* ABC, 1988.

Mallory, *Lady Mobster,* ABC, 1988.

Reid Chapman, *Snow Kill,* USA, 1990.

Also appeared in *Favorite Son,* 1988, and as Renza, *High Rise,* 1990.

TELEVISION APPEARANCES; EPISODIC

Driscoll, *Our Five Daughters,* NBC, 1962.

Also appeared on *Dynasty, Hotel,* and *Murder, She Wrote.*

TELEVISION APPEARANCES; PILOTS

Dale Hannigan, *Night Games,* NBC, 1974.*

D

DAILY, Bill 1928-

PERSONAL: Born August 30, 1928, in Des Moines, IA; children: Kimberly, Patrick. *Education:* Attended Goodman Theater College, Chicago.

ADDRESSES: Agent—Tom Korman, Agency for the Performing Arts, 9000 Sunset Blvd., Suite 1200, Los Angeles, CA 90069.

CAREER: Actor, producer, director, and writer. Performed in nightclubs. *Military service:* Served in U.S. Army.

CREDITS:

FILM APPEARANCES

Navigator, *The Barefoot Executive,* Buena Vista, 1971.

TELEVISION APPEARANCES; SERIES

Captain (then Major) Roger Healey, *I Dream of Jeannie,* NBC, 1965-70.
Howard Borden, *The Bob Newhart Show,* CBS, 1972-78.
Curtis Shea, *Aloha Paradise,* ABC, 1981.
Dr. Henry Hanratty, *Small and Frye,* CBS, 1983.
James Shepherd, *Starting from Scratch,* syndicated, 1988.

Also appeared on *Club 60,* 1957 (also see below).

TELEVISION APPEARANCES; PILOTS

Walter Grainger, *Rendezvous Hotel,* CBS, 1979.
Charles, *Valentine Magic on Love Island,* NBC, 1980.
Gregg Elliott, *Alone at Last,* NBC, 1980.
Ron Hart, *Inside O.U.T.,* CBS, 1984.

TELEVISION APPEARANCES; EPISODIC

Pete Peterson, *The Mary Tyler Moore Show,* CBS, 1972.
Larry Dykstra, *ALF,* NBC, 1987-89.

Carl, *Hooperman,* ABC, 1988.
Sam Leary, *Newhart,* CBS, 1990.

Also appeared on *The Comedy Factory,* ABC, 1985.

TELEVISION APPEARANCES; MOVIES

Peter Garrity, *In Name Only,* ABC, 1969.
Jack Murphy, *Murder at the Mardi Gras,* CBS, 1978.
Captain Roger Healey, *I Dream of Jeannie . . . Fifteen Years Later,* NBC, 1985.

TELEVISION WORK

Also worked as staff director for NBC.

WRITINGS:

Writer for television program *Club 60,* 1957.*

*   *   *

DANA, Bill 1924-

PERSONAL: Born October 5, 1924, in Quincy, MA.

CAREER: Actor, writer, nightclub performer, and comedian.

CREDITS:

FILM APPEARANCES

Archie Brody, *The Busybody,* Paramount, 1967.
Jack Schacht, *The Harrad Summer,* Cinerama, 1974.
Jonathon Levinson Seigle, *The Nude Bomb* (also known as *The Return of Maxwell Smart*), Universal, 1980.
Jose Jimenez, *The Right Stuff,* Warner Bros., 1983.

TELEVISION APPEARANCES; SERIES

Jose Jimenez, *The Steve Allen Show,* NBC, 1956-59.
Jose Jimenez, *The Spike Jones Show,* CBS, 1960.
Jose Jimenez, *The New Steve Allen Show,* ABC, 1961.
Jose Jimenez, *The Bill Dana Show,* NBC, 1963-65.
Host, *The Las Vegas Show,* United Network, 1967.
Mr. Plitzky, *No Soap, Radio,* ABC, 1982.
Bernardo, *Zorro and Son,* CBS, 1983.

TELEVISION APPEARANCES; PILOTS

Melvin Kaplan, *Female Instinct,* NBC, 1972.
Sergeant Pete Agopian, *Rosetti and Ryan: Men Who Love Women,* NBC, 1977.

TELEVISION APPEARANCES; EPISODIC

Spotlight, CBS, 1967.
Showtime, CBS, 1968.
Jose Jimenez, *Steve Allen's Laugh-Back,* syndicated, 1976.

Also appeared as Jose Jimenez, *The Milton Berle Show, Make Room for Daddy* (also known as *The Danny Thomas Show*), *The Ed Sullivan Show, Too Close for Comfort, Facts of Life, Hollywood Palace, St. Elsewhere,* and *The Golden Girls;* appeared as Wendell Dalaban, *Too Close for Comfort;* appeared on the syndicated show *Comedy Break.*

TELEVISION APPEARANCES; MOVIES

Melvin Kaplan, *The Snoop Sisters,* NBC, 1972.
Ed Small, *A Guide for the Married Woman,* ABC, 1978.
Himself, *Murder in Texas,* NBC, 1981.

TELEVISION APPEARANCES; SPECIALS

Murder at NBC—A Bob Hope Special, NBC, 1966.
Shoot-in-Bob Hope Special, NBC, 1967.
A Look at the Light Side, NBC, 1969.
The Bob Hope Show, NBC, 1969.
Windows, Doors, and Keyholes, NBC, 1972.
Mitzi and a Hundred Guys, CBS, 1975.

Also appeared on *The Television Academy Hall of Fame,* 1986; *Comic Relief II,* 1987; *The Smothers Brothers Thanksgiving Special,* 1988; *The Smothers Brothers Comedy Special,* 1988; *The Smothers Brothers Thanksgiving Special,* 1988; *Smothers Brothers Comedy Hour . . . Fun 'n' Games,* 1989; *Smothers Brothers Comedy Hour . . . Ghosts, Governments and Other Scary Things,* 1989; *Smothers Brothers Comedy Hour . . . Lonesome Doves and Lonely Guys,* 1989; *Smothers Brothers Comedy Hour . . . The Dangerous Comedy Liaisons,* 1989; and *I've Had It Up To Here.*

TELEVISION PRODUCER

The Milton Berle Show (series), NBC, 1948-59, ABC, 1966-67.

The Spike Jones Show (series), CBS, 1960.
Don Knotts Nice Clean Decent Wholesome Hour (special), CBS, 1970.
Car Wash (pilot), NBC, 1979.

WRITINGS:

SCREENPLAYS

(With Arne Sultan and Leonard B. Stern) *The Nude Bomb* (also known as *The Return of Maxwell Smart*), Universal, 1980.

TELEVISION SERIES

(With others) *The Spike Jones Show,* CBS, 1960.
(With others) *The New Steve Allen Show,* NBC, 1961.
The Bill Dana Show, NBC, 1963-65.
(With Bob Hinkley, Bernie Kukoff, Jack Haniahan, and Howard Leeds) *The Las Vegas Show,* United Network, 1967.
(With David Panich, Gene Farmer, John Barbour, and George Schlatter) *Speak Up America,* NBC, 1980.

TELEVISION EPISODES

(With others) *The Milton Berle Show,* NBC, 1948-59, ABC, 1966-67.
All in the Family, CBS, 1972.
(With others) *Donny and Marie,* ABC, 1977.

TELEVISION SPECIALS

(With Al Wasserman) *A Look at the Light Side,* NBC, 1969.
(With Jerry Mayer and Don Knotts) *Don Knotts Nice Clean Decent Wholesome Hour,* CBS, 1970.
(With Arne Sultan, Earl Barrett, and Leonard B. Stern) *Windows, Doors, and Keyholes,* NBC, 1972.

Also writer for *The Smothers Brothers Comedy Special,* 1988; and *The Smothers Brothers Thanksgiving Special,* 1988.*

*   *   *

DANIELS, William   1927-

PERSONAL: Full name, William David Daniels; born March 31, 1927, in Brooklyn, NY; son of David (a builder) and Irene Daniels; married Bonnie Bartlett (an actress), June 30, 1951; children: Michael, Robert. *Education:* Attended Lodge Private Tutoring, New York City; Northwestern University, B.S.S., 1950; studied acting and directing with Lee Strasberg at Actors' Studio. *Avocational interests:* Chess.

ADDRESSES: Agent—c/o The Artists Agency, 10000 Santa Monica Blvd., Suite 305, Los Angeles, CA 90067.

CAREER: Actor. *Military service:* U.S. Army, 1945-47; became staff sergeant.

MEMBER: Actors' Equity Association, Screen Actors Guild, American Federation of Television and Radio Artists.

AWARDS, HONORS: Clarence Derwent Award and *Village Voice* Obie Award, distinguished performance, 1959-60, for *The Zoo Story;* Argentina Drama Critics Award, best performance, 1962, for *The Zoo Story;* Emmy Award, outstanding lead actor in a drama series, 1986, for *St. Elsewhere.*

CREDITS:

STAGE APPEARANCES

(Debut) John and Clarence, *Life with Father,* Empire Theatre, New York City, 1939.

Richard the Second, City Center Theatre, New York City, 1951.

Sub Lieutenant Granger, R.N., *Seagulls over Sorento,* John Golden Theatre, New York City, 1952.

The Man Who Corrupted Hadleyburg, Forest Theatre, Philadelphia, PA, 1953.

The Man Who Had All the Luck, John Drew Theatre, East Hampton, NY, 1954.

Ladies in Retirement, John Drew Theatre, 1954.

Don Parritt, *The Iceman Cometh,* Circle in the Square, New York City, 1956.

Jimmy Porter, *Look Back in Anger,* 41st Street Theatre, New York City, 1958.

Cooper, *The Legend of Lizzie,* 54th Street Theatre, New York City, 1959.

Peter, *The Zoo Story* (also see below), Provincetown Playhouse, New York City, 1960.

Albert Amundsen, *A Thousand Clowns,* Eugene O'Neill Theatre, New York City, 1962.

Dr. Evans, *Dear Me, the Sky Is Falling,* Music Box Theatre, New York City, 1963.

Dale Harding, *One Flew over the Cuckoo's Nest,* Cort Theatre, New York City, 1963.

Warren Smith, *On a Clear Day, You Can See Forever,* Mark Hellinger Theatre, New York City, 1965.

Joseph, *Daphne in Cottage D,* Longacre Theatre, New York City, 1967.

John Adams, *1776,* 46th Street Theatre, New York City, 1969.

Fredrik Egerman, *A Little Night Music,* Shubert Theatre, New York City, 1973.

Also performer with "The Daniels Family," New York, NY, during 1930s.

MAJOR TOURS

Brick, *Cat on a Hot Tin Roof,* U.S. cities, 1957-58.

Also toured in *The Zoo Story, I Am a Camera,* and *Suddenly Last Summer,* South America, 1961.

STAGE WORK

Assistant director, *Oh Dad, Poor Dad, Mama's Hung You in the Closet and I'm Feelin' So Sad,* Phoenix Theatre, New York City, 1962.

FILM APPEARANCES

Mr. Clakins, *Ladybug, Ladybug,* Francis/United Artists, 1963.

Albert, *A Thousand Clowns,* United Artists, 1965.

Mr. Braddock, *The Graduate,* Lawrence Turman/ Embassy Pictures, 1967.

Wynn Quantrill, *The President's Analyst,* Panpiper/ Paramount, 1967.

Howard Manchester, *Two for the Road,* Twentieth Century-Fox, 1967.

Mr. Crowell, *Marlowe,* Metro-Goldwyn-Mayer, 1969.

John Adams, *1776,* Columbia, 1972.

Austin Tucker, *The Parallax View,* Paramount, 1974.

Pugh, *Black Sunday,* Paramount, 1977.

George Summers, *Oh God!,* Warner Brothers, 1977.

Mr. Crawford, *The One and Only,* First Artists/ Paramount, 1978.

Crawford, *Sunburn,* Tuesday/Paramount, 1979.

Arthur LeStrange, *The Blue Lagoon,* Columbia, 1980.

Julius Gerber, *Reds,* Paramount, 1981.

Judge Harold Bedford, *Blind Date,* Tri-Star, 1987.

Sam, *Her Alibi,* Warner Brothers, 1989.

TELEVISION APPEARANCES; SERIES

Carter Nash (Captain Nice), *Captain Nice,* NBC, 1967.

John Quincy Adams, *The Adams Chronicles,* PBS, 1976.

Lieutenant Commander Kenneth Kitteridge, *The Nancy Walker Show,* ABC, 1976-77.

District Attorney Walter W. Cruikshank, *Freebie and the Bean,* CBS, 1980-81.

Dr. Mark Craig, *St. Elsewhere,* NBC, 1982-88.

Voice of KITT (the car), *Knight Rider,* NBC, 1982-86.

TELEVISION APPEARANCES; EPISODIC

The Somerset Maugham Theatre, ABC, 1952.

Profiles in Courage, NBC, 1965.

Sebastian Parnell, the Celestial Messenger, "Heaven on Earth", *Comedy Theatre,* NBC, 1979.

Ted Benjamin, *Private Benjamin,* CBS, 1981-83.

Also appeared on *Deja View,* 1985; *The Nurses,* CBS; *East Side/West Side,* CBS; *The Defenders,* CBS; *For the People,* CBS; and *Naked City,* ABC.

TELEVISION APPEARANCES; MINI-SERIES

Samuel Adams, *The Bastard/Kent Family Chronicles,* ABC, 1978.

G. Gordon Liddy, *Blind Ambition,* CBS, 1979.
John Adams, *The Rebels,* ABC, 1979.

TELEVISION APPEARANCES; PILOTS

Roger Bates, *Murdock's Gang,* CBS, 1973.
Elliot Borden, *The Fabulous Dr. Fable,* ABC, 1973.
Dr. Morseby, *One of Our Own,* NBC, 1975.
Lawrence Stepwell III, *Big Bob Johnson and His Fantastic Speed Circus,* NBC, 1978.
C. Donald Devlin, *Boston and Kilbride,* CBS, 1979.
Frederick Carswell, *The Wonderful World of Philip Malley,* CBS, 1981.
Warren Berlinger, *Nuts and Bolts,* ABC, 1981.
Dr. DeVega, *Rooster,* ABC, 1982.
Dr. Mark Craig, *St. Elsewhere,* NBC, 1982.
Voice of KITT, *All That Glitters,* NBC, 1984.

TELEVISION APPEARANCES; MOVIES

Leonard Alexander, *A Case of Rape,* NBC, 1974.
Matt Hodges, *Sarah T.—Portrait of a Teenage Alcoholic,* NBC, 1975.
Bissell, *Francis Gary Powers: The True Story of the U-2 Spy Incident,* NBC, 1976.
Marshall Snowden, *Killer on Board,* NBC, 1977.
Dr. Bonifant, *The Return of the Incredible Hulk,* CBS, 1977.
Father Veller, *Sergeant Matlovich vs. The U.S. Air Force,* NBC, 1978.
Freeman Stribling, *City in Fear,* ABC, 1980.
Bishop Koeckmann, *Damien: The Leper Priest,* NBC, 1980.
Henry Burns, *The Million Dollar Face,* NBC, 1981.
Walter Lamb, *Rehearsal for Murder,* CBS, 1982.
Draper Wright, *Drop-Out Father,* CBS, 1982.
Mr. Haywood Dutton, *The Little Match Girl,* NBC, 1987.

Also appeared as Clifford Beane, *Instant Family,* 1977; Frederick Carswell, *The Wonderful World of Philip Malley,* 1981; Richard H. Copleston, *All Night Long,* 1981; narrator, *The Princess Who Never Laughed,* 1986; and David Slaney, *Howard Beach: Making the Case for Murder,* 1989.

OTHER TELEVISION APPEARANCES

That Was the Year that Was (special), NBC, 1976.
Major Reno, *The Court-Martial of George Armstrong Custer* (special), NBC, 1977.
Detective Lieutenant Fine, *Clara* (play), A & E, 1991.

Also appeared on the special *The Night of 100 Stars,* 1985.*

DaRE, Aldo
See Ray, Aldo

*   *   *

DAVI, Robert

PERSONAL: Born in Brooklyn, NY; married Jeri McBride (separated); children: Sean Christen. *Education:* Studied acting at the Actors Studio and with Stella Adler. *Avocational interests:* Boxing.

ADDRESSES: Agent—c/o Steve Tellez, Agency for the Performing Arts, 9000 Sunset Blvd., Suite 1200, Los Angeles, CA 90069.

CAREER: Actor and opera singer.

CREDITS:

STAGE APPEARANCES

Benny, *Broadway,* Wilbur Theatre, Boston, MA, 1978.

Also performed with Lyric Opera Company in Long Island, NY.

FILM APPEARANCES

Nino, *City Heat,* Warner Brothers, 1984.
Jake, *The Goonies,* Warner Brothers, 1985.
Max, *Raw Deal,* De Laurentiis Entertainment Group, 1986.
Chopper, biker, *Wild Thing,* Atlantic Releasing, 1987.
Aldo Palucci, mob boss, *Traxx,* De Laurentiis Entertainment Group, 1988.
Big Johnson, *Die Hard,* Twentieth Century-Fox, 1988.
Tony Moretti, *Action Jackson,* Lorimar, 1988.
Franz Sanchez, *License to Kill,* United Artists, 1989.
Maniac Cop 2, Shapiro Glikenhaus, 1990.

Also appeared in *1984.*

TELEVISION APPEARANCES; MOVIES

Mickey Sinardos, *Contract on Cherry Street,* NBC, 1977.
Dickie, *And Your Name Is Jonah,* CBS, 1979.
First resident, *Rage,* NBC, 1980.
Bobby Jim, *The $5.20 an Hour Dream,* CBS, 1980.
Hubbard, *Alcatraz: The Whole Shocking Story,* NBC, 1980.
White Hot: The Mysterious Murder of Thelma Todd, NBC, 1991.

Also appeared as Salim Ajami, *Terrorist on Trial: The United States v. Salim Ajami,* 1988; Detective Jack "Harley" Kessler, *Deceptions,* 1990; and Sergeant Frank Ramos, *Peacemaker,* 1990.

OTHER TELEVISION APPEARANCES

Guard, *From Here To Eternity* (mini-series), NBC, 1979.

William Quantrill, *The Legend of the Golden Gun* (pilot), NBC, 1979.

Lieutenant Elbone, *Nick and the Dobermans* (pilot), NBC, 1980.

Vito Genovese, *The Gangster Chronicles* (series), NBC, 1981.

Albert Cerrico, *Wiseguy* (episodic), CBS, 1987 and 1990.

Also appeared on *Hill Street Blues.*

OTHER SOURCES:

PERIODICALS

Starlog, November, 1989.
US, August 21, 1989.*

* * *

DAVIES, Howard   1945(?)-

PERSONAL: Born c. 1945 in Durham, England; father, a miner. *Education:* Studied drama at Bristol University.

CAREER: Stage director. Birmingham Repertory Company, Birmingham, England, assistant stage manager, 1968; Bristol Old Vic Company, Bristol, England, associate director, 1972-74; The Warehouse, London, England, artistic director, beginning in 1977; associate director and dramaturg, Royal Shakespeare Company, beginning in 1977.

AWARDS, HONORS: Drama Desk Award, Outstanding Director, and Antoinette Perry Award nomination, Best Director, both 1987, for *Les Liaisons Dangereuses.*

CREDITS:

STAGE DIRECTOR, EXCEPT WHERE NOTED

Narrow Road to the Deep North, Bristol Old Vic Company, Bristol, England, c. 1972-74.
Troilus and Cressida, Bristol Old Vic Company, c. 1972-74.
Long Day's Journey into Night, Bristol Old Vic Company, c. 1972-74.
Endgame, Early Morning, Bristol Old Vic Company, c. 1972-74.
Fears and Miseries of the Third Reich, Bristol Old Vic Company, c. 1972-74.
Woyzek, Bristol Old Vic Company, c. 1972-74.
Afore Night Come, Bristol Old Vic Company, c. 1972-74.
Spring Awakening, Bristol Old Vic Company, c. 1972-74.
The Beast, Royal Shakespeare Company (RSC), The Place, London, 1974.
The Caucasian Chalk Circle, Birmingham Repertory Company, Birmingham, England, 1974.
Struggles against the Iron Heel, Birmingham Repertory Company, 1974.

Assistant director, *Summerfolk,* RSC, Aldwych Theatre, London, 1974, then Brooklyn Academy of Music, Brooklyn, NY, 1975.
Man Is Man, RSC, Round House Theatre Downstairs, London, 1976.
The Iceman Cometh, RSC, Aldwych Theatre, 1976.
Schweyk in the Second World War, RSC, The Other Place, Stratford-on-Avon, England, 1976, then The Warehouse, London, 1977.
Bingo, RSC, The Other Place, 1976, then The Warehouse, 1977.
The Days of the Commune, RSC, Aldwych Theatre, 1977.
Bandits, RSC, The Warehouse, 1977.
The Bundle, RSC, The Warehouse, 1977.
(With John Caird) *The Adventures of Awful Knawful,* RSC, The Warehouse, 1978.
The Jail Diary of Albie Sachs, RSC, The Warehouse, 1978, then The Other Place, 1979.
Piaf, RSC, The Other Place, 1978, then The Warehouse, later Aldwych Theatre, both 1979.
The Innocent, RSC, The Warehouse, 1979.
No Limits to Love, RSC, The Warehouse, 1980.
Outskirts, RSC, The Warehouse, 1981.
The Fool, RSC, The Warehouse, 1981.
Piaf, Plymouth Theatre, New York City, 1981.
Good, RSC, The Warehouse, 1981, then Booth Theatre, New York City, 1982.
Henry VIII, RSC, Barbican Theatre, London, 1984.
Mother Courage, RSC, Barbican Theatre, 1984.
Soft Cons, RSC, The Pit, London, 1984.
The Time of Your Life, RSC, The Pit, 1984.
Troilus and Cressida, RSC, Royal Shakespeare Theatre, Stratford-on-Avon, 1985.
The Party, RSC, The Pit, 1985.
Les Liaisons Dangereuses, RSC, The Other Place, 1985, The Pit, 1986, Ambassadors Theatre, London, 1986, then Music Box Theatre, New York City, 1987.
Flight, RSC, The Other Place, 1986.
The Shaughraun, Olivier Theatre, London, 1988.
Cat on a Hot Tin Roof, National Theatre, London, 1988.
The Secret Rapture, Lyttelton Theatre, London, 1988.
The Crucible, National Theatre, then Olivier Theatre, 1990.

MAJOR TOURS

Directed *Much Ado about Nothing,* Royal Shakespeare Company, British cities.

TELEVISION WORK

Stage director, *Piaf* (special), 1982.

OTHER SOURCES:

PERIODICALS

Times (London), July 28, 1977.*

DAVIS, Carl   1936-

PERSONAL: Born October 28, 1936, in New York, NY; son of Isadore and Sara (Perlmutter) Davis; married Jean Boht (an actress), December 28, 1970 (one source says 1971); children: two daughters. *Education:* Attended Queen's College, New England Conservatory, Tanglewood Music Festival, and Bard College; received B.A. *Avocational interests:* Cooking, gardening and collecting graphics.

ADDRESSES: Office—Eaton Music, 8 West Eaton Place, London SW1X 8LS, England; c/o Paul Wing, 35 Priory Road, London N8, England.

CAREER: Composer. Robert Shaw Chorale, pianist, 1955-56; repetiteur for Santa Fe Opera, Santa Fe, NM, 1958, and New York City Opera, New York City, 1958-59; Sundergrade Music (publishing company), founder with Terry Oates, 1979; Bournemouth Pops, Bournemouth, England, conductor, 1984—; London Philharmonic Orchestra, conductor, 1987—.

AWARDS, HONORS: British Academy of Film and Television Arts Awards for original television music, 1980, for *Merchant of Venice, Fair Stood the Wind for France, Oppenheimer, Hollywood, The Misanthrope, The Sailor's Return,* and *The Old Curiosity Shop,* and for film score, 1981, for *The French Lieutenant's Woman;* Chevalier de l'Ordre des Arts et des Lettres, 1983.

CREDITS:

FILM APPEARANCES

Praise Marx and Pass the Ammunition, Mithras, 1970.

Also appeared in *Killer of Sheep,* 1977.

FILM WORK

Production assistant, *The Secret Policeman's Other Ball,* Miramax, 1981.
Music director, *Champions,* Embassy, 1983.
Music director, *King David,* Paramount, 1985.
Music conductor, *The Rainbow,* Vestron, 1989.

Also researcher, *The Late Great Planet Earth,* 1978.

TELEVISION APPEARANCES

Passion and Paradise, ABC, 1989.

TELEVISION WORK

Music director, *The Birth of the Beatles* (movie), ABC, 1979.
Music arranger, *Unknown Chaplin* (special), PBS, 1986.

Also music conductor, *Our Mutual Friend,* 1978; music director, *The American Film Institute Salute to Lillian Gish,* 1984.

RECORDINGS:

Composer for albums *The World at War,* Decca; *The Prince Regent,* Decca; *Champions; The Far Pavilions; Fire and Ice; The Silents.*

WRITINGS:

COMPOSER, EXCEPT WHERE NOTED; STAGE

Diversions (revue), produced in New York City, 1958.
Twists, produced in London, 1962.
The Merchant of Venice, produced at National Theatre, London, 1970.
Much Ado about Nothing, produced by Royal Shakespeare Company (RSC), 1971.
King Lear, produced in London, 1971.
Pericles, produced in London, 1973.
The Marriage of Figaro, produced at National Theatre, 1974.
A Month in the Country, produced at Chichester Theatre Festival, Chichester, England, 1974, produced in the West End, 1974.
Pilgrim, produced in Cranford, U.K., 1975.
Summerfolk, produced in Brooklyn, NY, 1975.
The Zykovs, produced by RSC, 1976.
Ivanov, produced by RSC, 1976.
The Devil's Disciple, produced by RSC, 1976.
Saint Joan, produced at Old Vic Theatre, 1977.
Saratoga, produced by RSC, 1978.
Antonio, produced in Nottingham, England, 1979.
The Relapse, produced at Old Vic Theatre, 1981.
Dances of Love and Death (ballet), produced in Edinburgh, Scotland, 1981.
(Also creator with Barry Humphries) *Last Night of the Poms—An Educational Sonorama with Music* (ballet), produced in London, 1981.
Pericles, produced in New York City, 1983.
The Tempest, produced at Old Vic Theatre, 1988.
(With Paul McCartney) *Liverpool Oratorio,* produced at Liverpool Cathedral, Liverpool, England, 1991.

Also composer for *Forty Years On,* 1969; *The Tempest,* 1970; *Council of Love,* 1970; *The Projector,* 1971; *Fire and Ice* (ballet), 1986; *The Portrait of Dorian Gray* (ballet), 1987; *A Simple Man* (ballet), 1987; *The Vaccies.*

COMPOSER; FILM

The Bofors Gun, Universal, 1968.
The Only Way, UMC, 1970.
Praise Marx and Pass the Ammunition, Mithras, 1970.
Up the Chastity Belt, Associated London/International Co-Productions, 1971.
The Lovers, British Lion, 1972.
Rentadick, Virgin, 1972.
(With George Howe) *What Became of Jack and Jill?* (also known as *Romeo and Juliet 1971—A Gentle Tale of*

Sex, Violence, Corruption, and Murder), Twentieth Century-Fox, 1972.

The National Health, or Nurse Norton's Affair, Columbia, 1973.

Man Friday, AVCO-Embassy, 1975.

What's Next?, Children's Film Foundation/Rank, 1975.

The Sailor's Return, Osprey, 1978.

The French Lieutenant's Woman, United Artists, 1981.

Praying Mantis, Channel Four, 1982.

The Weather in the Streets, Rediffusion/BBC-TV/Britannia TV, 1983.

Champions, Embassy, 1984.

George Stevens: A Filmmaker's Journey, Castle Hill, 1985.

King David, Paramount, 1985.

Crime of Honor, Academy Home Entertainment, 1987.

The Girl in a Swing, J & M, 1988.

The Rainbow, Vestron, 1989.

Scandal, Miramax, 1989.

Also composer for *The Aerodrome,* 1983; *The Song for Europe,* 1985; *Skulduggery,* 1989. Composer of new scores for silent films *Napoleon,* 1980; *Lines on London,* 1980; *The Crowd,* 1981; *Flesh and the Devil,* 1982; *Show People,* 1982; *Broken Blossoms,* 1983; *The Wind,* 1983; *The Thief of Bagdad,* 1984; *The Big Parade,* 1985; *Greed,* 1985; *The General,* 1987; *Ben Hur,* 1987; *Intolerance.*

COMPOSER; TELEVISION MINI-SERIES

The World at War, Thames, 1972.

The Mayor of Casterbridge, BBC, then *Masterpiece Theatre,* PBS, 1978.

Our Mutual Friend, BBC, then *Masterpiece Theatre,* PBS, 1978.

Hollywood, Thames, 1980.

Oppenheimer, PBS, 1982.

"The Tales of Beatrix Potter," *Masterpiece Theatre,* PBS, 1984.

Pride of Place: Building the American Dream, PBS, 1986.

COMPOSER; TELEVISION MOVIES

The Birth of the Beatles, ABC, 1979.

The Far Pavilions, HBO, 1984.

Sakharov, HBO, 1984.

Spymaker: The Secret Life of Ian Fleming, TNT, 1990.

Also composer for *Catholics,* 1973; *Murrow,* 1986.

COMPOSER; TELEVISION SPECIALS

The Snow Goose, NBC, 1971.

Big Henry and the Polka Dot Kid, NBC, 1976.

Unknown Chaplin, PBS, 1986.

Buster Keaton: A Hard Act to Follow, PBS, 1987.

Once in a Lifetime, BBC, then *Great Performances,* PBS, 1988.

Harold Lloyd: The Third Genius, PBS, 1989.

Also composer for *Staying On,* 1981; *Silas Marner,* 1987; *Paul Gauguin: The Savage Dream,* 1989.

OTHER

Also composer for *The Naked Civil Servant,* 1975; *Marie Curie,* 1977; *The Commanding Sea,* 1981; *The Pickwick Papers,* 1985; *Oscar,* 1985; *The Day the Universe Changed,* 1985; *Late Starter,* 1985; *Hotel du Lac,* 1986; *See It Now,* 1986; *Treasure Island; The Merchant of Venice; Fair Stood the Wind for France; The Misanthrope; The Old Curiosity Shop.* Composer for television series *That Was the Week That Was; The First Eden.*

OTHER SOURCES:

PERIODICALS

Soundtrack, December, 1987.*

*   *   *

DAVIS, Jeff 1950-

PERSONAL: Born April 14, 1950, in Philadelphia, PA; son of John Wallace (a surgeon) and Gail (Gardner) Davis. *Education:* Northwestern University, B.A., 1972.

CAREER: Lighting and scenic designer. Light design for industrial films for Johnson & Johnson Co., Care Bears, and Strawberry Shortcake; associate designer to Jo Mielziner; lighting assistant to Tharon Musser, Ken Billington, Richard Nelson, and John McLain. Actor at New Jersey Shakespeare Festival, Madison, NJ, 1987-88.

MEMBER: United Scenic Artists, Local 829.

CREDITS:

STAGE LIGHTING DESIGNER, EXCEPT AS NOTED

Ride the Winds, Bijou Theatre, New York City, 1974.

(Also scenic designer) *Death of a Salesman,* Walnut Street Theatre, Philadelphia, PA, 1974.

Fire!, All Angels Church, Lab Theatre, New York City, 1974.

Agnes and Joan, All Angels Church, Lab Theatre, 1975.

I Paid My Dues, Astor Place Theatre, New York City, 1976.

The Man Who Came to Dinner, Circle in the Square, New York City, 1980.

Chase a Rainbow, Theatre Four, New York City, 1980.

Album, Cherry Lane Theatre, New York City, 1980.

The Slab Boys, Hudson Guild Theatre, New York City, 1980.

Judgement, Theatre at St. Peter's Church, New York City, 1980.

Hoagy, Bix, and Wolfgang Beethoven Bunkhaus, Indiana Repertory Theatre, Indianapolis, IN, 1981.

Head over Heels, Harold Clurman Theatre, New York City, 1981.

Baseball Wives, American Renaissance Theatre, New York City, 1982.

The Me Nobody Knows, South Street Theatre, New York City, 1984.

Love Letter on Blue Paper, Hudson Guild Theatre, 1984.

Miss Liberty, Goodspeed Opera House, East Haddam, CT, 1984.

Carla's Song, Perry Street Theatre, New York City, 1984.

Candida, Stagewest, West Springfield, MA, 1984.

Godspell, Ford's Theatre, Washington, DC, 1985.

Anything Goes, Studio Arena Theatre, Buffalo, NY, 1985.

The Torch-Bearers, Hartman Theatre, Stamford, CT, 1985.

Romance Language, Playwrights Horizons, New York City, 1985.

Cliffhanger, Lamb's Theatre, New York City, 1985.

Fallen Angels, Hartman Theatre, 1986.

The Musical Comedy Murders, Longacre Theatre, New York City, 1987.

I Never Sang for My Father, John F. Kennedy Center for the Performing Arts, Washington, DC, 1987-88.

Two into One, Paper Mill Playhouse, Milburn, NJ, 1987-88.

Division Street, Philadelphia Drama Guild, Philadelphia, 1987-88.

I Never Sang for My Father, Center Theatre Group, Ahmanson Theatre, Los Angeles, 1987-88.

Born Yesterday, Morris A. Mechanic Theatre, Baltimore, MD, then Forty-sixth Street Theatre, New York City, 1988.

Also worked in lighting at Syracuse Stage, 1974-75, Huntington Theatre Company, Boston, MA, 1983-84, Portland Stage Company, Portland, ME, 1985-86, American Shakespeare Festival, Stratford, CT, Cincinnati Playhouse, Cincinnati, OH, and Berkshire Theatre Festival, Stockbridge, MA; associate designer for *Blues in the Night,* Rialto Theatre, New York City, *Fiddler on the Roof,* New York State Theatre, New York City, and *Oh Brother!,* ANTA Theatre, New York City; lighting designer for *Becoming Memories,* South Street Theatre, *Portrait of Jennie,* Henry Street Settlement, New York City, *Dancin' in the Streets,* Ford's Theatre, Jose Limon Dance Company, Annabelle Gamson, and for U.S. tours of *Fiddler on the Roof, Morning's at Seven,* and *The River Niger* (and lighting supervisor); lighting supervisor for *Annie,* Shubert Theatre, and *The Oldest Living Graduate,* Wilshire Theatre, both Los Angeles.*

DAVIS, Ossie   1917-

PERSONAL: Born December 18, 1917, in Cogdell, GA; son of Kince Charles (a railway construction engineer) and Laura (Cooper) Davis; married Ruby Ann Wallace (an actress and writer under name Ruby Dee), December 9, 1948; children: Nora, Guy, LaVerne. *Education:* Attended Howard University, 1935-38, and Columbia University, 1948; trained for the stage with Paul Mann and Lloyd Richards.

ADDRESSES: Office—Emmalyn II Productions, P.O. Box 1318, New Rochelle, NY 10802. *Agent*—Artists Agency, 10000 Santa Monica Blvd, Suite 305, Los Angeles, CA 90067. *Manager*—Marian Searchinger Associates Inc., 327 Central Park W., New York, NY 10025.

CAREER: Actor, playwright, and director. Worked as janitor, shipping clerk, and stock clerk in New York City, 1938-41; began acting career with Rose McClendon Players; chairman of the board for Institute for New Cinema Artists; founder with wife, Ruby Dee, of Emmalyn II Productions. *Military service:* U.S. Army, Medical Corps and Special Services, 1942-45.

MEMBER: Actors' Equity Association, Screen Actors Guild, American Federation of Radio and Television Artists, Director's Guild of America, National Association for the Advancement of Colored People (advisory board), Southern Christian Leadership Conference (advisory board), Congress of Racial Equality, Masons.

AWARDS, HONORS: First Mississippi Freedom Democratic Party Citation, 1965; Emmy Award nomination, best actor in a special, 1969, for "Teacher, Teacher," *Hallmark Hall of Fame,* and nomination, c. 1978, for *King;* Antoinette Perry Award nomination, best musical, 1970, for *Purlie;* Frederick Douglass Award from New York Urban League, for "distinguished leadership toward equal opportunity," 1970; Paul Robeson Citation from Actor's Equity Association, 1975, for "outstanding creative contributions in the performing arts and in society at large"; Coretta Scott King Book Award from American Library Association and Jane Addams Children's Book Award from Jane Addams Peace Association, both 1979, for *Escape to Freedom;* Jury Award from Neil Simon Awards, 1983, for "For Us the Living," *American Playhouse;* National Association for the Advancement of Colored People, Image Award for best performance by a supporting actor for *Do the Right Thing* and Hall of Fame Award for outstanding artistic achievement, both 1989.

CREDITS:

STAGE APPEARANCES

Joy Exceeding Glory, Rose McClendon Players, Harlem, NY, 1941.

(Broadway debut) Jeb Turner, *Jeb,* Martin Beck Theatre, 1946.

Rudolph, *Anna Lucasta,* American Negro Theatre Playhouse, New York City, 1948.

Trem, *The Leading Lady,* National Theatre, New York City, 1948.

John Hay, *The Washington Years,* National Theatre, 1948.

Stewart, *The Smile of the World,* Lyceum Theatre, New York City, 1949.

Lonnie Thompson, *Stevedore,* Equity Library Theatre, New York City, 1949.

Jacques, *The Wisteria Trees,* Martin Beck Theatre, 1950.

Jo, *The Royal Family,* City Center Theatre, New York City, 1951.

Gabriel, *The Green Pastures,* Broadway Theatre, New York City, 1951.

Al, *Remains to Be Seen,* Morosco Theatre, New York City, 1951.

Dr. Joseph Clay, *Touchstone,* Music Box Theatre, New York City, 1953.

A lieutenant, *No Time for Sergeants,* Alvin Theatre, New York City, 1955.

Jacques, *The Wisteria Trees,* City Center Theatre, 1955.
Cicero, *Jamaica,* Imperial Theatre, New York City, 1957.
Walter Lee Younger, *A Raisin in the Sun,* Ethel Barrymore Theatre, New York City, 1959.

Title role, *Purlie Victorious,* Cort Theatre, New York City, 1961.

Sir Radio, *Ballad for Bimshire,* Mayfair Theatre, New York City, 1963.

The Talking Skull, White Barn Theatre, Westport, CT, 1965.

Johannes, *The Zulu and the Zayda,* Cort Theatre, 1965.

Take It from the Top, New Federal Theatre, New York City, 1979.

Midge, *I'm Not Rappaport,* Booth Theatre, New York City, 1986.

Also appeared in *Zora Is My Name!,* Howard University, Washington, DC, and *Ain't Supposed to Die a Natural Death,* New York City.

MAJOR TOURS

Rudolf, *Anna Lucasta,* U.S. cities, 1947.
Walter Lee Younger, *A Raisin in the Sun,* U.S. cities, 1959.
A Treasury of Negro World Writing, U.S. cities, 1964.

STAGE WORK

Stage manager, *The World of Sholom Aleichem,* City Center Theatre, 1955.
Producer (with Bernard Waltzer and Page Productions), *Ballad for Bimshire,* Mayfair Theatre, 1963.
Director, *The Talking Skull,* White Barn Theatre, 1965.

Director, *Bingo,* AMAS Repertory Theatre, New York City, 1985.

Also director of *Goldbrickers of 1944,* Liberia, 1944, and *Take It from the Top,* 1979.

FILM APPEARANCES

(Film debut) John, *No Way Out,* Twentieth Century-Fox, 1950.
Cab driver, *Fourteen Hours,* Twentieth Century-Fox, 1951.
The Joe Louis Story, United Artists (UA), 1953.
Reverend Purlie, *Gone Are the Days* (also known as *The Man from C.O.T.T.O.N.* and *Purlie Victorious*), Hammer Bros., 1963.
Father Gillis, *The Cardinal,* Columbia, 1963.
Capshaw, *Shock Treatment,* Arcola/Fox, 1964.
Jacko King, *The Hill,* Seven Arts/Metro-Goldwyn-Mayer, 1965.
Nelson Davis, *A Man Called Adam,* Trace-Mark/Embassy Pictures Corporation, 1966.
Joseph Winfield Lee, *The Scalphunters,* Bristol-Norlan/UA, 1968.
Jedidiah Hooker, *Sam Whiskey,* Brighton Pictures/UA, 1969.
Luke, *Slaves,* Theatre Guild-Walter Reade/Continental, 1969.
Eulogist, *Malcolm X,* Warner Bros., 1972.
Elder Johnson, *Let's Do It Again,* First Artists/Warner Bros., 1975.
Ernest Motapo, *Countdown at Kusini,* Columbia, 1976.
Captain Geibarger, *Hot Stuff,* Rastar-Mort Engelberg/Columbia, 1979.
Raymond, *Harry and Son,* Orion, 1984.
Dr. Sanders, *The House of God,* UA, 1984.
Captain Moradian, *Avenging Angel,* Republic Entertainment International/New World, 1985.
Coach Odom, *School Daze,* Columbia, 1988.
Da Mayor, *Do the Right Thing,* Universal, 1989.
Reverend Purify, *Jungle Fever,* Universal, 1991.

Also appeared in *Nothing Personal,* 1979; as himself, *Making of "Do the Right Thing,"* 1989; Marshall, *Joe Versus the Volcano,* 1990; and *Love Supreme.*

FILM WORK; DIRECTOR

Cotton Comes to Harlem, UA, 1970.
Kongi's Harvest, Calpenny Films Nigeria, 1971.
Black Girl, Cinerama, 1972.
Gordon's War, Twentieth Century-Fox, 1973.
(And producer) *Countdown at Kusini,* Columbia, 1976.

TELEVISION APPEARANCES; MOVIES

James Lucas, *The Sheriff,* ABC, 1971.
Narrator, *Freedom Road,* NBC, 1979.

Blane Whitfield, *All God's Children,* ABC, 1980.
Chuffy Russell, *Don't Look Back,* ABC, 1981.
Boxer Oz Jackson, *B. L. Stryker: The Dancer's Touch,* ABC, 1989.

Also appeared as Oz in *Auntie Sue, Blind Chess, The King of Jazz,* and *Royal Gambit,* all 1989; and as Oz in *Night Train, Plates, Grand Theft Hotel,* and *High Rise,* all 1990. Appeared as narrator in *The Red Shoes,* 1990.

TELEVISION APPEARANCES; SPECIALS

The Green Pastures, Showtime USA, 1951.
Title role, "The Emperor Jones," *Kraft Television Theatre,* NBC, 1955.
Tell It on the Mountain, CBS, 1965.
Charles Carter, "Teacher, Teacher," *Hallmark Hall of Fame,* NBC, 1969.
Today Is Ours, CBS, 1974.
Dr. Fredericks, *Billy: Portrait of a Street Kid,* NBC, 1977.
Mr. Eolin, *A Piece of Cake,* NBC, 1977.
"For Us the Living," *American Playhouse,* PBS, 1983.
Host, *Martin Luther King: The Dream and the Drum,* PBS, 1986.
Eyes on the Prize II, PBS, 1990.
Zora Is My Name, PBS, 1990.

Also appeared as narrator, *And Every Man Is Free: A Tribute to Langston Hughes,* 1984; narrator, *Treemonisha,* 1986; Dred Scott, *The Blessings of Liberty,* 1987; Jay, Bruce Castleberry, and Reggie Bates, *Alice in Wonder,* 1987; host with Robert Terrell, *A Letter to Booker T.,* 1987; and *The Twenty-Second Annual NAACP Image Awards,* 1990.

TELEVISION APPEARANCES; EPISODIC

The Creative Person, PBS, 1965.

Also appeared in *The Sheriff, N.Y.P.D., The Fugitive,* and *12 O'Clock High,* all ABC; *The Defenders, Look Up and Live, Slattery's People, Hawaii Five-O, Doctors/Nurses,* and *Car 54, Where Are You?,* all CBS; and *Night Gallery, The Name of the Game, The Outsider, Run for Your Life, Eternal Light,* and *Bonanza,* all NBC.

OTHER TELEVISION APPEARANCES

"Seven Times Monday," *Play of the Week,* WNTA, 1960.
Host, *The Negro People* (series), PBS, 1965-67.
Lieutenant Wagner, *The Outsider* (pilot), NBC, 1967.
Osmond Portifoy, *Night Gallery* (pilot), NBC, 1969.
Martin Luther King, Sr., *King* (mini-series), NBC, 1978.
Dad Jones, *Roots: The Next Generation* (mini-series), ABC, 1979.
Evening Shade (series), CBS, 1990—.

Also appeared as co-host, *With Ossie and Ruby* (series), PBS.

TELEVISION WORK; SPECIALS

Director and producer, *Today Is Ours,* CBS, 1974.
Executive producer, *Martin Luther King: The Dream and the Drum,* PBS, 1986.

Executive producer and director of *Crown Dick,* 1987; producer and director of *A Letter to Booker T.* and *My Man Bovanne,* both 1987; producer of *The 85-Year-Old Swinger, Alice in Wonder, Crazy Hattie Enters the Ice Age, Mama,* and *Refrigerator,* all 1987, and *A Walk through the Twentieth Century with Bill Moyers.*

RADIO APPEARANCES

Host (with Ruby Dee), *The Ossie Davis and Ruby Dee Story Hour,* National Black Network, 1974-75.

RECORDINGS:

The Poetry of Langston Hughes, Caedmon, 1969.
The Best Poems of Countee Cullen, Caedmon, 1972.
The Black Cinema: Foremost Representatives of the Black Film World Air Their Views, Center for Cassette Studies, 1975.

Also participated in recording *Simple Stories,* Caedmon.

WRITINGS:

STAGE

Goldbrickers of 1944, produced in Liberia, 1944.
Alice in Wonder (one-act), produced in New York City, 1952, revised and expanded version produced as *The Big Deal* in New York City, 1953.
Purlie Victorious, produced on Broadway, 1961.
Curtain Call, Mr. Aldredge, Sir (produced in Santa Barbara, CA, 1968), published in *The Black Teacher and the Dramatic Arts: A Dialogue, Bibliography and Anthology,* edited by William R. Reardon and Thomas D. Pawley, Negro Universities Press, 1970.
(With Philip Rose, Peter Udell, and Gary Geld) *Purlie* (musical; produced on Broadway, 1970), Samuel French, 1971.
Escape to Freedom: A Play about Young Frederick Douglass (produced in New York City, 1976), Viking, 1978.
Langston: A Play, produced in New York City, 1982.
(With Hy Gilbert) *Bingo,* produced at AMAS Repertory Theatre, 1985.

Also author of *Last Dance for Sybil.*

FILM

Gone Are the Days (adapted from Davis's *Purlie Victorious;* also known as *Purlie Victorious* and *The Man from C.O.T.T.O.N.*), Trans Lux, 1963.
(With Arnold Perl) *Cotton Comes to Harlem* (based on a novel by Chester Himes), UA, 1970.

TELEVISION

"School Teacher," *East Side/West Side* (episode), CBS, 1963.

"Slavery," *The Negro People* (episode), PBS, 1965.

Today Is Ours (special), CBS, 1974.

(With Ladi Ladebo and Al Freeman, Jr.) *Countdown at Kusini* (based on a story by John Storm Roberts), Columbia, 1976.

Also writer for episodes of *Just Say the Word,* 1969; *The Eleventh Hour* and *Bonanza,* both NBC; *N.Y.P.D.;* and for special *Alice in Wonder,* 1987.

OTHER

(Contributor) *Anger, and Beyond: The Negro Writer in the United States,* Harper, 1966.

(Contributor) *Soon, One Morning: New Writing by American Negroes, 1940-1962,* Knopf, 1968.

"Ain't Now But It's Going to Be" (song), *Cotton Comes to Harlem,* UA, 1970.

(With Ruby Dee) *Glowchild, and Other Poems,* Third Press, 1972.

(With others) *The Black Cinema: Foremost Representatives of the Black Film World Air Their Views,* Center for Cassette Studies, 1975.

Escape to Freedom, Viking, 1979.

Contributor to periodicals and journals, including *Negro History Bulletin, Negro Digest,* and *Freedomways.*

OTHER SOURCES:

BOOKS

Dictionary of Literary Biography, Gale, Volume 7: *Twentieth-Century American Dramatists,* 1981, Volume 38: *Afro-American Writers after 1955: Dramatists and Prose Writers,* 1985.

Funke, Lewis, *The Curtain Rises: The Story of Ossie Davis,* Grosset & Dunlap, 1971.

*   *   *

DAY-LEWIS, Daniel 1957-

PERSONAL: Born April 20, 1957, in London, England; son of Cecil Day-Lewis (a poet) and Jill Balcon (an actress). *Education:* Trained with the Bristol Old Vic Theatre School. *Avocational interests:* Soccer, motorcycling.

ADDRESSES: Agent—Gene Parseghian, Triad Artists, 888 7th Ave., Suite 1602, New York, NY 10106. *Contact*—Julian Belfrage, 60 St. James St., London SW1, England.

CAREER: Actor.

AWARDS, HONORS: New York Film Critics Circle Award, Best Supporting Actor, 1986, for *My Beautiful Laundrette* and *A Room with a View;* Montreal Film Festival Award, Best Actor, New York Film Critics Circle Award, Best Actor, Los Angeles Film Critics Award, Best Actor, and Academy Award, Best Actor, all 1989, for *My Left Foot.*

CREDITS:

FILM APPEARANCES

Vandal (nonspeaking role), *Sunday Bloody Sunday,* United Artists, 1971.

Colin, *Gandhi,* Columbia, 1982.

John Fryer, *The Bounty,* Orion, 1984.

Cecil Vyse, *A Room with a View,* Cinecom, 1986.

Johnny, *My Beautiful Laundrette,* Orion, 1986.

Max, *Nanou,* Umbrella/Arion, 1986.

Tomas, *The Unbearable Lightness of Being,* Orion, 1988.

Henderson Dores, *Stars and Bars,* Columbia, 1988.

Fergus O'Connell, *Eversmile, New Jersey,* Los Films de Camino/J & M, 1989.

Christy Brown, *My Left Foot,* Granada/Miramax, 1989.

STAGE APPEARANCES

Guy Bennett, *Another Country,* Queen's Theatre, London, 1982.

Vladimir Vladimirovich Mayakovsky, *Futurists,* National Theatre Company, Cottesloe Theatre, London, 1986.

Title role, *Hamlet,* National Theatre Company, Olivier Theatre, London, 1989.

Also appeared in touring productions for the Royal Shakespeare Company, including *Romeo and Juliet* and *A Midsummer Night's Dream,* c. 1983-84; appeared in British productions of *Dracula,* Little Theatre Company, and *Look Back in Anger;* appeared in productions for the National Youth Theatre and the Bristol Old Vic Theatre.

TELEVISION APPEARANCES

How Many Miles to Babylon? (special), BBC, 1981.

Franz Kafka, *The Insurance Man* (movie), BBC, 1985.

My Brother Jonathan, BBC, 1985.

Also appeared in other BBC productions, including the television movie *A Frost in May.*

OTHER SOURCES:

PERIODICALS

People, February 22, 1988.

Premiere, February, 1988.

Sunday Times (London), April 1, 1990.

DEE, Ruby 1924(?)-

PERSONAL: Born Ruby Ann Wallace, October 27, 1924 (some sources say 1923), in Cleveland, OH; daughter of Marshall Edward (a cook; some sources say a road porter) and Emma (a teacher; maiden name, Benson) Wallace; married Ossie Davis (an actor and writer), December 9, 1948; children: Nora, LaVerne, Guy. *Education:* Hunter College, B.A., 1945; studied and apprenticed at American Negro Theatre, 1941-44; also studied with Morris Carnovsky, 1958-60 and Actors Workshop with Paul Mann and Lloyd Richards. *Avocational interests:* Painting, music, sewing.

ADDRESSES: Office—c/o Emmalyn II Productions, P.O. Box 1318, New Rochelle, NY 10802.

CAREER: Actress and writer. Emmalyn II Productions, founder with husband, Ossie Davis.

MEMBER: Actors' Equity Association, Screen Actors Guild, American Federation of Television and Radio Artists, Negro American Labor Council, Hunter Alumnae Association of Artists for Freedom, Ladies Auxiliary to Brotherhood of Sleeping Car Porters (honorary member), National Association for the Advancement of Colored People, CORE, Student Non-Violent Co-ordinating Committee, Southern Christian Leadership Conference.

AWARDS, HONORS: Emmy Award nomination for best actress, 1964, for role in episode of *East Side/West Side;* (with Ossie Davis) Frederick Douglass Award of the Urban League, 1970; *Village Voice* Obie Award, and Drama Desk Award, both 1971, for *Boseman and Lena;* Operation PUSH Martin Luther King Jr. Award, 1972; Drama Desk Award, 1973, for *The Wedding Band;* (with Ossie Davis) Actors' Equity Association Paul Robeson Citation, 1975, for outstanding creative contributions in the performing arts and in society at large; ACE Award, 1983, for role as Mary Tyrone in television movie *Long Day's Journey into Night;* inducted to Theatre Hall of Fame, 1988; NAACP Image Award for best performance by an actress, 1989, for her role in the film *Do the Right Thing;* Literary Guild Award, 1989, for *Two Ways to Count to Ten.* Honorary doctorates from Fairfield University, Iona College, and Virginia State University.

CREDITS:

STAGE APPEARANCES

Natural Man, American Negro Theatre, New York City, 1941.

Starlight, American Negro Theatre, 1942.

Three's A Family, American Negro Theatre, 1943.

(Broadway debut) A native, *South Pacific* (drama), Cort Theatre, New York City, 1943.

Ruth, *Walk Hard,* American Negro Theatre, 1944.

Libby George, *Jeb,* Martin Beck Theatre, New York City, 1946.

Title role, *Anna Lucasta,* Mansfield Theatre, New York City, 1946.

Marcy, *A Long Way from Home,* Maxine Elliot's Theatre, New York City, 1948.

Mrs. Ellen McClellan, *The Washington Years,* American Negro Theatre Playhouse, 1948.

Evelyn, *The Smile of the World,* Lyceum Theatre, New York City, 1949.

Defending Angel, *The World of Sholom Aleichem,* Barbizon Plaza Theatre, New York City, 1959.

Ruth Younger, *A Raisin in the Sun,* Ethel Barrymore Theatre, New York City, 1959.

Luttiebelle Gussie Mae Jenkins, *Purlie Victorious,* Cort Theatre, 1961.

Cordelia, *King Lear,* American Shakespeare Festival, Stratford, CT, 1965.

Kate, *The Taming of the Shrew,* American Shakespeare Festival, 1965.

The Talking Skull, White Barn Theatre, Westport, CT, 1965.

Julia Augustine, *The Wedding Bund,* Lydia Mendelssohn Theatre, Ann Arbor, MI, 1966.

Cassandra, *Agamemmon,* Ypsilanti Greek Theatre, Ypsilanti, MI, 1966.

Iris, *The Birds,* Ypsilanti Greek Theatre, 1966.

Oresteia, Ypsilanti Greek Theatre, 1966.

Lena, *Boseman and Lena,* Circle in the Square, New York City, 1970.

The Imaginary Invalid, Walnut Street Theatre, Philadelphia, PA, 1971.

Julia Augustine, *The Wedding Band,* New York Shakespeare Festival (NYSF) Public Theatre, New York City, 1972.

Gertrude, *Hamlet,* NYSF, Delacorte Theatre, 1975.

Lead role, *Twin-Bit Gardens* (musical play; also known as *Take It From the Top*; also see below), New Federal Theatre, New York City, 1979.

Mattie Cooper, *Checkmates,* 46th Street Theatre, New York City, 1988.

Amanda Wingfield, *The Glass Menagerie,* Kreeger Theatre, Washington, D.C., 1989.

Also appeared at Arena Stage, Washington, D.C., 1987-88; appeared in *Arsenic & Old Lace* and *John Loves Mary,* 1946.

MAJOR TOURS

Title role, *Anna Lucasta,* U.S. cities, 1944.

(With husband, Ossie Davis) *A Treasury of Negro World Writing* (poetry readings), U.S. cities, 1964.

STAGE DIRECTOR

Twin-Bit Gardens (musical play; also known as *Take It From the Top*), New Federal Theatre, 1979.
Zora Is My Name!, Howard University, 1983.

FILM APPEARANCES

(Film debut) Rae Robinson, *The Jackie Robinson Story,* Eagle Lion, 1950.
Connie, *No Way Out,* Twentieth Century-Fox, 1950.
Rachel, *The Tall Target,* Metro-Goldwyn-Mayer (MGM), 1951.
Irma Jackson, *Go, Man, Go!,* United Artists, 1954.
Lucy Tyler, *Edge of the City* (also known as *A Man Is Ten Feet Tall*), MGM, 1957.
Elizabeth, *St. Louis Blues,* Paramount, 1958.
Christine the Maid, *Taking a Giant Step,* Shelia/United Artists, 1959.
Ruth, *Virgin Island* (also known as *Our Virgin Island*), Countryman/Films-Around the World, 1960.
Ruth Younger, *A Raisin In the Sun,* Paman-Doris/Columbia, 1961.
Thief, *The Balcony,* City Film Corporation/Continental, 1963.
Luttiebelle, *Gone Are the Days* (also known as *The Man from C.O.T.T.O.N.;* based on Ossie Davis's *Purlie Victorious*), Hammer, 1963, later released as *Purlie Victorious.*
Laurie, *Uptight,* Marluikin/Paramount, 1965.
Joan Robinson, *The Incident,* Moned/Fox, 1968.
Netta's Mother, *Black Girl,* Cinerama, 1972.
Rught, *Buck and The Preacher,* Columbia, 1972.
Leah Matanzina, *Countdown at Kusini,* Tan International Ltd. of Nigeria-Gipp Productions/Columbia, 1976.
Female, *Cat People,* RKO, 1982.
Mother Sister, *Do the Right Thing,* Universal, 1989.
Lucinda Purify, *Jungle Fever,* Universal, 1991.

TELEVISION APPEARANCES; SERIES

Martha Frazier, *The Guiding Light,* CBS, 1967.
Alma Miles, *Peyton Place,* ABC, 1968-69.
Watch Your Mouth, PBS, 1978.
With Ossie and Ruby, National Black Network, 1981.

TELEVISION APPEARANCES; MINI-SERIES

Queen Haley, *Roots: The Next Generation,* ABC, 1979.
Keckley, *Gore Vidal's Lincoln,* NBC, 1988.

TELEVISION APPEARANCES; EPISODIC

"Actor's Choice," *Camera Three,* CBS, 1960.
The Fugitive, ABC, 1963.
"Go Down Moses," *The Great Adventure,* CBS, 1963.
"Express Stop to Lenox Ave.," *The Nurses,* CBS, 1963.
"No Hiding Place," *East Side/West Side,* CBS, 1964.
The Eternal Light, NBC, 1964.
The Defenders, CBS, 1965.
"Slavery," *The History of the Negro People,* NET, 1965.
The Sheriff, ABC, 1971.
Police Woman, NBC, 1975.

TELEVISION APPEARANCES; MOVIES

Lucinda, *Deadlock,* NBC, 1969.
Sue Anne Lucas, *The Sheriff,* ABC, 1971.
Ruth Campanella, *It's Good To Be Alive,* CBS, 1974.
Grandmother Baxter, *I Know Why the Caged Bird Sings,* CBS, 1979.
Irene Whitfield, *All God's Children,* ABC, 1980.
Mary Tyrone, *Long Day's Journey into Night,* ABC Cable, 1983.
Faye Williams, *The Atlanta Child Murders,* CBS, 1985.
Sidney Sheldon's Windmills of the Gods, CBS, 1988.
Decoration Day, NBC, 1990.

TELEVISION APPEARANCES; SPECIALS

Narrator and Zora Neale Hurston, "Zora Is My Name!," *American Playhouse,* PBS, 1990.
(With Davis) *Martin Luther King: The Dream and the Drum,* PBS, 1990.

TELEVISION APPEARANCES; PLAYS

"Seven Times Monday," *Play of the Week,* WNTA, 1960.
"Black Monday," *Play of the Week,* WNTA, 1961.
Shakespeare in Love and War, Repertory Theatre, 1965.
"Neighbors," *Armchair Theatre,* ABC (Manchester, England), 1966.
"To Be Young, Gifted and Black," *NET Playhouse,* PBS, 1972.

TELEVISION WORK

Co-producer of programs for television, including *Today Is Ours,* CBS; and (with Davis and Bill Moyers) *A Walk through the 20th Century,* CBS.

RADIO APPEARANCES; SERIES

This Is Norah Drake, CBS, 1955.
The Ossie Davis and Ruby Dee Story Hour, National Black Network, 1974-75.

RECORDINGS:

(With Davis) *The Poetry of Langston Hughes,* Caedmon, 1969.

Also has recorded poems and stories.

VIDEOS

(With Davis) *Hands Upon the Heart,* 1991.

WRITINGS:

(With Jules Dassin and Julian Mayfield) *Uptight* (screenplay; adapted from Liam O'Flaherty's novel *The Informer*), Paramount, 1968.

(Editor) *Glowchild, and Other Poems,* Third Press, 1972.

Twin-Bit Gardens (musical play; also known as *Take It From the Top*), produced Off-Broadway at New Federal Theatre, 1979.

My One Good Nerve (short stories, poetry and humor), Third World Press, 1987.

(Reteller) *Two Ways to Count to Ten* (juvenile), Holt, 1988.

"Zora Is My Name," *American Playhouse* (television play), PBS, 1990.

(Reteller) *The Tower to Heaven* (juvenile), Holt, 1991.

OTHER

Contributor to *Voices of the Black Theatre.* Author of columns for newspapers and magazines, including *New York Amsterdam News;* associate editor, *Freedomways* magazine.

SIDELIGHTS: Favorite roles: Luttiebell in *Purlie Victorious,* Lena in *Boseman and Lena,* Cleopatra in *Antony and Cleopatra.*

*   *   *

DeLUISE, Dom   1933-

PERSONAL: Born August 1, 1933, in Brooklyn, NY; son of John (a civil servant) and Vicenza "Jennie" (DeStefano) DeLuise; married Carol Arata (an actress; professional name, Carol Arthur), November 23, 1965; children: Peter John, Michael Robert, David Dominick. *Education:* Attended Tufts College. *Avocational interests:* Furniture refinishing, herb gardening.

ADDRESSES: Office—EBM, 132 South Rodeo Dr., Beverly Hills, CA 90212. *Contact*—(business affairs) Terry Crays, P.O. Box 1801, Pacific Palisades, CA 90272.

CAREER: Actor and commercial spokesman.

CREDITS:

STAGE APPEARANCES; PLAYS

(Off-Broadway debut) Struthion, *The Jackass,* Barbizon-Plaza Theatre, 1960.

Corporal Billy Jester, *Little Mary Sunshine,* Orpheum Theatre, then Players Theatre, both New York City, 1961.

Ensemble, *Another Evening with Harry Stoones* (revue), Gramercy Arts Theatre, New York City, 1961.

Bob Acres, *All in Love,* Martinique Theatre, New York City, 1961.

The King, *Half-Past Wednesday,* Orpheum Theatre, 1962.

(Broadway debut) Muffin T. Ragamuffin, *The Student Gypsy; or, The Prince of Liederkrantz,* 54th Street Theatre, 1963.

Mr. Faddish, *Too Much Johnson,* Phoenix Theatre, New York City, 1964.

Mr. Psawyer, *Here's Love,* Shubert Theatre, New York City, 1964.

Barney Cashman, *Last of the Red Hot Lovers,* Eugene O'Neill Theatre, New York City, 1971.

Also appeared in *The School for Scandal, Hamlet,* and *Stalag 17,* all Cleveland Playhouse, Cleveland, OH; and *Mixed Company,* Provincetown, MA; starred in the cabaret act *An Evening with Dom DeLuise* in Las Vegas, NV, and Atlantic City, NJ.

STAGE APPEARANCE; OPERA

Public opinion, *Orpheus in the Underworld,* Los Angeles Opera Company, 1989.

Froesch, *Die Fledermaus,* Metropolitan Opera of New York, 1990 and 1991.

MAJOR TOURS

Appeared in *Luv,* U.S. cities.

STAGE WORK; DIRECTOR

Same Time Next Year Burt Reynolds Theatre, Jupiter, FL, 1980.

Butterflies Are Free, Burt Reynolds Theatre, Jupiter, FL, 1980.

Brighton Beach Memoirs, Burt Reynolds Theatre, Jupiter, FL, 1986.

FILM APPEARANCES

(Film debut) Sergeant Collins, *Fail Safe,* Columbia, 1964.

Marvin Rollins, *Diary of a Bachelor,* American International, 1964.

Julius Pritter, *The Glass Bottom Boat,* Metro-Goldwyn-Mayer (MGM), 1966.

Kurt Brock, *The Busybody,* Paramount, 1967.

J. Gardner Monroe, *What's So Bad about Feeling Good?,* Universal, 1968.

Father Fyodor, *The Twelve Chairs,* UMC, 1969.

Bill Bird, *Norwood,* Paramount, 1970.

Irwin, *Who Is Harry Kellerman and Why Is He Saying Those Terrible Things about Me?,* National General, 1971.

Azzecca, *Every Little Crook and Nanny,* MGM, 1972.

Buddy Bizarre, *Blazing Saddles,* Warner Brothers, 1974.

Gambetti, *The Adventures of Sherlock Holmes's Smarter Brother,* Twentieth Century-Fox, 1975.

Dom Bell, *Silent Movie,* Twentieth Century-Fox, 1976.

Zitz, *The World's Greatest Lover,* Twentieth Century-Fox, 1977.

Pepe Domascus, *The Cheap Detective,* Columbia, 1978.

Dan Turner, *Sexette,* Crown International, 1978.

Marlon Borunki, *The End,* United Artists, 1978.

Ernie Fortunato, *Hot Stuff,* Columbia, 1979.

Bernie (the Hollywood agent), *The Muppet Movie,* Associated Film Distribution, 1979.

Dominick DiNapoli, *Fatso,* Twentieth Century-Fox, 1980.

Walter Holmes, *The Last Married Couple in America,* Universal, 1980.

Doc, *Smokey and the Bandit II* (also known as *Smokey and the Bandit Ride Again*), Columbia, 1980.

Shadrach, *Wholly Moses,* Columbia, 1980.

Victor/Captain Chaos, *The Cannonball Run,* Twentieth Century-Fox, 1981.

Emperor Nero, *History of the World, Part One,* Twentieth Century-Fox, 1981.

Melvin P. Thorpe, *The Best Little Whorehouse in Texas,* Universal, 1982.

Voice of Jeremy, *The Secret of NIMH* (animated), Metro-Goldwyn-Mayer/United Artists (MGM/UA), 1982.

Victor/Captain Chaos, *Cannonball Run II,* Warner Brothers, 1984.

The Pope, *Johnny Dangerously,* Twentieth Century-Fox, 1984.

Voice of Tiger, *An American Tail* (animated), Universal, 1986.

Aunt Kate, *Haunted Honeymoon,* Orion, 1986.

Voice of Pizza the Hutt, *Space Balls,* MGM/UA, 1987.

Police Chief, *Un tassinaro, a New York* (also known as *A Taxi Driver in New York*), Italian International Film, 1987.

Big Bad Joe, *Going Bananas* (also known as *My African Adventure*), Cannon, 1987.

Voice of Fagin, *Oliver and Company* (animated), Buena Vista, 1988.

Gutterman, *Loose Cannons,* Tri-Star, 1989.

Voice of Itchy, *All Dogs Go to Heaven* (animated), United Artists, 1989.

Also appeared in *Benito.*

FILM WORK

Director, *Hot Stuff,* Columbia, 1979.

TELEVISION APPEARANCES; SERIES

Regular, *The Entertainers,* CBS, 1964-65.

Regular, *The Dean Martin Summer Show,* NBC, 1966.

Host, *The Dom DeLuise Show,* CBS, 1968.

Regular, *The Glen Campbell Goodtime Hour,* CBS, 1971-72.

Regular, *The Dean Martin Show,* NBC, 1972-73.

Voice of Mr. Evictus, *The Roman Holidays* (animated), NBC, 1972-73.

Stanley Belmont, *Lotsa Luck!,* NBC, 1973-74.

Dominick DeLuca, *The Dom DeLuise Show,* syndicated, 1987.

Also appeared as Dominick the Great on *The Garry Moore Show,* CBS.

TELEVISION APPEARANCES; EPISODIC

Dr. Edward Dudley, *The Munsters,* CBS, 1966.

Please Don't Eat the Daisies, NBC, 1966.

The Girl from U.N.C.L.E., NBC, 1966.

"This Is Sholom Aleichem," *Experiment in Television,* NBC, 1969.

The Ghost and Mrs. Muir, ABC, 1969.

The Golddiggers, syndicated, 1971.

Medical Center, CBS, 1974.

Guilt, *Amazing Stories,* NBC, 1985.

Vito, *Easy Street,* NBC, 1987.

Win, Lose, or Draw, syndicated, 1987.

Uncle Dominic, *21 Jump Street,* Fox, 1989.

Toby Beaumont, "Die Laughing," *B. L. Stryker,* ABC, 1989.

TELEVISION APPEARANCES; SPECIALS

The Arthur Godfrey Special, NBC, 1972.

The Arthur Godfrey Portable Electric Medicine Show, NBC, 1972.

Dean Martin's Red Hot Scandals of 1926, NBC, 1976.

Dean Martin's Red Hot Scandals, Part 2, NBC, 1977.

Dean Martin Celebrity Roast: Frank Sinatra, NBC, 1978.

Dean Martin Celebrity Roast: George Burns, NBC, 1978.

Ann-Margret's Hollywood Movie Girls, ABC, 1980.

Dean Martin's Comedy Classics, NBC, 1981.

Baryshnikov in Hollywood, CBS, 1982.

The Best Little Special in Texas, CBS, 1982.

Dean Martin at the Wild Animal Park, NBC, 1982.

Magic with the Stars, NBC, 1982.

Host, *Dom DeLuise and Friends,* ABC, 1983.

Dean Martin Celebrity Roast: Joan Collins, NBC, 1984.

Host, *Dom DeLuise and Friends, Part II,* ABC, 1984.

The Funniest Joke I Ever Heard, ABC, 1984.

Host, *Dom DeLuise and Friends, Part III,* ABC, 1985.

Host, *Dom DeLuise and Friends, Part IV,* ABC, 1986.

NBC News Report on America: Life in the Fat Lane, NBC, 1987.

Dinah Comes Home Again, Nashville Network, 1990.

Also appeared in *The Bar-rump Bump Show,* 1964; *Hollywood: The Gift of Laughter,* 1982; *Henry's Cat,* 1986; *Friday Night Surprise!,* 1988; and *Superstars and Their Moms,* 1989.

OTHER TELEVISION APPEARANCES

Logan Delp, *Evil Roy Slade* (pilot), NBC, 1972.

Murray West, *Only with Married Men* (movie), ABC, 1974.

Roger Hanover, *Happy* (movie), CBS, 1983.

TELEVISION WORK

Executive producer, *Happy* (movie), CBS, 1983.

WRITINGS:

TELEVISION

Dom DeLuise and Friends, Part III, ABC, 1985.
Dom DeLuise and Friends, Part IV, ABC, 1986.

OTHER

Eat This . . . It Will Make You Feel Better: Mama's Italian Home Cooking and Other Favorites of Family and Friends (cookbook), Simon & Schuster, 1988.
Charlie the Caterpillar (children's book), Simon & Schuster, 1990.

Also coauthor of the film *Benito.*

OTHER SOURCES:

PERIODICALS

Jersey Journal, April 28, 1988.

*   *   *

DEMY, Jacques   1931-

PERSONAL: Born June 5, 1931, in Pont Chateau, France; son of Raymond and Marie Louise (Leduc) Demy; married Agnes Varda (a filmmaker and director), 1962; children: one son, one daughter. *Education:* College de Nantes, Ecole des Beaux-Arts, and Ecole Nationale de Photographie et Cinematographie, Paris. *Avocational interests:* Painting and flying.

CAREER: Director and screenwriter. Director of stage plays in Salzburg, Austria, and Paris, France; assistant to animator Paul Grimault on commercials, 1952; assistant to filmmaker Georges Rouquier, 1954; director of short films.

AWARDS, HONORS: Golden Palm Award, Cannes Film Festival, 1964, for *Les Parapluies de Cherbourg;* Prix Louis Delluc, 1964; Chevalier des Arts et des Lettres; Ordre Nationale du Merite; Grand Prix National, 1982.

CREDITS:

FILM APPEARANCES

Policeman, *Les Quatres cent coups* (also known as *The Four Hundred Blows*), Janus, 1959.

Also appeared as guest at a party, *Paris nous appartient,* 1960.

FILM DIRECTOR

(And screenwriter) *Donna Di Vita* (also known as *Lola*), Films Around the World, 1961.
Paris nous appartient (also known as *Paris Belongs to Us* and *Paris Is Ours*), Merlyn, 1962.
(And screenwriter with Roger Peyrefitte) "La Luxure," episode of *Les Sept peches capitaux* (also known as *Seven Deadly Sins* and *Seven Capital Sins*), Embassy Pictures, 1962.
(And screenwriter) *La Baie des anges* (also known as *Bay of Angels*), Pathe, 1964.
(And screenwriter) *Les Parapluies de Cherbourg* (also known as *Die Regenschirme von Cherbourg* and *The Umbrellas of Cherbourg*), Landau, 1964.
(And screenwriter) *Les Demoiselles de Rochefort* (also known as *The Young Girls of Rochefort*), Warner Brothers/Seven Arts, 1968.
(And screenwriter with Adrien Joyce, and producer) *The Model Shop,* Columbia, 1969.
(And screenwriter with Andrew Birkin and Mark Peploe) *The Pied Piper of Hamelin* (also known as *The Pied Piper*), Paramount, 1972.
(And screenwriter) *Peau d'ane* (also known as *Donkey Skin*), Janus Films, 1975.
(And screenwriter with Patricia Lousiana Knop) *Lady Oscar,* Toho, 1979.
(And screenwriter and composer of lyrics) *Parking,* American, 1985.

Also director of *La Naissance du jour,* 1980; and assistant director, with Rouquier, of *Lourdes et ses miracles,* 1954; *Arthur Honegger,* 1955; and *S.O.S. Noronha,* 1956. Director, with Jean Masson, of *Ars,* 1959, and *La Mere et l'infant,* 1959. Director and screenwriter of *Le Sabotier du val de Loire,* 1956; *Le Bel indifferent,* 1957; *Le Musee Grevin,* 1958; *L'Evenement le plus important depuis que l'homme a marche sur la lune* (also known as *A Slightly Pregnant Man*), 1973; *Une Chambre en ville* (also known as *A Room in Town*), 1982; *Trois places pour le 26* (also known as *Three Seats for the 26th*), 1988; and *La Table tournante,* 1988.

WRITINGS:

Contributor of articles to periodicals, including *Film Comment* and *Films and Filming.**

*   *   *

De WITT, Joyce   1949-

PERSONAL: Born April 23, 1949, in Wheeling, WV. *Education:* Ball State University, B.A., theatre; University of California, Los Angeles, M.F.A., acting.

ADDRESSES: Contact—c/o The Lantz Office, 9255 Sunset Blvd., Suite 505, Los Angeles, CA 90069.

CAREER: Actress. Performer and director in dinner theatre musicals; appeared in summer theatrical productions in Rockford, IL.

CREDITS:

TELEVISION APPEARANCES; SERIES

Janet Wood, *Three's Company,* ABC, 1977-84.

TELEVISION APPEARANCES; MOVIES

Jilly Weston, *With This Ring,* ABC, 1978.

TELEVISION APPEARANCES; EPISODIC

Appeared on *Baretta,* ABC; *Finder of Lost Loves,* ABC; and *The Tony Randall Show.*

TELEVISION APPEARANCES; SPECIALS

Battle of the Network Stars, ABC, 1976.
All Star Family Feud, ABC, 1978.
U.S. Against the World II, ABC, 1978.
Celebrity Challenge of the Sexes, CBS, 1979.
The Celebrity Football Classic, NBC, 1979.
Perry Como's Christmas in New Mexico, ABC, 1979.
Cheryl Ladd . . . Looking Back—Souvenirs, ABC, 1980.
John Ritter: Being of Sound Mind and Body, ABC, 1980.
Steve Martin: Comedy Is Not Pretty, NBC, 1980.
Battle of the Network Stars, ABC, 1980.
Host, *Saturday's the Place,* CBS, 1984.
The Real Trivial Pursuit, ABC, 1985.

TELEVISION APPEARANCES; PILOTS

Sharon, *Risko,* CBS, 1976.
Most Wanted, ABC, 1979.
The B.B. Beegle Show, syndicated, 1980.*

*   *   *

DINSDALE, Reece

PERSONAL: Born in Normanton, Yorkshire, England.

ADDRESSES: Manager—Louis Hammond Management, Golden House, 29 Great Pulteney St., London W1, England.

CAREER: Actor.

CREDITS:

STAGE APPEARANCES

Pascal Fawlgate, *Beethoven's Tenth,* Vaudeville Theatre, London, 1983.
Terry, *Red Saturday,* New End Theatre, London, 1983, then Theatre Upstairs, London, 1984.

Private Jimmy Crompton, *Woundings,* Royal Exchange Theatre, Manchester, England, 1986.
David Craig, *Observe the Sons of Ulster Marching towards the Somme,* Hampstead Theatre, London, 1986.
Martin, *Old Year's Eve,* Royal Shakespeare Company, The Pit, London, 1987.

FILM APPEARANCES

Mal Stanton, *Winter Flight,* Enigma/Goldcrest, 1984.
P. C. Penny, *A Private Function,* Island Alive, 1985.

TELEVISION APPEARANCES; SERIES

Home to Roost, ITV, 1989.

TELEVISION SERIES; EPISODIC

Title role, "Fearnot," *The Storyteller,* NBC, 1987.

Also appeared in *Bergerac,* BBC; *Minder,* Euston Film; *Robin of Sherwood; Knife Edge; Out on the Floor; Threads;* and *Glamour Night.*

TELEVISION APPEARANCES; MINI-SERIES

Albert, *Agatha Christie's "Partners in Crime,"* London Weekend Television, then *Mystery!,* PBS, 1986.
Albert, *The Secret Adversary,* London Weekend Television, then *Mystery!,* PBS, 1987.
Haggard, ITV, 1990.
Grand Duke Peter, *Young Catherine,* TNT, 1991.*

*   *   *

DONAT, Peter   1928-

PERSONAL: Born Pierre Collingwood Donat, January 20, 1928, in Kentville, Nova Scotia, Canada; son of Philip Ernst (a landscape gardener) and Marie (Bardet) Donat; married Michael Learned (an actress), September 8, 1956 (divorced, 1974); married Maria C. DeJong (a writer), February 9, 1983; children: (first marriage) Caleb, Christopher, Lucas. *Education:* Acadia University, B.A. and B.S., 1950; graduate work at the Yale University School of Drama, 1950-51; studied singing with Homer G. Mowe, 1950-53; studied for the theatre with Curt Conway, 1954-55; studied voice with Iris Warren, 1961. *Avocational interests:* Tennis, photography, swimming, and writing.

ADDRESSES: Office—c/o American Conservatory Theatre, 450 Geary Street, San Francisco, CA 94102. *Agent*—The Gersh Agency, 222 N. Canon Drive, Suite 202, Beverly Hills, CA 90210.

CAREER: Actor and writer. Company member, American Conservatory Theatre, San Francisco, CA, 1971—.

MEMBER: Actors' Equity Association, American Federation of Television and Radio Artists, Screen Actors

Guild, Association of Canadian Television and Radio Artists.

AWARDS, HONORS: Theatre World Award, 1957, for *The First Gentleman;* Radiant American Artist Award from American Conservatory Theatre, 1983.

CREDITS:

STAGE APPEARANCES

Valentine, *You Never Can Tell,* Provincetown Playhouse, Provincetown, MA, 1951.

Byron, *An Innocent in Time,* Provincetown Playhouse, MA, 1951.

Randall, *Heartbreak House,* Provincetown Playhouse, MA, 1951.

Faukland, *The Rivals,* Provincetown Playhouse, MA, 1951.

Doctor, *The Straw,* Provincetown Playhouse, MA, 1951.

Lysander, *A Midsummer Night's Dream,* Margo Jones Theatre, Dallas, TX, 1951.

Pastor, *The Father,* Margo Jones Theatre, 1952.

Poet, *A Gift for Cathy,* Margo Jones Theatre, 1952.

Tony, *You Can't Take It with You,* Pocono Playhouse, Mountainhome, PA, 1952.

Gaston, *Gigi,* Pocono Playhouse, 1952.

Dangerous Corner, Falmouth Playhouse, Falmouth, MA, 1952.

(Broadway debut) Arthur Fenwick, *Highlights of the Empire,* Empire Theatre, New York City, 1953.

Dr. Nicholas Agi, *The Swan,* Pocono Playhouse, then Falmouth Playhouse, both 1953.

Metellus Cimber, *Julius Caesar,* American Shakespeare Festival, Stratford, CT, 1955.

(Off-Broadway debut) Amphitryon, *A God Slept Here,* Provincetown Playhouse, New York City, 1957.

Prince Leopold, *The First Gentleman,* Belasco Theatre, New York City, 1957.

Dorilant, *The Country Wife,* Adelphi Theatre, New York City, 1957.

Florizel, *The Winter's Tale,* Stratford Shakespearean Festival, Stratford, ON, Canada, 1958.

Sir Richard Vernon, *Henry IV, Part One,* Stratford Shakespearean Festival, 1958.

Graham, *The Entertainer,* Royale Theatre, New York City, 1958.

The President's son, *The Goodwill Ambassador,* Olympia Theatre, Dublin, Ireland, 1959.

Tusenbach, *The Three Sisters,* Fourth Street Theatre, New York City, 1959.

Demetrius, *A Midsummer Night's Dream,* Stratford Shakespearean Festival, 1960.

Chatillon, *King John,* Stratford Shakespearean Festival, 1960.

Longaville, *Love's Labour's Lost,* Stratford Shakespearean Festival, 1961.

Earl of Surrey, *Henry VIII,* Stratford Shakespearean Festival, 1961.

Morris Townsend, *The Heiress,* Crest Theatre, Toronto, ON, Canada, 1961.

Christian, *Cyrano de Bergerac,* Stratford Shakespearean Festival, 1962.

Hortensio, *The Taming of the Shrew,* Stratford Shakespearean Festival, 1962.

Ferdinand, *The Tempest,* Stratford Shakespearean Festival, 1962.

Troilus, *Troilus and Cressida,* Stratford Shakespearean Festival, 1963.

Christian, *Cyrano de Bergerac,* Stratford Shakespearean Festival, 1963.

Antipholus of Syracuse, *The Comedy of Errors,* Stratford Shakespearean Festival, 1963.

Oliver, *The Chinese Prime Minister,* Royale Theatre, New York City, 1964.

Frank O'Keefe, *Return to the Mountain,* Royal Alexandra Theatre, Toronto, 1964.

Pistol, *Falstaff (Henry IV, Part Two),* Stratford Shakespearean Festival, 1965.

Cassius, *Julius Caesar,* Stratford Shakespearean Festival, 1965.

An Evening's Frost, American Conservatory Theatre (ACT), San Francisco, CA, 1968.

Under Milk Wood, ACT, 1968.

My Son God, ACT, 1968.

Deedle, Deedle Dumpling, ACT, 1968.

Staircase, ACT, 1969.

The Architect and the Emperor of Assyria, ACT, 1969.

Hadrian VII, ACT, 1970.

The Importance of Being Earnest, ACT, 1970.

Six Characters in Search of an Author, ACT, 1970.

The Merchant of Venice, ACT, 1970.

Caesar, *Caesar and Cleopatra,* ACT, 1971.

George Mason, *The Selling of the President,* ACT, 1971.

An Enemy of the People, ACT, 1971.

The Way of the World, Long Wharf Theatre, New Haven, CT, 1972.

Sleuth, ACT, 1972.

Pontagnac, *There's One in Every Marriage,* Avon Theatre, Stratford Shakespearean Festival, 1971, then Royale Theatre, 1972.

Title role, *Cyrano de Bergerac,* ACT, 1972.

Torvald Helmer, *A Doll's House,* ACT, 1973.

The Crucible, ACT, 1973.

The Cherry Orchard, ACT, 1974.

Title role, *Cyrano de Bergerac,* ACT, 1974.

(London debut) Alexander Ben Claiborne, *A Touch of Spring,* Comedy Theatre, 1975.

Equus, ACT, 1975-76.

Man and Superman, ACT, 1976.

The Master Builder, ACT, 1977.

A Month in the Country, ACT, 1978.

Piet, *A Lesson from Aloes,* Mark Taper Forum, Los Angeles, 1980.

The Holdup, ACT, 1982.

Duke, *As You Like It,* Old Globe Theatre, San Diego, CA, 1982-83.

The Government Inspector, Stratford Shakespearean Festival, 1985.

Gus Jordan, *Diamond Lil,* ACT, Geary Theatre, San Francisco, 1988.

Zeus, *Feathers,* ACT, Geary Theatre, San Francisco, 1988.

Also appeared in productions of *Le Bourgeois Gentilhomme* and *Edward II,* both Wellesley, MA, 1957.

MAJOR TOURS

(Stage debut) Oswald, *Ghosts,* and Manningham, *Angel Street,* Nova Scotia Players, tour of Canadian cities, 1950.

Peter Crewe, *Jane,* U.S. and Canadian cities, 1952.

Paul, *My Three Angels,* U.S. cities, 1953.

STAGE WORK

Director, *The Winter's Tale,* National Shakespeare Festival, Old Globe Theatre, San Diego, CA, 1978.

FILM APPEARANCES

David Burnham, *Lost Lagoon,* United Artists, 1958.

Car salesman, *Glory Boy* (also known as *My Old Man's Place* and *The Old Man's Place*), Cinerama, 1971.

Questadt, *The Godfather, Part II,* Paramount, 1974.

Reed Channing, *The Hindenburg,* Universal, 1975.

Inspector McDermott, *Russian Roulette,* AVCO-Embassy, 1975.

Sills, *A Different Story,* AVCO-Embassy, 1978.

Arthur St. Claire, *F.I.S.T.,* United Artists, 1978.

Don Jacovich, *The China Syndrome,* Columbia, 1979.

Dr. Philip Godard, *Mirrors* (also known as *Marianne*), First American, 1982.

Harley Dennis, *Ladies and Gentlemen, the Fabulous Stains,* Paramount, 1982.

Will Campbell, *Bay Boy,* Orion, 1984.

Don Maranzella, *High Point,* New World, 1984.

Lee Briscoe, *Massive Retaliation,* One Pass-Hammermark, 1984.

Novak, *Lune de Miel,* AAA-Revcom, 1985.

Ferenzy, *Unfinished Business,* American Film Institute, 1987.

Kerner, *Tucker: The Man and His Dream,* Paramount, 1988.

Sparky, *Skin Deep,* Twentieth Century-Fox, 1989.

Larrabee, *The War of the Roses,* Twentieth Century-Fox, 1989.

TELEVISION APPEARANCES; SERIES

Stephen Markley, *The Brighter Day,* CBS, 1955.

Bert Stanton, *As the World Turns,* CBS, 1959.

Vince Conway, *Moment of Truth,* NBC, 1965.

Arthur Raymond, *Rich Man, Poor Man—Book II,* ABC, 1976-77.

Elmo Tyson, *Flamingo Road,* NBC, 1981-82.

TELEVISION APPEARANCES; EPISODIC

Camera Three, CBS, 1957.

Title role, "Hamlet," *Look Up and Live,* CBS, 1964.

Zakhar Bardin, "Enemies," *Theatre in America,* PBS, 1974.

Title role, "Cyrano de Bergerac," *Theatre in America,* PBS, 1974.

Dr. Miles Pearson, *Dallas,* CBS, 1978.

Dexter, *Fortune Dane,* ABC, 1986.

Maurice Goodman, *The Days and Nights of Molly Dodd,* NBC, 1988.

Sergei Chaloff, *Murder, She Wrote,* CBS, 1989.

TELEVISION APPEARANCES; MOVIES

David Ormsby-Gore, *The Missiles of October,* ABC, 1974.

Peter Helms, *Last Hours Before Morning,* NBC, 1975.

Dr. Bryce, *The First 36 Hours of Dr. Durant,* ABC, 1975.

Colonel H. Norman Schwarzkopf, *The Lindbergh Kidnapping Case,* NBC, 1976.

Clair Montrose, *Captains and the Kings,* NBC, 1976.

John McCain, Jr., *Delta County U.S.A.,* ABC, 1977.

Mr. Durant, *Hanging by a Thread,* NBC, 1979.

Noel Adamson, *Happiness Is a Warm Clue* (also known as *The Return of Charlie Chan*), NBC, 1979.

Wayne Harrington, *The Suicide's Wife,* CBS, 1979.

Ted, *Fun and Games,* ABC, 1980.

Richard Byrne, *Golden Gate,* ABC, 1981.

Dr. Whedon, *A Matter of Life and Death,* CBS, 1981.

Edward James, *The Princess and the Cabbie,* CBS, 1981.

Harold, *Rona Jaffe's "Mazes and Monsters,"* CBS, 1982.

Admiral Beasley, *Earth*Star Voyager,* ABC, 1988.

Also appeared as Walker Garretson in *Things That Go Bump in the Night,* 1989.

TELEVISION APPEARANCES; SPECIALS

(Television debut) Playboy, "There Once Was a Diamond Ring," *Robert Montgomery Presents,* NBC, 1953.

Tusenbach, *The Three Sisters,* CBS, 1960.

Hjalmar, *The Wild Duck,* CBS, 1962.

Painter, *The Doctor's Dilemma,* CBS, 1962.

Scoundrel, *The Diary of a Scoundrel,* CBS, 1962.

Heartbreak House, WNET, 1966.

David, *Five-Finger Discount,* NBC, 1977.

George, "Return Engagement," *The Hallmark Hall of Fame,* NBC, 1978.

Also appeared as the narrator in *The Creation of Omo,* 1987.

RADIO APPEARANCES; SERIES

Stephen Markley, *The Brighter Day,* CBS, 1955.

WRITINGS:

TELEVISION PROGRAMS; ADAPTOR

"Emma," *Kraft Television Theatre,* NBC, 1953.
The Master Builder, CBC-TV, 1963.
Traveller without Luggage, CBC-TV, 1981.

Also adaptor with wife, Maria DeJong, of *Dr. Chekhov.**

*   *   *

DOWNIE, Penny

CAREER: Actress.

CREDITS:

STAGE APPEARANCES

Lady Anne, *Richard III,* Royal Shakespeare Company (RSC), Barbican Theatre, London, 1985.
Peggy Smith, *Today,* RSC, The Pit, London, 1985.
The God's Daughter (Agnes), *Dreamplay,* RSC, The Pit, London, 1985.
Struggle, *Crimes in Hot Countries,* RSC, The Pit, London, 1985.
Ann, *The Castle,* RSC, The Pit, London, 1985.
Sarah Sprackling, *The Art of Success,* RSC, The Pit, 1987.
Hermione and Perdita, *The Winter's Tale,* RSC, Barbican Theatre, 1987.
Lady Macduff, *Macbeth,* RSC, Barbican Theatre, 1987.
Queen Margaret, *The Plantagenets,* RSC, Stratford-on-Avon, 1988.

FILM APPEARANCES

Cindy, *Crosstalk,* Greater Union Organization, 1982.
Chrissie, *Wetherby,* Metro-Goldwyn-Mayer/United Artists, 1985.
Madelaine, *Lionheart* (also known as *Lionheart: The Children's Crusade*), Orion, 1987.

TELEVISION APPEARANCES

Sarah Copeland, *Campaign* (mini-series), BBC, then *Dramaworks,* Arts and Entertainment, 1988.
Inspector Kate Miskin, *A Taste for Death* (mini-series), Anglia Television, then *Mystery!,* PBS, 1990.

Also appeared as Kerry Vincent, *Prisoner: Cell Block H,* syndicated.*

DUNNE, Dominick   1925(?)-

PERSONAL: Born October 29, 1925 (some sources say 1926), in Hartford, CT; son of Richard, (a heart surgeon) and Dorothy B. Dunne; married Ellen Griffin, April 24, 1954 (divorced); children: Griffin, Alexander, Dominique (deceased). *Education:* Williams College, B.A., 1949. *Politics:* Democrat. *Religion:* Catholic.

ADDRESSES: Agent—James Oliver Brown, Curtis Brown Ltd., 575 Madison Ave., New York, NY 10022.

CAREER: Producer, television executive, journalist, and author. Previously worked as a stage manager at NBC, producer for CBS Studio One, executive producer at 20th Century-Fox, and vice president at Four Star (television company). *Military service:* U.S. Army, served during World War II; received Bronze Star.

CREDITS:

FILM PRODUCER, EXCEPT WHERE INDICATED

Panic in Needle Park, Twentieth Century-Fox, 1971.
(With Frank Perry) *Play It As It Lays,* Universal, 1972.
Ash Wednesday, Paramount, 1973.
Executive producer, *The Boys in the Band,* Leo/Cinema Center/National General, 1970.

TELEVISION WORK

Producer (with Richard Goldstone and Art Wallace), *Adventures in Paradise,* ABC, 1959-62.
Producer, *The Users,* ABC, 1978.

Also served as stage manager for *The Howdy Doody Show,* NBC; and *Robert Montgomery Presents,* NBC.

WRITINGS:

The Winners: Part II of Joyce Haber's The Users, (novel), Simon & Schuster, 1982.
The Two Mrs. Grenvilles (novel), Crown, 1985.
Fatal Charms, and Other Tales of Today (essays), Crown, 1986.
People Like Us (novel), Crown, 1988.
An Inconvenient Woman (novel), Crown, 1990.
The Mansions of Limbo, Crown, 1991.

Contributor to *New York Times Book Review.* Also a contributing editor for *Vanity Fair* magazine, 1984——.

ADAPTATIONS: The Two Mrs. Grenvilles was presented as an NBC television mini-series in 1987 starring Ann-Margret and Claudette Colbert. *People Like Us* was presented as an NBC television miniseries in 1990 starring Connie Sellecca, Dennis Farina, and Eva Marie Saint.

OTHER SOURCES:

PERIODICALS

Publishers Weekly, June 28, 1985.
TV Guide, May 12, 1990.*

*   *   *

DURY, Ian 1942-

PERSONAL: Born in 1942 in Billericay, Essex, England. *Education:* Attended Walthamstow Art College and the Royal College of Art.

CAREER: Actor, composer, and writer. Founder of band Kilburn and the High Roads; founder of band Blockheads.

CREDITS:

STAGE APPEARANCES

Byline Browne, *Apples,* English Stage Company, Royal Court Theatre, London, 1989.

FILM APPEARANCES

Teddy Bryant, *Number One,* Stageforum, 1984.
Meat Hook, *Pirates,* Cannon, 1986.
The Jester, *Rocinante,* Cinema Action, 1986.
Bones, *Hearts of Fire,* Lorimar, 1987.
Crippled acrobat, *O Paradissos anigi me antiklidi* (also known as *Red Ants*), Greek Film Center/Ann, 1987.
Weasel, *The Raggedy Rawney,* Island, 1988.
Terry Fitch, *The Cook, the Thief, His Wife, and Her Lover,* Recorded Films, 1989.

Also appeared as singer "Sweet Gene Vincent," *Radio On,* 1979; Harry Winfield, *Brennende Betten,* 1988; and Barman, *Bearskin: An Urban Fairytale,* 1989. Appeared in *Concert for Kampuchea,* 1980.

FILM WORK

Contributor of songs to films *Take It or Leave It,* 1981, *Real Genius,* Tri-Star, 1985, and *Brennende Betten,* 1988.

RECORDINGS:

(With Kilburn and the High Roads) *Handsome,* Pye, 1975.
(With Blockheads) *New Boots and Panties,* Stiff Records, 1977.
(With Kilburn and the High Roads) *Wot a Bunch,* Warner Brothers, 1978.
(With Blockheads) *Do It Yourself,* Stiff Records, 1979.
Laughter, Stiff Records, 1980.
Lord Upminster, Polydor, 1981.

Singles with Blockheads include "What A Waste," 1978, "Hit Me With Your Rhythm Stick," 1978, and "Reasons to Be Cheerful, Part Three," 1979.

WRITINGS:

(Composer of music and lyrics with Micky Gallagher and Charles Jankel) *Serious Money* (musical), New York Shakespeare Festival, Public Theatre, New York City, 1987.
(Author of book and lyrics) *Apples* (musical), English Stage Company, Royal Court Theatre, London, 1989.*

*   *   *

d'USSEAU, Arnaud 1916-1990

PERSONAL: Born April 18, 1916, in Los Angeles, CA; died of stomach cancer, January 29, 1990, in New York, NY; son of Leon (a film director and producer) and Ottola (an actress; maiden name, Nesmith) d'Usseau; married Susan Wells (an artist; died 1973); married Marie Christine; children: (second marriage) one son, one daughter. *Education:* Graduated from Beverly Hills High School.

CAREER: Playwright and screenwriter. Worked as book clerk and set dresser; writer for the United Press in Arizona during the early 1930s; writing instructor at New York University and the School of Visual Arts, New York City; scriptwriter for U.S. Office of War Information's Overseas Motion Picture Bureau. *Military service:* U.S. Army, Signal Corps Photographic Center, Long Island, NY, 1943-45, became sergeant.

MEMBER: Dramatists Guild (former council member).

AWARDS, HONORS: Page One Award from Newspaper Guild for *Tomorrow the World.*

WRITINGS:

PLAYS

(With James Gow) *Tomorrow the World,* produced on Broadway, 1943.
(With Gow) *Deep Are the Roots,* produced in New York City, 1945.
(With Gow) *Legend of Sarah,* produced in New York City, 1950.
(With Dorothy Parker) *Ladies of the Corridor,* produced on Broadway, 1953.

Also author of *Bledsoe* and, with Gow, *How Like an Angel.*

SCREENPLAYS

(With Richard Collins) *One Crowded Night,* RKO, 1940.
(With Collins) *Lady Scarface,* RKO, 1941.

(With Gow) *Repent at Leisure,* RKO, 1941.
Just off Broadway, Twentieth Century-Fox, 1942.
The Man Who Wouldn't Die, Twentieth Century-Fox, 1942.
Who Is Hope Schuyler?, Twentieth Century-Fox, 1942.
(With Julian Halvey) *Horror Express* (also known as *Panico en el Transiberiano* and *Panic on the Trans-Siberian Express*), Benmar Scotia, 1972.
Psychomania (also known as *The Death Wheelers*), Scotia International, 1974.

ADAPTATIONS: Tomorrow the World was adapted for film by Ring Lardner, Jr., and Leopold Atlas, United Artists, 1944.

OBITUARIES AND OTHER SOURCES:

PERIODICALS

Hollywood Reporter, February 1, 1990.
Variety, February 7, 1990.*

*   *   *

DUTTON, Charles   1951-

PERSONAL: Born January 30, 1951, in Baltimore, MD. *Education:* Attended Hagerstown Junior College; received degree from Towson State University, 1978; attended Yale School of Drama.

CAREER: Actor. American Conservatory Theatre, San Francisco, CA, guest artist, 1986-87.

AWARDS, HONORS: Theatre World Award, 1984, Antoinette Perry Award nomination, 1985, and Outer Critics' Circle Award nomination, all for *Ma Rainey's Black Bottom;* Antoinette Perry Award nomination for best leading actor and Drama Desk nomination for best actor, both 1990, for *The Piano Lesson.*

CREDITS:

STAGE APPEARANCES

Rip Van Winkle or "The Works," Yale Repertory Theatre, New Haven, CT, 1981.
Beef, No Chicken, Yale Repertory Theatre, 1981.
Astopovo, Yale Repertory Theatre, 1982-83.
Levee, trumpeter, *Ma Rainey's Black Bottom,* Yale Repertory Theatre, then Cort Theatre, New York City, 1984.
Title role, *Othello,* Yale Repertory Theatre, 1986, then American Conservatory Theatre, San Francisco, CA, 1986-87.
Herald Loomis, *Joe Turner's Come and Gone,* Yale Repertory Theatre, 1986, then American Conservatory Theatre, San Francisco, CA, 1986-87.
Boy Willie, *The Piano Lesson,* Huntington Theatre Company, Boston, MA, 1987-88, later New York City.
Ira Aldridge, *Splendid Mummer* (one-man show), American Place Theatre, New York City, 1988.

Also appeared in *A Day of Absence, Pantomime,* and *Fried Chicken and Invisibility.*

FILM APPEARANCES

Jake, *Jacknife,* Cineplex Odeon, 1989.

Also appeared in *No Mercy* and *Crocodile Dundee II.*

TELEVISION APPEARANCES

Assistant district attorney, *Apology* (movie), HBO, 1986.
Colby, *Runaway,* Wonderworks, PBS, 1989.

Also appeared on the television series *Miami Vice, The Equalizer,* and *Cagney and Lacey* and in the movie *The Murder of Mary Phagan.*

OTHER SOURCES:

PERIODICALS

Premiere, July, 1988.*

E

EBERT, Roger 1942-

PERSONAL: Full name, Roger Joseph Ebert; born June 18, 1942, in Urbana, IL; son of Walter H. and Annabel (Stumm) Ebert. *Education:* University of Illinios, B.S., 1964; also attended University of Cape Town, South Africa, 1965; University of Chicago, 1966-67. *Avocational interests:* Drawing, painting, art collecting.

ADDRESSES: Office—c/o *Chicago Sun-Times,* 401 North Wabash, Chicago, IL 60611.

CAREER: Film critic and writer. *News Gazette,* Champaign-Urbana, IL, staff reporter, 1958-66; *Chicago Sun Times,* Chicago, IL, film critic, 1967—; *New York Post,* New York City, film critic 1986—. *US Magazine,* film critic, 1978-79. Ebert Company, Ltd., president 1981—. Chicago City College, instructor in English, 1967-68; University of Chicago, lecturer in film criticism, 1969—; Columbia College, lecturer, 1973-74 and 1977-80. National Endowment for the Arts and Humanities, consultant, 1972-77; juror at film festivals.

MEMBER: American Newspaper Guild, National Society of Film Critics,Writers Guild of America (West), Arts Club of Chicago, Cliff Dwellers Club of Chicago, University of Illinois Alumni Association (member of board of directors 1975—), Phi Delta Theta, Sigma Delta Chi.

AWARDS, HONORS: Overseas Press Club Award, 1963; award from Chicago Headline Club, 1963; Rotary fellow, 1965; Stick o' Type Award, Chicago Newspaper Guild, 1973; Pulitzer Prize for distinguished criticism, 1975, for reviews and essays in *Chicago-Sun Times;* Chicago Emmy Award, 1979.

CREDITS:

TELEVISION APPEARANCES

Host (with Gene Siskel), *Sneak Previews,* PBS, 1978-82.

Film critic, *NBC News,* NBC, 1980-83.
Host (with Siskel), *At the Movies* (also known as *Movie Views*), PBS, 1982-86.
Host (with Siskel), *Siskel & Ebert* (also known as *Siskel & Ebert & the Movies*), syndicated, 1986—.

Also film critic for WMAQ-TV, Chicago, 1980-83; and WLS-TV, Chicago, 1984—.

RADIO APPEARANCES

Movie News, ABC, 1982-85.

Also contributor to the program *Critics at Large,* WBBM, Chicago.

WRITINGS:

An Illini Century, University of Illinois Press, 1967.
Beyond the Valley of the Dolls (film), Twentieth Century-Fox, 1970.
(With Russ Meyer), *Beneath the Valley of the Ultra Vixens* (film), RM Films, 1979.
A Kiss Is Still a Kiss, Andrews & McMeel, 1984.
Roger Ebert's Movie Home Companion, Andrews & McMeel, 1985.
(With Daniel Curley) *The Perfect London Walk,* Andrews & McMeel, 1986.

Contributor to periodicals, including *Esquire, Oui, Film Comment, American Film, Critic,* and *Rolling Stone.*

OTHER SOURCES:

PERIODICALS

Chicago Tribune, September 6, 1979.
Los Angeles Times, August 31, 1982.
New York Times Book Review, December 16, 1984.
People, August 20, 1984.*

EDELMAN, Gregg   1958-

PERSONAL: Born September 12, 1958, in Chicago, IL. *Education:* Graduated from Northwestern University.

CAREER: Actor and singer.

AWARDS, HONORS: Antoinette Perry Award nomination, leading actor in a musical, 1989, for *City of Angels.*

CREDITS:

STAGE APPEARANCES

(Broadway debut) Person of Argentina, *Evita,* Broadway Theatre, 1979-80.

Bustopher Jones, Asparagus, Growltiger, *Cats,* Winter Garden Theatre, New York City, 1982.

Timothy, *Weekend,* Theatre at Saint Peter's Church, New York City, 1983.

A Londoner, *Oliver!,* Mark Hellinger Theatre, New York City, 1984.

Amateurs, Cincinnati Playhouse in the Park, Cincinnati, OH, 1985.

Georgia Avenue, Godspeed Opera House, East Haddam, CT, 1986.

Tano Bitko, *The Shop on Main Street,* Jewish Repertory Theatre, New York City, 1986.

Clifford Bradshaw, *Cabaret,* Imperial Theatre, New York City, then Minskoff Theatre, New York City, 1988.

Stine, *City of Angels,* Virginia Theatre, New York City, 1989.

Also appeared as title role, *Arthur;* Hoagy Carmichael, *Hoagy;* George, *She Loves Me;* Billy, *Anything Goes.* Appeared in *Babes in Arms,* Lincoln Center, New York City; *Forbidden Broadway.*

MAJOR TOURS

Person of Argentina, *Evita,* U.S. cities, 1980.
Mike Doonesbury, *Doonesbury,* U.S. cities, 1984.
Clifford Bradshaw, *Cabaret,* U.S. cities, 1987.

FILM APPEARANCES

Science teacher, *Manhattan Project,* Twentieth Century-Fox, 1986.
Chris, *Crimes and Misdemeanors,* Orion, 1989.
Phil, *Green Card,* Buena Vista, 1990.

TELEVISION APPEARANCES; EPISODIC

Appeared in *Another World,* NBC; *One Life to Live,* ABC.

OTHER TELEVISION APPEARANCES

Appeared in *Spencer for Hire* (series), ABC.

EDEN, Barbara   1934-

PERSONAL: Born Barbara Jean Huffman, August 23, 1934, in Tucson, AZ; daughter of Harrison Connor and Alice Mary (Franklin) Huffman; married Michael Ansara (an actor), January 17, 1958 (divorced, 1974); married Charles Donald Fegert (a publishing executive), September 3, 1977 (divorced, 1982); children: (first marriage) Matthew Michael Ansara. *Education:* Attended San Francisco City College; studied at the San Francisco Conservatory of Music and the Elizabeth Holloway School of Theatre.

CAREER: Actress. President, Mi-Bar Productions; member of board of directors, Security First National Bank of Chicago.

CREDITS:

FILM APPEARANCES

Back from Eternity, Universal, 1956.
Molly, *The Wayward Girl,* Republic, 1957.
Katey, *A Private's Affair,* Twentieth Century-Fox, 1959.
Roslyn Pierce, *Flaming Star,* Twentieth Century-Fox, 1960.
Clemmie, *From the Terrace,* Twentieth Century-Fox, 1960.
Lucy Hall, *Twelve Hours To Kill,* Twentieth Century-Fox, 1960.
Sally Hobson, *All Hands On Deck,* Twentieth Century-Fox, 1961.
Cathy Conners, *Voyage to the Bottom of the Sea,* Twentieth Century-Fox, 1961.
Susan Gale, *Five Weeks in a Balloon,* Twentieth Century-Fox, 1962.
Greta Heinrich, *The Wonderful World of the Brothers Grimm,* Metro-Goldwyn-Mayer (MGM), 1962.
Lissa, *The Yellow Canary,* Twentieth Century-Fox, 1963.
Sylvia, *The Brass Bottle,* Universal, 1964.
Laura Rogers, *The New Interns,* Columbia, 1964.
Augie Poole, *Ride the Wild Surf,* Columbia, 1964.
Angela Benedict, *Seven Faces of Dr. Lao,* MGM, 1964.
Pia Pacelli, *Quick, Let's Get Married* (also known as *The Confession* and *Seven Different Ways*), Golden Eagle, 1965.
Justin Pirot, *The Amazing Dobermans,* Golden, 1976.
Stella Johnson, *Harper Valley P.T.A.,* April Fools Production, 1978.
Anxious tunnel person, *Jaws 3-D,* Universal, 1983.
Maggie, *Chattanooga Choo Choo,* April Fools Production, 1984.

Also appeared as Carol Walker, *Swingin' Along* (also known as *Double Trouble*), 1962.

TELEVISION APPEARANCES; SERIES

Loco Jones, *How to Marry a Millionaire,* syndicated, 1957-59.

Jeannie, *I Dream of Jeannie,* NBC, 1965-70.

Stella Johnson, and a saleswoman, *Harper Valley P.T.A.,* NBC, 1981-82.

Barbara McCray, "Brand New Life," *The Magical World of Disney,* NBC, 1989–90.

TELEVISION APPEARANCES; MINI-SERIES PILOTS

The Hellcats, ABC, 1967.

Barbara Morris, *The Barbara Eden Show,* ABC, 1973.

Liz Stonestreet, *Stonestreet: Who Killed the Centerfold Model,* NBC, 1977.

Also appeared in the pilot for *Howdy.*

TELEVISION APPEARANCES; MOVIES

Dr. Jane Bowers, *The Feminist and the Fuzz,* ABC, 1971.

Liza Crocker, *A Howling in the Woods,* NBC, 1971.

Dina Hunter, *The Woman Hunter,* CBS, 1972.

Francine Gregory, *Guess Who's Been Sleeping in My Bed?,* ABC, 1973.

Ann Collins, *The Stranger Within,* ABC, 1974.

Lucy Colbert, *Let's Switch,* ABC, 1975.

Ellen Dowling, *How to Break Up a Happy Divorce,* NBC, 1976.

Lee Rawlins, *The Girls in the Office,* ABC, 1979.

Mary Beth Allen, *Return of the Rebels,* CBS, 1981.

Jeanie and Jeannie II, *I Dream of Jeannie . . . 15 Years Later,* NBC, 1985.

Jeannie, *I Dream of Jeannie . . . 20 Years After,* NBC, 1986.

Laura Harding, *The Stepford Children,* NBC, 1987.

Kathy McCormick, *The Secret Life of Kathy McCormick* (also see below), NBC, 1988.

Brenda Andersen, *Your Mother Wears Combat Boots,* NBC, 1989.

Her Wicked Ways, CBS, 1990.

Also appeared in *A Woman Scorned,* 1991.

TELEVISION APPEARANCES; SPECIALS

Lalume, *Kismet,* ABC, 1967.

Romp, ABC, 1968.

Guest, *The Bob Hope Show,* NBC, 1968, 1970, 1971, and 1972.

The Engelbert Humperdinck Special, ABC, 1969.

Host, *The Wonderful World of Girls,* NBC, 1970.

Gene Kelly's Wonderful World of Girls, NBC, 1970.

Changing Scene, ABC, 1971.

Host, *Love Is . . . Barbara Eden,* NBC, 1972.

Telly . . . Who Loves Ya' Baby?, CBS, 1976.

Texaco Presents The Bob Hope All-Star Comedy Special from Australia, NBC, 1978.

ABC's Silver Anniversary Celebration, 25 and Still the One, ABC, 1978.

Festival of the Stars: Mexico, CBS, 1978.

Bob Hope's All-Star Look at TV's Prime Time Wars, NBC, 1980.

Men Who Rate a "10," NBC, 1980.

Bob Hope's All-Star Comedy Look at the Fall Season: It's Still Free and Worth It, NBC, 1981.

Bob Hope's Women I Love—Beautiful But Funny, NBC, 1982.

The Bob Hope Christmas Show, NBC, 1985.

Host, *52nd Annual King Orange Jamboree Parade,* NBC, 1985.

Ringmaster, *11th Annual Circus of the Stars,* CBS, 1986.

All Star Party for Clint Eastwood, CBS, 1986.

NBC's 60th Anniversary Celebration, NBC, 1986.

Happy Birthday Hollywood, ABC, 1987.

Bob Hope's USO Christmas from the Persian Gulf— Around the World in Eight Days, NBC, 1988.

Bob Hope Christmas Special from Waikoloa, Hawaii, NBC, 1989.

Host, *101st Tournament of Roses Parade,* NBC, 1990.

Also guest host for *The Big Show,* 1980, *It's Only Human,* 1981, and *The 38th Annual Emmy Awards,* 1986.

OTHER TELEVISION APPEARANCES

(Television debut) *Cross Roads,* ABC, 1955.

"Country Club Dance," *I Love Lucy,* CBS, 1957.

The Fantasy Film World of George Pal (documentary), LCA Video, 1986.

Guest, *The Oprah Winfrey Show,* ABC, 1987.

Also appeared in *The West Point Story,* 1956.

TELEVISION WORK

Co-producer, *The Secret Life of Kathy McCormick* (movie), NBC, 1988.*

*   *   *

EDLUND, Richard   1940-

PERSONAL: Born December 6, 1940, in Fargo, ND. *Education:* Attended University of Southern California.

ADDRESSES: Contact—P.O. Box 2230, Hollywood, CA 90078.

CAREER: Special visual effects designer and producer. Designer with Industrial Light and Magic, 1975-83; designer with Entertainment Effects, 1983—; founder, designer, and producer, Big Boss Films Corporation; producer of training films while in the Navy. Letter designer for Candy Apple Neon; photographer; cable car driver. *Military service:* U.S. Navy.

AWARDS, HONORS: Emmy Award, Outstanding Individual Achievement (Creative Technical Crafts division), 1979, for *Battlestar Galactica;* Academy Awards (with others), Best Visual Effects, 1977, for *Star Wars,* and 1981, for *Raiders of the Lost Ark;* Special Achievement Awards from Academy of Motion Picture Arts and Sciences (with others), 1980, for *The Empire Strikes Back,* and 1983, for *Return of the Jedi;* Academy Award nominations (with others), Best Visual Effects, 1982, for *Poltergeist,* 1984, for *Ghostbusters* and *2010,* and 1988, for *Die Hard;* Scientific and Engineering Award from the Academy of Motion Picture Arts and Sciences, 1986, for the Zoom Aerial 65mm Optical Printer.

CREDITS:

FILM WORK; SPECIAL VISUAL EFFECTS DESIGNER, EXCEPT WHERE INDICATED

Miniature effects photographer and special visual effects designer (with John Dykstra, Grand McCune, and Robert Blalack), *Star Wars,* Twentieth Century-Fox, 1977.

Miniature effects photographer, *The China Syndrome,* Columbia, 1979.

(With Brian Johnson, Dennis Muren, and Bruce Nicholson) *The Empire Strikes Back,* Twentieth Century-Fox, 1980.

(With Nicholson, Kit West, and Joe Johnson) *Raiders of the Lost Ark,* Paramount, 1981.

(With Nicholson and Michael Wood) *Poltergeist,* Metro-Goldwyn-Mayer (MGM)/United Artists (UA), 1982.

(With Muren, West, Roy Arbogast, and Ken Ralston) *Return of the Jedi,* Twentieth Century-Fox, 1983.

(With John Bruno, Mark Vargo, and Chuck Gaspar) *Ghostbusters,* Columbia, 1984.

(With Henry Millar) *2010,* MGM/UA, 1984.

Special visual effects producer (with Michael Lantieri, Darrell Pritchett, Clayton Pinney, and Albert Lanutti), *Fright Night,* Columbia, 1985.

Special visual effects producer, *Big Trouble in Little China,* Twentieth Century-Fox, 1986.

Poltergeist II (also known as *Poltergeist II: The Other Side*), MGM/UA, 1986.

Special visual effects producer, *Solar Babies,* MGM/UA, 1986.

The Boy Who Could Fly, Twentieth Century-Fox, 1986.

Legal Eagles, Universal, 1986.

Special visual effects producer, *Date with an Angel,* De-Laurentiis Group, 1987.

Masters of the Universe, Cannon, 1987.

Special visual effects producer (with Phil Cory), *The Monster Squad,* Tri-Star, 1987.

Special visual effects producer, *Leonard, Part Six,* Columbia, 1987.

Elvira, Mistress of the Dark, New World, 1988.

Big Top Pee-Wee, Paramount, 1988.

Special visual effects producer with others, *Die Hard,* Twentieth Century-Fox, 1988.

Special visual effects producer, *Vibes,* Columbia, 1988.

Special water unit photography director, *Farewell to the King* (also known as *Goodbye to the King* and *L'adieu au roi*), Orion, 1989.

(Also producer) *Solar Crisis* (also known as *Crisis 2050*), Inter-Ocean, 1990.

Ghost, Paramount, 1990.

Also special visual effects designer, *Earth Star*Voyager,* 1988.

TELEVISION WORK; SERIES

Special visual effects photographer, *Battlestar Galactica,* ABC, 1978-80.

Opening segment production designer and producer, *Tales from the Crypt,* HBO, 1989—.

TELEVISION WORK; EPISODIC

Special visual effects designer, "Collection Completed," "Lover Come Hack to Me," and "Only Sin Deep," *Tales from the Crypt,* HBO, 1989.*

*   *   *

EDWARDS, Ben   1916-

PERSONAL: Full name, George Benjamin Edwards; born July 5, 1916, in Union Springs, AL; son of William Thomas (in business) and Sarah (McLaurine) Edwards; married Jane Greenwood (a costume designer), September 21, 1963. *Education:* Attended Feagin School of Dramatic Arts, 1934-36; attended Kane School of Art, 1935-36. *Avocational interests:* Book collecting, hunting, fishing.

ADDRESSES: Contact—United Scenic Artists, 1540 Broadway, New York, NY 10036.

CAREER: Set, costume, and lighting designer, and producer. *Military service:* U.S. Army, 1942-46; became lieutenant.

MEMBER: United Scenic Artists (president for seven years), Players Club (art committee), League of New York Theatres.

AWARDS, HONORS: Variety Drama Critics' Poll, 1960, for *Heartbreak House.*

CREDITS:

STAGE WORK; SET DESIGNER, EXCEPT WHERE NOTED

Mrs. Moonlight, Barter Theatre, Abingdon, VA, 1935-39.

Pursuit of Happiness, Barter Theatre, 1935-39.

Smilin' Through, Barter Theatre, 1935-39.

Beyond the Hills, Barter Theatre, 1935-39.

The Silver Cord, Barter Theatre, 1935-39.

Diff'rent, New York State Federal Theatre, Works Progress Administration Project, Maxine Elliott's Theatre, New York City, 1938.

Pygmalion, New York State Federal Theatre, Works Progress Administration Project, Maxine Elliott's Theatre, 1938.

Coriolanus, New York State Federal Theatre, Works Progress Administration Project, Maxine Elliott's Theatre, 1938.

Captain Jinks of the Horse Marines, New York State Federal Theatre, Works Progress Administration Project, Maxine Elliott's Theatre, 1938.

Another Sun, National Theatre, New York City, 1940.

Medea, National Theatre, 1947, and New York City Center Theatre, 1949.

Sundown Beach, Belasco Theatre, New York City, 1948.

(With William De Forest) *Diamond Lil,* Coronet Theatre, New York City, 1949.

(And costume designer) *The Taming of the Shrew* and *Julius Caesar,* Woodstock Playhouse, Woodstock, NY, 1949.

Costume designer, *Legend of Sarah,* Fulton Theatre, New York City, 1950.

Costume designer, *The Bird Cage,* Coronet Theatre, 1950.

Captain Brassbound's Conversion, New York City Center Theatre, 1950.

The Royal Family, New York City Center Theatre, 1951.

King Richard II, New York City Center Theatre, 1951.

The Taming of the Shrew, New York City Center Theatre, 1951.

Costume designer, *Desire Under the Elms,* ANTA Theatre, New York City, 1952.

(And costume designer) *Sunday Breakfast,* Coronet Theatre, 1952.

(And lighting designer) *The Time of the Cuckoo,* Empire Theatre, New York City, 1952.

Costume designer, *The Emperor's Clothes,* Ethel Barrymore Theatre, New York City, 1953.

(And lighting and costume designer) *The Remarkable Mr. Pennypacker,* Coronet Theatre, 1953.

(And lighting designer) *Lullaby,* Lyceum Theatre, New York City, 1954.

Sing Me No Lullaby, Phoenix Theatre, New York City, 1954.

(And lighting and costume designer) *The Traveling Lady,* Playhouse Theatre, New York City, 1954.

(And costume designer) *Anastasia,* Lyceum Theatre, 1954.

(And lighting designer) *Tonight in Samarkand,* Morosco Theatre, New York City, 1955.

The Honeys, Longacre Theatre, New York City, 1955.

(And lighting designer) *Someone Waiting,* John Golden Theatre, New York City, 1956.

(And lighting designer) *The Ponder Heart,* Music Box Theatre, New York City, 1956.

(And lighting and costume designer) *The Waltz of the Toreadors,* Coronet Theatre, 1957.

The Dark at the Top of the Stairs, Music Box Theatre, 1957.

(And lighting designer) *Jane Eyre,* Belasco Theatre, 1958.

(And lighting and costume designer) *A Touch of the Poet,* Helen Hayes Theatre, New York City, 1958.

The Disenchanted, Coronet Theatre, 1958.

(And lighting designer) *God and Kate Murphy,* Fifty-Fourth Street Theatre, New York City, 1959.

(And lighting designer) *Heartbreak House,* Billy Rose Theatre, New York City, 1959.

Lighting designer, *Ages of Man,* Forty-Sixth Street Theatre, New York City, 1959.

(And lighting designer) *Face of a Hero,* Eugene O'Neill Theatre, New York City, 1960.

Midgie Purvis, Martin Beck Theatre, New York City, 1961.

(And producer with Louis Allen) *Big Fish, Little Fish,* ANTA Theatre, 1961.

(And lighting designer) *Purlie Victorious,* Cort Theatre, New York City, 1961.

(And lighting designer) *A Shot in the Dark,* Booth Theatre, New York City, 1961.

(And lighting designer) *The Aspern Papers,* The Playhouse Theatre, 1962.

(And producer) *Harold,* Cort Theatre, New York City, 1963.

(And producer with Lewis Allen) *The Ballad of the Sad Cafe,* Martin Beck Theatre, 1963.

Hamlet, Lunt-Fontanne Theatre, New York City, 1964.

Costume designer, *The Changeling,* Repertory Theatre of Lincoln Center, Washington Square Theatre, New York City, 1964.

(And lighting designer) *The Family Way,* Lyceum Theatre, 1965.

(And lighting designer, and producer with Elaine Perry) *A Race of Hairy Men!,* Henry Miller's Theatre, New York City, 1965.

Family Things, Falmouth Playhouse, Falmouth, MA, and Westport Country Playhouse, Westport, CT, 1965.

(With George Jenkins) Production supervisor, *The Royal Hunt of the Sun,* ANTA Theatre, 1965.

(And lighting designer) *Where's Daddy?,* Billy Rose Theatre, 1966.

(And lighting designer) *Nathan Weinstein, Mystic, Connecticut,* Brooks Atkinson Theatre, New York City, 1966.

(And lighting designer) *How's the World Treating You?,* Music Box Theatre, 1966.

(With Jean Rosenthal, and lighting designer) *The Freaking Out of Stephanie Blake,* Eugene O'Neill Theatre, 1967.

More Stately Mansions, Broadhurst Theatre, 1967.

Twelfth Night, and *The Master Builder,* Minnesota Theatre Company, Tyrone Guthrie Theatre, Minneapolis, MN, 1968.

(And lighting designer) *The Mother Lover,* Booth Theatre, 1969.

Purlie, Broadway Theatre, New York City, 1970, then Billy Rose Theatre, 1972.

(And lighting designer) *Hay Fever,* Helen Hayes Theatre, 1970.

(And lighting designer) *Look Away,* Playhouse Theatre, 1973.

(And lighting designer) *Finishing Touches,* Plymouth Theatre, New York City, 1973.

A Moon for the Misbegotten, Morosco Theatre, 1973, and Ahmanson Theatre, 1975.

(And lighting designer) *The Headhunters,* John F. Kennedy Center for the Performing Arts, Washington, DC, 1974.

(And lighting designer) *Figures in the Sand,* Theatre at St. Clements, New York City, 1974.

Long Day's Journey Into Night, John F. Kennedy Center for the Performing Arts, 1975-76, then Brooklyn Academy Opera House, New York City, 1976.

A Matter of Gravity, Broadhurst Theatre, 1976, and Ahmanson Theatre, 1976-77.

(And lighting designer) *A Texas Trilogy,* Broadhurst Theatre, 1976.

(And lighting designer) *Anna Christie,* Imperial Theatre, New York City, 1977.

(And lighting designer) *A Touch of the Poet,* Helen Hayes Theatre, 1977.

(And lighting designer) *An Almost Perfect Person,* Belasco Theatre, 1977.

The West Side Waltz, Ethel Barrymore Theatre, 1981-82.

To Grandmother's House We Go, Biltmore Theatre, New York City, 1981.

Medea, Cort Theatre, 1982, and Clarence Brown Theatre, Knoxville, TN, 1982.

Death of a Salesman, Broadhurst Theatre, 1984.

The Iceman Cometh, Lunt-Fontanne Theatre, 1985.

Lillian, Ethel Barrymore Theatre, 1986.

Opera Comique, John F. Kennedy Center for the Performing Arts, 1986-87.

Long Day's Journey into Night, Yale Repertory Theatre, New Haven, CT, 1987-88.

The Chosen, Second Avenue Theatre, New York City, 1987-88.

Long Day's Journey Into Night, Neil Simon Theatre, New York City, 1988.

Also set designer for Studio Arena Theatre, Buffalo, NY, 1969-70 and 1976-77.

MAJOR TOURS

Set and lighting designer, *What Do You Really Know About Your Husband?,* U.S. cities, 1967.

Set and lighting designer, *Finishing Touches,* U.S. cities, 1973-74.

Set designer, *A Matter of Gravity,* U.S. cities, 1976-77.

Set designer, *The West Side Waltz,* U.S. cities, 1980-81.

FILM WORK

Production designer, *Lovers and Other Strangers,* Cinerama, 1970.

Art director, *Jennifer on My Mind,* United Artists, 1971.

Art director, *Last of the Red Hot Lovers,* Paramount, 1972.

Production designer, *Class of '44,* Warner Brothers, 1973.

Production designer, *Fort Apache, The Bronx,* Twentieth Century-Fox, 1981.

Production designer, *Hanky-Panky,* Columbia, 1982.

Production designer, *Sweet Liberty,* Universal, 1986.

Also worked as visual consultant on *Fast Forward,* 1985.

TELEVISION WORK; SERIES

Production designer, *The Ed Wynn Show,* NBC, 1952.

Production designer, *Armstrong Circle Theatre,* CBS, 1955.

Art director, *Fame,* NBC, 1982.

Production designer, *Bagdad Cafe,* CBS, 1990.

TELEVISION WORK; MOVIES

Art director, *Mayflower: The Pilgrim's Adventure,* CBS, 1979.

Art director, *The Royal Romance of Charles and Diana,* CBS, 1982.

Art director, *Jacobo Timerman: Prisoner Without a Name, Cell Without a Number,* NBC, 1983.

Production designer, *Kennedy,* NBC, 1983.

Production designer, *A Special Friendship,* CBS, 1987.

Production designer, *Liberace: Behind the Music,* CBS, 1988.

Production designer, *Everybody's Baby: The Rescue of Jessica McClure,* ABC, 1989.

TELEVISION WORK; SPECIALS

Art director, *The World of Magic,* NBC, 1975.

Art director, *Breaking Up,* ABC, 1978.

Art director, *Home to Stay,* CBS, 1978.

Also art director of *The Easter Promise,* 1975; *The Rivalry,* 1975; and *Addie and the King of Hearts,* 1976. Production designer for *Phobia,* 1980; *Heartbreak House,* 1986; *Ike,* 1986; *The Kingdom Chums: Little David's Ad-*

venture, 1986; *Winston Churchill,* 1986; *Lyndon Johnson,* 1987; and *An Enemy of the People,* 1990. Sculptor for *Apology,* 1986.

OTHER SOURCES:

PERIODICALS

Theatre Crafts, August/September, 1989.*

* * *

EICHELBERGER, Ethyl 1945-1990

PERSONAL: Born James Roy, July 17, 1945, in Pelkin, IL; name legally changed in 1975; took his own life, August 14, 1990, in Staten Island, NY; son of Amish parents. *Education:* Attended Knox College, Galesburg, IL; studied at American Academy of Dramatic Arts.

CAREER: Actor, director, writer, and hairstylist. Performance artist. Adrian Hall's Trinity Square Repertory Co., Providence, RI, actor for seven years; Ridiculous Theatre Co., New York City, actor and wigmaker. Has performed in London, Sydney, Amsterdam, Florence, Edinburgh.

AWARDS, HONORS: Village Voice Obie Award, 1982-83, for *Lucrezia Borgia;* New York Dance and Performance Award (Bessie), 1987, for *Collective Work;* Villager Award.

CREDITS:

STAGE APPEARANCES

Scrub Woman, La Fleur, Bertha, *Caprice,* Ridiculous Theatrical Company, Performing Garage, New York City, 1976.
Gunther and Fricka, *Der Ring Gott Farblonjet,* Ridiculous Theatrical Company, Truck & Warehouse Theatre, New York City, 1977.
Hamilcar Barca, *Salammbo* (also see below), Ridiculous Theatrical Company, 1985-86.
Mrs. Nurdiger, *The Artificial Jungle,* Ridiculous Theatrical Company, 1986-87.
Emilia, Abbess at Espesus, Courtesan, *The Comedy of Errors,* Vivian Beaumont Theatre, New York City, 1987.
Ballad Singer, *The Threepenny Opera,* Lunt-Fontanne Theatre, New York City, 1989.
Berkeley, *Buzzsaw Berkeley,* WPA Theatre, New York City, 1989.
Measure for Measure, Mitzi E. Newhouse Theatre, New York City, 1990.

Also appeared in *Lucrezia Borgia,* 1982-83; solo performance, *Collective Work,* New York City, 1987; King, Fool, and Cordelia in *Leer; Hamlet* and *Oedipus Rex,*

Knox College; *Change in A Void Moon,* Pyramid Club, New York City; President Lincoln and Mary Todd, *The Lincolns,* Lincoln Center, New York City.

STAGE WORK; HAIRSTYLIST

Cloud 9, Lucille Lortel Theatre, New York City, 1981.
America Kicks Up Its Heels, Playwrights Horizons, New York City, 1983.
Wigs, *Vieux Carre,* WPA Theatre, 1983.
The Mystery of Irma Vep, Ridiculous Theatrical Company, 1984-85.
Salammbo, Ridiculous Theatrical Company, 1985-86.
The Artificial Jungle, Ridiculous Theatrical Company, 1986-87.

FILM APPEARANCES

As himself, *The Doors,* 1991.

TELEVISION APPEARANCES

Encyclopedia, HBO, 1988.

Also appeared as Abbess and Courtesan, *The Comedy of Errors* (special), 1987.

WRITINGS:

PLAYS

Author of *Leer* (a one-man comic rendition of Shakespeare's *Lear*); *Dilbert Dingle-Dong* (an adaptation of Moliere's *George Dandin*); *Hamlette* (an adaptation of Shakespeare's *Hamlet* for female in title role); *Das Vedanya Mama* (a variation on Chekov's plays); *Fiasco* (based on "The Royal Family"); *Ariadne Obnoxious* (a comic parody of the Strauss opera *Ariadne auf Naxos*); and other comedies for Ridiculous Theatrical Company.

OBITUARIES AND OTHER SOURCES:

PERIODICALS

Daily News, August 14, 1990.
New York Times, August 14, 1990.*

* * *

ELLENSHAW, Peter 1913-

PERSONAL: Born 1913, in London, England; son of Harrison Ellenshaw (a film special effects technician).

CAREER: Special effects technician, art director, producer and director. Special effects technician for Alexander Korda, 1930s, and for Walt Disney Studios, 1950—; ride designer, Disneyland, Pasadena, CA. Painter; has had his works exhibited at Hammer Gallery, New York City. *Military service:* Royal Air Force, World War II.

AWARDS, HONORS: Academy Awards for Special Visual Effects, 1964, for *Mary Poppins,* and 1971, for *Bedknobs and Broomsticks.*

CREDITS:

SPECIAL EFFECTS FILM TECHNICIAN

Kidnapped, Buena Vista, 1960.
The Absent Minded Professor, Buena Vista, 1960.
In Search of the Castaways, Buena Vista, 1962.
Son of Flubber, Buena Vista, 1963.
Summer Magic, Buena Vista, 1963.
Mary Poppins, Buena Vista, 1964.
The Fighting Prince of Donegal, Buena Vista, 1964.
(With Eustace Lycett) *Lieutenant Robin Crusoe, U.S.N.,* Buena Vista, 1966.
(With Lycett) *The Happiest Millionaire,* Buena Vista, 1967.
(With Lycett and Robert Matley) *Black Beard's Ghost,* Buena Vista, 1968.
(With Lycett) *The Love Bug,* Buena Vista, 1968.

Also special effects technician of *The Thief of Bagdad,* 1940; *A Matter of Life and Death* (also known as *Stairway to Heaven*), 1940; *Black Narcissus,* 1947; *Quo Vadis,* 1951; *The Story of Robin Hood and His Merrie Men,* 1952; *The Sword and the Rose,* 1952; *Rob Roy the Highland Rogue,* 1953; *Davy Crockett, King of the Wild Frontier,* 1954; *The Great Locomotive Chase,* 1956; *The Light in the Forest,* 1958; *Pollyanna,* 1960; *Spartacus,* 1960; *The Adventures of Bullwhip Giffin,* 1967; *The Gnome-Mobile,* 1967; *Monkeys, Go Home!,* 1967; *Never a Dull Moment,* 1968; and *The Man Who Could Work Miracles.*

OTHER FILM WORK

Art director, *Treasure Island,* RKO Radio Pictures, 1950.
Art director, *20,000 Leagues Under the Sea,* Buena Vista, 1954.
Producer and director, *Johnny Tremain,* Buena Vista, 1957.
Art director (with John Mansbridge), *Bedknobs and Broomsticks,* Buena Vista, 1971.
Producer, director, and production designer, *The Island at the Top of the World,* Buena Vista, 1974.
Producer, director, production designer, and miniature effects creator and supervisor, *The Black Hole,* Buena Vista, 1979.

Matte painting supervisor, *Superman IV: The Quest for Peace,* 1987.*

*   *   *

ELVIRA
See PETERSON, Cassandra

EPSTEIN, Alvin   1925-

PERSONAL: Born May 14, 1925, in New York City; son of Harry (a doctor) and Goldie (Rudnick) Epstein. *Education:* Attended High School of Music and Art, 1942 and Queen's College, 1943; attended Biarritz American University, France, 1945; studied dance with Martha Graham in New York City, 1946-47, and ballet with Olga Preobrajenska in Paris, 1948-49; studied mime at Etienne Decroux School of Mime, Paris, 1947-51, and acting with Sanford Meisner in New York City, 1951-52; Actors' Studio, observer, 1955-57. *Avocational interests:* Playing the piano and harpsichord.

ADDRESSES: Agent—c/o David Kalodner, APA, 7th Ave. and 57th St., New York, NY 10106.

CAREER: Actor, director, and teacher. Conducted mime classes at Chamber Theatre School, Tel Aviv, 1952-53, Neighborhood Playhouse School of the Theatre, 1957-58, Circle in the Square School of the Theatre, 1961, and Barnard College Summer Theatre. Directed experimental group established through Ford Foundation grant, 1961-62. Co-founder of the Berkshire Theatre Festival, Stockbrige, MA, 1966. Salzburg American Seminar on the American Theatre fellow, 1972. Acting and directing instructor at the Yale School of Drama, 1967-77. Associate director of the Yale Repertory Theatre, 1968-77. Trumbull College fellow, Yale University. Artistic Director of the Guthrie Theatre, 1978-79. Faculty member, Aspen Music Festival, 1980 and 1981. Faculty member, American Repertory Theatre Insitute, 1988—. Member of board of directors, Theatre Communications Group, 1975-77. *Military service:* Served in the U.S Army, Coast and Field Artillery, ETO, 1943-46.

MEMBER: Actors' Equity Association, American Federation of Television and Radio Artists, Screen Actors' Guild.

AWARDS, HONORS: Variety Drama Critics Poll, Most Promising Actor nomination, 1956, for *Waiting for Godot* and *King Lear;* Ford Foundation grant, 1960; Creative Arts Award, Brandeis University, 1966; Obie Award, 1967, for role of Sergeant in *Dynamite Tonite.*

CREDITS:

STAGE APPEARANCES

(Stage debut) Lord Rivers, *Richard III,* Biarritz American University, U.S. Army, 1945.
(New York debut) Wint Selby, *Ah, Wilderness!,* Equity Library Theatre, Lenox Hill Playhouse, 1946.
Arthur Jarvis, *Lost in the Stars,* Habima Theatre, Tel-Aviv, Israel, c. 1953-55.
Victor Karenin, *The Living Corpse,* Habima Theatre, c. 1953-55.

The Messiah, *The Golem,* Habima Theatre, c. 1953-55.

Tony, *The Mother,* Habima Theatre, c. 1953-55.

Donalbain, *Macbeth,* Habima Theatre, c. 1953-55.

The Snake, *Legend of 3 and 4,* Habima Theatre, c. 1953-55.

Willy Keith, *The Caine Mutiny Court Martial,* Habima Theatre, c. 1953-55.

Count Carlo di Nolli, *Henry IV,* Habima Theatre, c. 1953-55.

The Fool, *King Lear,* Habima Theatre, c. 1953-55.

Marcel Marceau and His Partners, Phoenix Theatre, then Ethel Barrymore Theatre, New York City, 1955.

The Fool, *King Lear,* City Center Theatre, New York City, 1956.

Lucky, *Waiting for Godot,* John Golden Theatre, New York City, 1956.

Puck, *A Midsummer Night's Dream,* Empire State Music Festival, Ellenville, NY, 1956.

O'Killigain, *Purple Dust,* Cherry Lane Theatre, New York City, 1956.

Satan, *Adam,* White Barn Theatre, Westport, CT, 1956.

The Devil, *L'Histoire du Soldat,* Kaufman Auditorium, New York City, 1957.

Johnny Casside, *Pictures in the Hallway,* Festival Theatre, Ravinia, IL, 1957.

The Ragpicker, *The Madwoman of Chaillot,* Boston Summer Theatre, MA, 1957.

Spy, *Romanoff and Juliet,* Shubert Theatre, Boston, MA, 1957.

Vicomte Octave de Clerambard, *Clerambard,* Rooftop Theatre, New York City, 1957.

Clov, *Endgame,* Cherry Lane Theatre, New York City, 1958.

Claudius, *The Golden Six,* York Playhouse, New York City, 1958.

Narrator, *The Play of Daniel,* Chapel of the Intercession, New York City, 1959.

Feste, *Twelfth Night,* Cambridge Drama Festival, MA, 1959.

Ensemble, *From A to Z* (revue), Plymouth Theatre, New York City, 1960.

Narrator, *The Play of Daniel,* St. George's Church, New York City, 1961.

Luc Delbert, *No Strings,* Fifty-Fourth Street Theatre, New York City, 1962.

Sergeant, *Dynamite Tonite,* Actors Studio, New York City, 1963.

Constable Kentinov, Alexander Lomov, and Trotsky, *The Passion of Josef D.,* Ethel Barrymore Theatre, New York City, 1964.

Brecht on Brecht, Playhouse in the Park, Philadelphia, PA, 1964.

Title role, *Enrico IV,* Henry Miller Theatre, Milwaukee, WI, 1964, then Harper Theatre, Chicago, IL, 1964.

A Wen and *Orange Souffle* (double bill), Loft, New York City, 1965.

Bob McKelloway, *Mary, Mary,* Bucks County Playhouse, New Hope, PA, 1965.

Various roles, *Postmark Zero,* Brooks Atkinson Theatre, New York City, 1965.

M. Berenger, *Pedestrian in the Air,* Goodman Theatre, Chicago, 1966.

Mr. Antrobus, *The Skin of Our Teeth,* Berkshire Theatre Festival, Stockbridge, MA, 1966.

Shylock, *The Merchant of Venice,* Berkshire Theatre Festival, 1966.

Sergeant, *Dynamite Tonite,* Yale Repertory, New Haven, CT, 1966, later Martinique Theatre, New York City, 1967.

Henry David Thoreau, *At This Hour,* Nassau Community College, Long Island, NY, 1967.

Theseus and Oberon, *A Midsummer Night's Dream,* Theatre de Lys, New York City, 1967.

Ensemble, *The World of Kurt Weill* (revue), Ravinia Festival, Chicago, 1967, then Bijou Theatre, New York City, 1979.

Arthur Landau, *The Latent Heterosexual,* Huntington Hartford Theatre, Los Angeles, CA, 1968.

William Clark Brackman, *God Bless,* Yale Repertory Theatre, 1968.

Various roles, *Story Theatre—Grimm's Fairy Tales,* Yale Repertory Theatre, 1968.

Ensemble, *A Kurt Weil Cabaret* (revue with Martha Schlamme), Yale Repertory Theatre, 1968, then Guthrie Theatre, Minneapolis, MN, 1977, then Bijou Theatre, New York City, 1979, then Aspen Music Festival, 1979 and 1980, then Roundabout Stage One, New York City, 1981, then Harold Clurman Theatre, 1984-85, later Israel Festival, Jerusalem, 1985.

The Golden Goose, Yale Repertory Theatre, 1968-69.

Various roles, *Metamorphoses,* Yale Repertory Theatre, 1969.

Dionysus, *The Bacchae,* Yale Repertory Theatre, 1969.

Title role, *Greatshot,* Yale Repertory Theatre, 1969.

Ensemble, *Whores, Wars and Tin Pan Alley* (revue with Schlamme), The Bitter End, New York City, 1969, then Sheridan Square Playhouse, later Macloren Playhouse, Hollywood, CA, 1970.

Maurice, *Crimes and Crimes,* Yale Repertory Theatre, 1970.

Khlestakov, *The Government Inspector,* Yale Repertory Theatre, 1970.

Title role, *Don Juan,* Yale Repertory Theatre, 1970.

Various roles, *Olympian Games,* Yale Repertory Company at John Drew Theatre, Easthampton, NY, 1970.

Three Stories by Philip Roth, Yale Repertory Company at John Drew Theatre, 1970.

The questioner, *A Place Without Doors* (English translation of *L'Amante Anglaise*), Long Wharf Theatre, New Haven, CT, 1970, and Staircase Theatre, New York City, 1970.

Dr. Nakamura, *Happy End,* Yale Repertory Theatre, 1971-72.

Title role, *Gimpel the Fool,* Yale Repertory Theatre, 1971.

The questioner, *A Place Without Doors,* Goodman Theatre, 1971-72.

Pietro, *If I Married You for the Fun of It,* Yale Repertory Theatre, 1972.

Husband, *Life Is A Dream,* Yale Repertory Theatre, 1972.

Title role, *Macbett,* Yale Repertory Theatre, 1973.

Prospero, *The Tempest,* Yale Repertory Theatre, 1973.

Warrington and the judge, *Lear* (by Edward Bond), Yale Repertory Theatre, 1973.

Various characters, *Watergate Classics,* Yale Repertory Theatre, 1973.

Kirilov, *The Possessed,* Yale Repertory Theatre, 1974.

Aekos, *The Frogs,* Yale Repertory Theatre, 1974.

Sergeant, *Dynamite Tonite!,* Yale Repertory Theatre, 1976.

Shakespeare, *Bingo: Scenes of Money and Death,* Yale Repertory Theatre, 1976.

Title role, *Ivanov,* Yale Repertory Theatre, 1976.

Grandfather, *White Marriage,* Yale Repertory Theatre, 1977.

Kochkariev, *Marriage,* Guthrie Theatre, Minneapolis, MN, 1977.

(With Martha Schlamme) *Schlamme and Epstein Sing Bernstein and Blitzstein,* Aspen Music Festival, HB Studio, New York City, and American Repertory Theatre, 1981.

Blondin, *Crossing Niagara,* Manhattan Theatre Club/Downstage, New York City, 1981.

Vershinin, *Three Sisters,* American Repertory Theatre, Cambridge, MA, 1982.

Pastor Manders, *Ghosts,* American Repertory Theatre, 1982.

Sir Peter Teazle, *School for Scandal,* American Repertory Theatre, 1982.

Reader, *Ohio Impromptu* Harold Clurman Theatre, New York City, 1983-84, and Mark Taper Forum New Theatre For Now, 1984, then Israel Festival, Jerusalem, 1985.

Director/Protagonist, *Catastrophe,* Harold Clurman Theatre, 1983-84, and Mark Taper Forum New Theatre For Now, 1984, then Israel Festival, 1985.

What Where, Harold Clurman Theatre, 1983-84, and Mark Taper Forum New Theatre For Now, 1984, then Israel Festival, 1985.

The Value of Names, Hartford Stage Company, CT, 1983-84.

Various roles, *Dead End Kids: A History of Nuclear Power,* Mark Taper Forum New Theatre for Now, 1983-84.

Hamm, *Endgame,* Samuel Beckett Theatre, and Cherry Lane Theatre, New York City, then New Mayfair Theatre, Santa Monica, CA, all 1984, later Israel Festival, Jerusalem, 1985.

Androcles, *Androcles and the Lion,* Hartford Stage Company, 1985-86.

Dr. Bonfant, *The Waltz of the Toreadors,* Roundabout Theatre, New York City, 1985-86.

Soloist, *Songs of Innocence and Experience,* Brooklyn Academy of Music, New York City, 1987.

Mr. Bonaparte, *Golden Boy,* Williamstown Theatre Festival, MA, 1987.

Mr. ShuFu, *The Good Woman of Setzuan,* American Repertory Theatre, 1987.

Father, *Six Characters in Search of an Author,* American Repertory Theatre, 1987.

Henry Howe, *Right You Are if You Think You Are,* American Repertory Theatre, 1987.

Sang in Lotte Lenya Tribute, *Kurt Weill Festival,* Merkin Hall, New York City, 1987.

Serebriakoff, *Uncle Vanya,* American Repertory Theatre, 1988.

Father, *Six Characters,* Joyce Theatre, New York City, 1988.

Glagoliev, *Platonov,* American Repertory Theatre, 1988.

Senator Bunting, Representative Moss, and Wylie Slaughter, *Mastergate,* American Repertory Theatre, 1988.

Various roles, *In Twilight,* American Repertory Theatre, 1989.

Harpagon, *The Miser,* American Repertory Theatre, 1989.

Jonathan Jeremiah Peachum, *The Threepenny Opera,* National Theatre, Washington, D.C., and Lunt-Fontanne Theatre, New York City, 1989.

Marquis de Sade, *Marat/Sade,* Williamstown Theatre Festival, 1990.

Herman Glogauer, *Once in a Lifetime,* American Repertory Theatre, 1990.

Arnold Rubek, *When We Dead Awaken,* American Repertory Theatre, 1991.

Gloucester, *King Lear,* American Repertory Theatre, 1991.

MAJOR TOURS

Lord Rivers, *Richard III,* Biarritz American University, U.S. Army, European cities, 1945-46.

Sganarelle, *The Doctor in Spite of Himself,* U.S. cities, 1951.

Ensemble, *A Kurt Weill Cabaret* (revue), United States, South America, and Israel, 1967-85.

A Place Without Doors, U.S. cities, 1971.

King Stag, American Repertory Theatre, Madrid, Spain, 1988.

Also toured with the French Mime Theatre of Etienne Decroux, Europe and the Middle East, 1947-51. Toured with *Marcel Marceau and His Partners,* 1955.

STAGE WORK; DIRECTOR

On the Harmfulness of Tobacco, National Theatre of the Deaf, Waterford, CT, 1967, then Hunter College Playhouse, New York City, 1967, later the Forum, Lincoln Center, New York City, 1968, and closing in Los Angeles, 1968.
The Rivals, Yale Repertory Theatre, 1970-71.
The Seven Deadly Sins, Yale Repertory Theatre, 1970-71.
Macbett, Yale Repertory Theatre, 1973.
In the Clap Shack, Yale Repertory Theatre, 1973.
(With Moni Yakim) *The Tempest,* Yale Repertory Theatre, 1973.
The Rise and Fall of the City of Mahagonny, Yale Repertory Theatre, 1974.
Colette, Berkshire Theatre Festival, Stockbridge, MA, 1974.
A Midsummer Night's Dream, Yale Repertory Theatre, 1975.
(With Walt Jones) *Dynamite Tonite!,* Yale Repertory Theatre, 1975.
Troilus and Cressida, Yale Repertory Theatre, 1976.
Julius Caesar, Yale Repertory Theatre, 1976.
The Pretenders, Guthrie Theatre, 1977-79.
The Rivals, Guthrie Theatre, 1977-79.
The Beggars Opera, Guthrie Theatre, 1977-79.
A Midsummer Night's Dream, American Repertory Theatre, 1979 and 1980-81.
The Seven Deadly Sins, American Repertory Theatre, 1980-81.
The Marriage of Figaro, American Repertory Theatre, 1980-81.
The Boys From Syracuse, American Repertory Theatre, 1982 and 1983.
Old Times, Williamstown Theatre Festival, 1983.
Endgame, Samuel Beckett Theatre, Cherry Lane Theatre, and New Mayfair Theatre, all 1984, then Israel Festival, 1985.
The Importance of Being Earnest, Yale Repertory Theatre, 1985-86.
Heartbreak House, Yale Repertory Theatre, 1987.

STAGE WORK: ARTISTIC DIRECTOR AT GUTHRIE THEATRE, 1978-79

Boy Meets Girl.
Hamlet.
A Christmas Carol.
The Beggars Opera.
Bonjour la Bonjour.
The Pretenders.
Teibele and Her Demon.
Right of Way.
Marriage.
Monsieur de Moliere.

OTHER STAGE WORK

Set designer, *Ah, Wilderness!,* Lenox Hill Playhouse, 1947.
Assistant director, *Miss Julie,* and *The Stronger* (double bill), Phoenix Theatre, 1956.

TELEVISION APPEARANCES

(Television debut) "The Ballad of Yermo Red," *Studio One,* CBS, 1956.
Phillip Manning, *The Doctors* (series), NBC, 1981-82.
Lou Rosenberg, *Doing Life* (movie), NBC, 1986.

Also host of *From China to U.S.,* 1978. Appeared as Son, "Therese Raquin," *Play of the Week,* WNET; Lucky, "Waiting for Godot," *Play of the Week,* WNET; Noah, "Prayers From the Ark," *Look Up and Live,* CBS. Also appeared in *Terezin Requiem,* CBS; *Story Theatre—Grimm's Fairy Tales,* PBS; *Lamp Unto My Feet,* CBS; *The Eternal Light,* CBS; *Omnibus,* NBC; *The Ed Sullivan Show,* CBS; *Ellery Queen,* NBC; *Accent,* CBS; *Histoire du Soldat;* and in various TV dramas, 1956—.

RECORDINGS:

Recorded *Waiting for Godot* (original cast), Columbia Records; *Pictures in the Hallway,* Spoken Arts Records; *Blitzstein by Blitzstein,* Caedmon Records; *The Soldier's Tale,* Kapp Records; *No Strings* (original cast), RCA Victor. Also recorded a series of plays by Samuel Beckett for radio, 1988-90.

SIDELIGHTS: Favorite roles: Lucky in *Waiting for Godot,* and Pirandello's Henry IV.

*   *   *

EVE, Trevor   1951-

PERSONAL: Born July 1, 1951, in Staffordshire, England (some sources say Wales).

ADDRESSES: Agent—John Kimble, Triad Artists, 10100 Santa Monica Blvd., 16th Floor, Los Angeles, CA 90068; Julian Belfrage Associates, 68 St. James's St., London SW1, England.

CAREER: Actor.

AWARDS, HONORS: Society of West End Theatres (SWET) Award, and Olivier Award, both for Best Actor, 1981-82, for *Children of a Lesser God.*

CREDITS:

STAGE APPEARANCES

Paul McCartney, *John, Paul, George, Ringo . . . and Bert,* Lyric Theatre, London, 1974.

Riccardo, *Filumena,* Lyric Theatre, 1977.

James Leeds, *Children of a Lesser God,* Mermaid Theatre, then Albery Theatre, both London, 1981.

Leo Lehrer, *The Genius,* Royal Court Theatre, London, 1983.

Dexter, *High Society,* Victoria Palace Theatre, London, 1987.

Man, Beast, and Virtue, National Theatre, Cottesloe Theatre, London, 1989.

FILM APPEARANCES

Jonathan Harker, *Dracula,* Universal, 1979.

Matinee idol, *Scandal,* Miramax, 1989.

TELEVISION APPEARANCES; SERIES

Eddie Shoestring, *Shoestring,* 1979-81, then Entertainment Channel, 1982.

Professor Jonathon MacKensie, *Shadow Chasers,* ABC, 1985-86.

Also appeared in *A Sense of Guilt,* BBC-1.

TELEVISION APPEARANCES; EPISODIC

Richard, *A Wreath of Roses,* Granada, 1988, then *Masterpiece Theatre,* PBS, 1989.

Ricky Fortune, *Dear John,* NBC, 1989.

TELEVISION APPEARANCES; MOVIES

Jem Meryn, *Jamaica Inn,* syndicated, 1985.

Louis da Franchi, *The Corsican Brothers,* CBS, 1985.

Denys Finch Hatton, *Beryl Markham: A Shadow on the Sun,* CBS, 1988.

Parnell, BBC, 1990.

Also appeared in *The Portrait,* 1975; *Hindle Wakes,* 1976; *London Belongs to Me,* 1977; and *A Brothers Tale.*

OTHER TELEVISION APPEARANCES

Tom Schwartz, *Lace* (mini-series), ABC, 1984.

Tripper Day, *Life on the Flipside* (pilot), NBC, 1988.*

F

FAIN, Sammy 1902-1989

PERSONAL: Full name Samuel Feinberg; born June 17, 1902, in New York, NY; died of a heart attack, December 6, 1989, University of California at Los Angeles Medical Center; son of Abraham (a reverend and cantor) and Mania (Glass) Feinberg; married Sally Fox, June 18, 1941 (divorced 1949); children: Frank. *Education:* Attended public schools in New York City.

CAREER: Composer and musician. Self-taught piano player. Staff pianist for Jack Mills, music publisher; recording contract with Columbia's Harmony Records; solo performer on many New York radio stations.

MEMBER: American Society of Composers, Authors and Publishers, American Guild of Authors and Composers, Composers and Lyricists Guild of America, American Federation of Television and Radio Artists, Masonic Order.

AWARDS, HONORS: Shared Academy Award with Paul Francis Webster, 1953, for song "Secret Love," from *Calamity Jane;* Academy Award with Webster, 1955, for title song, *Love Is a Many Splendored Thing;* Academy Award nominations for songs, "That Old Feeling," "April Love," "Tender is the Night," and "Strange Are the Ways of Love"; Diploma Di Benenerenza, Hall of Artists, Nice, France, 1956; Augosto Messinese Gold Award, Messina, Italy, 1956; Academy award nomination with Webster for "A Very Special Love," from *Marjorie Morningstar;* Laurel Awards for song "A Very Precious Love," and music from *A Certain Smile,* 1959; named an honorary Kentucky Colonel, 1961; Songwriters Hall of Fame, 1972; American Society of Composers, Authors and Producers Country Music Award, 1974; career award, ASCAP, 1989, for achievement as "one of America's premier composers of popular songs."

CREDITS:

STAGE APPEARANCES

(With Artie Dunn) *Fain and Dunn* (vaudeville act), 1928-32.

FILM APPEARANCES

Buttercup Baumer, *Dames,* Warner Brothers, 1934.

TELEVISION APPEARANCES; SPECIALS

Guest, *Johnny Carson Presents the Sun City Scandals '72,* National Broadcasting Company, Inc. (NBC-TV), 1972.

Also appeared in *The Music Makers: An ASCAP Celebration of American Music at Wolf Trap,* 1987.

WRITINGS:

STAGE MUSIC; COMPOSER

(Broadway debut) *Everybody's Welcome,* Sam S. Shubert Theatre, New York City, 1931.
(With Irving Kahal) Additional songs, *Right This Way,* Forty-Sixth Street Theatre, New York City, 1938.
Hellzapoppin, Forty-Sixth Street Theatre, 1938.
George White's Scandals (also see below), Alvin Theatre, New York City, 1939.
Ed Wynn's Boys and Girls Together, Broadhurst Theatre, New York City, 1940.
Songs, *Sons o' Fun,* Winter Garden Theatre, New York City, 1941.
Toplitzky of Notre Dame, Century Theatre, New York City, 1946.
(And collaborator with E. Y. Harburg) *Flahooley,* Broadhurst Theatre, 1951.
(And collaborator with Dan Shapiro) *Ankles Aweigh!,* Mark Hellinger Theatre, New York City, 1955.

Contributor, *Catch a Star!*, Plymouth Theatre, New York City, 1955.

Contributor, *Ziegleld Follies*, Winter Garden Theatre, 1957.

(And collaborator with Paul Francis Webster) *Christine*, Forty-Sixth Street Theatre, 1960.

Around the World in Eighty Days, St. Louis Municipal Opera, MO, 1962, then Marine Theatre, Jones Beach, Long Island, NY, 1963-64.

(And collaborator with Alan and Marilyn Bergman) *Something More*, produced on Broadway, 1964.

FILM MUSIC; COMPOSER WITH IRVING KAHAL

"Lonely Lane" and "Men of Calvert," *College Coach*, Warner Brothers, 1933.

"By a Waterfall," *Footlight Parade*, Warner Brothers, 1933.

Harold Teen (also known as *The Dancing Fool*), Warner Brothers, 1934.

"Good Green Acres of Home," "Ev'ry Day," "Don't Go on a Diet," "Winter Overnight," "There's a Different You in Your Heart," and "Seltzer Theme Song," *Sweet Music*, Warner Brothers, 1935.

Also composed songs with Kahal, including "Let a Smile Be Your Umbrella," "I Can Dream Can't I," "Nobody Knows What a Red-Headed Mama Can Do," "Second Star to the Right," "That Old Feeling," "Something I Dreamed Last Night," "Are You Havin' Any Fun," "Dear Hearts and Gentle People," "Wedding Bells Are Breaking Up that Old Gang of Mine," and "Was That the Human Thing to Do."

FILM MUSIC; COMPOSER WITH PAUL FRANCIS WEBSTER

Calamity Jane, Warner Brothers, 1953.

Lucky Me, Warner Brothers, 1954.

Title song, *Love Is a Many Splendored Thing*, Twentieth Century-Fox, 1955.

Theme song, *April Love*, Twentieth Century-Fox, 1957.

Theme song, *Gift of Love*, Twentieth Century-Fox, 1958.

"A Very Special Love," *Marjorie Morningstar*, Warner Brothers, 1958.

Theme song, *A Certain Smile*, Twentieth-Century Fox, 1958.

Mardi Gras, Twentieth Century-Fox, 1958.

Theme song, *Imitation of Life*, Universal, 1959.

Joy in the Morning, Metro-Goldwyn-Mayer (MGM), 1964.

"Paris Lullaby," *Made in Paris*, MGM, 1966.

Theme song, *The Teacher* (also known as *The Seductress*), Crown International, 1974.

Theme song, *The Specialist*, Crown International, 1975.

OTHER FILM COMPOSITIONS

Young Man of Manhattan, Paramount, 1930.

"When I Take My Sugar to Tea," *Monkey Business*, Paramount, 1931.

(With others) *The Big Pond*, Paramount, 1930.

Goin' to Town, Paramount, 1935.

(With Lew Brown) "Our Penthouse on Third Avenue," "Love Is Never out Of Season," "It Goes to Your Feet," "If I Didn't Have You," "Take the World off Your Shoulders," and "It's the Doctor's Orders," *New Faces of 1937*, RKO Radio Pictures, 1937.

(With Brown) "That Old Feeling," *Vogues of 1938*, United Artists, 1938.

(With Ted Kohler) "And There You Are," *Weekend at the Waldorf*, MGM, 1945.

(With others) *Anchors Aweigh*, MGM, 1945.

(With Jack Yellen) "I Want to Be a Drummer in the Band," "How Did You Get out Of My Dreams?," "I Wake up in the Morning," and "Who Killed Vaudeville?," *George White's Scandals*, RKO Radio Pictures, 1945.

(With Ralph Freed) "The Fire Chief's Daughter," "There Are Two Sides to Every Girl," "Down by the Ocean," "Nellie Martin," "After the Show," "G'wan Your Mudder's Callin," *Two Sisters from Boston*, MGM, 1946.

(With Howard Dietz) "The Dickey Bird Song," *Three Daring Daughters*, MGM, 1947.

(With Jack Barnett) "It's Bigger Than Both Of Us" and "Early Morning Song," *The Milkman*, Universal, 1950.

(With others) *Call Me Mister*, Twentieth Century-Fox, 1951.

(With others) *Alice in Wonderland*, RKO Radio Pictures, 1951.

(With Sammy Cahn) "The Elegant Captain Hook," "the Second Star to the Right," "What Makes the Red Man Red?" "You Can Fly, You Can Fly," "Your Mother and Mine," *Peter Pan*, RKO Radio Pictures, 1953.

(With Jerry Seelan) "Living the Life I Love," "What Are New Yorkers Made Of?" "Hush-a-bye," "Oh Moon," "I Hear the Music Now," *The Jazz Singer*, Warner Brothers, 1953.

(With Cahn) *Three Sailors and a Girl*, Warner Brothers, 1953.

(With Charles O'Curran and Webster) *Hollywood or Bust*, Paramount, 1956.

Theme song, *Tender is the Night*, Twentieth Century-Fox, 1962.

(With Harold Adamson) *The Incredible Mr. Limpet*, Warner Brothers, 1964.

Theme song, *The Stepmother*, Magic Eye, 1972.

"The Wild and Wooly West," *The Parallax View*, Paramount, 1974.

"The Dark Side of Love," *Dr. Minx*, Warner Brothers, 1975.

"Someone's Waiting for You," *The Rescuers*, Disney, 1977.

"Love Is A Many Splendored Thing," *Grease*, Paramount, 1978.

"Love Is A Many Splendored Thing," *Heartbeat*, Warner Brothers, 1979.

"I'll Be Seeing You," *Yanks*, Universal, 1979.

"Katie," *Just You and Me, Kid*, Columbia, 1979.

"A New Kind of Love," *Raging Bull*, United Artists, 1980.

"Secret Love" and "A Very Special Love," *Heartbreak Ridge*, Warner Brothers, 1986.

"You Brought A New Kind of Love to Me," *Children of a Lesser God*, Paramount, 1986.

(With others) *Radio Days*, Orion, 1987.

"Love Is A Many Splendored Thing," *Cookie*, Warner Brothers, 1989.

"I'll Be Seeing You," *Crimes and Misdemeanors*, Orion, 1989.

"I'll Be Seeing You," *New York Stories*, Buena Vista, 1989.

Also composer of songs that appeared in other films, including "Love Is A Many Splendored Thing," in *Shifshuf Naim*, 1981; "I'll Be Seeing You," in *Bad Timing*, 1980; and "Secret Love," in *Before Stonewall*, 1984.

TELEVISION MUSIC; COMPOSER

Score, *A Diamond for Carla*, Columbia Broadcasting System, Inc. (CBS-TV), 1960.

Score, *A Special Valentine with Family Ciros*, NBC, 1978.

Songs used on various television programs, 1972—.

OTHER

Sammy Fain's Songbook, H. Leonard Publishing Corp., 1990.

OBITUARIES AND OTHER SOURCES:

PERIODICALS

Variety, December 13, 1989.*

*   *   *

FARRELL, Charles   1900(?)-1990

PERSONAL: Born August 9, 1900 (some sources say 1901 or 1902), in Onset Bay, MA; died of cardiac arrest, May 6, 1990, in Palm Springs, CA; married Virginia Valli, 1931 (died, September, 1968). *Education:* Attended Boston University.

CAREER: Actor. Mayor of Palm Springs, CA, 1948-53. Co-founded and operated the Palm Springs Racquet Club. *Military service:* U.S. Navy, 1942-45.

CREDITS:

FILM APPEARANCES

The Ten Commandments, Paramount, 1923.

The Commodore, *Old Ironsides*, Paramount, 1926.

Timmy, *Sandy*, Paramount, 1926.

Chico, *Seventh Heaven*, Twentieth Century-Fox, 1927.

Stewart Van Brunt, *The Rough Riders*, Paramount, 1927.

Allen Pender, *The River*, Twentieth Century-Fox, 1928.

Gino, *Street Angel*, Twentieth Century-Fox, 1928.

Timothy Osborn, *Lucky Star*, 1929.

Jack Cromwell, *Sunny Side Up*, Twentieth Century-Fox, 1929.

Lem Tustine, *City Girl*, Twentieth Century-Fox, 1930.

Happy Days, Twentieth Century-Fox, 1930.

Eddie Granger, *High Society Blues*, Twentieth Century-Fox, 1930.

Title role, *Liliom*, Twentieth Century-Fox, 1930.

Charles Peters, *The Princess and the Plumber*, Twentieth Century-Fox, 1930.

Legionnaire, *Song of Soho*, First National, 1930.

Major Andrews, *Body and Soul*, Twentieth Century-Fox, 1931.

Jerry Beaumont, *Delicious*, Twentieth Century-Fox, 1931.

Poner, *The Flying Fool*, Wardour, 1931.

George Wollmer, *The Gables Mystery* (also known as *The Man at Six*), Powers, 1931.

John Merrick, *Heartbreak*, Twentieth Century-Fox, 1931.

Wharton, *The House Opposite*, Pathe, 1931.

Chicago Joe, *The Limping Man* (also known as *Creeping Shadows*), Powers, 1931.

Stephen Randolph, *The Man Who Came Back*, Twentieth Century-Fox. 1931.

John Lonsdale, *Merely Mary-Ann*, Twentieth Century-Fox, 1931.

Peter Piper, *After Tomorrow*, Twentieth Century-Fox, 1932.

Tommy Tucker, *The First Year*, Twentieth Century-Fox, 1932.

Bookmaker, *Lucky Ladies*, Warner Brothers/First National, 1932.

Digger, *Money for Nothing*, Pathe, 1932.

Frederick Garfield, Jr., *Tess of the Storm Country*, Twentieth Century-Fox, 1932.

Williams, *Tonight's the Night* (also known as *Tonight's the Night—Pass It On*), Wardour, 1932.

One of the strangers, *Wild Girl* (also known as *Salomy Jane*), Twentieth Century-Fox, 1932.

Smiler, *Why Saps Leave Home*, Power, 1932.

Tom Duncan, *Girl without a Room*, Paramount, 1933.

Martin, *Night and Day* (also known as *Jack's The Boy*), Gaumont, 1933.

Jimmy Morrell, *The Big Shakedown,* Warner Brothers, 1934.

Chris Thring, *Change of Heart,* Twentieth Century-Fox, 1934.

Title role, *Larry Davis,* Universal, 1935.

Himself, *Two Hearts in Harmony,* British International/Pickers, 1935.

Red Wagon, First Division, 1936.

Louis Brown, *Boys Will Be Boys,* Gaumont, 1936.

Sandy Nelson, *The Flying Doctor,* General Film Distributors, 1936.

Niba, *Forbidden Heaven,* Republic, 1936.

Howard Elliott, *Trouble Ahead* (also known as *Falling in Love*), Times, 1936.

Spike, *Under Proof,* Twentieth Century-Fox, 1936.

Briant Gaunt, *Bombs over London* (also known as *Midnight Menace*), Grosvenor, 1937.

Scales, *Romance and Riches* (also known as *The Amazing Quest of Ernest Bliss; Riches and Romance;* and *Amazing Adventure*), Grand National, 1937.

Palmer, *Scotland Yard Commands* (also known as *The Lonely Road*), Grand National, 1937.

Captain Lawrence, *Flight to Fame,* Columbia, 1938.

Jeff Hale, *Just Around the Corner,* Twentieth Century-Fox, 1938.

Jackson, *Meet Mr. Penny,* Associated British Films, 1938.

Eric Molander, *Moonlight Sonata,* United Artists, 1938.

Dave, *Night Journey,* Butchers Film Service, 1938.

Spike Nelson, *Jail Birds,* Butchers Film Service, 1939.

Logan, *Treachery on the High Seas* (also known as *Not Wanted on Voyage*), Film Alliance, 1939.

Tov Katch, *The Rebel Son,* United Artists, 1939.

Bud, *Tail Spin,* Twentieth Century-Fox, 1939.

Walker, *Convoy,* Associated British Films, 1940.

The Deadly Game, Monogram, 1941.

Jim Benson, *Bell-Bottom George,* Columbia, 1943.

Meet Sexton Blake, Anglo-American, 1944.

Johnny in the Clouds (also known as *The Way to the Stars*), United Artists, 1945.

Don Dooley, *Don Chicago,* Anglo, 1945.

This Man Is Mine, Columbia, 1946.

Curley, *I Became a Criminal* (also known as *They Made Me a Fugitive* and *They Made Me a Criminal*), Warner Brothers, 1947.

Jack, *The Turners of Prospect Road,* Grand National, 1947.

Beer, *Night and the City,* Twentieth Century-Fox, 1950.

Felling, *Madame Louise,* Butchers Film Service, 1951.

Arthur, *There Was a Young Lady,* Butchers Film Service, 1953.

Percy, *Final Appointment,* Monarch, 1954.

Posh Peterson, *The Hornet's Nest,* GFD-Rank, 1955.

Basher, *See How They Run,* British Lion, 1955.

Percy Simspon, *Stolen Assignment,* British Lion, 1955.

Shiv Maitland, *Death over My Shoulder,* Orb, 1958.

Percy Simspon, *The Diplomatic Corpse,* R.F.D. Production, 1958.

Bartender, *The Sheriff of Fractured Jaw,* Twentieth Century-Fox, 1958.

Karver, *The Strange Case of Dr. Manning* (also known as *Morning Call*), Republic, 1958.

Mungo Peddey, *Hidden Homicide,* Republic, 1959.

Charlie Stevens, *Operation Cupid,* Rank, 1960.

Joe Cole, *The Girl Hunters,* Colorama, 1963.

Chimes at Midnight (also known as *Campanada's a Media Noche* and *Falstaff*), Peppercorn, 1967.

Policeman, *Oh! What a Lovely War,* Paramount, 1969.

Landlord, *The Vampire Lovers,* American International, 1970.

Seller, *Countess Dracula,* Twentieth Century-Fox, 1972.

Also appeared in *Wings of Youth,* 1925, and as Andoniram Schlump, *Aggie Appleby, Maker of Men* (also known as *Cupid in the Rough*), 1933.

TELEVISION APPEARANCES; SERIES

Vernon Albright, *My Little Margie,* CBS, 1952, then NBC, 1953.

Himself, *The Charlie Farrell Show,* CBS, 1950, then NBC, 1957.

RADIO APPEARANCES

Appeared on *Seventh Heaven,* CBS, and *My Little Margie,* CBS.

OBITUARIES AND OTHER SOURCES:

PERIODICALS

Hollywood Reporter, May 11, 1990.
Variety, May 16, 1990.*

*   *   *

FENTON, George

CAREER: Composer. Church organist.

AWARDS, HONORS: British Academy of Film and Television Arts Awards for original television music, 1981, for *Bergerac, Going Gently, The History Man,* and *BBC News Theme,* 1983, for *An Englishman Abroad, Saigon—Year of the Cat, Loving Walter, Walter and June, The Ghost Writer, Breakfast Time, Natural World,* and *Village Earth,* and 1986, for *The Monocled Mutineer;* Academy Award nominations for best original score, 1983, for *Gandhi,* 1988, for *Cry Freedom,* and 1989, for *Dangerous Liaisons;* Academy Award nomination for best song, 1988, for *Cry Freedom.*

CREDITS:

STAGE APPEARANCES

Mr. Gardner, *Butley,* Criterion Theatre, London, 1971.
The Pleasure Principle, Theatre Upstairs, London, 1973.
A gentleman, *Twelfth Night,* Royal Shakespeare Company (RSC), Aldwych Theatre, London, 1975.

FILM WORK

Composer with Ravi Shankar, and music director, *Gandhi,* Columbia, 1982.
Composer and music director, *Bloody Kids,* Palace/BFI, 1983.
Composer and music director, *Runners,* Hanstall, 1983.
Composer and music director, *84 Charing Cross Road,* Columbia, 1987.

Also composer and music director, *Hussy,* 1979, composer and music director, *Billy the Kid and the Green Baize Vampire,* 1985, and music supervisor, *White of the Eye,* 1987.

TELEVISION APPEARANCES

Performer of the song "Cry Freedom," *The 60th Annual Academy Awards Presentation,* 1988.

WRITINGS:

FILM SCORES

(With Michael Feast and David Dundas) *Private Road,* Maya Films, 1971.
(With Ravi Shankar) *Gandhi,* Columbia, 1982.
Bloody Kids, Palace/BFI, 1983.
Runners, Hanstall, 1983.
The Company of Wolves, Cannon, 1985.
Clockwise, Universal/Cannon, 1986.
(With Jonas Gwangwa) *Cry Freedom,* Universal, 1987.
84 Charing Cross Road, Columbia, 1987.
White Mischief, Columbia, 1987.
A Handful of Dust, New Line, 1988.
The Dressmaker, Film Four, 1988.
High Spirits, Tri-Star, 1988.
Dangerous Liaisons, Warner Brothers, 1988.
Ghoulies II, Empire, 1988.
We're No Angels, Paramount, 1989.
Memphis Belle, Warner Brothers, 1990.
The Long Walk Home, Miramax, 1990.

Also composer of music for *Hussy,* 1979, *Billy the Kid and the Green Baize Vampire,* 1985, and *Past Caring,* 1985.

STAGE MUSIC

Much Ado about Nothing, National Theatre Company, Olivier Theatre, London, 1981.
A Month in the Country, National Theatre, Olivier Theatre, 1981.

The Duchess of Malfi, Royal Exchange Theatre Company, Round House Theatre, London, 1981.
Don Juan, National Theatre, Cottesloe Theatre, London, 1981.
Good, RSC, Warehouse Theatre, 1981, then Booth Theatre, New York City, 1982.
Antony and Cleopatra, RSC, The Pit, London, 1983.
Macbeth, RSC, Barbican Theatre, London, 1983.
Mother Courage, RSC, Barbican Theatre, 1984.
Bengal Lancer, Lyric Hammersmith Theatre, London, 1985.

TELEVISION MUSIC

The Monocled Mutineer, BBC, 1986, then KCET, 1990.
Trials of Life (twelve-part series), BBC, 1990, then TNT, 1991.

Also composer of music for *Bergerac, Going Gently, The History Man,* and *BBC News Theme,* all 1981; *Parole* (television movie), 1982; *An Englishman Abroad, Loving Walter, Saigon—Year of the Cat, Walter and June, The Ghost Writer* (television special), *Breakfast Time, Natural World,* and *Village Earth,* all 1983; and *The Jewel in the Crown* (special), 1984.

OTHER SOURCES:

PERIODICALS

The Hollywood Reporter, 1989.*

*   *   *

FERRER, Miguel

PERSONAL: Son of Jose Ferrer (an actor and director) and Rosemary Clooney (a singer and actress).

ADDRESSES: Agent—McCartt-Oreck-Barrett, 10390 Santa Monica Blvd., Beverly Hills, CA 90212. *Manager*—Green/Siegel Management, 1140 N. Alta Loma Dr., No. 105, Los Angeles, CA 90069.

CAREER: Actor.

CREDITS:

FILM APPEARANCES

Dragon, *Lovelines,* Tri-Star, 1984.
First officer (U.S.S. Excelsior), *Star Trek III: The Search for Spock,* Paramount, 1984.
Roget, *Flashpoint,* Tri-Star, 1984.
Robert Morton, *Robocop,* Orion, 1987.
Snyder, *Deepstar Six,* Tri-Star, 1989.
Biker, *Valentino Returns,* Skouras, 1989.
Ralph Hess, *The Guardian,* Universal, 1990.
Amador, *Revenge,* Columbia, 1990.

Also appeared as Angel, *Heartbreaker,* 1981, and as Pete, *Truckin' Buddy McCoy,* 1984.

TELEVISION APPEARANCES; MOVIES

Paul Kiley, *C.A.T. Squad: Python Wolf* (movie), NBC, 1988.

Scott, *Guts and Glory: The Rise and Fall of Oliver North* (movie), CBS, 1989.

Todd, *Shannon's Deal* (movie), NBC, 1989.

Tony Riva, *Drug Wars: The Camarena Story,* NBC, 1990.

Also appeared as Martin, *Downpayment on Murder* (movie), 1987.

TELEVISION APPEARANCES; EPISODIC

Ferguson, *Ohara,* ABC, 1987.

Virgilio, *Houston Knights,* CBS, 1987.

Scott Kappas, "Chariots of Fire," *Hooperman,* ABC, 1988.

Ramon Pendroza, *Miami Vice,* NBC, 1989.

Albert Rosenfield, *Twin Peaks,* ABC, 1990-91.

OTHER TELEVISION APPEARANCES

Rex, *Badlands 2005* (pilot), ABC, 1988.

Also appeared as Mick, *Kung Fu: The Next Generation* (series), 1987, and as the friend, *The Thing from the Grave* (special), 1990.

STAGE APPEARANCES

Peter, *Light up the Sky,* Coconut Grove Playhouse, Coconut Grove, Florida, 1983-84.

STAGE WORK

Stage director for Coconut Grove Playhouse, 1984-85.*

*   *   *

FIRTH, Colin   1960-

PERSONAL: Born September 10, 1960, in Grayshott, Hampshire, England; son of educators. *Education:* Attended Drama Centre, London.

ADDRESSES: Agent—Julian Belfrage Associates, 68 St. James's St., London SW1, England.

CAREER: Actor.

AWARDS, HONORS: Royal Television Society Award, best actor, and British Academy of Film and Television Arts Award nomination, both for *Tumbledown.*

CREDITS:

STAGE APPEARANCES

The Lonely Road, Old Vic Theatre, London, 1985.

Eben, *Desire under the Elms,* Greenwich Theatre, London, 1987.

The Caretaker, Comedy Theatre, London, 1991.

Also appeared as Guy Bennett, *Another Country,* London; and in *The Doctor's Dilemma,* Churchill Theatre, Bromley, England.

FILM APPEARANCES

Tommy Judd, *Another Country,* Orion, 1984.

Young Alexander, *1919,* British Film Institute/Channel 4, 1984.

Tom Birkin, *A Month in the Country,* Orion, 1987.

Adrian Le Duc, *Apartment Zero,* Skouras, 1988.

Vicomte DeValmont, *Valmont,* Orion, 1990.

Smith, *Wings of Fame,* Cannon, 1990.

Also appeared as Joe in *Femme Fatale,* 1991.

TELEVISION APPEARANCES; MINI-SERIES

Richard Herncastle, *Lost Empires,* Granada, then *Masterpiece Theatre,* PBS, 1987.

TELEVISION APPEARANCES; MOVIES

Armand Duval, *Camille,* CBS, 1984.

Colin as an adult, *The Secret Garden,* CBS, 1987.

Lieutenant Robert Lawrence, *Tumbledown,* BBC, 1988, then Arts & Entertainment, 1990.

TELEVISION APPEARANCES; SPECIALS

Rene Wilcox, "Tales from the Hollywood Hills: Pat Hobby Teamed with Genius," *Great Performances,* PBS, 1987.

"Milos Forman: Portrait," *American Masters,* PBS, 1989.

Also appeared in *Dutch Girls,* LWT.

*   *   *

FISHER, Linda   1943-

PERSONAL: Born September 30, 1943, in Lindsay, CA; daughter of James Howard (an Air Force pilot) and Doris (Lundgren) Fisher; married Richard Paul Cressen (a psychologist), November, 1976. *Education:* University of Texas, B.F.A., 1966; Yale University, M.F.A., 1969.

ADDRESSES: Office—139 West 82nd St., New York, NY 10024. *Agent*—Scott Hudson, 19 West 44th St., New York, NY 10036; and Marti Blumenthal, 11726 San Vicente Blvd., Los Angeles, CA 90049.

CAREER: Costume designer. Costume designer for theatres, including Arena Stage, 1969-71, 1974-75, 1976-77; Hartford Stage Company, 1970-71, 1972-73, 1974-76, 1977-78, 1980-81; McCarter Theatre, Princeton, NJ,

1972-73; Long Wharf Theatre, 1972-73, 1975-76, 1977-78, 1979-80, 1981-82, 1984-85; Center Stage, 1973-74, 1983-84; Milwaukee Repertory Theatre, Milwaukee, WI, 1976-77, 1981-82; Syracuse Stage, Syracuse, NY, 1977-78; Hartman Theatre Company, Stamford, CT, 1977-78, 1979-80; and Philadelphia Drama Guild, Philadelphia, PA, 1980-82.

MEMBER: United Scenic Artists, Costume Designers' Guild.

CREDITS:

STAGE WORK; COSTUME DESIGNER

Little Malcolm and His Struggle against the Eunuchs, Yale Drama School, New Haven, CT, 1968.

Three Sisters, Yale Repertory Theatre, 1968.

White Lies/Black Comedy, Williamstown Summer Theatre, 1968.

Wait until Dark, Williamstown Summer Theatre, 1968.

The Seagull, Williamstown Summer Theatre, 1968, 1974, and McCarter Theater, 1973.

How to Succeed, Williamstown Summer Theatre, 1968, then Pacific Conservatory of the Performing Arts, 1978.

The Trial of A. Lincoln, Hartford Stage Company, Hartford, CT, 1969-70.

The Unseen Hand and *Forensic and the Navigators* (double-bill), Astor Place Theatre, New York City, 1970.

Chemmy Circle, Arena Stage, Washington, DC, 1970.

Ring Round the Moon, Hartford Stage Company, 1970.

A Lovely Sunday for Creve Coeur, Hudson Guild Theatre, New York City, 1970.

The Brass Butterfly, Chelsea Theatre Center, Brooklyn Academy of Music, Brooklyn, NY, 1971.

Wipe-Out Games, Arena Stage, 1971.

Pantagleize, Arena Stage, 1971.

A Public Prosecutor Is Sick of It All, Arena Stage, 1972.

What Price Glory?, Long Wharf Theatre, New Haven, CT, 1972.

Charley's Aunt, Hartford Stage Company, 1972, then Academy Festival Theatre, Lake Forest, IL, 1979.

A Streetcar Named Desire, Hartford Stage Company, 1972.

Tooth of Crime, McCarter Theater, Princeton, NJ, 1972.

Uncle Vanya, Williamstown Summer Theatre, 1972, then Center Stage, Baltimore, MD, 1973, later Academy Festival Theatre, 1979, and Hartman Theatre, 1980.

Juno and the Paycock, Hartford Stage Company, 1973.

The Karl Marx Play, American Place Theatre, New York City, 1973.

Nobody's Earnest, Williamstown Summer Theatre, 1973.

What the Butler Saw, Williamstown Summer Theatre, 1973.

The Entertainer, McCarter Theater, 1973.

The Daughter-in-Law, McCarter Theater, 1974.

The Rivals, Williamstown Summer Theatre, 1974.

You Never Can Tell, McCarter Theater, 1974.

Hay Fever, Center Stage, 1974.

The Show-Off, Long Wharf Theatre, 1975.

Guys and Dolls, Pacific Conservatory of the Performing Arts, 1975.

Boccaccio, Edison Theatre, New York City, 1975.

A Raisin in the Sun, Hartford Stage Company, 1975.

Afternoon Tea, Hartford Stage Company, 1975.

He Who Gets Slapped, Pacific Conservatory of the Performing Arts, 1975.

The Animal Kingdom, Hartman Theatre, Stamford, CT, 1976.

Gypsy, Pacific Conservatory of the Performing Arts, 1976.

Much Ado about Nothing, Pacific Conservatory of the Performing Arts, 1976.

The Utter Glory of Morrissey Hall, Pacific Conservatory of the Performing Arts, 1976.

Envoi Messages, Indiana Repertory Theatre, 1976.

Catsplay, Arena Stage, 1977.

The Plough and the Stars, Syracuse Stage, Syracuse, NY, 1977.

Volpone, Milwaukee Repertory Theatre, Milwaukee, WI, 1977.

Purlie, Pacific Conservatory of the Performing Arts, 1977.

Enrico IV, Pacific Conservatory of the Performing Arts, 1977.

Winter's Tale, Pacific Conservatory of the Performing Arts, 1978.

Rib Cage, Manhattan Theatre Club, New York City, 1978.

Awake and Sing, Hartford Stage Company, 1978.

Eve, Hartford Stage Company, 1978.

They'd Come to See Charlie, Hartford Stage Company, 1978.

Catchpenny Twist, Hartford Stage Company, 1978-79.

Bonjour la, Bonjour, Hartford Stage Company, 1978-79.

S.S. Glencairn/Sea Plays, Long Wharf Theatre, 1979.

The Days Between, Playhouse Repertory Theatre, New York City, 1979.

Two Small Bodies, Playwrights' Horizons, 1979.

Old World, Hartford Stage Company, 1979.

The Interview, Academy Festival Theatre, 1979.

Hillbilly Women, Long Wharf Theatre, 1979.

Morning's at Seven, Academy Festival Theatre, 1979, then Lyceum Theatre, New York City, 1980, later Center Theatre Group, Ahmanson Theatre, Los Angeles, 1981.

Shout across the River, Phoenix Theatre, Marymount Manhattan Theatre, New York City, 1980.

The Rainmaker, Berkshire Theatre Festival, 1980.

Caretaker, Long Wharf Theatre, 1980.

Vikings, Manhattan Theatre Club, 1980.

Ardele, Hartford Stage Company, 1980.
Working, American Stage Festival, 1980.
The Lady from Dubuque, Hartford Stage Theatre, 1980.
Watch on the Rhine, Center Stage, 1980.
Sally and Marsha, Pepsico Festival, Purchase, NY, 1981.
Sally's Gone, She Left Her Name, Center Stage, 1981, then Perry Street Theatre, New York City, 1985.
After the Prize, Phoenix Theatre, Marymount Manhattan Theatre, 1981.
The Captivity of Pixie Shedman, Phoenix Theatre, Marymount Manhattan Theatre, 1981.
Gaslight, American Stage Festival, 1981.
Of Mice and Men, Philadelphia Drama Guild, 1981.
Philadelphia, Here I Come, Philadelphia Drama Guild, 1981.
Rose, Cort Theatre, New York City, 1981.
Two for the Seesaw, Berkshire Theatre Festival, 1981.
An Enemy of the People, Alaska Repertory Theatre, Anchorage/Fairbanks, AK, 1982.
Foxfire, Ethel Barrymore Theatre, New York City, 1982.
(With others) *Good,* Booth Theatre, New York City, 1982.
Greater Tuna, Circle in the Square Downtown, New York City, 1982, then Ford's Theatre, Washington, DC, 1984.
The Great Magoo, Hartford Stage Company, 1982.
Last Looks, Center Stage, 1982.
Palace of Amateurs, Berkshire Theatre Festival, 1982.
The Carmone Brothers Italian Food Products Corp.'s Annual Pasta Pageant, Long Wharf Theatre, 1982.
Surprise at Campobello, Berkshire Theatre Festival, 1982.
Secret Injury, Secret Revenge, Milwaukee Repertory Theatre, 1982.
The Workroom, Center Stage, 1982.
Becoming Memories, South Street Theatre, 1983.
Summer, Manhattan Theatre Club, 1983.
The Philanthropist, Manhattan Theatre Club, 1983.
A Backer's Audition, Manhattan Theatre Club, 1983.
Old Times, Stage One, New York City, 1983-84.
Painting Churches, Second Stage Company, Lamb's Theatre, New York City, 1983-84, then Birmingham Theatre, Birmingham, MI, 1984.
Fables for Friends, Playwrights Horizons, New York City, 1984.
Messiah, Manhattan Theatre Club, 1984.
Cat on a Hot Tin Roof, Centre Stage, Toronto, 1984.
In Celebration, Manhattan Theatre Club, The Space at City Center, New York City, 1984.
Homesteaders, Long Wharf Theatre, 1984.
Oliver Oliver, Long Wharf Theatre, 1984.
Ohio Tip-Off, Center Stage, 1984.
South Pacific, Dorothy Chandler Pavilion/Music Center, Los Angeles, 1985.
Not about Heroes, Lucille Lortel Theatre, New York City, 1985.

Crystal Clear, Long Wharf Theatre, 1985.
Bedroom Farce, Center Stage, 1985.
The Member of the Wedding, Berkshire Theatre Festival, 1985.
Top Girls, Playhouse in the Park, Cincinnati, OH, 1986.
A Little Night Music, Berkshire Theatre Festival, 1986.
I Never Sang for My Father, Eisenhower Theatre, Kennedy Center for the Performing Arts, Washington, DC, 1987, then Center Theatre Group, Ahmanson Theatre, 1987-88.
Harvey, Guthrie Theatre, 1989.
The March on Russia, Hudson Guild Theatre, 1990.

Also costume designer for *A Tuna Christmas,* 1989; *X-Notes on a Private Mythology,* Yale Drama School; *You Can't Take It With You,* Yale Drama School; and workshop productions of *Subject to Fits,* New York Public Theatre, 1971; and *Goose and Tom-Tom,* New York Public Theatre, 1980. Associate costume designer for American production of *All's Well That Ends Well,* Royal Shakespeare Company, 1983.

FILM WORK; COSTUME DESIGNER

Rachel River, Taurus Entertainment, 1987.
Heart of Midnight, Samuel Goldwyn, 1988.
Necessary Parties, Wonderworks, 1988.
Just Like in the Movies, Alon Kasha, 1988.

TELEVISION WORK; MOVIES; COSTUME DESIGNER

A Sunday Dinner, Showtime, 1982.
Mornings at Seven, CBS, 1982.
The Mysterious Stranger, PBS, 1982.
Greater Tuna, HBO, 1984.
The Final Verdict, TNT, 1991.

OTHER TELEVISION WORK; COSTUME DESIGNER

Private History of a Campaign That Failed (special), PBS, 1981.
"Pudd'nhead Wilson," *American Playhouse,* PBS, 1984.
(Credit sequence) *Saturday Night Live* (series), NBC, 1986-88.
The Cavanaughs (pilot), CBS, 1986.
Mabel and Max (pilot), CBS, 1987.

*   *   *

FLEISCHER, Charles 1950-

PERSONAL: Born August 27, 1950, in Washington, DC. *Education:* Studied acting at Goodman Theatre, Chicago, IL.

CAREER: Actor and comedian. Was a performer at The Comedy Store in Los Angeles, CA, during the 1980s.

CREDITS:

FILM APPEARANCES

Charlie, *Die Laughing,* Warner Brothers, 1980.

David Maddow, *The Hand,* Warner Brothers, 1981.

Prisoner, *Night Shift,* Warner Brothers, 1982.

Dr. King, *A Nightmare on Elm Street,* New Line Cinema, 1984.

Voice of Bee Bee, *Deadly Friend,* Warner Brothers, 1986.

Voices of Roger Rabbit, Benny the Cab, Greasy, and Psycho, *Who Framed Roger Rabbit?,* Buena Vista, 1988.

Voice of Roger Rabbit, *Roger Rabbit & the Secrets of Toontown,* Buena Vista, 1988.

Ron the pharmacist, *Bad Dreams,* Twentieth Century-Fox, 1988.

Tummy Trouble, Buena Vista, 1989.

Song performer, *Disorganized Crime,* Buena Vista, 1989.

Terry, *Back to the Future II,* Universal, 1989.

Rollercoaster Rabbit, Buena Vista, 1990.

Reporter, *Dick Tracy,* Touchstone Pictures, 1990.

TELEVISION APPEARANCES; SERIES

Regular, *Keep on Trucking,* ABC, 1975.

Regular, *The Richard Pryor Show,* NBC, 1977.

Lighting Jack Rappaport, a struggling comedian, *Sugar Time,* ABC, 1977.

Regular, *Wacko,* CBS, 1977.

Carvelli, and a sweathog, *Welcome Back Kotter,* ABC, 1978-79.

Everett Degroot, the gardener, *Aloha Paradise,* ABC, 1981.

Dennis, the bellboy, *Checking In,* CBS, 1981.

Regular, *Thicke of the Night,* syndicated, 1983-84.

Benson, *Sonny Spoon,* NBC, 1988.

TELEVISION APPEARANCES; EPISODIC

Guest, *Laugh-In,* NBC, 1972.

Walker, *Knight Rider,* NBC, 1985.

Also appeared in *One Night Stand,* 1989.

TELEVISION APPEARANCES; SPECIALS

Stagehand, *Mickey's 60th Birthday Special,* NBC, 1988.

The Magical World of Disney, NBC, 1988.

4th Annual American Comedy Awards, ABC, 1990.

Disneyland's 35th Anniversary Celebration, NBC, 1990.

Also appeared as Dr. Bernard in *George Burns Comedy Week,* 1985; Mr. Amsterdam in *Fast Times,* 1986; *Life's Most Embarrassing Moments,* and *Live! Dick Clark Presents,* both 1988; *The Prince's Trust Gala,* 1989; and *Be Careful What You Ask For,* 1990.

OTHER TELEVISION APPEARANCES

Miles Savantini, *Blue Jeans* (pilot), ABC, 1980.

Brick, *The Death of Richie* (movie), NBC, 1977.*

*   *   *

FLUELLEN, Joel   1908-1990

PERSONAL: Full name, Joel M. Fluellen; born December 1, 1908, in Monroe, LA; found dead, February 9, 1990, after committing suicide in Los Angeles, CA. *Education:* Studied acting with Morris Carnovsky, Hume Cronyn, Charles Laughton, and Madame Ouspenskaya.

CAREER: Actor. Appeared on stage in New York City and Los Angeles. Organized the First Meaningful Theater for Black Actors in Los Angeles' Negro Art Theater, 1950.

MEMBER: Screen Actors Guild, Actors' Equity Association, NAACP Performers Charity Club.

AWARDS, HONORS: Black Filmmakers Award, 1975.

CREDITS:

FILM APPEARANCES

Waiter in club car, *Without Reservations,* RKO Radio Pictures, 1946.

Porter, *This Love of Ours,* Universal, 1946.

Mumbo Jumbo, *White Pongo,* Producers Releasing Corp., 1946.

Charlie, *The Burning Cross,* Screen Guild, 1947.

Waiter, *Family Honeymoon,* Universal, 1948.

Father, *Force of Evil,* Metro-Goldwyn-Mayer, 1948.

Mack Robinson, *The Jackie Robinson Story,* Eagle-Lion, 1950.

Mess boy, *You're in the Navy Now* (also known as *Tea Kettle*), Twentieth Century-Fox, 1951.

Fisherman, *Affair in Trinidad,* Columbia, 1952.

Rangori the witch doctor, *Jungle Gents,* Allied Artists, 1954.

Bill, *Duffy of San Quentin* (also known as *Men Behind Bars*), Warner Brothers, 1954.

Al, *Riot in Cell Block 11,* Allied Artists, 1954.

Sam, *Sitting Bull,* United Artists, 1954.

Molu, *Lord of the Jungle,* Allied Artists, 1955.

Summertime, *Lucy Gallant* (also known as *Oil Town*), Paramount, 1955.

Enoch, *Friendly Persuasion,* Allied Artists, 1956.

Cab driver, *Oh, Men! Oh, Women!,* Twentieth Century-Fox, 1957.

Pete, *The Decks Ran Red,* Metro-Goldwyn-Mayer, 1958.

Arobi, *Monster from the Green Hell,* Distributors Corp. of America, 1958.

Bragg, *Run Silent, Run Deep,* United Artists, 1958.

Minister, *Imitation of Life,* Universal, 1959.

Robbins, *Porgy and Bess,* Columbia, 1959.

Bobo, *A Raisin in the Sun,* Columbia, 1961.

Clerk of the court, *The Young Savages,* United Artists, 1961.

Dr. Sam, *He Rides Tall,* Universal, 1964.

Cody Marsh, *Roustabout,* Paramount, 1964.

Abram, *The Skin Game* (also known as *Skin Games*), William Mishkin, 1965.

Lester Johnson, *The Chase,* Columbia, 1966.

Uncle Rob, *The Learning Tree* (also known as *Learn, Baby, Learn*), Winger Enterprises, 1969.

Tick, *The Great White Hope,* Twentieth Century-Fox, 1970.

Nathaniel, *Thomasine and Bushrod,* Columbia, 1974.

Mr. Holland, *The Bingo Long Traveling All-Stars and Motor Kings,* Universal, 1976.

Jimmy Judson, *Casey's Shadow,* Columbia, 1978.

Appeared in *The Moonlighter,* Warner Brothers, 1953; *White Goddess,* Lippert, 1953; and *Man Friday,* Avco Embassy, 1975.

TELEVISION APPEARANCES; EPISODIC

"The Navigator," *One Step Beyond,* ABC, 1959.

"The Case of the Pillow," *The Dick Van Dyke Show,* CBS, 1964.

"A Show of Hands," *The Dick Van Dyke Show,* CBS, 1965.

Also appeared in *The FBI; I Spy; Gidget; Tarzan; Laramie; The Invaders; Ben Casey; The Iron Horse; The Wild Wild West; Breaking Point; Death Valley Days; Slattery's People; Ramar of the Jungle; The Great Adventure; Alfred Hitchcock Presents; Marcus Welby; Columbo;* and *Hill Street Blues.*

TELEVISION APPEARANCES; SPECIALS

Appeared in *The Christmas Story* and *Miss Jane Pittman.*

OBITUARIES AND OTHER SOURCES:

PERIODICALS

Hollywood Reporter, February 6, 1990.
New York Times, February 7, 1990.*

*   *   *

FLYNN, Barbara

CAREER: Actress.

CREDITS:

STAGE APPEARANCES

Jane, *Two and Two Make Sex,* Cambridge Theatre, London, 1973.

Phillipa Haymes, *A Murder Is Announced,* Vaudeville Theatre, London, 1977.

Sylvia Craven, *The Philanderer,* National Theatre Company, Lyttelton Theatre, London, 1978.

Ursula, *Short List,* Hampstead Theatre, London, 1983.

Barbara, *The Perfectionist,* Hampstead Theatre, London, 1983.

Helen Schwartz, *Tales from Hollywood,* National Theatre Company, Olivier Theatre, London, 1983.

Title role, *Antigone,* National Theatre Company, Cottesloe Theatre, London, 1983.

FILM APPEARANCES

Private nurse, *Britannia Hospital,* Universal, 1982.

TELEVISION APPEARANCES; EPISODIC

Monica Height, "The Silent World of Nicholas Quinn," *Inspector Morse,* Central Television, then *Mystery!* PBS, 1988.

OTHER TELEVISION APPEARANCES

Belinda, *Season's Greetings* (special), BBC, then Arts and Entertainment, 1988.

Also appeared in the series *A Very Peculiar Practice.**

*   *   *

FORD DAVIES, Oliver

CAREER: Actor and director.

AWARDS, HONORS: Olivier Award, best actor, 1990, for *Racing Demon.*

CREDITS:

STAGE APPEARANCES

Frederick and Duke Senior, *As You Like It,* Birmingham Repertory Company, Vaudeville Theatre, London, 1967.

Major Blake, "We Were Dancing," Mr. Edwards, "Red Peppers," and Charles Winter, "Family Album," *Tonight at Eight,* Hampstead Theatre Club, London, 1970.

Mr. Morland, *Mary Rose,* 69 Theatre Company, Shaw Theatre, London, 1972.

Montjoy, *Henry V,* Royal Shakespeare Company (RSC), Royal Shakespeare Theatre, Stratford-on-Avon, England, 1975, then Aldwych Theatre, London, 1976, later Brooklyn Academy of Music, Opera House, Brooklyn, NY, 1976.

Sir Michael and Sheriff, *Henry IV, Part One,* RSC, Royal Shakespeare Theatre, 1975, then Aldwych Theatre, 1976.

Morton and Wart, *Henry IV, Part Two,* RSC, Royal Shakespeare Theatre, 1975, then Aldwych Theatre, 1976.

Duke of Somerset, *Henry VI, Part One,* RSC, Royal Shakespeare Theatre, 1977, then Aldwych Theatre, 1978.

Duke of Somerset, *Henry VI, Part Two,* RSC, Royal Shakespeare Theatre, 1977, then Aldwych Theatre, 1978.

Montjoy, *Henry V,* RSC, Royal Shakespeare Theatre, 1977, then Aldwych Theatre, 1978.

Duke Senior, *As You Like It,* RSC, Royal Shakespeare Theatre, 1977, then Aldwych Theatre, 1978.

Junius Brutus, *Coriolanus,* RSC, Royal Shakespeare Theatre, 1977, then Aldwych Theatre, 1978 and 1979.

Eadweard Muybridge, *Snap,* New End Theatre, London, 1981.

Nestor, *Troilus and Cressida,* RSC, Aldwych Theatre, 1981.

Timofey Mereschun, *The Love-Girl and the Innocent,* RSC, Aldwych Theatre, 1981.

Mr. Mulligan, *The Shadow of a Gunman,* RSC, Warehouse Theatre, London, 1981.

Senator, *Timon of Athens,* RSC, Warehouse Theatre, 1981.

Yevgeny Apollonich Milonov, *The Forest,* RSC, The Other Place, Stratford-on-Avon, 1981, then Warehouse Theatre, 1981, later Aldwych Theatre, 1982.

Provost, *Measure for Measure,* RSC, Royal Shakespeare Theatre, 1983, then Barbican Theatre, 1984.

Marullus and Titinius, *Julius Caesar,* RSC, Royal Shakespeare Theatre, 1983, then Barbican Theatre, 1984.

Gardiner, *King Henry VIII,* RSC, Royal Shakespeare Theatre, 1983, then Barbican Theatre, 1984.

Jean D'Armagnac, *The Devils,* RSC, The Pit, London, 1984.

Gilbert Wedgecroft, *Waste,* RSC, The Pit, then Lyric Theatre, London, both 1985.

Dunc, *The Light Rough,* Hampstead Theatre, 1986.

Scaramure, *Il Candelaio* (also known as *The Candlemaker*), RSC, The Pit, 1986.

Norton Quinn, *Principia Scriptoriae,* RSC, The Pit, 1986.

Fouquier-Tinville, *The Danton Affair,* RSC, Barbican Theatre, 1986.

Hugh Evans, *The Merry Wives of Windsor,* RSC, Barbican Theatre, 1987.

Matt Sandovat, *The Hole in the Top of the World,* Orange Tree Theatre, London, 1987.

Lionel, *Racing Demon,* National Theatre Company, Cottesloe Theatre, then Olivier Theatre, both London, 1990.

STAGE WORK

Director, *Brotherhood,* Orange Tree Theatre, London, 1985.

FILM APPEARANCES

Anthony Clegg, *Defence of the Realm,* Rank/Warner Brothers, 1985.

Mr. Woods, *Scandal,* Miramax, 1989.

TELEVISION APPEARANCES; MINI-SERIES

J. D. Casswell, *Cause Celebre,* Anglia Television, then *Mystery!,* PBS, 1988.

Tweed, *A Very British Coup,* Channel Four, then *Masterpiece Theatre,* PBS, 1989.

Father Barnes, *A Taste for Death,* Anglia Television, then *Mystery!,* PBS, 1990.*

*   *   *

FOWLDS, Derek   1937-

PERSONAL: Born September 2, 1937, in London, England.

ADDRESSES: Agent—Barry Burnett Organization, Suite 42, Grafton House, Golden Sq., London W1, England; Caroline Dawson and Belinda Wright, CDA, Apartment 20, 47 Courtfield Rd., London SW7 4DB, England.

CAREER: Actor.

CREDITS:

STAGE APPEARANCES

John Keller, *The Miracle Worker,* Wyndham's Theatre, West End, 1961.

Tod Roberts, *The Pander Touch,* Lyric Theatre, London, 1961.

Anthony Stewart, *Race Against Time,* Lyric Theatre, 1961.

Bill Turner, *Empress with Teapot,* Royal Court Theatre, London, 1961.

Les Thornton, *How Are You, Johnnie?,* Vaudeville Theatre, London, 1963.

252 Wingate (Chas), *Chips with Everything,* Royal Court Theatre, then Plymouth Theatre, New York City, both 1963.

Melchior Gabor, *Spring Awakening,* Royal Court Theatre, 1965.

Gary, *Spitting Image,* Hampstead Theatre Club, then Duke of York's Theatre, both London, 1968.

Father Penny, *Child's Play,* Queen's Theatre, London, 1971.

Anthony, *A Private Matter,* Vaudeville Theatre, 1973.

Terry, "Mother Figure," Martin, "Between Mouthfuls," Stewart, "Gosforth's Fete," and Ernest, "A Talk in the Park," *Confusions,* Apollo Theatre, London, 1976.

Runnicier, *No Sex Please, We're British,* Strand Theatre, West End, 1979-80.

Colclough, *Mindkill,* Greenwich Theatre, London, 1982.

John Smith, *Run for Our Wild,* Criterion Theatre, West End, 1986.

Also appeared in *Rattle of a Simple Man,* Sydney, Australia, 1987-88.

FILM APPEARANCES

Carson, *We Joined the Navy* (also known as *We're in the Navy Now*), Warner Brothers/Pathe, 1962.

Doctor in Distress, Rank, 1963.

Murchinson, *East of Sudan,* BLC, 1964.

Bash, *Tamahine,* Metro-Goldwyn-Mayer (MGM), 1964.

Johann, *Frankenstein Created Woman,* Seven Arts-Hammer/Twentieth Century-Fox, 1965.

Maxime, *Hotel Paradiso,* MGM, 1966.

Geoffrey, *School for Unclaimed Girls* (also known as *House of Unclaimed Women* and *The Smashing Bird I Used to Know*), Grand National, 1973.

Captain Peters, *The 'Copter Kids,* Children's Film Foundation, 1976.

Dan, *Beyond the Fog* (also known as *Tower of Evil* and *Horror on Snape Island*), Independent-International, 1981.

Dutch, *Round the Bend,* Rank, 1991.

TELEVISION APPEARANCES; SERIES

Bernard Wooley, *Yes, Minister,* BBC, then PBS, 1982.

Also appeared as Bernard Wooley, *Yes, Prime Minister,* BBC, then PBS; appeared in *The Basil Brush Show,* 1969-73, and *Affairs of the Heart.*

TELEVISION APPEARANCES; EPISODIC

Inspector Morse, ITV, then *Mystery!* PBS, 1990.

Also appeared in "Captain Video's Story," *Armchair 30;* appeared in *Robin's Nest, Edward VII, Captive Audience, The Doll, Strangers, My Son, My Son, Rings on Their Fingers, Rules of Enjoyment, Die Kinder, Van der Volk, Perfect Strangers,* and *Intensive Care.*

* * *

FRAKER, Bill
  See FRAKER, William A.

* * *

FRAKER, William
  See FRAKER, William A.

FRAKER, William A. 1923-
  (Bill Fraker, William Fraker)

PERSONAL: Born in 1923 in Los Angeles, CA; son of a Hollywood studio photographer; married; wife's name, Denise; children: Bill, Jr. *Education:* Received B.A. from University of Southern California Film School.

ADDRESSES: P.O. Box 2230, Hollywood, CA 90078.

CAREER: Cinematographer and director. Worked as camera operator for Conrad Hall; worked in television as camera operator, assistant, and director of photography; worked on television commercials and inserts beginning in mid-1950s. *Military service:* Served in U.S. Coast Guard during World War II.

MEMBER: American Society of Cinematographers (past president).

AWARDS, HONORS: Academy Award nominations, cinematography, 1977, for *Looking for Mr. Goodbar,* 1978, for *Heaven Can Wait,* c. 1983, for *WarGames,* and c. 1985, for *Murphy's Romance,* visual effects (with A. D. Flowers and Gregory Jein) and cinematography, both 1979, for *1941.*

CREDITS:

FILM APPEARANCES

The cellist, *Dusty and Sweets McGee,* Warner Bros., 1971 (also see below).

Cinematographer, *Irreconcilable Differences,* Warner Bros., 1984 (also see below).

FILM WORK; CINEMATOGRAPHER

Fade In, Paramount, 1967.

Games, Universal, 1967.

(As Bill Fraker) *The Fox,* Warner Bros., 1967.

The President's Analyst, Paramount, 1967.

Rosemary's Baby, Paramount, 1968.

Bullitt, Warner Bros., 1968.

Paint Your Wagon, Paramount, 1969.

Dusty and Sweets McGee, Warner Bros., 1971.

The Day of the Dolphin, Avco Embassy, 1973.

Rancho Deluxe, United Artists (UA), 1975.

(As William Fraker; with Haskell Wexler and Bill Butler), *One Flew over the Cuckoo's Nest,* UA, 1975.

Aloha, Bobby and Rose, Columbia, 1975.

Coonskin (animated), Bryanston, 1975.

The Killer inside Me, Warner Bros., 1976.

(With Butler) *Lipstick,* Paramount, 1976.

Gator, UA, 1976.

Exorcist II: The Heretic, Warner Bros., 1977.

(With nine others) *Close Encounters of the Third Kind,* Columbia, 1977.

Looking for Mr. Goodbar, Paramount, 1977.

American Hot Wax, Paramount, 1978.
Heaven Can Wait, Paramount, 1978.
Old Boyfriends, Avco Embassy, 1979.
1941, Universal, 1979.
Divine Madness, Warner Bros., 1980.
The Hollywood Knights, Columbia, 1980.
Sharky's Machine, Warner Bros., 1982.
The Best Little Whorehouse in Texas, Universal, 1982.
WarGames, Metro-Goldwyn-Mayer (MGM)-UA, 1983.
Irreconcilable Differences, Warner Bros., 1984.
Protocol, Warner Bros., 1984.
Murphy's Romance, Columbia, 1985.
Fever Pitch, MGM-UA, 1985.
(As William Fraker) *SpaceCamp,* Twentieth Century-Fox, 1986.
Burglar, Warner Bros., 1987.
Baby Boom, MGM-UA, 1987.
Chances Are, Tri-Star, 1989.
An Innocent Man, Buena Vista, 1989.
The Freshman, Tri-Star, 1990.

Also cinematographer and coproducer for *Forbid Them Not,* 1961.

FILM WORK; DIRECTOR

Monte Walsh, National General, 1970.
A Reflection of Fear (also known as *Labyrinth*), Columbia, 1973.
The Legend of the Lone Ranger, Universal/Associated Film Distribution, 1981.

FILM WORK; CAMERA OPERATOR

Father Goose, Universal, 1964.
The Wild Seed (also known as *Fargo*), Universal, 1965.
Morituri (also known as *The Saboteur: Code Name "Morituri"* and *The Saboteur*), Twentieth Century-Fox, 1965.
The Professionals, Columbia, 1966.

TELEVISION WORK

Cinematographer, *Frank's Place* (series), CBS, 1987.
Director, *B. L. Stryker: The Dancer's Touch* (movie), ABC, 1989.
Cinematographer, *Checkered Flag,* ABC, 1990.

Also worked as loader, *The Lone Ranger* (series), ABC; assistant and cameraman, *The Adventures of Ozzie and Harriet* (series), ABC; and worked on series *Stony Burke,* ABC, *Outer Limits,* ABC, and *Daktari,* CBS.

OTHER SOURCES:

PERIODICALS

American Cinematographer, May, 1978; May, 1979; July, 1980; April, 1984; October, 1984.
American Film, April, 1979.

Film Comment, March-April, 1984.

*   *   *

FRANKEL, Kenneth   1941-

PERSONAL: Born December 10, 1941, in Cleveland, OH; son of Elmer M. and Doris (Folph) Frankel. *Education:* Northwestern University, B.S., 1963.

ADDRESSES: Office—c/o Long Wharf Theatre, 222 Sargent Dr., New Haven, CT 06511.

CAREER: Director and actor. Served as assistant director to Tyrone Guthrie; affiliated with Minnesota Theatre Company, Minneapolis, MN, 1965; Barter Theatre, Abingdon, VA, 1972, 1973, and guest artist, 1975; McCarter Theatre Company, Princeton, NJ, guest director, 1975-76 and 1976-77, and director, 1977-78 and 1979-80; Long Wharf Theatre, New Haven, CT, director, 1975-76, 1977-79, 1980-82, and associate artistic director, 1984-85, 1986-87; Actors Theatre of Louisville, Louisville, KY, director, 1976-77; Milwaukee Repertory Theatre, Milwaukee, WI, director, 1977-78; Folger Theatre Group, Washington, DC, stage director, 1979-80; and Dallas Shakespeare Festival, artistic director, 1981.

MEMBER: Society of Stage Directors and Choreographers, Affiliate Artists.

AWARDS, HONORS: Village Voice Obie Award, 1983, for *Quartermaine's Terms.*

CREDITS:

STAGE APPEARANCES

(Broadway debut) Waiter, *Dinner at Eight,* Alvin Theatre, 1966.

STAGE DIRECTOR

When You Comin' Back, Red Ryder?, Circle Repertory Company, then Eastside Playhouse, New York City, both 1973.
Kerouac, The New Dramatists, Inc., New York City, 1976.
Visions of Kerouac, Lion Theatre Company, New York City, 1976.
The Arbor, Manhattan Theatre Club, New York City, 1979.
Spokesong; or, The Common Wheel, Circle in the Square Theatre, New York City, 1979.
Romeo and Juliet, Dallas Shakespeare Festival, Dallas, TX, 1981.
Pal Joey, Long Wharf Theatre, New Haven, CT, 1982-83.
Quartermaine's Terms, Playhouse 91, New York City, 1983.

Old Times, Roundabout Theatre, New York City, 1983-84.

Accent on Youth, Long Wharf Theatre, 1984.

Love Letters on Blue Paper, Hudson Guild Theatre, New York City, 1984.

Before the Dawn, American Place Theatre, New York City, 1985.

The Hands of Its Enemy, Manhattan Theatre Club, City Center Theatre, New York City, 1986.

The Downside, Long Wharf Theatre, 1987.

Macbeth, Mark Hellinger Theatre, New York City, 1988.

Fighting Chance, Long Wharf Theatre, 1988.

Also director of *In White America,* Cleveland, OH.

MAJOR TOURS; DIRECTOR

A Christmas Carol, U.S. cities, 1982-83.

Macbeth, U.S. cities, 1988.

Also directed touring company of *The Lion in Winter,* U.S. cities.*

* * *

FUNT, Allen 1914-

PERSONAL: Born September 16, 1914, in New York City.

ADDRESSES: Office—DGA, 110 West 57th St., New York, NY 10019.

CAREER: Producer, performer and writer. *Military service:* U.S. Army, served during World War II.

CREDITS:

FILM WORK; PRODUCER AND DIRECTOR

What Do You Say to a Naked Lady?, 1970, and *Money Talks,* 1972.

TELEVISION APPEARANCES; SERIES

Host, *Candid Microphone,* ABC, 1948-49, CBS, 1949-51, name changed to *Candid Camera,* ABC, 1951-56, CBS, 1957-67, syndicated as *The New Candid Camera,* 1974-80.

The Garry Moore Show, CBS, 1959-60.

TELEVISION APPEARANCES; SPECIALS; HOST

The Candid Camera Special, NBC, 1981.

Candid Camera Looks at the Difference between Men and Women, NBC, 1983.

Candid Camera: The First 40 Years, CBS, 1987.

Also appeared on *Buster Keaton: A Hard Act To Follow,* 1987, *Candid Camera Christmas Special,* 1987, *Candid Camera Eat! Eat! Eat!,* 1989, *Candid Camera on Wheels,* 1989, *Candid Camera Shopping Spree,* 1990, *Candid Cam-*

era . . . Funny Money, 1990, *Candid Camera . . . Funt's Favorite Funnies,* 1990, *Candid Camera . . . Smile, You're On Vacation!,* 1990, *Candid Camera . . . Getting Physical,* 1990, and *Candid Camera Goes To the Doctor,* 1990.

TELEVISION APPEARANCES; EPISODIC

The Jerry Lewis Show, NBC, 1960.

OTHER TELEVISION APPEARANCES

Host, *It's Only Human* (pilot), NBC, 1981.

TELEVISION WORK; EXECUTIVE PRODUCER AND DIRECTOR

Candid Camera Looks at the Difference between Men and Women, NBC, 1983.

Also *Candid Kids,* 1985, *Candid Camera Eat! Eat! Eat!,* 1989, *Candid Camera on Wheels,* 1989, *Candid Camera Shopping Spree,* 1990, *Candid Camera . . . Funny Money,* 1990, *Candid Camera . . . Funt's Favorite Funnies,* 1990, *Candid Camera . . . Smile, You're On Vacation!,* 1990, *Candid Camera . . . Getting Physical,* 1990, and *Candid Camera Goes To the Doctor,* 1990.

OTHER TELEVISION WORK

Producer, director, *Candid Microphone,* ABC, 1948-49, CBS, 1949-51.

Producer, *Candid Camera,* ABC, 1951-56, (with Julio Di Benedetto) CBS, 1960-67.

Producer, *Tell It to the Camera,* CBS, 1962.

Executive producer, *Candid Camera,* syndicated, 1974-80.

Producer, director, *It's Only Human* (pilot), NBC, 1981.

Executive producer, *The Candid Camera Special,* NBC, 1981.

Also producer, *Candid Camera Christmas Special,* 1987, and executive producer, *Candid Camera: The First 40 Years,* 1987.

RADIO APPEARANCES

Appeared on *Candid Microphone.*

WRITINGS:

FILM

Writer for *What Do You Say to a Naked Lady?,* 1970, and *Money Talks,* 1972.

TELEVISION SPECIALS

Writer for *Candid Camera . . . Funny Money, Candid Camera Comedy Shopping Spree, Candid Camera . . . Getting Physical,* and *Candid Camera . . . Smile, You're On Vacation!,* all 1990.

RADIO

Writer (with others) for *Truth or Consequences.*

G

GALLAGHER, Peter   1955-

PERSONAL: Born August 19, 1955, in Yonkers, NY; married Paula Harwood (a music video producer); children: James. *Education:* Received degree in economics from Tufts University; studied at Actor's Studio with Robert Lewis.

ADDRESSES: Agent—International Creative Management, 40 West 57th St., New York, NY 10155.

CAREER: Actor.

AWARDS, HONORS: Theatre World Award, 1982, for *A Doll's Life;* Clarence Derwent Award, 1984-85, for *The Real Thing;* Antoinette Perry Award nomination, c. 1986, for *Long Day's Journey into Night.*

CREDITS:

STAGE APPEARANCES

Danny Zuko, *Grease,* Eden Theatre, Broadhurst Theatre, and finally Royale Theatre, New York City, 1972, then Paper Mill Playhouse, Milburn, NJ, 1977.
Caligula, Robert Lewis Acting Company, New York City, 1978.
Romeo and Juliet, Long Wharf Theatre, New Haven, CT, 1980.
Another Country, Long Wharf Theatre, 1982, then Boston Shakespeare Company, MA.
Otto, *A Doll's Life,* Mark Hellinger Theatre, New York City, 1982.
Morgan Evans, *The Corn Is Green,* Lunt-Fontanne Theatre, New York City, 1983.
Billy, *The Real Thing,* Plymouth Theatre, New York City, 1984.
Mr. Darcy, *Pride and Prejudice,* Long Wharf Theatre, 1985.

Edmund Tyrone, *Long Day's Journey into Night,* Broadhurst Theatre, 1986.

Also appeared in *Hair,* 1977.

FILM APPEARANCES

Caesare, *The Idolmaker,* United Artists, 1980.
Michael Papa's, *Summer Lovers,* Filmways/Orion, 1982.
Jack Dolan, *Dreamchild,* Universal, 1983.
Kai, *My Little Girl,* Hemdale, 1987.
Brother Tony, *High Spirits,* Tri-Star, 1988.
John Millaney, *sex, lies, and videotape,* Outlaw, 1989.
Matt, *The Cabinet of Dr. Ramirez,* MediaScope, 1991.

Also appeared in *Late for Dinner,* 1990, and *Tune in Tomorrow.*

TELEVISION APPEARANCES; SERIES

John Skagska, *Skag,* NBC, 1980.

TELEVISION APPEARANCES; EPISODIC

Tommy Baron, *Private Eye,* NBC, 1987.
Charlie Castle, "The Big Knife," *American Playhouse,* PBS, 1988.

TELEVISION APPEARANCES; MOVIES

Nick, *Terrible Joe Moran,* CBS, 1984.
Lieutenant Commander Challee, *The Caine Mutiny Court Martial,* CBS, 1988.
Leo Frank, *The Murder of Mary Phagan,* NBC, 1988.
Aaron Copler, *I'll Be Home for Christmas,* NBC, 1988.
David West, *Love and Lies,* ABC, 1990.

TELEVISION APPEARANCES; SPECIALS

Phil Gray, *A Different Twist,* 1984.

Also appeared in *Private Contentment,* 1982.

OTHER SOURCES:

PERIODICALS

Premiere, October, 1990.*

*　　*　　*

GANZ, Tony

PERSONAL: Born in New York, NY. *Education:* Studied film at Harvard University.

CAREER: Producer. Formerly associated with PBS, Charles Fries Productions, and Ron Howard Productions.

CREDITS:

FILM WORK; PRODUCER, EXCEPT WHERE NOTED

(With Deborah Blum; and second-unit director), *Gung Ho,* Paramount, 1986.
Executive producer, *No Man's Land,* Orion, 1987.
(With Blum), *Clean and Sober,* Warner Brothers, 1988.
(With Blum), *Vibes,* Columbia, 1988.

TELEVISION WORK: MOVIES. EXCEPT WHERE NOTED

Associate producer, *Foster and Laurie,* CBS, 1975.
Associate producer, *The Hatfields and the McCoys,* ABC, 1975.
Associate producer, *The Call of the Wild,* NBC, 1976.
Associate producer, *The Greatest Thing That Almost Happened,* CBS, 1977.
Associate producer, *Intimate Strangers,* ABC, 1977.
Associate producer, *Crash,* ABC, 1978.
Associate producer, *The Winds of Kitty Hawk,* NBC, 1978.
Producer, *Bitter Harvest,* NBC, 1981.
Executive producer (with Irv Wilson), *Into Thin Air,* CBS, 1985.

Executive producer of the series *Maximum Security,* 1985, and *Gung Ho,* 1986; producer of the series *American Dream Machine.**

*　　*　　*

GARBER, Victor 1949-

PERSONAL: Born March 16, 1949, in London, Ontario, Canada.

ADDRESSES: Agent—Arlene Forster, Triad Artists Inc., 10100 Santa Monica Blvd., 16th Floor, Los Angeles, CA 90067.

CAREER: Actor.

AWARDS, HONORS: Theatre World Award, 1973, for *Ghosts;* Antoinette Perry Award nomination, best actor in a play, 1978, for *Deathtrap,* best actor in a musical, 1982, for *Little Me,* and best actor in a play, 1989, for *Lend Me a Tenor;* Drama Desk Award nomination, 1986, for *You Never Can Tell;* Obie Award, *Village Voice,* 1988, for *Wenceslas Square.*

CREDITS:

STAGE APPEARANCES

(Off-Broadway debut) Osvald Alving, *Ghosts,* Roundabout Theatre, 1973.
Ensemble, *Godspell,* Royal Alexandra Theatre, then Playhouse Theatre, both Toronto, Ontario, Canada, 1972.
Gaston, *The Waltz of the Toreadors,* Philadelphia Drama Guild, Philadelphia, PA, 1973.
The Soldier's Tale, Long Wharf Theatre, New Haven, CT, 1974.
The Knight of the Burning Pestle, Long Wharf Theatre, 1974.
Don Juan, Yale Repertory Theatre, New Haven, CT, 1975.
Lurk, *Joe's Opera,* St. Clement's Church Theatre, New York City, 1975.
Sammy, *Cracks,* Theatre de Lys, New York City, 1976.
As You Like It, American Shakespeare Theatre, Stratford, CT, 1976.
The House of Mirth, Long Wharf Theatre, 1976.
Daarlin' Juno, Long Wharf Theatre, 1976.
The Autumn Garden, Long Wharf Theatre, 1976.
Valere, *Tartuffe,* Circle in the Square, New York City, 1977.
Clifford Anderson, *Deathtrap,* Music Box Theatre, New York City, 1978.
Anthony Hope, *Sweeney Todd,* Uris Theatre, New York City, 1979.
Vernon Gersch, *They're Playing Our Song,* Imperial Theatre, New York City, 1981.
Noble Eggleston, Val du Val, Fred Poitrine, and Noble Junior, *Little Me,* Eugene O'Neill Theatre, New York City, 1982.
Valere, *The Miser,* Old Globe Theatre, San Diego, CA, 1982.
John, *The Importance of Being Earnest,* Old Globe Theatre, 1982.
Garry Lejeune, *Noises Off,* Brooks Atkinson Theatre, New York City, 1983-84, then Center Theatre Group, Ahmanson Theatre, Los Angeles, 1984.
Valentine, *You Never Can Tell,* Circle in the Square, 1986-87.
Various roles, *Wenceslas Square,* New York Shakespeare Festival, Public Theatre, New York City, 1988.
Richard Dudgeon, *The Devil's Disciple,* Circle in the Square, 1988.

Max, *Lend Me a Tenor,* Morris Mechanic Theatre, Baltimore, MD, then Royale Theatre, New York City, both 1989.

Also appeared with the Santa Fe Festival Theatre, Santa Fe, NM.

MAJOR TOURS

Vernon Gersch, *They're Playing Our Song,* U.S. cities, 1979-81.

FILM APPEARANCES

Jesus, *Godspell,* Columbia, 1973.

TELEVISION APPEARANCES; EPISODIC

Ryan's Four, ABC, 1983.
Kevin, "A Day in Beaumont," *Twilight Zone,* CBS, 1986.
Dennis Widmer, *The Days and Nights of Molly Dodd,* NBC, 1987-88, then Lifetime, 1989.

TELEVISION APPEARANCES; MOVIES

Jerry Sharma, *Private Session,* NBC, 1985.
Title role, *Liberace: Behind the Music,* CBS, 1988.

TELEVISION APPEARANCES; SPECIALS

Voice of Christian, *Cyrano de Bergerac* (animated), ABC, 1974.
Lafayette, "Valley Forge," *The Hallmark Hall of Fame,* NBC, 1975.
Jack of Hearts, *Jack: A Flash Fantasy,* PBS, 1977.
Valere, *Tartuffe,* PBS, 1978.
Jack Chesney, *Charley's Aunt,* Entertainment Channel, 1983.

Also appeared as Arthur in *Ah, Wilderness!,* 1976; and Ernest Hemingway in *The White House.*

OTHER TELEVISION APPEARANCES

Teddy Wheeler, *The Best of Families* (mini-series), PBS, 1977.
Jackson Beaudine, *I Had Three Wives* (series), CBS, 1985.
John White, *Roanoak* (mini-series), PBS, 1986.*

*   *   *

GARBO, Greta   1905-1990

PERSONAL: Full name Greta Lovisa Gustafasson; born September 18, 1905, in Stockholm, Sweden; immigrated to the United States, 1925; naturalized U.S. citizen, 1951; died of an undisclosed illness, April 15, 1990, in a New York Hospital, New York, NY; daughter of Swen and Louvisa Gustafasson. *Education:* Attended Royal Dramatic Theatre School, Stockholm, 1922-24; National Theatre, 1924.

CAREER: Actress.

AWARDS, HONORS: Academy Award nominations, best actress, 1929, for *Anna Christie,* and 1930, for *Romance;* New York Film Critics Award, best actress, 1935, for *Anna Karenina;* Academy Award nomination, best actress, 1937, for *Camille;* Academy Award nomination, best actress, 1939, for *Ninotchka;* Special Academy Award, 1954.

CREDITS:

FILM APPEARANCES

Felicitas von Eltz, *Flesh and the Devil,* Metro-Goldwyn-Mayer (MGM), 1926.
Elena, *The Temptress,* MGM, 1926.
Leonora, *The Torrent* (also known as *Ibanez' Torrent*), MGM, 1926.
Anna Karenina, *Love,* MGM, 1927.
Marianne, *The Divine Woman,* MGM, 1928.
Tania, *The Mysterious Lady,* MGM, 1928.
Tania, *A Woman of Affairs,* MGM, 1929.
Irene, *The Kiss,* MGM, 1929.
A Man's Man, MGM, 1929.
Arden Stuart, *The Single Standard,* MGM, 1929.
Lili Sterling, *Wild Orchids,* MGM, 1929.
Title role, *Anna Christie,* MGM, 1930.
Rita Cavallini, *Romance,* MGM, 1930.
Yvonne, *Inspiration,* MGM, 1931.
Title role, *Mata Hari,* MGM, 1931.
Title role, *Susan Lenox—Her Fall And Rise* (also known as *The Rise of Helga; Rising To Fame*), MGM, 1931.
Zara, *As You Desire Me,* MGM, 1932.
Grusinkaya, *Grand Hotel,* MGM, 1932.
Title role, *Queen Christina,* MGM, 1933.
Katherine Koerber Fane, *The Painted Veil,* MGM, 1934.
Title role, *Anna Karenina,* MGM, 1935.
Marguerite, *Camille,* MGM, 1937.
Marie Walewska, *Conquest* (also known as *Marie Walewska*), MGM, 1937.
Lena Yakushova Ninotchka, *Ninotchka,* MGM, 1939.
Karin Borg Blake/Katherine Borg, *Two-Faced Woman,* MGM, 1941.

Made film debut as an extra in *A Fortune Hunter* (also known as *En lychoriddare*), 1921; also appeared in *Mr. and Mrs. Stockholm, How Not To Dress* (also known as *Herr och fru Stockholm*), 1922; *Our Daily Bread,* 1922; Greta Nordberg, *Peter The Tramp* (also known as *Luffar-Petter*), 1922; Countess Elisabeth Dohna, *The Atonement of Gosta Berling* (also known as *Gosta Berlings Saga*), 1924; Greta Rumfort, *Joyless Street* (also known as *Die Freundlose Gasse*), 1925.

SIDELIGHTS: During her lifetime, the reclusive star was reported by biographer John Bainbridge to have, "granted no interviews, signed no autographs, attended no premieres, answered no fan mail."*

* * *

GARDE, Betty 1905-1989

PERSONAL: Born September 19, 1905, in Philadelphia, PA; died December 25, 1989, in Hollywood, CA; daughter of Charles Pierie Garde and Katherine M. (Cropper) Garde; married Frank Lennon (a master electrician; deceased, 1987). *Education:* Attended West Philadelphia High School.

CAREER: Actress.

CREDITS:

STAGE APPEARANCES

(Stage debut) Maid, *Nice People,* Broadway Theatre, Philadelphia, PA, 1922.

(Broadway debut) Alma Borden, *Easy Come, Easy Go,* Cohan Theatre, 1925.

Gloria Hall, *The Social Register,* Fulton Theatre, New York City, 1931.

Millie, *The Best People,* Waldorf Theatre, New York City, 1933.

Emma Wallace, *The Primrose Path,* Biltmore Theatre, New York City, 1939.

Aunt Eller, *Oklahoma!,* St. James Theatre, New York City, 1943.

Sarah Rock, *A Little Evil,* Playhouse Theatre, Wilmington, DE, 1952.

Aunt Eller, *Oklahoma!,* New York City Center, 1958 and 1963.

Mrs. Gordon, Agatha Sue, I Love You, Henry Miller's Theatre, New York City, 1966.

Dante, *Stephen D,* East 74th Street Theatre, New York City, 1967.

Mrs. Greenhouse, *The Sponsor,* Peachtree Playhouse, Atlanta, GA, 1975.

Also appeared as Liliom, *Madame Muscat,* Westport, CT, 1941; Frosine, *The Miser,* Downtown National Theatre, 1955. Company member, Mae Desmond Players, Philadelphia, PA, 1922-24; played leading roles with the Wright Players, MI, 1927-30.

MAJOR TOURS

Gertrude Lennox, *Meet the Wife,* U.S. Army installations overseas, 1945.

Also appeared as Julia Winters, *The Poor Nut,* 1926. Appeared in *The Nervous Wreck; Easy Come, Easy Go.*

FILM APPEARANCES

(Film debut) *The Lady Lies,* Astoria Studios, 1929.

Florence Cole, *Queen High,* Paramount, 1930.

Madge Sloane, *Damaged Love,* Worldwide Sonart, 1931.

Hattie Henery, *Girl Habit,* Paramount, 1931.

Dorothy White, *Secrets of a Secretary,* Paramount, 1931.

Kitty Stark, *Caged,* Warner Brothers, 1950.

Mirna, *The Prince Who Was a Thief,* Universal, 1951.

Mrs. O'Dell, *One Desire,* Universal, 1955.

Miss Bettenhausen, *The Wonderful World of the Brothers Grimm,* Metro-Goldwyn-Mayer, 1962.

Also appeared in *Call Northside 777,* 1948; *Cry of the City,* 1948.

TELEVISION APPEARANCES; SERIES

Regular, *Kobb's Korner,* CBS, 1948.

Regular, *Easy Aces,* Dumont, 1949.

Abigail Millikan, *The World of Mr. Sweeny,* NBC, 1954.

Mattie Lane, *The Edge of Night,* CBS, 1956, and ABC, 1975.

Aggie Larkin, *The Real McCoys,* ABC, 1962, and CBS, 1963.

OTHER TELEVISION APPEARANCES

Hands of Murders (episodic), Dumont, 1949.

Starlight Theater (episodic), CBS, 1950.

Guest star, "A Woman's Work is Never Done", *Honeymooners,* CBS, 1955.

One Step Beyond (episodic), ABC, 1959.

Aunt Sadie, *All the Way Home* (special), NBC, 1971.

Also appeared in *Twilight Zone, Hallmark Hall of Fame,* and *The Untouchables.*

RADIO APPEARANCES

The Eddie Cantor Show, Lux Radio Theatre, 1935-37.

Also appeared as Belle, *Lorenzo Jones.* Appeared in *Mrs. Wiggs of the Cabbage Patch; My Son and I; Gangbusters; The Kate Smith Show; The Aldrich Family; Orson Welles's Mercury Theatre of the Air; Jack Pearl Show; NBC Theater of the Air; Easy Aces.* Did voiceover for Jergens commercial on Walter Winchell program.

OBITUARIES AND OTHER SOURCES:

PERIODICALS

Variety, January 10, 1990.*

* * *

GARDNER, Ava 1922-1990

PERSONAL: Full name, Ava Lavinnia Gardner; born December 24, 1922, in Grabton (some sources say Smithfield), NC; died of respiratory problems and a stroke, January, 1990, in London, England; buried in North Carolina; daughter of Jonas Bailey (a tobacco and cotton farmer) and Mary Elizabeth (a boarding house manager) Gardner; married Mickey Rooney (an actor), 1942 (divorced, 1943); married Artie Shaw (a musician and bandleader), 1945 (divorced, 1946); married Frank Sinatra (a singer and actor), 1951 (divorced, 1957). *Education:* Attended Atlantic Christian College.

CAREER: Actress.

AWARDS, HONORS: Academy Award nomination, best actress, 1954, for *Mogambo.*

CREDITS:

FILM APPEARANCES

Girl, *H.M. Pulham Esq.,* Metro-Goldwyn-Mayer (MGM), 1941.

Girl bit, *Calling Dr. Gillespie,* MGM, 1942.

Girl, *Joe Smith, American* (also known as *Highway to Freedom*), MGM, 1942.

Car Hop, *Kid Glove Killer,* MGM, 1942.

Girl, *Reunion in France* (also known as *Mademoiselle France; Reunion*) MGM, 1942.

Ringsider, *Sunday Punch,* MGM, 1942.

Girl in car, *This Time for Keeps,* MGM, 1942.

Girl, *We Were Dancing,* MGM, 1942.

Betty Williams, *Ghosts on the Loose* (also known as *Ghosts in the Night; The East Side Kids Meet Bela Lugosi*), Monogram, 1943.

Katy Chotnik, *Hitler's Madman* (also known as *Hitler's Hangman*), MGM, 1943.

Girl role, *DuBarry Was a Lady,* MGM, 1943.

Girl role, *Pilot No. 5,* MGM, 1943.

Girl role, *Swing Fever,* MGM, 1943.

Girl role, *Young Ideas,* MGM, 1943.

Hat Check Girl, *Lost Angel,* MGM, 1944.

Gloria Fullerton, *Maisie Goes to Reno* (also known as *You Can't Do That to Me*), MGM, 1944.

Jean Brown, *Three Men in White,* MGM, 1944.

Rockette Girl, *Two Girls and a Sailor,* MGM, 1944.

Hilda Spotts, *She Went to the Races,* MGM, 1945.

Kitty Collins, *The Killers,* Universal, 1946.

Mary, *Whistle Stop,* United Artists, 1946.

Jean Ogilvie, *The Hucksters,* MGM, 1947.

Linda, *Singapore,* Universal, 1947.

Venus, Goddess of Love/Venus Jones, *One Touch of Venus,* Universal, 1948.

Elizabeth Hinton, *The Bribe,* MGM, 1949.

Isabel Lorrison, *East Side, West Side,* MGM, 1949.

Pauline Ostrovski, *The Great Sinner,* MGM, 1949.

Barbara Beaurevel, *My Forbidden Past,* RKO Radio Pictures, 1951.

Pandora Reynolds, *Pandora and the Flying Dutchman,* MGM, 1951.

Julie LaVerne, *Show Boat,* MGM, 1951.

Martha Ronda, *Lone Star,* MGM, 1952.

Cynthia, *The Snows of Kilimanjaro,* Twentieth Century-Fox, 1952.

The Movie Star, *The Band Wagon,* MGM, 1953.

Queen Guinevere, *Knights of the Round Table,* MGM, 1953.

Eloise Y. Kelly, *Mogambo,* MGM, 1953.

Cordelia Cameron, *Ride Vaquero!,* MGM, 1953.

Maria Vargas, *The Barefoot Contessa,* United Artists, 1954.

Spectator, *Around the World in Eighty Days,* United Artists, 1956.

Victoria Jones, *Bhowani Junction,* MGM, 1956.

Lady Brett Ashley, *The Sun Also Rises,* Twentieth Century-Fox, 1957.

Lady Susan Ashlow, *The Little Hut,* MGM, 1957.

Duchess of Alba, *The Naked Maja,* United Artists, 1959.

Moira Davidson, *On the Beach,* United Artists, 1959.

Soledad, *The Angel Wore Red,* MGM, 1960.

Baroness Natalie Ivanoff, *55 Days at Peking,* Allied Artists, 1963.

Maxine Faulk, *The Night of the Iguana,* MGM, 1964.

Eleanor Holdbrook, *Seven Days in May,* Paramount, 1964.

Sarah, *The Bible. . . In The Beginning,* Twentieth Century-Fox, 1966.

Empress Elizabeth, *Mayerling,* MGM, 1968.

Michaela, *The Devil's Widow* (also known as *Tamlin*), British International Pictures, 1972.

Lily Langtry, *The Life and Times of Judge Roy Bean,* National General, 1972.

Remy Graff, *Earthquake,* Universal, 1974.

Katina Petersen, *Permission to Kill,* AVCO-Embassy, 1975.

Luxury, *The Blue Bird,* Twentieth Century-Fox, 1976.

Nicole, *The Cassandra Crossing,* AVCO-Embassy, 1976.

Miss Logan, *The Sentinel,* Universal, 1977.

Maggie, *City on Fire,* AVCO-Embassy, 1979.

Beth Richards, *The Kidnapping of the President,* Crown International, 1980.

Mabel Dodge, *Priest of Love,* Filmways, 1981.

Also appeared in *Fancy Answers* (short), 1941, *Mighty Lak a Goat* (short), 1942, *We Were Dancing,* 1942, and *Regina,* 1982.

TELEVISION APPEARANCES

Ruth Galveston, *Knots Landing* (series), CBS, 1985.

Agrippina, *A.D.* (mini-series), NBC, 1985.

Minnie Littlejohn, *The Long Hot Summer* (movie), NBC, 1985.

Kadin, *Harem* (movie), ABC, 1986.

WRITINGS:

(With Alan Burgess) *Ava: The Autobiography of Ava Gardner,* Bantam, 1990.

OBITUARIES AND OTHER SOURCES:

BOOKS

Bernard, Andre, *Ava Gardner,* [Paris], 1976.
Gardner, Ava and Alan Burgess, *Ava: The Autobiography of Ava Gardner,* Bantam, 1990.
Kass, Judith M., *Ava Gardner,* [New York], 1979.
Parish, James R., and others, *The Hollywood Beauties,* Arlington House, 1978.
Rampling, Matthew, *Ava Gardner,* [Paris], 1981.
Romero, Jerry, *Sinatra's Women,* Manor Books, 1976.

PERIODICALS

Cine Review, August 26, 1982.
Ecran, August/September, 1974.
Films In Review, June/July, 1965.
New York Times, January 26, 1990.
Radio Times, March 27, 1982.
Variety, January 31, 1990.*

*　　*　　*

GARNER, James   1928-

PERSONAL: Born James Scott Bumgarner, April 7, 1928, in Norman, OK; married Lois Clarke, August 17, 1956; children: Kimberly, Gretta, Scott. *Education:* Attended University of Oklahoma; studied acting at Herbert Berghof Studios, New York.

ADDRESSES: Agent—Robinson, Lutrell, and Associates, 141 El Camino Drive, Suite 110, Beverly Hills, CA 90212.

CAREER: Actor and producer. Founder and president, Cherokee Productions. Has also worked as a salesman, oil field worker, carpet layer, swim trunks model, lifeguard, and truck driver; pace car driver in the Indianapolis 500 in 1975 and 1979. *Military service:* Merchant Marines, U.S. Army; served during Korean conflict; received Purple Heart.

AWARDS, HONORS: Golden Globe Award, most promising newcomer, 1958; Emmy Award, outstanding lead actor in a drama series, 1976, for *The Rockford Files; Advertising Age* Star Presenter of the Year, 1978; Emmy Award nomination and Golden Globe Award nomination, both 1984, for *Heartsounds;* Academy Award nomination, best actor, 1986, for *Murphy's Romance;* Emmy Award (with Peter K. Duchow), outstanding special, 1987, for *Hallmark Hall of Fame* special "Promise"; Emmy Award nominations, outstanding supporting actor

in a mini-series or special, and (with Duchow) outstanding drama/comedy special, both 1989, for *Hallmark Hall of Fame* special "My Name Is Bill W."; inducted into the Academy of Television Arts and Sciences' Hall of Fame, 1991.

CREDITS:

FILM APPEARANCES

Tumblers, *Joan of Arc,* RKO Radio Pictures, 1948.
Preston, *The Girl He Left Behind,* Warner Brothers, 1956.
Major Joe Craven, *Toward the Unknown* (also known as *Brink of Hell*), Warner Brothers, 1956.
Captain Mike Baily, *Sayonara,* Warner Brothers, 1957.
Maitland, *Shoot-Out at Medicine Bend,* Warner Brothers, 1957.
Major William Darby, *Darby's Rangers* (also known as *Young Invaders*), Warner Brothers, 1958.
Bret Maverick, *Alias Jesse James,* United Artists, 1959.
Ken, *Up Periscope,* Warner Brothers, 1959.
Cash McCall, *Cash McCall,* Warner Brothers, 1960.
Dr. Joe Cardin, *The Children's Hour* (also known as *The Loudest Whisper*), United Artists, 1961.
Fred Williams, *Boys' Night Out,* Metro-Goldwyn-Mayer (MGM), 1962.
Hendley "The Scrounger," *The Great Escape,* United Artists, 1963.
Nicholas Arden, *Move Over Darling,* Twentieth Century-Fox, 1963.
Dr. Gerald Boyer, *The Thrill of It All,* Universal, 1963.
Henry Tyroon, *The Wheeler Dealers* (also known as *Separate Beds*), Filmways, 1963.
Lieutenant Commander Charles Madison, *The Americanization of Emily,* MGM, 1964.
Casey, *The Art of Love,* Universal, 1965.
Major Jefferson Pike, *36 Hours,* MGM, 1965.
Jess Remsberg, *Duel at Diablo,* United Artists, 1966.
William Beddoes, *A Man Could Get Killed* (also known as *Welcome, Mr. Beddoes*), Universal, 1966.
Mr. Buddwing, *Mr. Buddwing* (also known as *Woman without a Face*), MGM, 1966.
Wyatt, *Hour of the Gun,* United Artists, 1967.
Grif Henderson, *How Sweet It Is,* New General Pictures, 1968.
Ben Morris, *The Pink Jungle,* Universal, 1968.
Philip Marlow, *Marlow,* MGM, 1969.
Jason McCullough, *Support Your Local Sheriff,* United Artists, 1969.
Luther Sledge, *A Man Called Sledge,* Columbia, 1971.
Quincy Drew, *The Skin Game,* Warner Brothers, 1971.
Latigo Smith, *Support Your Local Gunfighter,* United Artists, 1971.
Police Chief Abel Marsh, *They Only Kill Their Masters,* MGM, 1972.
Clint Keys, *One Little Indian,* Buena Vista, 1973.

Lincoln Costain, *The Castaway Cowboy,* Buena Vista, 1974.
Health (also known as *H.E.A.L.T.H.*), Twentieth Century-Fox, 1980.
Jake Berman, *The Fan,* Paramount, 1981.
King, *Victor/Victoria,* United Artists, 1982.
Zack, *Tank,* Universal, 1984.
Murphy Jones, *Murphy's Romance,* Columbia, 1985.
Wyatt Earp, *Sunset,* Tri-Star, 1988.

Also appeared in *Hawaiian Cowboy.*

TELEVISION APPEARANCES; SERIES

Bret Maverick, *Maverick,* ABC, 1957-62.
Title role, *Nichols,* NBC, 1971-72.
Jim Rockford, *The Rockford Files,* NBC, 1974-79.
Title role, *Bret Maverick,* NBC, 1981-82.
Jim Doyle, *Man of the People,* NBC, 1991—.

TELEVISION APPEARANCES; MOVIES, EXCEPT WHERE NOTED

Jim Rockford, *The Rockford Files,* NBC, 1974.
Bret Maverick, *The New Maverick,* ABC, 1978.
George Adams, *The Long Summer of George Adams,* NBC, 1982.
Dr. Harold Lear, *Heartsounds,* ABC, 1984.
Al Mackay, *The Glitter Dome,* HBO, 1984.
Norman Grant, *Space* (mini-series), CBS, 1987.

TELEVISION APPEARANCES; SPECIALS

The Bing Crosby Special, ABC, 1959.
The Bob Hope Show, NBC, 1960.
The Bob Hope Show, NBC, 1961.
The Bob Hope Show, NBC, 1963.
The Bob Hope Show, NBC, 1965.
Superstunt, NBC, 1977.
The American Film Institute Salute to Henry Fonda, CBS, 1978.
Host, *60 Years of Seduction,* ABC, 1981.
Bret Maverick, *Lily for President,* CBS, 1982.
Bob Beuhler, "Promise," *Hallmark Hall of Fame,* CBS, 1986 (also see below).
Dr. Bob, "My Name Is Bill W.," *Hallmark Hall of Fame,* ABC, 1989 (also see below).
"Decoration Day," *Hallmark Hall of Fame,* NBC, 1990.

Also appeared on *The Twelfth Annual People's Choice Awards,* 1986, *60th Annual Academy Awards Presentation,* 1988, *A Conversation with Dinah,* 1989, *Dinah Comes Home Again,* 1990, and *Cheyenne.*

TELEVISION APPEARANCES; EPISODIC

Conflict, ABC, 1956.
Young Maverick, CBS, 1979.

TELEVISION WORK

Executive producer (with Peter K. Duchow), "Promise," *Hallmark Hall of Fame* (special), ABC, 1986.
Executive producer (with Duchow), "My Name Is Bill W.," *Hallmark Hall of Fame* (special), ABC, 1989.

Also director of episodes of *Maverick,* ABC, and *The Rockford Files,* NBC.

STAGE APPEARANCES

The Caine Mutiny Court-Martial, Plymouth Theatre, New York City, New York City, 1954.*

*   *   *

GASPARD, Ray
See GASPARD, Raymond L.

*   *   *

GASPARD, Raymond L.   1949-
(Ray Gaspard)

PERSONAL: Born July 9, 1949, in Chicago, IL; son of Joseph Henry (a postal worker) and Charlie Etta (a registered nurse; maiden name, Taylor) Gaspard; children: Charlotte. *Education:* Attended Columbia University.

ADDRESSES: Office—Westside Arts Theatre, 407 West 43rd Street, New York, NY 10036.

CAREER: Producer. Producer and director, Westside Arts Theatre, New York City, 1980—.

MEMBER: Off-Broadway League.

CREDITS:

STAGE WORK

Producer, *We Won't Pay, We Won't Pay,* Westside Arts Theatre, New York City, 1980.
(As Ray Gaspard) Producer, *I Can't Keep Running in Place,* Westside Arts Theatre, 1981.
Associate producer, *Woza Albert,* Criterion Theatre, London, 1983.
Producer (with Martin Markinson, Mary Card, and Woodie King, Jr.), *Dinah! Queen of the Blues,* Westside Arts Center, Cheryl Crawford Theatre, New York City, 1983.
Associate producer, *Three Ways Home,* Astor Place Theatre, New York City, 1988.

Co-producer, *Woza Albert,* Empty Space Theatre, Seattle, WA, and Annenberg Center, Philadelphia, PA.

FILM APPEARANCES

(As Ray Gaspard) Harper, *Screams of a Winter Night,* Dimension, 1979.*

* * *

GAY, John   1924-

PERSONAL: Born April 1, 1924, in Whittier, CA. *Education:* Attended Los Angeles City College.

CAREER: Writer.

AWARDS, HONORS: Academy Award nomination (with Terence Rattigan), best screenplay based on material from another medium, 1958, for *Separate Tables;* Writers Guild of America Award nominations, 1977, for both *Kill Me If You Can* and *Hallmark Hall of Fame* movie "The Courtship of George Armstrong Custer," 1982, for *The Long Summer of George Adams,* and 1989, for *Inherit the Wind;* Emmy Award nomination, 1984, for *Fatal Vision.*

CREDITS:

TELEVISION APPEARANCES; SERIES

As himself, *Apartment 3-C,* syndicated, 1949.
As himself, *Mr. and Mrs. Mystery,* CBS, 1949.

WRITINGS:

STAGE

Christophe, produced by Chelsea Theatre Group, New York City, 1965.
Summer Voices, produced at Circle Theatre, Los Angeles, CA, 1977.
Diversions and Delights, produced by Eugene O'Neill Theatre, New York City, 1978, and Playhouse Theatre, London, 1990.

FILM

Run Silent, Run Deep, United Artists, 1958.
(With Terence Rattigan) *Separate Tables,* United Artists, 1958.
The Happy Thieves, United Artists, 1961.
(With Robert Ardrey) *The Four Horsemen of the Apocalypse,* Metro-Goldwyn-Mayer (MGM), 1962.
Uncredited contributor, *Mutiny on the Bounty,* MGM, 1962.
The Courtship of Eddie's Father, MGM, 1963.
The Hallelujah Trail, United Artists, 1965.
Uncredited contributor, *Texas Across the River,* Universal, 1966.
The Last Safari, Paramount, 1967.
No Way To Treat a Lady, Paramount, 1968.
The Power, MGM, 1968.
Soldier Blue, AVCO/Embassy, 1970.

Sometimes a Great Notion (also known as *Never Give an Inch*), Universal, 1971.
(With Terry Malick) *Pocket Money,* National General, 1972.
Hennessy, American International, 1975.
A Matter of Time, American International, 1976.
(With Stanley Price) *Golden Rendezvous,* Film Trust, 1977.

TELEVISION MOVIES, EXCEPT WHERE NOTED

Prairie Night, Kraft-TV, 1955.
The Sentry, Kraft-TV, 1956.
"The Day Before Atlanta," *Playhouse 90,* CBS, 1958.
"Out of Dust," *Playhouse 90,* CBS, 1959.
"To the Sound of Trumpets," *Playhouse 90,* CBS, 1960.
All My Darling Daughters, ABC, 1972.
My Darling Daughters' Anniversary, ABC, 1973.
The Red Badge of Courage, NBC, 1974.
Thing In Their Season, CBS, 1974.
The Chadwick Family, ABC, 1974.
Adventures of the Queen, CBS, 1975.
The Amazing Howard Hughes, CBS, 1977.
Captains Courageous, ABC, 1977.
Kill Me If You Can, NBC, 1977.
Les Miserables, CBS, 1978.
Transplant, CBS, 1979.
A Private Battle, CBS, 1980.
A Tale of Two Cities, CBS, 1980.
Stand By Your Man, CBS, 1981.
Berlin Tunnel 21, CBS, 1981.
The Bunker, CBS, 1981.
Dial M for Murder, NBC, 1981.
Ivanhoe, CBS, 1982.
The Hunchback of Notre Dame, CBS, 1982.
The Long Summer of George Adams, NBC, 1982.
Witness for the Prosecution, CBS, 1982.
A Piano for Mrs. Cimino, CBS, 1982.
Fatal Vision, NBC, 1984.
Samson and Delilah, ABC, 1984.
Doubletake, CBS, 1985.
The Manhunt for Claude Dallas, CBS, 1986.
Six Against the Rock, NBC, 1987.
Sidney Sheldon's Windmills of the Gods (mini-series), CBS, 1988.
Around the World in Eighty Days (mini-series), NBC, 1989.
Inherit the Wind, NBC, 1989.
Blind Faith (mini-series), NBC, 1990.

Also wrote *Uncle Tom's Cabin,* Showtime.

TELEVISION SPECIALS

"The Court Martial of George Armstrong Custer," *Hallmark Hall of Fame,* NBC, 1977.

"Shadow of a Doubt," *Hallmark Hall of Fame,* NBC, 1991.

Also wrote *Outlaw, And the Band Played On,* and *Giant.*

*   *   *

GILBERT, Bruce 1947-

PERSONAL: Full name, Bruce Regan Gilbert; born March 28, 1947, in Los Angeles, CA; son of Ross Gilbert and Laurie Barrett (Safren) Cole; married Ellen Ruth Bernstein, April 15, 1979; children: Jordan Robert, Spencer. *Education:* Attended Boston University, 1965-67; University of California, Berkeley, B.A., 1969. *Avocational interests:* Flying, skiing, and writing.

ADDRESSES: Office—9336 West Washington Blvd., Culver City, CA 90230. *Agent*—Creative Artists Agency, 9830 Wilshire Blvd., Beverly Hills, CA 90212.

CAREER: Producer. President, American Filmworks, 1980—. Worked at Pacific Film Archive, Berkeley, CA, and film production department, San Francisco State University; story editor, feature film division, Cine-Artists; partner with Jane Fonda and IPC Films Inc. Founder of progressive pre-school in the San Francisco area.

MEMBER: Academy of Motion Picture Arts and Sciences.

AWARDS, HONORS: Golden Globe Award and Academy Award nomination, both Best Picture, 1981, for *On Golden Pond.*

CREDITS:

FILM WORK

Associate producer, *Coming Home* (also see below), United Artists, 1978.
Executive producer, *The China Syndrome,* Columbia, 1979.
Producer, *Nine to Five,* Twentieth Century-Fox, 1980.
Producer, *On Golden Pond,* Universal, 1981.
Producer, *Rollover,* Warner Brothers, 1981.
Producer, *The Morning After,* Twentieth Century-Fox, 1986.

Also director of *Another World.*

TELEVISION WORK

Executive producer (with Jane Fonda and James Komack), *Nine to Five* (series), ABC, 1982.
Executive producer, *The Dollmaker* (movie), ABC, 1984.

WRITINGS:

(With others) *Coming Home* (screenplay), United Artists, 1978.

Also wrote screenplay *The Grand Tour,* based on the novel *Trinity's Child.**

*   *   *

GILBERT, Lewis 1920-

PERSONAL: Born March 6, 1920, in London, England; married Hylda Henrietta Tafler; children: two sons.

ADDRESSES: Contact—Baker Rooke, Clement House, 99 Aldwych, London WC2 BJY, England.

CAREER: Film director, producer, and writer. Began work as a child film actor; worked as an assistant director with various production companies, including London Films, Mayflower, Associated British Films, and RKO Radio Pictures, 1930-39; writer and director for Gainsborough Pictures, c. 1948, and Argyle Productions, 1950; also worked as a director for Nettlefold Films, Ltd. *Military service:* Royal Air Force; attached to U.S. Air Corps Film Unit as assistant director to William Keighley, 1939-44.

AWARDS, HONORS: Michael Balcon Award, directing, British Academy of Film and Television Arts, 1990, for *Shirley Valentine;* Best Film, British Film Academy, for *Reach for the Sky;* Best Film, British Academy of Film and Television Arts, for *Educating Rita.*

CREDITS:

FILM DIRECTOR, EXCEPT WHERE INDICATED

The Little Ballerina, Universal, 1951 (also see below).
Scarlet Thread, Butchers, 1951.
Once a Sinner, Hoffberg, 1952.
Albert, R.N. (also known as *Break to Freedom*), Eros, 1953.
Hundred Hour Hunt (also known as *Emergency Call*), Butchers, 1953.
Johnny on the Run, Associated British Films, 1953.
The Slasher (also known as *Cosh Boy*), Lippert, 1953.
Time Gentlemen Please!, Mayer-Kingsley, 1953.
The Good Die Young, Independent Film Distributors, 1954.
The Sea Shall Not Have Them, United Artists (UA), 1955.
The Admirable Crichton (also known as *Paradise Lagoon*), Columbia, 1957.
Reach for the Sky, J. Arthur Rank, 1957.
Carve Her Name with Pride, J. Arthur Rank, 1958.
Cast a Dark Shadow, Eros, 1958.
A Cry from the Street, Eros, 1959.
Ferry to Hong Kong, J. Arthur Rank, 1959 (also see below).
(And producer) *Light Up the Sky,* British Lion, 1960.
Sink the Bismarck!, Twentieth Century-Fox, 1960.
Loss of Innocence (also known as *The Greengage Summer*), Columbia, 1961.

Damn the Defiant! (also known as *H.M.S. Defiant*), Columbia, 1962.

The Seventh Dawn, UA, 1964.

(And producer) *Alfie,* Paramount, 1966.

You Only Live Twice, UA, 1967.

(And producer) *The Adventurers,* Paramount, 1970 (also see below).

(And producer) *Friends,* Paramount, 1971 (also see below).

(And producer) *Paul and Michelle,* Paramount, 1974.

Operation Daybreak (also known as *Price of Freedom*), Warner Bros., 1976.

(And producer) *Seven Nights in Japan,* Paramount, 1976.

The Spy Who Loved Me, UA, 1977.

Moonraker, UA, 1979.

(And producer) *Educating Rita,* Columbia, 1983.

(And producer with William P. Cartlidge) *Not Quite Jerusalem,* J. Arthur Rank, 1985.

(And producer) *Shirley Valentine,* Paramount, 1990.

Also director and producer of *Stepping Out,* 1991. Director of documentaries for G.B. Instructional, 1944-47, including *The Ten Year Plan, Sailors Do Care,* and *Arctic Harvest* (also see below); assistant director, *Target for Today.*

FILM APPEARANCES

Jem, *Dick Turpin,* Gaumont, 1933.

Over the Moon, UA, 1940.

Also appeared in *Divorce of Lady X,* 1937.

WRITINGS:

FILMS

(With Denis Waldock) *Marry Me!,* General Films Distributors, 1949.

The Little Ballerina, Universal, 1951.

Ferry to Hong Kong, J. Arthur Rank, 1959.

Emergency, Butchers, 1962.

The Adventurers, Paramount, 1970.

Friends, Paramount, 1971.

Paul and Michelle, Paramount, 1974.

Also author of documentaries for G.B. Instructional, 1944-47, including *The Ten Year Plan, Sailors Do Care,* and *Arctic Harvest.*

*   *   *

GIOVANNI, Paul   1940-1990

PERSONAL: Born October 25, 1940, in Atlantic City, NJ; died of complications from pneumonia, June 20, 1990, in New York, NY. *Education:* Attended St. Joseph College and Catholic University.

CAREER: Actor, director and playwright. Composer for theatre and film. Theatre instructor and director at University of South Carolina, 1988-90.

AWARDS, HONORS: Antoinette Perry Award nomination, best director, 1979, for *The Crucifer of Blood.*

CREDITS:

STAGE APPEARANCES

The Boy, *The Fantasticks,* Sullivan Street Playhouse, New York City, 1960.

Luck, *West of the Moon,* Grammercy Arts, New Playwrights Theatre, New York City, 1961.

Ensemble, *Viet Rock,* Martinique Theatre, New York City, 1966.

Also appeared in *The Crucifer of Blood* (Broadway debut), Helen Hayes Theatre, New York City. Appeared in productions at the Arena Stage, Washington, DC, 1971-72.

STAGE WORK; DIRECTOR

Equus, Studio Arena Theatre, 1976.

The Crucifer of Blood, Studio Arena Theatre, then Helen Hayes Theatre, both 1978 (also see below).

Love's Labour's Lost, Folger Shakespeare Theatre, Washington, DC, 1986-87.

A Man for All Seasons, Roundabout Theatre, New York City, 1986-87.

Also director of *Black Comedy/White Liars,* London.

MAJOR TOURS

Toured as director of *Amadeus,* U.K. cities.

FILM WORK

Song performer, "Corn Rigs," *The Wicker Man,* Warner Brothers, 1974.

Production manager assistant, *Golden Eighties,* 1986, and production manager, *A Soldier's Tale,* 1988.

WRITINGS:

Composer, *The Wicker Man* (film), Warner Brothers, 1974.

The Crucifer of Blood (play), produced at Studio Arena Theatre, then Helen Hayes Theatre, both 1978.

OBITUARIES AND OTHER SOURCES:

PERIODICALS

New York Times, June 20, 1990.*

CONTEMPORARY THEATRE, FILM, AND TELEVISION • *Volume 9*

GODDARD, Paulette   1911(?)-1990

PERSONAL: Full name, Pauline Marion Goddard Levee; born June 3, 1911 (some sources say 1905), in Great Neck, NY; died of heart failure, April 23, 1990, in Switzerland; married Edgar James (a lumber magnate), 1927 (divorced, 1929); married Charlie Chaplin (an actor, director and writer), 1936 (divorced, 1942); married Burgess Meredith (an actor), 1944 (divorced, 1949); married Erich Maria Remarque (a writer), 1958 (died, 1970). *Education:* Mount Saint Dominic's Academy, Caldwell, NJ.

CAREER: Actress. Professional model; performed on radio.

AWARDS, HONORS: Academy Award nomination, Best Supporting Actress, 1943, for *So Proudly We Hail.*

CREDITS:

STAGE APPEARANCES

Winterset, Abbey Theatre, Dublin, 1947.

Also appeared in her stage debut as Ziegfeld Girl, "Peaches," *No Fooling,* 1927.

MAJOR TOURS

USO tour, Far East, 1944.

FILM APPEARANCES

Girl Habit, Paramount, 1931.
Girl at Party, *The Mouthpiece,* Warner Brothers, 1932.
The 1932 Goldwyn Girls, *The Kid from Spain,* United Artists (UA), 1932.
(First major screen appearance) Gamine, *Modern Times* (silent feature), UA, 1936.
Nana, *Dramatic School,* Metro-Goldwyn-Mayer (MGM), 1938.
Leslie Saunders, *The Young In Heart,* UA, 1938.
Joyce Norman, *The Cat and the Canary,* Paramount, 1939.
Miriam Aarons, *The Women,* MGM, 1939.
Hannah (a laundress), *The Great Dictator,* UA, 1940.
Mary Carter, *The Ghost Breakers,* Paramount, 1940.
Louvette Corbeau, *Northwest Mounted Police,* Paramount, 1940.
Ellen Miller, *Second Chorus,* Paramount, 1940.
Anita Dixon, *Hold Back the Dawn,* Paramount, 1941.
Gwen Saunder, *Nothing But the Truth,* Paramount, 1941.
Molly McCorkle, *Pot O' Gold* (also known as *Golden Hour*), UA, 1941.
Celia Huston, *The Forest Rangers,* Paramount, 1942.
Sidney Royce, *The Lady Has Plans,* Paramount, 1942.
Loxi Claiborne, *Reap the Wild Wind,* Paramount, 1942.
Sweater, Sarong and Peekaboo Bang, *Star Spangled Rhythm,* Paramount, 1942.
Toni Gerard, *The Crystal Ball,* UA, 1943.

Lt. Joan O'Doul, *So Proudly We Hail,* Paramount, 1943.
Eva Morgan, *I Love a Soldier,* Paramount, 1944.
Jane Rogers, *Standing Room Only,* Paramount, 1944.
Duffy's Tavern, Paramount, 1945.
Title role, *Kitty,* Paramount, 1945.
Celestine, *Diary of a Chambermaid,* UA, 1946.
Mary Morely, *Suddenly It's Spring,* Paramount, 1947.
Abigail Martha "Abby" Hale, *Unconquered,* Paramount, 1947.
Variety Girl, Paramount, 1947.
Ellen Crane, *Hazard,* Paramount, 1948.
Mrs. Cheveley, *An Ideal Husband,* British Lion, 1948.
Martha Pease, *On Our Merry Way* (also known as *A Miracle Can Happen*), UA, 1948.
Title role, *Anna Lucasta,* Columbia, 1949.
Lucretia Borgia, *Bride of Vengeance,* Paramount, 1949.
Maria Dolores, *The Torch* (also known as *Bandit General*), Eagle Lion, 1950.
Kyra, *Babes in Baghdad,* UA, 1952.
Tanya, *Charge of the Lancers,* Columbia, 1953.
Betty Barnes, *Paris Model,* Columbia, 1953.
Jezebel, *Sins of Jezebel,* Lippert, 1953.
Mona, *Vice Squad* (also known as *The Girl in Room 17*), UA, 1953.
Angie Vickers, *The Unholy Four* (also known as *The Stranger Came Home*), Lippert, 1954.
Maria Grazia Ardengo, *Time of Indifference* (also known as *Indifferenti; Les Deux Rivales*), Continental Distributing, 1965.

Also appeared in *The Locked Door,* and *Berth Marks* (short), both 1929; *City Streets,* 1931; *Show Business,* (short), *Young Ironsides* (short), *Girl Grief,* and *Pack Up Your Troubles,* all 1932; Tuttle, *Roman Scandals,* 1933; and *Kid Millions,* 1934.

TELEVISION APPEARANCES; SERIES

Sherlock Holmes, syndicated, 1954.
Norma Treat, *The Snoop Sisters,* NBC, 1972.

TELEVISION APPEARANCES; EPISODIC

Performer, *Ford Television Theatre,* NBC, 1952, and ABC, 1956.
Performer, *On Trial,* CBS, 1956.
Performer, *The Errol Flynn Theatre,* Dumont, 1957.

OTHER TELEVISION APPEARANCES

Sylvia Fowler, *The Women* (special), NBC, 1955.
Norma Treat, *The Snoop Sisters* (also known as *Female Instinct;* pilot), NBC, 1972.

OBITUARIES AND OTHER SOURCES:

PERIODICALS

Films in Review, August/September, 1974.

New York Times, April 24, 1990.*

*   *   *

GOING, John 1936-

PERSONAL: Born November 28, 1936, in Lancaster, PA; son of John J. (a credit manager) and Marin C. (Morton) Going. *Education:* Catholic University, B.A. (cum laude), 1958; University of Minnesota, M.A., 1964.

ADDRESSES: Agent—c/o Bret Adams, 448 West 44th St., New York, NY 10036.

CAREER: Director. Assistant to Sir Tyrone Guthrie, Guthrie Theatre, 1963; associate professor of drama, 1964-69, drama department head, 1968-69, associate artistic director, 1965-68, acting artistic director, 1968-69, Edgecliff College; resident director, Cleveland Playhouse, 1969-71; resident director, Cherry County Playhouse, 1969-72; associate artistic director, Alaska Repertory Theatre, 1982-83; acting artistic director, Alaska Repertory Theatre, 1983-84. *Military service:* Served in the U.S. Army, Honor Guard Company, Specialist Fourth Class, 1960-62.

MEMBER: Society of Stage Directors and Choreographers, Actors' Equity Association.

AWARDS, HONORS: Phi Beta Kappa.

CREDITS:

STAGE DIRECTOR

Harvey, Cleveland Playhouse, c. 1969-71.
The Country Wife, Cleveland Playhouse, c. 1969-71.
Red's My Color; What's Yours?, Cleveland Playhouse, c. 1969-71.
The Taming of the Shrew, Cleveland Playhouse, c. 1969-71.
The Threepenny Opera, Cleveland Playhouse, c. 1969-71.
Summer and Smoke, Cleveland Playhouse, c. 1969-71.
Lysistrata, Cleveland Playhouse, c. 1969-71.
You Know I Can't Hear You When the Water's Running, Cleveland Playhouse, c. 1969-71.
The Devil's Disciple, Cleveland Playhouse, c. 1969-71.
Plaza Suite, Cleveland Playhouse, c. 1969-71.
The Man Who Came to Dinner, Mummers Theatre, Oklahoma City, OK, 1971.
The Odd Couple, Meadow Brook Theatre, Rochester, MI, 1971.
Private Lives, Little-Theatre-on-the-Square, 1971.
Champagne Complex, Little-Theatre-on-the-Square, 1971.
I Do, I Do, Little Theatre-on-the-Square, 1972.
Forty Carats, Little Theatre-on-the-Square, 1972.
Butterflies Are Free, Elitch Gardens, 1972.

(New York debut) *A Breeze From the Gulf,* Eastside Playhouse, 1973.
The Mousetrap, Olney Theatre, 1973.
A Breeze From the Gulf, Bucks Country Playhouse, PA, 1973.
Dear Liar, Homestead Theatre, Hot Springs, VA, 1973.
The Imaginary Invalid, Repertory Theatre of St. Louis, MO, 1973.
Harvey, Cincinnati Playhouse in the Park, OH, 1973.
Plain and Fancy, American Heritage Festival, Lancaster, PA, 1974.
The Sunshine Boys, Manitoba Theatre Centre, Winnipeg, Canada, 1974.
The Servant of Two Masters, Indiana Repertory Theatre, Indianapolis, IN, 1974.
Tonight at 8:30, Olney Theatre, 1974.
The Play's the Thing, Academy Festival, 1974.
Come Blow Your Horn, Showplace, 1975.
The Little Foxes, Indiana Repertory Theatre, 1975, and Syracuse Stage Company, NY, 1975.
One Flew Over the Cuckoo's Nest, Pittsburgh Public Theatre, PA, 1975.
Biography, Barter Theatre, Abingdon, VA, 1975.
Relatively Speaking, Cincinnati Playhouse in the Park, 1975.
Life with Father, Royal Poinciana Playhouse, 1975.
Send Me No Flowers, Royal Poinciana Playhouse, 1976.
Uncle Vanya, Olney Theatre, 1976.
Oliver, Cincinnati Playhouse in the Park, 1976.
The Threepenny Opera, Barter Theatre, 1976.
Blithe Spirit, Syracuse Stage Company, 1976.
The Tavern, Indiana Repertory Theatre, 1976.
The Last Meeting of the White Knights of the Magnolia, Indiana Repertory Theatre, 1976.
A Streetcar Named Desire, Syracuse Stage Company, 1977.
Tartuffe, Syracuse Stage Company, 1977.
You Never Can Tell, Pittsburgh Public Theatre, 1977.
Candida, Hartford Stage Company, 1977.
The Show Off, Seattle Repertory Theatre, WA, 1977.
Vanities, Barnato Theatre, Johannesburg, South Africa, 1977, and Cincinnati Playhouse in the Park, 1977.
The Royal Family, Cincinnati Playhouse in the Park, 1978.
Peg O'My Heart, American Stage Festival, 1978.
Peter Pan, Alliance Theatre, Atlanta, GA, 1978.
The Animal Kingdom, Hartman Theatre Company, Stamford, CT, 1978.
Juno's Swans, Ensemble Studio, New York City, 1978.
Vanities, Syracuse Stage Company, 1978.
She Stoops to Conquer, Syracuse Stage Company, 1978.
The Importance of Being Earnest, Indiana Repertory Theatre, 1979.

Period of Adjustment, Advent Theatre, Nashville, TN, 1979.

Misalliance, Barter Theatre, 1979.

Mister Roberts, Pittsburgh Public Theatre, 1979.

The Sea Gull, Pittsburgh Public Theatre, 1979.

Hedda Gabler, Cincinnati Playhouse in the Park, 1979.

Man of La Mancha, Cincinnati Playhouse in the Park, 1979.

The Cherry Orchard, Cincinnati Playhouse in the Park, 1980.

Toys in the Attic, Indiana Repertory Theatre, 1980.

Philadelphia Here I Come, Philadelphia Drama Guild, PA, 1981.

Mirandolina, Michigan Ensemble Theatre, MI, 1981.

The Man Who Came to Dinner, Alaska Repertory Theatre, 1981.

Tintypes, Cincinnati Playhouse in the Park, 1981.

Inherit the Wind, Cincinnati Playhouse in the Park, 1982.

Major Barbara, Alaska Repertory Theatre, 1982.

Cat on a Hot Tin Roof, Syracuse Stage Company, 1982.

The Miser, Syracuse Stage Company, 1982.

The Rivals, Alley Theatre, Houston, TX, 1982.

Lola, York Theatre Company, New York City, 1982.

Lunch Hour, Cherry County Playhouse, 1982.

The Philadelphia Story, Alaska Repertory Theatre, 1983.

You Can't Take it With You, Empire State Institute of Performing Arts, Albany, NY, 1983.

Uncle Vanya, Alley Theatre, 1984.

The 1940's Radio Hour, Repertory Theatre of St. Louis, 1984-85.

Inherit the Wind, Paper Mill Playhouse, Millburn, NJ, 1984-85.

Biloxi Blues, Paper Mill Playhouse, 1987.

Also directed at South Coast Repertory Theatre, Costa Mesa, CA, 1980-81.

MAJOR TOURS

My Daughter, Your Son, 1971, *Butterflies Are Free,* 1973, *Send Me No Flowers,* 1975-76, *The Best Man,* 1976, *Come Blow Your Horn,* 1977-78, *Vanities,* 1978, and *Children,* 1980.*

*   *   *

GOLDSTONE, James   1931-

PERSONAL: Born June 8, 1931, in Los Angeles, CA; son of Jules C. (an attorney) and Anita M. (Rosenberg) Goldstone; married Ruth Liebling, June 21, 1953; children: Peter, Jeffrey, Barbara. *Education:* Dartmouth College, B.A., English literature, 1953; Bennington College, M.A., drama, 1957; studied film editing with Merrill White.

CAREER: Director. Film editor, 1950—; television writer and story editor, 1957—. *Military service:* U.S. Army, 1953-55.

MEMBER: Academy of Motion Picture Arts and Sciences (member of directors' executive committee, 1985—), Academy of Television Arts and Sciences, Directors Guild of America (co-chairman of president's committee, 1986—), Film Editors Union, Writers Guild of America (member of board of directors, directors' council, and creative rights negotiating committee).

AWARDS, HONORS: Emmy Award nomination, Outstanding Directorial Achievement in Drama, 1970, for *A Clear and Present Danger;* Gold Medal from the Virgin Islands International Film Festival, 1975, for "Eric," *The Hallmark Hall of Fame;* Christopher Award, 1975, for *Journey from Darkness;* Emmy Award, Outstanding Directing in a Limited Series or a Special, and Gold Medal from the New York Film Festival, both 1981, for *Kent State.*

CREDITS:

FILM DIRECTOR

Jigsaw, Universal, 1968.

A Man Called Gannon, Universal, 1969.

Winning, Universal, 1969.

Brother John, Columbia, 1971.

The Gang That Couldn't Shoot Straight, Metro-Goldwyn-Mayer (MGM), 1971.

Red Sky at Morning, Universal, 1971.

They Only Kill Their Masters, MGM, 1972.

Swashbuckler (also known as *The Scarlet Buccaneer*), Universal, 1976.

(And executive producer) *Rollercoaster,* Universal, 1977.

When Time Ran Out, Warner Brothers, 1980.

TELEVISION DIRECTOR; PILOTS

"Where No Man Has Gone Before," *Star Trek,* NBC, 1966.

Scalplock (pilot for *Iron Horse*), ABC, 1966.

Code Name: Heraclitus (broadcast as an episode of *The Bob Hope Chrysler Theatre*), NBC, 1967.

Ironside, NBC, 1967.

A Clear and Present Danger (pilot for *The Senator*), NBC, 1970.

The Oath: The Sad and Lonely Sundays (pilot for a proposed series to be titled *The Oath*), ABC, 1976.

TELEVISION DIRECTOR; EPISODIC

"The Sixth Finger," *Outer Limits,* ABC, 1963.

"The Inheritors," *Outer Limits,* ABC, 1964.

Amos Burke—Secret Agent, ABC, 1965.

"What Are Little Girls Made Of?," *Star Trek,* 1966.

Also directed episodes of *Perry Mason,* CBS; *Sea Hunt,* syndicated; *Dennis the Menace,* CBS; *Death Valley Days,* syndicated; *Bat Masterson,* NBC; *Dr. Kildare,* NBC; *The Eleventh Hour,* NBC; *The Fugitive,* ABC; *Route 66,* CBS; *The Bob Hope Chrysler Theatre,* NBC; *Voyage to the Bottom of the Sea,* ABC; *The Man from U.N.C.L.E.,* NBC; *Star Trek,* NBC; and *The Senator,* NBC.

TELEVISION DIRECTOR; MOVIES

Shadow Over Elveron, NBC, 1968.
Cry Panic, ABC, 1974.
Things in Their Season, CBS, 1974.
(And producer) *Dr. Max,* CBS, 1974.
Journey from Darkness, NBC, 1975.
Kent State, NBC, 1981.
Charles and Diana: A Royal Love Story, ABC, 1982.
Rita Hayworth: The Love Goddess, CBS, 1983.
Calamity Jane, CBS, 1984.
Ernest Hemingway's "The Sun Also Rises," NBC, 1984.
Sentimental Journey, CBS, 1984.
Dreams of Gold: The Mel Fisher Story, CBS, 1986.
Earth*Star Voyager, ABC, 1988.

OTHER TELEVISION WORK; DIRECTOR

Court of Last Resort, NBC, 1957.
"Eric," *The Hallmark Hall of Fame* (special), NBC, 1975.
Studs Lonigan (mini-series), NBC, 1979.*

*   *   *

GOODMAN, John   1952-

PERSONAL: Born June 20, 1952, in St. Louis, MO; married Annabeth Hartzog, 1989. *Education:* Southwest Missouri State University, B.F.A. (theatre arts), 1975.

ADDRESSES: Agent—The Gersh Agency, 232 North Canon Dr., Beverly Hills, CA 90210.

CAREER: Actor. Previously appeared in television commercials.

AWARDS, HONORS: Emmy Award nominations, outstanding lead actor in a comedy series, 1989 and 1990, for *Roseanne.*

CREDITS:

TELEVISION APPEARANCES; SERIES

Dan Connor, *Roseanne,* ABC, 1988—.

TELEVISION APPEARANCES; MOVIES

Fred, *The Face of Rage,* ABC, 1983.
Raymond, *Heart of Steel,* ABC, 1983.
Hugh Rayburn, *Murder Ordained* (also released as *Broken Commandments* and *Kansas Gothic*), CBS, 1987.

TELEVISION APPEARANCES; EPISODIC

Hal Winter, *The Equalizer,* CBS, 1987.
Donald Chase, *Moonlighting,* ABC, 1987.

TELEVISION APPEARANCES; SPECIALS

The Third Annual American Comedy Awards, ABC, 1989.
ABC's Comedy Sneak Peek, ABC, 1989.
The Fourth American Comedy Awards, ABC, 1990.
The 16th Annual People's Choice Awards, CBS, 1990.
The 62nd Annual Academy Awards Presentation, ABC, 1990.
Happy Birthday, Bugs: 50 Looney Years, CBS, 1990.
Host, *Tom & Jerry's 50th Birthday Bash,* TBS, 1990.

OTHER TELEVISION APPEARANCES

Newt "Tub" Murray, *Chiefs* (mini-series), CBS, 1983.
Joe, *After Midnight* (pilot), ABC, 1988.

Also appeared in *Mystery of Moro Castle,* HBO; and *The Paper Chase.*

FILM APPEARANCES

(Film debut) Herbert, *Eddie Macon's Run,* Universal, 1983.
Commando, *The Survivors,* Columbia, 1983.
Cop in diner, *C.H.U.D.,* New World, 1984.
Coach Harris, *Revenge of the Nerds,* Twentieth Century-Fox, 1984.
Frank, *Maria's Lovers,* Cannon, 1985.
Otis, *Sweet Dreams,* Tri-Star, 1985.
Louis Fyne—"The Dancing Bear," *True Stories,* Warner Brothers, 1986.
Detective Andre De Soto, *The Big Easy,* Columbia, 1987.
Detective Nyswander, *Burglar,* Warner Brothers, 1987.
Gale, *Raising Arizona,* Twentieth Century-Fox, 1987.
Duke Earl, *The Wrong Guys,* New World, 1988.
John Krytsick, *Punchline,* Columbia, 1988.
Edward Lawrence, *Everybody's All-American,* Warner Brothers, 1988.
Al Yackey, *Always,* Universal, 1989.
Sherman, *Sea of Love,* Universal, 1989.
Ed Munn, *Stella* (also released as *Stella Dallas*), Buena Vista, 1990.
Delbert McClintock, *Arachnophobia* (also released as *Along Came a Spider*), Buena Vista, 1990.
Title role, *King Ralph,* Universal, 1990.
Charlie Meadows, *Barton Fink,* Twentieth Century-Fox, 1991.

STAGE APPEARANCES

(Off-Broadway debut) *A Midsummer Night's Dream,* Equity Library Theatre, 1978.
The Robber Bridegroom, Ford's Theatre Society, Washington, DC, 1978.

Private Wars and Lone Star, Center Stage, Baltimore, MD, 1979.

Lady of the Diamond, Studio Arena Theatre, Buffalo, NY, 1980.

Jack, *The Chisholm Trail Went Through Here,* Manhattan Theatre Club In-the-Works, New York City, 1981.

Sir Walter Blunt, *Henry IV, Part One,* New York Shakespeare Festival, Delacorte Theatre, New York City, 1981.

Davis, *Ghosts of the Loyal Oaks,* WPA Theatre, New York City, 1981.

Winninger, "Half a Lifetime," *Triple Feature,* Manhattan Theatre Club, 1983.

The Palace of Amateurs, Plaza Theatre, Dallas, TX, 1983.

Ted, "At Home," *One-Act Play Marathon '84,* Ensemble Studio Theatre, New York City, 1984.

Pap Finn and Sheriff Bell, *Big River,* Eugene O'Neill Theatre, 1985.

Enobarbus, *Antony and Cleopatra,* Los Angeles Theatre Center, Los Angeles, CA, 1987.*

*   *   *

GORDON, Gale   1906-

PERSONAL: Born Charles T. Aldrich, Jr., February 20, 1906, in New York City; son of Charles (a vaudeville performer) and Gloria (an actress; maiden name, Gordon) Aldrich.

ADDRESSES: Agent—Contemporary Artists, 132 Lasky Dr., Suite B, Beverly Hills, CA 90212.

CAREER: Actor.

AWARDS, HONORS: Radio Hall of Fame award.

CREDITS:

STAGE APPEARANCES

Made stage debut as cast member of *The Dancers.*

FILM APPEARANCES

Caldwalder, *Here We Go Again,* RKO Radio Pictures, 1942.

Station Clerk, *A Woman of Distinction,* Columbia, 1950.

H. J. Bellows, *Here Come the Nelsons* (also known as *Meet the Nelsons*), Universal, 1952.

Evans, *Francis Covers the Big Town,* Universal, 1953.

Osgood Conklin, *Our Miss Brooks,* Warner Bros., 1956.

Colonel Thorwald, *Rally 'Round the Flag, Boys!,* Twentieth Century-Fox, 1958.

Congressman Mandeville, *Don't Give Up the Ship,* Paramount, 1959.

Raven, *The Thirty Foot Bride of Candy Rock,* Columbia, 1959.

Bob Mayberry, *Visit to a Small Planet,* Paramount, 1960.

Commander Bintle, *All Hands on Deck,* Twentieth Century-Fox, 1961.

Oliver Dunning, *All in a Night's Work,* Paramount, 1961.

Colonel, *Dondi,* Allied Artists, 1961.

Captain Weiskopf, *Sergeant Deadhead* (also known as *Sergeant Deadhead the Astronut*), American International, 1965.

R. W. Hepworth, *Speedway,* Metro-Goldwyn-Mayer, 1968.

Walter, *The 'Burbs,* Universal, 1989.

Made film debut as dress extra for Greta Garbo in *The Temptress,* 1926.

TELEVISION APPEARANCES; SERIES

Osgood Conklin, *Our Miss Brooks,* CBS, 1952-56.

Mr. Heckendorn, *Make Room for Daddy,* ABC, then CBS, 1953-64.

Harvey Box, *The Brothers,* CBS, 1956-57.

Bascomb Bleacher, *Sally,* NBC, 1958.

John Wilson, *Dennis the Menace,* CBS, 1959-63.

Uncle Paul Porter, *Pete and Gladys,* CBS, 1960-62.

Theodore J. Mooney, *The Lucy Show,* CBS, 1962-68.

Harrison Otis Carter, *Here's Lucy,* CBS, 1968-74.

Judge, *It Takes Two,* ABC, 1982-83.

Curtis McGibbon, *Life with Lucy,* ABC, 1986.

TELEVISION APPEARANCES; PILOTS

Emil Sinclair, *For the Love of Mike,* CBS, 1962.

Warren Packard, *Where There's Smokey,* CBS, 1966.

The Abbott, *Bungle Abbey,* NBC, 1981.

TELEVISION APPEARANCES; EPISODIC

Mr. Littlefield, *I Love Lucy,* CBS, 1952.

Also appeared in *My Favorite Husband,* CBS, and *The Love Boat.*

TELEVISION APPEARANCES; SPECIALS

Anthony Baxter, *The Royal Follies of 1933,* NBC, 1967.

Mr. Harvey, *The Lucille Ball Comedy Hour,* CBS, 1967.

Guest, *The Lucille Ball Special,* CBS, 1977.

As himself, *Lucy Moves to NBC,* NBC, 1980.

RADIO APPEARANCES;

Appeared in series *Flash Gordon,* 1935; appeared as Mayor La Trivia, *Fibber McGee and Molly;* the harried sponsor, *The Phil Harris-Alice Faye Show;* Atterbury, *My Favorite Husband.*

*   *   *

GORDON, Serena   1963-

PERSONAL: Born September 3, 1963, in London, England; daughter of Ian Strathearn (a property consultant) and Nicola Mary (a magistrate; maiden name, Norman) Gordon. *Education:* Attended Bryanston Blanford-Dorset school, 1979-82; studied at Royal Academy of Dramatic Arts, 1983-85. *Religion:* Church of England. *Avocational interests:* Watching movies, traveling.

ADDRESSES: Agent—Duncan Heath Associates Ltd., Paramount House, 162/170 Wardour Street, London W1V 3AT, England.

CAREER: Actress.

MEMBER: British Actor's Equity.

AWARDS, HONORS: Time Out and Standard Theatre awards, 1989, for *Valued Friends.*

CREDITS:

STAGE APPEARANCES

(Stage debut) Helena, *A Midsummer Night's Dream,* Regents Park Open Air Theatre, London, 1985.

Diana Messerschmann, *Ring 'Round the Moon,* Regents Park Open Air Theatre, 1985.

Diana Rivers, *Jane Eyre,* Chichester Festival Theatre, Chichester, England, 1986.

Townswoman, *The Plague,* Chichester Festival Theatre, 1986.

Mrs. Lacey, *Keats in Chichester,* Chichester Festival Theatre, 1986.

Marion, *Valued Friends,* Hampstead Theatre, London, c. 1989.

Amanda, *Look, Look,* Aldwych Theatre, London, 1990.

Also appeared as Olivia in *Twelfth Night,* and as Ariel in *The Tempest,* both Chichester Festival Theatre.

MAJOR TOURS

Elizabeth, *The Circle,* major British cities, 1990.

FILM APPEARANCES

(Film debut) Gladys Olcott, *Maurice,* Merchant Ivory Production, 1987.

TELEVISION APPEARANCES

(Television debut) Prunella Rumsay, *Queenie* (movie), ABC, 1987.

Anabel, *The Shell Seekers* (movie), ABC, 1989.

Jane Longbridge, *Judith Krantz's Till We Meet Again* (movie), CBS, 1989.

Tricia Mabbott, *Kinsey* (series), BBC, 1991.

Also appeared as Lucie Manette, *A Tale of Two Cities* (special), 1989; and as Annie Rose, *After the War* (special), 1990.

SIDELIGHTS: Favorite roles: Annie Rose, *After the War.*

GORELIK, Mordecai   1899-1990

PERSONAL: Also known as Max; born August 25, 1899, in Shchedrin, Minsk, Russia (now U.S.S.R); died of cancer, March 7, 1990, in Sarasota, FL; son of Morris and Bertha (Dirskin) Gorelik; married Frances Strauss, 1935 (deceased); married Loraine Kabler, 1972; children: one son, one daughter. *Education:* Pratt Institute, graduated, 1920; studied design with Robert Edmond Jones, Norman Bel Geddes, and Serge Soudeikin. *Avocational interests:* Fishing.

CAREER: Designer, director, writer, and educator. Scene painter, stage technician, Provincetown Playhouse, 1920-21; faculty member, School of the Theatre, New York City, 1921-22, American Academy of Dramatic Arts, 1926-32, Drama Workshop of the New School for Social Research, 1940-41, Biarritz American University, 1945-46, University of Toledo, 1956, New York University, 1956, University of Hawaii, 1959, Bard University, 1959, Brigham Young University, 1961, California State College, 1964, San Jose State University, 1965, Long Island University, 1972, and University of Southern California, 1975; Southern Illinois University, research professor in theatre, 1960-72, professor emeritus, 1972-90. Consultant in theatre for U.S. Military Government in Germany, 1949. *Military service:* Student Army Corps, 1917.

MEMBER: United Scenic Artists, American Educational Theatre Association, Speech Communication Association, American Theatre Research Association.

AWARDS, HONORS: Guggenheim fellowship, 1936-37; Rockefeller Foundation grant, 1949-51, for study of European theatre; Fulbright scholarship, 1967, for study of Australian theatre; Theta Alpha Phi medal of honor, 1971.

CREDITS:

STAGE DESIGNER, EXCEPT AS NOTED

King Hunger, Players Club, Philadelphia, PA, 1924.
Processional, Garrick Theatre, New York City, 1925.
The Last Love, Schildkraut Theatre, New York City, 1926.
Nirvana, Greenwich Village Theatre, New York City, 1926.
The Moon Is a Gong, Cherry Lane Theatre, New York City, 1926.
Loudspeaker, 52nd Street Theatre, New York City, 1927.
The Final Balance, Provincetown Playhouse, New York City, 1928.
God, Man and the Devil, Yiddish Art Theatre, New York City, 1928.
Uncle Moses, Yiddish Art Theatre, New York City, 1930.
1931, Mansfield Theatre, New York City, 1931.

Success Story, Maxine Elliott's Theatre, New York City, 1932.

Big Night, Maxine Elliott's Theatre, 1933.

Little Ol' Boy, Playhouse Theatre, New York City, 1933.

Men in White, Broadhurst Theatre, New York City, 1933.

All Good Americans, Henry Miller's Theatre, New York City, 1933.

Gentlewoman, Cort Theatre, New York City, 1934.

Sailors of Cattaro, Civic Repertory Theatre, New York City, 1934.

Mother, Civic Repertory Theatre, 1935.

The Young Go First, Park Theatre, 1935.

Golden Boy, Belasco Theatre, New York City, 1937, then St. James Theatre, London, 1938.

Tortilla Flat, Henry Miller's Theatre, New York City, 1938.

Casey Jones, Fulton Theatre, New York City, 1938.

Thunder Rock, Mansfield Theatre, 1938.

Rocket to the Moon, Belasco Theatre, 1938.

The Quiet City, Belasco Theatre, 1939.

Night Music, Belasco Theatre, 1940.

Walk Into My Parlor, Sayville Theatre, New York City, 1941.

Volpone, Actors Laboratory Theatre, Los Angeles, 1944, Rooftop Theatre, New York City, 1957.

(And director) *Doctor Knock,* Biarritz American University, Paris, France, 1945.

All My Sons, Coronet Theatre, New York City, 1947.

(And director) *Paul Thompson Forever,* Actors Laboratory Theatre, 1947.

Desire Under the Elms, ANTA Theatre, New York City, 1952.

(And director) *Danger—Men Working,* Circle Workshop, New York City, 1952.

(And director) *The Flowering Peach,* Belasco Theatre, 1954.

A Hatful of Rain, Lyceum Theatre, New York City, 1955.

(And director) *Born Yesterday,* University of Toledo, Toledo, OH, 1956.

The Sin of Pat Muldoon, Cort Theatre, 1957.

Guests of the Nation, Theatre Marquee, New York City, 1958.

A Distant Bell, Eugene O'Neill Theatre, New York City, 1960.

(And director) *The Annotated Hamlet,* Southern Illinois University, Carbondale, IL, 1961.

(And director) *The Dybbuk,* Brigham Young University, Provo, UT, 1961.

The House of Bernarda Alba, Southern Illinois University, 1962.

Marseilles, Southern Illinois University, 1962.

Good Woman of Setzuan, Southern Illinois University, 1964.

(And director) *The Dybbuk,* San Jose State College, San Jose, CA, 1965.

Also designer and director for *The Front Page,* 1947; *The Firebugs,* California State University, 1964; *Rainbow Terrace,* California State University, 1966. Designer of *Waiting for Lefty.*

MAJOR TOURS

Designer, *Saint Joan,* U.S. cities, 1954.

FILM PRODUCTION DESIGNER

None But the Lonely Heart, RKO Radio Pictures, 1944.

Our Street, Republic Pictures, 1944.

Days of Glory, RKO Radio Pictures, 1944.

Salt to the Devil, Eagle/Lion, 1949.

L'Ennemi publique no. 1 (also known as *Most Wanted Man*), Cite Films, 1954.

WRITINGS:

PLAYS

Paul Thompson Forever, produced at Southern Illinois University, 1947.

The Annotated Hamlet produced at California State University, 1961.

(Translator) Max Frisch, *Firebugs* (produced at California State University, 1964, produced at Martinique Theatre, New York City, 1968), Hill & Wang, 1963.

Rainbow Terrace, produced at California State University, 1966.

Toward a Larger Theatre: Seven Plays by Mordecai Gorelik (includes *Yes and No, Andrus, or the Vision, Rainbow Terrace, The Feast of Unreason, Mrs. Disaster, The Big Day, Paul Thompson Forever,* and *Toward a Larger Theatre*), University Press of America, 1988.

Also author of *Megan's Son.*

OTHER

New Theatres for Old, Samuel French, 1940.

Contributor to periodicals.*

*   *   *

GRAFF, Ilene

PERSONAL: Born February 28 in Brooklyn, NY. *Education:* Graduated from Ithaca College.

ADDRESSES: Agent—Bob Gersh, The Gersh Agency, P.O. Box 5617, Beverly Hills, CA 91210.

CAREER: Actress.

CREDITS:

TELEVISION APPEARANCES; SERIES

Alicia Lewis, *Lewis and Clark,* NBC, 1981-82.
Marsha Owens, *Mr. Belvedere,* ABC, 1985-90.

OTHER TELEVISION APPEARANCES

Penny Whitaker, *Supertrain* (episodic), NBC, 1979.
Annabell Davis, *Beulah Land* (mini-series), NBC, 1980.
Angel Katie Fredericks, *Heaven On Earth* (pilot), NBC, 1981.
Kitty Spettigue, *Charley's Aunt* (special), The Entertainment Channel, 1983.
Melinda York, *13 Thirteenth Avenue* (pilot), CBS, 1983.
Jane Lassister, *The Earthlings* (pilot), ABC, 1984.
Marilyn, *Jury Duty: The Comedy* (movie), ABC, 1990.

STAGE APPEARANCES

(Broadway debut) Fran, *Promises, Promises,* Shubert Theatre, 1968.
Sandy Dumbrowski, *Grease,* Eden Theatre, Broadhurst Theatre, and Royale Theatre, all New York City, 1972.
Bonnie, *Truckload,* Lyceum Theatre, New York City, 1975.
Cleo, *I Love My Wife,* Ethel Barrymore Theatre, New York City, 1977.*

*   *   *

GRAFF, Randy   1955-

PERSONAL: Born May 23, 1955, in Brooklyn, NY. *Education:* Graduated from Wagner College.

ADDRESSES: Agent—Harris and Goldberg Talent Agency, 2121 Avenue of the Stars, Suite 950, Los Angeles, CA 90067.

CAREER: Actress.

AWARDS, HONORS: Outer Critics Circle Award nomination, 1987, for *Les Miserables;* Antionette Perry Award, Best Featured Actress in a Musical, and Drama Desk Award, both 1990, for *City of Angels.*

CREDITS:

STAGE APPEARANCES

(Off-Broadway debut) *Pins and Needles,* Roundabout Theatre, 1978.
Something Wonderful, Westchester Regional Theatre, Harrison, NY, 1979.
Rosalia, *Sarava,* Mark Hellinger Theatre, 1979.
Coming Attractions, Playwrights Horizons, Mainstage Theatre, New York City, 1980.
Keystone, McCarter Theatre, Princeton, NJ, 1981.

A . . . . My Name Is Alice, Village Gate Theatre, New York City, 1984.
Amateurs, Cincinnati Playhouse in the Park, Cincinnati, OH, 1985.
Fiorello!, Goodspeed Opera House, East Haddam, CT, 1985.
Absurd Person Singular, Philadelphia Drama Guild, Philadelphia, PA, 1986.
Fantine, *Les Miserables,* Broadway Theatre, New York City, 1987.
Oolie and Donna, *City of Angels,* Virgina Theatre, New York City, 1989.

Also appeared in *Eighty Days,* La Jolla Playhouse, La Jolla, CA; as Rizzo in *Grease,* Royale Theatre; and in *Jerry's Girls, Station Joy,* and *Once on a Summer's Day,* all in New York City.

TELEVISION APPEARANCES; PILOTS

Marlene Hobart, *The Ed Begley, Jr. Show,* CBS, 1989.
Gail, *Working It Out,* NBC, 1990.

TELEVISION APPEARANCES; EPISODIC

Appeared in *The Guiding Light,* CBS; *Donahue,* NBC; *The Tonight Show,* NBC; and *Kate and Allie,* CBS.*

*   *   *

GREENBERG, Edward M.   1924-

PERSONAL: Born July 22, 1924, in New York, NY; son of Herman M. (in sales) and Bess (a legal secretary; maiden name, Levy) Greenberg; married Sara Dillon (an actress and singer), April 30, 1957; children: Elizabeth, David. *Education:* City College (now of the City University of New York), B.S.S., 1948; University of Wisconsin, M.A., 1949; studied at the New School Dramatic Workshop with Erwin Piscator.

ADDRESSES: Office—c/o Municipal Theatre Association, St. Louis, Forest Park, St. Louis, MO 63112; Department of Drama, Theatre, and Dance, Queens College, Flushing, NY 11360.

CAREER: Director, producer, and writer. Queens College, instructor, 1951-57, professor of theatre, 1971—, director of Colden Center for the Performing Arts, 1975-80; City College (now of the City University of New York), instructor in department of speech, 1953-55; Los Angeles Civic Light Opera, founder and director of musical theatre workshop, 1963-70. *Military service:* U.S. Army, Signal Corps, 1942-46; served in Pacific theatre of operations.

MEMBER: Actors' Equity Association, International Society of Performing Arts Administrators, Society of Stage Directors and Choreographers, Players Club.

CREDITS:

STAGE WORK

Director, *The King and I*, New York State Theatre, New York City, 1964.

Director, *The Merry Widow*, New York State Theatre, 1964.

Director, *Carousel*, New York State Theater, 1965.

Director, *Kismet*, New York State Theater, 1965.

Assistant stage manager at Music Circus, Hyannis, MA, 1950; director at summer theatres in cities including Milwaukee, WI, and Jacksonville and Miami, FL, 1951-55; Municipal Opera of St. Louis, MO, director, 1957-59, executive producer, 1971—; director at Jones Beach Marine Theatre, NY, 1960, Richard Rodgers Music Theatre of Lincoln Center, New York City, 1964-65, and White House Conference on Children—Stage and Television Production, 1970; resident director and associate producer at civic light opera associations in Los Angeles and San Francisco, CA, 1960-70.

MAJOR TOURS

Director, *Drood!*, U.S. cities, 1988.

TELEVISION DIRECTOR

(With Dick McDonough) *Roberta*, NBC, 1958.

(With Bob Bum) "Archy and Mehitabel," *Play of the Week*, syndicated, 1960.

WRITINGS:

Author of adaptations of the plays *The Merry Widow* and *The Student Prince*.

*   *   *

GREENE, James   1926-

PERSONAL: Born James Nolan, December 1, 1926, in Lawrence, MA; son of Timothy (a police officer) and Martha (Greene) Nolan; married Betty Miller, December 5, 1955. *Education:* Emerson College, B.A., 1950.

ADDRESSES: Agent—Susan Smith & Associates, 121 North San Vicente Blvd., Beverly Hills, CA 90211; and 192 Lexington Ave., New York, NY 10016. *Manager*—Schumer-Oubre Management, Ltd., 1697 Broadway, New York, NY 10019.

CAREER: Actor. *Military service:* U.S. Navy Air Force, 1943-45.

CREDITS:

STAGE APPEARANCES

(Broadway debut) Capulet servant, *Romeo and Juliet*, Broadhurst Theatre, 1951.

Gunner, *Misalliance*, Sheridan Square Playhouse, New York City, 1961.

Husband, *Danton's Death*, Vivian Beaumont Theater, New York City, 1965.

Henderson, *You Can't Take It With You*, Lyceum Theatre, New York CIty, 1965.

Snake, *The School for Scandal*, Lyceum Theatre, 1966.

Butler, *Right You Are . . .* , Lyceum Theatre, 1966.

Gentleman, *The Wild Duck*, Lyceum Theatre 1967.

Henderson, *You Can't Take It With You*, Lyceum Theatre, 1967.

Karatayev, *War and Peace*, Lyceum Theatre, 1967.

Mr. Gill, *The Show-Off*, Lyceum Theatre, then Shubert Theatre, Boston, MA, both 1968.

Innocenti, *Pantagleize*, Lyceum Theatre, 1968.

Captain Harfeather, *Ring Round the Bathtub*, Martin Beck Theatre, New York City, 1972.

Poor man, *Don Juan*, Lyceum Theatre, 1972.

Postmaster, *The Government Inspector*, Phoenix Theatre Sideshows, Edison Theatre, New York City, 1973.

Client, *Baba Goya*, American Place Theatre, New York City, 1973.

Douglas Shearwater, *Shearwater*, Festival of Short Plays, American Place Theatre, 1974.

MacRune's Guevara, Phoenix Sideshows, Playhouse II, New York City, 1975.

Otherwise Engaged, Goodman Theatre, Chicago, IL, 1977-78.

Suitcase Sam, *One Crack Out*, Marymount Manhattan Theatre, New York City, 1978.

Archie, *Artichoke*, Manhattan Theatre Club, New York City, 1979.

Ben, *Just a Little Bit Less Than Normal*, Manhattan Theatre Club, 1979.

Brabantio, *Othello*, New York Shakespeare Festival, Delacorte Theatre, New York City, 1979.

The prosecution, *Salt Lake City Skyline*, Public/Anspacher Theatre, New York City, 1980.

Timon of Athens, Yale Repertory Theatre, New Haven, CT, 1979-80.

Jess, *Summer*, Hudson Guild Theatre, New York City, 1980, then Royal Poinciana Playhouse, Palm Beach, FL, 1981.

James Hyland, *The Rope Dancers*, Theatre East, New York City, 1981.

Doctor, *Foxfire*, Ethel Barrymore Theatre, New York City, 1982.

Great Days, American Place Theatre, 1983.

Jacob Brackish, *Park Your Car in Harvard Yard*, Manhattan Theatre Club/Downstage, 1984.

Richie, *Pigeons on the Walk*, Actors Outlet Theatre Center, New York City, 1984.

Roy, *Play Memory*, Longacre Theatre, New York City, 1984.

Nagg, *Endgame,* Samuel Beckett Theatre, New York City, 1984.

Ephraim Cabot, *Desire Under the Elms,* Hartford Stage Company, Hartford, CT, 1984-85.

The Common Pursuit, Long Wharf Theatre, New Haven, CT, 1984-85.

Old Mahon, *The Playboy of the Western World,* Roundabout Theatre, New York City, 1985.

James Cameron (Jimmy Tomorrow), *The Iceman Cometh,* Lunt-Fontanne Theatre, New York City, 1985.

Petey, *The Birthday Party,* Huntington Theatre Company, Boston, MA, 1985-86.

Bejart, *La Bete,* Eugene O'Neill Theatre, New York City, 1991.

Also appeared with American Shakespeare Festival, Stratford, CT, 1969; appeared in *The Death and Life of Jesse James,* New Theatre for Now, "In the Works: II" Festival; *Memory,* McCarter Theatre, Princeton, NJ; *Ragged Mountain Elegies,* Petersborough Playhouse, NY; *Man Is Man,* State University of New York; *American Gothic; The King and the Duke; The Hostage; Plays for Bleecker Street; Moon in the Yellow River; Girl on Via Flaminia; Compulsion; Inherit the Wind; Shadow of a Gunman; Andersonville Trial; Night Life; Nourish the Beast; Frugal Repast; Bella Figura; The Carnival of Glorie; Down River; In White America; Incident at Vichy; The Changeling; Marco Millions; After the Fall; Fathers and Sons; The Arbor; The Freak; Great God Brown.*

MAJOR TOURS

Alain, *The School for Wives,* North American cities, 1971.

FILM APPEARANCES

(Film debut) Pool player, *The Hustler,* Twentieth Century-Fox, 1961.

Mad Dog Coll, Columbia, 1961.

Gravey Combs, *The Traveling Executioner,* Metro-Goldwyn-Mayer, 1970.

Pound, United Artists, 1970.

Frank McLowrey, *Doc,* United Artists, 1971.

Crazy Joe, Columbia, 1974.

Reverend Kern, *The Bug,* Paramount, 1975.

Hellsgate rancher, *The Missouri Breaks,* United Artists, 1976.

Captain James William Boyd, *The Lincoln Conspiracy,* Sun Classics, 1977.

Mailman, *Ghost Story,* Universal, 1981.

Doorman, *Hanky Panky,* Columbia, 1982.

A Little Sex, Universal, 1982.

Soup for One, Warner Bros., 1982.

Chilly's friend, *Body Rock,* New World, 1984.

Body Rock, New World, 1984.

British prisoner, *Empire of the Sun,* Warner Bros., 1987.

Also appeared in *Some Sunny Day* and *Trust Me.*

TELEVISION APPEARANCES; MOVIES

Stan Restin, *The Spell,* NBC, 1977.

E. Howard Hunt, *Blind Ambition,* CBS, 1979.

Mr. McCormick, *Thin Ice,* CBS, 1981.

Appeared as Higgs, *Kenny Rogers as "The Gambler" III—The Legend Continues,* 1987; Leek, *Pals,* 1987; Flanders, *Terrorist on Trial: The United States vs. Salim Ajami,* 1988; Nathan Sanders, *Silent Whispers,* 1988; Scotti Bagwell, *Case Closed,* 1988; Bert Spindler, *Columbo Goes to the Guillotine,* 1989; appeared in *Freedom Fighter,* 1987; *Perfect Witness,* 1989.

TELEVISION APPEARANCES; SERIES

Davey McQuinn, *The Days and Nights of Molly Dodd,* NBC, 1987-88.

Also appeared in *Another World,* NBC; *The Edge of Night; Love of Life; The Tony Randall Show; Good Times; Hollywood Television Theatre.*

TELEVISION APPEARANCES; SPECIALS

Truett, *Sandburg's Lincoln,* NBC, 1974.

Appeared as Jeb, *Robbers, Rooftops and Witches,* 1982; Padre, *Mapp and Lucia,* 1986; in *Quiet on the Set! Behind the Scenes at "Molly Dodd,"* 1990.

TELEVISION APPEARANCES; EPISODIC

"Mr. Edith Bunker," *All in the Family,* CBS, 1976.

Defense counsel, "Service of All the Dead," *Inspector Morse,* 1988.

OTHER TELEVISION APPEARANCES

Shane O'Manion, *The Manions of America* (mini-series), ABC, 1981.

Father Ryan, *Rage of Angels* (mini-series), NBC, 1983.*

* * *

GREENWOOD, Bruce

PERSONAL: Born in Vancouver, British Columbia, Canada. *Education:* Studied acting at the University of British Columbia.

ADDRESSES: Agent—Alan Iezman, William Morris Agency, 151 El Camino Dr., Beverly Hills, CA 90212. *Publicist*—Jay Schwartz, Baker/Winokur/Ryder Public Relations, 9348 Civic Center Dr., Suite 407, Beverly Hills, CA 90210.

CAREER: Actor. Previously a lead singer and rhythm guitarist in a blues/rock band, diamond driller, and crew member of a sailboat in Greece.

CREDITS:

STAGE APPEARANCES

Appeared in *Scapino* and *Bent*.

STAGE WORK

Prop manager (with Clark Taylor), *Red, Hot, and Blue,* Equity Library Theatre, New York City, 1984.

Stage manager (with Jay McManigal and James McLaurin), *Sh-Boom!,* AMAS Repertory Theatre, New York City, 1986.

FILM APPEARANCES

Technician, *Bear Island,* Columbia, 1980.
Fifth guardsman, *First Blood,* Orion, 1982.
Herman Buhl, *The Climb,* Cinetel/Cineplex Odeon, 1987.
Todd, *The Malibu Bikini Shop* (also known as *The Bikini Shop*), International Film Marketing, 1987.
John Ripley, *Another Chance,* Moviestore Entertainment, 1988.
Jerome, *Wild Orchid,* Triumph Releasing/Vision International, 1990.

TELEVISION APPEARANCES; MOVIES

Dana Harrington, *Peyton Place: The Next Generation,* NBC, 1985.
Corbet St. James V/Cinco, *Destination: America,* ABC, 1987.
Jerry Dove, *In the Line of Duty: The F.B.I. Murders,* NBC, 1988.
Colonel Helmut Von Schraeder and Daniel Grossman, *Twist of Fate,* NBC, 1989.
Richard Berk, *Spy,* USA, 1989.
Stewart Horton, *Perry Mason: The Case of the All-Star Assassin,* NBC, 1989.
Dennis Wilson, *The Story of the Beach Boys: Summer Dreams,* ABC, 1990.

TELEVISION APPEARANCES; EPISODIC

Mitchell Gordon/Dr. Griffin, *Matlock,* NBC, 1987.
Carson Warfield, *Jake and the Fatman* CBS, 1987.

Also appeared in *The Hitchhiker,* HBO, 1983; and *Jessie,* ABC, 1984.

OTHER TELEVISION APPEARANCES

Jack Gage, *Legmen* (series), NBC, 1984.
Dr. Seth Griffin, *St. Elsewhere* (series), NBC, 1986-88.

RECORDINGS:

ALBUMS

Executive produced Norman Foote's *Some People* (children's songs).*

GRIMES, Tammy 1934-

PERSONAL: Full name, Tammy Lee Grimes; born January 30, 1934, in Lynn, MA; daughter of Nicholas Luther (a farmer, innkeeper, and country club manager) and Eola Willard (a spiritualist and naturalist; maiden name, Niles) Grimes; married Christopher Plummer (an actor), August 16, 1956 (divorced, 1960); married Jeremy Slade (an actor; divorced, 1964); children: (first marriage) Amanda. *Education:* Attended Stephens College; studied for the theatre with Sanford Meisner at the Neighborhood Playhouse; studied voice with Marjorie Schloss. *Religion:* Protestant. *Avocational interests:* Drawing, baking bread, walking, traveling.

ADDRESSES: Agent—Don Buchwald, 10 East 44th Street, New York, NY 10017; Fifi Oscard Associates Inc., 19 West 44th Street, New York, NY 10036.

CAREER: Actress. Westport Country Playhouse, Westport, CT, apprentice, 1954; night club performer at clubs, including Downstairs-at-the-Upstairs, New York City, 1958; Hollywood Palace, Las Vegas, NV, 1967; Freddy's, New York City, 1981; and Les Mouche, New York City, 1981; has entertained at the White House, Washington, DC, 1966; concert performer.

MEMBER: American Society for the Prevention of Cruelty to Animals (ASPCA), Whale Protection Society, Save the Seals Foundation, Landmarks Preservation Society, Save the Theatres, and Whitney Museum.

AWARDS, HONORS: Theatre World Award, 1959, for *Look after Lulu;* Comaedia Matinee Club Award and Antoinette Perry Award, Best Supporting or Featured Actress in a Musical, both 1961, for *The Unsinkable Molly Brown;* Antoinette Perry Award, Best Actress in a Drama, and *Variety's* New York Drama Critics Poll Award, both 1970, for *Private Lives;* National Endowment for the Arts Award, 1981.

CREDITS:

STAGE APPEARANCES

Three Men on a Horse, Falmouth Playhouse, MA, 1952.
Cockney juror, *The Verdict,* Westport Country Playhouse, Westport, CT, 1954.
(Broadway debut) Cherie, *Bus Stop,* Music Box Theatre, 1955.
Eshtemoa, *Jonah and the Whale,* Neighborhood Playhouse, New York City, 1955.
Ensemble, *The Littlest Revue,* Phoenix Theatre, New York City, 1956.
Flounder, *Clerambard,* Rooftop Theatre, New York City, 1957.
Mopsa, *The Winter's Tale,* Stratford Shakespeare Festival, Stratford, Ontario, Canada, 1958.

Mistress Quickly, *Henry IV, Part I,* Stratford Shakespeare Festival, Stratford, Ontario, Canada, 1958.

Lulu D'Arville, *Look after Lulu,* Henry Miller's Theatre, New York City, 1959.

Maria, *Twelfth Night,* Cambridge Festival Theatre, Cambridge, MA, 1959.

Actors Benefit, Palladium, 1960.

Moll, *The Cradle Will Rock* (opera), New York City Center, New York City, 1960.

Molly Tobin, *The Unsinkable Molly Brown,* Winter Garden Theatre, New York City, 1960.

Cyrenne, *Rattle of a Simple Man,* Booth Theatre, New York City, 1963.

Elvira Condimene, *High Spirits,* Alvin Theatre, New York City, 1964.

Sharon McLonergan, *Finian's Rainbow,* Hyatt Music Theatre, Burlingame, CA, 1965.

Ruth Arnold, *The Warm Peninsula,* Royal Poinciana Playhouse, Palm Beach, FL, 1966.

Ensemble, *The Decline and Fall of the Entire World as Seen through the Eyes of Cole Porter* (revue), Huntington Hartford Theatre, Los Angeles, CA, 1967.

Fran Walker, *The Only Game in Town,* Broadhurst Theatre, New York City, 1968.

Amanda Prynne, *Private Lives,* Billy Rose Theatre, New York City, 1969.

The Imaginary Invalid, Philadelphia Drama Guild, Walnut Street Theatre, 1971.

Kate, *The Taming of the Shrew,* Philadelphia Drama Guild, Walnut Street Theatre, Philadelphia, PA, 1974.

The Play's the Thing, Academy Festival, Lake Forest, IL, 1974.

Title role, *Gabrielle,* Studio Arena Theatre, Buffalo, NY, 1974, then Ford's Theatre Society, Washington, DC, 1975.

Pamela Fox, *Perfect Pitch,* John F. Kennedy Center for the Performing Arts, Eisenhower Theatre, Washington, DC, 1975.

Vicky, *My Fat Friend,* Royal Poinciana Playhouse, 1975.

Ensemble, *A Musical Jubilee* (revue), St. James Theatre, New York City, 1975.

Lydia Cruttwell, *In Praise of Love,* Westport Country Playhouse, 1975.

Hannah Warren, "Visitor from New York," Diana Nichols, "Visitors from London," and Gert Franklin, "Visitors from Chicago," all in *California Suite,* Eugene O'Neill Theatre, New York City, 1976.

Title role, *Molly,* Hudson Guild Theatre, New York City, 1978.

Elmire, *Tartuffe,* Circle in the Square, New York City, 1978.

Lillian Hellman, *Are You Now or Have You Ever Been,* Promenade Theatre, New York City, 1978.

The Neighborhood Playhouse at Fifty: A Celebration, Shubert Theatre, New York City, 1978.

Paula Cramer, *Trick,* Playhouse Theatre, New York City, 1979.

Marian, *Father's Day,* American Place Theatre, New York City, 1979.

Natalya Petrovna, *A Month in the Country,* McCarter Theatre Company, Princeton, NJ, 1979, then Roundabout Theatre, New York City, 1979.

Dorothy Brock, *42nd Street,* Winter Garden Theatre, 1980, Majestic Theatre, New York City, 1981.

The Millionairess, Hartman Theatre, Stamford, CT, 1981.

Madame Arcati, *Blithe Spirit,* Stratford Shakespeare Festival, Stratford, Ontario, Canada, 1982.

Lila Halliday, *Sunset,* Village Gate Theatre, New York City, 1983.

Over My Dead Body, Hartford Theatre, Hartford, CT, 1984.

Julia Baker, *Paducah,* American Place Theatre, 1985.

Madame St. Pe, *The Waltz of the Toreadors,* Roundabout Theatre, 1985.

Ensemble, *Waitin' in the Wings* (revue), Triplex Theatre, New York City, 1986.

Lady Bracknell, *The Importance of Being Earnest,* Yale Repertory Theatre, New Haven, CT, 1986.

Madame Alexandra, *Mademoiselle Colombe,* Theatre Off Park, New York City, 1987.

Tammy Grimes: A Concert in Words and Music (one-woman show), York Theatre Company, Church of the Heavenly Rest, New York City, 1988.

Vee Talbott, *Orpheus Descending,* Neil Simon Theatre, New York City, 1989.

Also appeared as Sabrina, *The Skin of Our Teeth,* 1950; appeared in *Actors and Actresses,* 1983, and *Pal Joey in Concert,* New York City. Appeared with the Potter's Field Theatre Company, New York City, 1979-80.

MAJOR TOURS

Title role, *The Amazing Adele,* U.S. cities, 1955-56.

Agnes Sorel, *The Lark,* U.S. cities, 1956.

Molly Tobin, *The Unsinkable Molly Brown,* U.S. cities, 1962, 1974.

Doreen, *The Private Ear,* and Belinda, *The Public Eye* (double-bill), U.S. cities, 1965.

Cyrenne, *Rattle of a Simple Man,* Californian cities, 1965.

Ruth Arnold, *The Warm Peninsula,* U.S. cities, 1971.

Amanda Prynne, *Private Lives,* U.S. cities, 1974.

Vicky, *My Fat Friend,* U.S. cities, 1974.

Title role, *Molly,* U.S. cities, 1975.

Love Letters, U.S. cities, 1991.

FILM APPEARANCES

Angela Sparrow, *Three Bites of the Apple,* Metro-Goldwyn-Mayer, 1967.

Helene, *Play It as It Lays,* Universal, 1972.

Audrey Van Santen, *Somebody Killed Her Husband,* Columbia, 1978.

Narrator, *Just Crazy about Horses* (documentary), Fred Baker, 1978.

Erna, *The Runner Stumbles,* Twentieth Century-Fox, 1979.

Sydney Channing, *Can't Stop the Music,* Associated Film Distribution, 1980.

Voice of Molly Grue, *The Last Unicorn* (animated), ITC, 1982.

Herself, *The Stuff,* New World, 1985.

Joy Hackley, *America,* ASA, 1986.

Sarah Baily-Lewis, *Mr. North,* Samuel Goldwyn Company, 1988.

Georgette, *Slaves of New York,* Tri-Star, 1989.

Also appeared in *Arthur!! Arthur?,* 1970.

TELEVISION APPEARANCES; SERIES

Tammy Ward, *The Tammy Grimes Show,* ABC, 1966.

TELEVISION APPEARANCES; EPISODIC

"The Bride Cried," *The U.S. Steel Hour,* CBS, 1955.

"Babe in the Woods," *Studio One,* CBS, 1957.

"Forty-Five Minutes from Broadway," *Omnibus,* NBC, 1959.

Mehitabel, "Archy and Mehitabel," *Play of the Week,* syndicated, 1960.

Daisy Strong, "The Datchel Diamonds," *The Dow Hour of Great Mysteries,* NBC, 1960.

Wife, "The Fourposter," *Golden Showcase,* CBS, 1962.

The Virginian, NBC, 1963.

Route 66, CBS, 1963.

Burke's Law, ABC, 1964.

Destry, ABC, 1964.

The Trials of O'Brien, CBS, 1965.

Tarzan, NBC, 1967.

The Smothers Brothers Comedy Hour, CBS, 1967.

The Outcasts, ABC, 1969.

Love, American Style, ABC, 1971.

The Snoop Sisters, NBC, 1974.

Also appeared on *The Ed Sullivan Show,* CBS; *The Andy Williams Show,* NBC; *The Garry Moore Show,* CBS; *Celebrity Game,* CBS; *Mr. Broadway,* CBS; *To Tell the Truth,* CBS; *The Dan Martin Show,* NBC; *The Danny Kaye Show,* CBS; *The Gypsy Rose Lee Show,* ABC; *Dateline: Hollywood,* ABC; *The Las Vegas Show,* syndicated; *The Pat Boone Show,* NBC; *Everybody's Talking,* ABC; *St. Elsewhere,* NBC; and *Kraft Television Theatre.*

TELEVISION APPEARANCES; MOVIES

Denise Gray, *The Other Man,* NBC, 1970.

Mrs. Pinder, *The Horror at 37,000 Feet,* CBS, 1973.

Amy Carlton, *You Can't Go Home Again,* CBS, 1979.

Paula, *An Invasion of Privacy,* CBS, 1983.

TELEVISION APPEARANCES; SPECIALS

Cafe singer, *Holiday,* NBC, 1956.

Heaven Will Protect the Working Girl, NBC, 1956.

Hazel, *Gift of the Magi,* CBS, 1958.

Hollywood Sings, NBC, 1960.

Homily Clock, "The Borrowers," *The Hallmark Hall of Fame,* NBC, 1973.

Voice of Albert Mouse, *'twas the Night before Christmas* (animated), CBS, 1974.

That Was the Year That Was, NBC, 1976.

Elmire, "Tartuffe," *Great Performances,* PBS, 1978.

Voice of Princess, "The Incredible Book Escape," *CBS Library,* CBS, 1980.

Mother Estelle, *Royal Match,* CBS, 1985.

Narrator, *The Emperor's Eye: Art and Power in Imperial China* (documentary), PBS, 1989.

Also appeared on *The Spy Who Returned from the Dead,* 1974.

RECORDINGS:

ALBUMS

The Littlest Revue (original cast recording), Painted Smiles, 1956.

42nd Street (original cast recording), RCA, 1980.

Also recorded *The Unsinkable Molly Brown* (original cast recording), *High Spirits* (original cast recording), *Tammy Grimes,* and *The Unsinkable Tammy Grimes,* all produced by Columbia.

TAPED READINGS

Fifteen Rabbits: A Celebration of Life, Higglety Pigglety Pop! or There Must Be More to Life, Kenny's Window, Where the Wild Things Are and Other Stories, The Golden Key, Prince Rabbit and Other Stories, Jenny and the Cat Club and Jenny's First Party, When Jenny Lost Her Scarf and Jenny's Adopted Brothers, Hector McSnector and the Mail-Order Christmas Witch, Lilly and Willy and the Mail Order Witch, The Complete Adventures of Olga Da Polga, Strega Nona's Magic Lessons and Other Stories, and *A Rose for Emily and Wash,* all produced by Caedmon.

OTHER SOURCES:

PERIODICALS

Theater Week, December 18-24, 1989.*

GRODIN, Charles 1935-

PERSONAL: Born April 21, 1935, in Pittsburgh, PA; son of Ted (in sales) and Lana (a volunteer for disabled veterans) Grodin; married Julia (divorced); married Elissa, March, 1985; children: Marion. *Education:* Attended University of Michigan, 1953; graduated from Pittsburgh Playhouse School, c. 1956; studied acting with Lee Strasberg and Uta Hagen in New York City.

ADDRESSES: Office—c/o Jim Berkus, Leading Artists Inc., 445 North Bedford Dr., Penthouse, Beverly Hills, CA 90210.

CAREER: Actor, director, producer, and writer.

MEMBER: American Federation of Television and Radio Artists, Actors' Equity Association, Screen Actors Guild.

AWARDS, HONORS: Golden Globe Award, 1973, for *The Heartbreak Kid;* Outer Critics Circle Award, 1975, for *Same Time Next Year;* Actors Fund Award of Merit, 1975; Emmy Award, Outstanding Writing in a Comedy-Variety or Music Special, 1977, for *The Paul Simon Special.*

CREDITS:

STAGE APPEARANCES

(Broadway debut) Robert Pickett, *Tchin-Tchin,* Plymouth Theatre, 1962.

Perry Littlewood, *Absence of a Cello,* Ambassador Theatre, New York City, 1964.

Tandy, *Steambath,* Truck and Warehouse Theatre, New York City, 1970.

George, *Same Time Next Year,* Brooks Atkinson Theatre, New York City, 1975.

Night of 100 Stars, Radio City Music Hall, New York City, 1982.

MAJOR TOURS

Appeared as George, *Same Time Next Year,* U.S. cities.

STAGE WORK; DIRECTOR, EXCEPT WHERE NOTED

Hooray! It's a Glorious Day . . . And All That, Theatre Four, New York City, 1966.

Lovers and Other Strangers, Brooks Atkinson Theatre, 1968.

(And producer) *Thieves,* Broadhurst Theatre, New York City, 1974.

(And producer) *Unexpected Guests,* Little Theatre, New York City, 1977.

FILM APPEARANCES

Bob, *Sex and the College Girl,* Entertainment Enterprises, 1964.

Dr. Hill, *Rosemary's Baby,* Paramount, 1968.

Lenny Cantrow, *The Heartbreak Kid,* Palomar/Twentieth Century-Fox, 1972.

Chesser, *11 Harrowhouse* (also known as *Anything for Love*), Twentieth Century-Fox, 1974.

Fred Wilson, *King Kong,* Paramount, 1976.

Martin Cramer, *Thieves,* Brut/Paramount, 1977.

Tony Abbott, *Heaven Can Wait,* Paramount, 1978.

Warren Yeager, *Real Life,* Paramount, 1979.

Jake, *Sunburn,* Tuesday/Paramount, 1979.

Homer, *It's My Turn,* Rastar-Martin Elfand/Columbia, 1980.

Ira, *Seems Like Old Times,* Columbia, 1980.

Nicky Holiday, *The Great Muppet Caper,* Universal, 1981.

Vance Kramer, *The Incredible Shrinking Woman,* Lija/Universal, 1981.

Warren Evans, *The Lonely Guy,* Universal, 1984.

Buddy, *The Woman in Red,* Woman in Red Productions/Orion, 1984.

Herb Derman, *Movers and Shakers,* Metro-Goldwyn-Mayer/United Artists, 1985.

George Lollar, *The Last Resort,* Concorde-Cinema Group-Trinity, 1986.

Jim Harrison, CIA agent, *Ishtar,* Columbia/Delphi V, 1987.

Also appeared as Aardvark, *Catch-22,* 1970; Jonathan Mardukas, *Midnight Run,* 1988; George Maitlin, *The Couch Trip,* 1988; Mr. Glerman, *You Can't Hurry Love,* 1988. Appeared in *All of Me,* 1984; *Club Sandwich,* 1986; *Greetings from LA,* 1987; *Taking Care of Business,* 1990.

FILM WORK; PRODUCER

Sorceress, New World Pictures, 1983.

(With William Asher, Richard Carrothers, and Dennis D. Hennessey), *Movers and Shakers,* Metro-Goldwyn-Mayer/United Artists, 1985.

TELEVISION APPEARANCES; SPECIALS

Bill Foster, *Paradise,* CBS, 1974.

The Paul Simon Special, NBC, 1977.

Him, *Love, Sex . . . and Marriage,* ABC, 1983.

Lord Fancourt Babberly, *Charley's Aunt,* The Entertainment Channel, 1988.

Also appeared as Jake, *Grown Ups,* 1985; appeared in *King Kong: The Living Legend,* 1986; *The American Comedy Awards,* 1989; *What's Up Dr. Ruth,* 1989; *The Muppets at Walt Disney World,* 1990.

TELEVISION APPEARANCES; EPISODIC

"Black Monday," *Play of the Week,* WNTA, 1961.

"Autumn Garden," *Sunday Showcase,* CBS, 1966.

Also appeared in *The Defenders,* CBS; *Camera Three,* CBS; *Armstrong Circle Theatre,* NBC; *The Nurses,* CBS;

My True Story, CBS; *Love of Life,* CBS; *Trials of O'Brien,* CBS.

OTHER TELEVISION APPEARANCES

Matt Crane, *The Young Marrieds* (series), ABC, 1964-66.
Michael, *Just Me and You* (movie), NBC, 1978.
Jim Benson, *The Grass is Always Greener over the Septic Tank* (movie), CBS, 1978.
Cane Kensington, *Fresno* (mini-series), CBS, 1986.

TELEVISION WORK

Director and producer, *Acts of Love and Other Comedies,* (Marlo Thomas special), ABC, 1973.
Director and producer, *Paradise,* CBS, 1974.

Also director, *Songs of America* (Simon and Garfunkel special), 1969; producer and director of episodes of *Candid Camera.*

WRITINGS:

(Author of book and lyrics with Maurice Teitelbaum) *Hooray! It's a Glorious Day . . . And All That* (play), produced at Theatre Four, 1966.
One of the All Time Greats (play), produced in Nyack, NY, 1972.
(With Jeffrey Bloom) *11 Harrowhouse* (film adapted from the novel of the same title; also known as *Anything for Love*), Twentieth Century-Fox, 1974.
(With others) *The Paul Simon Special* (television special), NBC, 1977.
Love, Sex . . . and Marriage (television special), ABC, 1983.
Movers and Shakers (film), Metro-Goldwyn-Mayer/ United Artists, 1985.

Also writer for episodes of *Candid Camera.**

*   *   *

GUARDINO, Harry   1925-

PERSONAL: Born December 23, 1925, in Brooklyn, NY; father, a musician. *Education:* Attended the Dramatic Workshop.

ADDRESSES: Agent—The Agency, 10351 Santa Monica Blvd., Suite 211, Los Angeles, CA 90025. *Manager*— Mimi Weber Management, 9738 Arby Dr., Beverly Hills, CA 90210.

CAREER: Actor.

MEMBER: Academy of Motion Picture Arts and Sciences.

AWARDS, HONORS: Antoinette Perry Award nomination, c. 1960, for *One More River;* Golden Globe Award, 1962, for *The Pigeon That Took Rome.*

CREDITS:

STAGE APPEARANCES

End as a Man, Theatre de Lys, New York City, 1953.
Chuck, *A Hatful of Rain,* Lyceum Theatre, New York City, 1955.
Pompey, *One More River,* Ambassador Theatre, New York City, 1960.
Bernie Slovenk, *Natural Affection,* Booth Theatre, New York City, 1963.
Bowden Hapgood, *Anyone Can Whistle,* Majestic Theatre, New York City, 1964.
Alvaro Mangiacavallo, *The Rose Tattoo,* City Center Theatre, New York City, 1966.
Chicken, *The Seven Descents of Myrtle,* Ethel Barrymore Theatre, New York City, 1968.
Sam Craig, *Woman of the Year,* Palace Theatre, New York City, 1981.

MAJOR TOURS

Sam Craig, *Woman of the Year,* U.S. cities, 1982.

FILM APPEARANCES

Lieutenant Roberts, *Purple Heart Diary* (also known as *No Time for Tears*), Columbia, 1951.
Lieutenant Collet, *Sirocco,* Columbia, 1951.
Lou Callan, *Flesh and Fury,* Universal, 1952.
Second hood, *The Big Tip-Off,* Allied Artists, 1955.
Detective, *Hold Back Tomorrow,* Universal, 1955.
Angelo, *Houseboat,* Paramount, 1958.
Tony Valani, *The Five Pennies,* Paramount, 1959.
Forstman, *Pork Chop Hill,* United Artists, 1959.
Branco, *Five Branded Women,* Paramount, 1960.
Barabbas, *King of Kings,* Metro-Goldwyn-Mayer (MGM), 1961.
Sergeant Larkin, *Hell Is for Heroes,* Paramount, 1962.
Sergeant Joseph Contini, *The Pigeon That Took Rome,* Paramount, 1962.
Alec Burnett, *Rhino,* MGM, 1964.
Sam Trimble, *The Adventures of Bullwhip Griffin,* Buena Vista, 1967.
Danny O'Neill, *Valley of Mystery,* Universal, 1967.
Arthur Belding, *Jigsaw,* Universal, 1968.
Lee Harris, *The Hell with Heroes,* Universal, 1968.
Detective Rocco Bonaro, *Madigan,* Universal, 1968.
Jack, *Treasure of San Gennaro* (also known as *Operazione San Gennaro, Operation San Gennaro,* and *Unser Boss Ist Eine Dame*), Paramount, 1968.
Johnny, *Lovers and Other Strangers,* Cinerama, 1970.
Bressler, *Dirty Harry,* Warner Bros., 1971.
Romeo Bonino, *Red Sky at Morning,* Universal, 1971.
Captain Streeter, *They Only Kill Their Masters,* MGM, 1972.
Johnny Torrio, *Capone,* Twentieth Century-Fox, 1975.

Chops, *Whiffs,* Twentieth Century-Fox, 1975.
Lieutenant Bressler, *The Enforcer,* Warner Bros., 1976.
Detective Deal, *St. Ives,* Warner Bros., 1976.
Lieutenant Keefer, *Rollercoaster,* Universal, 1977.
Uncle Nono, *Matilda,* American International, 1978.
Valenti, *Goldengirl,* AVCO-Embassy, 1979.
James Beekman, *Any Which Way You Can,* Warner Bros., 1980.

TELEVISION APPEARANCES; SERIES

Danny Taylor, *The Reporter,* CBS, 1964.
Title role, *Monty Nash,* syndicated, 1971.
Hamilton Burger, *The New Adventures of Perry Mason,* CBS, 1973-74.

TELEVISION APPEARANCES; PILOTS

Sergeant Solly Piccolini, *Police Story,* NBC, 1973.
Captain Casey Reardon, *Get Christie Love!,* ABC, 1974.
Al Lanier, *Street Killing,* ABC, 1976.
Ralph Bancini, *Having Babies,* ABC, 1976.
Bert Harrison, *Pleasure Cove,* NBC, 1979.
Sam Walsh, *On Our Way,* CBS, 1985.
Lee Gordon, *The Lonely Profession.* NBC, 1987.

TELEVISION APPEARANCES; EPISODIC

"The Deadly Silence," *The Kaiser Aluminum Hour,* NBC, 1957.
"The Mother Bit," *Studio One,* CBS, 1957.
"Last Request," *Alfred Hitchcock Presents,* CBS, 1957.
"A Touch of Evil," *Suspicion,* NBC, 1958.
"Chez Rouge," *Desilu Playhouse,* CBS, 1959.
"Made in Japan" and "The Killers of Mussolini," *Playhouse 90,* CBS, 1959.
"The Canvas Bullet," *Naked City,* ABC, 1959.
"The Wild Reed," *Staccato,* NBC, 1959.
"One-Armed Bandit," *The Untouchables,* ABC, 1960.
"Perilous Passage" and "The O'Hara's Ladies," *Overland Trail,* NBC, 1960.
"The Nick Moses Story," *The Untouchables,* ABC, 1961.
"The Left Side of Canada," *Cain's Hundred,* NBC, 1962.
"Chez Rouge," *Kraft Mystery Theatre,* NBC, 1962.
"The Sea Witch," *The Dick Powell Theatre,* NBC, 1962.
Dr. Kildare, NBC, 1962.
"The Masked Marine," *Alcoa Premiere,* ABC, 1962.
"Wheresoever I Enter," *The Lloyd Bridges Show,* CBS, 1962.
"Babes in Wall Street," *Target: The Corrupters,* ABC, 1962.
"Hey Moth, Come Eat the Flat," *Route 66,* CBS, 1962.
"Which Man Will Die?" and "Advice to the Lovelorn and Shopworn," *The Eleventh Hour,* NBC, 1963.
"No Naked Ladies in Front of Giavanni's House," *Naked City,* ABC, 1963.
"Lion on Fire," *The Greatest Show on Earth,* ABC, 1963.

"It's Metal Work in a Bar," *Bob Hope Presents the Chrysler Theatre,* NBC, 1963.
Mayor Roger Brother, "Human Factor," *The Outer Limits,* ABC, 1963.
Ben Casey, ABC, 1964.
The Virginian, NBC, 1965.
Run for Your Life, NBC, 1966.
The Name of the Game, NBC, 1968 and 1971.
The Lonely Profession, NBC, 1969.
Hawaii Five-O, CBS, 1969, 1970, and 1975.
"Escape to Terror," *The FBI,* ABC, 1970.
"The Dark World of Harry Anders," *Men at Law,* CBS, 1971.
Love, American Style, ABC, 1971.
"The Miracle at Camafeo," *Night Gallery* (also known as *Rod Serling's "Night Gallery"*), NBC, 1972.
Medical Center, CBS, 1972.
McCloud, NBC, 1973.
Moving Target, ABC, 1973.
Evil Touch, syndicated, 1973.
Police Story, NBC, 1974.
Manhunter, CBS, 1974.
Kojak, CBS, 1974 and 1975.
McCoy, NBC, 1975.
The Streets of San Francisco, ABC, 1976.
Police Chief Bender, *Bender,* CBS, 1979.
True Confessions, syndicated, 1986.
Al Shafer, *Hotel,* ABC, 1986.
Haskell Drake, *Murder, She Wrote,* CBS, 1986.
Rheinholt, *Adderly,* CBS, 1987.
Angelo Spinelli, *The Law and Harry McGraw,* CBS, 1988.
Commander Bill Ryan, *Hunter,* NBC, 1989.

Also appeared in *Vega$,* ABC; *Magnum, P.I.,* CBS; *Barnaby Jones,* CBS; appeared as Frank Delvecchio, *Lovers and Other Strangers,* 1983.

TELEVISION APPEARANCES; MOVIES

Howard Drumm, *The Last Child,* ABC, 1971.
Walt Connors, *Partners in Crime,* NBC, 1973.
Mel Thomas, *Indict and Convict,* ABC, 1974.
Ron Polito, *Contract on Cherry Street,* NBC, 1977.
Jerry Olson, *Evening in Byzantium,* syndicated, 1978.
Collins, *The Sophisticated Gents,* NBC, 1981.
Nick Donatello, *The Neon Empire,* Showtime, 1990.*

*   *   *

GUILLAUME, Robert   1937-

PERSONAL: Born November 30, 1937, in St. Louis, MO; married, 1985; wife's name, Donna; children: four. *Education:* Attended St. Louis University and Washington University, St. Louis, MO; studied opera and musical theatre in Cleveland, OH.

ADDRESSES: Manager—Hilly Elkins, 8306 Wilshire Blvd. #438, Beverly Hills, CA 90211.

CAREER: Actor and producer.

MEMBER: American Federation of Television and Radio Artists, Screen Actors Guild.

AWARDS, HONORS: Emmy Award, Outstanding Supporting Actor in a Comedy or Comedy-Variety Series, 1978-79, for *Soap,* and Outstanding Lead Actor in a Comedy or Comedy-Variety Series, 1984-85, for *Benson;* recipient of four NAACP Image Awards.

CREDITS:

STAGE APPEARANCES

(Broadway debut) Ako, *Kwamina,* Fifty-Fourth Street Theatre, 1961.

Carl, *Fly Blackbird,* Mayfair Theatre, New York City, 1962.

Ensemble, *Jacques Brel Is Alive and Well and Living in Paris,* Village Gate Theatre, New York City, 1968, then Charles Playhouse, Boston, MA, 1969-70.

Frankie, *No Place to Be Somebody,* Arena Stage, Washington, DC, 1969-70.

Karl, *The Life and Times of J. Walter Smintheus,* Theatre de Lys, New York City, 1970.

Fire in the Mindhouse, Center Stage, Baltimore, MD, 1970-71.

Allan, *Charlie Was Here and Now He's Gone,* Eastside Playhouse, New York City, 1971.

Title role, *Purlie,* Shubert Theatre, Philadelphia, PA, 1971, then Billy Rose Theatre, New York City, 1972.

Benito Cereno, Goodman Theatre, Chicago, IL, 1975-76.

Marshall, *Apple Pie,* New York Shakespeare Festival, Public/Anspacher Theatre, New York City, 1976.

Don Juan, Goodman Theatre, 1977.

Nathan Detroit, *Guys and Dolls,* Broadway Theatre, New York City, 1976.

Night of 100 Stars, Radio City Music Hall, New York City, 1982.

Made stage debut as Billy Bigelow, *Carousel.* Also appeared in *Golden Boy, Tambourines to Glory, Finian's Rainbow, Music! Music!, Othello, Porgy and Bess,* and *Miracle Play,* all New York City. Also performer in cabaret show at Riverside Resort, Las Vegas, NV, 1987. Appeared in title role, *The Phantom of the Opera,* Los Angeles, CA, 1990.

FILM APPEARANCES

Jordan Gaines, *Super Fly T.N.T.,* Paramount, 1973.
Fred, *Seems Like Old Times,* Columbia, 1980.

Martin Luther King, *Prince Jack,* Castle Hill, 1985.
V.A. Officer, *They Still Call Me Bruce,* Shapiro/Jihee Productions, 1987.
Philmore Walker, *Wanted: Dead or Alive,* New World Pictures, 1987.
Dr. Frank Napier, *Lean On Me,* Warner Brothers, 1989.

TELEVISION APPEARANCES; SERIES

Benson, *Soap,* ABC, 1977-79.
Benson Dubois, *Benson,* ABC, 1979-86.
Dr. Edward Sawyer, *The Robert Guillaume Show* (also see below), ABC, 1989.

TELEVISION APPEARANCES; EPISODIC

"Chain Letter," *All in the Family,* CBS, 1975.
Frank Stoner, *Hotel,* ABC, 1986.
Leon, *Sister Kate,* ABC, 1989.
Sam, *Carol & Company,* NBC, 1990.

Also appeared on *Dinah; Jim Nabors' Show; Sanford & Son; Marcus Welby, M.D.;* and *The Jeffersons.*

TELEVISION APPEARANCES; MOVIES

Larry Cooper, *The Kid from Left Field,* NBC, 1979.
Professor Mills, *The Kid with the 200 I.Q.* (also see below) NBC, 1983.
John Grin, *John Grin's Christmas* (also see below), ABC, 1986.
Harlan Wade, *Perry Mason: The Case of the Scandalous Scoundrel,* NBC, 1987.
Carter Guthrie, *Fire and Rain,* USA, 1989.
Eugene St. Clair, *The Penthouse,* ABC, 1989.

TELEVISION APPEARANCES; SPECIALS

Jack Lemmon in 'S Wonderful, 'S Marvelous, 'S Gershwin, NBC, 1972.
ABC's Silver Anniversary Celebration—25 and Still the One, ABC, 1978.
Dean Martin Celebrity Roast: Jack Klugman, NBC, 1978.
Rich Little's Washington Follies, ABC, 1978.
Benson, *Soap Retrospective II,* ABC, 1978.
Presenter, *The Tony Awards,* CBS, 1978.
The Singer, *Bob Hope Special: Bob Hope in the Star-Makers,* NBC, 1980.
The Donna Summer Special, ABC, 1980.
Hal Linden's Big Apple, ABC, 1980.
Magic with the Stars, NBC, 1982.
Texaco Star Theatre: Opening Night, NBC, 1982.
Host, *The World's Funniest Commercial Goofs,* ABC, 1983.
Title role, *Purlie,* PBS, 1983.
The 38th Annual Tony Awards, ABC, 1985.
Host, *Passion and Memory,* PBS, 1986.
We the People 200: The Constitutional Gala, CBS, 1987.

"The Music Makers: An ASCAP Celebration of American Music at Wolf Trap," *Great Performances*, PBS, 1987.

Host, *Living the Dream: A Tribute to Dr. Martin Luther King*, syndicated, 1988.

The Debbie Allen Special, ABC, 1989.

The 22nd Annual NAACP Image Awards, syndicated, 1990.

Also appeared in *Life's Most Embarrassing Moments*, 1985; *The 37th Annual Prime Time Emmy Awards*, 1985; *The 15th Annual People's Choice Awards*, 1989; and *Mel and Susan Together*.

OTHER TELEVISION APPEARANCES

Blake, *The Kid with the Broken Halo* (pilot), NBC, 1982.

Host, *It Hurts Only When You Laugh* (pilot), NBC, 1983.

Frederick Douglass, *North and South* (mini-series), ABC, 1985.

TELEVISION WORK

Executive producer (with Phil Margo), *The Kid with the 200 I.Q.* (movie), NBC, 1983.

Executive producer and director, *John Grin's Christmas* (special), ABC, 1986.

Executive producer, *The Robert Guillaume Show* (series), ABC, 1989.

Co-executive producer and host, *SST: Screen, Stage, Television* (special), ABC, 1989.

Also executive producer of *The Fantastic World of D. C. Collins* (movie), 1984.*

*   *   *

GUY, Jasmine   1964(?)-

PERSONAL: Born March 10, c. 1964, in Boston, MA; daughter of William Guy (a Baptist minister and college instructor in religion and philosophy) and Jaye (a high school English teacher; maiden name, Resendes) Rudolph. *Education:* Studied at Alvin Ailey Dance Theatre.

ADDRESSES: Office—NBC, Inc., 30 Rockefeller Plaza, New York, NY 10020. *Agent*—Carla Hacken, International Creative Management, 40 West 57th St., New York, NY 10019.

CAREER: Actress, dancer, and singer. Performed with Atlanta Ballet Junior Company and Alvin Ailey Dance Theatre.

AWARDS, HONORS: NAACP Image Awards, best actress in a comedy series, 1988, 1989, and 1990, for *A Different World*.

CREDITS:

TELEVISION APPEARANCES; SERIES

Whitley Gilbert, *A Different World*, NBC, 1987—.

TELEVISION APPEARANCES; EPISODIC

Appeared in ten episodes of *Fame*, and in *The Equalizer*, CBS; *Loving*, ABC; and *Ryan's Hope*, ABC; appeared on the game shows *Hollywood Squares* and *Win, Lose, or Draw*.

TELEVISION APPEARANCES; SPECIALS

Charlie, "Runaway," *WonderWorks*, PBS, 1989.

Best Catches, CBS, 1989.

16th Annual Black Filmmakers Hall of Fame, syndicated, 1989.

The 21st Annual NAACP Image Awards, NBC, 1989.

The 3rd Annual Soul Train Music Awards, syndicated, 1989.

The 41st Annual Emmy Awards, Fox, 1989.

The 3rd Annual American Comedy Awards, ABC, 1989.

The 22nd Annual NAACP Image Awards, NBC, 1990.

The Fifth Annual Stellar Gospel Music Awards, syndicated, 1990.

The 63rd Annual Academy Awards Presentation, ABC, 1991.

OTHER TELEVISION APPEARANCES

Bank teller, *At Mother's Request* (mini-series), CBS, 1987.

Teresa Hopkins, *A Killer Among Us* (movie), NBC, 1990.

Appeared in the pilot of *Fame*.

FILM APPEARANCES

Dina, *School Daze*, Columbia, 1988.

Dominique LaRue, *Harlem Nights*, Paramount, 1989.

Song performer, *Gremlins 2: The New Batch*, Warner Bros., 1990.

STAGE APPEARANCES

A crow, a Kalidah, and a citizen of the Emerald City, *The Wiz*, Majestic Theatre, New York City, 1975, later Lunt-Fontanne Theatre, New York City, 1984.

Mickey, waitress, and Annie (understudy), *Leader of the Pack*, Ambassador Theatre, New York City, 1985.

Diana Ross, Tina Turner, and Annette Funicello, *Beehive*, Village Gate Upstairs, New York City, 1986.

Toured with *The Wiz*, United States and Japan; and *Bubbling Brown Sugar*, Europe.

RECORDINGS:

ALBUMS

Jasmine Guy, Warner Bros., 1990.

Also recorded *Leader of the Pack* (original cast recording), Elektra; *Beehive* (cast album); and *School Daze* (sound track).

OTHER SOURCES:

PERIODICALS

Ebony, June, 1988.

*   *   *

GUZMAN, Claudio 1927-

PERSONAL: Full name, Claudio Elias Guzman; born August 2, 1927, in Rancagua, Chile; came to United States, 1951; son of Guillermo and Maria Elena (Jimenez) Guzman; married Anna Maria Alberghetti (divorced, 1972); married Micki McAuliffe, December 23, 1981; children: (first marriage) Alejandra, Pilar. *Education:* Received diploma in architecture from Catholic University of Chile. *Avocational interests:* Polo, sailing, painting.

CAREER: Set designer, director, producer, and architect. Desilu Productions, Los Angeles, CA, actor, 1950-53, set designer, 1954-55; worked as a director, producer, and production designer of television series and movies, 1955-71; Santiago TV Channel 7, Santiago, Chile, director and producer, beginning in 1981. Architect for eight Roman Catholic churches in Rancagua, Chile, 1985.

MEMBER: Directors Guild of America, Pirque Polo club (founder, president, 1983).

AWARDS, HONORS: Emmy Award nomination, best art direction in a filmed show, 1954, for *The Ray Bolger Show;* Emmy award, best art direction in a film, 1959, for *Bernadette;* Emmy Award nominations, best children's informational series, 1977 and 1978, for *Villa Alegre.*

CREDITS:

TELEVISION WORK; SERIES

Art director, *The Ray Bolger Show* (also known as *Where's Raymond?*), CBS, c. 1954.
Director (with Rod Amateau, Don Weis, James Sheldon, Gary Nelson, and Bruce Bilson), *The Patty Duke Show,* ABC, 1963-66.
Producer (with Sidney Sheldon) and director (with others), *I Dream of Jeannie,* NBC, 1965-70.

Director and producer, *The Good Life,* NBC, 1971-72.
Executive producer, producer, and creator, *Villa Alegre,* PBS, 1974-77.
Director (with others), *Three for the Road,* CBS, 1975.
Director (with H. Wesley Kenney, Walter C. Miller, and Al Schwartz), *Far Out Space Nuts,* CBS, 1975-77.

TELEVISION WORK; EPISODIC

Director (with others), *California Fever,* CBS, 1979.
Director (with others), *Here's Boomer,* NBC, 1980.
Director (with others), *Harper Valley P.T.A.,* NBC, 1981.
Director, *Starman,* ABC, 1986-87.

Also directed, with others, episodes of *The Dick Van Dyke Show,* CBS, and *The Desilu Playhouse,* CBS.

TELEVISION WORK; MOVIES

Art director and production designer, *Bernadette,* CBS, 1957.
Producer, *The Feminist and the Fuzz,* ABC, 1971.
Production designer, *And I Alone Survived,* NBC, 1978.
Director (with Joan Darling), *Willa,* CBS, 1979.
Director and production designer, *The Hostage Tower,* CBS, 1980.
Production designer, *Sidney Sheldon's "Windmills of the Gods,"* CBS, 1988.

Also production designer, *Rainbow Drive* (movie), 1990; worked on films produced in Chile, including *La Madre Tia,* and *Via Los Romos.*

OTHER TELEVISION WORK

Director, *The Desilu Revue* (special), CBS, 1959.
Director, *The Two of Us* (pilot), CBS, 1966.
Director, *For Lovers Only* (pilot), ABC, 1982.

TELEVISION APPEARANCES; MOVIES

Rosa, *Agatha Christie's "Murder In Three Acts",* CBS, 1986.

FILM WORK

Art director (with Rolland Brooks), *The Caretakers* (also known as *Border Lines*), United Artists, 1963.
Art director, *Touched by Love* (also known as *To Elvis with Love*), Columbia, 1980.

Also directed *Linda Lovelace for President.**

H

HALE, Alan, Jr. 1918-1990

PERSONAL: Born March 8, 1918, in Los Angeles, CA; died of cancer of the thymus, January 2, 1990, in Los Angeles, CA; cremated; son of Alan Hale (an actor) and an actress; married; wife's name, Naomi; children: three sons, one daughter.

CAREER: Actor. For fifteen years Hale was co-owner of Alan Hale's Lobster Barrel, West Hollywood, CA, a restaurant where he greeted customers; at the time of his death he was running Alan Hale's Leisure Quality, a travel agency. *Military service:* U.S. Coast Guard; served during World War II.

CREDITS:

FILM APPEARANCES

(Film debut) *Wild Boys of the Road,* Warner Brothers/First National, 1933.
Tiny, *All-American Co-ed,* United Artists (UA), 1941.
Pilot, *Dive Bomber,* Warner Brothers/First National, 1941.
Cadet, *I Wanted Wings,* Paramount, 1941.
Olesen, *Eagle Squadron,* Universal, 1942.
Red, *Rubber Racketeers,* Monogram, 1942.
Tom Hall, *To the Shores of Tripoli,* Twentieth Century-Fox, 1942.
Cruston, *Top Sergeant,* Universal, 1942.
Sight setter, *Wake Island,* Paramount, 1942.
Union checker, *No Time for Love,* Paramount, 1943.
Boy, *Watch on the Rhine,* Warner Brothers, 1943.
Courier, *Monsieur Beaucaire,* Paramount, 1946.
Mike Mitchell, *Sweetheart of Sigma Chi,* Monogram, 1946.
Whitey, *It Happened on Fifth Avenue,* Monogram, 1947.
Sarge, *Sarge Goes to College,* Monogram, 1947.

Oklahoma Cutter, *The Spirit of West Point,* Film Classics, 1947.
M.P., *Homecoming,* Metro-Goldwyn-Mayer (MGM), 1948.
Marty, *One Sunday Afternoon,* Warner Brothers, 1948.
The Music Man, Monogram, 1948.
Marshal Riggs, *Riders in the Sky,* Columbia, 1949.
Matt Kimbrough, *Rim of the Canyon,* Columbia, 1949.
Ben Luber, *The Blazing Sun,* Columbia, 1950.
Joe, *Four Days Leave,* Film Classics, 1950.
First brother, *The Gunfighter,* Twentieth Century-Fox, 1950.
Harry Shay, *Kill the Umpire,* Columbia, 1950.
Chris, *Short Grass,* Monogram, 1950.
Bull Gilbert, *The West Point Story* (also known as *Fine and Dandy*), Warner Brothers, 1950.
Schaeffer, *The Whipped* (also known as *The Underworld Story*), UA, 1950.
Porthos, *At Sword's Point* (also known as *Sons of the Musketeers*), RKO, 1951.
Slim Haskins, *Home Town Story,* MGM, 1951.
Joe Boyd, *Honeychile,* Republic, 1951.
Vance, *Sierra Passage,* Monogram, 1951.
Wetherby, *Arctic Flight,* Monogram, 1952.
Tiny, *The Big Trees,* Warner Brothers, 1952.
Porthos, *Lady in the Iron Mask,* Twentieth Century-Fox, 1952.
Olof, *The Man behind the Gun,* Warner Brothers, 1952.
Tiny, *Mr. Walkie Talkie,* Lippert, 1952.
Mizzell, *Springfield Rifle,* Warner Brothers, 1952.
George Oliphant, *Wait 'til the Sun Shines, Nellie,* Twentieth Century-Fox, 1952.
Fleming, *Captain John Smith and Pocahontas,* UA, 1953.
Jack Larson, *Destry,* Universal, 1954.
Patrick Gayton, *The Iron Glove,* Columbia, 1954.
Bob Ollinger, *The Law vs. Billy the Kid,* Columbia, 1954.
Johnny Stark, *Rogue Cop,* MGM, 1954.

Kirk, *Silver Lode,* RKO, 1954.
Captain Kidd and the Slave Girl, UA, 1954.
Will Crabtree, *The Indian Fighter,* UA, 1955.
Anderson, *A Man Alone,* Republic, 1955.
Luke Radford, *Many Rivers to Cross,* MGM, 1955.
Wentz, *The Sea Chase,* Warner Brothers, 1955.
Robert Neary, *Young at Heart,* Warner Brothers, 1955.
Lynch, *Canyon River,* Allied Artists, 1956.
Rocky, *The Cruel Tower,* Allied Artists, 1956.
Denny, *The Killer Is Loose,* UA, 1956.
The Three Outlaws, Associated, 1956.
Deke, *Affair in Reno,* Republic, 1957.
Tom Cullen, *All Mine to Give* (also known as *The Day They Gave Babies Away*), Universal, 1957.
Mess sergeant, *Battle Hymn,* Universal, 1957.
Cole Younger, *True Story of Jesse James* (also known as *The James Brothers*), Twentieth Century-Fox, 1957.
Frank Henshaw, *The Lady Takes a Flyer,* Universal, 1958.
Malone, *Up Periscope,* Warner Brothers, 1959.
Buddy Schaeffer, *Thunder in Carolina,* Howco, 1960.
Sheriff John Millard, *The Long Rope,* Twentieth Century-Fox, 1961.
Sheriff, *The Crawling Hand,* American International, 1963.
Paul Fisher, *The Swingin' Maiden* (also known as *The Iron Maiden*), Anglo-Amalgamated/Columbia, 1963.
Sergeant Beauregard Davis, *Advance to the Rear* (also known as *Company of Cowards*), MGM, 1964.
Leach, *Bullet for a Badman,* Universal, 1964.
Stone, *Hang 'em High,* UA, 1968.
Tobaccy, *There Was a Crooked Man,* Warner Brothers, 1970.
Billy Jack Whitehorn, *Tiger by the Tail,* Commonwealth, 1970.
Sheriff, *The Giant Spider Invasion,* Group I, 1975.
Porthos, *Behind the Iron Mask* (also known as *The Fifth Musketeer*), Columbia, 1977.
Harry the Hat, *The North Avenue Irregulars,* Buena Vista, 1979.
Desk sergeant, *Johnny Dangerously,* Twentieth Century-Fox, 1984.
McVicker, *Hambone and Hillie,* New World, 1984.
Back to the Beach, Paramount, 1987.

Also appeared in *It Happens Every Spring,* 1949; *The Yellow-Haired Kid,* 1952; *Trail Blazers,* 1953; *Evidence of Power,* 1979; *The Great Monkey Rip-Off,* 1979; *Angels' Brigade;* and *The Red Fury.*

TELEVISION APPEARANCES; SERIES

Title role, *Biff Baker, U.S.A.,* CBS, 1952-53.
Title role, *Casey Jones,* syndicated, 1957.
Jonas Grumby (The Skipper), *Gilligan's Island,* CBS, 1964-67.

Big Tom, *The Good Guys,* CBS, 1968-70.
Voice of Jonas Grumby, *The New Adventures of Gilligan* (animated), ABC, 1974-77.
Voice of Jonas Grumby, *Gilligan's Planet* (animated), CBS, 1982-83.

TELEVISION APPEARANCES; MOVIES

Jonas Grumby, *Rescue from Gilligan's Island,* NBC, 1978.
Jonas Grumby, *The Castaways on Gilligan's Island,* NBC, 1979.
Jonas Grumby, *The Harlem Globetrotters on Gilligan's Island,* NBC, 1981.

TELEVISION APPEARANCES; EPISODIC

"Johnny Risk," *Alcoa Theatre,* NBC, 1958.
The Loretta Young Theatre, NBC, 1958.
Jeff Pruitt, *The Andy Griffith Show,* CBS, 1962.

Also appeared as Kiley's father, *Marcus Welby, M.D.,* ABC; appeared in *Crossroads,* ABC, *Fireside Theatre,* NBC, *Matinee Theatre,* NBC, *The Lucy Show,* CBS, *Murder, She Wrote,* CBS, *Green Acres, Hazel, Wagon Train, Cheyenne, Maverick, Route 66, The Jack Benny Show,* and *The Law and Harry McGraw.*

OTHER TELEVISION APPEARANCES

Chief Barney Blaney, *Mighty O* (pilot), CBS, 1962.
Ernie Watson, *Come a Running* (pilot), CBS, 1963.
Walter, "The Fortunate Painter," *Rex Harrison Presents Short Stories of Love,* NBC, 1974.
Guest, *When the West Was Fun: A Western Reunion* (special), ABC, 1979.

Also appeared as Mayor, *The Revenge of Red Chief* (special), 1979; appeared in *Friday Night Surprise!* (special), 1989.*

*　　*　　*

HARRIS, Richard 1933(?)-

PERSONAL: Full name, Richard St. John Harris (one source says Richard R. St. Johns Harris); born October 1, 1933 (some sources say 1930 or 1932), in Limerick, Ireland; immigrated to England; son of Ivan (a flour mill owner) and Mildred (Harty) Harris; married Joan Elizabeth Rees-Williams (a former actress), February 9, 1957 (divorced, 1969); married Ann Turkel, 1974 (divorced, 1981); children: (first marriage) three sons. *Education:* Attended Sacred Heart Jesuit College; trained for the stage at London Academy of Music and Dramatic Arts, 1956, and Joan Littlewood's International Theatre Workshop, late 1950s. *Politics:* Socialist. *Religion:* Roman Catholic.

ADDRESSES: Office—Namco Booking, 165 West Forty-sixth St., Suite 1202, New York, NY, 10036. *Contact*—

c/o New World Pictures Worldwide Publicity, 1440 South Sepulveda Blvd., Los Angeles, CA 90025.

CAREER: Actor, director, producer, vocalist, and poet. Appeared on television in England and the United States during late 1950s; affiliated with Associated British Picture Corporation beginning in 1958. Performed and toured in concert as singer and poetry reader. Appeared on stage with the Chieftains, Carnegie Hall, New York City, 1988.

MEMBER: Knights of Malta.

AWARDS, HONORS: Best actor nomination for *The Iron Harp;* Best Actor Award from Cannes International Film Festival and Academy Award nomination for best actor, both 1963, and highest honors at Italian, Czechoslovakian, and Russian film festivals, all for *This Sporting Life;* Golden Globe Award, best motion picture actor in a musical/comedy, 1968, for *Camelot;* Grammy Award nominations, album of the year for *A Tramp Shining,* and best contemporary pop male vocalist for "MacArthur Park," both 1968; Emmy Award nomination for best actor in a single performance, 1971-72, for *The Snow Goose;* Grammy Award for best spoken word recording, 1973, for *Jonathan Livingston Seagull;* Golden Globe Award nomination for best actor and Academy Award nomination for best actor, both 1990, for *The Field.*

CREDITS:

STAGE APPEARANCES

Mickser, *The Quare Fellow,* Theatre Royal, Stratford, England, 1956 (also see below).

Louis, *A View from the Bridge,* Comedy Theatre, London, 1956.

Ross, *Macbeth,* Theatre Royal, 1957-58.

Paulino, *Man, Beast, and Virtue,* Lyric Theatre, London, 1958.

Tommy Ledou, *The Pier,* Bristol Old Vic Theatre, London, 1958.

Sebastian Dangerfield, *The Ginger Man,* Fortune Theatre, London, 1959.

Sergeant Collins and George, *Fings Ain't Wot They Used T' Be,* Theatre Royal, 1959.

Malheureux, *The Dutch Courtesan,* Theatre Royal, 1959.

Aksenti Ivanovitch, *The Diary of a Madman,* Royal Court Theatre, London, 1963 (also see below).

King Arthur, *Camelot,* Winter Garden Theatre, New York City, 1981-82.

Also appeared as King Arthur in productions of *Camelot,* as Monsignor Gusmao in *And the Wind Blew,* as Bernard Shaw in *Love and Lectures,* and in *Richard's Cork Leg,* American Theatre Arts, Hollywood, CA.

MAJOR TOURS

Macbeth, Joan Littlewood's Theatre Workshop, European cities, 1958.

King Arthur, *Camelot,* U.S. cities, 1980-82.

(And director) King Arthur, *Camelot,* U.S. and Canadian cities, 1984-86.

Also toured European cities in *Henry IV.*

STAGE WORK

Producer and director, *Winter Journey* (also known as *The Country Girl*), Irving Theatre, England, 1956.

Producer, *The Quare Fellow,* Theatre Royal, 1956.

Producer, *The Diary of a Madman,* Royal Court Theatre, 1963.

FILM APPEARANCES

Terence O'Brien, *Shake Hands with the Devil,* United Artists (UA), 1959.

Higgins, *The Wreck of the Mary Deare,* Metro-Goldwyn-Mayer (MGM), 1959.

Sean Reilly, *The Night Fighters* (also known as *A Terrible Beauty*), UA, 1960.

Corporal Johnstone, *The Long and the Short and the Tall* (also known as *Jungle Fighters*), Warner Brothers-Pathe, 1961.

Barnsby, *The Guns of Navarone,* Columbia, 1961.

Lover, *Alive and Kicking,* Seven Arts, 1962.

John Mills, *Mutiny on the Bounty,* MGM, 1962.

Frank Machin, *This Sporting Life,* Continental Distributing, 1963.

Corrado Zeller, *Red Desert* (also known as *Il Deserto Rosso* and *Le Desert Rouge*), Rizzoli Film, 1965.

Robert, *Three Faces of a Woman,* Dino De Laurentiis, 1965.

Captain Benjamin Tyreen, *Major Dundee,* Columbia, 1965.

Knut Straud, *The Heroes of Telemark,* Columbia, 1965.

Cain, *The Bible . . . in the Beginning,* Twentieth Century-Fox, 1966.

Rafer Hoxworth, *Hawaii,* UA, 1966.

Christopher White, *Caprice,* Twentieth Century-Fox, 1967.

King Arthur, *Camelot,* Warner Brothers Seven Arts, 1967.

James McParlan/McKenna, *The Molly Maguires,* Paramount, 1970.

Lord John Morgan, *A Man Called Horse,* National General Pictures, 1970.

Oliver Cromwell, *Cromwell,* Columbia, 1970.

Eitan, *Bloomfield* (also known as *The Hero;* also see below), World Film Sales, 1971.

Zachary Bass, *Man in the Wilderness,* Warner Brothers, 1971 (also see below).

Kilpatrick, *Deadly Trackers,* Warner Brothers, 1973.

Fallon, *Juggernaut,* UA, 1974.

Harry Crown, *99 and 44/100% Dead* (also known as *Call Harry Crown*), Twentieth Century-Fox, 1974.

Eugene Striden, *Echoes of a Summer* (also known as *The Last Castle;* also see below), Cine Artists, 1976.

John Morgan, *The Return of a Man Called Horse,* UA, 1976 (also see below).

King Richard, *Robin and Marian,* Columbia, 1976.

Captain Nolan, *Orca* (also known as *Orca—Killer Whale*), Paramount, 1977.

Dr. Jonathon Chamberlain, *The Cassandra Crossing,* Avco Embassy, 1977.

Gulliver, *Gulliver's Travels,* Sunn Classic, 1977.

John Carter, *Golden Rendezvous,* Golden Rendezvous, 1977.

Rafer Janders, *The Wild Geese,* Allied Artists, 1978.

Danny Travis, *The Last Word* (also known as *Danny Travis*), International, 1979.

Falk, *The Ravagers,* Columbia, 1979.

David Swansey, *A Game for Vultures,* New Line Cinema, 1980.

Parker, *Tarzan, The Ape Man,* UA, 1981.

John Morgan—Man Called Horse, *Triumphs of a Man Called Horse,* Jensen Farley, 1983.

Louis Kinney, *Highpoint,* New World, 1984.

Martin Steckert, *Martin's Day,* MGM-UA, 1985.

Mr. Peachum, *Mack the Knife,* Twenty-first Century Releasing, 1989.

Bull McCabe, *The Field,* Avenue Pictures, 1990.

Also appeared in *The Three Penny Opera,* 1988, *The Numbers, A Knight in New York, Your Ticket Is No Longer Valid,* and *Outlaws.*

FILM WORK

Director, *Bloomfield* (also known as *The Hero*), World Film Sales, 1971.

Executive producer, *Echoes of a Summer* (also known as *The Last Castle*), Cine Artists, 1976.

Executive producer, *The Return of a Man Called Horse,* UA, 1976.

TELEVISION APPEARANCES; SPECIALS

Ricardo, *Victory,* NBC, 1960.

The Peggy Fleming Show, NBC, 1968.

Philip Rhayader, *The Snow Goose,* NBC, 1971.

Burt Bacharach in Shangri-La, ABC, 1973.

King Arthur, *Camelot,* HBO, 1982.

Freedomfest: Nelson Mandela's Seventieth Birthday Celebration, Fox Broadcasting Company, 1988.

Lerner & Loewe: Broadway's Last Romantics, PBS, 1988.

Also appeared in television plays, 1956-58, including *The Iron Harp,* 1957.

OTHER TELEVISION APPEARANCES

Inspector Jules Maigret, *Maigret* (movie), syndicated, 1988.

Also appeared on *Dupont Show of the Month* (series), CBS.

RECORDINGS:

"MacArthur Park," Dunhill, 1968.

Other recordings include "Didn't We," 1969; "My Boy," 1971; *The Prophet Kahil Gibran,* Atlantic; *A Tramp Shining,* MCA; *His Greatest Performances,* MCA; *Jonathan Livingston Seagull,* Dunhill; and *MacArthur Park and This Time.*

WRITINGS:

(Adaptor with Lindsay Anderson) *The Diary of a Madman* (play), Royal Court Theatre, 1963.

(With Wolf Mankowitz) *Bloomfield* (screenplay; also known as *The Hero*), World Film Sales, 1971.

I, in the Membership of My Days: Poems, M. Joseph, 1973 (also see below).

Honor Bound: A Novel, St. Martin's, 1982.

Also author of numerous poems.

MUSICAL COMPOSITIONS

"The Last Castle" from *Echoes of a Summer* (also known as *The Last Castle*), Cine Artists, 1976.

"Zach Bass Theme" from *Man in the Wilderness,* Warner Brothers, 1971.

ADAPTATIONS: *I, in the Membership of My Days: Poems* was recorded with Harris's sons assisting in the reading.

OTHER SOURCES:

PERIODICALS

Premiere, February, 1991.*

* * *

HARRISON, Rex   1908-1990

OBITUARY NOTICE—See index for *CTFT* sketch: Born Reginald Carey Harrison, March 5, 1908, in Huyton, Lancashire, England; died of pancreatic cancer, June 2, 1990, in New York, NY. Stage and screen actor and writer. In a career spanning more than six decades, Harrison was popular for his portrayals of sophisticated and debonair Englishmen. He will be best remembered, perhaps, for his role as Professor Henry Higgins in both the stage and film versions of *My Fair Lady.* Harrison's role in the musical—an adaptation of George Bernard Shaw's *Pygmalion* that opened on Broadway in 1956 and ran for more than

2700 performances—earned the actor a Tony Award. For his work in the 1964 movie adaptation, Harrison received a Golden Globe Award, a New York Film Critics Award, and that year's Academy Award for best actor.

Harrison began his acting career with the Liverpool Repertory Theater, which he joined at age sixteen. After touring with various British productions for the next several years, Harrison made his London debut to favorable press in the 1931 play *Getting George Married.* Additional stage roles in the 1930s led Harrison to parts in films, and his work in the 1948 *Anna and the King of Siam,* his first American movie, was widely praised. Returning to the stage in the late 1940s, Harrison received his first Tony for his appearance in *Anne of a Thousand Days.* Among Harrison's numerous other credits are the films *The Ghost and Mrs. Muir, Cleopatra,* and *Doctor Doolittle,* as well as the 1980s play *Heartbreak House.* Harrison recounted his life as an actor in his 1974 autobiography *Rex;* he also published a book of poems titled *If Love Be Love.*

OBITUARIES AND OTHER SOURCES:

PERIODICALS

Los Angeles Times, June 3, 1990.
Times (London), June 4, 1990.
Washington Post, June 3, 1990.

*   *   *

HARTMAN, Lisa   1956-

PERSONAL: Born June 1, 1956, in Houston, TX; father, an actor and singer; mother, a television producer. *Education:* Graduated from High School of Performing Arts, New York City.

ADDRESSES: Manager—James Pregnolato, Anonymous Management, 804 Broom Way, Los Angeles, CA 90049.

CAREER: Actress and singer. Previously a nightclub performer.

CREDITS:

FILM APPEARANCES

Faith, *Deadly Blessing,* United Artists, 1981.
Jennie, *Where the Boys Are,* Tri-Star, 1984.

Also appeared in *Just Tell Me You Love Me,* 1979; and *Seventeenth Bride,* 1985.

TELEVISION APPEARANCES; SERIES

Tabitha Stevens, *Tabitha,* ABC, 1977-78.
Ciji Dunne, *Knots Landing,* CBS, 1982-83.
Kate Flannery, *High Performance,* ABC, 1983.
Cathy Geary, *Knots Landing,* CBS, 1983-86.

TELEVISION APPEARANCES; EPISODIC

Shelby Russell, *Matlock,* NBC, 1988-89.

TELEVISION APPEARANCES; PILOTS

Tabitha Stevens, *Tabitha,* ABC, 1977.
Host, *The Lisa Hartman Show,* ABC, 1979.
Darcy Winfield/Marie Winfield, *Scared Silly,* ABC, 1982.
Crystal Kramer, *Valentine Magic on Love Island,* NBC, 1980.

TELEVISION APPEARANCES; MOVIES

Stewardess, *Murder at the World Series,* ABC, 1977.
Crystal, *Where the Ladies Go,* ABC, 1980.
Nikki, *Gridlock* (also released as *The Great American Traffic Jam*), NBC, 1980.
Amanda Rider, *Beverly Hills Cowgirl Blues,* CBS, 1985.
Autumn McAvan Norton, *Roses Are for the Rich,* CBS, 1987.
Sarah Dutton, *Full Exposure: The Sex Tapes Scandal,* ABC, 1989.
Laura Parks, *The Operation,* CBS, 1990.
Sally Delaney, *The Take,* USA, 1990.
Fire! Trapped on the 37th Floor, ABC, 1991.
Not of This World, CBS, 1991.

Also appeared in *Bare Essentials,* CBS.

TELEVISION APPEARANCES; SPECIALS

Hollywood Foreign Press Association's 35th Annual Golden Globe Awards, NBC, 1978.
Night of 100 Stars II, ABC, 1985.
Host, *Miss Teen USA,* CBS, 1985.
American Video Awards, ABC, 1985.
The Twelfth Annual People's Choice Awards, CBS, 1986.
Hollywood Women, syndicated, 1988.
The Magic of David Copperfield X: The Bermuda Triangle, CBS, 1988.
Ninth Annual Emmy Awards for Sports, syndicated, 1988.
The 24th Annual Academy of Country Music Awards, NBC, 1989.

OTHER TELEVISION APPEARANCES

Neeley O'Hara, *Jacqueline Susann's "Valley of the Dolls"* (mini-series), CBS, 1981.
Peggy, "Student Exchange," *Disney Sunday Movie* (episode), ABC, 1987.

Also appeared in *On Stage America,* syndicated, 1984.

RECORDINGS:

ALBUMS

Lisa Hartman, CBS/Kirshner, 1977.
Letterock, RCA, 1982.

Also recorded *Hold On, I'm Comin'* 1979; and *Til My Heart Stops,* 1988.*

*   *   *

HARVEY, Anthony 1931-

PERSONAL: Born June 3, 1931, in London, England; son of Geoffrey Harrison and Dorothy (Leon) Harvey. *Education:* Attended the Royal Academy of Dramatic Art. *Avocational interests:* Gardening.

ADDRESSES: Office—Arthur Greene, 101 Park Ave., 43rd Floor, New York, NY 10178. *Agent*—Fred Milstein, William Morris Agency, 1350 Avenue of the Americas, New York, NY 10019 and 31 Soho Square, London W1, England.

CAREER: Director and film editor. Previously an actor with the Crown Film Unit, 1949.

MEMBER: Academy of Motion Picture Arts and Sciences, Directors Guild of America.

AWARDS, HONORS: Best new director award from the Cannes Film Festival, 1966, for *The Dutchman;* Directors Guild of America Award, outstanding directorial achievement for feature films, 1968, for *The Lion in Winter;* Academy Award nomination, best director, and Golden Globe Award nomination, both 1969, for *The Lion in Winter;* Directors Guild of America Award nominations, for *The Glass Menagerie* and *The Patricia Neal Story;* first prize from the London Film Festival, for *The Glass Menagerie.*

CREDITS:

FILM APPEARANCES

Ptolemy, *Caesar and Cleopatra,* Rank/United Artists (UA), 1946.

FILM WORK; EDITOR

Private's Progress, British Lion, 1956.
Brothers in Law, British Lion, 1957.
Happy Is the Bride, Kassler, 1958.
I'm All Right, Jack, British Lion, 1959.
The Angry Silence, British Lion, 1960.
Man in a Cocked Hat (also known as *Carlton-Browne of the F.O.*), Boulting Brothers/Show, 1960.
The Millionairess, Twentieth Century-Fox, 1960.
The L-Shaped Room, Columbia, 1962.
Lolita, Metro-Goldwyn-Mayer (MGM), 1962.
Dr. Strangelove: Or How I Learned to Stop Worrying and Love the Bomb, Columbia, 1964.
The Spy Who Came in from the Cold, Paramount, 1965.
(And director) *Dutchman,* Continental, 1966.
The Whisperers, UA/Lopert, 1967.

FILM WORK; DIRECTOR

The Lion in Winter, AVCO-Embassy, 1968.
They Might Be Giants, Universal, 1971.
The Abdication, Warner Brothers, 1974.
Eagle's Wing, Rank, 1979.
Players, Paramount, 1979.
Richard's Things, New World, 1981.
The Ultimate Solution of Grace Quigley (also known as *Grace Quigley*), MGM/UA/Cannon, 1984.

TELEVISION WORK; DIRECTOR

The Glass Menagerie (movie), ABC, 1973.
The Disappearance of Aimee (movie), NBC, 1976.
(With Anthony Page) *The Patricia Neal Story* (movie), CBS, 1981.
Svengali (movie), CBS, 1983.*

*   *   *

HAVEL, Vaclav 1936-

PERSONAL: Born October 5, 1936, in Prague, Czechoslovakia; son of Vaclav M. (a property owner) and Bozena (Vavreckova) Havel; married Olga Splichalova, 1964. *Education:* Attended technical college, 1955-57, and Academy of Art, Prague, 1962-67.

CAREER: Writer. Worker in a chemical factory; ABC Theatre, Prague, Czechoslovakia, stagehand, 1959-60; Theatre on the Balustrade Prague, stagehand, 1960-61, assistant to the artistic director, 1961-63, literary manager, 1963-68, and resident playwright, 1968; elected president of Czechoslovakia by parliament, 1989—. *Military service:* Served in the Czech Army.

MEMBER: PEN, Union of Writers (Czechoslovakia), Charter 77 (human rights movement; spokesman), Committee for the Defence of the Unjustly Persecuted (VONS).

AWARDS, HONORS: Austrian Stage Prize for European Literature, 1968; Obie Award, distinguished playwriting, *Village Voice,* 1970, for *The Increased Difficulty of Concentration,* 1984, for *A Private View;* Jan Palach Prize, 1981; Erasmus Prize for theater, 1986; Los Angeles Drama Critics Award, 1988, for *Largo Desolato;* prize from German Booksellers Association, 1989; Olof Palme Prize, 1989; Simon Bolivar Prize, UNESCO, 1990; honorary degree, Columbia University, 1990; President's Award, PEN Center U.S.A. West, 1990.

CREDITS:

FILM APPEARANCES

Appeared as himself in *Liberte,* 1989.

WRITINGS:

PLAYS

(With Ivan Vyskocil) *Autostop* (title means "Hitchhike"), first produced in Prague, 1961.

Zahradni slavnost (first produced at Theatre on the Balustrade, Prague, 1963), [Czechoslovakia], 1964, translation by Vera Blackwell published as *The Garden Party,* J. Cape, 1969.

Vyrozumeni (first produced at Theatre on the Balustrade, 1965, produced at Anspacher Theatre, Off-Broadway, 1968), Dilia, 1965, translation by Blackwell published as *The Memorandum,* J. Cape, 1967.

Protokoly (title means "Protocols"; contains *Zahradni slavnost, Vyrozumeni,* two essays, and poems), Mlanda Fronta, 1966.

Ztizena noznost soustredoni (first produced at Theatre on the Balustrade, 1968), Dilia, 1968, translation by Blackwell published as *The Increased Difficulty of Concentration* (produced at Forum Theatre, Lincoln Center, New York City, 1969), J. Cape, 1972.

Hry 1970-76, (includes *Spiklenci, Zebracka opera, Horsky hotel, Audience,* and *Vernisaz*), Sixty-Eight Publishing House (Toronto), 1977.

Audience [and] *Vernisaz,* translations by Blackwell published as *Sorry: Two Plays,* Methuen, 1978, translation by Jan Novak produced as *Free Advice From Prague (Audience and Unveiling)* at Northlight Theatre, Evanston, IL, 1986-87, *Audience* also produced at Walnut Street Theatre, Philadelphia, PA.

A Private View (contains one-act plays, *Interview, A Private View,* and *The Protest*), translation by Blackwell produced at New York Shakespeare Festival (NYSF), Public/Martinson Theatre, New York City, 1983-84, produced as *The Vanek Plays,* London, 1990.

Temptation (first produced in Vienna, Austria, 1985; also produced by Royal Shakespeare Company, England; translation by Winn produced at Public/Wilma Theatre, New York City, 1989), translation by George Thiener, Faber, 1988, Grove, 1989.

Largo Desolato (produced in Bristol, England; translation by Marie Winn produced by NYSF, Public/Susan Stein Shiva Theatre, New York City, 1986), translation by Tom Stoppard, Grove, 1987.

Also author of *The Conspirators,* 1971, an adaptation of *The Beggars Opera,* 1972, *The Mountain Hotel,* 1974, *Protest* (one-act), 1978, and *The Guardian Angel.*

OTHER

Lemonade Joe, (screenplay; also known as *Limonadovy Joe* and *Konska Opera*), Allied Artists, 1966.

(With others) *The Power of the Powerless: Citizens against the State in Central Eastern Europe,* edited by John Keane, M. E. Sharpe, 1985.

Vaclav Havel; or, Living in Truth, edited by Jan Vladislav, Faber, 1987.

Letters to Olga: June 1979 to September 1982, translated by Paul Wilson, Knopf, 1988.

Disturbing the Peace, Knopf, 1990.

Long Distance Interrogation, Knopf, 1990.

Open Letters: Selected Writings, Knopf, 1991.

Also author of monograph on writer and painter Joseph Capek, 1963, and *Slum Clearance,* 1987. Work included in anthologies, including *Three Eastern European Plays,* Penguin, 1970.*

*   *   *

HAYMER, John
See HAYMER, Johnny

*   *   *

HAYMER, Johnny   1920-1989
(John Haymer)

PERSONAL: Born in 1920 in St. Louis, MO; died of cancer, November 18, 1989, in Los Angeles, CA; wife's name, Helen; children: Susan, James, Robert. *Education:* Received degree from University of Missouri.

CAREER: Actor and stand-up comedian. Performed in nightclubs around the country as part of the Sears and Haymer comedy team; comedy writer for television shows featuring Sid Caesar, Steve Allen, Perry Como, Ed Sullivan, and Jackie Gleason; appeared in more than one hundred television commercials; worked as commercial spokesman for Standard Shoes.

CREDITS:

FILM APPEARANCES

Teen-Age Strangler, Anjay, 1967.

Sergeant Pozzallo, *The Secret War of Harry Frigg,* Universal, 1968.

John Bishop, *The Organization,* United Artists, 1971.

(As John Haymer) Rodeo cook, *Evel Knievel,* Fanfare, 1971.

(As John Haymer) *The Four Deuces,* Avco-Embassy, 1976.

Logan's Run, Metro-Goldwyn-Mayer/United Artists, 1976.

Comic, *Annie Hall,* United Artists, 1977.

Race official, *Herbie Goes to Monte Carlo,* Buena Vista, 1977.

American Hot Wax, Paramount, 1978.

Dr. Rennert, *Real Life,* Paramount, 1979.

Crenna, *. . . And Justice for All,* Columbia, 1979.

Paul Bernal, *Open House,* Intercontinental, 1987.

Also appeared as board member, *Win, Place or Steal,* 1975.

TELEVISION APPEARANCES; SERIES

Supply Sergeant Zale, *M*A*S*H,* CBS, 1977-79.
Walter Pinkerton, *Madame's Place,* syndicated, 1982.
Voice characterizations, *Alvin and the Chipmunks* (animated), NBC, beginning in 1983.

Also appeared as Gunther, *No Soap, Radio,* 1982; performed voice characterizations on *G.I. Joe,* 1984.

TELEVISION APPEARANCES; EPISODIC

The Dick Van Dyke Show, CBS, 1966.
First commissioner, *Golden Girls,* NBC, 1986.
Announcer, *Cagney and Lacey,* CBS, 1986.
Leon Schwartz, *Simon and Simon,* CBS, 1988.
Police chief, *Sonny Spoon,* NBC, 1988.
Rudy Vanelli, *Annie McGuire,* CBS, 1988.
Barney Ross, *Life Goes On,* ABC, 1989.
Mr. Blake, *Ann Jillian,* NBC, 1990.

Also appeared on *The Facts of Life, Three's Company, One Day at a Time, Get Smart, Gunsmoke,* and *Star Trek.*

TELEVISION APPEARANCES; MOVIES

Rocco, *Mongo's Back in Town,* CBS, 1971.
Reporter Poole, *Attack on Terror: The FBI Versus the Ku Klux Klan,* CBS, 1975.
Haberson, *The Comedy Company,* CBS, 1978.
Nazi official, *Ring of Passion,* NBC, 1978.
The Best Place to Be, NBC, 1979.
Stan, *The Ray Mancini Story,* CBS, 1985.
Full Exposure: The Sex Tapes Scandal, NBC, 1989.

OTHER TELEVISION APPEARANCES

Brown, *Operation Greasepaint* (pilot), CBS, 1968.
The Magician, NBC, 1973.
Voice characterization, "Five Weeks in a Balloon," *Famous Classic Tales* (animated special), CBS, 1977.
Voice of Gregor, *Mr. and Mrs. Dracula* (pilot), ABC, 1980.

STAGE APPEARANCES

Appeared in *Meet the People and New Faces of 1956,* New York City; *Social Security,* San Bernardino Civic Light Opera, San Bernardino, CA; and productions of *Anyone Can Whistle, Man of La Mancha, Irma La Douce, South Pacific, Damn Yankees,* and *Flower Drum Song.*

MAJOR TOURS

Jacquot, *Carnival,* U.S. cities, 1961-62.

OBITUARIES AND OTHER SOURCES:

PERIODICALS

Variety, November 22, 1989.*

*   *   *

HEAP, Douglas   1934-

PERSONAL: Born August 7, 1934, in Buckhurst Hill, London, England; son of Clifford Vernon (a miniature theatre entertainer) and Alexandra Jessica (a miniature theatre entertainer; maiden name, Richmond) Heap; married Jennifer Pennell (a painter and propmaker); children: Martin, Simon. *Education:* Attended Claysmore School, 1946-52; Byam Shaw School of Drawing and Painting, 1952-55. *Avocational interests:* Cricket, crosswords.

CAREER: Designer. Royal Academy of Dramatic Art, London, England, head of design, 1969-86.

CREDITS:

STAGE DESIGNER, EXCEPT AS NOTED

Bid Time Return, Vanbrugh Theatre, Royal Academy of Dramatic Art, London, 1958.
Boesman and Lena, Theatre Upstairs, London, 1971.
AC/DC, English Stage Company, Royal Court Theatre, London, 1971.
Within Two Shadows, English Stage Company, Royal Court Theatre, 1971.
Crete and Sergeant Pepper, English Stage Company, Royal Court Theatre, 1972.
The Old Ones, English Stage Company, Royal Court Theatre, 1972.
The Freedom of the City, English Stage Company, Royal Court Theatre, 1973.
X, English Stage Company, Royal Court Theatre, 1974.
Play Mas, English Stage Company, Royal Court Theatre, 1974.
Sizwe Banzi Is Dead, Long Wharf Theatre, New Haven, CT, then Edison Theatre, New York City, 1974.
The Island, Long Wharf Theatre, then Edison Theatre, 1974.
Loot, English Stage Company, Royal Court Theatre, 1975.
Pygmalion, Nottingham Repertory Theatre, Nottingham, England, 1976.
The Father, Old Tote Theatre, Sydney, Australia, 1977.
Shirt Sleeves in Summer, English Stage Company, Royal Court Theatre, 1977.
Ascent of Mount Fuji, Hampstead Theatre Club, London, 1977.
A and R, Royal Shakespeare Company, Donmar Theatre, London, 1978.

Piaf, The Other Place, Stratford-upon-Avon, England, then Donmar Theatre, 1978.

The Turn of the Screw, Kent Opera, Kent, England, 1979.

L'Amore Dei Tre Re, Wexford Opera, Wexford, England, 1979.

Edgar, Wexford Opera, 1980.

Ariadne Aux Naxos, English National Opera, London, 1980.

Enjoy, Vaudeville Theatre, London, 1980.

Dreyfus, Hampstead Theatre Club, 1982.

Run For Your Wife, Guildford Theatre, England, 1982, then Shaftesbury Theatre, London, 1983.

Pygmalion, Shaftesbury Theatre, 1983.

On the Razzle, Shaftesbury Theatre, 1984.

Just between Ourselves, Palace Theatre, London, 1985.

Leaving Home, Soho Poly Theatre, London, 1987.

Private Means, Soho Poly Theatre, 1987.

Pygmalion, Plymouth Theatre, New York City, 1987.

It Runs In the Family, Guildford Theatre, 1987.

Barnaby and the Old Boys, Clwyd Theatre, London, 1987, then Nuffield Theatre, Southampton, and Vaudeville Theatre, London, 1989.

Paris Match, Clwyd Theatre, 1988, then Garrick Theatre, London, 1989.

Stop the World—I Want to Get Off, Lyric Theatre, London, 1989.

(Co-designer) *Blitz Experience,* Imperial War Museum, London, 1989.

Art director, *Spitting Image,* Expo Osaka, Japan, 1990.

Getting On, Palace Theatre, 1990.

Out of Order, Shaftesbury Theatre, 1990.

Bread, Pavilion Theatre, Bournemouth, England, 1990.

Also designer for *Lady Be Good,* Sheffield, England, 1988; and *Driving Miss Daisy,* Tel Aviv, Israel, 1990.

*   *   *

HELLER, Paul   1927-
(Paul M. Heller)

PERSONAL: Full name, Paul Michael Heller; born September 25, 1927, in New York, NY; son of Alex Gordon (an inventor) and Anna (an activist; maiden name, Rappaport) Heller; married Georganne Aldrich (divorced, 1981); children: Michael Peter. *Education:* Studied engineering at Drexel Institute of Technology (now Drexel University), 1944-45; Hunter College (now of the City University of New York), B.A., 1950.

ADDRESSES: Office—Paul Heller Productions, 1666 North Beverly Dr., Beverly Hills, CA 90210.

CAREER: Producer. Set designer for theatre, film, and television productions, 1952-61; president, MPO Pictures Inc., 1964-69; production executive, Warner Brothers, 1970-71; founder (with Fred Weintraub), Sequoia Pictures Inc., 1972; president, Paul Heller Productions Inc., 1978—; president, Intrepid Productions. Chairman of board of directors, Plumstead Theatre Society and Community Film Workshop Council, both New York City. Instructor in motion picture and television production, New York University, 1964-66; instructor, American Film Institute; guest lecturer, Columbia University. *Military service:* U.S. Army, Signal Corps; received Presidential Unit Citation.

MEMBER: Screen Actors Guild, Directors Guild of America, Actors' Equity Association, United Scenic Artists, American Film Institute (founding member, Committee of 100), Human-Dolphin Foundation, Lotos Club.

AWARDS, HONORS: Venice Film Festival award, Best First Work, Mar Del Plata Festival Award, Best Film, and French Film Academy Award nomination, all 1962, for *David and Lisa;* Mar Del Plata Festival Award, Best Film, 1964, for *The Eavesdropper;* Academy Award nomination, Best Picture, 1989, for *My Left Foot;* French Film Academy Award, Best Foreign Film, for *Secret Ceremony;* special award from National Association for Mental Health.

CREDITS:

FILM PRODUCER, EXCEPT WHERE INDICATED

Production designer, *Happy Anniversary,* United Artists, 1959.

(As Paul M. Heller; also art director) *David and Lisa,* Continental, 1962.

(As Paul M. Heller) *The Eavesdropper,* Royal Films International, 1966.

Come Spy with Me, Twentieth Century-Fox, 1967.

Executive producer, *Secret Ceremony,* Universal, 1968.

Executive producer, *The New York Experience* (multimedia show), Trans-Lux Corporation, 1973.

(With Fred Weintraub) *Enter the Dragon,* Warner Brothers, 1973.

(With Weintraub) *Black Belt Jones,* Warner Brothers, 1974.

(With Weintraub) *Golden Needles* (also known as *Chase for the Golden Needles*), American International, 1974.

(As Paul M. Heller; with Weintraub) *Truck Turner,* American International, 1974.

(With Weintraub) *The Ultimate Warrior,* Warner Brothers, 1975.

(With Weintraub) *Dirty Knight's Work* (also known as *Trial By Combat, A Choice of Weapons,* and *Choice of Arms*), Gamma III, 1976.

(With Weintraub) *Hot Potato,* Warner Brothers, 1976.

(With Weintraub) *The Pack* (also known as *The Long Dark Night*), Warner Brothers, 1977.

Executive producer, *Outlaw Blues,* Warner Brothers, 1977.

(With Weintraub) *Checkered Flag or Crash,* Universal, 1978.

(With Weintraub) *The Promise* (also known as *Face of a Stranger*), Universal, 1979.

(With Martha Scott) *First Monday in October,* Paramount, 1981.

Withnail and I, Cineplex Odeon, 1987.

Executive producer, *My Left Foot,* Miramax, 1989.

Also producer of *Crash,* 1976; executive producer, *South Street Venture* (multimedia show).

STAGE WORK

Stage manager, *Angel in the Pornshop,* Booth Theatre, New York City, 1951.

TELEVISION WORK

Executive producer, *Falcon's Gold* (pilot), Showtime, 1982.

Producer, *Wait Until Dark* (special), HBO, 1982.

Also executive producer of the special *Pygmalion,* 1983.*

*   *   *

HELLER, Paul M.
    See HELLER, Paul

*   *   *

HEMMING, Lindy   1948-

PERSONAL: Born August 21, 1948, in Wales; daughter of Alan (a wood-carver) and Jean Margery (a lecturer and teacher; maiden name, Alexander) Hemming; married R. Grace, 1970 (divorced); children: Alexandra Grace, Daniel Grace. *Education:* Attended Llandovery School, Wales; trained as an orthopedic nurse, 1964-68; trained at the Royal Academy of Dramatic Arts. *Politics:* Socialist. *Religion:* None.

ADDRESSES: Agent—Louisa Stevenson, Prestige Talent Agency, Bugle House, 21A Noel St., London W1V 3PD, England.

CAREER: Costume designer.

AWARDS, HONORS: Antoinette Perry Award nomination, best costume designer, 1983, for *All's Well That Ends Well;* British Academy of Film and Television Sciences award nomination, 1987, for *Porterhouse Blue.*

CREDITS:

STAGE COSTUME DESIGNER

Alpha Alpha, Open Space Theatre, London, 1972.
Clouds, Hampstead Theatre Club, London, 1976.
Death of a Salesman, National Theatre, London, 1979.
Juno and the Paycock, Royal Shakespeare Company, 1982.
All's Well That Ends Well, Royal Shakespeare Company, 1983.
Mother Courage, Royal Shakespeare Company, 1984.
Sisterly Feelings, National Theatre, 1984.
Schweyk in the Second World War, National Theatre, 1985.
Pravda, National Theatre, 1986.
A Small Family Business, National Theatre, 1987.
Waiting for Godot, National Theatre, 1988.
Perdition, Royal Court Theatre, London, 1988.
Steel Magnolias, Lyric Theatre, London, 1989.
Exclusive, Strand Theatre, London, 1990.

Also costume designer for *King,* London, 1990; for other plays at Hampstead Theatre Club; and for West End productions of *Donkeys Years, Taking Steps, Chorus of Disapproval, Clouds, GlooJoo, Brighton Beach Memoirs,* and *A View from the Bridge,* 1978-89.

FILM COSTUME DESIGNER

Meantime, Portman Productions, 1983.
Loose Connections, Greenpoint, 1984.
(With Mary Jane Reyner) *Comfort and Joy,* Universal, 1984.
My Beautiful Laundrette, Working Title, 1985.
(With Jane Greenwood) *84 Charing Cross Road,* Brooks Films, 1985.
(With Greenwood) *Wetherby,* Greenpoint, 1986.
High Hopes, Portman Productions, 1987.
When the Wales Came, Cygnet, 1988.
Queen of Hearts, T.V.S. Films, 1989.
The Krays, Fugitive T.V. and Films, 1990.
Life is Sweet, Thin Man Films, 1990.
Hear My Song, Limelight Windmill Lane, 1990.
Blame it on the Bellboy, Hollywood Pictures, 1991.

TELEVISION COSTUME DESIGNER

Abigail's Party, BBC, 1980.

Also designer for *Short and Curlies,* 1987, and *Porterhouse Blue* (series), 1988.

SIDELIGHTS: Lindy Hemming commented: "I was motivated to work in the area of costume by being interested in how people look and behave in all circumstances—and by love of theatre and film drama. Now my children are growing up and I'm beginning to travel and see how people live and behave elsewhere."

*   *   *

HENRY, Buck   1930-

PERSONAL: Born Henry Zuckerman December 9, 1930, in New York, NY; son of Paul (a stockbroker and former air force general) and Ruth (an actress; maiden name, Taylor) Zuckerman. *Education:* Attended Harvard Military Academy and Choate School; Dartmouth College, B.A., English, 1952.

ADDRESSES: Office—760 North La Cienega Blvd., Los Angeles, CA 90069. *Agent*—William Morris Agency, 151 El Camino, Beverly Hills, CA 90212.

CAREER: Writer, director, and actor. Performed with the Premise Improvisational Theatre Company, New York City, 1961-62; creator of television series *Captain Nice*, NBC, 1967, (with Mel Brooks) *Get Smart!*, NBC, 1965-69, and *Quark*, NBC, 1978. *Military service:* U.S. Army, 7th Army Repertory Company, 1952-54; served as helicopter mechanic.

MEMBER: Writers Guild of America, Screen Actors Guild, Actors Equity Association, Directors Guild, Academy of Motion Picture Arts and Sciences.

AWARDS, HONORS: Emmy Award (with Leonard Stern), outstanding writing achievement in comedy, 1966, for "Ship of Spies," *Get Smart!;* Academy Award nomination (with Calder Willingham), best screenplay—adaptation, 1967, and British Academy Award for best script, New York Film Critics Award, and Writers Guild of America Award, all 1968, all for *The Graduate;* Screen Writers Guild Award, 1972, for *What's Up, Doc?;* Academy Award nomination for best director (with Warren Beatty), 1978, for *Heaven Can Wait.*

CREDITS:

STAGE APPEARANCES

Fortress of Glass, Circle in the Square, New York City, 1952.
Artie, *House of Blue Leaves,* Pasadena Playhouse, Pasadena, CA, 1987.
Wylie, *Kingfish,* Los Angeles Theatre Center, Los Angeles, 1988, then Public Theatre, New York City, 1988.

Also appeared in *Bernardine,* New York City, 1952; *The Premise* (improvisation), Off-Broadway, 1961-62.

MAJOR TOURS

(Stage debut) A Day son, *Life With Father,* U.S. cities, 1948.
No Time for Sergeants, U.S. cities, 1956.

FILM APPEARANCES

(Film debut) T. R. Kingston, *The Troublemaker,* Janus, 1964.
Hotel clerk, *The Graduate,* Embassy, 1967.
Stockade commandant, *The Secret War of Harry Frigg,* Universal, 1968.
Lieutenant Colonel Korn, *Catch 22,* Filmways, 1970.
Larry Tyne, *Taking Off,* Universal, 1971.
Oliver Farnsworth, *The Man Who Fell to Earth,* Cinema V, 1976.
The escort, *Heaven Can Wait,* Paramount, 1978.
Art Kopple, *Old Boyfriends,* Avco-Embassy, 1979.
Father Sandstone, *First Family,* Warner Bros., 1980.
Jack Dawn, *Gloria,* Columbia, 1980.
Mr. Leech, *Eating Raoul,* Twentieth Century-Fox, 1982.
Preston, "Rigoletto" segment, *Aria,* Virgin Vision, 1987.
Lloyd Stoole, *Rude Awakening,* Orion, 1989.
Defending Your Life, Warner Bros., 1991.

Also appeared in *Is There Sex After Death?,* 1971, and the short film *The Absent-Minded Waiter,* 1979.

FILM DIRECTOR

(With Warren Beatty) *Heaven Can Wait,* Paramount, 1978.
First Family, Warner Bros., 1980.

TELEVISION APPEARANCES; EPISODIC

The George Segal Show, NBC, 1974.
Host, *That Was the Year That Was,* NBC, 1976.

Also appeared as guest host, *The Dick Cavett Show,* 1970, and *Saturday Night Live,* NBC; appeared on *Falcon Crest,* CBS, and *Alfred Hitchcock Presents.*

TELEVISION APPEARANCES; SERIES

The Steve Allen Show, ABC, 1961.
That Was the Week That Was, NBC, 1964-65.
The New Show (series), NBC, 1984.

OTHER TELEVISION APPEARANCES

A Last Laugh at the '60s (special), ABC, 1970.

Also appeared as Felix, *The Owl and the Pussycat* (pilot), 1970.

TELEVISION WORK; SERIES

Story editor, *Get Smart!,* NBC, 1965-69.
Executive producer, *Captain Nice,* NBC, 1967.
Director, "Hunger Chic," *Trying Times,* KCET, 1989.

WRITINGS:

SCREENPLAYS

(With Theodore J. Flicker) *The Troublemaker,* Janus, 1964.

(With Calder Willingham) *The Graduate* (adapted from Charles Webb's novel of the same title), Embassy, 1967.

Candy (adapted from Terry Southern and Mason Hoffenberg's novel of the same title), Cinerama, 1968.

Catch 22 (adapted from Joseph Heller's novel of the same title), Filmways, 1970.

The Owl and the Pussycat (adapted from a play by Bill Manhoff), Columbia, 1970.

Taking Off, Universal, 1971.

(With David Newman and Robert Benton) *What's Up, Doc?,* Warner Bros., 1972.

The Day of the Dolphin (based on the novel by Robert Merle), Avco-Embassy, 1973.

First Family, Warner Bros., 1980.

Protocol, Warner Bros., 1984.

TELEVISION SCRIPTS

The Steve Allen Show, ABC, 1961.

(With Bob Howard) *The Bean Show,* CBS, 1964.

That Was the Week That Was, NBC, 1964-65.

Get Smart!, NBC, 1965-69.

Captain Nice, NBC, 1967.

Quark, NBC, 1978.

The New Show, NBC, 1984.

Also writer for *The Garry Moore Show,* 1958-67, and *Alfred Hitchcock Presents,* 1985.

OTHER SOURCES:

BOOKS

Dictionary of Literary Biography, Volume 26: *American Screenwriters,* Gale, 1984.

PERIODICALS

American Film, December, 1980.

Focus on Film, summer, 1972.

Life, June 12, 1970.

New York Times Magazine, July 19, 1970.

*   *   *

HERMAN, Pee-Wee 1952-
(Paul Reubens)

PERSONAL: Original surname Rubenfeld; born in 1952 in Peekskill, NY; son of Milton and Judy Rubenfeld (proprietors of a retail lamp store). *Education:* Studied acting at Northwestern University summer program for gifted high school students; attended Boston University and California Institute of the Arts.

ADDRESSES: Agent—Agency for the Performing Arts, 9000 Sunset Blvd., Suite 1200, Los Angeles, CA 90069.

CAREER: Comedian and actor. Created Pee-Wee Herman character in the late 1970s; performed, with Charlotte McGinnis, in vaudeville-style act called the Hilarious Betty and Eddie in clubs; performed with The Groundlings, a Los Angeles improvisational theatre group; has done voice-overs for cartoon shows and animated features; also worked variously as a busboy, brush salesman, and cook.

AWARDS, HONORS: Elmer Award, *Harvard Lampoon,* 1985, for lifetime achievement in comedy; Emmy Award nominations, best children's series, best performer in a children's series, best directing in a children's series (with John Paragon), and Emmy Awards, achievement in art direction, set decoration and scenic design (with others), and achievement in graphics and title design, all 1991, for *Pee-Wee's Playhouse.*

CREDITS:

STAGE APPEARANCES

Pee-Wee Herman, *The Pee-Wee Herman Show,* Groundling Theater, Los Angeles, CA, 1980, then Roxy Theater.

FILM APPEARANCES; UNDER NAME PAUL REUBENS

(Film debut) Waiter, *The Blues Brothers,* Universal, 1980.

Howie Hamburger, *Cheech and Chong's Nice Dreams* (also known as *Nice Dreams*), Columbia, 1981.

Pandemonium (also known as *Thursday the Twelfth*), Metro-Goldwyn-Mayer, 1981.

Paul Mall and voice of Max, *Flight of the Navigator,* Buena Vista, 1986.

FILM APPEARANCES; UNDER NAME PEE-WEE HERMAN

Desk clerk, *Cheech and Chong's Next Movie* (also known as *High Encounters [of the Ultimate Kind]*), Universal, 1980.

Meatballs, Part II, Tri-Star Pictures, 1984.

Pee-Wee's Big Adventure, Warner Brothers, 1985.

(And performer of song "Surfin' Bird") *Back to the Beach,* Paramount, 1987.

Big Top Pee-Wee, Paramount, 1988.

FILM WORK

Producer, *Big Top Pee-Wee,* Paramount, 1988.

TELEVISION APPEARANCES; SERIES

Pee-Wee's Playhouse, CBS, 1986—.

Also appeared as voice of Freaky Frankenstone, *The Flinstones.*

TELEVISION APPEARANCES; SPECIALS

Buckshot, ABC, 1980.

The Pee-Wee Herman Show, HBO, 1981.

Child educator, *Lily for President,* CBS, 1982.
Rock 'n' Wrestling Saturday Spectacular, CBS, 1985.
Wildest West Show of the Stars, CBS, 1986.
Pee-Wee's Playhouse, CBS, 1986.
A Special Evening of Pee-Wee's Playhouse, CBS, 1987.
It's Howdy Doody Time: A Forty-Year Celebration (also known as *Howdy Doody's Fortieth Birthday Special* and *Howdy Doody's Fortieth Anniversary*), syndicated, 1987.
Dolly (also known as *The Dolly Show*), ABC, 1987.
The American Comedy Awards (also known as *First Annual American Comedy Awards*), ABC, 1987.
Fourteenth Annual Daytime Emmy Awards, ABC, 1987.
Sixtieth Annual Academy Awards Presentation, ABC, 1988.
Pee-Wee's Playhouse Christmas Special, CBS, 1988.
Sesame Street Special, PBS, 1988.

TELEVISION APPEARANCES; EPISODIC

Guest, *The Late Show with Joan Rivers,* syndicated, 1987.

Also appeared on *The Gong Show; Late Night with David Letterman;* and *Saturday Night Live.*

TELEVISION WORK; UNDER NAME PAUL REUBENS

Executive producer, director (with John Paragon), title designer, and set decorator (with others), *Pee-Wee's Playhouse,* CBS, 1986—.

WRITINGS:

FILM SCREENPLAYS; UNDER NAME PAUL REUBENS

(With Phil Hartman and Michael Varhol) *Pee-Wee's Big Adventure,* Warner Brothers, 1985.
(With George McGrath) *Big Top Pee-Wee,* Paramount, 1988.

TELEVISION

Writer for Steve Martin's *Twilight Theater.*

OTHER SOURCES:

BOOKS

Contemporary Newsmakers, Volume 2, 1987.

PERIODICALS

Interview, December, 1983; September, 1985.
People, August 13, 1984; August 12, 1985.
Rolling Stone, February 12, 1987.
Us, August 26, 1985.*

*   *   *

HICKS, Barbara
CAREER: Actress.

CREDITS:

STAGE APPEARANCES

Mrs. Turner, *My Place,* Comedy Theatre, London, 1962.
Pauline, *Miss Pell Is Missing,* Criterion Theatre, London, 1962.
Agnes Webster, *Portrait of Murder,* Savoy Theatre, London, 1963.
Clara, *Hay Fever,* National Theatre Company, Old Vic Theatre, London, 1964.
Goodwife Ann Putnam, *The Crucible,* National Theatre Company, Old Vic Theatre, 1965.
Peasant woman, *Mother Courage and Her Children,* National Theatre Company, Old Vic Theatre, 1965.
Nurse to Miss Prue, *Love for Love,* National Theatre Company, Old Vic Theatre, 1965.
Feklusha, *The Storm,* National Theatre Company, Old Vic Theatre, 1966.
Miss Ramsden, *Man and Superman,* National Theatre Company, Olivier Theatre, London, 1981.
Miss Benita Mullet, *Tons of Money,* National Theatre Company, Lyttelton Theatre, London, 1986.
Yvonne, *A Small Family Business,* National Theatre Company, Olivier Theatre, 1987.

FILM APPEARANCES

Mrs. Thompson, *Fuss Over Feathers* (also known as *Conflict of Wings*), British Lion, 1954.
Panic in the Parlour (also known as *Sailor Beware!*), Distributors Corporation of America, 1957.
Hester, *Hell, Heaven, or Hoboken,* National Trade Association, 1958.
Miss Roberts, *Hand in Hand,* Columbia, 1960.
Woman, *His and Hers,* Eros, 1961.
Mrs. Stainton, *Murder She Said* (also known as *Meet Miss Marple*), Metro-Goldwyn-Mayer (MGM), 1961.
P.T. instructor, *Petticoat Pirates,* Warner Brothers/Pathe, 1961.
Margery, *A Matter of Who,* MGM, 1962.
Sergeant Merrified, *Operation Bullshine,* Seven Arts/Manhattan Films International, 1963.
Police secretary, *The Third Secret,* Twentieth Century-Fox, 1964.
Mrs. Duberly's Maid, *The Charge of the Light Brigade,* United Artists, 1968.
Miss Coke, *The Wildcats of St. Trinian's,* Enterprise, 1980.
Woman on waste ground, *Memoirs of a Survivor,* EMI, 1981.
Flewitt's secretary, *Evil Under the Sun,* Universal, 1982.
Miss Tinker, *Brittania Hospital,* Universal, 1982.
Mrs. Terrain, *Brazil,* Universal, 1985.
Stenographer, *Morons From Outer Space,* Universal, 1985.

Residents association lady, *We Think the World of You,* Film Four International/Cinecom International, 1988.

Ms. Clinch, *Wilt* (also known as *The Misadventures of Mr. Wilt*), Rank Film Distributors, 1989, released in the United States by Samuel Goldwyn, 1990.

The Witches, Warner Brothers, 1990.

TELEVISION APPEARANCES; MINI-SERIES

Miss Hartnell, "Murder at the Vicarage," *Agatha Christie's Miss Marple,* BBC, then *Mystery!,* PBS, 1989.

Cissy, *Oranges Are Not the Only Fruit,* BBC-2, 1990, then Arts and Entertainment, 1991.*

* * *

HILFERTY, Susan

PERSONAL: Education: Received B.F.A. in fashion design from Syracuse University; attended Yale University School of Drama.

CAREER: Costume and set designer. Instructor at Parsons School of Design, New York City.

CREDITS:

STAGE WORK; COSTUME DESIGNER, EXCEPT WHERE NOTED

The Palace of Amateurs, Plaza Theatre, Dallas, TX, 1983-84.

The Three Moscowteers, Goodman Theatre, Chicago, IL, 1983-84.

Mensch Meier, Manhattan Theatre Club, New York City, 1984.

All Night Long, McGinn/Cazale Theatre, New York City, 1984.

Coastal Disturbances, Second Stage, New York City, 1986-87, then Circle in the Square, New York City, 1987.

A Place with the Pigs, Yale Repertory Theatre, New Haven, CT, 1986, then in London and South Africa, 1988.

The Comedy of Errors, Lincoln Center Theatre Company, Vivian Beaumont Theatre, New York City, 1987.

Zero Positive, New York Shakespeare Festival, Public Theater, LuEsther Hall, New York City, 1988.

The Road to Mecca, Promenade Theatre, New York City, 1988.

Two Rooms, La Jolla Playhouse, Warren Theatre, San Diego, CA, 1988.

80 Days, La Jolla Playhouse, Mandell Weiss Theatre, 1988.

The Misanthrope, La Jolla Playhouse, 1989.

Down the Road, La Jolla Playhouse, Warren Theatre, 1989.

(And set designer) *My Children! My Africa!,* Market Theatre, Johannesburg, South Africa, 1989.

Set designer at Yale Repertory Theatre, 1979-80. Costume designer of productions at Berkeley Repertory Theatre, including *Twelfth Night* and *Tooth of Crime's Crow;* designer of *A Lesson from Aloes,* 1980, and *The Blood Knot,* 1980; costume designer of *Ubu* and *Ron Giovanni* for the Lincoln Center Theater Company; *The Tempest, The Matchmaker, Figaro Gets a Divorce,* and *Gillette* for the La Jolla Playhouse; *Approaching Zanzibar, Sister and Miss Lexie,* and *My Sister in This House* for the Second Stage; *Skirmishes* for the Manhattan Theatre Club; *Nothing Sacred* for the ACT in San Francisco, CA; *Twelfth Night* and *Tooth of Crime's Crow* for the Berkeley Repertory Theatre; and *Uncle Vanya* for Center Stage in Baltimore, MD. Has also worked on productions for the Goodman Theatre, Indiana Repertory Theatre, GeVa Theatre, Berkshire Theatre Festival, Whole Theatre Company, Roundabout Theatre Company, White Barn Theatre, and The Juilliard School; designer of productions for Alvin Ailey's dance company.

FILM WORK

Costume designer, *The Home of the Brave,* Cinecom, 1986.

OTHER SOURCES:

PERIODICALS

Theatre Crafts, January, 1990.*

* * *

HOLM, Ian   1931-

PERSONAL: Full name, Ian Holm Cuthbert; born September 12, 1931, in Goodmayes, Ilford, Essex, England; son of James Harvey (a doctor) and Jean Wilson (Holm) Cuthbert; married Lynn Mary Shaw, 1955 (divorced, 1965); married Sophie Baker, 1982; children: (first marriage) one son, three daughters; (second marriage) one son. *Education:* Studied for the stage at the Royal Academy of Dramatic Art. *Avocational interests:* Tennis, walking with a dog.

CAREER: Actor. Member of Shakespeare Memorial Theatre, 1954-55, later the Royal Shakespeare Company, 1958-67.

AWARDS, HONORS: Evening Standard Best Actor Award, 1965, for *Henry V;* Antoinette Perry Award, Best Supporting Actor, 1967, for *The Homecoming;* British Academy of Film and Television Arts Award, Best Supporting Actor, 1968, for *The Bofors Gun;* Academy Award nomination for Best Supporting Actor, British

Academy of Film and Television Arts Award for Best Supporting Actor, and Cannes International Film Festival Award for Best Supporting Actor, all 1981, all for *Chariots of Fire;* Award for Cable Excellence, National Cable Television Association, Best Actor in a Theatrical or Dramatic Special, 1988, for *The Browning Version;* Commander, Order of the British Empire.

CREDITS:

STAGE APPEARANCES

(Stage debut) Spear carrier, *Othello,* Shakespeare Memorial Theatre, Stratford-on-Avon, England, 1954.

Donalbain, *Macbeth,* Shakespeare Memorial Theatre, 1955.

Mutius, *Titus Andronicus,* Shakespeare Memorial Theatre, 1955.

(London debut) Rupert Bliss, *Love Affair,* Lyric (Hammersmith), 1956.

Peter, *Romeo and Juliet,* Shakespeare Memorial Theatre, 1958.

Sebastian, *Twelfth Night,* Shakespeare Memorial Theatre, 1958.

Verges, *Much Ado About Nothing,* Shakespeare Memorial Theatre, 1958.

Puck, *A Midsummer Night's Dream,* Shakespeare Memorial Theatre, 1959.

Fool, *King Lear,* Shakespeare Memorial Theatre, 1959.

Lorenzo, *The Merchant of Venice,* Shakespeare Memorial Theatre, 1960.

Gremio, *The Taming of the Shrew,* Shakespeare Memorial Theatre, 1960.

Trofimov, *The Cherry Orchard,* Aldwych Theatre, London, 1961.

First Judge, *Ondine,* Aldwych Theatre, 1961.

Mannoury, *The Devils,* Aldwych Theatre, 1961.

Little Monk, *Becket,* Aldwych Theatre, 1961.

Gremio, *The Taming of the Shrew,* Royal Shakespeare Company (RSC), Stratford-upon-Avon, 1962.

Claudio, *Measure for Measure,* RSC, 1962.

Puck, *A Midsummer Night's Dream,* RSC, 1962.

Troilus, *Troilus and Cressida,* Aldwych Theatre, 1962.

Ariel, *The Tempest,* RSC, 1963.

Richard, *Edward IV,* RSC, 1963.

Title role, *Richard III,* RSC, 1963.

Henry, Prince of Wales, *Henry IV, Part One,* RSC, 1964.

Henry, Prince of Wales, *Henry IV, Part Two,* RSC, 1964.

Title role, *Henry V,* RSC, 1964.

Richard, *Edward IV,* Aldwych Theatre, 1964.

Title role, *Richard III,* Aldwych Theatre, 1964.

Lenny, *The Homecoming,* Aldwych Theatre, 1965.

Malvolio, *Twelfth Night,* RSC, 1966.

Romeo, *Romeo and Juliet,* RSC, 1967.

(Broadway debut) Lenny, *The Homecoming,* Music Box Theatre, 1967.

Manfred, *The Friends,* Round House Theatre, London, 1970.

Nelson, *A Bequest to the Nation,* Haymarket Theatre, London, 1970.

Buddy, *Caravaggio Buddy,* Traverse Theatre Club, Edinburgh, Scotland, 1972.

Hatch, *The Sea,* Royal Court Theatre, London, 1973.

Dave, *Other People,* Hampstead Theatre, London, 1974.

Voinitsky, *Uncle Vanya,* Hampstead Theatre, 1979.

Appeared at Worthing Repertory Theatre, 1956, and in a reading of *The Investigator,* Aldwych Theatre, 1965.

MAJOR TOURS

Mutius, *Titus Andronicus,* European cities, 1956.

FILM APPEARANCES

Flynn, *The Bofors Gun,* Universal, 1968.

Grubeshov, *The Fixer,* Metro-Goldwyn-Mayer (MGM), 1968.

Puck, *A Midsummer Night's Dream,* Eagle, 1969.

President Poincare, *Oh! What a Lovely War,* Paramount, 1969.

Yakovlev, *Nicholas and Alexandra,* Columbia, 1971.

David Riccio, *Mary, Queen of Scots,* Universal, 1971.

Martin Lynch-Gibbon, *A Severed Head,* Columbia, 1971.

Lenny, *The Homecoming,* American Film Theatre, 1971.

George Buckle, *Young Winston,* Columbia, 1972.

Nicholas Porter, *Juggernaut,* United Artists (UA), 1974.

King John, *Robin and Marian,* Columbia, 1976.

Mohammed, *Shout at the Devil,* American International, 1976.

El Krim, *March or Die,* Columbia, 1977.

Ash, *Alien,* Twentieth Century-Fox, 1979.

Sam Mussabini, *Chariots of Fire,* Twentieth Century-Fox, 1981.

Napoleon, *Time Bandits,* Avco Embassy, 1981.

Ernest, *The Return of the Soldier,* Twentieth Century-Fox, 1983.

Captain Phillippe D'Arnot, *Greystoke: The Legend of Tarzan, Lord of the Apes,* Warner Bros., 1984.

Ben Singleton, *Laughter House* (also known as *Singleton's Pluck*), Film Four International, 1984.

Kurtzmann, *Brazil,* Universal, 1985.

Desmond Cussen, *Dance With a Stranger,* Twentieth Century-Fox, 1985.

Reverend Charles Dodgson, *Dreamchild,* Universal, 1985.

Stanley Pilborough, *Wetherby,* MGM/UA, 1985.

Ken, *Another Woman,* Orion, 1988.

Captain Fluellen, *Henry V,* Samuel Goldwyn, 1989.

Polonius, *Hamlet,* Warner Bros., 1990.

TELEVISION APPEARANCES; MOVIES

Zerah, *Jesus of Nazareth,* NBC, 1977.

Dural, *The Man in the Iron Mask,* NBC, 1977.

Gatekeeper, *The Thief of Baghdad,* NBC, 1978.
Thenardier, *Les Miserables,* CBS, 1978.
Himmelstoss, *All Quiet on the Western Front,* CBS, 1979.
J. Bruce Ismay, *S.O.S. Titanic,* ABC, 1979.
Dr. Joseph Goebbels, *Inside the Third Reich,* ABC, 1982.
Bernard Samson, *Game, Set and Match,* Granada TV, 1988, then *Mystery Theatre,* PBS, 1989.

TELEVISION APPEARANCES; SPECIALS

Narrator, *Arena: Bette Davis—The Benevolent Volcano,* BBC, 1983.
The Browning Version, Arts & Entertainment, 1987.
Title role, *The Tailor of Gloucester,* ITV, 1989, then *Great Performances,* KCET, 1990.
Narrator, *Stalin* (documentary), ITV, 1990.
Doctor, "Uncle Vanya," *Great Performances,* BBC/WNET, 1991.

Also appeared as Eustace Edgehill, *Mr. and Mrs. Edgehill,* 1985, and Hercule Poirot, *Murder by the Book.*

OTHER TELEVISION APPEARANCES

"Draw Me a Pear," *The Dick Van Dyke Show* (episode), CBS, 1965.
Heinrich Himmler, *Holocaust* (mini-series), NBC, 1978.
"The Stuff of Madness," *Mistress of Suspense* (episode), ITV, 1990.

Also appeared in *The Lost Boys,* 1979, *We, The Accused,* 1980, *The Bell,* 1981, and *Strike,* 1981; appeared as narrator, *Battle for the Falklands,* and Wedderburn, *The Rebel.*

RADIO APPEARANCES

Jasper, "The Mystery of Edwin Drood," *Classic Serial,* Radio 4, 1990.

SIDELIGHTS: Favorite roles: Richard III, Puck in *A Midsummer Night's Dream,* and Gremio in *The Taming of the Shrew.* *

*   *   *

HONG, James   1929(?)-

PERSONAL: Born c. 1929 in Minneapolis, MN. *Education:* Attended University of Minnesota—Twin Cities; received bachelor of engineering degree from University of Southern California; trained for the stage at Jeff Corey's School of Acting; studied acting at the Professional Theatre Workshop.

ADDRESSES: Agent—Guy Lee, Bessie Loo Agency, 8235 Santa Monica Blvd., Suite 202, Los Angeles, CA 90046.

CAREER: Actor. North Star Entertainment, Inc. (film production company), president, 1989—; East West Play-

ers (Asian American repertory company), Los Angeles, CA, co-founder. Has appeared in television commercials for several companies and products, including American Express, Safeway, Crest, and Pacific Telephone. Member of advisory commission, State of California Motion Picture Council. Formerly worked as an engineer for the Los Angeles Road Department and as a comedian. *Military service:* Served in the armed forces; served as head of live entertainment at Camp Rucker, AL, and at Ft. McClellan.

MEMBER: Screen Actors' Guild (member, board of directors), Association of Asian/Pacific American Artists (past president and charter member).

CREDITS:

FILM APPEARANCES

(Film debut) Fifth brother, *Love Is a Many-Splendored Thing,* Twentieth Century-Fox, 1955.
Communist soldier, *Soldier of Fortune,* Twentieth Century-Fox, 1955.
Young communist guard, *Blood Alley,* Batjac, 1955.
Policeman, *Flight to Hong Kong,* United Artists (UA), 1956.
Hep Cat, *Hell on Frisco Bay,* Warner Bros., 1956.
Charlie, *China Gate,* Twentieth Century-Fox, 1957.
Nationalist officer, *Seventh Sin,* Metro-Goldwyn-Mayer (MGM), 1957.
Japanese draftsman, *Blood and Steel,* Twentieth Century-Fox, 1959.
General, *Never So Few,* MGM, 1959.
Headwaiter, *Flower Drum Song,* Universal, 1961.
Dr. Yang, *The Satan Bug,* UA, 1965.
Ho Lee, *Destination Inner Space,* Magna, 1966.
Price Phanong, *One Spy Too Many,* MGM, 1966.
Victor Shu, *The Sand Pebbles,* Twentieth Century-Fox, 1966.
Sam Archibald, *The Bamboo Saucer,* NTA, 1966.
Computer scientist, *Colossus: The Forbin Project* (also known as *The Forbin Project* and *Colossus, 1980*), Universal, 1969.
Ti Chong, *The Hawaiians* (also known as *Master of the Islands*), UA, 1970.
David Tao, *The Carey Treatment,* MGM, 1972.
Khan, *Chinatown,* Paramount, 1974.
Wong, *Bound for Glory,* UA, 1976.
Swens, *The World's Greatest Lover,* Twentieth Century-Fox, 1977.
Captain Oldman, *Go Tell the Spartans,* Avco Embassy, 1978.
Bing Wong, *The In-Laws,* Warner Bros., 1979.
Japanese General, *Airplane!,* Paramount, 1980.
Oriental, *So Fine,* Warner Bros., 1981.
Coroner Wong, *True Confessions,* UA, 1981.

Chew, *Blade Runner,* Warner Bros., 1982.

Kwan, *Yes, Giorgio,* UA, 1982.

Grocer, *Breathless,* Orion, 1983.

General Tran, *Missing in Action,* Cannon, 1984.

Miyashima, *Ninja III—The Domination,* MGM-UA-Cannon, 1984.

David Lo Pan, *Big Trouble in Little China,* Twentieth Century-Fox, 1986.

Dr. Hong, *The Golden Child,* Paramount, 1986.

Snotty, *Revenge of the Nerds II: Nerds in Paradise,* Twentieth Century-Fox, 1987.

Shin, *Black Widow,* Twentieth Century-Fox, 1987.

Gung Tu, *China Girl,* Great American Vestron, 1987.

Kwo, *Vice Versa,* Columbia, 1988.

Quan, *Tango and Cash,* Warner Bros., 1989.

Tony Yang, Sr., *The Jitters,* Gaga Communications, 1989.

Tax Season, Prism, 1989.

Dr. Po, *The Vineyard,* New World, 1989 (also see below).

Khan, *The Two Jakes,* Paramount, 1990.

The Perfect Weapon, Paramount, 1991.

Also appeared in *The Hour of the Bath,* 1961; *In a Foreign Quarter,* 1962; *The Two-Headed Man,* 1972; *Black-Belt Brother,* 1973; *Double Trouble,* 1975; appeared as Detective Stoner, *Caged Fury* (also see below), 1990; and appeared in *Shadowzone, Too Much Sun, Crimelord, Missing Pieces, Mystery Date,* and *Joker's Wild,* all 1990.

FILM WORK

Director, *The Vineyard,* New World, 1989.

Also worked as associate producer, *Caged Fury,* 1990; director, *The Girl Next Door.*

TELEVISION APPEARANCES; SERIES

Barry Chan, *The New Adventures of Charlie Chan,* syndicated, 1957-58.

Duck Ho Cho, *Mickey Spillane's Mike Hammer,* CBS, 1984-85.

TELEVISION APPEARANCES; PILOTS

Hsiang, *Kung Fu,* ABC, 1972.

Prior, *Judge Dee and the Monastery Murders,* ABC, 1974.

Clarence Woo, *Winner Take All,* CBS, 1977.

Wang Theron, *Mandrake,* NBC, 1979.

Desk clerk, *The Hustler of Muscle Beach,* ABC, 1980.

Chinese grocer employing Michael, *Brothers,* CBS, 1980.

Yutong, *Cannon: The Return of Frank Cannon,* CBS, 1980.

Benson Liu, *Inspector Perez,* NBC, 1983.

Mr. Key, *Blade in Hong Kong,* CBS, 1985.

Also appeared in *Rocket Boy,* 1984; appeared as the reverend, *Club Fed,* 1989; and appeared in *Tequila and Bonner,* 1991.

TELEVISION APPEARANCES; EPISODIC

Lum Chen, *Tombstone Territory,* ABC, c. 1958.

Have Gun—Will Travel, CBS, 1961.

Perry Mason, CBS, 1962.

The Lloyd Bridges Show, CBS, 1962.

Ensign O'Toole, NBC, 1962.

Day in Court, ABC, 1963.

Li Kwan, *The Outer Limits,* ABC, 1963.

Seventy-Seven Sunset Strip, ABC, 1963.

Kentucky Jones, NBC, 1964.

Slattery's People, CBS, 1964.

I Spy, NBC, 1965.

Ben Casey, ABC, 1965.

The Man from U.N.C.L.E., NBC, 1965.

The FBI, ABC, 1965.

The Fugitive, ABC, 1965.

The Donna Reed Show, ABC, 1965.

The Wackiest Ship in the Army, NBC, 1965.

I Dream of Jeannie, NBC, 1965.

Anna and the King, CBS, 1972.

All in the Family, CBS, 1975.

Frank Chen, *Jigsaw John,* NBC, 1976.

Wang, *Switch,* CDS, 1977-78.

Taxi, ABC, 1979.

Bring 'em Back Alive, CBS, c. 1983.

Chang, *Hunter,* NBC, 1985.

General Chow, *The A-Team,* NBC, 1985.

Mr. Nguyen, *Cagney and Lacey,* CBS, 1985.

Lee Wenying, *MacGyver,* ABC, 1986.

Ralph Lee, *Crazy Like a Fox,* CBS, 1986.

Thomas Ping, *Who's the Boss?,* ABC, 1986.

Commissioner Chu, *MacGyver,* ABC, 1987.

Han Quing, *Magnum P.I.,* CBS, 1987.

Quang, *Tour of Duty,* CBS, 1987.

Tanaka, *Miami Vice,* NBC, 1987.

Vin Mong, *Stingray,* NBC, 1987.

Mr. Luc, *Outlaws,* CBS, 1987.

Chang Shin Li, *Beauty and the Beast,* CBS, 1988.

Colonel Trang, *Tour of Duty,* CBS, 1988.

Sirit Bansari, *The Equalizer,* CBS, 1988.

Hiram, *Jake and the Fatman,* CBS, 1989.

Jimmie Twan, *Tour of Duty,* CBS, 1989.

Mr. Chieko, *Booker,* Fox, 1990.

Nasty Boys, NBC, 1990.

Also appeared in episodes of many other series, including *Square Cop,* 1962; *Wagon Train,* 1962; *This Is the Life,* 1963; *The Mickey Rooney Show,* 1964; appeared in *Dragnet, Bonanza, Sky King, Hart to Hart, Charlie's Angels, Hardy Boys, Maude, The Bionic Woman, Wonder Woman, Starsky and Hutch, The Streets of San Francisco, The Rockford Files, The Rookies, S.W.A.T., Harry O, Baretta, Khan, McMillan and Wife, Rhoda, Barnaby Jones, The Young Lawyers, Family Affair, The Bob Newhart*

Show, Kung Fu, Ironside, Mission: Impossible, SFX, The Bill Cosby Show, Fantasy Island, Dallas, The Dukes of Hazzard, Lou Grant, Soap, Diff 'rent Strokes, Code Red, T. J. Hooker, The Fall Guy, Airwolf, It's a Living, Double Dare, St. Elsewhere, Here's Lucy, Hawaii Five-0, Dynasty, Falcon Crest, Gideon Oliver, and *General Hospital.*

TELEVISION APPEARANCES; MOVIES

Major Thon, *The Forgotten Man,* ABC, 1971.
Police surgeon, *A Tattered Web,* CBS, 1971.
Vanished, NBC, 1971.
Supervisor, *Pueblo,* CBS, 1973.
Dr. Wilde, *Sunshine,* CBS, 1973.
U Thant, *The Missiles of October,* ABC, 1974.
Larry Lee, *Panic in Echo Park,* NBC, 1977.
Quan Dong, *My Husband Is Missing* (also known as *The Reach of Love*), NBC, 1978.
Japanese man, *Last of the Good Guys,* CBS, 1978.
Ho Chin, *Dr. Scorpion,* ABC, 1978.
Nguyen, *When Hell Was in Session,* NBC, 1979.
Old man, *The Letter,* ABC, 1982.
Professor Chen, *China Rose,* CBS, 1983.
Mr. Li, *Leap of Faith,* CBS, 1988.
Dr. Dentworth, *The Karen Carpenter Story,* CBS, 1989.
Colonel Chan, *The Brotherhood of the Rose,* NBC, 1989.
Inspector Quang, *Last Flight Out,* NBC, 1990.

Also appeared in *Earth II,* 1970; appeared as Mr. Yu, *Harry's Hong Kong,* 1987; and appeared in *Caring.*

OTHER TELEVISION APPEARANCES

CBS Playhouse (special), CBS, 1966.
Father, *Jade Snow* (special), PBS, 1976.
Phags-Pa, *Marco Polo* (mini-series), NBC, 1982.

Also appeared in *Paper Angels,* 1985; appeared as Reverend Sung and Reverend Jimmy Tuin, *Camp California,* 1989; Mark Chu, *Bamboo Cross;* Shimako, *CBS Playhouse 90;* Hyashi, *Navy Log;* Kilo, *Man Called "X";* Tuen, *Faith Till Death;* Sammy and Lin Quon, *Crusaders;* restaurant owner, *Millionaire Series;* Kim, *The First 100 Days;* soldier, *Cavalry in China;* Lee, *Cavalcade Theatre;* Corporal Ikura, *Yellow Bellow;* appeared in *The Cold Touch* and two *NBC Matinee* specials, as Kim, "The Lighted Window" and Indonesian rebel, "Daughter of Mata Hari."

TELEVISION WORK

Director, *Year of the Dog* (special; also see below), NBC, 1970.

STAGE APPEARANCES

Wigmaker and Bandit, *Rashomon,* East West Players, Los Angeles, 1965 (also see below).
Year of the Dragon, East West Players, 1975.

STAGE WORK

Producer, *Rashomon,* East West Players, 1965.

WRITINGS:

Year of the Dog (television special), NBC, 1970.
(With others) *The Vineyard* (screenplay), New World Pictures, 1989.

Also collaborator on screenplays *Perfect Match,* 1968, *Connections,* 1972, and *The Girls Next Door,* 1977.

*   *   *

HOOKS, Kevin   1958-

PERSONAL: Born September 19, 1958, in Philadelphia, PA; son of Robert Hooks (an actor and director).

CAREER: Actor and director.

CREDITS:

FILM APPEARANCES

David Lee Morgan, *Sounder,* Twentieth Century-Fox, 1972.
Aaron, *Aaron Loves Angela,* Paramount, 1975.
Tiger, *A Hero Ain't Nothin' but a Sandwich,* New World, 1977.
Jasper MacGruder, *Take Down,* Buena Vista, 1979.
Duane, *Innerspace,* Warner Bros., 1987.

STAGE APPEARANCES

Lance Corporal Promus, *The Hooch,* Louis Abrons Arts for Living Center, 1984.
Nick, *Jonah and the Wonder Dog,* Negro Ensemble Company, 1986.

TELEVISION APPEARANCES; SERIES

Morris Thorpe, *The White Shadow,* CBS, 1978-81.
Mayor Carl Burke, *He's the Mayor,* ABC, 1986.

TELEVISION APPEARANCES; PILOTS

Junior, *Just an Old Sweet Song,* CBS, 1976.
Nate Simmons, Jr., *Down Home,* CBS, 1978.
Eddie Holmes, *For Members Only,* CBS, 1983.

TELEVISION APPEARANCES; MOVIES

Hoover Sissle, *The Greatest Thing That Almost Happened,* CBS, 1977.
Nat Blake, *Can You Hear the Laughter? The Story of Freddie Prinze,* CBS, 1979.

Also appeared in *Friendly Fire,* 1979.

OTHER TELEVISION APPEARANCES

Young Emmett, *Backstairs at the White House* (miniseries), NBC, 1979.
Himself, *Celebrity Challenge of the Sexes 5* (special), CBS, 1980.

TELEVISION DIRECTOR; EPISODIC

A Year in the Life, NBC, 1987.
21 Jump Street, Fox, 1988.
China Beach, ABC, 1988.
Almost Grown, CBS, 1989.
Midnight Caller, NBC, 1989.
Young Riders, ABC, 1989-90.
Doogie Howser, MD, ABC, 1990.
Equal Justice, ABC, 1990.

Also directed episodes of *Teen Father,* 1986; *Heart of the City,* 1986; *Mariah,* 1987; *Once a Hero,* 1987; *Probe,* 1988; *Fine Romance,* 1989; and *Nightingales,* 1989.

OTHER TELEVISION WORK; DIRECTOR

(With others) *St. Elsewhere,* NBC, 1982.
Roots: The Gift (movie), ABC, 1988.

Also codirected *Cutter to Houston* (series), 1983; directed *Class Act: A Teacher's Story* (special), 1987, "The Pass," *Vietnam War Story,* 1987, *Heat Wave* (movie), 1990, and *Home Sweet Homeless* (special).*

*   *   *

HOWELLS, Ursula   1922-

PERSONAL: Born September 17, 1922, in London, England; daughter of Herbert Norman and Dorothy Eveline (Goozee) Howells; married James Davy Dodd (divorced); married Anthony Pelissier. *Education:* Studied for the theatre with Anthony Hawtrey at the Dundee Repertory Theatre, Dundee, Scotland. *Avocational interests:* Reading, gardening, dressmaking.

ADDRESSES: Manager—International Creative Management Ltd., 388 Oxford St., London W1, England.

CAREER: Actress. Company member, Dundee Repertory Theatre, Dundee, Scotland, 1939-42, and Oxford Repertory Company, Oxford, U.K., 1942-44.

CREDITS:

STAGE APPEARANCES

(Stage debut) Joan Greenleaf, *Bird in Hand,* Dundee Repertory Theatre, Dundee, Scotland, 1939.
(London debut) Henrietta Turnbull, *Quality Street,* Embassy Theatre, 1945.
Peggy McNab, *Father Malachy's Miracle,* Embassy Theatre, 1945.

Judith Drave, *No Room at the Inn,* Embassy Theatre, 1945.
Elizabeth Wimpole, *Fit for Heroes,* Whitehall Theatre, London, 1945.
Judy Dawson, *Frieda,* Westminster Theatre, London, 1946.
Gloria Palfrey, *Peace Comes to Peckham,* Embassy Theatre, 1946.
Shirley Marsh, *Away from It All,* Embassy Theatre, 1946.
Anne Tower, *Jane,* Aldwych Theatre, London, 1947.
Nancy Tennant, *Honour and Obey,* Saville Theatre, London, 1947.
Kay Llewellyn, *Humoresque,* Q Theatre, London, 1948.
Fiona Spender, *Master of Arts,* Strand Theatre, London, 1949.
Marguerite, *Madam Tic-Tac,* Winter Garden Theatre, London, 1950.
(Broadway debut) Miss Smith, *Springtime for Henry,* John Golden Theatre, 1951.
Leopoldine von Schellendorffer, *High Balcony,* Embassy Theatre, 1952.
Mary Dallas, *Night of the Fourth,* King's Theatre, Edinburgh, Scotland, 1953.
Mary Ashbury, *The Big Killing,* Princes Theatre, London, 1962.
Katie Newton, *The Gimmick,* Gaiety Theatre, Dublin, Ireland, then Criterion Theatre, London, both 1962.
Leonora, *Doctors of Philosophy,* New Arts Theatre, London, 1962.
Margaret Conyngham, *Shout for Life* (originally titled *Sergeant Dower Must Die*), Vaudeville Theatre, London, 1963.
Leila, *Return Ticket,* Duchess Theatre, London, 1965.
Cynthia Randolph, *Dear Octopus,* Haymarket Theatre, London, 1967.
Eleanor, *The Lion in Winter,* Thorndike Theatre, Leatherhead, England, 1969.
Ruth, *Blithe Spirit,* Globe Theatre, London, 1970.
Clare, *Two and Two Make Sex,* Cambridge Theatre, London, 1974.

MAJOR TOURS

Margaret Conyngham, *Sergeant Dower Must Die,* U.K. cities, 1963.

FILM APPEARANCES

(Film debut) Harriet Marshall, *Flesh and Blood,* British Lion, 1951.
Peggy, *The Horse's Mouth* (also known as *The Oracle*), General Films Distributors, 1953.
Hon. Ursula, *I Believe in You,* Universal, 1953.
Brenda Lucas, *The Gilded Cage,* Eros, 1954.
Pam, *The Weak and the Wicked,* Associated British Films/Allied Artists, 1954.

Miss Pargiter, *The Constant Husband,* British Lion, 1955.

Antonia Pitt, *They Can't Hang Me,* Independent Film Distributors/British Lion, 1955.

Handcuffs, London, Eros, 1955.

Pat Anstey, *Keep It Clean,* Eros, 1956.

Mary Dennis, *Track the Man Down,* Republic, 1956.

Lucille Ainsworth, *Account Rendered,* R.F.D. Productions, 1957.

Eileen, *The Fighting Wildcats* (also known as *West of Suez*), Republic, 1957.

Mrs. Elliot, *The Third Key,* (also known as *The Long Arm*), Rank, 1957.

Louise, *Two Letter Alibi,* British Lion, 1962.

Joanna Druten, *80,000 Suspects,* Rank, 1963.

Madame Perrault, *The Sicilians,* Butchers Film Service, 1964.

Deirdre, *Dr. Terror's House of Horrors,* Regal Films, 1965.

Estelle, *Assignment K,* Columbia, 1968.

Miss Chambers, *Torture Garden,* Columbia, 1968.

Maggie Thwaites, *Crossplot,* United Artists, 1969.

Mumsy, *Mumsy, Nanny, Sonny, and Girly* (also known as *Girly*), Cinerama, 1970.

May Swift, *Time after Time,* BBC-TV/Arts & Entertainment/Australian Broadcasting, 1985.

TELEVISION APPEARANCES

Case of the Frightened Lady, BBC, 1948.

Frances, *The Forsyte Saga* (mini-series), BBC, then *Masterpiece Theatre,* PBS, 1969-70.

Barbara Mossman, *Father Dear Father* (series), syndicated, 1977.

Mrs. Gradgrind, "Hard Times," *Great Performances* (special), PBS, 1977.

Headmistress, *The Cold Room* (movie), HBO, 1984.

Also appeared in *Cousin Bette,* 1972; *Bon Voyage,* 1987; *A Murder Is Announced,* 1987; *The Kraft Mystery Theatre,* NBC; *The Small Back Room; A Woman Comes Home; For Services Rendered; Mine Own Executioner;* and *The Cocktail Party.*

SIDELIGHTS: Favorite roles: Celia in *The Cocktail Party,* Eleanor in *The Lion in Winter,* and Nina in *The Seagull.**

*   *   *

HULCE, Thomas 1953-
(Tom Hulce)

PERSONAL: Born December 6, 1953, in Whitewater, WI (some sources say Plymouth, MI). *Education:* Attended North Carolina School of the Arts.

ADDRESSES: Agent—Brian Lourd, Creative Artists Agency, 9830 Wilshire Blvd., Beverly Hills, CA 90212.

Manager—Bill Treusch Associates, 853 Seventh Ave., New York, NY 10019.

CAREER: Actor and director.

AWARDS, HONORS: Academy Award nomination and Donatello Award, both best actor, 1984, for *Amadeus;* Golden Globe Award nomination, best actor in a mini-series or motion picture, 1990, for *Murder in Mississippi.*

CREDITS:

STAGE APPEARANCES

(Broadway debut) Alan Strang, *Equus,* Plymouth Theatre, 1975.

Bert, *A Memory of Two Mondays,* Phoenix Theatre, The Playhouse, New York City, 1976.

Candida, Hartford Stage Company, Hartford, CT, 1977.

Innocent Thoughts and Harmless Intentions, Playwrights Horizons, New York City, 1977.

Octavius Caesar, *Julius Caesar,* Brooklyn Academy of Music, LePercq Space, Brooklyn, NY, 1978.

Summerfolk, Long Wharf Theatre, New Haven, CT, 1979.

The Sea Gull, Manitoba Theatre Center, Winnipeg, Manitoba, 1980.

Romeo and Juliet, Long Wharf Theatre, 1981.

Sanford Putnam, *Twelve Dreams,* New York Shakespeare Festival, Public Theatre, New York City, 1982.

Daniel Rocket/"Snood," *The Rise and Rise of Daniel Rocket,* Playwrights Horizons, 1982.

Ned Weeks, *The Normal Heart,* Long Wharf Theatre, New Haven, CT, 1986.

(As Tom Hulce) Lewis Carroll, *Haddock's Eyes,* Music-Theatre Group, St. Clements Church Theatre, New York City, 1987.

Drew Paley, *Eastern Standard,* Seattle Repertory Theatre, Seattle, WA, 1988.

Bazarov, *Nothing Sacred,* Mark Taper Forum, Los Angeles, 1988.

Lawyer, *A Few Good Men,* Music Box Theatre, New York City, 1990.

Also appeared with the Milwaukee Repertory Theatre, Milwaukee, WI, 1978-79; appeared in *The Glass Menagerie,* Chautauqua, NY, 1985.

STAGE WORK

Directed *Sleep around Town,* Playwrights Horizons, New York City.

FILM APPEARANCES

(Film debut) Hanley, *9/30/55,* Universal, 1977.

Larry "Pinto" Kroger, *National Lampoon's Animal House,* Universal, 1978.

Artie Shoemaker, *Those Lips, Those Eyes,* United Artists, 1980.

(As Tom Hulce) Wolfgang Amadeus Mozart, *Amadeus,* Orion, 1984.

Jonathan, *Echo Park,* Atlantic, 1986.

C. C. Drood, *Slamdance,* Island/Zenith, 1987.

Title role, *Shadowman,* Hungry Eye, 1988.

Dominick Luciano, *Dominick and Eugene,* Orion, 1988.

Larry, *Parenthood,* Universal, 1989.

Gary Wallace, *Black Rainbow,* Palace/Goldcrest, 1989.

(As Tom Hulce) *The Inner Circle,* Columbia, 1991.

TELEVISION APPEARANCES; SPECIALS

Edward Whitman, *Song of Myself,* CBS, 1976.

Freddie Putnam, *Emily, Emily,* NBC, 1977.

The National AIDS Awareness Test: What Do You Know about Acquired Immune Deficiency Syndrome?, syndicated, 1987.

OTHER TELEVISION APPEARANCES

Young Frank, "Forget-Me-Not-Lane," *Theatre in America* (episode), PBS, 1975.

The Adams Chronicles (mini-series), PBS, 1976.

Title role, "The Rise and Rise of Daniel Rocket," *American Playhouse* (episode), PBS, 1986.

Quinn, "John Henry," *Shelley Duvall's Tall Tales and Legends,* Showtime, 1987.

(As Tom Hulce) Mickey Schwerner, *Murder in Mississippi* (movie), NBC, 1990.

OTHER SOURCES:

PERIODICALS

Daily News, March 20, 1988.

Hollywood Reporter, October 3, 1988.*

*   *   *

HULCE, Tom
   See HULCE, Thomas

*   *   *

HUNT, Linda   1945-

PERSONAL: Born April 2, 1945, in Morristown, NJ. *Education:* Attended Interlochen Arts Academy; trained for the stage at Goodman Theatre and School of Drama.

ADDRESSES: Agent—Cynthia Wilkerson, Triad Artists, 10100 Santa Monica Blvd., 16th Floor, Los Angeles, CA 90067.

CAREER: Actress.

MEMBER: Actors' Equity Association, Screen Actors Guild.

AWARDS, HONORS: Academy Award, best supporting actress, 1983, for *The Year of Living Dangerously;* Antoinette Perry Award nomination, best actress in a play, 1984, for *End of the World.*

CREDITS:

STAGE APPEARANCES

Player Queen, *Hamlet,* New York Shakespeare Festival (NYSF), Delacorte Theatre, New York City, 1972.

The Soldier's Tale and *The Knight of the Burning Pestle* (double-bill), Long Wharf Theatre, New Haven, CT, 1974.

Hamlet, Center Theatre Group, Mark Taper Forum, Los Angeles, 1974.

(Off-Broadway debut) Constantine, *Down by the River Where Waterlilies Are Disfigured Every Day,* Circle Repertory Company, Circle Repertory Theatre, New York City, 1975.

(Broadway debut) Norah, *Ah, Wilderness!,* Circle in the Square, New York City, 1975.

The Rose Tattoo, Long Wharf Theatre, 1977.

Five Finger Exercise, Philadelphia Drama Guild, Philadelphia, PA, 1977.

The Recruiting Officer, Long Wharf Theatre, 1978.

Elizabeth Dead (one-woman show), Music-Theatre Group/Lenox Arts Center, Cubiculo Theatre, New York City, 1980.

Mother Courage and Her Children, Boston Shakespeare Company, Boston, MA, 1983.

Pope Joan and Louise, *Top Girls,* NYSF, Public Theatre, New York City, 1983.

Joan of Arc, *Little Victories,* American Place Theatre, New York City, 1983.

Audrey Wood, *End of the World,* Music Box Theatre, New York City, 1983.

Aunt Dan, *Aunt Dan and Lemon,* NYSF, Public Theatre, 1985.

Charlotta, *The Cherry Orchard,* Brooklyn Academy of Music, Majestic Theatre, Brooklyn, NY, 1988.

Also appeared in productions for the Long Wharf Theatre, 1971-73; appeared in *Metamorphosis in Miniature,* New York City, 1983; and *The Tennis Game.*

FILM APPEARANCES

(Film debut) Mrs. Oxheart, *Popeye,* Paramount, 1980.

Billy Kwan, *The Year of Living Dangerously,* Metro-Goldwyn-Mayer/United Artists, 1982.

Shadout Mapes, *Dune,* Universal, 1984.

Dr. Prance, *The Bostonians,* Almi, 1984.

Katina, *Eleni,* Warner Bros., 1985.

Stella, *Silverado,* Columbia, 1985.

Alice B. Toklas, *Waiting for the Moon,* Skouras, 1987.

Hooper, *She-Devil,* Orion, 1989.

Miss Schlowski, *Kindergarten Cop*, Universal, 1990.

TELEVISION APPEARANCES; SPECIALS

Norah, *Ah, Wilderness!*, PBS, 1976.
Rose Hudd, *The Room*, ABC, 1987.
Narrator, *Chico Mendes: Voice of the Amazon*, TBS, 1989.
Host, *Distant Lives*, Learning Channel, 1990.

OTHER TELEVISION APPEARANCES

Mona, *Fame*, NBC, 1978.
Mrs. Sanders, *The Room Upstairs* (movie), CBS, 1987.*

*   *   *

HUNT, Marsha   1917-
(Marsha A. Hunt)

PERSONAL: Born Marcia Virginia Hunt, October 17, 1917, in Chicago, IL; daughter of Earl (a lawyer, insurance company executive, and Social Security administrator) and Minabel (a voice teacher, accompanist, and organist) Hunt; married Jerry Hooper (a film director), November 23, 1938 (divorced, 1945); married Robert Presnell, Jr. (a writer), February 10, 1946; children: one stepson. *Education:* Graduated from Horace Mann School for Girls, New York City, 1934; attended Theodora Irvine's Studio for the Theatre, New York City, 1934-35.

CAREER: Actress. Worked as a John Powers fashion model in New York City; mistress of ceremonies on cerebral palsy telethons in various U.S. cities, 1951-56; conducted weekly drama workshop at San Fernando Valley Youth Foundation Center and sponsored Summer Teen-Age Drama Workshop at San Fernando Valley State College, both 1959-60; worked as fund-raiser for the March of Dimes, Easter Seals, Red Cross, and on behalf of refugees of the Korean War, beginning in 1960. Worked with United Service Organizations in Hollywood Canteen and performed for service men in the United States and Canada. *Wartime service:* Women's Ambulance and Defense Corps, served in World War II; became staff sergeant. Office of War Information, sold U.S. War Bonds and made radio transcriptions in French during World War II.

MEMBER: Screen Actors Guild (member of board of directors, 1945-46), Actors Equity Association, American Federation of Television and Radio Artists, British Actors Equity Association, Australian Actors Equity Association, San Fernando Valley Youth Foundation (board of directors), Community Relations Conference of Southern California (board of directors), U.S. Committee for Refugees (board of directors), United Nations Association (president of San Fernando Valley chapter, 1961-62; World Refugee chairman).

AWARDS, HONORS: Citation for meritorious service from U.S. Committee for Refugees, 1961; humanitarian awards from chapters of Hadassah, Humanists, Mount Holyoke College Alumnae of Southern California, Women's International League for Peace and Freedom, and City of Hope.

CREDITS:

FILM APPEARANCES

(Film debut) Mary Lee Calvert, *The Virginia Judge*, Paramount, 1935.
Claire Patterson, *The Accusing Finger*, Paramount, 1936.
Harriet Lindsay, *The Arizona Raiders*, Paramount, 1936.
Sylvia Smith, *College Holiday*, Paramount, 1936.
Jane Belding, *Desert Gold*, Paramount, 1936.
Donna Westlake, *Easy to Take*, Paramount, 1936.
Julia Atwater, *Gentle Julia*, Twentieth Century-Fox, 1936.
Patricia Blakeford, *Hollywood Boulevard*, Paramount, 1936.
Julia Clemmens, *Annapolis Salute* (also known as *Salute to Romance*), Allied Artists, 1937.
Bit, *Easy Living*, Paramount, 1937.
Nellie, *Born to the West* (also known as *Hell Town*), Paramount, 1937.
Nora Barry, *Murder Goes to College*, Paramount, 1937.
Amy Morgan, *Thunder Trail* (also known as *Thunder Pass*), Paramount, 1937.
Valerie, *Come On, Leathernecks*, Republic, 1938.
Susan Bowen, *The Hardys Ride High*, Metro-Goldwyn-Mayer (MGM), 1939.
Kitty Crusper, *Joe and Ethel Turp Call on the President*, MGM, 1939.
Martha Sharon, *The Long Shot*, Grand National, 1939.
Barbara, *Star Reporter*, Monogram, 1939.
Betty Ainsbridge, *These Glamour Girls*, MGM, 1939.
Lucy Morgan, *Winter Carnival*, United Artists (UA), 1939.
Barbara Braun, *Ellery Queen, Master Detective*, Columbia, 1940.
Claire, *Flight Command*, MGM, 1940.
Eleanor Worth, *Irene*, RKO Radio Pictures, 1940.
Mary Bennett, *Pride and Prejudice*, MGM, 1940.
Charlotte, *Blossoms in the Dust*, MGM, 1941.
Agatha Hall, *The Trial of Mary Dugan*, MGM, 1941.
Hope Thompson, *Cheers for Miss Bishop*, UA, 1941.
Pauline Miller, *I'll Wait for You*, MGM, 1941.
Katherine Logan, *The Penalty*, MGM, 1941.
Gail Fenton, *Unholy Partners*, MGM, 1941.
Martha Lindstrom, *The Affairs of Martha* (also known as *Once Upon a Thursday*), MGM, 1942.
Mary Smith, *Joe Smith, American* (also known as *Highway to Freedom*), MGM, 1942.
Jane Mitchell, *Kid Glove Killer*, MGM, 1942.

Leila Tree, *Panama Hattie,* MGM, 1942.
Regina, *Seven Sweethearts,* MGM, 1942.
Flo Norris, *Cry Havoc,* MGM, 1943.
Diana Steed, *The Human Comedy,* MGM, 1943.
Freddie, *Pilot Number Five,* MGM, 1943.
Guest star, *Thousands Cheer,* MGM, 1943.
Sylvia, *Bride By Mistake,* RKO Radio Pictures, 1944.
Katie Mallory, *Lost Angel,* MGM, 1944.
Rosalind, *Music for Millions,* MGM, 1944.
Marja Pacierkowski, *None Shall Escape,* Columbia, 1944.
Evie O'Connor, *A Letter for Evie,* MGM, 1945.
Constance Scott, *The Valley of Decision,* MGM, 1945.
Nora Ryan, *Carnegie Hall,* UA, 1947.
Martha Gray, *Smash-Up, The Story of a Woman* (also known as *A Woman Destroyed*), Universal, 1947.
Francine Taylor, *The Inside Story,* Republic, 1948.
Ann Martin, *Raw Deal,* Reliance, 1948.
Secretary-receptionist, *Jigsaw* (also known as *Gun Moll*), UA, 1949.
Title role, *Mary Ryan, Detective,* Columbia, 1949.
Martha Wier, *Take One False Step,* Universal, 1949.
Marcia Tilayou, *Actors and Sin,* UA, 1952.
Susan Bonnard, *The Happy Time,* Columbia, 1952.
Judy Anderson, *Diplomatic Passport,* Eros, 1954.
Anne Dobson, *No Place to Hide,* Allied Artists, 1956.
Katy, *Back from the Dead,* Twentieth Century-Fox, 1957.
Edith Brennan, *Bombers B-52,* (also known as *No Sleep Till Dawn*), Warner Bros., 1957.
Jessie Bartley, *Blue Denim* (also known as *Blue Jeans*), Twentieth Century-Fox, 1959.
Kate Miller, *The Plunderers,* Allied Artists, 1960.
Joe's Mother, *Johnny Got His Gun,* Cinemation, 1971.
Leah Wheat, *Welcome to the Club,* Columbia, 1971.
Gaynor, *Dracula A.D. 1972* (also known as *Dracula Today*), Warner Bros., 1972.
Song performer, *Fade to Black,* American Cinema, 1980.
Malibu party guest, *Rich and Famous,* MGM/UA, 1981.
Amanda, *Brittania Hospital,* Universal, 1982.
Nurse Jo, *The Sender,* Paramount, 1982.
(As Marsha A. Hunt) Mariana, *The Howling II . . . Your Sister Is a Werewolf,* Thorn-EMI, 1985.

Also appeared as Salena, *Tank Malling,* 1989.

STAGE APPEARANCES

(New York debut) Ann, *Joy to the World,* Plymouth Theatre, New York City, 1948.
Title role, *Laura,* Penthouse Theatre, Atlanta, GA, 1950, later Redmont Hotel, Birmingham, AL, 1951.
Judith Anderson, *The Devil's Disciple,* City Center Theatre, then Royale Theatre, both New York City, 1950.
Minerva Pinney, *Legend of Sarah,* Penthouse Theatre, 1951.
Gilda, *Design for Living,* Hilltop Theatre in the Round, Baltimore, MD, 1951.

Irene Elliott, *Affairs of State,* La Jolla Playhouse, La Jolla, CA, 1952.
Sybil, *Private Lives,* Tenthouse Theatre, Palm Springs, CA, 1953.
Barbara, *Major Barbara,* Glen Aire Country Club, Los Angeles, 1953.
Alice, *Anniversary Waltz,* Carthay Circle Theatre, Los Angeles, 1955.
Susan, *The Little Hot,* Princess Theatre, Melbourne, Australia, 1955.
Mrs. Stephen Douglas, *The Rivalry,* Beverly Hilton Hotel, Beverly Hills, CA, 1957.
Isolde Poole, *The Tunnel of Love,* Coconut Playhouse, Miami, FL, 1957, then National Theatre, New York City, 1958.
Anna, *The King and I,* Sacramento Music Circus, Sacramento, CA, 1958.
Content Lowell, *Marriage-Go-Round,* Opera House, Monterey, CA, then Circque Playhouse, Seattle, WA, later Pasadena Playhouse, Pasadena CA, all 1961.
Mary Follet, *All the Way Home,* Playhouse-in-the-Park, Philadelphia, PA, 1961.
Mary Rhodes, *The Complaisant Lover,* Avondale Playhouse, Indianapolis, IN, then Lobero Theatre, Santa Barbara, CA, 1962.
Lady Utterwood, *Heartbreak House,* Theatre Group, Schoenberg Hall, University of California at Los Angeles, 1963.
Meg Tynan, *The Paisley Convertible,* Henry Miller's Theatre, New York City, 1967.

Also appeared as Ann, *Goodbye Again,* Princeton, NJ, then Marblehead, MA, 1948; appeared in *The Man with a Load of Mischief,* Cape May, NJ, 1948; appeared as Hannie, *Borned in Texas,* 1950; Nancy Fallon, *A Roomful of Roses,* Cincinnati, OH, 1956; title role, *Laura,* Hartford, CT.

MAJOR TOURS

Celia Coplestone, *The Cocktail Party,* U.S. cities, 1951.
Jennet, *The Lady's Not for Burning,* U.S. cities, 1952-54.
Susan, *The Little Hot,* U.S. cities, 1956.
Isolde Poole, *The Tunnel of Love,* U.S. cities, 1958.

TELEVISION APPEARANCES; EPISODIC

Cosmopolitan Theater, syndicated, 1951.
No Warning, NBC, 1958.
Francesca Fields, *The Outer Limits,* ABC, 1964.
All in the Family, CBS, 1973.
Barney Miller, ABC, 1978.

Also appeared as Katie's Aunt Cecile, *My Three Sons,* ABC, CBS; appeared in *Danger,* CBS; *Silver Theater,* CBS; *Sure as Fate,* CBS; and *Studio One,* CBS.

Claire Andrews, *Action* (pilot), CBS, 1957.

Jennifer Peck, *Peck's Bad Girl* (series), CBS, 1959.

Dr. Sara Martin, *The Man from Denver* (pilot), CBS, 1959.

Mrs. Varney, *Fear No Evil* (movie), NBC, 1969.

Dr. Gehlen, *Jigsaw* (pilot), ABC, 1972.

Marge, *Terror among Us* (movie), CBS, 1981.

TELEVISION WORK

Producer of *A Call from the Stars* (documentary), c. 1959.*

*   *   *

HUNT, Marsha A.
See HUNT, Marsha

*   *   *

HURD, Gale Anne   1955-

PERSONAL: Born October 25, 1955, in Los Angeles, CA; father, an investor; married James Cameron (a director), 1985 (divorced, 1989). *Education:* Received degree from Stanford University, 1977.

CAREER: Producer and writer. New World Pictures, Los Angeles, CA, executive assistant, director of advertising and publicity, 1977; founder and owner, Pacific Western Productions, 1982—; founder and owner, No Frills Productions; created Gale Anne Hurd production grants for American Film Institute's Directing Workshop for Women. Juror, U.S. Film Festival, Salt Lake City, UT, 1988, and Focus Student Film Awards, 1989.

MEMBER: American Film Institute (board of trustees), Hollywood Women's Political Committee, Phi Beta Kappa.

AWARDS, HONORS: Grand Prix, Avoriaz Film Festival, c. 1984, for *The Terminator;* Special Merit Award, National Association of Theater Owners, and Hugo Award for best dramatic presentation, World Science Fiction Society, 1987, both for *Aliens;* Saturn nomination, c. 1988, for *Alien Nation.*

CREDITS:

FILM WORK

Production assistant, *Humanoids from the Deep,* New World Pictures, 1980.

Producer (with Roger Corman), *Smokey Bites the Dust,* New World Pictures, 1981.

Producer, *The Terminator,* Orion Pictures, 1984.

Producer, *Aliens,* Twentieth Century-Fox, 1986.

Producer (with Richard Kobritz), *Alien Nation,* Twentieth Century-Fox, 1988.

Producer, *Bad Dreams,* American Entertainment Partners II-No Frills/Twentieth Century-Fox, 1988.

Producer, *The Abyss,* Twentieth Century-Fox, 1989.

Also executive producer of *Tremors,* 1990, and *Downtown,* 1990.

TELEVISION APPEARANCES

Appeared on television special *The New Hollywood.*

WRITINGS:

(With James Cameron and William Wisher, Jr.), *The Terminator* (screenplay), Orion Pictures, 1984.

OTHER SOURCES:

PERIODICALS

American Film, June, 1989.

People, August 11, 1986.

Time, July 28, 1986.*

*   *   *

HUTTON, Robert   1920-

PERSONAL: Real name, Robert Bruce Winne; born June 11, 1920, in Kingston, NY. *Education:* Attended Blair Academy.

CAREER: Actor and director.

CREDITS:

FILM APPEARANCES

Guard, *Northern Pursuit,* Warner Bros., 1943.

Slim, *Hollywood Canteen,* Warner Bros., 1944.

Dick Lawrence, *Janie,* Warner Bros., 1944.

John (age 20-28), *Roughly Speaking,* Warner Bros., 1945.

Ira Enright, *Too Young to Know,* Warner Bros., 1945.

Dick Lawrence, *Janie Gets Married,* Warner Bros., 1946.

Donn Masters, *Always Together,* Warner Bros., 1947.

Bob Hutton, *Love and Learn,* Warner Bros., 1947.

Christopher Fortune, *Time out of Mind,* Universal, 1947.

"Doc" Vickers, *Smart Girls Don't Talk,* Warner Bros., 1948.

Warren James, *Wallflower,* Warner Bros., 1948.

Herbert Fletcher, *And Baby Makes Three,* Columbia, 1949.

Bill Kirby, *The Man on the Eiffel Tower,* RKO Radio Pictures, 1949.

Johnny Younger, *The Younger Brothers,* Warner Bros., 1949.

Gil McRoberts, *Beauty on Parade,* Columbia, 1950.

Lieutenant Vermont, *New Mexico,* United Artists (UA), 1951.

Ames, *The Racket,* RKO Radio Pictures, 1951.

Lieutenant Morgan, *Slaughter Trail,* RKO Radio Pictures, 1951.

Private Conchie Bronte, *The Steel Helmet,* Lippert, 1951.
Lieutenant Steve Smith, *Gobs and Gals* (also known as *Cruising Casanovas*), Republic, 1952.
Stratford Carver, *Tropical Heatwave,* Republic, 1952.
Charlie Johnson, *Paris Model,* Columbia, 1953.
Raphael, *Casanova's Big Night,* Paramount, 1954.
Dr. Peter Kirk, *The Big Bluff,* UA, 1955.
Brad Cameron, *Scandal Incorporated,* Republic, 1956.
Dr. Phil Merritt, *The Man without a Body,* Eros, 1957.
Chuck Collins, *Thunder over Tangier* (also known as *Man from Tangier*), Republic, 1957.
Professor John Carrington, *The Colossus New York,* Paramount, 1958.
Lieutenant Jerry Seabrook, *Outcasts of the City,* Republic, 1958.
Sloane, *Showdown at Boot Hill,* Twentieth Century-Fox, 1958.
Dr. John Lamont, *Invisible Invaders,* UA, 1959.
Rupert, *Cinderfella,* Paramount, 1960.
Tom, *The Jail Breakers,* American International, 1960.
Maddo, *Wild Youth* (also known as *Naked Youth*), Cinema Associates, 1961.
Tom Gregory (the aviator), *The Slime People* (also see below), Hansen, 1963.
Joe Adams, *The Secret Door,* Allied Artists, 1964.
Calvin Adams, *The Sicilians,* Butchers, 1964.
Commander, *Finders Keepers,* UA, 1966.
Rock Stewart, *Carnaby M.D.* (also known as *Doctor in Clover*), J. Arthur Rank, 1967.
Dr. Curtis Temple, *They Came from beyond Space,* Embassy, 1967.
Eric Lutgens, *The Vulture,* Paramount, 1967.
President's aide, *You Only Live Twice,* UA, 1967.
Bruce Benton, *Torture Garden,* Columbia, 1968.
Guest, *Cry of the Banshee,* American International, 1970.
Dr. Richard Warren, *Trog,* Warner Bros., 1970.
Mr. Baker, *Tales from the Crypt,* Cinerama, 1972.

FILM WORK

Director, *The Slime People,* Hansen, 1963.

TELEVISION APPEARANCES; EPISODIC, EXCEPT WHERE NOTED

Gruen Guild Playhouse, ABC, 1951-52.
Schaefer Century Theatre, syndicated, 1952.
Your Jeweler's Showcase, CBS, 1952.
TV Reader's Digest, ABC, 1955.
Ambassador Richards, *QB VII* (movie), 1974.*

*　　*　　*

HYTNER, Nicholas 1956-

PERSONAL: Full name, Nicholas Robert Hytner; born May 7, 1956; son of Benet and Joyce Hytner. *Education:* Received M.A. from Trinity Hall, Cambridge.

ADDRESSES: Office—Royal National Theatre, London, England.

CAREER: Director. Associate director, Royal Exchange Theatre, Manchester, England, 1985-89; associate director, Royal National Theatre, London, England, 1989—.

AWARDS, HONORS: Laurence Olivier Award and *Evening Standard* Award, both 1985, for *Xerxes; Evening Standard* Award and Critics Circle Award, both for best director, 1989; Antoinette Perry Award nomination for best direction of a musical, 1991, for *Miss Saigon.*

CREDITS:

STAGE DIRECTOR

King Priam, Kent Opera, Kent, England, 1983.
Rienzi, English National Opera, 1983.
Alice, Leeds Playhouse, London, England, 1984.
Xerxes, English National Opera, 1985.
As You Like It, Royal Exchange Theatre, Manchester, England, 1985.
The Country Wife, Royal Exchange Theatre, 1986.
Edward II, Royal Exchange Theatre, 1986.
Don Carlos, Royal Exchange Theatre, 1987.
Guilio Cesare, Paris Opera, Paris, 1987.
Measure for Measure, Royal Shakespeare Company (RSC), Stratford–upon–Avon, England, 1987, then London, 1988.
The Magic Flute, English National Opera, Coliseum, London, England, 1988.
The Knot Garden, Royal Opera House, Covent Garden, London, c. 1988.
The Tempest, RSC, Stratford-upon-Avon, 1988, then Barbican Theatre, London, 1989.
Ghetto, Royal National Theatre, London, 1989.
Julius Caesar, Houston Grand Opera, Houston, TX, 1989.
Le Nozze de Figaro, Geneva Opera, Geneva, Switzerland, 1989.
Miss Saigon, Theatre Royal Drury Lane, London, 1989, then Broadway Theatre, New York City, 1991.
King Lear, RSC, Royal Shakespeare Theatre, Stratford-upon-Avon, 1990.
Volpone, Almeida Theatre, 1990.
The Wind in the Willows, National Theatre, London, 1990.
The Madness of George III, National Theatre, 1991.

Also directed *The Scarlet Pimpernel,* Chichester, England, then London, 1985; and *Mumbo Jumbo,* 1987.

OTHER SOURCES:

PERIODICALS

New Statesman & Society, March 23, 1990.
New York Times, August 27, 1989.

I

IBBETSON, Arthur 1922-

PERSONAL: Born September 8, 1922, in England.

CAREER: Cinematographer.

AWARDS, HONORS: Emmy Award, Outstanding Cinematography for a Limited Series or a Special, 1981, for *Little Lord Fauntleroy.*

CREDITS:

FILM CINEMATOGRAPHER, EXCEPT AS INDICATED

The Blue Lagoon, Universal, 1949.

(With George Stretton and Bill Alan) *Floodtide,* General Film Distributors, 1949.

(With Stretton and Alan) *Poet's Pub,* General Film Distributors, 1949.

(With Alan and Cyril Bristow) *Stop Press Girl,* General Film Distributors, 1949.

Island of Desire (also known as *Saturday Island*), RKO Radio Pictures, 1952.

(With Ted Scaife) *Melba,* United Artists (UA), 1953.

The Horse's Mouth, UA, 1958.

Special effects, *The Key,* Open Road/Columbia, 1958.

The Bridal Path, British Lion, 1959.

The Angry Silence, British Lion, 1960.

Tunes of Glory, Lopert, 1960.

The Canadians, Twentieth Century-Fox, 1961.

The League of Gentlemen, Kingsley, 1961.

Whistle Down the Wind, Pathe-America, 1961.

Lisa (also known as *The Inspector*), Twentieth Century-Fox, 1962.

There Was a Crooked Man, Lopert/UA, 1962.

I Could Go on Singing, UA, 1963.

Murder at the Gallop, Metro-Goldwyn-Mayer (MGM), 1963.

(With Ted Moore) *Nine Hours to Rama* (also known as *Nine Hours to Live*), Twentieth Century-Fox, 1963.

The Chalk Garden, Universal, 1964.

Die, Die, My Darling (also known as *Fanatic*), Columbia, 1965.

The Fighting Prince of Donegal, Buena Vista, 1966.

Gypsy Girl (also known as *Sky West and Crooked*), Continental Distributors, 1966.

The Wild Affair, Goldstone, 1966.

A Countess from Hong Kong, Rank/Universal, 1967.

Inspector Clouseau, UA, 1968.

A Matter of Innocence, Universal, 1968.

Where Eagles Dare, MGM, 1968.

Anne of the Thousand Days, Universal, 1969.

The Walking Stick, MGM, 1970.

When Eight Bells Toll, Winkast/Cinerama, 1971.

The Railway Children, Universal, 1971.

Willy Wonka and the Chocolate Factory, Paramount, 1971.

A Doll's House, Paramount, 1973.

11 Harrowhouse (also known as *Anything for Love*), Twentieth Century-Fox, 1974.

Out of Season (also known as *Winter Rates*), Athenaeum-EMI, 1975.

The Sell Out, Distrib Venture, 1976.

A Little Night Music, New World, 1977.

The Medusa Touch, Warner Brothers, 1978.

All Things Bright and Beautiful (also known as *It Shouldn't Happen to a Vet*), World, 1979.

The Prisoner of Zenda, Universal, 1979.

Hopscotch, AVCO/Embassy, 1980.

(With Lazlo George) *Nothing Personal,* American International Pictures, 1980.

The Bounty, Orion, 1984.

Santa Claus: The Movie, Tri-Star, 1985.

TELEVISION CINEMATOGRAPHER; MOVIES, EXCEPT AS INDICATED

Frankenstein: The True Story, NBC, 1972.

Brief Encounter, NBC, 1974.
Spectre, NBC, 1977.
Little Lord Fauntleroy, CBS, 1980.
Witness for the Prosecution, CBS, 1982.
(In Africa) *Master of the Game* (mini-series), CBS, 1984.
Babes in Toyland, NBC, 1986.*

*　　*　　*

IMI, Tony   1937-

PERSONAL: Born March 27, 1937, in London, England.

ADDRESSES: Manager—Stella Richards, Stella Richards Management, 42 Hazlebury Rd., London SW6 2ND, England.

CAREER: Cinematographer.

CREDITS:

FILM CINEMATOGRAPHER, EXCEPT WHERE INDICATED

(With Kenneth Hodges) *Inadmissible Evidence,* Paramount, 1968.
Junket 89, Children's Film Foundation, 1970.
The Body, Metro-Goldwyn-Mayer, 1970.
Dulcima, Cinevision, 1971.
Long Ago Tomorrow (also known as *The Raging Moon*), Cinema V, 1971.
Universal Soldier, Ionian, 1971.
It's a 2'6" Above the Ground World (also known as *The Love Ban*), British Lion, 1972.
The Likely Lads, EMI, 1976.
The Slipper and the Rose (also known as *The Story of Cinderella*), Universal, 1976.
Additional photographer, *The Confessional* (also known as *House of Mortal Sin*), Atlas, 1977.
Brass Target, United Artists, 1978.
Breakthrough (also known as *Sergeant Steiner*), Maverick Pictures, 1978.
International Velvet, United Artists, 1978.
It's Not the Size That Counts (also known as *Percy's Progress*), Joseph Brenner, 1979.
Ffolkes (also known as *Sea Hijack* and *Assault Force*), Universal, 1980.
The Sea Wolves, Paramount, 1981.
Night Crossing, Buena Vista, 1982.
Nate and Hayes (also known as *Savage Islands*), Paramount, 1983.
Enemy Mine, Twentieth Century-Fox, 1985.
Not Quite Jerusalem, Rank, 1985.
Empire State, Virgin/Miracle, 1987.
Buster, Tri-Star, 1988.
Wired, Taurus Entertainment, 1989.
Fire Birds, Buena Vista, 1990.

Also cinematographer for *I Am a Dancer,* 1972; *American Roulette,* 1988; and *Options,* 1989.

TELEVISION CINEMATOGRAPHER; MOVIES

Death Penalty, NBC, 1980.
A Tale of Two Cities, CBS, 1980.
For Ladies Only, NBC, 1981.
Dreams Don't Die, ABC, 1982.
Little Gloria . . . Happy at Last, NBC, 1982.
Inside the Third Reich, ABC, 1982.
My Body, My Child, ABC, 1982.
(With Charles Rosher) *Princess Daisy,* NBC, 1983.
A Christmas Carol, CBS, 1984.
Pope John Paul II, CBS, 1984.
Sakharov, HBO, 1984.
Reunion at Fairborough, HBO, 1985.
Oceans of Fire, CBS, 1986.
The Last Days of Frank and Jesse James, NBC, 1986.
Babycakes, CBS, 1989.

Also cinematographer for *Ernest Hemingway's "The Old Man and the Sea,"* 1990, *The Last to Go,* 1990, and *Our Sons,* 1991.

OTHER TELEVISION WORK; CINEMATOGRAPHER

(With Mike Whitcutt) *Come Out, Come Out, Wherever You Are* (special), ABC, 1974.
Nicholas Nickleby (special), syndicated, 1983.
The Return of Sherlock Holmes (mini-series), Granada, then *Mystery!,* PBS, 1987.
Queenie (mini-series), ABC, 1987.

Also cinematographer for the special *Maggie,* 1986.

*　　*　　*

IRELAND, Jill   1941-1990

OBITUARY NOTICE—See index for *CTFT* sketch: Full name, Jill Dorothy Ireland; born April 24, 1941, in London, England; died of cancer, May 18, 1990, in Malibu, CA. Actress and dancer. An actress with extensive film and television credits, Jill Ireland was best known for her co-starring roles opposite her husband, actor Charles Bronson. Together they established a long film partnership that saw them appear together in many successful action-crime films.

Trained as a dancer, Ireland began her career performing in London music halls at the age of fifteen. She also toured Europe with the Monte Carlo Ballet. Soon after, she began acting, joining the Rank Organization's acting ensemble. She made her film debut dancing in *Oh Rosalinda!* (1955), and subsequently she appeared in numerous Rank films, including *There's Always a Thursday* (1957), *Hell Drivers* (1957), *Three Men in a Boat* (1958), and *The Big Money* (1962). Among the group of actors in Rank's ensemble was David McCallum, with whom Ireland made pictures and whom she married in 1957. To further their careers, in 1962 they both moved to Hollywood. Ireland continued to act in films, but she mainly performed on television, where she made guest appearances on such shows as *Star Trek, The Man from U.N.C.L.E., Ben Casey,* and *Night Gallery.* Ireland divorced McCallum in 1967 and married Charles Bronson the following year. Starting with *Villa Rides* (1968), the couple's film successes encompassed fifteen movies, including *The Valachi Papers* (1972), *Love and Bullets* (1979), and *Death Wish II* (1982). In 1984, after being diagnosed with breast cancer, Jill Ireland underwent a mastectomy. She received chemotherapy and radiation treatment, which put the cancer in remission. In spite of the cancer, she continued to work and made the films *Assassination* (1987) and *Caught* (1987). She also wrote an autobiography entitled *Life Wish* (1987), which detailed her recovery from the mastectomy and her ongoing battle with breast cancer. The book was widely praised for its inspirational and encouraging stance. In addition, Ireland toured the United States as a spokesperson for the American Cancer Society. Her lectures advised women with breast cancer to keep fighting and to live with dignity and self-respect. Ireland received the Medal of Courage from President Ronald Reagan in 1988 after she appeared before a Congressional Committee concerning cancer patients' medical expenses. Upon her death Jill Ireland was regarded as a symbol of courage for women fighting breast cancer.

OBITUARIES AND OTHER SOURCES:

PERIODICALS

Daily News, May 19, 1990.
New York Times, May 19, 1990.
Variety, May 23, 1990.

*   *   *

ISRAEL, Neal   1945(?)-

PERSONAL: Born c. 1945; married Lori Lieberman (a singer-songwriter; marriage dissolved); married Amy Heckerling (a director), July, 1984. *Education:* Attended Hofstra University.

CAREER: Actor, producer, director and writer. Formerly directed commercials; worked in promotion for CBS.

CREDITS:

FILM APPEARANCES

Tunnelvision, Worldwide, 1976.
Cracking Up, American International Pictures, 1977.
Dr. Zillman, *Johnny Dangerously,* Twentieth Century-Fox, 1984.

FILM WORK

Director (with Brad Swirnoff) and executive producer, *Tunnelvision,* Worldwide, 1976.

Director, *Americathon,* United Artists, 1979.
Director, *Bachelor Party,* Twentieth Century-Fox, 1984.
Director, *Moving Violations,* Twentieth Century-Fox, 1985.

Also executive producer of *Spurting Blood.*

TELEVISION WORK

Producer, *Marie* (series), NBC, 1980.
Producer, *Twilight Theater* (pilot), NBC, 1982.
Producer, *Twilight Theater II* (pilot), NBC, 1982.
Director, *Combat High* (movie), NBC, 1986.
Executive producer (with Don Johnson), *Life on the Flipside* (movie), NBC, 1988.
Director, *The Cover Girl and the Cop* (movie), NBC, 1989.

STAGE WORK

Production assistant, *The Education of H*Y*M*A*N K*A*P*L*A*N,* Alvin Theatre, New York City, 1968.
Director, *Frank Gagliano's City Scene,* Fortune Theatre, New York City, 1969.

WRITINGS:

SCREENPLAYS

(With Michael Mislove) *Tunnelvision,* Worldwide, 1976.
Cracking Up, American International Pictures, 1977.
(With Mislove and Monica Johnson) *Americathon,* United Artists, 1979.
(With Pat Proft) *Bachelor Party,* Twentieth Century-Fox, 1984.
(With Proft and Hugh Wilson) *Police Academy,* Warner Brothers, 1984.
(With Proft and Peter Torokvei) *Real Genius,* Tri-Star, 1985.
(With Proft) *Moving Violations,* Twentieth Century-Fox, 1985.
(With Larry Siegel) *Buy and Cell,* Altar/Empire, 1989.

Also author of *It's Alive III, Sketches* and *Spurting Blood.*

TELEPLAYS

The Mac Davis Show (series), NBC, 1976.
(With Proft) *Ringo* (special), NBC, 1978.
(With Jeffrey Barron, Jim Staahl and Jim Fisher) *Twilight Theater* (pilot), NBC, 1982.
(With Proft, Barron, John London, Ron Engleman, Carmen Finestra, Marshall McManus, and Kevin Kelton) *Twilight Theater II* (pilot), NBC, 1982.

Also author of *Lola Falana Special.*

OTHER SOURCES:

PERIODICALS

People, May 13, 1985.*

J

JACKSON, Gordon   1923-1990

PERSONAL: Full name, Gordon Cameron Jackson; born December 19, 1923, in Glasgow, Scotland; died after a brief illness, January 1, 1990, in London, England; son of Thomas and Margaret (Fletcher) Jackson; married Rona Anderson (an actress), 1951; children: two sons. *Avocational interests:* Music, gardening.

CAREER: Actor. Radio performer after 1939; worked as a draftsman before acting career.

AWARDS, HONORS: Officer of Order of the British Empire; British Actor of the Year Award, 1974, Royal Television Society Award, 1975, and Emmy Award, Outstanding Single Performance by a Supporting Actor in a Comedy or Drama Series, 1976, all for "Upstairs, Downstairs," *Masterpiece Theatre;* Australian Logie Award, 1981, for *A Town Like Alice.*

CREDITS:

STAGE APPEARANCES

(Stage debut) Dudley, *George and Margaret,* MSU Theatre, Rutherglen, Scotland, 1943.

(London debut) Able Seaman McIntosh, *Seagulls Over Sorrento,* Apollo Theatre, 1951.

Young Actor (Ismael), *Moby Dick,* Duke of York's Theatre, London, 1955.

Narrator, *The Soldier's Tale,* Sadler's Wells Theatre, London, 1958.

Banquo, *Macbeth,* Royal Court Theatre, London, 1966.

Narrator, *The Soldier's Tale,* Edinburgh Festival, Edinburgh, Scotland, 1967.

Mr. Booker, *Wise Child,* Garrick Theatre, London, 1967.

Baxter, *This Story of Yours,* Royal Court Theatre, 1968.

Horatio, *Hamlet,* Round House Theatre, London, 1969.

(Broadway debut) Horatio, *Hamlet,* Lunt-Fontanne Theatre, New York City, 1969.

Alfred, *The Signalman's Apprentice,* Oxford Playhouse, Oxford, England, 1969.

Tesman, *Hedda Gabler,* Stratford Theatre, Stratford, ON, Canada, 1970.

Creon, *Oedipus,* Young Vic Theatre, London, 1970.

Narrator, *The Soldier's Tale,* Young Vic Theatre, 1970.

Interrogator, *The Lovers of Viorne,* Royal Court Theatre, 1971.

Rodney, *Veterans,* Royal Court Theatre, 1972.

Banquo, *Macbeth,* Aldwych Theatre, London, 1975.

Title role, *Noah,* Chichester Festival, Chichester, England, 1976.

Malvolio, *Twelfth Night,* Chichester Festival, 1976.

Superintendent Battle, *Cards on the Table,* Vaudeville Theatre, London, 1981.

Father Tim Farley, *Mass Appeal,* Lyric Hammersmith Theatre, London, 1982.

Also appeared in *Death Trap,* 1981.

MAJOR TOURS

David, *What Every Woman Knows,* British cities, 1973.

FILM APPEARANCES

(Film debut) Jock, *Somewhere in France* (also released as *The Foreman Went to France*), United Artists (UA), 1941.

Fred Blake, *Millions Like Us,* General Film Distributors, 1943.

Young'un, *Nine Men,* UA, 1943.

John Jamieson, *San Demetrio, London,* Ealing Studios, 1947.

Johnny Duncan, *Against The Wind,* General Film Distributors, 1948.

Lt. Lennox, *The Captive Heart,* Ealing Studios, 1948.

David Shields, *Floodtide,* General Film Distributors, 1949.

Tom Kennedy, *Massacre Hill* (also released as *Eureka Stockade*), General Film Distributors, 1949.

Jock Melville, *Stop Press Girl,* General Film Distributors, 1949.

George Campbell, *Tight Little Island* (also released as *Whiskey Galore*), Universal, 1949.

Mac, *Bitter Springs,* British Empire Films, 1950.

David Sutton, *Pink String and Sealing Wax,* Ealing, 1950.

Paul Tracey, *Happy Go Lovely,* RKO Radio Pictures, 1951.

The Lady with a Lamp (also released as *The Lady with the Lamp*), British Lion, 1951.

Hiker, *Castle In The Air,* AB-Pathe, 1952.

Hector McPhere, *Meet Mr. Lucifer,* General Film Distributors, 1953.

Inspector Goldie, *Death Goes to School,* International Artists/Eros, 1953.

Florian, *The Delavine Affair,* Monarch, 1954.

Malta Story, British Film Makers/UA, 1954.

Ralph, *The Love Lottery,* General Film Distributors, 1954.

Burne, *Passage Home,* General Film Distributors, 1955.

Leonard, *Windfall,* Eros, 1955.

Percy, *Blonde Bait,* Associated Film Distributing Corporation, 1956.

District Officer, *Pacific Destiny,* British Lion, 1956.

TV Producer, *The Creeping Unknown* (also released as *The Quatermass Xperiment*), UA, 1956.

John Merritt, *Abandon Ship!* (also released as *Seven Waves Away*), Columbia, 1957.

Harry, *The Baby and the Battleship,* British Lion, 1957.

Bert Harris, *The Black Ice,* Archway, 1957.

Dougal Maclean, *Let's Be Happy,* Allied Artists, 1957.

Jimmy Norris, *Violent Stranger* (also released as *Man In The Shadow*), Anglo Amalgamated, 1957.

Carnoustie Bligh, *Panic In The Parlour* (also released as *Sailor Beware*), Romulus/Distributors Corporation of America, 1957.

Chalky, *Blind Spot* (short), Butchers Film Service, 1958.

Scottie, *Hell Drivers,* Rank, 1958.

George Campbell, *Mad Little Island* (also released as *Rockets Galore*), Rank, 1958.

Don Wescott, *Three Crooked Men,* Paramount, 1958.

Constable Alec, *The Bridal Path,* British Lion, 1959.

Sgt. Malcolm, *Devil's Bait,* R.F.D. Productions, 1959.

Leading Seaman Johnson, *The Navy Lark,* Twentieth Century-Fox, 1959.

Sgt. MacKenzie, *Yesterday's Enemy,* Columbia, 1959.

Police Sergeant, *Chance Meeting* (also released as *Blind Date*), Paramount, 1960.

Roger Fenton, *The Price of Silence,* Exclusive International, 1960.

Bill Donovan, *Snowball,* Rank, 1960.

Captain Jimmy Cairns, *Tunes of Glory,* Lopert, 1960.

Farmer, *Greyfriars Bobby,* Buena Vista, 1961.

Captain Bateson, *Trouble In Sky* (also released as *Cone of Silence*), Universal, 1961.

Tom, *Two Wives at One Wedding,* Paramount, 1961.

Edward Birkett, *Mutiny on the Bounty,* Metro-Goldwyn-Mayer (MGM), 1962.

MacDonald, *The Great Escape,* UA, 1963.

Vahlin, *The Long Ships* (also released as *Dugi Brodavi*), Columbia, 1964.

Daylight Robbery, CFF, 1964.

Operation Crossbow (also released as *The Great Spy Mission*), MGM, 1965.

Jock Carswell, *The Ipcress File,* Universal, 1965.

McDougal, a pilot, *Those Magnificent Men in Their Flying Machines or How I Flew From London to Paris in 25 Hours and 11 Minutes* (also released as *Those Magnificent Men in Their Flying Machines*), Twentieth Century-Fox, 1965.

James McAfee, *Cast a Giant Shadow,* UA, 1966.

Captain Leeds, *The Fighting Prince of Donegal,* Buena Vista, 1966.

Captain Engel, *The Night of The Generals* (also known as *La Nuit De Geneaux*), Columbia, 1967.

Triple Cross, Cineurop/Warner Brothers, 1967.

Stern, *Danger Route* (also released as *The Eliminator*), UA, 1968.

Horatio, *Hamlet,* Columbia, 1969.

Mr. Mallory, *On The Run,* Children's Film Fund, 1969.

Gordon Lowther, *The Prime of Miss Jean Brodie,* Twentieth Century-Fox, 1969.

Mr. Ransome, *Run Wild, Run Free,* Columbia, 1969.

Nephew's Friend, *Scrooge,* National General, 1970.

Charles Stewart, *Kidnapped,* American International Pictures, 1971.

Detective Sgt. Brian Hardison, *Russian Roulette,* AVCO/Embassy, 1975.

Dr. Marston, *Golden Rendezvous,* Film Trust-Milton Okun, 1977.

Dr. Johnson, *The Medusa Touch,* ITC/Warner Brothers, 1978.

Tom Harker, *The Shooting Party,* European Classics, 1985.

Sir Anthony Phelps, *Gunpowder,* Lazer Entertainment Productions, 1987.

Bruce, *The Whistle Blower,* Hemdale, 1987.

Beyond Therapy, Sandcastle/New World, 1987.

Also appeared in *As Long as You're Happy.*

TELEVISION APPEARANCES

Angus Hudson, "Upstairs, Downstairs," *Masterpiece Theatre* (series), PBS, 1970-75.

Commander Teddy Cavandish, *Madame Sin* (movie), ABC, 1972.

Inspector Cabell, *Spectre* (movie), NBC, 1977.

Fielding, *The Last Giraffe* (movie), CBS, 1979.

Strachan, "A Town Like Alice," *Masterpiece Theatre* (mini-series), PBS, 1980.

Professor Bramston, *Shaka Zulu* (mini-series), syndicated, 1986.

James Clavell's Noble House, NBC, 1988.

Harry, *The Lady and the Highway Man* (movie), CBS, 1989.

Arthur Winslow, "The Winslow Boy," *Great Performances,* PBS, 1989.

Also appeared as Cowley, *The Professionals* (series), 1977-81; appeared in an episode of *Hart to Hart,* ABC. Appeared in mini-series *Masks of Death,* 1984, and as Cairey, *Look to the Lady,* 1989. Appeared in *Sesame Street Special,* 1988, and *My Brother Tom.**

* * *

JACKSON, Nagle   1936-

PERSONAL: Full name, Paul Nagle Jackson; born April 28, 1936, in Seattle, WA; son of Paul J. (an English professor) and Gertrude J. (Dunn) Jackson; married Sandra S. Suter (an actress and singer), September 15, 1963; children: Rebecca, Hillary. *Education:* Whitman College, A.B., 1958; studied mime with Etienne Decroux in Paris, France; studied at the Directors' Workshop, Circle in the Square Theatre.

ADDRESSES: Office—c/o McCarter Theatre Company, 91 University Pl., Princeton, NJ 08540.

CAREER: Actor, director, and writer. Worked as a folk singer in Seattle, WA, 1959; American Conservatory Theatre, San Francisco, CA, stage director, 1967-70; Milwaukee Repertory Theatre, Milwaukee, WI, artistic director, 1971-77; McCarter Theatre, Princeton, NJ, artistic director, 1979—. Has taught acting at American Conservatory Theatre and University of Washington, Seattle.

MEMBER: Dramatists Guild, Society of Stage Directors and Choreographers.

AWARDS, HONORS: Fulbright Fellowship, Paris, France, 1958; Outstanding Young Man Award, Junior Chamber of Commerce.

CREDITS:

STAGE APPEARANCES

(Stage debut) Speed, *Two Gentlemen of Verona,* Oregon Shakespeare Festival, Ashland, OR, 1957.

Feste, *Twelfth Night,* Oregon Shakespeare Festival, 1959.

Earl of Salisbury, *King John,* Oregon Shakespeare Festival, 1959.

Lucio, *Measure for Measure,* Oregon Shakespeare Festival, 1959.

Octavius Caesar, *Antony and Cleopatra,* Oregon Shakespeare Festival, 1959.

(New York debut) Boy, *Measure for Measure,* New York Shakespeare Festival, Delacorte Theatre, New York City, 1960.

Player King, *Hamlet,* Oregon Shakespeare Festival, 1961.

Bertram, *All's Well That Ends Well,* Oregon Shakespeare Festival, 1961.

Earl of Westmoreland, *Henry IV, Part I,* Oregon Shakespeare Festival, 1961.

Face, *The Alchemist,* Oregon Shakespeare Festival, 1961.

Ensemble, *Dime a Dozen* (revue), Plaza 9 Room, Plaza Hotel, New York City, 1962.

Ensemble, *Struts and Frets* (revue), Julius Monk's, Chicago, IL, 1963.

Ensemble, *Baker's Dozen* (revue), Plaza 9 Room, Plaza Hotel, 1964.

Ensemble, *Bits and Pieces,* (revue), Plaza 9 Room, Plaza Hotel, 1964.

Benedick, *Much Ado About Nothing,* Oregon Shakespeare Festival, 1965.

Autolycus, *The Winter's Tale,* Oregon Shakespeare Festival, 1965.

Hume and Lieutenant, *Henry IV, Part II,* Oregon Shakespeare Festival, 1965.

Ensemble, *The Decline and Fall of the Entire World as Seen Through the Eyes of Cole Porter* (revue), Little Fox Theatre, San Francisco, CA, 1966, then Huntington Hartford Theatre, Los Angeles, CA, 1967.

Demetrius, *A Midsummer Night's Dream,* Oregon Shakespeare Festival, 1966.

Lewis XI, *Henry IV, Part III,* Oregon Shakespeare Festival, 1966.

Hortensio, *The Taming of the Shrew,* Oregon Shakespeare Festival, 1967.

Octavius, *Antony and Cleopatra,* Oregon Shakespeare Festival, 1967.

Stage Manager, *Your Own Thing,* Marines Memorial Theatre, San Francisco, CA, 1968.

Also appeared in *The Maske of the New World,* 1959.

STAGE DIRECTOR

Volpone, Oregon Shakespeare Festival, 1965.

Two Gentlemen of Verona, Oregon Shakespeare Festival, 1966.

Pericles, Prince of Tyre, Oregon Shakespeare Festival, 1967.

Little Murders, American Conservatory Theatre, San Francisco, CA, 1969.

In White America, American Conservatory Theatre, 1969.

Room Service, American Conservatory Theatre, 1969.

Little Malcolm and His Struggle Against the Eunuchs, American Conservatory Theatre, 1970.

Richard II, Oregon Shakespeare Festival, 1970.

The Tempest, Shakespeare Festival, Washington, DC, 1970.

The Miser, Seattle Repertory Theatre, WA, 1970.

The Misanthrope, Mummers Theatre, Oklahoma City, OK, 1971.

Blithe Spirit, Hartford Stage Company, Hartford, CT, 1971.

The Taming of the Shrew, Old Globe Theatre, San Diego, CA, 1971.

Cat Among the Pigeons, Milwaukee Repertory Theatre, Todd Wehr Theatre, Milwaukee, WI, 1971.

Mystery Plays, Milwaukee Repertory Theatre, 1971.

Measure for Measure, Milwaukee Repertory Theatre, 1972.

Journey of the Fifth Horse, Milwaukee Repertory Theatre, 1972.

Two Gentleman of Verona, Milwaukee Repertory Theatre, 1972.

All Together Now, Milwaukee Repertory Theatre, 1973.

Prisoner of the Crown, Milwaukee Repertory Theatre, 1973.

Our Town, Milwaukee Repertory Theatre, 1974.

The Tragical Historie of Doctor Faustus, Milwaukee Repertory Theatre, 1974.

An Occasional Piece Suitable to Openings of Theaters, Milwaukee Repertory Theatre, Court Street Theatre, 1974.

King Lear, Milwaukee Repertory Theatre, 1974.

Passing Charlie Greeley, Milwaukee Repertory Theatre, 1974.

The Visions of Simone Machard, Milwaukee Repertory Theatre, 1975.

The National Health, American Conservatory Theatre, 1977.

Travesties, American Conservatory Theatre, 1978.

The Utter Glory of Morrissey Hall, McCarter Theatre, Princeton, NJ, 1978, then Mark Hellinger Theatre, New York City, 1979.

Hay Fever, American Conservatory Theatre, 1979.

Custer, McCarter Theatre, 1981.

Cat among Pigeons, American Conservatory Theatre, 1982.

Hamlet, McCarter Theatre, 1982-83.

At This Evening's Performance, McCarter Theatre, 1982-83.

The Three Sisters, McCarter Theatre, 1982-83.

A Christmas Carol, McCarter Theatre, 1983.

The School for Wives, McCarter Theatre, 1984-85.

Faustus in Hell, McCarter Theatre, 1984-85.

The Boys Next Door, McCarter Theatre, 1985-86.

Fallen Angels, Hartman Theatre, Stamford, CT, 1986.

Opera Comique, American Conservatory Theatre, 1985-86, then John F. Kennedy Center for the Performing Arts, Eisenhower Theatre, Washington, DC, 1986-87.

Our Town, McCarter Theatre, 1986-87.

Don't Trifle with Love, McCarter Theatre, 1986-87.

Napoleon Nightdreams, McCarter Theatre, 1986-87.

The Middle Ages, McCarter Theatre, 1987-88.

Stepping Out, McCarter Theatre, 1987-88.

The Glass Menagerie, Gorky Theater, Leningrad, U.S.S.R., 1988.

Pvt. Wars, McCarter Theatre Company, Oslo, Norway, 1989.

Romeo and Juliet, Trondelag Theater, Trondheim, Norway, 1990.

Also director at Repertory Theatre of St. Louis, MO, 1969-70; Seattle Repertory Theatre, 1970-71; National Shakespeare Festival, San Diego, CA, 1971 and 1979; and American Conservatory Theatre, 1978-79, 1980-81, 1984-85, and 1985-86.

MAJOR TOURS

Director, *Romeo and Juliet,* The Acting Company, U.S. cities, 1979.

TELEVISION APPEARANCES

Guest, *The Jack Paar Show,* NBC, 1964.

We Interrupt This Season (special), NBC, 1967.

WRITINGS:

PLAYS

Adaptor, *Mystery Plays,* Milwaukee Repertory Theatre, Milwaukee, WI, 1971.

All Together Now, Milwaukee Repertory Theatre, 1973.

An Occasional Piece Suitable to Openings of Theaters, Milwaukee Repertory Theatre, 1974.

Chamber Piece, Court Street Theatre, Milwaukee, WI, 1976.

Adaptor, *A Christmas Carol,* Milwaukee Repertory Theatre, 1977.

(With Clark Gesner) *The Utter Glory of Morrissey Hall* (musical), Mark Hellinger Theatre, New York City, 1979.

At This Evening's Performance, McCarter Theatre, Princeton, NJ, 1982.

Adaptor, *Faustus in Hell,* McCarter Theatre, 1984-85.

Opera Comique, American Conservatory Theatre, San Francisco, CA, 1985-86.

Adaptor, *Tale of Two Cities,* American Conservatory Theatre, 1989.

SIDELIGHTS: Nagle Jackson, with his 1988 production of *The Glass Menagerie,* was the first U.S. director invited to work in the Soviet Union.

JAMES, Jessica   1931(?)-1990

PERSONAL: Born October 31, 1931 (one source says 1933), in Los Angeles, CA; died of cancer, May 7, 1990, in Los Angeles, CA; daughter of Jessie (a producer) and Evelyn (a singer and dancer; maiden name, Bauerman) James; children: Donald Burke, Bambi Sue Camerman. *Education:* Attended University of Southern California; studied acting with Pat Randall and George Morrison and opera with Galli Gurci.

CAREER: Actress and singer. Started performing in operas in Los Angeles, CA, at the age of five; performed as a showgirl and comedienne in Las Vegas, NV, with her own group, "Jessie & the James Boys."

MEMBER: Actors' Equity Association.

CREDITS:

STAGE APPEARANCES

(Broadway debut) Joanne, *Company,* Alvin Theatre, New York City, 1970.
Roz, *Hothouse,* Circle Repertory Theatre, New York City, 1974.
Elma, *Winter Chicken,* Manhattan Theatre Club, New York City, 1974.
13 Rue De L'Amour, Studio Arena Theatre, Buffalo, NY, 1974-75.
Bunny Weinberger, *Gemini,* Playwrights Horizons, New York City, 1976, then Circle Repertory Company, 1977, later The Little Theatre, New York City, 1977-78.
Maggie Jones, *42nd Street,* Winter Garden Theatre, New York City, 1980, then Majestic Theatre, New York City, 1981.
Belle (Today), *Little Me,* Eugene O'Neill Theatre, New York City, 1982.

Also appeared in *Nourish the Beast, Loss of Innocence, Rebirth Celebration of the Human Race,* and *Silver Bee,* all New York City; and in *Annie Get Your Gun, Funny Girl,* and *Brigadoon.*

FILM APPEARANCES

Jan, *Heaven with a Gun,* Metro-Goldwyn-Mayer (MGM), 1969.
Vicki, *So Fine,* Warner Brothers, 1981.
Mrs. Simmons, *Diner,* MGM/United Artists (MGM/UA), 1982.
Hilda Kendricks, *I, the Jury,* Twentieth Century-Fox, 1982.
Soup for One, Warner Brothers, 1982.
Easy Money, Orion, 1983.
Geri, *Spring Break,* Columbia, 1983.
Helen, *Power,* Twentieth Century-Fox, 1986.
Mrs. Dice, *Illegally Yours,* MGM/UA, 1988.

Mrs. Porter, *Alien Nation,* Twentieth Century-Fox, 1988.
Bessie, *Immediate Family,* Columbia, 1989.

Also appeared in *Underground and Emigrants,* 1976; *The Lemon Sisters,* 1990; and *Sam's Spa.*

TELEVISION APPEARANCES

Millworker, *Daddy, I Don't Like It Like This* (movie), CBS, 1978.
Mrs. Wittemberry, *Nurse* (pilot), CBS, 1980.
Mrs. Bogart, *Running Out* (movie), CBS, 1983.
Eddie's mother, *Diner* (pilot), CBS, 1983.
Dottie, *Major Dad* (episode), CBS, 1989.
Aggie Potter, *Starting Now* (series), CBS, 1989.
Congresswoman Millicent Bane, *Murphy Brown* (episode), CBS, 1990.

Also appeared in episodes of *St. Elsewhere,* NBC; *Edge of Night,* CBS; *One Life to Live,* ABC; *Generations,* NBC; and *Grand Slam,* 1989.*

*   *   *

JARMAN, Derek   1942-

PERSONAL: Born January 31, 1942; son of Lance and Elizabeth Evelyn (Puttock) Jarman. *Education:* Attended Slade School, and King's College, University of London.

ADDRESSES: Contact—c/o British Film Institute, 29 Rathbone Pl., London WC2, England.

CAREER: Director, designer, producer, actor, and writer. Artist, with exhibitions at Edward Totah Gallery, Lission Gallery, I.C.A., and Richard Salmon Ltd.

CREDITS:

STAGE WORK

Designer, *Jazz Calendar,* Royal Ballet, 1968.
Designer, *Don Giovanni,* English National Opera, 1968.

Also designer for *The Rake's Progress,* Teatro Communale, Florence, Italy, and *Thruway,* Ballet Rambert. Director and designer, *L'ispirazione* (opera), 1988.

FILM APPEARANCES

Patrick Proktor, *Prick Up Your Ears,* Civilhand Zenith/Goldwyn, 1987.

Also appeared as himself, *Derek Jarman: You Know What I Mean,* 1988, and as narrator, *Cactus Land,* 1988; appeared in *Nighthawks,* 1978, and *Ostia,* 1987.

FILM WORK

Director, *Jubilee,* Cinegate, 1978.
Director, *Caravaggio,* British Film Institute/Cinevista, 1986.

Director, "Sequence 9: Louise," *Aria,* RVP/Virgin Vision, 1987.

Director (with others) and cinematographer, *The Last of England,* Tartan Pictures, 1987.

Director, *War Requiem,* Anglo International, 1989.

Also producer, cinematographer, and editor, *In the Shadow of the Sun,* 1981, and producer, cinematographer, and director, *Imagining October,* 1984. Director of *Sebastiane,* 1978, *The Tempest,* 1979, *T.G.—Psychic Rally in Heaven,* 1981, *The Dream Machine,* 1982, *Waiting for Waiting for Godot,* 1982, *The Angelic Conversation,* 1985, and *The Garden,* 1990. Designer for *The Devils,* 1971, and *Savage Messiah,* Russ-Arts/MGM, 1972.

WRITINGS:

SCREENPLAYS

Jubilee, Cinegate, 1978.

Caravaggio (British Film Institute/Cinevista, 1986), Thames & Hudson, 1986.

"Sequence 9: Louise," *Aria,* RVP/Virgin Vision, 1987.

(With others) *The Last of England* (Tartan Pictures, 1987), Constable, 1987.

(Author of narrative text) *War Requiem* (Anglo International, 1989), Faber, 1989.

Also author of *Sebastiane,* 1975, *The Tempest,* 1979, *Imagining October,* 1984, *The Angelic Conversation,* 1985, and *The Garden,* 1990.

OTHER

Dancing Ledge, Quartet Books, 1984.

Also author of *Modern Nature,* Century Hutchinson.

* * *

JARMUSCH, Jim   1953-

PERSONAL: Born in 1953 in Akron, OH. *Education:* Attended Columbia University; studied with director Nicholas Ray at the New York University Film School.

CAREER: Director, actor, composer, and writer.

AWARDS, HONORS: Prizes in West Germany and Portugal for *Permanent Vacation;* International Critics Prize, Rotterdam Film Festival, c. 1983, for *The New World;* Golden Leopard award, International Film Festival of Locarno, Camera d'Or, best new director, Cannes Film Festival, and best film, National Society of Film Critics, all 1984, for *Stranger Than Paradise.*

CREDITS:

FILM WORK

Sound recorder, *Underground USA,* New Cinema, 1980.

Director and editor, *Stranger Than Paradise* (includes *The New World*), Samuel Goldwyn, 1984 (also see below).

Director, *Down by Law,* Island Pictures, 1986 (also see below).

Director, *Mystery Train,* Orion Classics, 1989 (also see below).

Also director, editor, and producer, *Permanent Vacation,* 1980 (also see below); production assistant, *Lightning Over Water,* 1980; sound recorder, *Burroughs,* 1983; camera operator, *Sleepwalk,* 1986; director, *Coffee and Cigarettes,* 1986 (also see below); director, *Coffee and Cigarettes Part Two,* 1988 (also see below).

FILM APPEARANCES

Appeared in *Fraulein Berlin,* 1982; as Mr. Dade, *Straight to Hell,* 1987; *Candy Mountain,* 1987; *Helsinki Napoli All Night Long,* 1988; and as car dealer in New York, *Leningrad Cowboys Go America,* 1989.

WRITINGS:

SCREENPLAYS

Stranger Than Paradise, Samuel Goldwyn, 1984.
Down by Law, Island Pictures, 1986.
Mystery Train, Orion Classics, 1989.

Also author and composer of *Permanent Vacation,* 1980; author of *Coffee and Cigarettes,* 1986, and *Coffee and Cigarettes Part Two,* 1988. Composed scores for *The State of Things* and *Reverse Angle.**

* * *

JEFFRIES, Lionel   1926-

PERSONAL: Full name, Lionel Charles Jeffries; born in 1926 in Forest Hill, London, England.

ADDRESSES: Contact—c/o Dennis Selinger, International Creative Management, 388/396 Oxford St., London W1 9HE, England.

CAREER: Actor, director, and screenwriter. *Military service:* Served with Oxford and Bucks Light Infantry and Royal West African Frontier Force in Burma, World War II; became captain; awarded Burma Star.

AWARDS, HONORS: Kendal Award, Royal Academy of Dramatic Art, 1947; Fleet Street Award for Best Actor, 1953, for *The Enchanted;* British Academy Award nomination, 1960, for *The Man with the Green Carnation; Box Office* Blue Ribbon Awards for best actor, 1965, for *The Truth about Spring,* and 1967, for *Camelot;* Golden Globe nomination, 1966, for *The Spy with the Cold Nose;* Christopher Award, 1971, for *The Railway Children;* Gold Ear Award for best European film, 1973, for *Baxter;* Gold

Medal for Best Screenplay, International Science Fiction and Fantasy Film Festival, Paris, 1974, for *The Amazing Mr. Blunden.*

CREDITS:

STAGE APPEARANCES

Carrington V.C., Westminster Theatre, London, 1949.

The Enchanted, Arts Theatre, London, 1952.

Blood Wedding, Arts Theatre, London, 1952.

Brouhaha, Aldwych Theatre, London, 1952.

Horace Vandergelder, *Hello, Dolly!,* Triumph Apollo/Birmingham Repertory Theatre, then Prince of Wales Theatre, London, 1984.

Bishop of Lax, *See How They Run,* Theatre of Comedy Company, Shaftesbury Theatre, London, 1984.

The manager, *Two Into One,* Theatre of Comedy Company, Shaftesbury Theatre, 1984.

Putz, *Rookery Nook,* Theatre of Comedy Company, Shaftesbury Theatre, 1986.

Colonel Pickering, *Pygmalion,* Plymouth Theatre, New York City, 1987.

Lieutenant Ekdal, *The Wild Duck,* Sir Peter Hall Company, Phoenix Theatre, London, 1990.

FILM APPEARANCES

Brennan, *The Black Rider,* Balblair Butcher, 1954.

Harry, *The Colditz Story,* British Lion, 1955.

George Pogson, *No Smoking,* Eros, 1955.

Mr. Frobisher, *Will Any Gentleman?,* Stratford, 1955.

Arthur Lee, *Windfall,* Eros, 1955.

Maitre d'hotel, *All for Mary,* Rank, 1956.

Lieutenant Graham McDaniel, *Bhowani Junction,* Metro-Goldwyn-Mayer (MGM), 1956.

Eyewitness, Rank, 1956.

Bert Benton, *Jumping for Joy,* Rank, 1956.

Dr. Peyron, *Lust for Life,* MGM, 1956.

Blake, *The Creeping Unknown* (also known as *The Quatermas Xperiment*), Hammer, 1956.

George, *The Baby and the Battleship,* British Lion, 1957.

Keith, *Decision Against Time* (also known as *The Man in the Sky*), MGM, 1957.

Dr. Hatchett, *Doctor at Large,* Rank, 1957.

Monkton, *High Terrace,* RKO/Allied Artists, 1957.

Elvin Main, *Hour of Decision,* Eros, 1957.

Wilson, *Up in the World,* Rank, 1957.

Walter Froy, *Behind the Mask,* GW, 1958.

Joe Mangan, *Blue Murder at St. Trinian's,* British Lion, 1958.

Colonel, *Dunkirk,* MGM, 1958.

Tourist, *Girls at Sea,* Seven Arts, 1958.

Major Proudfoot, *Law and Disorder,* Continental Distributing, 1958.

Interrogator, *Orders to Kill,* United Motion Pictures, 1958.

Fritz, *The Revenge of Frankenstein,* Columbia, 1958.

Steady Barker, *Up the Creek,* Dominant, 1958.

Gregory Mason, *Bobbikins,* Twentieth Century-Fox, 1959.

Geoffrey Windsor, *The Circle* (also known as *The Vicious Circle*), Kassler, 1959.

Bertie, *Idol on Parade,* Columbia, 1959.

Pet shop man, *Nowhere to Go,* MGM, 1959.

Dr. Goovaerts, *The Nun's Story,* Warner Brothers, 1959.

Sergeant Thompson, *The Jazz Boat* (also known as *Jazzboat*), Columbia, 1960.

Marsh, *Let's Get Married,* Eros, 1960.

Marquis of Queensberry, *The Man With the Green Carnation* (also known as *The Trials of Oscar Wilde* and *The Green Carnation*), Kingsley, 1960.

Ian Howard, *Please Turn Over,* Columbia, 1960.

Ames, *Tarzan the Magnificent,* Paramount, 1960.

Monsieur Brun, *Fanny,* Warner Brothers, 1961.

Sidney Crout, *Two-Way Stretch,* International/Show Corporation of America, 1961.

Luke Billings, *The Hellions,* Columbia, 1962.

Inspector Hook, *Kill or Cure,* MGM, 1962.

Genie, *Life Is a Circus,* Schoenfeld, 1962.

Lester Gibbons, *Mrs. Gibbons' Boys,* British Lion, 1962.

Inspector Oliphant, *The Notorious Landlady,* Columbia, 1962.

Evans, *Operation Snatch,* Continental Distributing, 1962.

Dr. Ezra Mungo, *Call Me Bwana,* United Artists, 1963.

Inspector Parker, *The Wrong Arm of the Law,* Continental Distributing, 1963.

Colonel Judd, *The Crimson Blade* (also known as *The Scarlet Blade*), Columbia, 1964.

Cavor, *First Men in the Moon,* Columbia, 1964.

Aziz, *The Long Ships* (also known as *Dugi Brodovi*), Columbia, 1964.

Captain Sidney de Courly Rhumstone, *Murder Ahoy,* MGM, 1964.

Inspector Hobart, Baron von Lukenberg, President Esteda, and Earl of Aldershot, *The Secret of My Success,* MGM, 1965.

Cark, *The Truth About Spring,* Universal, 1965.

Sergeant-Major McGregor, *You Must Be Joking!,* Columbia, 1965.

Parker, *Arrivederci, Baby!,* Paramount, 1966.

Stanley Farquhar, *The Spy with a Cold Nose,* Embassy, 1966.

King Pellinore, *Camelot,* Seven Arts, 1967.

Airport Commander, *Oh Dad, Poor Dad, Mama's Hung You in the Closet and I'm Feelin' So Sad,* Paramount, 1967.

Sir Charles Dillworthy, *Those Fantastic Flying Fools* (also known as *Jules Verne's Rocket to the Moon* and *Blast Off*), American International, 1967.

Grandpa Potts, *Chitty Chitty Bang Bang*, United Artists, 1968.

Colonel, *Sudden Terror* (also known as *Eyewitness*), National General, 1970.

Mr. Creighton, *Lola* (also known as *Twinky*), American International, 1971.

Inspector Willoughby, *Who Slew Auntie Roo?* (also known as *Whoever Slew Auntie Roo?* and *Gingerbread House*), American International, 1971.

Krafstein, *Royal Flash*, Twentieth Century-Fox, 1975.

What Changed Charley Farthing? (also known as *Bananas Boat*), Stirling Gold, 1976.

Voice of Womble, *Wombling Free*, Rank, 1977.

General Sapt, *The Prisoner of Zenda*, Universal, 1979.

Berthie Hargreaves, *Better Late Than Never*, Warner Brothers, 1983.

Jarvis Huntley-Pike, *A Chorus of Disapproval*, South Gate Entertainment, 1989.

Also appeared in *Journey to the Moon* and *Menage a Trois*.

FILM DIRECTOR

The Railway Children, Universal, 1971.
The Amazing Mr. Blunden, Hemisphere, 1973.
Baxter, National General, 1973.
Wombling Free, Rank, 1977.
The Water Babies, Pethurst International, 1979.

TELEVISION APPEARANCES

Mr. Jekyll, *Jekyll & Hyde* (movie), ABC, 1990.
Ending Up (special), ITV, 1990.
First and Last, BBC-TV, 1990.
Boon, ITV, 1990.

Also appeared as Mr. Snoddy, *Danny, the Champion of the World* (movie), 1989, and in *Morse*, 1990, and *Father Charlie, Tom, Dick, and Harriet, Cream in My Coffee*, and *Minder*.

WRITINGS:

SCREENPLAYS

The Railway Children, Universal, 1971.
The Amazing Mr. Blunden, Hemisphere, 1973.
Wombling Free, Rank, 1977.

*   *   *

JENKINS, David   1937-

PERSONAL: Born July 30, 1937, in Hampton, VA; son of F. Raymond and Cecelia (Chandler) Jenkins; married Leigh Rand (a stage designer). *Education:* Attended Earlham College; Yale University, M.F.A.

CAREER: Designer and art director.

CREDITS:

STAGE SET DESIGNER, EXCEPT AS INDICATED

Set and light designer, *A Musical Timepiece*, Equity Library Theatre, Library and Museum of Performing Arts, New York City, 1970.

The Importance of Being Earnest, McCarter Theatre, Princeton, NJ, 1971.

The Homecoming, McCarter Theatre, 1971.

Child's Play, Trinity Square Repertory Company, Providence, RI, 1971.

The Way of the World, Long Wharf Theatre, New Haven, CT, 1972.

The Tooth of Crime, McCarter Theatre, 1972.

The Changing Room, Long Wharf Theatre, 1972, then Morosco Theatre, New York City, 1973.

Scenes from American Life, Goodman Memorial Theatre, Chicago, IL, 1972.

The Tempest, McCarter Theatre, 1973.

Romersholm, McCarter Theatre, 1973.

One Flew Over the Cuckoo's Nest, Arena Stage, Kreeger Theatre, Washington, DC, 1973.

The Freedom of the City, Goodman Memorial Theatre, 1973, then Alvin Theatre, New York City, 1974.

The Widowing of Mrs. Holroyd, Long Wharf Theatre, 1973.

Tom, Arena Stage, Kreeger Theatre, 1973.

In Celebration and *Relatively Speaking* (double-bill), Arena Stage, Kreeger Theatre, 1974.

The Sea, Goodman Memorial Theatre, 1974.

Boccaccio, Arena Stage, Kreeger Theatre, 1974.

Mother Courage and Her Children, McCarter Theatre, 1975.

Afore Night Come, Long Wharf Theatre, 1975.

Rodgers and Hart, Helen Hayes Theatre, New York City, 1975.

Gorky, American Place Theatre, New York City, 1975.

Tartuffe, Center Stage, Baltimore, MD, 1976.

Checking Out, Longacre Theatre, New York City, 1976.

Saint Joan, Circle in the Square, New York City, 1977.

Says I, Says He, Marymount Manhattan Theatre, New York City, 1979.

Strangers, John Golden Theatre, New York City, 1979.

The Elephant Man (also see below), Booth Theatre, New York City, 1979.

Mary Stuart, Circle Repertory Theatre, New York City, 1979-80.

Hamlet, Circle Repertory Theatre, New York City, 1979-80.

The Art of Dining, New York Shakespeare Festival (NYSF), Public/Newman Theatre, New York City, 1979.

I Ought to Be in Pictures (also see below), Center Theatre Group, Mark Taper Forum, Los Angeles, CA, 1979, then Eugene O'Neill Theatre, New York City, 1980.

Piaf, Plymouth Theatre, New York City, 1981.

Special Occasions, Music Box Theatre, New York City, 1982.

The Good Parts, Astor Place Theatre, New York City, 1982.

Poor Little Lambs, Theatre at St. Peter's Church, New York City, 1982.

Weekends Like Other People, Marymount Manhattan Theatre, 1982.

Lullabye and Goodnight, NYSF, Public/Newman Theatre, 1982.

The Queen and the Rebels, Plymouth Theatre, 1982.

Total Abandon, Perry Street Theatre, 1982, then Booth Theatre, 1983.

Accidental Death of an Anarchist, Center Theatre Group, Mark Taper Forum, 1982-83.

Quartermaine's Terms, Long Wharf Theatre, then Playhouse 91, New York City, 1982-83.

Preppies, Promenade Theatre, New York City, 1983.

Blue Plate Special, Manhattan Theatre Club, New York City, 1983.

And a Nightingale Sang . . . , Mitzi E. Newhouse Theatre, New York City, 1984.

Short Eyes, The Second Stage, New York City, 1984.

Husbandry, Manhattan Theatre Club, 1984.

Fugue, Long Wharf Theatre, 1985-86.

The Real Thing, Center Theatre Group, Mark Taper Forum, 1985-86.

Stardust, Theatre Off Park, New York City, then Biltmore Theatre, 1986-87.

The Common Pursuit, Promenade Theatre, 1986-87.

Progress, Long Wharf Theatre, 1986-87.

Talk Radio, NYSF, Public/Martinson Theatre, 1987.

Stepping Out, John Golden Theatre, 1987.

Sherlock's Last Case, Nederlander Theatre, New York City, then John F. Kennedy Center for the Performing Arts, Washington, DC, 1987-88.

The Student Prince, New York City Opera, New York State Theatre, New York City, 1987.

Bunker Reveries, Roundabout Theatre, New York City, 1987.

The Music Man, New York City, 1988.

Other People's Money, Hartford Stage Company, Minetta Lane Theatre, New York City, 1989.

Also set designer at PAF Playhouse, Huntington Station, NY, 1972-73; American Shakespeare Festival, Stratford, CT, 1975; McCarter Theatre, 1976-77; Long Wharf Theatre, 1975-82, 1984-85; Hartford Stage Company, Hartford, CT, 1976-77, 1980-81; Goodman Memorial Theatre, 1977-78; Milwaukee Repertory Theatre, Milwaukee, WI, 1978-79, 1982-83; Cincinnati Playhouse, Cincinnati, OH, 1980-81; and Arena Stage, 1983-85.

MAJOR TOURS

Set designer, *Children of a Lesser God,* U.S. cities, 1980-82.

Set designer, *The Elephant Man,* U.S. cities, 1980-81.

Set designer, *I Ought to Be in Pictures,* U.S. cities, 1980-81.

FILM WORK

Production designer, *I'm Dancing as Fast as I Can,* Paramount, 1982.

TELEVISION WORK

Set designer, "The Trial of Bernhard Goetz," *American Playhouse,* PBS, 1988.*

*   *   *

JOFFE, Charles H.   1929-

PERSONAL: Born July 16, 1929, in Brooklyn, NY; son of Sid and Esther (Gordon) Joffe; married Carol Shapiro; children: Suzanne, Nicole. *Education:* Syracuse University, B.S.

CAREER: Producer and talent manager. Partner, Rollins & Joffe (talent management agency), New York City.

MEMBER: Academy of Motion Picture Arts and Sciences, American Film Institute.

AWARDS, HONORS: Academy Award, Best Picture, 1977, for *Annie Hall.*

CREDITS:

FILM PRODUCER

Don't Drink the Water, AVCO/Embassy, 1969.

Take the Money and Run, Cinerama, 1969.

(With Jack Grossberg) *Bananas,* United Artists (UA), 1971.

Everything You Always Wanted to Know About Sex, But Were Afraid to Ask, UA, 1972.

Love and Death, UA, 1975.

Annie Hall, UA, 1977.

Interiors, UA, 1978.

Manhattan, UA, 1979.

(With Harold Schneider), *The House of God,* UA, 1984.

FILM EXECUTIVE PRODUCER

Play It Again, Sam, Paramount, 1972.

Sleeper, UA, 1973.

The Front, Columbia, 1976.

Stardust Memories, UA, 1980.

Arthur, Orion/Warner Brothers, 1981.

A Midsummer Night's Sex Comedy, Orion/Warner Brothers, 1982.

Zelig, Orion/Warner Brothers, 1983.

Broadway Danny Rose, Orion, 1984.

Purple Rose of Cairo, Orion, 1985.

Hannah and Her Sisters, Orion, 1986.

September, Orion, 1987.

Radio Days, Orion, 1987.

(With Rollins) *Another Woman,* Orion, 1988.

Crimes and Misdemeanors, Orion, 1989.

"Oedipus Wrecks," *New York Stories,* Touchstone/Buena Vista, 1989.

TELEVISION WORK

Producer (with Rollins), *The Woody Allen Special,* NBC, 1969.

Executive producer (with Larry Brezner), *Good Time Harry* (series), NBC, 1980.

Executive producer (with Brezner), *The Acorn People* (movie), NBC, 1981.

Executive producer (with Brezner and Buddy Morra), *Cheers* (series), NBC, 1982.

Executive producer (with Brezner and Morra), *Star of the Family* (series), ABC, 1982-83.

STAGE PRODUCER

(With David Merrick and Jack Rollins) *Don't Drink the Water,* Morosco Theatre, New York City, 1966.

(With Merrick and Rollins) *Play It Again, Sam,* Broadhurst Theatre, New York City, 1969.*

*   *   *

JOHNSON, Alan

CAREER: Actor, choreographer and director.

AWARDS, HONORS: Emmy Awards for Outstanding Achievement in Choreography, 1972, for *Jack Lemmon in S' Wonderful, 'S Marvelous, 'S Gershwin,* and 1980, for *Shirley MacLaine . . . Every Little Movement;* Antoinette Perry Award nomination, Best Choreography, 1989, for *Legs Diamond.*

CREDITS:

STAGE APPEARANCES

Dancer, *No Strings,* Fifty-Fourth Street Theatre, New York City, 1962.

Ensemble, *Hallelujah Baby!,* Martin Beck Theatre, New York City, 1967.

The Merry Wives of Windsor, Globe Playhouse, Los Angeles, CA, 1977-78.

STAGE CHOREOGRAPHER, EXCEPT AS INDICATED

Ballad for a Firing Squad, Theatre de Lys, New York City, 1968.

Shirley MacLaine, Palace Theatre, New York City, 1976.

So Long 174th Street, Harkness Theatre, New York City, 1976.

The First, Martin Beck Theatre, 1981.

Shirley MacLaine on Broadway, Gershwin Theatre, New York City, 1984.

And director, *Ann Reinking . . . Music Moves Me,* Joyce Theatre, New York City, 1984-85.

West Side Story (major tour), U.S. and Canadian cities, 1987-88.

Legs Diamond, Mark Hellinger Theatre, New York City, 1989.

Also choreographer for tour of *Can-Can,* U.S. cities.

FILM APPEARANCES

Doctor, *Steele Justice,* Atlantic Releasing Corporation, 1987.

FILM WORK

Choreographer, *The Producers,* Embassy Pictures Corporation, 1967.

Choreographer, *Blazing Saddles,* Warner Brothers, 1974.

Choreographer, *Young Frankenstein,* Twentieth Century-Fox, 1974.

Choreographer, *The Adventures of Sherlock Holmes' Smarter Brother,* Twentieth Century-Fox, 1975.

Choreographer, *The World's Greatest Lover,* Twentieth Century-Fox, 1977.

Choreographer and associate producer, *History of the World, Part 1,* Twentieth Century-Fox, 1981.

Director, *To Be or Not To Be,* Twentieth Century-Fox, 1983.

Director, *Solarbabies,* Metro-Goldwyn-Mayer/United Artists, 1986.

TELEVISION APPEARANCES

Appeared in the movie *People Like Us,* 1990.

TELEVISION CHOREOGRAPHER; SPECIALS, EXCEPT AS INDICATED

George M!, NBC, 1970.

Jack Lemmon in 'S Wonderful, 'S Marvelous, 'S Gershwin, NBC, 1972.

Jack Lemmon—Get Happy, NBC, 1973.

Shirley MacLaine: If They Could See Me Now, CBS, 1974.

(With Kevin Carlisle) *Cos,* ABC, 1976.

Shirley MacLaine Special: Where Do We Go From Here, CBS, 1977.

Three Girls Three, NBC, 1977.

CBS On the Air, CBS, 1978.

(With Bill Hargate) *Happy Birthday, Las Vegas,* ABC, 1978.
Paul Anka in Monte Carlo, CBS, 1978.
Ann–Margret's Hollywood Movie Girls, ABC, 1980.
Shirley MacLaine. . . Every Little Movement, CBS, 1980.
Portrait of a Showgirl (movie), CBS, 1982.
Shirley MacLaine: Illusions, CBS, 1982.
Night of 100 Stars, ABC, 1982.

Also choreographer for *Walt Disney . . .One Man's Dream,* 1981; *The Shirley MacLaine Show,* 1985; *The Fifty-Ninth Annual Academy Awards Presentation,* 1987; *The Forty-First Annual Tony Awards,* 1987; *Broadway Sings: The Music of Jule Styne,* 1987; *The Fortieth Annual Emmy Awards,* 1988; *The Forty-Second Annual Tony Awards,* 1988; *Irving Berlin's 100th Birthday,* 1988; and *The Forty-Third Annual Tony Awards,* 1989.*

* * *

JONES, Davy 1946-

PERSONAL: Full name, David Jones; born December 30, 1946, in Manchester, England.

ADDRESSES: Agent—Bauman, Hiller, & Associates, 5750 Wilshire Blvd., #512, Los Angeles, CA 90038.

CAREER: Actor and singer. Appeared on British television in the early 1960s; member of the Monkees, 1966-69; appeared with Micky Dolenz and others in Monkees reunion concerts in the 1970s; beginning in 1985, appeared with original Monkees members Dolenz and Peter Tork in a Monkees reunion tour.

AWARDS, HONORS: Antoinette Perry Award nomination, 1963, for *Oliver!;* (with the Monkees) Comeback of the Year, *Rolling Stone* Magazine Music Awards Readers' Poll, 1986.

CREDITS:

STAGE APPEARANCES

Artful Dodger, *Oliver!,* Imperial Theatre, New York City, 1963-65.
Pickwick, Forty-Sixth Street Theatre, New York City, 1965.
Oblio, *The Point,* Mermaid Theatre, London, 1977.

TELEVISION APPEARANCES; SERIES

Davy Jones, *The Monkees* (series), NBC, 1966-68.

TELEVISION APPEARANCES; EPISODIC

Malcolm O'Dell, *My Two Dads,* 1988 and 1989.
Jerry Vicuna, *Sledge Hammer!,* ABC, 1988.

Also appeared on episodes of *Ben Casey, The Brady Bunch,* and *Love, American Style.*

OTHER TELEVISION APPEARANCES

33 1/3 Revolutions Per Monkee (special), NBC, 1969.
The Peapicker in Piccadilly (special), NBC, 1969.
Lubbock, *Hunter* (pilot), CBS, 1973.
Record executive, "It's Only Rock & Roll," *Afterschool Special,* ABC, 1991.

Also appeared on *The American Music Awards,* 1987.

FILM APPEARANCES

(With the Monkees) *Head,* Columbia, 1973.

Also appeared in *Hot Channels,* 1973; *Illusions of a Lady,* 1973; *Not Just Another Woman,* 1973; and *Devil's Due,* 1973.

RECORDINGS:

WITH THE MONKEES

The Monkees, Colgems/RCA, 1967.
More of the Monkees, Colgems/RCA, 1967.
Headquarters, Colgems/RCA, 1967.
Pisces, Aquarius, Capricorn & Jones, Colgems/RCA, 1967.
The Birds The Bees & The Monkees, Colgems/RCA, 1968.
Instant Replay, Colgems/RCA, 1969.
Greatest Hits, Colgems, 1969.
Head, Colgems/RCA, 1969.
Changes, Colgems, 1970.

Other "Greatest Hits" collections also released. Singles include "I'm a Believer," "(I'm Not Your) Steppin' Stone," "Last Train to Clarksville," "A Little Bit Me, A Little Bit You," "Pleasant Valley Sunday," "Words," and "Daydream Believer," all 1967; "Valeri," and "D. W. Washburn," both 1968.*

* * *

JORDAN, Glenn 1936-

PERSONAL: Born April 5, 1936, in San Antonio, TX. *Education:* Harvard University, B.A., 1957; attended Yale School of Drama, 1957-58.

ADDRESSES: Office—9401 Wilshire Blvd., Beverly Hills, CA 90212. *Agent*—c/o Bill Haber, Creative Artists Agency, 9830 Wilshire Blvd., Beverly Hills, CA 90212.

CAREER: Director and producer. Founding producing director, *New York Television Theatre,* Channel 13, PBS.

AWARDS, HONORS: Emmy Awards, for producing and directing, 1970, for *New York Television Theatre* and *Actor's Choice,* for outstanding limited series, 1975, for *Benjamin Franklin,* for outstanding drama/comedy special and outstanding directing in a mini-series or a special, both 1987, for "Promise," *Hallmark Hall of Fame,* and nominations for outstanding directing in a drama series—single episode, 1975, for "The Ambassador," *Benjamin Franklin,* for outstanding directing in a limited series or a special, 1979, for *Les Miserables,* and for outstanding drama special, 1981, for *The Women's Room;* Peabody awards, 1975, for *Benjamin Franklin,* 1984, for *Heartsounds,* and 1987, for "Promise," *Hallmark Hall of Fame;* Directors Guild Award, for best direction in a dramatic series, 1976, for "Rites of Friendship," *Family,* and nomination, c. 1978, for *Les Miserables;* Christopher Awards, c. 1978, for *Les Miserables,* c. 1979, for *Son-Rise: A Miracle of Love,* 1983, for *Lois Gibbs and the Love Canal,* and 1987, for *Promise;* Golden Globe Award, for producing and directing, 1987, for "Promise," *Hallmark Hall of Fame;* Humanitas awards for *Son-Rise: A Miracle of Love* and *Promise.*

CREDITS:

TELEVISION DIRECTOR; MOVIES

Frankenstein, ABC, 1973.
The Picture of Dorian Gray, ABC, 1973.
Shell Game, CBS, 1975.
One of My Wives Is Missing, ABC, 1976.
Sunshine Christmas, NBC, 1977.
Delta County, U.S.A., ABC, 1977.
In the Matter of Karen Ann Quinlan, NBC, 1977.
The Court Martial of General Custer, NBC, 1978.
Les Miserables, CBS, 1978.
Son-Rise: A Miracle of Love, NBC, 1979.
The Family Man, CBS, 1979.
(And supervising producer) *The Women's Room,* ABC, 1980.
The Princess and the Cabbie, CBS, 1981.
Lois Gibbs and the Love Canal, CBS, 1982.
Heartsounds, ABC, 1984.
Toughlove, ABC, 1985.
Dress Gray, NBC, 1986.
Something in Common, CBS, 1986.
(And producer) *Echoes in the Darkness,* CBS, 1987.
(And producer) *Jesse,* CBS, 1988.
(And producer) *Challenger,* ABC, 1989.
(And producer) *Sarah, Plain and Tall,* CBS, 1990.
(And producer) *Aftermath,* CBS, 1991.
(And producer) *The Boys,* ABC, 1991.

TELEVISION DIRECTOR; SERIES

The Young Dr. Kildare, syndicated, 1972.
(With others) *Family,* ABC, 1976.
(With Peter Levin, Seymore Robbie, and Robert Stevens) *The Best of Families,* PBS, 1977.

(With Bob Sand, Bo Kaprall, and Cindy Levin; and producer) *Friends,* ABC, 1979.

TELEVISION DIRECTOR; SPECIALS

"The Displaced Person," *American Short Story,* PBS, 1977.
(And producer) "Promise," *Hallmark Hall of Fame,* CBS, 1986.
"Home Fires Burning," *Hallmark Hall of Fame,* CBS, 1989.

Also director of *Something in Common,* 1986, *A Prowler in the Heart,* ABC, and *Eccentricities of a Nightingale;* director and producer of *Paradise Lost,* PBS, *Making Money and Thirteen Other Very Short Plays,* and *Dragon Country.*

TELEVISION DIRECTOR; OTHER

Delta County U.S.A. (pilot), ABC, 1962.
(With George Lefferts and Lewis Freedman; and producer) *Benjamin Franklin* (mini-series), CBS, 1974.
The Oath: Thirty-three Hours in the Life of God (pilot), ABC, 1976.

Also producer and director of *Actor's Choice,* PBS, and director of episode "The Typist," *Hollywood Television Theatre.*

STAGE DIRECTOR

The Disintegration of James Cherry, Eugene O'Neill Theatre Center, Waterford, CT, 1970.
The Disintegration of James Cherry, Forum Theatre, New York City, 1970.
A Streetcar Named Desire, Cincinnati Playhouse in the Park, Cincinnati, OH, 1973.
All My Sons, Huntington Hartford Theatre, Los Angeles, CA, 1975.
Actors and Actresses, Hartman Theatre, Stamford, CT, 1983.

Also director of *Another Evening with Harry Stoones,* New York City, 1961; *A Taste of Honey,* 1968; *Rosencrantz and Guildenstern Are Dead,* 1969; *A Delicate Balance,* Williamstown Theatre Festival, Williamstown, MA; *A Cry of Players,* Brandeis University; *Keep Tightly Closed in a Cool, Dry Place,* La Mama Experimental Theatre Company, New York City.

FILM DIRECTOR

Only When I Laugh, Columbia, 1981.
The Buddy System, Twentieth Century-Fox, 1984.
Mass Appeal, Universal, 1984.

K

KANIN, Michael 1910-

PERSONAL: Born February 1, 1910 in Rochester, NY; son of David (a builder) and Sadie (Levine) Kanin; married Fay Mitchell (a playwright), April 7, 1940; children: Josh. *Education:* Attended Arts Students League, 1928, and New York School of Design, 1929. *Avocational interests:* Painting, sculpture, books, music.

CAREER: Playwright, director, and producer. Worked as commercial and scenic artist, musician, and entertainer, 1927-37; contributor to fiction magazines.

MEMBER: American National Theater and Academy, Academy of Motion Picture Arts and Sciences, Dramatists Guild, Writers Guild of America (member of board, 1943-44; treasurer, 1944-45; organized Affiliated Committee for Television), Screen Writers Guild (member of executive board, 1933-34; treasurer, 1944-45), American Theater Association, American College Theatre Festival, International Sculpture Center.

AWARDS, HONORS: Academy Award, best original screenplay, 1942, for *Woman of the Year,* nomination, 1958, for *Teacher's Pet;* Writers Guild of America award nomination, 1958, for *Teacher's Pet;* American College Theatre Festival, Bronze Medal, 1972, Silver Medal, 1973; special citation, City of Los Angeles, for encouraging youth in the theater, 1974; Valentine Davies Award, 1989.

CREDITS:

STAGE PRODUCER

(With Aldrich and Myers) *Goodbye, My Fancy,* Morosco Theatre, New York City, 1948.
Seidman and Son, Belasco Theatre, New York City, 1962.

FILM WORK

Producer, *A Double Life,* Universal, 1948.

Director, *When I Grow Up,* Eagle Lion, 1951.
Associate producer, *The Outrage,* Metro-Goldwyn-Mayer, 1964.

WRITINGS:

PLAYS

(With Harry Ingram) *We, the Willoughbys,* produced in Stockbridge, MA, 1939.
(With wife, Fay Kanin) *His and Hers* (produced in New York City, 1954), Samuel French, 1954.
(With Kanin) *Rashomon* (based on stories by Ryanosuke Akutagawa; produced on Broadway, 1959), Random House, 1959.
(With Kanin) *The Gay Life,* produced on Broadway, 1961.
(With Ben Starr) *M. Lord and Lady,* first produced in Los Angeles, CA, 1974.

FILMS

Panama Lady, RKO, 1939.
(With Joe Pagano) *They Made Her a Spy,* RKO, 1939.
(With Jerry Cady) *Anne of Windy Poplars,* RKO, 1940.
(With Kanin and Allen Rivkin) *Sunday Punch,* Metro-Goldwyn-Mayer (MGM), 1940.
(With Ring Lardner, Jr.) *Woman of the Year,* MGM, 1942.
(With Lardner, Alexander Esway, and Robert D. Andrews) *The Cross of Lorraine,* MGM, 1943.
Centennial Summer, Twentieth Century-Fox, 1946.
Honeymoon (also released as *Two Men and a Girl*), RKO, 1947.
When I Grow Up, Eagle-Lion, 1951.
(With Kanin) *My Pal Gus,* Twentieth Century-Fox, 1952.
(With Kanin, Ruth Goetz, and Augustus Goetz) *Rhapsody,* MGM, 1954.
(With Kanin) *The Opposite Sex,* MGM, 1956.

(With Kanin) *Teacher's Pet*, Paramount, 1958.

(With Kanin) *The Right Approach*, Twentieth Century-Fox, 1961.

(With Kanin, Alec Coppel, Sandro Continenza, and Dominique Fabre), *The Swordsman of Sienna*, MGM, 1962.

The Outrage, (based on his play *Rashomon*), MGM, 1964.

(With Ben Starr) *How to Commit Marriage*, Cinerama, 1969.

Cabbages and Kings, Talent Associates, 1975.

Also wrote *The Source* (based on a novel by James A. Michener) with Fay Kanin.

ADAPTATIONS: Woman of the Year was adapted as a stage musical with book by Peter Stone, music by John Kander, and lyrics by Fred Ebb, produced on Broadway, 1981, U.S. tour, 1983-84.

*   *   *

KARLEN, John   1933-

PERSONAL: Original name John Adam Karlewicz; born May 28, 1933, in New York, NY; son of Adam Marion and Helen-Agnes (Balondowicz) Karlewicz; married Elizabeth Marie Silicato, January 20, 1963. *Education:* Trained for the stage at the American Academy of Dramatic Arts.

ADDRESSES: Agent—The Gersh Agency, 222 North Canon Dr., Beverly Hills, CA 90210.

CAREER: Actor. Member of Theatre Company of Boston, 1966-67, and Yale Repertory Theatre Company, 1967-68.

AWARDS, HONORS: Emmy Award, outstanding supporting actor in a drama series, 1986, for *Cagney and Lacey.*

CREDITS:

STAGE APPEARANCES

Postmark Zero, Brooks Atkinson Theatre, New York City, 1965.

Mr. Stein, "Suburban Tragedy" and Joe, "Young Marrieds Play Monopoly," *Monopoly,* Establishment Theatre Company, Stage 73, New York City, 1966.

'Tis Pity She's a Whore, Yale Repertory Theatre, New Haven, CT, 1967.

Also appeared in productions of *Sweet Bird of Youth, The Milk Train Doesn't Stop Here Anymore, Invitation to a March, Luther, Arturo Ui,* and *All in Good Time,* all New York City.

FILM APPEARANCES

Stefan Chiltern, *Daughters of Darkness* (also known as *Le Rouge aux levres*), Gemini, 1971.

Alex Jenkins, *Night of Dark Shadows* (also known as *Curse of Dark Shadows*), Metro-Goldwyn-Mayer (MGM), 1971.

Lenny, *A Small Town in Texas,* American International, 1976.

Detective, *Pennies from Heaven,* MGM, 1981.

Bucky "Dr. Spirit" Berkshire, *Gimme an 'F',* Twentieth Century-Fox, 1984.

Bob Russell, *Impulse,* Twentieth Century-Fox, 1984.

Mr. Nash, *Racing with the Moon,* Paramount, 1984.

Max, *Native Son,* Cinecom, 1986.

Also appeared in *Killer's Delight,* 1978.

TELEVISION APPEARANCES; SERIES

Willie Loomis and Desmond Collins, *Dark Shadows,* ABC, 1966.

Harvey Lacey, *Cagney and Lacey,* CBS, 1982-88.

Lieutenant Stan Akers, *Snoops,* CBS, 1989.

TELEVISION APPEARANCES; PILOTS

Werner, *Cool Million* (also known as *The Mask of Marcella*), NBC, 1972.

The Police Story, NBC, 1973.

Richard Copell, *Delancey Street: The Crisis Within,* NBC, 1975.

Kessler, *Colorado C.I.,* CBS, 1978.

Duane Haley, *The Long Days of Summer,* ABC, 1980.

TELEVISION APPEARANCES; EPISODIC

"Mike Goes Skiing," *All in the Family,* CBS, 1977.

Adam Simon, *The New Mike Hammer,* CBS, 1987.

Lieutenant McGinn, *Murder, She Wrote,* CBS, 1989.

Nathan Pollack, *227,* NBC, 1989.

Nathan Pollack, *Jackee,* NBC, 1989.

Also appeared in episodes of *Hill Street Blues,* NBC; *Lou Grant,* CBS; *Trapper John, M.D.,* CBS; *Quincy M.E.,* NBC; *The Waltons,* CBS; *Police Story,* NBC; *Kojak,* CBS; *Hawaii Five-O,* CBS; *The Streets of San Francisco,* ABC.

TELEVISION APPEARANCES; MOVIES

Pete Manning, *The Night of Terror,* ABC, 1972.

Otto Roget, *Frankenstein,* ABC, 1973.

Herbie Bush, *Shirts/Skins,* ABC, 1973.

Alan Campbell, *The Picture of Dorian Gray,* ABC, 1973.

Tony Redecci, *Melvin Purvis: G-Man* (also known as *The Legend of Machine Gun Kelly*), ABC, 1974.

Sam Cowley, *The Kansas City Massacre,* ABC, 1975.

Thomas Anman, *Trilogy of Terror,* ABC, 1975.

Charlie Powers, *The Last Ride of the Dalton Gang,* NBC, 1979.

Marty, *The Return of Mod Squad,* ABC, 1979.
Coach Ritter, *American Dream,* ABC, 1981.
Uncle George, *Rosie: The Rosemary Clooney Story,* CBS, 1982.
DiSalvo, *Hostage Flight,* NBC, 1985.
Simon Chapel, *The Return of Mickey Spillane's "Mike Hammer,"* CBS, 1986.
Mr. Geffin, *Welcome Home, Bobby,* CBS, 1986.
Mike Burnette, *Daddy,* ABC, 1987.
Albert, *Downpayment on Murder,* NBC, 1987.
Burnout (also known as *Police Story*), ABC, 1988.
Charlie Wingo, *The Cover Girl and the Cop,* NBC, 1989.
Al, *Babycakes,* CBS, 1989.

TELEVISION APPEARANCES; SPECIALS

Ned, *The Patriots,* NBC, 1973.
Bill Leggett, "My Dear Uncle Sherlock," *ABC Short Story Specials,* ABC, 1977.
Host, *CBS All American Thanksgiving Day Parade,* CBS, 1986.
Joe Farrell, "Date Rape," *ABC Afterschool Special,* ABC, 1988.

OTHER TELEVISION APPEARANCES

Captain Connelly, *The Winds of War* (mini-series), ABC, 1983.*

*   *   *

KARLIN, Fred 1936-

PERSONAL: Born June 16, 1936, in Chicago, IL. *Education:* Received B.A. from Amherst College.

CAREER: Composer, arranger, writer, and conductor. Composer and arranger for Benny Goodman and Harry James orchestras.

AWARDS, HONORS: Academy Award, Best Song, 1970, for "For All We Know," from *Lovers and Other Strangers;* Emmy Award, Outstanding Original Music Score, 1974, for *The Autobiography of Miss Jane Pittman.*

CREDITS:

FILM WORK

Music director, *Yours, Mine and Ours,* United Artists, 1968 (also see below).

WRITINGS:

FILM SCORES

Up the Down Staircase, Warner Brothers, 1967.
Yours, Mine and Ours, United Artists, 1968.
The Stalking Moon, National General, 1969.
The Sterile Cuckoo, Paramount, 1969.
The Baby Maker, National General, 1970.

Cover Me Babe, Twentieth Century-Fox, 1970.
Lovers and Other Strangers, Cinerama, 1970.
Believe in Me, Metro-Goldwyn-Mayer (MGM), 1971.
The Marriage of a Young Stockbroker, Twentieth Century-Fox, 1971.
Every Little Crook and Nanny, MGM, 1972.
The Little Ark, National General, 1972.
Westworld, MGM, 1973.
Chosen Survivors, Columbia, 1974.
The Gravy Train (also known as *The Dion Brothers*), Columbia, 1974.
Mixed Company, United Artists, 1974.
The Spikes Gang, United Artists, 1974.
The Take, Columbia, 1974.
Baby Blue Marine, Columbia, 1976.
Futureworld, American International Pictures, 1976.
(With Norman Gimbel), *Joe Panther,* Artists Creation, 1976.
Leadbelly, Paramount, 1976.
Greased Lightning, Warner Brothers, 1977.
Mean Dog Blues, American International Pictures, 1978.
California Dreaming, American International Pictures, 1979.
The Ravagers, Columbia, 1979.
Cloud Dancer, Blossom, 1980.
Loving Couples, Twentieth Century-Fox, 1980.
Vasectomy: A Delicate Matter, Seymour Borde and Associates, 1986.

Also composer for *Zandy's Bride,* 1974; and *Attack of the Phantoms,* 1980.

TELEVISION MOVIE SCORES

Mr. and Mrs. Bo Jo Jones, ABC, 1971.
The Man Who Could Talk to Kids, ABC, 1973.
The Autobiography of Miss Jane Pittman, CBS, 1974.
Bad Ronald, ABC, 1974.
Born Innocent, NBC, 1974.
It Couldn't Happen to a Nicer Guy, ABC, 1974.
Punch and Jody, NBC, 1974.
Death Be Not Proud, ABC, 1975.
The Dream Makers, NBC, 1975.
Dawn: Portrait of a Teenage Runaway, NBC, 1976.
Wanted: The Sundance Woman, ABC, 1976.
Woman of the Year, CBS, 1976.
Alexander: The Other Side of Dawn, NBC, 1977.
Billy: Portrait of a Street Kid, CBS, 1977.
Christmas Miracle in Caufield, U.S.A., NBC, 1977.
Green Eyes, ABC, 1977.
The Hostage Heart, CBS, 1977.
The Life and Assassination of the Kingfish, NBC, 1977.
Minstrel Man, CBS, 1977.
The Death of Richie, NBC, 1977.
Having Babies II, ABC, 1977.
Intimate Strangers, ABC, 1977.

The Trial of Lee Harvey Oswald, ABC, 1977.
Deadman's Curve, CBS, 1978.
Forever, CBS, 1978.
The Girl Called Hatter Fox, CBS, 1978.
Leave Yesterday Behind, ABC, 1978.
The Awakening Land: The Saga of An American Woman, NBC, 1978.
KISS Meets the Phantom of the Park, NBC, 1978.
Bud and Lou, NBC, 1978.
Forever, CBS, 1978.
The Gift of Love, ABC, 1978.
Just Me and You, NBC, 1978.
Lady of the House, NBC, 1978.
Long Journey Back, ABC, 1978.
More Than Friends, ABC, 1978.
The Waverly Wonders, NBC, 1978.
Who'll Save Our Children, CBS, 1978.
And Baby Makes Six, NBC, 1979.
And Your Name Is Jonah, CBS, 1979.
Ike, ABC, 1979.
Paris, CBS, 1979.
Samurai, ABC, 1979.
Sex and the Single Parent, CBS, 1979.
Strangers: The Story of a Mother and Daughter, CBS, 1979.
This Man Stands Alone, NBC, 1979.
Topper, ABC, 1979.
Transplant, CBS, 1979.
Vampire, ABC, 1979.
Walking through the Fire, CBS, 1979.
The Last Giraffe, CBS, 1979.
Baby Comes Home, CBS, 1980.
Fighting Back, ABC, 1980.
Mom, the Wolfman and Me, syndicated, 1980.
My Kidnapper, My Love, NBC, 1980.
Once Upon a Family, CBS, 1980.
The Plutonium Incident, CBS, 1980.
The Secret War of Jackie's Girls, NBC, 1980.
Sophia Loren: Her Own Story, NBC, 1980.
A Time for Miracles, ABC, 1980.
Homeward Bound, CBS, 1980.
Marriage Is Alive and Well, NBC, 1980.
Bitter Harvest, NBC, 1981.
Broken Promise, CBS, 1981.
The Five of Me, CBS, 1981.
Jacqueline Susann's Valley of the Dolls 1981, CBS, 1981.
Jessica Novak, CBS, 1981.
The Marva Collins Story, CBS, 1981.
Miracle on Ice, ABC, 1981.
Thornwell, CBS, 1981.
We're Fighting Back, CBS, 1981.
Deadly Encounter, CBS, 1982.
The First Time, ABC, 1982.
Inside the Third Reich, ABC, 1982.

Not in Front of the Children, CBS, 1982.
Gift of Love: A Christmas Story, CBS, 1983.
In Defense of Kids, CBS, 1983.
Night Partners, CBS, 1983.
One Cooks, the Other Doesn't, CBS, 1983.
Policewoman Centerfold, NBC, 1983.
Baby Sister, ABC, 1983.
Calamity Jane, CBS, 1984.
Love Leads the Way, The Disney Channel, 1984.
Final Jeopardy, NBC, 1985.
Hostage Flight, NBC, 1985.
Kids Don't Tell, CBS, 1985.
Robert Kennedy and His Times, CBS, 1985.
Dream West, CBS, 1986.
The Facts of Life Down Under, NBC, 1987.
A Place to Call Home, CBS, 1987.
Celebration Family, ABC, 1987.
What Price Victory, ABC, 1988.
Lady Mobster, ABC, 1988.
Dadah Is Death, CBS, 1988.
Bridge to Silence, CBS, 1989.
Fear Stalk, CBS, 1989.

Also composer of music score for *Leave Yesterday Behind,* 1978, *Flour Babies,* 1990, and *Murder C.O.D.,* 1990.

OTHER TELEVISION SCORES

Lucan (series), ABC, 1977.
The Man from Atlantis (series), NBC, 1977.
Life Goes to War: Hollywood and Homefront (special), NBC, 1977.
McLaren's Riders (pilot), CBS, 1977.
The World of Darkness (pilot), 1977.
The World Beyond (pilot), CBS, 1978.
Roll of Thunder, Hear My Cry (mini-series), ABC, 1978.
Kaz (series), CBS, 1978.
Blind Ambition (parts 3 and 4 of mini-series), CBS, 1979.
Catalina C-Lab (pilot), NBC, 1982.
Full House (pilot), CBS, 1983.
Inspector Perez (pilot), NBC, 1983.
Lovers and Other Strangers (pilot), ABC, 1983.
Wishman (pilot), ABC, 1983.
Off the Rack (pilot), ABC, 1984.

Also wrote scores for *Hollywood: The Gift of Laughter,* 1982; and *Hardesty House,* 1986.

OTHER

Also author, with Rayburn Wright, of *On the Track: A Guide to Contemporary Film Scoring,* Schirmer.*

KATZKA, Gabriel 1931-1990

PERSONAL: Born January 25, 1931, in Brooklyn, NY; died of a heart attack, February 19, 1990, in New York, NY; son of Emil Katzka (a lawyer); married Carol Ward Dudley; children: Edward Dudley. *Education:* Graduated from Kenyon College.

CAREER: Producer. President, Vista Organization (film and television production company).

CREDITS:

STAGE WORK

Production associate, *An Evening with Mike Nichols and Elaine May,* John Golden Theatre, New York City, 1960-61.

Production associate, *Beyond the Fringe,* John Golden Theatre, 1962-63.

Associate producer, *The School for Scandal,* Majestic Theatre, New York City, 1963.

Associate producer, *Man and Boy,* Brooks Atkinson Theatre, New York City, 1963.

Producer (with Alexander Cohen and Gustave Berne), *Karmon Israeli Dancer,* Royale Theatre, New York City, 1963.

Producer (with Berne and Saint-Subber), *Barefoot in the Park,* Biltmore Theatre, New York City, 1963-67.

Production associate, *Hamlet,* Lunt-Fontanne Theatre, New York City, 1964.

Production associate, *Beyond the Fringe '65,* Ethel Barrymore Theatre, New York City, 1964-65.

Producer (with Berne, Saint-Subber, Theodore Mann, and Joseph E. Levine), *Hughie,* Royale Theatre, 1964-65.

Producer (with Cohen), *Baker Street,* Broadway Theatre, New York City, 1965.

Producer (with Berne, Saint-Subber, Mann, and Levine), *And Things That Go Bump in the Night,* Henry Miller's Theatre, New York City, 1965.

Producer (with Berne, Levine, and Ulu Grosbard), *A View from the Bridge,* Sheridan Square Playhouse, New York City, 1965-66.

Producer (with Cohen and Edward L. Schuman), *Comedians,* Music Box Theatre, New York City, 1976.

Producer (with Cohen and Schuman), *Anna Christie,* Imperial Theatre, New York City, 1977.

MAJOR TOURS

Production associate, *Beyond the Fringe,* U.S. and Canadian cities, 1964-65.

Producer (with Berne and Saint-Subber), *Barefoot in the Park,* U.S. and Canadian cities, 1964-66.

Producer (with Berne), *The Porcelain Year,* U.S. cities, 1965.

FILM PRODUCER, EXCEPT WHERE INDICATED

Marlowe, Metro-Goldwyn-Mayer (MGM), 1969.
Soldier Blue, AVCO-Embassy, 1970.
(With Sidney Beckerman) *Kelly's Heroes,* MGM, 1970.
Executive producer, *Sleuth,* Twentieth Century-Fox, 1972.
The Taking of Pelham 1, 2, 3, United Artists, 1974.
Executive producer, *The Parallax View,* Paramount, 1974.
Executive producer, *Mr. Billion,* Twentieth Century-Fox, 1977.
Production consultant, *A Bridge Too Far,* United Artists, 1977.
(With Herb Jaffe) *Who'll Stop the Rain?,* United Artists, 1978.
(With Steven Bach) *Butch and Sundance: The Early Days,* Twentieth Century-Fox, 1979.
Executive producer (with Sandy Howard), *Meteor,* American International, 1979.
(With Harvey Bernhard) *The Beast Within,* United Artists, 1982.
(With Jaffe) *The Lords of Discipline,* Paramount, 1983.
(With John Schlesinger) *The Falcon and the Snowman,* Orion, 1985.

TELEVISION EXECUTIVE PRODUCER; SERIES

Philip Marlowe, Private Eye, HBO, 1983-86.
(With Gerald I. Isenberg) *Mariah,* ABC, 1987.

TELEVISION EXECUTIVE PRODUCER; PILOTS

(With Pat Nardo) *Rita,* CBS, 1986.

TELEVISION EXECUTIVE PRODUCER; MOVIES

(With Patricia Johnston and Stanley Chase) *The Courage of Kavik, the Wolf Dog,* NBC, 1980.
(With Stuart Miller) *Isabel's Choice,* CBS, 1981.
(With Frank Konigsberg) *Ellis Island,* CBS, 1984.
(With Bob Markell) *At Mother's Request,* CBS, 1987.
(With Miller) *Lady in a Corner,* NBC, 1989.

OBITUARIES AND OTHER SOURCES:

PERIODICALS

New York Times, February 21, 1990.
Variety, February 28, 1990.*

*　　　　*　　　　*

KAYE, Judy 1948-

PERSONAL: Born December 11, 1948, in Phoenix, AZ; daughter of Jerome Joseph (a physician) and Shirley Edith (Silverman) Kaye. *Education:* Attended University of California, Los Angeles, and Arizona State University. *Poli-*

tics: Democrat. *Religion:* Jewish. *Avocational interests:* Golf, tennis, skiing.

ADDRESSES: Agent—Bret Adams, Ltd., 448 West 44th St., New York, NY 10036.

CAREER: Actress and singer. Has appeared in concert with orchestras, including the New York Philharmonic, London Symphony, Pittsburgh Symphony, Boston Symphony, and Concordia Symphony.

AWARDS, HONORS: Frank Sinatra Award, UCLA, 1968; Natalie Wood Award, UCLA, 1969; Theatre World Award, Los Angeles Drama Critic's Circle Award, and Drama Desk Award nomination, 1979, all for *On the Twentieth Century;* Antoinette Perry Award, best featured actress in a musical, and Drama Desk Award nomination, both 1988, both for *The Phantom of the Opera.*

CREDITS:

STAGE APPEARANCES

(Stage debut) Chorus, *Melodyland,* Anaheim, CA, 1967.

Lucy, *You're a Good Man, Charlie Brown,* Los Angeles Civic Opera, Los Angeles, CA, 1968.

(Broadway debut) Rizzo, *Grease,* Royale Theatre, 1977.

Agnes, then Lily Garland, *On the Twentieth Century,* St. James Theatre, New York City, 1978.

Principal, *Moony Shapiro Songbook,* Morosco Theatre, New York City, 1981.

Saroyana, *Oh Brother!,* ANTA Theatre, New York City, 1981.

Hey, Look Me Over! A Tribute to the Work of Cy Coleman, Avery Fisher Hall, New York City, 1981.

Principal, *Can't Help Singing: A Salute to Jerome Kern,* St. Regis-Sheraton/King Cole Room, New York City, 1982.

Virginia McVay, *Four to Make Two,* Actors Repertory Theatre, New York City, 1982.

Ellen, *Love,* Audrey Wood Theatre, New York City, 1984.

Principal, *Side By Side By Sondheim,* Paper Mill Playhouse, Millburn, NJ, 1984-85.

Molly Malloy, *Windy City,* Paper Mill Playhouse, 1985-86.

Lucille Early, *No, No, Nanette,* Carnegie Hall, New York City, 1986.

Annie, *Annie Get Your Gun,* Paper Mill Playhouse, 1987.

Teresa, *Magdalena,* Alice Tully Hall, New York City, 1987.

Carlotta Giudicelli, *The Phantom of the Opera,* Majestic Theatre, New York City, 1988.

Also appeared as Babe Williams, *The Pajama Game,* New York City Opera, NY; Dorothy, *Wizard of Oz,* Arizona State University; Barbara, *Apple Tree,* Los Angeles, CA; Judy, *Godspell,* Los Angeles Civic Opera; Henny, *Awake and Sing,* Los Angeles, CA; Sheila, *Hair,* Sacramento

Music Circus, CA; Agnes, *I Do, I Do,* Dallas Civic Light Opera, TX; Leah, *The Dybbuk,* Arizona Civic Theatre; Kate, *Kiss Me Kate,* Sacramento, CA; Maria, *The Sound of Music,* Cincinnati Opera, OH, and Sacramento, CA; Pistache, *Can-Can,* St. Louis MUNY Opera, MO; Hodel, *Fiddler on the Roof,* Sacramento, CA, Honolulu, HI, and Los Angeles Civic Light Opera, Los Angeles, CA; Flor, *Half a Sixpence,* Melodyland, Anaheim, CA; Martha, *1776,* San Bernadino Civic Light Opera; Mrs. Lovett, *Sweeney Todd,* Michigan Opera; Julie Jordan, *Carousel,* Candlelight Dinner Theatre; Dinah, *Trouble in Tahiti,* Anchorage Opera; Eurydice, *Orpheus in the Underworld,* Santa Fe Opera; Lalume, *Kismet,* Canadian Opera; Nellie, *South Pacific,* Minnesota Opera; Musetta, *La Boheme,* Santa Fe Opera; and Annie, *Annie Get Your Gun,* Greater Miami Opera. Appeared in *The Amazing Flight of the Gooney Bird* and *Laura Nyro Revue,* New Theatre for Now, "In the Works: II" Festival, Los Angeles Center Theatre Group, 1975; *Desire Under the Elms* (opera), New York City; *The Merry Widow,* Paper Mill Playhouse, NJ, and Portland Opera Company; *Eileen in Concert, Sweethearts in Concert,* and *Sweet Adeline,* all Town Hall, New York City, NY.

MAJOR TOURS

Betty Rizzo, *Grease,* opening Shubert Theatre, Boston, MA, 1972.

Mary Magdalene, *Jesus Christ Superstar,* U.S. cities, 1972.

Lily Garland, *On the Twentieth Century,* opening Fisher Theatre, Detroit, MI, 1979, and closing Orpheum Theatre, San Francisco, CA, 1979, and also opening Coconut Grove Playhouse, Miami, FL, 1986, and closing Scranton, PA, 1987.

FILM APPEARANCES

(Film debut) Baby, *Just Tell Me What You Want,* Warner Brothers, 1980.

TELEVISION APPEARANCES; SERIES

Mr. Deeds Goes to Town, ABC 1969.

TELEVISION APPEARANCES; EPISODIC

Appeared on episodes of *The Doctors,* NBC; *The Today Show,* NBC; *Kojak,* CBS; *The Merv Griffin Show,* CBS; *Insight; The Donald O'Connor Show,* NBC; and *Matt Lincoln,* ABC.

TELEVISION APPEARANCES; SPECIALS

Fol-De-Rol, ABC, 1972.

Also appeared on *The Boston Pops,* PBS; *In Performance at the White House,* PBS; and *The Arte Johnson Special.*

TELEVISION APPEARANCES; PILOTS

This Week in Nemtin, CBS, 1972.

Also appeared on *Me on the Radio.*

* * *

KEITH, Brian 1921-

PERSONAL: Full name, Brian Michael Keith; born November 14, 1921, in Bayonne, NJ; son of Robert Lee (an actor) and Helena (an actress; maiden name, Shipman) Keith; married Victoria Lei Aloha Young (an artist), 1968; children: Mimi, Bobby, Daisy. *Religion:* Roman Catholic. *Avocational interests:* Fishing.

ADDRESSES: Agent—Guild Management, 9911 W. Pico Blvd., Los Angeles, CA 90035; and James McHugh Agency, 8150 Beverly Blvd., Suite 303, Los Angeles, CA 90048.

CAREER: Actor. President of Miguel Productions, Inc. *Military service:* U.S. Marine Corps, aerial gunner, 1942-45.

MEMBER: Screen Actors Guild, Actor's Equity Association, Directors Guild of America, American Federation of Television and Radio Artists.

CREDITS:

STAGE APPEARANCES

(Stage debut) *Heyday,* Shubert Theatre, New Haven, CT, 1946.
(Broadway debut) Mannion, *Mister Roberts,* Alvin Theatre, 1948.
Ilyich, *Darkness at Noon,* Alvin Theatre, 1951.
Lash, *Out West of Eighth,* Ethel Barrymore, New York City, 1951.
Title role, *Da,* Morosco Theatre, New York City, 1978.

Also appeared in *Moon Is Blue,* Chicago, 1951; and as Jezebel's husband, *The Emperor of Babylon,* Boston, 1952.

FILM APPEARANCES

(Film debut) Captain North, *Arrowhead,* Paramount, 1953.
Jim Kimmerly, *Alaska Seas,* Paramount, 1954.
Tony, *Jivaro* (also known as *Lost Treasure of the Amazon*), Paramount, 1954.
Captain Brady, *The Bamboo Prison,* Columbia, 1955.
Brick, *Five against the House,* Columbia, 1955.
Vince Striker, *Tight Spot,* Columbia, 1955.
Colonel Wilkison, *The Violent Men* (also known as *Rough Company*), Columbia, 1955.
John, *Nightfall,* Columbia, 1956.
Paul Duncan, *Storm Center,* Columbia, 1956.
Jim Fremont, *Chicago Confidential,* United Artists, 1957.
Sheridan, *Dino,* Allied Artists, 1957.
Hell Canyon Outlaws, Republic, 1957.

Captain Clark, *Run of the Arrow,* Universal, 1957.
Lieutenant Spencer, *Appointment with a Shadow,* Universal, 1958.
Captain Edwards, *Desert Hell,* Twentieth Century-Fox, 1958.
Clett, *Fort Dobbs,* Warner Brothers, 1958.
Jack McCracken, *Sierra Baron,* Twentieth Century-Fox, 1958.
Bill Harmon, *Villa!,* Twentieth Century-Fox, 1958.
Mitch, *Violent Road* (also known as *Hell's Highway*), Warner Brothers, 1958.
Mike Flannagan, *The Young Philadelphians* (also known as *The City Jungle*), Warner Brothers, 1959.
William Dunn, *Ten Who Dared,* Buena Vista, 1960.
Yellowleg, *The Deadly Companions,* Pathe-American, 1961.
Mitch Evans, *The Parent Trap,* Buena Vista, 1961.
Major General John Vanneman, *Moon Pilot,* Buena Vista, 1962.
Uncle Beck Coates, *Savage Sam,* Buena Vista, 1963.
Paul Barton, *The Pleasure Seekers,* Twentieth Century-Fox, 1964.
John G. McElroy, *The Raiders* (also known as *The Plainsman*), Universal, 1964.
Cam Calloway, *Those Calloways,* Buena Vista, 1964.
Sheriff Pete Williams, *A Tiger Walks,* Buena Vista, 1964.
Frank Wallingham, *The Hallelujah Trail,* United Artists, 1965.
Jonas Cord, *Nevada Smith,* Paramount, 1966.
Alexander Bowen, *The Rare Breed,* Universal, 1966.
Link Mattocks, *The Russians Are Coming, The Russians Are Coming,* United Artists, 1966.
General Hallenby, *Way . . . Way Out,* Twentieth Century-Fox, 1966.
Lieutenant Colonel Morris Langdon, *Reflections in a Golden Eye,* Warner Brothers, 1967.
Jake Iverson, *With Six You Get Eggroll* (also known as *A Man in Mommy's Bed*), National General Pictures, 1968.
Francis X, *Gaily, Gaily* (also known as *Chicago, Chicago*), United Artists, 1969.
Connerly, *Krakatoa, East of Java* (also known as *Volcano*), Cinerama, 1969.
Captain Jack Connor, *The McKenzie Break,* United Artists, 1970.
Warrant Officer Nace, *Suppose They Gave a War and Nobody Came* (also known as *War Games*), Cinerama, 1970.
John McCanless, *Scandalous John,* Buena Vista, 1971.
Colonel Morgan, *Something Big,* National General Pictures, 1971.
Theodore Roosevelt, *The Wind and the Lion,* United Artists, 1975.

George Tanner, *The Yakuza* (also known as *Brotherhood of the Yakuza*), Warner Brothers, 1975.

Captain Harper, *Joe Panther*, Artists Creation, 1976.

H. H. Cobb, *Nickelodeon*, Columbia, 1976.

Jocko, *Hooper*, Warner Brothers, 1978.

Dr. Alexei Dubov, *Meteor*, American International Pictures, 1979.

U.S. shuttle captain, *Moonraker*, United Artists, 1979.

Henry, *The Mountain Men*, Columbia, 1980.

Police chief, *Charlie Chan and the Curse of the Dragon Queen*, American Cinema, 1981.

Papa, *Sharky's Machine*, Warner Brothers, 1982.

Colonel Halloran, *Death before Dishonor*, New World Pictures, 1987.

Buckshot Roberts, *Young Guns*, Twentieth Century-Fox, 1988.

The Passage, Spectrum, 1988.

Dr. Harry, Jake's father, *Welcome Home*, Columbia, 1989.

Also appeared as Byron Monroe, *After the Rain*, 1988.

TELEVISION APPEARANCES; SERIES

Matt Anders, *Crusader*, CBS, 1955-56.

Dave Blassingame, *The Westerner*, NBC, 1960.

"Uncle Bill" Davis, *Family Affair*, CBS, 1966-71.

Sean Jamison, *The Little People*, NBC, 1972-73.

Dr. Sean Jamison, *The Brian Keith Show*, NBC, 1973-74.

Lew Archer, *Archer*, NBC, 1975.

Steven Halliday/Fox, *The Zoo Gang*, NBC, 1975.

General Lee Stonecipher, *How the West Was Won*, ABC, 1977.

Judge Milton C. Hardcastle, *Hardcastle and McCormick*, ABC, 1983-86.

Professor Roland G. Duncan, *Pursuit of Happiness*, ABC, 1987.

B. L. McCutcheon, *Heartland*, CBS, 1989.

TELEVISION APPEARANCES; MOVIES

Geoff Smith, *Second Chance*, ABC, 1972.

Tank Logan, *The Quest*, NBC, 1976.

Arnold Curtis, *The Loneliest Runner*, NBC, 1976.

Joe Quinlan, *In the Matter of Karen Ann Quinlan*, NBC, 1977.

Elijah Weatherby, *The Seekers*, HBO, 1979.

Mauritz Stiller, *Moviola: The Silent Lovers*, NBC, 1980.

Secretary General Gorny, *World War III*, NBC, 1982.

Chief Whalen, *Cry for the Strangers*, CBS, 1982.

Davy Crockett, *The Alamo: Thirteen Days to Glory*, NBC, 1987.

Frank Wellman, Sr., *Perry Mason: The Case of the Lethal Lesson*, NBC, 1989.

David Henderson, *Lady in a Corner*, NBC, 1989.

Also appeared as General Newmeyer, *B.R.A.T. Patrol*, 1986.

TELEVISION APPEARANCES; MINI-SERIES

Shadrock, *Elfego Baca*, ABC, 1958.

Axel Dumire, *Centennial*, NBC, 1978.

Andrew Blake, *The Chisholms*, CBS, 1979.

TELEVISION APPEARANCES; EPISODIC

Guest, *Studio One*, CBS, 1949.

The Lux Video Theater, CBS, 1950-54, NBC, 1954.

Robert Montgomery Presents Your Lucky Strike Theater, NBC, 1950.

Ford Television Theater, NBC, 1952-56, ABC, 1956.

Campbell Sound Stage, NBC, 1952.

The United States Steel Hour, ABC, 1953-55, CBS, 1955.

The Elgin Hour, NBC, 1954.

Climax!, CBS, 1954.

Studio 57, DuMont, 1954.

Zane Grey Theater, CBS, 1956.

Great Adventure, CBS, 1963.

Kraft Suspense Theater, NBC, 1963.

OTHER TELEVISION APPEARANCES

Dave Blassingame, *Winchester* (pilot), CBS, 1959.

Allan Jacobson, *The Court Martial of George Armstrong Custer* (special), NBC, 1977.

The ABC All-Star Spectacular (special), ABC, 1985.

Also appeared on the specials *All-Star Party for Clint Eastwood*, 1986, and *All-Star Party for Joan Collins*, 1987.

SIDELIGHTS: Favorite roles: Da.*

*   *   *

KENSIT, Patsy   1968-

PERSONAL: Born March 4, 1968, in London, England; daughter of James (an antiques dealer) and Margie (a publicist) Kensit; married Dan Donovan (a musician), 1988.

ADDRESSES: Agent—Duncan Heath Associates, Paramount House, 162-170 Wardour St., London W1V 3AT, England.

CAREER: Actress. Member, Royal Shakespeare Company, 1983. Lead singer of musical group Eighth Wonder; songwriter.

CREDITS:

FILM APPEARANCES

(Film debut) Pamela Buchannan, *The Great Gatsby*, Paramount, 1974.

Penny, *Alfie Darling*, EMI, 1975.

Mytyl, *The Blue Bird*, Twentieth Century-Fox, 1976.

Sarah Sellinger, *Hanover Street,* Columbia, 1979.
(And singer of "Having It All") Crepe Suzette, *Absolute Beginners,* Orion, 1986.
Linda Washbrook, *A Chorus of Disapproval,* South Gate Entertainment, 1989.
(And singer of "I'm Not Scared") Rika Van Den Haas, *Lethal Weapon II,* Warner Brothers, 1989.
Chicago Joe and the Showgirl (also known as *Chicago Joe*), New Line Cinema, 1990.
Katie, *Twenty-One,* Triton, 1991.

Also appeared in *The Atlantic.*

TELEVISION APPEARANCES; MINI-SERIES

Estella, *Great Expectations,* Entertainment Channel, 1982.
Emma Prince, *Tycoon: The Story of a Woman,* syndicated, 1983.

OTHER TELEVISION APPEARANCES

Pollyanna Harrington, *The Adventures of Pollyanna* (pilot), CBS, 1982.
Emilie du Caillaud, *The Corsican Brothers* (movie), CBS, 1985.

Also appeared in specials, including as young Diana, *Diana,* 1985; *The Noel Edmunds Show,* 1986; Eppie in *Silas Marner,* 1987; *Arms and the Man,* BBC; and *Frost in May.*

WRITINGS:

FILM; SONGWRITER

Wrote and performed "Having It All," for *Absolute Beginners;* and "I'm Not Scared" for *Lethal Weapon II.*

OTHER SOURCES:

PERIODICALS

Premiere, May, 1991.*

*   *   *

KIEL, Richard   1939-

PERSONAL: Born September 13, 1939, in Detroit, MI; married; wife's name, Diane (a publicity assistant); children: three sons, one daughter.

ADDRESSES: Agent—c/o Joshua Gray Agency, 6736 Laurel Canyon, North Hollywood, CA 91606.

CAREER: Actor and producer. Spokesperson for companies, including Toys R Us, Viacom Cable Television, and SBE Citizen Band Radios; actor in television commercials, including ones for Tough Act, Eggo Waffles, Teledyne Water-Pik, Chevrolet, Midas Mufflers, Austin Ma-

rina Cars, Nabisco Shredded Wheat, Glico Milk, Sharp Electronics, Fayva Shoes, and Sierra on Line.

CREDITS:

FILM APPEARANCES

Solarite, *The Phantom Planet,* American International Pictures, 1961.
Eegah, *Eegah!,* Fairway-International Films, 1962.
Pinhead, *The Magic Sword,* United Artists, 1962.
The Giant, *House of the Damned,* Twentieth Century-Fox, 1963.
Chinook Pete, *Lassie's Great Adventure,* Twentieth Century-Fox, 1963.
Strong Man, *Roustabout,* Paramount, 1964.
Kolos, *The Human Duplicators,* Crest, 1965.
Las Vegas Hillbillys, Woolner Brothers, 1966.
Otto, *A Man Called Dagger,* Metro-Goldwyn-Mayer, 1967.
Beany, *Skidoo,* Paramount, 1968.
Samson, *The Longest Yard,* Paramount, 1974.
Milo Pewett, *Flash and the Firecat,* Sebastian, 1976.
Reace/Goldtooth, *Silver Streak,* Twentieth Century–Fox, 1976.
Jaws, *The Spy Who Loved Me,* United Artists, 1977.
Drazac, *Force Ten From Navarone,* American International Pictures, 1978.
Duke, *They Went That-A-Way and That-A-Way,* International Picture Show, 1978.
Golob One, *The Humanoid* (also known as *L'Umanoide*), Columbia, 1979.
Jaws, *Moonraker,* United Artists, 1979.
Eddie, *So Fine,* Warner Brothers, 1981.
Captain Howdy, *Hysterical,* EMB, 1983.
Arnold, *Cannon Ball Run II,* Warner Brothers, 1984.
Club, *Pale Rider,* Warner Brothers, 1985.
The Giant of Thunder Mountain, New Generation Entertainment, 1991.

Also appeared as Irving, *Think Big,* 1990, and in *Dead Head Miles, The Nutty Professor, Gus, On a Clear Day, Brainstorm, Bigfoot, The Nasty Rabbit, The Phoenix, Aces Go Places III, The Racketeers,* and *Two on a Guillotine.*

FILM WORK

Executive producer (with John Herklotz), *The Giant of Thunder Mountain,* New Generation Entertainment, 1991.

TELEVISION APPEARANCES; SERIES

Voltaire, *The Wild Wild West,* CBS, 1965.
Malak, *Land of the Lost,* NBC, 1974.
Van Dyke and Company, NBC, 1976.
Lola, ABC, 1976.

TELEVISION APPEARANCES; EPISODIC

Master Styx, *Thriller*, NBC, 1960.
Superboy, syndicated, 1988.

Also appeared in "To Serve Man," *Twilight Zone;* as Cracks, *My Mother the Car;* as Duff Brannigan, *Klondike;* as Big Mike, *Phantom;* and on *Simon & Simon, The Rifleman, I Spy, 30 Minutes at Gunsight, Laramie, The Escape, Honey West, King of Diamonds, I Dream of Jeannie, Lassie, It Takes a Thief, Nightstalker, Fall Guy, Switch, The Monkeys, Starsky & Hutch, Gilligan's Island, Emergency, The Hardy Boys, Daniel Boone,* and *Young Daniel Boone.*

TELEVISION APPEARANCES; MOVIES

Nori, *Now You See it, Now You Don't*, NBC, 1968.
Moose Moran, *The Barbary Coast*, ABC, 1975.

Also appeared on *The Boy Who Stole the Elephant;* and as a giant Indian, *Lassie's Journey.*

OTHER TELEVISION APPEARANCES

Appeared on *Circus of the Stars* (special), 1979; on *Man from UNCLE* (pilot); on *The Danny Kaye Show;* on *The Peter Marshall Show;* on *The Steve Allen Show;* on *The Kooky Castle Show;* on *The Paul Bunyon Show;* and on a *National Geographic* special about Bigfoot.

Appeared on talk shows, including *The Mike Douglas Show, The Merv Griffin Show, The Today Show, Good Morning America, David Letterman, Regis Philbin, AM Los Angeles, Good Morning Los Angeles, AM San Francisco,* as well as several foreign talk shows; appeared on game shows, including *Win, Lose, or Draw, Hollywood Squares, Tattle Tales, Match Game, Celebrity Family Feud, All Star Family Feud,* and *Bullseye.*

TELEVISION WORK

Produced the children's special *The Paul Bunyon Show* (also see below).

WRITINGS:

Wrote the children's special *The Paul Bunyon Show.*

*   *   *

KIM, Willa

PERSONAL: Born in Los Angeles, CA; daughter of Shoon Kwam and Nora Kim; married William Pene du Bois (a designer). *Education:* Attended the Chouinard Institute of Art.

CAREER: Costume and set designer. Costume designer with the New Theatre for Now, Mark Taper Forum, Los

Angeles, 1969-70; and Goodman Theatre, Chicago, IL, 1978-79. Frequent costume and set designer for the Feld Ballet, Joffrey Ballet, American Ballet Theatre, and the San Francisco Ballet.

AWARDS, HONORS: Obie Award, *Village Voice*, 1964-65, for *The Old Glory;* Drama Desk Award, 1969-70, for *Promenade* and *Operation Sidewinder;* Maharam Award, Drama Desk Award, and the Annual *Variety* New York Drama Critics Poll Award, all 1971-72, all for *The Screens;* Antoinette Perry Award nomination, best costume design, 1975, for *Goodtime Charley;* Antoinette Perry Award nomination, best costume design, 1978, for *Dancin';* Antoinette Perry Award, best costume design, 1981, for *Sophisticated Ladies;* Emmy Award, 1981, for *The Tempest;* Asian Woman of Achievement Award, Asian American Professional Women, 1983; Antoinette Perry Award nomination, best costume designer, 1986, for *Song and Dance;* Antoinette Perry Award nomination, and Drama Desk Award nomination, both best costume design, both 1989, for *Legs Diamond;* Antoinette Perry Award, best costume design, 1991, for *The Will Rogers Follies.*

CREDITS:

STAGE WORK; COSTUME DESIGNER

Red Eye of Love, Provincetown Playhouse, New York City, 1961.
Fortuna, Maidman Playhouse, New York City, 1962.
The Saving Grace, Writer's Stage Theatre, New York City, 1963.
Have I Got a Girl for You!, Music Box Theatre, New York City, 1963.
Funnyhouse of a Negro, East End Theatre, New York City, 1964.
Dynamite Tonight, York Playhouse, New York City, 1964.
A Midsummer Night's Dream, New York Shakespeare Festival (NYSF), Mobile Theatre, New York City, 1964.
The Old Glory, American Place Theatre, St. Clement's Church, New York City, 1964.
Helen, Bouwerie Lane Theatre, New York City, 1964.
The Day the Whores Came Out to Play Tennis and *Sing to Me Through Open Windows* (double-bill), Players Theatre, New York City, 1965.
The Stag King (opera), Santa Fe Opera Company, Santa Fe, NM, 1965.
Malcolm, Theatre 1966, Shubert Theatre, New York City, 1966.
The Office, Henry Miller's Theatre, New York City, 1966.
(With Howard Bay) *Chu Chem,* Locust Theatre, Philadelphia, PA, 1966.
Hail Scrawdyke!, Booth Theatre, New York City, 1966.

Scuba Duba, New Theatre, New York City, 1967.
The Ceremony of Innocence, American Place Theatre, St. Clement's Church, 1967.
Promenade, Promenade Theatre, New York City, 1969.
Papp, American Place Theatre, St. Clement's Church, 1969.
Operation Sidewinder, Repertory Theatre of Lincoln Center, Vivian Beaumont Theatre, New York City, 1970.
Sunday Dinner, American Place Theatre, St. Clement's Church, 1970.
The Screens, Chelsea Theatre Center, Brooklyn Academy of Music, Brooklyn, NY, 1971.
Sleep, American Place Theatre, 1972.
Lysistrata, Brooks Atkinson Theatre, New York City, 1972.
The Chickencoop Chinaman, American Place Theatre, 1972.
Jumpers, Kennedy Center for the Performing Arts, Washington, D.C., then Billy Rose Theatre, New York City, both 1974.
Goodtime Charley, Palace Theatre, New York City, 1975.
The Old Glory, A Trilogy, American Place Theatre, 1976.
Dancin', Broadhurst Theatre, New York City, 1978.
The Grinding Machine, American Place Theatre, 1978.
Bosoms and Neglect, Longacre Theatre, New York City, 1979.
Sophisticated Ladies, Lunt-Fontanne Theatre, New York City, 1981.
Family Devotions, NYSF, Public Theatre, 1981.
Lydie Breeze, American Place Theatre, 1982.
Chaplin, Dorothy Chandler Pavilion Theatre, Los Angeles, 1983.
Elizabeth and Essex, York Theatre Company, Church of the Heavenly Rest, New York City, 1984.
Song and Dance, Royale Theatre, New York City, 1985.
Long Day's Journey into Night, Broadhurst Theatre, 1986.
The Front Page, Lincoln Center Theatre, Vivian Beaumont Theatre, 1986.
Legs Diamond, Mark Hellinger Theatre, New York City, 1989.
The Will Rogers Follies, Palace Theatre, 1991.

Also costume designer for ballets, *Birds of Sorrow,* 1962; *Gamelan,* Lennigrad, U.S.S.R., 1963, U.S., 1965; and *Game of Noah,* Netherlands, 1965, U.S., 1965. Costume and set designer for ballets, *Daphnis et Chloe, Papillon, Scenes for the Theatre, A Song for Dead Warriors, Shinju, Rodin, Dream Dances;* and for operas, *The Magic Flute,* Santa Fe Opera Company, *Le Rossignol,* and *Help, Help, the Gobolinks.*

MAJOR TOURS; COSTUME DESIGNER

Dancin', U.S. cities, 1979-83, European cities, 1980-84.
Sophisticated Ladies, U.S. cities, 1982.
Song and Dance, U.S. cities, 1987.

FILM WORK; COSTUME DESIGNER

(With Judianna Makovsky), *Gardens of Stone,* Tri-Star, 1987.

TELEVISION WORK; COSTUME DESIGNER; SPECIALS

"St. Patrick's Day," *Esso Repertory Theatre,* PBS, 1964.
"The Forced Marriage" and "The Beautiful People," *Esso Repertory Theatre,* PBS, 1965.
(And set designer) *A Song for Dead Warriors* PBS, 1984.
Julie Andrews: The Sound of Christmas (also known as *The Sound of Christmas*), ABC, 1987.
"Long Day's Journey into Night," *Showtime on Broadway,* Showtime, 1987, *American Playhouse,* PBS, 1988.

Also costume designer for *The Tempest,* 1981, and *Le Rossignol,* PBS.

*   *   *

KING, Mabel

PERSONAL: Original name Donnie Mabel Elizabeth Washington; born December 25, in Charleston, SC; daughter of Rosalie Washington; married Melvin King (marriage ended).

ADDRESSES: Manager—Gene Yusem, P.O. Box 67B/69, Los Angeles, CA 90067.

CAREER: Actress. Made professional debut at age 7, singing at Carnegie Hall; singer with the Sincere Four, a gospel group; recorded songs for Rama Records; night club performer at the Apollo and Paramount theatres, both in New York City; appeared with the Theatre National Populaire, Paris, France; toured the U.S. and Europe as a singer. Factory worker.

CREDITS:

STAGE APPEARANCES

Ernestina, *Hello, Dolly!,* St. James Theatre, New York City, 1964-68.
Mrs. Bowser, *Don't Play Us Cheap,* Ethel Barrymore Theatre, New York City, 1972.
Evillene, *The Wiz,* Majestic Theatre, New York City, 1975.
Grandma, *It's So Nice to Be Civilized,* Martin Beck Theatre, New York City, 1980.

Also appeared in productions of *A Race with the Wind, The Women,* and *Anna Lucasta,* all in New York City.

MAJOR TOURS

Maria, *Porgy and Bess,* U.S. cities, 1966.

FILM APPEARANCES

Queen of Myrthia, *Ganja and Hess* (also known as *Double Possession* and *Blood Couple*), Kelly/Jordan, 1973.
Bertha, *The Bingo Long Traveling All-Stars and Motor Kings,* Universal, 1976.
Madam Amy, *Scott Joplin,* Universal, 1977.
Evillene, *The Wiz,* Universal, 1978.
Mother, *The Jerk,* Universal, 1979.
Mabel, *The Gong Show Movie,* Universal, 1980.
Mabel Queen, *Getting Over,* Continental, 1981.
Gramma, *Scrooged,* Paramount, 1988.
Mrs. Bowser, *Don't Play Us Cheap,* Movin' On, 1990.

TELEVISION APPEARANCES; SERIES

Mabel Thomas, *What's Happening!!,* ABC, 1976-79.

TELEVISION APPEARANCES; EPISODIC

The Mike Douglas Show, syndicated, 1977.
Barney Miller, ABC, 1979.
Jennifer, *Amazing Stories,* NBC, 1986.
Odessa, *The Colbys,* ABC, 1986.
Mae Nina, *Wiseguy,* CBS, 1988.

TELEVISION APPEARANCES; SPECIALS

Mrs. Trussker, "All the Money in the World," *ABC Weekend Specials,* ABC, 1983.
Grandmother, *NBC Presents The AFI Comedy Special,* NBC, 1987.

OTHER TELEVISION APPEARANCES

Mama Johnson, *The Jerk, Too* (pilot), NBC, 1984.

RADIO APPEARANCES

Appeared on *Allen Freed's Rock 'n' Roll Show.**

* * *

KING, Perry 1948-

PERSONAL: Born April 30, 1948, in Alliance, OH; son of a physician; separated; children: Louise. *Education:* Received B.A. in theatre from Yale University; studied acting with John Houseman at the Juilliard School of Drama. *Avocational interests:* Restoring old cars and motorcycles; auto racing.

ADDRESSES: Agent—Creative Artists Agency, 9830 Wilshire Blvd., Beverly Hills, CA 90212.

CAREER: Actor.

AWARDS, HONORS: Golden Globe nomination, best supporting actor, for *The Hasty Heart;* won several auto races, including 1986 Long Beach Grand Prix Toyota Pro-Celebrity Race.

CREDITS:

STAGE APPEARANCES

Curly, *Knuckle,* Phoenix, NY, 1975.

Also appeared as lead, *Child's Play,* Morosco Theatre (New York debut); Cassio, *Othello,* Washington, DC; John, *Eccentricities of a Nightingale,* Los Angeles, CA; and Bassanio, *The Merchant of Venice,* Old Globe, Los Angeles, CA; *Jesse James,* New York City; and *The Trouble with Europe,* New York City.

FILM APPEARANCES

(Film debut) Joel Delaney, *The Possession of Joel Delaney,* Paramount, 1972.
Robert Pilgrim, *Slaughterhouse-Five,* Universal, 1972.
Chico Tyrell, *The Lords of Flatbush,* Columbia, 1974.
Hammond, *Mandingo,* Paramount, 1975.
Dale Sword, *The Wild Party,* American International Pictures, 1975.
Steve Edison, *Lipstick,* Paramount, 1976.
Baxter Slate, *The Choirboys,* Universal, 1977.
Albert, *A Different Story,* Avco Embassy, 1978.
Kip Moore, *Search and Destroy,* Film Ventures International, 1981.
Andy Norris, *Class of 1984,* United Film Distribution, 1982.
Paul McCormack, *The Killing Hour,* Lansbury-Berun, 1982.
Steve Brooks, *Switch,* Warner Brothers, 1991.

Also appeared as LT, *Andy Warhol's Bad,* 1976; *Striking Back,* 1981; and *The Clairvoyant.*

TELEVISION APPEARANCES; SERIES

Dan Underwood, *The Quest,* ABC, 1982.
Cody Allen, *Riptide,* NBC, 1984-86.

Also appeared as Dr. Matt Haley, *The Knife & Gun Club,* 1990; played the voice of Samson in the animated program *Samson & Delilah;* and *The Whirlwind.*

TELEVISION APPEARANCES; MINISERIES

Rory Armagh, *Captains and the Kings,* NBC, 1976.
Lee Bishop, *The Innocent and the Damned,* NBC, 1979 (also known as *Aspen,* originally aired 1977).
Russ Currier, *The Last Convertible,* NBC, 1979.
Cutter Amberville, *I'll Take Manhattan,* CBS, 1987.

Also appeared in *Vice Queen of the Sunset Strip,* 1987; and *Mama's Boys,* 1988.

TELEVISION APPEARANCES; MOVIES

Rocco Laurie, *Foster and Laurie,* CBS, 1975.
Dr. Edwin Alexander, *The Cracker Factory,* ABC, 1979.
Colonel Zachary Willis, *Love's Savage Fury,* ABC, 1979.

Lieutenant John Armstrong, *City in Fear* (also known as *Panic on Page One*), ABC, 1980.

Roy Matson, *Inmates: A Love Story,* ABC, 1981.

John Macy, *Helen Keller: The Miracle Continues,* Operation Prime Time, 1984.

Nick MacKenzie, *Stranded,* NBC, 1986.

Sergeant Charles Stoker, *Shakedown on Sunset Strip,* CBS, 1988.

Philip Weber, *The Man Who Lived at The Ritz,* syndicated, 1988.

Kenneth Caldwell, *Perfect People,* ABC, 1988.

Major Hicks, *Disaster at Silo 7,* ABC, 1988.

Herbert Pulitzer, *Roxanne: The Prize Pulitzer,* NBC, 1989.

Also appeared in *The Hasty Heart,* Showtime; *The Hemingway Play,* PBS; *Big Truck;* and *Poor Clare.*

TELEVISION APPEARANCES; PILOTS

Jordan Kingsley, *Golden Gate,* ABC, 1981.

Cody Allen, *Four Eyes,* NBC, 1984.

Scott Kallen, *Half 'n' Half,* ABC, 1988.

TELEVISION APPEARANCES; SPECIALS

Tenth Annual Circus of the Stars, CBS, 1985.

The NBC All-Star Hour, NBC, 1985.

NBC's 60th Anniversary Celebration, NBC, 1986.

It's Howdy Doody Time: A 40-Year Celebration, NBC, 1987.

Also appeared in the specials *The 37th Annual Prime Time Emmy Awards,* 1985; *The Valvoline National Driving Test,* CBS, 1989; and *The Second Annual Valvoline National Driving Test,* 1990.

TELEVISION APPEARANCES; EPISODIC

Appeared in episodes of *Medical Center,* CBS; *Hawaii Five-O,* CBS; *Apples's Way;* and *Cannon.*

RADIO APPEARANCES

Appeared as Hans Solo, *Star Wars,* National Public Radio; appeared in several dramas for *Earplay,* National Public Radio.*

*   *   *

KNEALE, Nigel   1922-

PERSONAL: Full name, Thomas Nigel Kneale; born April 28, 1922, in Barrow-in-Furness, Lancashire, England; son of William Thomas (a journalist) and Lilian (Kewley) Kneale; married Anne Judith Kerr (a writer), May 8, 1954; children: Tacy, Matthew. *Education:* Attended Royal Academy of Dramatic Art, 1946-48. *Politics:* "None." *Religion:* "None."

ADDRESSES: Agent—Douglas Rae Ltd., 28 Charing Cross Road, London WC2H ODB, England.

CAREER: Writer. Staff writer, BBC, London, England, 1951-55; free-lance writer, 1955—.

AWARDS, HONORS: Somerset Maugham Award, 1950, for *Tomato Cain.*

WRITINGS:

Tomato Cain and Other Stories, Collins, 1949, Knopf, 1950.

Quatermass and the Pit: A Play for Television in Six Parts, Penguin, 1960.

Quatermass II: A Play for Television in Six Parts, Penguin, 1960.

The Quatermass Experiment: A Play for Television in Six Parts, Penguin, 1960.

(Editor) *Ghost Stories of M. R. James,* Folio Society, 1973.

The Year of the Sex Olympics and Other TV Plays, Ferret Fantasy, 1976.

Quatermass, Hutchinson, 1979.

SCREENPLAYS

(With Richard Landau and Val Guest) *The Creeping Unknown* (also known as *The Quatermass Experiment*), United Artists, 1956.

The Abominable Snowman of the Himalayas, Twentieth Century-Fox, 1957.

(With V. Guest) *Enemy From Space* (also known as *Quatermass II*), United Artists, 1957.

(With John Osborne) *Look Back in Anger,* Warner Brothers, 1959.

(With J. Osborne) *The Entertainer,* Bryanston-British Lion, 1960.

(With Edmund H. North) *HMS Defiant: Damn the Defiant,* Columbia, 1962.

(With Jan Read) *First Men in the Moon,* Columbia, 1964.

The Devil's Own (also known as *The Witches*), Twentieth Century-Fox, 1967.

Five Million Years to Earth (also known as *Quatermass and the Pit*), Twentieth Century-Fox, 1968.

Quatermass Conclusion, Euston, 1980.

Also author of *The Woman in Black,* 1989, and a four-part film series, *Stanley and the Women,* 1991.

TELEVISION PLAYS, EXCEPT WHERE NOTED

The Quatermass Experiment, BBC, 1953.

1984, BBC, 1954.

The Creature, BBC, 1955.

Quatermass II, BBC, 1955.

Mrs. Wickens in the Fall, BBC, 1956.

Quatermass and the Pit, BBC, 1959.

The Road, BBC, 1963.

The Crunch, BBC, 1964.

The Year of the Sex Olympics, BBC, 1967.
Bam! Pow! Zapp!, BBC, 1969.
Wine of India, BBC, 1970.
Murrain, BBC, 1975.
Beasts (series of six plays: *Buddyboy; During Barty's Party; Special Offer; The Dummy; Baby; What Big Eyes*), ATV, 1976.

Also author of *The Chopper,* 1971; *The Stone Tape,* 1972; *Jack and the Beanstalk,* 1974; *Quatermass,* 1979; *Ladies Night,* 1986; and *Gentry,* 1988. Author of the series *Kinvig,* 1981.

L

LAKE, Ricki 1969(?)-

PERSONAL: Born c. 1969 in New York City.

ADDRESSES: Agent—Jane Berliner, Creative Artists Agency, 9830 Wilshire Blvd., Beverly Hills, CA 90212.

CAREER: Actress. Performed in cabarets and on commercials.

CREDITS:

FILM APPEARANCES

Bridesmaid, *Working Girl,* Twentieth Century-Fox, 1988.
Tracy Turnblad, *Hairspray,* New Line Cinema, 1988.
Donna, *Last Exit to Brooklyn,* Cinecom, 1989.
Pia, *Cookie,* Warner Brothers, 1989.
Pepper, *Cry-Baby,* Imagine Entertainment, 1990.

TELEVISION APPEARANCES; SERIES

Holly Pellagrino, *China Beach,* ABC, 1990.

TELEVISION APPEARANCES; EPISODIC

Made television debut on *Kate and Allie;* also appeared on *Fame.*

TELEVISION APPEARANCES; SPECIALS

Carmen, "A Family Again," *ABC Family Theater,* ABC, 1988.
Ricky Ross, *Starting Now,* CBS, 1989.
Performer and presenter, *61st Annual Academy Awards,* ABC, 1989.
Voice, *Rick Moranis in Gravedale High* (also known as *Gravedale High*), NBC, 1990.

OTHER TELEVISION APPEARANCES

Grace Johnson, *Babycakes* (movie; also known as *Sugarbaby* and *Big Girls Don't Cry*), CBS, 1989.
Tammie Davis, *The Chase* (movie), NBC, 1991.

Appeared in the pilot for *Starting Now,* CBS.

STAGE APPEARANCES

Lurene, *A Girl's Guide to Chaos,* Tiffany Theatre, West Hollywood, CA, 1990.

Appeared off-Broadway in *The Early Show* and *Youngsters,* c. 1983.

OTHER SOURCES:

PERIODICALS

Interview, January, 1988.
Mademoiselle, April, 1990.
Village Voice, March 1, 1988.*

* * *

LAMOS, Mark 1946-

PERSONAL: Born March 10, 1946, in Melrose Park, IL; son of Gustav (a horticulturalist) and Ruth (an office manager; maiden name Oechslin) Lamos; married Sharon Anderson, 1970 (divorced, 1977). *Education:* Northwestern University, B.S., 1969.

ADDRESSES: Office—c/o Hartford Stage Company, 50 Church St., Hartford, CT 06103. *Agent*—International Creative Management, 40 West 57th St., New York, NY 10019.

CAREER: Actor, director, administrator, and writer. Goodman Theatre, Chicago, IL, company member, 1971-72; Tyrone Guthrie Theatre, Minneapolis, MN, company member, 1974-77; Arizona Theatre Company, Tucson, AZ, stage director and artistic director, 1978-80; California Shakespearean Festival, Visalia, CA, artistic director, 1980; Hartford Stage Company, Hartford, CT, artistic director, 1980—.

AWARDS, HONORS: Received honorary degrees from Connecticut College and University of Hartford, both 1990; Antoinette Perry Award nomination for direction of a play, 1991, for *Our Country's Good.*

CREDITS:

STAGE APPEARANCES

(Stage debut) Joe, *Lovers,* Academy Festival Theatre, Lake Forest, IL, 1969.

Young Brendan Behan, *Borstal Boy,* Academy Festival Theatre, Lake Forest, IL, 1969.

Another Part of the Forest, Ivanhoe Theatre, Chicago, IL, 1970-71.

(Broadway debut) Private Bowers, *Love Suicide at Schofield Barracks,* ANTA Theatre, 1971.

Abel, *The Creation of the World and Other Business,* Shubert Theatre, New York City, 1972.

Christian de Neuvillette, *Cyrano,* Palace Theatre, New York City, 1973.

Title role, *Hamlet,* Old Globe Theatre, San Diego, CA, 1977.

Rex, *City Sugar,* Marymount Manhattan Theatre, New York City, 1978.

Feste, *Twelfth Night,* American Shakespeare Theatre, Stratford, CT, 1978.

Octavius, *Man and Superman,* Circle in the Square, New York City, 1978.

A Month in the Country, McCarter Theatre, Princeton, NJ, 1978-79.

Title role, *Anatol,* Hartford Stage Company, Hartford, CT, 1984.

Dr. Rank, *A Doll's House,* Hartford Stage Company, 1986.

Jack Worthing, *The Importance of Being Earnest,* Hartford Stage Company, 1989.

MAJOR TOURS

Solomon Rothschild, *The Rothschilds,* U.S. cities, 1972.

STAGE DIRECTOR

Dear Liar, Guthrie Theatre, 1976.
Mackerel, Hartford Stage Company/The Old Place, 1977.
The Threepenny Opera, Arizona Theatre Company, 1978.
The Seagull, Arizona Theatre Company, 1979.
Twelfth Night, Arizona Theatre Company, 1979.
The Beaux Stratagem, Hartford Stage Company, 1980.
Cymbeline, Hartford Stage Company, 1981.
Undiscovered Country, Hartford Stage Company, 1981.
Antony and Cleopatra, Hartford Stage Company, 1981.
Kean, Hartford Stage Company, 1982.
The Greeks, Hartford Stage Company, 1982.

The Great Magoo, Hartford Stage Company, 1982.
The Portage to San Cristobal of A. H., Hartford Stage Company, 1983.
The Misanthrope, Hartford Stage Company, 1983.
As You Like It, Hartford Stage Company, 1983.
Don Giovanni, St. Louis Opera, St. Louis, MO, 1983.
Arabella, Santa Fe Opera, Santa Fe, NM, 1983.
The Merchant of Venice, Stratford Festival, Stratford, Canada, 1984.
The Three Sisters, Hartford Stage Company, 1984.
Anatol, Hartford Stage Company, 1984.
Passion Play, Hartford Stage Company, 1985.
The Tempest, Hartford Stage Company, 1985.
Twelfth Night, Hartford Stage Company, 1985.
The Voyage of Edgar Allan Poe, Stora Teatern, Goteborg, Sweden, 1985.
Distant Fires, Hartford Stage Company, 1986.
On The Verge, Hartford Stage Company, 1986.
The Gilded Age, Hartford Stage Company, 1986.
Pericles, Hartford Stage Company, 1987.
Morocco, Hartford Stage Company, 1987.
Hamlet, Hartford Stage Company, 1987.
The School for Wives, La Jolla Playhouse, La Jolla, CA, 1987.
The Aspern Papers, Dallas Opera, Dallas, TX, 1988.
Desire Under the Elms, Pushkin Drama Theatre, Moscow, U.S.S.R., 1988.
Hedda Gabler, Hartford Stage Company, 1988.
The School for Wives, Hartford Stage Company, 1988.
A Midsummer Night's Dream, Hartford Stage Company, 1988.
(New York debut) *Measure for Measure,* Mitzi E. Newhouse Theater, Lincoln Center, 1989.
Peer Gynt, Hartford Stage Company, 1989.
The Importance of Being Earnest, Hartford Stage Company, 1989.
The Illusion, Hartford Stage Company, 1990.
The Miser, Hartford Stage Company, 1990.
La Boheme, Hartford Stage Company, 1990.
Our Country's Good, Hartford Stage Company, 1990.
The Master Builder, Hartford Stage Company, 1991.
Julius Caesar, Hartford Stage Company, 1991.
(Broadway debut) *Our Country's Good,* Nederlander Theater, New York City, NY, 1991.
Il Re Pastore, Glimmerglass Opera Theater, 1991.

FILM APPEARANCES

(Film debut) *Longtime Companion,* American Playhouse Theatrical Films, 1989.

TELEVISION APPEARANCES

Sir Benjamin Backbite, "School for Scandal," *Great Performances, Theatre in America,* PBS, 1975.

WRITINGS:

Some Other Time (play), Equity Library Theatre, Library and Museum of Performing Arts, New York City, 1970.

OTHER SOURCES:

PERIODICALS

New York Times, March 5, 1989.

*   *   *

LANDERS, Harry 1921-

PERSONAL: Born April 3, 1921, in New York, NY.

CAREER: Actor.

CREDITS:

FILM APPEARANCES

Owney, *C-Man,* Film Classics, 1949.
Bert, *Guilty Bystander,* Film Classics, 1950.
Tully, *Undercover Girl,* Universal, 1950.
Mr. Universe, Eagle-Lion, 1951.
Lt. Bowers, *Phantom from Space,* United Artists (UA), 1953.
Go-Go, *The Wild One,* Columbia, 1953.
Jack Slade, Allied Artists, 1953.
Ralph, *Drive a Crooked Road,* Columbia, 1954.
Young man, *Rear Window,* Paramount, 1954.
Grey Wolf, *The Indian Fighter,* UA, 1955.
Fiddler, *The Black Whip,* Twentieth Century-Fox, 1956.
The Ten Commandments, Paramount, 1956.
Andy, *Mister Cory,* Universal, 1957.
Captain Joe Foss, *The Gallant Hours,* UA, 1960.
Pilot, *In Enemy Country,* Universal, 1968.
Heff, *Charro,* National General, 1969.

FILM WORK

Associate producer, *DUBEAT-E-O,* H-Z-H, 1984.

TELEVISION APPEARANCES; SERIES

Dr. Ted Hoffman, *Ben Casey,* ABC, 1961-68.

OTHER TELEVISION APPEARANCES

Eric, *Poor Mr. Campbell* (pilot), CBS, 1962.
Dr. Bradford, *Mad Bull* (movie), CBS, 1977.
Dr. Ted Hoffman, *The Return of Ben Casey* (movie), syndicated, 1988.

TELEVISION WORK

Director (with others), *Ben Casey* (episodes), ABC, 1961-66.*

LANDESMAN, Heidi

PERSONAL: Married Rocco Landesman (a producer).

CAREER: Stage designer and producer. Loretto-Hilton Repertory Theatre, St. Louis, MO, stage designer, 1977-78.

AWARDS, HONORS: Obie Award for design from *Village Voice,* 1982-83, for *A Midsummer Night's Dream* and *Painting Churches;* Antoinette Perry awards, best musical and best scenic design, 1985, for *Big River;* Antoinette Perry Award and Drama Desk Award nomination, both best scenic design, and Antoinette Perry Award nomination and Drama Desk Award nomination (both with others), both best musical, all 1991, for *The Secret Garden.*

CREDITS:

STAGE DESIGNER, EXCEPT AS NOTED

Oh! What a Lovely War!, Playwrights Horizons, New York City, 1978.
Leave It to Beaver Is Dead, New York Shakespeare Festival (NYSF), Public Theatre, New York City, 1979.
Holeville, Brooklyn Academy of Music, Attic Theatre, New York City, 1979.
Table Settings, Playwrights Horizons, 1980.
Split, Second Stage Theatre, New York City, 1980.
The Marriage Dance, Brooklyn Academy of Music, Lepercq Space, 1980.
Treats, Indiana Repertory Theatre, Indianapolis, IN, 1981.
How It All Began, NYSF, Public Theatre, 1981.
Randy Newman's Maybe I'm Doing It Wrong, Production Company Theatre, New York City, 1981.
Penguin Touquet, NYSF, Public Theatre, 1981.
A Midsummer Night's Dream, Acting Company, Public Theatre, 1981.
Twelve Dreams, NYSF, Public Theatre, 1981.
A Midsummer Night's Dream, NYSF, Delacorte Theatre, 1982.
Pastorale, Second Stage, 1982.
Maybe I'm Doing It Wrong, Astor Place Theatre, New York City, 1982.
(And costumes) *'Night, Mother,* American Repertory Theatre, Cambridge, MA, 1982, then John Golden Theatre, New York City, 1983-84.
Painting Churches, Second Stage, South Street Theatre, then Lamb's Theatre, New York City, 1983.
Big River: The Adventures of Huckleberry Finn, American Repertory Theatre, 1983-84.
(And producer, with others) *Big River,* Eugene O'Neill Theatre, New York City, 1985.
Costumes, *'Night, Mother,* Mark Taper Forum, Los Angeles, 1985.
Miami, Mark Taper Forum, 1986.

Hunting Cockroaches, Manhattan Theatre Club, New York City, 1987.

Producer (with others) *Into the Woods,* Martin Beck Theatre, New York City, 1987.

Romeo and Juliet, NYSF, Public Theatre, 1988.

Emily, Manhattan Theatre Club, City Center Stage, New York City, 1988.

Producer, *Urban Blight,* Manhattan Theatre Club, City Center Theatre, 1988.

(And producer, with others) *The Secret Garden,* St. James Theatre, New York City, 1991.*

*   *   *

LANE, Charles 1905-
(Charles Levison)

PERSONAL: Born in 1905, San Francisco, CA; wife's name, Ruth; children: two. *Avocational interests:* Listening to opera, playing golf.

ADDRESSES: Agent—J. Carter Gibson Agency, 9000 Sunset Boulevard, Suite 801, Los Angeles, CA 90069.

CAREER: Actor. Performed Shakespeare, Chekhov, and Coward at Pasadena Playhouse, Pasadena, CA, during the 1930s.

CREDITS:

STAGE APPEARANCES

Cooper, *Love in E-Flat,* Brooks Atkinson Theatre, New York City, 1967.

FILM APPEARANCES

Desk clerk, *Smart Money,* Warner Brothers, 1931.

Desk clerk, *The Mouthpiece,* Warner Brothers, 1932.

Doctor, *The Bowery,* Twentieth Century-Fox, 1933.

Grand Slam, Warner Brothers, 1933.

Society reporter, *Gold Diggers of 1933,* Warner Brothers, 1933.

Process server, *Private Detective Sixty-Two* (also known as *Man Killer*), First National/Warner Brothers, 1933.

Reporter, *Twenty Million Sweethearts,* First National/Warner Brothers, 1934.

Defense attorney, *Crime of Dr. Forbes,* Twentieth Century-Fox, 1936.

State examiner, *It Had to Happen,* Twentieth Century-Fox, 1936.

Rickert, *Thirty-Six Hours to Kill* (also known as *Thirty-Six Hours to Live*), Twentieth Century-Fox, 1936.

Cleaner, *Three Men on a Horse,* First National/Warner Brothers, 1936.

Shyster, *Ticket to Paradise,* Republic, 1936.

Doctor, *Ali Baba Goes to Town,* Twentieth Century-Fox, 1937.

Grote, *Interns Can't Take Money* (also known as *You Can't Take Money*), Paramount, 1937.

Gilroy, *Danger—Love at Work,* Twentieth Century-Fox, 1937.

District attorney, *Venus Makes Trouble,* Columbia, 1937.

Horace Smith, *We're on the Jury,* RKO, 1937.

Fingers, *Trapped by G-Men* (also known as *The River of Missing Men*), Columbia, 1937.

Donald Gower, *Always in Trouble,* Twentieth Century-Fox, 1938.

Albee, *Boy Slaves,* RKO, 1938.

Dr. Abbott, *City Girl,* Twentieth Century-Fox, 1938.

Weaver, *Cocoanut Grove,* Paramount, 1938.

Booking agent, *In Old Chicago,* Twentieth Century-Fox, 1938.

Joy of Living, RKO, 1938.

Auctioneer, *Kentucky,* Twentieth Century-Fox, 1938.

Joe the photographer, *Professor Beware,* Paramount, 1938.

Dr. Olson, *Thanks for Everything,* Twentieth Century-Fox, 1938.

Manager of cleaning establishment, *Three Loves Has Nancy,* Metro-Goldwyn-Mayer (MGM), 1938.

Henderson, *You Can't Take It with You,* Columbia, 1938.

Reporter, *The Cat and the Canary,* Paramount, 1939.

Labor representative, *Fifth Avenue Girl,* RKO, 1939.

Drake, *Golden Boy,* Columbia, 1939.

Adler, *Television Spy,* Paramount, 1939.

District attorney, *Inside Story,* Twentieth Century-Fox, 1939.

Carpenter, *Lucky Night,* MGM, 1939.

Hotel clerk, *Miracles for Sale,* MGM, 1939.

Nosey, *Mr. Smith Goes to Washington,* Columbia, 1939.

Rufe Reynolds, *News Is Made at Night,* Twentieth Century-Fox, 1939.

Kress, *Rose of Washington Square,* Twentieth Century-Fox, 1939.

Voice of studio chief, *Second Fiddle,* Twentieth Century-Fox, 1939.

Psychiatrist, *They All Come Out,* MGM, 1939.

Captain Sabin, *Thunder Afloat,* MGM, 1939.

The Flying Irishman, RKO, 1939.

Charlie Graham, *Buck Benny Rides Again,* Paramount, 1940.

Phil, *The Crooked Road,* Republic, 1940.

Freeman Taylor, *Dancing on a Dime,* Paramount, 1940.

Reporter, *Doctor Takes a Wife,* Columbia, 1940.

Lecturer, *Edison, the Man,* MGM, 1940.

Dr. Prouty, *Ellery Queen, Master Detective,* Columbia, 1940.

Director, *The Great Profile,* Twentieth Century-Fox, 1940.

Horner, *It's a Date,* Universal, 1940.

Assistant district attorney, *Johnny Apollo,* Twentieth Century-Fox, 1940.

Mitchell, *The Leather-Pushers,* Universal, 1940.

Johnson, *On Their Own,* Twentieth Century-Fox, 1940.

Horace Grimley, *Queen of the Mob,* Paramount, 1940.

Mr. Bernard Schwartz, *Rhythm on the River,* Paramount, 1940.

Train passenger, *Texas Rangers Ride Again,* Paramount, 1940.

Perkins, *We Who Are Young,* MGM, 1940.

Salesman, *You Can't Fool Your Wife,* RKO, 1940.

Blondie Plays Cupid, Columbia, 1940.

Primose Path, RKO, 1940.

City for Conquest, First National/Warner Brothers, 1941.

Meet John Doe, Warner Brothers, 1941.

Buy Me That Town, Paramount, 1941.

The Big Store, MGM, 1941.

Larson, *Ball of Fire,* RKO, 1941.

Auctioneer, *Barnacle Bill,* Butcher's Film Service, 1941.

Dr. Prouty, *Ellery Queen and the Perfect Crime* (also known as *The Perfect Crime*), Columbia, 1941.

Dr. Prouty, *Ellery Queen's Penthouse Mystery,* Columbia, 1941.

Growley, *The Invisible Woman,* Universal, 1941.

Club secretary, *Look Who's Laughing,* RKO, 1941.

Man, *Never Give a Sucker an Even Break* (also known as *What a Man*), Universal, 1941.

Detective Smith, *Obliging Young Lady,* RKO, 1941.

Morgan, *Repent at Leisure,* RKO, 1941.

Dixon, *Sealed Lips,* Universal, 1941.

Ryan, *Sing Another Chorus,* Universal, 1941.

Rollo, *Sis Hopkins,* Republic, 1941.

Mortician, *Three Girls about Town,* Columbia, 1941.

Announcer, *You're the One,* Paramount, 1941.

Dudes Are Pretty People, United Artists, 1942.

A Gentleman at Heart, Twentieth Century-Fox, 1942.

Garage manager, *About Face,* United Artists, 1942.

Mr. Brooks, *Are Husbands Necessary?,* Paramount, 1942.

Airport official, *Flying Tigers,* Republic, 1942.

Braun, *Friendly Enemies,* United Artists, 1942.

Pierce, *The Great Man's Lady,* Paramount, 1942.

Editor, *Home in Wyomin',* Republic, 1942.

Florist Keating, *I Wake up Screaming* (also known as *Hotspot*), Twentieth Century-Fox, 1942.

Government man, *Lady in a Jam,* Universal, 1942.

K. K. Miller, *The Lady Is Willing,* Columbia, 1942.

Virgil Hickling, *The Mad Martindales,* Twentieth Century-Fox, 1942.

Superintendent, *Pardon My Sarong,* Universal, 1942.

Martin Manning, *Ride 'em Cowboy,* Universal, 1942.

Gould Beaton, *Tarzan's New York Adventure,* MGM, 1942.

Spotter, *They All Kissed the Bride,* MGM, 1942.

Mott, *Thru Different Eyes,* Twentieth Century-Fox, 1942.

Cynic, *Yokel Boy* (also known as *Hitting the Headlines*), Republic, 1942.

Comstock, *Mr. Lucky,* RKO, 1943.

Reporter, *Arsenic and Old Lace,* Warner Brothers, 1944.

Hack Hagen, *A Close Call for Boston Blackie* (also known as *Lady of Mystery*), Columbia, 1946.

Real estate salesman, *It's a Wonderful Life,* RKO, 1946.

Nick Steele, *Invisible Informer,* Republic, 1946.

Dr. Steiner, *Just before Dawn,* Columbia, 1946.

Detective Burns, *Mysterious Intruder,* Columbia, 1946.

Quiz master, *The Show-Off,* MGM, 1946.

Ben Tilwell, *Swell Guy,* Universal, 1946.

Jackson, *The Farmer's Daughter,* RKO, 1947.

Hotel clerk, *Intrigue,* United Artists, 1947.

Landlord, *It Happened on Fifth Avenue,* Monogram, 1947.

McCormack, *Louisiana,* Monogram, 1947.

Lipton, *Roses Are Red,* Twentieth Century-Fox, 1947.

Professor Collins, *Apartment for Peggy,* Twentieth Century-Fox, 1948.

Prosecuting attorney, *Call Northside 777* (also known as *Calling Northside 777*), Twentieth Century-Fox, 1948.

Fenmore, *The Gentleman from Nowhere,* Columbia, 1948.

Man in black, *Moonrise,* Republic, 1948.

Mr. Evans, *Out of the Storm,* Republic, 1948.

Desk clerk at Robbie's apartment building, *Race Street,* RKO, 1948.

Reporter, *Smart Woman,* Monogram/Allied Artists, 1948.

Blink Moran, *State of the Union* (also known as *The World and His Wife*), MGM, 1948.

Woodruff, *Miss Grant Takes Richmond* (also known as *Innocence Is Bliss*), Columbia, 1949.

Mr. DeHaven, *Mother Is a Freshman* (also known as *Mother Knows Best*), Twentieth Century-Fox, 1949.

Mr. Pflum, *You're My Everything,* Twentieth Century-Fox, 1949.

Peterson, *Borderline,* Universal, 1950.

Tax agent, *For Heaven's Sake,* Twentieth Century-Fox, 1950.

Erickson, *Riding High,* Paramount, 1950.

Love That Brute, Twentieth Century-Fox, 1950.

Frederick Waterman, *Criminal Lawyer,* Columbia, 1951.

Burchard, *Here Comes the Groom,* Paramount, 1951.

Pulvermacher, *I Can Get It for You Wholesale* (also known as *Only the Best*), Twentieth Century-Fox, 1951.

Man, *The Sniper,* Columbia, 1952.

Professor Obispo, *The Affairs of Dobie Gillis,* MGM, 1953.

Rosenberg, *The Juggler,* Columbia, 1953.

Examiner Delapp, *Remains to Be Seen,* MGM, 1953.

Judge Warner, *God Is My Partner,* Twentieth Century-Fox, 1957.

Bill Hadley, *Top Secret Affair* (also known as *Their Secret Affair*), Warner Brothers, 1957.

Roy, *Teacher's Pet,* Paramount, 1958.

Atwood, *But Not for Me,* Paramount, 1959.

Bigelow, *The Mating Game,* MGM, 1959.

Standard Bates, *The Thirty Foot Bride of Candy Rock,* Columbia, 1959.

Constable Locke, *The Music Man,* Warner Brothers, 1962.

Airport manager, *It's a Mad, Mad, Mad, Mad World,* United Artists, 1963.

Hiram Cosgrove, *Papa's Delicate Condition,* Paramount, 1963.

Denby, *The Carpetbaggers,* Paramount, 1964.

Jack Bailey, *Good Neighbor Sam,* Columbia, 1964.

Strife editor, *John Goldfarb, Please Come Home,* Twentieth Century-Fox, 1964.

Director, *Looking for Love,* MGM, 1964.

The New Interns, Columbia, 1964.

Coach Jones, *Billie,* United Artists, 1965.

Jenkins, *The Birds and the Bees,* Paramount, 1965.

Whitlow, *The Ghost and Mr. Chicken,* Universal, 1966.

Judge, *The Ugly Dachshund,* Buena Vista, 1966.

Mr. Scroggins, *The Gnome-Mobile,* Buena Vista, 1967.

Mr. Duckworth, *Did You Hear the One about the Traveling Saleslady?,* Universal, 1968.

Dr. Shapiro, *What's so Bad about Feeling Good?,* Universal, 1968.

Voice of Lawyer, *The Aristocats* (animated), Buena Vista, 1970.

Mr. Beeman, *Get to Know Your Rabbit,* Warner Brothers, 1972.

Pennington, "Baxter's Beauties of 1933," and judge, "Dynamite Hands," *Movie Movie,* Warner Brothers, 1978.

J. J., *The Little Dragons,* Aurora, 1980.

Donovan, *Dead Kids* (also known as *Strange Behavior*), South Street, 1981.

Professor Hollister, *Strange Invaders,* Orion, 1983.

Amos Abbott, *Murphy's Romance,* Columbia, 1985.

Father O'Shea, *Date with an Angel,* De Laurentiis Entertainment Group, 1987.

Also appeared in *Band of Outlaws,* 1936.

FILM APPEARANCES (AS CHARLES LEVISON)

Four Eyes, *Blonde Crazy* (also known as *Larceny Lane*), Warner Brothers, 1931.

Circulation manager, *Advice to the Lovelorn,* United Artists, 1933.

Agent, *My Woman,* Columbia, 1933.

Author, *42nd Street,* Warner Brothers, 1933.

Max Jacobs, *Twentieth Century,* Columbia, 1934.

I'll Fix It, Columbia, 1934.

Broadway Bill (also known as *Strictly Confidential*), Columbia, 1934.

Here Comes the Band, MGM, 1935.

Author, *Two for Tonight,* Paramount, 1935.

Hallor, *Mr. Deeds Goes to Town,* Columbia, 1936.

Willard, *The Milky Way,* Paramount, 1936.

Neighborhood House, 1936.

Easy to Take, Paramount, 1936.

TELEVISION APPEARANCES; SERIES

Mr. Fosdick, *Dear Phoebe,* NBC, 1954-55.

Mr. Barnsdahl, *The Lucy Show,* CBS, 1962-63.

Homer Bedloe, *Petticoat Junction,* CBS, 1963-68.

Maxwell, *The Pruitts of Southampton,* ABC, 1966-67.

Voice characterization, *The Adventures of Huckleberry Finn* (animated/live-action), NBC, 1968-69.

Dale W. Busch, *Karen,* ABC, 1975.

TELEVISION APPEARANCES; PILOTS

Garrity, *Tom and Jerry* (broadcast as an episode of *Screen Director's Playhouse*), NBC, 1955.

Mr. Martin, *The Soft Touch,* CBS, 1962.

Roundtree, *Hitched,* NBC, 1973.

Ned Cooper, *Love Nest,* CBS, 1975.

Chief, *Return of the Beverly Hillbillies,* CBS, 1981.

George McCloskey, *Side by Side,* ABC, 1984.

TELEVISION APPEARANCES; EPISODIC

Father in hospital waiting room, *I Love Lucy,* CBS, 1953.

Casting agent, *I Love Lucy,* CBS, 1953.

Mr. Hickox, *I Love Lucy,* CBS, 1954.

Mr. Snead, *So This Is Hollywood,* NBC, 1955.

Passport office clerk, *I Love Lucy,* CBS, 1956.

Mr. Peckinpaugh, "Mr. Bevis," *The Twilight Zone,* CBS, 1960.

McKeever and the Colonel, NBC, 1962.

The Beverly Hillbillies, CBS, 1962.

Mr. Frisby, *The Andy Griffith Show,* CBS, 1964.

Wendy and Me, ABC, 1965.

The Donna Reed Show, ABC, 1966.

Bert Bennington, *Love on a Rooftop,* ABC, 1966, 1967.

Town banker, *F Troop,* ABC, 1966.

He and She, CBS, 1967.

Nanny and the Professor, ABC, 1970, 1971.

Rhoda, CBS, 1974.

Chico and the Man, NBC, 1975.

Retired detective, *The Last Precinct,* NBC, 1986.

Mr. Cooper, *Hunter,* NBC, 1987.

Richard Welty, *St. Elsewhere,* NBC, 1987.

Waiter, *L.A. Law,* NBC, 1989.

Dark Shadows, NBC, 1991.

Shannon's Deal, NBC, 1991.

Also appeared as Harry Purvis, *The Real McCoys;* Lawrence Finch, *Dennis the Menace,* CBS. Appeared on *The George Burns and Gracie Allen Show,* CBS; *Bewitched,* ABC; *The Flying Nun,* ABC; *Get Smart,* NBC; *Gomer*

Pyle, CBS; *Green Acres,* CBS; *Guestward Ho!,* ABC; *The Many Loves of Dobie Gillis* (also known as *Dobie Gillis*), CBS; *Mr. Ed,* CBS; *The Munsters,* CBS; *The Odd Couple,* ABC; *Bachelor Father;* and *How to Marry a Millionaire.*

TELEVISION APPEARANCES; MOVIES

Philbrick, *The Great Man's Whiskers,* NBC, 1973.
Dr. Quinoness, *Sybil,* NBC, 1976.
Arnold Reinhammer, *Sunset Limousine,* CBS, 1983.
Admiral Standley, *The Winds of War* (mini-series), ABC, 1983.
Professor Van Der Graff, *When the Bough Breaks,* NBC, 1986.
Admiral Standley, *War and Remembrance* (mini-series), ABC, 1988.

TELEVISION APPEARANCES; SPECIALS

E. Ronald Mallu, *Soap Retrospective II,* ABC, 1978.
Walter Becker, "The $1000 Bill," *ABC Weekend Specials,* ABC, 1978.

WRITINGS:

FILM

(With Lester Lee) *Love at First Sight,* Chesterfield, 1930.

*   *   *

LANG, Charles   1902-
(Charles Lang, Jr.; Charles B. Lang, Charles B. Lang, Jr.)

PERSONAL: Full name, Charles Bryant Lang, Jr.; born March 27, 1902, in Bluff, UT. *Education:* Studied law at University of Southern California.

ADDRESSES: c/o American Society of Cinematographers, 1782 North Orange Dr., Hollywood, CA 90028.

CAREER: Cinematographer. Realart Studio, 1919-22, laboratory assistant and assistant cameraman; Preferred Picture Corp., still photographer, c. early 1920s; Paramount, beginning in mid-1920s, director of photography, 1929-52.

MEMBER: American Society of Cinematographers.

AWARDS, HONORS: Academy Award, cinematography, 1933, for *A Farewell to Arms;* Academy Award nominations, cinematography, 1931, for *The Right to Love,* 1969, for *Bob and Carol and Ted and Alice,* and 1972, for *Butterflies Are Free;* Academy Award nominations, black-and-white cinematography, 1940, for *Arise, My Love,* 1941, for *Sundown,* 1943, for *So Proudly We Hail,* 1944, for *The Uninvited,* 1947, for *The Ghost and Mrs. Muir,* 1948, for *A Foreign Affair,* 1952, for *Sudden Fear,* 1954, for *Sa-*

brina, 1955, for *Queen Bee,* 1958, for *Separate Tables,* 1959, for *Some Like It Hot,* and 1960, for *The Facts of Life;* Academy Award nomination, color cinematography, 1961, for *One-Eyed Jacks; Theatre World* Award, 1944-45; Lifetime Achievement Award, American Society of Cinematographers, 1990.

CREDITS:

FILM CINEMATOGRAPHER, EXCEPT AS NOTED

(Assistant) *Are You a Failure?,* Preferred, 1923.
(Assistant) *The Virginian,* Preferred, 1925.
(With Jack Stevens) *The Night Patrol,* FBO, 1926.
(With Stevens) *The Stalking Moon,* FBO, 1926.
The Shopworn Angel, Paramount, 1928.
Innocents of Paris, Paramount, 1929.
(With others) *Half Way to Heaven,* Paramount, 1929.
Anybody's Woman, Paramount, 1930.
Behind the Makeup, Paramount, 1930.
For the Defense, Paramount, 1930.
The Light of Western Stars, Paramount, 1930.
Sarah and Son, Paramount, 1930.
Seven Days Leave (also known as *Medals*), Paramount, 1930.
Shadow of the Law, Paramount, 1930.
Street of Chance, Paramount, 1930.
Tom Sawyer, Paramount, 1930.
Caught, Paramount, 1931.
Magnificent Lie, Paramount, 1931.
Newly Rich (also known as *Forbidden Adventure*), Paramount, 1931.
Once a Lady, Paramount, 1931.
The Right to Love, Paramount, 1931.
Unfaithful, Paramount, 1931.
The Vice Squad, Paramount, 1931.
Devil and the Deep, Paramount, 1932.
A Farewell to Arms, Paramount, 1932.
No One Man, Paramount, 1932.
Thunder Below, Paramount, 1932.
Tomorrow and Tomorrow, Paramount, 1932.
He Learned about Women, Paramount, 1933.
A Bedtime Story, Paramount, 1933.
Cradle Song, Paramount, 1933.
Gambling Ship, Paramount, 1933.
She Done Him Wrong, Paramount, 1933.
The Way to Love, Paramount, 1933.
Death Takes a Holiday, Paramount, 1934.
Mrs. Wiggs of the Cabbage Patch, Paramount, 1934.
She Loves Me Not, Paramount, 1934.
We're Not Dressing, Paramount, 1934.
(With Ernest Schoedsack) *Lives of a Bengal Lancer,* Paramount, 1935.
Mississippi, Paramount, 1935.
Peter Ibbetson, Paramount, 1935.
(With Victor Milner) *Desire,* Paramount, 1936.

Angel, Paramount, 1937.

Tovarich, Warner Bros., 1937.

(As Charles Lang, Jr.) *Souls at Sea,* Paramount, 1937.

(As Charles Lang, Jr.) *Spawn of the North,* Paramount, 1938.

(As Charles Lang, Jr.) *You and Me,* Paramount, 1938.

Dr. Rhythm, Paramount, 1938.

The Cat and the Canary, Paramount, 1939.

Gracie Allen Murder Case, Paramount, 1939.

Midnight, Paramount, 1939.

(As Charles Lang, Jr.) *Zaza,* Paramount, 1939.

Adventure in Diamonds, Paramount, 1940.

Arise, My Love, Paramount, 1940.

Buck Benny Rides Again, Paramount, 1940.

The Ghost Breakers, Paramount, 1940.

Women without Names, Paramount, 1940.

(As Charles Lang, Jr.) *Dancing on a Dime,* Paramount, 1940.

Nothing but the Truth, Paramount, 1941.

Skylark, Paramount, 1941.

Sundown, United Artists (UA), 1941.

(As Charles Lang, Jr.) *The Shepherd of the Hills,* Paramount, 1941.

Are Husbands Necessary?, Paramount, 1942.

The Forest Rangers, Paramount, 1942.

The Ghost and Mrs. Muir, Twentieth Century-Fox, 1942.

The Lady Has Plans, Paramount, 1942.

So Proudly We Hail, Paramount, 1943.

True to Life, Paramount, 1943.

(As Charles Lang, Jr.) *No Time for Love,* Paramount, 1943.

Here Come the Waves, Paramount, 1944.

I Love a Soldier, Paramount, 1944.

Standing Room Only, Paramount, 1944.

The Uninvited, Paramount, 1944.

(As Charles Lang, Jr.) *Practically Yours,* Paramount, 1944.

(As Charles Lang, Jr.) *Miss Susie Slagle's,* Paramount, 1945.

(As Charles Lang, Jr.) *The Stork Club,* Paramount, 1945.

(As Charles Lang, Jr.) *Blue Skies,* Paramount, 1946.

(As Charles Lang, Jr.; with Stuart Thompson) *Cross My Heart,* Paramount, 1946.

(With Edward Cronjager) *Desert Fury,* Paramount, 1947.

(As Charles B. Lang, Jr.) *Where There's Life,* Paramount, 1947.

(As Charles B. Lang, Jr.) *A Foreign Affair,* Paramount, 1948.

(As Charles B. Lang, Jr.) *Miss Tatlock's Millions,* Paramount, 1948.

(As Charles B. Lang, Jr.) *My Own True Love,* Paramount, 1948.

(As Charles B. Lang, Jr.) *The Great Lover,* Paramount, 1949.

(As Charles B. Lang, Jr.) *Rope of Sand,* Paramount, 1949.

(As Charles B. Lang, Jr.) *Copper Canyon,* Paramount, 1950.

(As Charles B. Lang, Jr.) *Fancy Pants,* Paramount, 1950.

(As Charles B. Lang; with Milner) *September Affair,* Paramount, 1950.

(As Charles B. Lang) *The Big Carnival* (also known as *Ace in the Hole* and *The Human Interest Story*), Paramount, 1951.

(As Charles B. Lang, Jr.) *Branded,* Paramount, 1951.

(As Charles B. Lang, Jr.) *Peking Express,* Paramount, 1951.

(As Charles B. Lang, Jr.) *Red Mountain,* Paramount, 1951.

(As Charles B. Lang, Jr.) *The Mating Season,* Paramount, 1951.

(With others) *Mr. Belvedere Rings the Bell,* Twentieth Century-Fox, 1951.

(As Charles B. Lang, Jr.) *Aaron Slick from Punkin Crick* (also known as *Marshmallow Moon*), Paramount, 1952.

(As Charles B. Lang, Jr.) *The Atomic City,* Paramount, 1952.

(As Charles Lang, Jr.) *Sudden Fear,* RKO Radio Pictures, 1952.

The Big Heat, Columbia, 1953.

Salome, Columbia, 1953.

It Should Happen to You, Columbia, 1954.

Phffft!, Columbia, 1954.

(As Charles Lang, Jr.) *Sabrina* (also known as *Sabrina Fair*), Paramount, 1954.

Female on the Beach, Universal, 1955.

The Man from Laramie, Columbia, 1955.

(As Charles Lang, Jr.) *Queen Bee,* Columbia, 1955.

Autumn Leaves, Columbia, 1956.

The Solid Gold Cadillac, Columbia, 1956.

(As Charles Lang, Jr.) *The Rainmaker,* Paramount, 1956.

(As Charles Lang, Jr.) *Gunfight at the O.K. Corral,* Paramount, 1957.

(As Charles Lang, Jr.) *Loving You,* Paramount, 1957.

(As Charles B. Lang, Jr.) *Wild Is the Wind,* Paramount, 1957.

The Matchmaker, Paramount, 1958.

(As Charles Lang, Jr.) *Separate Tables,* UA, 1958.

(As Charles B. Lang, Jr.) *Last Train from Gun Hill,* Paramount, 1959.

(As Charles Lang, Jr.) *Some Like It Hot,* UA, 1959.

(As Charles Lang, Jr.) *The Facts of Life,* UA, 1960.

(As Charles Lang, Jr.) *The Magnificent Seven,* UA, 1960.

(As Charles Lang, Jr.) *Strangers When We Meet,* Columbia, 1960.

(As Charles Lang, Jr.) *Blue Hawaii,* Paramount, 1961.

(As Charles Lang, Jr.) *One-Eyed Jacks,* Paramount, 1961.

(As Charles Lang, Jr.) *Summer and Smoke,* Paramount, 1961.

(As Charles Lang, Jr.) *A Girl Named Tamiko,* Paramount, 1962.

(As Charles Lang, Jr.; with Joseph LaShelle, William Daniels, Milton Krasner, and Harold Wellman) *How the West Was Won,* Cinerama, 1962.

Critic's Choice, Warner Bros., 1963.

The Wheeler Dealers (also known as *Separate Beds*), MGM, 1963.

(As Charles Lang, Jr.) *Charade,* Universal, 1963.

Sex and the Single Girl, Warner Bros., 1964.

(As Charles Lang, Jr.) *Father Goose,* Universal, 1964.

(As Charles Lang, Jr.) *Paris When It Sizzles,* Paramount, 1964.

Inside Daisy Clover, Warner Bros., 1965.

How to Steal a Million, Twentieth Century-Fox, 1966.

(With Paul Beeson) *Not with My Wife, You Don't!,* Warner Bros., 1966.

The Flim-Flam Man (also known as *One Born Every Minute*), Twentieth Century-Fox, 1967.

Hotel, Warner Bros., 1967.

Wait until Dark, Warner Bros., 1967.

A Flea in Her Ear, Twentieth Century-Fox, 1968.

Bob and Carol and Ted and Alice, Columbia, 1969.

(As Charles B. Lang) *Cactus Flower,* Columbia, 1969.

How to Commit Marriage, Cinerama, 1969.

The Stalking Moon, National General, 1969.

A Walk in the Spring Rain, Columbia, 1970.

(As Charles B. Lang) *Doctors' Wives,* Columbia, 1971.

(As Charles B. Lang) *The Love Machine,* Columbia, 1971.

(As Charles B. Lang) *Butterflies Are Free,* Columbia, 1972.

(As Charles B. Lang) *Forty Carats,* Columbia, 1973.

Also worked as an assistant for *The Golden Princess,* 1925, and as cinematographer for *Ritzy,* 1927.

OTHER SOURCES:

PERIODICALS

American Cinematographer, January, 1958; September, 1959; December, 1961; May, 1964; March, 1974; August, 1975.

Film Comment, summer, 1972.

Films in Review, October, 1970.

Focus on Film, Number 13, 1973.

Saturday Evening Post, July 22, 1933.*

* * *

LANG, Charles, Jr.
  See LANG, Charles

LANG, Charles B.
  See LANG, Charles

* * *

LANG, Charles B., Jr.
  See LANG, Charles

* * *

LANGELLA, Frank   1940-

PERSONAL: Born January 1, 1940, in Bayonne, NJ; son of Frank Langella (a business executive); married Ruth Weil (a magazine editor) June 14, 1977. *Education:* Attended Syracuse University, 1959; studied acting with Seymour Falk and Wyn Handman, dance with Anna Sokolow, and voice at Kersting Studios.

CAREER: Actor; Alfie Productions (theatre production company), founder. Toured Europe with a folksinging group, 1959-60; apprenticed for the stage at Pocono Playhouse, Mountain Home, PA; member of the original Lincoln Center repertory training company, 1963; member of the company of the Cleveland Playhouse, OH, 1967-68 season; appeared with Long Island Festival Repertory Theatre, Mineola, NY, 1968; Yale Repertory Theatre, New Haven, CT, 1971-72. Member of board of directors of Berkshire Festival, beginning in 1970.

MEMBER: Actors' Equity Association, Screen Actors Guild.

AWARDS, HONORS: Syracuse Critics Award, best actor, 1959; Obie awards, 1965, for *The Old Glory,* 1966, for *Good Day,* and 1966, for *The White Devil;* National Society of Film Critics Award, 1970, for *The Diary of a Mad Housewife;* Antoinette Perry Award, supporting or featured (dramatic) actor, and Drama Desk Award, both 1975, both for *Seascape;* Antoinette Perry Award nomination, Actor (Play) and Drama League Award, Distinguished Performance, both, 1978, for *Dracula;* Emmy Award nomination, outstanding individual achievement (performer) in informational programming, 1983, for *I, Leonardo: A Journey of the Mind.*

CREDITS:

STAGE APPEARANCES

Heinzie, *Pajama Game,* Erie Playhouse, PA, 1960.

Eugene Gant, *Look Homeward, Angel,* Erie Playhouse, PA, 1960.

Malcolm, *Macbeth,* Erie Playhouse, PA, 1960.

(New York debut) Michel, *The Immoralist,* Bouwerie Lane Theatre, 1963.

Title role, *Benito Cereno,* as part of double bill, *The Old Glory,* American Place at St. Clement's, New York City, 1964.

Young man, *Good Day,* Cherry Lane Theatre, New York City, 1965.

Flamineo, *The White Devil,* Circle in the Square, New York City, 1965.

Jamie, *Long Day's Journey into Night,* Long Wharf Theatre, New Haven, CT, 1966.

Juan, *Yerma,* Vivian Beaumont Theatre, Repertory Company of Lincoln Center, New York City, 1966.

The Skin of Our Teeth, Berkshire Theatre Festival, Stockbridge, MA, 1966.

The Cretan Woman, Berkshire Theatre Festival, 1966.

Title role, *Dracula,* Berkshire Theatre Festival, 1967.

Achilles, *Iphigenia at Aulis,* Circle in the Square, New York City, 1967.

Urbain Grandier, *The Devils,* Mark Taper Forum, Los Angeles, CA, 1967.

Will (Shakespeare), *A Cry of Players,* Berkshire Theatre Festival, then Vivian Beaumont Theatre, 1968.

Title role, *Cyrano de Bergerac,* Williamstown Theatre, Williamstown, MA, 1971.

Oberon, *A Midsummer Night's Dream,* Tyrone Guthrie Theatre, Minneapolis, MN, 1972.

Loveless, *The Relapse,* Tyrone Guthrie Theatre, Minneapolis, MN, 1972.

Hoss, *The Tooth of Crime,* McCarter Theatre, Princeton, NJ, 1972.

Petruchio, *The Taming of the Shrew,* Studio Arena, Buffalo, NY, 1973.

The Seagull, Williamstown Theatre, 1974.

(Broadway debut) Leslie, *Seascape,* Shubert Theatre, New York City, then Shubert Theatre, Los Angeles, CA, 1975.

Ring Round the Moon, Williamstown Theatre, 1975.

Prince Friedrich Arthur of Homburg, *The Prince of Homburg,* Chelsea Theater Center, Brooklyn Academy of Music, New York City, 1976.

Title role, *Dracula,* Martin Beck Theatre, New York City, 1977.

Title role, *Cyrano de Bergerac,* Williamstown Theatre, 1980.

Salieri, *Amadeus,* Broadhurst Theatre, New York City, 1982.

Jim, *Passion,* Longacre Theatre, New York City, 1983.

Otto, *Design for Living,* Circle in the Square, 1984.

Quentin, *After the Fall,* Playhouse 91, New York City, 1984.

Eddie, *Hurlyburly,* Ethel Barrymore Theatre, New York City, 1985.

Sherlock Holmes, *Sherlock's Last Case,* Nederlander Theatre, New York City, 1987.

Sherlock Holmes, *Sherlock's Last Case,* John F. Kennedy Center for the Performing Arts, Washington, DC, 1987-88.

Le Vicomte de Valmont, *Les Liaisons Dangereuses,* Ahmanson Theatre, Los Angeles, CA, c. 1988.

Prospero, *The Tempest,* Roundabout Theatre, New York City, 1989.

Also appeared as First Man, *A Thurber Carnival,* and Paul Verrall, *Born Yesterday,* both at New Playhouse, Syracuse, NY; Caesar, *Caesar and Cleopatra,* title role, *George Dandin,* Mr. Martin, *The Bald Soprano,* and Choubert, *Victims of Duty,* all at Syracuse Repertory Theatre; professor, *The Lesson,* and Jack, *Jack, or the Submission,* both at Tufts Arena, Medford, MA; Joe Pond, *Charm,* milkman, *Under the Yum Yum Tree,* both Cape Playhouse, Dennis, MA; Tom, *The Glass Menagerie,* Rudolpho, *A View from the Bridge,* and Donald Gresham, *The Moon is Blue,* all at Charles Playhouse, Boston, MA; Richard Rich, *A Man for All Seasons,* Rudolpho, *A View from the Bridge,* and old actor, *The Fantastics,* all at Williamstown Theatre; son (flier), *The Good Woman of Setzuan,* Caesar, *Caesar and Cleopatra,* and Iago, *Othello,* all at Directors Workshop, Sheridan Square Playhouse, New York City; title role, *Telemachus,* New Dramatists, New York City; Valentine, *Love for Love,* Maidman Theatre, New York City; Cliff, *Look Back in Anger,* Key Playhouse, New York City; Satan and Cain, *Man,* Key Theatre.

STAGE DIRECTOR

John and Abigail, Berkshire Theatre Festival, 1969.
Passione, Morosco Theatre, 1980.

STAGE PRODUCER

Has produced *After the Fall* Off-Broadway; and *Sherlock's Last Case* on Broadway.

FILM APPEARANCES

(Film debut) Ostap Bender, *The Twelve Chairs,* UMC, 1970.

George Prager, *Diary of a Mad Housewife,* Universal, 1970.

Philip, *The Deadly Trap,* National General, 1972.

Tomas de la Plata, *The Wrath of God,* Metro-Goldwyn-Mayer (MGM), 1972.

Title role, *Dracula,* Universal, 1979.

Harry Crystal, *Those Lips, Those Eyes,* United Artists, 1980.

Ahmed Khazzan, *Sphinx,* Orion/Warner Brothers, 1981.

Harold Canterbury, *The Men's Club,* Atlantic Releasing, 1986.

Skeletor, *Masters of the Universe,* Cannon, 1987.

James Tiernan, *And God Created Woman,* Vestron, 1988.

Also appeared in *House under the Trees*, 1971, and *Universe*, Cannon, 1987.

TELEVISION APPEARANCES; EPISODIC

Trials of O'Brien, CBS, 1965.
Love Story, NBC, 1973.
Benjamin Franklin, CBS, 1974.

TELEVISION APPEARANCES; SPECIALS

Jesus, *CBS Easter Sunday Special*, CBS, 1965.
Konstantine Treplev, "The Seagull," *Theater in America/ Great Performances*, PBS, 1975.
Prince, "The Prince of Homburg," *Theater in America/ Great Performances*, PBS, 1977.
Title role, *Sherlock Holmes*, HBO, 1981.
I, Leonardo: A Journey of the Mind, PBS, c. 1982.

OTHER TELEVISION APPEARANCES

"Good Day," *Experiment in Television*, NBC, 1965.
Don Diego/Zorro, *The Mark of Zorro* (movie), ABC, 1974.
Frederic Auguste Bartholdi, *Liberty* (movie), NBC, 1986.
Title role, "Dr. Paradise," *CBS Summer Playhouse* (pilot), CBS, 1988.

Also appeared in *Benito Cereno*, 1965; as John, *Eccentricities of a Nightingale*, 1976; *The Ambassador;* and *The American Woman*.

RECORDINGS:

Narration for performance by Daniel Nagrin Company, *The Peloponnesian War*.

WRITINGS:

Author of article in the *New York Times*.

OTHER SOURCES:

PERIODICALS

Hollywood Reporter, November 14, 1988.
New York Times, September 17, 1989.*

*　　　*　　　*

LARSON, Jack 1933-

PERSONAL: Born February 8, 1933, in Los Angeles, CA.

ADDRESSES: Contact—8721 Sunset Blvd., Suite 203, Los Angeles, CA 90069.

CAREER: Actor and producer.

CREDITS:

FILM APPEARANCES

Shorty, *Fighter Squadron*, Warner Brothers, 1948.

Dusty, *Redwood Forest Trail*, Republic Pictures, 1950.
Charleston Bits, *On the Loose*, RKO Radio Pictures, 1951.
Will, *Starlift*, Warner Brothers, 1951.
O'Doole, *Battle Zone*, Allied Artists, 1952.
Angelo, *Kid Monk Baroni*, Real Art, 1952.
John Jenkins, *Star of Texas*, Allied Artists, 1953.
Three Sailors and a Girl, Warner Brothers, 1953.
Eddie, *Johnny Trouble*, Warner Brothers, 1957.
Performer, *Teenage Millionaire*, United Artists, 1961.
Pete Mundy, *The Young Swingers*, Twentieth Century-Fox, 1963.
Max's Doctor, *Nothing in Common*, Tri-Star, 1986.
Lawyer, *Beaches*, Touchstone, 1988.

Also appeared in *Montgomery Clift*. 1982.

FILM WORK

Associate producer, *Mike's Murder*, Warner Brothers, 1984.
Coproducer, *Perfect*, Columbia, 1985.
Associate producer, *Bright Lights, Big City*, Metro-Goldwyn-Mayer, 1988.

TELEVISION APPEARANCES; EPISODIC

The Dick Van Dyke Show, CBS, 1963.

OTHER TELEVISION APPEARANCES

Jimmy Olsen, *The Adventures of Superman* (series), syndicated, 1951-57.

Also appeared on the special *Superman's 50th Anniversary: A Celebration of the Man of Steel*, 1988.*

*　　　*　　　*

LAURENTS, Arthur 1918-

PERSONAL: Born July 14, 1918, in Brooklyn, NY; son of Irving (an attorney) and Ada (a teacher; maiden name, Robbins) Laurents. *Education:* Cornell University, B.A., 1937. *Avocational interests:* Skiing, tennis, travel.

ADDRESSES: Agent—Shirley Bernstein, Paramuse Artists Associates, 1414 Sixth Ave., New York, NY 10019.

CAREER: Writer and director. *Military service:* U.S. Army, 1940-45; became sergeant.

MEMBER: Dramatists Guild (member of council), Screen Writers Guild, PEN, Society of Stage Directors and Choreographers, Motion Picture Academy of Arts and Sciences.

AWARDS, HONORS: Citation from Secretary of War and *Variety* Radio Award, 1945, for *Assignment Home;* National Institute of Arts and Letters grant for literature, 1946, for *Home of the Brave;* corecipient, Sidney Howard

Memorial Award, 1946, for *Home of the Brave;* Antoinette Perry Award, best musical, 1967, for *Hallelujah, Baby!;* Drama Desk Award, 1974, for revival of *Gypsy,* and 1978, for *My Mother Was a Fortune Teller;* Writers Guild of America Award, 1978, Golden Globe Award, National Board of Review Best Picture Award, and Screenwriters Guild Award, all for *The Turning Point;* Antoinette Perry Award for best director of a musical, 1984, and Sydney Drama Critics Award for Directing, 1985, both for *La Cage aux Folles;* Theatre Hall of Fame.

CREDITS:

STAGE DIRECTOR

Invitation to a March, Music Box Theatre, New York City, 1960 (also see below).

I Can Get for You Wholesale, Sam S. Shubert Theatre, New York City, 1962.

Anyone Can Whistle, Majestic Theatre, New York City, 1964 (also see below).

The Enclave, Washington Theatre Club, Washington, DC, then Theatre Four, New York City, 1973 (also see below).

Gypsy, Piccadilly Theatre, London, UK, 1973, then Winter Garden Theatre, New York City, 1974; and St. James Theatre, New York City, 1990 (also see below).

My Mother Was a Fortune Teller, Hudson Guild Theatre, New York City, 1978 (also see below).

Scream, Alley Theatre, Houston, TX, 1978 (also see below).

The Madwoman of Central Park West, Studio Arena Theatre, Buffalo, NY, and 22 Steps Theatre, New York City, 1979 (also see below).

La Cage aux Folles, Palace Theatre, New York City, 1983, and Music Hall, Dallas, TX, 1987.

Birds of Paradise, Promenade Theatre, New York City, 1987.

Also director of *So What Are We Gonna Do Now?,* 1982.

MAJOR TOURS

Director, *The Time of the Cuckoo,* U.S. cities, 1953 (also see below).
Director, *Gypsy,* U.S. cities, 1974 and 1989.
Director, *La Cage aux Folles,* Australia, 1985, U.S. cities, 1986, London, 1986.

FILM WORK

(With Herbert Ross) Producer, *The Turning Point,* Twentieth Century-Fox, 1977.

WRITINGS:

PLAYS

Home of the Brave (Belasco Theatre, New York City, 1945; produced in London as *The Way Back*), Random House, 1946.

Heartsong, Shubert Theatre, New Haven, CT, 1947.

The Bird Cage (Coronet Theatre, New York City, 1950), Dramatists Play Service, 1950.

The Time of the Cuckoo (Empire Theatre, New York City, 1952), Random House, 1953 (also see below).

A Clearing in the Woods (Belasco Theatre, 1957), Random House, 1957, revised edition, Dramatists Play Service, 1960.

West Side Story (musical; National Theatre, Washington, DC, then Winter Garden Theatre, New York City, 1957), Random House, 1958.

Gypsy (musical; based on Gypsy Rose Lee's memoirs of the same title; Broadway Theatre, New York City, 1959), Random House, 1960.

Invitation to a March (Music Box Theatre, 1960), Random House, 1961.

Anyone Can Whistle (musical; Majestic Theatre, 1964), Random House, 1965.

Do I Hear a Waltz? (musical; based on Laurents's *The Time of the Cuckoo;* Forty-Sixth Street Theatre, New York City, 1965), Random House, 1966.

Hallelujah, Baby! (musical; Martin Beck Theatre, New York City, 1967), Random House, 1967.

The Enclave (Washington Theatre Club, Washington, DC, then Theatre Four, 1973), Dramatists Play Service, 1974.

Scream, Alley Theatre, Houston, TX, 1978.

(With Phyllis Newman) *My Mother Was a Fortune Teller,* Hudson Guild Theatre, 1978, produced as *The Madwoman of Central Park West,* 22 Steps Theatre, NY, 1979.

A Loss of Memory (one-act; Southampton College Theatre, NY, 1981), Chilton, 1983.

Plays also published in anthologies and periodicals.

SCREENPLAYS

(With Frank Partos and Millen Brand) *The Snake Pit* (based on Mary Jane Ward's novel), Twentieth Century-Fox, 1948.

Rope (based on Patrick Hamilton's play), Warner Brothers, 1948.

(With Philip Yordan) *Anna Lucasta* (based on Yordan's play), Columbia, 1949.

Caught, Enterprise Pictures, 1949.

(With Carl Foreman) *Home of the Brave,* United Artists, 1949.

Anastasia (based on Marcelle Maurette's play), Twentieth Century-Fox, 1956.

Bonjour Tristesse (based on Francoise Sagan's novel), Columbia, 1958.

(With Ernest Lehman) *West Side Story,* United Artists, 1961.

(With Leonard Spigelgass) *Gypsy,* Warner Brothers, 1962.

(With David Lean and H. E. Bates) *Summertime* (also known as *Summer Madness*), United Artists, 1965.

The Way We Were, Columbia, 1973.

The Turning Point, Twentieth Century-Fox, 1977.

TELEVISION

The Light Fantastic; Or, How to Tell Your Past, Present and Maybe Future through Social Dancing (special), NBC, 1967.

RADIO

Author of the radio plays *Now Playing Tomorrow,* 1939; *Western Electric Communicade,* 1944; *The Last Day of the War,* 1945; and *The Face,* 1945. Author of episodes of *Hollywood Playhouse, Dr. Christian, The Thin Man, Manhattan at Midnight,* 1939-40; and *The Man Behind the Gun, Army Service Force Presents, Assignment Home, This is Your FBI,* 1943-45.

NOVELS

The Way We Were, Harper, 1972.

The Turning Point, New American Library, 1977.

* * *

LAWRENCE, Marc 1910-

PERSONAL: Born February 17, 1910, in New York City; son of Israel Simon and Minerva Norma (Sugarman) Goldsmith; married Fanya Foss, October 7, 1942; children: Michael, Antoinette. *Education:* Attended City College of New York, 1928-30.

ADDRESSES: Office—14016 Bora Bora Way, #119, Marina Del Rey, CA 90291.

CAREER: Actor, director and producer. Consultant, Ursus Production Company.

MEMBER: American Federation of Television and Radio Artists, Screen Actors Guild, Directors Guild of America, Academy of Motion Picture Arts and Sciences.

AWARDS, HONORS: Award from the Hollywood Achievement Society, 1982.

CREDITS:

FILM APPEARANCES

Hoodlum, *If I Had a Million,* Paramount, 1932.

Connors, *White Woman,* Paramount, 1933.

Don't Bet on Blondes, Warner Brothers, 1935.

Men of the Hour, Columbia, 1935.

Lefty, *Dr. Socrates,* Warner Brothers, 1935.

Hood at lodge, *G-Men,* Warner Brothers, 1935.

Dint Coleman, *Counterfeit,* Columbia, 1936.

Grivon, *Under Two Flags,* Twentieth Century-Fox, 1936.

Johnny Sampson, *The Cowboy Star,* Columbia, 1936.

Valet, *Desire,* Paramount, 1936.

Mike Magellon, *The Final Hour,* Columbia, 1936.

Barker, *Love on a Bet,* RKO, 1936.

Dorn, *Night Waitress,* RKO, 1936.

Pete, *Road Gang* (also known as *Injustice*), First National/Warner Brothers, 1936.

Griffin, *Trapped by Television,* Columbia, 1936.

Thomas Mitchell, *Charlie Chan on Broadway,* Twentieth Century-Fox, 1937.

Edwin Mitchell, *Counsel for Crime,* Columbia, 1937.

Blast Reardon, *Criminals of the Air,* Columbia, 1937.

Calkins, *A Dangerous Adventure,* Columbia, 1937.

Whitehat, *I Promise to Pay,* Columbia, 1937.

Slater, *Motor Madness,* Columbia, 1937.

Rusty Morgan, *Murder in Greenwich Village,* Columbia, 1937.

Blackie, *Racketeers in Exile,* Columbia, 1937.

Venetti, *San Quentin,* First National/Warner Brothers, 1937.

Kid Crow, *The Shadow,* Columbia, 1937.

Pete Brower, *What Price Vengeance?,* Rialto, 1937.

Poule, *Adventure in Sahara,* Columbia, 1938.

Johnnie McCoy, *Charlie Chan in Honolulu,* Twentieth Century-Fox, 1938.

Milton Miltis, *Convicted,* Columbia, 1938.

Eddie Girard, *I Am the Law,* Columbia, 1938.

Jack Hawkins, *Penitentiary,* Columbia, 1938.

Lawlor, *Squadron of Honor,* Columbia, 1938.

Stevens, *There's That Woman Again* (also known as *What a Woman*), Columbia, 1938.

Happy Nelson, *While New York Sleeps,* Twentieth Century-Fox, 1938.

Frank Daniels, *Who Killed Gail Preston?,* Columbia, 1938.

Slick Eastman, *Beware Spooks,* Columbia, 1939.

Buck, *Blind Alley,* Columbia, 1939.

Halstead, *Code of the Streets,* Universal, 1939.

Veneill, *Dust Be My Destiny,* Warner Brothers, 1939.

Bill Corsley, *Ex-Champ* (also known as *Golden Gloves*), Universal, 1939.

Chuck Brown, *Homicide Bureau,* Columbia, 1939.

Floyd, *Housekeeper's Daughter,* United Artists, 1939.

Joe, *Romance of the Redwoods,* Columbia, 1939.

Heavy leader, *The Lone Wolf Spy Hunt* (also known as *The Lone Wolf's Daughter*), Columbia, 1939.

"Piggy" Ceders, *Sergeant Madden,* Metro-Goldwyn-Mayer (MGM), 1939.

Sutter, *S.O.S. Tidal Wave* (also known as *Tidal Wave*), Republic, 1939.

Prosecutor, *Brigham Young—Frontiersman* (also known as *Brigham Young*), Twentieth Century-Fox, 1940.

Steve McBirney, *Charlie Chan at the Wax Museum,* Twentieth Century-Fox, 1940.

Lefty Sloane, *Invisible Stripes,* Warner Brothers, 1940.

John Bates, *Johnny Apollo,* Twentieth Century-Fox, 1940.

Tony, *Love, Honor, and Oh, Baby,* Universal, 1940.

Lofty Kyler, *The Man Who Talked too Much,* Warner Brothers, 1940.

"Happy" Dugan, *The Golden Fleecing,* MGM, 1940.

Tony, *The Great Profile,* Twentieth Century-Fox, 1940.

Mike, *Public Enemies,* Republic, 1941.

Bert LaVerne, *Blossoms in the Dust,* MGM, 1941.

Joe, *A Dangerous Game,* Universal, 1941.

Charlie Smith, *Hold That Ghost* (also known as *Oh, Charlie*), Universal, 1941.

Lefty Landers, *Lady Scarface,* RKO, 1941.

Frank DeSoto, *The Man Who Lost Himself,* Universal, 1941.

Sleeper, *The Monster and the Girl,* Paramount, 1941.

Hammud, *Sundown,* United Artists, 1941.

Louie, *Tall, Dark, and Handsome,* Twentieth Century-Fox, 1941.

Pete Matthews, *The Shepherd of the Hills,* Paramount, 1941.

Horace Dunston, *Call of the Canyon,* Republic, 1942.

Joe Aiello, *Nazi Agent* (also known as *Salute to Courage*), MGM, 1942.

McGaffey, *'Neath Brooklyn Bridge,* Monogram, 1942.

Tommy, *This Gun for Hire,* Paramount, 1942.

Trigger, *Yokel Boy* (also known as *Hitting the Headlines*), Republic, 1942.

Gordon Finch, *Eyes of the Underworld,* Universal, 1943.

Farnley, *The Ox-Bow Incident* (also known as *Strange Incident*), Twentieth Century-Fox, 1943.

Vincent Belga, *Submarine Alert,* Paramount, 1943.

Phil, *Hit the Ice* (also known as *Oh Doctor*), Universal, 1943.

Pedro, *The Princess and the Pirate,* RKO, 1944.

Alcoa, *Rainbow Island,* Paramount, 1944.

Valdez, *Tampico,* Twentieth Century-Fox, 1944.

Doc, *Dillinger,* Monogram, 1945.

Cliff Anson, *Don't Fence Me In,* Republic, 1945.

Disko, *Flame of the Barbary Coast,* Republic, 1945.

Luigi, *Cloak and Dagger,* Warner Brothers, 1946.

Joe Reed, *Club Havana,* Producers Releasing Corporation, 1946.

Pete, *Life with Blondie,* Columbia, 1946.

Pete, *The Virginian,* Paramount, 1946.

Corio, *Captain from Castile,* Twentieth Century-Fox, 1947.

Sioto, *Unconquered,* Paramount, 1947.

Duke, *Yankee Fakir,* Republic, 1947.

Nick Palestro, *I Walk Alone,* Paramount, 1948.

Ziggy, *Key Largo,* Warner Brothers, 1948.

Red Stubbins, *Out of the Storm,* Republic, 1948.

Dean, *Calamity Jane and Sam Bass,* Universal, 1949.

Angelo Agostini, *Jigsaw* (also known as *Gun Moll*), United Artists, 1949.

Vince, *Tough Assignment,* United Artists, 1949.

Frankie, *Abbott and Costello in the Foreign Legion,* Universal, 1950.

Cobby, *The Asphalt Jungle,* MGM, 1950.

Caesar Xavier Serpi, *The Black Hand,* MGM, 1950.

Samad, *The Desert Hawk,* Universal, 1950.

Angus Macready, *Hurricane Island,* Columbia, 1951.

Ben Ali, *My Favorite Spy,* Paramount, 1951.

Diomedes, *Helen of Troy,* Warner Brothers, 1956.

William Connors, *Kill Her Gently,* Columbia, 1958.

Johnny Colini, *Johnny Cool,* United Artists, 1963.

William Billie, *Johnny Tiger,* Universal, 1966.

Sergeant Barril, *Savage Pampas* (also known as *Pampa Salvaje*), Comet, 1967.

Goldminer, *Custer of the West,* Cinerama, 1968.

Jacobs, *Krakatoa, East of Java* (also known as *Volcano*), Cinerama, 1969.

Carnival Barker, *The Five Man Army* (also known as *Un Esercito di cinque uomini*), MGM, 1970.

Priest, *The Kremlin Letter,* Twentieth Century-Fox, 1970.

Diamonds Are Forever, United Artists, 1971.

Chiarelli, *Frasier, The Sensuous Lion,* LCS, 1973.

Rodney, *The Man with the Golden Gun,* United Artists, 1974.

Erhard, *Marathon Man,* Paramount, 1976.

Louie, *A Piece of the Action,* Warner Brothers, 1977.

Stiltskin, *Foul Play,* Paramount, 1978.

Webster, *Goin' Coconuts,* Osmond, 1978.

Swap Meet, Dimension, 1979.

Carmine, *Hot Stuff,* Columbia, 1979.

Tony Torpedo, *Super Fuzz* (also known as *Supersnooper*), AVCO-Embassy, 1981.

Zambrini, *Daddy's Deadly Darling* (also known as *Daddy's Girl* and *The Pigs*), Aquarius, 1984.

Weiss and Dieter, *Night Train to Terror,* Visto International, 1985.

Vinnie "The Cannon" DiMoti, *The Big Easy,* Columbia, 1987.

Michael Fazio, *Blood Red,* Hemdale, 1989.

Also appeared in *Cataclysm,* 1980, and *Dream No Evil,* 1984; and in several films made in Italy, France, and Spain.

FILM WORK

Producer (with John Derek) and director, *Nightmare in the Sun,* Zodiak, 1964.

Producer and director, *Daddy's Deadly Darling* (also known as *Daddy's Girl* and *The Pigs*), Aquarius, 1984.

TELEVISION APPEARANCES

Stefano Magaddino, *Honor Thy Father* (movie), CBS, 1973.

Franks, *Switch* (movie; also known as *Las Vegas Roundabout*), CBS, 1975.

Joe Cincinatti, *Border Pals* (pilot), ABC, 1981.

Daniel Ginelli, *Terror at Alcatraz* (pilot), NBC, 1982.

Sam Marlini, *The A-Team* (episodic), NBC, 1986.

Abe the Just, *Shannon's Deal* (episodic), NBC, 1990.

Gabriel's Fire, NBC, 1990.

Star Trek, syndicated, 1990.

STAGE APPEARANCES

Appeared in productions of *Sour Mountain, Waiting for Lefty, Golden Boy, The Survivor,* and *A View from the Bridge.*

WRITINGS:

Daddy's Deadly Darling (screenplay; also known as *Daddy's Girl* and *The Pigs*), Aquarius, 1984.

*　　*　　*

LAWSON, Denis   1947-

PERSONAL: Born September 27, 1947.

ADDRESSES: Agent—James Sharkey Associates, Third Floor, Suite 15, Golden Sq., London W1R 3A6, England.

CAREER: Actor. Affiliated with two production companies, Knock Productions and Lawrence Henry Productions.

AWARDS, HONORS: Most Promising Actor award from *Drama,* c. 1980.

CREDITS:

STAGE APPEARANCES

Martius, *Titus Andronicus,* Round House Theatre, London, 1971.

England's Ireland, Portable Theatre Company, Round House Theatre, 1972.

Another Kaspar, *Kaspar,* Almost Free Theatre, London, 1973.

Jason, M. Dumas, M. Pitou Armand, and Prince Henri de Ligne, *Sarah B. Divine,* Jeannetta Cochrane Theatre, London, 1973.

Warder Mullins, *Kidnapped at Christmas,* Dolphin Theatre Company, Shaw Theatre, London, 1975.

Brother David, *The Dog Ran Away,* Hampstead Theatre Club, London, 1977.

Stephen, *Censored Scenes From King Kong,* Open Space Theatre, London, 1977.

Luigi, *We Can't Pay? We Won't Pay!,* Half Moon Theatre, London, 1978.

Patrick, *A Greenish Man,* Bush Theatre, London, 1978.

Fifty Words—Bits of Lenny Bruce, King's Head Theatre, 1979.

Joey, *Pal Joey,* Half Moon Theatre, then Albery Theatre, London, 1980-81.

Jim Lancaster, *Mr. Cinders,* King's Head Theatre, then Fortune Theatre, both London, 1983.

Bellmour, *The Lucky Chance,* Royal Court Theatre, London, 1984.

Max, *Lend Me a Tenor,* Globe Theatre, London, 1986.

Colin, *Ashes,* Bush Theatre, 1986-87.

Algernon Moncrieff, *The Importance of Being Earnest,* Royalty Theatre, London, 1987.

Jonathon Balton, *The Film Society,* Hampstead Theatre Club, 1988.

Mosca, *Volpone,* Almeida Theatre, London, 1990.

FILM APPEARANCES

Dave Woodford, *Providence,* Cinema V, 1977.

Wedge (Red Two), *Star Wars,* Twentieth Century-Fox, 1977.

Wedge (Rogue Three), *The Empire Strikes Back,* Twentieth Century-Fox, 1980.

Gordon Urquhart, *Local Hero,* Warner Brothers, 1983.

Wedge, *Return of the Jedi,* Twentieth Century-Fox, 1983.

Keith, *The Chain,* Rank, 1985.

TELEVISION APPEARANCES

Claude, *The Man in the Iron Mask* (movie), NBC, 1977.

Love after Lunch (movie), BBC, 1986.

Bernard, *One Way Out* (movie), BBC, 1988.

Dominic Rossi, *The Justice Game I* (mini-series), BBC, 1988.

Dominic Rossi, *The Justice Game II* (mini-series), BBC, 1989.

Also appeared as Eddy in the mini-series *Dead Head,* 1985, and as John in the mini-series *That Uncertain Feeling,* 1986.

*　　*　　*

LAWSON, Leigh   1943-

PERSONAL: Born July 21, 1943, in Atherstone, Warwickshire, England; married Twiggy (an actress and model), 1988; children: one son (with Hayley Mills, an actress); one stepdaughter, Carly. *Education:* Attended Royal Academy of Dramatic Arts.

ADDRESSES: Agent—Duncan Heath Associates, Paramount House, 162/170 Wardour St., W1V 3AT London, England.

CAREER: Actor. Member of the National Theatre Company of Great Britain, London, and a theatrical repertory company in Coventry, England.

CREDITS:

STAGE APPEARANCES

Ivan Kaliayev, *The Price of Justice,* Mermaid Theatre, London, 1972.
Louis Dubedat, *The Doctor's Dilemma,* Greenwich Theatre, London, 1981.
Aubrey Tanqueray, *The Second Ms. Tanqueray,* National Theatre, Lyttelton Theatre, London, 1981.
Yonadab, National Theatre, Olivier Theatre, London, 1985.
Antonio, *The Merchant of Venice,* Phoenix Theatre, London, then (Broadway debut) 46th Street Theatre, New York City, both 1989.

Also appeared in *From the Balcony,* National Theatre.

FILM APPEARANCES

Bernardo, *Brother Sun, Sister Moon,* Paramount, 1973.
Ghost Story, Stephen Weeks, 1974.
Michael, *The Tiger Lily,* Gala, 1975.
Captain James Black, *Des Teufels Advokat* (also known as *The Devil's Advocate*), Rank, 1977.
Tony Cerdan, *Golden Rendezvous,* Rank, 1977.
Percy, *It's Not the Size that Counts* (also known as *Percy's Progress*), Joseph Brenner, 1979.
Alec d'Urberville, *Tess,* Columbia, 1980.
Marke, *Tristan und Isolde* (opera; also known as *Tristan and Isolde*), Veith von Fuerstenberg, 1981.
Humphrey, *Sword of the Valiant—The Legend of Gawain and the Green Knight,* Cannon, 1984 (also see below).
Ronnie Blum, *Madame Sousatzka,* Universal, 1988.

Also appeared in *The God King; Fire and Sword; Black Carrion;* and *The Captain's Doll.*

TELEVISION APPEARANCES; MINI-SERIES

Dicks, *QB VII,* ABC, 1974.
Count Charles de Chazalle, *Lace,* ABC, 1984.
Uncle Morgan, *Queenie,* CBS, 1987.

TELEVISION APPEARANCES; EPISODIC

Space 1999, syndicated, 1977.

TELEVISION APPEARANCES; MOVIES

Alfred Pratt, *Love Among the Ruins,* ABC, 1975.
Jimmy Lorrimer, *Agatha Christie's "Murder Is Easy,"* CBS, 1982.

Troubetzkoy, *Poor Little Rich Girl: The Barbara Hutton Story,* NBC, 1987.
Michael's friend, *Tears in the Rain,* Showtime, 1988.
Robert, *Deadline: Madrid* (also known as *Deadline*), ABC, 1988.

OTHER TELEVISION APPEARANCES

Murder Is a One-Act Play (special; also known as *Death of Sister Mary*), ABC, 1974.
The Duchess of Duke Street (series), BBC, 1976, then *Masterpiece Theatre,* PBS, 1978.
Title role, *Kinsey* (series), BBC-1, 1991—.

Also appeared in the series *Travelling Man,* ITV; appeared in the specials *Thriller,* 1975; *Big Brother; Black Beauty; Trapped; Song of Songs; William; Disraeli; Why Didn't They Ask Evans?;* and *Journey into the Shadows.*

WRITINGS:

Sword of the Valiant—The Legend of Gawain and the Green Knight (screenplay), released by Cannon, 1984.*

*   *   *

LAWSON, Richard

PERSONAL: Born March 7, in Loma Linda, CA.

ADDRESSES: Agent—Joe Funicello, International Creative Management, 8899 Beverly Boulevard, Los Angeles, CA 90048.

CAREER: Actor.

CREDITS:

STAGE APPEARANCES

The Final Concert Tour of Mickey Colossus, Philadelphia Company, Philadelphia, PA, 1978.
Frankie, *The Mighty Gents,* New York Shakespeare Festival, Mobile Theatre, New York City, 1979.
The Final Concert Tour of Mickey Colossus, Center Theatre Group/New Theatre for Now, Mark Taper Forum, Los Angeles, CA, 1983-84.
Eddie, *Fool for Love,* Los Angeles Theatre Center, Los Angeles, CA, 1985.
Levee, *Ma Rainey's Black Bottom,* Los Angeles Theatre Center, 1987.
Syl, *Checkmates,* Westwood Playhouse, Los Angeles, CA, 1987.
Wates, *Hapgood,* James A. Doolittle Theatre, Los Angeles, CA, 1989.
Bernard, *The Talented Tenth,* Manhattan Theatre Club, Stage I, New York City, 1989.

MAJOR TOURS

Melvin Smeltz, *No Place to Be Somebody,* U.S. cities, 1970-71.

FILM APPEARANCES

Homosexual, *Dirty Harry,* Warner Brothers, 1971.
Willis, *Scream Blacula Scream,* American International, 1973.
Sugar, *Willie Dynamite,* Universal, 1973.
Baron Samedi, *Sugar Hill* (also known as *Voodoo Girl* and *The Zombies of Sugar Hill*), American International, 1974.
The Black Street Fighter (also known as *Black Fist*), New Line, 1976.
Policeman, *Audrey Rose,* United Artists, 1977.
Pat, *Coming Home,* United Artists, 1978.
Hector Mantilla, *The Main Event,* Warner Brothers, 1979.
Ryan, *Poltergeist,* Metro-Goldwyn-Mayer/United Artists, 1982.
Ed Price, *Streets of Fire,* Universal/RKO, 1984.
Cornell, *Stick,* Universal, 1985.

Also appeared in *Bogard,* 1975.

TELEVISION APPEARANCES; SERIES

Detective O. Z. Tate, *Chicago Story,* NBC, 1982.
Nick Kimball, *Dynasty,* ABC, 1986-87.
Detective Nathaniel Hawthorne, *The Days and Nights of Molly Dodd,* Lifetime, 1988—.

TELEVISION APPEARANCES; PILOTS

Ken Dillard, *Crossfire,* NBC, 1975.
Most Wanted, ABC, 1976.
Caleb Holiday, *The Buffalo Soldiers,* NBC, 1979.
Nick Scott, *Silent Whisper* (broadcast as an episode of *CBS Summer Playhouse*), CBS, 1988.

TELEVISION APPEARANCES; EPISODIC

Medical Center, CBS, 1975.
The Streets of San Francisco, ABC, 1975.
Get Christie Love!, ABC, 1975.
All in the Family, CBS, 1979.
Monroe Henderson, *Remington Steele,* NBC, 1985.
Dr. Jonathan Williams, *Amen,* NBC, 1987.
Blake Simpson, *227,* NBC, 1988.
McGill, *Wiseguy,* CBS, 1988.
Jesse Colton, *MacGyver,* ABC, 1989.

TELEVISION APPEARANCES; MOVIES

James Harris, *Charleston,* NBC, 1979.
R. C. Stiles, *The Jericho Mile,* ABC, 1979.
Gene Davis, *The Golden Moment—An Olympic Love Story,* NBC, 1980.
Dr. Ben Taylor, *V,* NBC, 1983.

Adam Prentice, *Johnnie Mae Gibson: FBI,* CBS, 1986.
Dr. Duran, *Under the Influence,* CBS, 1986.
C. Gabriel Dash, *Double Your Pleasure,* NBC, 1989.
Sergeant Frank McDermott, *The Forgotton,* USA, 1989.

TELEVISION APPEARANCES; SPECIALS

Officer Venchek, *Lead Foot,* syndicated, 1982.
Dr. Julius Pepper, *The Faculty,* ABC, 1986.*

*   *   *

LEEDS, Phil

PERSONAL: Born in New York, NY; son of a post office clerk; married Toby Brandt. *Education:* Attended City College of New York.

CAREER: Actor. Comedian in nightclubs throughout the United States. Peanut vendor, Yankee Stadium and the Polo Grounds, both New York City. *Military service:* U.S. Army, 1943-46, served in Special Services; became sergeant.

MEMBER: Actors' Equity Association, American Guild of Variety Artists, American Federation of Television and Radio Artists, Screen Actors Guild.

CREDITS:

STAGE APPEARANCES

(Debut) Ensemble, *Of V We Sing* (revue), Concert Theatre, New York City, 1942.
Ensemble, *Let Freedom Sing* (revue), Longacre Theatre, New York City, 1942.
Dr. Francel, *Make a Wish,* Winter Garden Theatre, New York City, 1951.
Curtain Going Up, Forrest Theatre, Philadelphia, PA, 1952.
Theophile and Boris Adzinidzinadze (understudy), *Can-Can,* Shubert Theatre, New York City, 1953.
Joe Scalan and Gypsy, *The Matchmaker,* Royale Theatre, New York City, 1955.
Soldier, *Romanoff and Juliet,* Plymouth Theatre, New York City, 1957.
The Girls Against the Boys, Alvin Theatre, New York City, 1959.
Uncle, *Christine,* 46th Street Theatre, New York City, 1960.
Simeon Moodis, *Smiling, the Boy Fell Dead,* Cherry Lane Theatre, New York City, 1961.
Sandor, *Bells Are Ringing,* State Fair Music Hall, Dallas, TX, 1961.
Peppy, *The Merry Widow,* South Shore Music Circus, Cohasset, MA, 1961.
Song of Norway, State Fair Music Hall, 1961.

Oliver Badger, *The Banker's Daughter,* Jan Hus Playhouse, New York City, 1962.

Chinese laundry man and Hymie the waiter, *Nowhere to Go But Up,* Winter Garden Theatre, 1962.

William Morris, *Sophie,* Winter Garden Theatre, 1963.

Victor Talsey, *Nobody Loves an Albatross,* Lyceum Theatre, New York City, 1963.

Louis Lamont, Dominique You, and Louis the Guide, *Mardi Gras,* Marine Theatre, Jones Beach, NY, 1965.

Benoit Pinglet, *Hotel Passionato,* East 74th Street Theatre, New York City, 1965.

Ali Hakim, *Oklahoma!,* State Fair Music Hall, 1966.

Max Kane, *Dinner at Eight,* Alvin Theatre, New York City, 1966.

Lieutenant Miles Practice, *Little Murders,* Broadhurst Theatre, New York City, 1967.

Harry Gold, *Inquest,* Music Box Theatre, New York City, 1970.

Harrison Fairchild III, town drunk, Dr. Krauss, chief, chorus boy, and Uncle Larry, *Hurry, Harry,* Ritz Theatre, New York City, 1972.

The Sunshine Boys, American Conservatory Theatre, San Francisco, CA, 1973.

Hysterium, *A Funny Thing Happened on the Way to the Forum,* Coconut Grove Playhouse, Miami, FL, 1983.

MAJOR TOURS

Mr. Sawyer, *Here's Love,* U.S. cities, 1964.

Launce, *Two Gentlemen of Verona,* New York Shakespeare Festival, U.S. and Canadian cities, 1973.

FILM APPEARANCES

Dr. Shand, *Rosemary's Baby,* Paramount, 1968.

Sam, *Don't Drink the Water,* AVCO-Embassy, 1969.

Dog catcher, *Won Ton Ton, the Dog Who Saved Hollywood,* Paramount, 1976.

Chief monk, *History of the World, Part I,* Twentieth Century-Fox, 1981.

Sammy Pinkers, *Beaches,* Buena Vista, 1988.

Saturday the 14th Strikes Back, Concorde, 1988.

Pesheles, *Enemies, a Love Story,* Twentieth Century-Fox, 1989.

Also appeared as Jerry Shea, *Cat Chaser,* 1988; and in *Soap Dish; He Said, She Said;* and *Frankie and Johnny.*

TELEVISION APPEARANCES; SERIES

Regular, *Front Row Center,* Dumont, 1949-50.

Vladimir, *Ivan the Terrible,* CBS, 1976.

TELEVISION APPEARANCES; PILOTS

What's Up?, NBC, 1971.

Lou, *Hereafter,* NBC, 1975.

Repairman, *The Bureau,* NBC, 1976.

Everett Buhl, *Featherstone's Nest,* CBS, 1979.

Singer and Sons, NBC, 1990.

Also appeared in *Civil Wars.*

TELEVISION APPEARANCES; EPISODIC

The Dick Van Dyke Show, CBS, 1962.
Barney Miller, ABC, 1975, 1977, 1979, 1980, and 1981.
All in the Family, CBS, 1976 and 1978.
Sid, *Good Time Harry,* NBC, 1980.
Dr. Barnes, *You Again?,* NBC, 1986.
Russell Hansen, *Cagney and Lacey,* CBS, 1987.
Alan, *The Famous Teddy Z,* CBS, 1990.
Jack, *ALF,* NBC, 1990.

Also appeared on *The Milton Berle Show,* NBC; *The Jimmy Durante Show,* NBC; *The Jackie Gleason Show,* CBS; *I Love Lucy,* CBS; *The Jack Paar Show,* NBC; *Car 54, Where Are You?,* NBC; *The Patty Duke Show,* ABC; *The Tonight Show,* NBC; *For the People,* CBS; *The Trials of O'Brien,* CBS; *The Hero,* NBC; *The Monkees,* NBC; *The Odd Couple,* ABC; *Happy Days,* ABC; *Alice,* CBS; *Three's Company,* ABC; *thirtysomething,* ABC; *Coach; Gabriel's Fire;* and *Doctor, Doctor.*

TELEVISION APPEARANCES; MOVIES

Eddie, *Murder by Natural Causes,* CBS, 1979.

TELEVISION APPEARANCES; SPECIALS

What's Up America?, NBC, 1971.

Also appeared as Uncle Max, *The Haunting of Harrington House,* 1981; Mr. Brownstein, *Wings,* 1983; appeared on *This Proud Land,* ABC; and *Pins and Needles,* NET.

RADIO APPEARANCES

Guest comedian, *The Jane Pickens Show* (episodic), NBC, 1947.*

*   *   *

LEGRAND, Michel 1932-

PERSONAL: Full name, Michel Jean Legrand; born February 24, 1932, in Paris, France; son of Raymond (a musician) and Marcelle Legrand; married Christine Bouchard, 1958; children: Herve, Benjamin, Eugenie. *Education:* Received diploma from Conservatoire Nationale Superieur de Musique, Paris, France, 1951. *Avocational interests:* Boating, flying, tennis, and horseback riding.

ADDRESSES: Office—c/o Jim DiGiovanni, 157 West 57th Street, New York, NY 10019.

CAREER: Composer, musician, director, and writer. Leader of Michel Legrand Orchestra; conductor and arranger for Maurice Chevalier; jazz pianist, Pittsburgh

Symphony Orchestra, Minneapolis Symphony Orchestra, Buffalo Philharmonic Orchestra.

MEMBER: Dramatists Guild, Songwriters Guild of America, American Federation of Musicians, American Federation of Television and Radio Artists, American Society of Composers, Authors, and Producers, Academy of Motion Picture Arts and Sciences.

AWARDS, HONORS: Academy awards, best song, 1968, for "Windmills of Your Mind," best musical score, 1971, for *Summer of '42,* and best original song score and adaptation score, 1983, for *Yentl;* British Academy Award, best score, 1971, for *Summer of '42;* Grammy awards, best instrumental composition, 1971, for "Theme from *Summer of '42,*" best arrangement accompanying a vocalist, 1972, for "What Are You Doing the Rest of Your Life," best instrumental composition, 1972, for *Brian's Song,* best instrumental composition, 1975, for "Images," and best jazz-big band album, 1975, for *Images.*

CREDITS:

STAGE APPEARANCES

Andy Williams with Michel Legrand, Uris Theatre, New York City, 1974.

FILM APPEARANCES

Bob, *Cleo de 5 a 7* (also known as *Cleo from 5 to 7*), Rome Paris Film, 1961.

FILM WORK; MUSIC DIRECTOR, EXCEPT AS NOTED

Les Parapluies de Cherbourg (also known as *The Umbrellas of Cherbourg;* also see below), Laundau, 1964.
Ice Station Zebra (also see below), Filmways/MGM, 1968.
La Dame dans l'auto avec des lunettes et fusil (also known as *The Lady in the Car with Glasses and a Gun;* also see below), Columbia, 1970.
Le Mans (also see below), National General, 1971.
Summer of '42 (also see below), Warner Brothers, 1971.
One Is a Lonely Number (also known as *Two Is a Happy Number;* also see below), MGM, 1972.
Portnoy's Complaint (also see below), Warner Brothers, 1972.
Director, *Five Days in June* (also see below), AAA, 1988.

TELEVISION APPEARANCES; SPECIALS

The Maurice Chevalier Show, NBC, 1956.
The Dick Van Dyke Special, CBS, 1968.
Ann-Margaret Smith, NBC, 1975.
The Shirley Bassey Special, syndicated, 1981.

TELEVISION WORK

Director, "Michel's Mixed-Up Musical Bird," *ABC Afterschool Specials* (also see below), ABC, 1978.

RECORDINGS:

Performer for albums, including *Images,* recorded with Phil Woods and the Michel Legrand Orchestra; arranger for albums, including *I Love Paris.*

WRITINGS:

STAGE MUSIC

Music, musical concepts and arrangements, *Brainchild,* Forrest Theatre, Philadelphia, PA, 1974.
Music, orchestrations and arrangements, *The Umbrellas of Cherbourg,* New York Shakespeare Festival, Public Theatre, New York City, 1979.

FILM MUSIC

Cleo de 5 a 7 (also known as *Cleo from 5 to 7*), Rome Paris Film, 1961.
Lola, Films Around the World, 1961.
Une Femme est une femme (also known as *A Woman Is a Woman*), Pathe Contemporary, 1961.
(With Francis Lemarque) *Le cave se rebiffe il re dei faisari* (also known as *Money, Money, Money* and *The Counterfeiters of Paris*), Cite/CCM/Metro-Goldwyn-Mayer (MGM), 1962.
Eva the Devils' Woman (also known as *Eva*), Paris Film/Interopa, 1962.
"Anger," "Gluttony," "Lust," "Envy," and "Laziness," *Les Sept Peches capitaus* (also known as *I sette peccati capitali; Seven Capital Sins*), Embassy, 1962.
Le Coeur Battant (also known as *The French Game*), Atlantic, 1963.
Love Is a Ball (also known as *All This and Money Too*), United Artists, 1963.
Vivre sa vie (also known as *My Life to Live*), Union/Pathe Contemporary, 1963.
Les Baie des Anges (also known as *Bay of Angels*), Pathe, 1964.
Les Parapluies de Cherbourg (also known as *The Umbrellas of Cherbourg*), Laundau, 1964.
Bande a part (also known as *Band of Outsiders*), Royal, 1966.
Une Ravissante Idiote (also known as *The Ravishing Idiot; Agent 38-24-36; The Wary-Blooded Spy; Adorable Idiot; Bewitching Scatterbrain; A Ravishing Idiot*), Seven Arts, 1966.
La Vie de chateau (also known as *A Matter of Resistance*), Royal, 1967.
Tender Vouyou (also known as *Un avventuriero a Tahiti; Tender Scoundrel*), Embassy, 1967.
How To Save a Marriage—and Ruin Your Life (also known as *Band of Gold*), Columbia, 1968.
Ice Station Zebra, Filmways/MGM, 1968.
A Matter of Innocence (also known as *Pretty Polly*), Universal, 1968.

Le Plus Vieux Metier du monde (also known as *L'amore attraverso i secoli; Das alteste Gewerbe der Welt; The Oldest Profession*), Goldstone/VIP, 1968.

Sweet November, Warner Brothers/Seven Arts, 1968.

The Thomas Crown Affair (also known as *Thomas Crown and Company; The Crown Caper*), United Artists, 1968.

Les Demoiselles de Rochefort (also known as *The Young Girls of Rochefort*), Warner Brothers/Seven Arts, 1968.

Castle Keep, Columbia, 1969.

The Happy Ending, United Artists, 1969.

Play Dirty (also known as *Written on the Sand*), United Artists, 1969.

La Dame dans l'auto avec des lunettes et fusil (also known as *The Lady in the Car with Glasses and a Gun*), Columbia, 1970.

Pieces of Dreams, United Artists, 1970.

Wuthering Heights, American International, 1970.

The Go-Between, Columbia, 1971.

Le Mans, National General, 1971.

Summer of '42, Warner Brothers, 1971.

A Time for Loving (also known as *Paris Was Made for Lovers*), London Screen Plays, 1971.

Lady Sings the Blues, Paramount, 1972.

One Is a Lonely Number (also known as *Two Is a Happy Number*), MGM, 1972.

Portnoy's Complaint, Warner Brothers, 1972.

Breezy, Universal, 1973.

Cops and Robbers, United Artists, 1973.

A Doll's House, World Film Services, 1973.

Forty Carats, Columbia, 1973.

Impossible Object (also known as *Story of a Love Story*), Valoria, 1973.

The Nelson Affair (also known as *Bequest to the Nation*), Universal, 1973.

Un Homme est Mort (also known as *The Outside Man*), United Artists, 1973.

Our Time (also known as *Death of Her Innocence*), Warner Brothers, 1974.

The Three Musketeers, Twentieth Century-Fox, 1974.

Peau d'ane (also known as *Donkey Skin*), Janus, 1975.

Additional music, *The Four Musketeers* (also known as *The Revenge of Milady*), Twentieth Century-Fox, 1975.

Le Sauvage (also known as *Lovers Like Us; The Savage*), Gaumont, 1975.

Sheila Levine Is Dead and Living in New York, Paramount, 1975.

Gable and Lombard, Universal, 1976.

Ode to Billy Joe, Warner Brothers, 1976.

Gulliver's Travels (animated/live-action), Sunn Classic, 1977.

The Other Side of Midnight, Twentieth Century-Fox, 1977.

Lady Oscar, Toho, 1979.

Falling in Love Again, International Picture Show of Atlanta, 1980.

(With Jun Fukamachi) *Hinotori,* Toho, 1980.

The Hunter, Paramount, 1980.

The Mountain Men, Columbia, 1980.

Atlantic City (also known as *Atlantic City U.S.A.*), Paramount, 1981.

Best Friends, Warner Brothers, 1982.

(With Francis Lai) *Bolero,* Double 13, 1982.

Le Cadeau (also known as *The Gift*), Samuel Goldwyn Company, 1983.

Never Say Never Again, Warner Brothers, 1983.

Yentl, MGM/United Artists (MGM/UA), 1983.

Un Amour en Allemagne (also known as *Eine Liebe in Deutschland; A Love in Germany*), Triumph, 1984.

Secret Places, Twentieth Century-Fox, 1984.

La Flute a six schtroumnpfs (also known as *The Smurfs and the Magic Flute*), Atlantic Releasing, 1984.

Partir revenir (also known as *Going and Coming Back*), Films 13/Union Generale Cinematographique/Top 1/FR 3, 1985.

Palace, Wonderland/Third Wave/Rapid, 1985.

Parking, American, 1985.

Paroles et musiques (also known as *Love Songs; Words and Music*), SpectraFilm, 1986.

Club Recontres (also known as *Lonely Hearts Club*), AMLF, 1987.

Spirale (also known as *Spiral*), Union Generale Cinematographique, 1987.

Switching Channels, Tri-Star, 1988.

Five Days in June, AAA, 1988.

Also composer for *Beau fixe* (short), 1953; *Les Amants du Tage,* 1955; *Le Triporteur,* 1957; *Raffles sur la ville,* 1957; *Chamants garcons,* 1958; *Chien de pique,* 1960; *Terrain vague,* 1960; *Les Portes claquent,* 1960; *L'Amerique insolite* (also known as *L'Amerique vue par un francais*), 1960; *Cause toujours mon lapin,* 1961; *Me faire ca a moi,* 1961; *Une Grosse Tete,* 1961; *Comme un poisson dans l'eau,* 1961; *L'Empire de la nuit,* 1961; *Le Gentleman d'Epsom,* 1963; *Le Joli Mai,* 1963; *Monnaie de singe,* 1965; *L'Or et le plomb,* 1965; *Qui etes-vous, Polly Magoo,* 1965; *Quand passent les faisans,* 1965; *L'Homme a Buick,* 1967; *La Piscine* (also known as *The Swimming Pool*), 1969; *The Plastic Dome of Norma Jean,* 1970; *Les Maries de l'an II,* 1970; *Le Decharge,* 1970; *Appellez-moi Mathilde,* 1970; *Un Peu de soleil dans l'eau froide,* 1971; *La Poudre d'escampette* (also known as *French Leave*), 1971; *The Picasso Summer,* 1972; *Barbe-Bleue* (also known as *Bluebeard*), 1972; *Les Feux de la chandeleur* (also known as *Hearth Fires*), 1972; *La Vieille Fille* (also known as *The Old Maid*), 1972; *Pas folle la guepe,* 1972; *La Gang des otages,* 1973;

L'Evenement le plus important depuis que l'homme a marche sur la lune (also known as *A Slightly Pregnant Man*), 1973; *Verites et mensonges,* 1973; *F for Fake,* 1975; *Jalousie 1976* (also known as *Le Voyage de noces* and *Honeymoon Trip*), 1976; *On peut le dire sans se facher* (also known as *La Belle Emmerdeuse; One Can Say It Without Getting Angry; The Beautiful Nuisance*), 1977; *Les Fabuleuses aventures du legendaire baron de Munchauisen* (also known as *The Fabulous Adventures of the Legendary Baron Munchausen*), 1978; *Mon premier amour,* 1978; *Les Routes du sud,* 1979; "La Trentaine," "Allez Viens," "Bien Sur," "Prends le Temps," "D'egal a Egal," "Feline," "Et Que Je T'aime," *Qu-est-ce qui fait courir David?* (also known as *What Makes David Run?*), 1982; *Train d'enfer,* 1984; "Lonesome No More," *Slapstick of Another Kind,* 1984; *Micki & Maude,* 1984; and *Trois places pour le 26* (also known as *Three Seats for the 26th*), 1988.

MUSIC FOR TELEVISION MOVIES

Brian's Song, ABC, 1971.
The Adventures of Don Quixote, BBC, 1973.
It's Good to Be Alive, CBS, 1974.
Cage Without a Key, CBS, 1975.
A Woman Called Golda, Paramount Pictures Television, 1982.
The Jesse Owens Story, Paramount Pictures Television, 1984.
Promises to Keep, CBS, 1985.
As Summers Die, HBO, 1986.
Crossings, ABC, 1986.
Sins, CBS, 1986.
Not a Penny More, Not a Penny Less, BBC, then TNT, 1990.

Also composer for *Casanova,* 1987.

MUSIC FOR TELEVISION SPECIALS

"Blind Sunday," *ABC Holiday Weekend Specials,* ABC, 1976.
"Michel's Mixed-Up Musical Bird," *ABC Afterschool Specials,* ABC, 1978.

Also composed music for *Evening at the Pops* ("The Way He Makes Me Feel"), 1988; *Time Warner Presents the Earth Day Special* ("One Day"), 1990.

OTHER

(With George Mendoza) *Michel's Mixed-Up Musical Bird* (children's book), Bobbs-Merrill, 1978.
(With Pierre Uytterhoeven and Benjamin Legrand) *Five Days in June* (screenplay), AAA, 1988.

Also translator, French lyrics, *Darling Lili* (film), 1970.

LEIDER, Jerry 1931-

PERSONAL: Full name, Gerald J. Leider; born May 28, 1931, in Camden, NJ; son of Myer and Minnie L. Leider; married Susan Trustman, December 21, 1968; children: Matthew Trustman, Kenneth Harold. *Education:* Syracuse University, B.A., 1953; University of Bristol, M.A., 1954.

ADDRESSES: Office—ITC Entertainment Group, Inc., 12711 Ventura Blvd., Studio City, CA 91604. *Agent*—Tony Fantozzi, William Morris Agency, 151 El Camino, Beverly Hills, CA 90212.

CAREER: Producer and executive. Affiliated with MCA Inc., 1955; CBS-TV, director of special programs, 1960-61, director of program sales, 1961-62; Ashley Famous Agency, Inc., New York City, vice president, television operation, 1962-69; Warner Brothers Television, Burbank, CA, president, 1969-74; Warner Brothers Pictures, Rome, Italy, executive vice president of foreign production, 1975-76; GJL Productions, Los Angeles, CA, president, 1977-82; ITC Productions, Inc., Studio City, CA, president, 1982-87; ITC Entertainment Group, Studio City, president and CEO, 1987—. Member of Board of Visitors of College of Visual and Performing Arts, Syracuse University.

MEMBER: American Film Institute, Academy of Television Arts and Sciences, Hollywood Radio and Television Society (board of directors; president, 1975-76), Academy of Motion Picture Arts and Sciences, Caucus for Producers, Writers and Directors (member of steering committee).

AWARDS, HONORS: Fulbright fellow, 1954; Arents Alumni Medal, Syracuse University, 1979.

CREDITS:

STAGE WORK; PRODUCER

Producer of *Ages of Man,* New York and London, 1956-59; *Shinbone Alley* and *The Visit,* both New York City; and *Garden District.*

FILM WORK

Producer, *The Jazz Singer,* Associated Film, 1980.
Sophie's Choice, Universal, 1982.
Producer, *Trenchcoat,* Buena Vista, 1983.
Where the Boys Are, Tri-Star, 1984.
Dark Crystal, Universal, 1984.
The Evil That Men Do, Tri-Star, 1984.

Other film work includes *Wild Horse Hank,* 1979.

TELEVISION WORK

Executive producer, *And I Alone Survived,* NBC, 1978.

Executive producer (with Burt Nodella), *Willa*, CBS, 1979.

Executive producer, *The Hostage Tower*, CBS, 1980.

Other television work includes *Skeezer, Jane Doe, The Scarlet and the Black, The Haunting Passion, Sunset Limousine, Secrets of a Married Man, Letting Go, A Time to Live, The Girl Who Spelled Freedom, Unnatural Causes,* and *Poor Little Rich Girl.**

*   *   *

LENARD, Mark   1927-

PERSONAL: Born October 15, 1927, in Chicago, IL; married; wife's name, Ann (an actress); children: one daughter. *Education:* Received B.A. from University of Michigan; attended Carnegie Institute of Technology, Biarritz (France), American University, and New School for Social Research; studied acting with Lee Strasberg, Uta Hagen, and Mira Rostava.

ADDRESSES: Agent—Lew Sherrell Agency, 7060 Hollywood Blvd., Suite 610, Los Angeles, CA 90028.

CAREER: Actor. Appeared with Center Theatre Group, Ahmanson Theatre, Los Angeles, CA, 1966-68, and with Actors Theatre of Louisville, Louisville, KY, 1972-73. *Military service:* Served in U.S. Army.

MEMBER: Actors Equity Association, American Federation of Television and Radio Artists, Screen Actors Guild.

CREDITS:

FILM APPEARANCES

The Greatest Story Ever Told, United Artists, 1964.
Hang 'Em High, United Artists, 1968.
Navy Officer, *Annie Hall,* United Artists, 1977.
Klingon Captain, *Star Trek: The Motion Picture,* Paramount, 1979.
Ambassador Sarek, *Star Trek III: The Search for Spock,* Paramount, 1984.
Ambassador Sarek, *Star Trek IV: The Voyage Home,* Paramount, 1986.

Also appeared in *The Radicals,* 1989.

TELEVISION APPEARANCES; SERIES

Nathan Walsh, *Search for Tomorrow,* CBS, 1959-60.
Dr. Ernest Gregory, *Another World,* NBC, 1964.
Aaron Stempel, *Here Come the Brides,* ABC, 1968.
Urko, *The Planet of the Apes,* CBS, 1974.
Emperor Thorval, *The Secret Empire,* NBC, 1979.

TELEVISION APPEARANCES; MOVIES

Mr. Chandler, *Outrage,* ABC, 1973.
Mr. Bloom, *Getting Married,* CBS, 1978.

TELEVISION APPEARANCES; EPISODIC

Sarek, *Star Trek,* NBC, 1966.
The Bob Newhart Show, CBS, 1977.

Also appeared on *The Defenders,* CBS; *The Nurses,* CBS; *Iron Horse,* ABC; and *Mission: Impossible,* CBS.

OTHER TELEVISION APPEARANCES

Jusac, *The Three Musketeers* (special), CBS, 1960.
The Power and the Glory, CBS, 1961.

Also appeared on *Directions '65,* ABC; *Lamp Unto My Feet,* CBS; and *Jericho,* CBS.

STAGE APPEARANCES

Richard, *Exiles,* Renata Theatre, New York City, 1957.
(Understudy) *The Square Root of Wonderful,* National Theatre, New York City, 1957.
George, *A Clearing in the Woods,* Sheridan Square Playhouse, New York City, 1959.
Conrad, *Much Ado About Nothing,* Lunt-Fontanne Theatre, New York City, 1959.
Platanov, *A Country Scandal,* Greenwich Mews, New York City, 1960.
Duke of Vienna, *Measure for Measure,* New York Shakespeare Festival, New York City, 1960.
Loevborg, *Hedda Gabler,* Fourth Street Theatre, New York City, 1960.
Malchiel, *Gideon,* Plymouth Theatre, New York City, 1961-62.
Rudolfo Pascal, *We Take the Town,* Shubert Theatre, New Haven, CT, then Shubert Theatre, Philadelphia, PA, both 1962.
Dr. Katz, *My Mother, My Father and Me,* Plymouth Theatre, 1963.
(Standby) Sloane, *A Case of Libel,* Longacre Theatre, New York City, 1963.
Alfred Allmers, *Little Eyolf,* Actors Playhouse, New York City, 1964.
Captian Delano, *Benito Cereno,* Theatre de Lys, New York City, 1965.
Reverend T. Lawrence Shannon, *The Night of the Iguana,* Purdue University Theatre, West Lafayette, IN, 1965.
Rosmersholm, McCarter Theatre, Princeton, NJ, 1972-73.
Magritte Skies, Playwrights Horizons Theatre, New York City, 1976.

Made stage debut as Digger in *The Hasty Heart;* also appeared in *The Climate of Eden.*

MAJOR TOURS

Freud, *A Far Country,* U.S. cities, 1962-63.*

LEVIN, Ira 1929-

PERSONAL: Born August 27, 1929, in New York, NY; son of Charles (a toy importer) and Beatrice (Schlansky) Levin; married Gabrielle Aronsohn, August 20, 1960 (divorced, 1968); married Phyllis Finkel, August 26, 1979 (divorced, 1981); children: (first marriage) Adam, Jared, Nicholas. *Education:* Attended Drake University, 1946-48; New York University, A.B., 1950.

ADDRESSES: Agent—Harold Ober Associates, 425 Madison Ave., New York, NY 10017.

CAREER: Writer. Wrote training films for the U.S. Army. *Military service:* U.S. Army Signal Corps, 1953-55.

MEMBER: Dramatists Guild (council member, 1981—), Authors Guild, American Society of Composers, Authors, and Publishers.

AWARDS, HONORS: Edgar Allan Poe Award, Mystery Writers of America, 1953, for *A Kiss Before Dying,* and 1980, for *Deathtrap.*

WRITINGS:

NOVELS

A Kiss Before Dying, Simon & Schuster, 1953.
Rosemary's Baby, Random House, 1967.
This Perfect Day, Random House, 1970.
The Stepford Wives, Random House, 1972.
The Boys from Brazil, Random House, 1976.
Sliver, Bantam, 1991.

STAGE

No Time for Sergeants (adapted from the novel by Mac Hayman; Alvin Theatre, New York City, 1955, Her Majesty's Theatre, London, U.K., 1956), Random House, 1956.
Interlock (ANTA Theatre, New York City, 1958), Dramatists Play Service, 1958.
Critic's Choice (Ethel Barrymore Theatre, New York City, 1960), Random House, 1961.
General Seeger (Lyceum Theatre, New York City, 1962), Dramatists Play Service, 1962.
Drat! The Cat!, Martin Beck Theatre, New York City, 1965.
Dr. Cook's Garden, Belasco Theatre, New York City, 1967.
Veronica's Room (Music Box Theatre, New York City, 1973), Random House, 1974.
Break a Leg (U.R.G.E.N.T. Theatre, New York City, 1974, Palace Theatre, New York City, 1979), Samuel French, 1981.
Deathtrap (Music Box Theatre, 1978), Random House, 1979.

Cantorial (Lamb's Theatre, New York City, 1989), Samuel French, 1990.

ADAPTATIONS: Adaptations of Levin's novels and plays include the feature films *A Kiss before Dying,* United Artists, 1956; *No Time for Sergeants,* Warner Brothers, 1958; *Critic's Choice,* Warner Brothers, 1963; *Rosemary's Baby,* Paramount, 1968; *The Stepford Wives,* Columbia, 1975; *The Boys from Brazil,* Twentieth Century-Fox, 1978; *Deathtrap,* Warner Brothers, 1982; *A Kiss before Dying,* Universal, 1991; and the television movie *Dr. Cook's Garden,* ABC, 1971.

*   *   *

LEVISON, Charles
See LANE, Charles

*   *   *

LINCOLN, Geoffrey
See MORTIMER, John

*   *   *

LIPSCOMB, Dennis 1942-

PERSONAL: Born March 1, 1942, in Brooklyn, NY. *Education:* Received undergraduate degree from Clarkson Technical College; M.A., University of Iowa; attended London Academy of Music and Dramatic Art.

ADDRESSES: Agent—Harris & Goldberg, 2121 Avenue of the Stars, #950, Los Angeles, CA 90067. *Publicist*—Baker/Winokur/Ryder, 9348 Civic Center Dr., #404, Beverly Hills, CA 90210.

CAREER: Actor.

CREDITS:

STAGE APPEARANCES

The Survival of St. Joan, Studio Arena Theatre, Buffalo, NY, 1970-71.
Twelfth Night, North Shore Shakespeare Festival, Beverly, MA, 1971.
(Off-Broadway debut) Faulkland, *The Rivals,* Roundabout Theatre/Stage One, New York City, 1974-75.
Richard II, *The Tragedy of King Richard II,* Champlain Shakespeare Festival, Burlington, VT, 1976.
Lawrence Duncan, *The Boss,* Brooklyn Academy of Music, Brooklyn, NY, then Playwrights Horizons, New York City, 1976.
As You Like It, Theatre Venture '76, Beverly, MA, 1976.
Hamlet, Great Lakes Shakespeare Festival, Lakewood, OH, 1977.

The Taming of the Shrew, Great Lakes Shakespeare Festival, 1977.

Cackleson, *The Crazy Locomotive,* Brooklyn Academy of Music, 1977.

Gregory and chief watch, *Romeo and Juliet,* Circle in the Square, New York City, 1977.

Two Gentlemen of Verona, Great Lakes Shakespeare Festival, 1978.

Understudy, George and Jacob, *Night and Day,* Ania Theatre, New York City, 1979.

MAJOR TOURS

Carr Gomm, conductor, Pinhead manager, policeman, Will, and Lord John, *The Elephant Man,* U.S. cities, 1979-81.

FILM APPEARANCES

Harlan, *Union City,* Kinesis, 1980.

Arthur Brady, *Love Child,* Warner Brothers, 1982.

Lyle Watson, *Wargames,* Metro-Goldwyn-Mayer/United Artists, 1983.

Will Smythe, *Eyes of Fire,* Elysian, 1984.

Captain Taylor, *A Soldier's Story,* Columbia, 1984.

Lloyd, *Crossroads,* Columbia, 1986.

Johnny B. Goode, *Amazing Grace and Chuck,* Tri-Star, 1987.

Commander Perkins, *The First Power,* Orion, 1990.

Also appeared as Cleve Doucet, *Sister, Sister,* 1987, and as George Miller, *Retribution,* 1987.

TELEVISION APPEARANCES; MOVIES

Reverend Walker, *The Day After,* ABC, 1983.

Finch, *The Blue Yonder,* (also known as *Time Flyer*), Disney Channel, 1985.

Chief Ron McDonald, *Slow Burn,* Showtime, 1986.

Michael Light, *Perry Mason: The Case of the Sinister Spirit,* NBC, 1987.

Andrew Hutchinson, *Guilty of Innocence: The Lenell Geter Story,* CBS, 1987.

Ivan Fletcher, *She Knows Too Much,* NBC, 1989.

Prime Target, NBC, 1989.

TELEVISION APPEARANCES; SERIES

Sid Royce (Elvis Prim), *Wiseguy,* CBS, 1987.

Mayor Findley, *In the Heat of the Night,* NBC, 1988.

Also appeared as Carl Martin, *Our Family Honor,* 1985.

TELEVISION APPEARANCES; EPISODIC

Mob boss, *Midnight Caller,* NBC, 1989.

Reverend Tobias Bennett, *Highway to Heaven,* NBC, 1989.

Harland Keyvo, *The Famous Teddy Z,* CBS, 1989-90.

Also appeared as Val Webster, *Amazing Stories,* 1987; appeared in *Moonlighting* and *Call to Glory.*

TELEVISION APPEARANCES; PILOTS

Jed Carter, *Farrell for the People,* NBC, 1982.

Les McCall, *Diary of a Perfect Murder,* NBC, 1986.

Mayor Findley, *In the Heat of the Night,* NBC, 1988.*

*   *   *

LIPTON, Peggy   1947(?)-

PERSONAL: Born August 30, 1947 (some sources say 1948), in New York, NY; daughter of Harold (a corporate lawyer) and Rita (an artist) Lipton; married Quincy Jones (a music producer), September 14, 1974 (divorced 1987); children: Kidada, Rashida (daughters). *Avocational interests:* New Age spiritualism, hatha-yoga.

CAREER: Actress. Worked previously as a model, singer, and songwriter.

AWARDS, HONORS: Golden Globe Award, best television actress in a drama, 1971, for *The Mod Squad.*

CREDITS:

FILM APPEARANCES

Mom, *The Purple People Eater,* Concorde, 1988.

Kathleen Crowe, *Kinjite: Forbidden Subjects,* Cannon, 1989.

TELEVISION APPEARANCES; SERIES

Joanna, *The John Forsythe Show,* NBC, 1965-66.

Julie Barnes, *The Mod Squad,* ABC, 1968-73.

Norma Jennings, *Twin Peaks,* ABC, 1990.

OTHER TELEVISION APPEARANCES

Julie Barnes, *The Return of the Mod Squad* (movie), ABC, 1979.

Assistant district attorney, *Addicted to His Love* (movie; also known as *Sisterhood*), ABC, 1988.

Twin Peaks and Cop Rock: Behind the Scenes (special), ABC, 1990.

RECORDINGS:

ALBUMS

Singer on album *Peggy Lipton.*

WRITINGS:

SONGS

Wrote song "L.A. Is My Lady," recorded by Frank Sinatra.

OTHER SOURCES:

PERIODICALS

People Weekly, September 8, 1986; April 4, 1988.*

*   *   *

LOCKHART, June 1925-

PERSONAL: Born June 25, 1925, in New York, NY; daughter of Gene (an actor) and Kathleen (an actress) Lockhart; children: Anne Kathleen, June Elizabeth. *Education:* Graduated from Westlake School for Girls.

ADDRESSES: Manager—Patricia Newby Management, 9021 Melrose Ave., #207, Los Angeles, CA 90069.

CAREER: Actress. Member of board of directors of First Federal Savings Bank of California, 1980—; corporate spokesperson for Purina, Pets for People, and General Electric; lecturer.

AWARDS, HONORS: Antoinette Perry Award for Best Debut Performance, 1948, *Theatre World* Award, 1948, Donaldson Award, and Woman of the Year in Drama Award, Associated Press, all for *For Love or Money;* Emmy Award nomination, for *Lassie.*

CREDITS:

FILM APPEARANCES

Belinda Cratchit, *A Christmas Carol,* Metro-Goldwyn-Mayer (MGM), 1938.
Isabelle, *All This and Heaven Too,* Warner Brothers, 1940.
Vance, *Adam Had Four Sons,* Columbia, 1941.
Rose York, *Sergeant York,* Warner Brothers, 1941.
Stella Bainbridge, *Miss Annie Rooney,* United Artists (UA), 1942.
Daughter, *Forever and a Day,* RKO Radio Pictures, 1943.
Lucille Ballard, *Meet Me in St. Louis,* MGM, 1944.
Betsy at age 18, *The White Cliffs of Dover,* MGM, 1944.
Sarah Swanson, *Keep Your Powder Dry,* MGM, 1945.
Priscilla, *Son of Lassie,* MGM, 1945.
Babs Norvell, *Easy to Wed,* MGM, 1946.
Phyllis Allenby, *She-Wolf of London,* Universal, 1946.
Twink Weatherby, *The Yearling,* MGM, 1946.
Barbara Carlin, *Bury Me Dead,* Eagle-Lion, 1947.
Mary Lou, *It's a Joke Son,* Eagle-Lion, 1947.
Tony's wife, *T-Men,* Eagle-Lion, 1947.
Mrs. Cargill, *Time Limit,* Health/UA, 1957.
Ruth Martin, *Lassie's Great Adventure,* Wrather/Twentieth Century-Fox, 1963.
Mrs. Gillespie, *Butterfly,* Analysis, 1982.
Mrs. Bigelow, *Strange Invaders,* EMI/Orion, 1983.
Eunice St. Clair, *Troll,* Empire, 1986.
Archie's mother, *Rented Lips,* Cineworld, 1988.
Janet Kingsley, *The Big Picture,* Columbia, 1989.

C.H.U.D. II: Bud the Chud, Vestron, 1989.

Also appeared (voice only) in *Peter No Tail.*

TELEVISION APPEARANCES; MOVIES

Hope, *But I Don't Want to Get Married,* ABC, 1970.
Mrs. Fowler, *Who is the Black Dahlia?,* NBC, 1975.
Mrs. Lockridge, *Curse of the Black Widow,* ABC, 1977.
Constance Schuyler, *The Gift of Love,* ABC, 1978.
Ruth Moore, *Walking Through the Fire,* CBS, 1979.
Liz Hawkins, *The Capture of Grizzly Adams,* NBC, 1982.
Mrs. Claus, *The Night They Saved Christmas,* ABC, 1984.
Esther, *Perfect People,* ABC, 1988.
Winnie, *A Whisper Kills,* ABC, 1988.

TELEVISION APPEARANCES; SERIES

Panelist, *Who Said That?,* NBC, then ABC, 1952-55.
Ruth, *Lassie,* CBS, 1958-64.
Maureen Robinson, *Lost in Space,* CBS, 1965-68.
Dr. Janet Craig, *Petticoat Junction,* CBS, 1968-70.
Alice Davidson, *The Greatest American Hero,* ABC, 1981-83.
Maria Rameriz, *General Hospital,* ABC, beginning 1984.
Ruth, *The New Lassie,* syndicated, beginning 1989.

TELEVISION APPEARANCES; EPISODIC

Light's Out, NBC, 1946-52.
Ford Theatre Hour, NBC, 1948-51.
Studio One, CBS, 1948-58.
Prudential Family Playhouse, CBS, 1950-51.
Robert Montgomery Presents Your Lucky Strike Theatre, NBC, 1950-57.
Panelist, *It's News to Me,* CBS, 1951-54.
Ford Television Theatre, NBC then ABC, 1952-57.
The U.S. Steel Hour, ABC, 1953-55, then CBS, 1955-63.
The General Electric Theatre, CBS, 1953-62.
Substitute hostess, *Home,* NBC, 1954-57.
Climax!, CBS, 1954-58.
The Elgin Hour, NBC, 1954-55.
Star Tonight, ABC, 1955-56.
The Alcoa Hour, NBC, 1955-57.
The Kaiser Aluminum Hour, NBC, 1956-57.
On Trial, CBS, 1956-57.
Panelist, *To Tell the Truth,* CBS, 1956-67.
The Joseph Cotten Show, NBC, 1957-58, then CBS, 1959.
Shirley Temple's Storybook, NBC, then ABC, 1958-61.
Panelist, *Password,* CBS, 1961-67.
Voice of Martha Day, *These Are the Days,* ABC, 1974-76.
Darkroom, ABC, 1982.
Dr. Sylvia Heywood, *Dynasty II: The Colbys,* ABC, 1985.

Also appeared on *Magnum, P.I.,* CBS.

TELEVISION APPEARANCES; SPECIALS

The March of Dimes Fashion Show, CBS, 1948.

Amy March, *Little Women,* CBS, 1949.
Katherine Telford, *ABC's Matinee Today,* ABC, 1978.
Emily, *Peking Encounter,* syndicated, 1982.

Also appeared as hostess for *Miss USA Pageant,* CBS, 6 years; *Miss Universe Pageant,* CBS, 6 years; *Rose Parade,* CBS, 8 years; and *Thanksgiving Parade,* CBS, 5 years. Appeared on *The 38th Annual Emmy Awards,* 1986.

OTHER TELEVISION APPEARANCES

Panelist, *Password* (pilot), CBS, 1961.
Katherine Telford, *ABC's Matinee Today* (pilot), ABC, 1973.
Nora, *The Bait* (pilot), ABC, 1973.
Irene Evans, *Loose Change* (mini-series), NBC, 1978.

Also appeared on *Pound Puppies* (voice only), 1986; *True Confessions,* 1986; *Breaking the Habit;* and *Take My Word For It.* Appeared as Helen Hocker, *Dinky Hocker,* 1979; Mo Donovan, *Never Say Goodbye,* 1988; and Debbie Whitmire, *Somerset Gardens,* 1989.

STAGE APPEARANCES

Delia, *Bedroom Farce,* Center Theatre Group, Ahmanson Theatre, Los Angeles, CA, 1979-80.

Made stage debut in *Peter Ibbetson,* Metropolitan Opera House, New York City; made Broadway debut as Janet, *For Love or Money,* 1947. Also appeared in *The Pleasure of His Company,* San Antonio, TX; *No Sex Please, We're British,* Stage West, Los Angeles; *Murder at the Howard Johnson's,* Union Plaza Theatre, Las Vegas, NV; *Once More With Feeling,* Lawrence Welk Village Theatre; *Forty Carats;* and *Butterflies Are Free.*

MAJOR TOURS

Clairee, *Steel Magnolias,* U.S. cities, 1989-90.

Also appeared in *Bedroom Farce,* U.S. cities; and *Once More With Feeling,* U.S. cities.

*   *   *

LUFT, Lorna   1952-

PERSONAL: Born November 21, 1952, in Hollywood, CA; daughter of Sid Luft (a producer) and Judy Garland (an actress and singer); married Jake Hooker.

ADDRESSES: Agent—Diane Roberts, Gersh Agency, 222 North Canon Dr., Beverly Hills, CA 90210. *Manager*—Jake Hooker, Hooker Enterprises International, 8285 Sunset Blvd., Suite 10, Los Angeles, CA 90046.

CAREER: Actress and singer. Nightclub performer.

AWARDS, HONORS: Stereo Review Record of the Year award, 1991, for *Girl Crazy.*

CREDITS:

STAGE APPEARANCES

Judy Garland at Home at the Palace (concert), Palace Theatre, New York City, 1967.
(Broadway debut) *Promises, Promises,* Shubert Theatre, 1971.
Peppermint Patty, *Snoopy,* Lambs Theatre, New York City, 1983.
Terry, *Extremities,* Westside Arts Center/Cheryl Crawford Theatre, New York City, 1983.
Gooch, *Mame,* Burt Reynolds Theatre, Jupiter, FL, 1987.
Hollywood Celebration (concert), Hollywood Roosevelt Cinegrill, 1989.
Rainbow & Stars, Rockefeller Center, New York City, 1990-91.
Tribute to Cole Porter, Carnegie Hall, New York City, then London Paladium, London, England, 1991.

Also appeared in *The Singers' Salute to the Songwriter,* Dorothy Chandler Pavilion, Los Angeles, CA.

MAJOR TOURS

Sonia Walsk, *They're Playing Our Song,* U.S. cities, 1981-82.

Also appeared in touring productions of *Grease, Girl Crazy, Extremities, Little Shop of Horrors, Jerry Herman's Broadway,* and *The Unsinkable Molly Brown,* all U.S. cities.

FILM APPEARANCES

Paulette Rebchuck, *Grease II,* Paramount, 1982.
Carol, *Where the Boys Are '84,* Tri-Star, 1984.

TELEVISION APPEARANCES; MINI-SERIES

Doris, *Fear Stalk,* CBS, 1989.

TELEVISION APPEARANCES; EPISODIC

Lilly Kegler, *Trapper John, M.D.,* CBS, 1985.
Sheila Cunningham, "Children's Zoo," *The Twilight Zone,* NBC, 1985.
Peaches Markowitz, *Hooperman,* ABC, 1988.
Patsy Dumont, *Murder, She Wrote,* CBS, 1990.

Also appeared in *Tales From the Dark Side,* syndicated; and *The Cosby Show,* NBC.

TELEVISION APPEARANCES; SPECIALS

Host, *Judy Garland: The Concert Years,* PBS, 1985.
Standing Room Only: Liza in London, HBO, 1986.
Happy Birthday Hollywood, ABC, 1987.
Lifetime Salutes Mom, Lifetime, 1987.
The Wonderful Wizard of Oz: Fifty Years of Magic, CBS, 1990.

RECORDINGS:

Girl Crazy, Elektra, 1990.

Also recorded *Lorna Luft,* Epic, *Grease II* (soundtrack), Capitol, *Where the Boys Are,* Silver Blue Records, and *Born Again,* Dessca Records.

*   *   *

LUNDGREN, Dolph   1959-

PERSONAL: Born in 1959 in Stockholm, Sweden; son of a parliamentary economist. *Education:* Attended Washington State University, Massachusetts Institute of Technology, and Royal Institute of Technology, Stockholm, Sweden; earned master's degree (chemical engineering), University of Sydney.

CAREER: Actor. Represented Sweden in heavyweight martial arts championships. Worked previously as a bouncer, bodyguard, and instructor in hand-to-hand combat.

AWARDS, HONORS: Fulbright scholar at Massachusetts Institute of Technology; winner of British Open kickboxing championships, 1980-81, and Australian Open, 1982.

CREDITS:

FILM APPEARANCES

(Film debut) Venz, *A View to Kill,* Metro-Goldwyn-Mayer (MGM)/United Artists (UA), 1985.
Drago, *Rocky IV,* MGM/UA, 1985.
He-Man, *Masters of the Universe,* Cannon, 1987.
Frank Castle, *The Punisher,* New World Pictures, 1989.
Jack Caine, *I Come in Peace* (also known as *Death Angel, Dark Angel,* and *Lethal Contact*), Triumph Releasing, 1990.
The Eleventh Station (also known as *Cover-Up*), Capitol, 1990.
Lieutenant Nikolai, *Red Scorpion,* Shapiro Glickenhaus, 1990.

TELEVISION APPEARANCES; SPECIALS

Bob Hope's Royal Command Performance From Sweden, NBC, 1986.

OTHER SOURCES:

PERIODICALS

Amazing Heroes, May 15, 1989.
People, December 9, 1985.*

LYMAN, Dorothy   1947-

PERSONAL: Born April 18, 1947, in Minneapolis, MN; daughter of Hector H. (a stockbroker) and Violet E. (Brightwell) Lyman; married Joachim Tillinger, December 1, 1971 (divorced, 1978); children: Emma, Sebastian. *Education:* Graduated from Sarah Lawrence College.

ADDRESSES: Agent—Jacksina and Freedman, 1501 Broadway, New York, NY 10036.

CAREER: Actress, director, and producer. Operator of Directors Theatre, Los Angeles, CA.

MEMBER: League of Professional Theatre Women.

AWARDS, HONORS: Emmy Awards, outstanding supporting actress in a daytime drama series, 1981-82, and outstanding actress in a daytime drama series, 1982-83, both for *All My Children.*

CREDITS:

TELEVISION APPEARANCES; MOVIES

Dr. Nancy Brannigan, *Summer Fantasy,* NBC, 1984.
Mom, *Ollie Hopnoodle's Haven of Bliss,* PBS, 1988.
Ruth Mortimer, *The People across the Lake,* NBC, 1988.
Millie Schector, *Camp Cucamonga,* NBC, 1990.

TELEVISION APPEARANCES; SERIES

Julie Stark, *A World Apart,* ABC, 1970-71.
Elly Jo Jamison, *The Edge of Night,* CBS, 1972-73.
Sister Margaret, *One Life to Live,* ABC, 1975.
Gwen Parrish Frame, *Another World,* NBC, 1976-80.
Opal Gardner, *All My Children,* ABC, 1981-83.
Naomi Oates Harper, *Mama's Family,* NBC, 1983-85, syndicated, 1986-87.
Rebecca Whitmore, *Generations,* NBC, 1989.

TELEVISION APPEARANCES; EPISODIC

Appeared on *Alf,* NBC.

TELEVISION APPEARANCES; PILOTS

Johnnie Baylor, *Hearts Island,* NBC, 1985.

STAGE APPEARANCES

(Off-Broadway debut) First interviewer, "Interview," *America Hurrah,* Pocket Theater, 1967-68.
Niagara Falls, Mark Taper Forum, Los Angeles, CA, 1968.
The American Hamburger League, The New Theatre of Brooklyn, New York City, 1969.
Director's assistant, *Pequod,* Mercury Theatre, New York City, 1969.
A Doll's House, Playhouse Theatre, New York City, 1971.
Hedda Gabler, Playhouse Theatre, 1971.

Liza, "Killer's Head," *Killer's Head and Action,* American Place Theatre, New York City, 1975.

The House of Mirth, Long Wharf Theatre, New Haven, CT, 1975-76.

"On the Inside," *On the Outside and On the Inside,* Long Wharf Theatre, 1975-76.

Action, American Place Theatre, 1976.

Cindy, *Fefu and Her Friends,* American Place Theatre, 1978.

Laurie, *Later,* Marymount Manhattan Theatre, New York City, 1979.

Maude Mix, *A Coupla White Chicks Sitting Around Talking,* Astor Place Theatre, New York City, 1980-81 (also see below).

Jan Morrison, *Dancing in the End Zone,* Ritz Theatre, New York City, 1985.

Also appeared in productions of *Shrivings,* London, 1969, and *Rosencrantz and Guildenstern Are Dead,* Florida, 1970.

MAJOR TOURS

Cast member, *The Serpent,* Open Theatre, European cities, 1968.

Director, *A Coupla White Chicks Sitting Around Talking,* U.S. cities, 1985-86.

STAGE DIRECTOR; EXCEPT WHERE INDICATED

A Coupla White Chicks Sitting Around Talking, Astor Place Theatre, 1980-81.

Frugal Repast, Actors and Directors Theatre, New York City, 1981.

Peep, South Street Theatre, New York City, 1981.

Loving Reno, New York Theatre Studio, 1983.

Produced *The Sum of Us* at Directors Theatre, Los Angeles, CA.

FILM APPEARANCES

Jean, *300 Year Weekend,* ABC Cinerama, 1971.

Night of the Juggler, Columbia, 1980.*

M

MacDOWELL, Andie   1958(?)-

PERSONAL: Full name, Anderson MacDowell; born c. 1958 in Gaffney, SC; daughter of Paula MacDowell (a schoolteacher); married Paul Qualley (a model); children: Justin, Rainy (son). *Education:* Attended Winthrop College; studied acting with Shakespeare and Company.

ADDRESSES: Agent—Risa Shapiro, International Creative Management, 8899 Beverly Blvd., Los Angeles, CA 90048. *Publicist*—Linda Brown, P/M/K, 8436 W. 3rd St., No. 650, Los Angeles, CA 90048.

CAREER: Actress. Model for newspaper advertisements, Columbia SC, and Elite Modeling Agency, New York City, and for commercials.

AWARDS, HONORS: Female star of tomorrow award, Motion Picture Bookers Club, 1989, Achievement Award, best actress, Los Angeles Film Critics Association, 1989, and Independent Spirit Award, best actress, Independent Feature Project/West, 1990, all for *sex, lies, and videotape;* Golden Globe nomination, best actress in a musical or comedy, 1990, for *Green Card.*

CREDITS:

FILM APPEARANCES

(Film debut) Jane Porter, *Greystoke: The Legend of Tarzan, Lord of the Apes,* Warner Brothers, 1984.
Dale Biberman, *St. Elmo's Fire,* Columbia, 1985.
Ann Milaney, *sex, lies, and videotape,* Miramax, 1989.
Bronte Parish, *Green Card,* Touchstone, 1990.
Tina, *The Object of Beauty,* Avenue Pictures, 1991.
Anna Baragli, *Hudson Hawk,* Tri-Star, 1991.

TELEVISION APPEARANCES

Anthea, *Sahara's Secret* (mini-series), RAI (Italy), 1988.
First Person with Maria Shriver (special), NBC, 1990.

Rich and Famous: 1990 World's Best (special), syndicated, 1990.

OTHER SOURCES:

PERIODICALS

New York, July 17, 1989.
Premiere, February, 1991.*

*   *   *

MACKINTOSH, Cameron   1946-

PERSONAL: Born October 17, 1946, in Enfield, Middlesex, England; son of Ian Robert (a jazz trumpeter and timber merchant) and Diana Gladys (a production secretary; maiden name, Tonna) Mackintosh. *Education:* Attended Prior Park College (Somerset, England); studied for the stage at Central School of Speech and Drama for one year. *Religion:* Roman Catholic.

ADDRESSES: Office—Cameron Mackintosh Ltd., Number One, Bedford Sq., London WC1, England.

CAREER: Producer. Worked odd jobs backstage with touring companies. Previously affiliated with Andrew Lloyd Webber.

MEMBER: Society of West End Theatres (executive officer), Dramatist League.

AWARDS, HONORS: New York Drama Critics Circle Award (with WPA Theatre, David Geffen, and the Shubert Organization) for Best Musical, 1983, Outer Critic's Circle Award, and Drama Desk Award, all for *Little Shop of Horrors;* Antoinette Perry Awards for Best Musical, 1983 for *Cats* (with the Really Useful Company, David Geffen, and the Shubert Organization), 1987 for *Les Miserables,* and 1988 for *Phantom of the Opera;* Antoinette

Perry Award nomination, best musical 1991, for *Miss Saigon.*

CREDITS:

STAGE PRODUCER

Little Woman, Jeannetta Cochrane Theatre, London, 1967.

Anything Goes, Saville Theatre, London, 1969.

Trelawney, Sadler's Wells Theatre, then Prince of Wales Theatre, both London, 1972.

The Card, Queens Theatre, London, 1973.

Winnie the Pooh, Phoenix Theatre, London, 1974 and 1975.

Owl and the Pussycat Went to See, Westminster Theatre, London, 1975.

Godspell, Phoenix Theatre, 1975, then Her Majesty's Theatre, 1977, later Shaftsbury Theatre, then Duke of York's Theatre, all London, 1978.

Side by Side by Sondheim, Wyndham's Theatre, then Garrick Theatre, both London, 1976.

Oliver!, Albery Theatre, 1977-80, then Aldwych Theatre, both London, 1983.

Diary of a Madam, Phoenix Theatre, 1977.

After Shave, Apollo Theatre, London, 1977.

Out on a Limb, Vaudeville Theatre, London, 1977.

Gingerbread Man, Old Vic Theatre, London, 1978.

My Fair Lady, Adelphi Theatre, London, 1979.

Gingerbread Man, Old Vic Theatre, 1979, then Royalty Theatre, 1980, later Westminster Theatre, all London, 1981.

Tomfoolery, Criterion Theatre, London, 1980.

Jeeves Takes Charge, Fortune Theatre, London, 1981.

(With Hinks Shimberg) *Tomfoolery,* Village Gate Upstairs, New York City, 1981-82 (also see below).

(With the Really Useful Company and the Shubert Organization) *Cats,* New London Theatre, London, 1981—, then (also with David Geffen) Winter Garden Theatre, New York City, 1982—.

Song and Dance, Palace Theatre, London, 1982.

(With WPA Theatre, David Geffen, and the Shubert Organization) *Little Shop of Horrors,* WPA Theatre, New York City, 1982, then Orpheum Theatre, New York City, 1982-87.

Blondel, Old Vic Theatre, then Aldwych Theatre, both London, 1983.

Little Shop of Horrors, Comedy Theatre, London, 1983.

Abbacadabra, Lyric Hammersmith Theatre, London, 1983.

The Boyfriend, Old Vic Theatre, 1984.

(With Carole J. Shorenstein, James M. Nederlander, and the Southbrook Group) *Oliver!,* Mark Hellinger Theatre, New York City, 1984.

(With the Shubert Organization, F. W. M. Producing Group, and the Really Useful Company) *Song and Dance,* Royale Theatre, New York City, 1985-86.

(With Royal Shakespeare Co.) *Les Miserables,* Palace Theatre, London, c. 1985—, then Broadway Theatre, New York City, 1987-90, later Imperial Theatre, New York City, 1990—.

Phantom of the Opera, Her Majesty's Theatre, 1986—, then Majestic Theatre, New York City, 1988—.

Miss Saigon, Drury Lane Theatre, London, 1989—, then Broadway Theatre, 1991—.

Just So, Tricycle Theatre, London, 1990.

Five Guys Named Moe, Lyric Theatre, London, 1990.

Also producer of *The Reluctant Debutante,* Henley, England, 1967; *Relatively Speaking,* Canada, 1974; *Little Whiff of Windsor,* South Africa, 1975; *Side by Side by Sondheim,* Canada, 1976, then Ireland, 1977; *Lauder,* South Africa, 1976, then Australia, later New Zealand, 1977; *Tomfoolery,* Ireland, 1981; *My Fair Lady,* Canada, 1982; *Oklahoma!,* Australia, 1982; *Tomfoolery,* South Africa, 1982; *Oliver!,* Scandinavia, 1982, then Canada, 1983, later Australia, 1984; *Song and Dance,* Australia, 1983; *Little Shop of Horrors,* South Africa, 1984; and *Follies,* London, c. 1987.

Producer of various productions of *Cats, Phantom of the Opera,* and *Les Miserables* throughout the world.

MAJOR TOURS; PRODUCER

Cats, U.S. cities, 1983—.

Also producer of touring productions of *Cats, Phantom of the Opera,* and *Les Miserables* worldwide.

MAJOR TOURS; BRITISH CITIES; PRODUCER, EXCEPT WHERE INDICATED

Stage manager, *Oliver!,* 1965.

Little Woman, 1967.

Murder at the Vicarage, 1969.

Rebecca, 1969.

At Home with the Dales, 1970.

Salad Days, 1972.

Butley, 1973.

Winnie the Pooh, 1973-74.

Time and Time Again, 1974.

Godspell, 1974-80.

The Owl and the Pussycat Went to See, 1974, 1975, and 1976.

Relatively Speaking, 1974-75.

An Inspector Calls, 1974.

Private Lives, 1974.

Bell, Book and Candle, 1974.

A Merry Whiff of Windsor, 1975.

Beyond the Fringe, 1975.

Rock Nativity, 1975.

So Who Needs Marriage, 1975.
John, Paul, George and Ringo, 1975-76.
Touch of Spring, 1976.
Virginia Woolf, 1976.
Lauder, 1976,
Oliver!, 1977 and 1983.
Side by Side by Sondheim, 1978-79.
My Fair Lady, 1978 and 1981-82.
Rocky Horror Show, 1979-80.
Gingerbread Man, 1979.
Oklahoma!, 1980.

TELEVISION APPEARANCES

Bob Hope Lampoons Show Business (special), NBC, 1990.
The South Bank Show, London Weekend Television, 1990.

WRITINGS:

Adaptor (with Robin Ray), *Tomfoolery,* Village Gate Upstairs, 1981-82.

OTHER SOURCES:

PERIODICALS

Hollywood Reporter, September 21, 1989.
New York Times, December 7, 1986; September 17, 1989; January 10, 1990.
Time, April 22, 1991.
Variety, August 15, 1990.

*   *   *

MacLACHLAN, Kyle   1959(?)-

PERSONAL: Born February 22, 1959 (some sources say 1960), in Yakima, WA. *Education:* University of Washington, Seattle, B.F.A. (theater).

CAREER: Actor. Performed with Oregon Shakespeare Festival, Ashland; guest artist, Playmakers Repertory Company, Chapel Hill, NC.

AWARDS, HONORS: Golden Globe Award, best actor in a drama series, 1990, for *Twin Peaks.*

CREDITS:

TELEVISION APPEARANCES; SERIES

Dale Cooper, *Twin Peaks,* ABC, 1990.

TELEVISION APPEARANCES; MOVIES

Father Bobby O'Connor, *Dream Breakers* (also known as *The O'Connors*), CBS, 1989.

OTHER TELEVISION APPEARANCES

Co-host, *Red, Hot, and Blue* (special), ABC, 1990.

Twin Peaks and Cop Rock: Behind the Scenes (special), ABC, 1990.
"Carrion Death," *Tales from the Crypt: Trilogy,* HBO, 1991.

FILM APPEARANCES

Paul Atreides, *Dune,* Universal, 1984.
Jeffrey Beaumont, *Blue Velvet,* DiLaurentiis Entertainment Group, 1986.
Lloyd Gallagher, *The Hidden,* New Line Cinema/Heron Communications, 1987.
Trout, *Don't Tell Her It's Me* (also known as *The Boyfriend School*), Hemdale, 1990.
Ray Manzarek, *The Doors,* Tri-Star, 1991.

STAGE APPEARANCES

Terrence Beebe, *The Palace of Amateurs,* Minetta Lane Theatre, New York City, 1988.*

*   *   *

MADONNA   1958(?)-

PERSONAL: Full name, Madonna Louise Veronica Ciccone; born August 16, 1958 (some sources say 1959, 1960, or 1961), in Bay City, MI; daughter of Silvio (an engineer) and Madonna Ciccone; married Sean Penn (an actor), August 16, 1985 (divorced, 1989). *Education:* Attended University of Michigan, 1976-78; studied dance with Alvin Ailey American Dance Theater, 1979, and with Pearl Lang.

ADDRESSES: Office—c/o Sire Records, 75 Rockefeller Plaza, New York, NY 10019. *Agent*— Creative Artists Agency, 9830 Wilshire Blvd., Beverly Hills, CA 90212.

CAREER: Singer, actress, dancer, and musician. Performer with various popular music groups during early 1980s, including Breakfast Club, Millionaires, Modern Dance, Emmy, and Madonna.

AWARDS, HONORS: Grammy Award nomination for best female pop performance, 1986, for "Crazy for You," from the movie *Vision Quest.*

CREDITS:

FILM APPEARANCES

A Certain Sacrifice, Commtron, 1980.
Nightclub performer, *Vision Quest,* Warner Brothers, 1985.
Susan, *Desperately Seeking Susan,* Orion, 1985.
Gloria Tatlock, *Shanghai Surprise,* Metro-Goldwyn-Mayer (MGM), 1986.
Nikki Finn, *Who's That Girl,* Warner Brothers, 1987.
Hortense Hathaway, *Bloodhounds of Broadway,* Columbia, 1989.

Breathless Mahoney, *Dick Tracy,* Buena Vista, 1990.
Truth or Dare (documentary), Miramax, 1991.

FILM WORK

Executive producer, *Truth or Dare,* Miramax, 1991.

STAGE APPEARANCES

(Broadway debut) Karen, *Speed-the-Plow,* Royale Theatre, 1988.

TELEVISION APPEARANCES; SPECIALS

The Thirteenth Annual American Music Awards, ABC, 1986.
MTV's 1989 Video Music Awards, MTV, 1989.
MTV Rewind, MTV, 1989.
Madonna—Live! Blond Ambition World Tour, HBO, 1990.
MTV's 1990 Video Music Awards, MTV, 1990.
Sex in the '90s, CBS, 1990.
The Sixty-Third Annual Academy Awards Presentation, ABC, 1991.

Also appeared on *American Bandstand's 33 1/3 Celebration,* 1985, and *Disney's D-TV Valentine,* 1986.

RECORDINGS:

ALBUMS

Madonna, Sire, 1983.
Like a Virgin, Sire, 1984.
True Blue, Sire, 1986.
You Can Dance, Sire, 1987.
Like a Prayer, Sire, 1989.
I'm Breathless: Music from and Inspired by the Film "Dick Tracy," Sire, 1990.

Author or coauthor of numerous songs.

VIDEOS

Madonna, WEA, 1984.
Madonna Live: The Virgin Tour, WEA, 1985.
Madonna Ciao Italia: Live from Italy, WEA, 1988.

Also appeared in numerous shorter videos.

OTHER SOURCES:

BOOKS

Contemporary Musicians, Volume 4, Gale, 1991.
Contemporary Newsmakers, Volume 2, Gale, 1985.

PERIODICALS

Entertainment Weekly, May 11, 1990; May 25, 1990.
Rolling Stone, June 13, 1991.*

MAKAROVA, Natalia   1940-

PERSONAL: Born November 21 (one source says 28), 1940, in Leningrad, U.S.S.R., immigrated to England, 1970; daughter of Kapitalina Petrova; married first husband (a dancer), divorced; married second husband (a film director), divorced; (some sources say married and divorced one other husband); married Edward Karkar (an industrialist), 1976; children: Andrei Michel. *Education:* Graduated from Vaganova Ballet School after six years; graduated from Leningrad Choreographic School, 1959. *Avocational interests:* Oil and watercolor painting.

ADDRESSES: Office—London Festival Ballet, 39 Jay Mews, London SW7 2ES, England; American Ballet Theatre, 888 Seventh Ave., New York, NY 10019.

CAREER: Ballet dancer, choreographer of staged ballets, and actress. Ballerina with Leningrad Kirov Ballet, 1959-70, appearing in numerous countries, including Austria, 1969, Italy, and England; performed at International Festival of Ballet, London, 1964; principal dancer with American Ballet Theatre, 1970-72, 1976-80, and 1981; partner with Anthony Dowell, Royal Ballet; worked with Mikhail Baryshnikov, American Ballet Theatre; head of Makarova and Company, 1980; associate artist with London Festival Ballet, 1985—. Guest dancer with numerous companies throughout the world, 1972—, including Royal Ballet, 1972, London Festival Ballet, 1984, Paris Opera Ballet, National Ballet of Canada, Royal Danish Ballet, and Maurice Bejart Company.

AWARDS, HONORS: Gold medal, Second International Ballet Competition, Varna, Bulgaria, 1965; named honored artist of the Russian Federation, 1969; special Theatre World Award, 1982-83, Antoinette Perry Award for Best Actress in a Musical, 1983, and Laurence Olivier Award for Best Actress in a Musical, 1984, all for *On Your Toes;* London Evening Standard Award, 1985, for *Eugene Onegin;* other dance awards.

CREDITS:

STAGE APPEARANCES

Title role, *Giselle,* Kirov Ballet, London, 1961.
Odette-Odile, *Swan Lake,* Kirov Theatre, Leningrad, U.S.S.R., 1964.
Guest appearance, *Giselle,* Netherlands National Ballet, Amsterdam, Netherlands, 1966.
Giselle, American Ballet Theatre, City Center, New York City, 1970.
The River, American Ballet Theatre, Lincoln Center for the Performing Arts, New York City, 1971.
The Miraculous Mandarin, American Ballet Theatre, Lincoln Center for the Performing Arts, 1971.
Juliet, *Romeo and Juliet,* American Ballet Theatre, Lincoln Center for the Performing Arts, 1971.

(Broadway debut) Vera Baronova, *On Your Toes,* Virginia Theatre, New York City, 1983-84, then London, 1984.
On Your Toes, Dorothy Chandler Pavilion, Los Angeles, c. 1985.
Eugene Onegin, National Ballet of Canada, 1988.
Romeo and Juliet, Covent Garden, London, 1989.
Eugene Onegin, Kirov Theatre, 1989.

Also performed at Royal Opera House, Covent Garden, 1961; appeared with Kirov Ballet in London, 1970. Appeared in *The Blue Angel,* 1985; in benefit performance, British Columbia, Canada, 1987; and in *Swan Lake,* Kirov Ballet, c. 1988. Appeared with American Ballet Theatre in *Lilac Garden, Coppelia, La Sylphide, Les Sylphides,* and *Swan Lake.* Also appeared in other productions, including *Fountains of Bakhchisarai, Masquerade, Cinderella, Sleeping Beauty, Raymonda, The Firebird, A Month in the Country, Don Quixote, Manon, Carmen, Epilogue, Contradance,* and *Other Dances.*

MAJOR TOURS

Title role, *Giselle,* Kirov Ballet, U.S. cities, 1961.
Odette, *Swan Lake,* Kirov Ballet, U.S. cities, 1964.

STAGE WORK

Choreographer and director, *La Bayadere,* American Ballet Theatre, 1980.

TELEVISION APPEARANCES; EPISODIC

The Ed Sullivan Show, CBS, 1970.

TELEVISION APPEARANCES; SPECIALS

Title role, *Giselle,* PBS, 1977.
Natasha Special, BBC, 1985.
Ballerina, BBC, 1987.
Swan Lake, Arts & Entertainment, 1989 (also see below).

Also appeared as Odette-Odile in *Swan Lake,* 1976, and as dancer in "Don Quixote," *American Ballet Theatre,* 1978. Appeared in *The Cowboy, the Craftsman and the Ballerina,* 1981; *The Magic of Dance,* 1982; and *Makarova: Class of Her Own,* 1984.

OTHER TELEVISION APPEARANCES

Appeared with Rudolf Nureyev on BBC in early 1970s.

TELEVISION WORK

Choreographer and stage director, *Swan Lake* (special), Arts & Entertainment, 1989.

WRITINGS:

A Dance Autobiography, Knopf, 1979.

Contributor to *Sunday Telegraph* (London).

OTHER SOURCES:

PERIODICALS

New York Times, February, 1989.*

* * *

MANDEL, Howie 1955-

PERSONAL: Born November 29, 1955, in Toronto, Ontario, Canada; son of a lighting manufacturer and realtor; married, wife's name, Terry; children: Jackelyn, Al.

ADDRESSES: Agent—Ben Bernstein, Triad Artists, 10100 Santa Monica Blvd., 16th Floor, Los Angeles, CA 90067. *Publicist*—Paul Burditch, Guttman & Pam, 8500 Wilshire Blvd., No. 801, Beverly Hills, CA 90211.

CAREER: Comedian and actor. Worked as door-to-door carpet salesman and later as owner of carpet stores, c. 1975-79; owner of a novelty business. Performed at Comedy Store, Los Angeles, CA, and at nightclubs in Atlantic City, Las Vegas, New York City, and Los Angeles.

CREDITS:

TELEVISION APPEARANCES; SERIES

The Shape of Things, NBC, 1982.
Laugh Trax, syndicated, 1982.
Dr. Wayne Fiscus, *St. Elsewhere,* NBC, 1982-88.
Howie, *Howie and Rose,* CBS, 1991.

TELEVISION APPEARANCES; SPECIALS

Voices of Animal, Skeeter, and Bunson Honeydew, *Jim Henson's Muppet Babies and Monsters,* CBS, 1984.
Cinemax Comedy Experiment, Cinemax, 1985.
37th Annual Emmy Awards, ABC, 1985.
Presenter, *American Video Awards,* ABC, 1985.
On Location: Howie Mandel, HBO, 1986.
Young Comedians All-Star Reunion, HBO, 1986.
38th Annual Emmy Awards, NBC, 1986.
Waldo, *The Princess Who Never Laughed,* Showtime, 1986.
39th Annual Emmy Awards, Fox, 1987.
"Howie From Maui—Live!," *HBO Comedy Hour,* HBO, 1987.
Comedy Store 15th Year Class Reunion (also known as *Comedy Store Reunion*), NBC, 1988.
Comic Relief III, HBO, 1989.
Hooray for Howiewould!, Showtime, 1990.
Voice of Bobby, *Bobby's World,* Fox, 1990.
Fourth Annual American Comedy Awards, ABC, 1990.
Jerry, *Between Cars,* HA! TV Comedy Network, 1990.
Ernie Lapidus, *Good Grief,* Fox, 1990.

Also presented *The Watusi Tour,* HBO; hosted the *Juno Music Awards,* 1987.

TELEVISION APPEARANCES; EPISODIC

Make Me Laugh, syndicated, 1979-80.

Also appeared on *The Tonight Show, The Merv Griffin Show, Norm Crosby Comedy Show, An Evening at the Improv,* and *The Max Headroom Show.*

OTHER TELEVISION APPEARANCES

Rock Comedy (pilot for *Laugh Trax*), syndicated, 1982.
Welcome to the Fun Zone (pilot), NBC, 1984.
Humpty Dumpty, *Mother Goose Rock 'n' Rhyme* (movie), Disney, 1990.

TELEVISION WORK

Executive producer, *On Location: Howie Mandel,* HBO, 1986 (also see below).

FILM APPEARANCES

Matt Lloyd, *Gas,* Paramount, 1981.
Larry Pound, *Funny Farm,* Mutual, 1982.
Dennis Powell, *A Fine Mess,* Columbia, 1986.
The Canadian Conspiracy, Shtick Productions, 1986.
Bobo Shand, *Walk Like a Man* (also known as *Bobo the Dog Boy*), Metro-Goldwyn-Mayer (MGM)/United Artists (UA), 1987.
Maurice, *Little Monsters,* MGM/UA, 1989.
Voice of Gizmo, *Gremlins II: The New Batch,* Warner Brothers, 1990.

Also voice of Omni, *Once Upon a Star.*

RECORDINGS:

ALBUMS

Howie Mandel Fits Like a Glove, Warner Brothers, 1986.

Also recorded *The Watusi Tour.*

VIDEOS

Howie Mandel's North American Watusi Tour, Paramount, 1987.

WRITINGS:

TELEVISION SPECIALS

Welcome to the Fun Zone, NBC, 1984.
On Location: Howie Mandel, HBO, 1986.

OTHER SOURCES:

PERIODICALS

Hollywood Reporter, October, 1987.*

MASTERS, Ben 1947-

PERSONAL: Born May 6, 1947, in Corvallis, OR. *Education:* Graduate of the University of Oregon.

CAREER: Actor.

CREDITS:

STAGE APPEARANCES

(Broadway debut) American Bluejacket, *Captain Brassbound's Conversion,* Ethel Barrymore Theatre, 1972.
Gaston, *The Waltz of the Toreadors,* Circle in the Square, New York City, 1973.
Mourning Becomes Electra, Goodman Theatre Center, Chicago, IL, 1975.
Long Day's Journey Into Night, Massachusetts Center Repertory Company, Boston, MA, 1977.
Yasha, *The Cherry Orchard,* New York Shakespeare Festival, Vivian Beaumont Theatre, New York City, 1977.
The Further Adventures of Sally, Center Stage, Baltimore, MD, 1981.
Philip, *Key Exchange,* Orpheum Theatre, New York City, 1981.
Codename Lazar, *Plenty,* Plymouth Theatre, New York City, 1983.

Also appeared in *The Boys in the Band* 1970; and *What the Butler Saw.*

MAJOR TOURS

Gaston, *The Waltz of the Toreadors,* U.S. cities, 1974.

TELEVISION APPEARANCES; EPISODIC

Vic Strang, *Another World,* NBC, 1982.

TELEVISION APPEARANCES; SERIES

Nick Malloy, *Muggsy,* NBC, 1977.
Dr. Leo Rosetti, *Heartbeat,* ABC, 1988.

Also appeared in *Until She Talks,* 1983.

TELEVISION APPEARANCES; PILOTS

Felix Needham, *One of Our Own,* NBC, 1975.
Pete, *Making It,* NBC, 1976.
Craig Bryant, *Mobile Medics,* CBS, 1977.

TELEVISION APPEARANCES; MOVIES

Joe Norman, *Loose Change,* NBC, 1978.
Mark, *The Shadow Box,* ABC, 1980.
Tony Bernhardt, *The Neighborhood,* NBC, 1983.
Larry Dobbins, *Illusions,* CBS, 1983.
Kleber Cantrell, *Celebrity,* NBC, 1984.
Detective Mike Fisher, *The Deliberate Stranger,* NBC, 1986.
Jack Stark, *Kate's Secret,* NBC, 1986.

Jonathan Patrick Kelly, *Riviera,* ABC, 1987.
Linc Bartlett, *Noble House,* NBC, 1988.
Thomas Kydd, *Street of Dreams,* CBS, 1988.

FILM APPEARANCES

Charles, *Mandingo,* Paramount, 1975.
Dr. Garry, *All That Jazz,* Twentieth Century-Fox, 1979.
Philip, *Key Exchange,* Twentieth Century-Fox/TCL, 1985.
Michael Hansen, *Dream Lover,* United Artists, 1986.
Congressman Steve Marcus, *Making Mr. Right,* Orion, 1987.*

*   *   *

MATHERS, Jerry   1948-

PERSONAL: Born June 2, 1948, in Sioux City, IA; divorced. *Education:* University of California, Berkeley, B.A. (philosophy), 1974.

ADDRESSES: Agent—Peter Young, Triad Artists, 10100 Santa Monica Blvd., 16th Floor, Los Angeles, CA 90067. *Publicist*—Milton Kahn, Milton Kahn Associates, 9229 Sunset Blvd., Suite 305, Los Angeles, CA 90069.

CAREER: Actor. Worked as a bank loan officer and real estate salesman.

CREDITS:

TELEVISION APPEARANCES; SERIES

Theodore (Beaver) Cleaver, *Leave It to Beaver,* CBS, 1957-58, ABC, 1958-63.
Theodore (Beaver) Cleaver, *The New Leave It to Beaver,* Disney, 1985-86, TBS, 1986—.

TELEVISION APPEARANCES; MOVIES

Deputy Henry Thomas Watts, *The Girl, the Gold Watch, and Dynamite,* syndicated, 1981.
Theodore (Beaver) Cleaver, *Still the Beaver,* CBS, 1983.

TELEVISION APPEARANCES; PILOTS

Beaver, "It's a Small World" (pilot for *Leave It to Beaver;* also known as "Wally and the Beaver"), *Studio '57,* syndicated, 1957.
Mr. Sirota, *High School, U.S.A.,* NBC, 1984.

TELEVISION APPEARANCES; SPECIALS

Guest, *Dick Clark's Good ol' Days: From Bobby Sox to Bikinis,* NBC, 1977.
Getting the Last Laugh, ABC, 1985.
It's Howdy Doody Time: A Forty-Year Celebration (also known as *Howdy Doody's Fortieth Birthday Special*), syndicated, 1987.
Lifetime Salutes Mom, Lifetime, 1987.

Honorary cochairman, *March of Dimes Telethon,* 1986.

TELEVISION APPEARANCES; EPISODIC

(Television debut) *The Ed Wynn Show,* CBS, 1950.
Lux Video Theatre Show, CBS, 1954.

Also appeared in episodes of *Saturday Night Live,* NBC; *Flying High,* CBS; *Fourth Network; Batman; My Three Sons;* and *Lassie.*

FILM APPEARANCES

David Myer, *This Is My Love,* RKO Radio Pictures, 1954.
Bernie at age five, *The Seven Little Foys,* Paramount, 1955.
Arnie Rogers, *The Trouble with Harry,* Paramount, 1955.
Norman Taylor, *That Certain Feeling,* Paramount, 1956.
Petey, *The Shadow on the Window,* Columbia, 1957.
Steve, *The Deep Six,* Warner Brothers, 1958.
Back to the Beach, Paramount, 1987.
Down the Drain, Moonstone, 1990.

Also appeared in *Men of the Fighting Lady.*

OTHER SOURCES:

PERIODICALS

People, summer, 1989.*

*   *   *

MATLIN, Marlee   1965-

PERSONAL: Born Marlee Beth Matlin, August 24, 1965, in Morton Grove, IL; rendered deaf at eighteen months by the childhood disease roseola; daughter of Donald and Libby Matlin. *Education:* Attended William Rainey Harper College as a criminal justice major.

ADDRESSES: Agent—Carla Hacken, International Creative Management, 8899 Beverly Boulevard, Los Angeles, CA 90048. *Publicist*—c/o Brad Cafarelli, Bragman and Company, 8693 Wilshire Blvd., Penthouse Suite, Beverly Hills, CA 90211.

CAREER: Actress. As a child, appeared in such plays as *The Wizard of Oz, Peter Pan,* and *Mary Poppins* throughout Illinois, Indiana, and Nebraska, produced by a theatre group associated with the Chicago-area Center on Deafness. National spokesperson for the National Captioning Institute. Member of board of trustees, international and Southern California chapters of Starlight Foundation. Affiliated with The Pediatric Aids Foundation, The Children's Museum (Boston and New Orleans), Very Special Arts, Special Olympics, United Friends of the Children, Camp Ronald McDonald, The Marlee Matlin Deaf Children's Theatre Fund, Big Sisters of Los Angeles, Adam

Walsh Child Resource Center, and Amber Swarz-Garcia Foundation.

MEMBER: Young Artists United.

AWARDS, HONORS: Academy Award, 1986, and Golden Globe Award, 1987, both for best actress, for *Children of a Lesser God* (film); Jefferson Award, greatest public service performed by an individual thirty-five years or under, 1988, American Institute for Public Service; Rose Award, 1989, The Jewish Home for the Aging of Greater Los Angeles. Victory Award, National Rehabilitation Hospital; Distinctive Service Award, Gallaudet University Alumni Association; Ciak Award; Deafness Research Foundations's Media Award; Women of Achievement Award, The Women's Group/Friends of Tel Hashomer. Inducted into the Governor's Hall of Fame for People with Disabilities, California Department of Rehabilitation. Honorary Ph.D.s from Marymount Manhattan College and Gallaudet University.

CREDITS:

STAGE APPEARANCES

Appeared in Immediate Theater Company's Chicago production of *Children of a Lesser God.*

FILM APPEARANCES

Sarah Norman, *Children of a Lesser God,* Paramount, 1986.
Ellen Martin, *Walker,* Universal, 1987.
Maria, *L'Homme au masque d'or* (also known as *The Man in the Golden Mask*), World Marketing Films, 1990.
Jeanette, *The Linguini Incident,* Rank Films, 1990.

TELEVISION APPEARANCES; SPECIALS

Special Olympics Opening Ceremony Special, ABC, 1987.
Golden Globe Awards (87), syndicated, 1987.
59th Annual Academy Awards Presentation, ABC, 1987.
Funny, You Don't Look 200 (variety), ABC, 1987.
Happy Birthday Hollywood, ABC, 1987.
60th Annual Academy Awards Presentation, ABC, 1988.
Golden Globe Awards (88), syndicated, 1988.
All-Star Tribute to Kareem Abdul-Jabbar, NBC, 1989.
The American Comedy Awards (89) (also known as *The Third Annual American Comedy Awards*), ABC, 1989.
Robert Wuhl's World Tour (also known as *HBO Comedy Hour*), HBO, 1990.
The Wonderful Wizard of Oz: 50 Years of Magic, CBS, 1990.
The Creative Spirit, PBS, 1991.

OTHER TELEVISION APPEARANCES

Peggy Lawrence, *Bridge to Silence* (movie), CBS, 1989.
Tess Kaufman, *Reasonable Doubts* (series), NBC, 1991.

Also appeared in *We Didn't Start the Fire,* a music video.

OTHER SOURCES:

PERIODICALS

Daily News (New York), November 29, 1987.
Parade, May 22, 1988.

*   *   *

MAZURKI, Mike   1909-

PERSONAL: Born December 25, 1909, in Tarnopal, Austria. *Education:* Manhattan College, NY, B.A., 1930.

CAREER: Actor. Worked as a wrestler before acting.

CREDITS:

FILM APPEARANCES

Belle of the Nineties, Paramount, 1934.
Coolie, *The Shanghai Gesture,* United Artists (UA), 1941.
Dr. Renault's Secret, Twentieth Century-Fox, 1942.
Jake Kilrain, *Gentleman Jim,* Warner Brothers-First National, 1942.
Japanese Wrestler, *Behind the Rising Sun,* RKO Radio Pictures, 1943.
Kurt, *Bomber's Moon,* Twentieth Century-Fox, 1943.
Shadow, *Henry Aldrich Haunts a House,* Paramount, 1943.
Bouncer, *It Ain't Hay* (also known as *Money For Jam*), Universal, 1943.
Workman, *Mission to Moscow,* Warner Brothers, 1943.
Wrestler, *Swing Fever,* Metro-Goldwyn-Mayer (MGM), 1943.
Olaf, *Thank Your Lucky Stars,* Warner Brothers, 1943.
Metropolus, *The Canterville Ghost,* MGM, 1944.
Fighter, *Lost Angel,* MGM, 1944.
Cullie, *The Missing Juror,* Columbia, 1944.
Pirate, *The Princess and the Pirate,* RKO Radio Pictures, 1944.
Bouncer, *Shine On, Harvest Moon,* Warner Brothers, 1944.
Policeman, *Summer Storm,* UA, 1944.
Man, *The Thin Man Goes Home,* MGM, 1944.
Klondike Pete, *Abbott and Costello in Hollywood,* MGM, 1945.
Splitface, *Dick Tracy,* RKO Radio Pictures, 1945.
Bigtree Collins, *Dakota,* Republic, 1945.
Humphrey Rafferty, *The Horn Blows at Midnight,* Warner Brothers, 1945.
Moose Malloy, *Murder, My Sweet* (also known as *Farewell, My Lovely*), RKO Radio Pictures, 1945.
Rafferty's Fighter, *Nob Hill,* Twentieth Century-Fox, 1945.
Swaine, *The Spanish Main,* RKO Radio Pictures, 1945.

Sam Cragg, *The French Key,* Republic, 1946.

Patsy Clark, *Live Wires,* Monogram, 1946.

Harry Pontos, *Mysterious Intruder,* Columbia, 1946.

Little Joe, *Killer Dill,* Screen Guild, 1947.

Bruno, *Nightmare Alley,* Twentieth Century-Fox, 1947.

Yusuf, *Sinbad the Sailor,* RKO Radio Pictures, 1947.

Dave Bone, *Unconquered,* Paramount, 1947.

Dan, *I Walk Alone,* Paramount, 1948.

Chuck, *The Moose Hangs High,* Eagle-Lion, 1948.

Jake, *Relentless,* Columbia, 1948.

Hoppe, *Abandoned,* (also known as *Abandoned Woman*), Universal, 1949.

Heavy Man, *Come to the Stable,* Twentieth Century-Fox, 1949.

Rhino, *The Devil's Henchmen,* Columbia, 1949.

Mac Mozolla, *Neptune's Daughter,* MGM, 1949.

Person, *Rope of Sand,* Paramount, 1949.

Leader of Philistine soldiers, *Samson and Delilah,* Paramount, 1949.

Sidney Winant, *Dark City,* Paramount, 1950.

"Lunk" Boxwell, *He's a Cockeyed Wonder,* Columbia, 1950.

Strangler, *Night and the City,* Twentieth Century-Fox, 1950.

"Moose" Hendricks, *Criminal Lawyer,* Columbia, 1951.

Charles, *The Light Touch,* MGM, 1951.

Monkara, *My Favorite Spy,* Paramount, 1951.

Ape Danowski, *Pier 23,* Lippert, 1951.

Roshko, *Ten Tall Men,* Columbia, 1951.

Death House Foreman, *The Egyptian,* Twentieth Century-Fox, 1954.

Big Han, *Blood Alley,* Warner Brothers, 1955.

Bigfoot Mason, *Davy Crockett, King of the Wild Frontier,* Buena Vista, 1955.

Chief Policeman, *Kismet,* MGM, 1955.

Mike, *New Orleans Uncensored* (also known as *Riot on Pier 6*), Columbia, 1955.

Arnie Wendler, *New York Confidential,* Warner Brothers, 1955.

Character, *Around the World in Eighty Days,* UA, 1956.

Flat Mouth, *Comanche,* UA, 1956.

Louie, *Man in the Vault,* RKO Radio Pictures, 1956.

Ross, *Hell Ship Mutiny,* Republic, 1957.

Rak, *The Man Who Died Twice,* Republic, 1958.

Some Like It Hot, UA, 1959.

Man in motel room, *The Facts of Life,* UA, 1960.

Blonde "movie siren", *The Errand Boy,* Paramount, 1961.

Big Mike, *Pocketful of Miracles,* UA, 1961.

Slave captain, *Five Weeks in a Balloon,* Twentieth Century-Fox, 1962.

Bookie, *Swingin' Along* (also known as *Double Trouble*), Twentieth Century-Fox, 1962.

Igor, *Zotz!,* Columbia, 1962.

Sargeant Menkowicz, *Donovan's Reef,* Paramount, 1963.

Chad, *Four for Texas,* Warner Brothers, 1963.

Minor, *It's a Mad, Mad, Mad, Mad World,* UA, 1963.

The Disorderly Orderly, Paramount, 1964.

First Sargeant Stanislaus Wichowsky, *Cheyenne Autumn,* Warner Brothers, 1964.

Ivy Bliss, *Requiem for a Gunfighter,* Embassy Pictures, 1965.

Tunga Khan, *Seven Women,* MGM, 1966.

Mountain ox, *The Adventures of Bullwhip Griffin,* Buena Vista, 1967.

Randall, *The Wild McCullochs,* American International, 1975.

Trapper, *Challenge to Be Free* (also known as *Mad Trapper of the Yukon*), Garnett, 1976.

Studio guard, *Won Ton Ton, The Dog Who Saved Hollywood,* Paramount, 1976.

Handler, *One Man Jury,* Cal-Am Artists, 1978.

Himself, *The Man With Bogart's Face* (also known as *Sam Marlow, Private-Eye*), Twentieth Century-Fox, 1980.

Bruno, *Doin' Time,* Warner Brothers, 1985.

Old man at hotel, *Dick Tracy,* Buena Vista, 1990.

Also appeared as Apollo in *The Magic of Lassie,* 1978; as Moiv in *Gas Pump Girls,* 1979; as the gatekeeper in *Aligator,* 1980; and as Dutch in *Amazon Women on the Moon,* 1987.

TELEVISION APPEARANCES

Clon, *It's About Time* (series), CBS, 1966-67.

Julius, *Chicago Teddy Bears* (series), CBS, 1971.

Tidy, *Mad Bull* (movie), CBS, 1977.

Crazy Horse, *The Incredible Rocky Mountain Race* (movie), NBC, 1977.

Logan, *The Adventures of Huckleberry Finn* (movie), NBC, 1981.

Joe Malcheski, *Revenge of the Gray Gang* (pilot), NBC, 1981.*

* * *

McDIARMID, Ian

ADDRESSES: Agent—Duncan Heath Associates, Paramount House, 162/170 Wardour St., London W1V 3AT, England.

CAREER: Actor and director.

CREDITS:

STAGE APPEARANCES

Pronos, *And They Put Handcuffs on the Flowers,* Open Space Theatre, London, 1973.

J. Finnay (the Worm), *In the Jungle of the Cities,* The Place Theatre, London, 1973.

Second servant, *Macbeth*, Belgrade Theatre, Coventry, U.K., 1973, then Bankside Globe Theatre, London, 1973.

Elbow, *Measure for Measure*, Royal Shakespeare Company (RSC), Stratford-on-Avon, U.K., 1974.

Sergeant, *Macbeth*, RSC, Aldwych Theatre, London, 1975.

Ross, *Macbeth*, RSC, The Other Place Theatre, Stratford-on-Avon, U.K., 1976.

Turner, *Destiny*, RSC, The Other Place Theatre, 1976.

Comic, *Dingo*, RSC, The Other Place Theatre, 1976.

Goebbels and Bruttschneider, *Schweyk in the Second World War*, RSC, The Other Place Theatre, 1976, then Warehouse Theatre, London, 1977.

Don John, *Much Ado About Nothing*, RSC, Royal Shakespeare Theatre, Stratford-on-Avon, U.K., 1976, then Aldwych Theatre, 1977.

McPhee, *That Good Between Us*, RSC, Warehouse Theatre, 1977.

Ross and porter, *Macbeth*, RSC, Warehouse Theatre, 1977.

Rigault, *The Days of the Commune*, RSC, Aldwych Theatre, 1977.

Comic, *Dingo*, RSC, Warehouse Theatre, 1978.

Ivanov, *Every Good Boy Deserves Favour*, Mermaid Theatre, London, 1978.

Hendrick Hofgen, *Mephisto*, Oxford Playhouse Company, Round House Theatre, London, 1981.

Trench and Terry, *The Worlds*, New Half Moon Theatre, London, 1981.

Ezra Pound, *Ezra*, New Half Moon Theatre, London, 1981.

Professor, *Insignificance*, Royal Court Theatre, London, 1982.

John Tagg, *The Party*, RSC, The Pit, London, 1985.

Chorus, *Henry V*, RSC, Barbican Theatre, London, 1985.

Monster, "Red, Black, and Ignorant," first man, "Tin Can People," and officer and middle-aged man, "Great Peace," *The War Plays*, RSC, The Pit, 1985.

Hacker, *Crimes in Hot Countries*, RSC, The Pit, 1985.

Stucley, *The Castle*, RSC, The Pit, 1985.

Tom Downchild, *Downchild*, RSC, The Pit, 1985.

King Edward II, *Edward II*, Royal Exchange Theatre, Manchester, U.K., 1986.

Cambyses, old farmer, and Llyr, *The Saxon Shore*, Almeida Theatre Company, Almeida Theatre, London, 1986.

Gustav, *Creditors*, Almeida Theatre Company, Almeida Theatre, 1986.

Maximilien Robespierre, *The Danton Affair*, RSC, Barbican Theatre, 1986.

King Philip II of Spain, *Don Carlos*, Royal Exchange Theatre, 1987.

Bradley, *The Black Prince*, Aldwych Theatre, 1989.

Vulpine Volpone, *Volpone*, Almeida Theatre Company, Almeida Theatre, 1990.

STAGE DIRECTOR

Don Juan, Royal Exchange Theatre, 1988.
The Possibilities, Almeida Theatre Company, Almeida Theatre, 1988.

FILM APPEARANCES

Vicar, *The Likely Lads*, EMI, 1976.

Dr. Richter, *The Awakening*, Warner Brothers, 1980.

Reg Smeeton, *Sir Henry at Rawlinson End*, Charisma, 1980.

Brother Jacopus, *Dragonslayer*, Paramount, 1981.

Burglar, *Richard's Things*, New World, 1981.

Professor Andreev, *Gorky Park*, Rank, 1983.

Emperor Palpatine, *Return of the Jedi*, Twentieth Century-Fox, 1983.

Arthur, *Dirty Rotten Scoundrels*, Orion, 1988.

TELEVISION APPEARANCES; MOVIES

Chernobyl: The Final Warning, TNT, 1991.*

*   *   *

McDONNELL, Mary   1953(?)-

PERSONAL: Born in 1953 (some sources say 1952) in Wilkes Barre, PA (some sources say Ithaca, NY); married Randle Mell (an actor); children: Olivia. *Education:* Graduate of State University of New York College at Fredonia.

ADDRESSES: Agent—Perri Kipperman, Bresler, Kelly, Kipperman, 15760 Ventura Blvd., Suite 1730, Encino, CA 91436.

CAREER: Actress. Guest artist, Actors Theatre of Louisville, 1982.

AWARDS, HONORS: Obie Award, performance, *Village Voice*, 1980-81, for *Still Life;* Golden Globe Award nomination and Academy Award nomination, both best supporting actress, 1990, for *Dances With Wolves*.

CREDITS:

FILM APPEARANCES

Lady Capulet, *Garbo Talks*, Metro-Goldwyn-Mayer/United Artists, 1984.

Elma Radnor, *Matewan*, Cinecom, 1987.

Paula Warsaw, *Tiger Warsaw*, Sony, 1988.

Stands With a Fist, *Dances With Wolves*, Orion, 1990.

STAGE APPEARANCES

(New York City debut) Shelly, *Buried Child*, Theatre de Lys, 1978, then Circle Repertory Theatre, New York City, 1979.

Sylvia Plath, *Letters Home,* American Place Theatre, New York City, 1979.

Cheryl, *Still Life,* American Place Theatre, 1981.

Mary Alice, *The Death of a Miner,* Portland Stage Company, Portland, ME, 1981-82, then American Place Theatre, 1982.

Nessa, *A Weekend Near Madison,* Actors Theatre of Louisville, Louisville, KY, 1982, then Astor Place Theatre, New York City, 1983.

Red River, Goodman Theatre, Chicago, IL, 1982-83.

Simone Engel, *Black Angel,* Circle Repertory Theatre, 1982-83.

Jill, *All Night Long,* McGinn/Cazale Theatre, New York City, 1984.

Three Sisters, Guthrie Theatre, Minneapolis, MN, 1984-85.

Linda Rotunda, *Savage in Limbo,* Double Image Theatre, New York City, 1985.

Stitchers and Starlight Talkers, Yale Repertory Theatre, New Haven, CT, 1985-86.

Mary Ann White, *Execution of Justice,* Virginia Theatre, New York City, 1986.

Nora, *A Doll House,* Hartford Stage Company, Hartford, CT, 1986-87.

Sharon, *Three Ways Home,* Astor Place Theatre, 1988.

Heidi, *The Heidi Chronicles,* Plymouth Theatre, New York City, 1990.

Also appeared as Olivia, *Twelfth Night;* as Fanny Wilton, *John Gabriel Borkman;* and in *National Anthems.*

TELEVISION APPEARANCES; SERIES

Dr. Eve Sheridan, *E.R.,* CBS, 1984-85.

TELEVISION APPEARANCES; MOVIES

Terri, *Money on the Side,* ABC, 1982.

Gabriella Estrada, *Courage,* CBS, 1986.

Alexandra Bergson, *O, Pioneers!,* PBS, 1991.*

*   *   *

McGILLIS, Kelly   1958-

PERSONAL: Born in 1958, in Newport Beach, CA; daughter of a doctor and a housewife; married Boyd Black (a writer; marriage ended); married Barry Tubb (an actor; marriage ended); married Fred Tillman (a yacht broker), January, 1989. *Education:* Attended Pacific Conservatory of Performing Arts and Juilliard School of Drama.

CAREER: Actress.

CREDITS:

STAGE APPEARANCES

Understudy for the role of Dona Elvire, *Don Juan,* New York Shakespeare Festival, Delacorte Theatre, New York, NY, 1982.

Nina, *A Seagull,* John F. Kennedy Center for the Performing Arts, Washington, DC, 1985-86.

Portia, *The Merchant of Venice,* Folger Shakespeare Theatre, Washington DC, 1988.

Viola, *Twelfth Night,* Folger Shakespeare Theatre, 1989.

Title role, *Mary Stuart,* Folger Shakespeare Theatre, 1990.

Mistress Alice Ford, *The Merry Wives of Windsor,* Folger Shakespeare Theatre, 1990.

Also appeared in *Three Sisters, Love for Love, Six Characters in Search of an Author,* and *The Winter's Tale.*

FILM APPEARANCES

Geneva Spofford, *Reuben, Reuben,* Twentieth Century-Fox, 1983.

Rachel Lapp, *Witness,* Paramount, 1985.

Charlotte Blackwood, *Top Gun,* Paramount, 1986.

Annie Packert and Ally Chandler, *Made in Heaven,* Lorimar, 1987.

Anda, *Dreamers* (also known as *Once We Were Dreamers*), Hemdale, 1987.

Emily Crane, *The House on Carroll Street,* Orion, 1988.

Kathryn Murphy, *The Accused,* Paramount, 1988.

Collie Wright, *Winter People,* Columbia, 1989.

Also appeared in *Promised Land, Reckless Endangerment, Down with the Lions, Cat Chaser,* and *Before and After Death.*

TELEVISION APPEARANCES; MOVIES

Katherine Dennison Breen, *Sweet Revenge,* CBS, 1984.

Jennifer Coles, *Private Sessions,* NBC, 1985.

TELEVISION APPEARANCES; SPECIALS

Host, *The Juilliard School at 80,* PBS, 1985.

Host, *Santabear's First Christmas* (animated), ABC, 1986.

Narrator, *Santabear's Highflying Adventure* (animated), CBS, 1987.

Host, *The Legend of Sleepy Hollow* (animated), Showtime, 1988.

That's What Friends Are For: AIDS Concert '88, Showtime, 1988.

Host, *Against Her Will* (documentary), Lifetime, 1989.

Narrator, *Thumbelina* (animated), Showtime, 1989.

Also appeared on *Kennedy Center Honors: A Celebration of the Performing Arts,* 1989.

OTHER SOURCES:

PERIODICALS

Hollywood Reporter, March, 1988.
New York Times, October 12, 1989.
Premiere, March, 1988.*

*   *   *

McINTYRE, Dennis   1943(?)-1990

PERSONAL: Born c. 1943 in Detroit, MI; died of stomach cancer, February 1, 1990, in New York, NY; son of Kathleen McIntyre. *Education:* Attended University of Michigan and Carnegie-Mellon University.

CAREER: Playwright and educator. Taught playwriting seminar at University of Michigan.

WRITINGS:

PLAYS

Children in the Rain, Cherry Lane Theatre, New York City, 1970.
Modigliani, Astor Place Theatre, New York City, 1979.
Split Second, INTAR Stage 2, then Negro Ensemble Company, New York City, 1984.
Established Price, Philadelphia Festival Theatre, PA, 1987.
National Anthems, Long Wharf Theatre, New Haven, CT, 1989.

OBITUARIES AND OTHER SOURCES:

PERIODICALS

New York Times, February 2, 1990.
Variety, February 7, 1990.*

*   *   *

McTEER, Janet   1961-

PERSONAL: Born May 8, 1961, in Newcastle, England; daughter of Alan and Jean McTeer. *Education:* Royal Academy of Dramatic Art.

ADDRESSES: Agent—Michael Poster, Duncan Heath Associates, Ltd., Paramount House, 162/170 Wardour Street, London W1V 3AT, England

CAREER: Actress.

AWARDS, HONORS: Royal Television Society Best Performance Award, and Rhems Television Best Actress Award, for *Precious Bane;* Bancroft Gold Medal, Royal Academy of Dramatic Art.

CREDITS:

STAGE APPEARANCES

(Stage debut) A cough, *Mother Courage and Her Children,* Nottingham Playhouse, England, 1984.
(London debut) Mary, *Grace of Mary Traverse,* Royal Court Theatre, 1985.
Hippolyta and Tatania, *A Midsummer's Night Dream,* Royal Shakespeare Company (RSC), Stratford-upon-Avon, England, 1986.
Victoria, *Worlds Apart,* RSC, The Other Place, Stratford, 1986, then The Pit, London, 1987.
Katerina, *The Storm,* RSC, The Pit, 1987.
Greenland, English Stage Company, Royal Court Theatre, 1988.

Also appeared as Imogen, *Cymbeline,* Rosalind, *As You Like It,* and Masha, *The Three Sisters,* all Manchester Royal Exchange Theatre, England

FILM APPEARANCES

Van Arkady's Secretary, *Half Moon Street* (also known as *Escort Girl*), Twentieth Century-Fox, 1986.
Hazel, *Hawks,* Skouras, 1988.

TELEVISION APPEARANCES

Prue Sarn, *Precious Bane* (movie), BBC, 1988, then *Masterpiece Theatre,* PBS, 1989.
Juliet, *Yellowbacks* (movie), BBC, 1989.

Also appeared in television movies as Vita Sackville-West, *Portrait of a Marriage,* BBC; Caroline, *Sweet Nothings,* BBC; and Celeste, *Proust,* BBC.

*   *   *

MESSICK, Don   1926-

PERSONAL: Full name, Donald E. Messick; born September 7, 1926; son of Binford Earl (a housepainter) and Lena Birch (Hughes) Messick; married Helen Marie McHugh; children: Timothy, Charles. *Education:* Trained for the stage at the William Ramsay Street School of Acting.

ADDRESSES: Agent—Charles H. Stern Agency, 11725 Wilshire Blvd., Suite 2320, Los Angeles, CA 90025.

CAREER: Voice actor. *Military service:* U.S. Army.

MEMBER: American Federation of Television and Radio Artists, Screen Actors Guild, Pacific Pioneer Broadcasters (charter member).

AWARDS, HONORS: Honorary award for excellence, International Animated Film Society.

CREDITS:

FILM APPEARANCES; VOICE-ACTOR

Boo Boo, Ranger Smith, *Hey There, It's Yogi Bear,* Columbia, 1964.

Bamm Bamm (and others), *The Man Called Flintstone,* Columbia, 1966.

Geoffrey, *Charlotte's Web,* Paramount, 1973.

Gears, *The Transformers: The Movie,* Deg, 1986.

Also appeared as Astro in *The Jetsons: The Movie,* 1990.

TELEVISION APPEARANCES; SERIES; VOICE-ACTOR

(And puppeteer) *The Buffalo Billy Show,* CBS, 1950-51.

Ruff, Professor Gizmo, narrator, *The Ruff and Reddy Show,* NBC, 1957-64.

Pixie, Boo Boo Bear, Ranger John Smith, *The Huckleberry Hound Show,* syndicated, 1958.

Tadpole, *Spunky and Tadpole,* syndicated, 1958.

Boo Boo Bear, Ranger John Smith, *Yogi Bear,* syndicated, 1958.

Ruff, Professor Gizmo, narrator, *Ruff 'n' Reddy,* NBC, 1959.

Dino, Bamm Bamm, Hoppy, Arnold, *The Flintstones,* ABC, 1960-66.

The Beany and Cecil Show, syndicated, 1961, then ABC, 1964-66.

Astro, *The Jetsons,* ABC, 1962.

Twiddles, *Wally Gator,* syndicated, 1962.

Ricochet Rabbit, *The Magilla Gorilla Show,* syndicated, 1964.

So So, *The Peter Potamus Show,* syndicated, 1964.

Bandit, *The Adventures of Johnny Quest,* ABC, 1964-65, then CBS, 1967-70, later NBC, 1971-72.

Atom Ant, *The Atom Ant/Secret Squirrel Show,* NBC, 1965-68.

Countdown, Pupstar, *Space Kiddettes,* NBC, 1966-67.

Multiman, *Frankenstein Jr. and the Impossibles,* CBS, 1966-68.

Falcon 7 (a superhero), Vapor Man, *Birdman* (also known as *Birdman and the Galaxy Trio*), NBC, 1967-68.

Gloop, Gleep, *The Herculoids,* CBS, 1967-69.

Scooby the Seal, *Moby Dick and the Mighty Mightor,* CBS, 1967-69.

Muttley, Ring-A-Ding, Little Gruesome, *The Wacky Races,* CBS, 1968-70.

Shagg Rugg, *The Banana Splits Adventure Hour,* NBC, 1968-70.

Tag (Gary's dog), *The Adventures of Gulliver,* ABC, 1969-70.

Zippy, Pockets, Dum Dum, Snoozy, *The Perils of Penelope Pitstop,* CBS, 1969-71.

Haddy, *The Cattanooga Cats,* ABC, 1969-71.

Muttley, Klunk, Zilly, *Dastardly and Muttley in Their Flying Machines,* CBS, 1969-71.

Scooby Doo, *Scooby Doo, Where Are You?,* ABC, 1969-74.

Animal voices, *Doctor Doolittle,* 1970-72.

Sebastian, *Josie and the Pussycats,* CBS, 1970-76.

The Barkleys, NBC, 1972-73.

Schleprock, *The Flintstone Comedy Hour,* CBS, 1972-74.

Sebastian, Bleep, *Josie and the Pussycats in Outer Space,* CBS, 1972-74.

Chu Chu the Dog, *The Amazing Chan and The Chan Clan,* CBS, 1972-74.

Robot, Brack, *Lost in Space,* ABC, 1973.

Bravehart, *Inch High, Private Eye,* NBC, 1973-74.

Boo Boo Bear, Touche Turtle, Squiddly Diddly, Ranger Smith, Atom Ant, *Yogi's Gang,* ABC, 1973-75.

Spot, *Hong Kong Phooey,* ABC, 1974-76, then NBC, 1978.

Scooby Doo, Boo Boo, Pixie, Mumbly, Dalton Brothers, *The Scooby Doo/Dynomutt Hour,* CBS, 1976.

Jabberjaws, ABC, 1977.

Hotdog, *The Bang-Shang Lalaplooza Show,* NBC, 1977-78.

Clyde, *The C.B. Bears,* CBS, 1977-78.

Boo Boo Bear, Pixie, Scooby Doo, Creeply Son, Mumbly, Dirty Dalton, *Scooby's All Star Laff-A-Lympics,* ABC, 1977-78.

Scarecrow, *The World's Greatest Super Heroes,* ABC, 1978-80.

Godzuki, *Godzilla* (also known as *The Godzilla Power Hour* and *The Godzilla Super 90*), NBC, 1978-1981.

Bamm Bamm, Dino, *The New Fred and Barney Show,* NBC, 1979.

Scooby Doo, Scrappy Doo, *The Scooby Doo and Scrappy Doo Show,* ABC, 1979.

Snip, *Jack Frost,* NBC, 1980.

Schleprock, *Flintstone Family Adventures,* NBC, 1980-81.

Toad, Fly, *The Drak Pak,* CBS, 1980-82.

Bamm Bamm, Vulture, *The Flintstones,* NBC, 1981-82.

Marmaduke, *The Heathcliff and Marmaduke Show,* ABC, 1981-82.

Azrael the Cat, Papa Smurf, *The Smurfs,* NBC, 1981-82.

TELEVISION APPEARANCES; SPECIALS; VOICE-ACTOR

Rudolph's Shiny New Year, ABC, 1976.

The Hobbit, NBC, 1977.

Whiskers, *The First Easter Rabbit,* CBS, 1978.

Roman Soldier, *Nestor, The Long-Eared Christmas Donkey,* ABC, 1978.

Bamm Bamm, *Fred and Barney Meet the Thing,* NBC, 1979.

Azrael, Horse, Papa Smurf, *The Smurfs Christmas Special,* NBC, 1986.

Papa Smurf, *'Tis the Season to Be Smurfy,* NBC, 1987.

Cartoon All-Stars to the Rescue, ABC, CBS, NBC, and various cable networks, 1990.

Also appeared as Boo Boo Bear on *Casper's First Christmas,* 1979; as Boo Boo Bear, Ranger Smith, and Pixie on

Yogi Bear's All-Star Comedy Christmas Caper, 1982; and on *Hanna-Barbera's 50th: A Yabba Dabba Doo Celebration,* 1989.

TELEVISION APPEARANCES; MOVIES; VOICE-ACTOR

Appeared as Scooby Doo, Scrappy Doo, and Hound on *Scooby Doo Meets the Boo Brothers,* 1987; as Astro on *Rockin' with Judy Jetson,* 1988; and as Boo Boo and Ranger Smith on *Yogi's Great Escape,* 1988.

TELEVISION APPEARANCES; EPISODIC; VOICE-ACTOR

Killer, Gorgeous Cat, Captain Parker, *Gidget Makes the Wrong Connection,* ABC, 1973.
Gleep, Gloop, Astro, *Space Stars,* NBC, 1981-82.

OTHER TELEVISION APPEARANCES; VOICE-ACTOR

Appeared on *Jeannie,* 1973; on *Bailey's Comets,* 1973; on *The First Christmas Snow,* 1975; on *The Oddball Couple,* 1975; as Godzooky on *The All-New Popeye Hour,* 1978; on *The Funtastic World of Hanna-Barbera,* 1981; on *The Jokebook,* 1982; as Azrael, Papa Smurf, and Vulture on *My Smurfy Valentine,* 1983; on *The Wrong-Way Kid,* 1983; on *The Get Along Gang,* 1984; on *Mighty Orbots,* 1984; on *Pink Panther and Sons,* 1984; on *The Transformers,* 1984; as Wally Wooster and Dippy Duck on *The Duck Factory,* 1984; on *Goltar and the Golden Lance,* 1985; on *The New Jetsons,* 1985; on *The Paw Paws,* 1985; on *Yogi's Treasure Hunt,* 1985; as Azrael and Papa Smurf on *Smurfily Ever After,* 1985; as Scooby Doo and Scrappy Doo on *Thirteen Ghosts of Scooby Doo,* 1985; as Scooby Doo on *Scooby Doo's Mystery Funhouse,* 1985; as Pepe on *Foofur,* 1986; on *The New Adventures of Johnny Quest,* 1987; on *Popeye and Son,* 1987; as Scooby Doo on *A Pup Named Scooby Doo,* 1988; and as Hamton J. Pig on *Tiny Toon Adventures.*

RADIO APPEARANCES

WBOC, Salsbury, MD, 1941-43.
Raggedy Andy, *The Raggedy Ann Show,* 1946.

SIDELIGHTS: Don Messick once told *CTFT* that he began his career as a performer at age thirteen, when he developed his own act as a ventriloquist in rural Maryland.*

*   *   *

MICHAELS, Lorne   1944-

PERSONAL: Born Lorne Lipowitz, November 17, 1944, in Toronto, Canada; son of Florence (Becker) Lipowitz; married Rosie Shuster (divorced); married Susan Forristal, 1981 (divorced); married Alice Barry, April, 1991. *Education:* University of Toronto, 1966.

ADDRESSES: Office—Broadway Video, 1619 Broadway, New York, NY 10019; NBC, 30 Rockefeller Plaza, 9th Floor, New York, NY 10020.

CAREER: Writer and producer. CBC, writer and producer of comedy specials, 1968; NBC, Los Angeles, CA, writer, 1968-75, producer of television series and specials, 1975—. Broadway Video, New York City, chairman of the board, 1979—.

MEMBER: American Federation of Television and Radio Artists, Writers Guild of America (board member), Astoria Foundation.

AWARDS, HONORS: Emmy Awards, best writing in comedy-variety, variety, or music for a special program (with others), 1974, for *Lily,* outstanding writing in a comedy-variety or music special (with others), 1976, for *The Lily Tomlin Special,* outstanding producer of a comedy-variety or music series, 1976, for *Saturday Night Live,* outstanding writing in a comedy-variety or music series for a single episode of a regular or limited series (with others), 1977 and 1989, for *Saturday Night Live,* outstanding writing in a comedy-variety or music special (with others), 1978, for *The Paul Simon Special;* San Francisco Film Award, 1976; four Writers Guild of America Awards.

CREDITS:

TELEVISION WORK; SERIES

Creator and producer, *Saturday Night Live* (also known as *NBC's Saturday Night*), NBC, 1975-81, 1985— (also see below).
Executive producer, *The Coneheads* (animated), NBC, 1983.
Producer, *The New Show,* NBC, 1984 (also see below).
Creator and executive producer, *Michelob Presents Sunday Night* (also known as *Michelob Presents Night Music* and *Sunday Night*), NBC, 1987—.
Executive producer, *The Kids in the Hall* (also known as *On Location*), HBO, 1988—.

TELEVISION WORK; SPECIALS

Producer, *Perry Como's Winter Show,* NBC, 1973, broadcast as *The Perry Como Winter Show,* CBS, 1973 (also see below).
Producer, *Flip Wilson . . . of Course,* NBC, 1974 (also see below).
Producer, *Lily,* ABC, 1975 (also see below).
Producer, *The Lily Tomlin Special,* ABC, 1975 (also see below).
Producer, *The Beach Boys Special,* NBC, 1976 (also see below).
Producer, *The Paul Simon Special,* NBC, 1977 (also see below).

Producer, *The Rutles: All You Need Is Cash,* NBC, 1978 (also see below).

Producer, *Steve Martin's Best Show Ever,* NBC, 1981.

Executive producer, *Simon and Garfunkel: The Concert in Central Park,* HBO, 1981.

Executive producer, *Bob & Ray & Jane, Laraine & Gilda,* NBC, 1981.

Executive producer, *Randy Newman at the Odeon,* Showtime, 1983.

Executive producer, *Simon and Garfunkel in Concert,* HBO, 1983.

Executive producer, *Big Shots in America,* NBC, 1985.

Executive producer, *Bugs Bunny/Looney Tunes All-Star 50th Anniversary,* CBS, 1986.

Executive producer, *Rolling Stone Magazine's 20 Years of Rock 'n' Roll* (also known as *Rolling Stone Magazine's 20th Anniversary Special*), ABC, 1987.

Executive producer, *The Rolling Stones' 30 Years of Rock 'n' Roll,* ABC, 1988.

Executive producer, *Superman's 50th Anniversary: A Celebration of the Man of Steel,* CBS, 1988.

Executive producer, *The 40th Annual Emmy Awards,* Fox, 1988.

Creator, *Coca-Cola Presents Live: The Hard Rock* (also known as *Live: The Hard Rock*) NBC, 1988.

Executive producer, *Saturday Night Live's 15th Anniversary,* NBC, 1989.

Executive producer, *Rolling Stones: Terrifying* (also known as *Rolling Stones: The Steel Wheels Concert* and *The Rolling Stones*), Showtime, 1989.

Executive producer, *Saturday Night Live Goes Commercial,* NBC, 1991.

TELEVISION APPEARANCES

Lily, CBS, 1973.
The Canadian Conspiracy, CBC, 1986.

Has also appeared on numerous episodes of *Saturday Night Live,* NBC.

FILM WORK

Producer, *Nothing Lasts Forever,* Metro-Goldwyn-Mayer/United Artists, 1984.

Producer, *Three Amigos,* Orion, 1987 (also see below).

Also executive producer of *Mr. Mike's Mondo Video,* 1979.

STAGE WORK

Producer (with others), *Appearing Nitely,* Biltmore Theatre, New York City, 1977.

Producer and director, *Gilda Radner Live from New York,* Winter Garden Theatre, New York City, 1979 (also see below).

WRITINGS:

TELEVISION SERIES

The Beautiful Phyllis Diller Show, NBC, 1968.
Rowan and Martin's Laugh-In, NBC, 1968-69.
Saturday Night Live (also known as *NBC's Saturday Night*), NBC, 1975-81, 1985—.
The New Show, NBC, 1984.

TELEVISION SPECIALS

Lily, CBS, 1973.
Perry Como's Winter Show, NBC, 1973, broadcast as *The Perry Como Winter Show,* CBS, 1973.
Flip Wilson . . . of Course, NBC, 1974.
Lily, ABC, 1975.
The Lily Tomlin Special, ABC, 1975.
The Beach Boys Special, NBC, 1976.
The Paul Simon Special, NBC, 1977.
The Rutles: All You Need Is Cash, NBC, 1978.

SCREENPLAYS

(With Steve Martin and Randy Newman) *Three Amigos,* Orion, 1987.

STAGE

(With others) *Gilda Radner Live from New York,* Winter Garden Theatre, New York City, 1979.

*　　*　　*

MINER, Stephen
See MINER, Steve

*　　*　　*

MINER, Steve　1951-
(Stephen Miner)

PERSONAL: Born June 18, 1951, in Chicago, IL.

ADDRESSES: Office—c/o Kirk Orlando, Paramount Images, 5555 Melrose Ave., Hollywood, CA 90038.

CAREER: Director and producer. Director of commercials, Paramount Images.

AWARDS, HONORS: Directors Guild of America award and Emmy Award nominations, best director and best comedy series, all 1988, for *The Wonder Years.*

CREDITS:

TELEVISION DIRECTOR; SERIES

(And supervising producer) *The Wonder Years,* ABC, 1988—.
Elvis (also known as *Elvis: Good Rockin' Tonight*), ABC, 1990.

TELEVISION DIRECTOR; EPISODIC

"B-Men," *CBS Summer Playhouse,* CBS, 1989.

FILM DIRECTOR, EXCEPT WHERE INDICATED

(And producer) *Friday the 13th Part II,* Paramount, 1981.
Friday the 13th Part III (also see below), Paramount, 1982.
House, New World, 1986.
Soul Man, New World, 1986.
(And producer) *Warlock,* Trimark, 1991.
Wild Hearts Can't Be Broken, Walt Disney Pictures, 1991.

Director, producer, and editor of industrial, educational, and sport films.

OTHER FILM WORK

(As Stephen Miner) Editor and co-producer, *Here Come the Tigers* (also known as *Manny's Orphans*), American International, 1978.
Unit production manager and associate producer, *Friday the 13th,* Paramount, 1980.

Production assistant for *Last House on the Left,* 1970; film editor for *The Case of the Full Moon Murders,* 1973, and *The Case of the Smiling Stiffs,* 1974.

FILM APPEARANCES

Newscaster, *Friday the 13th Part III,* Paramount, 1982.*

*   *   *

MOORE, Alvy   1925-

PERSONAL: Born in 1925.

ADDRESSES: Agent—Mary Murphy Agency, 6014 Greenbush Ave., Van Nuys, CA 91401.

CAREER: Actor and producer. Formed a film production company with L. Q. Jones.

MEMBER: American Federation of Television and Radio Artists, Screen Actors Guild, Actors' Equity.

CREDITS:

FILM APPEARANCES

Quartermaster, *Okinawa,* Columbia, 1952.
Friend, *You for Me,* Metro-Goldwyn-Mayer (MGM), 1952.
Carlson, *China Venture,* Columbia, 1953.
Aide, *Destination Gobi,* Twentieth Century-Fox, 1953.
Anderson, *Gentlemen Prefer Blondes,* Twentieth Century-Fox, 1953.
Private Stone, *The Glory Brigade,* Twentieth Century-Fox, 1953.
Zippy, *The War of the Worlds,* Paramount, 1953.

Pigeon, *The Wild One,* Columbia, 1953.
Secret of the Incas, Paramount, 1954.
Smitty, *Return from the Sea,* Allied Artists, 1954.
Gator, *Riot in Cell Block 11,* Allied Artists, 1954.
Virgil, *Susan Slept Here,* RKO, 1954.
Katy's boyfriend, *There's No Business Like Show Business,* Twentieth Century-Fox, 1954.
Willie, *An Annapolis Story* (also known as *The Blue and the Gold*), Allied Artists, 1955.
Roy, *Five against the House,* Columbia, 1955.
Grimes, *Screaming Eagles,* Allied Artists, 1956.
Luke Coslow, *Designing Woman,* MGM, 1957.
Willy Williams, *The Persuader,* Allied Artists, 1957.
Private Marvin Brewer, *The Perfect Furlough* (also known as *Strictly for Pleasure*), Universal, 1958.
Jim Lipscott, *Everything's Ducky,* Columbia, 1961.
Dizzy Bellew, *Twist Around the Clock,* Columbia, 1961.
Johnson, *The Wackiest Ship in the Army,* Columbia, 1961.
George, *For Love or Money,* Universal, 1963.
Waiter, *Move over, Darling,* Twentieth Century-Fox, 1963.
Sutter T. Finley, *Three Nuts in Search of a Bolt,* Harlequin International, 1964.
The Devil's Bedroom, Manson, 1964.
Officer Jones, *Love and Kisses,* Universal, 1965.
Maxwell, *One Way Wahini* (also known as *One Way Wahine*), United Screen Arts, 1965.
Ralph, *A Very Special Favor,* Universal, 1965.
For Pete's Sake!, World-Wide, 1966.
Gas station mechanic, *The Gnome-Mobile,* Buena Vista, 1967.
Dr. Ralph Hayes, *The Witchmaker* (also known as *Legend of Witch Hollow*), Excelsior, 1969.
Tobey, *The Brotherhood of Satan,* Columbia, 1971.
Bill Morris, *The Late Liz,* Gateway, 1971.
Herbie Rides Again, Buena Vista, 1974.
Committee member, *A Boy and His Dog,* LQJAF, 1975.
Sheriff Frank, *Dr. Minx,* Dimension, 1975.
Bailiff, *The Specialist,* Crown, 1975.
Al, *Scream,* Vestron, 1981.
Mortuary, Film Ventures, 1983.
Jimbo, *They're Playing with Fire,* New World, 1984.
Voice of Grandpa Little, *Here Come the Littles* (animated), Atlantic Releasing, 1985.
Chili salesman, *The Horror Show,* MGM/United Artists, 1989.
Intruder (also known as *Night Crew: The Final Checkout* and *Nightcrew*), Phantom, 1989.

Also appeared in *Ms. 45* (also known as *Angel of Vengeance*), 1980; *The Heart is a Rebel,* World-Wide; and *The Stranger in the House.*

FILM WORK

Associate producer, *The Devil's Bedroom,* Manson, 1964.

Associate producer, *The Witchmaker* (also known as *Legend of Witch Hollow*), Excelsior, 1969.

Producer (with L. Q. Jones), *The Brotherhood of Satan*, Columbia, 1971.

Producer, *A Boy and His Dog*, LQJAF, 1975.

Also produced *The World of Little League.*

TELEVISION APPEARANCES; SERIES

Narrator, *Border Collie* (broadcast as a segment of *The Mickey Mouse Club*), ABC, 1955.

Reporter, *What I Want to Be* (broadcast as a segment of *The Mickey Mouse Club*), ABC, 1955.

Hank Kimball, *Green Acres*, CBS, 1965-71.

TELEVISION APPEARANCES; PILOTS

Andy, *Johnny Come Lately*, CBS, 1960.

Otis Platt, *Hooray for Love*, CBS, 1963.

Reverend, *Lacy and the Mississippi Queen*, NBC, 1978.

Claude Pomerantz, *Stephanie*, CBS, 1981.

Jonas, *The Wonderful World of Philip Malley*, CBS, 1981.

Also appeared in *Grand Hotel* and *Con Men.*

TELEVISION APPEARANCES; EPISODIC

Voyage to the Bottom of the Sea, ABC, 1965.

The Dick Van Dyke Show, CBS, 1965.

My Mother the Car, NBC, 1965, 1966.

Birdie Fletcher, *Hardcastle and McCormick*, ABC, 1986.

Delivery man, *Newhart*, CBS, 1989.

Also appeared as salesman, *The Andy Griffith Show*, CBS; Dillard Crumbley III, *My Little Margie;* Howie, *Pete and Gladys*, CBS; "Love and the Lost Dog" and "Love and the Amateur Night," *Love American Style*, ABC; *Nanny and the Professor*, ABC; *Peter Loves Mary*, NBC; *The Beverly Hillbillies*, CBS; *Dennis the Menace*, CBS; *The Donna Reed Show*, ABC; *Gomer Pyle*, CBS; *Hazel*, CBS; *The Munsters*, CBS; and in numerous other series, including *Navy Log*, *Bachelor Father*, *Space Patrol*, *Wagon Train*, *Dragnet*, *Surf Side Six*, *Burke's Law*, *The Virginian*, *How the West Was Won*, *Trapper John*, *Fantasy Island*, *The Waltons*, *Little House on the Prairie*, *Daniel Boone*, and *The Joey Bishop Show.*

TELEVISION APPEARANCES; MOVIES

George's father, *Cotton Candy*, NBC, 1978.

Room clerk, *Kate Bliss and the Ticker Tape Kid*, ABC, 1978.

First mayor, *Little House: The Last Farewell*, NBC, 1984.

Little White Lies (also known as *First Impressions*), NBC, 1989.

Hank Kimball, *Return to Green Acres*, CBS, 1990.

TELEVISION APPEARANCES; SPECIALS

Voice characterizations, *Liberty and the Littles* (animated), ABC, 1986.

STAGE APPEARANCES

Appeared as Hornbeck, *Inherit the Wind*, Pasadena Playhouse, Pasadena, CA; as next door neighbor, *Send Me No Flowers*, Santa Barbara Playhouse, Santa Barbara, CA; and as shore patrolman and Pulver, *Mr. Roberts*, U.S. cities. Also appeared in various productions at Cain Park Theatre, Cleveland, OH, Ogunquit Playhouse, Ogunquit, ME, and Mansion Theatre, Odessa, TX.

* * *

MORTIMER, John 1923-
(Geoffrey Lincoln)

PERSONAL: Full name, John Clifford Mortimer; born April 21, 1923, in Hampstead, London, England; son of Clifford (a barrister) and Kathleen May (Smith) Mortimer; married Penelope Ruth Fletcher (a writer), 1949 (divorced, 1972); married Penelope Gollop, 1972; children: (first marriage) Sally, Jeremy; (second marriage) Rosamond; stepchildren: Madelon Lee, Caroline, Julia, Deborah. *Education:* Brasenose College, Oxford, B.A., 1947. *Avocational interests:* Cooking, gardening, going to the theatre, and working.

ADDRESSES: Agent—A.D. Peters, Two Chambers, Chelsea Harbour, London SW10 0XF, England.

CAREER: Writer. Barrister-at-Law, London, England, 1948—; named to Queen's Counsel, 1966; Master of the Bench, Inner Temple, 1975. Scriptwriter for Crown Film Units during World War II; drama critic for *New Statesman, Evening Standard,* and *Observer,* 1972. President of Berkshire, Buckinghamshire, and Oxfordshire Naturalists' Trust, 1984—.

MEMBER: League of Dramatists (chairman), Garrick Club.

AWARDS, HONORS: Italia Prize, 1957, for *The Dock Brief;* Writers Guild of Great Britain award, best original teleplay, 1969, for *A Voyage round My Father;* Golden Globe Award nomination, 1969, for *John and Mary;* British Academy of Film and Television Arts Writers Award, 1980; Emmy Award nomination, writing—limited series or special, 1981-82, for *Brideshead Revisited: Et in Arcadia Ego;* Commander, Order of the British Empire, 1986. D.Litt., Susquehanna University, 1985, University of St. Andrews, 1987, University of Nottingham, and Brunel University; LL.D., Exeter University, 1986.

CREDITS:

FILM WORK

Associate producer, *Lunch Hour*, London Films, 1962 (also see below).

WRITINGS:

PLAYS

The Dock Brief [and] *What Shall We Tell Caroline?* (double bill; Lyric Opera House, Hammersmith, England, then Garrick Theatre, London, 1958), published with *I Spy* as *Three Plays*, Elek, 1958, Grove Press, 1962 (also see below).

I Spy (Salisbury Playhouse, Salisbury, England, 1959), published in *Three Plays*, Elek, 1958, Grove Press, 1962.

The Wrong Side of the Park (Cambridge Theatre, then St. Martin's Theatre, London, 1960), Heinemann, 1960.

Collect Your Hand Baggage (London Academy of Music and Dramatic Art, London, 1962), Samuel French, 1960.

Lunch Hour (Salisbury Playhouse, 1960, then Criterion Theatre, London, 1961), published in *Lunch Hour and Other Plays* (includes *David and Broccoli*), Methuen, 1960.

Two Stars for Comfort (Garrick Theatre, 1962), Methuen, 1962.

Translator, *A Flea in Her Ear* (National Theatre Company, Old Vic Theatre, London, 1966), Samuel French, 1968 (also see below).

The Judge (Deutsches Schauspielhaus, Hamburg, Germany, then Cambridge Theatre, 1967), Methuen, 1967.

Translator, *Cat among the Pigeons* (Prince of Wales' Theatre, London, 1969, then Milwaukee Repertory Theatre, Milwaukee, WI, 1971), Samuel French, 1970.

Come As You Are (includes *Mill Hill, Bermondsey, Gloucester Road,* and *Marble Arch;* New Theatre, London, 1970), Methuen, 1971.

A Voyage round My Father (Greenwich Theatre, 1970, then Haymarket Theatre, London, 1971), Methuen, 1971 (also see below).

Translator, *The Captain of Koepenick* (National Theatre Company, Old Vic Theatre, 1971), Methuen, 1971.

Adaptor, *I, Claudius,* Queen's Theatre, London, 1972.

Collaborators (Duchess Theatre, London, 1973), Methuen, 1973.

Heaven and Hell (includes *The Fear of Heaven,* Samuel French, 1978, and *The Prince of Darkness,*), Greenwich Theatre, 1977.

Translator, *The Lady from Maxim's* (National Theatre Company, Lyttleton Theatre, London, 1977), Heinemann, 1977.

The Bells of Hell (Garrick Theatre, 1977), Samuel French, 1978.

John Mortimer's Casebook (includes *The Dock Brief, The Prince of Darkness,* and *Interlude*), Young Vic Theatre, London, 1982.

When That I Was, Arts Centre, Ottawa, Ontario, Canada, 1982.

Translator, *A Little Hotel on the Side* (National Theatre Company, Olivier Theatre, London, 1984), published in *Three Boulevard Farces,* Penguin, 1985.

Also author with others of *Conflicts,* produced in London, 1971.

TELEVISION PLAYS, EXCEPT WHERE NOTED

Call Me a Liar, BBC, 1958.

David and Broccoli, BBC, 1960.

The Encyclopaedist, BBC, 1961.

The Choice of Kings, Associated Rediffusion, 1966.

The Exploding Azalea, Thames Television, 1966.

The Head Waiter, BBC, 1966.

The Other Side, BBC, 1967.

Desmond (BBC, 1968), published in *The Best Short Plays 1971,* Chilton, 1971.

Infidelity Took Place, BBC, 1968.

Married Alive, CBS, 1970.

Only Three Can Play, Independent Broadcasting Authority, 1970.

Alcock and Gander, Thames Television, 1972.

Swiss Cottage, BBC, 1972.

Knightsbridge (BBC, 1972), Samuel French, 1973.

Rumpole of the Bailey, BBC, then PBS, 1975 (also see below).

Will Shakespeare, Associated Television, 1978 (also see below).

Unity, BBC, 1978.

Rumpole of the Bailey (series), BBC, then PBS, 1978, 1979, and 1987.

(Adaptor) *Brideshead Revisited* (mini-series), Granada Television, then PBS, 1981.

Paradise Postponed, Thames Television, 1986 (also see below).

Summer's Lease (mini-series), BBC, then PBS, 1989 and 1991.

Also author of *A Voyage round My Father,* 1982, *The Ebony Tower,* 1984, and *The Dock Brief.* Adapted several Graham Greene stories for television, including *A Little Place off Edgware Road, The Blue Film, The Destructors, The Case for the Defense, Chagrin in Three Parts, The Invisible Japanese Gentlemen, Special Duties,* and *Mortmain,* all Thames Television, 1975-76.

SCREENPLAYS

(With Lewis Gilbert and Vernon Harris) *Ferry to Hong Kong,* Rank, 1959.

(With Truman Capote and William Archibald) *The Innocents,* Twentieth Century-Fox, 1961.

Guns of Darkness, Warner Brothers, 1962.

(With others) *I Thank a Fool,* Metro-Goldwyn-Mayer, 1962.

Lunch Hour, London Films, 1962.

The Running Man, Columbia, 1963.

(With wife, Penelope Mortimer) *Bunny Lake is Missing,* Columbia, 1965.

A Flea in Her Ear, Twentieth Century-Fox, 1968.

John and Mary, Twentieth Century-Fox, 1969.

Also author of *Maschenka,* 1987.

RADIO PLAYS

Like Men Betrayed, BBC, 1955.

No Hero, BBC, 1955.

The Dock Brief, BBC, 1957.

Three Winters, BBC, 1958.

Personality Split, BBC, 1964.

Education of an Englishman, BBC, 1964.

A Rare Device, BBC, 1965.

Mr. Luby's Fear of Heaven, BBC, 1976.

Edwin (broadcast, 1982), published in *Edwin and Other Plays,* Penguin, 1984.

Also author of *A Voyage round My Father,* 1963.

OTHER

Charade (novel), Lane, 1948, Viking, 1986.

Rumming Park (novel), Lane, 1949.

Answer Yes or No (novel), Lane, 1950, published as *Silver Hook,* Morrow, 1950.

Like Men Betrayed (novel), Collins, 1953, Lippincott, 1954.

Three Winters (novel), Collins, 1956.

Narrowing Stream (novel), Collins, 1956, Viking, 1989.

(As Geoffrey Lincoln) *No Moaning at the Bar,* Bles, 1957.

(With first wife, Penelope Ruth Mortimer) *With Love and Lizards* (travel), M. Joseph, 1957.

Will Shakespeare, Hodder & Stoughton, 1977, published as *Will Shakespeare: The Untold Story,* Delacorte, 1978.

Rumpole of the Bailey (stories), Penguin, 1980.

Regina v. Rumpole (stories), Allen Lane, 1981.

The Trials of Rumpole (stories), Penguin, 1981.

Clinging to the Wreckage: A Part of Life (autobiography), Ticknor & Fields, 1982.

Rumpole's Return (stories), Penguin, 1982.

In Character (interviews), Allen Lane, 1983.

Editor, *Famous Trials,* Penguin, 1984.

Rumpole and the Golden Thread (stories), Penguin, 1984.

Rumpole for the Defence (stories), Penguin, 1984.

A First Rumpole Omnibus (stories), Penguin, 1984.

Paradise Postponed (novel), Viking, 1986.

Character Parts (interviews; originally published in *Sunday Times*), Penguin, 1987.

The Second Rumpole Omnibus (stories), Penguin, 1987.

Summer's Lease, Viking, 1988.

Rumpole's Last Case, Penguin, 1988.

Titmuss Regained, Viking, 1990.

Also author of a scenario for ballet, *Home,* 1968, and *Rumpole and the Age of Miracles,* 1988. Adaptor of two Son et Lumiere scripts, *Hampton Court,* 1964, and *Brighton Pavilion,* 1965.

*   *   *

MURCH, Walter

PERSONAL: Full name, Walter S. Murch. *Education:* Attended Johns Hopkins University; graduate study at University of Southern California—Los Angeles.

ADDRESSES: 11010 Santa Monica Blvd., Los Angeles, CA 90067.

CAREER: Sound technician, film editor, screenwriter, and director.

AWARDS, HONORS: British Academy Award, 1974, for *The Conversation;* Academy Award nominations, best sound (with Arthur Rochester), 1974, for *The Conversation,* best film editing (with Richard Chew), 1977, for *Julia,* and (with Richard Marks, Gerald B. Greenberg, and Lisa Fruchtman), 1979, for *Apocalypse Now,* and award, best sound (with Mark Berger, Richard Beggs, and Nat Boxer), 1979, for *Apocalypse Now,* nominations for best editing, 1991, for *Ghost* and (with Barry Malkin and Fruchtman) *The Godfather, Part III.*

CREDITS:

FILM WORK

Sound technician, *The Rain People,* Warner Bros., 1969.

Sound technician (with others), *Gimme Shelter,* Cinema V, 1970.

Sound technician and (with George Lucas) screenwriter, *THX 1138,* Warner Bros., 1971.

Sound technician, *The Godfather,* Paramount, 1972.

Sound technician, *American Graffiti,* Universal, 1973.

Sound technician (with Arthur Rochester) and editor (with Richard Chew), *The Conversation,* Paramount, 1974.

Sound technician, *The Godfather, Part II,* Paramount, 1974.

Sound technician, *The Great Gatsby,* Paramount, 1974.

Editor, *Julia,* Twentieth Century-Fox, 1977.

Sound technician (with Mark Berger, Richard Beggs, and Nat Boxer) and editor (with Richard Marks, Gerald B. Greenberg, and Lisa Fruchtman), *Apocalypse Now,* United Artists, 1979.

Sound technician (with Mark Berger and Dale Strumpell), *Dragonslayer,* Paramount, 1981.

Documentary editorial researcher, *The Right Stuff,* Ladd, 1984.

Screenwriter (with Gill Dennis) and director, *Return to Oz,* Buena Vista, 1985.

Special creative consultant, *The Adventures of Mark Twain* (animated), Atlantic, 1985.

Editor (with B. J. Sears, Vivien Gilliam, and Steven Rotter), *The Unbearable Lightness of Being,* Orion, 1988.

Sound technician and editor, *Ghost,* Paramount, 1990.

Editor (with Barry Malkin and Lisa Fruchtman), *The Godfather, Part III,* Paramount, 1990.

OTHER SOURCES:

PERIODICALS

Cinefantastique, July, 1985.
Cinefex, Number 3, 1980.
Los Angeles Times, August 30, 1981.
San Francisco Chronicle, April 6-12, 1988.

N

NANCE, Jack

ADDRESSES: Agent—BDP and Associates, 10637 Burbank Blvd., North Hollywood, CA 90212.

CAREER: Actor.

CREDITS:

FILM APPEARANCES

Hippie, *Fools,* Cinerama, 1970.
Ace, *Jump,* Cannon, 1971.
Gary Salt, *Hammet,* Warner Brothers, 1982.
Aram Strossell, *City Heat,* Warner Brothers, 1984.
Nefud, *Dune,* Universal, 1984.
Priest, *Johnny Dangerously,* Twentieth Century-Fox, 1984.
Wolfgang, *Ghoulies,* Empire, 1985.
Paul, *Blue Velvet,* DiLaurentiis, 1986.
Detective, *Barfly,* Cannon, 1987.
Doctor, *The Blob,* Tri-Star, 1988.
Officer Samuels, *Colors,* Orion, 1988.
Julian Ward, *The Hot Spot,* Orion, 1990.
OO Spool, *Wild at Heart,* Manifesto, 1990.

Also appeared as Henry Spencer in *Eraserhead,* 1977, and in *Catch Me If You Can,* 1989.

TELEVISION APPEARANCES; SERIES

Pete Martell, *Twin Peaks,* ABC, 1990-91.

TELEVISION APPEARANCES; MOVIES

Tricks of the Trade, CBS, 1988.

STAGE APPEARANCES

Appeared in *The Collected Works of Billy the Kid,* "In the Works" Festival, Mark Taper Forum, Los Angeles, CA.*

NEAR, Timothy 1945-

PERSONAL: Born February 23, 1945, in Los Angeles, CA. *Education:* Graduated from San Francisco State College; studied acting at the London Academy of Music and Dramatic Arts.

CAREER: Actress, director, and writer. Center Theatre Group, New Theatre for Now, Los Angeles, CA, performer, 1972-73; Stage West Theatre, West Springfield, MA, resident director, 1977-85, artistic director, 1984-85; Repertory Theatre of St. Louis, St. Louis, MO, director, 1983-87; Guthrie Theatre, Minneapolis, MN, director, 1985-86; Alliance Theatre Company, Atlanta, GA, associate artistic director, 1986-87.

AWARDS, HONORS: Obie Award for best performance, *Village Voice,* 1980-81, for *Still Life.*

CREDITS:

STAGE APPEARANCES

Voice of Leye, *The Dybbuk,* and dental assistant, *Priscilla, Princess of Power* (double-bill), Brooklyn Academy of Music, Brooklyn, NY, 1975.
When We Dead Awaken, Stage West Theatre, West Springfield, MA, 1977.
The Hot L Baltimore, Stage West Theatre, 1977.
The Three Sisters, Stage West Theatre, 1978.
Vanities, Stage West Theatre, 1978.
(Off-Broadway debut) Lorraine Dugan, *Just the Immediate Family,* Hudson Guild Theatre, 1978.
How the Other Half Loves, Stage West Theatre, 1979.
Nadine, *Still Life,* American Place Theatre, New York City, 1981.

STAGE DIRECTOR

Artichoke, Stage West Theatre, 1982.
A Streetcar Named Desire, Stage West Theatre, 1983.

All My Sons, Stage West Theatre, 1984.
The Unexpected Guest, Stage West Theatre, 1984.
The Rainmaker, Stage West Theatre, 1984.
The Glass Menagerie, Stage West Theatre, 1985.
A Doll's House, Stage West Theatre, 1985.
Ghost on Fire, La Jolla Playhouse, La Jolla, CA, 1985.
Annulla, An Autobiography, Repertory Theatre of St. Louis, St. Louis, MO, 1985, then Alliance Theatre Company, Atlanta, GA, 1987.
All My Sons, Repertory Theatre of St. Louis, 1986.
The Little Foxes, Repertory Theatre of St. Louis, 1987.
An American Doll's House, Alliance Theatre Company, 1987.

FILM APPEARANCES

Waitress, *Cisco Pike,* Columbia, 1971.
Marcja, *Breakfast in Bed,* William Haugse, 1978.

TELEVISION APPEARANCES

Appeared on an episode of *The Odd Couple,* ABC.

WRITINGS:

PLAYS

(Adaptor with Rae Allen) *A Christmas Carol,* Stage West Theatre, West Springfield, MA, 1977, then Ford's Theatre, Washington, DC, 1980, 1984.
(With Peter Elbling) *A Bagful of Stories,* Stage West Theatre, 1978.*

*   *   *

NELSON, Judd   1959-

PERSONAL: Born in 1959, in Portland, ME. *Education:* Attended Haverford/Bryn Mawr College; studied acting at the Stella Adler Conservatory.

ADDRESSES: Agent—David Schiff, Creative Artists Agency, 9830 Wilshire Blvd., Beverly Hills, CA 90212. *Publicist*—Lili Ungar/Allen Burry, PMK Public Relations Inc., 8436 W. 3rd St., No. 650, Los Angeles, CA 90048. *Manager*—Loree Rodkin, Rodkin Company, 8600 Melrose Ave., Los Angeles, CA 90069.

CAREER: Actor.

CREDITS:

STAGE APPEARANCES

Henry Hitchcock, *Sleeping Dogs,* Mark Taper Forum, Los Angeles, CA, 1986.
Sling/Bartender, *Planet Fires,* Mark Taper Forum, 1986.
Orphans, Burt Reynolds Dinner Theatre, Jupiter, FL, 1986.
Paulie, *Temple,* American Jewish Theatre, New York City, 1988.

Also appeared as Mozart, *Mozart and Salieri;* Roy, *Domino Courts;* Don Juan, *The Stone Guest.* Appeared in productions for the Shoestring Theatre Company, 1976-78.

FILM APPEARANCES

(Film debut) Eddie Keaton, *Making the Grade,* Metro-Goldwyn-Mayer/Cannon/United Artists, 1984.
John Bender, *The Breakfast Club,* Universal, 1985.
Phil Hicks, *Fandango,* Warner Brothers (Warner Bros.), 1985.
Alex, *St. Elmo's Fire,* Columbia, 1985.
Billy Turner, *Blue City,* Paramount, 1986.
Voice of Hot Rod/Rodimus Prime, *Transformers: The Movie,* DeLaurentiis Entertainment Group (DEG), 1986.
Robin Weathers, *From the Hip,* DEG, 1987.
Buck Taylor, *Relentless,* New Line Cinema, 1989.
Officer Nick Peretti, *New Jack City,* Warner Bros., 1991.

TELEVISION APPEARANCES; MOVIES

Joe Hunt, *Billionaire Boys Club,* NBC, 1987.
Lieutenant Pete Dunham, *Out of the Ashes,* NBC, 1990.

OTHER TELEVISION APPEARANCES

Funny, You Don't Look 200 (special), ABC, 1987.
Unauthorized Biography: Jane Fonda, syndicated, 1988.*

*   *   *

NEUFELD, Mace   1928-

PERSONAL: Full name, Mace Alvin Neufeld; born July 13, 1928; son of Philip M. (a stockbroker) and Margaret Ruth (Braun) Neufeld; married Helen Katz (a designer), February 28, 1954; children: Bradley David, Glenn Jeremy, Nancy Ann. *Education:* Yale University, B.A., 1949; postgraduate study at New York University, 1958-60. *Politics:* Democrat.

ADDRESSES: Office—Paramount Pictures, 5555 Melrose Ave., Los Angeles, CA 90038.

CAREER: Film company executive and producer. Photographer for various New York City publications, 1943-45; production assistant to Raymond E. Nelson, 1949-50; Ray Bloch Associates, Inc. (production and personal management company), New York City, founder and owner, 1951-59; BNB Productions, New York City, partner, 1959-70; Neufeld-Davis Productions, Inc., Beverly Hills, CA, partner, 1981—; Neufeld-Rehme Productions, partner, 1989—.

MEMBER: Academy of Motion Picture Arts and Sciences, Academy of Television Arts and Sciences, American Society of Composers, Authors, and Publishers, Producers League, American Film Institute (trustee, 1978—), Yale Club, Regency Club.

AWARDS, HONORS: Photograph of the Year award, New York *World Telegram-Sun,* 1944; grand prize, Eastman Kodak National Salon of Photography, 1945; Emmy nomination, and Golden Globe for best mini-series, 1982, both for *East of Eden.*

CREDITS:

FILM WORK

Executive producer, *The Omen,* Twentieth Century-Fox, 1976.

Co-producer, *Damien—Omen II,* Twentieth Century-Fox, 1977.

Producer, *The Frisco Kid,* Warner Brothers, 1979.

Associate producer, *Omen III—The Final Conflict,* Twentieth Century-Fox, 1981.

Executive producer, *The Funhouse,* Universal, 1981.

Producer, *The Aviator,* Metro-Goldwyn-Mayer, 1985.

Executive producer, *Transylvania 6-5000,* New World, 1985.

Executive producer, *No Way Out,* Orion, 1987.

Producer, *The Punisher,* New World, 1989.

Producer, *The Hunt for Red October,* Paramount, 1990.

Producer, *Flight of the Intruder,* Paramount, 1991.

Producer, *Necessary Roughness,* Paramount, 1991.

TELEVISION WORK; SERIES

Production executive, *The Kids from C.A.P.E.R.,* NBC, 1976.

Executive producer, *The Captain and Tennille,* ABC, 1976.

Producer, *Quark,* NBC, 1978.

Executive producer, *The American Dream,* ABC, 1981.

TELEVISION WORK; MINI-SERIES

Executive producer, *East of Eden,* ABC, 1981.

Producer, *The Far Pavilions,* HBO, 1984.

Executive producer, *A Death in California,* ABC, 1985.

TELEVISION WORK; MOVIES

Executive producer, *Angel on My Shoulder,* ABC, 1980.

Executive producer, *Omen IV: The Awakening,* FBC, 1991.

Executive producer (with Doris Keating), *White Hot: The Mysterious Murder of Thelma Todd,* NBC, 1991.

OTHER TELEVISION WORK

Executive producer, *Cagney and Lacy* (pilot), CBS, 1981.

Executive producer, *The Magic Planet* (special), ABC, 1983.

STAGE WORK

Producer, *The Flying Karamazov Brothers,* Ritz Theatre, New York City, 1983.

OTHER SOURCES:

PERIODICALS

Hollywood Reporter, March 18, 1991.

*   *   *

NEWHART, Bob   1929-

PERSONAL: Born September 5, 1929, in Oak Park, IL; married Virginia Quinn, January 12, 1964; children: four *Education:* Loyola University, B.S., 1952.

ADDRESSES: Office—315 S. Beverly Dr., Beverly Hills, CA 90212.

CAREER: Actor and comedian. Worked briefly as an accountant. Performed in productions for a theatrical stock company in Oak Park, IL. *Military service:* U.S. Army, 1952-54.

AWARDS, HONORS: Emmy Award, outstanding lead actor in a musical/comedy series, and Peabody Award, both 1961, for *The Bob Newhart Show;* Grammy Award, best comedy performance (spoken word), 1962, for *The Button-Down Mind Strikes Back;* Sword of Loyola Award, 1976; Emmy Award nominations, outstanding writing achievement in comedy, 1962, for *The Bob Newhart Show,* outstanding lead actor in a comedy series, 1984, 1985, and 1986, all for *Newhart.*

CREDITS:

STAGE APPEARANCES

Night of 100 Stars II, Radio City Music Hall, New York City, 1985.

FILM APPEARANCES

Pvt. Driscoll, *Hell Is for Heroes,* Paramount, 1962.

Willard C. Gnatpole, *Hot Millions,* Metro-Goldwyn-Mayer, 1968.

Maj. Major, *Catch-22,* Filmways, 1970.

Dr. Mason Hume, *On A Clear Day You Can See Forever,* Paramount, 1970.

Merwin Wren, *Cold Turkey,* United Artists, 1971.

Voice of Bernard, *The Rescuers* (animated), Walt Disney Productions (Disney), 1977.

President Manfred Link, *First Family,* Warner Bros., 1980.

Regret, *Little Miss Marker,* Universal, 1980.

Voice of Bernard, *The Rescuers Down Under* (animated), Disney, 1990.

TELEVISION APPEARANCES; SERIES

The Bob Newhart Show, NBC, 1961-62.
The Entertainers, CBS, 1964.
Bob Hartley, *The Bob Newhart Show,* CBS, 1972-78.
Dick Loudon, *Newhart,* CBS, 1982-90.

TELEVISION APPEARANCES; SPECIALS

The Perry Como Christmas Show, NBC, 1964.
A Salute to Stan Laurel, CBS, 1965.
The Perry Como Thanksgiving Special, NBC, 1967.
A Funny Thing Happened on the Way to Hollywood, NBC, 1967.
The Jack Paar Special, NBC, 1967.
A Last Laugh at the 60s, ABC, 1970.
Don Rickles: Alive and Kicking, CBS, 1972.
Ed McMahon and Friends . . . Discover Wet at Cypress Gardens, NBC, 1972.
The Rowan and Martin Special, NBC, 1973.
The Don Rickles Show, CBS, 1975.
Perry Como's Springtime Special, CBS, 1975.
Ladies and Gentlemen . . . Bob Newhart, CBS, 1980.
Ladies and Gentlemen . . . Bob Newhart, Part II, CBS, 1980.
Ringmaster, *Circus of the Stars,* CBS, 1981.
Dean Martin's Comedy Classics, NBC, 1981.
Circus of the Stars, CBS, 1982.
Thirty-Ninth Annual Emmy Awards, Fox, 1987.
The Tonight Show Starring Johnny Carson: The 28th Anniversary Special, NBC, 1990.
CBS Comedy Bloopers, CBS, 1990.
Grand Marshall, *Tournament of Roses Parade,* CBS, 1991.

Also appeared on *Thirty-Seventh Annual Emmy Awards,* 1985; *Rickles on the Loose,* 1987; *Jerry Lewis MDA Telethon,* 1990; *The Montreal International Comedy Festival,* 1990; *The Parenthood Game.*

TELEVISION APPEARANCES; MOVIES

Marvin Ellison, *Thursday's Game,* ABC, 1974.
Walter Burton, *Marathon,* CBS, 1980.

Also appeared as God, *Packy,* 1987.

OTHER TELEVISION APPEARANCES

The Colgate Comedy Hour (pilot), NBC, 1967.

Also appeared on *The Hollywood Palace,* ABC; *The Jack Paar Show,* NBC; *The Tonight Show,* NBC; *Don Adams' Screen Test,* syndicated.

RECORDINGS:

Recorded *The Button-Down Mind of Bob Newhart,* 1961; *The Button-Down Mind Strikes Back,* 1962.

SIDELIGHTS: Newhart's first job was as a copywriter for the Fred Niles Film company; he was also a law clerk at the U.S. Gypsum Company.*

*   *   *

NEWMAN, Randy   1943-

PERSONAL: Born November 28, 1943, in Los Angeles, CA; son of Irving and Adele Newman; married Roswitha (a boutique owner), 1967 (separated); children: Amos, Eric, John. *Education:* Received B.A. in music composition from University of California, Los Angeles.

CAREER: Singer, composer, and musician.

AWARDS, HONORS: Grammy Award nominations, for best arrangement, 1969, for "Is That All There Is," and for best film score, 1982, for *Ragtime;* Academy Award nominations, for best score and best song, 1981, for *Ragtime,* and for best score, 1991, for *Avalon.*

CREDITS:

FILM APPEARANCES

Song performer, "Gone Dead Train," *Performance* (also see below), Warner Brothers, 1970.
Singing Bush, *The Three Amigos* (also see below), Orion, 1986.

Also performer of "I'm In Love Again," *Shag,* 1988.

FILM WORK

Music director, *Performance,* Warner Brothers, 1970.

TELEVISION APPEARANCES; SPECIALS, EXCEPT AS NOTED

Host, *Randy Newman at the Odeon,* Showtime, 1983.

Also appeared as song performer, "LA You Belong to Me," *Half-Nelson,* 1985; song performer, "Kingfish," *The Life and Assassination of the Kingfish* (movie), 1977; song performer, "I Love To See You Smile," *Sixty-Second Annual Academy Awards Presentations,* 1990. Also performed for *Funny, You Don't Look 200,* 1987; and *Rolling Stone Magazine's 20 Years of Rock 'n' Roll,* 1987.

RECORDINGS:

Randy Newman, Reprise, 1968.
Twelve Songs, Reprise, 1970.
Randy Newman Live, Reprise, 1972.
Sail Away, Reprise, 1972.
Good Old Boys, Reprise, 1974.
Little Criminals, Reprise, 1977.
Born Again, Reprise, 1979.
Trouble in Paradise, Reprise, 1983.
Land of Dreams, Reprise, 1988.

Composer or arranger for recordings by others, including "Is That All There Is," for Peggy Lee, and "Mama Told me (Not to Come)," for Three Dog Night.

WRITINGS:

STAGE

Songs, *Rosenbloom,* Center Theatre Group, Mark Taper Forum, Los Angeles, CA, 1970.

Music and lyrics, *Randy Newman's Maybe I'm Doing It Wrong,* Production Company Theatre, 1981, then Astor Place Theatre, New York City, 1982.

FILM

Music, *Cold Turkey,* United Artists, 1971.
Music, lyrics, *The Pursuit of Happiness,* Columbia, 1971.
Music, lyrics, *Ragtime,* Paramount, 1981.
Music, *The Natural,* Tri-Star, 1984.
(With Charles Bernstein) Music, lyrics, *April Fool's Day,* Paramount, 1986.
Music, lyrics, and (with Steve Martin and Lorne Michaels) screenplay, *The Three Amigos,* Orion, 1986.
Music, *Parenthood,* Universal, 1989.
Music, *Avalon,* Tri-Star, 1990.

Also author of songs, "I Don't Want to Hear It Anymore," *Love & Money,* 1980; additional music, *Huey Long,* 1985; "Naked Man," *Mr. Love,* 1985; arranger, "Is That All There Is?," *After Hours,* 1985; "Mama Told Me (Not to Come)," *April Fool's Day,* 1986; "You Can Leave Your Hat On," *9 1/2 Weeks,* 1986; "Guilty," *Singing the Blues in Red,* 1986; "I Love LA," *Down and Out in Beverly Hills,* 1986; "It's Money That I Love," *Surrender,* 1987; "Short People," *Harry and the Hendersons,* 1987; *Overboard,* 1987; "I Think It's Going To Rain," *Beaches,* 1988; "I Love LA," *The Naked Gun—From the Files of Police Squad!,* 1988; *Her Alibi,* 1989.

TELEVISION

Music, *Whatever Happened to Dobie Gillis* (pilot), CBS, 1977.

Also wrote song "Fallin' in Love," *The Marshall Chronicles,* 1990.*

*   *   *

NGEMA, Mbongeni   1955-

PERSONAL: Name pronounced "moan-*gay*-nee en-*gay*-ma"; born in 1955 in Verulam, South Africa. *Education:* Attended schools in South Africa.

CAREER: Director, playwright, actor, and musician. Worked for various companies in South Africa as a manual laborer; played guitar for plays in Durban, South Af-

rica; worked at the Stable Theatre with Kessie Govender; founder of Committed Artists (acting troupe), 1983.

AWARDS, HONORS: Obie Award Special Citation (shared with Percy Mtwa and Barney Simon), *Village Voice,* 1983-84, for *Woza Albert!;* Antoinette Perry Award nomination, Best Director of a Play, 1987, for *Asinamali!;* Antoinette Perry Award nominations, Best Director of a Musical and Best Score for a Musical, 1988, both for *Sarafina!;* Drama Desk Award nomination, Best Orchestration, 1991, for *Township Fever.*

CREDITS:

STAGE APPEARANCES

Appeared in *Isigcino* (stage debut), 1976, and in *Mama and the Load.*

STAGE DIRECTOR

Asinamali! (also see below), New Heritage Repertory Theater, New York City, 1986, then Center Theatre Group, Mark Taper Forum, Los Angeles, CA, 1986, staged as part of *Woza Afrika: A Festival of South African Theatre,* Lincoln Center, Mitzi E. Newhouse Theatre, New York City, 1986, then Jack Lawrence Theatre, New York City, 1987.
Sarafina! (also see below), Lincoln Center Theatre, Mitzi E. Newhouse Theatre, 1987, then Cort Theatre, New York City, 1988.
(With Richard Gant) *Sheila's Day,* Crossroads Theatre, New Brunswick, NJ, 1989, then Ford's Theatre, Washington, DC, 1990.

Also director of *The Last Generation.*

RECORDINGS:

Recorded album, *Time to Unite.*

WRITINGS:

PLAYS

(With Percy Mtwa and Barney Simon) *Woza Albert!,* New York City, 1984.
(And composer of musical score) *Asinamali!,* New York City, 1986, staged as part of *Woza Afrika: A Festival of South African Theatre,* New York City, 1986.
(And composer, with Hugh Masekela, of musical score) *Sarafina!,* Lincoln Center, New York City, 1987.

Also author of *The Last Generation,* and *Township Fever,* a musical.

OTHER SOURCES:

BOOKS

Contemporary Literary Criticism, Volume 57, Gale, 1990.

PERIODICALS

Christian Science Monitor, February 28, 1989.*

*　　　*　　　*

NUYTTEN, Bruno   1945-

PERSONAL: Born in 1945, in Paris, France; father a physician, mother a pharmacist; children: (with Isabelle Adjani) Barnabe Nuytten. *Education:* Attended Institut des Hautes Etudes Cinematographiques, Paris, France, and Institut des Arts du Spectacle, Brussels, Belgium.

CAREER: Cinematographer, director, and screenwriter.

AWARDS, HONORS: Prize for artistic contribution, Cannes Film Festival, 1982, for *Invitation au voyage;* Academy Award nomination for best foreign-language film, 1990, for *Camille Claudel;* awards for best cinematography, British Academy of Film and Television Arts, for *Jean de Florette* and *Manon des sources;* Cesar awards, for *Tchao Pantin, The Best Way to Walk,* and *Barocco;* Cesar Award nominations, for *Les Soeurs Bronte, Possession, La Vie est un roman, Fort Saganne, Jean de Florette,* and *Manon des sources.*

CREDITS:

FILM WORK; CINEMATOGRAPHER, EXCEPT AS NOTED

Camera operator, first assistant, *Nathalie Granger,* French Consulate/Moullet et Compagnie, 1972.

Les Valseuses (also known as *The Waltzers* and *Going Places*), Societe Nouvelle Productions/Almi Cinema V/Interama, 1973.

L'Asassin musicien (also known as *The Musician Killer*), Sunchild Productions, 1975.

India Song, Artificial Eye, 1975.

La Meilleure Facon de marcher (also known as *The Best Way to Walk*), AMLF/Oppidan, 1975.

Souvenirs d'en France (also known as *French Provincial* and *Inside Memories of France*), AMLF, 1975.

Barocco, Films la Boetie, 1976.

Le Camion (also known as *The Truck*), Cinema 9/Films Moliere, 1977.

L'Exercice du pouvoir, Camera One, 1977.

Mon Coeur est rouge (also known as *My Heart Is Red*), Films Moliere, 1977.

Les Soeurs Bronte (also known as *The Bronte Sisters*), Gaumont International/Roissy, 1978.

French Postcards, Paramount, 1979.

Zoo-Zero, Panoceanic Films, 1979.

The Best Way, Filmoblic, 1980.

Brubaker, Twentieth Century-Fox, 1980.

La Tortue sur le dos (also known as *Like a Turtle on Its Back*), World Marketing Films/New Line Cinema, 1981.

Garde a vue (also known as *The Inquisitor*), Gala Film Distributors, 1981.

Possession, New Realm Distributors/Limelight International, 1981.

Hotel des Ameriques (also known as *Hotel of the Americans*), Parafrance, 1982.

Tchao Pantin (also known as *So Long, Stooge*), Roissy/AMLF/European Classics, 1983.

La Vie est un roman (also known as *Life Is a Bed of Roses*), Spectrafilm, 1983.

Les Enfants (also known as *The Children*), Productions Berthemont, 1984.

Fort Saganne, Roissy/AAA, 1984.

La Pirate (also known as *The Pirate*), AMLF/Films du Scorpion, 1984.

Detective, Spectrafilm/Union Generale Cinematographique, 1985.

Jean de Florette, AMLF/Orion Classics, 1986.

Manon des sources (also known as *Manon of the Spring*), Orion Classics/Cannon Releasing/AMLF/Roissy, 1986.

Double Messieurs (also known as *Double Gentlemen*), Mallia Films/Saltzgeber/Mutual Reception, 1986 (also see below).

Director, *Camille Claudel,* Pathe Releasing/Gaumont/Orion Classics/Roissy, 1988 (also see below).

Also cinematographer for *Invitation au voyage,* c. 1982.

WRITINGS:

SCREENPLAYS

(With Jean-Francois Stevenin and Jackie Berroyer) *Double Messieurs* (also known as *Double Gentlemen*), Mallia Films/Saltzgeber/Mutual Reception, 1986.

(With Marilyn Goldin) *Camille Claudel,* Pathe Releasing/Gaumont/Orion Classics/Roissy, 1988.*

O

O'CONNOR, Carroll 1924-

PERSONAL: Born August 2, 1924, in New York, NY; married; wife's name, Nancy; children: Hugh. *Education:* National University at Dublin, B.A., 1952; University of Montana, M.A., English and speech, 1956.

CAREER: Actor, producer, director, and writer.

AWARDS, HONORS: Golden Globe Award, best television actor in a musical/comedy series, 1972, for *All in the Family;* Emmy Awards, outstanding lead actor in a comedy series, 1971, 1976, 1977, and 1978, all for *All in the Family;* George Foster Peabody Broadcasting Award, 1980, for *Edith's Death* (an episode of *Archie Bunker's Place*); Emmy Award, outstanding lead actor in a drama series, 1989, for *In the Heat of the Night;* NAACP Image Award, and Golden Globe nomination, best actor in a drama series, both 1990, for *In the Heat of the Night.*

CREDITS:

STAGE APPEARANCES

(Broadway debut) Jim, *Brothers,* Music Box Theatre, New York City, 1983.
Bob, *Home Front,* Royale Theatre, New York City, 1985.

Also appeared in productions for Dublin's Gate Theatre, 1949-52. Appeared in *Ulysses in Nighttown* (Off-Broadway debut), 1957; *The Big Knife.*

FILM APPEARANCES

Mr. Harper, *Johnny Frenchman,* Universal, 1946.
Bernie Breck, *By Love Possessed,* United Artists (UA), 1961.
Matt Keenan, *A Fever in the Blood,* Warner Bothers (Warner Bros.), 1961.
Fire Chief, *Parrish,* Warner Bros., 1961.
Hamilcar Q. Glure, *Lad: A Dog,* Warner Bros., 1962.

Hinton, *Lonely Are the Brave,* Universal, 1962.
Casca, *Cleopatra,* Twentieth Century-Fox, 1963.
Lt. Comdr. Burke, *In Harm's Way,* Paramount, 1965.
Charles Bromley, *Hawaii,* UA, 1966.
Gen. Parker, *Not with My Wife, You Don't!,* Warner Bros., 1966.
Gen. Bolt, *What Did You Do in the War, Daddy?,* UA, 1966.
Brewster, *Point Blank,* Metro-Goldwyn-Mayer (MGM), 1967.
Paul Jerez, *Warning Shot,* Paramount, 1967.
Sheriff John Copperud, *Waterhole No. Three,* Paramount, 1967.
Maj. Gen. Hunter, *The Devil's Brigade,* UA, 1968.
Frank Austin, *For Love of Ivy,* Cinerama, 1968.
Lester Locke, *Death of a Gunfighter,* Universal, 1969.
Lt. Christy French, *Marlowe,* MGM, 1969.
Ride a Northbound Horse, Walt Disney Productions, 1969.
Gen. Colt, *Kelly's Heroes,* MGM, 1970.
Joe Gray, *Doctor's Wives,* Columbia, 1971.
Willie, *Law and Disorder,* Columbia, 1974.

Also appeared in *Belle Sommers,* 1962.

TELEVISION APPEARANCES; SERIES

Alcoa Premiere, ABC, 1962.
The Dick Powell Show, NBC, 1962.
Great Adventure, CBS, 1963.
The DuPont Show of the Week, NBC, 1964.
Archie Bunker, *All in the Family,* CBS, 1971-79.
Archie Bunker, *Archie Bunker's Place,* CBS, 1979-83.
Chief Bill Gillespie, *In the Heat of the Night,* NBC, 1988—.

Also appeared in *The Outer Limits,* ABC; *Profiles in Courage,* NBC; *People,* CBS; *Voyage to the Bottom of the Sea,* ABC.

TELEVISION APPEARANCES; SPECIALS

Major Hoople/Daddy Warbucks/Joe, *Funny Papers*, CBS, 1972.
Don Rickles: Alive and Kicking, CBS, 1972.
Jon P. Wintergreen, *Of Thee I Sing*, CBS, 1972.
Keep U.S. Beautiful, CBS, 1973.
Show Business Salute to Milton Berle, NBC, 1973.
Husband, *Three for the Girls*, CBS, 1973.
Frank Skeffington, *The Last Hurrah*, NBC, 1977.
CBS: On the Air, CBS, 1978.
The American Comedy Awards, ABC, 1987.
The Television Hall of Fame, Fox, 1990.
All in the Family 20th Anniversary Special, CBS, 1991.

Also appeared in *Acting: Lee Strasberg and the Actor's Studio*, 1981.

TELEVISION APPEARANCES; MOVIES

Myles Donovan, *Fear No Evil*, NBC, 1969.
Frank Nolan, *Brass*, CBS, 1985.
Lewis May, *Convicted*, ABC, 1986.
Cardinal Cody, *The Father Clements Story*, NBC, 1987.

TELEVISION APPEARANCES; PILOTS

Dr. Lyman Savage, *Luxury Liner*, NBC, 1963.
A Walk in the Night, CBS, 1971.
Tom Snyder's Celebrity Spotlight, NBC, 1980.

TELEVISION WORK; EXECUTIVE PRODUCER, EXCEPT WHERE INDICATED

(And creator) *Bronk*, CBS, 1975-76.
The Banana Company, CBS, 1977.
Bender, CBS, 1979.
(And director) *Gloria Comes Home* (pilot for *Gloria*), CBS, 1982.
Director, *The Red Foxx Show*, ABC, 1986.
In the Heat of the Night, NBC, 1989—.

WRITINGS:

STAGE

Author of *The Ladies of Hanover Tower* (three-act play).

TELEVISION SERIES

Closing theme, *All in the Family* ("Remembering You"), CBS, 1971.
The Red Foxx Show, ABC, 1986.
In the Heat of the Night, NBC, 1988-89.*

*   *   *

OLDMAN, Gary 1958-

PERSONAL: Born March 21, 1958, in London, England; father, a welder; mother, a homemaker. *Education:* Rose Buford College of Speech and Drama, B.A., theatre arts, 1979; trained for the stage at Greenwich Young People's Theatre.

ADDRESSES: Agent—Martha Luttrell and Tracey Jacobs, International Creative Management, 8899 Beverly Blvd., Los Angeles, CA 90048; and Duncan Heath Associates, Paramount House, 162/170 Wardour St., London W1V 3AT, England.

CAREER: Actor. Member of Theatre Royal, York, England.

AWARDS, HONORS: Drama Magazine Award, Best Actor, British Theatre Association, 1985, and Fringe Award, Best Newcomer, *Time Out* Magazine, 1985-86, both for *The Pope's Wedding;* British Academy of Film and Television Arts Award nomination, Best Actor, 1988, for *Prick up Your Ears.*

CREDITS:

FILM APPEARANCES

Sid Vicious, *Sid and Nancy*, Samuel Goldwyn, 1986.
Joe Orton, *Prick up Your Ears*, Samuel Goldwyn, 1987.
Martin, *Track 29*, Island, 1988.
Johnny, *We Think the World of You*, Cinecom, 1988.
Ben Chase, *Criminal Law*, Tri-Star, 1988.
Emmett Foley, *Chattahoochee*, Hemdale, 1990.
State of Grace, Orion, 1990.
Rosencrantz, *Rosencrantz and Guildenstern Are Dead*, Cinecom, 1991.

Also appeared in *Before and After Death* and *Exile*.

STAGE APPEARANCES

Massacre at Paris, Glasgow Citizens Theatre, Glasgow, Scotland, 1980.
Chinchilla, Glasgow Citizens Theatre, 1980.
Desperado Corner, Glasgow Citizens Theatre, 1980.
A Waste of Time, Glasgow Citizens Theatre, 1980.
Soldier, *Summit Conference*, Lupton Theatre Company, Lyric Theatre, London, 1982.
P. C. Naylor, *Rat in the Skull*, Royal Court Theatre, London, 1984.
Scopey, *The Pope's Wedding*, Royal Court Theatre, 1984.
Son, "Red, Black, and Ignorant," third man, "Tin Can People," and son and man, "Great Peace," *The War Plays*, Royal Shakespeare Company (RSC), the Pit, London, 1985.
Major Carp and Petko, *The Desert Air*, RSC, the Pit, 1985.
Sordido, *Women Beware Women*, Royal Court Theatre, 1986.
Jack, *Real Dreams*, RSC, 1986.
Jake Todd and Billy Corman, *Serious Money*, Royal Court Theatre, 1987.

Also appeared in *Minnesota Moon,* and as Len in *Saved,* both London.

MAJOR TOURS

Appeared in *Massacre at Paris, Chinchilla, Desperado Corner,* and *A Waste of Time,* all with the Glasgow Citizens Theatre, European and South American cities.

TELEVISION APPEARANCES; MOVIES

Daniel, *Remembrance,* Channel 4, released in the United States by Mainline, 1982.
Coxy, *Meantime,* Channel 4, 1983, released in the United States by Film 4, 1984.
Derek, *Honest, Decent, and True,* BBC, released in the United States in 1985.

Also appeared in *Morgan's Boy,* and as P. C. Naylor in *Rat in the Skull.*

OTHER SOURCES:

PERIODICALS

American Film, April, 1988.*

*　　　*　　　*

OLIN, Ken   1954-

PERSONAL: Born July 30, 1954, in Chicago, IL; father, a deputy director of the Peace Corps; married Patricia Wettig (an actress), 1982; children: Clifford, Roxanne. *Education:* Received B.A. in English literature from the University of Pennsylvania; studied acting with Warren Robertson and Stella Adler. *Avocational interests:* Basketball, baseball, distance running, and weightlifting.

ADDRESSES: Agent—Bob Gersh, The Gersh Agency, 232 N. Canon Drive, Beverly Hills, CA 90210.

CAREER: Actor and director.

CREDITS:

TELEVISION APPEARANCES; SERIES

Rocky Padillo, *The Bay City Blues,* NBC, 1983.
Detective Harry Garibaldi, *Hill Street Blues,* NBC, 1984-85.

Father Christopher, *Falcon Crest,* CBS, 1985-86.
Michael Steadman, *thirtysomething,* ABC, 1987-91.

TELEVISION APPEARANCES; EPISODIC

Perry Revere, *Murder, She Wrote,* CBS, 1986.
Mark Fredericks, *Hotel,* ABC, 1987.

Also appeared in *The Hitchhiker.*

TELEVISION APPEARANCES; MOVIES

Board member, *Women at West Point,* CBS, 1979.
David Frank, *Flight 90: Disaster on the Potomac,* NBC, 1984.
Jay Savage, *There Must Be a Pony,* ABC, 1986.
Henry Fox, *Tonight's the Night,* ABC, 1987.
Nathan Lammerman, *I'll Take Manhattan* (mini-series), CBS, 1987.
Curtis "Manny" Mandell, *Cop Killer,* ABC, 1988.
Jim Sandler, *A Stoning in Fulham County,* NBC, 1988.

TELEVISION APPEARANCES; SPECIALS

Battle of the Network Stars XVIII, ABC, 1985.
Narrator, *More Than Broken Glass: Memories of Kristallnacht,* PBS, 1988.
The 15th Annual People's Choice Awards, CBS, 1989.

TELEVISION WORK; EPISODIC

Director, *thirtysomething,* ABC, 1989-90.

STAGE APPEARANCES

(Off-Broadway debut) Al Corley, *Taxi Tales,* Century Theatre, 1978.
Streamers, Theatre-by-the-Sea, Portsmouth, NH, 1979.
Major Barbara, Alaska Repertory Theatre, Anchorage/Fairbanks, AK, 1982.
Stanley Kowalski, *A Streetcar Named Desire,* Theatre-by-the-Sea, 1982.

Also appeared in *Lorenzaccio,* New York City.

FILM APPEARANCES

Young James, *Ghost Story,* Universal, 1981.
Ray, *Queen's Logic,* New Visions, 1991.*

P-Q

PALTROW, Bruce 1943-

PERSONAL: Born November 26, 1943, in New York, NY; married Blythe Danner (an actress); children: Gwyneth, Jake. Education: B.F.A., Tulane University.

ADDRESSES: Contact—304 21st St., Santa Monica, CA 90402.

CAREER: Producer, director, and writer. Affiliated with Paltrow Group NYLA. Creator of television series The White Shadow, Tattinger's, and Nick and Hillary.

CREDITS:

TELEVISION WORK; MOVIES

Producer, Shirts/Skins, ABC, 1973.

TELEVISION WORK; SERIES

Producer, Big City Boys, 1978.
Executive producer, The White Shadow, CBS, 1978-81.
Executive producer, St. Elsewhere, NBC, 1982-88.
Executive producer, Tattinger's, NBC, 1988.
Executive producer, Nick and Hillary, NBC, 1989.

Also director of various episodes of The White Shadow, CBS, and St. Elsewhere, NBC.

TELEVISION WORK; PILOTS

Director, You're Gonna Love It Here, CBS, 1977.
Producer, Big City Boys, CBS, 1978.
Director, Operating Room, NBC, 1979.
Director, Tattinger's, NBC, 1988.

FILM WORK

Producer, director, A Little Sex, Universal, 1982.

STAGE WORK

Producer, Someone's Coming Hungry, Pocket Theatre, New York City, 1969.

WRITINGS:

Shirts/Skins (television movie), ABC, 1973.

Also writer of television episodes for You're Gonna Love It Here, Operating Room, St. Elsewhere, and Tattinger's.*

*   *   *

PAN, Hermes 1910(?)-1990

PERSONAL: Born December 10, 1910 (some sources say 1905, 1911, or 1913), in Memphis, TN; died in September, 1990, in Beverly Hills, CA; son of Pantelis and Mary (Huston) Panagiotopulos. Education: Studied at Miss Georgia Brown's Private School, Nashville, TN. Religion: Roman Catholic.

CAREER: Dancer and choreographer. Dancer in Broadway musicals, 1927-30.

AWARDS, HONORS: Academy Award nomination, best dance direction, 1935, for "Piccolino" and "Top Hat" numbers from Top Hat, and 1936, for "Bo Jangles" number from Swing Time; Academy Award, best dance direction, 1937, for "Fun House" number from Damsel in Distress; Emmy Award, best choreography, 1958, for An Evening with Fred Astaire; National Film Award for achievement in cinema, 1980; Joffrey Ballet Award, 1986.

CREDITS:

FILM APPEARANCES

Specialty dancer, My Gal Sal, Twentieth Century-Fox, 1942.

Specialty number, *Pin Up Girl,* Twentieth Century-Fox, 1944.

Lily's dance partner, *A Life of Her Own,* Metro-Goldwyn-Mayer (MGM), 1950.

Specialty sailor dance, *Kiss Me Kate,* MGM, 1953.

(Role of) choreographer, *Pal Joey,* Columbia, 1957.

Also appeared in *George Stevens: A Filmmaker's Journey,* 1985.

FILM CHOREOGRAPHER

(With Fred Astaire and Dave Gould) *The Gay Divorcee,* RKO Radio Pictures, 1934.

I Dream Too Much, RKO Radio Pictures, 1935.

In Person, RKO Radio Pictures, 1935.

Old Man Rhythm, RKO Radio Pictures, 1935.

(With Astaire) *Roberta,* RKO Radio Pictures, 1935.

(With Astaire) *Top Hat,* RKO Radio Pictures, 1935.

(With Astaire) *Follow the Fleet,* RKO Radio Pictures, 1936.

Swing Time, RKO Radio Pictures, 1936.

A Woman Rebels, RKO Radio Pictures, 1936.

(With Astaire) *A Damsel in Distress,* RKO Radio Pictures, 1937.

(With Harry Losee) *Shall We Dance,* RKO Radio Pictures, 1937.

(With Astaire) *Carefree,* RKO Radio Pictures, 1938.

Radio City Revels, RKO Radio Pictures, 1938.

The Story of Vernon and Irene Castle, RKO Radio Pictures, 1939.

Second Chorus, Paramount, 1940.

Blood and Sand, Twentieth Century-Fox, 1941.

Moon Over Miami, Twentieth Century-Fox, 1941.

Rise and Shine, Twentieth Century-Fox, 1941.

Sun Valley Serenade, Twentieth Century-Fox, 1941.

That Night in Rio, Twentieth Century-Fox, 1941.

Weekend in Havana, Twentieth Century-Fox, 1941.

Footlight Serenade, Twentieth Century-Fox, 1942.

(With Val Raset) *My Gal Sal,* Twentieth Century-Fox, 1942.

Roxie Hart, Twentieth Century-Fox, 1942.

Song of the Islands, Twentieth Century-Fox, 1942.

Springtime in the Rockies, Twentieth Century-Fox, 1942.

Coney Island, Twentieth Century-Fox, 1943.

(With Raset) *Hello, Frisco, Hello,* Twentieth Century-Fox, 1943.

Sweet Rosie O'Grady, Twentieth Century-Fox, 1943.

Irish Eyes Are Smiling, Twentieth Century-Fox, 1944.

Pin Up Girl, Twentieth Century-Fox, 1944.

Diamond Horseshoe (also known as *Billy Rose's Diamond Horseshoe*), Twentieth Century-Fox, 1945.

Blue Skies, Paramount, 1946.

I Wonder Who's Kissing Her Now, Twentieth Century-Fox, 1947.

The Shocking Miss Pilgrim, Twentieth Century-Fox, 1947.

That Lady in Ermine, Twentieth Century-Fox, 1948.

The Barkleys of Broadway, Metro-Goldwyn-Mayer (MGM), 1949.

Let's Dance, Paramount, 1950.

Three Little Words, MGM, 1950.

Excuse My Dust, MGM, 1951.

Texas Carnival, MGM, 1951.

Lovely to Look At, MGM, 1952.

Kiss Me Kate, MGM, 1953.

(With Jose Greco) *Sombrero,* MGM, 1953.

The Student Prince, MGM, 1954.

Hit the Deck, Metro, 1955.

Jupiter's Darling, MGM, 1955.

(With Eugene Loring) *Meet Me in Las Vegas,* MGM, 1956.

Pal Joey, Columbia, 1957.

(With Loring) *Silk Stockings,* MGM, 1957.

The Blue Angel, Twentieth Century-Fox, 1959.

Never Steal Anything Small, Universal, 1959.

Porgy and Bess, Columbia, 1959.

Can-Can, Twentieth Century-Fox, 1960.

Flower Drum Song, Universal, 1961.

(With Astaire) *The Pleasure of His Company,* Paramount, 1961.

Cleopatra, Twentieth Century-Fox, 1963.

My Fair Lady, Warner Brothers, 1964.

The Pink Panther, United Artists, 1964.

The Great Race, Warner Brothers, 1965.

Finian's Rainbow, Seven Arts, 1968.

Darling Lili, Paramount, 1970.

Lost Horizon, Columbia, 1973.

Also choreographed *Aiutami a sognare.*

TELEVISION APPEARANCES; SPECIALS

The Television Academy Hall of Fame (also known as *The Sixth Annual Television Academy Hall of Fame*), Fox Broadcasting Company, 1990.

You're the Top: The Cole Porter Story (also known as *American Masters*), PBS, 1990.

The Fred Astaire Songbook (also known as *Great Performances*), PBS, 1991.

Rita Hayworth: Dancing into the Dream (also known as *Crazy about the Movies*), Cinemax, 1991.

TELEVISION CHOREOGRAPHER

An Evening with Fred Astaire, NBC, 1958.

OBITUARIES AND OTHER SOURCES:

PERIODICALS

Time, October 1, 1990.*

PASDAR, Adrian

PERSONAL: Born in Pittsfield, MA; son of a physician. *Education:* Attended University of Central Florida; studied with People's Light and Theatre Co. and the Lee Strasberg Theatre Institute.

ADDRESSES: Agent—Judy Hofflund, International Talent Agency, 6253 Hollywood Blvd., No. 230, Hollywood, CA 90028. *Publicist*—Michelle Marx, 9044 Melrose Ave., Los Angeles, CA 90069.

CAREER: Actor.

CREDITS:

FILM APPEARANCES

(Film debut) Chipper, *Top Gun,* Paramount, 1986.
Darstar, *Solarbabies,* Metro-Goldwyn-Mayer/United Artists, 1986.
Timmy Boyle, *Streets of Gold,* Twentieth Century-Fox, 1986.
Caleb, *Near Dark,* DEG, 1987.
Dar, *Made in U.S.A.,* DEG, 1988.
Vito, *Cookie,* Warner Brothers, 1989.
Michael Chatham, *Vital Signs,* Twentieth Century-Fox, 1990.
Ben Arnon, *Torn Apart* (also known as *Forbidden Love*), Cori, 1990.

TELEVISION APPEARANCES; EPISODIC

Paul, "Big Time", *American Playhouse,* PBS, 1989.

TELEVISION APPEARANCES; MOVIES

Jimmy Capone/Richard Hart, *The Lost Capone,* TNT, 1990.

STAGE APPEARANCES

Appeared in *The Glass Menagerie, Shadow Box, Hotters, Barefoot in the Park, Sorry, Wrong Number, Cold Foot,* and *Monkey's Paw* at various regional theaters.*

*   *   *

PATAKI, Michael   1938-
(Mike Pataki)

PERSONAL: Born January 16, 1938, in Youngstown, OH.

CAREER: Actor and director.

CREDITS:

FILM APPEARANCES

10 North Frederick, Twentieth Century-Fox, 1958.
Private Hagstrom, *The Young Lions,* Twentieth Century-Fox, 1958.

Mimes, *Easy Rider,* Columbia, 1969.
J. C., *Five the Hard Way* (also known as *The Sidehackers*), Crown International, 1969.
(As Mike Pataki) Joe, *The Return of Count Yorga,* American International Pictures, 1971.
Snake, *The Dirt Gang,* American International Pictures, 1972.
Grave of the Vampire (also known as *Seed of Terror*), Entertainment Pyramid, 1972.
State Senator Sills, *Sweet Jesus, Preacher Man,* Metro-Goldwyn-Mayer (MGM), 1973.
Sergeant, *The Bat People* (also known as *It Lives by Night*), American International Pictures, 1974.
The Last Porno Flick (also known as *The Mad, Mad Moviemakers*), Bryanston, 1974.
Wilson, *Airport 77,* Universal, 1977.
Michael Drake, *Dracula's Dog* (also known as *Zoltan, Hound of Dracula*), Crown International, 1978.
District Attorney Dino Fulgoni, *The Onion Field,* Avco Embassy, 1979.
The Last Word (also known as *Danny Travis*), International, 1979.
Mobster, *Love at First Bite,* American International Pictures, 1979.
Munk, *Raise the Titanic,* Associated Film Distribution, 1980.
Harry Iverson, *The Glove* (also known as *Blood Mad*), Pro International, 1980.
Sam, *Dead and Buried,* Avco Embassy, 1981.
Principal, *Graduation Day,* Scope 111, 1981.
George Martin, *Sweet Sixteen,* Century International, 1983.
Jim Wilson, *Remo Williams: The Adventure Begins,* Orion, 1985.
Nicoli Koloff, *Rocky IV,* MGM/United Artists, 1985.
Coach Soranhoff, *American Anthem,* Columbia, 1986.
Murphy, *The Underachievers,* Lightning, 1987.
Dr. Hoffman, *Halloween 4: The Return of Michael Myers,* Galaxy, 1990.

Also appeared as Paul, *Last Foxtrot in Burbank,* 1973; as Detective Barbera, *Spider-Man,* 1977, and *Spider-Man Strikes Back,* 1978; as Rex, *R.S.V.P.,* 1984; and as Professor Drewton, *Hollywood Hot Tubs 2: Educating Crystal,* 1990. Appeared in *Brute Corps,* 1972, *Carnal Madness,* 1975, and *Delinquent Schoolgirls,* 1975.

FILM WORK

Director, *Mansion of the Doomed* (also known as *The Terror of Dr. Chancey*), Group I, 1976.

Also director of *The Other Cinderella,* 1976.

TELEVISION APPEARANCES; SERIES

Charlie Dreyfuss, *Paul Sand in Friends and Lovers*, CBS, 1974.

Sgt. Pete Gallagher, *Get Christie Love!*, ABC, 1974.

Police Captain Barbera, *The Amazing Spider-Man*, CBS, 1978.

Vladimir Gimenko, *Phyl and Mikhy*, CBS, 1980.

TELEVISION APPEARANCES; MINI-SERIES

General Eshnev, *Harold Robbins' "The Pirate"*, CBS, 1978.

TELEVISION APPEARANCES; PILOTS

Pete Cardiff, *They Call It Murder*, NBC, 1971.

Sergeant Ross, *Benny and Barney: Las Vegas Undercover*, NBC, 1977.

Kelso, *The Chopped Liver Brothers*, ABC, 1977.

Captain Barbera, *Spider-Man*, CBS, 1977.

Peter Lacey, *Samurai*, ABC, 1979.

Detective Rizzo, *The Eyes of Texas*, NBC, 1980.

Sergeant Michael Bruno, *Wendy Hooper—U.S. Army*, NBC, 1981.

Cab driver, *Terror at Alcatraz*, NBC, 1982.

TELEVISION APPEARANCES; EPISODIC

All in the Family, CBS, 1973 and 1977.

Barney Miller, ABC, 1978.

Also appeared as Pedro, *The Flying Nun*, ABC.

TELEVISION APPEARANCES; MOVIES

Indict and Convict, ABC, 1974.

Stranger, *The Call of the Wild*, NBC, 1976.

Robert Najarian, *When Every Day Was the Fourth of July*, NBC, 1978.

Ike Pappas, *Ruby and Oswald* (also known as *Four Days in Dallas*), CBS, 1978.

Tony, *Superdome* (also known as *Two Minute Warning*), ABC, 1978.

Arnold Denker, *Survival of Dana*, CBS, 1979.

Tate, *Disaster on the Coastliner*, ABC, 1979.

Squeek Squalis, *Marciano*, ABC, 1979.

Darold, *High Noon, Part II: The Return of Will Kane*, CBS, 1980.

Sheriff Grover, *Cowboy*, CBS, 1983.

Valery, *The Cowboy and the Ballerina*, CBS, 1984.

TELEVISION WORK

Director, *The Nancy Drew Mysteries* (episodes), ABC, 1977-78.

STAGE APPEARANCES

Suphkin, *The Jumping Fool*, Fortune Theatre, New York City, 1970.

Ten Com. Zip Com. Zip, Center Theatre Group, New Theatre for Now, 1971-72.*

*   *   *

PATAKI, Mike
 See PATAKI, Michael

*   *   *

PECK, Bob   1945-

PERSONAL: Full name Robert Peck; born August 23, 1945, in Leeds, England; son of Ernest Lambert and Millicent (McBain) Peck; married Gillian Mary Baker (an actress), September 11, 1982; children: Hannah Louise, George Edward. *Education:* Received diploma in Art and Design, Leeds College of Art, 1967.

ADDRESSES: Agent—Markham & Froggatt Ltd., 4 Windmill St., London W1, England.

CAREER: Actor. Member of repertory theatres in Birmingham, Scarborough, and Exeter, England, 1969-74; member of Royal Shakespeare Company, 1975-84, and National Theatre Company, 1985.

AWARDS, HONORS: British Academy of Film and Television Arts Award for Best Television Actor, 1985, for *Edge of Darkness*.

CREDITS:

STAGE APPEARANCES

(London debut) Abercrombie, *Life Class*, Royal Court Theatre, London, 1974.

Lord Mowbray, *Henry IV, Parts One and Two*, Royal Shakespeare Company (RSC), Royal Shakespeare Theatre, Stratford-on-Avon, England, 1975, then Aldwych Theatre, London, 1976.

Earl of Kent, *King Lear*, RSC, Royal Shakespeare Theatre, 1976.

Camillo, *The Winter's Tale*, RSC, Royal Shakespeare Theatre, 1976.

Uria Shelley, *Man Is Man*, RSC, Round House Theatre Downstairs, London, 1976.

Richard Cleaver, *Destiny*, RSC, The Other Place, Stratford-on-Avon, 1976, then Aldwych Theatre, 1977.

Himmler, SS man, guard, and soldier, *Schweyk in the Second World War*, RSC, The Other Place, 1976, then The Warehouse, London, 1977.

Borachio, *Much Ado About Nothing*, RSC, Royal Shakespeare Theatre, 1976, Aldwych Theatre, 1977.

Macduff, *Macbeth*, RSC, The Other Place, 1976, then The Warehouse, 1977, later Young Vic Theatre, London, 1978.

Wilcox and Purvis, *Bandits,* RSC, The Warehouse, 1977.

Ferryman, *The Bundle,* RSC, The Warehouse, 1977.

Papa, *The Days of the Commune,* RSC, Aldwych Theatre, 1977.

Sir Wilful Witwoud, *The Way of the World,* RSC, Aldwych Theatre, 1978.

George Page, *The Merry Wives of Windsor,* RSC, Royal Shakespeare Theatre, 1979.

Cloten, *Cymbeline,* RSC, Royal Shakespeare Theatre, 1979.

Iago, *Othello,* RSC, Royal Shakespeare Theatre, 1979.

Vassily Vassilich Soliony, *The Three Sisters,* The Other Place, 1979.

C. S. M. Rivers, *The Accrington Pals,* RSC, The Warehouse, 1981.

(Broadway debut) Sir Mulberry Hawke and John Browdie, *The Life and Adventures of Nicholas Nickleby,* RSC, Plymouth Theatre, New York City, 1981.

Domitrius Enobarbus, *Antony and Cleopatra,* RSC, The Pit, London, 1983.

Title role, *Lear,* RSC, The Pit, 1983.

Title role, *Macbeth,* RSC, Barbican Theatre, London, 1983.

Caliban, *The Tempest,* RSC, Barbican Theatre, 1983.

Pavel Lermontov, *Maydays,* RSC, Barbican Theatre, 1983.

Guy Jones, *A Chorus of Disapproval,* Olivier Theatre, London, 1985.

The Road to Mecca, Lyttelton Theatre London, then Cottesloe Theatre, London, 1985.

Also appeared in productions of plays by Arthur Miller, Young Vic Theatre, 1989-90.

MAJOR TOURS

The Three Sisters, RSC, British cities, 1978.

Twelfth Night, RSC, British cities, 1978.

Title role, *Lear,* RSC, European cities, 1984.

FILM APPEARANCES

Rohl, *Parker,* Virgin, 1985.

Amos Jones, *On the Black Hill,* British Film Institute, 1987.

John Graham, *The Kitchen Toto,* Cannon, 1987.

Byron, *Slipstream,* Entertainment Film, 1989.

Detective Inspector Atherton, *Ladder of Swords,* Film Four, 1989.

Also appeared in "Art and Socialism" segment, *Against the Grain,* 1983.

TELEVISION APPEARANCES

Sunset Across the Bay, BBC, 1974.

Sir Mulberry Hawke and John Browdie, *Nicholas Nickleby* (special), syndicated, 1983.

Ronald Craven, *Edge of Darkness* (series), BBC, 1985.

James Westgate, *After Pilkington* (movie), BBC, 1987.

One Way Out, BBC, 1989.

Centre Point, Channel 4 TV, 1990.

"Children Crossing," *Screen Two* (episode), BBC, 1990.

RADIO APPEARANCES; EPISODIC

The Fuhrer's envoy, "1953," *The Friday Play,* BBC Radio-3, 1990.

*   *   *

PEERCE, Larry   1935(?)-

PERSONAL: Born c. 1935 in Bronx, NY; son of Jan Peerce (a singer).

ADDRESSES: Agent—Geoff Brandt, Geoff Brandt Co., 12700 Ventura Blvd., Studio City, CA 91604.

CAREER: Director.

CREDITS:

FILM DIRECTOR

One Potato, Two Potato, Cinema V, 1964.

The Incident, Twentieth Century-Fox, 1967.

Goodbye, Columbus, Paramount, 1969.

The Sporting Club, Avco Embassy, 1971.

A Separate Peace, Paramount, 1972.

Ash Wednesday, Paramount, 1973.

The Other Side of the Mountain, Universal, 1974.

Two-Minute Warning, Universal, 1976.

The Other Side of the Mountain Part 2, Universal, 1977.

(And executive producer) *The Bell Jar,* Avco Embassy, 1979.

Why Would I Lie?, Metro-Goldwyn-Mayer/United Artists, 1980.

Love Child, Warner Brothers, 1982.

Hard To Hold, Universal, 1983.

Wired, Taurus, 1989.

Also directed *The Big T.N.T. Show,* 1966.

TELEVISION DIRECTOR; MOVIES

The Stranger Who Looks Like Me, ABC, 1974.

I Take These Men, CBS, 1983.

Love Lives On, ABC, 1985.

The Fifth Missile, NBC, 1986.

Prison for Children (also known as *Find a Safe Place* and *A Prison of Children*), CBS, 1987.

Queenie, ABC, 1987.

Elvis and Me, ABC, 1988.

The Neon Empire, Showtime, 1988.

The Court-Martial of Jackie Robinson, TNT, 1990.

Menu For Murder (also known as *Murder at the PTA Luncheon*), CBS 1990.*

PERRIN, Vic
　See PERRIN, Victor

*　　*　　*

PERRIN, Victor　1916-1989
　(Vic Perrin)

PERSONAL: Born in 1916 in Menomonee Falls, WI; died of cancer, July 4, 1989; second wife's name, Rita; children: George; (stepson) Steven. *Education:* Received degree from University of Wisconsin, 1940; studied Shakespeare with Charles Laughton.

CAREER: Actor. Radio announcer for NBC and the Blue Network. Spokesman for several companies, including Porsche and World Vision, and official voice of "The Spaceship Earth" at the Exxon pavilion at Walt Disney World's Epcot Center.

CREDITS:

FILM APPEARANCES

Andrew, *Outrage,* RKO Radio Pictures, 1950.
Elevator operator, *Don't Bother to Knock,* Twentieth Century-Fox, 1952.
Little Harry, *The System,* Warner Brothers, 1953.
(As Vic Perrin) Scenic designer, *Forever Female,* Paramount, 1953.
Bar-M Rider, *Riding Shotgun,* Warner Brothers, 1953.
Adolph Alexander, *Dragnet,* Warner Brothers, 1954.
Dr. Hart, *Black Tuesday,* United Artists, 1955.
The Bubble (also known as *The Fantastic Invasion of Planet Earth*), Arch Oboler 3-D, 1967.
(As Vic Perrin) Hector, *The Klansman,* Paramount, 1974.
(As Vic Perrin) Finch, *Black Oak Conspiracy,* New World, 1977.

TELEVISION APPEARANCES; SERIES; AS VIC PERRIN

Control voice, *The Outer Limits* (also see below), ABC, 1963-65.
The New Adventures of Huckleberry Finn, NBC, 1968-69.
Voice of Sinestro, *The World's Greatest Super Heroes,* ABC, 1978-80.
Voice of Vultan, *Flash Gordon—The Greatest Adventure of All,* NBC, 1983.

Also appeared as voice of Dr. Zin in *Jonny Quest,* and *The New Adventures of Jonny Quest,* 1987.

TELEVISION APPEARANCES; EPISODIC; AS VIC PERRIN

The Adventures of Superman, ABC, 1953.
Martian No. 2, "People Are Alike All Over," *The Twilight Zone,* CBS, 1960.
State trooper, "Ring-A-Ding Girl," *The Twilight Zone,* CBS, 1963.

Intercom voice, "The Human Factor," *Outer Limits,* ABC, 1963.
Voice of Mr. Schumacher, "The Hundred Days of The Dragon," *Outer Limits,* ABC, 1963.
Voice of Zanti prisoner, "The Zanti Misfits," *Outer Limits,* ABC, 1963.
Scanner unit voice, "Moonstone," *Outer Limits,* ABC, 1964.
Sharpies voice, "Fun and Games," *Outer Limits,* ABC, 1964.
Helmet voice, "Soldier," *Outer Limits,* ABC, 1964.
Tharn, "Mirror, Mirror," *Star Trek,* NBC, c. 1966-69.
Voice of Metron, "Arena," *Star Trek,* NBC, c. 1966-69.
Voice of Nomad, "The Changeling," *Star Trek,* NBC, c. 1966-69.
Land of the Giants, ABC, 1969.
Inch High, Private Eye, NBC, 1973.
Jabberjaw, ABC, 1976.

Also appeared in *Dragnet,* ABC; *Frontier,* NBC; *Daniel Boone,* 1981; *Rocky Jones, Space Ranger,* and *Gunsmoke.*

OTHER TELEVISION APPEARANCES; AS VIC PERRIN

Don Negler, *Dragnet* (pilot), NBC, 1969.
Narrator, *The UFO Incident* (movie; also known as *Interrupted Journey*), NBC, 1975.
Doctor, *The Abduction of Saint Anne* (movie), ABC, 1975.
Voice of Vultan, *Flash Gordon—The Greatest Adventure of All* (pilot), NBC, 1983.

Also appeared as Barney, *For The Defense* (pilot), 1954.

RADIO APPEARANCES, SERIES

Appeared as Ross Farnsworth, *One Man's Family;* as Clyde Beatty, *The Clyde Beatty Show;* as Sergeant Gorse, *Fort Laramie;* and on *Dragnet.*

OBITUARIES AND OTHER SOURCES:

PERIODICALS

Hollywood Reporter, July 10, 1989.
Starlog, June, 1990.*

*　　*　　*

PERRY, Frank　1930-

PERSONAL: Born in New York, NY, in 1930; married Barbara Goldsmith. *Education:* Apprenticed at the Westport, CT, Country Playhouse.

ADDRESSES: Office—Corsair Pictures, 1740 Broadway, New York, NY 10019.

CAREER: Motion picture producer, director, editor, and writer. Worked variously as a theatre manager, production manager, and managing director. Actor's Studio, New York City, director/observer, 1955; Theatre Guild, New York City, producer, 1955-56; Corsair Pictures, New York City, began as producer, became president and chief executive officer. Harvard University, lecturer on film; New York University Graduate Film School and Columbia University, adjunct professor of film. Board of directors, Lincoln Center Theatre; executive committee, Actors Studio. *Military service:* U.S. Army, 1952-54.

MEMBER: American Academy of Arts and Sciences.

CREDITS:

STAGE WORK; DIRECTOR

Ladies at the Alamo, Martin Beck Theatre, New York City, 1977.

FILM DIRECTOR; EXCEPT WHERE INDICATED

Art director, *Island Women,* United Artists (UA), 1958.
David and Lisa, Continental, 1962.
(And producer) *Ladybug, Ladybug,* UA, 1963.
(And producer) *The Swimmer,* Columbia, 1968.
Last Summer, Allied Artists, 1969.
(And producer) *Truman Capote's Trilogy,* Allied Artists, 1969.
(And producer) *Diary of a Mad Housewife,* Universal, 1970.
(And producer) *Doc,* UA, 1972.
(And producer) *Play It As It Lays,* Universal, 1972.
Man On a Swing, Paramount, 1974.
Rancho Deluxe, UA, 1975.
Mommie Dearest, Paramount, 1981.
Monsignor, Twentieth Century-Fox, 1982.
(And producer) *Compromising Positions,* Paramount, 1985.
(And producer) *Hello Again,* Buena Vista, 1987.

FILM APPEARANCES

Chef, *Rio Rita,* Metro-Goldwyn-Mayer, 1942.
Mr. Grimbly, *My Side of the Mountain,* Paramount, 1969.
Sub Captain, *The Neptune Factor,* Twentieth Century-Fox, 1973.

Also appeared in *Bush Pilot,* 1947; *Accident,* 1983.

TELEVISION DIRECTOR, EXCEPT WHERE INDICATED; MOVIES

(And producer) *A Christmas Memory,* ABC, 1966.
(And producer) *Thanksgiving Visitor,* ABC, 1968.
Dummy, CBS, 1979.

TELEVISION DIRECTOR; SERIES

Skag, NBC, 1980.

WRITINGS:

SCREENPLAYS

Mommie Dearest, Paramount, 1981.

*   *   *

PETERSON, Cassandra   1951-
(Elvira)

PERSONAL: Born September 17, 1951, in Manhattan, KS; daughter of an insurance salesman and a costume shop owner; married Mark Pierson (a personal manager), 1981. *Avocational interests:* Italian cooking, gardening, and animal rights.

ADDRESSES: Manager—Eric Gardner, Panacea Entertainment, 2705 Glendower Ave., Los Angeles, CA 90027; and Mark Pierson, Creative Minds Mgt., P.O. Box 38246, Los Angeles, CA 90038.

CAREER: Actress, comedienne, singer, screenwriter and dancer. Dunes Hotel, Las Vegas, NV, dancer and showgirl, 1969-70; lead singer in rock and roll band on tour in Italy, c. 1971-72; singer and dancer in revue "Mama's Boys" on American nightclub circuit during the 1970s; performer with Los Angeles-based improvisational comedy group the Groundlings during the late 1970s; created character Elvira, 1981.

AWARDS, HONORS: Count Dracula Society Award; Academy of Science Fiction, Fantasy and Horror Films award, 1984; Elvira Day declared in city of Los Angeles, March 9, 1984, and in city of Atlanta, October 26, 1985; named honorary mayor of city of West Hollywood, 1986.

CREDITS:

FILM APPEARANCES

Dinner party guest, *Coast to Coast,* Paramount, 1980.
Hostage, *Cheech and Chong's Next Movie,* Universal, 1980.
Neighbor, *King of the Mountain,* Universal, 1981.
Busty nurse, *Jekyll and Hyde . . . Together Again,* Paramount, 1982.
O'Malley's girl, *The Sting II,* Universal, 1983.
Girl with lugs, *Stroker Ace,* Warner Brothers, 1983.
Biker mama, *Pee-Wee's Big Adventure,* Warner Brothers, 1985.
Sheri, *Echo Park,* Atlantic, 1986.
Angie Stoddard, *Balboa,* Vestron Video, 1986.
Sorais, *Allan Quatermain and the Lost City of Gold,* Cannon, 1987.
Elvira, *Elvira: Mistress of the Dark,* New World, 1988.

Also appeared in *Roma* (also known as *Fellini's Roma*), 1972.

Life's Most Embarrassing Moments III, ABC, 1984.
The Paragon of Comedy, Showtime, 1984.
Elvira's Halloween Special, MTV, 1984.
Bob Hope Lampoons Television 1985, NBC, 1985.
Elvira's Halloween Special, MTV, 1986.
Friday Night Surprise!, NBC, 1989.

Dance hall girl, *Beyond Westworld,* CBS, 1980.
Host, *Elvira's Movie Macabre,* KHJ-Los Angeles, 1981-83, nationally syndicated, 1983—.

Also appeared in guest supporting acting roles on numerous television series, including *Alice, CHIPs, The Fall Guy, Happy Days, House Calls, Fantasy Island, thirtysomething, Totally Hidden Video, Saturday Night Live,* and *St. Elsewhere.*

Associate producer, *Elvira's Movie Macabre,* KHJ-Los Angeles, 1981-83, nationally syndicated, 1983—.

WRITINGS:

Elvira's Movie Macabre, KHJ-Los Angeles, 1981-83, nationally syndicated, 1983—.
(With John Paragon and Sam Egan) *Elvira: Mistress of the Dark* (screenplay), New World, 1988.

OTHER SOURCES:

Detroit Free Press, October 31, 1986.
Hollywood Reporter, January 7, 1987.
Maclean's, November 11, 1985.
Newsweek, August 8, 1988.
New York Post, May 25, 1987.
People, November 4, 1985; May 5, 1986.
Time, August 8, 1988.
Us, November 4, 1985.
USA Weekend, October 31-November 2, 1986.

*   *   *

PETRIE, Daniel   1920-

PERSONAL: Full name Daniel Mannix Petrie; born November 26, 1920, in Glace Bay, Nova Scotia, Canada; son of William Mark (a businessman) and Mary Anne (Campbell) Petrie; married Dorothea Grundy (a producer), October 27, 1946; children: Daniel Mannix Jr., Donald Mark, Mary Susan and June Anne (twins). *Education:* St. Francis Xavier University, Nova Scotia, B.A., 1942; Co-

lumbia University, M.A., 1945; attended Northwestern University, 1947-48.

ADDRESSES: Office—c/o Creative Artists Agency, 9830 Wilshire Blvd., Beverly Hills, CA 90212.

CAREER: Director, actor, screenwriter. Creighton University, Omaha, NE, assistant professor, 1948-49; member of faculty, American Film Institute, 1979-83; chairman, Center for Advanced Film and Television Studies, American Film Institute; guest lecturer at University of Southern California, and University of Iowa. *Military service:* Royal Canadian Army, Artillery, 1942-43; became lieutenant.

MEMBER: Academy of Motion Picture Arts and Sciences, Writers Guild of America, Directors Guild of America, National Academy of Television Arts and Sciences, Society of Stage Directors and Choreographers.

AWARDS, HONORS: Christopher Award for direction, for "The Prince and the Pauper"; Directors Guild of America Award for direction, 1961, for *A Raisin in the Sun;* Television Directors Guild of America Awards, 1963, for *The Benefactor,* 1969, for *Silent Night, Lonely Night,* and 1970, for *Hands of Love;* Western Heritage Award for Outstanding Western Television, 1972, for *Hec Ramsey;* L.H.D., St. Francis Xavier University, Nova Scotia, 1973; Emmy Award nomination, 1976, for *Harry Truman Plain Speaking;* Emmy Award for Direction, Peabody Award, and Critics Circle Award, all 1976, all for *Eleanor and Franklin;* Directors Guild of American Awards, 1976, for *Eleanor and Franklin* and *Eleanor and Franklin: The White House Years;* Emmy Award for Outstanding Special, and Peabody Award, both 1977, both for *Sybil;* Emmy Award for Direction, 1977, for *Eleanor and Franklin: The White House Years;* Directors Guild Award, 1984, for *The Dollmaker;* Emmy Award nomination, 1985, for *The Execution of Raymond Graham;* Cable Award, 1986, for *Half a Lifetime;* Emmy Award and Golden Globe Award nominations, 1989, for *My Name Is Bill W.*

CREDITS:

(Broadway debut) Charlie, *Kiss Them for Me,* Belasco Theatre, New York City, 1945.
Understudy, then Nels, *I Remember Mama* (tour), U.S. cities, 1946-47.

A Shadow of My Enemy, American National Theatre Academy, New York City, 1957.
The Cherry Orchard, Sombrero Playhouse, Phoenix, AZ, then Royal Poinciana Playhouse, Palm Beach, FL, 1959.

Who'll Save the Ploughboy?, Phoenix Theatre, New York City, 1962.

Mornin' Sun, Phoenix Theatre, 1963.

Conversations in the Dark, Walnut Street Theatre, Philadelphia, 1963-64, 1972.

Monopoly (four short plays, *Make Like a Dog, Suburban Tragedy, Princess Rebecca Birnbaum,* and *Young Married Play Monopoly*), Stage 73, New York City, 1966.

Volpone, Philadelphia Drama Guild, Philadelphia, 1971.

Also director of *A Lesson from Aloes,* 1981.

FILM APPEARANCES

Kalijak Director, *Into the Night,* Universal, 1985.

FILM DIRECTOR, EXCEPT AS INDICATED

The Bramble Bush, Warner Brothers, 1960.

A Raisin in the Sun, Columbia, 1961.

The Main Attraction, Metro-Goldwyn-Mayer, 1962.

Stolen Hours, United Artists, 1963.

The Idol, Embassy, 1965.

The Spy with a Cold Nose, Embassy, 1966.

The Neptune Factor (also known as *An Underwater Odyssey* and *The Neptune Disaster*), Twentieth Century-Fox, 1972.

Buster and Billie, Columbia, 1973.

Lifeguard, Paramount, 1974.

The Betsy, Allied Artists, 1978.

Resurrection, Universal, 1980.

Fort Apache, The Bronx, Twentieth Century-Fox, 1981.

Six Pack, Twentieth Century-Fox, 1982.

Bay Boy, Orion, 1984.

(And producer) *Square Dance,* Island, 1986.

Rocket Gilbraltar, Columbia, 1988.

Cocoon: The Return, Twentieth Century-Fox, 1988.

TELEVISION APPEARANCES; EPISODIC

The Golden Age of Television, PBS, 1981.

TELEVISION DIRECTOR; MOVIES

Victory, NBC, 1960.

Silent Night, Lonely Night, NBC, 1969.

Big Fish, Little Fish, PBS, 1970.

A Howling in the Woods, NBC, 1971.

A Stranger in Town, ABC, 1972.

Moon of the Wolf, ABC, 1972.

Trouble Comes to Town, ABC, 1973.

Mousey (released theatrically in England as *Cat and Mouse*), ABC, 1974.

Returning Home, ABC, 1975.

Harry Truman Plain Speaking, PBS, 1976.

Sybil, NBC, 1976.

Eleanor and Franklin, ABC, 1976.

Eleanor and Franklin: The White House Years, ABC, 1977.

The Quinns, ABC, 1977.

The Dollmaker, ABC, 1984.

The Execution of Raymond Graham, 1985.

Half a Lifetime, HBO, 1986.

(And producer) "My Name Is Bill W.," *Hallmark Hall of Fame,* ABC, 1989.

TELEVISION DIRECTOR; SERIES

Panhandle Pete and Jennifer, NBC, 1950-51.

The Billy Rose Show, ABC, 1950-51.

Assignment: Manhunt, NBC, 1951-52.

Short, Short Drama, NBC, 1952-53.

TELEVISION DIRECTOR; PILOTS

The City, ABC, 1971.

Hec Ramsey (also known as *The Century Turns*), NBC, 1972.

The Gun and the Pulpit, ABC, 1974.

TELEVISION DIRECTOR; EPISODIC

Somerset Maugham Theatre, ABC, 1951.

Treasury Men in Action, NBC, 1952.

Excursion, CBS, 1953.

Omnibus, CBS, 1953.

Revlon Mirror Theatre, CBS, 1953.

Justice, NBC, 1954.

Armstrong Circle Theatre, NBC, 1954.

Elgin Theatre Hour, ABC, 1955.

The Alcoa Hour, NBC, 1956.

The U.S. Steel Hour, ABC, then CBS, 1955-58.

DuPont Show of the Month, CBS, 1958-61.

"The Benefactor," *The Defenders,* CBS, 1962.

"One Day in the Life of Ivan Denisovich," *Bob Hope Chrysler Show,* NBC, 1963.

East Side/West Side, CBS, 1963.

San Francisco International Airport, NBC, 1970.

McMillan and Wife, NBC, 1971.

Also director of episodes of *The Man and the City,* 1971, *N.Y.P.D.,* ABC, *Marcus Welby, M.D.,* ABC, *Medical Center,* CBS, *The Lawyers,* NBC, and *Ironside,* NBC.

OTHER TELEVISION WORK

Director, *Hawkins Falls* (special), NBC, 1950.

Also producer for episodes of *Studs' Place,* NBC, 1950.

WRITINGS:

The Bay Boy (screenplay), 1984.*

PETRIE, George O.

ADDRESSES: Agent—Gage Group, Inc., 9255 Sunset Blvd., Suite 515, Los Angeles, CA 90069.

CAREER: Actor.

CREDITS:

FILM APPEARANCES

O'Shea, *Boomerang,* Twentieth Century-Fox, 1947.
Sidney, *Four Days Leave,* Film Classics, 1950.
Chalais, *At Sword's Point* (also known as *Sons of the Musketeers*), RKO Radio Pictures, 1951.
George, *Gypsy,* Warner Brothers, 1962.
Joe Scanlon, *Hud,* Paramount, 1963.
Mr. Harrington, *Wall of Noise,* Warner Brothers, 1963.
Crowley, *He Rides Tall,* Universal, 1964.
What's So Bad About Feeling Good?, Universal, 1968.
The Molly Maguires, Paramount, 1970.
Hotel receptionist, *Telefon,* United Artists (UA), 1977.
Doctor in Las Vegas, *The Other Side of the Mountain—Part 2,* Universal, 1978.
Dr. Savianno, *Wavelength,* New World, 1983.
Martin Page, *Planes, Trains, and Automobiles,* Paramount, 1987.
Everett Sloane, *Baby Boom,* UA, 1987.

TELEVISION APPEARANCES; MOVIES

President MacCloud, *The Deadly Season,* CBS, 1977.
Charles Kraus, *Tail Gunner Joe,* NBC, 1977.
Chaim Zadok, *Raid on Entebbe,* NBC, 1977.
Hank, *A Fire in the Sky,* NBC, 1978.
With This Ring, ABC, 1978.
Sifty, *Goldie and the Boxer,* NBC, 1979.
Warren Porter, *Silent Victory: The Kitty O'Neil Story,* CBS, 1979.
City in Fear (also known as *Panic on Page One*), ABC, 1980.
Fraser, *The Dream Merchants,* syndicated, 1980.
Frank, *Goldie and the Boxer Go to Hollywood,* NBC, 1981.
Dad, *Million Dollar Infield,* CBS, 1981.
Dr. Landowska, *The Day After,* ABC, 1983.
Uncle Louie, *Something in Common* (also known as *Love 40*), CBS, 1986.

TELEVISION APPEARANCES; SERIES

The Jackie Gleason Show, CBS, 1952-54, 1957-59, and 1966-69.
Nathan Walsh, *Search for Tomorrow,* CBS, 1954-58.
The Honeymooners, CBS, 1955-56.
Dr. Peter Frey, *As the World Turns,* CBS, 1958-61.
Peter Quinn, *The Edge of Night,* CBS, 1964-74.
Harve Smithfield, *Dallas,* CBS, 1978-91.
Scoop Webster, *Hard Copy,* CBS, 1987.

TELEVISION APPEARANCES; EPISODIC

Dr. Quentin Tanner, *Knight Rider,* ABC, 1985.
Joe Ewell, *St. Elsewhere,* NBC, 1986.
Judge, "Shadow Play," *The Twilight Zone,* CBS, 1986.
Don Aiuppo, *Wiseguy,* CBS, 1989.
Lester, *Dear John,* NBC, 1990.
Father Jasper, *Newhart,* CBS, 1990.
Grandpa Romano, *Who's the Boss?,* ABC, 1990.
Bruno Petrell, *Max Monroe: Loose Cannon,* NBC, 1990.

Also appeared as Edgar Flaherty, *Tough Cookies,* 1986; Harold Masur, *Heart Beat,* 1989; and George Haskell, *Leave It to Beaver,* CBS and ABC. Appeared in *Hill St. Blues, House Calls, The Love Boat, Hawaiian Eye, Hawaii Five-O, Little House on the Prairie, Another World, Days of Our Lives, General Hospital, Medical Center, Gunsmoke, Wild, Wild West, Streets of San Francisco, Switch, Hart to Hart, Maude, Petrocelli, One Day at a Time, Ironside,* and *How the West Was Won.*

OTHER TELEVISION APPEARANCES

McNamara's Band (pilot), ABC, 1977.
Admiral Hatfield, *Operation Petticoat* (pilot; also known as *Life in the Pink*), ABC, 1977.
Panic in Echo Park (pilot), NBC, 1977.
Skag (pilot), NBC, 1980.
Court clerk, *The Blue and the Gray* (mini-series), CBS, 1982.
Jackie Gleason: The Great One (special), CBS, 1988.

RADIO APPEARANCES

Appeared in title roles in *The Amazing Mr. Malone, The Falcon,* and *Gregory Hood.*

*   *   *

PHOENIX, River   1970-

PERSONAL: Born August 23, 1970, in Madras, OR; son of John (a carpenter) and Arlyn Phoenix.

ADDRESSES: Agent—Iris Burton Agency, 1450 Belfast Dr., Los Angeles, CA 90069.

CAREER: Actor. Worked in commercials as a child.

AWARDS, HONORS: National Board of Review award and Academy Award nomination, both for best supporting actor, 1988, for *Running On Empty.*

CREDITS:

FILM APPEARANCES

(Film debut) Wolfgang Muller, *Explorers,* Paramount, 1985.
Charlie Fox, *The Mosquito Coast,* Warner Brothers, 1986.
Chris Chambers, *Stand By Me,* Columbia, 1986.

Jeff Grant, *Little Nikita,* Columbia, 1988.

Title role, *A Night in the Life of Jimmy Reardon,* Twentieth Century-Fox, 1988.

Danny Pope, *Running On Empty,* Warner Brothers, 1988.

Young Indy, *Indiana Jones and the Last Crusade,* Paramount, 1989.

Devo, *I Love You to Death,* Tri-Star, 1990.

TELEVISION APPEARANCES; MOVIES

Jeffie at age eleven, *Celebrity,* NBC, 1984.

Robert Kennedy, Jr., *Robert Kennedy and His Times,* Part 3, CBS, 1985.

Philip Brogan, *Surviving,* ABC, 1985.

OTHER TELEVISION APPEARANCES

Guthrie McFadden, *Seven Brides for Seven Brothers* (series), CBS, 1982-83.

Also played Brian Ellsworth in *Backwards: The Riddle of Dyslexia,* 1984.

OTHER SOURCES:

PERIODICALS

Daily News (New York), March 17, 1988.
Premiere, April, 1988.
Sunday Star-Ledger (Newark), March 27, 1988.*

*   *   *

PIMLOTT, Steven

PERSONAL: Education: Attended University of Cambridge.

ADDRESSES: Agent—Harriet Cruickshank, 97 Old South Lambeth Rd., London SW8 1XU, England.

CAREER: Director.

CREDITS:

STAGE WORK; DIRECTOR, EXCEPT WHERE NOTED

Staff producer, *Rigoletto,* English National Opera, 1976-77.

Staff producer, *A Night in Venice,* English National Opera, 1976-77.

Staff producer, *La Boheme,* English National Opera, 1976-77.

Staff producer, *Gianni Schicchi,* English National Opera, 1976-77.

Staff producer, *Werther,* English National Opera, 1976-77.

The Seraglio, English National Opera, spring tour, 1978.

L'Enfant et les sortileges, Rotterdam Philharmonic/ Swingle 2, 1978.

Turnadot, Abbey Opera, 1978.

La Boheme, Opera North, 1978.

Tosca, Opera North, c. 1978-83.

Nabucco, Opera North, c. 1978-83.

Bartered Bride, Opera North, c. 1978-83.

Werther, Opera North, c. 1978-83.

Cavalleria Rusticana, Opera North, c. 1978-83.

I Pagliacci, Opera North, c. 1978-83.

Ring around the Moon, Royal Exchange Theatre, Manchester, England, 1983.

(With Jim Broadbent) *A Winter's Tale,* Crucible Theatre, Sheffield, England, 1987-88.

The Park, Crucible Theatre, 1987-88.

Samson and Dalila, Bregenz Festival, Austria, 1988.

Sunday in the Park with George, National Theatre, London, 1990.

Joseph and the Amazing Technicolor Dreamcoat, Palladium, London, 1991.

Also directed *Amadeus* and *Entertaining Mr. Sloane,* Harrogate Theatre, London; *Deathtrap,* Northcott Theatre, Exeter, England; *A Patriot For Me* and *On the Razzle,* Playhouse Theatre, Leeds, England; *The Daughter in Law,* Sheffield; *Carousel,* Royal Exchange Theatre; *Carmen Jones* and *Twelfth Night,* Crucible Theatre; *Don Giovanni,* Victorian State Opera, Australia; *Manon Lescaut,* Australian Opera; *La Traviata,* Jerusalem Festival; *Les Miserables,* Cameri Theatre, Israel; *The York Mystery Plays* (with Victor Banerjee); *Carmen,* Earl's Court Theatre, London, then Tokyo; *Tosca* and *Werther,* Royal Opera House; and *The Pearl Fishers,* Scottish Opera.

*   *   *

PINCHOT, Bronson   1959-

PERSONAL: Full name, Bronson Alcott Pinchot; born May 20, 1959, in New York, NY; son of a bookbinder and Rosina Pinchot (a typist). *Education:* Yale University, B.A. (theater; with honors), 1981. *Avocational Interests:* Collecting antique painted Scandinavian furniture.

ADDRESSES: Office—ABC-TV, 1330 Avenue of the Americas, New York, NY 10019.

CAREER: Actor. Member, Theater at Monmouth Company, Monmouth, ME, 1978.

CREDITS:

TELEVISION APPEARANCES; SERIES

Dennis Kemper, *Sara,* NBC, 1985.

Balki Bartokomous, *Perfect Strangers,* ABC, 1986—.

TELEVISION APPEARANCES; SPECIALS

Charles Dickens, *Dave Thomas: The Incredible Time Travels of Henry Osgood* (also known as *Showtime Comedy Spotlight*), Showtime, 1986.

The 39th Annual Emmy Awards, Fox, 1987.
The 1st Annual American Comedy Awards, ABC, 1987.
The Twelfth Annual Circus of the Stars, CBS, 1987.
The 14th Annual People's Choice Awards, CBS, 1988.
Host, *The ABC Perfectly Strange Saturday Morning Preview,* ABC, 1989.
ABC's Comedy Sneak Peak, ABC, 1989.
The 16th Annual People's Choice Awards, CBS, 1990.

TELEVISION APPEARANCES; MOVIES

Photographer, *Between Two Women,* ABC, 1986.
Sanford Lagelfost, Jorge Jiminez, Arthur Lloyd, and Magda, *Jury Duty: The Comedy,* ABC, 1990.

TELEVISION APPEARANCES; EPISODIC

Appeared on *Amazing Stories,* NBC, and *Saturday Night Live,* NBC, and *George Burns Comedy Week.*

FILM APPEARANCES

(Film debut) Barry, *Risky Business,* Warner Brothers, 1983.
Alfred Schultz, *The Flamingo Kid,* Twentieth Century-Fox, 1984.
Serge, *Beverly Hills Cops,* Paramount, 1984.
Lloyd, *After Hours,* Warner Brothers, 1985.
Bobby McGee, *Second Sight,* Warner Brothers, 1989.

Also appeared as Brad in *Hot Resort,* 1986.

STAGE APPEARANCES

Appeared in the Off-Broadway productions *Poor Little Lambs* and *Mr. Joyce Is Leaving Paris.**

*   *   *

PLANA, Tony   1953-

PERSONAL: Born April 19, 1953, in Havana, Cuba; married Ada Maris (an actress); children: one son. *Education:* Loyola Marymount University, B.A., drama and literature; studied acting at Royal Academy of Dramatic Arts, London.

ADDRESSES: *Agent*—Pearl Wexler, Paul Kohner Inc., 9169 Sunset Blvd., Los Angeles, CA 90069.

CAREER: Actor.

AWARDS, HONORS: Five Dramalogue Awards for stage performances.

CREDITS:

STAGE APPEARANCES

(Broadway debut) Rudy Reyna, *Zoot Suit,* Winter Garden Theatre, New York City, 1979.

Second murderer, *Richard III,* Center Theater Group, Mark Taper Forum, Los Angeles, 1983.
Miguel, *Rum and Coke,* South Coast Repertory, Costa Mesa, CA, 1985, then (Off-Broadway debut) Public Theatre, New York City, 1986.
Sarge, *The Boys of Winter,* Biltmore Theatre, New York City, 1985.
Charlie Bacon and His Family, South Coast Repertory, 1986.
Dr. Danny Lucchesi, *Fugue,* Syracuse Stage, Syracuse, NY, 1987.
The Captain, *Widows,* Mark Taper Forum, 1991.

Also appeared with the California Shakespearean Festival, Visalia, CA, 1980; as Puck, *A Midsummer Night's Dream,* the Devil, *Peer Gynt,* and Tilly, *He Who Gets Slapped,* all Pacific Conservatory of the Performing Arts, Santa Maria, CA; and as Sirhan Sirhan, *Sirhan and RFK: A Murder Mystery,* Melrose Theatre, Los Angeles.

FILM APPEARANCES

Seed of Innocence (also known as *Teen Mother*), Cannon, 1980.
Rudy Reyna, *Zoot Suit,* Universal, 1981.
Reza Hadda, *Mystique* (also known as *Circle of Power*), Mehlman, 1981.
National Guard general, *Love and Money,* Paramount, 1982.
Emiliano Della Serra, *An Officer and a Gentleman,* Paramount, 1982.
Del Amo, *Nightmares,* Universal, 1983.
Low rider, *Valley Girl,* Atlantic, 1983.
Chicano, *Deal of the Century,* Warner Brothers, 1983.
Carlos, *El Norte,* Cinecom International/Island Alive, 1984.
Ramos, *City Limits,* Atlantic, 1985.
Ruben Trevino, *Latino,* Cinecom International, 1985.
Chico, *The Best of Times,* Universal, 1986.
Major Max, *Salvador,* Hemdale, 1986.
Jefe, *Three Amigos,* Orion, 1986.
Feo, *Born in East L.A.,* Universal, 1987.
Miguel, *Disorderlies,* Warner Brothers, 1987.
Voice of Omar Cabezas, *Fire from the Mountain* (documentary), Common Sense Foundation, 1987.
Gene Rodriguez, *Break of Dawn,* Cinewest, 1988.
Father Manuel Morantes, *Romero,* Four Seasons Entertainment, 1989.
Buy and Cell, Empire, 1989.
Beniamino, *One Good Cop,* Hollywood Pictures, 1991.

TELEVISION APPEARANCES; PILOTS

Vostonovich, *Callahan,* ABC, 1982.

TELEVISION APPEARANCES; EPISODIC

Guerrara, *Miami Vice,* NBC, 1988.

Jorge, *It's Garry Shandling's Show,* Showtime, 1988.
Antonio Cruz, *The Equalizer,* CBS, 1989.
Edwardo Montoya, *Snoops,* CBS, 1989.
Rivera, *L.A. Law,* NBC, 1989.
Sal Tortino, *Falcon Crest,* CBS, 1989.
Horner, *Beauty and the Beast,* CBS, 1990.
Samuel Delacruz, "Sweet 15," *Wonderworks,* PBS, 1990.
Hunter, NBC, 1990.

Also appeared in *Baretta,* ABC; *Barnaby Jones,* CBS; *Quincy, M.E.,* NBC; *Hill Street Blues,* NBC; and *Remington Steele,* NBC.

TELEVISION APPEARANCES; MOVIES

Alberto "Toto" Corona, *Streets of L.A.,* CBS, 1979.
Senor Rueda, *Madame X,* NBC, 1981.
Dentist, *Sadat,* syndicated, 1983.
Julio, *Listen to Your Heart,* CBS, 1983.
White Man Runs Him, *Kenny Rogers as "The Gambler" III—The Legend Continues,* CBS, 1987.
Mike Hernandez, *The Case of the Hillside Stranglers,* NBC, 1989.
Commandante Pavon Reyes, *Drug Wars: The Camarena Story,* NBC, 1990.
F.B.I. Agent Alonso, *So Proudly We Hail,* CBS, 1990.*

*   *   *

POST, Markie 1950-

PERSONAL: Born November 4, 1950, in Palo Alto, CA; daughter of Richard (a nuclear physicist) and Marylee (a poet) Post; married Michael Ross; children: Kate. *Education:* Received B.A. from Lewis and Clark College; earned a theatre degree from Pomona College.

ADDRESSES: Agent—Gary Rado, William Morris Agency, 151 El Camino Dr., Beverly Hills, CA 90212. *Publicist*—Jon Carrasco, Sterling/Winters Co., 9044 Melrose Ave, 3rd Floor, Los Angeles, CA 90069.

CAREER: Actress. Researcher for the series *Split Second.*

CREDITS:

TELEVISION APPEARANCES; SERIES

Barbara Jane Bookman, *Semi-Tough,* ABC, 1980.
Chris Brennan, *The Gangster Chronicles,* NBC, 1981.
Terri Michaels (also known as Terri Shannon), *The Fall Guy,* ABC, 1982-85.
Christine Sullivan, *Night Court,* NBC, 1985—.

TELEVISION APPEARANCES; MOVIES

Jan Thacker, *Not Just Another Affair,* CBS, 1982.
Delia Langtree, *Triplecross,* ABC, 1986.
Linda Moon, *Glitz,* NBC, 1988.
Maria, *Tricks of the Trade,* CBS, 1988.

TELEVISION APPEARANCES; SPECIALS

The 21st Annual Academy of Country Music Awards, NBC, 1986.
60th Annual Macy's Thanksgiving Day Parade, NBC, 1986.
The Wildest West Show of the Stars, CBS, 1986.
Host, *The 98th Tournament of the Roses Parade,* NBC, 1987.
The 23rd Annual Academy of Country Music Awards, NBC, 1988.
Disney's Magic in the Magic Kingdom, NBC, 1988.
The Chipmunks: Rockin' Through the Decades, NBC, 1990.

TELEVISION APPEARANCES; PILOTS

Julie Ramsdell, *Massarati and the Brain,* ABC, 1982.
Terry Shannon, *How Do I Kill a Thief—Let Me Count the Ways,* ABC, 1982.
Sally Leadbetter, *Six Pack,* NBC, 1983.
Courtney Hollander, *Scene of the Crime,* NBC, 1984.

TELEVISION APPEARANCES; EPISODIC

Guest, *Comedy Break,* Showtime, 1985.

Also appeared on episodes of *Frankie and Annette—The Second Time Around, Hotel, Fantasy Island, Matt Houston, The Love Boat, Hart To Hart, Eight Is Enough, The A-Team,* and *Cheers.*

TELEVISION WORK

Associate producer of *Double Dare* (series), 1976-77

STAGE APPEARANCES

Appeared in *Joe Egg, The Fantasticks, The Hairy Ape,* and *Guys and Dolls.**

*   *   *

PRESSMAN, Edward R. 1943-

PERSONAL: Born in 1943 in New York, NY; son of Jack (a toy company executive) and Lynn Pressman; married Annie McEnroe (an actress), May, 1983; children: Sammy Jack. *Education:* B.A., Stanford University; attended London School of Economics.

ADDRESSES: Office—445 North Bedford Dr., Penthouse, Beverly Hills, CA 90210.

CAREER: Producer. Founder, with director Paul Williams, of Pressman-Williams Enterprises; founder of Edward R. Pressman Film Corp.

CREDITS:

FILM WORK

Producer, *Out of It,* United Artists (UA), 1969.

Producer, *The Revolutionary,* UA, 1970.

Producer, *Dealing: Or The Berkeley-to-Boston Forty-Brick Lost-Bag Blues,* Warner Bros., 1971.

Producer, *Sisters* (also known as *Blood Sisters*), American International, 1973.

Executive producer, *Badlands,* Warner Bros., 1973.

Producer, *Phantom of the Paradise,* Twentieth Century-Fox, 1974.

Executive producer, *Paradise Alley,* Universal, 1978.

Executive producer, *Despair,* Gala Film Distributors, 1978.

Producer (with Michele Rappaport), *Old Boyfriends,* Avco Embassy, 1979.

Executive producer, *Victoria,* Svensk Filmindustri, 1979.

Executive producer, *Heart Beat,* Columbia-EMI-Warner, 1979.

Producer, *You Better Watch Out,* Edward R. Pressman Film Corp., 1980.

Producer, *The Hand,* Warner Bros., 1981.

Executive producer, *Flicks* (also known as *Loose Joints*), United Film Distribution, 1981.

Executive producer, *Das Boot* (also known as *The Boat*), Columbia, 1981.

Executive producer, *Conan the Barbarian,* Universal, 1982.

Executive producer, *The Pirates of Penzance,* Universal, 1982.

Executive producer, *Crimewave* (also known as *The XYZ Murders* and *Broken Hearts and Noses;* also see below), Embassy, 1985.

Producer (with Joseph Papp), *Plenty,* Twentieth Century-Fox, 1985.

Executive producer, *Half Moon Street,* Twentieth Century-Fox, 1986.

Executive producer, *True Stories,* Warner Bros., 1986.

Executive producer, *Good Morning Babylon,* Vestron, 1986.

Executive producer, *Masters of the Universe,* Cannon, 1987.

Executive producer, *Walker,* Universal, 1987.

Producer, *Wall Street,* Twentieth Century-Fox, 1987.

Producer, *Cherry 2000,* Orion, 1988.

Executive producer, *Paris by Night,* Cineplex Odeon, 1988.

Producer, *Talk Radio,* Universal, 1988.

Producer, *Blue Steel,* Metro-Goldwyn-Mayer/UA, 1989.

Executive producer, *Martians Go Home,* Taurus Entertainment, 1990.

Producer (with Oliver Stone), *Reversal of Fortune,* Warner Bros., 1990.

Executive producer, *To Sleep with Anger,* Samuel Goldwyn, 1990.

Executive producer, *Waiting for the Light,* Triumph, 1990.

Producer (with Michael Hausman), *Homicide,* Triumph, 1991.

FILM APPEARANCES

Ernest Trend, *Crimewave,* Embassy, 1985.

OTHER SOURCES:

PERIODICALS

New York Times Magazine, September 29, 1987.

*   *   *

PROWSE, Juliet   1936-

PERSONAL: Born September 25, 1936, in Bombay, India; immigrated to United States, 1959, naturalized citizen, 1980; married Eddie James; married John McCook; children: (second marriage) Seth. *Education:* Attended Royal Academy of Dance, Johannesburg, South Africa.

ADDRESSES: Agent—Fred Moch/Jeff Witjas/Sam Haskell, William Morris Agency, 151 El Camino Dr., Beverly Hills, CA 90012. *Manager*—Mark Mordoh, 9200 Sunset Blvd., Suite 905, Los Angeles, CA 90069.

CAREER: Actress and dancer.

CREDITS:

STAGE APPEARANCES

Charity, *Sweet Charity,* Caesars Palace, Las Vegas, NV, 1966-67.

Hey, Look Me Over!, Avery Fisher Hall, New York City, 1981.

Also appeared in *Kismet,* London, England. Toured in productions of *Sweet Charity, Irma La Douce, On A Clear Day You Can See Forever, Mame, The Pajama Game,* and *Follies.*

FILM APPEARANCES

Claudine, *Can-Can,* Twentieth Century-Fox, 1960.

Lili, *G.I Blues,* Paramount, 1960.

Francina, *The Fiercest Heart,* Twentieth Century-Fox, 1961.

Ursula Poe, *The Right Approach,* Twentieth Century-Fox, 1961.

Rena, *Second Time Around,* Twentieth Century-Fox, 1961.

Wife, *An American Wife,* SADI, 1965.

Marion Davis, *Dingaka,* Embassy, 1965.

Norah, *Who Killed Teddy Bear?,* Magna, 1965.

Jenny, *Run for Your Wife*, Allied Artists, 1966.

Mona Carroll/Mona McCluskey, *Mona McCluskey*, NBC, 1965-66.
On Parade, NBC, 1964.
Showtime, CBS, 1968.
Samantha Bricker, *The Love Boat*, ABC, 1977.
The Shape of Things, NBC, 1982.

Frank Sinatra, ABC, 1959.
The Bob Hope Show, NBC, 1961.
Remember How Great?, NBC, 1961.
The Bob Hope Show, NBC, 1962.
Hollywood Melody, NBC, 1962.
Favorite Songs, NBC, 1964.
The Don Knotts Special, CBS, 1967.
The Bob Hope Show, NBC, 1968.
Bing Crosby and Carol Burnett: Together Again for the First Time, NBC, 1969.
Danny Thomas Looks At Yesterday, Today, and Tomorrow, CBS, 1970.
Don Knotts' Nice, Clean, Decent, Wholesome Hour, CBS, 1970.
The Klowns, ABC, 1970.
Don Rickles: Alive and Kicking, CBS, 1972.
Stars and Stripes Show, NBC, 1975.
The Paul Lynde Comedy Hour, ABC, 1978.
Musical Comedy Tonight, PBS, 1981.
Women of Russia (documentary), syndicated, 1981.
Night of 100 Stars II, ABC, 1985.
Thirty-Ninth Annual Tony Awards, CBS, 1985.
Fortieth Annual Tony Awards, CBS, 1986.
Championship Ballroom Dancing, PBS, 1986.
Championship Ballroom Dancing, PBS, 1987.
Las Vegas: All-Star 75th Anniversary Celebration, ABC, 1987.
Championship Ballroom Dancing, PBS, 1990.
The Mother/Daughter USA Pageant, syndicated, 1990.
America's Dance Honors, ABC, 1990.

Also appeared in *Twelfth Annual Circus of the Stars*, 1977, and *Placido Domingo: Stepping Out With the Ladies*.

Martha Foster, *Second Chance*, ABC, 1972.*

*   *   *

PYLE, Denver   1920-

PERSONAL: Born May 11, 1920, in Bethune, CO; children: David, Tony. *Education:* Attended Colorado State University.

CAREER: Actor, director, and writer. *Military service:* Served in U.S. Navy.

CREDITS:

(Debut) Masher, *The Guild of Janet Ames*, Columbia, 1947.
Carl, *Devil Ship*, Columbia, 1947.
Easy Jarrett, *The Man from Colorado*, Columbia, 1948.
Night Clerk, *Marshal of Amarillo*, Republic Pictures, 1948.
Hutchins, *Train to Alcatraz*, Republic Pictures, 1948.
Lefty, *Flame of Youth*, Republic Pictures, 1949.
Rex, *Hellfire*, Elliot-McGowan/Republic Pictures, 1949.
Hutch, *Red Canyon*, Universal, 1949.
Ed Quinn, *Streets of San Francisco*, Republic Pictures, 1949.
Youth, *Too Late for Tears*, United Artists (UA), 1949.
Rim of the Canyon, Columbia, 1949.
Al, *Customs Agent*, Columbia, 1950.
Whip, *Dynamite Pass*, RKO, 1950.
"Jumpy" Jordon, *Federal Agent at Large*, Republic Pictures, 1950.
Turner, *The Flying Saucer*, Colonial/Film Classics, 1950.
George, *The Old Frontier*, Republic Pictures, 1950.
Bowie French, *Hills of Utah*, Columbia, 1951.
Nick Algren, *Million Dollar Pursuit*, Republic Pictures, 1951.
Lacey, *Rough Riders of Durango*, Republic Pictures, 1951.
Allen, *Desert Passage*, RKO, 1952.
Niko, *The Lusty Men*, RKO, 1952.
Hartley, *The Man from Black Hills*, Silvermine/Monogram, 1952.
Bud Karnes, *The Maverick*, Silvermine/Allied Artists, 1952.
Skip, *Oklahoma Annie*, Republic Pictures, 1952.
Canyon Ambush, Monogram, 1952.
Fargo, Silvermine/Monogram, 1952.
Vigilante Terror, Westwood/Allied Artists, 1953.
Bernie Malloy, *Goldtown Ghost Riders*, Columbia, 1953.
Bartender, *A Perilous Journey*, Republic Pictures, 1953.
Greeley, *Rebel City*, Silvermine/Allied Artists, 1953.
Tench, *Texas Bad Man*, Allied Artists, 1953.
Jonas Bailey, *Topeka*, Westwood/Allied Artists, 1953.
Reverend Moorehead, *Ride Clear of Diablo*, Universal, 1954.
Johnny Guitar, Republic Pictures, 1954.
Clint Reno, *Rage at Dawn* (also known as *Seven Bad Men*), RKO, 1955.
Harvey, *Run for Cover*, Paramount, 1955.
Dave Weed, *Ten Wanted Men*, Ranown/Columbia, 1955.

Thompson, *To Hell and Back,* Universal, 1955.

Top Gun, Fame/UA, 1955.

Yaqui Drums, Allied Artists, 1956.

Jim Bailey, *I Killed Wild Bill Hickok,* Wheeler, 1956.

Bert Killian, *The Naked Hills,* La Salle/Allied Artists, 1956.

Lieutenant Bradley, *Please Murder Me,* Distributors Corporation of America, 1956.

Dixon, *Seventh Cavalry,* Columbia, 1956.

Mickey Hill, *Destination 60,000,* Allied Artists, 1957.

Bill Dragger, *Domino Kid,* Columbia, 1957.

Ranger Captain, *Gun Duel in Durango* (also known as *Duel in Durango*), Peerless/UA, 1957.

Mr. Simpson, *Jet Pilot,* RKO/Universal, 1957.

Sheriff, *The Lonely Man,* Paramount, 1957.

Colonel Wiley, *China Doll,* UA, 1958.

Collins, *Fort Massacre,* UA, 1958.

Moore, *Good Day for Hanging,* Columbia, 1958.

Ollinger, *The Left Handed Gun,* Warner Brothers, 1958.

Mr. Bickford, *The Party Crashers,* Paramount, 1958.

Harrison, *Cast a Long Shadow,* UA, 1959.

Jagger Jo, *The Horse Soldiers,* Mirisch/UA, 1959.

Doc, *King of the Wild Stallions,* Allied Artists, 1959.

Gambler, *The Alamo,* Batjac/UA, 1960.

Senator Conrad, *Geronimo,* UA, 1962.

Amos Carruthers, *The Man Who Shot Liberty Valence,* Ford/Paramount, 1962.

Sheriff, *Terrified,* Bern-Field/Crown, 1963.

Senator Henry, *Cheyenne Autumn,* Warner Brothers, 1964.

Preacher Pope, *Mail Order Bride* (also known as *West of Montana*), Metro-Goldwyn-Mayer (MGM), 1964.

Sheriff, *The Great Race,* Warner Brothers, 1965.

Bull, *The Rounders,* MGM, 1965.

Pastor Bjoerling, *Shenandoah,* Universal, 1965.

Captain Hold, *Gunpoint,* Universal, 1966.

First Hunter, *Incident at Phantom Hill,* Universal, 1966.

Kelly, *Mara of the Wilderness* (also known as *Valley of the White Wolves*), Unicorn/Allied Artists, 1966.

Frank Hamer, *Bonnie and Clyde,* Warner Brothers, 1967.

Grandpa, *Tammy and the Millionaire,* Uni-Bet/Universal, 1967.

Alfie, *Welcome to Hard Times* (also known as *Killer on a Horse*), MGM, 1967.

Munice Carter, *Bandolero,* Twentieth Century-Fox, 1968.

Sig Evers, *Five Card Stud,* Paramount, 1968.

Junior Frisbee, *Something Big,* Stanmore Penbar/National General, 1971.

Grandpappy John, *Who Fears the Devil* (also known as *The Legend of Hillbilly John; My Name Is John*), Two's Company/Jack H, 1972.

Denver Cahill, *United States Marshal,* Warner Brothers, 1973.

Uncle Bene, *Escape to Witch Mountain,* Buena Vista, 1975.

Old Mountainman, *The Adventures of Frontier Fremont,* Sun Classics, 1976.

McLaughlin, *Buffalo Bill and the Indians or Sitting Bull's History Lesson,* UA, 1976.

Colonel Seymour Hawkins, *Hawmps!,* Mulberry Square, 1976.

Carl Barber, *Welcome to L.A.,* UA, 1976.

Arkansas, *Winter Hawk,* Howco International, 1976.

Galen Clark, *Guardian of the Wilderness,* Sunn Classic, 1977.

Return from Witch Mountain, Buena Vista, 1978.

TELEVISION APPEARANCES; SERIES

The Roy Rogers Show, CBS, 1951-64.

Ben Thompson, *The Life and Legend of Wyatt Earp,* ABC, 1955-56.

Sergeant Murchison, *Code Three,* syndicated, 1957.

Grandpa Tarleton, *Tammy,* ABC, 1965-66.

Buck Webb, *The Doris Day Show,* CBS, 1968-70.

Uncle Duncan, *Here Come the Brides,* ABC, 1968-70.

Dale Busch, *Karen,* ABC, 1975.

Mad Jack, *The Life & Times of Grizzly Adams,* NBC, 1977-78.

Uncle Jesse Duke, *The Dukes of Hazzard,* CBS, 1979-85.

Voice of Uncle Jesse, host, and narrator, *The Dukes* (animated), CBS, 1983.

TELEVISION APPEARANCES; PILOTS

Ben Bridgeman, *Hitched,* NBC, 1973.

Drunk, *Sidekicks,* CBS, 1974.

Morgan Luke Evans, *Mrs. R—Death among Friends* (also known as *Death among Friends*), NBC, 1975.

TELEVISION APPEARANCES; EPISODIC

Crown Theatre with Gloria Swanson, syndicated, 1953.

Medic, NBC, 1954-56.

Crossroads, ABC, 1955-57.

Thriller, NBC, 1960-62.

Briscoe Darling, *The Andy Griffith Show,* CBS, 1960-68.

Kraft Mystery Theater, NBC, 1961-63.

The Dick Van Dyke Show, CBS, 1963.

Bonanza, NBC, 1964.

Eben Connors, *Murder, She Wrote,* CBS, 1988.

Also appeared on *Crossroads,* ABC; *The Gene Autry Show;* and *You Are There.*

TELEVISION APPEARANCES; MOVIES

Amos Chapman, *Murder or Mercy,* ABC, 1974.

Briscoe Darling, *Return to Mayberry,* NBC, 1986.

TELEVISION APPEARANCES; SPECIALS

Dean Martin's Celebrity Roast: Dan Haggerty, NBC, 1977.

When the West Was Fun: A Western Reunion, ABC, 1979.

TELEVISION DIRECTOR; EPISODIC

The Doris Day Show, CBS, 1968-73.
(With others) *Dirty Sally,* CBS, 1974.
(With others) *The Dukes of Hazzard,* CBS, 1979-85.

WRITINGS:

(With Calvin Clements, Jay Simms, Leonard Katzman, Dale Eunson, and John Mantley) *Dirty Sally* (television episodes), CBS, 1974.*

*   *   *

QUIGLEY, William J.   1951-

PERSONAL: Born July 6, 1951, in New York, NY. *Education:* Wesleyan University, B.A.; Columbia University, M.S., 1983.

CAREER: Producer. Quigley Publishing Company, advertising circulation manager, 1973-74; school teacher in Kenya, 1974; Walter Reade Organization, assistant film buyer, 1975-77, vice-president, 1982; Vestron, Inc., senior vice-president, 1986, founder of Vestron Pictures, president, 1987-89. Grey Advertising, media planner.

CREDITS:

FILM WORK; EXECUTIVE PRODUCER

The Dead, Vestron, 1987.
Steel Dawn (also known as *Desert Warrior*), Vestron, 1987.
(With M.J. Peckos) *Burning Secret* (also known as *Brennendes Geheimnis* and *Brulant Secret*), Vestron, 1988.
(With Dan Ireland) *Salome's Last Dance* (also known as *Salome's Last Night*), Vestron, 1988.
(With Ireland) *The Lair of the White Worm,* Vestron, 1988.
(With Ireland) *Waxwork,* Vestron, 1988.
(With Ireland) *The Unholy,* Vestron, 1988.
(With Ireland) *The Rainbow,* Vestron, 1989.
(With Ireland) *Twister,* Vestron, 1989.
(With Ireland) *Sundown: The Vampire in Retreat* (also known as *Sundown*), Vestron, 1989.
(With Ireland) *Paint It Black* (also known as *Painted Black*), Vestron, 1990.*

*   *   *

QUILLAN, Eddie   1907-1990

PERSONAL: Born Edward Frances Quillan, March 31, 1907, in Philadelphia, PA; died of cancer, July 19, 1990, in Burbank, CA; son of Joseph Frances (a performer) and Sarah (a performer; maiden name, Owens) Quillan. *Education:* Received stage training while playing in family act. *Politics:* Democrat. *Religion:* Roman Catholic. *Avocational interests:* Golf, bowling.

CAREER: Actor. Began career as part of family variety act, *A Little Bit of Everything.*

MEMBER: American Federation of Television and Radio Artists, Screen Actors Guild.

AWARDS, HONORS: Screen Actors Guild Award for *Mutiny on the Bounty.*

CREDITS:

FILM APPEARANCES

Eddie Kehoe, vaudeville hoofer, *Show Folks,* Pathe, 1928.
"Goat," *The Godless Girl,* Pathe, 1929.
Eddie Able, *Geraldine,* Pathe, 1929.
Eddie, *Noisy Neighbors,* Pathe, 1929.
Joe Collins, *The Sophomore,* Pathe, 1929.
Eddie, *Big Money,* Pathe, 1930.
Willie, *Night Work,* Pathe, 1930.
Ray, *The Big Shot* (also known as *The Optimist*), RKO Radio Pictures-Pathe, 1931.
Bud Doyle, *Sweepstakes,* RKO Radio Pictures-Pathe, 1931.
Tommy Jordan, *The Tip-Off* (also known as *Looking for Trouble*), RKO Radio Pictures-Pathe, 1931.
Danny Churchill, *Girl Crazy,* RKO Radio Pictures, 1932.
Ted the Third, *Broadway to Hollywood* (also known as *Ring up the Curtain*), Metro-Goldwyn-Mayer (MGM), 1933.
Andy, *Strictly Personal,* Paramount, 1933.
Bob, *Hollywood Party,* MGM, 1934.
Gridiron Flash (also known as *The Luck of the Game*), Radio, 1935.
Ellison, *Mutiny on the Bounty,* MGM, 1935.
(As Edward Quillan) Tod Mason, *Gentleman from Louisiana,* Republic, 1936.
Mike Edwards, *Big City,* MGM, 1937.
Bill, *London by Night,* MGM, 1937.
Ellery Queen, *The Mandarin Mystery,* Republic, 1937.
Chick, *Swing, Sister, Swing,* Universal, 1938.
Anderson, *Allegheny Uprising* (also known as *The First Rebel*), RKO Radio Pictures, 1939.
Sammy, *The Family Next Door,* Universal, 1939.
Henry, *The Flying Irishman,* RKO Radio Pictures, 1939.
Ray Peters, *Hawaiian Nights,* Universal, 1939.
Conway, *Made for Each Other,* United Artists, 1939.
Adam Clay, *Young Mr. Lincoln,* Twentieth Century-Fox/Cosmopolitan, 1939.
Jack Norcross, *Dancing on a Dime,* Paramount, 1940.

Connie Rivers, *The Grapes of Wrath,* Twentieth Century-Fox, 1940.

Jerry Jones, *Dark Streets of Cairo,* Universal, 1940.

Titus Endover, *La Conga Nights,* Universal, 1940.

Joe, *Margie,* Universal, 1940.

Third sailor, *The Flame of New Orleans,* Universal, 1941.

Riley, *Flying Blind,* Paramount, 1941.

Skat, *Six Lessons from Madame La Zonga,* Universal, 1941.

Wally Pelton, *Too Many Blondes,* Universal, 1941.

Joe Olson, *Where Did You Get that Girl?,* Universal, 1941.

Eddie Wright, *Kid Glove Killer,* MGM, 1942.

Sticks O'Hara, *Priorities on Parade,* Paramount, 1942.

Pompadour Jones, *Alaska Highway,* Paramount, 1943.

Marvin Howe, *Follow the Band* (also known as *Trombone from Heaven*), Universal, 1943.

Jimmy Kelly, *Here Comes Kelly,* Monogram, 1943.

Corky Mills, *Hi Ya, Sailor,* Universal, 1943.

Harry the Horse, *It Ain't Hay* (also known as *Money for Jam*), Universal, 1943.

Jimmy Tracy, *Melody Parade,* Monogram, 1943.

Willie, *Dark Mountain,* Paramount, 1944.

Dynamo Carson, *Hi, Good-Lookin',* Universal, 1944.

Cochery, *The Imposter* (also known as *Strange Confession*), Universal, 1944.

Stubby, *Moonlight and Cactus,* Universal, 1944.

Charlie, *Slightly Terrific,* Universal, 1944.

Gus, *This Is the Life,* Universal, 1944.

Twilight on the Prairie, Universal, 1944.

Jeff Calhoun, *Dixie Jamboree,* Producers Releasing Corporation, 1945.

Ray Lawson, *Sensation Hunters,* Monogram, 1945.

Tony, *Song of the Sarong,* Universal, 1945.

George Cummings, *A Guy Could Change,* Republic, 1946.

Big Top, *Sideshow,* Monogram, 1950.

Sandy, *Brigadoon,* MGM, 1954.

The Ladies Man, Paramount, 1961.

Dingo, the phone repairman, *Who's Got the Action?,* Paramount, 1962.

Bellboy, *Move Over, Darling,* Twentieth Century-Fox, 1963.

Bartender, *Promises, Promises* (also known as *Promise Her Anything*), NTD, 1963.

Mailman, *Summer Magic,* Buena Vista, 1963.

Smitty, *Advance to the Rear* (also known as *Company of Cowards*), MGM, 1964.

Gunfight at Comanche Creek, Allied Artists, 1964.

M. C., *Viva Las Vegas* (also known as *Love in Las Vegas*), MGM, 1964.

Pianist, *The Bounty Killer,* Premiere, 1965.

Elevator operator, *The Ghost and Mr. Chicken,* Universal, 1966.

Cologne salesman, *A Guide for the Married Man,* Twentieth Century-Fox, 1967.

Salesman, *Did You Hear the One about the Traveling Saleslady?,* Universal, 1968.

Rev. Beckwith, *Angel in My Pocket,* Universal, 1969.

Old man, *How to Frame a Figg,* Universal, 1971.

TELEVISION APPEARANCES; SERIES

Angus, *The Rifleman,* ABC, 1958-63.

Grover Cleveland Fipple, *Valentine's Day,* ABC, 1964-65.

Horace Beesley, *The Addams Family,* ABC, 1964-66.

Eddie Edson, *Julia,* NBC, 1968-71.

Poco Loco, *Hell Town,* NBC, 1985.

Also appeared in *Moonlighting,* ABC, *Matlock,* NBC, *Police Woman,* and *Baretta.*

TELEVISION APPEARANCES; PILOTS

George Gobel Presents, ABC, 1963.

I and Claudie, CBS, 1964.

Emcee, *Cap'n Ahab,* CBS, 1965.

Max Lovechild, *Harry and Maggie,* CBS, 1975.

Seebring, *The Banana Company,* CBS, 1977.

Arthur, *Flatfoots,* NBC, 1982.

TELEVISION APPEARANCES; EPISODIC

Appeared in episodes of *Little House on the Prairie,* NBC, and *Highway to Heaven,* NBC.

TELEVISION APPEARANCES; MOVIES

Billy Lambert, *The Judge and Jake Wyler,* NBC, 1972.

Janitor, *She Lives,* ABC, 1973.

Counterman, *Hitchhike!,* ABC, 1974.

Hotel Clerk, *Melvin Purvis: G-Man,* ABC, 1974.

Rafferty, *Mad Bull,* CBS, 1977.

Watchman, *The Darker Side of Terror,* CBS, 1979.

Wino, *For the Love of It,* ABC, 1980.

Alfred Ammonet, *The Great Cash Giveaway Getaway,* NBC, 1980.

Old white man, *White Mama,* CBS, 1980.

Smitty, *Father of Hell Town,* NBC, 1985.

OBITUARIES AND OTHER SOURCES:

PERIODICALS

Los Angeles Times, July 24, 1990.*

R

RAPPAPORT, David 1951-1990

OBITUARY NOTICE—See index for *CTFT* sketch: Born November 23, 1951, in London, England; found dead near Los Angeles, CA, May 2, 1990, after committing suicide. Actor. Rappaport, a dwarf who held a degree in psychology from Bristol University in England, worked extensively in theatre, film, and television. He was perhaps best known for his recurring role on the NBC television series *L.A. Law,* in which he played a talented lawyer known as "Mighty Mouth." He also starred in the series *The Wizard,* which was broadcast on CBS from 1986 to 1987, and appeared on episodes of other series, including *Hardcastle and McCormick, Amazing Stories,* and *Mr. Belvedere.* His numerous British television credits include *File on Harry Jordan, The Young Ones,* and *Beauty and the Beast.* Among the films he appeared in were the 1981 comedy *Time Bandits, Cuba, Black Jack, Sword of the Valiant,* and *The Bride.* Rappaport also appeared in several British stage productions, including *Volpone, Dr. Faustus,* and *Exit the King.*

OBITUARIES AND OTHER SOURCES:

PERIODICALS

Los Angeles Times, May 4, 1990.
Variety, May 9, 1990.

*   *   *

RAWLINS, Adrian

PERSONAL: Son of Edward and Mavis (Leese) Rawlins. *Education:* Received B.A. from Crewe and Alsager College. *Avocational interests:* Cricket, travel.

ADDRESSES: Agent—Ken McReddie Ltd., 91 Regents St., London W1, England.

CAREER: Actor.

CREDITS:

STAGE APPEARANCES

(Stage debut) Jean, *Miss Julie,* Cafe Theatre, 1984.
Dromio, *Comedy of Errors,* Swan Theatre, Worcester, England, 1985.
Bobby, *American Buffalo,* Swan Theatre, Old Red Lion Theatre, Worcester, 1986.
(London debut) Rodolpho, *View from a Bridge,* National Theatre, 1987.
Roy Ruston, *A Small Family Business,* Olivier Theater, London, 1987.
Gentleman caller, *The Glass Menagarie,* Royal Exchange Theatre, Manchester, England, 1989.

FILM APPEARANCES

David Litvinoff, *Palm Beach,* Albie Thomas, 1979.
Maury Chaikin, *Double Negative,* 1980.
Bill, *Revolution,* Warner Brothers, 1985.
Edward Burton, *Mountains of the Moon,* Tri-Star, 1990.

TELEVISION APPEARANCES

Chris Chataway, *The Four Minute Mile,* BBC, 1988.
Arthur Kidd, *Woman in Black,* Central TV, 1989.
The Ginger Tree, BBC, 1989.
Christabel, BBC, 1989.

SIDELIGHTS: Favorite roles: Arthur Kidd in *Woman in Black.* Rawlins told *CTFT* that the films of Robert De Niro provided initial inspiration to try acting.

RAY, Aldo   1926-1991
(Aldo DaRe)

OBITUARY NOTICE—See index for *CTFT* sketch: Born Aldo DaRe, September 25, 1926, in Pen Argyl, PA; died of throat cancer and complications from pneumonia, March 27, 1991, in Martinez, CA. Actor. Ray gained fame for his portrayals of rough-edged soldiers in such films as *Battle Cry, Men in War, The Naked and the Dead,* and *The Green Berets.* Before he began acting, Ray enlisted in the Navy and fought in Japan during World War II. After the war he attended the University of California at Berkeley and served as town constable in Crockett, CA, before making his acting debut—using his original name—in the 1951 film *Saturday's Hero.* Beginning with his second film, *The Violent Ones,* the actor used the name Aldo Ray, and in the following four decades he appeared in more than sixty films. Though best known for his roles in war movies, Ray also appeared in such films as *Pat and Mike, We're No Angels, Miss Sadie Thompson,* and *God's Little Acre.* His television credits include the movies *Promise Him Anything* and *Women in White* as well as episodes of *The Virginian, Bonanza,* and *Falcon Crest.*

OBITUARIES AND OTHER SOURCES:

PERIODICALS

Hollywood Reporter, March 28, 1991.

*   *   *

REAVES-PHILLIPS, Sandra

PERSONAL: Born December 23 in Mullins, SC.

CAREER: Actress and singer. Has performed in concerts and at jazz festivals.

AWARDS, HONORS: Audelco Award, Outstanding Female Performer, for *Champeeen!,* 1985; nominated for Helen Hayes Award and National Association for the Advancement of Colored People (NAACP) Image Award.

CREDITS:

STAGE APPEARANCES

The Late Great Ladies of Blues and Jazz (one-woman show), John Houseman Theatre, New York City, 1982.
Mama Younger, *Raisin,* Crossroads Theatre, New Brunswick, NJ, 1983.
Harmony, *Basin Street,* New Federal Theatre, New York City, 1983.
Bessie Smith, *Champeeen!,* Harry DeJur Playhouse, 1983, then Henry Street Settlement Federal Theatre, 1985.
Freddie Banks, *American Dreams,* Negro Ensemble Company, Theatre Four, New York City, 1984.

Fat Momma, *Oh! Oh! Obesity!,* Louis Abrons Arts for Living Center, New Federal Theatre, New York City, 1984.
One Mo' Time, Crossroads Theatre Company, New Brunswick, NJ, c. 1985-86.
Big Bertha, *Further Mo',* The Village Gate, New York City, 1990.

Made Broadway debut as Mama Younger, *Raisin,* 1973. Also appeared as Ma Rainey, *Ma Rainey's Black Bottom,* Citadel Theatre; appeared in *Black and Blue,* Chatelet Theatre, Paris, France; *Blues in the Night; Sparrow in Flight; Stompin' at the Savoy; L'il Bit; Ragtime Blues; Karma;* and *Take Care.* Appeared in revues *Cavalcade of Stars,* Carnegie Hall; *Bold 'n Brassy Blues,* Hawaii; and *Heart to Heart.*

MAJOR TOURS

Appeared in *One, The Best Little Whorehouse in Texas,* and *The Late Great Ladies of Blues and Jazz,* all U.S. cities.

FILM APPEARANCES

Buttercup, *'Round Midnight,* Warner Brothers, 1986.
Mrs. Powers, *Lean on Me,* Warner Brothers, 1989.

TELEVISION APPEARANCES; SERIES

Appeared on *Another World,* NBC.

WRITINGS:

The Late Great Ladies of Blues and Jazz (one-woman show), produced at John Houseman Theatre, New York City, 1982.
(With Corliss Taylor-Dunn) *Opening Night* (musical), produced at AMAS Repertory Theatre, New York City, 1983.*

*   *   *

REEVES, Keanu   1965-

PERSONAL: Born in 1965 in Beirut, Lebanon. *Education:* Trained for the stage at Second City Workshop, Toronto, and Hedgerow Theatre.

ADDRESSES: Agent—Todd Smith, Creative Artists Agency, 9830 Wilshire Blvd., Beverly Hills, CA 90212.

CAREER: Actor. Appeared in television commercials.

CREDITS:

FILM APPEARANCES

Tommy, *Flying,* Golden Communications, 1986.
Hoover, *Youngblood,* Metro-Goldwyn-Mayer/United Artists, 1986.
Matt, *River's Edge,* Island, 1987.

Chris Townsend, *Permanent Record,* Paramount, 1988.
Winston Connelly, *The Night Before,* Kings Road, 1988.
Rupert Marshetta, *The Prince of Pennsylvania,* New Line Cinema, 1988.
Chevelier Danceny, *Dangerous Liaisons,* Warner Brothers, 1988.
18 Again, New World, 1988.
Ted "Theodore" Logan, *Bill and Ted's Excellent Adventure,* Orion, 1989.
Tod, *Parenthood,* Universal, 1989.
Marlon, *I Love You to Death,* Tri-Star, 1990.
Martin Loader, *Tune in Tomorrow,* Cinecom/Tri-Star, 1990.
Ted "Theodore" Logan, *Bill and Ted's Bogus Journey,* Orion, 1991.
Johnny Utah, *Point Break,* Twentieth Century-Fox, 1991.

Also appeared in *Prodigal.*

TELEVISION APPEARANCES; EPISODIC

Crackers, "Fast Food," *The Comedy Factory,* ABC, 1985.
Mick Riley, "Young Again," *Disney Sunday Movie,* ABC, 1986.
Joey, "Moving Day," *Trying Times,* PBS, 1988.
Kip, "Life under Water," *American Playhouse,* PBS, 1989.
Jesse, *The Tracey Ullman Show,* Fox, 1989.

TELEVISION APPEARANCES; MOVIES

First Stereo Teen, *Letting Go,* ABC, 1985.
Buddy Palmer, *Act of Vengeance,* HBO, 1986.
Alex/Jack Be Nimble, *Babes in Toyland,* NBC, 1986.
Eddie Talbot, *Under the Influence,* NBC, 1986.
Derek, *Brotherhood of Justice,* ABC, 1986.

OTHER TELEVISION APPEARANCES

Save the Planet (special), CBS, 1990.

Also appeared in *Hanging In* (television debut), CBC.

STAGE APPEARANCES

Appeared in *Wolf Boy* (stage debut), Toronto, Ontario; *For Adults Only;* and *Romeo and Juliet.*

OTHER SOURCES:

PERIODICALS

Rolling Stone, March 9, 1989.*

*   *   *

REUBENS, Paul
   See HERMAN, Pee-Wee

RITT, Martin   1914-1990

OBITUARY NOTICE—See index for *CTFT* sketch: Born March 2, 1914, in New York, NY; died of complications from heart disease, December 8, 1990, in Santa Monica, CA. Director, producer, and actor. Ritt gained prominence for making films that championed the oppressed and downtrodden. He began his career as a stage actor, joining Lee Strasberg's famous Group Theatre and appearing in such productions as *Golden Boy, The Gentle People,* and *Two on an Island.* He also began directing plays and achieved success in the 1940s with dramas, including *The Big People* and *Set My People Free.* In the late 1940s he started working in television and until 1951 appeared in more than one hundred fifty teleplays while also directing more than one hundred shows. In 1951, however, targeted by Senator Joseph McCarthy for alleged communist sympathies, Ritt was fired from his job with CBS. Unable to find work in television, he resumed his association with the Group Theatre and its Actors' Studio, before deciding to direct feature films. He made his first film, *Edge of the City,* in 1957 and in the following three decades found wide acclaim for such films as *The Long Hot Summer, The Molly Maguires, Sounder,* and *Hud,* which earned Ritt an Academy Award nomination for best director. One of his most successful films is *Norma Rae,* a 1979 picture about a textile worker's attempts to organize a union. Toward the end of his career Ritt directed *Murphy's Romance* and *Stanley and Iris* and resumed acting, appearing in such films as *The End of the Game* and *The Slugger's Wife.*

OBITUARIES AND OTHER SOURCES:

PERIODICALS

Hollywood Reporter, December 10, 1990.

*   *   *

ROBARDS, Sam   1962(?)-

PERSONAL: Born c. 1962.

CAREER: Actor.

CREDITS:

FILM APPEARANCES

Freddy, *Tempest,* Columbia, 1982.
Mike, *Not Quite Jerusalem,* Rank, 1984.
Kenneth Waggener, *Fandango,* Warner Brothers, 1985.
Moscowitz, *Bird,* Warner Brothers, 1988.
Rich Vanier, *Bright Lights, Big City,* Metro-Goldwyn-Mayer/United Artists, 1988.
Chaplain Kirk, *Casualties of War,* Columbia, 1989.

TELEVISION APPEARANCES; SERIES

Kevin Keegan, *TV 101,* CBS, 1988.
Larry Potter, *Get a Life!,* Fox, 1990—.

TELEVISION APPEARANCES; MOVIES

Daniel Timerman, *Jacobo Timerman: Prisoner without a Name, Cell without a Number,* NBC, 1983.
Stephen Walker, *Into Thin Air,* CBS, 1985.
Gene McKendry, *Pancho Barnes* (also known as *The Happy Bottom Riding Club*), CBS, 1988.

STAGE APPEARANCES

Boo, *Album,* Cherry Lane Theatre, New York City, 1980-81.
Saul, *Flux,* Second Stage, New York City, 1982.
The Philadelphia Story, Hartman Theatre, Stamford, CT, 1985-86.
Mr. Cherry, *Idiot's Delight,* John F. Kennedy Center for the Performing Arts, Washington, DC, 1986.
Tristram, *Taking Steps,* York Theatre Company, 1986.
Cootie, *Moonchildren,* Second Stage, 1988.*

*   *   *

ROBERTS, Julia   1967-

PERSONAL: Born in 1967 in Smyrna, GA; daughter of acting workshop proprietors.

ADDRESSES: Agent—Risa Shapiro and Elaine Goldsmith, International Creative Management, 40 West 57th St., New York, NY 10019.

CAREER: Actress.

AWARDS, HONORS: Independent Spirit Award nomination, best actress, 1988, for *Mystic Pizza;* Academy Award nomination and Golden Globe Award, best supporting actress, both 1989, both for *Steel Magnolias;* Academy Award nomination, best actress, and Golden Globe Award, best actress in a musical or comedy, both 1990, both for *Pretty Woman;* named Female Star of the Year, National Association of Theatre Owners, 1991.

CREDITS:

FILM APPEARANCES

Daisy Araujo, *Mystic Pizza,* Samuel Goldwyn, 1988.
Daryle Shane, *Satisfaction,* Twentieth Century-Fox, 1988.
Shelby Eatenton Latcherie, *Steel Magnolias,* Rastar/Tri-Star, 1989.
A call girl, *Off the Boulevard,* Touchstone Pictures, 1989.
Vivian Ward, *Pretty Woman,* Buena Vista, 1990.
Rachel Kinberg, *Flatliners* (also known as *L'Experience interdite, Linea Mortale* and *Morte Imminente*), Columbia, 1990.

Sara Waters/Laura Burney, *Sleeping with the Enemy* (also known as *Les Nuits avec mon ennemi* and *Feind in meinem Bett*), Twentieth Century-Fox, 1991.
Hilary O'Neil, *Dying Young,* Twentieth Century-Fox, 1991.

Also appeared as Marisa Collogero, *Blood Red,* filmed in 1986, released in 1989.

TELEVISION APPEARANCES; MOVIES

(Television debut) Candy Hutchins, *Baja Oklahoma,* HBO, 1988.

TELEVISION APPEARANCES; SPECIALS

The Sixty-Second Annual Academy Awards Presentation, ABC, 1990.
Barbara Walters Special, ABC, 1991.

OTHER SOURCES:

PERIODICALS

New York Times, March 18, 1990.
Vogue, April, 1990.*

*   *   *

ROBERTSON, Toby   1928-

PERSONAL: Born Sholto David Maurice Robertson, November 29, 1928, in Chelsea, London, England; son of David Lambert (a naval officer) and Felicity Douglas (a playwright; maiden name, Tomlin) Robertson; married Jane McCulloch, June, 1964 (divorced, 1981); children: Sebastian, Francesca, Sasha, Joshua. *Education:* Trinity College, Cambridge, B.A., 1952, M.A., 1981. *Avocational interests:* Painting, sailing.

ADDRESSES: Office—Theatr Clwyd, Clwyd CU7 1YA, N. Wales. *Agent*—International Creative Management, 388 Oxford St., London W1, England.

CAREER: Stage director. Actor, 1952-58. Prospect Theatre Company, England, artistic director, 1964-79; Circle Repertory Theatre, New York City, associate director, 1983-84; Theatr Clwyd, North Wales, U.K., artistic director, 1985—, founder of summer festival, 1986. Drama advisor, Argo Records, 1979—; professor of drama, Brooklyn College, Brooklyn, NY, 1981-83; member of faculty, British American Drama Academy, 1984—. *Military service:* 5th King's African Rifles.

MEMBER: Garrick Club (London).

AWARDS, HONORS: Wilson Memorial Lecture Award, Cambridge University, 1974; Officer of the Order of the British Empire, 1978; Obie Award from the *Village Voice,* best direction, 1980-81, for *Pericles.*

CREDITS:

STAGE DIRECTOR; BRITISH TOURING PRODUCTIONS FOR THE PROSPECT THEATRE COMPANY

The Soldier's Fortune, 1964.
You Never Can Tell, 1964.
The Confederacy, 1964.
The Importance of Being Earnest, 1964.
The Square, 1965.
Howard's End, 1965.
The Man of Mode, 1965.
Macbeth, 1966.
The Tempest, 1966.
The Gamecock, 1966.
A Murder of No Importance, 1967.
A Room with a View, 1967.
Twelfth Night, 1968.
No Man's Land, 1968.
The Beggar's Opera, 1968.
The Servant of Two Masters, 1968.
Edward II, 1969.
Much Ado About Nothing, 1970.
Boswell's Life of Johnson, 1970.
Venice Preserved, 1970.
King Lear, 1971.
Love's Labour's Lost, 1971.
Alice in Wonderland, 1971.
Richard III, 1972.
Ivanov, 1972.
Twelfth Night, 1973.
The Grand Tour, 1973.
Pericles, 1973.
The Royal Hunt of the Sun, 1973.
The Pilgrim's Progress, 1974.
A Month in the Country, 1974.

Several of Robertson's productions for the Prospect Theatre Company were performed in London and at the Edinburgh Festival of Music and Drama in Edinburgh, Scotland.

OTHER STAGE WORK; DIRECTOR

The Iceman Cometh, New Shakespeare Theatre, Liverpool, England, 1958.
The Lower Depths, Royal Shakespeare Company, London, 1960.
A Midsummer Night's Dream, Scottish Opera Company, 1972.
The Beggar's Opera, Phoenix Opera Company, 1972.
Hermiston, Scottish Opera Company, 1975.
The Marriage of Figaro, Scottish Opera Company, 1977.
War Music, Prospect Theatre Company, Old Vic Theatre, London, 1977.
Hamlet, Prospect Theatre Company, Old Vic Theatre, 1977.

Buster, Prospect Theatre Company, Old Vic Theatre, 1977.
Antony and Cleopatra, Prospect Theatre Company, Old Vic Theatre, 1977.
Twelfth Night, Prospect Theatre Company, Old Vic Theatre, 1978.
Great English Eccentrics, Prospect Theatre Company, Old Vic Theatre, 1978.
Ivanov, Prospect Theatre Company, Old Vic Theatre, 1978.
King Lear, Prospect Theatre Company, Old Vic Theatre, 1978.
Hamlet, Old Vic Theatre Company (formerly Prospect Theatre Company), Old Vic Theatre, 1979.
Romeo and Juliet, Old Vic Theatre Company, Old Vic Theatre, 1979.
The Government Inspector, Old Vic Theatre Company, Old Vic Theatre, 1979.
The Padlock, Old Vic Theatre Company, Old Vic Theatre, 1979.
The Trial of Queen Caroline, Old Vic Theatre Company, Old Vic Theatre, 1979.
Elisir D'Amore, Opera Company of Philadelphia, Philadelphia, PA, 1982.
Dido and Aeneas, Opera Company of Philadelphia, 1982.
Oedipus Rex, Opera Company of Philadelphia, 1982.
Night and Day, Huntington Theatre Company, Boston, MA, 1982-83.
Pericles, American Place Theatre, New York City, 1983.
The Tempest, Cleveland Play House, Cleveland, OH, 1983-84.
The Kiss, Wexford Opera Company, 1984.
Love's Labour's Lost, Circle Repertory Company, New York City, 1984.
Faust, Opera Company of Philadelphia, 1984.
The Barber of Seville, New York City Opera, 1984.
Barnaby and the Old Boys, Theatr Clwyd, North Wales, U.K., then Nuffield Theatre, Southampton, England, 1989.

Also director of *The Buskers,* 1959, *Pitlochry,* 1962, *Henry IV,* 1963, *Muir of Huntershill,* 1963, and *The Provok'd Wife,* 1964. Directed opera *A Midsummer Night's Dream,* Wiesbaden, Germany, 1984; directed *Richard II,* Folger Shakespeare Theatre, Washington, DC, and *Measure for Measure,* Beijing People's Arts Theatre, Beijing, China.

Director of productions at Theatr Clwyd between 1985 and 1989, including *Medea* (then Young Vic Theatre, London), *Taming of the Shrew* (then Haymarket Theatre, London), *You Never Can Tell* (then Haymarket Theatre), *Edward III, Captain Carvallo, The Revenger's Tragedy, The Old Devils,* and *Othello.*

MAJOR TOURS; DIRECTOR

Love's Labor's Lost, Prospect Theatre Company, Australian cities, 1971.

The Royal Hunt of the Sun, Prospect Theatre Company, Moscow, Leningrad, and Hong Kong, 1973.

Hamlet, Prospect Theatre Company, Elsinore, Denmark, and cities in Republic of China, 1979-80.

Also directed *Great English Eccentrics,* Moscow, Hong Kong, and Australian cities.

FILM WORK

Assistant director, *Lord of the Flies,* Continental, 1963.

TELEVISION WORK

Director of more than twenty-five productions for television, including *The Beggar's Opera, Richard II,* and *Edward II.*

*   *   *

ROCCO, Alex   1936-

PERSONAL: Born February 29, 1936, in Cambridge, MA; son of Alesandra Sam and Mary (Di Biasc) Petricone; married Sandra Elaine Garrett, March 24, 1966; children: Maryann Petricone, Marc Rocco, Jennifer Rocco, Lucien Rocco. *Education:* Attended public and private schools and Military Academy, Bordentown, NJ. Studied acting and speech with Leonard Nimoy. *Religion:* Bahai Faith.

ADDRESSES: Agent—The Gersh Agency, Inc., 222 North Cannon Dr., Suite 202, Beverly Hills, CA, 90210.

CAREER: Actor. Has also worked as a truck driver, and bartender in Hollywood's Rain Check Room. *Military service:* U.S. National Guard, 1952-55.

MEMBER: Screen Actors' Guild, American Federation of Television and Radio Artists, Actors Equity.

AWARDS, HONORS: Emmy Award, outstanding supporting actor in a comedy series, 1989, and two American Comedy Awards nominations, all for role as Al Floss in *The Famous Teddy Z.*

CREDITS:

STAGE APPEARANCES

Joan of Lorraine, Hartman Theatre Company, Stanford, CT, 1975-76.

FILM APPEARANCES

Cory Maddox, *Motor Psycho,* Eve Productions, 1965.

Diamond, *The St. Valentine's Day Massacre,* Twentieth Century-Fox, 1967.

Blood Mania, Crown International, 1971.

Stick, *Wild Riders* (also known as *Angels for Kicks*), Crown International, 1971.

Moe Greene, *The Godfather,* Paramount, 1972.

Lt. Danny Bassett, *Detroit 9000,* General, 1973.

Scalise, *The Friends of Eddie Coyle,* Paramount, 1973.

Miller, *The Outside Man* (also known as *Un Homme est Mort*), United Artists, 1973.

Man with ice cream, *Slither,* Metro-Goldwyn-Mayer (MGM), 1973.

Richard Thomkins, *Stanley,* Crown, 1973.

District Attorney, *Freebie and the Bean,* Warner Brothers, 1974.

Lt. DiNisco, *Three the Hard Way,* Allied Artists, 1974.

Earl, and (role of) Assistant Director, *Hearts of the West* (also known as *Hollywood Cowboy*), MGM/United Artists, 1975.

Vinnie and Blackjack Kibitzer, *Rafferty and the Gold Dust Twins* (also known as *Rafferty and the Highway Hustlers*), Warner Brothers, 1975.

Al, *Fire Sale,* Twentieth Century-Fox, 1977.

Danny, *Rabbit Test,* Avco Embassy, 1978.

Frank Rothman, *Voices,* MGM/United Artists, 1979.

Quinn, *Herbie Goes Bananas,* Buena Vista, 1980.

Jake, *The Stunt Man,* Twentieth Century-Fox, 1980.

Boss, *Nobody's Perfekt,* Columbia, 1981.

Jerry Anderson, *The Entity,* Twentieth Century-Fox, 1982.

Tony, *Cannonball Run II,* Warner Brothers, 1984.

Al (Jonathan's father), *Gotcha!,* Universal, 1985.

Firestone, *Stick,* Universal, 1985.

Gus Keller, *Dream a Little Dream,* Vestron, 1990.

Arnie Fromson, *Wired,* Taurus, 1990.

Other appearances include *Brute Corps,* 1972, *Bonnie's Kids,* 1973, *A Woman for All Men,* 1975, Lester, *P. K. and the Kid,* 1982, Barry Sleerik, *Return to Horror High,* 1986, Nathan DiAngelo, *Scenes from the Goldmine,* 1987, and Angelo, *Lady in White,* 1988.

TELEVISION APPEARANCES; MOVIES

Swifty, *Hustling,* Filmways, 1975.

Detective Charley Bronski, *The Blue Knight* (pilot), CBS, 1975.

Murray Zuckerman, *Husbands and Wives* (pilot), CBS, 1977.

Mel Duvall, *A Question of Guilt,* CBS, 1978.

Ralph Corliss, *The Grass Is Always Greener Over the Septic Tank,* CBS, 1978.

Jay, *The First Time,* ABC, 1982.

Bill Butler, *Badge of the Assassin,* CBS, 1985.

Orsini, *Braker,* ABC, 1985.

Arthur, "Changing Patterns," *CBS Summer Playhouse,* CBS, 1987.

Jerry Weiss, "Rock 'n' Roll Mom," *Disney Sunday Movie*, ABC, 1988.

Al Floss, *The Famous Teddy Z*, CBS, 1989.

Beverly Hills Get Rich Quick Murders (also known as *Bad Times in Beverly Hills, Your Money or Your Wife*, and *The Couch Potato Murders*), CBS, 1990.

Police Detective Locke, *A Quiet Little Neighborhood, A Perfect Little Murder* (also known as *Honey, Let's Kill the Neighbors* and *The Don and Judy Show*), NBC, 1990.

Other appearances include *Three for the Road* and Walter Summers, *How to Murder a Millionaire*, 1990.

TELEVISION APPEARANCES; SPECIALS

Frank, *Twigs*, CBS, 1975.

Guest, *Lily—Sold Out*, CBS, 1981.

The Thirty-Ninth Annual Emmy Awards (also known as *The Emmy Awards*), Fox Broadcasting, 1987.

Comic Relief III (also known as *Comic Relief*), HBO, 1989.

The Fourth Annual American Comedy Awards (also known as *The American Comedy Awards*), ABC, 1990.

OTHER TELEVISION APPEARANCES

Pete Karras, *Three for the Road* (series), CBS, 1975.

Harry Bell, *This Better Be It* (pilot), CBS, 1976.

Frank Millerson, *79 Park Avenue* (six-part mini-series; also known as *Harold Robbins' "79 Park Avenue"*), NBC, 1977.

Murray Zuckerman, *Husbands, Wives and Lovers* (series), CBS, 1978.

Charlie Polniaszek (Jo's father), *The Facts of Life* (series), NBC, 1979-80.

Gene Falcone (Pete's father), *The Best of Times* (pilot), CBS, 1983.

Casper Stieglitz, *An Inconvenient Woman* (four-hour mini-series), ABC, 1991.

Also appeared in episodes of *That Girl, Cannon, Kojak, Lotsa Luck, The Rookies*, and *Alan King's Final Warning*.

OTHER SOURCES:

PERIODICALS

TV Guide, September 23, 1989.

*   *   *

RONSTADT, Linda 1946-

PERSONAL: Full name, Linda Marie Ronstadt; born July 15, 1946, in Tucson, AZ; daughter of Gilbert and Ruthmary (Copeman) Ronstadt. *Education:* Attended University of Arizona, c. 1964.

ADDRESSES: Manager—Peter Asher Management, 644 N. Doheny Dr., Los Angeles, CA 90069.

CAREER: Singer and actress. Member of Stone Poneys recording group, 1964-68; solo artist, 1968—. Has made numerous concert tours in United States, Japan, Europe, Australia, and New Zealand; singer at concert for inauguration of U.S. President Jimmy Carter, 1977.

AWARDS, HONORS: Grammy awards, 1975, for best country vocal performance, female, for "I Can't Help It (If I'm Still in Love with You)," 1976, for best pop vocal performance, female, for *Hasten Down the Wind*, 1987, for best country performance by a group with vocal, for *Trio* (with Dolly Parton and Emmylou Harris), 1988, for best Mexican/American performance, for *Canciones de mi padre*, 1989, for best pop performance by a duo with vocal, for "Don't Know Much" (with Aaron Neville), 1990, for best pop performance by a duo with vocal, for "All My Life" (with Neville); American Music Award, 1978; Female Vocalist of the Year, *Rolling Stone* Readers' Poll, 1978; Album of the Year, Academy of Country Music, 1987, for *Trio;* Emmy Award, outstanding individual performance in a variety or music program, 1989, for "Linda Ronstadt's *Canciones de mi padre*."

CREDITS:

STAGE APPEARANCES

Mabel, *The Pirates of Penzance*, Delacorte Theater, New York City, 1980, then Uris Theater, New York City, 1981.

Mimi, *La Boheme*, Public/Anspacher Theater, New York City, 1984.

TELEVISION APPEARANCES; SPECIALS

Mad Love Concert, HBO, 1980.

Hostess, *Linda Ronstadt in Concert*, HBO, 1984.

Kate and Anna McGarrigle in Concert, PBS, 1986.

The Twenty-Eighth Annual Grammy Awards, CBS, 1986.

The Twentieth Annual Country Music Association Awards, CBS, 1986.

Disney's Golden Anniversary of "Snow White and the Seven Dwarfs," NBC, 1987.

Viva Miami! The Night of Super Sounds, CBS, 1989.

The Thirty-First Annual Grammy Awards, CBS, 1989.

Super Bowl Saturday Nite, CBS, 1990.

The Thirty-Second Annual Grammy Awards, CBS, 1990.

Host, *Women Song*, PBS, 1990.

TELEVISION APPEARANCES; EPISODIC

The Johnny Cash Show, ABC, 1969-71.

Motown Revue, NBC, 1985.

"George Gershwin Remembered," *American Masters,* PBS, 1987.

La Chata, Adelita, "Corridos! Tales of Passion and Revolution," *From San Francisco,* PBS, 1987.

"Linda Ronstadt's *Canciones de mi padre*," *Great Performances,* PBS, 1989.

"You're the Top: The Cole Porter Story," *American Masters,* PBS, 1990.

"Smokey Robinson," *Motown on Showtime,* Showtime, 1990.

FILM APPEARANCES

Concert performer, *FM,* Universal, 1978.

Mabel, *The Pirates of Penzance,* Universal, 1983.

The Return of Reuben Blades, Films Around the World, 1985.

Hail! Hail! Rock 'n' Roll!, Universal, 1987.

RECORDINGS:

ALBUMS

(With Stone Poneys) *Evergreen,* Capitol, 1967.

(With Stone Poneys) *Evergreen, Volume II,* Capitol, 1967.

(With Stone Poneys) *Linda Ronstadt, the Stone Poneys, and Friends, Volume III,* Capitol, 1968.

Hand Sown . . . Home Grown, Capitol, 1969.

Silk Purse, Capitol, 1970.

Linda Ronstadt, Capitol, 1972.

Don't Cry Now, Asylum, 1973.

Heart Like a Wheel, Capitol, 1974.

Different Drum, Asylum, 1974.

Prisoner in Disguise, Asylum, 1975.

Hasten Down the Wind, Asylum, 1976.

Linda Ronstadt's Greatest Hits, Asylum, 1976.

(With Stone Poneys) *The Stone Poneys Featuring Linda Ronstadt,* Capitol, 1976.

Simple Dreams, Asylum, 1977.

Blue Bayou, Asylum, 1977.

Retrospective, Asylum, 1977.

Living in the U.S.A., Asylum, 1978.

Mad Love, Asylum, 1980.

Linda Ronstadt's Greatest Hits, Volume II, Asylum, 1980.

Get Closer, Asylum, 1982.

What's New?, Asylum, 1983.

Lush Life, Asylum, 1984.

For Sentimental Reasons, Asylum, 1986.

Prime of Life, Asylum, 1986.

Rockfile, Asylum, 1986.

(With Dolly Parton and Emmylou Harris) *Trio,* Warner Bros., 1986.

'Round Midnight: The Nelson Riddle Sessions, Asylum, 1987.

Canciones de mi padre, Asylum, 1987.

Cry Like a Rainstorm, Howl Like the Wind, Elektra, 1989.

ROOKER, Michael   1955(?)-

PERSONAL: Born c. 1955 in Jasper, AL. *Education:* Goodman School of Drama, DePaul University, B.F.A., 1982.

ADDRESSES: Agent—Gersh Agency, 222 North Canon Dr., Suite 202, Beverly Hills, CA 90210.

CAREER: Actor.

CREDITS:

FILM APPEARANCES

(Film debut) Cop, *Streets of Fire,* Universal, 1984.

Henry, *Henry: Portrait of a Serial Killer,* Maljack, 1986.

Chick Gandil, *Eight Men Out,* Orion, 1988.

Frank Baily, *Mississippi Burning,* Orion, 1988.

Joe, *Rent-a-Cop,* King's Road, 1988.

Man at bar, *Above the Law,* Warner Brothers, 1988.

Karchy Laszlo, *Music Box,* Tri-Star, 1989.

Terry, *Sea of Love,* Universal, 1989.

Rowdy Burns, *Days of Thunder,* Paramount, 1990.

Also appeared in *Light of Day.*

TELEVISION APPEARANCES; MOVIES

Bosko, *L.A. Takedown* (also known as *Hanna*), NBC, 1989.

Detective John Quinn, *Sleep Well, Professor Oliver* (also known as *Gideon Oliver*), *ABC Mystery Movie,* ABC, 1989.

TELEVISION APPEARANCES; EPISODIC

Deputy Sheriff, *The Edge,* HBO, 1989.

STAGE APPEARANCES

Abundance, Manhattan Theatre Club, New York City, 1990.

Also appeared in *Union Boys, The Crack Walker,* and *Scheherazade* in Chicago, IL, and in *Not Your Average Serial Killer* in New York City.*

*   *   *

ROSENMAN, Leonard   1924-

PERSONAL: Born September 7, 1924, in Brooklyn, NY; son of a store owner. *Education:* Studied piano with Julius Herford and Bernard Abramowitsch; studied composition with Arnold Schoenberg, Roger Sessions, and Luigi Dallapiccola; attended University of California, Berkeley.

CAREER: Composer, conductor, and educator. Piano teacher in New York City, during 1950s; conductor in Rome, Italy, c. 1962-66; instructor at University of Southern California; musical director of New Muse chamber orchestra. *Military service:* Served in U.S. Army Air Force during World War II.

MEMBER: International Society for Contemporary Music (member of board of directors).

AWARDS, HONORS: Margaret Lee Crofts Scholarship for study at Tanglewood, 1952; Oscar awards for best adaptation score, 1975, for *Barry Lyndon,* and 1976, for *Bound for Glory;* Emmy awards for music composition for dramatic underscore of a special, 1977, for *Sybil,* and 1979, for *Friendly Fire.*

CREDITS:

FILM WORK

Music director, *The Outsider,* Universal, 1962 (also see below).

Music director, *Barry Lyndon,* Warner Bros., 1975 (also see below).

Music director, *Bound for Glory,* United Artists (UA), 1976 (also see below).

Music director, *The Lord of the Rings,* UA, 1978 (also see below).

Assistance, *The Telephone,* New World, 1988.

TELEVISION WORK

Music conductor, *Sherlock Holmes in New York,* NBC, 1976.

WRITINGS:

FILM MUSIC

The Cobweb, Metro-Goldwyn-Mayer (MGM), 1955.
East of Eden, Warner Bros., 1955.
Rebel without a Cause, Warner Bros., 1955.
Bombers B-52, Warner Bros., 1957.
Edge of the City, MGM, 1957.
The Young Stranger, Universal, 1957.
Lafayette Escadrille, Warner Bros., 1958.
Pork Chop Hill, UA, 1959.
The Bramble Bush, Warner Bros., 1960.
The Crowded Sky, Warner Bros., 1960.
The Plunderers, Allied Artists, 1960.
The Rise and Fall of Legs Diamond, Warner Bros., 1960.
The Chapman Report, Warner Bros., 1962.
Convicts Four, Allied Artists, 1962.
Hell is for Heroes, Paramount, 1962.
The Outsider, Universal, 1962.
A Covenant with Death, Warner Bros., 1966.
Fantastic Voyage, Twentieth Century-Fox, 1966.
Countdown, Warner Bros., 1968.
This Savage Land, Universal, 1969.
Beneath the Planet of the Apes, Twentieth Century-Fox, 1970.

A Man Called Horse, National General Pictures, 1970.
The Todd Killings, National General, 1971.
Battle for the Planet of the Apes, Twentieth Century-Fox, 1973.
Music adaptation, *Barry Lyndon,* Warner Bros., 1975.
Race with the Devil, Twentieth Century-Fox, 1975.
Birch Interval, Gamma III, 1976.
Music adaptation, *Bound for Glory,* UA, 1976.
The Car, Universal, 1977.
9/30/55, Universal, 1977.
An Enemy of the People, Warner Bros., 1978.
The Lord of the Rings, UA, 1978.
Promises in the Dark, Warner Bros., 1979.
Prophecy, Paramount, 1979.
Hide in Plain Sight, UA, 1980.
Additional music, incidental music, *The Jazz Singer,* Associated Film, 1980.
Making Love, Twentieth Century-Fox, 1982.
Cross Creek, Universal, 1983.
Heart of the Stag, New World, 1984.
Sylvia, MGM-United Artists Classics, 1985.
Additional music, *Star Trek IV: The Voyage Home,* Paramount, 1986.
Robocop 2, Orion, 1990.
Ambition, Miramax, 1991.

TELEVISION MUSIC; MOVIES

Banyon, NBC, 1971.
In Broad Daylight, ABC, 1971.
Vanished, NBC, 1971.
The Bravos, ABC, 1972.
The Cat Creature, ABC, 1973.
Judge Dee and the Monastery Murders, ABC, 1974.
Nakia, ABC, 1974.
The Phantom of Hollywood, CBS, 1974.
The First Thirty-Six Hours of Dr. Durant, ABC, 1975.
Sky Heist, NBC, 1975.
Kingston: The Power Play, NBC, 1976.
Lanigan's Rabbi, NBC, 1976.
Sybil, NBC, 1976.
Mary White, ABC, 1977.
The Possessed, NBC, 1977.
The Other Side of Hell, NBC, 1978.
Friendly Fire, ABC, 1979.
Nero Wolfe, ABC, 1979.
City in Fear, ABC, 1980.
Murder in Texas, NBC, 1981.
The Wall, CBS, 1982.
Celebrity, NBC, 1984.
Heartsounds, ABC, 1984.
The Return of Marcus Welby, M.D., ABC, 1984.
First Steps, CBS, 1985.
Promised a Miracle, CBS, 1988.
Where Pigeons Go to Die, NBC, 1990.

Aftermath: A Test of Love, CBS, 1991.

TELEVISION MUSIC; SERIES

Men from Shiloh, NBC, 1970.
Primus, syndicated, 1971.
Nakia, ABC, 1974.
Gibbsville, NBC, 1976.
Holmes and Yoyo, ABC, 1976.
Rafferty, CBS, 1977.
Joshua's World, CBS, 1980.

TELEVISION MUSIC; EPISODIC

"Miss Lonelyhearts," *American Playhouse,* PBS, 1983.

OTHER

Author of compositions for orchestra and chamber orchestra. Contributor of articles to periodicals, including *Film Music* and *Perspectives of New Music.*

SIDELIGHTS: In the early 1950s Leonard Rosenman was an aspiring composer who lived in New York City and supported himself by giving piano lessons. One of his students was an up-and-coming young actor named James Dean. When Dean broke into Hollywood by being cast in the film *East of Eden,* he told the director—Elia Kazan—about his music teacher. Kazan recruited Rosenman to score the picture, and the composer went on to an extended career in Hollywood, earning acclaim for bringing a modern, twentieth-century sound to the highly traditional world of film music.

OTHER SOURCES:

PERIODICALS

New York Times, August 29, 1982.*

*　　*　　*

ROSS, Frank   1904-1990

PERSONAL: Born August 12, 1904, in Boston, MA; died following brain surgery, February 18, 1990, in Los Angeles, CA; married Jean Arthur (an actress), 1932 (divorced, 1949); married Joan Caulfield (an actress), 1950 (divorced, 1959); married Joan Bradshaw; children: (second marriage) Kevin. *Education:* Graduated from Princeton University.

CAREER: Actor, producer, director, and writer. President of Frank Ross Inc.

AWARDS, HONORS: Academy Award nominations for best screenplay (with Richard Flournoy, Robert Russell, and Lewis Russell), 1943, for *The More the Merrier,* and for best picture, 1953, for *The Robe;* Academy Award for special work (with Mervyn LeRoy), 1945, for *The House I Live In.*

CREDITS:

FILM APPEARANCES

Ken, *The Saturday Night Kid,* FP/Paramount, 1929.
Lieutenant Graham, *Young Eagles,* Paramount, 1930.

FILM WORK; PRODUCER, EXCEPT AS NOTED

Associate producer, *Of Mice and Men,* United Artists (UA), 1939.
(With Norman Krasna) *The Devil and Miss Jones,* RKO Radio Pictures, 1941.
A Lady Takes a Chance, Frank Ross/RKO Radio Pictures, 1943.
(With Harold Hecht) *The Flame and the Arrow,* Warner Brothers, 1950.
Director and (with John Stillman) producer, *The Lady Says No,* UA, 1951.
The Robe, Twentieth Century-Fox, 1953.
Demetrius and the Gladiators, Twentieth Century-Fox, 1954.
The Rains of Ranchipur, Twentieth Century-Fox, 1955.
(With brother, Richard Ross) *Kings Go Forth,* UA, 1958.
One Man's Way, UA, 1964.
Mister Moses, UA, 1965.
Where It's At, UA, 1969.
(With Douglas Morrow) *Mauric* (also known as *Big Mo*), National General, 1973.

Also worked as director and (with Mervyn LeRoy) producer, *The House I Live In* (short), 1945.

TELEVISION WORK

Producer, *Sally* (series), NBC, 1957-58.

WRITINGS:

(With Richard Flournoy, Robert Russell, and Lewis Russell) *The More the Merrier* (screenplay), Columbia, 1943.
(With Sol Sak and Robert Russell) *Walk, Don't Run* (screenplay), Columbia, 1966.

OBITUARIES AND OTHER SOURCES:

PERIODICALS

Hollywood Reporter, February 22, 1990.
Variety, February 28, 1990.*

*　　*　　*

RUBEN, Joseph   1951-

PERSONAL: Full name, Joseph P. Ruben; born in 1951 in Briarcliff, NY. *Education:* Attended University of Michigan; received B.A. from Brandeis University.

CAREER: Director, writer, and producer.

CREDITS:

FILM DIRECTOR

(And producer) *The Sister-in-Law,* Crown International, 1975 (also see below).
(And producer) *The Pom Pom Girls,* Crown International, 1976 (also see below).
Joyride, American International, 1977 (also see below).
Our Winning Season, American International, 1978.
G.O.R.P., Filmways, 1980.
Dreamscape, Twentieth Century-Fox, 1984 (also see below).
The Stepfather, New Century/Vista, 1987.
True Believer, Columbia, 1990.
Sleeping with the Enemy, Twentieth Century-Fox, 1991.

TELEVISION DIRECTOR

(With Stan Lathan, Jack Bender, and Ralph Rosenblum) *Breaking Away* (series), ABC, 1980-81.
Eddie Dodd (series; based on his film, *True Believer*), ABC, 1991—.

STAGE WORK

Assistant to the director, *Bridegroom of Death—A Ceremony of Remembrance,* The Cubiculo, New York City, 1973.

WRITINGS:

SCREENPLAYS

The Sister-in-Law, Crown International, 1975.
(With Robert Rosenthal) *The Pom Pom Girls,* Crown International, 1976.
(With Peter Rainer) *Joyride,* American International, 1977.
(With David Lougherty and Chuck Russell) *Dreamscape,* Twentieth Century-Fox, 1984.*

*   *   *

RUDDY, Albert S.   1934-

PERSONAL: Full name, Albert Stotland Ruddy; born March 28, 1934, in Montreal, Quebec, Canada; son of Hy and Ruth (Ruddy) Stotland. *Education:* University of Southern California, B.S., architectural design, 1956.

ADDRESSES: *Office*—5451 Marathon St., Los Angeles, CA 90038.

CAREER: Film producer. Universal Studios, Los Angeles, CA, film producer, 1960-62; Screen Gems, Los Angeles, film producer, 1966-67; Alfrany Productions, Los Angeles, president, 1965-72; Albert S. Ruddy Productions, Los Angeles, president, 1972—. Abroe Construction Co.,

Cranford, NJ, construction supervisor, 1955-57; Systems Development Corp., Los Angeles, systems analyst, 1958-59.

MEMBER: Academy of Motion Picture Arts and Sciences, Producers Guild of America (director, 1973-74), Variety Club of Southern California.

AWARDS, HONORS: Academy Award, Golden Globe Award, David D'Donatello award from the president of Italy, and Heraldo Award from Mexican Film Board, all 1972, for *The Godfather;* Golden Globe Award, 1974, for *The Longest Yard.*

CREDITS:

FILM PRODUCER

Wild Seed, Universal, 1965.
Little Fauss and Big Halsy, Paramount, 1970.
Making It, Twentieth Century-Fox, 1971.
The Godfather, Paramount, 1972.
The Longest Yard, Paramount, 1974.
Coonskin, Bryanston, 1975.
Matilda, American International, 1978.
The Cannonball Run, Twentieth Century-Fox, 1981.
Megaforce, Twentieth Century-Fox, 1982.
Cannonball Run II, Warner Bros., 1984.
Lassiter, Warner Bros., 1984.
(With Andre Morgan) *Farewell to the King,* Orion, 1990.

Also producer of *Paramedics, Speed Zone,* and *Impulse.*

TELEVISION WORK

Creator, *Hogan's Heroes,* CBS, 1964-71.
Producer, *The Stockers* (pilot), NBC, 1981.*

*   *   *

RUEHL, Mercedes

PERSONAL: Born in Queens, NY. *Education:* Received B.A. in English from College of New Rochelle; studied acting with Uta Hagen and Tad Danielewski.

ADDRESSES: *Agent*—Susan Smith and Associates, 121 North San Vicente Blvd., Beverly Hills, CA 90211.

CAREER: Actress.

AWARDS, HONORS: Obie Award from the *Village Voice,* 1985; National Film Critics Award, best supporting actress, 1988; Clarence Derwent Award, 1989; Antoinette Perry Award, best performance by a leading actress in a play, Drama Desk Award, best actress in a play, Outer Critics Circle Award, best performance by an actress, all 1991, all for *Lost in Yonkers.*

CREDITS:

STAGE APPEARANCES

Vanities, Cincinnati Playhouse in the Park, Cincinnati, OH, and Indiana Repertory Theatre, Indianapolis, IN, both 1977-78.

Girl, *Billy Irish,* Actor's Collective, Ray Gordon Theatre, 1980.

Medea, *Medea,* Denver Center Theatre Company, Denver, CO, 1980-82.

Beatrice, *Much Ado about Nothing,* Denver Center Theatre Company, 1980-82.

Lena, *Misalliance,* Denver Center Theatre Company, 1980-82.

Laninia, *Androcles and the Lion,* Denver Center Theatre Company, 1980-82.

Dorine, *Tartuffe,* Denver Center Theatre Company, 1980-82.

Masha, *The Three Sisters,* McCarter Theatre Company, Princeton, NJ, 1982-83.

Fran, *The Day They Shot John Lennon,* 1982-83.

Joyce, *Flirtation,* T.O.M.I. Terrace Theatre, 1983.

Lucille, *June Moon,* Manhattan Punch Line, Lion Theatre, New York City, 1983-84.

Monday after the Miracle, Cincinnati Playhouse in the Park, 1983-84.

Patricia, *Coming of Age in Soho,* Public/Martinson Hall, New York City, 1985.

Joan Brennan, *The Marriage of Bette and Boo,* Public/Newman Theatre, New York City, 1985.

Clara, *I'm Not Rappaport,* American Place Theatre, New York City, 1985.

Karen, *American Notes,* Public/Susan Stein Shiva Theatre, New York City, 1988.

Bella, *Lost in Yonkers,* Richard Rodgers Theatre, New York City, 1991.

Also appeared in *Other People's Money,* 1989.

FILM APPEARANCES

Eve, *Heartburn,* Paramount, 1986.

Kay, *84 Charing Cross Road,* Columbia, 1987.

Advertising agency executive, *Radio Days,* Orion, 1987.

Sheila, *The Secret of My Success,* Universal, 1987.

Mrs. Baskin, *Big,* Twentieth Century-Fox, 1988.

Connie Russo, *Married to the Mob,* Orion, 1988.

Samantha, *Slaves of New York,* Tri-Star, 1989.

Dr. Elizabeth Baylor, *Crazy People,* Paramount, 1990.

Another You, Tri-Star, 1991.

The Fisher King, Tri-Star, 1991.

Made film debut as policewoman in *The Warriors,* 1979; also appeared in *Four Friends,* 1981, and *Leader of the Band,* 1987.

RUFFELLE, Frances 1966-

PERSONAL: Born in 1966 in London, England. *Education:* Trained for the stage at Sylvia Young Theatre School.

ADDRESSES: Agent—ICM Duncan Heath Associates Ltd., Paramount House, 162-170 Wardour St., London W1V 3AT, England.

CAREER: Actress.

AWARDS, HONORS: Antoinette Perry Award, Best Supporting or Featured Actress in a Musical, Helen Hayes Award, Outer Critics Circle Award, and *Theatre World* Award, all 1987, for *Les Miserables.*

CREDITS:

STAGE APPEARANCES

Princess Louisa, *The Sleeping Prince,* Haymarket Theatre, London, 1983.

Dinah, *Starlight Express,* Apollo Victoria Theatre, London, 1984.

Eponine, *Les Miserables,* Royal Shakespeare Company, London, 1985, then (Broadway debut) Broadway Theatre, 1987.

Delilah, *Apples,* English Stage Company, Royal Court Theatre, London, 1989.

Yonah, *Children of Eden,* Prince Edward Theatre, London, 1991.

Also appeared as narrator in touring company of *Joseph and the Amazing Technicolor Dreamcoat,* 1982.

FILM APPEARANCES

Roxanne, *The Wildcats of St. Trinians,* Wildcat, 1980.

Eunice, *Kipperbang* (also known as *P'tang Yang Kipperbang*), Metro-Goldwyn-Mayer/United Artists, 1982.

TELEVISION APPEARANCES; EPISODIC

Sylvie, *The Equalizer,* CBS, 1988.

RECORDINGS:

Featured on cast recordings of *Starlight Express,* 1984, and *Les Miserables,* 1986, 1987. Appeared on recordings *Mack and Mable in Concert,* 1988, *Save the Children Christmas Album,* 1989, and *Children of Eden,* 1990; also appeared on Christopher Cross's *Back of My Mind,* 1988, and Ian Dury's *Apples,* 1989.

*   *   *

RUSS, William 1951(?)-

PERSONAL: Born c. 1951 in New Orleans, LA.

ADDRESSES: Agent—Bresler Kelly Kipperman, 15760 Ventura Blvd., Suite 1730, Encino, CA 91436.

CAREER: Actor. Member of Arena Stage Theatre Company, Washington, DC, 1978-79.

CREDITS:

TELEVISION APPEARANCES; SERIES

Burt McGowen, *Another World*, NBC, 1978.
Wes Connelly, *Crime Story*, NBC, 1986.
Roger LoCocco, *Wiseguy*, CBS, 1988.
Redmond Dunne, *Capital News* (also known as *Power House* and *Powerhouse*), ABC, 1990.

TELEVISION APPEARANCES; MOVIES, EXCEPT WHERE NOTED

J. O. Powell, *Crisis at Central High*, CBS, 1981.
Frank Heller, *Rehearsal for Murder*, CBS, 1982.
J. D. Smith, *Command 5*, ABC, 1985.
Jody Varner, *The Long Hot Summer* (mini-series), NBC, 1985.
Josh, *Second Serve*, CBS, 1986.
Lloyd Murdoch, *Blood and Orchids*, CBS, 1986.
Will Travis, *Houston: The Legend of Texas*, CBS, 1986.
Jake Willis, *The Loner* (pilot), ABC, 1988.
Lieutenant Ben Farlow, *Nasty Boys*, NBC, 1989.
Carl Goodrich, *A Promise to Keep* (also known as *Promises to Keep* and *Angels Without Wings*), NBC, 1990.

Appeared as Rattlesnake in the special *Robbers, Rooftops and Witchers*, 1982.

TELEVISION APPEARANCES; EPISODIC

Also appeared as Evan in *Miami Vice.*

FILM APPEARANCES

Demesta, *Just You and Me, Kid*, Columbia, 1979.
Paul Gaines, *Cruising*, United Artists, 1980.
Jimbo, *The Border*, Universal, 1981.
Little Dick Raidler, *Cattle Annie and Little Britches*, Universal, 1981.
Slick Goodlin, *The Right Stuff*, Warner Bros., 1983.
Sonny, *Raw Courage* (also known as *Courage*), New World, 1984.
Merle Draggett, *Beer*, Orion, 1985.
Danny Quintz, *Wanted: Dead or Alive*, New World, 1987.
Rob Sweeney, *Dead of Winter*, Metro-Goldwyn-Mayer/United Artists, 1987.
Luke, *The Unholy*, Vestron, 1988.
Nick Bartkowski, *Disorganized Crime*, Buena Vista, 1989.
Roy Dean Bream, *One Cup of Coffee*, Miramax, 1989.

STAGE APPEARANCES

J. J., *The Last Christians*, New Dramatists, 1975.

Kid Champion, Public/Anspacher Theatre, New York City, 1975.
Cody, *Visions of Kerouac*, Lion Theatre Company, 1976.
Cody, *Kerouac*, New Dramatists, 1976.
Peter Cope, *The Shortchanged Review*, New York Shakespeare Festival, Mitzi E. Newhouse Theatre, New York City, 1976.
Zan, *G. R. Point*, Marymount Manhattan Theatre, New York City, 1977.
Cracks, Playwrights Horizons, Queens Festival Theatre, New York City, 1977.
Bradley, *Buried Child*, Theatre De Lys, New York City, 1978-79.
Murph, *Ice*, Manhattan Theatre Club, New York City, 1979.
Buck, *The Chisholm Trail Went Through Here*, Manhattan Theatre Club, 1981.
Cooper, *Ghosts of the Loyal Oaks*, WPA Theatre, New York City, 1981.
Mickey "Spider" McGuire, *The Brixto Recovery*, South Street Theatre, New York City, 1982.
Cassius, *Julius Caesar*, Alliance Theatre Company, Atlanta, GA, 1983-84.
Neil Toomey, *Ghost on Fire*, La Jolla Playhouse, 1986.
Eilert Louborg, *Hedda Gabler*, La Jolla Playhouse, 1988.

*   *   *

RUSSELL, Jane   1921-

PERSONAL: Born June 21, 1921, in Bemidji, MN; daughter of Roy William and Geraldine Russell; married Robert Station Waterfield, 1943 (divorced, 1967); married Roger Barrett, 1967 (deceased); married John Calvin Peoples, 1974; children: (first marriage, all adopted) Thomas, Tracy, Robert. *Education:* Studied at Max Reinhardt's Theatrical Workshop and Madame Ouspenskaya's School of Drama.

CAREER: Actress. Photographer's model, 1939-40; secretary and treasurer of Russ-Field Corp., 1954-59. President, World Adoption International Fund (WAIF); member of advisory committee, Los Angeles County Bureau of Adoptions.

AWARDS, HONORS: Golden Apple Star of the Year award, Hollywood Women's Press Club, 1955.

CREDITS:

FILM APPEARANCES

(Film debut) Rio, *The Outlaw*, RKO Radio Pictures, 1943.
Joan Kenwood, *Young Widow*, United Artists, 1946.
Calamity Jane, *The Paleface*, Paramount, 1948.

Mildred "Mibs" Goodhug, *Double Dynamite,* RKO Radio Pictures, 1951.

Lenore Brent, *His Kind of Woman,* RKO Radio Pictures, 1951.

Julie Benson, *Macao,* RKO Radio Pictures, 1951.

Linda Rollins, *The Las Vegas Story,* RKO Radio Pictures, 1952.

As herself, *Road to Bali,* Paramount, 1952.

Mike, *Son of Paleface,* Paramount, 1952.

Dorothy, *Gentlemen Prefer Blondes,* Twentieth Century-Fox, 1953.

Mary Carson, *The French Line,* RKO Radio Pictures, 1954.

Amanda, *Foxfire,* Universal, 1955.

Bonnie (Mimi) Jones, *Gentlemen Marry Brunettes,* United Artists, 1955.

Nella Turner, *The Tall Men,* Twentieth Century-Fox, 1955.

Theresa, *Underwater,* RKO Radio Pictures, 1955.

Annie Caldash, *Hot Blood,* Columbia, 1956.

Title role, *The Revolt of Mamie Stover,* Twentieth Century-Fox, 1956.

Laurel Stevens, *The Fuzzy Pink Nightgowns,* United Artists, 1957.

As herself, *Fate Is the Hunter,* Twentieth Century-Fox, 1964.

Nona Williams, *Johnny Reno,* Paramount, 1966.

Jill Stone, *Waco,* Paramount, 1966.

Mrs. Shorn, *Born Losers,* American International, 1967.

Alabama Tiger, *Darker Than Amber,* National General, 1970.

TELEVISION APPEARANCES; SERIES

Rose Hollister, *Yellow Rose,* NBC, 1983-84.

Also appeared in *Judge Roy Bean,* 1955.

TELEVISION APPEARANCES; EPISODIC

Robert Mitchum: The Reluctant Star (also known as *Crazy about the Movies*), Cinemax, 1991.

Also appeared in *Hollywood Stars' Screen Tests,* 1984, and *The Desilu Playhouse,* CBS.

OTHER TELEVISION APPEARANCES

Brandy Macreedy, *Macreedy's Woman* (pilot), NBC, 1958.

Hollywood: The Golden Years (special), Arts and Entertainment, 1988.

Also appeared in *Bob Hope Special: Bob Hope's Road to Hollywood,* 1983.

STAGE APPEARANCES

(Broadway debut) Joanne, *Company,* Alvin Theatre, New York City, 1971.

Night of 100 Stars, Radio City Music Hall, New York City, 1982.*

*   *   *

RUSSELL, Willy   1947-

PERSONAL: Full name, William Martin Russell; born August 23, 1947, in Whiston, Lancashire, England; son of shopkeepers; married Ann Margaret Seagroatt, 1969; children: one son, two daughters. *Education:* Attended Childwall College of Further Education, 1969-70; St. Katharine's College of Higher Education, Cert.Ed., 1973.

ADDRESSES: Office—W.R. Ltd., 43 Canning St., Liverpool L8 7NN, England. *Agent*—Margaret Ramsay Ltd., 14-A Goodwin's Court, London WC2N 4LL, England.

CAREER: Writer. Liverpool Playhouse, Liverpool, England, associate director, 1981-83, honorary director, 1983—; founding director, Quintet Films, beginning 1982. Teacher, Shorefields Comprehensive, 1973-74; writer in residence, C. F. Mott College of Education, Liverpool, 1976; fellow in creative writing, Manchester Polytechnic, 1977-79. Also worked as a hairdresser, 1963-68, and warehouse laborer, 1968-69. Folk song composer and singer, performing with Kirbytown Three in clubs, and on radio and television, since 1965.

AWARDS, HONORS: Arts Council bursary, 1974; *Evening Standard* Award, 1974; London Theatre Critics Award, 1974, for *John, Paul, George, Ringo. . . and Bert;* Laurence Olivier Award, 1980, for *Educating Rita;* Society of West End Theatre Award, 1980 and 1983; M.A., Open University, Milton Keynes, Buckinghamshire, 1983; Academy Award nomination, Best Screenplay, 1984, for *Educating Rita;* Ivor Novello Award, 1985; Laurence Olivier Award, Best Comedy of the Year, and Drama Desk Award nomination, Outstanding New Play, both 1989, both for *Shirley Valentine.*

CREDITS:

STAGE APPEARANCES

Narrator, *Blood Brothers,* Liverpool, England, 1985.
Narrator, *Shirley Valentine,* Liverpool, 1986.

STAGE WORK

Director, *Educating Rita,* Liverpool, 1981.

WRITINGS:

PLAYS

Keep Your Eyes Down, produced in Liverpool, England, 1971.

Blind Scouse (includes *Keep Your Eyes Down, Playground,* and *Sam O'Shanker* [also see below]), produced in Liverpool, 1972.

Tam Lin, produced in Liverpool, 1972.

Sam O'Shanker (revised version), produced in Liverpool, 1973.

When the Reds (adapted from Alan Plater's play *The Tigers Are Coming—O.K.?*), produced in Liverpool, 1973.

Terraces, published in *Second Playbill I,* Hutchinson, 1973, collection published in *Terraces,* 1979.

John, Paul, George, Ringo . . . and Bert, produced in Liverpool, 1974, produced on the West End, 1974.

The Cantril Tales, produced in Liverpool, 1975.

Breezeblock Park (produced in Liverpool, 1975, produced on the West End, 1977), Samuel French, 1978.

One for the Road (produced as *Painted Veg and Parkinson,* Manchester, England, 1976, produced as *Dennis the Menace,* Norwich, England, 1978, produced as *Happy Returns,* Brighton, England, 1978, produced as *One for the Road,* Nottingham, England, 1979), Samuel French, 1980, revised version (produced in Liverpool, 1986, and on the West End, 1987), 1985.

Stags and Hens (also see below; produced in Liverpool, 1978, produced in London, 1984), Samuel French, 1985.

Educating Rita (also see below; produced in London, 1980, produced on Broadway, 1987), Samuel French, 1981.

Blood Brothers (also see below; produced in Liverpool, 1981, revised version produced in Liverpool and on the West End, 1983), Hutchinson, 1986.

Our Day Out (revised from his teleplay; also see below; produced in Liverpool and London, 1983), Methuen, 1984.

Educating Rita, Stags and Hens, and Blood Brothers, Methuen, 1986.

Shirley Valentine (also see below), produced in Liverpool, 1986, produced in London, 1988, produced on Broadway, 1989.

Also author of *Single Spies,* produced in London.

SCREENPLAYS

Educating Rita (based on his play), Columbia, 1983.

(And composer of music) *Shirley Valentine* (based on his play), Paramount, 1989.

(And composer of music) *Dancin' Thru the Dark,* Palace and British Screen, 1990.

TELEPLAYS

Break In, 1975, published in *Scene Scripts 2,* Longman, 1978.

Our Day Out, 1977, published in *Act 1,* Hutchinson, 1979.

Lies, 1978, published in *City Life,* Hutchinson, 1980.

Politics and Terror, 1978, published in *Working,* Hutchinson, 1980.

Also author of *King of the Castle,* 1973, *The Death of a Young, Young Man,* 1975, *The Daughters of Albion,* 1979, *The Boy With the Transistor Radio,* 1980, and *One Summer* (series), 1983.

PUBLISHED MUSIC

I Will Be Your Love, RKO, 1974.

OOee boppa OOee boppa, RKO, 1974.

Dance the Night, Paternoster, 1980.

Blood Brothers, Paternoster-Russell Music, 1983.

The Show, Timeact-Russell Music-Paternoster, 1985.

Mr. Love (film score), Russell Music-Warner Brothers, 1986.

OTHER

I Read the News Today (radio play), 1976, published in *Home Truths,* Longman, 1982.

Sam O'Shanker: A Liverpool Tale (verse), Mersey Yarns (Liverpool), 1978.

OTHER SOURCES:

PERIODICALS

Drama (London), summer, 1983.

New York Times, February 12, 1989; February 17, 1989.*

*   *   *

RYAN, Fran

PERSONAL: Born November 29 in Los Angeles, CA.

ADDRESSES: Agent—Dade/Rosen/Schultz Agency, 15010 Ventura Blvd., Suite 219, Sherman Oaks, CA 91403.

CAREER: Actress.

CREDITS:

FILM APPEARANCES

Farm woman, *Scandalous John,* Buena Vista, 1971.

$1,000,000 Duck, Buena Vista, 1971.

Pickup on 101, American International, 1972.

Mrs. Toklas, *How to Seduce a Woman,* Cinerama, 1974.

Mrs. Stockley, *The Apple Dumpling Gang,* Buena Vista, 1975.

Lucy, *Big Wednesday,* Warner Brothers, 1978.

The Great Brain, Osmond, 1978.

Cafe owner, *Straight Time,* Warner Brothers, 1978.

Adrian's nurse, *Rocky II,* United Artists (UA), 1979.

Mrs. Samuel, *The Long Riders,* UA, 1980.

Dowager, *Stripes,* Columbia, 1981.

Mrs. Hinkle, *Take This Job and Shove It,* AVCO-Embassy, 1981.
Marie Davies, *Mystique,* Televicine International, 1981.
Miss Prudence Dutchbok, *Private School,* Universal, 1983.
Farmer Wilma, *Savannah Smiles,* Gold Coast, 1983.
Colonel, *Americana,* Crown, 1983.
Gert Long, *Tough Enough,* Twentieth Century-Fox, 1983.
Ma Blankenship, *Pale Rider,* Warner Brothers, 1985.
Louise, *The Sure Thing,* Embassy, 1985.
Ma, *Quiet Cool,* New Line Cinema, 1986.
Granny Plug, *Rebel Love,* Troma Team, 1986.
Fainting lady, *Stewardess School,* Columbia, 1986.
Eyes of Fire, Aquarius, 1986.
Mavis Talmadge, *Chances Are,* Tri-Star, 1989.
Ma, *Lucky Stiff,* New Line Cinema, 1989.
Out Cold, Hemdale, 1989.

STAGE APPEARANCES

Merton of the Movies, Center Theatre Group, Ahmanson Theatre, Los Angeles, CA, 1976.

TELEVISION APPEARANCES; SERIES

Aggie Thompson, *The Doris Day Show,* CBS, 1968.
Doris Ziffel, *Green Acres,* CBS, 1969-70.
Miss Goodbody, *The New Zoo Revue,* syndicated, 1972.
Gertrude Gouch, *Sigmund and the Sea Monsters,* NBC, 1973.
Miss Hannah, *Gunsmoke,* CBS, 1974-75.
Voice characterizations, *Hong Kong Phooey* (animated), ABC, 1974-76.
Mrs. Belmont, *No Soap, Radio,* ABC, 1982.
Tillie Russell, *The Wizard,* CBS, 1986-87.

Also appeared as Rosie Carlson, *Days of Our Lives,* NBC.

TELEVISION APPEARANCES; PILOTS

Marcus Welby M.D., ABC, 1969.
Panic in Echo Park, NBC, 1977.
Frieda Beezly, *Deadly Game,* NBC, 1977.
Nurse Bremmer, *Who's on Call?,* ABC, 1979.
Mother Maggie, *Father of Hell Town,* NBC, 1985.
Jeannie, *Nick Knight,* CBS, 1989.

TELEVISION APPEARANCES; EPISODIC

I Dream of Jeannie, NBC, 1970.
Mrs. Madison, *The Odd Couple,* ABC, 1970.
"Witches' Feast," *Rod Serling's "Night Gallery"* (also known as *Night Gallery*), NBC, 1971.
Barney Miller, ABC, 1977.
Taxi, ABC, 1982.
Mrs. Peevy, *Punky Brewster,* NBC, 1985.
Helen Webster, *The Colbys,* ABC, 1986.
Old woman, "Fuzzbucket," *Disney Sunday Movie,* ABC, 1986.

Mrs. Abbott, *Amazing Stories,* NBC, 1986.
Terry Sinclair, *Leo and Liz in Beverly Hills,* CBS, 1986.
Frau Himmler, *The New Mike Hammer,* CBS, 1987.
Ethel LaRue, *Night Court,* NBC, 1987.
Lil, *Highway to Heaven,* NBC, 1987.
Minnie, *Houston Knights,* CBS, 1987.
The Asp, *Murphy Brown,* CBS, 1988.
Dorothy Curtis, *Matlock,* NBC, 1989.
Rose Mulligan, *Murder, She Wrote,* CBS, 1989.
Housewife, *The Bradys,* NBC, 1990.
The Dave Thomas Comedy Show, CBS, 1990.

Also appeared as emergency room nurse, *The Bold Ones,* NBC; housekeeper, *The Beverly Hillbillies,* CBS; *The Bill Cosby Show,* NBC; *The Brady Bunch,* ABC.

TELEVISION APPEARANCES; MOVIES

Ellen Mott, *Stalk the Wild Child,* NBC, 1976.
Ethel, *Goldie and the Boxer,* NBC, 1979.
Mrs. Roman, *The Adventures of Nellie Bly,* NBC, 1981.
Aggie, *Johnny Belinda,* CBS, 1982.
Beatrice's mother, *Life of the Party: The Story of Beatrice,* CBS, 1982.
Judge Roberta Morgan, *Ghost Dancing,* ABC, 1983.
Millie Clark, *The Return of Marcus Welby, M.D.,* ABC, 1984.
Hannah, *Gunsmoke: Return to Dodge,* CBS, 1987.

OTHER TELEVISION APPEARANCES

Martha Stedman, "Liza's Pioneer Diary," *Visions* (special), PBS, 1976.
Pat Boone and Family (special), ABC, 1978.
Nina Carrolle, *Hollywood Wives* (mini-series), ABC, 1985.*

*   *   *

RYAN, Meg   1963-

PERSONAL: Born 1963 in Fairfield, CT; daughter of a casting director. *Education:* New York University.

ADDRESSES: Agent— International Creative Management, 8899 Beverly Blvd., Los Angeles, CA 90048.

CAREER: Actress. Has appeared in numerous television commercials.

AWARDS, HONORS: Golden Apple Award, Hollywood Women's Press Club, 1989, for female discovery of the year.

CREDITS:

FILM APPEARANCES

(Film debut) Debby at age eighteen, *Rich and Famous,* Metro-Goldwyn-Mayer/United Artists, 1981.

Lisa, *Amityville 3-D,* Orion, 1983.

Carole, *Top Gun,* Paramount, 1986.

Maggie Cavanaugh, *Armed and Dangerous,* Columbia, 1986.

Lydia Maxwell, *Inner Space,* Warner Brothers, 1987.

Bev, *Promised Land,* Vestron, 1987.

Sydney Fuller, *D.O.A.,* Buena Vista, 1988.

Donna Caldwell, *The Presidio,* Paramount, 1988.

Sally Albright, *When Harry Met Sally,* Columbia, 1989.

DeDe, Angelica and Patricia, *Joe Versus the Volcano* (also known as *Joe Against the Volcano*), Warner Brothers, 1990.

Pamela Courson, *The Doors,* Tri-Star, 1991.

TELEVISION APPEARANCES; SERIES

Jane, *One of the Boys,* NBC, 1982.

Betsy Stewart Montgomery, *As the World Turns,* CBS, 1982-84.

Megan Harper, *Charles in Charge,* CBS, 1984.

Cally Oaks, *Wildside,* ABC, 1985.

Voice of Dr. Blight, *Captain Planet and the Planeteers,* syndicated, 1990.

Narrator, *Red Riding Hood/Goldilocks* (also known as *Storybook Classics*), Showtime, 1990.

OTHER SOURCES:

PERIODICALS

Daily News (New York), January 22, 1988; March 16, 1988.

Rolling Stone, February 11, 1988.*

*   *   *

RYDELL, Chris
   See RYDELL, Christopher

RYDELL, Christopher
(Chris Rydell)

PERSONAL: Born in Hollywood, CA; son of Marc Rydell (a director) and Joanne Linville (an actress). *Education:* Attended Yale University and the State University of New York at Purchase; studied acting with Peggy Feury, Stella Adler, and Robert Lewis. *Politics:* Democrat. *Religion:* None. *Avocational interests:* Golfing, going to the beach, going to movies, "reading books about people who have done terrible things."

ADDRESSES: Agent—c/o Marilyn Heston/Victoria Miller, Baker-Winokur-Ryder, 9348 Civic Center Dr., Suite 407, Beverly Hills, CA 90210.

CAREER: Actor. Formerly worked as a busboy.

CREDITS:

FILM APPEARANCES

Boy fishing, *Cinderella Liberty,* Twentieth Century-Fox, 1973.

Harry and Walter Go to New York, Columbia, 1976.

(Under name Chris Rydell) Sumner Todd, *On Golden Pond,* Universal, 1981.

Bob Jensen, *Gotcha,* Universal, 1985.

Biker, *Mask,* Universal, 1985.

Charlie, *The Sure Thing,* Embassy Pictures, 1985.

Drunken sailor, *The Check Is in the Mail,* Ascot Entertainment Group, 1986.

(Under name Chris Rydell) Everett, *Dixie Lanes,* Miramax, 1988.

Oliver Hudson, *How I Got into College,* Twentieth Century-Fox, 1989.

Tom Lloynd, *Listen to Me,* Columbia, 1989.

Juan Gallardo, *Blood and Sand,* Overseas Film Group, 1989.

Also appeared in *Indian Summer.*

TELEVISION APPEARANCES; EPISODIC

Appeared as child molester, *Cagney and Lacey,* CBS; fraternity head, *Family Ties,* NBC; and atheist student, *The Bronx Zoo.*

S

SACHS, Andrew 1930-

PERSONAL: Born April 7, 1930, in Berlin, Germany; immigrated to England; son of Hans Emil (an insurance broker) and Katharina (Schrott-Fiecht) Sachs; married Melody Lang (an actress); children: William, John, Kate. *Avocational interests:* Wildlife, photography, art.

ADDRESSES: Agent—Richard Stone, 18/20 York Building, Adelphi, London WC2, England.

CAREER: Actor and writer. *Military service:* National Service, Royal Armoured Corps.

AWARDS, HONORS: Variety Club Award for Most Promising Artist, 1977, for *Fawlty Towers.*

CREDITS:

STAGE APPEARANCES

(Debut) Tony, *Frieda,* Delawarr Pavilion, Bexhill-on-Sea, England, 1947.
(London debut) Grobhchick, *Simple Spymen,* Whitehall Theatre, 1958-61.
Hamid, *Stand by Your Bedouin,* Garrick Theatre, London, 1967.
Private enquiry agent, *Uproar in the House,* Garrick Theatre, 1967.
Mr. Gudgeon, *Let Sleeping Wives Lie,* Garrick Theatre, 1967.
Ringer Lean, thong, and film director, *A Voyage 'round My Father,* Haymarket Theatre, London, 1971-72.
Mr. Shanks, *Habeas Corpus,* Lyric Theatre, London, 1973.
No Sex Please—We're British, Strand Theatre, London, 1975.
Gregory, *Reluctant Heroes,* Greenwich Theatre, London, 1976.

Armand Desroches, *Monsieur Perrichon's Travels,* Chichester Festival, Chichester, U.K., 1976.
Andrew Aguecheek, *Twelfth Night,* Chichester Festival, 1976.
Arnold Crouch, *Not Now, Darling,* Savoy Theatre, London, 1979.
Bones, *Jumpers,* Aldwych Theatre, London, 1985.
Brod, *Kafka's Dick,* Royal Theatre, London, 1986.

MAJOR TOURS

Morgan, *Reluctant Heroes,* British cities, 1955.
Polignac, *Dry Rot,* British cities, 1956.
Arnold Crouch, *Not Now, Darling,* South African cities, 1969.
Arnold Crouch, *Not Now, Darling,* Toronto, Canada, and Australian cities, 1981.
Augustin Jedd, *Dandy Dick,* British cities, 1981.

FILM APPEARANCES

(Debut) Dotheby Hall Boy, *Nicholas Nickleby,* Universal, 1947.
Walter Wagner, *Hitler: The Last Ten Days,* Tomorrow Entertainment, 1973.
Barry, *Frightmare,* Ellman, 1974.
Young man, *The Confessional* (also known as *House of Mortal Sin*), Atlas, 1977.
Waiter Guido, *What's up Nurse,* Variety, 1977.
Hospital inmate, *Revenge of the Pink Panther,* United Artists, 1978.
Gerard, *History of the World, Part I,* Twentieth Century-Fox, 1981.
Jason, *Consuming Passions,* Samuel Goldwyn/Vestron, 1988.
Voice of Ardeco, *Asterix et le coup du Menhir* (also known as *Asterix and the Big Fight, Asterix and the Stone's Throw,* and *Le Coupe de Menhir*), Gaumont/Palace, 1989.

Also appeared in *Romance with a Double Bass,* 1974.

TELEVISION APPEARANCES; SERIES

Manuel, *Fawlty Towers,* BBC, 1975, 1979.
Rainbow Safari, BBC Natural History Unit, 1981-84.

Also appeared in *Tom O'Connor,* 1984; *Flight of the Condor;* and *The Discovery of Animal Behavior.*

OTHER TELEVISION APPEARANCES

Trinculo, *The Tempest,* BBC, then PBS, 1980.

Also appeared as Mr. Polly, *The History of Mr. Polly,* 1980; Ernest, *Dead Ernest,* 1982. Appeared in *Six Proud Walkers,* BBC; *Buddenbrooks,* 1965; *Are You Being Served?,* 1977; *This Is Your Life,* 1980; *There Comes a Time,* 1984; *James and the Giant Peach; Rising Damp; Krek Bristle; Took and Company; Crown Court; The Tommy Cooper Show; The Dawson Watch; Lovely Couple; The Michael Parkinson Show; Play It Again; World about Us; It'll All Be over in Half an Hour; The Galactic Garden;* and *Point of View.*

WRITINGS:

Made in Heaven (play; based on his radio play), produced in Chichester, U.K., 1975.
The Stamp Collectors (play), produced in Worthing, U.K., 1977.

Also author of published collection *Three Melodramas,* 1977; author of teleplays *Robin Hood Junior,* BBC; *It's Your Move,* BBC; and (with others) *The Galactic Garden.* Author of radio plays *Till Death Do Us Join,* 1964; *Flat to Let,* 1964; *Pie and Pea Supper,* 1966; *Kidnapped,* 1967; *Time for a Coat,* 1967; *Philately Will Get You Nowhere,* 1971; *Made in Heaven,* 1971; *Home from Home,* 1972; *Cash Me a Portrait,* 1972; and *The Revenge,* 1978.*

*   *   *

ST. JACQUES, Raymond   1930-1990

PERSONAL: Born James Arthur Johnson March 1, 1930, in Hartford, CT; died August 27, 1990, in Los Angeles, CA; son of Vivienne Johnson (a medical technician); children: Raymond, Sterling. *Education:* Studied psychology and drama at Yale University; studied at Actors Studio, New York City, and American Shakespeare Festival Academy, NY and CT; also studied acting with Herbert Berghof in New York City.

CAREER: Actor, director, and producer. Worked variously as a dishwasher, houseboy, model, and Bloomingdale's salesman in New York City. Fencing director for American Shakespeare Festival, Stratford, CT, during the 1960s.

CREDITS:

STAGE APPEARANCES

Judge, *The Blacks,* St. Mark's Playhouse, New York City, 1961.

Also appeared in (Off-Broadway debut) *High Name Today,* c. 1954, *Night Life, The Cool World,* and *Seventh Heaven.*

STAGE WORK

Choreographer, *Romeo and Juliet,* Old Globe Theatre, San Diego, CA, 1966.

FILM APPEARANCES

(Film debut) *Black Like Me,* Continental, 1964.
Ubi, *Mister Moses,* United Artists, 1965.
Tangee, *The Pawnbroker,* Allied Artists/American International, 1965.
Hank, *Mister Buddwing,* Metro-Goldwyn-Mayer (MGM), 1966.
Cancasseur, *The Comedians,* MGM, 1967.
Doc McGee, *The Green Berets,* Warner Brothers, 1968.
James Lake, *If He Hollers, Let Him Go,* Cinerama, 1968.
Dr. Taylor, *Madigan,* Universal, 1968.
B.G., *Uptight,* Paramount, 1968.
David Rowe, *Change of Mind,* Cinerama, 1969.
Coffin Ed Johnson, *Cotton Comes to Harlem,* United Artists, 1970.
Coffin Ed Johnson, *Come Back Charleston Blue,* Warner Brothers, 1972.
Bill Mercer, *Cool Breeze,* MGM, 1972.
Imir, *The Final Comedown,* New World, 1972.
Blueboy Harris, *Book of Numbers,* Associated Exhibitors, 1973.
John Kumalo, *Lost in the Stars,* American Film Theatre, 1974.
Jimmy Newsom, *Born Again,* Associated Exhibitors, 1978.
Martin Luther King, Jr., *The Private Files of J. Edgar Hoover,* American International, 1978.
Bell, *Cuba Crossing,* Key West, 1980.
Randolph, *The Evil that Men Do,* Twenty First Century, 1984.
Ivory, *The Wild Pair* (also known as *Devil's Odds*), Trans World Entertainment, 1987.
Street preacher, *They Live,* Universal, 1988.
Frederick Douglass, *Glory,* Tri-Star, 1990.

Also appeared in *Sweet Dirty Tony,* 1981.

FILM WORK

(Directing debut) Producer and director, *Book of Numbers,* Associated Exhibitors, 1973.

TELEVISION APPEARANCES; SERIES

Solomon King, *Rawhide,* CBS, 1965-66.
Dr. Hooks, *Falcon Crest,* CBS, 1983-84.

Also appeared in *Superior Court.*

OTHER TELEVISION APPEARANCES

The drummer, *Roots* (mini-series), ABC, 1977.

Also appeared in *Dark Mansions, Sophisticated Gents,* and *Search for the Gods.**

*   *   *

SAIRE, Rebecca   1963-

PERSONAL: Born April 16, 1963, in Hertfordshire, England; father, a singer; mother, an actress.

ADDRESSES: Manager—Jean Diamond, London Management, 235 Regent St., London W1A 2JT, England.

CAREER: Actress.

CREDITS:

STAGE APPEARANCES

Princess Beatrice in 1897, *I and Albert,* Piccadilly Theatre, London, 1972.
May Edwards, *The Ticket-of-Leave Man,* National Theatre Company, Cottesloe Theatre, London, 1981.
Madeline Bray, Phib, Mrs. Kenwigs' sister, and Miss Ledrock, *The Life and Adventures of Nicholas Nickleby,* Royal Shakespeare Company (RSC), Stratford-on-Avon, then Newcastle, England, later Broadhurst Theatre, New York City, all 1986.
Ophelia, *Hamlet,* RSC, Barbican Theatre, London, 1989.
Zsofi, *Have,* RSC, The Pit, London, 1989.
Table of the Two Horsemen, Greenwich Theatre, London, 1990.

FILM APPEARANCES

Hettie, *The Quatermass Conclusion,* Thames Video Collection, 1979.
Cicely Nettleby, *The Shooting Party,* European Classics, 1985.

TELEVISION APPEARANCES; MINI-SERIES

Victoria, *Love in a Cold Climate,* Thames, then PBS, 1982.
Ruth, *A.D.* (also known as *Anno Domini*), NBC, 1985.
Amelia, *Vanity Fair,* BBC, then Arts and Entertainment, 1988.
Theresa Nolan, *A Taste for Death,* Anglia Television, then *Mystery!* PBS, 1990.

TELEVISION APPEARANCES; SPECIALS

Juliet, *Romeo and Juliet,* BBC, 1978, then PBS, 1979.

Also played in title role, *Virgin Mary;* appeared in *Quatermass.*

*   *   *

SAKS, Gene   1921-

PERSONAL: Born November 8, 1921, in New York City; son of Morris J. and Beatrix (Lewkowitz) Saks; married Bea Arthur (an actress), May 28, 1950 (divorced). *Education:* Cornell University, A.B., 1943; attended New School for Social Research; studied acting at Actors Studio with Lee Strasberg, Sanford Meisner, and David Pressman, and at the Dramatic Workshop.

CAREER: Actor and director.

AWARDS, HONORS: Antoinette Perry award nominations, best director of a musical, 1965, for *Half a Sixpence,* and 1966, for *Mame;* Antoinette Perry award nominations, best director of a play, 1975, for *Same Time Next Year,* and 1991, for *Lost in Yonkers;* Antoinette Perry Award, best director of musical, 1977, for *I Love My Wife;* New York Drama Critics Circle Award, best director of a play, 1983, for *Brighton Beach Memoirs;* Antoinette Perry awards, best director of a play, 1983, for *Brighton Beach Memoirs,* and 1985, for *Biloxi Blues;* Outer Critics Circle Award, best director, 1991, for *Lost in Yonkers.*

CREDITS:

STAGE APPEARANCES

(New York debut) Joxer, *Juno and the Paycock,* Cherry Lane Theatre, New York City, 1947.
The butler, *Topaze,* Morosco Theatre, New York City, 1947.
Old shepherd, *The Infernal Machine,* Provincetown Playhouse, New York City, 1948.
The German, *Yes Is For a Very Young Man,* Cherry Lane Theatre, 1949.
Chauffeur, *Personal Appearance,* Circle Theatre, Atlantic City, NJ, 1951.
Bill Page, *Voice of the Turtle,* Circle Theatre, 1951.
Wilbur, *For Love or Money,* Circle Theatre, 1951.
Missouri Legend, Circle Theatre, 1951.
Professor, *South Pacific,* Majestic Theatre, New York City, 1951, then City Center Theatre, New York City, 1955.
Citizen and servant, *Coriolanus,* Phoenix Theatre, New York City, 1954.
Wicked Duke, *The Thirteen Clocks,* Westport Country Playhouse, Westport, CT, 1954.
Billy Gordon, *Late Love,* Westchester Playhouse, Mt. Kisco, NY, 1954.
Ragnar Brovik, *The Master Builder,* Phoenix Theatre, 1955.

Charlie Reader, *The Tender Trap,* Westchester Playhouse, 1955.

Richard Sherman, *The Seven Year Itch,* Westchester Playhouse, 1956.

Del Rio, *The Gimmick,* Westport Country Playhouse, 1956.

Various roles, *Johnny Johnston,* Carnegie Hall Playhouse, New York City, 1956.

First God, *The Good Woman of Szechuan,* Phoenix Theatre, 1956.

Son-in-law, *Middle of the Night,* ANTA Theatre, New York City, 1957.

Captain, *The Infernal Machine,* Phoenix Theatre, 1958.

The professor, *Howie,* 46th-Street Theatre, New York City, 1958.

Various roles, *Album of Leaves,* Spoleto Festival, Italy, 1959.

Rabbi, *The Tenth Man,* Booth Theatre, New York City, 1959.

Norman Yarrow, *Love and Libel,* Martin Beck Theatre, New York City, 1960.

Morestan, *A Shot in the Dark,* Booth Theatre, 1961.

Leo Herman, *A Thousand Clowns,* Eugene O'Neill Theatre, New York City, 1962.

The Goodbye People, Berkshire Theatre Festival, Stockbridge, MA, 1971.

Also appeared as the vicar and poet W. H. Auden in *Dog beneath the Skin;* as the engineer in *Gas;* as title role in Pirandello's *Henry IV;* and as Renee St. Gaul in *The Watched Pot,* all 1947; as the park attendant in *Within the Gates* and as the doctor in *him,* both 1948; as the professor of religion in *Too Many Thumbs* and as Monsieur Jordan in *The Bourgeois Gentleman,* both 1949; as the second discusser in *Marty's Double* and as Sam in *All You Need Is One Good Break,* both Mansfield, NY, 1950.

MAJOR TOURS; DIRECTOR, EXCEPT AS INDICATED

Half a Sixpence, U.S. cities, 1966-67.
Mame, U.S. cities, 1968.
I Love My Wife, U.S. cities, 1977.
California Suite, U.S. cities, 1977-78.
Brighton Beach Memoirs, U.S. cities, 1983-85.
Bye-Bye Birdie, U.S. cities, 1991.

Also appeared as Stefanowski in *Mr. Roberts,* 1950-51, and directed *The Millionairess,* 1963.

STAGE WORK; DIRECTOR

Enter Laughing, Henry Miller's Theatre, New York City, 1963.

Nobody Loves an Albatross, Lyceum Theatre, New York City, 1963-64.

Half a Sixpence, Broadhurst Theatre, 1964, then Curran Theatre, San Francisco, CA, 1966, later Dorothy Chandler Pavilion, Los Angeles, CA.

Generation, Morosco Theatre, 1965.

Mame, Winter Garden Theatre, New York City, 1966.

A Mother's Kisses, Shubert Theatre, New Haven, CT, 1968, then Mechanic Theatre, Baltimore, MD.

Sheep on the Runway, Helen Hayes Theatre, New York City, 1970, then Washington, DC, 1970.

How the Other Half Loves, Royale Theatre, New York City, 1971.

Same Time Next Year, Brooks Atkinson Theatre, New York City, 1975-78, then Ambassador Theatre, New York City, 1978.

California Suite, Eugene O'Neill Theatre, 1976-77.

I Love My Wife, Ethel Barrymore Theatre, New York City, 1977-79.

Home Again, Home Again, Royal Alexandra Theatre, Toronto, Canada, then American Shakespeare Theatre, Stratford, CT, 1979.

Save Grand Central, Phoenix Theatre Company, Marymount Manhattan Theatre, New York City, 1980.

Special Occasions, Music Box Theatre, New York City, 1980 and 1982.

The Supporting Cast, Biltmore Theatre, New York City, 1981.

Brighton Beach Memoirs, Alvin Theatre, New York City, 1983-84.

Biloxi Blues, Neil Simon Theatre, New York City, 1985, then Fox Theatre, Atlanta, GA, 1986-87.

The Odd Couple, Broadhurst Theatre, 1985, then Center Theatre Group, Ahmanson Theatre, Los Angeles, CA, 1985.

Rags, Mark Hellinger Theatre, New York City, 1986.

Broadway Bound, Broadhurst Theatre, 1986-88.

A Month of Sundays, Ritz Theatre, New York City, 1987.

Rumors, Broadhurst Theatre, 1988.

The Man Who Came to Dinner, Barbican Theatre, London, 1989.

Lost in Yonkers, Richard Rodgers Theatre, New York City, 1991.

Also directed *Prince of Grand Street,* Philadelphia and Boston, 1978.

FILM APPEARANCES

Leo Herman, *A Thousand Clowns,* United Artists, 1965.
The Prisoner of Second Avenue, Warner Brothers, 1974.
Sidney Seltzer, *The One and Only,* Paramount, 1978.
Frantic patient, *Lovesick,* Warner Brothers, 1983.
Marcus Soloway, *The Goodbye People,* Embassy, 1984.

FILM WORK; DIRECTOR

Barefoot in the Park, Paramount, 1967.
The Odd Couple, Paramount, 1968.

Cactus Flower, Columbia, 1969.
Last of the Red Hot Lovers, Paramount, 1972.
Mame, Warner Brothers, 1974.
Brighton Beach Memoirs, Universal, 1986.
Tchin-Tchin, Independent CEP (France), 1989.

TELEVISION APPEARANCES

Psychiatrist, *Love, Sex, and Marriage* (special), ABC, 1983.

Also appeared in *The Actors Studio Series,* 1949, *U.S. Steel Hour, You Are There, Playwright 1955-56, Philco Playhouse, Circle Armstrong Theatre,* and *Producer's Showcase.*

TELEVISION WORK

Director, *Love, Sex, and Marriage* (special), ABC, 1983.

*   *   *

SARA, Mia   1968-

PERSONAL: Born in 1968 in Brooklyn, NY.

CAREER: Actress. Began career in television commercials.

CREDITS:

FILM APPEARANCES

Princess Lili, *Legend,* Universal, 1985.
Sloane Peterson, *Ferris Bueller's Day Off,* Paramount, 1986.
Alice Spangler, *Apprentice to Murder,* New World, 1988.
Melanie, *Shadows in the Storm,* Vidmark, 1988.

Also appeared as Gerlind in *Any Man's Death;* in *The Long Lost Friend,* and in *Imagination.*

TELEVISION APPEARANCES; MOVIES

Queenie Kelly, *Queenie,* ABC, 1987.
Delphine de Lancel, *Judith Krantz's Till We Meet Again* (also known as *Till We Meet Again*), CBS, 1989.

Also appeared as Cathy Thatcher in *Daughter of Darkness.*

TELEVISION APPEARANCES; EPISODIC

Fran, *Big Time, American Playhouse,* CBS, 1989.

Also appeared on *Alfred Hitchcock Presents,* and had a recurring role in *All My Children.**

SATO, Isao   1949-1990

PERSONAL: Born June 27, 1949, in Tokyo, Japan; died in an airplane crash, March 9, 1990; son of Toshio Hirai (a real estate salesman) and Kyoko Sato; married Shizue Kanemitsu, October 17, 1976 (divorced, 1979). *Education:* Attended Keio University, Japan; trained for the stage at Toho Musical Academy and Shiki Theatrical Company.

CAREER: Actor. Appeared in Tokyo, Japan, with Shiki Theatrical Company before coming to United States in 1975; appeared on radio and television.

MEMBER: Actors' Equity Association, Screen Actors Guild, American Federation of Television and Radio Artists.

AWARDS, HONORS: Shiki Theatre Award, most promising actor, 1971; Antoinette Perry Award nomination, best featured actor in a musical, 1976, for *Pacific Overtures.*

CREDITS:

STAGE APPEARANCES

(Stage debut) Soldier, *The Wizard of Oz,* Nissei Theatre, Tokyo, Japan, 1970.
Servant, *Nobunaga-Ki,* Nissei Theatre, 1971.
Title role, *Lelio,* Tokyo Bunka Kaikan, Tokyo, 1971.
Theo, *Piaf,* Nissei Theatre, 1971.
Narrator, *Soldier's Tale,* Tokyo Bunka Kaikan, 1972.
Servant, *Marriage of Figaro,* Dai-ichi Seimei Hall, Tokyo, 1972.
Fox, *Animal Conference,* Nissei Theatre, 1972.
First player and Player Queen, *Hamlet,* Nissei Theatre, 1972.
Theo, *Piaf,* Yubin-chokin Hall, 1972.
Balthazar, *Much Ado About Nothing,* Dai-ichi Seimei Hall, 1973.
Patrick Dennis, *Mame,* Nissei Theatre, 1973.
Theo, *Piaf,* Nissei Theatre, 1974.
Yukichi Fukuzawa, *John Manjiro,* Nissei Theatre, 1974.
Kayama, *Pacific Overtures,* Winter Garden Theatre, New York City, 1976.
Sup-tai, *Genghis Khan,* Imperial Theatre, Tokyo, 1977.
Eiko, *Utamaro,* Imperial Theatre, 1977.
I Love My Wife, Ethel Barrymore Theatre, New York City, 1977.
Title role, *Aladdin,* Orpheum Theatre, Vancouver, Canada, then Concert Hall, Winnipeg, Canada, 1978.
Chan Ch'uer and Fa-lian, *Fanshen,* A Contemporary Theatre, Seattle, WA, 1979.
Zeng Wenging, *Peking Man,* Horace Mann Theatre, New York City, 1980.

Second official, Dr. Peng, and bailiff, *Extenuating Circumstances,* Perry Street Theatre, New York City, 1981.

Ito, *Mame,* American Musical Theatre, New London, CT, 1985-86.

Also appeared as China Joe and Mrs. Smith, *Shot Thru the Heart,* Birmingham, MI, 1983, and in *A Bowler Hat,* New York City. Appeared in several New York Shakespeare Festival productions and touring shows.

MAJOR TOURS

Indian and pirate, *Peter Pan,* northern Japanese cities, 1971.

First player and Lucianus, *Hamlet,* northern Japanese cities, 1971.

Theo, *Piaf,* Japanese cities, 1972.

Young man, *A Girl from the Star,* northern Japanese cities, 1972.

Watchmaker, *Intermezzo,* northern Japanese cities, 1973.

Balthazar, *Much Ado About Nothing,* western Japanese cities, 1973.

Old man, *Twin Lotte,* northern Japanese cities, 1974.

Kayama, *Pacific Overtures,* U.S. cities, 1975-76.

Title role, *Aladdin,* U.S. cities, 1978-79.*

*   *   *

SCHOONMAKER, Thelma   1945-

PERSONAL: Born in 1945; married Michael Powell (a director), 1984 (died, 1990).

CAREER: Film editor.

AWARDS, HONORS: Academy Award, best editing, 1980, for *Raging Bull;* Academy Award nomination, best editing, 1990, for *GoodFellas.*

CREDITS:

FILM EDITOR

(With others) *Finnegan's Wake* (also known as *Passages From "Finnegan's Wake"*), Grove Press, 1965.

(With others) *The Virgin President,* New Line Cinema, 1968.

Who's That Knocking at My Door (also known as *I Call First* and *J.R.*), Joseph Brenner, 1968.

Raging Bull, Buena Vista, 1980.

The King of Comedy, Twentieth Century-Fox, 1983.

After Hours, Warner Brothers, 1985.

The Color of Money, Buena Vista, 1986.

The Last Temptation of Christ, Universal, 1988.

(With others) *New York Stories,* Buena Vista, 1989.

GoodFellas, Warner Brothers, 1990.

Also edited *Woodstock,* 1970.*

SCHROEDER, Barbet   1941-

PERSONAL: Born April 26, 1941, in Teheran, Iran; son of German parents. *Education:* Degree in philosophy, Sorbonne, Paris.

ADDRESSES: Agent—Sam Cohn, International Creative Management, 40 West 57th St., New York, NY 10019.

CAREER: Director, producer, actor, writer. Worked as a jazz tour operator in Europe and as a photojournalist in India; film critic for *Cahiers du Cinema* and *L'air de Paris,* 1958-63; formed own production company, Films du Losange, 1963.

AWARDS, HONORS: Academy Award nomination and Golden Globe nomination for best director, both 1990, both for *Reversal of Fortune.*

CREDITS:

FILM DIRECTOR, EXCEPT AS INDICATED

More, Cinema V, 1969.

La Vallee (also known as *The Valley*), Societe nouvelle de cinema, 1972.

General Idi Amin Dada (also known as *Idi Amin Dada;* documentary), Prestige Films, 1974.

Mistress (originally *Maitresse*), Gaumont International/Lagoon, 1975.

Koko, the Talking Gorilla (originally *Koko le gorille qui parle;* documentary), New Yorker, 1978.

Les Tricheurs (also known as *The Cheaters*), Films Galatee/Roissy Films, 1983.

The Charles Bukowski Tapes (four-part documentary), Lagoon Video, 1985.

(And producer with Fred Roos and Tom Luddy) *Barfly,* Cannon, 1987.

Reversal of Fortune, Warner Brothers, 1990.

Also director of *Sing-Song* (documentary).

FILM PRODUCER

Six in Paris (originally *Paris Vu Par . . . ,* 1965), New Yorker, 1968.

(With Pierre Cottrell), *My Night at Maud's* (originally *Ma Nuit chez Maud*), Pathe-Contemporary-Pathe, 1970.

(With Georges Beauregard), *La Collectionneuse* (also known as *The Collector*), Pathe, 1971.

Chloe in the Afternoon (originally *L'Amour, l'apres-midi*), Columbia, 1972.

(With Cottrell), *The Mother and the Whore* (originally *La maman et la putain*), NPF-CECRT, 1973.

Perceval (originally *Perceval le gallois*), New Yorker, 1978.

Improper Conduct (originally *Mauvaise Conduite*), New Yorker, 1983.

Also producer of *La Carriere de Suzanne* (short film), *Mediterrannee, Tu Imagines Robinson, Out One, Flocons d'Or, The Marquise of O, Le Passe-Montagne, The Rites of Death, Le Navire Night,* and *Le Pont du Nord.*

OTHER FILM WORK

Assistant to director Jean-Luc Godard, *The Soldiers* (originally *Les Carabiniers,* 1963), New Yorker, 1968.
Executive producer, *Claire's Knee,* Columbia, 1971.
Executive producer, *Celine and Julie Go Boating* (originally *Celine et Julie vont en bateau*), Les Films du Losange/Les Films Christian Fachner, 1974.
Co-producer, *Chinese Roulette,* New Yorker, 1977.
Co-producer, *The American Friend,* New Yorker, 1977.

FILM APPEARANCES

Car salesman, *The Soldiers* (originally *Les Carabiniers,* 1963), New Yorker, 1968.
Jean-Pierre, *Six in Paris* (originally *Paris Vu Par . . . ,* 1965), New Yorker, 1968.
Oliver, *Celine and Julie Go Boating* (originally *Celine et Julie vont en bateau*), Les Films du Losange/Les Films Christian Fachner, 1974.
Vittorio, *Roberte* (also known as *Robert*), Seine, 1978.
Wait until Spring, Bandini, Orion Classics, 1989.
Mean passerby, *The Golden Boat,* Golden Boat Productions, 1990.

WRITINGS:

SCREENPLAYS

(With Paul Gegauff) *More,* Cinema V, 1969.
La Vallee (also known as *The Valley*), Societe nouvelle de cinema, 1972.
Mistress (originally *Maitresse*), Gaumont International/ Lagoon, 1975.
Les Tricheurs (also known as *The Cheaters*), Films Galatee/Roissy Films, 1983.

FILM DOCUMENTARIES

General Idi Amin Dada (also known as *Idi Amin Dada*), Prestige Films, 1974.
Koko, the Talking Gorilla (originally *Koko le gorille qui parle*), New Yorker, 1978.*

* * *

SCHULTZ, Dwight

PERSONAL: Born in Baltimore, MD. *Education:* Received B.A. from Towson State University.

ADDRESSES: Agent—Paula Wagner/Pam Prince, Creative Artists Agency, 9830 Wilshire Blvd., Beverly Hills, CA 90212.

CAREER: Actor. Member of Baltimore Theatre Ensemble; McCarter Theatre Company, Princeton, NJ, 1972-74; Center Stage Company, Baltimore, MD, 1973-74; Loretto-Hilton Repertory Theatre Company, St. Louis, MO; and Alley Theatre Company, Houston, TX, 1975-76.

AWARDS, HONORS: Drama-Logue Award, 1980-81, for *The Crucifer of Blood.*

CREDITS:

TELEVISION APPEARANCES; SERIES

H.M. Murdock, *The A-Team,* NBC, 1983-87.

TELEVISION APPEARANCES; MOVIES

Schlatter, *Bitter Harvest,* NBC, 1981.
Dial M For Murder, NBC, 1981.
Mr. Ritchie, *Thin Ice,* CBS, 1981.
Richard Reese, *When Your Lover Leaves,* NBC, 1983.
Andrew Lloyd, *Perry Mason: The Case of the Sinister Spirit* (also known as *The Case of the Sinister Spirit*), NBC, 1987.
Tony Franklin, *Perry Mason: The Case of the Musical Murder* (also known as *The Case of the Musical Murder* and *Perry Mason: The Case of the Final Curtain*), NBC, 1989.
Clifford Gillette, *A Killer Among Us,* NBC, 1990.

TELEVISION APPEARANCES; SPECIALS

Basil, *Sherlock Holmes,* HBO, 1981.

FILM APPEARANCES

Director, *The Fan,* Paramount, 1981.
Dan Potter, *Alone in the Dark,* New Line Cinema, 1982.
J. Robert Oppenheimer, *Fat Man and Little Boy,* Paramount, 1989.
Norman Thompson, *The Long Walk Home,* Miramax, 1990.

STAGE APPEARANCES

(Off-Broadway debut) Soldier, *The Screens,* Chelsea Theatre Company, Brooklyn Academy of Music, New York City, 1971.
Jose Andrew Santos, *The Interrogation of Havana,* Chelsea Theatre Company, Brooklyn Academy of Music, 1971.
The Seagull, McCarter Theatre Company, Princeton, NJ, 1973.
Nicholas Slobok, *The Crazy Locomotive,* Chelsea Theatre Company, Brooklyn Academy of Music, 1977.
(Broadway debut) Charles Lang, *The Water Engine,* Plymouth Theatre, New York City, 1978.
Michael, *Funeral March for a One-Man Band,* Westbeth Theatre Center, 1978.

Major Alistair Ross, *The Crucifer of Blood,* Helen Hayes Theatre, New York City, 1978.

George Guthrie, *Night and Day,* ANTA Theatre, New York City, 1979.

Major Ross, *The Crucifer of Blood,* Center Theatre Group, Ahmanson Theatre, Los Angeles, CA, 1980.

Edward "Ned" Sheldon, *Ned and Jack,* Hudson Guild Theatre, New York City, 1981.

The Keeper, Philadelphia Drama Guild, Philadelphia, PA, 1982.

OTHER SOURCES:

PERIODICALS

National Review, November 10, 1989.*

*   *   *

SCHUMACHER, Joel   1939-

PERSONAL: Born August 29, 1939, in New York, NY; son of Francis and Marian (Kantor) Schumacher. *Education:* Parsons University, School of Design, B.A., 1965.

CAREER: Writer, director, and costume designer. Henri Bendel (department store), New York City, former design and display artist; former owner of boutique, Paraphernalia, and clothing and packaging designer for Revlon Group Inc. President of Joel Schumacher Productions.

CREDITS:

FILM WORK

Costume designer, *Play It as It Lays,* Universal, 1972.

Costume designer, *Sleeper,* United Artists, 1973.

Costume designer, *The Prisoner of Second Avenue,* Warner Bros., 1975.

Costume designer, *Interiors,* United Artists, 1978.

Director, *The Incredible Shrinking Woman,* Universal, 1981.

Director, *D.C. Cab,* Universal, 1983 (also see below).

Director, *St. Elmo's Fire,* Columbia, 1985 (also see below).

Director, *The Lost Boys,* Warner Bros., 1987.

Director, *Cousins,* Paramount, 1989.

Director, *Flatliners,* Columbia, 1990.

Director, *Dying Young,* Twentieth Century-Fox, 1991.

Also worked as a costume designer for *The Last of Sheila,* 1972, and *Blume in Love,* 1973.

TELEVISION WORK

Director, *The Virginia Hill Story* (movie), NBC, 1974 (also see below).

Director, *Amateur Night at the Dixie Bar and Grill* (movie), NBC, 1979 (also see below).

Executive producer, *Now We're Cookin'* (pilot), CBS, 1983 (also see below).

Executive producer (with Stefanie Staffin Kowal), *Slow Burn* (movie), Showtime, 1986.

Also production designer, *Killer Bees* (movie), 1974; executive producer, *Foxfire,* 1985; director of INXS music video, "Devil Inside."

STAGE WORK

Costume designer, *The Time of the Cuckoo,* Center Theatre Group, Ahmanson Theatre, Los Angeles, c. 1974.

WRITINGS:

SCREENPLAYS

Car Wash, Universal, 1976.

Sparkle (based on a story by Schumacher and Howard Rosenman), Warner Bros., 1976.

The Wiz (based on musical of the same title by William F. Brown and Charlie Smalls, which was based on *The Wonderful Wizard of Oz* by L. Frank Baum), Universal, 1978.

D.C. Cab (based on a story by Schumacher and Topper Carew), Universal, 1983.

(With Carl Kurlander), *St. Elmo's Fire,* Columbia, 1985.

TELEVISION MOVIES, EXCEPT WHERE NOTED

The Virginia Hill Story, NBC, 1974.

Amateur Night at the Dixie Bar and Grill, NBC, 1979.

Now We're Cookin' (pilot), CBS, 1983.*

*   *   *

SCOTT, Campbell

PERSONAL: Son of actors George C. Scott and Colleen Dewhurst. *Education:* Attended college in Wisconsin.

ADDRESSES: Agent—STE Representation Ltd., 9301 Wilshire Blvd., Suite 312, Beverly Hills, CA 90210.

CAREER: Actor.

CREDITS:

FILM APPEARANCES

Cop, *Five Corners,* Cineplex Odeon, 1987.

Bobby, *From Hollywood to Deadwood,* Nightfilm, 1988.

Willy, *Longtime Companion,* American Playhouse Theatrical Films, 1989.

Ain't No Way Back (also known as *No Way Back*), DSL Entertainment, 1990.

Tunner, *The Sheltering Sky,* Warner Brothers, 1990.

Victor Geddes, *Dying Young,* Twentieth Century-Fox, 1991.

TELEVISION APPEARANCES; MOVIES

Joseph P. Kennedy, Jr., *The Kennedys of Massachusetts* (also known as *The Fitzgeralds and the Kennedys*), ABC, 1990.

Southern boy, *The Perfect Tribute,* ABC, 1991.

STAGE APPEARANCES

Soldier, *The Queen and the Rebels,* Plymouth Theatre, New York City, 1982.

Brodie, *The Real Thing,* Plymouth Theatre, 1984.

George, *Our Town,* Seattle Repertory Theatre, Seattle, WA, 1984.

Sandy Tyrell, *Hay Fever,* Music Box Theatre, New York City, 1985.

Master Richard Rich, *A Man for All Seasons,* Roundabout Theatre, New York City, 1986.

Fritz, *Dalliance,* Long Wharf Theatre, New Haven, CT, 1986.

Parker Smith, *Copperhead,* WPA Theatre, New York City, 1987.

Ah, Wilderness!, Yale Repertory Theatre, New Haven, CT, 1987-88.

Long Day's Journey into Night, Yale Repertory Theatre, 1987-88.

Also appeared in *Paradise for the Worried.*

OTHER SOURCES:

PERIODICALS

Rolling Stone, June 14, 1990.*

*   *   *

SCOTT, Ridley   1939-

PERSONAL: Born in 1939 in South Shields, Northumberland, England. *Education:* Royal College of Art, London.

ADDRESSES: Contact—Hampstead Grove, London NW3, England; and R.S.A., 6-10 Lexington St., London W1, England.

CAREER: Director, producer. Set designer and director for British Broadcasting Corp.; director of almost three thousand commercials; partner with brother, Tony Scott, in Ridley Scott Associates (commercial production company).

AWARDS, HONORS: Venice Film Festival award for commercial work; award for "Best First Film," for *The Duellists.*

CREDITS:

FILM WORK

Director, *The Duellists,* Paramount, 1977.

Director, *Alien,* Twentieth Century-Fox, 1979.

Director, *Blade Runner,* Warner Brothers, 1982.

Director, *Legend,* Universal, 1985.

Executive producer, director, *Someone to Watch over Me,* Columbia, 1987.

Director, *Black Rain,* Paramount, 1989.

Producer (with Mimi Polk), director, *Thelma & Louise,* Metro-Goldwyn-Mayer, 1991.

TELEVISION WORK

Director of episodes of *Z Cars,* BBC, 1966; worked on *The Informer,* Rediffusion, 1966-67.*

*   *   *

SELTZER, David   1920(?)-

PERSONAL: Born c. 1920; children: four. *Education:* Attended Northwestern University.

ADDRESSES: Agent—Creative Artists Agency, 1888 Century Park E., Suite 1400, Los Angeles, CA 90067.

CAREER: Screenwriter, director, producer, and novelist. Began career working with Jacques Cousteau on documentaries.

AWARDS, HONORS: Emmy Award nominations, all 1970, achievement in news documentary programming—program and individual, for *Adventures at the Jade Sea,* achievement in cultural documentary programming—program, for *The Journey of Robert F. Kennedy;* Humanitas Prize, ninety-minute category, Human Family Educational and Cultural Institute, 1977, for *Green Eyes.*

CREDITS:

FILM WORK

Director, *Lucas,* Twentieth Century-Fox, 1986 (also see below).

Director, *Punchline,* Columbia, 1988 (also see below).

TELEVISION WORK

Producer, *Adventures at the Jade Sea* (documentary), CBS, c. 1970 (also see below).

Producer, *The Journey of Robert F. Kennedy* (documentary), ABC, c. 1970 (also see below).

Producer (with John Erman), *Green Eyes,* ABC, 1977 (also see below).

STAGE PRODUCER

F. Jasmine Addams (musical; based on Carson McCullers's story "The Member of the Wedding"), Circle in the Square, New York City, 1971.

(With David Black) *Lysistrata,* Brooks Atkinson Theatre, New York City, 1972.

WRITINGS:

FILMS

The Hellstrom Chronicle (documentary), Cinema 5, 1971.

(With David Shaw), *King, Queen, Knave* (based on Vladimir Nabokov's novel of the same title), Avco Embassy, 1972.

One Is a Lonely Number (also known as *Two Is a Happy Number;* based on Rebecca Morris's short story "The Good Humor Man"), Metro-Goldwyn-Mayer, 1972.

The Other Side of the Mountain, Universal, 1975.

The Omen (also known as *Birthmark*), Twentieth Century-Fox, 1976 (also see below).

Prophecy, Paramount, 1979 (also see below).

Six Weeks (based on Fred Mustard Stewart's novel of the same title), Universal, 1982.

Table for Five, Warner Brothers, 1983.

Lucas, Twentieth Century-Fox, 1986.

Punchline, Columbia, 1988.

(With Louis Venosta and Eric Lerner) *Bird on a Wire,* Universal, 1990.

TELEVISION

The Journey of Robert F. Kennedy (documentary), ABC, c. 1970.

Adventures at the Jade Sea (documentary), CBS, c. 1970.

Larry (adapted from Robert McQueen's book *Larry: Case History of a Mistake*), CBS, 1974.

(With David Sontag), *My Father's House,* ABC, 1975.

Green Eyes, ABC, 1977.

(With Thom Thomas), *Private Sessions,* NBC, 1985.

OTHER

The Omen (novelization of his screenplay of the same title), New American Library, 1976.

Prophecy (novelization of his screenplay of the same title), Ballantine, 1979.

Contributor to *Premiere.*

OTHER SOURCES:

PERIODICALS

Chicago Tribune, February 23, 1983; April 2, 1986; September 30, 1988; May 18, 1990.

Los Angeles Times, February 17, 1983; May 1, 1986; September 30, 1988; May 18, 1990.

New York Times, June 20, 1972; June 25, 1976; June 15, 1979; July 24, 1979; February 18, 1983; March 28, 1986; September 24, 1989; May 18, 1990.

New York Times Book Review, September 11, 1977.

Washington Post, March 12, 1983; October 7, 1988.

Washington Post Book World, August 22, 1976.*

SHANDLING, Garry 1949-

PERSONAL: Born November 29, 1949, in Chicago, IL; son of Irving (a print shop owner) and Muriel (a pet store proprietor) Shandling. *Education:* Earned a degree in marketing from University of Arizona.

ADDRESSES: Agent—Our Production Co., 1438 North Gower St., Los Angeles, CA 90028.

CAREER: Comedian and actor. Began career writing scripts for situation comedies.

AWARDS, HONORS: Four ACE (cable TV) Award nominations for *It's Garry Shandling's Show—25th Anniversary Special,* 1986; Television Critics Association Award, best comedy series, 1987, for *It's Garry Shandling's Show;* ACE Awards, best comedy series (with others), 1989 and 1990, and best actor in a comedy series, 1990, all for *It's Garry Shandling's Show.*

CREDITS:

TELEVISION APPEARANCES; SERIES

It's Garry Shandling's Show, Showtime, then Fox, 1986-90 (also see below).

TELEVISION APPEARANCES; SPECIALS

The Tonight Show Starring Johnny Carson: 19th Anniversary Special, NBC, 1981.

Garry Shandling—Alone in Las Vegas, Showtime, 1984 (also see below).

The Tonight Show Starring Johnny Carson: 23rd Anniversary Special, NBC, 1985.

It's Garry Shandling's Show—25th Anniversary Special, Showtime Comedy Spotlight, Showtime, 1986 (also see below).

Disneyland's Summer Vacation Party, NBC, 1986.

The 39th Annual Emmy Awards, Fox, 1987.

Caesar's 20th Birthday Celebration, Showtime, 1987.

The 40th Annual Emmy Awards, Fox, 1988.

The 2nd Annual American Comedy Awards, ABC, 1988.

The Comedy Store 15th Year Class Reunion (also known as *Class Reunion* and *Comedy Store Reunion*), NBC, 1988.

Merrill Markoe's Guide to Glamorous Living, Cinemax Comedy Experiment, Cinemax, 1988.

The Tonight Show Starring Johnny Carson: 26th Anniversary Special, NBC, 1988.

Comedy Celebration: The Comedy and Magic Club's 10th Anniversary, Showtime, 1989.

Comic Relief III, HBO, 1989.

The 32nd Annual Grammy Awards, CBS, 1990.

The 33rd Annual Grammy Awards, CBS, 1991.

Garry Shandling: Stand Up, HBO Comedy Hour, HBO, 1991 (also see below).

TELEVISION APPEARANCES; EPISODIC

Sunday Night with Larry King, NBC, 1990.

Appeared on several episodes of *The Tonight Show* and *Late Night With David Letterman.*

OTHER TELEVISION APPEARANCES

Michael Nesmith in Television Parts (pilot), NBC, 1985.
Jack, *Mother Goose Rock 'n' Rhyme* (movie), The Disney Channel, 1990.

TELEVISION WORK

Producer, *Garry Shandling—Alone in Las Vegas* (special), Showtime, 1984.
Executive producer, *It's Garry Shandling's Show—25th Anniversary Special, Showtime Comedy Spotlight,* Showtime, 1986.
Executive producer (with others) and creator, *It's Garry Shandling's Show* (series), Showtime, then Fox, 1986-90.

WRITINGS:

TELEVISION

Garry Shandling—Alone in Las Vegas (special), Showtime, 1984.
It's Garry Shandling's Show—25th Anniversary Special, Showtime Comedy Spotlight (special), Showtime, 1986.
It's Garry Shandling's Show (series), Showtime, then Fox, 1986-90.
Garry Shandling: Stand-Up, HBO Comedy Hour, HBO, 1991.

Writer for the series *Sanford and Son; Welcome Back, Kotter;* and *Three's Company.*

OTHER SOURCES:

PERIODICALS

Rolling Stone, February 26, 1990.*

*   *   *

SHANLEY, John Patrick   1950-

PERSONAL: Born in 1950 in New York, NY; father worked as a meat-packer and mother worked as a telephone operator; married Jayne Haynes (an actress) (divorced). *Education:* Graduated from New York University with degree in educational theater.

ADDRESSES: Office—c/o Warner Bros., 4000 Warner Blvd., Burbank, CA 91522.

CAREER: Playwright, screenwriter, and director. Also worked as a bartender and housepainter. *Military service:* Served in U.S. Marines.

MEMBER: Writers Guild of America.

AWARDS, HONORS: Writers Guild of America Award and Academy Award, both for best original screenplay, 1987, for *Moonstruck;* special-jury prize, Barcelona Film Festival, for *Five Corners.*

CREDITS:

FILM APPEARANCES

Celebrity party guest, *Crossing Delancey,* Warner Bros., 1988.

TELEVISION APPEARANCES

The New Hollywood (talk show), NBC, 1990.

FILM WORK

Associate producer, *Five Corners,* Cineplex Odeon, 1988 (also see below).
Director, *Joe versus the Volcano* (also known as *Joe against the Volcano*), Warner Bros., 1990 (also see below).

Also director of short film *I Am Angry,* c. 1988.

WRITINGS:

SCREENPLAYS

Moonstruck, Metro Goldwyn-Mayer, 1987.
Five Corners, Cineplex Odeon, 1988.
The January Man, Metro Goldwyn-Mayer, 1989.
Joe versus the Volcano (also known as *Joe against the Volcano*), Warner Bros., 1990.

Also author of television scripts.

STAGE PLAYS

Ketchup, staged reading, New Dramatists, New York City, c. 1980.
Rockaway, produced at Vineyard Theater, New York City, 1982.
Welcome to the Moon, produced at Ensemble Studio Theatre, New York City, 1982, published in *Welcome to the Moon and Other Plays,* Dramatists Play Service, 1985.
Danny and the Deep Blue Sea, produced at Circle in the Square, New York City, 1984, published as *Danny and the Deep Blue Sea: An Apache Dance,* Dramatists Play Service, 1984.
Savage in Limbo, produced at 47th Street Theater, New York City, 1985, published by Dramatists Play Service, 1986.

the dreamer examines his pillow, staged reading, O'Neill Playwrights Conference, New Haven, CT, 1985, then produced at Double Image Theater, New York City, 1986, published as *the dreamer examines his pillow: A Heterosexual Homily,* Dramatists Play Service, 1987.

Women of Manhattan, produced at Manhattan Theatre Club, City Center Theater, New York City, 1986.

All for Charity, in *Marathon '87: Evening B,* produced at Ensemble Studio Theatre, 1987.

Also author of *Italian-American Reconciliation,* New York City, 1988.

OTHER SOURCES:

PERIODICALS

American Film, September, 1989.
Chicago Tribune, March 9, 1990.
Los Angeles Times, February 5, 1986; March 5, 1988; February 9, 1989; March 9, 1990.
Maclean's, April 4, 1988.
National Review, March 4, 1988.
Newsweek, December 21, 1987.
New York, October 20, 1986; November 14, 1988.
New Yorker, January 25, 1988.
New York Times, October 14, 1982; November 24, 1982; September 26, 1985; May 5, 1986; December 16, 1987; December 27, 1987; April 10, 1988; January 13, 1989.
People, January 18, 1988.
Time, November 7, 1988; January 23, 1989.
Village Voice, January 5, 1988; February 2, 1988.*

* * *

SHAW, Fiona

PERSONAL: Born in Cork, Ireland; father, an eye surgeon. *Education:* Studied at Cork University; trained for the stage at Royal Academy of Dramatic Art.

ADDRESSES: Agent—Jeremy Conway Ltd., 109 Jermyn St., London SW1Y 6HB, England.

CAREER: Actress.

AWARDS, HONORS: Bancroft Gold Medal from Royal Academy of Dramatic Art, 1990; Olivier Award, best actress, 1990, for *Electra, As You Like It,* and *The Good Person of Sichuan.*

CREDITS:

STAGE APPEARANCES

Julia Melville, *The Rivals,* National Theatre Company, Olivier Theatre, London, 1983.

Mary Shelley, *Bloody Poetry,* Hampstead Theatre, London, 1984.
Celia, *As You Like It,* Royal Shakespeare Company (RSC), Stratford-on-Avon, England, then Barbican Theatre, London, both 1985.
Madame de Volanges, *Les Liaisons Dangereuses,* RSC, Stratford-on-Avon, 1985, then The Pit, London, 1986.
Tatyana Vasilyevna, *The Philistines,* RSC, Stratford-on-Avon, 1985, then The Pit, 1986.
Erika Bruckner, *Mephisto,* RSC, Barbican Theatre, 1986.
Prudence, *The New Inn,* RSC, Swan Theatre, Stratford-on-Avon, 1987.
Mistress Carol, *Hyde Park,* RSC, Swan Theatre, 1987, then The Pit, 1988.
Katherine, *The Taming of the Shrew,* RSC, Stratford-on-Avon, 1987, then Barbican Theatre, 1988.
Title role, *Mary Stuart,* Greenwich Theatre, London, 1988.
Title role, *Electra,* RSC, The Pit, 1988-89.
Rosalind, *As You Like It,* Old Vic Theatre, London, 1989.
Shen Teh/Shui Ta, *The Good Person of Sichuan,* National Theatre Company, Olivier Theatre, 1989-90.

Also appeared as Rosaline, *Love's Labour's Lost.*

MAJOR TOURS

Portia, *The Merchant of Venice,* RSC, British cities, 1986-87.
Beatrice, *Much Ado About Nothing,* RSC, British cities, 1986-87.

FILM APPEARANCES

Sister Felicity, *Sacred Hearts,* Reality/Film Four, 1984.
Dr. Eileen Cole, *My Left Foot,* Miramax, 1989.
Isabel Arundell, *Mountains of the Moon,* Tri-Star, 1990.
Miss Lomax, *Three Men and a Little Lady,* Touchstone, 1990.

TELEVISION APPEARANCES

Young Deirdre, *Love Song,* Anglia Television, then *Masterpiece Theatre,* PBS, 1987.

Also appeared in *Fireworks for Elspeth* and *Sacred Hearts.**

* * *

SHELTON, Ron   1945-

PERSONAL: Full name, Ronald W. Shelton; born September 15, 1945, in Whittier, CA; children: two daughters. *Education:* Westmont College, graduated, 1967; University of Arizona, Tucson, M.F.A., sculpture, 1974.

ADDRESSES: Contact—Directors Guild of America, 7950 Sunset Blvd., Los Angeles, CA 90046.

CAREER: Director and writer. Played for several minor league baseball teams before attending graduate school; worked at odd jobs during the 1970s; after receiving his master's degree, exhibited his sculpture, including a one-man exhibition at the Space Gallery.

AWARDS, HONORS: Writers Guild of America award, New York Film Critics Award, Los Angeles Film Critics Award, and National Film Critics Award, all for best original screenplay, all 1988, for *Bull Durham.*

CREDITS:

FILM WORK; DIRECTOR

Bull Durham, Orion, 1988.
Blaze, Buena Vista, 1990.

WRITINGS:

SCREENPLAYS

Under Fire, Orion, 1983.
The Best of Times, Universal, 1986.
Bull Durham, Orion, 1988.
Blaze, Buena Vista, 1990.

* * *

SHERIDAN, Jim   1949-

PERSONAL: Born in 1949 in Dublin, Ireland; married; wife's name, Fran. *Education:* Attended University College, Dublin, and New York University Institute of Film and Television.

ADDRESSES: Agent—Creative Artists Agency, 9830 Wilshire Blvd., Beverly Hills, CA 90212.

CAREER: Director, writer, and producer. Worked at the Lyric Theatre, Belfast, Ireland, Abbey Theatre, Dublin, Ireland, and English 7:84 Company; Project Arts Theatre, Dublin, director, 1976-80; New York Irish Arts Center, New York City, artistic director, 1982-87. Children's T Theatre Company, Dublin, founder.

AWARDS, HONORS: Edinburgh Festival Fringe Award, best play, 1983, for *Spike in the First World War;* Academy Award nominations, best adapted screenplay (with Shane Connaughton) and best director, both 1989, for *My Left Foot.*

CREDITS:

FILM WORK

Director, *My Left Foot,* Miramax, 1989 (also see below).
Producer (with Noel Pearson) and director, *The Field,* Avenue Pictures, 1990 (also see below).

STAGE WORK

Director, *Shadow of a Gunman,* Abbey Theatre, Dublin, 1981, then Actors Playhouse, Irish Arts Center, New York City, 1984.

WRITINGS:

SCREENPLAYS

(With Shane Connaughton) *My Left Foot* (based on the book by Christy Brown), Miramax, 1989.
(With Noel Pearson) *The Field* (based on a play by J. B. Keane), Avenue Pictures, 1990.

PLAYS

Mobile Homes (first produced at Project Arts Center, Dublin), Co-Op Books, 1978.

Also author of *Spike in the First World War,* c. 1983, and several other plays.*

* * *

SHIELDS, Brooke   1965-

PERSONAL: Born May 31, 1965, in New York, NY; daughter of Frank and Teri Shields. *Education:* Received degree from Princeton University, 1987; member of the theatre musical group Triangle.

ADDRESSES: Office—P.O. Box B, Haworth, NJ 07641.

CAREER: Model and actress. Began her modeling career as Ivory Snow baby when eleven months old; appeared on over 30 magazine covers in 1981; also appeared in Simplicity pattern books and in ads for Breck shampoo, Carter's pajamas, Colgate toothpaste, Band-Aids, J.C. Penny, and Sears.

AWARDS, HONORS: Star Presenter of the Year Award, 1980; United Service Organizations Woman of the Year Award, 1986; Face of the 80s Award, *Time* magazine.

CREDITS:

FILM APPEARANCES

(Film debut) Karen Spages, *Alice, Sweet Alice* (also known as *Communion* and *Holy Terror*), Allied Artists, 1978.
Violet, *Pretty Baby,* Paramount, 1978.
Tita Stepanowicz, *The King of the Gypsies,* Paramount, 1978.
Kate, *Just You and Me, Kid,* United Artists, 1979.
Brenda Louise Davenport/"Tilt", *Tilt,* Warner Brothers, 1979.
Wanda Nevada, *Wanda Nevada,* United Artists, 1979.
Jade Butterfield, *Endless Love,* Universal, 1980.
Emmeline, *The Blue Lagoon,* Columbia, 1980.
As herself, *The Muppets Take Manhattan,* Tri-Star, 1984.

Gordon Dale, *Sahara,* Metro-Goldwyn-Mayer/United Artists, 1984.

The Big Apple Movie, Edward Ditterline Entertainment, 1989.

Brenda Starr, *Brenda Starr,* Triumph, 1989.

Stewardess, *Speed Zone,* Orion, 1990.

Stevie Bloom, *Backstreet Dreams* (also known as *Back Street Dreams* and *Backstreet Strays*), Vidmark Entertainment, 1990.

Also appeared in *The Actor.*

STAGE APPEARANCES

Night of One Hundred Stars, Radio City Music Hall, New York City, 1982.

(Broadway debut) Suzanne, *The Eden Cinema,* UBU Repertory Theatre, Harold Clurman Theatre, New York City, 1986.

TELEVISION APPEARANCES; SERIES

Elizabeth Harrington, *The Doctors,* NBC, 1982.

TELEVISION APPEARANCES; MOVIES

(Television debut) Kristin, *The Prince of Central Park,* CBS, 1977.

Laura, *Wet Gold,* ABC, 1984.

Tara Holden, *The Diamond Trap* (also known as *The Great Diamond Robbery*), CBS, 1988.

TELEVISION APPEARANCES; SPECIALS

Ringmaster, *Circus of the Stars 4,* CBS, 1979.

Female team member, *Celebrity Challenge of the Sexes 5,* CBS, 1980.

Hostess, *Men Who Rate a Ten,* NBC, 1980.

Guest, *Bob Hope for President,* NBC, 1980.

Guest, *Bob Hope Special: Bob Hope's All-Star Look at TV's Prime Time Wars,* NBC, 1980.

Ringmaster, *Circus of the Stars 6,* CBS, 1981.

Guest, *Bob Hope Special: Bob Hope's Thirtieth Anniversary TV Special,* NBC, 1981.

Guest, *Bob Hope Special: Bob Hope's All-Star Comedy Birthday Party at West Point,* NBC, 1981.

Guest, *Bob Hope Special: Bob Hope's Spring Fling of Comedy and Glamour,* NBC, 1981.

Guest, *Bob Hope Special: Bob Hope's All-Star Birthday at Annapolis,* NBC, 1982.

Guest, *Bob Hope Special: Bob Hope's Star-Studded Spoof of the New TV Season—G Rated—With Glamour, Glitter & Gags,* NBC, 1982.

Guest, *Bob Hope Special: Bob Hope's Women I Love—Beautiful but Funny,* NBC, 1982.

Guest, *Bob Hope Special: The Bob Hope Christmas Special,* NBC, 1982.

Performer, *Circus of the Stars 7,* CBS, 1982.

Performer, *Circus of the Stars 8,* CBS, 1983.

Guest, *Bob Hope Special: Happy Birthday, Bob!,* NBC, 1983.

Guest, *Bob Hope Special: Bob Hope's Merry Christmas Show,* NBC, 1983.

Ringmaster, *Circus of the Stars 9,* CBS, 1984.

Guest, *Bob Hope Special: Bob Hope's USO Christmas Special in Beirut,* NBC, 1984.

Guest, *Bob Hope Special: Ho Ho Hope's Jolly Christmas Hour,* NBC, 1984.

Guest, *Bob Hope's Happy Birthday Homecoming,* NBC, 1985.

Guest, *Exotic People, Exotic Places,* syndicated, 1985.

Guest, *The Night of One Hundred Stars II,* ABC, 1985.

Guest, *The Bob Hope Christmas Show,* NBC, 1985.

Guest, *All-Star Tribute to Jimmy Doolittle,* syndicated, 1986.

Guest, *Bob Hope's Bagful of Christmas Cheer,* NBC, 1986.

Guest, *Bob Hope's High-Flying Birthday,* NBC, 1986.

Guest, *Bob Hope's Christmas Show—A Snow Job in Florida,* NBC, 1987.

Guest, *Bob Hope's High Flying Birthday Extravaganza,* NBC, 1987.

The Television Academy Hall of Fame (also known as *The Fourth Annual Television Academy Hall of Fame*), Fox Broadcasting Company (FBC), 1987.

The Fourteenth Annual People's Choice Awards, CBS, 1988.

Guest, *Hope News Network* (also known as *Bob Hope's News Network*), NBC, 1988.

United We Stand, syndicated, 1988.

Guest, *Happy Birthday, Bob—Fifty Stars Salute Your Fifty Years with NBC,* NBC, 1988.

Best Catches, CBS, 1989.

Guest, *Ooh-La-La, It's Bob Hope's Fun Birthday Spectacular from Paris's Bicentennial,* NBC, 1989.

Night of One Hundred Stars III (also known as *Night of One Hundred Stars*), NBC, 1990.

Guest, *Bob Hope's USO Road to the Berlin Wall and Moscow,* NBC, 1990.

Voices that Care, FBC, 1991.

Also appeared in *The All-Star Salute to Mother's Day,* 1981; guest, *Animals Are the Funniest People,* 1983; and guest, *Blondes vs. Brunettes, Salute to Lady Liberty,* and *The Funniest Joke I Ever Heard,* all 1984.

OTHER TELEVISION APPEARANCES

Also appeared on many talk shows, including *The Tonight Show with Joan Rivers* and *Entertainment Tonight.**

SIDNEY, Sylvia 1910-

PERSONAL: Born Sophia Kossow, August 8 (some sources say August 10), 1910, in New York, NY; daughter of Victor and Rebecca (Saperstein) Kossow; married Bennett Cerf (a publisher), October, 1935 (divorced, 1936); married Luther Adler (an actor), 1938 (divorced, 1946); married Carlton Alsop, 1947 (divorced, 1951); children: (second marriage) Jacob L. *Education:* Attended Theater Guild School, 1925; studied acting with Rouben Mamoulian, Alfred Lunt and Lynn Fontanne, and the Langners. *Avocational interests:* Needlepoint, reading, watching television, breeding pug dogs.

ADDRESSES: Publicist—c/o John Springer, 130 East Sixty-seventh St., New York, NY 10021.

CAREER: Actress.

MEMBER: Actors' Equity Association, Screen Actors Guild, American Federation of Television and Radio Artists, National Amyotrophic Lateral Sclerosis Foundation (board of directors).

AWARDS, HONORS: Emmy nomination, best actress in a single performance, 1963, for "The Madman," *The Defenders;* Academy Award nomination and National Board of Review Award, best supporting actress, 1974, for *Summer Wishes, Winter Dreams;* Golden Globe Award, best performance by an actress in a supporting role in a series, mini-series, or motion picture made for television, 1986, for *An Early Frost.*

CREDITS:

STAGE APPEARANCES

(Stage debut) *The Challenge of Youth,* Poli's Theatre, Washington, DC, 1926.
(Broadway debut) Anita, *The Squall,* Forty-eighth Street Theatre, New York City, 1926.
Annabelle Porter, *Crime,* Eltinge Theatre, New York City, 1927.
Mary Norton, *Mirrors,* Forrest Theatre, New York City, 1928.
Amy, *The Breaks,* Klaw Theatre, New York City, 1928.
Rosalie, *Gods of the Lightning,* Little Theatre, New York City, 1928.
Elizabeth Girard, *Nice Women,* Longacre Theatre, New York City, 1929.
Patricia, *Cross Roads,* Morosco Theatre, New York City, 1929.
Patsy Coster, *Many a Slip,* Little Theatre, 1930.
Dot, *Bad Girl,* Hudson Theatre, New York City, 1930.
Lola Hobbs, *To Quito and Back,* Guild Theatre, New York City, 1937.
Stella Goodman, *The Gentle People,* Belasco Theatre, New York City, 1939.

We Will Never Die (pageant), Madison Square Garden, New York City, 1943.
Alicia Christie, *Black Chiffon,* Hartman Theatre, Columbus, OH, then Locust Street Theatre, Philadelphia, PA, 1951.
Agnes, *The Fourposter,* Ethel Barrymore Theatre, New York City, 1951.
Fanny Benton, *The Gypsies Wore High Hats,* Falmouth Playhouse, Coonamessett, MA, 1952.
Anna, *A Very Special Baby,* Playhouse Theatre, New York City, 1956.
Mrs. Kolowitz, *Enter Laughing,* Henry Miller's Theatre, New York City, 1963.
Beatrice Wright, "Damn You, Scarlett O'Hara," and Leslie Ross, "All My Pretty Little Ones," in *Riverside Drive* (double-bill), Theatre de Lys, New York City, 1964.
Mrs. Banks, *Barefoot in the Park,* Biltmore Theatre, New York City, 1966.
Lady Bracknell, *The Importance of Being Earnest,* Oakland Repertory Theatre, CA, 1966.
Mrs. Hardcastle, *She Stoops to Conquer,* National Repertory Theatre, Ford's Theatre, Washington, DC, 1968.
Mrs. Venable, *Suddenly, Last Summer,* Ivanhoe Theatre, Chicago, IL, 1973.
A Family and a Fortune, Seattle Repertory Theatre, Seattle, WA, 1973-74.
Matty Seaton, *A Family and a Fortune,* Seattle Repertory Theatre, 1974.
Tessie, *Me Jack, You Jill,* John Golden Theatre, New York City, 1976.
Sabrina Fair, Arlington Park Theatre, Arlington Heights, IL, 1976-77.
Mrs. Wire, *Vieux Carre,* St. James Theatre, New York City, 1977.
Night of 100 Stars, Radio City Music Hall, New York City, 1982.

Also appeared as Prunella, Garrick Theatre, New York City, 1926; Fraulein Schneider, *Cabaret,* Wallingford, CT, 1970; and Mrs. Baker, *Butterflies Are Free,* St. Louis, MO, 1972. Appeared in *Morning's at 7* and *Come Along With Me,* both 1981; and *'Night Mother.*

MAJOR TOURS

Linda Brown, *Accent on Youth,* U.S. cities, 1941.
Mrs. Manningham, *Angel Street,* U.S. cities, 1942.
Title role, *Auntie Mame,* U.S. cities, 1958.
Mrs. Malaprop, *The Rivals,* National Repertory Theatre, U.S. cities, 1965-66.
Constance, the Madwoman of Passy, *The Madwoman of Chaillot,* National Repertory Theatre, U.S. cities, 1965-66.
The Trojan Women, National Repertory Theatre, U.S. cities, 1965-66.

Mrs. Banks, *Barefoot in the Park,* U.S. cities, 1966.
Mrs. Baker, *Come Blow Your Horn,* U.S. and Canadian cities, 1968.

Also toured as Eliza, *Pygmalion,* and in *Tonight at 8:30,* 1938; title role, *Jane Eyre,* 1943; *Joan of Lorraine,* 1947; *Kind Lady,* 1948; *O Mistress Mine,* 1948-49; *The Two Mrs. Carrolls,* 1949; *Pygmalion,* 1949; *Goodbye, My Fancy,* 1950; *Anne of the Thousand Days,* 1950; *The Innocents,* 1950-51; as Cora Flood, *The Dark at the Top of the Stairs,* stock tour, 1960; *The Silver Cord,* 1964; *Kind Lady,* 1964; and Regina, *The Little Foxes,* 1966.

FILM APPEARANCES

Valerie Briand, *Thru Different Eyes,* Twentieth Century-Fox, 1929.
Roberta Alden, *An American Tragedy,* Paramount, 1931.
Nan Cooley, *City Streets,* Paramount, 1931.
Patricia, *Confessions of a Co-ed,* Paramount, 1931.
Rose Maurrant, *Street Scene,* United Artists (UA), 1931.
Kathleen Storm, *Ladies of the Big House,* Paramount, 1932.
Cho-Cho San, *Madame Butterfly,* Paramount, 1932.
Guest star, *Make Me a Star,* Paramount, 1932.
Joan Prentice, *Merrily We Go to Hell* (also known as *Merrily We Go to . . .*), Paramount, 1932.
Helen Smith, *The Miracle Man,* Paramount, 1932.
Title role, *Jennie Gerhardt,* Paramount, 1932.
Mary Richards, *Pick-Up,* Paramount, 1933.
Nancy Lanea/Princess Catterina Theodora Margerita Zizzi, *Thirty-Day Princess,* Paramount, 1934.
Lillie Taylor, *Good Dame,* Paramount, 1934.
Linda Brown, *Accent on Youth,* Paramount, 1935.
Tonita Stormcloud, *Behold My Wife,* Paramount, 1935.
Title role, *Mary Burns, Fugitive,* Paramount, 1935.
June Tolliver, *The Trail of the Lonesome Pine,* Paramount, 1936.
Katherine Grant, *Fury,* Metro-Goldwyn-Mayer, 1936.
Drina, *Dead End* (also known as *Dead End* and *Cradle of Crime*), UA, 1937.
Sylvia Verloc, *Sabotage* (also known as *The Woman Alone* and *A Woman Alone*), Gaumont/Janus, 1937.
Joan Graham, *You Only Live Once,* UA, 1937.
Helen Dennis, *You and Me,* Paramount, 1938.
Mary Rogers, *One Third of a Nation,* Paramount, 1939.
Flo Lorraine, *The Wagons Roll at Night,* Warner Brothers/First National, 1941.
Iris Hilliard, *Blood on the Sun,* UA, 1945.
Margaret Wyndham Chase, *Mr. Ace,* UA, 1946.
Cassie Bowman, *The Searching Wind,* Paramount, 1946.
Cecily Harrington, *Love from a Stranger* (also known as *A Stranger Walked In*), Eagle-Lion, 1947.
Fantine, *Les Miserables,* Twentieth Century-Fox, 1952.
Elsie, *Violent Saturday,* Twentieth Century-Fox, 1955.
Hilda Carmichael, *Behind the High Wall,* Universal, 1956.

Mrs. Pritchett, *Summer Wishes, Winter Dreams,* Columbia, 1973.
Elizabeth Mullin, *God Told Me To* (also known as *Demon*), New World, 1976.
Miss Coral, *I Never Promised You a Rose Garden,* New World, 1977.
Aunt Marion, *Damien—Omen II,* Twentieth Century-Fox, 1978.
Donaldina Cameron, *Hammett,* Warner Brothers, 1982.
Margaret Smith, *Corrupt* (also known as *Order of Death*), New Line Cinema, 1984.
Juno, *Beetlejuice,* Warner Brothers, 1988.
The Exorcist III, Twentieth Century-Fox, 1990.

TELEVISION APPEARANCES; MOVIES

Elizabeth Gibson, *Do Not Fold, Spindle or Mutilate,* ABC, 1971.
Kitty, *The Secret Night Caller,* NBC, 1975.
Anne Barclay, *Winner Take All,* NBC, 1975.
Clara Josephs, *Death at Love House,* ABC, 1976.
Carrie Rill, *Snowbeast,* NBC, 1977.
Dora Block, *Raid on Entebbe,* NBC, 1977.
Lillian Gordon, *Siege,* CBS, 1978.
Cousin Polly, *F.D.R.—The Last Year,* NBC, 1980.
Felicity Thomas, *The Shadow Box,* ABC, 1980.
Sadie Ross, *A Small Killing,* CBS, 1981.
Marney, *Having it All,* ABC, 1982.
Beatrice McKenna, *An Early Frost,* NBC, 1985.
Margaret Finnegan, *Finnegan Begin Again,* HBO, 1985.
Fern, *Pals,* CBS, 1987.

TELEVISION APPEARANCES; SERIES

Star Stage, NBC, 1955-56.
Sister Mary Joel, *Ryan's Hope,* ABC, 1975.
Binnie Byrd Baylor, *Morningstar/Eveningstar,* CBS, 1986.

TELEVISION APPEARANCES; EPISODIC

Kraft Television Theater, NBC, 1947.
Theatre, NBC, 1952.
Playwrights '56, NBC, 1955.
"The Helen Morgan Story," *Playhouse 90,* CBS, 1957.

Appeared on *Climax,* 1953; *Naked City, Tales of Tomorrow, My Three Sons,* and *thirtysomething,* all ABC; *20th Century Hour, The June Allyson Show, G.E. Theatre, Route 66, Playhouse of Stars, Lux Video Theatre, The Nurses,* and as Adela, "The Madman," *The Defenders,* all CBS; *Philco Playhouse, The Eleventh Hour,* and *Star Stage,* all NBC; *Broadway Television Theatre,* independent; *Whiz Kids; Magnum, P.I.;* and *Trapper John, M.D.*

TELEVISION APPEARANCES; SPECIALS

In the Last Place (Yom Kippur special), CBS, 1963.
"Come Along with Me," *American Playhouse,* PBS, 1982.

Mrs. Downes, "Andre's Mother," *American Playhouse,* PBS, 1990.

TELEVISION APPEARANCES; PILOTS

Ruth, *Maureen,* CBS, 1976.
Lillian "Mama" Carlson, *WKRP in Cincinnati,* CBS, 1978.
Mrs. Flanner, *Sense of Humor,* PBS, 1982.

Also appeared as Alma Llewellyn, *The Gossip Columnist,* 1980.

OTHER TELEVISION APPEARANCES

Appeared in *Dark Victory, Kind Lady,* and *Angel Street,* all 1953; *Pals;* and *Sense of Humor.*

RADIO APPEARANCES

Miss Anima, "The Undecided Molecule," *Norman Corwin,* 1945.

WRITINGS:

(With Alfred Allen Lewis) *Sylvia Sidney's Needlepoint Book,* Reinhold, 1968.
(With Lewis) *The Sylvia Sidney Question and Answer Book on Needlepoint,* Galahad Books, 1974.

OTHER SOURCES:

PERIODICALS

Films in Review, January, 1966.
Monthly Film Bulletin (London), November, 1974.*

*   *   *

SILVER, Joel   1939-

PERSONAL: Born in 1939. *Education:* Attended New York University.

ADDRESSES: Office—Silver Pictures Company, 10201 West Pico Blvd., Los Angeles, CA 90035.

CAREER: Film producer and executive. Began as an assistant to producer Lawrence Gordon, and became president of the motion picture division of Lawrence Gordon Productions; formed Silver Pictures production company.

AWARDS, HONORS: Named NATO/Showest's producer of the year, 1990.

CREDITS:

FILM PRODUCER, EXCEPT WHERE INDICATED

(Associate producer) *Warriors,* Paramount, 1979.
(Co-producer) *Xanadu,* Universal, 1980.
48 Hours, Paramount, 1982.
(Executive producer) *Jekyll and Hyde . . . Together Again,* Paramount, 1982.

Streets of Fire, Universal-RKO Radio Pictures, 1984.
Brewster's Millions, Universal, 1985.
Commando, Twentieth Century-Fox, 1985.
Weird Science, Universal, 1985.
Jumpin' Jack Flash, Twentieth Century-Fox, 1986.
Lethal Weapon, Warner Brothers, 1987.
Predator, Twentieth Century-Fox, 1987.
Action Jackson, Lorimar, 1988.
Die Hard (also known as *Piege de cristal*), Twentieth Century-Fox, 1988.
Road House, Metro-Goldwyn-Mayer/United Artists, 1989.
Lethal Weapon 2, Warner Brothers, 1989.
The Adventures of Ford Fairlane (also known as *Las Aventuras de Ford Fairlane, Fuodo Fuearen No Boken,* and *Ford Fairlane*), Twentieth Century-Fox, 1990.
Predator 2, Twentieth Century-Fox, 1990.
Die Hard 2: Die Harder, Twentieth Century-Fox, 1990.
Hudson Hawk, Tri-Star, 1991.

FILM APPEARANCES

Director, *Who Framed Roger Rabbit,* Buena Vista, 1988.

TELEVISION APPEARANCES

The 23rd Annual NAACP Image Awards, NBC, 1991.

TELEVISION EXECUTIVE PRODUCER FOR HBO ANTHOLOGY "TALES FROM THE CRYPT"

"Collection Completed," 1989.
"Lover Come Hack To Me," 1989.
"Only Sin Deep," 1989.
" 'Til Death," 1990.
"Fitting Punishment," 1990.
"For Crying Out Loud," 1990.
"Four-Sided Triangle," 1990.
"Judy, You're Not Yourself Today," 1990.
"Korman's Kalamity," 1990.
"The Lower Berth," 1990.
"Mute Witness to Murder," 1990.
"My Brother's Keeper," 1990.
"The Sacrifice," 1990.
"The Secret," 1990.
"Television Terror," 1990.
"The Thing From the Grave," 1990.
"Three's A Crowd," 1990.
"The Ventriloquist's Dummy," 1990.
"Trilogy" (includes "Loved to Death," "Carrion Death," and "The Trap"), 1991.

OTHER SOURCES:

PERIODICALS

Premiere, December, 1990.
Rolling Stone, June 15, 1989.*

SINATRA, Frank 1915-

PERSONAL: Full name, Francis Alfred Sinatra; born December 12, 1915, in Hoboken, NJ; son of Anthony Martin and Natalie Della (Garaventi) Sinatra; married Nancy Barbato, February 4, 1939 (divorced, 1951); married Ava Gardner (an actress), November 7, 1951 (divorced, 1957); married Mia Farrow (an actress), July 19, 1966 (divorced, 1968); married Barbara Jane Blakeley Marx (a dancer), July 11, 1976; children: (first marriage) Nancy Sandra, Franklin Wayne, Christina. *Education:* Attended Drake Institute.

ADDRESSES: Office—c/o Nathan Golden, 8501 Wilshire Blvd., Suite 250, Beverly Hills, CA 90211; and Sinatra Enterprises, Goldwyn Studios, 1041 N. Formosa St., Los Angeles, CA 90046. *Publicist*—Burson-Marsteller, 3333 Wilshire Blvd., Los Angeles, CA 90010.

CAREER: Singer, actor, director, and producer. Worked as a copy boy and reporter covering college sports for *Jersey Observer,* during early 1930s; professional singer, 1936—; sang with The Hoboken Four, 1937; Rustic Cabin (restaurant), Englewood, NJ, singing M.C. and headwaiter, c. 1939; featured singer with Harry James's Music Makers, 1939-40, with The Tommy Dorsey Orchestra, 1940-42, and with Benny Goodman's Band, 1942; began solo career, 1942. Founded Reprise Records, c. 1960, and Artanis Co. Member of board of directors of Princess Grace Arts Advisory Committee.

MEMBER: Friars Club.

AWARDS, HONORS: Named top band vocalist by *Billboard,* 1941; *down beat,* top band vocalist, 1941, top vocalist, 1943, favorite male singer, 1946, most popular vocalist and top pop records personality, 1954; American Academy of Motion Picture Arts and Sciences, Special Academy Award, 1945, for *The House I Live In,* Academy Award for best supporting actor, 1953, for *From Here to Eternity,* Jean Hersholt Humanitarian Award, 1971; Grammy awards, for designing best album cover, 1958, for *Only the Lonely,* for album of the year and best male vocal performance, 1959, for *Come Dance with Me,* for album of the year, 1965, for *September of My Years,* for best male vocal performance, 1965, for "It Was a Very Good Year," for record of the year and best male vocal performance, 1966, for *Strangers in the Night,* and for album of the year, 1966, for *A Man and His Music;* Sylvania Television Award, 1959; National Academy of Recording Arts and Sciences, Lifetime Achievement Award, 1965, Trustee Award, 1980; George Foster Peabody Award, 1965; Cecil B. DeMille Award, Hollywood Foreign Press Association, 1971; Screen Actors Guild Award, 1972; Golden Apple Award for male star of the year, Hollywood Women's Press Club, 1977; Humanitarian Award, Variety Clubs International, 1980; Cross of Sci-

ence and the Arts, Austria, 1984; Presidential Medal of Freedom, 1985; honorary doctorate, Stevens Institute of Technology, 1985; Kennedy Center Honor, 1986; Lifetime Achievement Award, National Association for the Advancement of Colored People (NAACP), 1987.

CREDITS:

FILM

Cameo, *Las Vegas Nights,* Paramount, 1941.
Cameo, *Ship Ahoy,* Metro-Goldwyn-Mayer (MGM), 1942.
Frank, *Higher and Higher,* RKO, 1943.
Cameo, *Reveille with Beverly,* Columbia, 1943.
Glen, *Step Lively,* RKO, 1944.
Clarence Doolittle, *Anchors Aweigh,* MGM, 1945.
Cameo, *Till the Clouds Roll By,* MGM, 1946.
Danny Webson Miller, *It Happened in Brooklyn,* MGM, 1947.
Ricardo, *The Kissing Bandit,* MGM, 1948.
Father Paul, *The Miracle of the Bells,* RKO, 1948.
Chip, *On the Town,* MGM, 1949.
Dennis Ryan, *Take Me Out to the Ball Game,* MGM, 1949.
Johnny Dalton, *Double Dynamite* (also *It's Only Money*), RKO, 1951.
Title role, *Meet Danny Wilson,* Universal, 1952.
Angelo Maggio, *From Here to Eternity,* Columbia, 1953.
John Baron, *Suddenly,* United Artists (UA), 1954.
Nathan Detroit, *Guys and Dolls,* MGM, 1955.
Frankie Machine, *The Man with the Golden Arm,* UA, 1955.
Alfred Boone, *Not as a Stranger,* UA, 1955.
Charlie Y. Reader, *The Tender Trap,* MGM, 1955.
Barney Sloan, *Young at Heart,* Warner Bros., 1955.
Saloon pianist, *Around the World in Eighty Days,* UA, 1956.
Mike Connor, *High Society,* MGM, 1956.
Title role, *Johnny Concho,* UA, 1956 (also see below).
Cameo, *Meet Me in Las Vegas,* MGM, 1956.
Joe E. Lewis, *The Joker Is Wild,* Paramount, 1957.
Joey Evans, *Pal Joey,* Columbia, 1957.
Miguel, *The Pride and the Passion,* UA, 1957.
Lt. Sam Loggins, *Kings Go Forth,* UA, 1958.
Tony Manetta, *A Hole in the Head,* UA, 1959.
Tom C. Reynolds, *Never So Few,* MGM, 1959.
David Hirsh, *Some Came Running,* MGM, 1959.
Francois Durnais, *Can-Can,* Twentieth Century-Fox, 1960.
Danny Ocean, *Ocean's Eleven,* Warner Bros., 1960.
Cameo, *Pepe,* Columbia, 1960.
Harry, *Devil at Four O'Clock,* Columbia, 1961.
Bennett Marco, *The Manchurian Candidate,* UA, 1962.
Cameo, *The Road to Hong Kong,* UA, 1962.

First Sergeant Mike Merry, *Sergeants 3,* UA, 1962 (also see below).

Alan, *Come Blow Your Horn,* Paramount, 1963.

Zack Thomas, *Four for Texas,* Warner Bros., 1963.

Gypsy stableman, *The List of Adrian Messenger,* Universal, 1963.

Cameo, *Paris When It Sizzles,* Paramount, 1964.

Robbo, *Robin and the Seven Hoods,* Warner Bros., 1964 (also see below).

Dan Edwards, *Marriage on the Rocks,* Warner Bros., 1965.

Maloney, *None but the Brave,* Warner Bros., 1965 (also see below).

Col. Joseph L. Ryan, *Von Ryan's Express,* Twentieth Century-Fox, 1965.

Mark Brittain, *Assault on a Queen,* Paramount, 1966.

Vince, *Cast a Giant Shadow,* UA, 1966.

Cameo, *The Oscar,* Embassy, 1966.

Sam Caker, *The Naked Runner,* Warner Bros., 1967.

Title role, *Tony Rome,* Twentieth Century-Fox, 1967.

Joe Leland, *The Detective,* Twentieth Century-Fox, 1968.

Tony Rome, *Lady in Cement,* Twentieth Century-Fox, 1968.

Title role, *Dirty Dingus Magee,* MGM, 1970.

Edward Delaney, *The First Deadly Sin,* Filmways, 1980.

Cameo, *Canonball Run II,* Warner Bros., 1984.

Singing sword, *Who Framed Roger Rabbit,* Buena Vista, 1988.

Also presenter for *That's Entertainment,* 1974.

FILM WORK

Producer, *Johnny Concho,* UA, 1956.

Producer, *Sergeants 3,* UA, 1962.

Producer, *Robin and the Seven Hoods,* Warner Bros., 1964.

Director and producer, *None but the Brave,* Warner Bros., 1965.

TELEVISION APPEARANCES; SPECIALS

Billy Crocker, *Anything Goes,* NBC, 1954.

Stage Manager, *Our Town,* NBC, 1955.

Host, *The Frank Sinatra Show,* ABC, 1959.

Host, *The Frank Sinatra Timex Show,* 3 productions, ABC, 1959-60.

Host, *The Frank Sinatra Show,* NBC, 1965.

Host, *Frank Sinatra: A Man and His Music,* NBC, 1967.

Host, *Francis Albert Sinatra Does His Thing,* CBS, 1968.

Host, *Sinatra,* CBS, 1969 (also see below).

Guest, *Frank Sinatra, Jr., with His Family and Friends,* CBS, 1969.

Host, *Magnavox Presents Frank Sinatra,* NBC, 1973.

Star, *Sinatra—The Main Event,* ABC, 1974.

Host, *Sinatra and Friends,* ABC, 1977.

Host, *Sinatra—The First Forty Years,* NBC, 1980.

Host, *Sinatra: The Man and His Music,* NBC, 1981.

Host, *Sinatra: Concert for the Americas,* Showtime, 1982.

OTHER TELEVISION APPEARANCES

Host, *The Frank Sinatra Show* (series), CBS, 1950-52, then ABC, 1957-58.

Presenter (voice only), *The Matt Dennis Show* (series), NBC, 1955.

Deputy Inspector Frank Hovannes, *Contract on Cherry Street* (movie), NBC, 1977.

TELEVISION WORK

Executive producer, *Sinatra,* CBS, 1969.

RADIO APPEARANCES

Regular performer on *Your Hit Parade,* 1943-45.

RECORDINGS:

SELECTED ALBUMS

Songs for Young Lovers, Capitol, 1954.

Swing Easy, Capitol, 1954.

In the Wee Small Hours, Capitol, 1955.

Songs for Swingin' Lovers, Capitol, 1956.

Close to You, Capitol, 1957.

A Swingin' Affair, Capitol, 1957.

Where Are You?, Capitol, 1957.

A Jolly Christmas from Frank Sinatra, Capitol, 1957.

Come Fly with Me, Capitol, 1958.

Only the Lonely, Capitol, 1958.

Come Dance with Me, Capitol, 1959.

Look to Your Heart, Capitol, 1959.

No One Cares, Capitol, 1959.

Nice 'n' Easy, Capitol, 1960.

Sinatra's Swingin' Session, Capitol, 1961.

All the Way, Capitol, 1961.

Come Swing with Me, Capitol, 1961.

I Remember Tommy, Reprise, 1961.

Ring-A-Ding-Ding, Reprise, 1961.

Sinatra Swings, Reprise, 1961.

Point of No Return, Capitol, 1962.

Sinatra Sings of Love and Things, Capitol, 1962.

Sinatra and Strings, Reprise, 1962.

Sinatra and Swingin' Brass, Reprise, 1962.

All Alone, Reprise, 1962.

Sinatra-Basie, Reprise, 1963.

The Concert Sinatra, Reprise, 1963.

Sinatra's Sinatra, Reprise, 1963.

Frank Sinatra Sings "Days of Wine and Roses," "Moon River," and Other Academy Award Winners, Reprise, 1964.

Sinatra-Basie: It Might as Well Be Swing, Reprise, 1964.

Softly, As I Leave You, Reprise, 1964.

Sinatra '65, Reprise, 1965.

September of My Years, Reprise, 1965.

A Man and His Music, Reprise, 1965.
My Kind of Broadway, Reprise, 1966.
Moonlight Sinatra, Reprise, 1966.
Strangers in the Night, Reprise, 1966.
Sinatra-Basie: Sinatra at the Sands, Reprise, 1966.
That's Life, Reprise, 1966.
Francis Albert Sinatra and Antonio Carlos Jobim, Reprise, 1967.
Frank Sinatra and Frank and Nancy, Reprise, 1967.
Francis A. and Edward K., Reprise, 1968.
Cycles, Reprise, 1968.
My Way, Reprise, 1969.
A Man Alone, Reprise, 1969.
Watertown, Reprise, 1970.
Sinatra and Company, Reprise, 1971.
Ol' Blue Eyes Is Back, Reprise, 1973.
Some Nice Things I've Missed, Reprise, 1974.
The Main Event—Live from Madison Square Garden, Reprise, 1974.
Trilogy, Reprise, 1980.
She Shot Me Down, Reprise, 1981.
L.A. Is My Lady, QWest, 1984.

SELECTED SINGLES

"Night and Day," Bluebird, 1942.
"People Will Say We're in Love," Columbia, 1943.
"Nancy," Columbia, 1944.
"Ol' Man River," Columbia, 1944.
"I Should Care," Columbia, 1945.
"Put Your Dreams Away," Columbia, 1945.
"Day by Day," Columbia, 1945.
"The Things We Did Last Summer," Columbia, 1946.
"My One and Only Love," Capitol, 1953.
"Love and Marriage," Capitol, 1955.
"All the Way," Capitol, 1957.
"Strangers in the Night," Reprise, 1966.
"My Way," Reprise, 1969.
"New York, New York," Reprise, 1980.*

*   *   *

SINDEN, Jeremy   1950-

PERSONAL: Born June 14, 1950, in London, England; son of Donald Alfred (an actor) and Diana Catherine Mahony (an actress) Sinden; married Delia Lindsay (an actress), July 1, 1978; children: Kezia, Harriet. *Education:* Attended Lancing College; studied at London Academy of Music and Dramatic Art.

ADDRESSES: Agent—c/o Michael Anderson, International Creative Management, 388/396 Oxford St., London W1, England.

CAREER: Actor. Chairman of Catchfavour Ltd. (production company).

MEMBER: Actors' Benevolent Fund (councillor), British Actors Equity (councillor, 1978-84), Evelyn Norris Trust (trustee), Garrick Club, Croquet Association, Worshipful Company of Innholders.

AWARDS, HONORS: Emmy Award nomination for *Brideshead Revisited.*

CREDITS:

STAGE APPEARANCES

First Venetian officer, *Othello,* Royal Shakespeare Company (RSC), Stratford, 1971.
(London debut) Private Broughton, *Journey's End,* Mermaid Theatre, 1972.
Venetian soldier, *Othello,* Chichester Festival, 1975.
Station announcer, *Made in Heaven,* Chichester, 1975.
Guardsman and Spanish officer, *Cyrano de Bergerac,* Chichester, 1975.
David, *Lady Harry,* Savoy Theatre, London, 1978.
Graham, *The Philanthropist,* Chichester Festival Theatre, 1985.
Lord Goring, *An Ideal Husband,* Westminister Theatre, London, 1988.

Also appeared at Pitlocking Festival Theatre (stage debut), Scotland, 1969, and at Chichester Festival, 1975 and 1987, including performing as Lord Goring, *An Ideal Husband.* Appeared with RSC, 1970-72.

MAJOR TOURS

Cast member, *Conduct Unbecoming,* Canadian cities, 1983.

STAGE WORK

Assistant stage manager at Pitlocking Festival Theatre, 1969, and producer of *An Ideal Husband,* Chichester Festival.

FILM APPEARANCES

(Film debut) Gold Two, *Star Wars,* Twentieth Century-Fox, 1977.
President, Gilbert and Sullivan Society, *Chariots of Fire,* Twentieth Century-Fox, 1981.
Woodford, *Madame Sousatzka,* Universal, 1988.

Appeared as vorticist, *Mark Gertler Fragments of a Biography,* 1981; as business executive, *Doll's Eye,* 1982; and as Darcy, *Ascendancy,* 1982.

TELEVISION APPEARANCES; MOVIES

Appeared as Randolph, *Harem,* 1986.

TELEVISION APPEARANCES; SPECIALS

Brockman, "Lord Mountbatten: The Last Victory," *Masterpiece Theatre,* PBS, 1986.

"Have His Carcase," "Dorothy L. Sayers' Lord Peter Wimsey," *Mystery!,* PBS, 1987.
Brian Routh, "After the War," *Masterpiece Theatre,* PBS, 1990.

TELEVISION APPEARANCES; MINI-SERIES

(Television debut) Price, *The Expert,* BBC, 1976.
Danger UXB, Thames, 1978, then *Masterpiece Theatre,* PBS, 1981.
Boy Mulcaster, *Brideshead Revisited,* PBS, 1982.
Raikes, *The Far Pavilions,* HBO, 1984.

* * *

SINISE, Gary

CAREER: Actor and director. Cofounder and artistic director of Steppenwolf Theatre, Chicago, IL.

AWARDS, HONORS: Obie Award, Best Director, 1982-83, for *True West;* Antoinette Perry Award nomination, Best Featured Actor in a Play, and Drama Desk Award nomination, Best Actor in a Play, both 1990, for *The Grapes of Wrath.*

CREDITS:

STAGE APPEARANCES

Dopey, *Balm in Gilead,* Minetta Lane Theatre, New York City, 1985.
Billy, *Streamers,* Eisenhower Theatre, John F. Kennedy Center, Washington, DC, 1986.
Mick, *The Caretaker,* Circle in the Square, New York City, 1986.
The Grapes of Wrath, Cort Theatre, New York City, 1990.

Also appeared as Austin in *True West,* New York City.

STAGE WORK; DIRECTOR

True West, Cherry Lane Theatre, New York City, 1982.
Orphans, Cheryl Crawford Theatre, New York City, 1985.

FILM WORK; DIRECTOR

Miles from Home, Cinecom, 1988.

TELEVISION APPEARANCES; MOVIES

Motorcyclist, *Family Secrets,* NBC, 1984.
Ebby Thatcher, "My Name Is Bill W.," *Hallmark Hall of Fame,* ABC, 1989.

Appeared as Richard Ben-Veniste, *The Final Days,* 1989.

TELEVISION APPEARANCES; EPISODIC

Tony Rutherford, *Hunter,* NBC, 1990.

TELEVISION APPEARANCES; SPECIALS

Austin, "True West," *American Playhouse,* PBS, 1984.

TELEVISION WORK; EPISODIC; DIRECTOR

thirtysomething, ABC, 1989.

Also director of *Crime Story,* 1987.*

* * *

SKYE, Ione   1971-

PERSONAL: Full name, Ione Skye Leitch; born 1971, in London, England; daughter of Donovan Leitch (a singer and songwriter), and Enid Karl (a model).

CAREER: Actress.

CREDITS:

FILM APPEARANCES

Clarissa, *River's Edge,* Hemdale Releasing Corporation, 1987.
Deirdre Clark, *Stranded,* New Line, 1987.
Denise Hunter, *A Night in the Life of Jimmy Reardon,* 20th Century-Fox, 1988.
Diane Court, *Say Anything,* 20th Century-Fox, 1990.
Rachel Seth-Smith, *The Rachel Papers,* United Artists, 1990.
Kit, *Mindwalk,* Overseas Filmgroup, 1990.

TELEVISION APPEARANCES

Marie, "Carmilla," *Nightmare Classics,* Showtime, 1989.
Joanna Dibble, *It's Called the Sugar Plum* (one-act play), *General Motors Playwrights Theatre,* A & E, 1991.

Also appeared as Pauline in the 1987 television movie *Napoleon and Josephine: A Love Story.*

OTHER SOURCES:

PERIODICALS

People, August 3, 1987.
Premiere, December, 1987.
Us, October 2, 1989.*

* * *

SLATER, Christian   1969-

PERSONAL: Born August 18, 1969, in New York, NY; son of Mary Jo Slater (a casting executive) and Michael Hawkins (an actor). *Education:* Attended Dalton School, High School of the Performing Arts, and Professional Children's School.

ADDRESSES: Agent—Rick Kurtzman, Creative Artists Agency, 9830 Wilshire Blvd., Beverly Hills, CA 90212.

CAREER: Actor.

CREDITS:

FILM APPEARANCES

Binx Davy, *The Legend of Billy Jean,* Tri-Star, 1985.
Adso of Melk, *The Name of the Rose,* Twentieth Century-Fox, 1986.
Preston Tucker, Jr., *Tucker: The Man and His Dream,* Paramount, 1988.
Brian Kelly, *Gleaming the Cube,* Twentieth Century-Fox, 1989.
J.D., *Heathers,* New World, 1989.
Nick, *The Wizard,* Universal, 1989.
Andy, *Tales from the Dark Side: The Movie,* Paramount, 1990.
Arkansas Dave Rudabaugh, *Young Guns II,* Twentieth Century-Fox, 1990.
Mark Hunter, *Pump Up the Volume,* SCE Entertainment Corp., 1990.
Will Scarlett, *Robin Hood: Prince of Thieves,* Warner Brothers, 1991.
Charles "Lucky" Luciano, *Mobsters,* Universal, 1991.

TELEVISION APPEARANCES; SPECIALS

The kid, *The Edge,* HBO, 1989.
The 61st Annual Academy Awards Presentation, ABC, 1989.
The 63rd Academy Awards Presentation, ABC, 1991.
The 48th Annual Golden Globe Awards, TBS, 1991.
The 17th Annual People's Choice Awards, CBS, 1991.

Also appeared as Billy Beak in *The Haunted Mansion Mystery,* 1983.

TELEVISION APPEARANCES; MOVIES

Walt Willy, *Living Proof: The Hank Williams Jr. Story,* NBC, 1983.
Cliff Petrie, *Desperate for Love* (also known as *Dying for Love*), CBS, 1989.

TELEVISION APPEARANCES; SERIES

D.J. LaSalle, *Santa Barbara,* NBC, 1985.

Also appeared as Charlie in *Robbers, Rooftops and Witches,* 1982.

STAGE APPEARANCES

(Broadway debut) Winthrop Paroo, *The Music Man,* City Center, 1980.
(Off-Broadway debut) Jimmy, *Between Daylight and Boonville,* Wonderhorse Theatre, 1980.
Billy Mowcher, *Copperfield,* ANTA Theatre, New York City, 1981.
MacDuff's son, *Macbeth,* Circle in the Square, New York City, 1982.

Young Merlin and Arthur, *Merlin,* Mark Hellinger Theatre, New York City, 1983.
Bert, *Landscape of the Body,* Walter McGinn/John Cazale Theatre, Second Stage, New York City, 1984.
Steve Tierney, *Dry Land,* New Arts Theatre Company, Judith Anderson Theatre, New York City, 1986.

OTHER SOURCES:

PERIODICALS

Us, May 1, 1989.*

*   *   *

SMART, Jean 1951(?)-

PERSONAL: Born September 13, c. 1951, in Seattle, WA; married Richard Gilliand (an actor), 1987. *Education:* Received B.F.A. in theater from University of Washington, Seattle.

ADDRESSES: Agent—Michael Blake, International Creative Management, 8899 Beverly Blvd., Los Angeles, CA 90048.

CAREER: Actress. Member of Oregon Shakespeare Festival Company, 1975-77, Hartford Stage Company, Pittsburgh Public Theatre Company, and Intiman Theatre Company.

AWARDS, HONORS: New York Drama Desk Award nomination for the Off-Broadway production of *Last Summer at Bluefish Cove;* Los Angeles Drama Critics Circle Award, Dramalogue Award, and Los Angeles Drama Desk Award for the Los Angeles production of the same play.

CREDITS:

TELEVISION APPEARANCES; SERIES

Joan Reynolds, *Reggie,* ABC, 1983.
Shari, *Teachers Only,* ABC, 1983.
Charlene Frazier, *Designing Women,* CBS, 1986—.

TELEVISION APPEARANCES; SPECIALS

Marlene, *Piaf,* Entertainment Channel, 1982.
Deputy Warden Allison Brody, *Maximum Security,* HBO, 1985.
Princess Katerina, *Royal Match,* CBS, 1985.
Susan Singer, *A Place at the Table* (also known as *The Best Kept Secret, No Children Shall Go Hungry,* and *A Million Children*), NBC, 1988.
The Forty-first Annual Emmy Awards, Fox, 1989.
US Magazine—Live at the Emmys, Fox, 1989.
Charlene Frazier, *The Designing Women Special: Their Finest Hour,* CBS, 1990.

TELEVISION APPEARANCES; MOVIES

Virge, *Single Bars, Single Women,* ABC, 1984.
Valerie Thomas, *A Fight for Jenny,* NBC, 1986.
A Seduction in Travis County, CBS, 1991.

TELEVISION APPEARANCES; EPISODIC

Appeared on episodes of *Lime Street,* ABC, *Facts of Life,* NBC, *Goodnight, Beantown,* CBS, and *Remington Steele,* NBC.

FILM APPEARANCES

Doris, *Flashpoint,* Tri-Star, 1984.
Ella, *Protocol,* Warner Brothers, 1984.
Sister Marie, *Fire with Fire,* Paramount, 1986.
Dr. Criswell, *Project X,* Twentieth Century-Fox, 1987.

STAGE APPEARANCES

Equus, Seattle Repertory Theatre, Seattle, WA, 1976-77.
Much Ado about Nothing, Oregon Shakespeare Festival, Ashland, OR, 1976.
A Moon for the Misbegotten, Oregon Shakespeare Festival, 1977.
A Christmas Carol, ACT: A Contemporary Theatre, Seattle, WA, 1977-78 and 1978-79.
Terra Nova, Alaska Repertory Theatre, Anchorage/Fairbanks, AL, 1978-79.
Cat's Play, Seattle Repertory Theatre, 1978-79.
Saint Joan, Seattle Repertory Theatre, 1979-80.
Eve, *A History of the American Film,* Seattle Repertory Theatre, 1979-80.
Lil, *Last Summer at Bluefish Cove,* Actors Playhouse, New York City, 1980-81.
A History of American Film, Alliance Theatre Company, Atlanta, GA, 1980-81.
(Broadway debut) Marlene, *Piaf,* Plymouth Theatre, New York City, 1981.
Babs, *Mrs. California,* Mark Taper Forum and Los Angeles Public/Coronet Theatre, Los Angeles, CA, 1985-86.

Also appeared as Lil in *Last Summer at Bluefish Cove,* Fountain Theatre, Los Angeles, CA, and in *Strange Snow,* Coast Playhouse.

OTHER SOURCES:

PERIODICALS

TV Guide, March 11, 1989.*

*   *   *

SMITH, Liz   1925-

PERSONAL: Original name, Betty Smith; born December 11, 1925, in Scunthorpe, Lincolnshire, England; divorced, 1959; children: Robert, Sarah. *Education:* Trained for the stage at Little Theatre. *Politics:* "Anti-party politics." *Religion:* "Undecided." *Avocational interests:* Painting.

ADDRESSES: Agent—Jeremy Conway, 18-21 Jermyn St., London, England.

CAREER: Actress. Worked at Little Theatre in the 1950s; spent five years in improvisational theatre. Friend of the Royal Academy; president, North London Animal Aid. *Military service:* Royal Navy, World War II.

MEMBER: British Academy of Film and Television Arts.

AWARDS, HONORS: British Academy of Film and Television Arts Award, best supporting actress, 1984, and Italian film award, both for *A Private Function.*

CREDITS:

FILM APPEARANCES

(Film debut) Pat's mother, *Bleak Moments,* Contemporary, 1972.
Hotel manager, *The Stick Up,* Trident-Barber, 1977.
Mrs. Dodds, *All Things Bright and Beautiful* (also known as *It Shouldn't Happen to a Vet*), World, 1979.
Flora, *Agatha,* Warner Brothers, 1979.
Lady Philippa of Staines, *Sir Henry at Rawlinson End,* Charisma, 1980.
Mrs. Fairley, *The French Lieutenant's Woman,* United Artists (UA), 1981.
Landlady, *Give Us This Day,* Concord, 1982.
Maizie, *Britannia Hospital,* UA, 1982.
Lady in pub, *Crystal Gazing,* British Film Institute, 1982.
The Trail of the Pink Panther, Metro-Goldwyn-Mayer (MGM)/UA, 1982.
Martha, *Curse of the Pink Panther,* MGM/UA, 1983.
Mother, *A Private Function,* Island Alive, 1985.
Millie, *We Think the World of You,* Cinecom, 1988.
Mary Louise McKinney, *Apartment Zero,* Skouras, 1988.
Mrs. Plunkett, *High Spirits,* Tri-Star, 1988.
Mrs. Bangham, *Little Dorrit,* Cannon, 1988.
Mrs. Rigby, *Bert Rigby, You're a Fool,* Warner Brothers, 1989.
Grace, *The Cook, the Thief, His Wife, and Her Lover,* Miramax, 1990.

STAGE APPEARANCES

Mrs. Baildon, *Then and Now,* Hampstead Theatre, London, 1979.
Mrs. Northrop, *When We Are Married,* National Theatre, Lyttelton Theatre, London, 1979.
The mother, *Why Me?,* Strand Theatre, London, 1985.

Also appeared as Mother Superior in *Once a Catholic* (London debut), Wyndham's Theatre; and in *Enjoy,* Alan Bennett Theatre.

TELEVISION APPEARANCES; MOVIES

La Falourdel, *The Hunchback of Notre Dame,* NBC, 1977.
Mrs. Dilber, *A Christmas Carol,* CBS, 1984.
Mrs. Pendleton, *Harem,* ABC, 1986.

Also appeared in *Hard Labour.*

TELEVISION APPEARANCES; SPECIALS

Miss Meachum, *Separate Tables,* HBO, 1983.
"Young Charlie Chaplin," *WonderWorks,* PBS, 1988.

TELEVISION APPEARANCES; MINI-SERIES

Mary's mother, *The Life and Loves of a She-Devil* (also known as *She Devil*), Arts & Entertainment, 1987.

OTHER TELEVISION APPEARANCES

Appeared in numerous situation comedies.

*   *   *

SMUIN, Michael   1938-

PERSONAL: Born October 13, 1938, in Missoula, MT; married Paula Tracy (a dancer); children: Shane. *Education:* University of Montana, D.F.A., 1984; studied with Christensen Brothers and with the San Francisco Ballet.

CAREER: Choreographer, director, and dancer. Resident choreographer for American Ballet Theatre, New York City; free-lance dancer partnered with wife, Paula Tracy; director of San Francisco Ballet; co-chairman of National Endowment for the Arts Dance Advisory Panel, Washington, DC. Member of U.S. Dance Study Team, People's Republic of China, 1983.

AWARDS, HONORS: Antoinette Perry Award nomination, Best Direction of a Musical, and Outer Critics Circle Award, 1981, both for *Sophisticated Ladies; Dancemagazine* award, 1983; Antoinette Perry Award and Drama Desk Award, Best Choreography, both 1988, for *Anything Goes;* Emmy Awards for "Romeo and Juliet," "The Tempest," and "A Song for Dead Warriors," all *Dance in America—Great Performances.*

CREDITS:

STAGE APPEARANCES

Dancer with University of Utah Ballet, Salt Lake City, UT, 1955-57; San Francisco Ballet, San Francisco, CA, 1957-62 and 1973-84; and American Ballet Theatre, New York State Theatre, New York City, 1967.

STAGE WORK

Director, musical stager, and choreographer (with Donald McKayle), *Sophisticated Ladies,* Lunt-Fontanne Theatre, New York City, 1981.
Director and choreographer, *Chaplin,* Dorothy Chandler Pavilion, Los Angeles, 1983.
Choreographer, *Anything Goes,* Vivian Beaumont Theatre, Lincoln Center, New York City, 1987.

Also staged dance for Leslie Caron, Mikhail Baryshnikov, and Rudolf Nureyev, American Ballet Theatre/Paris Opera Ballet Gala at Metropolitan Opera House, New York City, 1986; producer, *Cinderella, Romeo and Juliet, The Tempest,* and *A Song for Dead Warriors,* all San Francisco Ballet; choreographer, *Pulcinella Variations,* American Ballet Theatre, Metropolitan Opera House; and director, *Faustus in Hell,* American Conservatory Theatre, San Francisco, CA. Director of many works for San Francisco Ballet, CA, and American Ballet Theatre, New York City.

MAJOR TOURS

Staged dance and musical numbers, *Candide,* U.S. cities, 1971.
Choreographer (with Donald McKayle), *Sophisticated Ladies,* U.S. cities, 1982.

FILM WORK

Choreographer, *Rumble Fish,* Universal, 1983.
Principal choreographer, *The Cotton Club,* Orion, 1984.
Choreographer, *Fletch Lives,* Universal, 1989.

Also technical adviser for *The Golden Child,* 1986.

TELEVISION WORK; EPISODIC

Choreographer, "A Song for Dead Warriors," *Dance in America—Great Performances,* PBS, 1984.
Choreographer, "Cinderella," *Dance in America—Great Performances,* PBS, 1985.

Choreographer for "Romeo and Juliet" and "The Tempest," both *Dance in America—Great Performances,* PBS.

TELEVISION WORK; SPECIALS

Director, *Jinx,* 1985; choreographer, "Delgadina," *Corridos! Tales of Passion and Revolution,* 1987; director, *Voice/Dance: Bobby McFerrin and the Tandy Beal Dance Company,* 1987; creator, *The Omo,* 1987; and director and choreographer for *Linda Ronstadt's Canciones de Mi Padre,* 1989, and *Aid and Comfort.**

*   *   *

SOBIESKI, Carol   1939-1990

OBITUARY NOTICE—See index for *CTFT* sketch: Full name, Carol O'Brien Sobieski; born March 16, 1939, in

Chicago, IL; died of amyloidosis, November 4, 1990, in Santa Monica, CA. Television writer and screenwriter. Sobieski was an accomplished author and adapter of scripts for television and motion pictures. She began writing for television series such as *Mister Novak, Peyton Place,* and *The Mod Squad* in the 1960s. In her more than twenty-five years in the business, the author established a reputation for skillfully rendering complex themes and characterizations. Her works have earned consistent praise for their realistic depiction of family crises and penetrating treatment of human growth and maturation. A three-time winner of Writers Guild awards, Sobieski penned the scripts for such television movies as *Sunshine,* about a young wife and mother who dies of cancer; *Amelia Earhart,* a biography of the American aviator who disappeared in 1937; and *The Women's Room,* an adaptation of Marilyn French's feminist novel. She also adapted the television miniseries *The Bourne Identity* from Robert Ludlum's spy novel of the same title and earned Emmy nominations for best script and program for her monologue *Harry Truman: Plain Speaking.* Sobieski's feature film credits include *Casey's Shadow,* about a womanizing country music singer; an adaptation of the legendary Broadway musical *Annie;* and *Winter People,* a Depression-era drama of conflict, retribution, and justice among feuding families in the Appalachians. Her final work, a Hallmark Hall of Fame television film titled *Sarah, Plain and Tall,* was slated for broadcast after her death.

OBITUARIES AND OTHER SOURCES:

PERIODICALS

Los Angeles Times, November 7, 1990.
New York Times, November 9, 1990.

* * *

SOULE, Olan   1909-

PERSONAL: Born February 28, 1909, in La Harpe, IL.

CAREER: Actor. Appeared on radio and in theatre productions; film actor in Hollywood, CA, beginning in 1940s.

CREDITS:

FILM APPEARANCES

Secretary, *The Lady Takes a Sailor,* Warner Brothers, 1949.
Ralph Newell, *Destination Big House,* Republic, 1950.
Simmons, *Peggy,* Universal, 1950.
Jimmy, *Cuban Fireball,* Republic, 1951.
Mr. Krull, *The Day the Earth Stood Still,* Twentieth Century-Fox, 1951.

Salesman, *You Never Can Tell* (also known as *You Never Know*), Universal, 1951.
Mr. Fenton, *The Atomic City,* Paramount, 1952.
Desk clerk, *Don't Bother to Knock,* Twentieth Century-Fox, 1952.
Hotel clerk, *Monkey Business,* Twentieth Century-Fox, 1952.
Lieutenant Quatermaster, *Never Wave at a WAC* (also known as *The Private Wore Skirts*), Independent Artists/RKO, 1952.
Glove salesman, *Stars and Stripes Forever* (also known as *Marching Along*), Twentieth Century-Fox, 1952.
Secretary, *The Story of Will Rogers,* Warner Brothers, 1952.
Clerk, *Call Me Madam,* Twentieth Century-Fox, 1953.
Ray Pinker, *Dragnet,* Mark VII, Ltd./Warner Brothers, 1954.
Captain Creavy, *Francis Joins the WACs,* Universal, 1954.
Lewis, *Human Desire,* Columbia, 1954.
Mr. Duncan, *Phffft!,* Columbia, 1954.
Major Martin Fielding, *Cult of the Cobra,* Universal, 1955.
Assistant hotel manager, *Daddy Long Legs,* Twentieth Century-Fox, 1955.
Catesby, *Prince of the Players,* Twentieth Century-Fox, 1955.
Dr. Pearson, *Queen Bee,* Columbia, 1955.
First reporter, *This Island Earth,* Universal, 1955.
Hugo Paige, *Shock Treatment,* Arcola/Twentieth Century-Fox, 1964.
Desk clerk, *The Cincinnati Kid,* Metro-Goldwyn-Mayer, 1965.
The Destructors, United Pictures-Harold Goldman Associates/Feature Film Corporation of America, 1968.
Harvey Underwood, *The Seven Minutes,* Twentieth Century-Fox, 1971.
Engineer, *The Towering Inferno,* Twentieth Century-Fox/Warner Brothers, 1974.
Rube Cluck, *The Apple Dumpling Gang,* Buena Vista, 1975.
Station man, *St. Ives,* Warner Brothers, 1976.
Cash McCall, Warner Brothers, 1960.
Thirteen West Street, Ladd Enterprises/Columbia, 1962.
The Bubble (also known as *The Fantastic Invasion of Planet Earth*), Arch Obder 3-D, 1967.
Fantastic Planet (also known as *La Planete sauvage*), Les Films Armorial/Service de Recherche Ortif/Ceskoslovensky Film Export, 1973.
The Shaggy D.A., Walt Disney/Buena Vista, 1976.

Also appeared in *Girl Happy.*

TELEVISION APPEARANCES; MOVIES

Saltillo, *The Six Million Dollar Man,* ABC, 1973.
Eli Bence, *The Legend of Lizzie Borden,* ABC, 1975.

Code Red, ABC, 1981.

TELEVISION APPEARANCES; SERIES

Aristotle "Tut" Jones, *Captain Midnight,* CBS, 1954-56.
Mr. McGunnis, *Have Gun, Will Travel,* CBS, 1957-63.
Mr. Pfeiffer, *My Three Sons,* ABC, 1961-63.
Fred Springer, *Arnie,* CBS, 1970-72.
Voice of Batman, *Super Friends* (animated), ABC, 1973-83.
Voice of Batman, *The All-New Superfriends Hour,* ABC, 1977.
Voice of Batman, *The New Super Friends Hour* (animated), ABC, 1977-78.
Voice of Batman, *The World's Greatest Super Heroes* (animated), ABC, 1978-80.

TELEVISION APPEARANCES; EPISODIC

I Love Lucy, CBS, 1955.
"The Navigator," *One Step Beyond,* ABC, 1959.
"Legacy of One," *One Step Beyond,* ABC, 1960.
Man from IRS, "The Man in the Battle," *The Twilight Zone,* CBS, 1960.
Mr. Smiles, "Caesar and Me," *The Twilight Zone,* CBS, 1964.

TELEVISION APPEARANCES; PILOTS

House on Greenapple Road, ABC, 1970.
Dr. Samuels, *The D.A.: Conspiracy to Kill,* NBC, 1971.
Hotel clerk, *Charlie Cobb: Nice Night for a Hanging,* NBC, 1977.
Hotel manager, *The 25th Man,* NBC, 1982.
Mr. Baxter, *The Jerk, Too,* NBC, 1984.

Also appeared in *Getaway Car,* 1958.

RADIO APPEARANCES

Appeared on *The First Nighter,* 1943-53; as Coach Hardy, *Jack Armstrong;* and as Ah Ha, *Little Orphan Annie.* *

*   *   *

SPACEY, Kevin   1959-

PERSONAL: Born July 26, 1959, in South Orange, NJ. *Education:* Attended Los Angeles Valley College; studied drama at Juilliard School.

ADDRESSES: Agent—Creative Artists Agency, 9830 Wilshire Blvd., Beverly Hills, CA 90212.

CAREER: Actor. Has appeared with Seattle Repertory Theatre, New York Shakespeare Festival, American National Theatre, and the Kennedy Center.

AWARDS, HONORS: Drama Desk Award, featured actor, and Antoinette Perry Award, featured actor in a play, both 1991, for *Lost in Yonkers.*

CREDITS:

TELEVISION APPEARANCES; SERIES

Mel Profitt, *Wiseguy,* CBS, 1987-88.

TELEVISION APPEARANCES; MOVIES

Wes Brent, *The Murder of Mary Phagan* (also known as *The Ballad of Mary Phagan*), NBC, 1988.
Jim Bakker, *Fall from Grace,* NBC, 1990.
Wade Black, *When You Remember Me* (also known as *The Legacy, The Legacy of Michael Patrick Smith,* and *The Amazing Legacy of Michael Patrick Smith*), ABC, 1990.

TELEVISION APPEARANCES; SPECIALS

Jamie, *Long Day's Journey into Night, Broadway on Showtime,* Showtime, 1987, then *American Playhouse,* PBS, 1988.
Clarence Darrow, *Darrow* (play), *American Playhouse,* PBS, 1991.

FILM APPEARANCES

(Film debut) Subway thief, *Heartburn,* Paramount, 1986.
Bob Speck, *Working Girl,* Twentieth Century-Fox, 1988.
Dwayne Hanson, *Rocket Gibraltar,* Columbia, 1988.
Mario, *Dad,* Universal, 1989.
Kirgo, *See No Evil, Hear No Evil,* Tri-Star, 1989.
Frank Curtain, *A Show of Force,* Paramount, 1990.
Osborne, *Henry and June,* Universal, 1990.

STAGE APPEARANCES

(Off-Broadway debut) Messenger, *Henry IV, Part One,* New York Shakespeare Festival, Delacorte Theatre, New York City, 1981.
Paul, *Barbarians,* Soho Repertory Theatre, New York City, 1982.
(Broadway debut) Oswald Alving, *Ghosts,* Brooks Atkinson Theatre, New York City, 1982.
The Mousetrap, Barter Theatre, Abingdon/Fairfax, VA, 1982-83.
The Misanthrope, Seattle Repertory Theatre, Seattle, WA, 1983-84.
As You Like It, Seattle Repertory Theatre, 1983-84.
Mickey, *Hurlyburly,* Ethel Barrymore Theatre, New York City, 1984-85.
Konstantin, *A Seagull,* John F. Kennedy Center for the Performing Arts, Eisenhower Theatre, Washington, DC, 1985-86.
James Tyrone, Jr., *Long Day's Journey into Night,* Broadhurst Theatre, New York City, 1986.
Mitch, *As It Is in Heaven,* Perry Street Theatre, New York City, 1987.
Bernie, *Right Behind the Flag,* Playwrights Horizons Theatre, New York City, 1988.

Ben Cook, *National Anthems,* Long Wharf Theatre, New Haven, CT, 1988–89.

Louie, *Lost in Yonkers,* Richard Rodgers Theatre, New York City, 1991.

Also appeared in productions of *Uncle Vanya,* and *The Robbers.*

OTHER SOURCES:

PERIODICALS

New York Times, March 3, 1991.

* * *

SPADER, James 1961-

PERSONAL: Born in 1961 in Boston, MA; married. *Education:* Attended Phillips Academy; trained for the stage at Michael Chekov Studio.

ADDRESSES: Agent—Toni Howard, International Creative Management, 8899 Beverly Blvd., Los Angeles, CA 90048.

CAREER: Actor. Previously worked as a truck driver and stable boy.

AWARDS, HONORS: Cannes Film Festival Award, best actor, 1989, for *sex, lies, and videotape.*

CREDITS:

FILM APPEARANCES

(Film debut) Keith Butterfield, *Endless Love,* Universal, 1981.
Dutra, *The New Kids,* Columbia, 1985.
Morgan Hiller, *Tuff Turf,* New World, 1985.
Steff McKee, *Pretty in Pink,* Paramount, 1986.
Ken Arrenberg, *Baby Boom,* Metro-Goldwyn-Mayer/United Artists, 1987.
Rip, *Less Than Zero,* Twentieth Century-Fox, 1987.
Richards, *Mannequin,* Twentieth Century-Fox, 1987.
Roger Barnes, *Wall Street,* Twentieth Century-Fox, 1987.
John and Rick Wesford, *Jack's Back,* Palisades, 1988.
DeForest, *The Rachel Papers,* United Artists, 1989.
Graham Dalton, *sex, lies, and videotape,* Outlaw, 1989.
Max Baron, *White Palace,* Universal, 1990.
Michael Boll, *Bad Influence,* Emerald Films International, 1990.
Tim Garrity, *True Colors,* Paramount, 1991.

TELEVISION APPEARANCES: MOVIES

Buddy Gant, *Cocaine: One Man's Seduction,* NBC, 1983.
Donny Tison, *A Killer in the Family,* ABC, 1983.
Lowell Everall, *Family Secrets,* NBC, 1984.
Joey, *Starcrossed,* ABC, 1985.

Also appeared in *The Gladiola Girls,* NBC.

OTHER TELEVISION APPEARANCES

Fenwick, *Diner* (pilot), CBS, 1983.
Jake Nichols, *The Family Tree* (series), NBC, 1983.

STAGE APPEARANCES

Appeared in productions of *Equus, A Streetcar Named Desire,* and *Veronica's Room;* also appeared with Actor's Studio, New York City.

OTHER SOURCES:

PERIODICALS

Premiere, November, 1987.*

* * *

SPINER, Brent

ADDRESSES: Agent—c/o The Gersh Agency, 232 North Canon Dr., Beverly Hills, CA 90210.

CAREER: Actor.

CREDITS:

STAGE APPEARANCES

Kil, *The Family,* Chelsea Theatre Center of Brooklyn, Westside Theatre, New York City, 1975.
Counselor two, *Marco Polo,* Phoenix Theatre, Marymount Manhattan Theatre, New York City, 1976.
Hank, *A History of the American Film,* ANTA Theatre, New York City, 1978.
Luke, *Leave It to Beaver Is Dead,* New York Shakespeare Festival (NYSF), Public Theatre, New York City, 1979.
AA, *Emigres,* Brooklyn Academy of Music, Attic Theatre, Brooklyn, NY, 1979.
Older son, *Table Settings,* Playwrights Horizons Theatre, New York City, 1980.
Konstantin Treplev, *The Sea Gull,* NYSF, Public Theatre, 1980.
Electrician, *Marvelous Gray,* Lion Theatre, New York City, 1982.
John, *The Philanthropist,* Manhattan Theatre Club, New York City, 1983.
The Cherry Orchard, Long Wharf Theatre, New Haven, CT, 1983.
Franz, *Sunday in the Park with George,* Playwrights Horizons Theatre, 1983, then Franz and Dennis, Booth Theatre, New York City, 1984.
The Duke, *Big River,* Eugene O'Neill Theatre, New York City, 1985.

Also appeared on Broadway as Aramis in *The Three Musketeers,* 1984.

FILM APPEARANCES

Leonard, *Rent Control,* Group S, 1981.
Preacher Mann, *Miss Firecracker* (also known as *Miss Firecracker Contest*), Corsair/Rank Film Distributors, 1989.

TELEVISION APPEARANCES; MOVIES

Hinnerman, *Crime of Innocence,* NBC, 1985.
Jim Stevens, *Manhunt for Claude Dallas,* CBS, 1986.
McMahon, *Family Sins,* CBS, 1987.

TELEVISION APPEARANCES; SERIES

Lieutenant Commander Data, *Star Trek: The Next Generation,* syndicated, 1987—.

TELEVISION APPEARANCES; EPISODIC

Franz and Dennis, "Sunday in the Park with George," *Broadway on Showtime,* Showtime, 1986, then *American Playhouse,* PBS, 1986.
Vaughn, *Hunter,* NBC, 1986.
Bob Wheeler, *Night Court,* NBC, 1986 and 1987.

Also appeared in *Cheers,* NBC.

TELEVISION APPEARANCES; PILOTS

Clinton C. Waddle, *Sylvan in Paradise,* NBC, 1986.
Brentwood Carter, *What's Alan Watching?* (also known as *Outrageous*), CBS, 1989.

TELEVISION APPEARANCES; MINI-SERIES

Tom Fink, *The Dain Curse,* CBS, 1978.
Allard Lowenstein, *Robert Kennedy and His Times,* CBS, 1985.*

*   *   *

STRAIGES, Tony

PERSONAL: Education: Studied design with John Priest, Eldon Elder, Ming Cho Lee, and Peter Feller.

CAREER: Designer.

AWARDS, HONORS: Antoinette Perry Award, 1984, for *Sunday in the Park with George.*

CREDITS:

STAGE DESIGNER

Glance of a Landscape, Playwrights Horizons Theatre, New York City, 1975.
Children, Virginia Museum Theatre Repertory Company, Richmond, VA, 1975.
Just the Immediate Family, Hudson Guild Theatre, New York City, 1978.
Icedancing, Minskoff Theatre, New York City, 1978.

Timbuktui, Mark Hellinger Theatre, New York City, 1978.
A History of the American Film, ANTA Theatre, New York City, 1978.
Richard the Third, Cort Theatre, New York City, 1979.
Don Juan Comes Back from the War, Manhattan Theatre Club, New York City, 1979.
Gertrude Stein Gertrude Stein Gertrude Stein, Circle Repertory Theatre, New York City, then Provincetown Playhouse, New York City, both 1979.
Vikings, Manhattan Theatre Club, 1980.
Harold and Maude, Martin Beck Theatre, New York City, 1980.
Talking With, Manhattan Theatre Club/Downstairs, 1982.
Waiting for Godot, American Repertory Theatre, Cambridge, MA, 1982.
The Great Magoo, Hartford Stage Company, Hartford, CT, 1982.
Summer, Manhattan Theatre Club/Downstairs, 1983.
Sunday in the Park with George, Playwrights Horizons Theatre, 1983, then Booth Theatre, New York City, 1984.
Diamonds, Circle in the Square, New York City, 1984.
Messiah, The Space at City Center, Manhattan Theatre Club, 1984.
On the Verge on the Geography of Yearning, Center Stage Theatre, Baltimore, MD, 1984.
Fighting Interntional Fat, Playwrights Horizons Theatre, 1985.
Women and Water, Arena Stage, 1986.
Long Day's Journey into Night, Broadhurst Theatre, New York City, 1986.
Into the Woods, Old Globe Theatre, San Diego, CA, 1986, then Martin Beck Theatre, 1987.
Coastal Disturbances, Second Stage Theatre, New York City, 1987.
Rumors, Broadhurst Theatre, 1988.
I Hate Hamlet, Walter Kerr Theatre, New York City, 1991.
Coppelia, American Ballet Theatre, Kennedy Center for the Performing Arts, Washington, DC, 1991.

Also designer for *Troilus and Cressida,* Yale Repertory Theatre; *Ghosts,* American Repertory Theatre; *On the Verge,* Center Stage Theatre; *Tennessee Williams: A Celebration,* Williamstown Theatre Festival, Williamstown, MA. Designer for Yale Repertory Theatre, New Haven, CT, 1974-77, 1978-79, and 1981-82; McCarter Theatre Company, Princeton, NJ, 1976-77; Arena Stage, 1976-81 and 1982-83; Tyrone Guthrie Theatre, Minneapolis, MN, 1978-79; American Repertory Theatre, 1979-82; and Center Stage Theatre, Baltimore, MD, 1983-84.

MAJOR TOURS

Designer, *Timbuktui,* U.S. cities, 1979.

TELEVISION DESIGNER

Sunday in the Park with George, PBS, 1986.
Long Day's Journey into Night, PBS, 1987.*

*   *   *

SUMMERHAYS, Jane

PERSONAL: Born October 11 in Salt Lake City, UT; married Richard Blumenthal (an attorney). *Education:* Received B.A. from University of Utah; Received M.A. from Catholic University of America.

ADDRESSES: Agent—Joan Fields, William Morris Agency, 1350 Avenue of the Americas, New York, NY 10019.

CAREER: Actress.

AWARDS, HONORS: Antoinette Perry Award nomination and Drama Desk Award, both Best Featured Actress in a Musical, 1987, for *Me and My Girl.*

CREDITS:

STAGE APPEARANCES

Sheila, *A Chorus Line,* Drury Lane Theatre, London, 1976, then Royal Alexandra Theatre, Toronto, Canada, 1977.
Lady Kay Wellington, *Oh, Kay!,* Royal Alexandra Theatre, then Kennedy Center Opera House, Washington, DC, both 1978.
(Broadway debut) Jane and understudy for Ann Miller, *Sugar Babies,* Mark Hellinger Theatre, New York City, 1980–82.
(Off-Broadway debut) Zelda Fitzgerald and Sylvia Beach, *Paris Lights,* American Place Theatre, 1980.
Ensemble, *Hey, Look Me Over!,* Avery Fisher Hall, New York City, 1981.
Sheila, *A Chorus Line,* Shubert Theatre, New York City, 1983.
Maria, *On Approval,* Roundabout Theatre, Susan Bloch Theatre, New York City, 1984.
Lady Jaqueline Carstone, *Me and My Girl,* Marquis Theatre, New York City, 1986.
Diana, *Lend Me a Tenor,* Royale Theatre, New York City, 1989.
Elizabeth, *Taking Steps,* Circle in the Square, New York City, 1991.

MAJOR TOURS

Nash at Nine, U.S. cities, 1975.

Understudy for Ann Miller, *Sugar Babies,* U.S. cities, 1985.

TELEVISION APPEARANCES; SPECIALS

Appeared in *Kennedy Center Honors: A Celebration of the Performing Arts,* 1986.

*   *   *

SUMNER, Geoffrey   1908-1989

PERSONAL: Born November 20, 1908, in Ilfracombe, Devon, U.K.; died in 1989, in Alderney, Channel Islands, England; son of Edmund and Kathleen Marion (Brook) Sumner; married Gwen Williams Roberts; children: three daughters. *Education:* Attended Clifton College and Tarka Training Farm.

CAREER: Actor and director. Worked as a pig breeder, mountaineer, and bobsled racer prior to theater career. *Military service:* H. M. Royal Artillery, served during World War II; became colonel.

CREDITS:

STAGE APPEARANCES

(Stage debut) Algie, *Sport of Kings,* Q Theatre, 1931.
(London debut) Flag Lieutenant, *Admirals All,* Shaftesbury Theatre, 1933.
Gilbert, *The Wind and the Rain,* Savoy Theatre, London, 1935.
Alec Merton, *Rise and Shine,* Drury Lane Theatre, London, 1936.
Captaine Corrie, *Mirabelle,* Q Theatre, 1937, then Vaudeville Theatre, London, 1938.
Armand de Perlichon, *Money Talks,* Lyceum Theatre, London, 1938.
Henry Westby, *Room for Two,* Comedy Theatre, London, 1938.
Tim Shields, *Tony Draws a Horse,* Criterion Theatre, London, 1939.
George Beesdale, *Mountain Air,* Comedy Theatre, 1948.
Sir Lindsay Cooper, *Uproar in the House,* Whitehall Theatre, London, 1967.
Lord Coverley de Beaumont, *The Jockey Club Stakes,* Duke of York's Theatre, London, 1971, then Cort Theater, New York City, 1973.
Dr. Gerald Drimmond, *Come Back to My Place,* Palace Theatre, Westcliff, U.K., 1973.
Dr. Gerald Drimmond, *There Goes the Bride,* Criterion Theatre, then Ambassadors' Theatre, London, 1975.
Sir William Boothroyd, *Lloyd George Knew My Father,* Redgrave Theatre, Farnham, U.K., 1975.

Also appeared as Marquis of Candover, *The Jockey Club Stakes,* South Africa, 1972; and in *Rookery Nook* and *Wife Begins at Forty.*

MAJOR TOURS

Jerry, *While Parents Sleep,* U.K. cities, 1932.
Gilbert Bodley, *Not Now Darling,* South African cities, 1968-69.
Sir Tristram Marden, *Dandy Dick,* U.K. cities, 1970.
Sir William Boothroyd, *Lloyd George Knew My Father,* U.K. cities, 1974.

STAGE WORK

Director, *The Jockey Club Stakes,* South Africa, 1972.

FILM APPEARANCES

(Film debut) Captain Corrie, *Too Many Husbands,* Liberty, 1938.
Announcer, *She Couldn't Say No,* Associated British Films, 1939.
Law and Disorder, British Consolidated/RKO Radio Pictures, 1940.
Murder in the Night (also known as *Murder in Soho*), Associated British Films/Film Alliance, 1940.
Captain Curry, *One Night in Paris* (also known as *Premiere*), Alliance, 1940.
Jack Farrell, *Dark Secret,* Nettleford, 1949.
Humphrey Beagle, *Helter Skelter,* Gainsborough/General Films Distributors, 1949.
A peer, *While the Sun Shines,* International Screenplays-Associated British Films/Monogram-Stratford, 1950.
Major, *The Dark Man,* Independent Artists/General Films Distributors, 1951.
Wingo, *A Tale of Five Women* (also known as *A Tale of Five Cities*), United Artists, 1951.
Lord Tillbrook, *Travellers Joy,* Gainsborough/General Films Distributors, 1951.
Those People Next Door, Film Studios Manchester/Eros, 1952.
Major, *Island Rescue* (also known as *Appointment with Venus*), British Film Makers/Universal, 1952.
Sir Charles Spanniell, *Mr. Lord Says No* (also known as *The Happy Family*), London Independent/Souvaine, 1952.
Pike, *Mr. Potts Goes to Moscow* (also known as *Top Secret*), Transocean/Stratford, 1953.
Teddy, *Always a Bride,* General Films Distributors, 1954.
Lecturer, *Doctors in the House,* General Films Distributors, 1954.
Colonel Audacious, *The Flying Eye,* British Films/British Lion-Children's Film Foundation, 1955.
The Silken Affair, Dragon/RKO Radio Pictures, 1957.
Major Upshott-Bagley, *I Only Asked,* Hammer-Granada/Columbia, 1958.

Governor, *Band of Thieves,* Filmvale/RFD, 1962.
His Father, *Cul-de-Sac,* Sigma/Filmways, 1966.
Gerald Drimond, *There Goes the Bride,* Vanguard, 1980.

Also appeared as Magistrate, *Side By Side,* 1975; and in *Mine Own Executioner.*

TELEVISION APPEARANCES

Appeared on *The Army Game* (series), U.K. television; *Strictly Personal* (series); and *Home and Beauty* (play).

OBITUARIES AND OTHER SOURCES:

PERIODICALS

Variety, October 11, 1989.*

*   *   *

SUTHERLAND, Kiefer   1966(?)-

PERSONAL: Full name, Kiefer William Frederick Dempsey George Rufus Sutherland; born December 21, 1966 (some sources say 1967), in London, England; son of Donald Sutherland (an actor), and Shirley Douglas (an actress); married Camelia Kath, September 12, 1986 (marriage ended); children: Michelle Kath, Sarah. *Education:* Attended a Canadian boarding school.

ADDRESSES: Agent—Ron Meyer/Jay Moloney, Creative Artists Agency, 9830 Wilshire Blvd., Beverly Hill, CA 90212.

CAREER: Actor. Left school to become an actor at the age of fifteen.

AWARDS, HONORS: Genie award nomination, 1984, for performance in *Bay Boy.*

CREDITS:

STAGE APPEARANCES

(Stage debut), *Throne of Straw,* Los Angeles Odyssey Theatre, 1977.

Also appeared in productions of *Minnesota Moon,* and *America Modern.*

FILM APPEARANCES

Max Dugan Returns, Walt Disney Productions, 1983.
Donald Campbell, *Bay Boy,* Orion, 1984.
Tim, *At Close Range,* Orion, 1986.
Brooks, *Crazy Moon,* Cinegem, 1986.
Ace Merrill, *Stand by Me,* Columbia, 1986.
Brian Mars, deputy, *The Killing Time,* New World, 1987.
Danny Rivers, *Promised Land,* Vestron, 1987.
David, *The Lost Boys,* Warner Bros., 1987.
Josiah "Doc" Sculock, *Young Guns,* 20th Century-Fox, 1988.

Scott, *1969,* Atlantic, 1988.

Tad Allagash, *Bright Lights, Big City,* Metro Goldwyn Mayer-United Artists, 1988.

Buster McHenry, *Renegades,* Universal, 1989.

Josiah "Doc" Sculock, *Young Guns II,* 20th Century-Fox, 1990.

John Buckner, *Flashback,* Paramount, 1990.

Karl Hulten, Ricky Allen, *Chicago Joe and the Showgirl* (also known as *Chicago Joe*), New Line Cinema, 1990.

Nelson Wright, *Flatliners,* Columbia, 1990.

Voice of Nutcracker and Hans, *The Nutcracker Prince,* Warner Bros., 1990.

Also appeared in *Article 99,* 1991.

TELEVISION APPEARANCES

(Television debut), Kevin Richter, *Trapped in Silence* (movie), CBS, 1986.

Victor, *Brotherhood of Justice* (movie), ABC, 1986.

61st Annual Academy Awards (special), ABC, 1989.

TELEVISION APPEARANCES: EPISODIC

"The Mission," *Amazing Stories* (pilot), NBC, 1986.

OTHER SOURCES:

PERIODICALS

Hollywoood Reporter, January 11, 1988.
New York Post, August 18, 1986.
People, April 9, 1984.
Rolling Stone, February 25, 1988.
The Cable Guide, August, 1988.*

*   *   *

SWAYZE, Pat
 See SWAYZE, Patrick

*   *   *

SWAYZE, Patrick   1954(?)-
 (Pat Swayze)

PERSONAL: Full name, Patrick Wayne Swayze; born August 18, 1954 (one source says 1950; another source says 1955; other sources say 1952), in Houston, TX; son of Jesse Wayne (an engineering draftsman) and Patsy (a dancer, dance instructor, and choreographer) Swayze; married Lisa Niemi (a dancer and actress), 1976. *Education:* Studied dance with mother, Patsy Swayze; attended San Jacinto College for two years; studied with Harkness Ballet Company and Joffrey Ballet during the 1970s; trained as an actor with Warren Robertson and Milton

Katselas. *Avocational interests:* Carpentry, riding horses, dancing, and music.

ADDRESSES: Agent—Triad Artists, 10100 Santa Monica Blvd., No. 1600, Los Angeles, CA 90067.

CAREER: Actor, dancer, choreographer, singer, and songwriter. Performed at Alley Theater, Houston, TX; dancer with Buffalo Ballet, New York; principal dancer with Eliot Feld Dance Company, late 1970s. Worked as carpenter in New York and as house renovator in Los Angeles, CA. Head of Troph Productions.

AWARDS, HONORS: Won six Drama Critics awards (with wife, Lisa Niemi, and Nicholas Gunn), for *Without a Word;* Golden Globe Award nominations, Best Actor, 1987, for *Dirty Dancing,* and Best Actor in a Musical or Comedy, 1990, for *Ghost.*

CREDITS:

FILM APPEARANCES

Ace, *Skatetown, U.S.A.,* Columbia, 1979.

Darrel Curtis, *The Outsiders,* Warner Brothers, 1983.

Scott, *Uncommon Valor,* Paramount, 1983.

Jed Eckert, *Red Dawn,* UA, 1984.

Ernie "Slam" Webster, *Grandview, U.S.A.,* Warner Brothers, 1984 (also see below).

Derek Sutton, *Youngblood,* Metro-Goldwyn-Mayer (MGM)-United Artists (UA), 1986.

Nomad, *Steel Dawn,* Vestron-Silver Lion, 1987.

Johnny Castle, *Dirty Dancing,* Vestron, 1987 (also see below).

Chuck "Tiger" Warsaw, *Tiger Warsaw,* Sony, 1988.

Dalton, *Road House,* MGM-UA, 1989 (also see below).

Truman Gates, *Next of Kin,* Warner Brothers, 1989 (also see below).

Sam Wheat, *Ghost,* Paramount, 1990.

Bodhi, *Point Break,* Twentieth Century-Fox, 1991.

Performed "Raising Heaven (in Hell) Tonight" and "Cliff's Edge" in *Road House.*

FILM WORK

Choreographer with wife, Lisa Niemi, *Grandview, U.S.A.,* Warner Brothers, 1984.

TELEVISION APPEARANCES: MOVIES

Chuck, *The Comeback Kid,* ABC, 1980.

KC Barnes, *Return of the Rebels,* CBS, 1981.

Doug Zimmer, *Off Sides* (originally titled *Pigs vs. Freaks*), NBC, 1984.

Also appeared in *The New Season.*

TELEVISION APPEARANCES: EPISODIC

Host, *Saturday Night Live,* NBC, 1990.

Also appeared on "Life on Death Row" episode of *Amazing Stories* and as a soldier dying of leukemia on *M*A*S*H*, CBS.

TELEVISION APPEARANCES; SPECIALS

Texas 150: A Celebration Special, ABC, 1986.
Macy's Thanksgiving Day Parade, NBC, 1987.
The Thirtieth Annual Grammy Awards, CBS, 1988.
Sixtieth Annual Academy Awards Presentation, ABC, 1988.
An All-Star Celebration: The '88 Vote, ABC, 1988.
The American Music Awards, ABC, 1988.
The Barbara Walters Special, ABC, 1988.
The World's Greatest Stunts: A Tribute to Hollywood's Stuntmen, ABC, 1988.
Sixty-first Annual Academy Awards Presentation, ABC, 1989.
Superstars and Their Moms, Turner Broadcasting System, 1989.
Award presenter, *The Thirty-second Annual Grammy Awards*, CBS, 1990.
America's Dance Honors, ABC, 1990.
To Be Free: The National Literacy Honors from the White House, ABC, 1990.
Roy Orbison Tribute to Benefit the Homeless, Showtime, 1990 (also see below).
The Twenty-third Annual NAACP Image Awards, NBC, 1991.

Also performed "Love Hurts" on *Roy Orbison Tribute to Benefit the Homeless*.

TELEVISION APPEARANCES; MINI-SERIES

Orry Main, *North and South*, ABC, 1985.
Orry Main, *North and South, Book II*, ABC, 1986.

OTHER TELEVISION APPEARANCES

Bandit, *The Renegades*, ABC, (pilot), 1982, (series), 1983.

STAGE APPEARANCES

(Under name Pat Swayze) Servant, *Goodtime Charley*, Palace Theatre, New York City, 1975.

Also appeared in productions on and Off Broadway, including appearing as Danny Zuko in *Grease*, Broadway, beginning in 1978; *West Side Story;* and *Without a Word*, Beverly Hills Playhouse (also see below).

MAJOR TOURS

Toured North and Central American cities as Prince Charming, "Snow White," *Disney on Parade* (ice show), one year.

RECORDINGS:

SONGS

"Cliff's Edge," Very Tony Music Inc., 1989 (also see below).

Also recorded, with Wendy Fraser, "She's Like the Wind," on soundtrack album of *Dirty Dancing;* recorded, with Larry Gatlin, "Brothers," on soundtrack album of *Next of Kin.*

VIDEOS

Guest star, *Swayze Dancing*, First Run Productions, Inc., 1988.

WRITINGS:

Author, with wife, Lisa Niemi, and Nicholas Gunn, *Without a Word* (play), produced at Beverly Hills Playhouse.

COMPOSER OF MUSIC AND LYRICS

"Cliff's Edge," Very Tony Music Inc., 1989.
(With Stacy Widelitz) "She's Like the Wind," from *Dirty Dancing*, Vestron, 1987.

OTHER SOURCES:

PERIODICALS

People, September 10, 1984; August 6, 1990.
Us, May 29, 1989.*

* * *

SYLBERT, Anthea 1939-

PERSONAL: Born October 6, 1939, in New York, NY; married Paul Sylbert (a designer and director; marriage ended). *Education:* Received B.A. from Barnard College and M.A. from Parsons School of Design.

ADDRESSES: Office—Hawn-Sylbert Movie Company, 500 S. Buena Vista St., Anim. 1D-6, Burbank, CA 91521.

CAREER: Costume designer and producer. Warner Brothers, Hollywood, CA, vice president—special projects, 1977-78, vice president—production, 1978-81; United Artists, Hollywood, CA, senior vice president—production; partner (with Goldie Hawn) and executive vice president, Hawn-Sylbert Movie Company, Burbank, CA., 1982—.

AWARDS, HONORS: Academy Award nominations, 1974, for *Chinatown*, and 1977, for *Julia.*

CREDITS:

FILM WORK; COSTUME DESIGNER

The Tiger Makes Out, Columbia, 1967.
Rosemary's Baby, Paramount, 1968.

The Illustrated Man, Seven Arts, 1969.
John and Mary, Twentieth Century-Fox, 1969.
Some Kind of a Nut, United Artists, 1969.
Carnal Knowledge, AVCO-Embassy, 1971.
A New Leaf, Paramount, 1971.
The Steagle, AVCO-Embassy, 1971.
Bad Company, Paramount, 1972.
The Cowboys, Warner Brothers, 1972.
The Heartbreak Kid, Twentieth Century-Fox, 1972.
The Day of the Dolphin, AVCO-Embassy, 1973.
Chinatown, Paramount, 1974.
The Fortune, Columbia, 1975.
Shampoo, Columbia, 1975.
(With Anna Hill Johnstone) *The Last Tycoon,* Paramount, 1976.
(With Moss Mabry and Arny Lipin; and wardrobe consultant) *King Kong,* Paramount, 1976.
(And wardrobe consultant) *Julia,* Twentieth Century-Fox, 1977.
(With Thalia Phillips and Tony Scarano; and wardrobe consultant) *F.I.S.T.,* United Artists, 1978.

OTHER FILM WORK

Visual consultant, *Mikey and Nicky,* Paramount, 1976.
Producer, *Protocol,* Warner Brothers, 1984.
Producer (with Jerry Bick), *Swing Shift,* Warner Brothers, 1984.
Producer, *Wildcats,* Warner Brothers, 1986.
Producer (with Alexandra Rose), *Overboard,* Metro-Goldwyn-Mayer/United Artists, 1987.
Producer (with Herbert Ross), *My Blue Heaven,* Warner Brothers, 1990.
Executive producer, *Crisscross,* Pathe, 1991.
Executive producer, *The Mrs.,* Buena Vista, 1991.

Also worked on *One-Trick Pony,* Warner Brothers, 1980; *Personal Best,* Warner Brothers, 1982; *Jinx;* and *Stab.*

STAGE WORK; COSTUME DESIGNER

The Prisoner of Second Avenue, Center Theatre Group, Ahmanson Theatre, Los Angeles, CA, 1972-73.
The Real Thing, Plymouth Theatre, New York City, 1984-85.

MAJOR TOURS

Costume designer, *The Prisoner of Second Avenue,* U.S. cities, 1973-74.

*   *   *

SYLBERT, Dick
See SYLBERT, Richard

SYLBERT, Paul   1928-

PERSONAL: Born April 16, 1928, in New York, NY; father, a dressmaker; married; wife's name, Anthea (a production company head), marriage ended; children: one. *Avocational interests:* Fly-fishing.

CAREER: Production designer and art director. Painted scenery for television networks; worked in film beginning in early 1950s; designed opera sets at City Center Theatre, New York City.

AWARDS, HONORS: Academy Award (with Edwin O'Donovan), Best Art Direction, 1978, for *Heaven Can Wait.*

CREDITS:

FILM WORK; PRODUCTION DESIGNER, EXCEPT WHERE INDICATED

Art director, *The Wrong Man,* Warner Brothers, 1956.
(With brother, Richard Sylbert) *Baby Doll,* Warner Brothers, 1956.
(With brother, Richard Sylbert) *A Face in the Crowd,* Warner Brothers, 1957.
Art director (with Rolland M. Brooks and Howard Hollander), *Teenage Millionaire,* United Artists (UA), 1961.
The Tiger Makes Out, Columbia, 1967.
(And art director) *Riot,* Paramount, 1969.
Director, *The Steagle,* Avco Embassy, 1971.
The Drowning Pool, Warner Brothers, 1975.
One Flew over the Cuckoo's Nest, UA, 1975.
Mikey and Nicky, Paramount, 1976.
(And art director, with Edwin O'Donovan) *Heaven Can Wait,* Paramount, 1978.
Hardcore (also known as *The Hardcore Life*), Columbia, 1979.
Kramer vs. Kramer, Columbia, 1979.
Wolfen (also known as *The Wolfman*), Omni, 1979.
Resurrection, Universal, 1980.
Blow Out, Filmways, 1981.
Gorky Park, Rank, 1983.
Without a Trace, Twentieth Century-Fox, 1983.
Firstborn, Paramount, 1984.
The Pope of Greenwich Village, Metro-Goldwyn-Mayer/UA, 1984.
The Journey of Natty Gann, Buena Vista, 1985.
Ishtar, Columbia, 1987.
Nadine, Tri-Star, 1987.
The Pick-Up Artist, Twentieth Century-Fox, 1987.
Biloxi Blues, Universal, 1988.
Fresh Horses, Columbia, 1988.

WRITINGS:

SCREENPLAYS

The Steagle, Avco Embassy, 1971.
(With David Shaber) Night Hawks, Universal, 1981.

OTHER SOURCES:

PERIODICALS

People, January 30, 1984.*

* * *

SYLBERT, Richard 1928-
(Dick Sylbert)

PERSONAL: Born April 16, 1928, in New York, NY; father, a dressmaker; children: three. Education: Attended Tyler School of Art. Avocational interests: Fly-fishing.

CAREER: Production designer and art director. Painted scenery for television networks; worked in film beginning in early 1950s; vice president of production, Paramount Pictures, 1975-78.

AWARDS, HONORS: Academy Awards, Best Art Direction, 1966 for Who's Afraid of Virginia Woolf?, and 1990 for Dick Tracy; Academy Award nominations, Best Art Direction, 1974 for Chinatown, 1975 for Shampoo, 1981 for Reds, and 1984 for The Cotton Club.

CREDITS:

FILM WORK; PRODUCTION DESIGNER, EXCEPT WHERE INDICATED

Art director, Patterns (also known as Patterns of Power), United Artists (UA), 1956.
Crowded Paradise, Tudor, 1956.
(With brother, Paul Sylbert) Baby Doll, Warner Brothers, 1956.
Edge of the City (also known as A Man Is Ten Feet Tall), Metro-Goldwyn-Mayer (MGM), 1957.
(With brother, Paul Sylbert) A Face in the Crowd, Warner Brothers, 1957.
Art director, Wind across the Everglades, Warner Brothers, 1958.
Art director, The Fugitive Kind, UA, 1960.
(Under name Dick Sylbert) Murder, Inc., Twentieth Century-Fox, 1960.
Art director, Mad Dog Coll, Columbia, 1961.
Art director, Splendor in the Grass, Warner Brothers, 1961.
The Young Doctors, UA, 1961.
The Connection, Allen/Clarke, 1962.
(And art director) Long Day's Journey into Night, Embassy, 1962.

(And art director, with Phil Jeffries) The Manchurian Candidate, UA, 1962.
Art director, Walk on the Wild Side, Columbia, 1962.
(And art director) All the Way Home, Paramount, 1963.
Art director, Lilith, Columbia, 1964.
How to Murder Your Wife, UA, 1965.
Art director, The Pawnbroker, Landau Releasing Organization/Allied Artists/American International, 1965.
Associate producer, What's New, Pussycat? UA, 1965.
Who's Afraid of Virginia Woolf? Warner Brothers, 1966.
Grand Prix, MGM, 1966.
The Graduate, Embassy, 1967.
Rosemary's Baby, Paramount, 1968.
The April Fools, National General, 1969.
Visual arts consultant, The Illustrated Man, Warner Brothers, 1969.
Catch-22, Filmways, 1970.
Carnal Knowledge, AVCO-Embassy, 1971.
Fat City, Columbia, 1972.
Art director, The Heartbreak Kid, Twentieth Century-Fox, 1972.
The Day of the Dolphin, AVCO-Embassy, 1973.
Chinatown, Paramount, 1974.
The Fortune, Columbia, 1975.
Shampoo, Columbia, 1975.
Players, Paramount, 1979.
Reds, Paramount, 1981.
Frances, Universal, 1982.
Partners, Paramount, 1982.
Breathless, Orion, 1983.
The Cotton Club, Orion, 1984.
Under the Cherry Moon, Warner Brothers, 1986.
Shoot to Kill, Buena Vista, 1988.
Tequila Sunrise, Warner Brothers, 1988.
(And art director) Dick Tracy, Buena Vista, 1990.
Bonfire of the Vanities, Warner Brothers, 1990.
Mobsters, Universal, 1991.

STAGE WORK

Set designer, The Prisoner of Second Avenue, Eugene O'Neill Theatre, New York City, 1971, then Ahmanson Theatre, Los Angeles, 1972.

MAJOR TOURS

Set designer, The Prisoner of Second Avenue, U.S. cities, 1972-74.

TELEVISION WORK

Art director, Inner Sanctum (series), syndicated, 1951-53.
Production designer, Last Hours Before Morning (movie), NBC, 1975.
Set designer and creative consultant, Don Johnson's Music Video Feature (special), HBO, 1987.

OTHER SOURCES:

PERIODICALS

People, January 30, 1984.*

*   *   *

SZWARC, Jeannot   1939-

PERSONAL: Born November 21, 1939, in Paris, France; married Cara de Menaul (a film production coordinator); children: one son.

ADDRESSES: Office—Shapiro-Lichtman, 8827 Beverly Blvd., Los Angeles, CA 90048.

CAREER: Director.

MEMBER: Directors Guild of America.

CREDITS:

FILM WORK; DIRECTOR

Bug, Paramount, 1975.
Jaws II, Universal, 1978.
Somewhere in Time, Universal, 1980.
Enigma, Embassy, 1983.
Supergirl, Tri-Star, 1984.
Santa Claus—The Movie, Tri-Star, 1985.

Also directed *Extreme Close-Up,* 1978, and *Honor Bound.*

TELEVISION WORK; SERIES; DIRECTOR WITH OTHERS

The Virginian, NBC, 1962.
Ironside, NBC, 1967.
Marcus Welby, MD, ABC, 1969.
The Black Sheep Squadron, NBC, 1970.
Paris 7000, ABC, 1970.

The Men from Shiloh, 1970.
The Man and the City, ABC, 1971.
Alias Smith and Jones, ABC, 1971.
Sarge, NBC, 1972.
The New Adventures of Perry Mason, CBS, 1973.
The Six-Million-Dollar Man, ABC, 1973.
Toma, ABC, 1973.
The Rockford Files, NBC, 1974.
Baretta, ABC, 1975.

TELEVISION WORK; MOVIES; DIRECTOR

The Weekend Nun, ABC, 1972.
Night of Terror, ABC, 1972.
A Summer without Boys, ABC, 1973.
You'll Never See Me Again, ABC, 1973.
Lisa, Bright and Dark, 1973.
The Devil's Daughter, ABC, 1973.
Crime Club, CBS, 1975.
Code Name: Diamond Head, NBC, 1977.
Murders in the Rue Morgue, CBS, 1986.

Also directed *Grand Larceny,* 1989.

OTHER TELEVISION WORK; DIRECTOR, EXCEPT WHERE INDICATED

Production Assistant, *Code Name: Heraclitus* (pilot), NBC, 1967.
Night Gallery, NBC, 1971.
The Small Miracle (special), NBC, 1973.
The Hazard's People (pilot), CBS, 1976.
(With Melville Shavelson) *True Life Stories* (pilot), ABC, 1981.

Also directed *Supergirl: The Making of the Movie,* 1985; *Twilight Zone,* 1986; and *To Catch a Thief.**

T

TAMBLYN, Russ 1935-

PERSONAL: Born December 30, 1935, in Los Angeles, CA.

ADDRESSES: Agent—Thomas Jennings and Associates, 427 North Canon Dr., Suite 205, Beverly Hills, CA 90210.

CAREER: Actor. Actor in radio shows; appeared on stage with little theatre group; performed song-and-dance act in Los Angeles clubs and veterans' hospitals.

AWARDS, HONORS: Golden Globe Award, most promising male newcomer, 1956; Academy Award nomination, best supporting actor, 1957, for *Peyton Place.*

CREDITS:

FILM APPEARANCES

Student, *The Boy with the Green Hair,* RKO, 1949.

Bart Tare, age fourteen, *Gun Crazy* (also known as *Deadly Is the Female*), United Artists (UA), 1949.

Johnny Barrows, *The Kid from Cleveland,* Republic, 1949.

Saul, *Samson and Delilah,* Paramount, 1949.

Pietro, *Captain Carey, U.S.A.* (also known as *After Midnight*), Paramount, 1950.

Tommy Banks, *Father of the Bride,* Metro-Goldwyn-Mayer (MGM), 1950.

Tino, *The Vicious Years,* Film Classics, 1950.

Willie, *As Young as You Feel,* Twentieth Century-Fox, 1951.

Tommy Banks, *Father's Little Dividend,* MGM, 1951.

Willie Alexander, *The Winning Team,* Warner Brothers, 1952.

Paul Jamison, *Take the High Ground,* MGM, 1953.

Berrison, Jr., *Deep in My Heart,* MGM, 1954.

Gideon Pontabee, *Seven Brides for Seven Brothers,* MGM, 1954.

Danny Xavier Smith, *Hit the Deck,* MGM, 1955.

Shields, *Many Rivers to Cross,* MGM, 1955.

Eric Doolittle, *Fastest Gun Alive,* MGM, 1956.

Jimmy, *The Last Hunt,* MGM, 1956.

Tully, *The Young Guns,* Allied Artists, 1956.

Norman Page, *Peyton Place,* Twentieth Century-Fox, 1957.

Tony Baker/Mike Wilson, *High School Confidential* (also known as *The Young Hellions*), MGM, 1958.

Title role, *Tom Thumb,* MGM, 1958.

The kid, *Cimarron,* MGM, 1960.

Riff, *West Side Story,* UA, 1961.

Rebel soldier, *How the West Was Won,* MGM/Cinerama, 1962.

The Woodsman, *The Wonderful World of the Brothers Grimm,* MGM, 1962.

Lieutenant "Smitty" Smith, *Follow the Boys,* MGM, 1963.

Luke Sanderson, *The Haunting,* MGM, 1963.

Orm, *The Long Ships* (also known as *Dugi Brodovi*), Columbia, 1964.

Johnny, *Son of a Gunfighter* (also known as *El Hijo del Pistolero*), MGM, 1966.

Russ, *The Female Bunch* (also known as *A Time to Run*), Gilbreth, 1969.

Link, *Free Grass* (also known as *Scream Free*), Hollywood Star, 1969.

Anchor, *Satan's Sadists,* Independent-International, 1969.

Dr. Paul Stewart, *The War of the Gargantuas* (also known as *Furankenshutan No Kaijusanda Tai Gailah, Sanda Tai Gailah,* and *Duel of the Gargantuas*), Toho/Maron, 1970.

Member of Billy's gang, *The Last Movie* (also known as *Chinchero*), Universal, 1971.

Dracula vs. Frankenstein (also known as *Blood of Frankenstein*), Independent-International, 1971.

Ensign Tyson, *Don't Go near the Water,* MGM, 1975.

Raymond, *Win, Place, or Steal* (also known as *Three for the Money* and *Just Another Day at the Races*), Cinema National, 1975.

Black Heat, Independent-International, 1976.

Fred Kelly, *Human Highway,* Shakey, 1982.

Anchor, *Commando Squad,* Trans World Entertainment, 1987.

Cyclone, CineTel, 1987.

Professor Charles DeLonge, *Necromancer,* Bonnaire, 1989.

Hugh, *B.O.R.N.* (also known as *Body Organ Replacement Network*), Prism Entertainment, 1989.

Bill, *The Phantom Empire,* American Independent, 1989.

Aftershock, Crown International/Prism Entertainment, 1990.

Also appeared in *Reign of Terror, Retreat Hell,* and *Demon Sword.*

TELEVISION APPEARANCES; EPISODIC

"Silent Love, Secret Love," *The Greatest Show on Earth,* ABC, 1963.

"The Last Testament of Buddy Crown," *Channing,* ABC, 1963.

"Who Killed Rosie Sunset?" *Burke's Law,* ABC, 1965.

"Leopard on the Loose," *Tarzan,* NBC, 1966.

The Iron Horse, ABC, 1967.

"A Hard Case of the Blues," *The Name of the Game,* NBC, 1969.

"Ragged Edge," *Cade's County,* CBS, 1972.

The Quest, NBC, 1976.

Roger, *Rags to Riches,* NBC, 1987.

Quantum Leap, NBC, 1989.

TELEVISION APPEARANCES; SERIES

Dr. Lawrence Jacoby, *Twin Peaks,* ABC, 1990.

WRITINGS:

FILM

(With Bernard Shakey, Jean Fields, Dean Stockwell, and James Beshears) *Human Highway,* Shakey, 1982.*

*   *   *

TAYBACK, Vic 1930(?)-1990

PERSONAL: Born Victor Tabback, January 6, 1930 (some sources say 1929), in Brooklyn, NY; died of a heart attack, May 25, 1990, in Glendale, CA; son of Najeeb James and Helen (Hanood) Tabback; married Sheila McKay Barnard, 1962; children: Christopher. *Education:* Attended Glendale Community College; studied at the Frederick A. Speare School of Radio and Television Broadcasting.

CAREER: Actor. Worked as a bank teller and cab driver before beginning acting career. Founder, with Richard Chamberlain and Sally Kellerman, of Company of Angels Theatre, Los Angeles, CA. *Military service:* U.S. Navy.

AWARDS, HONORS: Emmy Award nomination, Best Supporting Actor in a Comedy Series, 1978, and Golden Globe awards, Best Actor in a Supporting Role, 1980 and 1981, for *Alice.*

CREDITS:

TELEVISION APPEARANCES; SERIES

Captain Barney Marcus, *Griff,* ABC, 1973-74.

Lieutenant Gubbins, *Khan,* CBS, 1975.

Mel Sharples, *Alice,* CBS, 1976-85.

Also appeared as the man in *Morning Star,* NBC.

TELEVISION APPEARANCES; PILOTS

Jeffrey Poland, *They Call It Murder,* NBC, 1971.

Avery Crest, *Call Home,* NBC, 1972.

Coach, *Cops,* CBS, 1973.

Bullets, *Two's Company,* CBS, 1973.

Mel Sharples, *Alice,* CBS, 1976.

Horembeb, *Through the Magic Pyramid,* NBC, 1981.

Ted Randall, *The Mysterious Two,* NBC, 1982.

TELEVISION APPEARANCES; EPISODIC

JoJo Krako, "A Piece of The Action," *Star Trek,* NBC, 1968.

The Mary Tyler Moore Show, CBS, 1971.

Pizuti, *The Super,* ABC, 1972.

Officer Haseejian, *The Streets of San Francisco,* ABC, 1972.

M*A*S*H, CBS, 1973.

All in the Family, CBS, 1974.

Barney Miller, ABC, 1975.

Loan shark, "Your Money or Your Wife," *Love Boat,* ABC, 1985.

Sal Domino, *Murder, She Wrote,* CBS, 1986.

Mo Schmidt, *Crazy Like a Fox,* NBC, 1986.

Also appeared as Gregorin, *Adderly,* 1987, and in episodes of *Bewitched, Bonanza, The Partridge Family, The Rookies,* and *Emergency.*

TELEVISION APPEARANCES; MOVIES

Policeman, *The Alpha Caper* (also known as *Inside Job*), ABC, 1973.

Kelso, *Partners in Crime,* NBC, 1973.

Neil Grogan, *The Blue Knight,* NBC, 1973.

Archie, *Dark Victory,* NBC, 1976.

Finch, *Little Ladies of the Night,* ABC, 1977.

Burt Carboni, *Getting Married,* CBS, 1978.

Harry Parkins, *Portrait of a Stripper,* CBS, 1979.

Floyd "Snake" Kraslowski, *Gridlock* (also known as *The Great American Traffic Jam*), NBC, 1980.
Harry Cohn, *Moviola: This Year's Blonde,* NBC, 1980.
Morris Brustein, *The Night the City Screamed,* ABC, 1980.
Tommy, *Rage,* NBC, 1980.
Abe Saperstein, *The Jesse Owens Story,* syndicated, 1984.
Harold, *The Three Kings,* ABC, 1987.

TELEVISION APPEARANCES; SPECIALS

Circus of the Stars, CBS, 1979.
Celebrity Challenge of the Sexes, CBS, 1980.

Also appeared on *Dean Martin Celebrity Roast,* 1984, *George Carlin—Playin' with Your Head,* 1986, and *Stand-Up Comics Take a Stand,* 1989.

TELEVISION WORK

Director of episodes of *Alice,* CBS.

FILM APPEARANCES

Fred, *Five Minutes to Live* (also known as *Door to Door Maniac*), Sutton, 1961.
Arms Cooper, *Surftide 77* (also known as *Call Surftide 77, Call Girl 77,* and *Surftide 777*), Olympic International, 1962.
Cye, *Love with the Proper Stranger,* Paramount, 1963.
Peter Ross, *Bullitt,* Warner Brothers/Seven Arts, 1968.
Chicken truck driver, *With Six You Get Eggroll,* National General, 1968.
Calvin Carruthers, *Blood and Lace,* Contemporary Filmmakers/Carlin, 1971.
Ralph Negri, *The Don Is Dead,* (also known as *Beautiful but Deadly*), Universal, 1973.
Yardman, *Emperor of the North Pole,* (also known as *Emperor of The North*), Universal, 1973.
Sergeant, *Papillon,* Allied Artists, 1973.
One, *The Gambler,* Paramount, 1974.
Mario, *Thunderbolt and Lightfoot,* United Artists, 1974.
Mel, *Alice Doesn't Live Here Anymore,* Warner Brothers, 1975.
Lieutenant Seidensticker, *Report to the Commissioner* (also known as *Operation Undercover*), United Artists, 1975.
Lucky Luciano, *Lepke,* Warner Brothers, 1975.
Goldie, *The Big Bus,* Paramount, 1976.
Big Joe, *No Deposit, No Return,* (also known as *Double Trouble*), Buena Vista, 1976.
Detective, *Mansion of the Doomed* (also known as *The Terror of Dr. Chaney*), Group I, 1976.
Eddie Roschak, *The Shaggy D.A.,* Buena Vista, 1976.
Wyatt, *Special Delivery,* American International, 1976.
Pete Zoony, *The Choirboys,* Universal, 1977.
Lieutenant DiMaggio, *The Cheap Detective,* Columbia Pictures, 1978.

Sargent Burge, *Weekend Warriors,* Movie Store, 1986.
Coach, *The Underachievers,* Lightning, 1988.
Criminal Act, Independent Networks, 1989.
Harry Bruckner, *Loverboy,* Tri-Star, 1989.
Voice of Carface, *All Dogs Go to Heaven* (animated), United Artists, 1989.

Also appeared as John Silver, *L'Ile au Tresor,* 1985; Lou, *Beverly Hills Bodysnatchers,* 1989; and George Samsa, *The Horseplayer,* 1990.

STAGE APPEARANCES

An Oasis in Manhattan, Venture Theatre, Burbank, CA, 1990.

Appeared in more than twenty-five stage works, including *Stalag 17, Death of a Salesman,* and *The Killing of Yablonski.*

OBITUARIES AND OTHER SOURCES:

PERIODICALS

Variety, May 30, 1990.*

*   *   *

THAW, John 1942-

PERSONAL: Born January 3, 1942, in Manchester, England; son of John Edward and Dorothy (Abblott) Thaw; married Sheila Hancock (an actress). *Education:* Trained for the stage at the Royal Academy of Dramatic Art. *Avocational interests:* Music, reading.

ADDRESSES: Agent—John Redway Ltd., 5 Denmark St., London WC2 H82P, England.

CAREER: Actor.

AWARDS, HONORS: British Academy of Film and Television Arts Award, best actor—television, 1990, for *Inspector Morse;* Vanbrugh Award and Liverpool Playhouse Award, both from the Royal Academy of Dramatic Art.

CREDITS:

STAGE APPEARANCES

(Stage debut) The Inspector, *A Shred of Evidence,* Liverpool Playhouse, Liverpool, England, 1960.
(London debut) The Professor, *The Fire Raisers,* Royal Court Theatre, 1961.
Sordido, *Women Beware Women,* Arts Theatre, London, 1962.
Robert Freeman, *Semi-Detached,* Saville Theatre, London, 1962.
Dicky, *So What about Love?,* Criterion Theatre, London, 1969.

Jimmy, *Random Happenings in the Hebrides,* Edinburgh Festival, Scotland, 1970.

Stranger, *The Lady from the Sea,* Greenwich Theatre, London, 1971.

George, *Friday,* Theatre Upstairs, London, 1971.

Sam Brown, *Collaborators,* Duchess Theatre, London, 1973.

Leary, *Fair Slaughter,* Royal Court Theatre, 1977.

Dick Wagner, *Night and Day,* Phoenix Theatre, London, 1978.

Serjeant Musgrave, *Serjeant Musgrave's Dance,* National Theatre Company, Cottesloe Theatre, London, 1981.

Cardinal Wolsey, *King Henry VIII,* Royal Shakespeare Company, Stratford-upon-Avon, England, 1983.

Sir Toby Belch, *Twelfth Night,* Royal Shakespeare Company, Stratford-upon-Avon, England, 1983.

Alfred Doolittle, *Pygmalion,* Theatre of Comedy, Shaftesbury Theatre, London, 1984.

MAJOR TOURS

Cast member, *Absurd Person Singular,* British cities, 1976.

FILM APPEARANCES

Bosworth, *The Loneliness of the Long Distance Runner* (also known as *Rebel with a Cause*), Continental Distributing, 1962.

Alan Roper, *Five to One,* Allied Artists, 1963.

David Jones, *Dead Man's Chest,* Allied Artists, 1965.

Featherstone, *The Bofors Gun,* Universal, 1968.

Terry Mitchell, *The Last Grenade,* Cinerama, 1970.

Dom, *Praise Marx and Pass the Ammunition,* Mithras, 1970.

Shavers, *Doctor Phibes Rises Again,* American International, 1972.

Detective Inspector Jack Regan, *Sweeney,* EMI, 1977.

Detective Inspector Jack Regan, *Sweeney 2,* EMI, 1978.

Dick Turner, *The Grass Is Singing* (also known as *Killing Heat*), Mainline, 1982.

Kieran Flynn, *Business as Usual,* Cannon, 1987.

Kruger, *Cry Freedom,* Universal, 1987.

TELEVISION APPEARANCES; EPISODIC

Jonathan Small, "The Sign of Four," *The Return of Sherlock Holmes II,* Granada, then *Mystery!,* PBS, 1988.

OTHER TELEVISION APPEARANCES

Detective Inspector Jack Sweeney, *The Sweeney* (series), syndicated, 1976.

Home to Roost, ITV, 1985-89.

Chief Inspector Morse, *Inspector Morse* (series), ITV, then *Mystery!,* PBS, 1988—.

Sir Arthur Harris, *Bomber Harris* (movie), BBC-1, 1989.

Also appeared in the series *Sir Francis Drake,* 1981-82; *Mitch,* 1983; *Redcap;* and *Thick as Thieves.* Appeared in *Macbeth; Nil Carborundum;* and *The Caucasian Chalk Circle.*

*   *   *

THEISS, Bill
See THEISS, William Ware

*   *   *

THEISS, William
See THEISS, William Ware

*   *   *

THEISS, William Ware
(Bill Theiss, William Theiss)

CAREER: Costume designer.

AWARDS, HONORS: Academy Award nominations, all best costume design, 1976, for *Bound for Glory,* 1979, for *Butch and Sundance: The Early Days,* and 1983, for *Heart Like a Wheel.*

CREDITS:

FILM COSTUME DESIGNER

Pretty Maids All in a Row, Metro-Goldwyn-Mayer, 1971.

(As Bill Theiss) *Harold and Maude,* Paramount, 1971.

Bound for Glory, United Artists, 1976.

Goin' South, Paramount, 1978.

(As Bill Theiss) *Who'll Stop the Rain?,* United Artists, 1978.

(As William Theiss) *Butch and Sundance: The Early Days,* Twentieth Century-Fox, 1979.

Heart Like a Wheel, Twentieth Century-Fox, 1983.

Kidco, Twentieth Century-Fox, 1984.

The Man With One Red Shoe, Twentieth Century-Fox, 1985.

STAGE COSTUME DESIGNER

Patio/Porch, Theatre Three, Dallas, TX, 1986.

TELEVISION COSTUME DESIGNER; SERIES

(As Bill Theiss) *Sidekicks,* ABC, 1986.

Star Trek: The Next Generation, syndicated, 1987.

TELEVISION COSTUME DESIGNER; PILOTS

I-Man (broadcast as an episode of *The Disney Sunday Movie*), ABC, 1986.

Double Agent (broadcast as an episode of *The Disney Sunday Movie*), 1987.

Waco and Rhinehart (also known as *U.S. Marshals: Waco and Rhinehart*), ABC, 1987.

TELEVISION COSTUME DESIGNER; EPISODIC

"2 1/2 Dads," *The Disney Sunday Movie*, ABC, 1986.
"The B.R.A.T. Patrol," *The Disney Sunday Movie*, ABC, 1986.
"Casebusters," *The Disney Sunday Movie*, ABC, 1986.
"The Deacon Street Deer," *The Disney Sunday Movie*, ABC, 1986.
"A Fighting Choice," *The Disney Sunday Movie*, ABC, 1986.
"Fuzzbucket," *The Disney Sunday Movie*, ABC, 1986.
"The Leftovers," *The Disney Sunday Movie*, ABC, 1986.
"Little Spies," *The Disney Sunday Movie*, ABC, 1986.
"Mr. Boogedy," *The Disney Sunday Movie*, ABC, 1986.
"My Town," *The Disney Sunday Movie*, ABC, 1986.
"Sunday Drive," *The Disney Sunday Movie*, ABC, 1986.
"The Thanksgiving Promise," *The Disney Sunday Movie*, ABC, 1986.
"Help Wanted: Kids," *The Disney Sunday Movie*, ABC, 1986.
"Bigfoot," *The Disney Sunday Movie*, ABC, 1987.
"Bride of Boogedy," *The Disney Sunday Movie*, ABC, 1987.
"You Ruined My Life," *The Disney Sunday Movie*, ABC, 1987.
"Young Harry Houdini," *The Disney Sunday Movie*, ABC, 1987.

TELEVISION COSTUME DESIGNER; MOVIES

Genesis II, CBS, 1973.*

*　　　*　　　*

THOMPSON, Lea   1961-

PERSONAL: Born May 31, 1961, in Rochester, MN.

ADDRESSES: Agent—Bob Gersh, The Gersh Agency, 222 N. Canon Dr., Suite 202, Beverly Hills, CA 90210.

CAREER: Actress. Dancer with Pennsylvania Ballet Company, American Ballet Theatre, and San Francisco Ballet. Starred in several Burger King commercials.

CREDITS:

FILM APPEARANCES

(Film debut) Kelly Ann Bukowski, *Jaws 3-D*, Universal, 1983.
Lisa, *All the Right Moves*, Twentieth Century-Fox, 1983.
Anita, *The Wild Life*, Universal, 1984.
Erica, *Red Dawn*, Metro-Goldwyn-Mayer/United Artists, 1984.
Marigold De La Hunt, *Going Undercover*, Miramax, 1984.
Lorraine Baines, *Back to the Future*, Universal, 1985.
Beverly Switzler, *Howard the Duck*, Universal, 1986.
Kathryn, *Space Camp*, Twentieth Century-Fox, 1986.

Amanda Jones, *Some Kind of Wonderful*, Paramount, 1987.
Stacy, *Casual Sex*, Universal, 1988.
Sybil, *The Wizard of Loneliness*, Skouras, 1988.
Lorraine McFly, *Back to the Future II*, Universal, 1989.
Maggie and Lorraine McFly, *Back to the Future III*, Universal, 1990.

TELEVISION APPEARANCES; MOVIES

Sally Matthews, *Nightbreaker* (also known as *Advance to Ground Break Zero*), TNT, 1989.
Peg Guthrie, *Montana*, TNT, 1990.

TELEVISION APPEARANCES; EPISODIC

Sylvia Vane, "Only Sin Deep," *Tales from the Crypt*, HBO, 1989.
Robert Wuhl's World Tour, HBO Comedy Hour, HBO, 1990.

TELEVISION APPEARANCES; SPECIALS

The 11th Annual ACE Awards, Bravo, 1990.*

*　　　*　　　*

THORPE-BATES, Peggy   1914-1989

PERSONAL: Born August 11, 1914, in London, England; died December 26, 1989; daughter of Edith Helena Leech and Thomas Thorpe-Bates; married Brian Oulton; children: two. *Education:* Attended the Cone School of Dancing and the Royal Academy of Dramatic Art.

CAREER: Actress.

MEMBER: British Actors Equity Association (executive council member).

CREDITS:

STAGE APPEARANCES

Isabel, *Henry V*, Shakespeare Memorial Theatre, Stratford-on-Avon, England, 1934.
Mrs. Dainty Fidget, *The Country Wife*, The Little Theatre, London, 1940.
Mary Tudor, *The Young Elizabeth*, Cambridge Repertory Players, Cambridge, England, 1951, then New Theatre, London, 1952.
Clytemnestra, *Sacrifice to the Wind*, Arts Theatre, London, 1955.
Mother Saybrook, *Lead Me Gently*, New Lindsey Theatre, London, 1956.
Gertrude Marescaud, *All in the Family*, BBC Repertory Company, The Strand Theatre, London, 1959.
Mrs. Ann Summer, *Lady Barker's Last Appearance*, The Pembroke Theatre, Croydon, England, 1960.

Joyce Glyn, *Unfinished Journey,* The Pembroke Theatre, 1961.

Mary Tyrone, *Long Day's Journey into Night,* The Guildford Theatre, London, 1962.

Mrs. George, *Getting Married,* Birmingham Repertory (Golden Jubilee), Birmingham, England, 1962.

Charity Hannigan, *Three Acts of Charity,* The Richmond Theatre, London, 1964.

Mrs. Porter, *A Public Mischief,* St. Martin's Theatre, London, 1965.

Phyllis, *The Thunderbolt,* Arts Theatre, 1966.

Mrs. Winifred Masters, *Dead Silence,* Whitehall Theatre, London, 1969.

The Duchess of York, *Richard II,* Edinburgh Festival, Edinburgh, Scotland, 1969, and Mermaid and Piccadilly Theatres, London, 1969-70.

Matron, *Forty Years On,* Birmingham Repertory, 1970.

Catherine Smith, *Mr. Sydney Smith Coming Upstairs,* The Harrogate Theatre, London, 1972.

Mrs. Weston, *Say Goodnight to Grandma,* The Palace Theatre, Westcliff, England, 1974.

Lady Boothroyd, *Lloyd George Knew My Father,* The Palace Theatre, 1974.

Bess Raleigh, *The Wisest Fool,* The Arnaud Theatre, Guildford, England, 1974.

Births, Marriages and Deaths, Assembly Hall, Hackney, England, 1975.

Mrs. Candle, *His First Wife,* Theatre at the Park, Bracknell, England, 1975.

Donna Lucia D'Alvadorez, *Charley's Aunt,* The Key Theatre, Peterborough, England, 1975.

Mrs. Higgins, *Pygmalion,* Leeds Playhouse, London, 1976.

Mrs. Caudle, *Up All Night,* Player's Theatre, London, 1976.

Mrs. Caudle, *Upstairs, Downstairs,* Stoke Newington Assembly Hall, London, 1976.

My Lady's Chamber, Stoke Newington Assembly Hall, Stoke, England, 1976.

Maman, *Uncle Vanya,* Royal Exchange, Manchester, England, 1977.

Lady Saltburn, *Present Laughter,* Royal Exchange, 1977.

Also appeared as the nurse in *Romeo and Juliet,* Thorndike, Leatherhead, England, 1965; Miss Smythe, *Move Over Mrs. Markham,* Thorndike, 1975; *Sybil: Her Infinite Variety, A Tribute to Sybil Thorndike,* Thorndike, 1977; Lady Elizabeth Mulhammer, *The Confidential Clerk,* Cheltenham Literary Festival, 1978. Repertory member, The Intimate Theatre, 1942; repertory member, Birmingham Repertory Theatre, 1946; guest appearances, Worthing, Windsor, and Oxford, 1947-48.

MAJOR TOURS

Queen Mary, *Crown Matrimonial,* South Africa, 1973.

Also toured as Doris in *Saloon Bar,* 1940-41; Joyce Glyn in *Unfinished Journey;* Duchess of York in *Richard II;* and Bess Raleigh in *The Wisest Fool;* also in *For Entertainment Only;*

FILM APPEARANCES

Mrs. Muswell, *In the Doghouse,* Rank/Zenith, 1964.

Hospital Sister, *Georgy Girl,* Everglades, Columbia, 1966.

Mrs. Stacey, *Thank You All Very Much,* Palomar-Amicus, 1969.

Mosquito Squadron, Oakmont/United Artists, 1970.

Also appeared as court lady in *Galileo,* 1974.

TELEVISION APPEARANCES

Appeared in numerous plays and serials, including *Sanctuary, Glittering Prizes,* and as Mrs. Rumpole in *Rumpole of the Bailey.* *

*   *   *

THORSON, Linda 1947-

PERSONAL: Born June 18, 1947, in Toronto, Ontario, Canada; father, a farmer; married Harry Bergthornson (a television cameraman; divorced); married Bill Boggs (a talk show host) November 18, 1984 (separated); children: (second marriage) Trevor. *Education:* Attended the Royal Academy of Dramatic Art.

ADDRESSES: Agent—c/o Century Artists Ltd., 9744 Wilshire Blvd., Suite 308, Beverly Hills, CA 90212.

CAREER: Actress.

AWARDS, HONORS: Theatre World Award, 1983, for *Steaming.*

CREDITS:

STAGE APPEARANCES

Frances Hunter, *No Sex Please—We're British,* Strand Theatre, London, 1971.

Belinda, *The Provok'd Wife,* Company Theatre, Greenwich Theatre, London, 1973.

Titania, *A Midsummer Night's Dream,* Open Air Theatre, London, 1974 and 1975.

Freddie, *The Club,* Regent Theatre, London, 1978.

Lucia Amory, *Black Coffee,* Alley Theatre, Houston, TX, 1979.

Artichoke, Alley Theatre, 1979.

The Sea Gull, Manitoba Theatre Center, Winnipeg, 1980.

The Beaux' Stratagem, Hartford Stage Company, Hartford, CT, 1980.

Loot, Studio Arena Theatre, Buffalo, NY, 1981.

The Play's the Thing, South Coast Repertory Theatre, Costa Mesa, CA, 1981.

(Broadway debut) Nancy, *Steaming,* Brooks Atkinson Theatre, 1982.

Belinda Blair, *Noises Off,* Brooks Atkinson Theatre, then Center Theatre Group, Ahmanson Theatre, Los Angeles, CA, both 1985.

Title role, *Zoya's Apartment,* Circle in the Square, New York City, 1990.

Also appeared with the Bristol Old Vic Company, Bristol, England; and with the Crucible Theatre, Sheffield, England.

FILM APPEARANCES

Billie Streeter, *Valentino,* United Artists, 1977.
Angela, *The Greek Tycoon,* Universal, 1978.
Brooke Parsons, *Curtains,* Jenson Farley, 1983.
Andrea, *Flanagan,* United Film Distributors, 1985.
Principal O'Neill, *Joey,* Satori Entertainment, 1985.
Grace, *Sweet Liberty,* Universal, 1986.

TELEVISION APPEARANCES; SERIES

Tara King, *The Avengers,* ABC, 1968-69.
Hilary Stonehill, *Marblehead Manor,* syndicated, 1987-88.

Also appeared in *One Life to Live,* ABC.

TELEVISION APPEARANCES; EPISODIC

Toni, "Lady Killer" (also known as "The Death Policy"), *Thriller,* ABC, 1973.
Lime Street, ABC, 1985.
St. Elsewhere, NBC, 1985 and 1986.
Karen Cooper, *Spenser: For Hire,* ABC, 1986.
Gregory, *Moonlighting,* ABC, 1986.
Ann Delvecchio, *The Bronx Zoo,* NBC, 1987.
Laura Browne, *Buck James,* ABC, 1988.
Janice Brattle, *Empty Nest,* NBC, 1989.

OTHER TELEVISION APPEARANCES

Cory Fuhrman, *The Lost Honor of Kathryn Beck* (movie), CBS, 1984.
Lady in class, *Gladiator* (pilot), ABC, 1986.
Pamela Blake, *Blind Justice* (movie), CBS, 1986.*

*   *   *

THRELFALL, David   1953-

PERSONAL: Born October 12, 1953, in Manchester, England. *Education:* Graduated from the Polytechnic School of Theatre; studied acting with the Manchester Youth Theatre.

ADDRESSES: Agent—James Sharkey Associates, Third Floor, 15 Golden Square, London SW1, England.

CAREER: Actor. Member of the Royal Shakespeare Company.

AWARDS, HONORS: Clarence Derwent Award, Society of West End Theatres (SWET) Award, and the DRAMA London Critics Award, all 1981; Antoinette Perry Award nomination, Best Featured Actor in a Play, 1982, for *The Life and Adventures of Nicholas Nickleby;* Emmy Award nomination, 1983, for *Nicholas Nickleby.*

CREDITS:

THEATER APPEARANCES

Blackie, *The Sons of Light,* Royal Shakespeare Company (RSC), Other Place Theatre, Stratford-on-Avon, England, 1977, then Warehouse Theatre, London, 1978.

Philip, *A Bed of Roses,* Royal Court Theatre, London, then Bush Theatre, London, 1978.

Fritz, *Savage Amusement,* RSC, Warehouse Theatre, 1978.

Jake, *A and R,* RSC, Warehouse Theatre, 1978.

Mike, *Shout Across the River,* RSC, Warehouse Theatre, 1978.

Abraham Slender, *The Merry Wives of Windsor,* RSC, Royal Shakespeare Theatre, Stratford-on-Avon, 1979.

Second lord attending Cloten, *Cymbeline,* RSC, Royal Shakespeare Theatre, 1979.

Viktor Viktorovitch, *The Suicide,* RSC, Other Place Theatre, 1979.

Mark Antony, *Julius Caesar,* RSC, Royal Shakespeare Theatre, 1979.

Smike, *The Life and Adventures of Nicholas Nickleby,* RSC, Plymouth Theatre, Stratford-on-Avon, 1981.

Mike, *Not Quite Jerusalem,* English Stage Company, Royal Court Theatre, 1982.

Apoo, *Topokana Martyrs' Day,* Bush Theatre, 1983.

Malcolm, *Selling the Sizzle,* Hampstead Theatre, London, 1986.

Title role, *Hamlet,* Oxford Playhouse Company, Assembly Hall, Edinburgh and Elsinore Festival, Edinburgh, Scotland, 1986.

Title role, *Riddley Walker,* Royal Exchange Theatre, Manchester, England, 1986.

Title role, *The Traveller,* Haymarket Theatre, Leicester, England, then Almeida Theatre, London, both 1987.

Title role, *Bussy D'Ambois,* Old Vic Theatre, London, 1988.

Title role, *Macbeth,* Royal Exchange Theatre, 1989.

Gregers Werle, *The Wild Duck,* Phoenix Theatre, London, 1990.

Mickey Robinson, *Your Home in the West,* Royal Exchange Theatre, 1991.

Also appeared in *Over a Barrel,* 1989.

FILM APPEARANCES

Jack Jenkins, *When the Whales Came* (also known as *Why the Whales Came*), Twentieth Century-Fox, 1989.

Leward Wicklow, *The Russia House,* Metro-Goldwyn-Mayer/United Artists, 1990.

Also appeared in *Red Monarch.*

TELEVISION APPEARANCES; EPISODIC

"He's Asking for Me," *Screenplay on Sunday,* BBC-2, 1990.

OTHER TELEVISION APPEARANCES

Smike, *Nicholas Nickleby* (mini-series; also known as *The Life and Adventures of Nicholas Nickleby*), syndicated, 1983.

Leslie Titmus, *Paradise Postponed* (series), ITV, then *Masterpiece Theatre,* PBS, both 1986.

Murderers Among Us: The Simon Wiesenthal Story (also known as *The Simon Wiesenthal Story*) HBO, 1989.

Nightingales (series), NBC, 1990.

Tom Rowse, *A Casualty of War* (movie), USA, 1990.

Also appeared in *A Murder of Quality,* 1990; *Titmuss Regained,* 1990; *King Lear,* BBC; *The Daughter-In-Law; The Gathering Seed; Scum; The Kiss of Death; Jumping the Queue; The Marksman; The Brylcream Boys; Dog Ends; Making Plays: Arena.*

*   *   *

THULIN, Ingrid   1929-
(Ingrid Tulean)

PERSONAL: Born January 27, 1929, in Solleftea, Sweden; daughter of Adam and Nanna (Larsson) Thulin; married Claes Sylwander, 1951 (marriage ended); married Harry Schein, 1956. *Education:* Attended Royal Dramatic Theatre School, Stockholm.

CAREER: Actress, writer, and film and stage director.

AWARDS, HONORS: Best Actress Award, Cannes International Film Festival, 1958, for *Nara livet (Brink of Life);* Best New Director, Chicago International Film Festival (Hugo award), 1983, for *Broken Sky.*

CREDITS:

FILM APPEARANCES

Marianne Borg, *Wild Strawberries,* Janus, 1956.

(As Ingrid Tulean) Brita, *Foreign Intrigue,* United Artists, 1956.

Manda Aman, *The Magician* (also known as *The Face*), Janus, 1957.

Cecilia Ellius, *Nara livet* (also known as *Brink of Life* and *So Close to Life*), Nordisk Tone Film, 1958.

Marguerite Laurier, *The Four Horsemen of the Apocalypse,* Metro-Goldwyn-Mayer (MGM), 1962.

Mother, *Agostino,* Baltea, 1962.

Marta Lundberg, *The Winter Light* (also known as *Nattvardsgaesterna*), Svensk Filmindustri, 1963.

Ester, *The Silence* (also known as *Tystnaden*), Janus, 1964.

Dr. Michele Wolf, *Return from the Ashes,* United Artists, 1965.

Irene, *Night Games,* AVCO/Embassy, 1966.

Marianne, *La Guerre est Finie* (also known as *Krigetar Slut* and *The War is Over*), Brandon, 1967.

Veronica Volger, *The Hour of the Wolf* (also known as *Varetimmen*), Svensk Filmindustri, 1968.

Elisabeth Hermann, *Fino a Farti Male* (also known as *Adelaide*), Sigma, 1969.

Thea Winkelmann, *Riten* (also known as *The Rite* and *The Ritual*), Janus, 1970.

Wife, *N.P.* (also known as *The Secret*), Zeta-a-Elle, 1971.

Karin, *Cries and Whispers* (also known as *Viskingar Och Rop*), New World, 1972.

Helene, *La Cage,* Lira-UGE-Parma, 1975.

Miriam, *Moses,* AVCO/Embassy, 1977.

Elena, *The Cassandra Crossing,* AVCO/Embassy, 1977.

Rakel, *After the Rehearsal,* Triumph, 1984.

Il Giorno Prima (also known as *The Day Before*), Columbia Pictures Italia, 1987.

Also appeared in *Havets Son,* 1941; *Kann dej som Hemma,* 1948; *Dit Vindarna Bar,* 1948; *Karleken segrar* (also known as *Love Will Conquer*), 1949; *Hjarter Kneki,* 1950; *Nar Karleken kim till Byn,* 1950; *Leva pa "Hoppet,"* 1951; *Mote med Livet,* 1952; *Kalle Karlsson fran Jularbo,* 1952; *En Skargardsnatt,* 1953; *Goingehov dingen,* 1953; *Tva Skona Juveler,* 1954; *I Rok och Dans,* 1954; *Hoppsan!,* 1955; *Danssalongen,* 1955; *Aldrig i livet,* 1957; *Donnaren,* 1960; *Sekstet* (also known as *Sextet*), 1963; as Nadine Anderson, *Die Lady* (also known as *Games of Desire* and *Frustration*), 1964; *Domani non siamo piu qui,* 1967; as cook, *Badarna* (also known as *I, a Virgin*), 1968; Baroness Sophie von Essenbeck, *La caduta degli dei* (also known as *The Damned*), 1969; *Un diablo bajo la Almohada,* 1970; *It Rained All Night the Day I Left,* 1970; Maria, *La Sainte Famille,* 1970; as Inez Crona, *En handful karelek* (also known as *A Handful of Love*), 1973; as investigator, *Monismanien 1995,* 1975; in *Il viaggio nella vertigini,* 1975; title role, *Madame Kitty* (also known as *Salon Kitty*), 1976; Tania, *Comincio il viaggio nella vertigini,* 1976; in *Agnes Will Die,* 1977; Ylva, *En och en* (also known as *One and One,* 1978; *Il Corsario,* 1983; *La Casa del Sorriso* ("The House of Smiles"), 1991; and *Rabbit Face.*

FILM DIRECTOR

(And writer) *Brusten Himmel* (also known as *Broken Sky*), Svenska Filminstitutet, c. 1982.

Also director of *Haengivelse,* 1965; (with Erland Josephson and Erland Nykvist) *En och en* (also known as *One and One* and *Devotion*).

TELEVISION APPEARANCES; EPISODIC

Espionage, NBC, 1964.

OTHER TELEVISION APPEARANCES

Miriam, *Moses—The Lawgiver* (mini-series), CBS, 1975.
Anita Hoffman, *Intermezzo* (special), NBC, 1961.
Mrs. Havemeyer, *Control* (movie), HBO, 1987.

Also appeared as Indra's daughter in *The Dream Play,* 1970.

STAGE APPEARANCES

(Broadway debut) Inga, *Of Love Remembered,* American National Theatre and Academy, New York City, 1967.

Made stage debut at Municipal Theatre, Norrkoping, Sweden; appeared in *Gigi, Peer Gynt, Two for the Seesaw, Twelfth Night,* and *Miss Julie,* all in Sweden.

*　　*　　*

TIPTON, Jennifer   1937-

PERSONAL: Born September 11, 1937, in Columbus, OH; daughter of Samuel Ridley and Isabel (Hanson) Tipton; married William F. Beaton, August 29, 1976. *Education:* Cornell University, B.A., 1958.

ADDRESSES: Office—11 West 18th St., New York, NY 10011.

CAREER: Lighting Designer. Yale University School of Drama, associate professor, 1981—.

AWARDS, HONORS: Antoinette Perry Award, best lighting design, and Drama Desk Award, 1977, for *The Cherry Orchard,* 1989, for *Jerome Robbins' Broadway,* and 1991, for *La Bete;* Joseph Jefferson Award, 1977; Obie Award, 1979, for sets and lighting, Jennifer Tipton Public Theater; nominated for Antoinette Perry Award, lighting design, 1981, for *Sophisticated Ladies;* Creative Arts Award, music and dance, Brandeis University, 1982; Kudos Award, 1983; New York Dance and Performance (Bessie) awards, choreographers and creators (with Dana Reitz), for *Circumstantial Evidence,* and for sustained achievement in lighting design, both 1987; Guggenheim fellowship, 1987; American Theatre Wing Design

Awards, 1987 and 1989; Drama Desk Award, lighting design, 1989, for *Long Day's Journey into Night, Waiting for Godot,* and *Jerome Robbins' Broadway;* Common Wealth Award, 1989.

CREDITS:

STAGE WORK; LIGHTING DESIGNER

Macbeth, American Shakespeare Festival, Stratford, CT, 1967.
The Grab Bag, Astor Place Theatre, New York City, 1968.
Richard II, American Shakespeare Festival, 1968.
Love's Labour's Lost, American Shakespeare Festival, 1968.
Our Town, American National Theater Academy (ANTA), New York City, 1969.
A Night Out, Park Avenue Community Theatre, New York City, 1971.
Dreyfus in Rehearsal, Ethel Barrymore Theatre, New York City, 1974.
The Killdeer, New York Shakespeare Festival (NYSF), Public/Newman Theater, New York City, 1974.
Macbeth, Mitzi E. Newhouse Theatre, New York City, 1974.
The Tempest, Mitzi E. Newhouse Theatre, 1974.
A Midsummer Night's Dream, Mitzi E. Newhouse Theatre, 1975.
The Misanthrope, St. James Theatre, New York City, 1975.
Murder among Friends, Biltmore Theatre, New York City, 1975.
Habeas Corpus, Martin Beck Theatre, New York City, 1975.
For Colored Girls Who Have Considered Suicide When the Rainbow is Enuf, Booth Theatre, New York City, 1976-77.
The Baker's Wife, Dorothy Chandler Pavilion, Los Angeles, CA, then Kennedy Center Opera House, Washington, DC, 1976.
Rex, Lunt-Fontanne Theatre, New York City, 1976.
The Cherry Orchard, Vivian Beaumont Theatre, New York City, 1977.
Agamemnon, NYSF, Delacorte Theatre, New York City, 1977.
Landscape of the Body, NYSF, Public Theatre, 1977.
Happy End, Brooklyn Academy of Music, Brooklyn, NY, then Martin Beck Theatre, New York City, 1977.
Marco Polo Sings a Solo, NYSF, Public Theatre, 1977.
Runaways, Plymouth Theatre, New York City, 1977.
Drinks before Dinner, Public/Newman Theater, 1978.
All's Well That Ends Well, NYSF, Delacorte Theatre, 1978.
The Taming of the Shrew, NYSF, Delacorte Theatre, 1978.
Museum, NYSF, Public Theatre, 1978.

Alice, Forrest Theatre, Philadelphia, PA, 1978.

Artichoke, Manhattan Theatre Club, New York City, 1979.

Bosoms and Neglect, Longacre Theatre, New York City, 1979.

The Goodbye People, Westport Country Theatre, Westport, CT, then Belasco Theatre, New York City, 1979.

Daddy Goodness, Forrest Theatre, 1979.

Justice, Playwrights Horizons Theatre, New York City, 1979.

The Jail Diary of Albie Sachs, Manhattan Theatre Club, 1979.

Julius Caesar, NYSF, Public Theatre, 1979.

Happy Days, NYSF, Public Theatre, 1979.

The Woods, NYSF, Public Theatre, 1979.

Two Part Inventions, Goodman Theatre, 1979.

Dispatches, NYSF, Public/Cabaret Theatre, 1979.

After the Season, Academy Festival Theatre, Lake Forest, IL, 1980.

A Month in the Country, Williamstown Theatre Festival, Williamstown, MA, 1980.

Lunch Hour, Ethel Barrymore Theatre, 1980.

Billy Bishop Goes to War, Morosco Theatre, then Theatre de Lys, New York City, later Mark Taper Forum, 1980.

The Sea Gull, Public/Newman Theater, 1980.

Mother Courage and Her Children, Public Theater, 1980.

The Pirates of Penzance, NYSF, Delacorte Theatre, 1980, then Uris Theatre, New York City, later Ahmanson Theatre, Los Angeles, CA, 1981.

Funny Face, Studio Arena Theatre, Buffalo, NY, 1980.

Baal, Goodman Theatre, 1980.

The Captivity of Pixie Shedman, Marymount Manhattan Theatre, New York City, 1981.

Sophisticated Ladies, Lunt-Fontanne Theatre, 1981.

Crossing Niagara, Manhattan Theatre Club, 1981.

Rip van Winkle or The Works, Yale Repertory Theater, New Haven, CT, 1981.

Zastrozzi, NYSF, Public Theatre, 1982.

Lydie Breeze, American Place Theatre, New York City, 1982.

As You Like It, Guthrie Theatre, Minneapolis, MN, 1982.

Falstaff, Los Angeles Opera, Los Angeles, CA, 1982.

The Wake of Jamey Foster, Eugene O'Neill Theatre, New York City, 1982.

Jungle Coup, Goodman Theatre, Chicago, IL, 1983.

The School for Scandal, American Repertory Theatre, Cambridge, MA, 1983.

Non Pasquale, NYSF, Delacorte Theatre, 1983.

Orgasmo Adulto Escapes from the Zoo, NYSF, Public Theatre, 1983.

Uncle Vanya, La Mama Experimental Theatre Company, New York City, 1983, then Classic Stage Company (CSC) Repertory Theatre, New York City, 1987.

Baby with the Bathwater, Playwrights Horizons, 1983.

Peer Gynt, Guthrie Theatre, 1983.

A Touch of the Poet, Yale Repertory Theater, 1983.

The Photographer, Brooklyn Academy of Music, 1983.

Measure for Measure, American Repertory Theatre, 1984.

The Misanthrope, Seattle Repertory Theatre, Seattle, WA, 1984.

The Ballad of Soapy Smith, NYSF, Public Theatre, 1984.

Hurlyburly, Goodman Theatre, then Promenade Theatre, New York City, later Ethel Barrymore Theatre, New York City, 1984.

Whoopi Goldberg, Lyceum Theatre, New York City, 1984.

The Sleep of Reason, Center Stage, Baltimore, 1984.

Six Characters in Search of an Author, American Repertory Theatre, 1984.

Endgame, Samuel Beckett Theatre, then Cherry Lane Theatre, New York City, 1984.

King Stag, American Repertory Theatre, 1984.

the CIVIL warS, Act III-E, IV, American Repertory Theater, 1985.

Singin' in the Rain, Gershwin Theatre, New York City, 1985.

The Juniper Tree, American Repertory Theatre, 1985.

Under Statements, Repertory Theatre of St. Louis, St. Louis, MO, 1985-86.

Little Eyolf, Yale Repertory Theatre, 1985.

The Balcony, American Repertory Theater, 1986.

Alcestis, American Repertory Theater, 1986.

Hamlet, NYSF, Public Theatre, 1986.

The Return of Pinocchio, Forty-Seventh Street Theatre, New York City, 1986.

Principia Scriptoriae, Manhattan Theatre Club, 1986.

Hamletmachine, New York University, 1986.

Worstword Ho, Mabou Mines, New York City, 1986.

Paradise Lost, Center Stage, Baltimore, MD, 1987.

The Misanthrope, Guthrie Theatre, 1987-88.

Leon and Lena (and Lenz), Guthrie Theatre, 1987.

Long Day's Journey into Night, Neil Simon Theatre, New York City, 1988.

Ah! Wilderness, Neil Simon Theatre, 1988.

Tannhaeuser, Chicago Lyric Opera, Chicago, IL, 1988.

Waiting for Godot, Mitzi E. Newhouse Theatre, 1988.

The Landscape of the Body, Goodman Theater, 1988.

Jerome Robbins' Broadway, Imperial Theatre, New York City, 1989.

The Screens, Guthrie Theatre, 1989.

Lulu, Berkeley Repertory Theater, Berkeley, CA, 1989.

A Walk in the Woods, Yale Repertory Theatre, then Booth Theatre, 1989.

The Winter's Tale, Goodman Theatre, 1990.

Alceste, Lyric Opera of Chicago, 1990.

Medea, Guthrie Theater, 1991.
Henry IV, NYSF, New York City, 1991.
Parsifal, Hamburg Opera, 1991.
La Bete, Eugene O'Neill Theatre, 1991.

Also lighting designer for *Horseman, Pass By,* Off-Broadway, 1969; *Circumstantial Evidence,* The Kitchen, 1987; *The Rimers of Eldritch,* Off-Broadway, 1988; *Suspect Terrain,* SUNY/Purchase, 1989; *Titus Andronicus,* NYSF, 1989; and *Brace-Up,* Wooster Group.

MAJOR TOURS; LIGHTING DESIGNER

For Colored Girls Who Have Considered Suicide When the Rainbow is Enuf, U.S. cities, 1977-78.

LIGHTING DESIGNER; DANCE PRODUCTIONS

Orbs, Holland Festival, 1965.
A Ballet behind the Bridge, Negro Ensemble Company, New York City, 1972.
Celebration: The Art of Pas de Deux, Jose Limon Dance Company, Spoleto, Italy, 1973.
The Dybbuk, New York City Ballet, New York City, 1974.
The Leaves Are Fading, American Ballet Theatre, 1975.
Don Quixote, American Ballet Theatre, 1976.
The Nutcracker, American Ballet Theater, 1976.
The Four Seasons, New York City Ballet, 1979.
Romeo and Juliet, Hartford Ballet, Hartford, CT, 1980, then Joffrey Ballet, 1984 and 1986.
Dances of Albion, Royal Ballet, London, 1980.
The Front Page, Goodman Theatre, 1981.
The Catherine Wheel, Twyla Tharp Dance Company, 1981.
Plenty, Goodman Theatre, 1981.
Svadebka, Netherlands Dance Theatre, The Hague, 1982.
Fire, Joffrey Ballet, New York City, 1982.
Sunset, Paul Taylor Dance Company, 1983.
Wiegelied, Netherlands Dans Theater, 1983.
Bach Partita, American Ballet Theater, 1983.
The Little Ballet, American Ballet Theatre, 1983.
Square Deal, Joffrey Ballet, 1983.
Fait Accompli, Twyla Tharp, Brooklyn Academy of Music, 1984.
Antique Epigraphs, New York City Ballet, 1984.
Brahms/Handel, New York City Ballet, 1984.
In Memory of . . . , New York City Ballet, 1985.
Roses, Paul Taylor Dance Company, 1985.
Giselle, Royal Ballet, London, 1985.
A Musical Offering, Paul Taylor Dance Company, 1986.
Quiet City, New York City Ballet, 1986.
L'Histoire du Soldat, Netherlands Dans Theater, 1986.
In the Upper Room, Twyla Tharp Dance, 1986.
La Ronde, National Ballet of Canada, 1987.
Songs/Ives, New York City Ballet, 1988.
The Informer, American Ballet Theater, 1988.

Swan Lake, American Ballet Theater, 1988.
To Comfort Ghosts, Dan Wagoner Dancers, 1988.
Speaking in Tongues, Paul Taylor Dance Company, 1989.
Tagore, National Ballet of Canada, 1989.
Die Materie, Dutch National Opera, 1989.
Brief Fling, American Ballet Theater, 1990.

Also lighting designer for *Airs Amnon v'Tamar, Export: OP Jazz,* and *Triad,* Kazuko Hirabayashi Dance Company, 1972. Lighting designer for Paul Taylor Dance Company, 1965; Twyla Tharp and Dancers, 1965; Pennsylvania Ballet Company, 1966; Harkness Ballet Company, 1967; Dan Wagoner Dancers, Les Grands Ballet Canadiens, 1968; Yvonne Rainer Company, City Center Joffrey Ballet, 1969; ANTA Theatre Dance Series, Elliot Feld Ballet Company, 1971-72; American Ballet Theatre, 1971; Houston Ballet Company, Delacorte Dance Festival, New York City, 1972; National Ballet Company, 1972; Hartford Ballet Company, 1973; San Francisco Ballet Company, 1974; Cleveland Ballet Company, 1976; Arena Stage, Washington, DC, 1979-80; Goodman Theatre, 1979-1980; Long Wharf Theatre, 1979-80; Guthrie Theatre, Minneapolis, MN, 1981-82, 1982-83, and 1987-88; Goodman Theatre, 1981-82; Yale Repertory Theatre, 1981-82, 1982-83, 1983-84, and 1987-88; Center Stage, 1983-84; American Repertory Theatre, 1984; and Repertory Theatre of St. Louis, MO, 1985.

OTHER SOURCES:

PERIODICALS

New York Times, April 14, 1991.
Theatre Crafts, April, 1983; October, 1990.

*   *   *

TOPOL 1935-

PERSONAL: Full name, Chiam Topol; born September 9, 1935, in Tel Aviv, Palestine (now Israel); son of Jacob and Rel (Goldman) Topol; married Galia Finkelstein, 1956; children: three.

CAREER: Actor, producer, and director.

AWARDS, HONORS: Golden Globe Award, Hollywood Foreign Press Association, 1965, for most promising newcomer, and 1972, for best actor in *Fiddler on the Roof;* Academy Award nomination for *Fiddler on the Roof;* Antoinette Perry Award nomination, leading actor in a musical, 1991, for *Fiddler on the Roof.*

CREDITS:

STAGE APPEARANCES

Tevye, *Fiddler on the Roof,* Gershwin Theatre, New York City, 1991.

Also appeared as Aimable, *The Baker's Wife.*

FILM APPEARANCES

Sallah Shabati, *Sallah,* Palisades International, 1965.

Abou Ibn Kader, *Cast a Giant Shadow,* United Artists, 1966.

Janovic, *Before Winter Comes,* Columbia, 1969.

Tevye, *Fiddler on the Roof,* United Artists, 1971.

Julian Cristoforou, *The Public Eye* (also known as *Follow Me*), Universal, 1972.

Title role, *Galileo,* American Film Theatre, 1975.

Dr. Hans Zarkov, *Flash Gordon,* Universal, 1980.

Columbo, *For Your Eyes Only,* United Artists, 1981.

Also appeared as Gadi, *Haternegol,* 1970; Effi Avidar, *Roman Behemshechim,* 1985.

FILM WORK

Producer, *Every Bastard a King,* Continental Distributing, 1968.

TELEVISION APPEARANCES

Michael, *The House on Garibuldi Street* (movie), ABC, 1979.

Berel Jastrow, *The Winds of War* (miniseries), ABC, 1983.

Dimitri Goldner, *Queenie,* ABC, 1987.

Berel Jastrow, *War and Remembrance* (miniseries), ABC, 1988.

WRITINGS:

Topol by Topol (autobiography), Weidenfeld & Nicolson, 1981.*

*   *   *

TREVOR, Claire   1909-

PERSONAL: Born Claire Wemlinger, March 8, 1909 (some sources say 1910 and 1912), in Bensonhurst, NY; married Clark Andrews (a producer), 1938 (divorced, 1942); married Cylos William Dunsmoore, 1943 (divorced, 1947); married Milton Bren (a producer), 1948; children: (second marriage) Charles Cylos. *Education:* Attended Columbia University; studied for the stage at American Academy of Dramatic Arts.

ADDRESSES: Manager—c/o Richard Lewis, 247 South Beverly Dr., Suite 102, Beverly Hills, CA 90212.

CAREER: Actress. Performer in theatre stock productions during the 1920s. Appeared in two short films for Vitaphone, 1929; Warner Brothers, St. Louis, MO, stock company member, 1930; Hampton Players, Southampton, NY, company member, 1931.

AWARDS, HONORS: Academy Award nomination, Best Supporting Actress, 1937, for *Dead End,* 1948, for *Key*

Largo, and 1954, for *The High and the Mighty;* Emmy Award, Best Single Performance by an Actress, 1957, for "Dodsworth," on *Producers Showcase.*

CREDITS:

STAGE APPEARANCES

(Stage debut) *The Seagull,* Robert Henderson's Repertory Players, Ann Arbor, MI, 1929.

(Broadway debut) Toby Van Buren, *Whistling in the Dark,* Ethel Barrymore Theatre, New York City, 1932.

Betty, *The Party's Over,* Vanderbilt Theatre, New York City, 1933.

Danielle Forbes, *The Big Two,* Booth Theatre, New York City, 1947.

MAJOR TOURS

Anne Rogers, *Goodbye Again,* U.S. cities, 1947.

June Buckridge/Sister George, *The Killing of Sister George,* U.S. cities, 1967-68.

FILM APPEARANCES

(Film debut) *Life in the Raw,* Twentieth Century-Fox, 1933.

Sally Johnson, *Jimmy and Sally,* Twentieth Century-Fox, 1933.

Jane Lee, *The Mad Game,* Twentieth Century-Fox, 1933.

Kay Ellison, *Baby, Take a Bow,* Twentieth Century-Fox, 1934.

Tony Bellamy, *Hold That Girl,* Twentieth Century-Fox, 1934.

The Last Trail, Twentieth Century-Fox, 1934.

Jerry Jordan, *Wild Gold,* Twentieth Century-Fox, 1934.

Janette Foster, *Black Sheep,* Twentieth Century-Fox, 1935.

Bette McWade, *Dante's Inferno,* Twentieth Century-Fox, 1935.

Title role, *Elinor Norton,* Twentieth Century-Fox, 1935.

Betty Ingals, *Spring Tonic,* Twentieth Century-Fox, 1935.

Carroll Aiken, *Career Woman,* Twentieth Century-Fox, 1936.

Jane Martin, *Fifteen Maiden Lane,* Twentieth Century-Fox, 1936.

Bonnie Brewster, *Human Cargo,* Twentieth Century-Fox, 1936.

Carol Barton, *My Marriage,* Twentieth Century-Fox, 1936.

Vicky Blake, *Navy Wife,* Twentieth Century-Fox, 1936.

Julia Carroll, *The Song and Dance Man,* Twentieth Century-Fox, 1936.

Nina Lind, *Star for a Night,* Twentieth Century-Fox, 1936.

Kitty Brant, *To Mary—With Love,* Twentieth Century-Fox, 1936.

Fay Loring, *Big Town Girl,* Twentieth Century-Fox, 1937.

Francie, *Dead End* (also known as *Cradle of Crime*), United Artists, 1937.

Dixie, *King of Gamblers* (also known as *Czar of the Slot Machines*), Paramount, 1937.

Lucy "Tex" Warren, *One Mile from Heaven,* Twentieth Century-Fox, 1937.

Marcia, *Second Honeymoon,* Twentieth Century-Fox, 1937.

Barbara Blanchard, *Time Out for Romance,* Twentieth Century-Fox, 1937.

Jo Keller, *The Amazing Dr. Clitterhouse,* Warner Brothers, 1938.

Christine Nelson, *Five of a Kind,* Twentieth Century-Fox, 1938.

Lee Roberts, *Valley of the Giants,* Warner Brothers, 1938.

Joan Bradley, *Walking Down Broadway,* Twentieth Century-Fox, 1938.

Janie, *Allegheny Uprising* (also known as *The First Rebel*), RKO, 1939.

Laura Benson, *I Stole a Million,* Universal, 1939.

Dallas, *Stagecoach,* United Artists, 1939.

Mary McCloud, *The Dark Command,* Republic, 1940.

"Gold Dust" Nelson, *Honky Tonk,* Metro-Goldwyn-Mayer (MGM), 1941.

"Mike" King, *Texas,* Columbia, 1941.

Connie Dawson, *The Adventures of Martin Eden,* Columbia, 1942.

Michelle Allaine, *Crossroads* (also known as *The Man Who Lost His Way*), MGM, 1942.

Ruth Dillon, *Street of Chance,* Paramount, 1942.

Countess Maletta, *The Desperadoes,* Columbia, 1943.

Ruth Jones, *Good Luck, Mr. Yates,* Columbia, 1943.

Dora Hand, *The Woman of the Town,* United Artists, 1943.

Lilah, *Johnny Angel,* RKO, 1945.

Velma/Mrs. Grayle, *Murder, My Sweet* (also known as *Farewell, My Lovely*), RKO, 1945.

Cynthia, *The Bachelor's Daughters* (also known as *Bachelor Girls*), United Artists, 1946.

Terry Cordeau, *Crack-Up,* RKO, 1946.

Helen Trent, *Born to Kill* (also known as *Lady of Deceit*), RKO, 1947.

Claire Hodgson, *The Babe Ruth Story,* Allied Artists, 1948.

Gaye Dawn, *Key Largo,* Warner Brothers, 1948.

Pat, *Raw Deal,* El-Reliance, 1948.

Marian Webster, *The Velvet Touch,* RKO, 1948.

Marguerite Seaton, *The Lucky Stiff,* United Artists, 1949.

Madeline Haley, *Borderline,* Universal, 1950.

Lily Fowler, *Best of the Badmen,* RKO, 1951.

Milly Farley, *Hard, Fast, and Beautiful,* RKO, 1951.

Connie Williams, *Hoodlum Empire,* Republic, 1952.

Mrs. Ansel Ames, *My Man and I,* MGM, 1952.

Nora Marko, *Stop, You're Killing Me,* Warner Brothers, 1952.

Josie Sullivan, *The Stranger Wore a Gun,* Columbia, 1953.

May Hoist, *The High and the Mighty,* Warner Brothers, 1954.

Lady Macbeth, *Lucy Gallant* (also known as *Oil Town*), Paramount, 1955.

Idonee, *Man without a Star,* Universal, 1955.

Marie, *The Mountain,* Paramount, 1956.

Rose Morgenstern, *Marjorie Morningstar,* Warner Brothers, 1958.

Clara Kruger, *Two Weeks in Another Town,* MGM, 1962.

Helen Baird, *The Stripper* (also known as *Woman of Summer*), Twentieth Century-Fox, 1963.

Edna, *How to Murder Your Wife,* United Artists, 1965.

Capetown Affair, Killarney, 1967.

Charlotte, *Kiss Me Goodbye,* Twentieth Century-Fox, 1982.

Also appeared in *Beauty's Daughter,* 1935.

TELEVISION APPEARANCES; EPISODIC

"Alias Nora Hale," *Ford Theatre,* NBC, 1953.

"Foggy Night," *G.E. Theatre,* CBS, 1954.

"Summer Memory," *Ford Theatre,* NBC, 1954.

Willy, CBS, 1954.

"No Sad Songs for Me," *Lux Video Theatre,* NBC, 1955.

"Billy and the Bride," *Stage Seven,* CBS, 1955.

"The Prowler," *Climax!,* CBS, 1956.

"Foolproof," *Schlitz Playhouse of Stars,* CBS, 1956.

"Dodsworth," *Producers Showcase,* NBC, 1956.

"Emergency Call," *G.E. Theatre,* CBS, 1956.

"If You Knew Elizabeth," *Playhouse 90,* CBS, 1957.

"Happy Hill" and "The C. L. Harding Story," *Desilu Playhouse,* CBS, 1959.

The Untouchables, ABC, 1959.

"The Revolt of Judge Lloyd," *U.S. Steel Hour,* CBS, 1960.

"A Crime for Mothers," *Alfred Hitchcock Theatre,* NBC, 1961.

Investigators, CBS, 1961.

Judith Harlan, *Murder, She Wrote,* CBS, 1987.

Grace Porter, *Norman Rockwell's "Breaking Home Ties"* (also known as *Breaking Home Ties*), ABC, 1987.

Wolf Trap Salutes Victor Borge: An 80th Birthday Celebration, PBS, 1990.

Also appeared in *The Love Boat,* ABC.

RADIO APPEARANCES

Lorelei Kilbourne, *Big Town* (series), CBS, 1937.*

TRINTIGNANT, Jean-Louis 1930-

PERSONAL: Full name, Jean-Louis Xavier Trintignant; born December 11, 1930, in France; son of Raoul Trintignant and Claire (Tourtin) Trintignant; married Colette Dacheville (an actress; professional name, Stephane Audran), 1954 (divorced); married Nadine Marquand (a director), 1960; children: one son, two daughters (one deceased). *Education:* Attended Faculte de Droit, Aix-en-Provence; studied acting with Charles Dullin and Tatania Balacgova.

CAREER: Actor and director. *Military service:* Served in military, 1956-59.

AWARDS, HONORS: Prix d'Interpretation de l'Academy, 1965, for *Mata Hari;* Best Actor, Berlin Film Festival, 1968, for *L'Homme qui ment;* Best Actor, Cannes Film Festival, 1969, for *Z;* Prix David de Donatello, Taormina Festival, 1972; Officer des Arts et des Lettres.

CREDITS:

FILM APPEARANCES

(Film debut) Jean-Louis, *If All the Guys in the World* (also known as *Si tous les gars du monde* and *Race for Life*), Christian-Jaque, 1955.

Michel, *And God Created Woman* (also known as *Et Dieu crea la femme* and *And Woman . . . Was Created*), Kingsley International, 1957.

Austerlitz (also known as *The Battle of Austerlitz*), Lux, 1960.

Guy, *The Game of Truth* (also known as *Le Jeu de la verite*), Concinor, 1961.

Danceny, *Dangerous Love Affairs* (also known as *Relazion: Periclose* and *Les Liaisons Dangereuses*), Astor, 1961.

Carlo Romanazzi, *Estate Violenta* (also known as *Ete Violent, Violent Summer,* and *The Widow Is Willing),* Around the World-Don Kay, 1961.

Paul, *Seven Capital Sins* (also known as *I Sette Peccati Capital* and *Les Sept Peches Capitaux*), Embassy Pictures, 1962.

Roberto Mariani, *The Easy Life* (also known as *Il Sorpasso*), Embassy Pictures, 1963.

Francois, *The French Game* (also known as *Le Coeur Battant*), Atlantic Pictures, 1963.

Eric, *Nutty, Naughty Chateu* (also known as *Chateu en Suede Il Castello in Svezin*), Lopert, 1964.

Captain Francois Lassalle, *Mata Hari* (also known as *Matta Hari Agent H-21* and *Mata Hari Agente Segreto H-21*), Magna Pictures, 1965.

Serge, *Is Paris Burning?* (also known as *Paris, brule t'il?*), Paramount, 1966.

Jean-Louis Duroc, *A Man and a Woman* (also known as *Un Homme et une femme*), Allied Artists, 1966.

Eric, *The Sleeping Car Murders* (also known as *Compartiment Tueurs*), Twentieth Century-Fox, 1966.

Pierre, *Journey Beneath the Desert* (also known as *L'Antinea L'amante della citta sepolta* and *L'Atlantide*), Embassy Pictures, 1967.

Paul Thomas, *The Heterosexuals* (*Les Biches*), Jack H. Harris, 1968.

Elias, himself, *Trans-Europ-Express,* Trans American, 1968.

Marco, *Plucked* (also known as *La Morte ha fatto l'uovo* and *La Mort a Ponduy un oeuf*), U-M, 1969.

Examining magistrate, *Z,* Cinema V, 1969.

Boris Varissa, *The Man Who Lies* (also known as *L'Homme qui ment*), Grove Press, 1970.

Jean-Louis, *My Night at Maud's* (also known as *My Night with Maud* and *Ma Nuit chez Maud*), Pathe Contemporary-Corinth, 1970.

Marcello, *The Conformist* (also known as *Il Conformist*), Paramount, 1971.

Simon, *The Crook* (also known as *Le Voyou*), United Artists, 1971.

Tony, *And Hope To Die* (also known as *La Course du lievre a travers ces champs*) Twentieth Century-Fox, 1972.

Stephane Carella, *Without Apparent Motive* (also known as *Sans Mobile Apparent*), Twentieth Century-Fox/Cinteleuro, 1972.

Darien, *The French Conspiracy* (also known as *L'Attentat*), Cine Globe, 1973.

Lucian, *The Outside Man* (also known as *Un Homme est mort*), United Artists, 1973.

Nicholas, *The French Way* (also known as *Love at the Top* and *Le Mouton Enrage*), Wormser, 1975.

Doctor, *The Desert of Tartars* (also known as *Le Desert des Tartares*), Gaumont, 1976.

Rulbert, *Malevil,* Union Generale Cinematographique, 1981.

Doctor, *Passion of Love* (also known as *Passione d'amore*), Putnam Square, 1982.

Blow to the Heart (also known as *Colpa al curore*), Other Cinema, 1983.

Monsieur Sauce, *La Nuit de Varennes,* Triumph, 1983.

Julien Vercel, *Confidentially Yours* (also known *Vivement dimanche!*), Artificial Eye, 1983.

The President, *Le Bon plaisir,* MK2, 1984.

Roland Riviere, *Going and Coming Back* (also known as *Partir revenir*), Union Generale Cinematographique, 1985.

Inspector Mayene, *L'Homme aux yeux d'argent,* AAA-Revom, 1985.

Scutzler, *Rendezvous,* SpectraFilm, 1985.

Fodo the teacher, *Volley for a Black Buffalo* (also known as *Sortuz egy fekete bivalyert*), MaFilm-Objektiv-Procinex, 1985.

Gilquin, *Nobody's Women* (also known as *Femmes de Personne*), European Classics, 1986.

Pierre, *The Woman of My Life* (also known as *La Femme de ma vie*), Union Generale Cinematographique, 1986.

Jean-Louis Duroc, *A Man and a Woman: Twenty Years Later* (also known as *Un Homme et une femme: Vingt ans deja*), Warner Brothers, 1986.

Paul, *Next Summer* (also known as *L'Ete prochain*), European Classics, 1986.

Paul, *The Ghost Valley* (also known as *La Vallee fantome*), MK2, 1987.

Holm, *Bunker Palace Hotel,* Bac Films, 1989.

Also appeared in *La Loi des rues,* 1956; *Club de femmes,* 1956; Georges, *La Millieme fenetre,* 1960; Jean-Marie, *Pleins feux sur l'assassin,* 1961; Clement, *Fire and Ice* (also known as *Le Combat dans l'ile*), 1961; Joseph, *Horace '62,* 1962; the poet, *Merveilleuse Angelique,* 1964; *La Bonne Occase,* 1965; *Un Jour a Paris,* 1965; *Fragilite, ton nom est jemme,* 1965; "La donna che vive va sola," *Io uccido, tu uccidi,* 1966; Francois, *Le Dix-septieme ciel,* 1966; Philippe, *La Longue marche,* 1966; Raphael, *Safari diamants,* 1966; Bernard, *Col cuore in gola* (also known as *With Baited Breath* and *Deadly Sweet*), 1967; Raphael, *Un Homme a abattre* (also known as *A Man to Kill*), 1967; Vincent, *Mon amour, mon amour,* 1967; Michele, *Metti, una sera a cena* (also known as *The Love Circle* and *One Night at Dinner*), 1969; Dr. De Marchi, *La matriarca* (also known as *The Libertine*), 1969; *Il grande silenzio,* 1969; *L'Opium et le baton,* 1969; *Cosi dolce cosi perversa,* 1969; *L'Homme au cerveau greffe,* 1971; Darien, *L'Attendat* (also known as *Plot* and *The French Conspiracy*), 1972; Laube, *Defense de savior* (also known as *Forbidden to Know*), 1973; Meyereu, *Le Train,* 1973; Michel, *Les Violons du bal,* 1974; David, *The Secret* (also known as *Le Secret*), 1974; Ferdinand, *L'Escapade,* 1974; Paul, *Le Voyage de noces,* 1975; Paul Varlin, *L'Agression* (also known as *Act of Agression*), 1975; Buisson, *Flic Story,* 1975; Senator, *Il pleut sur Santiago,* 1975; Massimo, *The Sunday Woman* (also known as *La donna della domenica*), 1975; Alex, *Les Passagers,* 1976; Rainier, *L'Argent des autres* (also known as *Other People's Money*), 1978; Victor, *Reperages* (also known as *Faces of Love*), 1978; Bruno, *L'Amercain,* 1979; *La Banquiere,* 1980; *Eaux profondes,* 1980; *David, Thomas et les Autres,* 1985; The General, *Le Moustachu,* (also known as *The Field Agent*), 1987; also appeared as Georges in *Les Pas Perdus;* and in *Glissements progressifs du plaisir.*

FILM WORK

Director of *Une Journee bien remplie* (also known as *A Well-Filled Day*), 1972, and *Le Maitre nageur,* 1979.

STAGE APPEARANCES

Made stage debut in *To Each According to His Hunger,* 1951; appeared as Mary Stuart, *Macbeth,* Comedie de Saint-Etienne; also appeared in *Jacques ou la Soumission, Hamlet, Bonheur, impaire et passe,* and *Deux sur la balancoire.*

OTHER SOURCES:

PERIODICALS

Films and Filming (London), October, 1960.*

*   *   *

TUCKER, Lael
    See WERTENBAKER, Timberlake

*   *   *

TULEAN, Ingrid
    See THULIN, Ingrid

*   *   *

TURTURRO, John   1957-

PERSONAL: Born February 28, 1957, in Brooklyn, NY; married Katherine Borowitz (an actress). *Education:* Attended State University of New York at New Paltz; studied at Yale School of Drama, 1983.

ADDRESSES: Agent—The Gersh Agency, 232 North Canon Dr., Beverly Hills, CA 90210.

CAREER: Actor.

AWARDS, HONORS: Theatre World Award, and Obie Award from the *Village Voice,* both 1985, for *Danny and the Deep Blue Sea;* Cannes Film Festival Award, best actor, 1991, for *Barton Fink.*

CREDITS:

FILM APPEARANCES

Raging Bull, United Artists, 1980.
First Guy, *Exterminator II,* Cannon, 1984.
Ted from Pinky's, *The Flamingo Kid,* Twentieth Century-Fox, 1984.
Carl Cody, *To Live and Die in L.A.,* Metro-Goldwyn-Mayer/United Artists, 1985.
Ray, *Desperately Seeking Susan,* Orion, 1985.

Neil Pepper, *Off Beat,* Touchstone, 1986.

Julian, *The Color of Money,* Buena Vista, 1986.

Willie, *Gung Ho,* Paramount, 1986.

Writer, *Hannah and Her Sisters,* Orion, 1986.

Aspanu Pisciotta, *The Sicilian,* Twentieth Century-Fox, 1987.

Heinz Sabatino, *Five Corners,* Cineplex Odeon, 1987.

Pino, *Do the Right Thing,* Universal, 1989.

Himself, *The Making of Do the Right Thing* (documentary), First Run Features, 1989.

State of Grace, Orion, 1990.

Mike Battaglia, *Men of Respect,* Sugar Entertainment, 1990.

Moe Flatbush, *Mo' Better Blues,* Universal, 1990.

Bernie, *Miller's Crossing,* Twentieth Century-Fox, 1990.

Title role, *Barton Fink,* Twentieth Century-Fox, 1991.

Paulie Carbone, *Jungle Fever,* Universal, 1991.

Lame Ducks, Paramount, 1991.

STAGE APPEARANCES

Astopovo, Yale Repertory Theatre, New Haven, CT, 1982.

Niccollo "Mac" Vittelli, *Steel on Steel,* West Side Y Arts Center, New York City, 1983.

Title role, *Danny and the Deep Blue Sea,* Humana Festival of New American Plays, Actors Theatre of Louisville, Louisville, KY, 1983.

(Off-Broadway debut) Title role, *Danny and the Deep Blue Sea,* Circle in the Square, New York City, 1984.

Understudy for Biff, Happy, and Stanley, *Death of a Salesman,* Broadhurst Theatre, New York City, 1984.

Jesse, *Chaos and Hard Times,* West Side Y Arts Center, 1985.

Sal, "Men Without Dates," *Marathon '85,* Ensemble Studio Theatre, New York City, 1985.

Mac, "The Workers Life," *Marathon '86,* Ensemble Studio Theatre, 1986.

Chino, "Nijinsky Choked His Chicken," and Angelo, "Poppa Dio!," *La Puta Vida Trilogy,* New York Shakespeare Festival, Public Theatre, New York City, 1987.

The Bald Soprano/The Leader, Open Space Theatre, New York City, 1987.

Also appeared in *Of Mice and Men; Jamie's Gang; The Tooth of Crime.*

TELEVISION APPEARANCES

Larry, *Mario Puzo's "The Fortunate Pilgrim"* (miniseries), NBC, 1988.

WRITINGS:

(With Brandon Cole) "The Worker's Life" (sketch), produced as *Marathon '86,* Ensemble Studio Theatre, New York City, 1986.*

U-V

ULLMAN, Tracey 1959(?)-

PERSONAL: Born December 30, 1959 (some sources say 1961), in Hackbridge, England; daughter of an attorney; married Allan McKeown (a producer), 1984; children: Mabel Ellen. *Education:* Attended Italia Conti Stage School for four years.

CAREER: Actress, musician, singer, and dancer. Toured with a dance troupe in Berlin as a teenager.

AWARDS, HONORS: London Theatre Critics Award for most promising actress, 1981, for *Four in a Million;* Best Light Entertainment Performance Award, British Academy of Film and Television Art, 1983, for *Three of a Kind;* Golden Globe Award for best actress in a television series, 1988, for *The Tracey Ullman Show;* Emmy Award corecipient for outstanding writing in a variety or music program, Academy of Television Arts and Sciences, 1990, for *The Tracey Ullman Show;* Emmy Award for outstanding individual performance, 1990 for *The Best of the Tracey Ullman Show;* Emmy award corecipient for outstanding variety, music or comedy program, 1990, for *The Tracey Ullman Show;* Best female television performer, American Comedy Awards, 1991, for *The Tracey Ullman Show;* Drama Desk Award nomination, solo performance, 1991, for *The Big Love.*

CREDITS:

STAGE APPEARANCES

Beverly, *Four in a Million* (improvisation), Royal Court Theatre, London, 1981.
The Big Love (one-woman show), Plymouth Theatre, New York City, 1991.

Also appeared in *Talent* at Everyman's Playhouse and West End theatre productions of *Elvis, Grease,* and *The Rocky Horror Picture Show.*

FILM APPEARANCES

Sandra, *Give My Regards To Broad Street,* Twentieth Century-Fox, 1984.
Alice Park, *Plenty,* Twentieth Century-Fox, 1985.
Fiona, *Jumpin' Jack Flash,* Twentieth Century-Fox, 1986.
Rosalie Boca, *I Love You To Death,* Tri-star Pictures, 1990.

Also appeared in *The Young Visitors,* 1984.

TELEVISION APPEARANCES; SERIES

Lisa Isaacs, *Mackenzie,* The Entertainment Channel, 1982.
The Tracey Ullman Show, Fox Broadcasting Corporation (Fox), 1987-90.

Also appeared in the BBC series *Girls on Top, Three of a Kind,* and *A Kick up the Eighties.*

TELEVISION APPEARANCES; SPECIALS

The 39th Annual Emmy Awards, Fox, 1987.
Comic Relief II, HBO, 1987.
The 40th Annual Emmy Awards, Fox, 1988.
The American Comedy Awards, ABC, 1988.
Tracey Ullman Backstage, Fox, 1988.
The 41st Annual Emmy Awards, Fox, 1989.
I, Martin Short, Goes Hollywood, HBO, 1989.
4th Annual American Comedy Awards, ABC, 1990.
The Best of the Tracey Ullman Show, Fox, c. 1990.
Big Bird's Birthday, or Let Me Eat Cake, PBS, 1991.

RECORDINGS:

ALBUMS

Produced the album *You Broke My Heart in Seventeen Places,* 1984.

OTHER SOURCES:

BOOKS

Newsmakers, Issue 3, Gale, 1988.

PERIODICALS

Ms., September, 1987.
Rolling Stone, May 10, 1984; August 27, 1987.*

*   *   *

UNDERWOOD, Blair

PERSONAL: Born August 25 in Tacoma, Washington. *Education:* Carnegie-Mellon University, B.F.A., theater.

ADDRESSES: *Contact*—Media Relations, National Broadcasting Company, Inc., 30 Rockefeller Plaza, New York, NY 10112.

CAREER: Actor. Head of own production company.

AWARDS, HONORS: Golden Globe nomination, best supporting actor in a series, mini-series, or motion picture, 1990, for *L.A. Law;* Image Award, best actor in a dramatic series, NAACP, 1990, for *Murder in Mississippi.*

CREDITS:

FILM APPEARANCES

Russell, *Krush Groove,* Warner Brothers, 1985.

TELEVISION APPEARANCES; SERIES

Bobby Blue, *One Life to Live,* ABC, 1986.
Terry Corsaro, *Downtown,* CBS, 1986-87.
Jonathan Rollins, *L.A. Law,* 1987—.

TELEVISION APPEARANCES; EPISODIC

Mark Roberts, *The Cosby Show,* NBC, 1985.
Reggie Brooks, *21 Jump Street,* Fox, 1987.

Also appeared as Stillman on *Scarecrow and Mrs. King,* 1987, and on *Knight Rider.*

TELEVISION APPEARANCES; MOVIES

Horace Bouchee, *The Cover Girl and the Cop,* NBC, 1989.
Bob Richardson, *Heat Wave,* TNT, 1990.
James Chaney, *Murder in Mississippi,* NBC, 1990.

TELEVISION APPEARANCES; SPECIALS

Unforgettable, KHV-TV, 1989.
Host, *101st Tournament of Roses Parade,* NBC, 1990.

Also appeared on *Mickey's 60th Birthday Special,* 1988; *That's What Friends Are For: Aids Concert '88,* 1988; Judge, *The 1988 Miss America Pageant,* 1988; *The 10th Annual American Black Achievement Awards,* 1989; *The*

21st Annual NAACP Image Awards, 1989; *61st Annual Academy Awards,* 1989; Host, *Legacy,* 1990; *MDA Jerry Lewis Telethon,* 1990; *Martin Luther King, Jr. Parade,* 1990; NBC team member, *Battle of the Network Stars XIX.* *

*   *   *

URQUHART, Robert   1922-

PERSONAL: Born October 16, 1922, in Ullapool, Scotland.

ADDRESSES: *Agent*—Norman Boyack, 9 Cork St., London W1, England.

CAREER: Actor and writer. *Military service:* Served in the Royal Merchant Navy, 1938-45.

CREDITS:

FILM APPEARANCES

(Film debut) Sheltie, *You're Only Young Twice,* Associated British Films, 1952.
Slater, *Paul Temple Returns,* Butchers Film Service, 1952.
Clifford Brett, *Tread Softly,* Apex, 1952.
Jim Frobisher, *The House of the Arrow,* Associated British Films/Pathe, 1953.
Frank, *Isn't Life Wonderful!,* Pathe, 1953.
Sir Gawaine, *Knights of the Round Table,* Metro-Goldwyn-Mayer (MGM), 1953.
Dr. Michael Flynn, *Tonight's the Night* (also known as *Happy Ever After* and *O'Leary Night*), Pathe, 1954.
Sir Philip, *The Warriors* (also known as *The Dark Avenger*), Allied Artists, 1955.
Peter Darwin, *You Can't Escape,* Associated British Films/Pathe, 1955.
Flight Lieutenant Fearnley, *Battle Hell* (also known as *Yangtse Incidents*), Herbert Wilcox, 1956.
Paul Krempe, *The Curse of Frankenstein,* Warner Brothers, 1957.
Jim Dobson, *White Huntress* (also known as *Golden Ivory*), American International, 1957.
Mike, *Dunkirk,* MGM, 1958.
Commander Clayton, *The Bulldog Breed,* Rank, 1960.
Bob Murray, *Danger Tomorrow,* Allied Artists, 1960.
Major Wilson, *Foxhole in Cairo,* British Lion, 1960.
Pearson, *The Break,* Planet, 1962.
George Crossfield, *Murder at the Gallop,* MGM, 1963.
Captain Hanley, *55 Days at Peking,* Allied Artists, 1963.
Brian Maitland, *In Trouble with Eve* (also known as *In Walked Eve* and *Trouble with Eve*), Borde, 1964.
George Brant, *The Syndicate,* Schoenfeld, 1968.
Hardwick, *The Limbo Line,* London Independent Producers, 1969.

Auctioneer, *Brotherly Love* (also known as *Country Dance*), MGM, 1970.

Johnson, *The Looking Glass War*, Columbia, 1970.

Major Kemble, *Mosquito Squadron*, United Artists, 1970.

Captain Lockhart, *The Dogs of War*, United Artists, 1980.

Headmaster, *The Dollar Bottom* (short film), CIC, 1981.

Evan Gorley-Peters, *Sharma and Beyond*, Cinecom, 1983.

Headmaster, *Kipperbang* (also known as *P'Tang, Yang, Kipperbang*), MGM/United Artists, 1984.

Detective Inspector Baird, *Restless Natives*, Oxford/Thorn/EMI, 1985.

Godfrey, *Playing Away*, Film Four International, 1986.

Journalist, *Testimony*, Enterprise, 1987.

D. C. McKinnon, *The Kitchen Toto*, Cannon, 1987.

Also appeared in *Walter Scott*, 1970, and *Murder in Mind*.

TELEVISION APPEARANCES

Attorney General, *A Tale of Two Cities* (movie), CBS, 1980.

Quartering Commandant, *Brideshead Revisited* (mini-series), Granada, 1980-81, then *Great Performances*, PBS, 1982.

Boythorn, *Bleak House* (mini-series), BBC, then Arts and Entertainment, later PBS, 1985.

Albrecht Hoffman, *Hitler's SS: Portrait in Evil* (movie), NBC, 1985.

Also appeared as Vic, *The Reporters*, 1972; *The Pathfinders*, 1972; *The Inheritors*, 1973; *Mr. Goodall*, 1974-76; *The Prime of Miss Jean Brodie*, 1978; *Enemy of the People*, 1978; *Plane Makers*; *Tamer Tamed*; *Infinite Shoeblack*; *Morning Departure*; *The Human Touch*; *The Iron Harp*; *Sleeping Clergyman*; *The Naked Lady*; *For Services Rendered*; *The Bright One*; *Jango*; *Murder Swamp*; *She Died Young*; *The Nearly Man*; *The Button Man*; *Happy Returns*; *Endless-Aimless*; *The Queens Arms*; and *Shostakovich*.

STAGE APPEARANCES

Chitterlow, *Half a Sixpence*, Broadhurst Theatre, New York City, 1966.

Elector Friedrich Wilhelm, *The Prince of Homburg*, National Theatre Company, London, 1982.

Father Dolan, *The Shaughraun*, National Theatre Company, 1988.

Made stage debut at Park Theatre, Glasgow, Scotland.

WRITINGS:

Author of teleplays, including *House of Lies, End of the Tether, Landfall,* and *The Touch of a Dead Hand.**

VelJOHNSON, Reggie
See VelJOHNSON, Reginald

   *   *   *

VelJOHNSON, Reginald 1952-
(Reggie VelJohnson)

PERSONAL: Born August 16, 1952, in Queens, NY. *Education:* Attended Long Island Institute of Music and Arts; received a B.A. in theater from New York University; studied under Lloyd Richards.

ADDRESSES: Agent—Jeralyn Bagdley, Bagdley Connor, 9229 Sunset Blvd., Suite 607, Los Angeles, CA 90069. *Publicist*—Lori DeWaal, The Garrett Co., 6922 Hollywood Blvd., Suite 407, Los Angeles, CA 90028.

CAREER: Actor. Member of Joseph Papp's Black/Hispanic Shakespeare Company; national spokesman for Big Brothers of America "Pass It On" Program.

CREDITS:

TELEVISION APPEARANCES; SERIES

Carl Winslow, *Perfect Strangers*, ABC, 1988-89.
Carl Winslow, *Family Matters*, ABC, 1989—.

TELEVISION APPEARANCES; MOVIES

John Van Horn, *Quiet Victory: The Charlie Wedemeyer Story*, CBS, 1988.

Barry Gates, *The Bride in Black* (also known as *The Bride Wore Black*), ABC, 1990.

Judge, *Jury Duty: The Comedy*, ABC, 1990.

TELEVISION APPEARANCES; SPECIALS

Attitudes, Lifetime, 1986.
ABC's Comedy Sneak Peak, ABC, 1989.
Carl Winslow, *The ABC Saturday Morning Preview*, ABC, 1990.

Also appeared in *The Party Machine*, *The Home Show*, and *Live from L.A. with Tanya Hart*, all 1991.

TELEVISION APPEARANCES; EPISODIC

Appeared on *The Joan Rivers Show*, 1989; *New York Views*, KABC News (Los Angeles), and *Good Morning America*, all 1990; *Into the Night Starring Rick Dees*, *Hollywood Insider*, *The Byron Allen Show*, *Entertainment Tonight*, *Ebony Jet Showcase*, *AM Los Angeles*, *Regis and Kathy Lee*, *BET Screen Scene*, *The Arsenio Hall Show*, and *Personalities*, all 1991; *I'll Skate*, PBS, *The Equalizer*, CBS, *227*, NBC, *Doing Life*, and *When Hell Freezes Over.*

FILM APPEARANCES

Morgue attendant, *Wolfen*, Warner Brothers, 1981.
The Cotton Club, Orion, 1984.

(As Reggie VelJohnson) Jail Guard, *Ghostbusters,* Columbia, 1984.

Ambulance driver, *Remo Williams: The Adventure Begins . . . ,* Orion, 1985.

Crocodile Dundee, Paramount, 1986.

Armed and Dangerous, Columbia, 1986.

Sergeant Al Powell, *Die Hard,* Twentieth Century-Fox, 1988.

Detective David Sutton, *Turner and Hooch,* Buena Vista, 1989.

Sergeant Al Powell, *Die Hard 2,* Twentieth Century-Fox, 1990.

STAGE APPEARANCES

Duchess, Humpty-Dumpty, and the King of Hearts, *But Never Jam Today,* Longacre Theatre, New York City, 1979.

Mary Rydell, *Inacent Black,* Biltmore Theatre, New York City, 1981.

The World of Ben Caldwell, Henry Street Settlement's New Federal Theatre, New York City, 1982.

Fat Daddy, *Oh! Oh! Obesity!,* Henry Street Settlement's New Federal Theatre, 1984.

Eli, *Spell #7,* Crossroads Theatre Company, New Brunswick, NJ, 1987-88.

Also appeared in *Staggerlee,* Second Avenue Theatre; *The Dream Team,* Goodspeed Opera House; and *Honky Tonk Nights.*

W

WALDO, Janet 1930-

PERSONAL: Born in 1930; married Robert E. Lee (a playwright), 1948; children: one son, one daughter.

CAREER: Actress.

CREDITS:

RADIO APPEARANCES; SERIES

Title role, *Meet Corliss Archer,* CBS, 1943, ABC, 1950, CBS, 1954.

Emmy Lou, *The Adventures of Ozzie and Harriet,* CBS, beginning 1944.

Regular, *The Eddie Bracken Show,* NBC, 1945, CBS, 1946.

Janet, *Young Love,* CBS, 1949-50.

Made radio commercials, 1990-91.

TELEVISION APPEARANCES; SERIES

Marge, *The Lucy Show,* CBS, 1962.

Judy Jetson, *The Jetsons* (animated), ABC, 1962, CBS, 1965, NBC, 1966.

Libby Freeman, *Valentine's Day,* ABC, 1964.

Voice of Anastasia Antnik, *The Atom Ant/Secret Squirrel Show* (animated), NBC, 1965.

Jenny, *Space Kiddettes* (animated), NBC, 1966.

Nancy, *Schazzan!* (animated), CBS, 1967.

Penelope Pitstop, *The Wacky Races* (animated), CBS, 1968.

Jenny Trent, *The Cattanooga Cats* (animated), ABC, 1969.

Penelope Pitstop, *The Perils of Penelope* (animated), CBS, 1969.

Josie, *Josie and the Pussycats* (animated), CBS, 1970.

Help! It's The Hair Bear Bunch (animated), CBS, 1971.

Josie, *Josie and the Pussycats In Outer Space* (animated), CBS, 1972.

Henrietta, *The Roman Holiday* (animated), NBC, 1972.

The Amazing Chan and the Chan Clan (animated), CBS, 1972.

Voice of Morticia and Grandmama Addams, *The Addams Family* (animated), NBC, 1973.

Speed Buggy (animated), CBS, 1973.

Inch High, Private Eye (animated), NBC, 1973.

Jabberjaw (animated), ABC, 1976.

Princess, *Battle of the Planets* (animated), syndicated, 1978.

Jokebook (animated), NBC, 1982.

TELEVISION APPEARANCES; EPISODIC

Guest, "The Young Fans," *I Love Lucy,* CBS, 1952.

Emmy Lou, *The Adventures of Ozzie and Harriet,* ABC, 1963.

Mother in law, *The Flintstones,* ABC, 1963.

OTHER TELEVISION APPEARANCES

Voice of Beauty, *Beauty and the Beast* (animated special), CBS, 1983.

Provided voice for Little Girl and Lady Bird, *The Tiny Tree* (animated), 1977; Miss Switch, *Miss Switch to the Rescue* (animated), 1981; *Daniel Boone* (animated), 1981; *Funtastic World of Hanna-Barbera Arena Show,* 1981; *The Puppy Saves the Circus* (animated), 1981; voice of Mrs. Jones, PA voice, and Lady in Street, *Yogi Bear's All-Star Comedy Christmas Caper* (animated), 1982; Voice of mother and of Old Lady, *The Secret World of Og* (animated), 1983; *The Little Prince* (animated), 1984; *Yogi's Treasure Hunt* (animated), 1985; Lilac, *Smurfily Ever After* (animated), 1985; Judy Jetson, *Rockin' with Judy Jetson* (animated movie), 1988; Hogatha, *The Smurfs* (animated), 1988-89; voice of Alice, *Alice in Wonderland* (animated), Hanna Barbera; voice of Princess and Harp, *Jack and the Beanstalk,* Hanna Barbera; also in *Yogi's First*

Christmas and *Shake, Rattle, and Roll*—"Fender Bender," Hanna Barbera.

FILM APPEARANCES

Hunted Men (also known as *Crime Gives Orders*), Paramount, 1938.

Cafe Society, Paramount, 1939.

Honeymoon in Bali (also known as *My Love for Yours*), Paramount, 1939.

Receptionist, *Our Neighbors—The Carters,* Paramount, 1939.

Stella, *The Star-Maker,* Paramount, 1939.

Ruth Phelps, *Tom Sawyer, Detective,* Paramount, 1939.

Gwen, *What a Life,* Paramount, 1939.

Simone, *Zaza,* Paramount, 1939.

Switch Board Operator, *The Farmer's Daughter,* Paramount, 1940.

Elsa, *Waterloo Bridge,* Metro-Goldwyn-Mayer, 1940.

Miss Willowboughy, *Those Were the Days* (also known as *Good Old School Days at Good Old Siwash*), Paramount, 1940.

Jan, *Silver Stallion,* Monogram, 1941.

Ellen Grant, *The Bandit Trail,* RKO Radio Pictures, 1941.

Mary Cook, *Land of the Open Range,* RKO Radio Pictures, 1941.

The Man Called Flintstone (animated; also known as *That Man Flintstone*), Columbia, 1966.

Fantastic Planet (animated; also known as *La Planete Sauvage*), Ceskoslovensky Film Export, 1973.

Voice of Tinette, *Heidi's Song* (animated), Paramount, 1982.

Jetsons: The Movie (animated), Universal, 1990.

STAGE APPEARANCES

Sister, *I Never Sang for My Father,* Theatre 40, Beverly Hills, CA, 1970.

Olivia, *Twelfth Night,* California Artists, 1991.

*   *   *

WALSH, J. T.

PERSONAL: Born in San Francisco, CA.

CAREER: Actor. Former salesman.

CREDITS:

FILM APPEARANCES

Man in bar, *Eddie Macon's Run,* Universal, 1983.

Deputy Anderson, *Hard Choices,* Screenland-Breakout, 1984.

Ed Smythe, *Hannah and Her Sisters,* Orion, 1986.

Jerome Cade, *Power,* Twentieth Century-Fox, 1986.

Sergeant Dickerson, *Good Morning, Vietnam,* Buena Vista, 1987.

Businessman, *House of Games,* Orion, 1987.

Wing, *Tin Men,* Buena Vista, 1987.

Hotel manager, *Things Change,* Columbia, 1988.

Maguire, *Tequila Sunrise,* Warner Brothers, 1988.

Allen Habel, *The Big Picture,* Columbia, 1989.

Bob Woodward, *Wired,* Taurus, 1989.

Dr. Santana, *Dad,* Universal, 1989.

Francis Mahoney, *Why Me?,* Triumph, 1990.

Charles F. Drucker, *Crazy People,* Paramount, 1990.

Quinn, *The Russia House,* Metro-Goldwyn-Mayer/United Artists, 1990.

Cole, *The Grifters,* Miramax, 1990.

Martin Swayzak, *Backdraft,* Universal, 1991.

Also appeared as Michael Tarlow, *Narrow Margin,* 1990.

TELEVISION APPEARANCES

Little Gloria . . . Happy at Last (movie), NBC, 1982.

Jacobo Timerman: Prisoner without a Name, Cell without a Number (movie), NBC, 1983.

Major Vegvary, *Right to Kill?* (movie), ABC, 1985.

TV announcer, *Tough Cookies,* CBS, 1986.

Captain Quail, *On the Edge,* NBC, 1987.

Colonel McKinney, *Sidney Sheldon's "Windmills of the Gods"* (movie), CBS, 1988.

STAGE APPEARANCES

Kit Carson, *Yucca Flats,* Manhattan Theatre Club, New York City, 1973.

Main man, *Alive and Well in Argentina,* Theatre at Saint Clement's, New York City, 1974.

Ensemble, *In Our Time,* Theatre at Saint Clement's, 1974.

Able, *Enter a Free Man,* St. Clement's Church, 1974.

Marvin, *Workers,* St. Clement's Church, 1975.

Palfrey, "Endecott and the Red Cross," and Man in periwig, "My Kinsman, Major Molineux," in *The Old Glory: A Trilogy* (triple-bill), American Place Theatre, New York City, 1976.

Bobby, *American Buffalo,* Saint Clement's Theatre, 1976.

Richard, *Rib Cage,* Manhattan Theatre Club, 1978.

Goose, *April 2, 1979: The Day the Blanchardville, N.C. Political Action and Poker Club Got the Bomb,* WPA Theatre, New York City, 1978.

Amazing Grace, New Dramatists, Inc., New York City, 1978.

Otherwise Engaged, Cincinnati Playhouse, Cincinnati, OH, 1978-79.

Good Evening, Stage West, West Springfield, MA, 1978-79.

Sir Roger Brakenbury, *Richard III,* Cort Theatre, New York City, 1979.

Dennis Quinlan, *Last Licks,* Longacre Theatre, New York City, 1979.

Ice, Manhattan Theatre Club, 1979.

Mary Barnes, Long Wharf Theatre, New Haven, CT, 1979-80.

Brewster, Rudy, Ryan, Stanislaus, and Sheriff, *The American Clock,* Harold Clurman Theatre, New York City, 1980.

Cymbeline, Hartford Stage Company, Hartford, CT, 1980-81.

Jim Beam, *Rose,* Cort Theatre, 1981.

The Suicide, Yale Repertory Theatre, New Haven, CT, 1980-81.

Macduff, *MacBeth,* Circle in the Square, New York City, 1982.

Kenneth Baxter, *This Story of Yours,* Long Wharf Theatre, 1981-82.

Edouard, *Lumiere,* Ark Theatre Company, New York City, 1982.

a/k/a Tennessee, South Street Theater, New York City, 1982.

Marcellus, Player, and English ambassador, *Hamlet,* New York Shakespeare Festival, Public Theater, 1982-83.

Winter, *Half a Lifetime,* Manhattan Theatre Club, 1983.

Frank, *Faith Healer,* Vineyard Theatre, New York City, 1983.

John Williamson, *Glengarry Glen Ross,* Goodman Theatre, Chicago, IL, 1983-84, then John Golden Theatre, New York City, 1984.

Title role, *Terry Neal's Future,* in *Marathon '86,* Ensemble Studio Theatre, New York City, 1985-86.

Dr. Bazelon and Manville, *The Day Room,* Manhattan Theatre Club, City Center Stage, 1987-88.

MAJOR TOURS

John Williamson, *Glengarry Glen Ross,* U.S. cities, 1986.*

* * *

WARD, Fred 1943-

PERSONAL: Born in 1943 in San Diego, CA. *Education:* Studied at Herbert Berghof Studios.

ADDRESSES: Agent—Jerry Scott, STE Representation, 9301 Wilshire Blvd., Suite 312, Beverly Hills, CA 90210. *Publicist*—Ken Amorosano Public Relations, 3327 Deronda Dr., Los Angeles, CA 90028.

CAREER: Actor. Member of Sam Shepherd's Magic Theatre. Formerly worked as a truck loader, a janitor, a logger, a cook, a crop picker, and a construction worker. *Military service:* Served in U.S. Air Force.

CREDITS:

FILM APPEARANCES

John Anglin, *Escape from Alcatraz,* Paramount, 1979.

Jack, *Carny,* United Artists, 1980.

Rifleman Lonnie Reece, *Southern Comfort,* Twentieth Century-Fox, 1981.

Title role, *Timerider: The Adventures of Lyle Swann,* Jensen-Farley, 1982.

Morgan, *Silkwood,* Twentieth Century-Fox, 1983.

Wilkes, *Uncommon Valor,* Paramount, 1983.

Gus Grissom, *The Right Stuff,* Warner Brothers, 1984.

Biscuits Toohey, *Swing Shift,* Warner Brothers, 1984.

Lou Fimple, *Secret Admirer,* Orion, 1985.

Sheldon, *UFOria,* Universal, 1985.

Title role, *Remo Williams: The Adventure Begins . . . ,* Orion, 1985.

The teacher, *Train of Dreams,* National Film Board, 1987.

Gary Marshetta, *The Prince of Pennsylvania,* New Line, 1988.

Roone Dimmick, *Big Business,* Buena Vista, 1988.

Sergeant Benjamin Dix, *Off Limits,* Twentieth Century-Fox, 1988.

Earl Basset, *Tremors* (also known as *Dead Silence*), Universal, 1990.

Henry Miller, *Henry and June,* Universal, 1990.

Pauling, *Backtrack* (also known as *Catchfire*), Live Entertainment, 1990.

Sergeant Hoke Mosely, *Miami Blues* (also see below), Orion, 1990.

Also appeared as Lenny in *Tilt,* 1979, and as Crouch in *The Price of Life,* 1988; also appeared in *No Available Witness, Warriors of the Wasteland,* and *Saigon.*

FILM WORK

Executive producer, *Miami Blues,* Orion, 1990.

TELEVISION APPEARANCES; MOVIES

Ned Christie, *Belle Starr,* CBS, 1980.

Lucky Boone, *Florida Straits,* HBO, 1986.

TELEVISION APPEARANCES; EPISODIC

"Noon Wine," *American Playhouse,* PBS, 1985.

STAGE APPEARANCES

Appeared in *The Glass Menagerie, One Flew Over the Cuckoo's Nest,* and *Find Your Way Home.**

* * *

WASHINGTON, Denzel 1954-

PERSONAL: Born December 28, 1954, in Mt. Vernon, NY; son of Denzel Washington (a minister); parents divorced; married Pauletta Pearson (an actress and singer); children: John David, Katia. *Education:* Received B.A. in journalism from Fordham University; studied acting at

American Conservatory Theatre, San Francisco, and in New York with Wynn Handman.

ADDRESSES: Agent—Ed Limato, International Creative Management, 8899 Beverly Blvd., Los Angeles, CA, 90048. *Publicist*—Lisa Kasteler, PMK Public Relations, Inc., 955 S. Carillo Dr., No. 200, Los Angeles, CA 90048.

CAREER: Actor.

AWARDS, HONORS: Obie Award (with Adolph Caesar and Larry Riley), distinguished ensemble performance, 1982, for *A Soldier's Play;* National Association for the Advancement of Colored People (NAACP) Image awards, actor, 1988, for *Cry Freedom,* and best performance by a supporting actor, 1990, for *Glory;* Golden Globe Award, best supporting actor, 1989, for *Glory;* Academy Award, best supporting actor, 1990, for *Glory;* Audelco Award for *When the Chickens Came Home to Roost.*

CREDITS:

TELEVISION APPEARANCES; SERIES

Dr. Phillip Chandler, *St. Elsewhere,* NBC, 1982-88.

TELEVISION APPEARANCES; MOVIES

Robert Eldridge, *Wilma,* NBC, 1977.
Kirk, *Flesh and Blood,* CBS, 1979.
Martin Sawyer, *License to Kill,* CBS, 1984.
Title role, *The George McKenna Story,* CBS, 1986.

OTHER TELEVISION APPEARANCES

Nineteenth Annual NAACP Image Awards, NBC, 1987.
Freedomfest: Nelson Mandela's Seventieth Birthday Celebration (rock 'n' roll concert), FBC, 1988.
Narrator, *Baka: People of the Forest* (National Geographic special), PBS, 1989.
Motown 30: What's Goin' On (music special), CBS, 1990.
Presenter, *Sixty-second Annual Academy Awards Presentation,* ABC, 1990.
Twenty-second Annual NAACP Image Awards, NBC, 1990.
Presenter, *Sixty-third Annual Academy Awards Presentation,* ABC, 1991.

Hosted *Twenty-third Annual NAACP Image Awards,* 1991.

STAGE APPEARANCES

Aediles, *Coriolanus,* New York Shakespeare Festival (NYSF), Delacorte Theater, New York City, 1979.
Tommy Paul, *One Tiger to a Hill,* Manhattan Theatre Club, New York City, 1980.
Pfc. Melvin Peterson, *A Soldier's Play,* Negro Ensemble Company, Theatre Four, New York City, 1981-82, then Goodman Theatre, Chicago, IL, 1982-83.

Pfc. Melvin Peterson, *A Soldier's Play,* Center Theatre Group, Mark Taper Forum, Los Angeles, CA, 1982-83.
Frank, *Every Goodbye Ain't Gone,* Louis Abrons Arts for Living Center, New Federal Theater, New York City, 1984.
Title role, *Richard III,* Delacorte Theater, New York City, 1991.
Malcolm Shabazz, *When the Chickens Came Home to Roost,* produced with *Zora* (double-bill), Louis Abrons Arts for Living Center, New Federal Theater, 1981.

Also appeared in *The Emperor Jones* (Off-Broadway debut), *Othello, Mighty Gents, Beckett, Spell #7, Ceremonies in Dark Old Men,* and *Split Second.* Appeared in *Checkmates,* Westwood Playhouse, Los Angeles, CA.

FILM APPEARANCES

Roger Porter, *Carbon Copy,* Avco Embassy, 1981.
Pfc. Melvin Peterson, *A Soldier's Story,* Columbia, 1984.
Arnold Billings, *Power,* Twentieth Century-Fox, 1986.
Stephen Biko, *Cry Freedom,* Universal, 1987.
Reuben James, *For Queen and Country,* Atlantic, 1988.
Xavier Quinn, *The Mighty Quinn,* Metro-Goldwyn-Mayer/United Artists, 1989.
Trip, *Glory,* Tri Star, 1990.
Bleek Gilliam, *Mo' Better Blues,* Universal, 1990.
Napoleon Stone, *Heart Condition,* New Line Cinema, 1990.

Also appeared in *Reunion,* 1988; *Mississippi Masala;* and *Ricochet.*

OTHER FILM APPEARANCES; MUSIC PERFORMER

"Cakewalk into Town," *The Mighty Quinn,* Metro-Goldwyn-Mayer/United Artists, 1989.
"Pop Top 40," *Mo' Better Blues,* Universal, 1990.

WRITINGS:

Author of book on the making of *Mo' Better Blues,* for Simon & Schuster.

OTHER SOURCES:

PERIODICALS

Hollywood Reporter, February 1, 1988.
New York, August 13, 1990.
New York Times, December 26, 1987.
Premiere, August, 1990.
Rolling Stone, December 3, 1987.
Sunday Star-Ledger, November 29, 1987.

WERTENBAKER, L. T.
See WERTENBAKER, Timberlake

*   *   *

WERTENBAKER, Lael
See WERTENBAKER, Timberlake

*   *   *

WERTENBAKER, Lael Tucker
See WERTENBAKER, Timberlake

*   *   *

WERTENBAKER, Timberlake 1909-
(Lael Tucker, L. T. Wertenbaker, Lael Wertenbaker, Lael Tucker Wertenbaker)

PERSONAL: Full name, Lael Louisiana Timberlake Tucker; born March 28, 1909, in Bradford, PA; daughter of Royal K. and Juliet (Luttrell) Tucker; married Charles Christian Wertenbaker (a writer and editor), 1942 (died, 1953); married Bramwell Fletcher (an actor), 1970; children: (first marriage) Christian Tucker, Lael Louisiana Timberlake. *Education:* Attended schools near St. Jean-de-Luz, France; attended University of Louisville, KY. *Politics:* Independent. *Religion:* Episcopalian.

ADDRESSES: Agent—c/o Michael Imison Playwrights, 28 Almeida St., London N1, England.

CAREER: Writer. Theatre Guild, Inc., New York City, treasurer and road agent, 1928-38; *Time* magazine, reporter, foreign correspondent, and war correspondent, 1938-47; Boston University, MA, visiting professor, 1974-76; lecturer, New School for Social Research, Massachusetts Institute of Technology, and at writer's conferences at Rollins College and Wesleyan University; consulting editor at McGraw-Hill Book Company, Putnam Publishing Group, and Little, Brown & Company; Thames Television Resident Writer at the Royal Court Theatre, London, England; Arts Council Resident Writer for Shared Experience Theatre Company. Vice president, History in Sound and Light Corporation; member, Monadnock Music (member of board of directors), National Repertory Theatre, MacDowell Colony, Ossabaw Island Foundation, and New Hampshire Commission on the Arts (member of advisory board). Taught French in Greece for one year.

MEMBER: Concern for Dying (member of advisory board); Overseas PEN Club.

AWARDS, HONORS: All-London Playwrights' Award for *The Third;* honorary doctorate, Keene State College, 1973; Arts Council of Great Britain grant, 1983; *Plays and Players* Most Promising Playwright Award, 1985, for *The Grace of Mary Traverse;* Laurence Olivier Award, best play, 1988, and Antoinette Perry Award nomination (with others), best play, 1991, both for *Our Country's Good;* Mrs. Giles Whiting Award for general body of work; *Evening Standard* Most Promising Playwright Award.

WRITINGS:

PLAYS

New Anatomies (produced at Women's Theatre Group, I.C.A. Theatre, London, 1981, and Space 603, The Directors Company, New York City, 1987), Faber, 1984.

Translator, "False Admissions" and "Successful Strategies," *Successful Strategies,* Lyric Studio Theatre, London, 1983.

Abel's Sister, produced at Theatre Upstairs, London, 1984, produced in New York City, 1985.

The Grace of Mary Traverse (produced at Royal Court Theatre, London, 1985), Faber, 1985.

Adaptor and translator, *Mephisto,* produced by Royal Shakespeare Company (RSC) at Barbican Theatre, London, 1986.

Our Country's Good, produced at Royal Court Theatre, 1988, then Center Theatre Group, Mark Taper Forum, Los Angeles, CA, and Wharf Theatre, Sydney Australia, 1989, later Nederlander Theatre, New York City, 1991.

The Love of the Nightingale (produced by RSC, 1989, produced by L.A. Theatre Works, Edgemar Theatre, Los Angeles, CA, 1990), published in *The Love and the Nightingale* [and] *The Grace of Mary Traverse,* Faber, 1990.

Also author of *This Is No Place for Tallulah Bankhead,* produced in London, England, 1978; *The Third,* produced in London, 1980; *Second Sentence,* produced in Brighton, England, 1980; *Breaking Through,* produced in London, 1980; *Case to Answer,* produced in London, 1980, then in Ithaca, New York, 1981; *Inside Out,* produced in Stoke-on-Trent, England, 1982; and *Home Leave,* produced in Ipswich, Suffolk, England, 1982.

Translator of Maurice Maeterlink's *Pelleas and Melisande* and Federico Garcia Lorca's *The House of Bernarda Alba.*

SCREENPLAYS

The Children, Film Four International, 1990.

Also author of *Do Not Disturb.*

RADIO PLAYS

Translator, *Leocadia* (broadcast, 1985), Methuen, 1987.

Also translator of *La Dispute,* 1987.

OTHER

(Under name Lael Tucker) *Lament for Four Virgins* (novel), 1952.

(Under name Lael Tucker) *Festival,* Random House, 1954.

(Under name Lael Tucker Wertenbaker) *Death of a Man,* Random House, 1957.

(Under name Lael Tucker Wertenbaker) *Mister Junior* (biography), Pageant, 1958.

(Under name Lael Tucker Wertenbaker; with Suzanne Gleaves) *Tip and Dip* (juvenile) Lippincott, 1960.

(Under name Lael Tucker Wertenbaker; with Gleaves) *Mercy Percy* (juvenile), Lippincott, 1961.

(Under name L. T. Wertenbaker; with Gleaves) *You and the Armed Services* (nonfiction), Simon & Schuster, 1961.

(Under name Lael Tucker Wertenbaker) *The Eye of the Lion* (novel), Little, Brown, 1965.

(Under name Lael Tucker Wertenbaker) *The Afternoon Women* (novel), Little, Brown, 1966.

(Under name Lael Tucker Wertenbaker; with Maudie Basserman) *The Hotchkiss School: A Portrait,* Time-Life, 1966.

(Under name Lael Wertenbaker; with editors of Time-Life Books) *The World of Pablo Picasso,* Time-Life, 1967.

(Under name Lael Wertenbaker) *Unbidden Guests* (novel), Little, Brown, 1970.

(Under name Lael Wertenbaker; with Jean Rosenthal) *The Magic of Light: The Craft and Career of Jean Rosenthal, Pioneer in Lighting for the Modern Stage,* Little, Brown, 1972.

(Under name Lael Wertenbaker) *Perilous Voyage* (novel), Little, Brown, 1975.

(Under name Lael Wertenbaker) *To Mend the Heart* (nonfiction), Viking, 1980.

*   *   *

WESTMORE, Michael
See WESTMORE, Michael G.

*   *   *

WESTMORE, Michael G.   1938-
(Michael Westmore, Mike Westmore)

PERSONAL: Full name, Michael George Westmore; born March 22, 1938, in Hollywood, CA; son of Montague George (a makeup artist) and Edith Adeline (McCarrier) Westmore; married Marion Christine Bergeson, December 4, 1966; children: Michael George, Michele, McKen-

zie. *Education:* University of California at Santa Barbara, B.A., 1961.

ADDRESSES: Office—Star Trek: The Next Generation, Paramount Pictures, 5555 Melrose Ave., Los Angeles, CA 90038.

CAREER: Makeup artist and special effects designer. Universal City Studios, Universal City, CA, staff makeup artist, 1961-64, assistant department head of makeup, 1964-70; free-lance makeup artist, various studios, Hollywood, CA, 1971—; founder and director, M. G. Westmore Ltd. (makeup lab for special makeup and effects), 1971—. Consultant, researcher, and lecturer in therapeutic cosmetics for medical associations; president, Hollywood Magic Cosmetics, 1985—; instructor at Los Angeles Valley College and University of California at Los Angeles. Exhibited work at California Museum of Science and Industry, 1981. *Military service:* U.S. Army, 1956.

MEMBER: International Alliance of Theatrical Stage Employees, Society of Make Up Artists, Academy of Motion Picture Arts and Sciences, Academy of Television Arts and Sciences, Makeup Artists and Hair Stylists Guild, Vikings of Scandia, Lambda Chi Alpha.

AWARDS, HONORS: Emmy awards, individual achievement in makeup, 1973 (with Marvin Westmore), for *Frankenstein,* 1976 (with Del Armstrong), for *Eleanor and Franklin,* 1984, for *Why Me?,* 1985, for *The Three Wishes of Billy Grier,* 1987, for *Amazing Stories* episode "Without Diana," and 1988, for *Star Trek: The Next Generation* episode "Conspiracy"; Emmy Award nominations, individual achievement in children's programming, 1976 (with Louis Phillippi), for *Land of the Lost,* and 1978, for *Once upon a Brothers Grimm;* Emmy Award nominations, individual achievement in makeup, 1977 (with Ed Butterworth and Charlie Schram), for *Million Dollar Rip-off,* 1978 (with Hank Edds and Lynn Reynolds), for *The Amazing Howard Hughes,* 1978 (with Frank C. Westmore), *A Love Affair: The Eleanor and Lou Gehrig Story,* 1983, for *The Day After,* 1986, for *Annihilator,* 1986, for *Amazing Stories* episode "Gather Ye Acorns," 1987, for *MacGyver,* 1988, for *Star Trek* episode "Coming of Age," 1988, for *Highway to Heaven* episode "I Was a Middle-Aged Werewolf," 1989, for *David,* and 1989, for *Star Trek* episode "A Matter of Honor"; admitted to Motion Picture Hall of Fame, 1981; Academy Award nominations, best makeup, 1984, for *2010,* and 1987, for *The Clan of the Cave Bear;* Academy Award (with others), best makeup, 1985, for *Mask.*

CREDITS:

FILM WORK; MAKEUP ARTIST, EXCEPT WHERE INDICATED

Flower Drum Song, Universal, 1961.
The List of Adrian Messenger, Universal, 1963.

(As Michael Westmore) *Harlow,* Magna, 1965.

Gambit, Universal, 1966.

The Andromeda Strain, Universal, 1971.

(As Mike Westmore) *Rocky,* United Artists, 1976.

(As Mike Westmore) *Trackdown,* United Artists, 1976.

(As Michael Westmore; with Christian Smith) *New York, New York,* United Artists, 1977.

F.I.S.T., United Artists, 1978.

Capricorn One, Warner Brothers, 1978.

Paradise Alley, Universal, 1978.

Circle of Iron (also known as *The Silent Flute*), Avco Embassy, 1979.

(As Michael Westmore) *Rocky II,* United Artists, 1979.

Raging Bull, United Artists, 1980.

True Confessions, United Artists, 1981.

Blade Runner, Warner Brothers, 1982.

First Blood, Orion, 1982.

Rocky III, Metro-Goldwyn-Mayer/United Artists, 1982.

Uncommon Valor, Paramount, 1983.

The Star Chamber, Twentieth Century-Fox, 1983.

(As Michael Westmore; with Michele Burke) *Iceman,* Universal, 1984.

(As Michael Westmore) Makeup supervisor, *2010,* United Artists, 1984.

(With John M. Elliot, Zoltan Elek, and Tommy Cole) *Mask,* Universal, 1985.

(With Michele Burke) *The Clan of the Cave Bear,* Warner Brothers, 1986.

(As Michael Westmore) Special makeup designer (with Mark Reedall), *Psycho III,* Universal, 1986.

(As Michael Westmore) Makeup conceptual designer, *Masters of the Universe,* Cannon, 1987.

Project X, Twentieth Century-Fox, 1987.

(As Michael Westmore) Makeup designer, *Roxanne,* Columbia, 1987.

(As Michael Westmore) Special effects makeup, *Stripped to Kill,* Concorde, 1987.

(As Michael Westmore) Special makeup designer, *Johnny Handsome,* Tri-Star, 1989.

Special makeup designer, *The Blood of Heroes,* New Line Cinema, 1990.

Rocky V, United Artists, 1990.

Texasville, Columbia, 1990.

Revenge, Columbia, 1990.

Also makeup artist for *Escape to Victory,* 1981; assistant editor, *Halloween V: The Revenge of Michael Meyers,* 1989.

TELEVISION WORK; MOVIES; MAKEUP ARTIST, EXCEPT WHERE INDICATED

(With Marvin Westmore) *Frankenstein,* ABC, 1973.

(With Del Armstrong) *Eleanor and Franklin,* ABC, 1976.

(With Ed Butterworth and Charlie Schram) *The Million Dollar Rip-off,* NBC, 1977.

(With Hank Edds and Lynn Reynolds), *The Amazing Howard Hughes,* CBS, 1977.

Deathmoon, CBS, 1978.

(With Frank C. Westmore) *A Love Affair: The Eleanor and Lou Gehrig Story,* NBC, 1978.

Once upon a Brothers Grimm, CBS, 1978.

Makeup creator, *The Day After,* ABC, 1983.

Special makeup designer, *Why Me?,* ABC, 1984.

(With others) *The Three Wishes of Billy Grier,* ABC, 1984.

Malice in Wonderland, CBS, 1985.

The Burning Bed, NBC, 1985.

The Rape of Richard Beck, ABC, 1985.

The Annihilator, NBC, 1986.

The Defiant Ones, ABC, 1986.

There Must Be a Pony, ABC, 1986.

OTHER TELEVISION WORK; MAKEUP ARTIST, EXCEPT WHERE INDICATED

Blackout (special), HBO, 1985.

Makeup supervisor, *Star Trek: The Next Generation* (syndicated), 1987—.

Makeup artist for television series *Amazing Stories,* NBC, *MacGyver,* ABC, *Night Gallery,* and *The Munsters;* makeup artist for special *Mabel and Max,* 1987, and special makeup for specials *David,* 1988, and *Remo Williams,* 1988. Also makeup artist for *Land of the Lost, Skullduggery, Redd Fox Show, Evolution of Man, Highway to Heaven, thirtysomething,* and *Cheers.*

WRITINGS:

The Art of Theatrical Makeup for Stage and Screen, McGraw, 1973.

Contributor of chapters on cosmetics to medical books concerning plastic surgery and the treatment of burn victims.

SIDELIGHTS: Michael G. Westmore's work has been exhibited in Atlantic City for Universal Studios, in the traveling special effects exhibit "The Makeup Artistry of Michael Westmore," 1987-91, and is included in the permanent exhibit "2010" at the American Museum of the Moving Image in Astoria, New York. Westmore is the thirteenth member of his family to pursue a career as a makeup artist in film and television.

OTHER SOURCES:

BOOKS

(Frank Westmore and Muriel Davidson) *Westmores of Hollywood,* Lippincott, 1976.

PERIODICALS

Theatre Crafts, August/September, 1990.

WESTMORE, Mike
See WESTMORE, Michael G.

*   *   *

WETTIG, Patricia 1951-

PERSONAL: Born December 4, 1951, in Cincinnati, OH; married Ken Olin (an actor), 1982; children: Clifford, Roxanne. *Education:* Graduated from Temple University; attended Ohio Wesleyan University and University of Aberdeen, Scotland; studied with Bill Esper at the Neighborhood Playhouse.

ADDRESSES: Agent—Bob Gersh, The Gersh Agency, 232 North Canon Dr., Beverly Hills, CA 90210.

CAREER: Actress. Previously a personal dresser to Shirley MacLaine; member of the Circle Repertory Company for seven years.

AWARDS, HONORS: Emmy Awards, best supporting actress in a drama, 1988, and best actress in a drama, 1990, both for *thirtysomething;* Golden Globe Award, best actress in a drama, 1990, for *thirtysomething.*

CREDITS:

TELEVISION APPEARANCES; SERIES

Joanne McFadden, *St. Elsewhere,* NBC, 1986.
Joanne Morrison, *St. Elsewhere,* NBC, 1987.
Nancy Weston, *thirtysomething,* ABC, 1987-1991.

TELEVISION APPEARANCES; EPISODIC

Mrs. Glasband, *L.A. Law,* NBC, 1987.

Also appeared in *Hill Street Blues,* NBC.

STAGE APPEARANCES

Crimes of the Heart, Loretto-Hilton Repertory Theatre, St. Louis, MO, 1979.
(Broadway debut) The girl, *Innocent Thoughts, Harmless Intentions,* Circle Repertory Company, Circle Repertory Theatre, New York City, 1980.
Rose, *The Woolgatherer,* Circle Repertory Company, Circle Repertory Theatre, 1980.
Girl, *Childe Byron,* Circle Repertory Company, Circle Repertory Theatre, 1981.
Olive, *A Tale Told,* Circle Repertory Company, Circle Repertory Theatre, 1981.
Janine, *Threads,* Circle Repertory Company, Circle Repertory Theatre, 1981.
Jennie Mae, *The Diviners,* Circle Repertory Company, Circle Repertory Theatre, 1981.
A Streetcar Named Desire, Theatre by the Sea, Portsmouth, NH, 1982.

The Dining Room, Astor Place Theatre, New York City, 1982.
Clear Glass Marbles, *Talking With,* Center Theatre Group, Taper Too Theatre, Los Angeles, CA, 1984.

FILM APPEARANCES

Guilty by Suspicion, Warner Brothers, 1991.
Barbara Robbins, *City Slickers,* Columbia, 1991.

OTHER SOURCES:

PERIODICALS

Entertainment Weekly, February 22, 1991.

*   *   *

WHALLEY, Joanne
See WHALLEY-KILMER, Joanne

*   *   *

WHALLEY-KILMER, Joanne 1964-
(Joanne Whalley)

PERSONAL: Born in 1964 in Salford, England; married Val Kilmer (an actor).

ADDRESSES: Agent—Brian Lourd, Creative Artists Agency, 9830 Wilshire Blvd., Beverly Hills, CA 90212.

CAREER: Actress.

AWARDS, HONORS: Olivier Award nomination, Best Actress, 1985; *Theatre World* Award, 1989, for *What the Butler Saw.*

CREDITS:

FILM APPEARANCES; AS JOANNE WHALLEY, EXCEPT WHERE INDICATED

Groupie, *Pink Floyd—The Wall,* Metro-Goldwyn-Mayer/United Artists (MGM/UA), 1982.
Christine, *Dance with a Stranger,* Twentieth Century-Fox, 1985.
Mary Hall, *The Good Father,* Skouras, 1986.
Cheryl, *No Surrender,* Norstar, 1986.
Sorsha, *Willow,* MGM/UA, 1988.
Anna, *Popielusko* (also known as *To Kill a Priest* and *Le Complot*), Columbia, 1989.
(As Joanne Whalley-Kilmer) Christine Keeler, *Scandal,* Miramax, 1989.
(As Joanne Whalley-Kilmer) Fay Forrester, *Kill Me Again,* MGM/UA, 1989.
The Big Man, Miramax, 1991.

STAGE APPEARANCES; AS JOANNE WHALLEY, EXCEPT WHERE INDICATED

Maria, *Bows and Arrows,* Young Writers' Festival, Royal Court Theatre, London, 1982.

Rita, *Rita, Sue, and Bob Too,* Young Writers' Festival, Royal Court Theatre, 1982.

Gilly Brown, *The Genius,* English Stage Company, Royal Court Theatre, 1983.

Title role, *Kate,* Bush Theatre, London, 1983.

Coquart and Esther van Gobseck, *The Crimes of Vautrin,* Joint Stock Theatre Company, Almeida Theatre, London, 1983.

June, *The Pope's Wedding,* Royal Court Theatre, 1984.

Pam, *Saved,* Royal Court Theatre, 1984.

Dewey Dell, *As I Lay Dying,* National Theatre Company, Cottesloe Theatre, London, 1985.

Bianca, *Women Beware Women,* Royal Court Theatre, 1986.

Masha, *Three Sisters,* Greenwich Theatre, London, 1987.

(As Joanne Whalley-Kilmer) Geraldine Barklay, *What the Butler Saw,* Manhattan Theatre Club, City Center Theatre, New York City, 1989.

TELEVISION APPEARANCES; MINI-SERIES; AS JOANNE WHALLEY

Emma Craven, *Edge of Darkness,* BBC, then PBS, 1986.

Nurse Mills, *The Singing Detective,* BBC, then *Channel Crossings,* PBS, 1988.

TELEVISION APPEARANCES; EPISODIC

Appeared in *Bergerac.*

OTHER TELEVISION APPEARANCES

(As Joanne Whalley) Fan, *A Christmas Carol* (movie), CBS, 1984.

Also appeared in the movies *A Kind of Loving; A Quiet Life; The Gentle Touch;* and *Reilly;* appeared in the series *Crown Court,* Granada.

OTHER SOURCES:

PERIODICALS

Premiere, March, 1991.*

* * *

WHITMAN, Stuart 1928-

PERSONAL: Born February 1, 1928, in San Francisco, CA. *Education:* Studied drama at Ben Bard Drama College and Los Angeles City College.

CAREER: Actor. Competed as a light heavyweight boxer. *Military service:* Army Corps of Engineers, 1945-46.

AWARDS, HONORS: Academy Award nomination, best actor, 1961, for *The Mark.*

CREDITS:

FILM APPEARANCES

When Worlds Collide, Paramount, 1951.

Zip Parker, *The All-American,* Universal, 1953.

Sergeant, *The Veils of Baghdad,* Universal, 1953.

Bernal Vaquaro, *Passion,* RKO, 1954.

Wickers, *Silver Lode,* RKO, 1954.

Captain, *Prisoner of War,* Metro-Goldwyn-Mayer (MGM), 1954.

Dove, *Rhapsody,* MGM, 1954.

Man on beach, *Interrupted Melody,* MGM, 1955.

Henri's squire, *Diane,* MGM, 1955.

Prentiss, *Girl in Black Stockings,* United Artists (UA), 1955.

Officer, *One Minute to Zero,* RKO, 1955.

Cavalry lieutenant, *Seven Men from Now,* Warner Brothers (Warner Bros.), 1956.

Johnny Smith, *War Drums,* UA, 1957.

Lab technician, *Crime of Passion,* UA, 1957.

Eddie Mason, *Hell Bound,* UA, 1957.

Johnny, *Johnny Trouble,* Warner Bros., 1957.

Hank Bishop, *Darby's Rangers,* Warner Bros., 1958.

Leroy Martin, *The Decks Ran Red,* MGM, 1958.

Dan O'Neill, *China Doll,* UA, 1958.

Charley Bongiorno, *10 North Frederick,* Twentieth Century-Fox, 1958.

Blackie Scantling, *Hound-Dog Man,* Twentieth Century-Fox, 1959.

Tom Ping, *These Thousand Hills,* Twentieth Century-Fox, 1959.

Charles Busch, *The Sound and the Fury,* Twentieth Century-Fox, 1959.

Joey Collins, *Murder, Inc.,* Twentieth Century-Fox, 1960.

Boaz, *The Story of Ruth,* Twentieth Century-Fox, 1960.

Bates, *The Fiercest Heart,* Twentieth Century-Fox, 1961.

Regret, *The Comancheros,* Twentieth Century-Fox, 1961.

Paolo, *Francis of Assisi,* Twentieth Century-Fox, 1961.

Jim Fuller, *The Mark,* Twentieth Century-Fox, 1961.

Principal keeper, *Convicts Four,* Allied Artists, 1962.

Lt. Sheen, *The Longest Day,* Twentieth Century-Fox, 1962.

Capt. Allan Morley, *The Day and the Hour,* MGM, 1963.

Capt. Haven, *Rio Conchos,* Twentieth Century-Fox, 1964.

Alex Forrester, *Signpost to Murder,* MGM, 1964.

Dale Nelson, *Shock Treatment,* Twentieth Century-Fox, 1964.

Orville Newton, *Those Magnificent Men in Their Flying Machines: Or How I Flew from London to Paris in 25 Hours and 11 Minutes,* Twentieth Century-Fox, 1965.

O'Brian, *Sands of the Kalihari,* Paramount, 1965.

Stephen Rojack, *An American Dream*, Warner Bros., 1966.

Prisoner, *Sweet Hunters*, General Productions, 1969.

Tex, *The Invisible Six*, Continental, 1970.

Capt. Lee Mitchell, *The Last Escape*, UA, 1970.

Griffin, *Captain Apache*, Scotia International, 1971.

Roy Bennett, *Night of the Lepus*, MGM, 1972.

Jim Bob, *Crazy Mama*, New World, 1975.

Shatter, *Call Him Mr. Shatter*, Hammer, 1976.

Sheriff Martin, *Eaten Alive*, Virgo International, 1976.

Vic, *Las Vegas Lady*, Crown International, 1976.

Mario Racconi, *Mean Johnny Barrows*, Atlas, 1976.

Deputy Rakes, *Tender Flesh*, Warner Bros., 1976.

Maniac!, New World, 1977.

Vince Kemper, *Ruby*, Twentieth Century-Fox, 1977.

Winifred Coxy, *The White Buffalo*, UA, 1977.

Charlie, *Run for the Roses*, Kodiak, 1978.

Delta Fox, Sebastian International, 1979.

Capt. Tony Terracino, *Cuba Crossing*, Key West, 1980.

Rev. James Johnson, *Guyana, Cult of the Damned*, Universal, 1980.

Father Cunningham, *Demonoid*, American Panorama, 1981.

Sam, *The Monster Club*, ITC, 1981.

Rev. Rivers, *Butterfly*, Analysis, 1982.

Dr. Latimer, *Omega Cop*, South Gate Entertainment, 1990.

Lt. Gallegher, *Smooth Talker*, Reivaj Films, 1990.

Narrator, *Ten To Chi To* (also known as *Heaven and Earth*), Triton Pictures, 1990.

Also appeared as Counselor, *Delta Fox*, 1977; Capt. Tony Siatta, *Strange Shadows in an Empty Room*, 1977; Capt. Pritchett, *Deadly Intruder*, 1985; and as George Larson, *Color of Evening*, 1991. Appeared in *Lost World of the Libra*, 1968; *The Only Way Out is Dead*, 1970; *Jamaican Gold*, 1971; *The Last Generation*, 1971; *Blazing Magnum*, 1976; *Oil*, 1976; *The Thoroughbreds*, 1977; *Treasure of the Amazon*, 1983; and *Vultures in Paradise*, 1984.

TELEVISION APPEARANCES; SERIES

U.S. Marshall Jim Crown, *Cimarron Strip*, CBS, 1967-71.

Also appeared on *Murder, She Wrote*, CBS.

TELEVISION APPEARANCES; EPISODIC

Ghost Story, NBC, 1972.
Superboy, syndicated, 1988.

Also appeared in *Bob Hope Presents the Chrysler Theatre*, NBC; *Four Star Playhouse*, CBS.

TELEVISION APPEARANCES; MOVIES

Dr. McCarter Purvis, *The Man Who Wanted to Live Forever*, ABC, 1970.

Admiral Michael Matthews, *City Beneath the Sea*, CBS, 1971.

Mark Hembric, *Revenge*, ABC, 1971.

Paul Carter, *The Woman Hunter*, CBS, 1972.

Lt. Marco, *Curse of the Cat Creature*, ABC, 1973.

Erik Seward, *The Man Who Died Twice*, CBS, 1973.

Terry Sullivan, *Harold Robbins' "The Pirate,"* CBS, 1978.

Deputy Shreeve, *Go West, Young Girl*, ABC, 1978.

Col. Elkart, *The Last Convertible*, NBC, 1979.

Rev. Blackthorn, *The Seekers*, HBO, 1979.

Dr. Ken Dalton, *Women in White*, NBC, 1979.

Marty Liss, *Condominium*, HBO, 1980.

Josh Rider, *Beverly Hills Cowgirl Blues*, CBS, 1985.

Luther Pelham, *Stillwatch*, CBS, 1987.

Dr. Hemingway, *Hemingway*, syndicated, 1988.

George Agnew, *Once Upon a Texas Train* (also known as *Texas Guns*), CBS, 1988.

Moving Target, USA, 1990.

Don Francisco, *Mob Boss*, syndicated, 1991.

TELEVISION APPEARANCES; PILOTS

Coach Freddie Gordon, *Starr, First Baseman*, CBS, 1965.

John McKennon, *Intertect*, ABC, 1973.

Host, *Roughcuts*, syndicated, 1984.

*   *   *

WILLIAMS, Anson   1949-

PERSONAL: Original name, Anson William Heimlick; born September 25, 1949, in Los Angeles, CA; married Lorrie Mahaffey (marriage ended); married Jackie Gerken (a television producer); children: (second marriage) Hannah Lily.

ADDRESSES: Manager—Denny Bond, Management III, 4570 Encino Ave., Encino, CA 91316.

CAREER: Actor, producer, director, and writer. Founder, with Jackie Gerken and Bill Novodar, of Enchantment Pictures.

CREDITS:

TELEVISION APPEARANCES; SERIES

Jimmy Fowler, *The Paul Lynde Show*, ABC, 1972.

Warren "Potsie" Weber, *Happy Days*, ABC, 1974-83.

Correspondent, *Inside America*, ABC, 1982.

TELEVISION APPEARANCES; MOVIES

Brian, "Lisa, Bright and Dark," *The Hallmark Hall of Fame*, NBC, 1973.

Rick Bellows, *I Married a Centerfold*, NBC, 1984.

TELEVISION APPEARANCES; PILOTS

Warren "Potsie" Weber, "Love and the Happy Days," (pilot for *Happy Days*), *Love, American Style*, ABC, 1972.
Host, *Anson and Lorrie*, NBC, 1981.
Twilight Theater, NBC, 1982.

TELEVISION APPEARANCES; SPECIALS

Top of the Month, syndicated, 1972.
Bing!... A 50th Anniversary Gala, CBS, 1977.
James Hewitt, *'twas the Night before Christmas*, NBC, 1977.
ABC's Silver Anniversary Celebration—25 and Still the One, ABC, 1978.
The All-Star Salute to Mother's Day, 1981.
Host, *Battle of the Video Games*, syndicated, 1983.

TELEVISION APPEARANCES; EPISODIC

The Chuck Barris Rah-Rah Show, NBC, 1978.

Also appeared on *Owen Marshall: Counselor at Law*, ABC.

TELEVISION EXECUTIVE PRODUCER

(With Ron Howard) *Skyward* (movie), NBC, 1980.
(With Howard) *Skyward Christmas* (pilot), NBC, 1981.
(With Howard) *Little Shots* (pilot), NBC, 1983.
(With Howard and Fred Tatashore), "The Lone Star Kid," *WonderWorks* (special), PBS, 1986.

TELEVISION DIRECTOR; MOVIES

Dream Date, NBC, 1989.
Little White Lies, NBC, 1989.
Your Mother Wears Combat Boots (also known as *Your Mother Wears Army Boots*) NBC, 1989.
A Quiet Little Neighborhood, a Perfect Little Murder, NBC, 1990.

TELEVISION DIRECTOR; SPECIALS

"No Greater Gift," *ABC Afterschool Special*, ABC, 1985.
"The Drug Knot," *CBS Schoolbreak Special*, CBS, 1986.

TELEVISION DIRECTOR; EPISODIC

L.A. Law, NBC, 1987.
Hooperman, ABC, 1987 and 1988.
The Slap Maxwell Story, ABC, 1987 and 1988.
Just the Ten of Us, ABC, 1988.

WRITINGS:

COMPOSER

(With Ron Rosen) *Anson and Lorrie*, NBC, 1981.

SCREENPLAYS

(With Josef Anderson) "No Greater Gift," *ABC Afterschool Special*, ABC, 1985.
(With Barbara Hiser) "The Lone Star Kid," *WonderWorks*, PBS, 1986.
(Coauthor) *The Magic of Michael Jackson*, Showtime, 1988.

OTHER

Also wrote episodes of *Simon and Simon*, CBS; *Fantasy Island*, ABC; and *Hart to Hart*, ABC.*

*   *   *

WILLIS, Bruce   1955-

PERSONAL: Born Walter Bruce Willis, March 19, 1955, in Germany; son of David (a mechanic and welder) and Marlene Willis; married Demi Moore (an actress), November 21, 1987, in Las Vegas, NV; children: Rumer Glenn and Scout LaRue (daughters).

ADDRESSES: Office—ABC Television, 2040 Avenue of the Stars, Los Angeles, CA 90067. *Agent*—Arnold Rifkin, Triad Artists, Inc., 10100 Santa Monica Blvd., Sixteenth Floor, Los Angeles, CA 90067. *Publicist*—Paul Bloch, Rogers & Cowan, 10000 Santa Monica Blvd., No. 400, Los Angeles, CA 90067.

CAREER: Actor and singer. Acted in commercials for Levi's 501 Jeans and Seagram's Golden Wine Coolers; member of First Amendment Comedy Theater; harmonica player with the Loose Goose band. Worked briefly at a chemical company, a nuclear power plant, and as a security guard; tended bar at Kamikaze and Cafe Central, New York City.

AWARDS, HONORS: People's Choice Award, best actor in a television series, 1986, for *Moonlighting;* Emmy Award, outstanding lead actor in a drama series, 1987, for *Moonlighting;* Golden Globe Award, best performance by an actor in a television series—comedy/musical, 1987, for *Moonlighting.*

CREDITS:

TELEVISION APPEARANCES; SERIES

David Addison, *Moonlighting*, ABC, 1985-89.

TELEVISION APPEARANCES; EPISODIC

Peter Jay Novins, "Shatterday," *Twilight Zone*, CBS, 1985.

Appeared on episodes of *Miami Vice* and *Hart to Hart*.

OTHER TELEVISION APPEARANCES

ABC All-Star Spectacular, ABC, 1985.

Whatta Year . . . 1986, ABC, 1986.

Bruno Radolini, *Bruce Willis: The Return of Bruno,* HBO, 1987 (also see below).

Performer of "Bruno's Bop," "Texas Woman," and "Respect Yourself," *The Pointer Sisters . . . Up All Night,* NBC, 1987.

The American Music Awards, ABC, 1987.

All-Star Tribute to Kareem Abdul-Jabbar, NBC, 1989.

Time Warner Presents the Earth Day Special, ABC, 1990.

Sinatra 75: The Best Is Yet to Come, CBS, 1990.

Seriously . . . Phil Collins (variety special), CBS, 1990.

Face to Face with Connie Chung (interview), CBS, 1990.

Appeared on *Thirty-seventh Prime Time Emmy Awards,* 1985, *Thirty-eighth Annual Emmy Awards,* 1986, *Thirty-ninth Annual Emmy Awards,* 1987, and *Sixty-first Annual Academy Awards Presentation,* 1989.

TELEVISION WORK

(Writer and executive producer) *Bruce Willis: The Return of Bruno,* HBO, 1987.

FILM APPEARANCES

(Debut) Walter Dennis, *Blind Date,* Tri-Star, 1987.

John McClane, *Die Hard,* Twentieth Century-Fox, 1988.

Tom Mix, *Sunset* (also see below), Tri-Star, 1988.

Emmett Smith, *In Country,* Warner Brothers, 1990.

Voice of Mikey, *Look Who's Talking,* Tri-Star, 1989.

Voice of Mikey, *Look Who's Talking Too,* Tri-Star, 1990.

John McClane, *Die Hard II: Die Harder,* Twentieth Century-Fox, 1990.

Peter Fallow, *Bonfire of the Vanities,* Warner Brothers, 1990.

Title role, *Hudson Hawk* (also see below), Tri-Star, 1991.

James Urbansky, *Mortal Thoughts,* Columbia, 1991.

Appeared as himself in *That's Adequate,* 1989.

FILM APPEARANCES; MUSIC PERFORMER

"Daddy's Coming Home," *Look Who's Talking Too,* Tri-Star, 1990.

FILM WORK

Coexecutive producer, *Sunset,* Tri-Star, 1988.

STAGE APPEARANCES

Sheriff, *Railroad Bill,* St. Peter's Hall, Labor Theater, New York City, 1981.

The Bayside Boys, Labor Theater, 1981.

Appeared as Brick, *Cat on a Hot Tin Roof,* Montclair State College, NJ (stage debut); in *Heaven and Earth,* New York City, 1977; as Eddie in *Fool for Love;* and in *The Bullpen.*

RECORDINGS:

The Return of Bruno, Motown Records, 1986.

If It Don't Kill You, It Just Makes You Stronger, Motown Records, 1989.

WRITINGS:

FILM

(With Robert Kraft) *Hudson Hawk,* Tri-Star, 1991.

OTHER SOURCES:

BOOKS

Contemporary Newsmakers 1986 Cumulation, Gale, 1987.

PERIODICALS

Sunday Star-Ledger, October 8, 1989.

Us, October 2, 1989.*

*   *   *

WILSON, Julie   1924(?)-

PERSONAL: Born October 21, 1924 (one source says 1925), in Omaha, NE; married Barron Polan (marriage ended); married second husband; children: (second marriage) Holt, Michael.

ADDRESSES: Contact—David Chase, Chase, La Rosa, CPA, 505 Eighth Ave., New York, NY 10018.

CAREER: Actress and singer. Performer in nightclubs throughout the world.

AWARDS, HONORS: Antoinette Perry Award nomination, best featured actress in a musical, 1989, for *Legs Diamond;* former Miss Nebraska.

CREDITS:

STAGE APPEARANCES

Ginny, *High Fidelity,* Walnut Street Theatre, Philadelphia, PA, 1961.

The Girl in the Freudian Slip, Booth Theatre, New York City, 1967.

Allie Walker, *Jimmy,* Winter Garden Theatre, New York City, 1969.

Woman, *Park,* Center Stage Theatre, Baltimore, MD, then John Golden Theatre, New York City, 1970.

Julie Wilson: From Weill to Sondheim—A Concert, Kaufman Theatre, New York City, 1987.

Flo, *Legs Diamond,* Mark Hellinger Theatre, New York City, 1989.

Title role, *Hannah 1939,* Vineyard Theatre, New York City, 1990.

Made Broadway debut in *Three to Make Ready,* 1946. Also appeared as Bianca, *Kiss Me, Kate;* Mama Rose,

Gypsy; in *Kismet* and *The Pajama Game,* New York City; in *Bells Are Ringing; South Pacific; Kiss Me, Kate;* and *Bet Your Life,* all London; and in *Two for the Seesaw; Showboat; Dames at Sea; Pal Joey;* and *Milicent's Castle.*

MAJOR TOURS

Joanne, *Company,* U.S. cities, 1972.

Also toured in *Earl Carroll's Vanities; Follies; Kiss Me, Kate; Babes in Arms; A Little Night Music;* and *The Gershwin Years,* all U.S. cities.

FILM APPEARANCES

Rosebud, *The Strange One* (also released as *End as a Man*), Columbia, 1957.
Ivy Corlane, *This Could Be the Night,* Metro-Goldwyn-Mayer, 1957.

TELEVISION APPEARANCES

Leslie, *The Bachelor* (special), NBC, 1956.
Lois Lane, "Kiss Me, Kate," *The Hallmark Hall of Fame* (special), NBC, 1958.

Appeared in episodes of *The Secret Storm;* "Come to Me," *Kraft Theatre; The Phil Silvers Show; The Jackie Gleason Show; The Perry Como Show; The Milton Berle Show; The Ed Sullivan Show; Person to Person.*

RECORDINGS:

ALBUMS

Albums include *Julie Wilson Sings the Stephen Sondheim Songbook, Julie Wilson Sings The Kurt Weill Songbook,* and *The Music of Irving Berlin,* all for DRG Records.*

*   *   *

WILTON, Penelope 1946-

PERSONAL: Born June 3, 1946, in Scarborough, England.

ADDRESSES: Agent—Julian Belfrage Associates, 60 St. James's St., London SW1, England; William Morris Agency, 31/32 Soho Square, London W1, England.

CAREER: Actress.

CREDITS:

STAGE APPEARANCES

Mary, *West of Suez,* Royal Court Theatre, London, 1971.
Araminta, *The Philanthropist,* Royal Court Theatre, then Ethel Barrymore Theatre, New York City, 1971.
Maud, *The Great Exhibition,* Hampstead Theatre Club, London, 1972.
Sophia, *The Director of the Opera,* Chichester Festival, Chichester, England, 1973.

Masha, *The Seagull,* Chichester Festival, 1973.
Dikson, *Something's Burning,* Mermaid Theatre, London, 1974.
Ruth, *The Norman Conquests,* Greenwich Theatre, London, 1974.
Dora Carrington, *Bloomsbury,* Phoenix Theatre, London, 1974.
Second woman, "Play," *Play and Others,* Royal Court Theatre, 1976.
Prudence Malone, *Plunder,* National Theatre Company, Lyttelton Theatre, London, 1978.
Julia Craven, *The Philanderer,* National Theatre Company, Lyttelton Theatre, 1978.
Emma, *Betrayal,* National Theatre Company, Lyttelton Theatre, 1978.
Barbara, *Tishoo,* Wyndham's Theatre, London, 1979.
Ann Whitefield and Dona Ana, *Man and Superman,* National Theatre Company, Olivier Theatre, London, 1981.
Beatrice, *Much Ado about Nothing,* National Theatre Company, Olivier Theatre, 1981.
Barbara Undershaft, *Major Barbara,* National Theatre Company, Lyttelton Theatre, 1982.
Marion French, *The Secret Rapture,* National Theatre Company, Lyttelton Theatre, 1988.
Hermione, *Andromache,* Old Vic Theatre, London, 1988.
Piano, National Theatre Company, Cottesloe Theatre, London, 1990.

FILM APPEARANCES

Sonia, *The French Lieutenant's Woman,* United Artists, 1981.
Virginia, *Country,* British Film Institute, 1981.
Alice Singleton, *Laughter House* (also known as *Singleton's Pluck*), Film Four International, 1984.
Pat Garden, *Clockwise,* Universal/Cannon, 1986.
Wendy Woods, *Cry Freedom,* Universal, 1987.

TELEVISION APPEARANCES

Annie, "The Norman Conquests," *Great Performances* (special), PBS, 1978.
Title role, *The Tales of Beatrix Potter,* BBC, then PBS, 1984.
Ever Decreasing Circles (series), BBC-1, 1989.
"Madly in Love," *4 Play* (episodic), Channel 4, 1990.

Also appeared in *King Lear,* 1975; *Joseph Andrews,* 1976; and *The Widowing of Mrs. Holroyd.*

RADIO APPEARANCES

"Redevelopment," *The Monday Play* (episodic), R4, 1989.
"Night and Day," *The Friday Play* (episodic), R3, 1990.
Virginia Woolf, *An Oddly Complete Understanding* (play), R4, 1990.*

WINCER, Simon

PERSONAL: Born in Australia.

CAREER: Director, producer.

AWARDS, HONORS: Emmy Award for Outstanding Direction, 1988-89, for *Lonesome Dove.*

CREDITS:

FILM WORK

Director, *Harlequin,* New Image, 1980.
Director, *The Day after Halloween* (also known as *Snapshot*), Group 1, 1981.
Executive producer, *The Man from Snowy River,* Twentieth Century-Fox, 1982.
Director, *Phar Lap* (also known as *Phar Lap—Heart of a Nation*), Twentieth Century-Fox, 1984.
Director, *D.A.R.Y.L.,* Paramount, 1985.
Producer (with Ian Jones), director, *The Lighthorsemen,* Cinecom, 1987.
Director, *Quigley Down Under,* Metro-Goldwyn-Mayer/United Artists, 1990.

Also executive producer, *One Night Stand,* 1983.

TELEVISION WORK

Director, *The Girl Who Spelled Freedom* (also known as *The Story of Linn Yann;* movie), ABC, 1986.
Director, *The Last Frontier* (movie), CBS, 1986.
Director, *Bluegrass* (movie), CBS, 1988.
Director, *Lonesome Dove* (mini-series), CBS, 1989.
Consultant, *The Adventures of the Black Stallion* (series), The Family Channel, 1990.

Also director of episodes of the syndicated series *Prisoner: Cell Block H,* 1980. Director of over 200 hours of Australian television programs, including *Cash and Company, Tandarra, Ryan, Against the Wind,* and *The Sullivans.**

*　　　*　　　*

WINCHELL, Paul   1922-

PERSONAL: Born December 21, 1922, in New York, NY; son of Sol and Clara (Fuchs) Winchell; children: Stephanie, Stacey Paul, April Terri. *Education:* Attended Columbia University, 1958-59; graduated from Acupuncture Research Institute College, 1974; National Christian University, D.Sc., 1975.

CAREER: Actor, director, writer, ventriloquist, and inventor. Invented an artificial heart in 1975 and donated it to the University of Utah.

AWARDS, HONORS: First prize, Major Bowes Radio Amateur Hour, 1936; named TV's Most Versatile Per-

former, *Look* magazine, 1952 and 1953; Academy Award, short subjects—cartoons, 1968, for *Winnie the Pooh and the Blustery Day;* Grammy Award, best recording for children, 1974, for *Winnie the Pooh and Tigger Too.*

CREDITS:

TELEVISION APPEARANCES; SERIES

Winchell and Mahoney Show, NBC, 1947.
Host, *Dunninger and Winchell,* CBS and NBC, 1949.
Host, *The Paul Winchell and Jerry Mahoney Speidel Show,* NBC, 1950-53.
Host, *Paul Winchell and Jerry Mahoney's What's My Name,* NBC, 1952-54.
Host, *Jerry Mahoney's Club House,* NBC, 1954.
Host, *Toyland Express,* ABC, 1955.
Host, *Circus Time,* ABC, 1956.
Host, *Five Star Comedy,* ABC, 1957.
Host, *The Paul Winchell Show,* ABC, 1957.
Homer Winch, *The Beverly Hillbillies,* CBS, 1962.
Voice of Knucklehead Smiff, *Cartoonsville* (animated), ABC, 1963.
Voice of Dick Dastardly, *The Wacky Races* (animated), CBS, 1968.
Voice of the General, *Dastardly and Muttley in Their Flying Machines* (animated), CBS, 1969.
Voices of Claude and Softy, *The Perils of Penelope Pitstop* (animated), CBS, 1969.
Fleegle, *The Banana Splits Adventure Hour,* NBC, 1970.
Voice of Bubi Bear, *Help! It's the Hair Bear Bunch* (animated), CBS, 1971.
Host, *Runaround,* NBC, 1972.
Voice of Goober, *Goober and the Ghost Chaser* (animated), ABC, 1973.
Voice of Fleabag, *The Oddball Couple* (animated), ABC, 1975.
Monty, *Adams of Eagle Lake,* ABC, 1975.
Voices of Woofer and Wimper, *The Clue Club* (animated), CBS, 1976.
Voice of Shake, *The C.B. Bears* (animated), CBS, 1977.
Voice of Woofer, *The Skate Birds* (animated), CBS, 1977.
Voice of Moe, *The Three Robonic Stooges* (animated), NBC, 1979.
Voice of Revs, *Wheelie and the Chopper* (animated), NBC, 1979.
Voice of the Father, *The Heathcliff and Marmaduke Show* (animated), ABC, 1981.
Voice of Gargamel, *The Smurfs* (animated), NBC, 1981.
Voice of Mayor Lumpkin, *Trollkins* (animated), CBS, 1981.

Also appeared in *Show Business Inc.,* 1947; *Meatballs and Spaghetti,* 1982; *The New Jetsons,* 1985; as voice of Zummi, *Disney's Adventures of the Gummi Bears,* 1985; voices of Zummi and Tigger, *Disney's Gummi Bears/*

Winnie the Pooh Hour, 1989; voice of Tigger, *The Adventures of Winnie the Pooh, The New Adventures of Winnie the Pooh,* 1988-89 and 1989-90; voice of Dick Dastardly, *Wake, Rattle and Roll,* "Fender Bender 500," 1990; voice of Turtle, *The Tiny Tree.*

OTHER TELEVISION APPEARANCES

Host, *The Paul Winchell Show* (pilot), CBS, 1956.

Appeared in *The Treasure Chest Murder* (movie), 1975; in specials as voice of Gargamel, *My Smurfy Valentine,* 1983, *Smurfily Ever After,* 1985, and *The Smurfs Christmas Special,* 1986; appeared in *Yogi's Treasure Hunt,* 1985; *Stooge Snapshots.*

TELEVISION PRODUCER; SERIES

The Paul Winchell and Jerry Mahoney Speidel Show, NBC, 1950.
Toyland Express, ABC, 1955.

FILM APPEARANCES

Winnie the Pooh and the Blustery Day, Walt Disney Productions/Buena Vista, 1968.
Voice of Chinese Cat, *The Aristocats* (animated), Buena Vista, 1970.
Schroeder, *Which Way to the Front,* Warner Bros., 1970.
Voice of Boomer, *The Fox and the Hound* (animated), Buena Vista, 1981.

Also appeared in *Stop, Look and Laugh,* 1959; *The Man from Clover Grove,* 1973; and *Winnie the Pooh and Tigger Too,* 1974.

RADIO APPEARANCES

Appeared on *Major Bowes Radio Amateur Hour,* 1936; had own radio show, beginning in 1943.

RECORDINGS:

Appeared on album *Winnie the Pooh and Tigger Too* with Sebastian Cabot and Sterling Holloway, c. 1974.

WRITINGS:

(With Carl Jampel, Stan Dreben, and Hannah Goodman) *The Paul Winchell and Jerry Mahoney Speidel Show* (television series), NBC, 1950.
(With Bud Burston) *Jerry Mahoney's Club House* (television series), NBC, 1954.

Also author of *Ventriloquism for Fun and Profit,* 1954, and (with Keith E. Kenyon) *Acupuncture Without Needles,* 1974.

SIDELIGHTS: Jerry Mahoney and Knucklehead Smiff puppets were donated to the Smithsonian Institution.*

WINFREY, Oprah   1954-

PERSONAL: Born January 29, 1954, in Kosciusko, MS; daughter of Vernon Winfrey (a barber and city councilman) and Vernita Lee (a maid). *Education:* Received B.A. from Tennessee State University.

ADDRESSES: Office—WLS-TV, 190 North State, Chicago, IL, 60601; (business address) P.O. Box 909715, Chicago, IL 60690.

CAREER: Talk show host, actress, producer. Worked as a reporter and newscaster for WVOL-Radio, Nashville, TN, during high school; reporter and news anchor for WTVF-TV, Nashville, during college; WJZ-TV, Baltimore, MD, news anchor, 1976-77; host of morning talk show *People Are Talking,* 1977-83; WLS-TV, Chicago, IL, host of talk show *A.M. Chicago,* 1984-85, renamed *The Oprah Winfrey Show,* 1985, syndicated, 1986—. Founder of Harpo Productions, 1986.

AWARDS, HONORS: Miss Black Tennessee, 1971; Academy Award nomination and Golden Globe nomination, 1986, for *The Color Purple;* Woman of Achievement Award, National Organization of Women, 1986; selected one of *Playgirl* magazine's ten most admired women, 1986; Emmy Awards, outstanding host of talk/service show, and outstanding direction, 1987, for *The Oprah Winfrey Show;* Emmy Awards, outstanding talk/service program, 1987 and 1988, for *The Oprah Winfrey Show;* Broadcaster of the Year Award, International Radio and Television Society, 1988; NAACP Image Awards, Entertainer of the Year, 1989, and best actress in a dramatic series, miniseries, or TV movie, for *The Women of Brewster Place,* 1989; NAACP Image Award (with Carole Isenberg), executive producer, best episode in a dramatic series, miniseries, or TV movie, for *The Women of Brewster Place;* NAACP Image Award, executive producer, best news/information series or special, 1989, for *Prime Time Oprah: No One Dies Alone;* Daytime Emmy awards, best talk/service show, and best talk/service show host, both 1991, for *The Oprah Winfrey Show.*

CREDITS:

TELEVISION APPEARANCES; TALK SHOWS

Host, *A.M. Chicago,* WLS-TV, 1984-85, renamed *The Oprah Winfrey Show* (also see below), 1985, syndicated, 1986—.

Hosted morning talk show, *People Are Talking,* 1977-83.

TELEVISION APPEARANCES; DRAMAS

Mattie Michael, *The Women of Brewster Place* (miniseries), ABC, 1989.
Mattie Michael, *Brewster Place* (series), ABC, 1990.

TELEVISION APPEARANCES; EPISODIC

Made guest appearance on *Gabriel's Fire*, ABC.

OTHER TELEVISION APPEARANCES

Host, *A Star-Spangled Celebration*, ABC, 1987.
The Dolly Show (variety), ABC, 1987.
NBC News Report on America: Life in the Fast Lane (news documentary), NBC, 1987.
Special Olympics Ceremonies, ABC, 1987.
Fifteenth Annual Daytime Emmy Awards, CBS, 1987.
Host, *Prime Time Oprah: No One Dies Alone* (also see below), syndicated, 1988.
The Twentieth Annual NAACP Image Awards, NBC, 1988.
The Barbara Walters Special (interview), ABC, 1988.
Living the Dream: A Tribute to Dr. Martin Luther King, syndicated, 1988.
Pee-wee's Playhouse Christmas Special, CBS, 1988.
People Magazine on TV (interview), CBS, 1988.
Tenth Annual American Black Achievement Awards, syndicated, 1989.
Host, *Just between Friends* (special; also see below), syndicated, 1989.
Sixteenth Annual Daytime Emmy Awards, NBC, 1989.
Diet America Challenge, CBS, 1989.
Host, *Seventeenth Annual Daytime Emmy Awards*, ABC, 1990.
America's All-Star Tribute to Oprah Winfrey, ABC, 1990.
Grammy Legends Show, CBS, 1990.
MDA Jerry Lewis Telethon (twenty-fifth anniversary MDA Jerry Lewis Telethon), syndicated, 1990.
Walt Disney Company Presents the American Teacher Awards, Disney Channel, 1990.

Hosted *Fourteenth Annual Daytime Emmy Awards*, 1987. Appeared on *Fifty-ninth Annual Academy Awards Presentation*, 1987, and *The Twenty-second NAACP Image Awards*, 1990.

TELEVISION WORK; EXECUTIVE PRODUCER, EXCEPT WHERE INDICATED

Supervising producer, *The Oprah Winfrey Show*, syndicated, 1986—.
Prime Time Oprah: No One Dies Alone, syndicated, 1988.
The Women of Brewster Place (miniseries), ABC, 1989.
Just between Friends (special), syndicated, 1989.
Brewster Place (series), ABC, 1990.

FILM APPEARANCES

Sofia, *The Color Purple*, Warner Brothers, 1985.
Mrs. Thomas, *Native Son*, Cinecom, 1986.
Herself, *Throw Momma from the Train*, Orion, 1988.
Listen Up: The Lives of Quincy Jones (documentary), Warner Brothers, 1990.

OTHER SOURCES:

BOOKS

Contemporary Newsmakers 1986 Cumulation, Gale, 1987.

PERIODICALS

Hollywood Reporter, 58th anniversary issue, 1989.
New York Times, March 12, 1989.
New York Times Magazine, June 11, 1989.*

*   *   *

WISBERG, Aubrey   1909(?)-1990

PERSONAL: Full name, Aubrey Lionel Wisberg; born October 20, 1909 (one source says 1912), in London, England; immigrated to United States, 1921, naturalized citizen; died of cancer, March 14, 1990, in New York, NY; son of Philip and Cynthia (Shuman) Wisberg; married Barbara Duberstein. *Education:* Attended New York University and Columbia University.

CAREER: Screenwriter, director, and producer. Associate producer for Edward Small Productions; founder and executive producer for Wisberg Productions; cofounder of American Pictures Corporation and Mid-Century Films. Radio and television dramatist in the United States, Australia, and England; radio diffusionist in Paris; journalist.

MEMBER: Writers Guild of America, West, Dramatists Guild, Authors League of America, Directors Guild of America.

AWARDS, HONORS: International Unity Award, Inter-Racial Society, for *The Burning Cross*.

CREDITS:

FILM WORK; PRODUCER

The Man From Planet X, Mid-Century/United Artists, 1951.
Captive Women, (also known as *1000 Years From Now* and *3000 A.D.*), RKO, 1952.
Captain John Smith and Pocahontas, United Artists, 1953.
Port Sinister, (also known as *Beast of Paradise Island* and *Beast of Paradise Isle*), RKO, 1953.
Problem Girls, Columbia, 1953.
Sword of Venus, (also known as *Island of Monte Cristo*), RKO, 1953.
Captain Kidd and the Slave Girl, Reliance/United Artists, 1954.
And director, *Dragon's Gold*, United Artists, 1954.
Return to Treasure Island, United Artists, 1954.
Murder Is My Beat, Allied Artists, 1955.
(With Jean Yarbrough) *The Women of Pitcairn Island*, Twentieth Century-Fox, 1957.

Hercules in New York (also known as *Hercules: The Movie*), RAF-United, 1970.

WRITINGS:

SCREENPLAYS

Submarine Raider, Columbia, 1942.

Counter Espionage, Columbia, 1942.

They Came to Blow Up America, Twentieth Century-Fox, 1943.

(With Kenneth Gamet) *Bomber's Moon,* Twentieth Century-Fox, 1943.

U-Boat Prisoner (adapted from a novel by Archie Gibbs), Columbia, 1944.

Adventures of Rusty, Columbia, 1945.

(With Gamet) *Betrayal From the East* (adapted from a novel by Alan Hynd), RKO, 1945.

Escape in the Fog, Columbia, 1945.

(Author of idea) Sam Hellman and James V. Kern, *The Horn Blows at Midnight,* Warner Bros., 1945.

The Power of the Whistler, Columbia, 1945.

(With Robert E. Kent) *The Falcon's Adventure,* RKO, 1946.

(With Eric Taylor) *Just Before Dawn* (adapted from a radio program by Max Marcin), Columbia, 1946.

(Author of story) Martin Berkeley and Ted Thomas, *Out of Depths,* Columbia, 1946.

Rendezvous 24, Twentieth Century-Fox, 1946.

(Author of story) Martin Berkeley and Dwight Babcock, *So Dark the Night,* Columbia, 1946.

(With George Bricker) *The Big Fix,* Producers Releasing Corporation/Universal, 1947.

The Wreck of the Hesperus (adapted from the poem by Henry Wadsworth Longfellow), Columbia, 1947.

The Burning Cross, Screen Guild, 1947.

(Author of story) Art Arthur, Ernest Haycox, and Rowland Leigh, *Heaven Only Knows* (also known as *Montana Mike*), United Artists, 1947.

Road to the Big House, Somerset/Screen Guild, 1947.

(With Jack Pollexfen) *Treasure of Monte Cristo,* Lippert/Screen Guild, 1949.

(With Pollexfen and Gerard Drayson Adams) *The Desert Hawk,* Universal, 1950.

(With Elizabeth Reinhardt and Lawrence Kimble) *Hit Parade of 1951,* Republic, 1950.

(Author of story with Pollexfen) Walter Ferris and Joseph Hoffman, *At Sword's Point* (also known as *Sons of the Musketeers*), RKO, 1951.

(With Pollexfen) *The Man From Planet X,* Mid-Century/United Artists, 1951.

(With Pollexfen) *Captive Women,* RKO, 1952.

(With Pollexfen) *Lady in the Iron Mask,* Twentieth Century-Fox, 1952.

(With Pollexfen) *The Neanderthal Man,* United Artists, 1953.

(With Pollexfen) *Captain John Smith and Pocahontas,* United Artists, 1953.

(With Pollexfen) *Port Sinister,* RKO, 1953.

(With Pollexfen) *Problem Girls,* Columbia, 1953.

(Author of story) Richard Schayer, *The Steel Lady* (also known as *Treasure of Kalifa*), United Artists, 1953.

(With Pollexfen) *Sword of Venus* (also known as *Island of Monte Cristo*), RKO, 1953.

(With Pollexfen) *Captain Kidd and the Slave Girl,* Reliance/United Artists, 1954.

(Author of story) Hal Kantor and Edmund Hartman, *Casanova's Big Night,* Paramount, 1954.

(With Pollexfen) *Dragon's Gold,* United Artists, 1954.

(With Pollexfen) *Return to Treasure Island,* United Artists, 1954.

Murder Is My Beat, Allied Artists, 1955.

(With Pollexfen) *Son of Sinbad,* RKO, 1955, re-released as *A Night in a Harem,* 1961.

The Women of Pitcairn Island, Twentieth Century-Fox, 1957.

Hercules in New York (also known as *Hercules: The Movie*), RAF-United, 1970.

Also screenwriter for *The Snow Devils,* 1965; *Target Minus Forty; Mission Mars; Ride the Wild Wind;* and *Evil in the Blood.*

OTHER

(With Harold Waters) *Bushman at Large,* Green Circle Books, 1937.

(With Waters) *This Is the Life,* Harrap, 1942.

(With Waters) *Patrol Boat 999,* Chilton, 1959.

Second Floor Front (play), first produced in Texas City, TX, 1979.

Also author of plays *Thirsty Death,* first produced at Biltmore Theatre, Los Angeles; *Angels With Horns; Whip Hand; Royal Flush; Destiny Obscure;* and *Virtue, Inc.* Contributor to *New York Daily News, Skipper,* and *Chicago Tribune.*

OBITUARIES AND OTHER SOURCES:

PERIODICALS

New York Times, March 15, 1990.*

*   *   *

WISEMAN, Joseph   1918-

PERSONAL: Born May 15, 1918, in Montreal, Quebec, Canada; son of Louis (in business) and Pearl Rubin (a seamstress; maiden name, Ruchwarger) Wiseman; married Nell Kinard, August 28, 1943 (divorced); married

Pearl Lang; children: one son, one daughter. *Education:* Attended City College of New York, 1935.

ADDRESSES: Agent—International Creative Management, 8899 Beverly Blvd., Los Angeles, CA 90048, and 40 West 57th St., New York, NY 10019.

CAREER: Actor. Performed concert readings of Yiddish and related literature in U.S. and Canada under auspices of B'nai B'rith, 1975-89. *Military service:* U.S. Army Signal Corps, 1942.

MEMBER: Actors' Equity Association, Screen Actors Guild, American Federation of Television and Radio Artists.

CREDITS:

STAGE APPEARANCES

(Stage debut) Moses, *Three Men on a Horse,* New Barn Theatre, Saugerties, NY, 1936.

The Milky Way, New Barn Theatre, 1936.

The Warrior's Husband, New Barn Theatre, 1936.

(Broadway debut) Union soldier, *Abe Lincoln in Illinois,* Plymouth Theatre, 1938.

Kulygin, *The Three Sisters,* Surrey Theatre, Maine, 1939.

News Boy, *The Grass Is Always Greener,* Surrey Theatre, 1939.

Beggar, second money changer, *Journey to Jerusalem,* National Theatre, New York City, 1940.

Corporal Mueller, *Candle in the Wind,* Shubert Theatre, New York City, 1941.

Andre Prozorov, *The Three Sisters,* Ethel Barrymore Theatre, New York City, 1942.

Second German soldier, *The Barber Had Two Sons,* Playhouse Theatre, New York City, 1943.

Stefano, *Storm Operation,* Belasco Theatre, New York City, 1944.

Champlain, *Joan of Lorraine,* Alvin Theatre, New York City, 1946.

Mardian, *Antony and Cleopatra,* Martin Beck Theatre, New York City, 1947.

Charlie, *Detective Story,* Hudson Theatre, New York City, 1949.

Juan de Escovedo, *That Lady,* Martin Beck Theatre, 1949.

Boris, *Within a Glass Bell,* Westport Country Playhouse, Westport, CT, 1950.

Edmund, *King Lear,* National Theatre, 1950.

Eddie Fuseli, *Golden Boy,* American National Theatre and Academy (ANTA), New York City, 1952.

Oliver Erwenter, *The Silver Whistle,* Westchester County Playhouse, Mount Kisco, NY, 1952.

Dick Dudgeon, *The Devil's Disciple,* Playhouse in the Park, Philadelphia, PA, 1952.

Sergius, *Arms and the Man,* Playhouse in the Park, 1953.

Inquisitor, *The Lark,* Longacre Theatre, New York City, 1955.

Stranger, *Susan and the Stranger,* Westchester County Playhouse, 1956.

Ferdinand, Duke of Calabria, *The Duchess of Malfi,* Phoenix Theatre, New York City, 1957.

Mr. Frank, *The Diary of Anne Frank,* Coconut Grove Playhouse, Miami, FL, 1958.

Amos, *The Queen and the Rebels,* Bucks County Playhouse, New Hope, PA, 1959.

Father, *Six Characters in Search of an Author,* Theatre Group, University of California at Los Angeles, 1961.

Bocadur, *Turn on the Night,* Playhouse in the Park, 1961.

Nota, *Naked,* Royal Court Theatre, London, 1963.

Chu Yin, *Marco Millions,* Lincoln Center Repertory Company, ANTA Theatre, New York City, 1964.

Le Duc, a doctor, *Incident at Vichy,* Lincoln Center Repertory Company, ANTA Theatre, 1964, then Huntington Hartford Theatre, Los Angeles, 1965.

Thomas, Archbishop of Canterbury, *Murder in the Cathedral,* American Shakespeare Festival, Stratford, CT, 1966.

Title role, *In the Matter of J. Robert Oppenheimer,* Center Theatre Group, Mark Taper Forum, Los Angeles, 1968, then Vivian Beaumont Theatre, New York City, 1969.

Astrov, *Uncle Vanya,* Center Theatre Group, Mark Taper Forum, 1969.

Bummidge, *The Last Analysis,* Circle in the Square, New York City, 1971.

Yako Bardin, *Enemies,* Vivian Beaumont Theatre, 1972.

The rabbi, *Zalmen; or, The Madness of God,* Arena Stage, Washington, DC, 1974, then Lyceum Theatre, New York City, 1976.

Fyodor Balyasnikov, *Balyasnikov,* Pittsburgh Public Theatre, Pittsburgh, PA, 1977-78.

The professor, *The Lesson,* Harold Clurman Theatre, New York City, 1978.

Prospero, *The Tempest,* Folger Theatre Group, Washington, DC, 1981-82.

Tadeus, *The Golem,* New York Shakespeare Festival (NYSF), Public Theatre, New York City, 1984.

Olbram, *Largo Desolato,* NYSF, Public Theatre, 1986.

Hirschman-Cabalist, *The Tenth Man,* Vivian Beaumont Theatre, 1989.

MAJOR TOURS

Bab and Cavalry Captain, *Abe Lincoln in Illinois,* U.S. cities, 1939-40.

Corporal Mueller, *Candle in the Wind,* U.S. cities, 1942-43.

Andre Prozorov, *The Three Sisters,* U.S. cities, 1942-43.

Mardian, *Antony and Cleopatra,* U.S. cities, 1947.

Juan de Escovedo, *That Lady,* U.S. cities, 1950.

Driver, *The Saturday Night Kid,* U.S. cities, 1957.

Dr. Rafael Taurez, *Sweet Love Remember'd,* U.S. cities, 1959.

FILM APPEARANCES

With These Hands, CLC, 1950.

Charles Geninini, *Detective Story,* Paramount, 1951.

Genflou, *Les Miserables,* Twentieth Century-Fox, 1952.

Fernando Aguirre, *Viva Zapata!,* Twentieth Century-Fox, 1952.

Dominic Guido, *Champ for a Day,* Republic, 1953.

Mijamin, *The Silver Chalice,* Warner Bros., 1954.

Carmish, *The Prodigal,* Metro-Goldwyn-Mayer, 1955.

Narrator, *Eliahu,* ORT, 1955.

Narrator, *Mella,* ORT, 1955.

Kovan, *The Garment Jungle,* Columbia, 1957.

Jim Barron, *Three Brave Men,* Twentieth Century-Fox, 1957.

Abe Kelsey, *The Unforgiven,* United Artists (UA), 1960.

Title role, *Dr. No,* UA, 1962.

Jean Marie Calbert, *The Happy Thieves* (also known as *Once a Thief*), UA, 1962.

Felix Ottensteen, *Bye Bye Braverman,* Warner Bros., 1968.

Rajeski, *The Counterfeit Killer,* Universal, 1968.

Louis Minsky, *The Night They Raided Minsky's* (also known as *The Night They Invented the Striptease*), UA, 1968.

Emilio Matteo, *Stiletto,* Embassy, 1969.

Lucas, *Lawman,* UA, 1971.

Salvatore Maranzano, *The Valachi Papers* (also known as *Joe Valachi: I Segretti di Cosa Nostra*), Columbia, 1972.

Uncle Benhy, *The Apprenticeship of Duddy Kravitz,* Paramount, 1974.

Colonel Haki, *Journey into Fear* (also known as *Burn Out*), Sterling Gold, 1976.

Jake Weinstein, *The Betsy,* Associated Artists, 1978.

Draco, *Buck Rogers in the 25th Century,* Universal, 1979.

Ben Ashir, *Jaguar Lives,* American International, 1979.

Also appeared as narrator in *Homage to Chagall—The Colours of Love* (documentary), 1977, and *Rise and Fall of the Borscht Belt,* 1985.

TELEVISION APPEARANCES; SERIES

Frontiers of Faith, NBC, 1950-60.

Manny Weisbord, *Crime Story,* NBC, 1986-88.

TELEVISION APPEARANCES; MINI-SERIES

Morris Cady, *QB VII,* ABC, 1974.

Jerahmed, *Masada,* ABC, 1981.

Antonio Granelli, *Rage of Angels,* NBC, 1983.

TELEVISION APPEARANCES; PILOTS

Pharaoh, *Great Bible Adventures,* ABC, 1966.

Ernest Grimes, *The Outsider,* NBC, 1967.

Balashev, *Men of the Dragon,* ABC, 1974.

TELEVISION APPEARANCES; EPISODIC

Paul Radin, "One More Pallbearer," *The Twilight Zone,* CBS, 1962.

The Loretta Young Show, NBC, 1964.

Desilu Playhouse, NBC, 1965.

The Untouchables, ABC, 1965.

Camera Three, CBS, 1965.

The Eternal Light, NBC, 1965.

Jesse James, ABC, 1966.

The Bob Hope Show, NBC, 1966.

Preview Tonight, ABC, 1966.

T.H.E. Cat, NBC, 1966.

Coronet Blue, CBS, 1967.

"Room with a View," *Rod Serling's Night Gallery* (also known as *Night Gallery*), NBC, 1970.

Theatre in America, PBS, 1975.

TELEVISION APPEARANCES; MOVIES

Fahdil Bondalok, *The Mask of Sheba,* NBC, 1970.

Dr. Peter Nordmann, *The Pursuit,* NBC, 1972.

Sam Druckman, *Murder at the World Series,* ABC, 1977.

Victor Castle, *Lady Mobster,* ABC, 1988.

Also appeared as Grudin, *Nightside,* 1973; appeared in *The Ghost Writer,* 1984; and appeared as Dr. Adler, *Seize the Day,* 1986.

TELEVISION APPEARANCES; SPECIALS

"Darkness at Noon," *Producers Showcase,* NBC, 1955.

Macbeth, CBS, 1959 and 1960.

The Lincoln Center Day, CBS, 1964.

Also appeared in *Arrowsmith, Billy Budd, The Dybbuk,* and *Antigone.*

*   *   *

WITHERS, Googie   1917-

PERSONAL: Born Georgette Lizette Withers, March 12, 1917, in Karachi, India (now Pakistan); daughter of Edgar Clements and Lizette Catarina Wilhelmina (van Wageningen) Withers; married John McCallum. *Education:* Studied for the stage with Italia Condi in London; studied at Helena Lehmiski Academy, Birmingham, England, and at the Buddy Bradley School of Dancing. *Avocational interests:* Interior decorating, music, books.

CAREER: Actress.

AWARDS, HONORS: British Academy of Film and Television Arts Award, best television actress, 1954; Sun Award, best actress, 1974; Officer of the Order of Australia, 1980; Annual Cable Excellence Award, best actress in a movie or mini-series, 1988, for *Time After Time.*

CREDITS:

STAGE APPEARANCES

(Stage debut) *The Windmill Man,* Victoria Palace, 1929.

Chorus, *Nice Goings On,* Strand Theatre, London, 1933.

Happy Week-End, Duke of York's Theatre, London, 1934.

This World of Ours, Gate Theatre, London, 1935.

Miss Worrall, *Duet in Floodlight,* Apollo Theatre, London, 1935.

Diana, *Ladies and Gentlemen,* Strand Theatre, 1937.

Sally Pilgrim, *Hand in Glove,* Richmond Theatre, London, 1937.

Alice Foster, *They Came to a City,* Globe Theatre, London, 1943.

Amanda Prynne, *Private Lives,* Apollo Theatre, 1945.

Lee, *Champagne for Delilah,* New Theatre, London, 1949.

Georgie Elgin, *Winter Journey,* St. James's Theatre, London, 1952.

Hester Collyer, *The Deep Blue Sea,* Duchess Theatre, London, 1952.

Jill Manning, *Waiting for Gillian,* St. James's Theatre, 1954.

Jessica, *Janus,* Aldwych Theatre, London, 1957.

Gertrude, *Hamlet,* Shakespeare Memorial Theatre, Stratford-on-Avon, England, 1958.

Beatrice, *Much Ado About Nothing,* Shakespeare Memorial Theatre, 1958.

Georgie Elgin, *Winter Journey,* Comedy Theatre, Melbourne, Australia, 1960.

Constance, *The Constant Wife,* Comedy Theatre, 1960.

(New York debut) Mary Rhodes, *The Complaisant Lover,* Ethel Barrymore Theatre, 1961.

Amy Preston, *Woman in a Dressing Gown,* Comedy Theatre, 1962.

Queen Marguerite, *Exit the King,* Edinburgh Festival, Scotland, and Royal Court Theatre, London, 1963.

Edith Cassidy, *Desire of the Moth,* Comedy Theatre, 1966.

Mrs. George, *Getting Married,* Strand Theatre, 1967.

Madame Ranevsky, *The Cherry Orchard,* Melbourne Theatre Company, 1971.

Mrs. Chevely, *An Ideal Husband,* Melbourne Theatre Company, 1971.

Lady Kitty, *The Circle,* Haymarket Theatre, London, 1976.

Lady Bracknell, *The Importance of Being Earnest,* Chichester Festival, Chichester, England, 1979.

Mrs. Conway, *Time and the Conways,* Chichester Festival, 1983.

Mrs. St. Maugham, *The Chalk Garden,* Chichester Festival, 1986.

Also appeared in productions for military troops in England and the British Liberation Army with Southern Command Entertainments, 1944; appeared in *School for Scandal,* London; and in productions of *Dandy Dick, Hay Fever,* and *Ring Round the Moon.*

MAJOR TOURS

Hester Collyer, *The Deep Blue Sea,* Australian and New Zealand cities, 1955.

Laura Foster, *Simon and Laura,* Australian and New Zealand cities, 1955.

Emma, *Roar Like a Dove,* Australian and New Zealand cities, 1959.

Georgie Elgin, *Winter Journey,* Australian and New Zealand cities, 1960.

The First Four Hundred Years (excerpts from Shakespeare), Australian and New Zealand cities, 1964.

Lady Piper, *Beekman Place,* Australian cities, 1965.

Relatively Speaking, Australian cities, 1968.

Plaza Suite, Australian and New Zealand cities, 1969-70.

The Kingfisher, Australian cities, 1978-79, and Middle Eastern cities.

Stardust, British cities, 1986.

Also toured as Amy Preston, *Woman in a Dressing Gown,* 1962; and as Edith Cassidy, *Desire of the Moth,* c. 1966.

FILM APPEARANCES

Sally, *The Girl in the Crowd,* First National/Warner Bros., 1934.

Daphne Tomkins, *All at Sea,* Twentieth Century-Fox, 1935.

Annie, *Dark World,* Twentieth Century-Fox, 1935.

Effie, *Her Last Affaire,* Producers Distributors Corp., 1935.

Minnie, *The Love Test,* Twentieth Century-Fox, 1935.

Dodie, *Windfall,* RKO, 1935.

Ninette, *Accused,* United Artists, 1936.

Miss Dupres, *Crime Over London,* United Artists, 1936.

Ella, *Crown vs. Stevens,* First National, 1936.

Elaine, *King of Hearts* (also known as *Little Gel*), Butchers Film Service, 1936.

Dora, *She Knew What She Wanted,* Wardour, 1936.

Mary, *Action for Slander,* United Artists, 1937.

Doreen, *Pearls Bring Tears,* Columbia, 1937.

Lottie, *Convict 99,* General Film Distributors, 1938.

Miki, *The Gaiety Girls* (also known as *Paradise For Two*), United Artists, 1938.

Pat, *If I Were Boss,* Columbia, 1938.

Lady Moya, *Kate Plus Ten,* General Film Distributors, 1938.

Blanche, *The Lady Vanishes,* Metro-Goldwyn-Mayer, 1938.

Jean Mason, *Paid in Error,* Columbia, 1938.

Elsie, *Strange Boarders,* Gainsborough Productions/GB, 1938.

Helen Firmstone, *You're the Doctor,* British Independent, 1938.

Dora, *She Couldn't Say No,* Associated British Films, 1939.

Mary Brown, *Trouble Brewing,* Associated British Films, 1939.

Dead Men Are Dangerous, Pathe, 1939.

Toots, *Bulldog Sees It Through,* ABPC, 1940.

Polly, *Busman's Honeymoon* (also known as *Haunted Honeymoon*), Metro-Goldwyn-Mayer, 1940.

Lola Matthews, *Murder in the Night* (also known as *Murder in Soho*), Film Alliance, 1940.

Laundry girl, *Girl in Distress* (also known as *Jeannie*), General Film Distributors, 1941.

Bobbie, *Back Room Boy,* General Film Distributors, 1942.

Joe de Vries, *One of Our Aircraft Is Missing,* United Artists, 1942.

Helen Hale, *On Approval,* English, 1944.

Alice, *They Came to a City,* Ealing, 1944.

Helene van Leyden, *The Silver Fleet,* Producers Releasing Corporation, 1945.

Joan Courtland, *Dead of Night,* Universal, 1946.

Title role, *The Loves of Joanna Godden,* General Film Distributors, 1947.

Rose Sandigate, *It Always Rains on Sunday,* Eagle-Lion, 1949.

Clare Marten, *Miranda,* Eagle-Lion, 1949.

Ms. Carol Gilbert, *Once Upon a Dream,* General Film Distributors, 1949.

Helen Nosseross, *Night and the City,* Twentieth Century-Fox, 1950.

Pearl Bono, *Pink String and Sealing Wax,* Pentagon, 1950.

Bumble Pelham, *Traveller's Joy,* General Film Distributors, 1951.

Betty Molloy, *Four Against Fate* (also known as *Derby Day*), British Lion, 1952.

Sitter in bath studio, *The Magic Box,* British Lion, 1952.

Dr. Sophie Dean, *White Corridors,* Jaro, 1952.

Mrs. Cadell, *Devil on Horseback,* British Lion, 1954.

Anne Stirling, *Port of Escape,* Renown, 1955.

Lady Godiva Rides Again, Carroll, 1955.

Meg Blake, *The Nickel Queen,* Woomera, 1971.

Also appeared in *Safe Harbor.*

TELEVISION APPEARANCES

Leda Klein, *Time After Time* (movie), BBC-TV/Arts & Entertainment/Australian Broadcasting Corp., 1985.

Ending Up (special), ITV, 1990.

Also appeared in *Hotel du Lac* (movie), 1986; as Mrs. Allen, *Northanger Abbey* (series), 1987; as Lady Armstrong, *Melba* (series), 1989; and in *Within These Walls* (series), *Amphitryon 38* (special), and *The Deep Blue Sea* (special).*

*   *   *

WOLFE, Ian 1896-

PERSONAL: Born November 4, 1896, in Canton, IL. *Avocational interests:* Writing poetry.

ADDRESSES: Agent—Progressive Artists Agency, 400 S. Beverly Drive, Suite 216, Beverly Hills, CA 90212.

CAREER: Actor. *Military service:* Served as a volunteer medical sergeant in World War I.

CREDITS:

FILM APPEARANCES

Harry Bevan, *The Barretts of Wimpole Street* (also known as *Forbidden Alliance*), Metro-Goldwyn-Mayer (MGM), 1934.

Van Arkel, *The Fountain,* Radio, 1934.

Swedish Consul, *The Mighty Barnum,* United Artists, 1934.

Kent, *Clive of India,* United Artists, 1935.

Maggs, *Mutiny on the Bounty,* MGM, 1935.

Pinky Geoffrey, *The Raven,* Universal, 1935.

Davidson, *$1,000 a Minute,* Republic, 1935.

Mad Love (also known as *The Hands of Orlac*), MGM, 1935.

The Last of the Mohicans, United Artists, 1936.

Priest, *Bold Caballero* (also known as *The Bold Cavalier*), Republic, 1936.

Hudson, *The Leavenworth Case,* Republic, 1936.

Apothecary, *Romeo and Juliet,* MGM, 1936.

Sanders, *The Devil Is Driving,* Columbia, 1937.

Leon, *The Emperor's Candlesticks,* MGM, 1937.

Izquierdo, *The Firefly,* MGM, 1937.

Nicholas Cabot, *League of Frightened Men,* Columbia, 1937.

Court official, *Maytime,* MGM, 1937.

Proprietor, *The Prince and the Pauper,* First National/Warner Brothers, 1937.

Conquest (also known as *Marie Walewska*), MGM, 1937.

A. LeMarchand, *Arsene Lupin Returns,* MGM, 1938.

Judge, *Blondie,* Columbia, 1938.

Herbert the jailer, *Marie Antoinette,* MGM, 1938.

Kirby's secretary, *You Can't Take It with You,* Columbia, 1938.

Poole, *Allegheny Uprising* (also known as *The First Rebel*), RKO, 1939.

Police judge, *Blondie Brings up Baby,* Columbia, 1939.

Wilkes, *Fast and Loose,* MGM, 1939.

Charles Wentworth, *On Borrowed Time,* MGM, 1939.

Bunting, *Orphans of the Street,* Republic, 1939.

Schmidt, *Society Lawyer,* MGM, 1939.

Fritz, *Tell No Tales,* MGM, 1939.

The Return of Dr. X, Warner Brothers, 1939.

Abe Lincoln in Illinois (also known as *Spirit of the People*), RKO, 1940.

Reading clerk, *The Earl of Chicago,* MGM, 1940.

Totten, *Earthbound,* Twentieth Century-Fox, 1940.

Stiles, *Foreign Correspondent,* United Artists, 1940.

Mayor, *Hudson's Bay,* Twentieth Century-Fox, 1940.

Judge, *We Who Are Young,* MGM, 1940.

Tax collector, *The Great Commandment,* Twentieth Century-Fox, 1941.

Doctor, *Love Crazy,* MGM, 1941.

Thin workman, *Paris Calling,* Universal, 1941.

Dr. Winston, *The Trial of Mary Dugan,* MGM, 1941.

Bombs over Burma, Producers Releasing Corporation, 1942.

Sir Charles Porter, *Eagle Squadron,* Universal, 1942.

Dentist, *Mrs. Miniver,* MGM, 1942.

Abbington's butler, *Nightmare,* Universal, 1942.

Lloyd, *Now, Voyager,* Warner Brothers, 1942.

Registrar, *Random Harvest,* MGM, 1942.

Robert, *Saboteur,* Universal, 1942.

Captain Larsen, *Secret Agent of Japan,* Twentieth Century-Fox, 1942.

Reggie, *We Were Dancing,* MGM, 1942.

Eustace L. Harley, *The Falcon and the Co-eds,* RKO, 1943.

Librarian, *Flesh and Fantasy,* Universal, 1943.

Hotel clerk, *Government Girl,* RKO, 1943.

Strawley, *Holy Matrimony,* Twentieth Century-Fox, 1943.

Professor Runnymead, *The Iron Major,* RKO, 1943.

Joseph, *The Moon Is Down,* Twentieth Century-Fox, 1943.

Antique store clerk, *Sherlock Holmes Faces Death,* Universal, 1943.

Antique store clerk, *Sherlock Holmes in Washington,* Universal, 1943.

Minister of the interior, *The Song of Bernadette,* Twentieth Century-Fox, 1943.

Corvette K-225 (also known as *The Nelson Touch*), Universal, 1943.

The Falcon in Danger, RKO, 1943.

Babes on Swing Street, Universal, 1944.

Pa Henderson, *Are These Our Parents?* (also known as *They Are Guilty*), Monogram, 1944.

Caleb, *Her Primitive Man,* Universal, 1944.

Sergeant clerk, *The Imposter* (also known as *Strange Confession*), Universal, 1944.

Second butler, *In Society,* Universal, 1944.

Jim Feeny, *Invisible Man's Revenge,* Universal, 1944.

Clerk, *The Merry Monahans,* Universal, 1944.

Edwards, *Murder in the Blue Room,* Universal, 1944.

Reporter, *Once upon a Time,* Columbia, 1944.

Professor Mellasagus, *Reckless Age,* Universal, 1944.

Drake, *The Scarlet Claw* (also known as *Sherlock Holmes and the Scarlet Claw*), Universal, 1944.

Amoss Hodder, *The Pearl of Death,* Universal, 1944.

Process server, *Seven Days Ashore,* RKO, 1944.

Skipper, *The White Cliffs of Dover,* MGM, 1944.

Oliver, *Blonde Ransom,* Universal, 1945.

Mayor, *The Brighton Strangler,* RKO, 1945.

Dr. Bellows, *Confidential Agent,* Warner Brothers/First National, 1945.

Ostrovski, *Counter-Attack* (also known as *One Against Seven*), Columbia, 1945.

Berton, *The Fighting Guardsman,* Columbia, 1945.

Vicar, *Love Letters,* Paramount, 1945.

Pleyel's clerk, *A Song to Remember,* Columbia, 1945.

Dr. Straus, *This Love of Ours,* Universal, 1945.

Professor Hopkins, *Zombies on Broadway* (also known as *Loonies on Broadway*), RKO, 1945.

Lord Mortimer, *The Bandit of Sherwood Forest,* Columbia 1946.

Sidney Long, *Bedlam,* RKO, 1946.

Man, *Dressed to Kill* (also known as *Sherlock Holmes and the Secret Code*), Universal, 1946.

Denison, *The Falcon's Adventure,* RKO, 1946.

Adam Wheelright, *The Notorious Lone Wolf,* Columbia, 1946.

Norton, *Tomorrow Is Forever,* RKO, 1946.

Charlie Gibbs, *Without Reservations,* RKO, 1946.

Jury foreman, *The Verdict,* Warner Brothers, 1946.

The Searching Wind, Paramount, 1946.

Gentleman Joe Palooka (also known as *Joe Palooka, Champ*), Monogram, 1946.

Three Strangers, First National/Warner Brothers, 1946.

Unexpected Guest, United Artists, 1946.

E. J. Lutz, *Dishonored Lady,* United Artists, 1947.

Doctor, *If Winter Comes,* MGM, 1947.

Black, *The Marauders,* United Artists, 1947.

Coroner, *Pursued,* Warner Brothers, 1947.

L. B. Crandall, *That Way with Women,* Warner Brothers, 1947.

Martin, *Wild Harvest,* Paramount, 1947.

Health officer, *Angel in Exile,* Republic, 1948.

Rector, *Johnny Belinda,* Warner Brothers, 1948.

Hobson, *Julia Misbehaves,* MGM, 1948.

Smith, *Mr. Blandings Builds His Dream House,* RKO/Selznick, 1948.

Deputy, *Silver River,* Warner Brothers, 1948.

Butler, *Three Daring Daughters* (also known as *The Birds and the Bees*), MGM, 1948.

Wallace, *Colorado Territory,* Warner Brothers, 1949.

Professor Lilliquist, *Joe Palooka in the Counter-Punch,* Monogram, 1949.

Hector Brown, *The Judge Steps Out* (also known as *Indian Summer*), RKO, 1949.

Hawkins, *They Live by Night* (also known as *Your Red Wagon* and *The Twisted Road*), RKO, 1949.

Chairman, *The Younger Brothers,* Warner Brothers, 1949.

Mr. Henderson, *Copper Canyon,* Paramount, 1950.

Dr. White, *Emergency Wedding* (also known as *Jealousy*), Columbia, 1950.

Mr. Adams, *The Magnificent Yankee* (also known as *The Man with Thirty Sons*), MGM, 1950.

President Webb, *The Petty Girl* (also known as *Girl of the Year*), Columbia, 1950.

Edward Warrender, *Please Believe Me,* MGM, 1950.

No Way Out, Twentieth Century-Fox, 1950.

Hutchins, *The Great Caruso,* MGM, 1951.

Uncle Adam, *Here Comes the Groom,* Paramount, 1951.

Signor Donner, *Mask of the Avenger,* Columbia, 1951.

Carrey, *On Dangerous Ground,* RKO, 1951.

Dr. Weyland, *A Place in the Sun,* Paramount, 1951.

Viceroy, *Captain Pirate* (also known as *Captain Blood, Fugitive*), Columbia, 1952.

Reverend Nash, *Captive City,* United Artists, 1952.

Presiding judge, *Les Miserables,* Twentieth Century-Fox, 1952.

Foster, *Something for the Birds,* Twentieth Century-Fox, 1952.

Mr. Bagley, *The Actress,* MGM, 1953.

Fante, *Houdini,* Paramount, 1953.

Ligarius, *Julius Caesar,* MGM, 1953.

Councilman Hurdwell, *Scandal at Scourie,* MGM, 1953.

Stranger, *Young Bess,* MGM, 1953.

Walde Daggett, *99 River Street,* United Artists, 1953.

Mr. Pope, *About Mrs. Leslie,* Paramount, 1954.

Roger Frane, *Her Twelve Men,* MGM, 1954.

Reverend Elcott, *Seven Brides for Seven Brothers,* MGM, 1954.

Theron, *The Silver Chalice,* Warner Brothers, 1954.

The Steel Cage, United Artists, 1954.

President Calvin Coolidge, *The Court-Martial of Billy Mitchell* (also known as *One-Man Mutiny*), Warner Brothers, 1955.

Lord Tremouille, *Diane,* MGM, 1955.

Fell, *The King's Thief,* MGM, 1955.

Tewkesbury, *Moonfleet,* MGM, 1955.

Lecturer, *Rebel without a Cause,* Warner Brothers, 1955.

Mr. Rojecki, *Sincerely Yours,* Warner Brothers, 1955.

Registrar, *Gaby,* MGM, 1956.

Carter, *Witness for the Prosecution,* United Artists, 1957.

Mr. Neely, *Pollyanna,* Buena Vista, 1960.

Burton White, *The Lost World,* Twentieth Century-Fox, 1960.

O'Hara, *All in a Night's Work,* Paramount, 1961.

Gruber, *The Wonderful World of the Brothers Grimm,* MGM, 1962.

Pierre, *Diary of a Madman,* United Artists, 1963.

Bishop Hardwick, *One Man's Way,* United Artists, 1964.

Dr. Edwards, *Games,* Universal, 1967.

PTO, *THX 1138,* Warner Brothers, 1971.

Mr. Loomis, *Homebodies,* AVCO-Embassy, 1974.

Priest, *The Terminal Man,* Warner Brothers, 1974.

Justice of the peace, *The Fortune,* Columbia, 1975.

Abner and Arnie, *Mr. Sycamore,* Film Venture, 1975.

Judge, *Mean Dog Blues,* ITC Entertainment/American International, 1978.

The Seniors, Cinema Shares, 1978.

Father Joseph, *The Frisco Kid,* Warner Brothers, 1979.

Commandant Caseway, *Up the Academy* (also known as *Mad Magazine's "Up the Academy"* and *The Brave Young Men of Weinberg*), Warner Brothers, 1980.

Mr. Partlow, *Reds,* Paramount, 1981.

Jinxed, MGM/United Artists, 1982.

Professor Brauer, *Creator,* Universal, 1985.

Mr. D'Amato, *Checking Out,* Warner Brothers, 1989.

Forger, *Dick Tracy,* Buena Vista, 1990.

Also appeared in *Son of Monte Cristo,* 1940; *Keep 'em Sailing,* 1942; *Famous Bonners,* 1942; *Mystery of the River Boat* (serial), 1944; and *California,* 1947.

TELEVISION APPEARANCES; EPISODIC

Judge, *The Defender* (broadcast as an episode of *Studio One*), CBS, 1957.

Strange Counsel (broadcast as an episode of *Colgate Theater*), NBC, 1958.

"Father Image," *One Step Beyond,* ABC, 1959.

Schwimmer, "Uncle Simon," *The Twilight Zone,* CBS, 1963.

Reverend Leighton, *The Andy Griffith Show,* CBS, 1966.

Love on a Rooftop, ABC, 1967.

Septimus, "Bread and Circuses," *Star Trek,* NBC, 1968.

Mr. Atoz, "All Our Yesterdays," *Star Trek,* NBC, 1969.

The Partridge Family, ABC, 1971.

The Mary Tyler Moore Show, CBS, 1975.

The New Original Wonder Woman, ABC, 1975.

All in the Family, CBS, 1977.

Barney Miller, ABC, 1977.

Taxi, ABC, 1979.

Cheers, NBC, 1982.

Barney Miller, ABC, 1982.

Searle, *The Fall Guy,* ABC, 1985.

Grandpa Charlie, "Grandpa's Ghost," *Amazing Stories,* NBC, 1986.

Rupert Simpson, *Scarecrow and Mrs. King,* CBS, 1986.

Also appeared in *Trouble in High Timber Country,* 1980, and as a judge in *Daniel Boone,* NBC.

TELEVISION APPEARANCES; MOVIES

Father McHugh, *The Devil's Daughter,* ABC, 1973.
Dr. Klauber, *James A. Michener's "Dynasty,"* NBC, 1976.
Dorset, *Mae West,* ABC, 1982.
LBJ: The Early Years, NBC, 1987.

TELEVISION APPEARANCES; SPECIALS

Harley Dibble, *America, You're On,* ABC, 1975.

STAGE APPEARANCES

The Barretts of Wimpole Street, Empire Theatre, New York City, 1931.
Parcival, *Winesburg, Ohio,* National Theatre, New York City, 1958.
Father General, *The Deputy,* Brooks Atkinson Theatre, New York City, 1964.
Murderous Angels, Center Theatre Group, Mark Taper Forum, Los Angeles, 1969.

Also appeared with the Center Theatre Group, Mark Taper Forum, 1967-70; and with the Theatre Group, University of California at Los Angeles, 1965-66.*

*　　　*　　　*

WOOD, G. 1919-

PERSONAL: Born December 31, 1919, in Forrest City, AR. *Education:* Graduated from Carnegie Institute of Technology and New York University.

CAREER: Actor, composer, lyricist, and director. *Military service:* U.S. Army, Special Services theatrical adviser.

CREDITS:

STAGE APPEARANCES

(Broadway debut) Carbon de Castel-Jaloux, *Cyrano de Bergerac,* New York City Theatre Company, New York City Centre, 1953.
Priest, *King Richard,* New York City Theatre Company, New York City Centre, 1953.
Ignatz, *Reuben Reuben,* Shubert Theatre, Boston, MA, 1955.
Poet, *Cradle Song,* Circle in the Square, New York City, 1955.
Briggs, *Thunder Rock,* Broadway Congregational Church, 1956.
Cymen, *Thor, with Angels,* Broadway Congregational Church, 1956.
Raquel, *Tobias and the Angel,* Broadway Congregational Church, 1957.
Fr. William Callifer, *The Potting Shed,* Broadway Congregational Church, 1958.

Frank Hedge, *A Box of Watercolors,* Broadway Congregational Church, 1959 (also see below).
Dr. Hobie Merganser, *Kittiwake Island,* Martinique Theatre, New York City, 1960.
Yevgeny Sergeyevitch Dorn, *The Seagull,* Belasco Theatre, New York City, 1964.
Thomas Putnam, *The Crucible,* Belasco Theatre, 1964.
Monsieur Argan, *The Imaginary Invalid,* ANTA Theatre, New York City, 1967.
Jamie, *A Touch of the Poet,* ANTA Theatre, 1967.
Albert Godby, *Still Life,* ANTA Theatre, 1967.
Solinus, *The Comedy of Errors,* National Repertory Theatre, Ford's Theatre, Washington, DC, 1968 (also see below).
Robert E. Lee, John Brown, and Abraham Lincoln, *John Brown's Body,* National Repertory Theatre, Ford's Theatre, 1968.
Mr. Hardcastle, *She Stoops to Conquer,* National Repertory Theatre, Ford's Theatre, 1968.
The Little Murders, American Conservatory Theatre, San Francisco, CA, 1969.
Exeter, *Henry V,* American Shakespeare Festival, ANTA Theatre, 1969.
Hadrian VII, American Conservatory Theatre, 1970.
The Latent Homosexual, American Conservatory Theatre, 1971.
George Smith, *The Selling of the President,* American Conservatory Theatre, 1971.
Paradise Lost, American Conservatory Theatre, 1972.
The Contractor, American Conservatory Theatre, 1972.
The Cherry Orchard, Milwaukee Repertory Theatre Company, 1972-73.
Horace, *All Together,* Milwaukee Repertory Theatre Company, 1973.
The Service for Joseph Axminster, Milwaukee Repertory Theatre Company, 1974.
The Little Foxes, Milwaukee Repertory Theatre Company, 1974.
General Mike O'Henry, *Who's Who in Hell,* Lunt-Fontanne Theatre, New York City, 1974.
The Duchess of Malfi, Center Theatre Group, Mark Taper Forum, Los Angeles, 1975-76.
Reverend Canon Chasuble, *The Importance of Being Earnest,* Circle in the Square, New York City, 1977.
The Tempest, Meadow Brook Theatre, Rochester, MI, 1977-78.
Signor Chapuys, *A Man for All Seasons,* Center Theatre Group, Ahmanson Theatre, Los Angeles, 1978-79.
The Taming of the Shrew, McCarter Theatre Company, Princeton, NJ, 1980-81.
A Christmas Carol, McCarter Theatre Company, 1980-81.
Custer, McCarter Theatre Company, 1980-81.
Putting on the Dog, McCarter Theatre Company, 1980-81.

Gonzalo, *The Tempest,* Old Globe Theatre, San Diego, CA, 1981-83.

Weller Martin, *The Gin Game,* Old Globe Theatre, 1981-83.

Duke Fredrick, *As You Like It,* Old Globe Theatre, 1981-83.

John Tarleton, *Misalliance,* Old Globe Theatre, 1981-83.

Oh, Coward!, Old Globe Theatre, 1981-83 (also see below).

Judge, Tremayne, *The Skin of Our Teeth,* Old Globe Theatre, 1983.

Doctor, *Wings,* Old Globe Theatre, 1983.

Darling, *Clap Your Hands,* Old Globe Theatre, 1983.

Feste, *Twelfth Night,* Old Globe Theatre, 1983.

John of Gaunt, *Richard II,* Old Globe Theatre, 1986-87.

Sir Edmund Milne, *The Petition,* Old Globe Theatre, 1986-87.

Much Ado About Nothing, Old Globe Theatre, 1986-87.

Company member, The Repertory Theatre, St. Louis, MO, 1969-70; National Shakespeare Festival, San Diego, CA, 1972, 1975, 1976, 1978, 1979, and 1981; A Contemporary Theatre, Seattle, WA, 1975-76; Milwaukee Repertory Theater, 1976-77; McCarter Theatre Company, Princeton, NJ, 1979-80; California Shakespearean Festival, Visalia, CA, 1980; Denver Center Theatre Company, Denver, CO, 1984-85.

MAJOR TOURS

Romainville, *Ring 'Round the Moon,* National Repertory Theatre Company, 1963.

Police Captain, *Liliom,* National Repertory Theatre Company, 1964-65.

Mr. Hardcastle, *She Stoops to Conquer,* National Repertory Theatre Company, 1964-65.

The God Poseidon, *The Trojan Women,* National Repertory Theatre Company, 1965-66.

Sir Anthony Absolute, *The Rivals,* National Repertory Theatre Company, 1965-66.

The President, *The Madwoman of Chaillot,* National Repertory Theatre Company, 1965-66.

STAGE WORK; DIRECTOR

Fumed Oak, National Repertory Theatre, ANTA Theatre, 1967.

The Comedy of Errors, National Repertory Theatre, Washington, DC, 1968.

Oh, Coward!, Old Globe Theatre, San Diego, CA, 1981-83.

FILM APPEARANCES

Police Captain Crandall, *Brewster McCloud,* Metro-Goldwyn-Mayer, 1970.

Psychiatrist, *Harold and Maude,* Paramount, 1971.

Chief F.B.I. agent, *Bank Shot,* United Artists, 1974.

TELEVISION APPEARANCES; EPISODIC

General Hamilton Hammond, *M*A*S*H,* CBS, 1970 and 1972.

OTHER TELEVISION APPEARANCES

Jim, *On Borrowed Time* (special), "The Hallmark Hall of Fame," NBC, 1957.

Pagonis, *Truman Capote's "The Glass House"* (movie), CBS, 1972.

Warren Morgan, *It Couldn't Happen to a Nicer Guy* (movie), ABC, 1974.

Police commissioner, *Holmes and Yoyo* (series), ABC, 1976-77.

WRITINGS:

STAGE, EXCEPT WHERE NOTED

Lyrics, *Shoestring '57,* Barbizon-Plaza Theatre, New York City, 1956.

Music and lyrics, *Kaleidoscope,* Provincetown Playhouse, 1957.

Music, lyrics, and book, *A Box of Watercolors,* Broadway Congregational Church, 1959.

Music and lyrics, "Three Cheers for the Tired Businessman," *Happy Medium,* Chicago Theatre, 1963.

Contributor, *Put It in Writing,* Theatre de Lys, 1963.

Music and lyrics, "The Old Eight-Ten" and "Merry Go-Round," *Baker's Dozen,* Plaza 9 Theatre, 1964.

Music, lyrics, and (with Carson McCullers and Theodore Mann) book, *F. Jasmine Addams,* Circle in the Square, New York City, 1971.

Author of revues *Sweetest and Lowest* and *Slings and Arrows.* Composed the song "My One and Only Love" for the feature film *Let's Get Lost,* 1988.*

*   *   *

WOODARD, Alfre   1953-

PERSONAL: Born November 8, 1953, in Tulsa, OK; married Roderick Spencer. *Education:* Boston University, B.F.A. (cum laude), 1974.

CAREER: Actress. Appeared with Arena Stage, Washington, DC, 1973-74; appeared with the Center Theatre Group's Improvisational Theatre Project, Mark Taper Forum, Los Angeles, CA, 1977-78.

AWARDS, HONORS: Academy Award nomination, best supporting actress, 1984, for *Cross Creek;* Golden Apple Award, best newcomer, 1984; Emmy Awards, best supporting actress in a drama series, 1984, for *Hill Street Blues* episode "Doris in Wonderland," and best guest performance in a drama series, 1987, for the pilot *L.A. Law;*

Emmy Award nominations, 1985 and (for best actress in a drama series) 1986, for *St. Elsewhere;* NAACP Image Awards, both best actress in a drama, 1988, for *Mandela,* and 1990, for *A Mother's Courage.*

CREDITS:

TELEVISION APPEARANCES; MOVIES, EXCEPT WHERE NOTED

Katie, *Freedom Road,* NBC, 1979.
Evelyn Evers, *The Sophisticated Gents,* NBC, 1981.
Kariha Ellsworth, *The Ambush Murders,* CBS, 1982.
Vickie Teegue, *Sweet Revenge,* CBS, 1984.
Maude DeVictor, *Unnatural Causes,* NBC, 1986.
Winnie Mandela, *Mandela,* HBO, 1987.
L.A. Law (pilot), NBC, 1987.
Andrea Crawford, *The Child Saver* (also known as *The Fierce Dreams of Jackie Watson*), NBC, 1988.
Jessica Filley, *Blue Bayou* (also known as *Orleans*), NBC, 1990.

TELEVISION APPEARANCES; EPISODIC

"The Trial of the Moke," *Great Performances,* PBS, 1978.
"Doris in Wonderland," *Hill Street Blues,* NBC, 1984.
Mattie Custer, "The Killing Floor," *American Playhouse,* PBS, 1984.

Also appeared on *Faerie Tale Theater.*

TELEVISION APPEARANCES; SERIES

Marsha Fulbright, *Tucker's Witch,* CBS, 1982-83.
Roz Dupree, *Sara,* NBC, 1985.
Dr. Roxanne Turner, *St. Elsewhere,* NBC, 1985-87.

TELEVISION APPEARANCES; SPECIALS

For Colored Girls Who Have Considered Suicide/When the Rainbow is Enuf, PBS, 1982.
Denise Powell, *The Line,* NBC, 1987.
The 20th Annual NAACP Image Awards, NBC, 1988.
The 9th Annual ACE Awards, HBO, 1988.
Title role, *A Mother's Courage: The Mary Thomas Story* (also known as *The Long Shot*), *Magical World of Disney,* NBC, 1989.
The 10th Annual ACE Awards, Black Entertainment Television, CBN, Discovery Channel, Lifetime, Nickelodeon, TBS, and USA, 1989.

Also appeared in *Words By Heart, For Love of a Soldier, Games Before We Forget, That Good Witch of Laurel Canyon, Palmerstown, Enos, White Shadow,* and *Two By South.*

FILM APPEARANCES

(Film debut) Rita, *Remember My Name,* Columbia, 1978.
Health (also known as *H.E.A.L.T.H.*), Twentieth Century-Fox, 1980.

Geechee, *Cross Creek,* Universal, 1983.
Esther, *Go Tell It on the Mountain,* Learning in Focus, 1984.
Patricia, *Extremities,* Atlantic, 1986.
Grace Cooley, *Scrooged,* Paramount, 1988.
Popeye Jackson, *Miss Firecracker,* Corsair, 1989.

STAGE APPEARANCES

(Understudy) *Me and Bessie,* Ambassador Theatre, then Edison Theatre, both New York City, 1975.
Terry, *So Nice, They Named It Twice,* New York Shakespeare Festival, Public/Other Stage, New York City, 1975-76.
For Colored Girls Who Have Considered Suicide/When the Rainbow is Enuf, Center Theatre Group, Mark Taper Forum, and Huntington Theatre, Los Angeles, CA, 1977.
"Precious Blood," *Two By South,* Los Angeles Actors Theatre, Los Angeles, 1981.
Elaine Le Fanu, *A Map of the World,* Public/Newman Theatre, New York City, 1985.

Also appeared in *Horatio* and *Saved,* both for Arena Stage, Washington, DC; and in *Split Second, Bugs Guns, Leander Stillwell, Vlast,* and *A Christmas Carol.* Appeared in an Australian touring production of *For Colored Girls Who Have Considered Suicide/When the Rainbow is Enuf.**

*   *   *

WOODVINE, John   1929-

PERSONAL: Born July 21, 1929, in Tyne Dock, Durham, England; son of John and Rose (Kelly) Woodvine; married Hazel Wright. *Education:* Attended grammar school in England; studied acting at Royal Academy of Dramatic Arts.

ADDRESSES: Agent—c/o Scott Marshall Ltd., 13 Queen's Gardens, London W2 England.

CAREER: Actor.

AWARDS, HONORS: Laurence Olivier Award, Comedy Performance of the Year, 1987, for *Henry IV, Part One* and *Part Two.*

CREDITS:

STAGE APPEARANCES

Vincentio, *The Taming of the Shrew,* Old Vic Theatre, London, 1954.
Macbeth, Old Vic Theatre, 1954.
Duke Senior, *As You Like It,* Old Vic Theatre, 1955.
Lord Chief Justice, *Henry IV, Part One,* Old Vic Theatre, 1955.

Lord Chief Justice, *Henry IV, Part Two,* Old Vic Theatre, 1955.

Tybalt, *Romeo and Juliet,* Old Vic Theatre, 1956.

Roderigo, *Othello,* Old Vic Theatre, 1956.

Careless, *The Double Dealer,* Old Vic Theatre, 1959.

Mowbray, *Richard II,* Old Vic Theatre, 1959.

Nym, *The Merry Wives of Windsor,* Old Vic Theatre, 1959.

Harry V. Esterbrook, *Inherit the Wind,* St. Martin's Theatre, London, 1960.

General Lew Wallace, *The Andersonville Trial,* Mermaid Theatre, London, 1961.

Vazquez, *'Tis Pity She's a Whore,* Mermaid Theatre, London, 1961.

Long John Silver, *Treasure Island,* Mermaid Theatre, London, 1961.

Pentheus, *The Bacchae,* Mermaid Theatre, London, 1964.

Title role, *Macbeth,* Mermaid Theatre, London, 1964.

Simon Eyre, *The Shoemaker's Holiday,* Mermaid Theatre, London, 1964.

Theseus, *Oedipus at Colonus,* Mermaid Theatre, London, 1965.

Cutler Walpole, *The Doctor's Dilemma,* Comedy Theatre, London, 1966.

Badger, *Toad of Toad Hall,* Comedy Theatre, 1966.

Jackie, *Close the Coalhouse Door,* Fortune Theatre, London, 1968.

Warrant Officer Ormsby, *Poor Horace,* Lyric Theatre, London, 1970.

Joe Wilson, *Joe Lives!* (one-man show), University Theatre, Newcastle, England, then Greenwich, England, 1971.

Sir Wilful Witwoud, *The Way of the World,* Actors' Company, Edinburgh Festival, Edinburgh, Scotland, 1974.

Orlvosky, *The Wood Demon,* Actors' Company, Brooklyn Academy of Music, New York City, 1974.

Earl of Kent, *King Lear,* Actors' Company, Brooklyn Academy of Music, 1974.

Sir Wilful Witwoud, *The Way of the World,* Actors' Company, Brooklyn Academy of Music, 1974.

Cardinal, *'Tis Pity She's a Whore,* Actors' Company, Wimbledon Theatre, Wimbledon, England, 1974.

Pontagnac, *Ruling the Roost,* Actors' Company, Wimbledon Theatre, 1974.

Staller, *Stallerhof,* Hampstead Theatre, London, 1975.

Gerald, *The Formation Dancers,* Arnaud Guildford Theatre, United Kingdom, 1975, Royal Shakespeare Company (RSC), 1976.

Duke of Cornwall, *King Lear,* RSC, 1977.

Capulet, *Romeo and Juliet,* RSC, 1977.

Dogberry, *Much Ado About Nothing,* RSC, 1977.

Polixenes, *The Winter's Tale,* RSC, 1977.

Banquo, *Macbeth,* RSC, 1977.

Dr. Pinch, *A Comedy of Errors,* RSC, 1977.

Subtle, *The Alchemist,* RSC, 1977.

Fainall, *The Way of the World,* Aldwych Theatre, London, 1978.

Alexander, *Every Good Boy Deserves Favour,* Mermaid Theatre, 1979.

Sir John Falstaff, *The Merry Wives of Windsor,* RSC, 1979-80.

Malvolio, *Twelfth Night,* RSC, 1979-80.

Title role, *Julius Caesar,* RSC, 1979-80.

Charles Merrythought, *The Knight of the Burning Pestle,* RSC, 1981.

Ralph Nickleby, *The Life and Adventures of Nicholas Nickleby,* RSC, then Plymouth Theatre, New York City, 1981.

Mr. Prince, *Rocket to the Moon,* Hampstead Theatre, then Apollo Theatre, London, 1982.

Gregor Hasek, *Between East and West,* Hampstead Theatre, 1987.

Sir John Falstaff, *Henry IV, Part One* and *Part Two,* All English Stage Company, Old Vic Theatre, London, 1987.

Gens, *Ghetto,* National Theatre Company, Olivier Theatre, London, 1989.

Dr. Gortler, *I Have Been Here Before,* Watford, England, 1990.

Chris, *Anna Christie,* Young Vic Theatre, London, 1990.

MAJOR TOURS

(Stage debut) Caspar Darde, *Captain Carvallo,* tour of service establishments, 1954.

Claudius, *Hamlet,* British cities, 1971.

FILM APPEARANCES

Bertie Irons, *The Walking Stick,* Metro-Goldwyn-Mayer, 1970.

Howard, *Young Winston,* Columbia, 1972.

Inspector Matt Fenrek, *Assault on Agathon,* Nine Network, 1976.

Dr. Hirsch, *An American Werewolf in London,* Universal, 1981.

Also appeared as Trincant, *The Devils,* 1971; appeared in *Darling,* 1964; and *Squaring the Circle,* 1983.

TELEVISION APPEARANCES

Ralph Nickleby, *Nicholas Nickleby* (special), syndicated, 1983.

Rupert Potter, "The Tale of Beatrix Potter" (mini-series), *Masterpiece Theatre,* PBS, 1984.

Christian Gilbranson, *Agatha Christie's Murder with Mirrors* (movie), CBS, 1985.

Chief Inspector, *Deceptions* (movie), NBC, 1985.

Mr. Stott, "And a Nightingale Sang" (episode), *Masterpiece Theatre,* PBS, 1989.

"A Tale of Two Cities," *Masterpiece Theatre* (mini-series), PBS, 1989.

Also appeared in specials as Master 488, *The Tripods*, 1985; Ross, *Edge of Darkness*, 1986; Dr. J. J. R. McLeod, *Glory Enough for All*, 1989; Tallon, *Danny, the Champion of the World*, 1989; appeared in series *The Dustbinmen*, *Elizabeth R*, and *Z Cars*.

SIDELIGHTS: Favorite roles: Simon Eyre in *The Shoemaker's Holiday*, Jackie in *Close the Coalhouse Door*, and Othello.*

* * *

WRIGHT, Amy 1950-

PERSONAL: Born April 15, 1950, in Chicago, IL. *Education:* Graduated from Beloit College.

ADDRESSES: Agent—Writers and Artists Agency, 11726 San Vicente Blvd., Suite 300, Los Angeles, CA 90049.

CAREER: Actress.

CREDITS:

STAGE APPEARANCES

Maria of Anjou, *Agnes and Joan*, Lab Theatre Company, All Angels Church, New York City, 1975.
Laura, *The Glass Menagerie*, Pittsburgh Public Theatre, Pittsburgh, PA, 1975.
One Flew over the Cuckoo's Nest, Pittsburgh Public Theatre, 1975.
Mary, *The Elusive Angel*, New Dramatists, Inc., New York City, 1976.
Jennifer, *A Safe Place*, New Dramatists, Inc., 1976.
Eva Jackson, *The Rimers of Eldritch*, Equity Library Theatre, New York City, 1976.
Title role, *Miss Julie*, Mrs. Y, *The Stronger*, and woman, *Creditors* (triple-bill), Hudson Guild Theatre, New York City, 1977.
Mrs. Y, *The Stronger*, and woman, *Creditors* (double-bill), New York Shakespeare Festival, Public Theatre, New York City, 1977.
Model, *Night Shift*, Playhouse Theatre, New York City, 1977.
The Little Foxes, Paper Mill Playhouse, Millburn, NJ, 1977.
Yucca, *My Cup Ranneth Over*, Circle Repertory Company Theatre, 1978.
Shirley Talley, *The Fifth of July*, Circle Repertory Company Theatre, New York City, 1978, then Center Theatre Group, Mark Taper Forum, Los Angeles,

1979, later New Apollo Theatre, New York City, 1980.
Connie, "Slacks and Tops," *Triple Feature*, Manhattan Theatre Club, New York City, 1983.
Shelby Dischinger, *Breakfast with Les and Bess*, Hudson Guild Theatre, 1983.
Poppy Norton-Taylor, *Noises Off*, Brooks Atkinson Theatre, New York City, 1983, then Center Theatre Group, Ahmanson Theatre, Los Angeles, 1984.
Words from the Moon, South Street Theatre, New York City, 1987.

Also appeared in productions of *Hamlet*, *Time Framed*, *Trifles*, *Terrible Jim Fitch*, and *Village Wooing*, all New York City.

FILM APPEARANCES

Cindy, *Not a Pretty Picture*, Other Cinema, 1975.
Bridesmaid, *The Deer Hunter*, Universal, 1978.
Ceil, *Girlfriends*, Warner Brothers, 1978.
Jackie, *The Amityville Horror*, American International, 1979.
Nancy, *Breaking Away*, Twentieth Century-Fox, 1979.
Sabbath Lily Hawks, *Wise Blood*, New Line, 1979.
Clara Jane, *Heartland*, Filmhaus, 1980.
Ann, *Inside Moves*, Associated Film Distributors, 1980.
Shelley, *Stardust Memories*, United Artists (UA), 1980.
Stacey, *Beer*, Orion, 1986.
Mary Ellen Gruenwald, *Off Beat*, Touchstone/Silver Screen Partners II, 1986.
Honey Boxe, irate neighbor, voice of Jennifer the answering machine, *The Telephone*, New World, 1988.
Rose Leary, *The Accidental Tourist*, Warner Brothers, 1988.
Ricki, *Crossing Delancey*, Warner Brothers, 1988.
Missy Mahoney, *Miss Firecracker*, Corsair, 1989.
Lurene, *Daddy's Dyin'. . . Who's Got the Will?* (also known as *Daddy's Dyin'*), Metro-Goldwyn-Mayer/UA, 1990.

TELEVISION APPEARANCES

Jean, *A Fine Romance* (pilot), CBS, 1983.
Dana Wendolowski, *Trapped in Silence* (movie), CBS, 1986.
Becky Whately, *Settle the Score* (movie; also known as *Hidden Rage* and *Blood Knot*), NBC, 1989.
Lucy, "Vaclav Havel's 'Largo Desolato,'" *Great Performances* (special), PBS, 1990.*

* * *

WRIGHT, Steven 1955-

PERSONAL: Born December 6, 1955, in New York City (some sources say Boston, MA); son of an electronics company executive and Dolly Wright. *Education:* Emerson College, B.A., 1978.

ADDRESSES: Agent—Marty Klein, Agency for the Performing Arts, Inc., 888 Seventh Ave., New York, NY 10106. *Publicity*—Sandy Friedman, Rogers & Cowan, Inc., 122 East 42nd St., New York, NY 10168. *Contact*—Bob Merlis, Warner Brothers (record label), 75 Rockefeller Plaza, New York, NY 10019.

CAREER: Comedian. Worked at several jobs, including parking cars and working in a warehouse; stand-up comedian, 1979—; performed mainly in New England until 1982; makes public appearances nationwide.

AWARDS, HONORS: Academy Award (with Dean Parisot), best live action film, short subject, 1988, for *The Appointments of Dennis Jennings.*

CREDITS:

TELEVISION APPEARANCES

(National debut) *Tonight Show,* NBC, 1982.
On Location: Steven Wright, HBO, 1985.
Comic Relief, HBO, 1986.
Comic Relief II, HBO, 1987.
Dwight Harper, *Get a Job,* PBS, 1987.
The Smothers Brothers Thanksgiving Special, CBS, 1988.
Comic Relief III, HBO, 1989.
Mike's Talent Show (variety show), Cinemax, 1989.
The Prince's Trust Gala (variety show), TBS, 1989.
Woodstock: Return to the Planet of the '60s (variety show), CBS, 1989.
Dennis Jennings, *The Appointments of Dennis Jennings* (also see below), HBO, 1989.
Comic Relief IV, HBO, 1990.
Wicker Chairs and Gravity (also see below), HBO, 1990.

Made nine appearances on *Tonight Show,* 1982-86. Also appeared on *Seventh Annual Young Comedians Show,* HBO, *Saturday Night Live, Late Night with David Letterman,* and *An Evening at the Improv.* Guest host on *Saturday Night Live* and Music Television (MTV).

FILM APPEARANCES

Larry Stillman, D.D.S., *Desperately Seeking Susan,* Orion, 1985.
Pruitt, *Stars and Bars,* Columbia, 1988.

Appeared in *Coffee and Cigarettes* (also see below), 1986; appeared as Sterling, *Men of Respect,* 1990.

RECORDINGS:

I Have a Pony (comedy album), Warner Brother Records, 1985.

WRITINGS:

The Appointments of Dennis Jennings (television script), HBO, 1989.

Also author of screenplay, *Coffee and Cigarettes,* 1986, and television script, *Wicker Chairs and Gravity,* 1990.

OTHER SOURCES:

BOOKS

Contemporary Newsmakers, issue 3, Gale, 1986.*

*   *   *

WUHL, Robert

PERSONAL: Surname pronounced "Wall"; born in Union, NJ. *Education:* Graduated from the University of Houston.

ADDRESSES: Agent—Lee Brillstein, International Creative Management, 8899 Beverly Blvd, Los Angeles, CA 90048. *Publicist*—Michelle Marx, Michelle Marx Inc., 9044 Melrose Ave., Los Angeles, CA 90069. *Manager*—Gail Stocker, 1025 North Kings Rd., No. 113, Los Angeles, CA 90069.

CAREER: Actor, writer, and comedian. Performs stand-up comedy throughout the United States with regular appearances at such New York City nightclubs as Catch a Rising Star, the Improv, and Caroline's; also appears at Atlantic City casinos; joke writer for Rodney Dangerfield's nightclub act.

CREDITS:

FILM APPEARANCES

Newbomb Turk, *The Hollywood Knights,* Columbia, 1980.
Mawby's regular, *Flashdance,* Paramount, 1983.
Marty Lee Dreiwitz, *Good Morning, Vietnam,* Buena Vista, 1987.
Benny Berbel, *Ray's Male Heterosexual Dance Hall,* Twentieth Century-Fox, 1988.
Larry, *Bull Durham,* Orion, 1988.
Alexander Knox, *Batman,* Warner Brothers, 1989.
Red Synder, *Blaze,* Buena Vista, 1989.
Waiter, *Wedding Band,* IRS Media, 1990.

TELEVISION APPEARANCES; PILOTS

Joel Larabee, *Rockhopper,* CBS, 1985.
Sid Barrows, *Sniff,* CBS, 1988.

TELEVISION APPEARANCES; EPISODIC

Barker, "Dig That Cat . . . He's Real Gone!," *Tales from the Crypt,* HBO, 1989.

TELEVISION APPEARANCES; SERIES

Appeared in *Moonlighting*, ABC; *L.A. Law*, NBC; *Falcon Crest*, CBS. Also appeared on *The Tonight Show Starring Johnny Carson*, NBC; *Late Night with David Letterman*, NBC; *The Merv Griffin Show*, syndicated.

TELEVISION APPEARANCES; SPECIALS

Arlo, *The Big Bang* (also known as *Robert Wuhl's The Big Bang* and *Cinemax Comedy Experiment*), Cinemax, 1986.
Comic Relief IV (also known as *Comic Relief '90*), HBO, 1990.
Time Warner Presents the Earth Day Special, ABC, CBS, and NBC, 1990.

Also appeared in *Wild Wuhl of Sports*, Playboy Channel.

TELEVISION WORK

Story editor, *Police Squad!* (series), ABC, 1982.

Director, *The Big Bang* (also known as *Robert Wuhl's The Big Bang* and *Cinemax Comedy Experiment*), Cinemax, 1986.

WRITINGS:

TELEVISION; PILOTS

(With Rod Warren and Eric Lieber) *Legends of the West: Truth and Tall Tales*, ABC, 1981.

TELEVISION; EPISODIC

Police Squad!, ABC, 1982.
Sledge Hammer!, ABC, 1987.

TELEVISION; SPECIALS

The Big Bang (also known as *Robert Wuhl's The Big Band* and *Cinemax Comedy Experiment*), Cinemax, 1986.
The 29th Annual Grammy Awards, CBS, 1987.
The 30th Annual Grammy Awards, CBS, 1988.
The 31st Annual Grammy Awards, CBS, 1989.
The 62nd Annual Academy Awards, ABC, 1990.
The 63rd Annual Academy Awards, ABC, 1991.*

Y-Z

YOUNG, Robert M. 1924-
(Robert Malcolm Young)

PERSONAL: Born November 22, 1924. *Education:* Attended Harvard University.

CAREER: Director, writer and cinematographer.

AWARDS, HONORS: Emmy Award, outstanding achievement in cultural documentary programming—individuals, 1971, for *The Eskimo: Fight for Life.*

CREDITS:

FILM DIRECTOR

(As Robert Malcolm Young) *Trauma,* Parade, 1962 (also see below).

(And cinematographer) *Alambrista!,* Filmhaus, 1977 (also see below).

Short Eyes (also released as *Slammer*), Paramount Film League, 1977.

Rich Kids, United Artists, 1979.

One-Trick Pony, Warner Bros., 1980.

The Ballad of Gregorio Cortez, Embassy Pictures, 1983.

(And cinematographer) *Extremities,* Atlantic, 1986.

Saving Grace, Columbia, 1986.

(And cinematographer) *Dominick and Eugene,* Orion, 1988.

(And cinematographer) *Triumph of the Spirit,* Triumph, 1989 (also see below).

Also director of *Keep It Up Downstairs,* 1976; *Deal,* 1977; and *The World Is Full of Married Men,* 1979.

TELEVISION WORK; AS ROBERT MALCOLM YOUNG

Director, *The Eskimo: Fight for Life* (documentary), CBS, c. 1970.

Also director of *Harry's Kingdom* (television movie), 1989; *We Are the Children; Sit-In;* and *Angola—Journey to a War;* director, producer and editor of documentary *The Inferno* (also known as *Cortile Cascino*); director and producer of documentary *Anatomy of a Hospital.*

WRITINGS:

TELEVISION MOVIES; AS ROBERT MALCOLM YOUNG

Locusts, ABC, 1974.

The Ghost of Flight 401, NBC, 1978.

Diary of a Hitchhiker, ABC, 1979.

(With Irving Pearlberg) *Women in White,* NBC, 1979.

Starflight: The Plane That Couldn't Land, ABC, 1983.

(With Sue Grafton and Steven Humphrey) *Agatha Christie's "Sparkling Cyanide,"* CBS, 1985.

TELEVISION SERIES; WITH OTHERS; AS ROBERT MALCOLM YOUNG

The FBI, ABC, 1965.

Marcus Welby, M.D., ABC, 1969.

The Streets of San Francisco, ABC, 1972.

The Waltons, CBS, 1972.

Harry O, ABC, 1974.

Trapper John, M.D., CBS, 1985.

Spenser: For Hire, ABC, 1985-87.

Blacke's Magic, NBC, 1986.

OTHER TELEVISION WRITINGS; AS ROBERT MALCOLM YOUNG

Amanda Fallon (pilot), NBC, 1972.

(With W. Sandfeur and Hal Kanter) *Beyond Witch Mountain* (pilot), CBS, 1982.

Also author of documentary *The Inferno* (also known as *Cortile Cascino*).

SCREENPLAYS

(As Robert Malcolm Young) *Trauma,* Parade, 1962.

(As Robert Malcolm Young) *Escape to Witch Mountain,* Buena Vista, 1975.

Alambrista!, Filmhaus, 1977.

(With others) *Triumph of the Spirit,* Triumph, 1989.*

* * *

YOUNG, Robert Malcolm
See YOUNG, Robert M.

* * *

ZADORA, Pia 1956–

PERSONAL: Born May 4, 1956, in New York City; daughter of Alphonse Schipani (a violinist) and Nina Zadora (a theatrical wardrobe supervisor); married Meshulam Riklis; children: Kady, Christopher. *Education:* Attended High School of Professional Arts and American Academy of Dramatic Arts.

ADDRESSES: Agent—International Creative Management, 8899 Beverly Blvd., Los Angeles, CA 90048. *Publicist*—Solters, Roskin, Friedman, Inc., 5455 Wilshire Blvd. #2200, Los Angeles, CA 90036.

CAREER: Actress and singer. Has sung at numerous night clubs and on concert tours.

AWARDS, HONORS: Golden Globe Award for new star of the year in a motion picture, 1982, and Newcomer of the Year Award from Montreal Film Festival, both for *Butterfly;* Golden Apple Discovery of the Year Award from Hollywood Women's Press Club, 1986.

CREDITS:

STAGE APPEARANCES

Penny (understudy), *The Garden of Sweets,* ANTA Theater, New York City, 1961.

Child, *We Take the Town,* Shubert Theater, New Haven, CT, then Shubert Theater, Philadelphia, PA, 1962.

Bielke, *Fiddler on the Roof,* Imperial Theater, New York City, 1964.

Gil (understudy), *Henry, Sweet Henry,* Palace Theater, 1967.

Ruby, *Dames at Sea,* Bouwerie Lane Theater, New York City, then Theatre DeLys, New York City, 1968-69.

Pia, *Applause,* U.S. cities, 1972-73.

Fanny, *Funny Girl,* Long Beach Civic Light Opera's Terrace Theatre, Long Beach, CA, 1991.

Also appeared in *The Mary Show* and *Heidi.*

FILM APPEARANCES

Girmar, *Santa Claus Conquers the Martians,* Embassy, 1964.

Kady, *Butterfly,* Analysis, 1982.

Jerilee, *The Lonely Lady,* Universal, 1983.

Beatnik Girl, *Hairspray,* New Line, 1988.

Dee Dee, *Voyage of the Rock Aliens,* Inter Planetary Curb, 1988.

Troop Beverly Hills, Columbia, 1989.

Also appeared as Bobbie Warren in *Fake-Out,* 1982.

TELEVISION APPEARANCES; MOVIES

Pajama Tops, Showtime, 1983.

Mother Goose Rock 'n' Rhyme, Disney Channel, 1990.

TELEVISION APPEARANCES; SPECIALS

Circus of the Stars, CBS, 1983.

Born America: A March of Dimes Television Event, syndicated, 1986.

Fame, Fortune, and Romance, ABC, 1986.

Las Vegas: An All-Star Seventy-Fifth Anniversary, ABC, 1987.

Our Kids and the Best of Everything, ABC, 1987.

Sixty-First Annual Macy's Thanksgiving Day Parade, NBC, 1987.

The Second Annual Star-Spangled Celebration, ABC, 1988.

Candid Camera on Wheels, CBS, 1989.

The Ice Capades Fiftieth Anniversary Special, ABC, 1990.

Twenty-Fifth Anniversary MDA-Jerry Lewis (Labor Day) Telethon, syndicated, 1990.

Night of 100 Stars III, NBC, 1990.

Also appeared in a set of five specials for French television.

RECORDINGS:

(With London Philharmonic Orchestra) *Pia and Phil,* CBS, 1986.

(With London Philharmonic Orchestra) *I Am What I Am,* CBS Associated, 1986.

Also released the recordings *Pia,* Curb/Elektra, and *Pia Z.,* CBS Associated.

* * *

ZAENTZ, Saul

PERSONAL: Born in Passaic, NJ.

ADDRESSES: Office—Saul Zaentz Company Film Center, 2600 Tenth St., Berkeley, CA 94710.

CAREER: Film producer. Owner and producer of Fantasy Records (music label), Berkeley, CA, during 1960s. Founder and head of Saul Zaentz Company Film Center.

AWARDS, HONORS: Academy Award (with Michael Douglas), best picture, 1975, for *One Flew over the Cuck-*

oo's Nest; producer of the year award (with Michael Douglas), National Association of Theatre Owners, 1976, for *One Flew over the Cuckoo's Nest;* Academy Award, best picture, 1984, for *Amadeus.*

CREDITS:

FILM WORK; PRODUCER EXCEPT WHERE INDICATED

Executive producer, *Payday,* Cinerama, 1972.
(With Michael Douglas) *One Flew over the Cuckoo's Nest,* United Artists, 1975.
(With Sy Gomberg) *Three Warriors,* Fantasy Films, 1977.
The Lord of the Rings (animated), United Artists, 1978.
Amadeus, Orion, 1984.
Executive producer, *The Mosquito Coast,* Warner Brothers, 1986.
The Unbearable Lightness of Being, Orion, 1988.

Also producer of *At Play in the Fields of the Lord.*

TELEVISION APPEARANCES

Milos Forman: Portrait, PBS, 1989.

*　　　*　　　*

ZAPATA, Carmen   1927-

PERSONAL: Born July 15, 1927, in New York, NY; daughter of Julio and Ramona (Roca) Zapata; married Roy A. Friedman, July, 1957 (divorced, 1963).

ADDRESSES: Agent—Fred Amsel and Associates, 6310 San Vicente Blvd., Suite 407, Los Angeles, CA 90048.

CAREER: Actress, producer, and writer. President and producer, Bilingual Foundation of the Arts, 1973—; singing comedienne in nightclub acts. Chairperson, Mexican-American Women's Conference, 1979. Member, Performing Tree, Los Angeles, CA; American National Theatre and Academy West; Inter-Cultural Exchange Commission, University of Southern California; California Theatre Council; Confederation of the Arts; and National Repertory Theatre Foundation, Los Angeles. Board member, Mayor's Commission on the Arts, Los Angeles; Mexican-American Opportunity Foundation, Monteray Park, CA; Los Angeles Boy Scouts of America; and Los Angeles-Mexico City Sister-City Affiliate Commission.

MEMBER: Actors Equity Association, Screen Actors Guild, American Federation of Television and Radio Artists, American Guild of Variety Artists.

AWARDS, HONORS: Nosotros Award, Best Actress, 1971; El Angel Award, Best Spanish Speaking Actress, 1973; Dramalogue Award, 1977, for *Blood Wedding,* and 1979, for *Fanlights;* Ruben Salazar Award from the National Council of La Raza, 1980; Silver Achievement Award from the Los Angeles Young Women's Christian Association (YWCA), 1981.

CREDITS:

TELEVISION APPEARANCES; SERIES

Josefina, *The Man and the City,* ABC, 1971-72.
Mayor, *Villa Alegre,* PBS, 1974-77.
Sophia Valdez, *Viva Valdez,* ABC, 1976.
Mrs. Chavez, *Hagen,* CBS, 1980.
Carmen Castillo, *Santa Barbara,* NBC, 1985—.

TELEVISION APPEARANCES; PILOTS

Mrs. Bellagio, *Flying High,* CBS, 1978.
Grandma Mallory, *The Tom Swift and Linda Craig Mystery Hour,* ABC, 1983.

TELEVISION APPEARANCES; EPISODIC

Mrs. Rodriquez, *Foley Square,* CBS, 1985.
Mrs. Rosales, *Downtown,* CBS, 1986.
Edna Walker, *Hunter,* NBC, 1987.
Judge Patterson, *Falcon Crest,* CBS, 1989.
Madame Olga, *Married with Children,* Fox, 1989.

Also appeared on *Flamingo Road,* NBC; *Marcus Welby, M.D.,* ABC; and *Charlie's Angels,* ABC.

TELEVISION APPEARANCES; MOVIES

Maria, *The Couple Takes a Wife,* ABC, 1972.
Miss Rodriguez, *The Girls of Huntington House,* ABC, 1973.
Esther, *My Darling Daughters' Anniversary,* ABC, 1973.
Elena de la Paz, *A Home of Our Own,* CBS, 1975.
Sara, *Winner Take All,* NBC, 1975.
Helena Mendoza, *Shark Kill,* NBC, 1976.
Connie, *Leave Yesterday Behind,* ABC, 1978.
Mrs. Garcia, *A Guide for the Married Woman,* ABC, 1978.
License clerk, *Like Normal People,* ABC, 1979.
Mrs. Ruiz, *Children of Divorce,* NBC, 1980.
Lorenza, *Homeward Bound,* CBS, 1980.
Judge Mercado, *Not Just Another Affair,* CBS, 1982.
Ms. Adkins, *Broken Angel* (also known as *Best Intentions*), ABC, 1988.

TELEVISION APPEARANCES; SPECIALS

Mrs. Martinez, "One Last Ride," *CBS Afterschool Playhouse,* CBS, 1980.
The Screen Actors Guild 50th Anniversary Celebration, CBS, 1984.
Consuelo, "Daniel and the Towers," *WonderWorks,* PBS, 1987.
Funny, You Don't Look 200, ABC, 1987.
Narrator, *In the Shadow of the Law* (documentary), PBS, 1988.

STAGE APPEARANCES

STAGE APPEARANCES

Uprooted, Center Theatre Group, Mark Taper Forum, Los Angeles, 1975.

Mother, *Blood Wedding* (also known as *Bodas de Sangre*), Bilingual Foundation of the Arts, Little Theatre, Los Angeles, 1985.

Also appeared with the Inner City Repertory Theatre, Los Angeles, 1975-76; appeared in productions of *Fanlights, Stop the World I Want to Get Off, Oklahoma!, Bloomer Girl, Carnival, Bye Bye Birdie,* and *No Strings.*

STAGE WORK

Producer, *La Celestina,* Bilingual Foundation of the Arts, Inner City Cultural Center, Los Angeles, 1978.

Producer, *The Young Lady from Tacna,* Bilingual Foundation of the Arts, Little Theatre, 1984.

FILM APPEARANCES

Juana, *Hail, Hero!,* National General, 1969.

Mrs. Harero, *Portnoy's Complaint,* Warner Brothers, 1972.

Pete 'n' Tillie, Universal, 1972.

Lottie, *Bad Charleston Charlie,* International Cinema, 1973.

Betty, *W* (also known as *I Want Her Dead*), Cinerama, 1974.

Marguerita, *Boss Nigger,* Dimension, 1974.

Maria, *I Will . . . I Will . . . for Now,* Twentieth Century-Fox, 1976.

Nurse, *Telefon,* Metro-Goldwyn-Mayer/United Artists, 1977.

Mrs. Landeros, *Boulevard Nights,* Warner Brothers, 1979.

Mama Figueroa, *How to Beat the High Cost of Living,* American International, 1980.

Mrs. Ramirez, *There Goes the Bride,* Vanguard, 1980.

Narrator, *Las Madres de la Plaza de Mayo* (documentary; also known as *La Ofrenda, Las Madres, The Day of the Dead,* and *The Mothers from the Plaza de Mayo*), First Run Features, 1985.

WRITINGS:

STAGE

(Translator, with Lina Montalvo) *The M.C.,* Bilingual Foundation of the Arts, Little Theatre, Los Angeles, 1984.

(Translator, with Michael Dewell) *Blood Wedding* (also known as *Bodas de Sangre*), Bilingual Foundation of the Arts, Little Theatre, 1985.

(Translator, with Dewell) *The Shoemaker's Prodigious Wife,* Bilingual Foundation of the Arts, Little Theatre, 1985.*

ZUCKER, David   1947-

PERSONAL: Born October 16, 1947, in Milwaukee, WI. *Education:* Attended University of Wisconsin, B.A., electrical engineering, 1970; studied with Ed Gein at the Method School.

ADDRESSES: Contact—Paramount Pictures, 5555 Melrose Ave., Los Angeles, CA 90038.

CAREER: Director, producer, and electrician. Zucker Brothers Productions, co-owner.

AWARDS, HONORS: Writers Guild award, best comedy, 1980, for *Airplane!.*

CREDITS:

FILM WORK

Executive producer and director, *Airplane!* (also see below), Paramount, 1980.

Executive producer and director (with brother, Jerry Zucker and Jim Abrahams), *Top Secret!* (also see below), Paramount, 1984.

Director (with J. Zucker and Abrahams), *Ruthless People,* Touchstone, 1986.

Executive producer and director, *The Naked Gun: From the Files of Police Squad!,* Paramount, 1988.

Director, *The Naked Gun 2 1/2: The Smell of Fear,* Paramount, 1991.

FILM APPEARANCES

Grumwald, Man, Second Technician, *The Kentucky Fried Movie,* United Film, 1977.

Ground Crewman, *Airplane!,* Paramount, 1980.

TELEVISION WORK

Executive producer (with J. Zucker and Abrahams), and director, *Police Squad!* (series), ABC, 1982.

Creator and executive producer, *Our Planet Tonight,* NBC, 1987.

WRITINGS:

FILM

(With J. Zucker and Abrahams) *The Kentucky Fried Movie,* United Film, 1977.

(With J. Zucker and Abrahams) *Airplane!,* Paramount, 1980.

(With J. Zucker, Abrahams, and Martyn Burke) *Top Secret!,* Paramount, 1984.

(With J. Zucker and Abrahams) *The Naked Gun: From the Files of Police Squad!,* Paramount, 1988.

(With Pat Proft) *The Naked Gun 2 1/2: The Smell of Fear,* Paramount, 1991.

TELEVISION

(With others), *Police Squad!* (series), ABC, 1982.
Our Planet Tonight, NBC, 1987.

OTHER

Author of lyrics, "Spend This Night with Me," *Top Secret!,* Paramount, 1984.*

*   *   *

ZWICK, Joel 1942-

PERSONAL: Born January 11, 1942, in Brooklyn, NY. *Education:* Graduate of Brooklyn College.

CAREER: Director, producer, actor, stage manager, and choreographer. Handled special movement for Trainer, Dean, Liepolt & Company, American Place Theatre, New York City, 1968.

CREDITS:

TELEVISION DIRECTOR; SERIES

(With others) *Laverne and Shirley* (comedy), ABC, 1977.
(With others) *Busting Loose* (comedy), CBS, 1977.
(With others) *The Ted Knight Show* (comedy), CBS, 1978.
(With others) *Mork and Mindy* (comedy), ABC, 1978-82.
(With others) *Makin' It* (comedy), ABC, 1979.
Struck by Lightning (comedy), CBS, 1979.
(With others) *Bosom Buddies* (comedy), ABC, 1980.
Goodtime Girls, ABC, 1980.
(With others; and supervising producer) *It's a Living,* ABC, 1980.
(And executive producer) *Hot W.A.C.S.* (comedy), ABC, 1981.
(With others) *Joannie Loves Chachi,* ABC, 1982.
(With others) *Star of the Family* (comedy), ABC, 1982-83.
(With others; and supervising producer) *The New Odd Couple* (comedy), ABC, 1982-83.
Webster (comedy), ABC, 1983.
Full House (comedy), ABC, 1987.

TELEVISION DIRECTOR; EPISODIC

Perfect Strangers (premiere), ABC, 1986.
Better Days (premiere), CBS, 1986.
Family Matters (premiere), ABC, 1989.
Going Places (premiere), ABC, 1990.

OTHER TELEVISION WORK; DIRECTOR

American 2100 (comedy pilot), ABC, 1979.
(And supervising producer) *Brothers* (pilot), Showtime, 1984.
Reno and Yolanda, (CBS Summer Playhouse special), CBS, 1987.
Adventures in Babysitting (comedy pilot), CBS, 1989.
Morning Glory (comedy pilot), ABC, 1989.
World According to Straw (comedy pilot), FBC, 1990.

STAGE APPEARANCES

(Off-Broadway debut) Aide, *MacBird!* (also see below), Village Gate, New York City, 1967.
Venerable Zwish, *Dance wi' Me, or "The Fatal Twitch"* (also see below), New York Shakespeare Festival (NYSF), Public Theater, 1971.
Bulldog Allen, *Dance with Me* (also see below), Mayfair Theatre, New York City, 1975.

STAGE DIRECTOR, EXCEPT WHERE INDICATED

Stage manager, *Macbird!,* Village Gate, 1967.
Dance wi' Me, or "The Fatal Twitch," NYSF, Public Theater, 1971.
(And choreographer) *Dance with Me,* Mayfair Theatre, 1975.
Cold Storage, American Place Theatre, New York City, 1977.
Esther, Promenade Theatre, New York City, 1977.

FILM DIRECTOR

Second Sight, Warner Brothers, 1989.*

Cumulative Index

To provide continuity with *Who's Who in the Theatre*, this index interfiles references to *Who's Who in the Theatre*, 1st-17th Editions, and *Who Was Who in the Theatre* (Gale, 1978) with references to *Contemporary Theatre, Film, and Television*, Volumes 1-9.

References in the index are identified as follows:

CTFT and volume number—*Contemporary Theatre, Film, and Television*, Volumes 1-9
WWT and edition number—*Who's Who in the Theatre*, 1st-17th Editions
WWasWT—*Who Was Who in the Theatre*

Aames, Willie 1960- CTFT-7
Aarons, Alexander A. ?-1943 ....WWasWT
Aarons, Alfred E. ?-1936 ....WWasWT
Abady, Josephine R. 1949- CTFT-4
Abarbanell, Lina 1880-1963 .....WWasWT
Abba, Marta 1907-1988 ....WWasWT
Abbas, Hector 1884-1942 ....WWasWT
Abbensetts, Michael 1938- CTFT-6
  Earlier sketch in WWT-17
Abbot, Rick
  See Sharkey, Jack CTFT-1
Abbott, George 1887- CTFT-5
  Earlier sketch in WWT-17
Abbott, John 1905- ....WWasWT
Abel, Lionel 1910- CTFT-1
Abel, Walter 1898-1987 ....CTFT-5
  Earlier sketch in WWT-17
Abeles, Edward S. 1869-1919 ....WWasWT
Abercrombie, Lascelles
  1881-1938 ....WWasWT
Abingdon, W. L. 1859-1918 .....WWasWT
Abingdon, William 1888-1959 ....WWasWT
Aborn, Milton 1864-? ....WWasWT
Abraham, F. Murray 1939- CTFT-4
  Earlier sketch in CTFT-1
Abraham, Paul ?-1960 ....WWasWT
Abrahams, A. E. 1873-1966 .....WWasWT
Abrahams, Doris Cole 1925- CTFT-5
  Earlier sketch in WWT-17
Abrahams, Jim 1944- CTFT-4
Abrahamsen, Daniel Charles
  1952- CTFT-1
Abravanel, Maurice 1903- CTFT-1
Abuba, Ernest 1947-.............CTFT-1
Achard, Marcel 1900-1974 ......WWasWT
Achurch, Janet 1864-1916 ....WWasWT
Ackerman, Bettye 1928- CTFT-1
Ackerman, Harry S. 1912-.........CTFT-3
Ackerman, Leslie CTFT-7
Ackerman, Robert Allan 1945- CTFT-9
Ackland, Joss 1928- CTFT-5
  Earlier sketch in WWT-17
Ackland, Rodney 1908- WWT-17
  Earlier sketch in WWasWT
Ackles, Kenneth V. 1916-1986 .....CTFT-4
Ackroyd, David 1940- CTFT-1
Acton-Bond, Acton ....WWasWT
Ada-May
  See May, Ada ....WWasWT
Adair, Jean ?-1953 ....WWasWT
Adam, Ken 1921- CTFT-1
Adam, Ronald 1896-1979 ....WWT-16
Adams, Brooke 1949-............CTFT-2

Adams, Casey
  See Showalter, Max CTFT-8
Adams, Dick 1889- ....WWasWT
Adams, Don 1926- CTFT-3
Adams, Edie CTFT-3
  Earlier sketch in WWT-17
Adams, Ida ?-1960 ....WWasWT
Adams, Julie CTFT-1
Adams, Mason CTFT-4
  Earlier sketch in CTFT-1
Adams, Maud 1945- CTFT-6
Adams, Maude 1872-1953 ....WWasWT
Adams, Miriam 1907- ....WWasWT
Adams, Molly CTFT-2
Adams, Polly CTFT-7
Adams, Robert ....WWasWT
Adams, Tony 1953- CTFT-2
Adams, W. Bridges
  See Bridges-Adams, W. ....WWasWT
Adams, Wayne 1930- CTFT-1
Addams, Dawn 1930-1985 ....CTFT-2
  Earlier sketch in WWT-17
Addinsell, Richard Stewart
  1904-1977 ....WWT-16
Addison, Carlotta 1849-1914 .....WWasWT
Addison, John 1920- CTFT-9
Addy, Wesley 1913- CTFT-8
  Earlier sketch in WWT-17
Ade, George 1866-1944 ....WWasWT
Adelman, Sybil 1942- CTFT-3
Aderer, Adolphe 1855-? ....WWasWT
Adjani, Isabelle 1955- CTFT-9
  Earlier sketch in CTFT-3
Adler, Jacob 1855-1962 ....WWasWT
Adler, Jerry 1929- CTFT-3
  Earlier sketch in WWT-17
Adler, Larry 1914- CTFT-4
Adler, Luther 1903-1984 ....CTFT-2
  Earlier sketch in WWT-17
Adler, Richard 1921- CTFT-4
  Earlier sketch in WWT-17
Adler, Stella 1902- CTFT-3
  Earlier sketch in WWT-17
Adlon, Percy 1935-...............CTFT-8
Adrian, Max 1903- ....WWasWT
Adrienne, Jean 1905- ....WWasWT
Adye, Oscar ....WWasWT
Agar, Dan 1881-1947 ....WWasWT
Agar, John 1921- CTFT-8
Agate, May 1892- ....WWasWT
Agutter, Jenny 1952- CTFT-2
Aherne, Brian 1902-1986 ....WWasWT
Ahlander, Thecla Ottilia 1855-? ..WWasWT

Ahlers, Anny 1906-1933 ....WWasWT
Aidem, Betsy 1957- CTFT-3
Aidman, Betty Linton CTFT-1
Aidman, Charles 1925- CTFT-1
Aiello, Danny 1933-.............CTFT-5
Ailey, Alvin 1931-1989 ....CTFT-1
Aimee, Anouk 1934(?)- CTFT-9
  Earlier sketch in CTFT-2
Ainley, Henry 1879-1967 ....WWasWT
Aitken, Maria 1945- CTFT-4
  Earlier sketch in WWT-17
Akalaitis, JoAnne 1937- CTFT-5
  Earlier sketch in WWT-17
Aked, Muriel 1887-1955 ....WWasWT
Akers, Karen 1945- CTFT-4
Akins, Claude 1926- CTFT-7
  Earlier sketch in CTFT-2
Albanesi, Meggie (Margherita)
  1899-1923 ....WWasWT
Albee, Edward 1928- CTFT-4
  Earlier sketch in WWT-17
Albert, Allan 1945- WWT-17
Albert, Ben 1876-? ....WWasWT
Albert, Eddie 1908- CTFT-8
  Earlier sketches in CTFT-2, WWT-17
Albert, Edward 1951-..............CTFT-7
  Earlier sketch in CTFT-1
Albert, William 1863-? ....WWasWT
Albert-Lambert, Raphael
  1865-? ....WWasWT
Albertson, Jack ?-1981 ....WWT-17
Albery, Bronson 1881-1971 .....WWasWT
Albery, Donald 1914-1988 ....CTFT-7
  Earlier sketch in WWT-17
Albery, Ian Bronson 1936- WWT-17
Albright, Hardie 1903-..........WWasWT
Alda, Alan 1936- CTFT-3
  Earlier sketches in CTFT-1, WWT-17
Alda, Robert 1914-1986 ....CTFT-3
  Earlier sketch in WWT-17
Alda, Rutanya CTFT-4
Alden, Hortense 1903- ....WWasWT
Alderson, Clifton 1864-1930 .....WWasWT
Alderton, John 1940- CTFT-5
  Earlier sketch in WWT-17
Aldin, Arthur 1872-? ....WWasWT
Aldredge, Theoni V. 1932- CTFT-4
  Earlier sketches in CTFT-1, WWT-17
Aldredge, Thomas
  See Aldredge, Tom CTFT-9
Aldredge, Tom 1928- CTFT-9
  Earlier sketch in CTFT-1
Aldrich, Charles T. 1872-? ......WWasWT

Aldrich, Janet 1956- CTFT-7
Aldrich, Richard 1902-1986 ....CTFT-3
  Earlier sketch in WWasWT
Aldrich, Robert 1918-1983 ....CTFT-2
Aldridge, Michael 1920- CTFT-3
  Earlier sketch in WWT-17
Aleandri, Emelise CTFT-2
Aleandro, Norma 1941- CTFT-9
Aletter, Frank 1926-..............CTFT-1
Alexander, Bill 1948- WWT-17
Alexander, C. K. 1923- WWT-17
Alexander, George 1858-1918 ....WWasWT
Alexander, Jane 1939- CTFT-4
  Earlier sketches in CTFT-1, WWT-17
Alexander, Janet ?-1961 ....WWasWT
Alexander, Jason 1959- CTFT-8
  Earlier sketch in CTFT-1
Alexander, John 1897- WWT-16
Alexander, Kathleen WWT-13
Alexander, Katherine 1901-......WWasWT
Alexander, Muriel 1898- ....WWasWT
Alexander, Robert A. 1929- CTFT-2
Alexander, Terence 1923- CTFT-6
  Earlier sketch in WWT-17
Alexandre, Rene 1885-1946 ......WWasWT
Alice, Mary CTFT-6
Alison, Dorothy 1925- CTFT-1
Allan, Elizabeth 1910-1990 ....WWT-14
Allan, Maud ....WWasWT
Allandale, Fred 1872-? ....WWasWT
Allen, A. Hylton 1879-? ....WWasWT
Allen, Adrienne WWT-14
Allen, Billie CTFT-1
Allen, Bob 1906-..................CTFT-4
Allen, Charles Leslie 1830-1917 ..WWasWT
Allen, Chesney 1896- ....WWasWT
Allen, Corey 1934- CTFT-8
Allen, Debbie 1950- CTFT-6
Allen, Dede 1924(?)- CTFT-9
Allen, Elizabeth 1934- CTFT-8
  Earlier sketch in WWT-17
Allen, Frank 1851-? ....WWasWT
Allen, H. Marsh WWT-6
Allen, Jack 1907- WWT-17
Allen, Jay Presson 1922- CTFT-7
  Earlier sketch in CTFT-1
Allen, Joan 1956- CTFT-7
Allen, John Piers 1912- WWT-17
Allen Jonelle 1944- CTFT-7
Allen, Karen 1951- CTFT-4
  Earlier sketch in CTFT-1
Allen, Kelcey 1875-1951 ....WWasWT
Allen, Nancy CTFT-5
  Earlier sketch in CTFT-2
Allen, Patrick 1927- WWT-17
Allen, Penelope CTFT-4
Allen, Peter 1944-................CTFT-9
Allen, Rae 1926- WWT-17
Allen, Ralph G. 1934- WWT-17
Allen, Roland
  See Ayckbourn, Alan CTFT-4
Allen, Sheila 1932- WWT-17
Allen, Steve 1921-................CTFT-4
Allen, Vera 1897- CTFT-1
  Earlier sketch in WWasWT
Allen, Viola 1869-1948 ....WWasWT
Allen, Woody 1935- CTFT-8
  Earlier sketches in CTFT-1, WWT-17
Allenby, Frank 1898-1953 ....WWasWT
Allenby, Peggy 1905-1967 ....WWasWT
Allensworth, Carl 1908-...........CTFT-6
Allers, Franz 1905-...............CTFT-1
Alley, Kirstie CTFT-5

Allgood, Sara 1883-1950 ....WWasWT
Allik, Vera Viiu CTFT-6
Allinson, Michael WWT-17
Allison, Nancy 1954- CTFT-4
Allister, Claud 1891-1967 ....WWasWT
Allmon, Clinton 1941- CTFT-1
Almberg, John 1940- CTFT-2
Almendros, Nestor 1930-...........CTFT-5
Almquist, Gregg 1948-.............CTFT-4
Alonso, Maria Conchita 1957- CTFT-7
Alpar, Gitta 1900- ....WWasWT
Alper, Jonathan 1950- CTFT-5
  Earlier sketch in WWT-17
Alswang, Ralph 1916-1979 ....WWT-17
Alt, Natalie ....WWasWT
Altman, Robert B. 1925- CTFT-7
  Earlier sketch in CTFT-2
Altman, Ruth ....WWasWT
Alvarado, Trini 1967-.............CTFT-7
Alvin, John 1917-.................CTFT-9
Alzado, Lyle 1949-................CTFT-8
Ambient, Mark 1860-1937 ....WWasWT
Ambrose, David 1943- CTFT-5
  Earlier sketch in CTFT-1
Ameche, Don 1908- CTFT-7
  Earlier sketches in CTFT-2, WWT-17
Ames, Florenz 1884-? ....WWasWT
Ames, Gerald 1881-1933 ....WWasWT
Ames, Leon 1901- ....WWasWT
Ames, Robert 1893-1931 ....WWasWT
Ames, Rosemary 1906- ....WWasWT
Ames, Winthrop 1871-1937 ......WWasWT
Amic, Henri 1853-? ....WWasWT
Amiel, Denys 1884-? ....WWasWT
Amos, John 1941-..................CTFT-4
Amram, David 1930-...............CTFT-1
Amsterdam, Morey 1908- CTFT-9
Ana-Alicia 1956- CTFT-8
Anders, Glenn 1890- ....WWasWT
Anderson, Craig CTFT-1
Anderson, Daphne 1922- WWT-17
Anderson, Harry 1952- CTFT-6
Anderson, Haskell V. III 1942-....CTFT-4
Anderson, J. Grant 1897- WWT-17
Anderson, John 1922- CTFT-9
Anderson, John (Hargis)
  1896-1943 ....WWasWT
Anderson, John Murray
  1886-1954 ....WWasWT
Anderson, Judith 1898- CTFT-4
  Earlier sketch in WWT-17
Anderson, Laurie 1947- CTFT-8
Anderson, Lawrence 1893-1939 ..WWasWT
Anderson, Lindsay 1923- CTFT-6
  Earlier sketch in CTFT-2
Anderson, Loni 1945(?)- CTFT-9
  Earlier sketch in CTFT-2
Anderson, Mary 1859-1940 ......WWasWT
Anderson, Maxwell 1888-1959 ...WWasWT
Anderson, Melissa Sue 1962-.......CTFT-2
Anderson, Melody CTFT-4
Anderson, Michael 1920-..........CTFT-8
Anderson, Michael, Jr. 1943- CTFT-6
Anderson, Richard 1926-...........CTFT-1
Anderson, Richard Dean 1950-....CTFT-8
Anderson, Robert Woodruff
  1917- WWT-17
Anderson, Rona 1928- WWT-17
Andersson, Bibi 1935-.............CTFT-7
Andersson, Harriet 1932-..........CTFT-8
Andreeva-Babakhan, Anna
  Misaakovna 1923-............WWasWT
Andress, Ursula 1936-.............CTFT-3

Andreva, Stella
  See Browne, Stella ....WWasWT
Andrew, Leo 1957-................CTFT-8
Andrews, Ann 1895-..............WWasWT
Andrews, Anthony 1948-..........CTFT-7
Andrews, Dana 1912-..............CTFT-4
  Earlier sketch in WWT-17
Andrews, Eamonn 1922-1987 ......CTFT-2
Andrews, George Lee 1942- CTFT-1
Andrews, Harry 1911-1989 ....CTFT-7
  Earlier sketches in CTFT-2, WWT-17
Andrews, Julie 1935-.............CTFT-7
  Earlier sketches in CTFT-1, WWasWT
Andrews, Maidie ....WWasWT
Andrews, Nancy 1924-1989 ....CTFT-8
  Earlier sketch in WWT-17
Andrews, Robert 1895- ....WWasWT
Andrews, Tige CTFT-3
Andrews, Tod 1920- ....WWasWT
Andros, Douglas 1931- CTFT-1
Angel, Heather 1909-1986 ....CTFT-4
  Earlier sketch in WWasWT
Angelus, Muriel 1909- ....WWasWT
Angers, Avril 1922- WWT-17
Anglim, Philip 1953- CTFT-4
  Earlier sketch in WWT-17
Anglin, Margaret 1876-1958 .....WWasWT
Annabella 1912- ....WWasWT
Annals, Michael 1938- WWT-17
Annaud, Jean-Jacques 1943- CTFT-3
Annis, Francesca 1944- CTFT-8
Ann-Margret 1941-................CTFT-9
  Earlier sketch in CTFT-3
Annunzio, Gabriele d'
  1863-1938 ....WWasWT
Anouilh, Jean 1910-1987 ....CTFT-5
  Earlier sketch in WWT-17
Ansara, Michael 1927-............CTFT-3
Ansell, John 1874-1948 ....WWasWT
Anson, A. E. 1879-1936 ....WWasWT
Anson, George William
  1847-1920 ....WWasWT
Anspach, Susan CTFT-3
Anspacher, Louis K. 1878-1947 ..WWasWT
Anspaugh, David 1946- CTFT-8
Anstey, Edgar 1907-1987 ....CTFT-5
  Earlier sketch in CTFT-4
Anstey, F. 1856-1934 ....WWasWT
Anstruther, Harold ....WWasWT
Anthony, Joseph 1912- WWT-17
Anthony, Michael 1920- CTFT-5
Antille, Lisa CTFT-3
Antoine, Andre 1857-1943 ....WWasWT
Anton, Susan 1951- CTFT-3
  Brief Entry in CTFT-2
Antona-Traversi, Camillo
  1857-1926 ....WWasWT
Antona-Traversi, Giannino
  1860-1934 ....WWasWT
Antonio, Lou 1934- CTFT-8
Antonioni, Michelangelo 1912- CTFT-6
Antony, Hilda 1886-? ....WWasWT
Antoon, A. J. 1944-..............CTFT-5
  Earlier sketch in WWT-17
Antrobus, John 1933-.............WWT-17
Apple, Gary 1955- CTFT-3
Applebaum, Gertrude H. CTFT-1
Appleby, Dorothy 1908-1990 ....WWasWT
Apted, Michael 1941-.............CTFT-5
  Earlier sketch in CTFT-1
Aranha, Ray CTFT-3
Arbeit, Herman 1925- CTFT-2
Arbenina, Stella 1887- ....WWasWT

Arbuckle, Maclyn 1866-1931 . . . . . WWasWT
Arbus, Allan 1918- CTFT-6
  Ealier sketch in CTFT-1
Arcenas, Loy 1953(?)- CTFT-9
Archer, Anne 1949- CTFT-6
Archer, Joe . . . . WWasWT
Archer, John 1915- . . . . WWasWT
Archer, John 1953- CTFT-2
Archer, William 1856-1924 . . . . . . WWasWT
Arden, Edwin Hunter
  Pendleton 1864-1918 . . . . WWasWT
Arden, Eve 1912-1990 . . . . CTFT-3
  Earlier sketch in WWT-17
Arden, John 1930- WWT-17
Ardrey, Robert 1908- . . . . WWasWT
Arell, Sherry H. 1950- CTFT-3
Arenal, Julie CTFT-2
Argent, Edward 1931- WWT-17
Argentina . . . . WWasWT
Argento, Dario 1940- CTFT-8
Argenziano, Carmen 1943- CTFT-8
Argyle, Pearl 1910- . . . . WWasWT
Aris, Ben 1937- CTFT-3
Arkell, Elizabeth . . . . WWasWT
Arkell, Reginald 1882-1959 . . . . . . WWasWT
Arkin, Adam 1956- CTFT-7
Arkin, Alan 1934- CTFT-2
  Earlier sketch in WWT-17
Arkoff, Samuel Z. 1918- CTFT-3
Arledge, Roone 1931- CTFT-4
Arlen, Harold 1905-1986 . . . . WWT-17
Arlen, Michael 1895-1956 . . . . WWasWT
Arlen, Stephen 1913- . . . . WWasWT
Arling, Joyce 1911- . . . . WWasWT
Arlington, Billy 1873-? . . . . WWasWT
Arliss, George 1868-1946 . . . . WWasWT
Armen, Rebecca 1957- CTFT-2
Armitage, Frank
  See Carpenter, John CTFT-8
Armitage, Richard ?-1986 . . . . CTFT-4
Armstrong, Anthony 1897- . . . . . . WWasWT
Armstrong, Barney 1870-? . . . . WWasWT
Armstrong, Bess 1953- CTFT-6
Armstrong, Curtis 1953- CTFT-8
Armstrong, Gillian 1950- CTFT-7
Armstrong, Paul 1869-1915 . . . . . . WWasWT
Armstrong, R.G. 1917- CTFT-8
Armstrong, Robert 1896- . . . . WWasWT
Armstrong, Will Steven
  1930-1969 . . . . WWasWT
Armstrong, William 1882-1952 . . . WWasWT
Arnatt, John 1917- WWT-17
Arnaud, Yvonne 1892-1958 . . . . . . WWasWT
Arnaz, Desi 1917-1986 . . . . CTFT-4
  Earlier sketch in CTFT-3
Arnaz, Desi, Jr. 1953- CTFT-1
Arnaz, Lucie 1951- CTFT-1
  Earlier sketch in WWT-17
Arness, James 1923- CTFT-3
Arnold, Danny 1925- CTFT-3
Arnold, Edward 1890-1956 . . . . . . WWasWT
Arnold, Franz 1878-1960 . . . . WWasWT
Arnold, Jeanne 1931- CTFT-8
Arnold, Phyl ?-1941 . . . . WWasWT
Arnold, Tom ?-1969 . . . . WWasWT
Arnold, Tom 1947- CTFT-4
  Earlier sketch in WWT-17
Arnott, James Fullarton
  1914-1982 . . . . CTFT-4
  Earlier sketch in WWT-17
Arnott, Mark 1950- CTFT-5
Arnott, Peter 1936- CTFT-3
Aronson, Boris 1900-1980 . . . . WWT-17

Aronstein, Martin 1936- CTFT-4
  Earlier sketch in WWT-17
Arquette, Rosanna 1959- CTFT-6
  Earlier sketch in CTFT-2
Arrabal, Fernando 1932- WWT-17
Arrambide, Mario 1953- CTFT-3
Arrowsmith, William 1924- CTFT-1
Arthur, Beatrice 1926- CTFT-4
  Earlier sketch in WWT-17
Arthur, Carol 1935- CTFT-1
Arthur, Daphne 1925- . . . . WWasWT
Arthur, Jean 1905- . . . . WWasWT
Arthur, Julia 1869-1950 . . . . WWasWT
Arthur, Paul 1859-1928 . . . . WWasWT
Arthur, Robert ?-1929 . . . . WWasWT
Arthur, Robert 1909-1986 . . . . CTFT-4
Arthur-Jones, Winifred WWT-6
Arthurs, George 1875-1944 . . . . . . WWasWT
Artus, Louis 1870-? . . . . WWasWT
Arundale, Grace (Kelly) . . . . WWasWT
Arundale, Sybil 1882-1965 . . . . . . WWasWT
Arundell, Dennis 1898-1936 . . . . . WWasWT
Asade, Jim 1936- CTFT-2
Ash, Gordon ?-1929 . . . . WWasWT
Ash, Maie 1888-? . . . . WWasWT
Ashby, Hal 1936-1988 . . . . CTFT-6
Ashby, Harvey CTFT-4
Ashcroft, Peggy 1907- CTFT-4
  Earlier sketch in WWT-17
Asher, Jane 1946- CTFT-8
  Earlier sketches in CTFT-2, WWT-17
Asher, William 1919- CTFT-9
Asherson, Renee WWT-17
Ashley, Elizabeth 1939- CTFT-8
  Earlier sketches in CTFT-1, WWT-17
Ashley, Iris 1909- . . . . WWasWT
Ashman, Howard 1950-1991 . . . . . CTFT-9
  Earlier sketch in CTFT-1
Ashmore, Basil 1951- WWT-17
Ashmore, Peter 1916- . . . . WWasWT
Ashton, Ellis 1919- CTFT-4
  Earlier sketch in WWT-17
Ashton, Frederick 1906- . . . . WWasWT
Ashton, John CTFT-6
Ashwell, Lena 1872-1957 . . . . WWasWT
Askey, Arthur Bowden 1900- WWT-17
Askin, Leon 1907- CTFT-2
Askin, Peter 1946- CTFT-5
Asner, Edward 1929- CTFT-6
  Earlier sketch in CTFT-1
Asquith, Anthony 1902-1968 . . . . . WWasWT
Asquith, Ward CTFT-3
Assante Armand 1949- CTFT-4
Asseyev, Tamara CTFT-3
Astaire, Adele 1898-1981 . . . . WWasWT
Astaire, Fred 1899-1987 . . . . CTFT-5
  Earlier sketches in CTFT-3, WWasWT
Astin, John 1930- CTFT-6
Astley, John . . . . WWasWT
Astredo, Humbert Allen CTFT-1
Atherton, William 1947- CTFT-4
  Earlier sketch in WWT-17
Athis, Alfred 1873-? . . . . WWasWT
Atienza, Edward 1924- WWT-17
Atkin, Nancy 1904- . . . . WWasWT
Atkins, Christopher 1961- CTFT-5
  Brief Entry in CTFT-2
Atkins, Eileen 1934- CTFT-4
  Earlier sketch in WWT-17
Atkins, Robert 1886-1972 . . . . WWasWT
Atkinson, Barbara 1926- CTFT-3
  Earlier sketch in WWT-17
Atkinson, Don 1940- CTFT-7

Atkinson, Harry 1866-? . . . . WWasWT
Atkinson, (Justin) Brooks
  1894-1984 . . . . WWT-17
Atkinson, Rosalind 1900-1977 . . . . . WWT-16
Atlas (William Hedley Roberts)
  1864-? . . . . WWasWT
Atlee, Howard 1926- CTFT-1
Attenborough, Richard 1923- CTFT-8
  Earlier sketches in CTFT-1, WWT-17
Atteridge, Harold R. 1886-1938 . . WWasWT
Attles, Joseph 1903- CTFT-1
Atwater, Edith 1911-1986 . . . . WWasWT
Atwill, Lionel 1885-1946 . . . . WWasWT
Auberjonois, Rene 1940- CTFT-8
  Earlier sketches in CTFT-2, WWT-17
Aubrey, James 1947- CTFT-3
  Earlier sketch in WWT-17
Aubrey, Madge 1902-1970 . . . . WWasWT
Auden, W. H. 1907-1973 . . . . WWasWT
Audley, Maxine 1923- CTFT-6
  Earlier sketch in WWT-17
Audran, Stephane 1932- CTFT-8
Augarde, Adrienne ?-1913 . . . . WWasWT
Augarde, Amy 1868-1959 . . . . WWasWT
Aukin, David 1942- WWT-17
Auletta, Robert 1940- CTFT-1
Aulisi, Joseph G. CTFT-8
  Earlier sketch in WWT-17
Ault, Marie 1870-1951 . . . . WWasWT
Aumont, Jean-Pierre 1909- CTFT-4
  Earlier sketch in WWT-17
Austin, Charles 1878-1944 . . . . WWasWT
Austin, Lyn 1922- CTFT-1
Austrian, Marjorie 1934- CTFT-4
Auteuil, Daniel 1950- CTFT-8
Avalon, Frankie 1940- CTFT-3
Avalos, Luis 1946- CTFT-5
Avedis, Howard CTFT-1
Averback, Hy 1920- CTFT-6
Avery, Margaret CTFT-8
Avnet, Jonathan 1949- CTFT-2
Avni, Ran 1941- CTFT-1
Avril, Suzanne . . . . WWasWT
Axelrod, George 1922- CTFT-4
Axton, Hoyt 1938- CTFT-3
Axworthy, Geoffrey 1923- WWT-17
Ayckbourn, Alan 1939- CTFT-4
  Earlier sketch in WWT-17
Ayer, Nat. D. ?-1952 . . . . WWasWT
Ayers, David H. 1924- CTFT-1
Ayers-Allen, Phylicia
  See Rashad, Phylicia CTFT-6
Aykroyd, Dan 1952- CTFT-6
Ayliff, Henry Kiell ?-1949 . . . . WWasWT
Aylmer, Felix 1889-1964 . . . . WWasWT
Aynesworth, Allan 1865-1959 . . . . WWasWT
Ayr, Michael 1953- CTFT-9
Ayres, Lew 1908- CTFT-3
Ayrton, Norman 1924- WWT-17
Ayrton, Randle 1869-1940 . . . . WWasWT
Azenberg, Emanuel 1934- CTFT-5
  Earlier sketch in WWT-17
Aznavour, Charles 1924- CTFT-2
Azzara, Candy 1947- CTFT-1

B

Babcock, Barbara CTFT-6
Babcock, Debra Lee 1956- CTFT-5
Babe, Thomas 1941- CTFT-5
  Earlier sketch in WWT-17
Babenco, Hector CTFT-6

Bacall, Lauren 1924- CTFT-7
   Earlier sketch in CTFT-1
Baccus, Stephen 1969- CTFT-1
Bach, Barbara CTFT-2
Bach, Catherine CTFT-5
   Brief Entry in CTFT-2
Bach, Reginald 1886-1941 ....WWasWT
Bacharach, Burt 1929- CTFT-3
Bachman, Richard
   See King, Stephen CTFT-8
Backus, Jim 1913-1989- CTFT-6
Backus, Richard 1945- CTFT-4
   Earlier sketch in WWT-17
Baclanova, Olga 1899- ....WWasWT
Bacon, Frank 1864-1922 ....WWasWT
Bacon, Jane 1895- ....WWasWT
Bacon, Kevin 1958- CTFT-5
   Brief Entry in CTFT-2
Bacon, Mai 1898- ....WWasWT
Baddeley, Angela 1904-1976 ......WWT-16
Baddeley, Hermione 1906-1986 .....CTFT-4
   Earlier sketch in WWT-17
Bade, Tom 1946- CTFT-1
Badel, Alan 1923- WWT-17
Badel, Sarah 1943- CTFT-5
   Earlier sketch in WWT-17
Badham, John 1939-...............CTFT-8
   Earlier sketch in CTFT-1
Baer, Marian 1924-...............CTFT-1
Baer, Max, Jr. 1937-..............CTFT-6
Bagden, Ronald 1953- CTFT-1
Bagley, Ben 1933-...............WWT-17
Bagneris, Vernel 1949- CTFT-9
Bagnold, Enid 1889-1981 ....WWT-17
Bailey, Frederick 1946- CTFT-1
Bailey, Gordon 1875- ....WWasWT
Bailey, H. C. 1878-1961 ....WWasWT
Bailey, John 1942- CTFT-5
Bailey, Pearl 1918-1990 ....CTFT-9
   Earlier sketches in WWT-17, CTFT-4
Bailey, Robin 1919- WWT-17
Bain, Barbara CTFT-3
Bain, Conrad 1923- CTFT-4
   Earlier sketch in WWT-17
Baines, Florence 1877-1918 ......WWasWT
Bainter, Fay 1891-1968 ....WWasWT
Baio, Scott 1961- CTFT-5
   Brief Entry in CTFT-2
Baird, Bil 1904-1987 ....CTFT-5
   Earlier sketch in WWT-17
Baird, Dorothea 1875-1933 ......WWasWT
Baird, Ethel ....WWasWT
Baird, Mary E. 1947- CTFT-1
Baker, Benny 1907- ....WWasWT
Baker, Blanche 1956- CTFT-1
Baker, Carroll 1931- CTFT-8
   Earlier sketch in CTFT-1
Baker, Elizabeth ?-1962 ....WWasWT
Baker, George 1885-? ....WWasWT
Baker, George 1931-..............CTFT-3
   Earlier sketch in WWT-17
Baker, George Pierce 1866-1935 ..WWasWT
Baker, Iris 1901- ....WWasWT
Baker, Joe Don 1936- CTFT-6
Baker, Josephine 1906-1975 ....WWT-16
Baker, Kathy 1950- CTFT-8
Baker, Kathy Whitton
   See Baker, Kathy CTFT-8
Baker, Kenny 1934-...............CTFT-8
Baker, Lee ?-1948 ....WWasWT
Baker, Mark 1946- WWT-17
Baker, Paul 1911-................CTFT-1

Baker, Raymond 1948- CTFT-6
   Earlier sketch in CTFT-1
Baker, Rick 1950-................CTFT-6
Baker, Rod 1945- CTFT-4
Baker, Word 1923-...............CTFT-1
Bakshi, Ralph 1938- CTFT-6
Bakula, Scott CTFT-7
Balaban, Bob 1945- CTFT-6
   Earlier sketch in CTFT-1
Balanchine, George 1904-1980 ....WWT-17
Balch, Marston 1901-.............CTFT-2
Balderston, John L. 1889-1954 ...WWasWT
Baldwin, Adam 1962- CTFT-7
Baldwin, Alec 1958- CTFT-5
Baldwin, James 1924-1987 ....CTFT-3
Balfour, Katharine 1920-1990 .....CTFT-4
Balin, Ina 1937-1990 ....CTFT-9
Ball, Lucille 1911-1989 ....CTFT-8
   Earlier sketch in CTFT-3
Ball, William 1931- CTFT-5
   Earlier sketch in WWT-17
Ballantyne, Paul 1909- CTFT-3
   Earlier sketch in WWT-17
Ballard, Carroll 1937- CTFT-8
Ballard, Kaye 1926- CTFT-3
   Earlier sketch in CTFT-1
Ballard, Lucien 1908-1988 ....CTFT-7
Ballet, Arthur H. 1924- WWT-17
Balsam, Martin 1919-.............CTFT-7
   Earlier sketches in CTFT-2, WWT-17
Balsam, Talia CTFT-7
Bamman, Gerry 1941- CTFT-3
Banbury, Frith 1912- CTFT-4
   Earlier sketch in WWT-17
Bancroft, Anne 1931-.............CTFT-7
   Earlier sketches in CTFT-1, WWT-17
Bancroft, George Pleydell
   1868-1956 ....WWasWT
Bancroft, Lady 1839-1921 ....WWasWT
Bancroft, Squire 1841-1926 ......WWasWT
Banerjee, Victor 1946- CTFT-9
   Earlier sketch in CTFT-3
Bangs, John Kendrick
   1862-1922 ....WWasWT
Bankhead, Tallulah 1903-1968 ...WWasWT
Banks, Jonathan CTFT-7
Banks, Leslie J. 1890-1952 ....WWasWT
Bannen, Ian 1928- CTFT-5
   Earlier sketch in WWT-17
Banner, Bob 1921-...............CTFT-3
Bannerman, Celia 1946-...........CTFT-5
   Earlier sketch in WWT-17
Bannerman, Kay 1919- CTFT-4
   Earlier sketch in WWT-17
Bannerman, Margaret 1896- .....WWasWT
Bannister, Harry 1893-1961 ......WWasWT
Bannon, Jack 1940- CTFT-6
Bantry, Bryan 1956-..............CTFT-1
Baraka, Amiri 1934-..............CTFT-7
   Earlier sketch in WWT-17
Baraka, Imamu Amiri
   See Baraka, Amiri CTFT-7
Baranski, Christine 1952-..........CTFT-4
   Earlier sketch in WWT-17
Barbeau, Adrienne CTFT-4
Barbee, Richard 1887- ....WWasWT
Barber, Frances 1957- CTFT-9
Barber, John CTFT-1
Barbera, Joseph 1911- CTFT-8
   Earlier sketch in CTFT-1
Barbor, H. R. 1893-1933 ....WWasWT
Barbour, Elly 1945- CTFT-2
Barbour, Joyce 1901- ....WWasWT

Barbour, Thomas 1921- CTFT-2
Barcelo, Randy 1946-.............CTFT-4
Bard, Wilkie 1874-? ....WWasWT
Bardon, Henry 1923- WWT-17
Bardot, Brigitte 1934- CTFT-3
Barge, Gillian 1940- WWT-17
Baring, Maurice 1874-1945 ......WWasWT
Barker, Bob 1923- CTFT-2
Barker, Clive 1931-.............WWT-17
Barker, Felix WWT-17
Barker, H. Granville-
   See Granville-Barker, Harley ...WWasWT
Barker, Helen Granville-
   See Granville-Barker, Helen ...WWasWT
Barker, Howard 1946- WWT-17
Barker, Ronnie 1929- CTFT-7
   Earlier sketch in WWT-17
Barkin, Ellen 1955- CTFT-6
Barkworth, Peter 1929- WWT-17
Barlog, Boleslaw 1906-..........WWasWT
Barlow, Billie 1862-1937 ....WWasWT
Barlow, H. J. 1892-1970 ....WWasWT
Barnabe, Bruno 1905- WWT-17
Barnard, Ivor 1887-1953 ....WWasWT
Barner, Barry K. 1906-1965 ......WWasWT
Barnes, Binnie 1905- ....WWasWT
Barnes, Clive 1927- CTFT-3
   Earlier sketch in WWT-17
Barnes, Fran 1931-...............CTFT-1
Barnes, Fred 1884-? ....WWasWT
Barnes, Howard 1904-1968 ......WWasWT
Barnes, J. H. 1850-1925 ....WWasWT
Barnes, Joanna 1934- CTFT-6
Barnes, Kenneth (Ralph)
   1878-1957 ....WWasWT
Barnes, Peter 1931- CTFT-5
   Earlier sketch in WWT-17
Barnes, Priscilla 1955- CTFT-9
Barnes, Wade 1917- CTFT-4
Barnes, Winifred 1894-1935 ......WWasWT
Barnett, Ken
   See Francis, Freddie CTFT-8
Barney, Jay 1913-1985 ....CTFT-1
Baron, Alec CTFT-5
Baron, Evalyn 1948-..............CTFT-2
Baronova, Irina 1919- ....WWasWT
Barr, Patrick 1908-1985 ....WWT-17
Barr, Richard 1917-1989 ....CTFT-7
   Earlier sketch in WWT-17
Barr, Roseanne 1952-.............CTFT-8
Barranger, Millie S. 1937- WWT-17
Barratt, Augustus ....WWasWT
Barratt, Watson 1884-1962 ......WWasWT
Barrault, Jean-Louis 1910-.......WWasWT
Barre, Gabriel 1957-.............CTFT-4
Barrett, Edith 1906-.............WWasWT
Barrett, George 1869-1935 ....WWasWT
Barrett, Leslie 1919-.............CTFT-4
   Earlier sketch in WWT-17
Barrett, Lester ....WWasWT
Barrett, Oscar 1875-1941 ....WWasWT
Barrett, Rona 1936- CTFT-4
Barrett, Wilson 1900-...........WWasWT
Barrie, Amanda 1939- WWT-17
Barrie, Barbara 1931-............CTFT-3
   Earlier sketch in WWT-17
Barrie, Frank 1939- WWT-17
Barrie, James Matthew
   1860-1937 ....WWasWT
Barrington, Rutland 1853-1922 ...WWasWT
Barris, Chuck 1929-.............CTFT-6
Barron, Marcus 1925-1944 ......WWasWT
Barron, Muriel 1906-...........WWasWT

Barrs, Norman 1917- CTFT-1
Barry, B. Constance 1913- CTFT-1
Barry, B. H. 1940- CTFT-5
  Earlier sketch in CTFT-1
Barry, Christine 1911- ....WWasWT
Barry, Gene 1922- CTFT-5
  Earlier sketch in CTFT-2
Barry, Jack 1918-1984 ....CTFT-2
Barry, Joan 1901-1989 ....WWasWT
Barry, John 1933- CTFT-4
Barry, Michael 1910-1988 ....CTFT-7
  Earlier sketch in WWT-17
Barry, Paul 1931- CTFT-5
  Earlier sketch in CTFT-1
Barry, Philip 1896-1949 ....WWasWT
Barry, Ray
  See Barry, Raymond J. CTFT-9
Barry, Raymond
  See Barry, Raymond J. CTFT-9
Barry, Raymond J. 1939- CTFT-9
  Earlier sketch in CTFT-1
Barry, Shiel 1882-1937 ....WWasWT
Barrymore, Diana 1921-1960 .....WWasWT
Barrymore, Drew 1975- CTFT-5
  Brief Entry in CTFT-2
Barrymore, Ethel 1879-1959 .....WWasWT
Barrymore, John 1882-1942 ......WWasWT
Barrymore, Lionel 1878-1954 ....WWasWT
Bart, Lionel 1930- CTFT-3
  Earlier sketch in WWT-17
Bart, Peter 1932- CTFT-2
Bartel, Paul 1938- CTFT-6
Bartenieff, George 1935- CTFT-1
Bartet, Jeanne Julia 1854- ....WWasWT
Barth, Cecil ?-1949 ....WWasWT
Bartholomac, Phillip H. ?-1947 ...WWasWT
Bartlett, Basil 1905- ....WWasWT
Bartlett, Bonnie CTFT-6
Bartlett, Clifford 1903-1936 .....WWasWT
Bartlett, D'Jamin 1948- CTFT-5
  Earlier sketch in WWT-17
Bartlett, Elise ....WWasWT
Bartlett, Hall 1925- CTFT-1
Bartlett, Michael 1901- ....WWasWT
Barton, Dora ?-1966 ....WWasWT
Barton, James 1890-1962 ....WWasWT
Barton, John 1928- CTFT-6
  Earlier sketch in WWT-17
Barton, Margaret 1926- ....WWasWT
Barton, Mary ?-1970 ....WWasWT
Barton, Peter CTFT-9
Barty, Billy 1924- CTFT-6
Barty, Jack 1888-1942 ....WWasWT
Baryshnikov, Mikhail 1948- CTFT-3
Basehart, Richard 1914-1984 .....CTFT-2
  Earlier sketch in WWT-17
Basinger, Kim 1953- CTFT-6
  Brief Entry in CTFT-2
Baskcomb, A. W. 1880-1939 .....WWasWT
Baskcomb, Lawrence 1883-1962 ..WWasWT
Bass, Alfie 1921-1987 ....CTFT-5
  Earlier sketch in WWT-17
Bass, George Houston 1938- CTFT-1
Bass, Kingsley B., Jr.
  See Bullins, Ed CTFT-7
Bassett, Alfred Leon 1870-? ......WWasWT
Bassett, Linda CTFT-8
Bataille, Henry 1872-1940 ....WWasWT
Bate, Anthony WWT-17
Bateman, Jason CTFT-5
  Brief Entry in CTFT-2
Bateman, Justine CTFT-5
  Earlier sketch in CTFT-2

Bateman, Leah 1892- ....WWasWT
Bateman, Miss 1842-1917 ....WWasWT
Bateman, Virginia Frances
  See Compton, Mrs. Edward ....WWasWT
Bateman, Zitlah 1900-1970 ......WWasWT
Bates, Alan 1934- CTFT-7
  Earlier sketches in CTFT-2, WWT-17
Bates, Bianche 1873-1941 ....WWasWT
Bates, Kathy 1948- CTFT-1
Bates, Michael 1920- WWT-16
Bates, Ralph 1940- CTFT-9
Bates, Sally 1907- ....WWasWT
Bates, Thorpe 1883-1958 ....WWasWT
Bateson, Timothy 1926- WWT-17
Bath, Hubert 1883- ....WWasWT
Batley, Dorothy 1902- ....WWasWT
Battles, John 1921- ....WWasWT
Batty, Archibald 1884-1961 ......WWasWT
Baty, Gaston 1885-1952 ....WWasWT
Bauer, Rocky
  See Bauer, Steven CTFT-8
Bauer, Steven 1956- CTFT-8
Bauersmith, Paula 1909-1987 .....CTFT-5
  Earlier sketch in WWT-17
Baughan, Edward Algernon
  1865-1938 ....WWasWT
Baughman, Renee CTFT-2
Baumann, K. T. CTFT-1
Baumgarten, Craig 1949- CTFT-1
Bava, Mario 1914- CTFT-8
Bawn, Harry 1872-? ....WWasWT
Bax, Clifford 1886-1962 ....WWasWT
Baxley, Barbara 1927-1990 ....CTFT-2
  Earlier sketch in WWT-17
Baxter, Alan 1908- ....WWasWT
Baxter, Anne 1923-1985 ....CTFT-3
  Earlier sketch in WWT-17
Baxter, Barry 1894-1922 ....WWasWT
Baxter, Beryl 1926- ....WWasWT
Baxter, Beverly 1891- ....WWasWT
Baxter, Cash 1937- CTFT-5
Baxter, Jane 1909- WWT-17
Baxter, Keith 1935- CTFT-4
  Earlier sketch in WWT-17
Baxter, Meredith 1947- CTFT-9
Baxter, Stanley 1926- WWT-17
Baxter, Trevor 1932- WWT-17
Baxter-Birney, Meredith
  See Baxter, Meredith CTFT-9
Bay, Howard 1912-1986 ....CTFT-4
  Earlier sketch in WWT-17
Baye, Nathalie 1948- CTFT-8
Bayes, Nora 1880-1928 ....WWasWT
Bayler, Terence 1930- CTFT-3
Bayley, Caroline 1890- ....WWasWT
Bayley, Hilda ?-1971 ....WWasWT
Baylis, Lilian 1874-1937 ....WWasWT
Bayliss, Peter WWT-17
Bayly, Caroline ....WWasWT
Baynton, Henry 1892-1951 ....WWasWT
Beach, Ann 1938- WWT-17
Beach, Gary 1947- CTFT-1
Beacham, Stephanie 1947- CTFT-4
  Earlier sketch in WWT-17
Beal, John 1909- WWT-17
Bealby, George 1877-1931 ....WWasWT
Beals, Jennifer 1963- CTFT-5
  Brief Entry in CTFT-2
Bean, Orson 1928- CTFT-3
  Earlier sketch in WWT-17
Beard, Winston
  See Goldman, James CTFT-8
Beardsley, Alice 1925- CTFT-1

Bearse, Amanda CTFT-8
Beasley, Allyce 1954- CTFT-7
Beaton, Cecil 1904-1980 ....WWT-16
Beatty, Harcourt ....WWasWT
Beatty, John Lee 1948- CTFT-6
  Earlier sketches in CTFT-2, WWT-17
Beatty, May ?-1945 ....WWasWT
Beatty, Ned 1937- CTFT-6
Beatty, Robert 1909- WWT-17
Beatty, Roberta 1891- ....WWasWT
Beatty, Warren 1938- CTFT-3
Beauchamp, John ?-1921 ....WWasWT
Beaufort, John 1912- WWT-17
Beaumont, Cyril William 1891-...WWasWT
Beaumont, Diana 1909-1964 ......WWasWT
Beaumont, Gabrielle 1942- CTFT-1
Beaumont, Hugh 1908-1982 ....WWasWT
Beaumont, John 1902- ....WWasWT
Beaumont, Muriel 1881-1957 ....WWasWT
Beaumont, Roma 1914- ....WWasWT
Becher, John C. 1915-1986 ....WWT-17
Beck, John 1943(?)- CTFT-9
Beck, Julian 1925-1985 ....CTFT-4
  Earlier sketch in WWT-17
Beck, Kimberly 1956- CTFT-9
Beck, Michael CTFT-3
Beckel, Graham CTFT-9
Beckerman, Bernard 1921- WWT-17
Beckett, Samuel 1906-1989 ....CTFT-9
  Earlier sketches in CTFT-4, WWT-17
Beckhard, Arthur J. ....WWasWT
Beckley, Beatrice Mary 1885-? ...WWasWT
Beckman, John c.1898-1989 ....CTFT-8
Beckwith, Reginald 1908-1965 ...WWasWT
Bedelia, Bonnie 1950- CTFT-3
Bedells, Phyllis 1893-1985 .....WWasWT
Bedford, Brian 1935- CTFT-2
  Earlier sketch in WWT-17
Beecher, Janet 1884-1955 ....WWasWT
Beerbohm, Clarence Evelyn
  ?-1917 ....WWasWT
Beerbohm, Max 1872-1956 ......WWasWT
Beere, Bernard (Mrs.) 1856-? ....WWasWT
Beers, Francine CTFT-1
Beery, Noah 1916- CTFT-3
Beet, Alice ?-1931 ....WWasWT
Begley, Ed 1901-1970 ....WWasWT
Begley, Ed, Jr. 1949- CTFT-4
Behan, Brendan 1923-1964 ......WWasWT
Behrman, Samuel Nathaniel
  1893-1973 ....WWasWT
Beim, Norman 1923- CTFT-1
Belafonte, Harry 1927- CTFT-5
  Earlier sketch in CTFT-1
Belafonte-Harper, Shari 1954- CTFT-6
Belasco, David 1853-1931 ....WWasWT
Beldon, Eileen 1901- WWT-17
Belfrage, Bruce 1901- ....WWasWT
Bel Geddes, Barbara 1922- CTFT-3
  Earlier sketch in WWT-17
Belgrader, Andrei 1946- CTFT-2
Belkin, Jeanna 1924- CTFT-1
Belknap, Allen R. 1941- CTFT-2
Bell, Ann 1939- WWT-17
Bell, Digby Valentine ?-1917 .....WWasWT
Bell, Enid 1888- ....WWasWT
Bell, James (Harliee) 1891- .....WWasWT
Bell, John 1940- WWT-17
Bell, Lynne 1944- CTFT-1
Bell, Mary Hayley 1914- ....WWasWT
Bell, Stanley 1881-1952 ....WWasWT
Bell, Tom 1932(?)- CTFT-9
Bella, Joseph F. 1940- CTFT-1

Bellamy, Franklyn 1886- . . . . WWasWT
Bellamy, Ralph 1904- CTFT-6
    Earlier sketches in CTFT-1, WWasWT
Bellaver, Harry 1905- CTFT-1
Belleville, Frederic de 1857- . . . . .WWasWT
Bellew, Kyrie 1887- . . . . .WWasWT
Bellonini, Edna 1903- . . . . .WWasWT
Belmondo, Jean-Paul 1933- CTFT-7
Belmore, Bertha 1882-1953 . . . . . .WWasWT
Belson, Jerry CTFT-7
Belushi, Jim 1954- CTFT-3
    Brief Entry in CTFT-2
Ben-Ami, Jacob 1890- . . . . .WWasWT
Ben-Ari, Neal 1952- CTFT-9
Benaventa, Jacinto 1866- . . . . .WWasWT
Benchley, Peter 1940- CTFT-5
Benchley, Robert C. 1889- . . . . . . .WWasWT
Bendall, Ernest Alfred
    1846-1924 . . . . .WWasWT
Benedict, Dirk 1945- CTFT-1
Benedict, Paul CTFT-3
Benedictus, David 1938- WWT-17
Benelli, Sem 1877-1949 . . . . .WWasWT
Bening, Annette 1958- CTFT-9
Benini, Ferruccio 1854-1925 . . . . .WWasWT
Benjamin, Allan 1949- CTFT-3
Benjamin, Louis 1922- WWT-17
Benjamin, Morris Edgar 1881-? . .WWasWT
Benjamin, P. J. 1951- CTFT-1
Benjamin, Richard 1938- CTFT-5
    Earlier sketch in CTFT-1
Bennett, Alan 1934- CTFT-8
    Earlier sketch in WWT-17
Bennett, Arnold 1867-1931 . . . . . .WWasWT
Bennett, Charles 1899- . . . . .WWasWT
Bennett, Faith . . . . .WWasWT
Bennett, Fran 1937- CTFT-1
Bennett, Harve 1930- CTFT-8
Bennett, Hywel 1944- CTFT-9
    Earlier sketch in WWT-17
Bennett, Jill 1931- WWT-17
Bennett, Joan 1910-1990 . . . . .CTFT-9
    Earlier sketches in CTFT-4, WWT-17
Bennett, Lelia . . . . .WWasWT
Bennett, Meg 1948- CTFT-7
Bennett, Michael 1943-1987 . . . . . . .CTFT-5
    Earlier sketch in WWT-17
Bennett, Peter 1917-1990(?) CTFT-9
    Earlier sketch in WWT-17
Bennett, Richard 1873-1944 . . . . .WWasWT
Bennett, Ruth CTFT-7
Bennett, Tony 1926- CTFT-6
Bennett, Vivienne 1905-1978 . . . . . .WWT-16
Bennett, Wilda 1894-1967 . . . . . . .WWasWT
Bennett-Gordon, Eve CTFT-2
Benrimo, J. Harry 1874-1942 . . . .WWasWT
Benson, Frank R. 1858-1939 . . . . .WWasWT
Benson, George 1911-1983 . . . . .CTFT-3
    Earlier sketch in WWT-17
Benson, Lady ?-1946 . . . . .WWasWT
Benson, Robby 1956- CTFT-8
Benson, Ruth 1873-1948 . . . . .WWasWT
Bent, Buena ?-1957 . . . . .WWasWT
Benthall, Michael 1919-1956 . . . . .WWasWT
Bentham, Frederick 1911- WWT-17
Bentley, Eric 1916- WWT-17
Bentley, Irene ?-1940 . . . . .WWasWT
Bentley, Will 1873-? . . . . .WWasWT
Benton, Barbi 1950- CTFT-9
Benton, Robert 1932- CTFT-3
Berendt, Rachel ?-1957 . . . . .WWasWT
Berenger, Tom 1950- CTFT-9
    Earlier sketch in CTFT-3

Berenson, Marisa 1948- CTFT-7
Berenson, Stephen 1953- CTFT-3
Beresford, Bruce 1940- CTFT-6
Beresford, Harry 1867-1944 . . . . .WWasWT
Berg, Barry 1942- CTFT-1
Berg, Gertrude 1899-1941 . . . . . . .WWasWT
Berg, Greg CTFT-4
Bergen, Candice 1946- CTFT-3
Bergen, Nella 1873-1919 . . . . .WWasWT
Bergen, Polly 1930- CTFT-6
Berger, Anna CTFT-7
Berger, Henning 1872- . . . . .WWasWT
Berger, Keith 1952- CTFT-2
Berger, Robert 1914- CTFT-1
Berger, Senta 1947- CTFT-1
Berger, Sidney L. 1936- CTFT-1
Berger, Stephen 1954- CTFT-1
Bergerat, Emile 1845-? . . . . .WWasWT
Bergere, Lee CTFT-8
Bergere, Valerie 1872-1938 . . . . . .WWasWT
Bergese, Micha 1945- CTFT-4
Berghof, Herbert 1909-1990 . . . . . . .CTFT-4
    Earlier sketch in WWT-17
Bergman, Ingmar 1918- CTFT-3
Bergman, Ingrid 1915-1982 . . . . .CTFT-1
    Earlier sketch in WWT-17
Bergman, J. Peter 1946- CTFT-1
Bergman, Sandahl CTFT-7
Bergner, Elisabeth 1900-1986 . . . . .WWT-17
Bergstrom, Hilda . . . . .WWasWT
Beringer, Esme 1875-1936 . . . . . . .WWasWT
Beringer, Mrs. Oscar 1856-1936 . .WWasWT
Beringer, Vera 1879-1964 . . . . . . .WWasWT
Berk, Tony ?-1988 . . . . .CTFT-2
Berkeley, Ballard 1904-1988 . . . . .WWasWT
Berkeley, Busby 1859-1976 . . . . . . .WWT-16
Berkeley, Reginald Cheyne
    1890-1935 . . . . .WWasWT
Berkeley, Wilma . . . . .WWasWT
Berkoff, Steven 1937- WWT-17
Berkson, Susan CTFT-3
Berle, Milton 1908- CTFT-3
    Earlier sketch in WWT-17
Berlin, Irving 1888-1989 . . . . .CTFT-8
    Earlier sketch in WWT-17
Berlind, Roger 1930- CTFT-1
Berliner, Ron 1958- CTFT-3
Berlinger, Warren 1937- CTFT-5
    Earlier sketch in WWT-17
Berlyn, Alfred 1860-1936 . . . . .WWasWT
Berman, Ed 1941- CTFT-5
    Earlier sketch in WWT-17
Berman, Shelley 1926- CTFT-6
Bermel, Albert 1927- CTFT-1
Bernard, Barney 1877-1924 . . . . . .WWasWT
Bernard, Jason 1938- CTFT-8
Bernard, Jean Jacques 1888- . . . . .WWasWT
Bernard, Kenneth 1930- CTFT-1
Bernard, Sam 1863-1927 . . . . .WWasWT
Bernard, Tristan 1866-1947 . . . . . .WWasWT
Bernede, Arthur . . . . .WWasWT
Bernette, Sheila WWT-17
Bernhard, Harvey 1924- CTFT-4
Bernhard, Sandra 1955- CTFT-6
Bernhardt, Melvin CTFT-2
    Earlier sketch in WWT-17
Bernhardt, Sarah 1845-1923 . . . . .WWasWT
Bernsen, Corbin 1954- CTFT-7
Bernstein, Aline 1882-1955 . . . . . .WWasWT
Bernstein, Elmer 1922- CTFT-4
Bernstein, Henry 1875-1953 . . . . .WWasWT
Bernstein, Jay 1937- CTFT-5

Bernstein, Leonard 1918- CTFT-3
    Earlier sketch in WWT-17
Bernstein, Walter 1919- CTFT-6
    Earlier sketch in CTFT-1
Beroza, Janet CTFT-2
Berr, Georges 1867-1942 . . . . .WWasWT
Berr De Turique, Julien
    1863-1923 . . . . .WWasWT
Berri, Claude 1934- CTFT-8
Berridge, Elizabeth 1962- CTFT-5
Berry, David 1943- CTFT-2
Berry, Eric 1913- WWT-17
Berry, James 1883-? . . . . .WWasWT
Berry, Ken 1933- CTFT-8
Berry, William Henry
    1870-1951 . . . . .WWasWT
Bertinelli, Valerie 1960- CTFT-3
Bertolazzi, Carlo 1870-? . . . . .WWasWT
Bertolucci, Bernardo 1940- CTFT-4
Bertram, Arthur 1860-1955 . . . . . .WWasWT
Bertram, Eugene 1872-1941 . . . . . .WWasWT
Bertrand, Sandra 1943- CTFT-1
Beruh, Joseph 1924-1989 . . . . .CTFT-8
    Earlier sketch in WWT-17
Besch, Bibi 1940- CTFT-6
    Earlier sketch in CTFT-1
Besier, Rudolf 1878-1942 . . . . .WWasWT
Bessell, Ted 1942- CTFT-9
Bessette, Denise 1954- CTFT-2
Best, Edna 1900-1974 . . . . .WWasWT
Bethencourt, Francis 1926- WWT-17
Bethune, Zina 1950(?)- CTFT-9
Bettelheim, Edwin 1865-1938 . . . . .WWasWT
Bettger, Lyle 1915- CTFT-1
Betti, Laura 1934- CTFT-8
Bettis, Valerie ?-1982 . . . . .WWT-17
Betts, Edward William 1881-? . . . .WWasWT
Betts, Ernest WWT-11
Bevan, Faith 1896- . . . . .WWasWT
Bevan, Isla 1910- . . . . .WWasWT
Beveridge, J. D. 1844-1926 . . . . . . .WWasWT
Beverley, Trazana 1945- CTFT-8
Bewes, Rodney 1937- WWT-17
Beyer, Elsie WWT-13
Beymer, Richard 1939- CTFT-9
Bibby, Charles 1878-1917 . . . . . . .WWasWT
Bicat, Tony 1945- WWT-17
Bickford, Charles A. 1891-1933 . .WWasWT
Bickford, David 1953- CTFT-4
Biehn, Michael 1957- CTFT-8
Biggs, Roxann CTFT-5
Bikel, Theodore 1924- CTFT-5
    Earlier sketch in WWT-17
Bilbrooke, Lydia 1888-1990 . . . . . .WWasWT
Bilhaud, Paul 1854-1933 . . . . .WWasWT
Bill, Tony 1940- CTFT-6
Billig, Robert 1947- CTFT-1
Billing, H. Chiswell 1881-1934 . . .WWasWT
Billings, Josh 1947- CTFT-5
Billingsley, Peter 1972- CTFT-7
Billington, Adeline 1825-? . . . . . . .WWasWT
Billington, Ken 1946- CTFT-4
    Earlier sketch in CTFT-1
Billington, Kevin 1934- WWT-17
Billington, Michael 1939- WWT-17
Bilowit, Ira J. 1925- CTFT-1
Binder, Steve CTFT-1
Bingham, Amelia 1869-1927 . . . . . .WWasWT
Bingham, Jeffrey 1946- CTFT-6
Bingham, Sallie 1937- CTFT-1
Binner, Margery 1908- . . . . .WWasWT
Binney, Constance 1900- . . . . .WWasWT
Binus, Judith 1944- CTFT-2

Binyon, Laurence 1869-1943 ..... WWasWT
Birch, Frank 1889-1956 .... WWasWT
Birch, Patricia WWT-17
Bird, David 1907- WWT-17
Bird, John 1936- WWT-17
Bird, Richard 1894-1986 .... WWasWT
Birkett, Viva 1887-1934 .... WWasWT
Birmingham, George A.
  1865-1950 .... WWasWT
Birney, David CTFT-5
  Earlier sketches in CTFT-1, WWT-17
Birney, Reed 1954- CTFT-1
Bishop, Alfred 1848-1928 .... WWasWT
Bishop, Andre 1948- CTFT-9
  Earlier sketch in CTFT-1
Bishop, Carole
  See Bishop, Kelly CTFT-5
Bishop, Conrad J. 1941- CTFT-1
Bishop, George Walter
  1886-1965 .... WWasWT
Bishop, Joey 1918- CTFT-7
Bishop, John
  See Willis, Ted CTFT-7
Bishop, Kate 1847-1923 .... WWasWT
Bishop, Kelly 1944- CTFT-5
  Earlier sketch in WWT-17
Bishop, Will 1867-1944 .... WWasWT
Bisno, Leslie 1953- CTFT-6
Bisoglio, Val 1926- CTFT-8
Bisset, Jacqueline 1944- CTFT-6
  Earlier sketch in CTFT-2
Bivens, Diane E. CTFT-1
Bixby, Bill 1934- CTFT-9
  Earlier sketch in CTFT-3
Black, Alfred 1913- .... WWasWT
Black, David 1931- WWT-17
Black, Dorothy 1899- .... WWasWT
Black, Dorothy 1913-1985 ....CTFT-2
  Earlier sketch in WWT-17
Black, George 1911-1970 .... WWasWT
Black, George 1890-1945 .... WWasWT
Black, Karen 1942- CTFT-4
Black, Malcolm 1928- CTFT-1
Black, Noel 1937- CTFT-2
Blackler, Betty 1929- .... WWasWT
Blackman, Eugene Joseph 1922- CTFT-1
Blackman, Fred J. 1879-1951 .... WWasWT
Blackman, Honor CTFT-4
  Earlier sketch in WWT-17
Blackmer, Sidney 1895- .... WWasWT
Blackmore, Peter 1909- .... WWasWT
Blacque, Taurean CTFT-8
Blades, Ruben 1948- CTFT-5
Blaine, Vivian 1921- CTFT-5
  Earlier sketch in WWT-17
Blair, Isla 1944- WWT-17
Blair, Joyce 1932- WWT-17
Blair, Linda 1959- CTFT-3
Blair, Lionel 1931- WWT-17
Blair, Pamela 1949- CTFT-2
Blaisdell, Nesbitt 1928- CTFT-3
Blake, Betty 1920- CTFT-1
Blake, Bobby
  See Blake, Robert CTFT-9
Blake, Charles H. 1916- CTFT-1
Blake, Harry 1866-? ....WWasWT
Blake, Josh 1975- CTFT-8
Blake, Robby
  See Blake, Robert CTFT-9
Blake, Robert 1933(?)- CTFT-9
  Earlier sketch in CTFT-3
Blakeley, James 1873-1915 ...... WWasWT
Blakelock, Denys 1901-1970 ..... WWasWT

Blakely, Colin 1930-1987 ....CTFT-4
  Earlier sketch in WWT-17
Blakely, Susan 1948- CTFT-6
Blakley, Ronee 1946- CTFT-7
Blakemore, Michael 1928- CTFT-6
  Earlier sketch in WWT-17
Blakiston, Clarence 1864-1943 ... WWasWT
Blanc, Mel 1908-1989 ....CTFT-8
Blanche, Ada 1862-1953 .... WWasWT
Blanche, Marie 1893- .... WWasWT
Bland, Alan 1897-1946 .... WWasWT
Bland, Joyce 1906-1963 .... WWasWT
Blaney, Charles E. ?-1944 .... WWasWT
Blaney, Norah .... WWasWT
Blatty, William Peter 1928- CTFT-4
Blavet, Emile 1838-? .... WWasWT
Blaxill, Peter 1931- CTFT-1
Blayney, May 1875-1953 .... WWasWT
Bleckner, Jeff CTFT-4
  Earlier sketch in WWT-17
Blessed, Brian 1937- CTFT-8
Bley, Maurice G. 1910- CTFT-4
Blick, Newton 1899-1965 .... WWasWT
Blier, Bernard 1916-1989 ....CTFT-8
Blier, Bertrand 1939- CTFT-8
Blinn, Holbrook 1872-1928 ...... WWasWT
Bliss, Helena 1917- WWT-17
Bloch, Robert 1917- CTFT-2
Bloch, Scotty CTFT-1
Block, Larry 1942- CTFT-8
  Earlier sketch in CTFT-2
Blomfield, Derek 1920-1964 ..... WWasWT
Blondell, Joan 1909-1979 .... WWT-16
Bloom, Claire 1931- CTFT-4
  Earlier sketch in WWT-17
Bloom, Lindsay 1955- CTFT-3
Bloom, Michael 1950- CTFT-4
Bloom, Verna CTFT-7
Bloomgarden, Kermit
  1904-1976 .... WWT-16
Blore, Eric 1887-1959 .... WWasWT
Blossom, Henry Martyn Jr.
  1866-1919 .... WWasWT
Blount, Helon 1929- CTFT-4
  Earlier sketch in WWT-17
Blount, Lisa CTFT-7
Blow, Sydney 1878-1961 .... WWasWT
Blum, Mark 1950- CTFT-8
Blumenfeld, Robert 1943- CTFT-3
Blumenkrantz, Jeff 1965- CTFT-8
Blundell, Graeme 1945- WWT-17
Bluth, Don CTFT-6
Blyden, Larry 1925-1975 .... WWT-16
Blyth-Pratt, Charles Edward
  1869-? .... WWasWT
Blyth-Pratt, Violet .... WWasWT
Blythe, Bobby 1894- .... WWasWT
Blythe, Coralie 1880-1928 ...... WWasWT
Blythe, John 1921- WWT-17
Blythe, Violet .... WWasWT
Bobadilla, Pepita .... WWasWT
Bobs, The Two .... WWasWT
Bochco, Steven 1943- CTFT-6
Bochner, Hart 1956- CTFT-2
Bochner, Lloyd 1924- CTFT-7
Bock, Jerry 1928- WWT-17
Bode, Milton 1860-1938 .... WWasWT
Bodie, Dr. Walford 1870-? ...... WWasWT
Bodom, Borgchild WWT-7
Boers, Frank, Jr.
  See Bonner, Frank CTFT-7
Bofshever, Michael 1950- CTFT-6
Boganny, Joe 1874-? .... WWasWT

Bogard, Travis 1918- CTFT-3
Bogarde, Dirk 1921(?)- CTFT-9
  Earlier sketch in WWasWT
Bogart, Humphrey 1899-1957 .... WWasWT
Bogart, Paul 1919- CTFT-1
Bogdanov, Michael 1938- WWT-17
Bogdanovich, Peter 1939- CTFT-4
  Earlier sketch in CTFT-1
Boggetti, Victor 1895- .... WWasWT
Bogin, Abba 1925- CTFT-1
Bogosian, Eric 1953- CTFT-7
Bohannon, Judy CTFT-2
Bohay, Heidi CTFT-3
Bohnen, Roman ?-1949 .... WWasWT
Boht, Jean 1936- CTFT-8
Bolam, James 1938- CTFT-5
  Earlier sketch in WWT-17
Boland, Mary 1885-1965 .... WWasWT
Bolasni, Saul CTFT-1
Boles, John 1900-1969 .... WWasWT
Boleslawski, Richard 1889-1937 .. WWasWT
Bolger, Ray 1904-1987 ....CTFT-3
  Earlier sketch in WWT-17
Bolm, Adolph 1887-1951 .... WWasWT
Bologna, Joseph 1938- CTFT-9
  Earlier sketch in CTFT-3
Bolt, Jonathan 1935- CTFT-3
Bolt, Robert 1924- CTFT-4
  Earlier sketch in WWT-17
Bolton, Guy Reginald
  1884-1979 .... WWT-16
Bond, Acton ?-1941 .... WWasWT
Bond, C. G. 1945- WWT-17
Bond, Derek 1920- CTFT-1
Bond, Edward 1934- CTFT-4
  Earlier sketch in WWT-17
Bond, Frederic 1861-1914 .... WWasWT
Bond, Gary 1940- CTFT-3
  Earlier sketch in WWT-17
Bond, Jessie 1853-1942 .... WWasWT
Bond, Lilian 1910- .... WWasWT
Bond, Sheila 1928- CTFT-1
  Earlier sketch in WWasWT
Bond, Sudie 1928-1984 ....CTFT-1
  Earlier sketch in WWT-17
Bondi, Beulah 1892-1981 .... WWasWT
Bondor, Rebecca CTFT-1
Bonerz, Peter 1938- CTFT-1
Bonet, Lisa CTFT-4
Bonfils, Helen 1889-1972 .... WWasWT
Bonham Carter, Helena 1966- CTFT-7
Bonnaire, Henri 1869-? .... WWasWT
Bonner, Frank 1942- CTFT-7
Bono, Sonny 1935- CTFT-7
Bonus, Ben ?-1984 .... WWT-17
Boockvor, Steve 1945- CTFT-1
Booke, Sorrell 1930- CTFT-4
  Earlier sketch in WWT-17
Boone, Debby 1956- CTFT-1
Boor, Frank ?-1938 .... WWasWT
Boorman, John 1933- CTFT-6
Boot, Gladys ?-1964 .... WWasWT
Booth, James 1933- WWT-17
Booth, Shirley 1907- CTFT-4
  Earlier sketch in WWT-17
Booth, Webster 1902- .... WWasWT
Boothby, Victoria CTFT-1
Boothe, Clare 1903-1987 .... WWasWT
Boothe, Power 1945- CTFT-1
Boothe, Powers 1949- CTFT-4
Bordoni, Irene ?-1953 .... WWasWT
Borell, Louis 1906- .... WWasWT

Borgnine, Ernest 1917- CTFT-7
 Earlier sketch in CTFT-2
Boris, Robert M. 1945- CTFT-5
Borlin, Jean ....WWasWT
Borrego, Jesse CTFT-5
Bosco, Philip 1930- CTFT-4
 Earlier sketches in CTFT-1, WWT-17
Bosley, Tom 1927- CTFT-4
 Earlier sketch in WWT-17
Bosse-Vingard, Harriet Sofie
 1878-? ....WWasWT
Bosson, Barbara 1939- CTFT-7
Bostock, Thomas H. 1899- ......WWasWT
Bostwick, Barry 1945- CTFT-5
 Earlier sketch in CTFT-2
Bott, Alan 1894- ....WWasWT
Bottin, Rob 1959(?)- CTFT-9
Bottomley, Gordon 1874-1948 ...WWasWT
Bottoms, Joseph 1954- CTFT-4
Bottoms, Timothy 1951- CTFT-3
Bottoms, Sam 1955- CTFT-4
Boucher, Victor 1879-1942 ......WWasWT
Bouchier, Chili 1909- CTFT-6
 Earlier sketch in WWT-17
Bouchier, Dorothy
 See Bouchier, Chili CTFT-6
Boucicault, Aubrey 1869-1913 ...WWasWT
Boucicault, Mrs. Dion
 1833-1916 ....WWasWT
Boucicault, Dion G. 1859-1929 ...WWasWT
Boucicault, Nina 1867-1950 .....WWasWT
Boughton, Rutland 1878-1960 ....WWasWT
Bould, Beckett 1880-? ....WWasWT
Boule, Kathryn 1949- CTFT-1
Boulter, Rosalyn 1916- ....WWasWT
Boulton, Guy Pelham 1890- .....WWasWT
Bourchier, Arthur 1863-1927 ....WWasWT
Bourne, Adeline ....WWasWT
Bourneuf, Philip 1912-1979 ......WWT-16
Bouwmeester, Louis 1842-? ......WWasWT
Bova, Joseph 1924- CTFT-4
 Earlier sketch in WWT-17
Bovasso, Julie 1930- CTFT-7
 Earlier sketch in WWT-17
Bovill, C. H. 1878-1918 ....WWasWT
Bovy, Berthe 1887- ....WWasWT
Bowden, Charles WWT-17
Bowen, John 1924- WWT-17
Bowen, Roger 1932- CTFT-7
Bower, Marian ?-1945 ....WWasWT
Bowers, Faubion 1917- CTFT-2
Bowers, Lally 1917-1984 ....WWT-17
Bowers, Robert Hood
 1877-1941 ....WWasWT
Bowes, Alice ?-1969 ....WWasWT
Bowes, Janet Elizabeth 1944- CTFT-1
Bowie, David 1947- CTFT-3
Bowles, Anthony 1931- WWT-17
Bowles, Paul 1910- CTFT-1
Bowles, Peter 1936- CTFT-6
 Earlier sketch in WWT-17
Bowman, Nellie 1878-? ....WWasWT
Boxer, (Cyril) John 1909- WWT-17
Boxleitner, Bruce 1950- CTFT-3
Boyd, Frank M. 1863-? ....WWasWT
Boyer, Charles 1899- ....WWasWT
Boyle, Billy 1945- WWT-17
Boyle, Katie 1926- CTFT-1
Boyle, Peter 1933(?)- CTFT-9
 Earlier sketch in CTFT-3
Boyle, William 1853-1923 ....WWasWT
Boyne, Clifton 1874-1945 ....WWasWT
Boyne, Leonard 1853-1920 ......WWasWT

Braban, Harvey 1883-? ....WWasWT
Bracco, Roberto 1863-1943 ......WWasWT
Brach, Gerard 1927- CTFT-6
Bracken, Eddie 1920- CTFT-3
 Earlier sketch in WWT-17
Bradbury, James H. 1857-1940 ...WWasWT
Braden, Bernard 1916- ....WWasWT
Braden, William 1939- CTFT-2
Bradfield, W. Louis 1866-1919 ...WWasWT
Bradley, Buddy 1908- ....WWasWT
Bradley, Lillian Trimble
 1875-1939 ....WWasWT
Brady, Leo 1917- CTFT-1
Brady, Scott 1924-1985 ....CTFT-2
Brady, Terence 1939- WWT-17
Brady, Veronica 1890-1964 ......WWasWT
Brady, William A. 1863-1950 ....WWasWT
Brady, William A. 1900-1935 ....WWasWT
Brae, June 1918- ....WWasWT
Braeden, Eric CTFT-8
Braga, Sonia 1951- CTFT-7
Bragaglia, Marinella ....WWasWT
Bragg, Bernard CTFT-3
Braham, Horace 1893-1955 ......WWasWT
Braham, Leonora 1853-1931 .....WWasWT
Braham, Lionel ....WWasWT
Braham, Philip 1881-1934 ....WWasWT
Brahms, Caryl WWT-17
Braine, John 1922-1986 ....CTFT-4
Braithwaite, Lilian 1873-1948 ....WWasWT
Brambell, Wilfrid 1912-1985 ......WWT-17
Branagh, Kenneth 1960- CTFT-9
Branch, Eileen 1911- ....WWasWT
Brand, Oscar 1920- CTFT-1
Brandauer, Klaus Maria 1944- CTFT-6
Brandes, Marthe (Brunschwig)
 1862-1930 ....WWasWT
Brando, Marlon 1924- CTFT-3
Brandon, Dorothy 1899?-1977 ...WWasWT
Brandon, Johnny CTFT-1
Brandon, Michael CTFT-7
Brandon-Thomas, Amy
 Marguerite 1890- ....WWasWT
Brandon-Thomas, Jevan 1898- ...WWasWT
Brandt, Ivan 1903- ....WWasWT
Brandt, Yanna Kroyt 1933- CTFT-3
Brasseur, Albert Jules 1862-? ....WWasWT
Bray, Yvonne de 1889- ....WWasWT
Brayton, Lily 1876-1953 ....WWasWT
Brecher, Egon 1885-1946 ....WWasWT
Breen, Helen 1902- ....WWasWT
Breen, Robert 1914-1990 ....CTFT-2
Breese, Edmund 1871-1936 ......WWasWT
Bregman, Martin 1926- CTFT-5
 Earlier sketch in CTFT-1
Brennan, Eileen 1935- CTFT-8
 Earlier sketch in CTFT-1
Brenner, David 1945- CTFT-2
Brenner, Dori CTFT-9
Brenner, Randy 1955- CTFT-3
Brent, Romney 1902-1976 ....WWasWT
Brenton, Howard 1942- CTFT-6
 Earlier sketch in WWT-17
Brereton, Austin 1862-1923 ......WWasWT
Bressack, Celia 1956- CTFT-3
Bresson, Robert 1907- CTFT-8
Brest, Martin 1951- CTFT-7
Brett, Jeremy 1933- CTFT-8
 Earlier sketches in CTFT-3, WWT-17
Brett, Stanley 1879-1923 ....WWasWT
Breuer, Lee 1937- CTFT-5
 Earlier sketch in WWT-17
Brewster, Towsend Tyler 1924- CTFT-1

Brian, Donald 1877-1948 ....WWasWT
Brice, Fanny 1891-1951 ....WWasWT
Brickman, Marshall 1941- CTFT-6
Bricusse, Leslie 1931- CTFT-9
 Earlier sketch in WWT-17
Bridge, Peter 1925- WWT-17
Bridges, Beau 1941- CTFT-3
Bridges, James 1936- CTFT-4
Bridges, Jeff 1951- CTFT-3
Bridges, Lloyd 1913- CTFT-3
Bridges, Robert 1937- CTFT-3
Bridges-Adams, W. 1889-1965 ...WWasWT
Bridgewater, Leslie 1893- ....WWasWT
Bridie, James 1888-1951 ....WWasWT
Brien, Alan 1925- WWT-17
Briercliffe, Nellie ?-1966 ....WWasWT
Brierley, David 1936- WWT-17
Briers, Richard 1934- CTFT-9
 Earlier sketch in WWT-17
Brieux, Eugene 1858-1932 ....WWasWT
Briggs, Hedley 1907-1968 ....WWasWT
Brighouse, Harold 1882-1958 ....WWasWT
Bright, Richard CTFT-4
Brightman, Stanley 1888-1961 ....WWasWT
Brighton, Pam 1946- WWT-17
Brill, Fran CTFT-8
 Earlier sketch in CTFT-1
Brillstein, Bernie CTFT-6
Brimley, Wilford 1934- CTFT-6
Brisbane, Katharine 1932- CTFT-4
 Earlier sketch in WWT-17
Brisson, Carl 1895-1965 ....WWasWT
Brisson, Frederick 1913-1984 .....WWT-17
Bristow, Charles 1928- WWT-17
Brittany, Morgan 1951- CTFT-7
Britton, Tony 1924- WWT-17
Broad, Jay 1930- CTFT-2
Broadhurst, George H.
 1866-1952 ....WWasWT
Broadhurst, Kent 1940- CTFT-2
Broccoli, Albert R. 1909- CTFT-6
Brockett, Oscar G. 1923- WWT-17
Brocksmith, Roy 1945- CTFT-2
Brockway, Amie 1938- CTFT-2
Broderick, Helen 1891-1959 .....WWasWT
Broderick, Matthew 1962- CTFT-4
Brodziak, Kenn 1913- WWT-17
Brogden, Gwendoline 1891- .....WWasWT
Brogger, Ivar 1947- CTFT-6
 Earlier sketch in CTFT-1
Brokaw, Tom 1940- CTFT-6
Brolin, James 1941- CTFT-7
Bromberg, J. 1904-1951 ....WWasWT
Bromka, Elaine 1950- CTFT-1
Bromley-Davenport, Arthur
 1867-1946 ....WWasWT
Bron, Eleanor WWT-17
Bronson, Charles 1920- CTFT-3
Brook, Clive 1887-1974 ....WWasWT
Brook, Faith 1922- CTFT-4
 Earlier sketch in WWT-17
Brook, Lesley 1917- ....WWasWT
Brook, Peter 1925- WWT-17
Brook, Sara WWT-17
Brook-Jones, Elwyn 1911-1962 ...WWasWT
Brooke, Cynthia 1875-1949 ......WWasWT
Brooke, Mrs. E. H. ?-1915 ....WWasWT
Brooke, Emily ?-1953 ....WWasWT
Brooke, Harold 1910- WWT-17
Brooke, Paul 1944- WWT-17
Brooke, Sarah ....WWasWT
Brookes, Jacqueline 1930- CTFT-7
 Earlier sketch in WWT-17

Brookfield, Charles Hallam
  Elton 1857-1913 ....WWasWT
Brooks, Albert 1947- CTFT-6
Brooks, Avery 1949- CTFT-9
Brooks, Charles David III
  1939- CTFT-3
Brooks, David 1920- CTFT-1
Brooks, James L. 1940- CTFT-3
Brooks, Jeff 1950- CTFT-1
Brooks, Joel CTFT-4
Brooks, Mel 1926- CTFT-6
  Earlier sketch in CTFT-1
Brooks, Norman G. 1926- CTFT-4
Brooks, Virginia Fox
  See Vernon, Virginia ....WWasWT
Broones, Martin 1892- ....WWasWT
Brosnan, Pierce 1953- CTFT-6
Brosten, Harve 1943- CTFT-2
Brotherson, Eric 1911-1989 ....CTFT-9
  Earlier sketch in WWT-17
Brouett, Albert ....WWasWT
Brough, Colin 1945- CTFT-1
Brough, Fanny Whiteside
  1854-1914 ....WWasWT
Brough, Mary 1863-1934 ....WWasWT
Brough, Mrs. Robert ?-1932 ...WWasWT
Broughton, Bruce 1945-.......CTFT-7
Broughton, Jessie 1885-? ....WWasWT
Broughton, Phyllis 1862?-1926 ...WWasWT
Broun, Heywood 1888-1939 .....WWasWT
Broun, Heywood Hale 1918- CTFT-1
Brown, Arvin 1940- CTFT-8
  Earlier sketches in CTFT-2, WWT-17
Brown, Barry M. 1942- CTFT-8
  Earlier sketch in CTFT-1
Brown, Blair 1948- CTFT-6
Brown, Bryan 1950- CTFT-7
Brown, David 1916- CTFT-3
Brown, Georg Stanford 1943- CTFT-7
Brown, Georgia 1933- CTFT-9
  Earlier sketch in WWT-17
Brown, Graham 1924- CTFT-9
Brown, Ivor 1891-1974 ....WWasWT
Brown, Jim 1936- CTFT-9
Brown, Joe E. 1892-1973 ....WWasWT
Brown, John Mason 1900-1969 ...WWasWT
Brown, John Russell 1923- WWT-17
Brown, Julie 1958- CTFT-9
Brown, Kenneth H. 1936- CTFT-4
  Earlier sketch in CTFT-2
Brown, Kermit 1939(?)- CTFT-9
  Earlier sketch in CTFT-1
Brown, Lew 1899-1958 ....WWasWT
Brown, Lionel 1888-1964 ....WWasWT
Brown, Louise ....WWasWT
Brown, Pamela 1917-1975 ......WWasWT
Brown, William F. 1928- CTFT-1
Brown, Zack 1949- CTFT-1
Browne, Coral 1913- CTFT-4
  Earlier sketch in WWT-17
Browne, E. Martin 1900-1980 .....WWT-17
Browne, Irene 1896-1965 ....WWasWT
Browne, Laidman 1896-1961 .....WWasWT
Browne, Louise ....WWasWT
Browne, Marjorie 1913- ....WWasWT
Browne, Maurice 1881-1955 .....WWasWT
Browne, Pattie 1869-1934 ......WWasWT
Browne, Roscoe Lee 1925- CTFT-4
  Earlier sketch in WWT-17
Browne, Stella 1906- ....WWasWT
Browne, W. Graham 1870-1937 ..WWasWT
Browne, Wynyard (Barry)
  1911-1964 ....WWasWT

Browning, Susan 1941-.........CTFT-4
  Earlier sketch in WWT-17
Brownlow, Kevin 1938- CTFT-5
Brown-Potter, Mrs.
  See Potter, Cora Urquhart .....WWasWT
Bruce, Brenda 1922-...............CTFT-9
  Earlier sketch in WWT-17
Bruce, Carol 1919- WWT-17
Bruce, Edgar K. 1893- ....WWasWT
Bruce, Nigel 1895-1953 ....WWasWT
Bruce, Shelley 1965-..............CTFT-1
Bruce, Susan 1957-...............CTFT-3
Bruce, Tonie Edgar 1892-1966 ...WWasWT
Bruce-Potter, Hilda 1888- ......WWasWT
Bruckheimer, Jerry CTFT-6
  Earlier sketch in CTFT-1
Bruford, Rose Elizabeth 1904- WWT-17
Brule, Andre ....WWasWT
Brune, Adrienne 1892- ....WWasWT
Brune, Clarence M. 1870-? ......WWasWT
Brune, Gabrielle 1912- ....WWasWT
Brune, Minnie Tittell 1883-? ....WWasWT
Bruning, Francesca 1907- ....WWasWT
Bruno, Albert 1873-1927 ....WWasWT
Brunton, Dorothy 1893- ....WWasWT
Brustein, Robert 1927- WWT-17
Bruton, Margo CTFT-6
Bryan, Dora 1924- CTFT-5
  Earlier sketch in WWT-17
Bryan, Hal 1891-1948 ....WWasWT
Bryan, Herbert George ?-1948 ...WWasWT
Bryan, Kenneth 1953-1986 ....CTFT-2
Bryan, Peggy 1916- ....WWasWT
Bryan, Robert 1934-..............CTFT-8
  Earlier sketch in WWT-17
Bryant, Charles 1879-1948 ......WWasWT
Bryant, J. V. 1889-1924 ....WWasWT
Bryant, Michael 1928- WWT-17
Bryantsev, Alexandr
  Alexandrovich 1883-1961 ......WWasWT
Bryceland, Yvonne CTFT-7
  Earlier sketch in WWT-17
Bryden, Bill 1942- CTFT-6
  Earlier sketch in WWT-17
Bryden, Ronald 1927- WWT-17
Brydone, Alfred 1863-1920 ......WWasWT
Bryer, Vera 1905- ....WWasWT
Bryggman, Larry 1938- CTFT-9
Bryning, John 1913- ....WWasWT
Brynner, Yul 1920-1985 ....CTFT-3
  Earlier sketch in WWT-17
Buchanan, Jack 1891-1957 ......WWasWT
Buchanan, Maud ....WWasWT
Buchanan, Thompson
  1877-1937 ....WWasWT
Buchholz, Horst 1933- CTFT-1
Buck, David 1936-1989 ....CTFT-8
  Earlier sketch in WWT-17
Buckham, Bernard 1882-1963 ....WWasWT
Bucklaw, Alfred ....WWasWT
Buckler, Hugh C. 1870-1936 .....WWasWT
Buckley, Betty 1947- CTFT-4
  Earlier sketch in CTFT-1
Buckley, May 1875-? ....WWasWT
Buckmaster, John 1915-.........WWasWT
Buckstone, J. C. 1858-1924 .....WWasWT
Buckstone, Rowland 1860-1922 ..WWasWT
Buckton, Florence 1893- ....WWasWT
Budries, David 1953- CTFT-1
Buell, Bill 1952- CTFT-1
Bufman, Zev 1930- CTFT-4
  Earlier sketch in WWT-17
Buist, Walter Scott 1860-? ......WWasWT

Bujold, Genevieve 1942- CTFT-3
Bulgakov, Leo 1889-1948 ....WWasWT
Bull, Peter 1912-1984 ....CTFT-1
  Earlier sketch in WWasWT
Bullard, Thomas 1944-..........CTFT-9
  Earlier sketch in CTFT-1
Bullins, Ed 1935- CTFT-7
  Earlier sketch in WWT-17
Bullock, Christopher 1934- WWT-17
Bullock, Donna 1955- CTFT-3
Bullock, Eldon 1952- CTFT-4
Bullock, John Malcolm
  1867-1938 ....WWasWT
Buloff, Joseph 1899-1985 ....WWT-17
Bunce, Alan 1903-1965 ....WWasWT
Bundy, William 1924- WWT-17
Bunnage, Avis WWT-17
Bunston, Herbert 1870-1935 .....WWasWT
Buono, Victor 1938-1981 ....CTFT-2
Burbidge, Douglas 1895-1959 ....WWasWT
Burbridge, Edward CTFT-4
  Earlier sketch in WWT-17
Burch, Shelly 1959- CTFT-2
Burchill, William ?-1930 ....WWasWT
Burden, Hugh 1913-1985 ....WWT-17
Burdon, Albert 1900- ....WWasWT
Burge, Stuart 1918- CTFT-8
  Earlier sketch in WWT-17
Burgess, Muriel 1926- CTFT-4
Burghoff, Gary 1943- CTFT-8
Burgis, Kathleen 1907- ....WWasWT
Burke, Alfred 1918- WWT-17
Burke, Billie 1885-1970 ....WWasWT
Burke, Chris 1965- CTFT-8
Burke, David 1934- WWT-17
Burke, Delta 1956- CTFT-7
Burke, Marie 1894- ....WWasWT
Burke, Patricia 1917- WWT-17
Burke, Tom 1890-1969 ....WWasWT
Burlingame, Lloyd WWT-17
Burnaby, G. Davy 1881-1949 ....WWasWT
Burnand, Francis Cowley
  1836-1917 ....WWasWT
Burne, Arthur 1873-1945 ....WWasWT
Burne, Nancy 1912-1954 ....WWasWT
Burnett, Carol 1933- CTFT-8
  Earlier sketches in CTFT-1, WWT-17
Burnett, Frances Hodgson
  1849-1924 ....WWasWT
Burnham, Barbara 1900- ....WWasWT
Burns, David 1902-1971 ....WWasWT
Burns, Eileen CTFT-6
Burns, George 1896- CTFT-9
  Earlier sketch in CTFT-3
Burns-Bisogno, Louisa 1936- CTFT-1
Burnside, R. H. 1870-1952 ......WWasWT
Burr, Anne 1920- ....WWasWT
Burr, Raymond 1917- CTFT-9
  Earlier sketch in CTFT-3
Burr, Robert WWT-17
Burrell, Daisy 1893- ....WWasWT
Burrell, John 1910- ....WWasWT
Burrell, Pamela 1945-...........CTFT-4
Burrell, Sheila 1922- WWT-17
Burrill, Ena 1908- ....WWasWT
Burroughs, Robert C. 1923- CTFT-3
Burrows, Abe 1910-1984 ....CTFT-2
  Earlier sketch in WWT-17
Burstyn, Ellen 1932-............CTFT-6
  Earlier sketch in CTFT-1
Burt, Laura 1872-1952 ....WWasWT
Burton, Frederick 1871-1975 .....WWasWT
Burton, Kate 1957-..............CTFT-2

Burton, Langhorne 1880-1949 .... WWasWT
Burton, Levar 1957- CTFT-7
Burton, Margaret 1924-1984 ......WWT-17
Burton, Percy 1878-1948 ....WWasWT
Burton, Richard 1925-1984 ....CTFT-2
   Earlier sketch in WWT-17
Burton, Richard P. 1878-? ....WWasWT
Burton, Tim 1960- CTFT-9
Bury, John 1925- WWT-17
Busch, Charles CTFT-6
Busey, Gary 1944- CTFT-6
   Earlier sketch in CTFT-1
Busfield, Timothy CTFT-8
Bush, Norman 1933- CTFT-4
Bushell, Anthony 1904- .... WWasWT
Buskirk, June Van
   See Van Buskirk, June ....WWasWT
Busley, Jessie 1869-1950 ....WWasWT
Busse, Margaret ....WWasWT
Bussert, Meg 1949- CTFT-1
Butcher, Ernest 1885-1965 ....WWasWT
Butkus, Dick 1942- CTFT-7
Butler, Richard William
   1844-1928 ....WWasWT
Butler, Robert CTFT-1
Butleroff, Helen 1950- CTFT-3
Butlin, Jan 1940- WWT-17
Butt, Alfred Bart 1878-1962 .....WWasWT
Butterworth, Charles 1896-1946 ..WWasWT
Butterworth, Clara ....WWasWT
Butti, Enrico Annibale
   1868-1912 ....WWasWT
Button, Jeanne 1930- WWT-17
Buttons, Red 1919- CTFT-6
Buttram, Pat 1917(?)- CTFT-9
Buzas, Jason 1952- CTFT-2
Buzo, Alexander 1944- WWT-17
Buzzell, Edward 1897- ....WWasWT
Buzzi, Ruth 1939- CTFT-3
Byerley, Vivienne WWT-17
Byers, (Bobbie) Catherine CTFT-1
Byford, Roy 1873-1939 ....WWasWT
Byington, Spring 1893-1971 ..... WWasWT
Byner, John CTFT-7
Byng, Douglas 1893- WWT-16
Byng, George W. ....WWasWT
Byrd, David CTFT-8
Byrd, Sam 1908-1955 ....WWasWT
Byrne, Cecily ....WWasWT
Byrne, David 1952- CTFT-6
Byrne, Gabriel CTFT-6
Byrne, John 1940- WWT-17
Byrne, Patsy 1933- WWT-17
Byrne, Peter 1928- WWT-17
Byron, Arthur 1872-1943 ....WWasWT
Byron, John 1912- ....WWasWT

C

Caan, James 1940- CTFT-7
Cabalero, Roxann
   See Biggs, Roxann CTFT-5
Cabot, Eliot 1899-1938 ....WWasWT
Cabot, Susan 1937-1986 ....CTFT-4
Cacaci, Joe CTFT-6
Cacoyannis, Michael CTFT-1
Cadell, Jean 1884-1967 ....WWasWT
Cadell, Simon 1950- CTFT-9
   Earlier sketch in CTFT-2
Cadman, Ethel 1886- ....WWasWT
Cadorette, Mary CTFT-5
Cady, Frank 1915- CTFT-9

Caesar, Adolph 1934-1986 ....CTFT-3
Caesar, Irving 1895- WWT-17
Caesar, Sid 1922- CTFT-9
   Earlier sketches in CTFT-1, WWT-17
Cage, Nicholas 1965- CTFT-5
   Brief Entry in CTFT-2
Cagney, James 1899-1986 ....CTFT-3
   Earlier sketch in WWT-10
Cagney, Jeanne 1919- ....WWasWT
Cahill, Lily 1886-1955 ....WWasWT
Cahill, Marie 1870-1933 .... WWasWT
Cahn, Sammy 1913- WWT-17
Cain, Henri 1857-? ....WWasWT
Cain, William 1931- CTFT-9
   Earlier sketch in CTFT-1
Caine, Derwent Hall 1892- ......WWasWT
Caine, Hall 1853-1931 ....WWasWT
Caine, Henry 1888-1914 ....WWasWT
Caine, Michael 1933- CTFT-6
Cairncross, James 1915- WWT-17
Cairney, John 1930- WWT-17
Cairns, Tom 1952- CTFT-9
Calabresi, Oreste 1857-? ....WWasWT
Calder-Marshall, Anna 1947- WWT-17
Calderisi, David 1940- WWT-17
Caldicot, Richard 1908- WWT-17
Caldwell, Anne 1876-1936 ....WWasWT
Caldwell, L. Scott CTFT-8
Caldwell, Marianne ?-1933 ......WWasWT
Caldwell, Zoe 1933- CTFT-1
   Earlier sketch in WWT-17
Calhern, Louis 1895-1956 ....WWasWT
Calhoun, Rory 1922- CTFT-9
Callahan, James T. 1930- CTFT-3
Callan, K. CTFT-1
Calleia, Joseph 1897-1975 ......WWasWT
Callow, Simon 1949- CTFT-8
   Earlier sketch in WWT-17
Calloway, Cab 1907- WWT-17
Calmour, Alfred C. 1857?-1912 ...WWasWT
Calthrop, Dion Clayton
   1878-1937 ....WWasWT
Calthrop, Donald 1888-1940 .....WWasWT
Calthrop, Gladys E. ....WWasWT
Calvert, Catherine 1890-1971 ...WWasWT
Calvert, Cecil G. 1871-? ....WWasWT
Calvert, Mrs. Charles
   1837-1921 ....WWasWT
Calvert, Louis 1859-1923 ....WWasWT
Calvert, Patricia 1908- ....WWasWT
Calvert, Phyllis 1915- WWT-17
Cameron, Donald 1889-1955 .....WWasWT
Cameron, James 1954- CTFT-3
Cameron, Kirk CTFT-5
Cameron, Violet 1862-1919 ......WWasWT
Camp, Hamilton 1934- CTFT-6
Camp, Joe 1939- CTFT-7
Campanella, Joseph 1927- CTFT-6
Campbell, Cheryl 1951- CTFT-8
Campbell, Douglas 1922- CTFT-6
   Earlier sketch in WWT-17
Campbell, Glen 1938- CTFT-1
Campbell, Judy 1916- WWT-17
Campbell, Ken 1941- WWT-17
Campbell, Margaret 1894- ...... WWasWT
Campbell, Mrs. Patrick
   1865-1940 ....WWasWT
Campbell, Patton 1926- WWT-17
Campbell, Stella Patrick
   1886-1940 ....WWasWT
Campbell, Violet 1892-1970 ......WWasWT
Campion, Clifford 1949- CTFT-4
Campion, Cyril 1894-1961 ....WWasWT

Campton, David 1924- WWT-17
Canby, Vincent 1924- CTFT-4
Candler, Peter 1926- CTFT-1
Candy, John 1950- CTFT-5
   Brief Entry in CTFT-2
Cannan, Denis 1919- WWT-17
Cannan, Gilbert 1884-1955 ......WWasWT
Cannell, Stephen J. 1941- CTFT-7
Cannon, Dyan 1937- CTFT-3
Canonero, Milena CTFT-9
Canova, Diana 1953- CTFT-1
Cantor, Arthur 1920- CTFT-7
   Earlier sketch in WWT-17
Cantor, Eddie 1892-1964 ....WWasWT
Capalbo, Carmen 1925- CTFT-1
Capecce, Victor CTFT-3
Capek, Karel 1890-1938 ....WWasWT
Caplin, Jeremy O. 1955- CTFT-3
Capra, Frank 1897-1991 ....CTFT-9
Capra, Frank, Jr. CTFT-3
Capri, Mark 1951- CTFT-4
Capshaw, Kate CTFT-5
   Brief Entry in CTFT-2
Captain Kangaroo
   See Keeshan, Robert J. CTFT-4
Capucine 1935(?)-1990 ....CTFT-9
Capus, Alfred 1858-1922 ....WWasWT
Cara, Irene 1959- CTFT-5
   Brief Entry in CTFT-2
Carambo, Cristobal 1950- CTFT-1
Carden, William 1947- CTFT-4
Cardinale, Claudia 1938- CTFT-4
Carew, James 1876-1938 ....WWasWT
Carey, Denis 1909-1986 ....CTFT-4
   Earlier sketch in WWT-17
Carey, Harry, Jr. 1921- CTFT-8
   Earlier sketch in CTFT-1
Carey, Joyce 1898- WWT-17
Carey, MacDonald 1913- CTFT-8
Carey, Ron 1935- CTFT-8
Carfax, Bruce 1905-1970 ....WWasWT
Cargill, Patrick 1918- WWT-17
Cariou, Len 1939- CTFT-3
   Earlier sketch in CTFT-1
Carle, Cynthia CTFT-1
Carle, Richard 1871-1941 ...... WWasWT
Carleton, Claire 1913- ....WWasWT
Carlier, Madeleine ....WWasWT
Carlin, George 1937- CTFT-7
Carlin, Lynn 1938- CTFT-1
Carlisle, Alexandra 1886-1936 ....WWasWT
Carlisle, Kevin 1935- CTFT-2
Carlisle, Kitty 1914- CTFT-3
   Earlier sketch in WWT-17
Carlisle, Margaret 1905- ....WWasWT
Carlisle, Sybil 1871-? ....WWasWT
Carlsen, John A. 1915- ....WWasWT
Carlton (Arthur Carlton Philps)
   1880-? ....WWasWT
Carlton, Bob 1950- CTFT-8
Carme, Pamela 1902- ....WWasWT
Carmel, Roger C. 1932-1986 ....CTFT-4
Carmichael, Ian 1920- CTFT-6
   Earlier sketch in WWT-17
Carminati, Tullio 1894-1971 .....WWasWT
Carmines, Al 1936- WWT-17
Carne, Judy 1939- CTFT-3
Carney, Art 1918- CTFT-4
   Earlier sketch in WWT-17
Carney, George 1887-1947 ....WWasWT
Carney, Kate 1870-1950 ....WWasWT
Carney, Kay 1933- CTFT-1
Carnovsky, Morris 1897- WWT-17

Caro, Warren 1907- WWT-17
Caron, Cecile ....WWasWT
Caron, Leslie 1931- CTFT-3
  Earlier sketch in WWasWT
Caron, Marguerite ....WWasWT
Carpenter, Carleton 1926- WWT-17
Carpenter, Constance 1906- WWT-17
Carpenter, Edward Childs
  1872-1950 ....WWasWT
Carpenter, Freddie 1908-1989 ......CTFT-8
  Earlier sketch in WWT-17
Carpenter, John 1948- CTFT-8
  Earlier sketch in CTFT-1
Carpenter, Maud ?-1967 ....WWasWT
Carr, Alexander 1878-1946 ......WWasWT
Carr, Allan 1941- CTFT-3
Carr, Darleen 1950- CTFT-8
Carr, F. Osmond 1858-1916 .....WWasWT
Carr, George ?-1962 ....WWasWT
Carr, Howard 1880-1960 ....WWasWT
Carr, Jane 1909-1957 ....WWasWT
Carr, Jane CTFT-5
Carr, Joseph W. Comyns
  1849-1916 ....WWasWT
Carr, Lawrence 1916-1969 ....WWasWT
Carr, Martin 1932- CTFT-2
Carr, Philip 1874-1957 ....WWasWT
Carr-Cook, Madge 1856-1933 ....WWasWT
Carradine, David 1936- CTFT-4
Carradine, John 1906-1988 ....CTFT-7
  Earlier sketches in CTFT-4, WWT-17
Carradine, Keith 1949- CTFT-1
Carradine, Robert 1954- CTFT-3
Carre, Fabrice 1855-? ....WWasWT
Carre, Michel 1865-? ....WWasWT
Carrera, Barbara 1945- CTFT-6
  Earlier sketch in CTFT-1
Carrick, Edward 1905- ....WWasWT
Carrick, Hartley 1881-1929 ......WWasWT
Carriere, Jean-Claude 1931- CTFT-8
Carrillo, Leo 1880-1961 ....WWasWT
Carrington, Ethel 1889-1962 .....WWasWT
Carrington, Murray 1885-1941 ...WWasWT
Carroll, David-James 1950- CTFT-1
Carroll, Diahann 1935- CTFT-3
Carroll, Earl 1893-1948 ....WWasWT
Carroll, Helena CTFT-1
Carroll, Leo G. 1892-1972 ....WWasWT
Carroll, Leo M. WWT-14
Carroll, Madeleine 1906-1987 ....WWasWT
Carroll, Nancy 1906-1965 ....WWasWT
Carroll, Pat 1927- CTFT-3
Carroll, Paul Vincent
  1900-1968 ....WWasWT
Carroll, Sydney W. 1877-1958 ....WWasWT
Carroll, Vinnette CTFT-5
  Earlier sketch in WWT-17
Carson, Charles 1885-1977 ....WWT-16
Carson, Mrs. Charles L. ?-1919 ..WWasWT
Carson, Doris 1910- ....WWasWT
Carson, Frances 1895- ....WWasWT
Carson, Jeannie 1929- WWT-17
Carson, John David CTFT-8
Carson, Johnny 1925-.............CTFT-3
Carson, Lionel 1873-1937 ....WWasWT
Carson, Murray 1865-1917 ......WWasWT
Carte, Mrs. D'Oyly ?-1948 .....WWasWT
Carte, Rupert D'Oyly
  See D'Oyly Carte, Rupert .....WWasWT
Carten, Audrey 1900- ....WWasWT
Carter, Desmond ?-1939 ....WWasWT
Carter, Dixie 1939- CTFT-5
Carter, Frederick 1900-1970 .....WWasWT

Carter, Hubert ?-1934 ....WWasWT
Carter, Mrs. Leslie 1862-1937 ....WWasWT
Carter, Lonnie 1942- CTFT-1
Carter, Lynda CTFT-5
  Brief Entry in CTFT-2
Carter, Margaret ....WWasWT
Carter, Mell 1894-1965 ....WWasWT
Carter, Nell 1948-...............CTFT-3
Carter, T. K. CTFT-4
Carter, Thomas CTFT-9
Carter-Edwards, James
  1840-1930 ....WWasWT
Carteret, Anna 1942- CTFT-5
  Earlier sketch in WWT-17
Cartlidge, Katrin 1961- CTFT-6
Carton, R. C. 1853-1938 ....WWasWT
Cartwright, Charles 1855-1916 ...WWasWT
Cartwright, Peggy 1912- ....WWasWT
Cartwright, Veronica 1950- CTFT-6
  Brief Entry in CTFT-2
Carus, Emma 1879-1927 ....WWasWT
Carver, James C. 1932- CTFT-3
Carver, Mary CTFT-1
Carver, Steven 1945- CTFT-1
Cary, Falkland 1897-1989 ....CTFT-8
  Earlier sketch in WWT-17
Caryll, Ivan 1861-1921 ....WWasWT
Casady, Cort 1947-...............CTFT-3
Casartelli, Gabrielle 1910- ....WWasWT
Casey, Bernie 1939- CTFT-7
Cash, Morny ....WWasWT
Cash, Rosalind 1938- CTFT-4
  Earlier sketch in WWT-17
Cason, Barbara 1933-.............CTFT-8
Cass, Henry 1902-1989 ....WWT-17
Cass, Peggy 1926- CTFT-3
  Earlier sketch in WWT-17
Cass, Ronald 1923-...............CTFT-5
  Earlier sketch in WWT-17
Cassavetes, John 1929-1989 ....CTFT-7
  Earlier sketch in CTFT-3
Cassel, Seymour 1937- CTFT-9
Cassidy, David 1950- CTFT-8
Cassidy, Jack 1927-1976 ....WWT-16
Cassidy, Joanna 1944- CTFT-6
Cassidy, Patrick 1961- CTFT-8
Cassidy, Shaun 1958- CTFT-3
Casson, Ann 1915-1990 ....WWasWT
Casson, Christopher 1912- ....WWasWT
Casson, John 1909-.............WWasWT
Casson, Lewis T. 1875-1969 .....WWasWT
Casson, Mary 1914- ....WWasWT
Cassutt, Michael 1954- CTFT-3
Castang, Veronica CTFT-1
Castellaneta, Dan CTFT-6
Castellano, Richard 1933-1988 .....CTFT-7
Castillo, Helen 1955- CTFT-4
Castle, John 1940- WWT-17
Cates, Madelyn CTFT-8
Cates, Phoebe CTFT-5
Catlett, Mary Jo 1938- CTFT-2
Catlett, Walter 1889-1960 ....WWasWT
Catling, Thomas 1838-1920 ......WWasWT
Cattley, Cyril 1876-1937 ....WWasWT
Cattrall, Kim 1956- CTFT-8
Caulfield, Maxwell 1959- CTFT-3
Cavanagh, Lilian ?-1932 ....WWasWT
Cavanagh, Paul 1895-1960 ....WWasWT
Cavanaugh, Michael CTFT-9
Cavani, Liliana 1936- CTFT-8
Cavett, Dick 1936-'..............CTFT-8
  Earlier sketch in CTFT-1
Cawthorn, Joseph 1867-1949 .....WWasWT

Cazenove, Christopher 1945-........CTFT-4
  Earlier sketch in WWT-17
Cecchetti, Enrico 1847-1928 .....WWasWT
Cecil, Henry 1902-1976 ....WWT-16
Cecil, Jonathan 1939-............WWT-17
Cecil, Sylvia 1906- ....WWasWT
Celestin, Jack 1894- ....WWasWT
Celli, Faith 1888-1942 ....WWasWT
Cellier, Antoinette 1913- ....WWasWT
Cellier, Frank 1884-1948 ....WWasWT
Cerito, Ada ....WWasWT
Cerny, Berthe ....WWasWT
Chabrol, Claude 1930- CTFT-8
Chacksfield, Frank CTFT-2
Chadbon, Tom 1946- CTFT-5
  Earlier sketch in WWT-17
Chagrin, Julian 1940-............WWT-17
Chaikin, Joseph 1935- CTFT-7
  Earlier sketch in WWT-17
Chaikin, Shami 1931- CTFT-1
Chaine, Pierre ....WWasWT
Challenor, (James) Bromley
  1884-1935 ....WWasWT
Chalzel, Leo 1901-1953 ....WWasWT
Chamberlain, George 1891- ......WWasWT
Chamberlain, Richard 1935- CTFT-5
  Earlier sketches in CTFT-1, WWT-17
Chamberlin, Lee CTFT-4
Chambers, Charles Haddon
  1860-1921 ....WWasWT
Chambers, Emma ....WWasWT
Chambers, H. Kellett
  1867-1935 ....WWasWT
Champion, Gower 1920-1980 .....WWT-17
Champion, Harry 1866-1942 .....WWasWT
Champion, Marge 1919- CTFT-1
Chan, Jackie 1955(?)- CTFT-9
Chancellor, Betty ....WWasWT
Chancellor, John 1927- CTFT-7
Chancellor, Joyce 1906-..........WWasWT
Chandler, Helen 1909-1965 ....WWasWT
Chandler, Jeffrey Alan CTFT-2
Chaney, Stewart 1910-1969 ......WWasWT
Chang, Tisa 1941-...............CTFT-1
Channing, Carol 1921-............CTFT-3
  Earlier sketch in WWT-17
Channing, Marvin 1944- CTFT-4
Channing, Stockard 1944- CTFT-7
  Earlier sketch in CTFT-1
Chansky, Dorothy 1951- CTFT-1
Chapin, Harold 1886-1915 ....WWasWT
Chapin, Louis Le Bourgeois
  1918-....................WWT-17
Chapin, Miles 1954- CTFT-1
Chaplin, Charles Spencer
  1889-1977 ....WWasWT
Chaplin, Geraldine 1944- CTFT-9
  Earlier sketch in CTFT-3
Chapman, Constance 1912- WWT-17
Chapman, David 1938- CTFT-7
  Earlier sketch in WWT-17
Chapman, Edward 1901-1986 ....WWasWT
Chapman, Graham 1941-1989 ......CTFT-8
Chapman, John R. 1927- CTFT-6
  Earlier sketch in WWT-17
Chapman, Lonny 1920- CTFT-4
Chapman, Michael 1935- CTFT-8
Chappell, William 1908- WWT-17
Chappelle, Frederick W. 1895- ...WWasWT
Charbonneau, Patricia CTFT-8
Charell, Erik 1895-.............WWasWT
Charles, Maria 1929- WWT-17
Charles, Pamela 1932- WWT-17

Charles, Walter 1945- CTFT-1
Charleson, Ian 1949-1989 ....CTFT-4
  Earlier sketches in CTFT-1, WWT-17
Charnin, Martin 1934-..............CTFT-2
  Earlier sketch in WWT-17
Chart, Henry Nye 1868-1934 ....WWasWT
Chartoff, Melanie CTFT-1
Chartoff, Robert CTFT-3
Charvay, Robert 1858-? ....WWasWT
Chase, Chevy 1943- CTFT-9
  Earlier sketch in CTFT-3
Chase, Ilka 1905-1978 ....WWT-16
Chase, Mary 1907-1981 ....WWT-17
Chase, Pauline 1885-1962 ....WWasWT
Chasen, Heather 1927-............CTFT-6
  Earlier sketch in WWT-17
Chater, Geoffrey 1921-...........WWT-17
Chatterton, Ruth 1893-1961 .....WWasWT
Chatwin, Margaret ?-1937 ....WWasWT
Chaves, Richard 1951- CTFT-8
Chayefsky, Paddy 1923-1981 ......CTFT-1
  Earlier sketch in WWT-17
Chaykin, Maury CTFT-7
Cheeseman, Peter 1932-..........WWT-17
Chekhov, Michael 1891-1955 ....WWasWT
Chelsom, Peter 1956-.............CTFT-3
Chelton, Nick 1946-..............CTFT-5
  Earlier sketch in WWT-17
Cheney, Sheldon 1886-1980 ......WWasWT
Cher 1946- CTFT-9
  Earlier sketch in CTFT-3
  Brief Entry in CTFT-2
Cherkasov, Nikolai 1903-1966 ....WWasWT
Cherrell, Gwen 1926-............WWT-17
Cherry, Charles 1872-1931 ......WWasWT
Cherry, Helen 1915-.............WWasWT
Cherry, Wal 1932-1986 ....WWT-17
Cheskin, Irving W. 1915-.........WWT-17
Chesney, Arthur 1882-1949 ......WWasWT
Chester, Betty 1895-1943 ....WWasWT
Chester, Nora CTFT-2
Chetham-Strode, Warren 1897-...WWasWT
Chetwyn, Robert 1933- WWT-17
Chevalier, Albert 1861-1923 .....WWasWT
Chevalier, Marcelle............WWasWT
Chevalier, Maurice 1888-1972 ....WWasWT
Chew, Lee CTFT-3
Child, Harold Hannyngton
  1869-1945 ....WWasWT
Childs, Gilbert ?-1931 ....WWasWT
Chiles, Linden CTFT-9
Chiles, Lois CTFT-7
Chirgwin, George H. 1854-1922 ..WWasWT
Chisholm, Robert 1898-1960 .....WWasWT
Chinoy, Helen Krich 1922- CTFT-1
Choate, Tim 1954- CTFT-1
Chodorov, Edward 1914-1988 ......CTFT-7
  Earlier sketches in WWT-17, WWasWT
Chodorov, Jerome 1911- WWT-17
Chomsky, Marvin J. 1929- CTFT-6
Chong, Rae Dawn CTFT-7
Chong, Tommy 1938- CTFT-5
  Brief Entry in CTFT-2
Chorpenning, Ruth 1905- ....WWasWT
Christianson, Catherine 1957- CTFT-5
Christians, Mady 1900-1951 .....WWasWT
Christie, Agatha 1890-1976 ....WWT-16
Christie, Audrey 1912-1989 ....WWT-17
Christie, Campbell 1893-1963 ....WWasWT
Christie, Dorothy 1896- ....WWasWT
Christie, George 1873-1949 ......WWasWT
Christie, Julie 1940(?)- CTFT-9
  Earlier sketch in CTFT-3

Christine, Virginia 1920- CTFT-1
Christopher, Dennis 1955-..........CTFT-3
Christy, Donald CTFT-2
Chudleigh, Arthur 1858-1932 ....WWasWT
Chung, Connie 1946- CTFT-9
Chung Ling Soo ....WWasWT
Church, Esme 1893-1972 ....WWasWT
Church, Tony 1930-...............CTFT-6
  Earlier sketch in WWT-17
Churchill, Berton 1876-1940 .....WWasWT
Churchill, Caryl 1938- CTFT-3
  Earlier sketch in WWT-17
Churchill, Diana (Josephine)
  1913- ....WWasWT
Churchill, Marguerite 1910- .....WWasWT
Churchill, Sarah 1914-1982 ....WWT-17
Churchill, Winston 1871-1947 ....WWasWT
Ciccone, Madonna
  See Madonna CTFT-3
Cilento, Diane 1933- CTFT-5
  Earlier sketch in WWT-17
Cimino, Michael 1940-............CTFT-6
  Earlier sketch in CTFT-2
Cinquevalli, Paul 1859-1918 .....WWasWT
Cizmar, Paula 1949-..............CTFT-1
Clair, Mavis 1916-..............WWasWT
Claire, Helen 1911-1974 ....WWasWT
Claire, Ina 1895-1985 ....WWasWT
Claire, Ludi 1927- CTFT-1
Claman, Barbara S. 1939- CTFT-1
Clancy, Deidre 1943- CTFT-5
  Earlier sketch in WWT-17
Clanton, Ralph 1914-............WWT-17
Clare, Mary 1894-1970 ....WWasWT
Clare, Tom 1876-? ....WWasWT
Clarence, O. B. 1870-1955 ....WWasWT
Claridge, Norman 1903- WWT-17
Clark, Alfred ....WWasWT
Clark, B. D. 1945-..............CTFT-3
Clark, Barrett H. 1890-1953 .....WWasWT
Clark, Bob 1941- CTFT-7
Clark, Bobby 1888-1960.........WWasWT
Clark, Brian 1932- CTFT-4
  Earlier sketch in WWT-17
Clark, Candy CTFT-1
Clark, China CTFT-2
Clark, Dick 1929-...............CTFT-3
Clark, E. Holman 1864-1925 .....WWasWT
Clark, Ernest 1912-.............WWT-17
Clark, Fred 1914-1968 ....WWasWT
Clark, John Pepper 1935- WWT-17
Clark, John Richard 1932- WWT-17
Clark, Mara 1930- CTFT-5
Clark, Marguerite 1887-1940 .....WWasWT
Clark, Marjory 1900- ....WWasWT
Clark, Matt 1936-...............CTFT-8
Clark, Peggy 1915-..............WWT-17
Clark, Perceval
  See Perceval-Clark, P. ....WWasWT
Clark, Roy 1933-...............CTFT-7
Clark, Susan 1944-..............CTFT-3
Clark, Wallis 1888-1961 ....WWasWT
Clarke, Caitlin 1952-............CTFT-8
Clarke, Cuthbert 1869-1953 .....WWasWT
Clarke, David 1908-.............CTFT-1
Clarke, George 1886-1946 ....WWasWT
Clarke, Mae 1907-..............WWasWT
Clarke, Nigel 1895- .'...........WWasWT
Clarke, Richard 1930-...........CTFT-5
Clarke, Rupert 1865-1926 ....WWasWT
Clarke-Smith, Douglas A.
  1888-1959 ....WWasWT
Clarkson, Joan 1903- ....WWasWT

Clarkson, Willie 1861-1934 ......WWasWT
Clary, Robert 1926-.............CTFT-1
Claudel, Paul 1868-1955 ....WWasWT
Claughton, Susan ....WWasWT
Clavell, James CTFT-1
Claver, Bob 1928-................CTFT-2
Clayburgh, Jill 1944- CTFT-5
  Earlier sketch in CTFT-2
Clayton, Herbert 1876-1931 ......WWasWT
Clayton, Jack 1921-.............CTFT-5
Clayton, Tony 1935-.............CTFT-4
Cleather, Gordon 1872-? ....WWasWT
Cleave, Arthur 1884-? ....WWasWT
Cleese, John 1939- CTFT-4
Clemens, Le Roy 1889-? ....WWasWT
Clement, Clay 1888-1956 ....WWasWT
Clement, Elfrida ....WWasWT
Clement-Scott, Joan 1907-1969 ...WWasWT
Clement-Scott, Margaret
  See Scott, Margaret Clement ...WWasWT
Clements, John 1910-1988 ....CTFT-6
  Earlier sketch in WWT-17
Clements, Miriam ....WWasWT
Clennon, David CTFT-8
Cliff, Laddie 1891-1937 ....WWasWT
Cliffe, H. Cooper 1862-1939 .....WWasWT
Clifford, Camille ....WWasWT
Clifford, Kathleen 1887-1962 .....WWasWT
Clift, Ernest Paul 1881-1963 .....WWasWT
Clift, Montgomery 1920-1966 ....WWasWT
Clifton, Bernard 1902-1970 ......WWasWT
Climenhaga, Joel 1922- CTFT-4
Clinger, Bijou 1955- CTFT-4
Clive, Colin 1900-1937 ....WWasWT
Clive, Vincent ?-1943 ....WWasWT
Close, Glenn 1947- CTFT-9
  Earlier sketch in CTFT-3
Closser, Louise 1872-? ....WWasWT
Clowes, Richard 1900-..........WWasWT
Clunes, Alec S. 1912-..........WWasWT
Clurman, Harold 1901-1980 ......WWT-17
Clyde, Jeremy 1941-.............CTFT-8
Coakley, Marion ....WWasWT
Coates, Carolyn CTFT-3
  Earlier sketch in WWT-17
Cobb, Lee J. 1911-1976 ....WWasWT
Cobb, Randall "Tex" CTFT-7
Coburn, Charles 1852-1945 ......WWasWT
Coburn, Charles (Douville)
  1877-1961 ....WWasWT
Coburn, D(onald) L. 1938- CTFT-1
Coburn, James 1928- CTFT-3
Coca, Imogene 1908-.............CTFT-9
  Earlier sketches in CTFT-2, WWT-17
Cocea, Alice 1899-.............WWasWT
Cochran, Charles (Blake)
  1872-1951 ....WWasWT
Cochrane, Frank 1882-1962......WWasWT
Coco, James 1929-1987 ....CTFT-3
  Earlier sketches in CTFT-1, WWT-17
Cocteau, Jean 1889-1963 ....WWasWT
Codrington, Ann 1895-..........WWasWT
Codron, Michael 1930-...........CTFT-2
  Earlier sketch in WWT-17
Cody, Iron Eyes 1915-............CTFT-1
Coe, Fred H. 1914-1979..........WWT-16
Coe, Peter 1929-1987 ....CTFT-5
  Earlier sketches in CTFT-3, WWT-17
Coe, Richard L. 1914- CTFT-1
Coen, Ethan 1958- CTFT-7
Coen, Joel 1955- CTFT-7
Coffey, Denise 1936- WWT-17
Coffin, C. Hayden 1862-1935 .....WWasWT

Coffin, Frederick (D.) 1943- CTFT-1
Cogan, David J. 1923- CTFT-1
Coghill, Nevill 1899-1980 ....WWT-17
Coghlan, Gertrude 1879-1952 ....WWasWT
Coghlan, Rose 1850-1932 ....WWasWT
Cohan, Charles 1886- ....WWasWT
Cohan, George M. 1878-1942 ....WWasWT
Cohan, Georgette 1900- ....WWasWT
Cohen, Alexander H. 1920- CTFT-5
Earlier sketches in CTFT-1, WWT-17
Cohen, Edward M. 1936- CTFT-9
Earlier sketch in CTFT-1
Cohen, Harry I. 1891-1987 ......WWasWT
Cohen, Larry 1947- CTFT-7
Cohenour, Patti 1952- CTFT-2
Coke, Peter (John) 1913- ....WWasWT
Colbert, Claudette 1905- CTFT-2
Earlier sketch in WWT-17
Colbin, Rod 1923- CTFT-2
Colbourne, Maurice 1894-1965 ...WWasWT
Colbron, Grace Isabel ?-1943 ....WWasWT
Cole, Dennis CTFT-4
Cole, Edith 1870-1927 ....WWasWT
Cole, Elizabeth
See Ashley, Elizabeth CTFT-8
Cole, Gary CTFT-8
Cole, George 1925- CTFT-9
Earlier sketch in WWT-17
Cole, Kay 1948- CTFT-4
Cole, Nora 1953- CTFT-2
Cole, Olivia 1942- CTFT-8
Coleby, Wilfred T. 1865-? ....WWasWT
Coleman, Cy 1929- CTFT-3
Earlier sketch in WWT-17
Coleman, Dabney 1932- CTFT-3
Coleman, Fanny 1840-1919 ......WWasWT
Coleman, Gary 1968- CTFT-3
Coleman, Jack 1958- CTFT-8
Coleman, Nancy 1917- CTFT-1
Coleman, Robert 1900- ....WWasWT
Coleridge, Ethel 1883-? ....WWasWT
Coleridge, Sylvia 1909- WWT-17
Colicos, John 1928- CTFT-8
Earlier sketch in WWT-16
Colin, Georges ....WWasWT
Colin, Jean 1905-1989 ....WWasWT
Colin, Margaret 1957- CTFT-7
Collamore, Jerome 1891- CTFT-1
Colleano, Bonar 1923-1958 ......WWasWT
Collet, Richard 1885-1946 ....WWasWT
Collette, Charles 1842-1924 ......WWasWT
Colley, Kenneth 1937- CTFT-9
Collier, Constance 1878-1955 ....WWasWT
Collier, Gaylan Jane 1924- CTFT-2
Collier, Patience 1910-1987 ....CTFT-5
Earlier sketch in WWT-17
Collier, William 1866-1944 ......WWasWT
Collinge, Patricia 1894-1974 .....WWasWT
Collins, A. Greville 1896- ....WWasWT
Collins, Arthur 1863-1932 ....WWasWT
Collins, Barry 1941- CTFT-5
Earlier sketch in WWT-17
Collins, Charles 1904-1964 ......WWasWT
Collins, Frank 1878-1957 ....WWasWT
Collins, Gary 1938- CTFT-6
Collins, Horace 1875-1964 ....WWasWT
Collins, Joan 1933- CTFT-8
Earlier sketch in CTFT-2
Collins, Jose 1887-1958 ....WWasWT
Collins, Pauline 1940- CTFT-8
Earlier sketch in WWT-17
Collins, Robert 1930- CTFT-1
Collins, Russell 1897-1965 ....WWasWT
Collins, Sewell 1876-1934 ....WWasWT
Collins, Stephen CTFT-3
Collins, Winnie 1896- ....WWasWT
Collison, David 1937- CTFT-5
Earlier sketch in WWT-17
Collison, Wilson 1892-1941 ......WWasWT
Colman, Henry CTFT-8
Colman, Ronald 1891-1958 ......WWasWT
Colon, Miriam 1945- CTFT-5
Earlier sketch in WWT-17
Colonna, Jerry 1904-1986 ....CTFT-4
Colt, Alvin 1916- CTFT-6
Earlier sketch in WWT-17
Colton, John B. 1889-1946 ......WWasWT
Columbu, Franco CTFT-4
Columbus, Chris CTFT-5
Comber, Bobbie 1886-1942 ......WWasWT
Combermere, Edward 1888- .....WWasWT
Comden, Betty 1919- CTFT-2
Earlier sketch in WWT-17
Comencini, Luigi 1916- CTFT-9
Commire, Anne CTFT-1
Company of Four ....WWasWT
Compton, Edward 1854-1918 ....WWasWT
Compton, Mrs. Edward
1853-1940 ....WWasWT
Compton, Fay 1894-1978 ....WWasWT
Compton, Katherine 1858-1928 ..WWasWT
Compton, Madge ?-1970 ....WWasWT
Compton, Viola 1886-1971 ......WWasWT
Comstock, F. Ray 1880-1949 ....WWasWT
Comstock, Nanette 1873-1942 ....WWasWT
Conaway, Jeff 1950- CTFT-5
Brief Entry in CTFT-2
Concannon, John N. 1946- CTFT-1
Conklin, Peggy 1912- ....WWasWT
Conn, Didi 1951- CTFT-9
Connell, F. Norreys 1874-1948 ...WWasWT
Connell, Jane 1925 ....CTFT-3
Earlier sketch in WWT-17
Connelly, Christopher
1941-1988 ....CTFT-7
Connelly, Edward J. 1855-1928 ...WWasWT
Connelly, Marc 1890-1980 ....WWT-17
Conners, Barry 1883-1933 ....WWasWT
Connery, Sean 1930- CTFT-3
Connolly, Michael 1947- CTFT-1
Connolly, Walter 1887-1940 .....WWasWT
Connor, Whitfield 1916-1988 ....CTFT-1
Connors, Chuck 1924- CTFT-6
Connors, Michael
See Connors, Mike CTFT-9
Connors, Mike 1925- CTFT-9
Connors, Touch
See Connors, Mike CTFT-9
Conquest, Arthur 1875-1945 .....WWasWT
Conquest, Fred 1870-1941 ....WWasWT
Conquest, George 1858-1926 .....WWasWT
Conquest, Ida 1876-1937 ....WWasWT
Conrad, Con 1891-1938 ....WWasWT
Conrad, Michael 1925-1983 ....CTFT-2
Conrad, Robert 1935- CTFT-3
Conrad, William 1920- CTFT-5
Earlier sketch in CTFT-2
Conreid, Hans 1917-1980 ....CTFT-2
Earlier sketch in WWT-17
Conroy, Frank 1890-1964 ....WWasWT
Conroy, Kevin 1955- CTFT-1
Considine, John CTFT-8
Constanduros, Mabel ?-1957 .....WWasWT
Conte, John 1915- ....WWasWT
Conti, Bill 1943- CTFT-4
Conti, Italia 1874-1946 ....WWasWT
Conti, Tom 1941- CTFT-3
Earlier sketch in WWT-17
Converse, Frank 1938- CTFT-9
Earlier sketch in CTFT-3
Converse-Roberts, William CTFT-7
Conville, David 1929- WWT-17
Convy, Bert 1934- CTFT-1
Earlier sketch in WWT-17
Conway, Gary CTFT-2
Conway, Harold 1906- ....WWasWT
Conway, Jackie 1922- CTFT-2
Conway, Kevin 1942- CTFT-6
Earlier sketches in CTFT-2, WWT-17
Conway, Tim 1933- CTFT-3
Conyngham, Fred 1909- ....WWasWT
Cooder, Ry 1947- CTFT-8
Coogan, Jackie 1914-1984 ....CTFT-1
Cook, Barbara 1927- CTFT-3
Earlier sketch in WWT-17
Cook, Donald 1901-1961 ....WWasWT
Cook, Elisha Jr. 1906- CTFT-8
Earlier sketch in WWasWT
Cook, James 1937- CTFT-3
Cook, Joe 1890-1959 ....WWasWT
Cook, Linda CTFT-3
Cook, Peter 1937- CTFT-4
Earlier sketch in WWT-17
Cook, Roderick 1932-1990 ....CTFT-1
Cook, T. S. 1947- CTFT-3
Cooke, Alistair 1908- CTFT-8
Cooke, Stanley 1869-1931 ....WWasWT
Cookman, Anthony Victor
1894-1962 ....WWasWT
Cookson, Georgina ....WWasWT
Cookson, Peter 1913-1990 ....CTFT-9
Coolidge, Martha 1946- CTFT-8
Coolus, Romain 1868-1952 ......WWasWT
Coombe, Carol 1911-1966 ....WWasWT
Cooney, Dennis 1938- CTFT-4
Cooney, Ray 1932- CTFT-1
Earlier sketch in WWT-17
Cooper, Anthony Kemble 1908- ..WWasWT
Cooper, Chris 1951- CTFT-7
Cooper, Daley 1872-? ....WWasWT
Cooper, Enid 1902- ....WWasWT
Cooper, Frank Kemble
1857-1918 ....WWasWT
Cooper, Frederick 1890-1945 ....WWasWT
Cooper, Giles 1918-1966 ....WWasWT
Cooper, Gladys 1888-1971 ....WWasWT
Cooper, Greta Kemble ....WWasWT
Cooper, Hal 1923- CTFT-6
Earlier sketch in CTFT-1
Cooper, Jackie 1922- CTFT-8
Earlier sketch in CTFT-2
Cooper, Lillian Kemble 1891- ....WWasWT
Cooper, Margaret Gernon ....WWasWT
Cooper, Melville 1896-1973 ......WWasWT
Cooper, Richard 1893-1947 ......WWasWT
Cooper, Susan 1935- CTFT-2
Cooper, T. G. 1939- CTFT-3
Cooper, Violet Kemble
1889-1961 ....WWasWT
Coote, Bert 1868-1938 ....WWasWT
Coote, Robert 1909-1982 ....WWT-17
Copeau, Jacques 1878-1949 ......WWasWT
Copeland, Joan 1922- CTFT-7
Earlier sketch in WWT-17
Copeland, Maurice 1911- CTFT-1
Copeland, Stewart 1952- CTFT-5
Copley, Paul 1944- WWT-17
Copley, Peter 1915- WWT-17
Coppel, Alec 1910-1972 ....WWasWT

Copperfield, David 1957- CTFT-7
Coppola, Carmine 1910- CTFT-7
Coppola, Francis Ford 1939-.......CTFT-6
  Earlier sketch in CTFT-1
Coquelin, Jean 1865-1944 ....WWasWT
Coram 1883-? ....WWasWT
Corbett, Glenn 1929(?)- CTFT-9
Corbett, Gretchen 1947- CTFT-5
  Earlier sketch in WWT-17
Corbett, Harry H. 1925-? WWT-17
Corbett, Leonora 1908-1960 .....WWasWT
Corbett, Thalberg 1864-? ....WWasWT
Corbin, John 1870-1959 ....WWasWT
Corby, Ellen 1913- CTFT-9
Corcoran, Jane ....WWasWT
Cord, Alex 1933(?)- CTFT-9
  Earlier sketch in CTFT-1
Cordell, Cathleen 1916- ....WWasWT
Cordes, Jim 1932-...............CTFT-4
Corey, Jeff 1914-...............CTFT-8
Corey, Wendell 1914-1968 ....WWasWT
Corfman, Caris 1955-.............CTFT-1
Corlett, William 1938-...........CTFT-2
Corman, Gene 1927- CTFT-9
  Earlier sketch in CTFT-1
Corman, Roger 1926-.............CTFT-7
  Earlier sketch in CTFT-2
Cornell, Katharine 1898-1974 ....WWasWT
Cornthwaite, Robert 1917- CTFT-1
Cornwell, Judy 1942- WWT-17
Correia, Don 1951-..............CTFT-7
Corri, Charles Montague 1861-? ..WWasWT
Corrigan, Emmett 1871-1932 ....WWasWT
Corsaro, Frank 1924-............CTFT-7
  Earlier sketch in WWT-17
Corson, Richard WWT-17
Cort, Bud 1950- CTFT-1
Corwin, Betty 1920- CTFT-2
Corwin, Norman 1910- CTFT-1
Corzatte, Clayton CTFT-4
Cosby, Bill 1937- CTFT-9
  Earlier sketch in CTFT-3
Cosell, Howard 1920- CTFT-6
Cosgrave, Peggy CTFT-8
Cossart, Ernest 1876-1951 ....WWasWT
Cossart, Valerie 1910- ....WWasWT
Cossins, James 1933- WWT-17
Costabile, Richard 1947- CTFT-3
Costa-Gavras 1933- CTFT-6
Costello, Tom 1863-1945 ....WWasWT
Costigan, Ken 1934-.............CTFT-9
  Earlier sketch in CTFT-1
Costner, Kevin 1955- CTFT-9
  Brief Entry in CTFT-5
Cotes, Peter 1912- WWT-17
Cotsirilos, Stephanie 1947-.........CTFT-1
Cotsworth, Staats 1908-1979 ......WWT-16
Cotten, Joseph 1905- CTFT-4
  Earlier sketch in WWT-17
Cottens, Victor de 1862-? ....WWasWT
Cotton, Oliver 1944-..............CTFT-9
  Earlier sketch in WWT-17
Cotton, Wilfred 1873-? ....WWasWT
Cottrell, Cherry 1909- .... WWasWT[
Cottrell, Richard 1936- CTFT-6
  Earlier sketch in WWT-17
Coullet, Rhonda CTFT-2
Coulouris, George 1903-1989 ......CTFT-8
  Earlier sketch in WWT-17
Counsell, John 1905-1987 ....WWT-17
Countryman, Michael 1955- CTFT-9
Couper, Barbara 1903- ....WWasWT
Court, Dorothy ....WWasWT

Courteline, Georges 1860-1929 ...WWasWT
Courtenay, Margaret 1923- WWT-17
Courtenay, Tom 1937-............CTFT-5
  Earlier sketches in CTFT-1, WWT-17
Courtenay, William 1875-1933 ...WWasWT
Courtleigh, William 1869-1930 ...WWasWT
Courtneidge, Cicely 1893-1980 ....WWT-17
Courtneidge, Robert 1859-1939 ...WWasWT
Courtneidge, Rosaline
  1903-1926 ....WWasWT
Courtney, Gordon 1895-1964 ....WWasWT
Courtney, Maud 1884-? ....WWasWT
Courtney, Richard 1927- CTFT-5
  Earlier sketch in WWT-17
Courtney, William Leonard
  1850-1928 ....WWasWT
Cousin Bubba
  See Emmons, Wayne CTFT-4
Cover, Franklin 1928- CTFT-8
Covington, Julie CTFT-4
  Earlier sketch in WWT-17
Cowan, Edie CTFT-1
Cowan, Maurice A. 1891- ....WWasWT
Coward, Noel 1899-1973 ....WWasWT
Cowen, Laurence 1865-1942 .....WWasWT
Cowie, Laura 1892-1969 ....WWasWT
Cowl, Jane 1890-1950 ....WWasWT
Cowley, Eric 1886-1948 ....WWasWT
Cox, Alan 1970- CTFT-6
Cox, Alex CTFT-5
Cox, Brian 1946- CTFT-9
  Earlier sketch in WWT-17
Cox, Constance 1915-............WWT-17
Cox, Courteney 1964- CTFT-7
Cox, Ronny 1938- CTFT-4
  Earlier sketch in CTFT-1
Coyle, J. J. 1928- CTFT-1
Coyne, Joseph 1867-1941 ....WWasWT
Coyote, Peter 1942- CTFT-6
Crabe, James 1931-1989 ....CTFT-2
Cracknell, Ruth 1925- WWT-17
Craggs, The ....WWasWT
Craig, Carl 1954- CTFT-2
Craig, Edith 1869-1947 ....WWasWT
Craig, Edward Gordon
  1872-1966 ....WWasWT
Craig, Helen 1912-1986 ....WWT-17
Craig, Michael 1928- WWT-17
Craig, Wendy 1934- WWT-17
Crane, Richard 1944-.............CTFT-6
  Earlier sketch in WWT-17
Crane, W. H. 1845-1928 ....WWasWT
Cranham, Kenneth 1944-.........WWT-17
Crauford, J. R. 1847-1930 ....WWasWT
Craven, Arthur Scott 1875-1971 ..WWasWT
Craven, Elise 1898-..............WWasWT
Craven, Frank 1880-1945........WWasWT
Craven, Gemma 1950- CTFT-2
  Earlier sketch in WWT-17
Craven, Tom 1868-1919 ....WWasWT
Craven, Wes 1939- CTFT-6
Crawford, Alice 1882- ....WWasWT
Crawford, Anne 1920-1956 ......WWasWT
Crawford, Cheryl 1902-1986 ......CTFT-4
  Earlier sketch in WWT-17
Crawford, Joanna 1942-..........CTFT-4
Crawford, Michael 1942-..........CTFT-3
  Earlier sketch in WWT-17
Crawford, Mimi ?-1966 ....WWasWT
Crawley, Tom 1940-.............CTFT-2
Creedon, Dennis 1880-? ....WWasWT
Cregan, David 1931- CTFT-6
  Earlier sketch in WWT-17

Crenna, Richard 1927-.............CTFT-3
Cressall, Maud 1886-1962 ....WWasWT
Crews, Laura Hope 1880-1942 ...WWasWT
Cribbins, Bernard 1928- CTFT-6
  Earlier sketch in WWT-17
Crichton, Charles 1910- CTFT-8
Crichton, Madge 1881-? ....WWasWT
Crichton, Michael 1942- CTFT-5
Crinkley, Richmond 1940-1989 .....CTFT-8
  Earlier sketch in WWT-17
Crisham, Walter ....WWasWT
Crisp, Quentin 1908- CTFT-6
Crispi, Ida ....WWasWT
Crist, Judith 1922- CTFT-1
Cristina, Ines 1875-? ....WWasWT
Cristofer, Michael 1945- CTFT-3
  Earlier sketch in WWT-17
Critt, C. J. 1954-.................CTFT-1
Crofoot, Leonard J. CTFT-1
Croft, Anne 1896-1959 ....WWasWT
Croft, Michael 1922-1986 ....WWT-17
Croft, Nita 1902- ....WWasWT
Croft, Paddy WWT-17
Croisset, Francis de 1877-1937 ...WWasWT
Croke, Wentworth 1871-1930 ...WWasWT
Croker, T. F. Dillon 1831-1912 ...WWasWT
Croker-King, C. H. 1873-1951 ...WWasWT
Crommelynck, Fernand
  1885-1970 ....WWasWT
Cromwell, John 1887-1979 ....WWT-17
Cronenberg, David 1943-..........CTFT-6
Cronin, Jane 1936-..............CTFT-3
Cronkite, Walter 1916- CTFT-6
Cronyn, Hume 1911- CTFT-7
  Earlier sketches in CTFT-1, WWT-17
Cronyn, Tandy 1945-.............CTFT-9
  Earlier sketch in CTFT-1
Crook, John ?-1922 ....WWasWT
Cropper, Anna 1938-............WWT-17
Cropper, Roy 1898-1954 ....WWasWT
Crosby, Denise CTFT-8
Crosby, Gary 1933- CTFT-7
Crosby, Mary CTFT-5
  Brief Entry in CTFT-2
Crosman, Henrietta 1865-1944 ...WWasWT
Cross, Ben 1947-...............CTFT-6
Cross, Beverley 1931-............CTFT-6
  Earlier sketch in WWT-17
Cross, Julian 1851-1925 ....WWasWT
Croswell, Anne CTFT-1
Crothers, Rachel 1878-1958 ......WWasWT
Crothers, Scatman 1910-1986 ......CTFT-3
Crouch, J. H. 1918-..............CTFT-1
Crouse, Lindsay 1948- CTFT-4
Crouse, Russel 1893-1966 ....WWasWT
Crow, Laura 1945- CTFT-5
Crowden, Graham 1922- CTFT-9
  Earlier sketch in WWT-17
Crowder, Jack
  See Rasulala, Thalmus CTFT-8
Crowe, Christopher 1948- CTFT-4
Crowley, Mart 1935- WWT-17
Crowley, Pat CTFT-8
Crowley, Patricia
  See Crowley, Pat CTFT-8
Crowther, Leslie 1933-...........WWT-17
Croxton, Arthur 1868-? ....WWasWT
Cruickshank, Andrew
  1907-1988 ....CTFT-7
  Earlier sketch in WWT-17
Cruickshank, Gladys 1902- ......WWasWT
Cruikshank, A. Stewart
  1877-1949 ....WWasWT

Cruikshank, Stewart 1908-1966 . . . WWasWT
Cruikshanks, Charles 1844-1928 . . WWasWT
Cruise, Tom 1962- CTFT-9
   Earlier sketch in CTFT-3
   Brief Entry in CTFT-2
Crutchley, Rosalie 1921- CTFT-8
   Earlier sketch in WWasWT
Cruttwell, Hugh 1918- WWT-17
Cryer, David 1936- WWT-17
Cryer, Gretchen 1935- CTFT-4
   Earlier sketch in WWT-17
Cryer, Jon 1965- CTFT-4
Crystal, Billy 1947- CTFT-3
Cuka, Frances 1936- CTFT-6
   Earlier sketch in WWT-17
Cukor, George 1899-1983 . . . . CTFT-1
Cullen, David 1942- CTFT-6
Culley, Frederick 1879-1942 . . . . . WWasWT
Culliton, Joseph 1948- CTFT-2
Culliver, Karen 1959- CTFT-2
Cullum, John 1930- CTFT-4
   Earlier sketch in WWT-17
Culp, Robert 1930- CTFT-3
Culver, Roland 1900-1984 . . . . WWT-17
Cumberland, Gerald 1879-1926 . . . WWasWT
Cumberland, John 1880-? . . . . WWasWT
Cummings, Bob 1910- CTFT-1
Cummings, Constance 1910- CTFT-4
   Earlier sketch in WWT-17
Cummings, Vicki 1913-1969 . . . . . WWasWT
Cummins, Peggy 1925- . . . . WWasWT
Cuningham, Philip 1865-? . . . . WWasWT
Cunliffe, Whit . . . . WWasWT
Cunningham, Robert 1866-? . . . . . WWasWT
Cunningham, Sarah 1919-1986 . . . . . CTFT-3
Cupito, Suzanne
   See Brittany, Morgan CTFT-7
Curel, Viscomte Francois de
   1854-1928 . . . . WWasWT
Currah, Brian Mason 1929- WWT-17
Curran, Leigh 1943- CTFT-5
Currie, Clive 1877-1935 . . . . WWasWT
Currie, Finlay 1878-1968 . . . . WWasWT
Currie, Glenne 1926- CTFT-1
Curry, Julian 1937- WWT-17
Curry, Tim CTFT-7
Curtin, Jane 1947- CTFT-3
Curtin, Valerie CTFT-7
Curtis, Jamie Lee 1958- CTFT-6
Curtis, Keene 1923- CTFT-2
   Earlier sketch in WWT-17
Curtis, Tony 1925- CTFT-9
   Earlier sketch in CTFT-3
Curwen, Patric 1884-1949 . . . . WWasWT
Curzon, Frank 1868-1927 . . . . WWasWT
Curzon, George 1898- . . . . WWasWT
Cusack, Cyril 1910- CTFT-7
   Earlier sketch in WWT-17
Cusack, Joan 1962- CTFT-7
Cusack, John 1966- CTFT-8
Cusack, Sinead 1948- CTFT-2
   Earlier sketch in WWT-17
Cushing, Catherine Chisholm
   1874-1952 . . . . WWasWT
Cushing, Peter 1913- CTFT-4
   Earlier sketch in WWT-17
Cushing, Tom 1879-1941 . . . . WWasWT
Cushman, Robert 1943- WWT-17
Cuthbert, Neil 1951- CTFT-6
   Earlier sketch in CTFT-1
Cuthbertson, Allan 1920-1988 . . . . . . CTFT-6
   Earlier sketch in WWT-17

Cuthbertson, Iain 1930- CTFT-2
   Earlier sketch in WWT-17
Cutler, Kate 1870-1955 . . . . WWasWT
Cutter, Lise CTFT-4
Cuvillier, Charles 1879-1955 . . . . . WWasWT
Cypher, Jon 1932- CTFT-9

D

Dabdoub, Jack 1925- CTFT-2
Dabney, Augusta CTFT-1
D'Abo, Maryam 1961- CTFT-7
da Costa, Liz 1955- CTFT-6
Da Costa, Morton 1914-1989 . . . . . . CTFT-6
   Earlier sketch in WWT-17
Dafoe, Willem 1955- CTFT-7
Dagnall, Ells 1868-1935 . . . . WWasWT
Dagnall, Thomas C. ?-1926 . . . . . . WWasWT
Dahl, Arlene 1928- CTFT-2
Dahl, Roald 1916- CTFT-6
Dailey, Dan 1915-1978 . . . . WWT-16
Dailey, Irene 1920- CTFT-3
   Earlier sketch in WWT-17
Daily, Bill 1928- CTFT-9
Dainton, Marie 1881-1938 . . . . WWasWT
D'Albert, George 1870-1949 . . . . . WWasWT
Dale, Alan 1861-1928 . . . . WWasWT
Dale, Grover 1935- CTFT-5
   Earlier sketch in WWT-17
Dale, James Littlewood 1886- . . . . WWasWT
Dale, Jim 1935- CTFT-3
   Earlier sketches in CTFT-1, WWT-17
Dale, Margaret 1880-1972 . . . . WWasWT
Dale, Margaret 1922- . . . . WWasWT
Dallas, J. J. 1853-1915 . . . . WWasWT
Dallas, Meredith Eugene 1916- CTFT-1
Dalmatoff, B. 1862-? . . . . WWasWT
D'Alroy, Evelyn ?-1915 . . . . WWasWT
Dalrymple, Jean 1910- WWT-17
Dalton, Abby 1935- CTFT-7
Dalton, Charles 1864-1942 . . . . . . WWasWT
Dalton, Doris 1910- . . . . WWasWT
Dalton, Dorothy 1893-1972 . . . . . . WWasWT
Dalton, Timothy 1944- CTFT-7
Daltrey, Roger 1944- CTFT-6
Dalva, Robert 1942- CTFT-1
Daly, Arnold 1875-1927 . . . . WWasWT
Daly, Blyth 1902- . . . . WWasWT
Daly, Dutch 1848-? . . . . WWasWT
Daly, James 1918-1978 . . . . WWT-16
Daly, Mark 1887-1957 . . . . WWasWT
Daly, Timothy 1956- CTFT-8
Daly, Tyne 1946- CTFT-6
Dames, Rob 1944- CTFT-4
Damon, Stuart 1937- CTFT-5
   Earlier sketch in WWT-17
Dana, Bill 1924- CTFT-9
Dana, F. Mitchell 1942- CTFT-2
   Earlier sketch in WWT-17
Dana, Henry 1855-1921 . . . . WWasWT
Dana, Leora 1923- WWT-17
Dance, Charles 1946- CTFT-4
   Earlier sketch in CTFT-2
Dance, George 1865-1932 . . . . WWasWT
Dane, Clemence 1888-1965 . . . . . . WWasWT
Dane, Ethel . . . . WWasWT
Dane, Marjorie 1898- . . . . WWasWT
Daneman, Paul 1925- WWT-17
Danforth, William 1867-1941 . . . . WWasWT
D'Angelo, Beverly CTFT-5
   Earlier sketch in CTFT-2
Dangerfield, Rodney 1922- CTFT-3

Daniel, T. 1945- CTFT-1
Danielewski, Tad CTFT-3
Daniell, Henry 1894-1963 . . . . WWasWT
Daniels, Bebe 1901-1971 . . . . WWasWT
Daniels, Danny 1924- CTFT-3
Daniels, Danny
   See Giagni, D. J. CTFT-4
Daniels, Frank 1860-1935 . . . . WWasWT
Daniels, Jeff CTFT-4
Daniels, Marc c.1912-1989 . . . . CTFT-8
Daniels, Ron 1942- CTFT-5
   Earlier sketch in WWT-17
Daniels, William 1927- CTFT-9
   Earlier sketch in CTFT-3
Danilova, Alexandra 1907- . . . . . . WWasWT
Danner, Blythe CTFT-5
   Earlier sketches in CTFT-1, WWT-17
Danning, Sybil CTFT-7
Dano, Royal 1922- CTFT-8
Dansey, Herbert 1870-1917 . . . . . . WWasWT
Danson, Ted 1947- CTFT-4
   Earlier sketch in CTFT-1
Dante, Joe CTFT-7
Danvers, Johnny 1870-1939 . . . . . . WWasWT
Danza, Tony 1951- CTFT-5
   Brief Entry in CTFT-2
D'Arbanville, Patti CTFT-7
Darby, Kim 1948- CTFT-3
Darbyshire, Iris 1905- . . . . WWasWT
Darden, Severn 1929- CTFT-8
DaRe, Aldo
   See Ray, Aldo CTFT-9
Dare, Daphne WWT-17
Dare, Phyllis 1890-1975 . . . . WWasWT
Dare, Zena 1887-1975 . . . . WWasWT
Darewski, Herman 1883-1929 . . . . WWasWT
Dark, Sidney 1874-1947 . . . . WWasWT
Darley, Herbert . . . . WWasWT
Darlington, William Aubrey
   1890-1979 . . . . WWT-16
Darlow, Cynthia 1949- CTFT-1
Darragh, Miss ?-1917 . . . . WWasWT
Darrell, Maisie 1901- . . . . WWasWT
Darren, James 1936- CTFT-3
Darthy, Gilda . . . . WWasWT
Darvas, Lili 1906-1974 . . . . WWasWT
D'Arville, Camille 1863-1932 . . . . WWasWT
Da Silva, Howard 1909-1986 . . . . CTFT-5
   Earlier sketch in WWT-17
Datas 1876-? . . . . WWasWT
Daubeny, Peter 1921-1975 . . . . WWasWT
Daunt, William 1893-1938 . . . . WWasWT
Dauphin, Claude 1903-1978 . . . . . . WWT-17
Davenport, Harry 1866-1949 . . . . . WWasWT
Davenport, Nigel 1928- CTFT-3
   Earlier sketch in WWT-17
Davey, Nuna 1902- . . . . WWasWT
Davey, Peter 1857-1946 . . . . WWasWT
Davi, Robert CTFT-9
David, Joanna 1947- CTFT-2
David, Keith CTFT-8
David, Worton ?-1940 . . . . WWasWT
Davidson, Gordon 1933- WWT-17
Davidson, John 1941- CTFT-7
Davidson, Richard M. 1940- CTFT-2
Davies, Acton 1870-1916 . . . . WWasWT
Davies, Ben 1858-1943 . . . . WWasWT
Davies, Betty-Ann 1910-1955 . . . . WWasWT
Davies, Edna 1905- . . . . WWasWT
Davies, Harry Parr 1914-1955 . . . . WWasWT
Davies, Howard 1945(?)- CTFT-9
Davies, Hubert Henry
   1869-1932 . . . . WWasWT

Davies, Marion 1897-1961 . . . . WWasWT
Davies, Robertson 1913- CTFT-4
  Earlier sketch in WWT-17
Daviot, Gordon 1897-1952 . . . . . . WWasWT
Davis, Allan 1913- WWT-17
Davis, Allen III 1929- CTFT-4
  Earlier sketch in CTFT-1
Davis, Ann B. 1926- CTFT-3
Davis, Ariel 1912- CTFT-1
Davis, Bette 1908-1989 . . . . .CTFT-8
  Earlier sketches in CTFT-1, WWT-17
Davis, Boyd 1885-1963 . . . . WWasWT
Davis, Brad 1949- CTFT-5
Davis, Carl 1936- CTFT-9
  Earlier sketch in WWT-17
Davis, Clayton 1948- CTFT-3
Davis, Clifton 1945- CTFT-6
Davis, Fay 1872-1945 . . . . WWasWT
Davis, Geena CTFT-5
Davis, Gilbert 1899- . . . . WWasWT
Davis, Hal 1950- CTFT-6
Davis, Jeff 1950- CTFT-9
  Earlier sketch in CTFT-1
Davis, Joan 1906-1961 . . . . WWasWT
Davis, Joe 1912-1984 . . . . WWT-17
Davis, Judy 1956- CTFT-7
Davis, Kevin 1945- CTFT-4
Davis, Luther 1921- CTFT-3
Davis, Mac 1942- CTFT-3
Davis, Michael 1936- CTFT-2
Davis, Newnham-N.
  See Newnham-Davis . . . . WWasWT
Davis, Ossie 1917- CTFT-9
  Earlier sketches in CTFT-2, WWT-17
Davis, Owen 1874-1956 . . . . WWasWT
Davis, Owen 1907-1949 . . . . WWasWT
Davis, Phoebe 1865-? . . . . WWasWT
Davis, R. G. 1933- CTFT-2
Davis, Ray C. CTFT-6
  Earlier sketch in WWT-17
Davis, Richard Harding
  1864-1916 . . . . WWasWT
Davis, Sammi CTFT-7
Davis, Sammy, Jr. 1925- CTFT-4
  Earlier sketch in WWT-17
Davis, Tom Buffen 1867-1931 . . . . WWasWT
Davis, William Boyd 1885-? . . . . . WWasWT
Davison, Bruce 1946- CTFT-4
Davison, Peter CTFT-8
Davys, Edmund 1947- CTFT-7
Dawber, Pam 1954- CTFT-4
  Earlier sketch in CTFT-1
Dawe, Thomas F. 1881-1928 . . . . . WWasWT
Dawe, Thomas F. 1881-1928 . . . . . WWasWT
Dawson, Anna CTFT-5
  Earlier sketch in WWT-17
Dawson, Beatrice 1908-1976 . . . . . . WWT-16
Dawson, Forbes 1860-? . . . . WWasWT
Dawson, Richard 1932- CTFT-8
Day, Doris 1924- CTFT-7
Day, Edith 1896-1971 . . . . WWasWT
Day, Frances 1908- . . . . WWasWT
Day, Linda 1938- CTFT-7
Day, Lynda
  See George, Lynda Day CTFT-8
Day, Marjorie 1889- . . . . WWasWT
Day, Richard Digby 1940- WWT-17
Day-Lewis, Daniel 1957- CTFT-9
  Brief Entry in CTFT-6
Dazey, Charles Turner
  1853-1938 . . . . WWasWT
Dazie, Mdlle. 1882-1952 . . . . WWasWT
Deacon, Brian 1949- CTFT-4

Deacon, Richard 1923-1984 . . . . . . .CTFT-2
Dean, Basil 1888-1978 . . . . WWasWT
Dean, Isabel WWT-17
Dean, Laura 1963- CTFT-3
Dean, Julia 1880-1952 . . . . WWasWT
Deane, Barbara 1886-? . . . . WWasWT
Deane, Tessa . . . . WWasWT
Dean, Julia 1880-1952 . . . . WWasWT
De Angelis, Rosemary 1933- CTFT-5
Deans, F. Harris 1886-1961 . . . . . . WWasWT
Dearden, Harold 1882-1962 . . . . . . WWasWT
Dearing, Peter 1912- . . . . WWasWT
Dearly, Max 1875-1943 . . . . WWasWT
Dearth, Harry 1876-1933 . . . . WWasWT
de Banzi, Lois CTFT-1
De Banzie, Brenda 1915- . . . . WWasWT
De Basil, Wassily ?-1951 . . . . WWasWT
De Bear, Archibald 1889-1970 . . . WWasWT
De Belleville, Frederic
  1857-1923 . . . . WWasWT
Debenham, Cicely 1891-1955 . . . . WWasWT
De Bray, Henry 1889-1965 . . . . . . WWasWT
De Burgh, Aimee ?-1946 . . . . WWasWT
Debuskey, Merle 1923- CTFT-4
DeCarlo, Yvonne 1924- CTFT-7
De Casalis, Jeanne 1897-1966 . . . . WWasWT
De Cordoba, Pedro 1881-1950 . . . WWasWT
De Cordova, Frederick 1910- CTFT-7
  Earlier sketch in CTFT-1
De Cordova, Rudolph
  1860-1941 . . . . WWasWT
Decourcelle, Pierre 1856-1926 . . . . WWasWT
De Courville, Albert P.
  1887-1960 . . . . WWasWT
DeDomenico, Richard 1936- CTFT-2
Dee, Ruby 1924(?)- CTFT-9
  Earlier sketches in CTFT-1, WWT-17
Deering, Olive 1919-1986 . . . . .CTFT-3
  Earlier sketch in WWT-17
De Foe, Louis Vincent
  1869-1922 . . . . WWasWT
De Fontenoy, Diane 1878-? . . . . . . WWasWT
De Fore, Don 1919- CTFT-4
De Frece, Lauri 1880-1921 . . . . . . WWasWT
De Frece, Walter 1870-? . . . . WWasWT
De Groot, Walter 1896-? . . . . WWasWT
De Hartog, Jan 1914- CTFT-2
de Havilland, Olivia 1916- CTFT-6
Dehelly, Emile 1871-? . . . . WWasWT
Dehn, Paul 1912-1976 . . . . WWT-16
Dehner, John 1915- CTFT-7
Dekker, Albert 1905-1962 . . . . WWasWT
De Koven, Reginald 1859-1920 . . . WWasWT
Delafield, E.M. 1890-1943 . . . . WWasWT
de la Giroday, Francois 1952- CTFT-2
de la Haye, Ina 1906- . . . . WWasWT
Delaney, Kim 1961- CTFT-7
Delaney, Shelagh 1939- CTFT-6
  Earlier sketch in WWT-17
De Lange, Herman 1851-1929 . . . . WWasWT
de la Pasture, Mrs. Henry
  1866-1945 . . . . WWasWT
De Lappe, Gemze 1922- CTFT-3
de la Roche, Elisa 1949- CTFT-4
de la Tour, Francis 1944- WWT-17
Delaunay, Louis 1854-? . . . . WWasWT
de Laurentiis, Dino 1919- CTFT-7
  Earlier sketch in CTFT-1
Delderfield, R. F. 1912-1972 . . . . . WWasWT
De Legh, Kitty 1887-? . . . . WWasWT
De Leon, Jack 1897-1956 . . . . WWasWT
Delerue, Georges 1924- CTFT-7
Delevines . . . . WWasWT

Delfont, Bernard 1909- WWT-17
de Liagre, Alfred 1904-1987 . . . . . . .CTFT-5
  Earlier sketch in WWT-17
Dell, Floyd 1887-1969 . . . . WWasWT
Dell, Gabriel 1919-1988 . . . . .CTFT-7
  Earlier sketch in WWT-17
Dell, Jeffrey 1899- . . . . WWasWT
Delorme, Hugues . . . . WWasWT
Deloy George 1953- CTFT-4
Delroy, Irene 1898- . . . . WWasWT
DeLuise, Dom 1933- CTFT-9
  Earlier sketch in CTFT-2
De Lungo, Tony 1892- . . . . WWasWT
Delysia, Alice 1889- . . . . WWasWT
Demarest William 1892-1983 . . . . . .CTFT-2
De Marney, Derrick 1906-1971 . . . WWasWT
De Marney, Terence 1909-1971 . . WWasWT
de Mille, Cecil B. 1881-1959 . . . . . WWasWT
de Mille, Agnes 1905- CTFT-3
  Earlier sketch in WWT-17
de Mille, William C. 1878-1955 . . WWasWT
Demme, Jonathan 1944- CTFT-5
De Montherlant, Henry 1896- . . . . WWasWT
De Mornay, Rebecca 1962- CTFT-3
  Brief Entry in CTFT-2
Dempsey, Patrick 1966- CTFT-7
Dempster, Hugh 1900-1987 . . . . . . WWasWT
De Munn, Jeffrey 1947- CTFT-7
Demy, Jacques 1931- CTFT-9
Dench, Judi 1934- CTFT-4
  Earlier sketch in WWT-17
Denes, Oscar 1893- . . . . WWasWT
Deneuve, Catherine 1943- CTFT-4
  Earlier sketch in CTFT-2
Denham, Isolde 1920- . . . . WWasWT
Denham, Maurice 1909- CTFT-3
  Earlier sketch in WWT-17
Denham, Reginald 1894- WWT-17
De Niro, Robert 1943- CTFT-4
  Earlier sketch in CTFT-1
Denison, Michael 1915- CTFT-4
  Earlier sketch in WWT-17
Denker, Henry 1912- CTFT-6
  Earlier sketch in WWT-17
Dennehy, Brian CTFT-4
Dennis, Sandy 1937- CTFT-1
  Earlier sketch in WWT-17
Dennison, Sally 1941- CTFT-3
Denny, Ernest 1862-1943 . . . . WWasWT
Denny, Reginald 1891-1967 . . . . . . WWasWT
Denny, William Henry
  1853-1915 . . . . WWasWT
Denoff, Sam 1928- CTFT-4
Dent, Alan 1905-1978 . . . . WWT-16
Denton, Frank 1878-1945 . . . . WWasWT
Denver, Bob 1935- CTFT-7
Denver, John 1943- CTFT-8
Denville, Alfred J. P. 1876-1955 . . WWasWT
DePalma, Brian 1940- CTFT-6
  Earlier sketch in CTFT-1
Depardieu, Gerard 1948- CTFT-8
Depre, Ernest 1854-? . . . . WWasWT
Derek, Bo 1956- CTFT-3
Derek, John 1926- CTFT-3
De Reyes, Consuelo 1893-1948 . . . WWasWT
Dern, Bruce 1936- CTFT-3
Dern, Laura 1967- CTFT-3
Derr, Richard 1917- . . . . WWasWT
Derricks, Cleavant CTFT-6
Derwent, Clarence 1884-1959 . . . . WWasWT
De Sanctis, Alfredo . . . . WWasWT
De Santis, Joe 1909-1989 . . . . .CTFT-1
Desborough, Philip 1883-? . . . . WWasWT

Descaves, Lucien 1861-1949 ..... WWasWT
Deschanel, Caleb 1944- CTFT-8
De Selincourt, Hugh 1878-1951 .. WWasWT
Desfontaines, Henri 1876-? ...... WWasWT
De Shields, Andre 1946- CTFT-7
  Earlier sketch in WWT-17
Desiderio, Robert CTFT-6
De Silva, N. 1868-1949 .... WWasWT
Desjardins, Maxime .... WWasWT
Deslys, Gaby 1884-1920 .... WWasWT
Desmond, Dan 1944- CTFT-5
Desmond, Florence 1905- .... WWasWT
DeSoto, Rosana CTFT-7
De Sousa, May 1887-1948 ...... WWasWT
Despres, Loraine CTFT-6
Despres, Suzanne 1875-1951 ..... WWasWT
Desprez, Frank 1853-1916 .... WWasWT
Desvallieres, Maurice
  1857-1926 .... WWasWT
De Sylva B. G. 1895-1950 ...... WWasWT
Deutsch, Benoit-Leon 1892- ..... WWasWT
Deutsch, Helen 1906- CTFT-4
De Vahl, Anders 1869-? .... WWasWT
Deval, Jacques 1895-1972 ...... WWasWT
De Valois, Ninette 1898- .... WWasWT
Devane, William 1937- CTFT-3
Devant, David 1863-? .... WWasWT
Deverell, John W. 1880-1965 .... WWasWT
Devereux, William ?-1945 ..... WWasWT
Devine, George 1910-1966 ...... WWasWT
DeVine, Lawrence 1935- CTFT-1
Devine, Loretta CTFT-3
DeVito, Danny 1944- CTFT-6
Devlin, Dean CTFT-4
Devlin, Jay 1929- CTFT-1
Devlin, William 1911-1987 ..... WWasWT
DeVore, Cain 1960- CTFT-6
Devore, Gaston 1859-? .... WWasWT
De Vries, Henry .... WWasWT
De Vries, Peter 1910- CTFT-1
De Warfaz, George 1889-1966 ... WWasWT
Dewell, Michael 1931- CTFT-5
  Earlier sketch in WWT-17
Dewhurst, Colleen 1926- CTFT-4
  Earlier sketch in WWT-17
Dewhurst, Keith 1931- CTFT-7
  Earlier sketch in WWT-17
De Winton, Alice .... WWasWT
De Witt, Joyce 1949- CTFT-9
De Wolfe, Billy 1907-1974 ...... WWasWT
De Wolfe, Elsie 1865-1950 ...... WWasWT
Dews, Peter 1929- CTFT-6
  Earlier sketch in WWT-17
Dexter, Aubrey 1898-1958 .... WWasWT
Dexter, John 1935-1990 .... WWT-17
Dey, Susan 1952- CTFT-5
  Brief Entry in CTFT-2
De Young, Cliff 1946- CTFT-4
Diaghileff, Serge 1872-1929 ..... WWasWT
Diamond, I. A. L. 1920-1988 .... CTFT-7
  Earlier sketch in CTFT-1
Diamond, Margaret 1916- WWT-17
Diamond, Selma 1921-1985 .... CTFT-2
Dicenta, Joaquin 1860-? .... WWasWT
DiCenzo, George CTFT-8
Dickens, C. Stafford 1896-1967 ... WWasWT
Dickerson, George CTFT-6
Dickey, Paul 1884-1933 .... WWasWT
Dickinson, Angie 1931- CTFT-6
  Earlier sketch in CTFT-2
Dickson, Dorothy 1896- .... WWasWT
Didring, Ernst 1868-1931 .... WWasWT

Diener, Joan 1934- CTFT-4
  Earlier sketch in WWT-17
Dietrich, Dena CTFT-1
Dietrich, Marlene 1900- WWT-17
Dietz, Howard 1896-1983 .... WWT-17
Digges, Dudley 1879-1947 ...... WWasWT
Diggs, Elizabeth 1939- CTFT-3
Dighton, John 1909- WWT-16
Dignam, Mark 1909-1989 .... WWT-17
Diller, Barry 1942- CTFT-3
Diller, Phyllis 1917- CTFT-1
Dillingham, Charles B.
  1868-1934 .... WWasWT
Dillman, Bradford 1930- CTFT-3
Dillon, Frances ?-1947 .... WWasWT
Dillon, John 1945- CTFT-1
Dillon, Kevin 1965- CTFT-8
Dillon, Matt 1964- CTFT-5
  Brief Entry in CTFT-2
Dillon, Melinda CTFT-3
Dillon, Mia CTFT-4
  Earlier sketch in CTFT-1
Dinallo, Gregory S. 1941- CTFT-8
Dinehart, Alan 1890-1944 .... WWasWT
Dinner, William CTFT-4
Dinsdale, Reece CTFT-9
Disher, Maurice Willson
  1893-1969 .... WWasWT
Dishy, Bob CTFT-5
  Earlier sketch in WWT-17
Dispenza, Joe 1961- CTFT-7
Ditrichstein, Leo 1865-1928 ...... WWasWT
Divine 1945-1988 .... CTFT-7
DiVito, Joanne 1941- CTFT-3
Dix, Beulah Marie 1876-1970 .... WWasWT
Dix, Dorothy 1892-1970 .... WWasWT
Dixey, Henry E. 1859-1943 ...... WWasWT
Dixon, Adele 1908- .... WWasWT
Dixon, Campbell 1895-1960 .... WWasWT
Dixon, Donna 1957- CTFT-6
Dixon, George
  See Willis, Ted CTFT-7
Dixon, Ivan 1931- CTFT-8
Dixon, Jean 1896-1981 .... WWasWT
Dixon, MacIntyre 1931- CTFT-8
D'Lugoff, Art 1924- CTFT-2
Dobie, Alan 1932- CTFT-6
  Earlier sketch in WWT-17
Doble, Frances 1902-1967 .... WWasWT
Dobson, Kevin CTFT-3
Dodd, Ken 1929- WWT-17
Dodd, Lee Wilson 1879-1933 .... WWasWT
Dodds, Jamieson 1884-1942 ..... WWasWT
Dodds, William CTFT-1
Dodge, Henry Irving 1861-1934 .. WWasWT
Dodimead, David 1919- WWT-17
Dodson, Jack 1931- CTFT-8
  Earlier sketch in CTFT-1
Dodson, John E. 1857-1931 ...... WWasWT
Dolin, Anton 1904-1983 .... WWasWT
Dolly, Jennie 1892-1941 .... WWasWT
Dolly, Rosie 1892-1970 .... WWasWT
Dolman, Richard 1895- .... WWasWT
Dombasle, Arielle 1957- CTFT-6
Donahue, Elinor 1937- CTFT-7
Donahue, Jack 1892?-1930 ...... WWasWT
Donahue, Phil 1935- CTFT-6
Donahue, Troy 1936- CTFT-8
Donald, James 1917- .... WWasWT
Donat, Peter 1928- CTFT-9
  Earlier sketch in CTFT-1
Donat, Robert 1905-1958 .... WWasWT
Donath, Ludwig 1907-1967 ...... WWasWT

Donehue, Vincent J. 1920-1966 ... WWasWT
Donenberg, Benjamin 1957- CTFT-2
Doniger, Walter CTFT-2
Donisthorpe, G. Sheila
  1898-1946 .... WWasWT
Donlan, Yolande WWT-17
Donleavy, J. P. 1926- WWT-17
Donlevy, Brian 1903-1972 ...... WWasWT
Donnay, Maurice 1859-? .... WWasWT
Donnell, Jeff 1921-1988 .... CTFT-1
Donnell, Patrick 1916- WWT-17
Donnelly, Candice 1954- CTFT-8
Donnelly, Donal 1931- CTFT-3
  Earlier sketch in WWT-17
Donnelly, Dorothy Agnes
  1880-1928 .... WWasWT
Donner, Clive 1926- CTFT-6
  Earlier sketch in WWT-17
Donner, Richard CTFT-5
Donohue, Jack 1912-1984 .... CTFT-2
  Earlier sketch in WWT-17
Donovan, Arlene CTFT-5
Doohan, James 1920- CTFT-8
Dooley, Paul 1928- CTFT-3
Dooley, Rae 1896-1984 .... WWasWT
Dooley, Ray 1952-1984 .... CTFT-1
Doran, Charles 1877-1964 ...... WWasWT
Dore, Alexander 1923- WWT-17
Dorgere, Arlette .... WWasWT
D'Orme, Aileen 1877-1939 ...... WWasWT
Dormer, Daisy 1889- .... WWasWT
Dorn, Dolores CTFT-1
Dorn, Harding 1923-1987 ... ...,. CTFT-3
Dornay, Jules .... WWasWT
Doro, Marie 1882-1956 .... WWasWT
Dorr, Dorothy 1867-? .... WWasWT
D'Orsay, Lawrance 1853-1931 ... WWasWT
Dorwart, David A. 1948- CTFT-2
Dorziat, Gabrielle .... WWasWT
Dossor, Alan 1941- WWT-17
Dotrice, Roy 1925- CTFT-3
  Earlier sketch in WWT-17
Doucet, Catherine Calhoun
  1875-1958 .... WWasWT
Douglas, Diana 1923- CTFT-1
Douglas, Eric 1962- CTFT-6
Douglas, Felicity WWT-17
Douglas, Gordon CTFT-2
Douglas, Juliet 1962- CTFT-8
Douglas, Kenneth ?-1923 .... WWasWT
Douglas, Kirk 1916- CTFT-7
  Earlier sketch in CTFT-1
Douglas, Melvin 1901-1980 .... CTFT-1
  Earlier sketch in WWT-17
Douglas, Michael 1944- CTFT-4
  Earlier sketch in CTFT-1
Douglas, Michael
  See Crichton, Michael CTFT-5
Douglas, Mike 1925- CTFT-6
Douglas, Robert 1909- .... WWasWT
Douglas, Sarah CTFT-4
Douglas, Tom 1903- .... WWasWT
Douglas, Torrington ?-1986 .... WWT-17
Douglas, Wallace 1911- WWT-17
Douglass, Albert 1864-1940 ...... WWasWT
Douglass, R. H. .... WWasWT
Douglass, Stephen 1921- WWT-17
Douglass, Vincent 1900-1926 .... WWasWT
Dourif, Brad 1950- CTFT-7
Dovey, Alice 1885-1969 .... WWasWT
Dow, Clara 1883-1969 .... WWasWT
Dow, Tony 1945- CTFT-2

Dowd, M'el CTFT-5
  Earlier sketch in WWT-17
Dowling, Eddie 1894-1976 ....WWasWT
Dowling, Joan 1928-1954 ....WWasWT
Dowling, Vincent 1929- CTFT-2
Down, Angela 1943- WWT-17
Down, Lesley-Anne 1954- CTFT-5
Downey, Robert CTFT-8
Downey, Robert Jr. 1965- CTFT-7
Downie, Penny CTFT-9
Downs, Hugh 1921- CTFT-5
Downs, Jane WWT-17
Doyle, Arthur Conan
  1859-1930 ....WWasWT
Doyle, David 1925- CTFT-7
Doyle, Jill 1965- CTFT-4
D'Oyly Carte, Rupert 1876-? .....WWasWT
Dragoti, Stan(ley G.) 1932- CTFT-1
Drake, Alfred 1914- WWT-17
Drake, Fabia 1904-1990 ....CTFT-8
  Earlier sketch in WWasWT
Drake, William A. 1899-1965 ....WWasWT
Draper, Polly CTFT-8
Draper, Ruth 1889-1956 ....WWasWT
Draycott, Wilfred 1848-? ....WWasWT
Drayton, Alfred 1881-1949 ......WWasWT
Dreiser, Theodore 1871-1945 ....WWasWT
Dresdal, Sonia 1909-1976 ....WWT-16
Dresser, Louise 1882-1965 ....WWasWT
Dressler, Eric 1900- ....WWasWT
Dressler, Marie 1869-1934 ....WWasWT
Drever, Constance ?-1948 ....WWasWT
Drew, John 1853-1927 ....WWasWT
Drewitt, Stanley 1878-? ....WWasWT
Drexler, Rosalyn CTFT-1
Dreyfuss, Henry 1904-1972 ......WWasWT
Dreyfuss, Richard 1947- CTFT-5
  Earlier sketches CTFT-1, WWT-17
Drinkwater, Albert Edwin
  ?-1923 ....WWasWT
Drinkwater, John 1882-1937 .....WWasWT
Drivas, Robert 1938-1986 ....CTFT-2
  Earlier sketch in WWT-17
Driver, Donald 1923?-1988 ....CTFT-7
  Earlier sketch in WWT-17
Driver, John 1947- CTFT-6
Drouet, Robert 1870-1914 ....WWasWT
Droomgoole, Patrick 1930- WWT-17
Druce, Hubert 1870-1931 ....WWasWT
Drulie, Sylvia CTFT-1
Drummond, Alice 1928- CTFT-3
  Earlier sketch in CTFT-1
Drummond, Dolores 1834-1926 ..WWasWT
Drury, Alan 1949- CTFT-5
  Earlier sketch in WWT-17
Drury, William Price 1861-1949 ..WWasWT
Dryden, Vaughan 1875-? ....WWasWT
Dryer, Fred 1946- CTFT-7
Du Bois, Raoul Pene 1914- WWT-17
Duberman, Martin Bauml
  1930- CTFT-1
Duberstein, Helen 1926- CTFT-4
Duchin, Peter 1937- CTFT-1
Duclow, Geraldine 1946- CTFT-4
Dudley, Bide 1877-1944 ....WWasWT
Dudley, Carol L. 1949- CTFT-2
Dudley, William 1947- CTFT-5
  Earlier sketch in WWT-17
Duell, William CTFT-3
Duff, Howard 1917-1990 ....CTFT-6
Duffield, Kenneth 1885-? ....WWasWT
Duffy, Julia 1951- CTFT-4
Duffy, Patrick 1949- CTFT-3

Duflos, Raphael?-1946 ....WWasWT
Dufour, Val 1927- CTFT-1
Dugan, Dennis 1946- CTFT-8
Duggan, Andrew 1923-1988 ....CTFT-7
Dukakis, Olympia 1931- CTFT-7
  Earlier sketch in CTFT-1
Duke, Ivy 1896- ....WWasWT
Duke, Patty 1946- CTFT-3
Duke, Vernon 1903-1969 ....WWasWT
Dukes, Ashley 1885-1959 ....WWasWT
Dukes, David 1945- CTFT-7
  Earlier sketch in CTFT-2
Du Kore, Lawrence 1933- CTFT-5
Dullea, Keir 1936- CTFT-4
  Earlier sketch in WWT-17
Dullin, Charles 1885-1949 ....WWasWT
Dullzell, Paul 1879-1961 ....WWasWT
Du Maurier, Daphne 1907-1989 ..WWasWT
du Maurier, Gerald 1873-1934 ...WWasWT
Dunaway, Faye 1941- CTFT-7
  Earlier sketches in CTFT-1, WWT-17
Duncan, Augustin 1873-1954 ....WWasWT
Duncan, Fiona CTFT-4
Duncan, Isadora 1880-1927 ......WWasWT
Duncan, Lindsay 1950- CTFT-7
Duncan, Malcolm 1881-1942 .....WWasWT
Duncan, Mary 1903- ....WWasWT
Duncan, Ronald 1914- WWT-17
Duncan, Rosetta 1900-1959 ......WWasWT
Duncan, Sandy 1946- CTFT-7
  Earlier sketches in CTFT-2, WWT-17
Duncan, Todd 1900- ....WWasWT
Duncan, Vivian 1899-1986 ....WWasWT
Duncan, William Cary
  1874-1945 ....WWasWT
Duncan-Petley, Stella 1975- CTFT-4
Dunfee, Jack 1901- ....WWasWT
Dunham, Joanna 1936- CTFT-6
  Earlier sketch in WWT-17
Dunham, Katherine 1910- WWT-17
Dunkels, Dorothy 1907- ....WWasWT
Dunkels, Marjorie 1916- ....WWasWT
Dunlop, Frank 1927- WWT-17
Dunlop, Vic Jr. CTFT-4
Dunn, Emma 1875-1966 ....WWasWT
Dunn, Geoffrey 1903- WWT-17
Dunn, Thomas G. 1950- CTFT-1
Dunne, Dominick 1925(?)- CTFT-9
Dunne, Griffin 1955- CTFT-4
Dunne, Irene 1904-1990 ....WWasWT
Dunning, Philip 1890-1957 ....WWasWT
Dunning, Ruth 1911- WWT-17
Dunnock, Mildred 1900- CTFT-8
  Earlier sketch in WWT-17
Dunsany, Lord 1878-1957 ....WWasWT
Dupree, Minnie 1875-1947 ....WWasWT
Duprez, Fred 1884-1938 ....WWasWT
Duprez, June 1918- ....WWasWT
Duquesne, Edmond 1855-? ....WWasWT
Durand, Charles 1912- CTFT-1
du Rand, le Clanche 1941- CTFT-1
Durang, Christopher 1949- CTFT-3
  Earlier sketches in CTFT-1, WWT-17
Durante, Jimmy 1893-1980 ....WWasWT
Duras, Marguerite 1914- CTFT-4
  Earlier sketch in WWT-17
Durning, Charles 1923- CTFT-5
Durrenmatt, Friedrich 1921- WWT-17
Dury, Ian 1942- CTFT-9
Du Sautoy, Carmen 1950- CTFT-5
  Earlier sketch in WWT-17
Duse, Eleonora 1858-1924 ....WWasWT
Dusenberry, Ann CTFT-8

Du Souchet, H. A. 1852-1922 ....WWasWT
Dussault, Nancy 1936- CTFT-4
  Earlier sketch in WWT-17
d'Usseau, Arnaud 1916-1990 ....CTFT-9
  Earlier sketch in WWasWT
Dutton, Charles 1951- CTFT-9
  Earlier sketch in CTFT-3
Duttine, John 1949- CTFT-2
Duval, Georges 1847-1919 ....WWasWT
Duvall, Robert 1931- CTFT-7
  Earlier sketch in CTFT-1
Duvall, Shelley 1949- CTFT-3
Dux, Emilienne 1874-? ....WWasWT
Duxbury, Elspeth 1909-1967 .....WWasWT
Dwyer, Ada ?-1952 ....WWasWT
Dwyer, Leslie 1906-1986 ....WWasWT
Dyall, Frank 1874-1950 ....WWasWT
Dyall, Valentine 1908-1985 ....WWT-17
Dyer, C.
  See Dyer, Charles CTFT-6
Dyer, Charles 1928- CTFT-6
  Earlier sketch in WWT-17
Dyer, Christopher 1947- WWT-17
Dyer, Raymond
  See Dyer, Charles CTFT-6
Dykstra, John CTFT-8
Dyrenforth, James ....WWasWT
Dysart, Richard A. CTFT-4
  Earlier sketch in WWT-17
Dzundza, George CTFT-6

E

Eadie, Dennis 1869-1928 ....WWasWT
Eagels, Jeanne 1894-1929 ....WWasWT
Eaker, Ira 1922- CTFT-1
Eames, Clare 1896-1930 ....WWasWT
Earle, Virginia 1875-1937 ....WWasWT
Eason, Mules 1915-1977 ....WWT-16
Easterbrook, Leslie CTFT-7
Eastman, Frederick 1859-1920 ...WWasWT
Easton, Richard 1933- CTFT-5
  Earlier sketch in WWT-17
Eastwood, Clint 1930- CTFT-6
  Earlier sketch in CTFT-1
Eaton, Mary 1902-1948 ....WWasWT
Eaton, Wallas 1917- WWT-17
Eaton, Walter Prichard
  1878-1957 ....WWasWT
Eaves, Hilary 1914- ....WWasWT
Ebb, Fred 1933- CTFT-5
  Earlier sketch in WWT-17
Ebersole, Christine CTFT-5
  Earlier sketch in CTFT-2
Ebert, Joyce 1933- CTFT-5
  Earlier sketch in WWT-17
Ebert, Roger 1942- CTFT-9
Ebsen, Buddy 1908- CTFT-3
Eccles, Donald 1908-1986 ....WWT-17
Eccles, Janet 1895-1966 ....WWasWT
Echegaray, Miguel 1848-1927 ....WWasWT
Echevarria, Rocky
  See Bauer, Steven CTFT-8
Eck, Scott 1957- CTFT-6
Eckart, Jean 1921- CTFT-3
  Earlier sketch in WWT-17
Eckart, William J. 1920- CTFT-4
  Earlier sketch in WWT-17
Eckstein, George 1928- CTFT-2
eda-Young, Barbara 1945- CTFT-5
  Earlier sketch in WWT-17
Eddinger, Wallace 1881-1929 ....WWasWT

Eddington, Paul 1927- CTFT-6
  Earlier sketch in WWT-17
Eddison, Robert 1908- WWT-17
Eddy, Nelson 1901-1967 ....WWasWT
Eddy, Teddy Jack
  See Busey, Gary CTFT-6
Ede, George 1931- CTFT-1
Edelman, Gregg 1958- CTFT-9
Edelman, Herbert 1933- CTFT-6
  Earlier sketch in CTFT-1
Eden, Barbara 1934- CTFT-9
  Earlier sketch in CTFT-3
Eden, Sidney 1936- CTFT-2
Edeson, Robert 1868-1931 ....WWasWT
Edgar, David 1948- CTFT-6
  Earlier sketch in WWT-17
Edgar, Marriott 1880-1951 ......WWasWT
Edgar-Bruce, Tonie
  See Bruce, Tonie Edgar ....WWasWT
Edgett, Edwin Francis
  1867-1946 ....WWasWT
Edgeworth, Jane 1922- WWT-17
Edginton, May ?-1957 ....WWasWT
Edgley, Michael 1943- CTFT-5
  Earlier sketch in WWT-17
Ediss, Connie 1871-1934 ....WWasWT
Edlin, Tubby (Henry) 1882-? .....WWasWT
Edlund, Richard 1940- CTFT-9
Edmead, Wendy CTFT-1
Edney, Florence 1879-1950 ......WWasWT
Edouin, Rose 1844-1925 ....WWasWT
Edwardes, Felix ?-1954 ....WWasWT
Edwardes, George 1852-1915 ....WWasWT
Edwardes, Olga 1917- ....WWasWT
Edwardes, Paula ....WWasWT
Edwards, Anthony CTFT-6
Edwards, Ben 1916- CTFT-9
  Earlier sketch in WWT-17
Edwards, Blake 1922- CTFT-6
  Earlier sketch in CTFT-1
Edwards, Burt 1928- CTFT-2
Edwards, G. Spencer ?-1916 .....WWasWT
Edwards, Henry 1883-1952 ......WWasWT
Edwards, Hilton 1903- WWT-17
Edwards, Julie
  See Andrews, Julie CTFT-7
Edwards, Maurice 1922- CTFT-1
Edwards, Osman 1864-1936 .....WWasWT
Edwards, Ralph CTFT-3
Edwards, Sherman 1919-1981 .....WWT-17
Edwards, Tom 1880-? ....WWasWT
Edwards, Vince 1928- CTFT-7
Egan, Michael 1895-1956 ....WWasWT
Egan, Michael 1926- CTFT-2
Egan, Peter 1946- CTFT-5
  Earlier sketch in WWT-17
Egbert, Brothers (Seth and
  Albert) ....WWasWT
Egerton, George 1860-1945 ......WWasWT
Eggar, Jack 1904- ....WWasWT
Eggar, Samantha 1939- CTFT-8
  Earlier sketch in CTFT-1
Eggert, Nicole CTFT-4
Eggerth, Marta 1916- CTFT-1
  Earlier sketch in WWasWT
Eichelberger, Ethyl 1945-1990 .....CTFT-9
Eichhorn, Lisa 1952- CTFT-6
Eigsti, Karl 1938- CTFT-5
  Earlier sketch in WWT-17
Eikenberry, Jill 1947- CTFT-5
Eilbacher, Lisa CTFT-6
Eisele, Robert 1948- CTFT-4
Eisinger, Irene 1906- ....WWasWT

Eisner, Michael D. 1942- CTFT-1
Ekberg, Anita 1931- CTFT-7
Ekland, Britt 1942- CTFT-7
Elam, Jack 1916- CTFT-6
  Earlier sketch in CTFT-2
Elcar, Dana 1927- CTFT-6
Elder, Eldon 1924- WWT-17
Elder, Lonne III 1931- CTFT-7
  Earlier sketch in WWT-17
Eldred, Arthur ?-1942 ....WWasWT
Eldridge, Florence 1901-1988 ....WWasWT
Elen, Gus 1862-1940 ....WWasWT
Elg, Taina 1930- CTFT-1
Elgar, Avril 1932- CTFT-5
  Earlier sketch in WWT-17
Elias, Hector WWT-17
Elias, Michael 1940- CTFT-4
Eliasberg, Jan 1954- CTFT-1
Elikann, Larry 1923- CTFT-2
Eliot, T. S. (Thomas Stearns)
  1888-1965 ....WWasWT
Eliscu, Fernanda 1882-1968 .....WWasWT
Elizondo, Hector 1936- CTFT-7
  Earlier sketches in CTFT-2, WWT-17
Elkins, Hillard 1929- WWT-17
Ellenshaw, Peter 1913- CTFT-9
Ellenstein, Robert 1923- CTFT-1
Ellerbe, Harry 1906- CTFT-1
Ellerbee, Linda 1944- CTFT-6
Ellinger, Desiree 1893-1951 .....WWasWT
Elliott, Alice 1946- CTFT-4
Elliott, Denholm 1922- CTFT-4
  Earlier sketch in WWT-17
Elliott, George 1899- ....WWasWT
Elliott, George H. 1884-? ....WWasWT
Elliott, Gertrude 1874-1950 .....WWasWT
Elliott, Madge 1898-1955 ....WWasWT
Elliott, Maxine 1871-1932 ......WWasWT
Elliott, Michael 1931-1984 ....WWT-17
Elliott, Michael (Allwyn) 1936- CTFT-1
Elliott, Patricia 1942- WWT-17
Elliott, Paul 1941- WWT-17
Elliott, Sam 1944- CTFT-3
Elliott, Stephen 1945- WWT-17
Elliott, Sumner Locke 1917- CTFT-1
Elliott, William 1885-1932 ......WWasWT
Ellis, Anita 1920- CTFT-3
Ellis, Anthony L. ?-1944 ....WWasWT
Ellis, Edith 1876-1960 ....WWasWT
Ellis, Edward 1872-1952 ....WWasWT
Ellis, Leslie 1962- CTFT-5
Ellis, Mary 1900- WWT-17
Ellis, Vivian WWT-17
Ellis, Walter 1874-1956 ....WWasWT
Elliston, Daisy 1894- ....WWasWT
Elliston, Grace 1881-1950 ....WWasWT
Elsie, Lily 1886-1962 ....WWasWT
Elsom, Isobel 1893- ....WWasWT
Elsom, John 1934- WWT-17
Elson, Anita 1898- ....WWasWT
Elston, Robert 1934-1987 ....CTFT-1
Eltinge, Julian 1883-1941 ....WWasWT
Elton, George 1875-1942 ....WWasWT
Elvey, Maurice 1887-1967 ....WWasWT
Elvin, Joe 1862-1935 ....WWasWT
Elvin, Violetta 1925- ....WWasWT
Elvira
  See Peterson, Cassandra CTFT-9
Elwes, Cary 1962- CTFT-7
Emerald, Connie ?-1959 ....WWasWT
Emerson, Faye 1917-1983 ....WWasWT
Emerson, John 1874-1956 ....WWasWT
Emerton, Roy 1892-1944 ....WWasWT

Emery, Gilbert 1875-1945 ....WWasWT
Emery, John 1905-1964 ....WWasWT
Emery, Katherine 1908- ....WWasWT
Emery, Pollie 1875-1958 ....WWasWT
Emery, Winifred 1862-1924 ......WWasWT
Emhardt, Robert 1901?- WWT-17
Emmet, Alfred 1908- WWT-17
Emmons, Beverly 1943- CTFT-2
Emmons, Wayne CTFT-4
Emney, Fred 1865-1917 ....WWasWT
Emney, Fred 1900- WWT-17
Emney, Joan Fred ....WWasWT
Emonts, Ann 1952- CTFT-1
Engar, Keith M. 1923- WWT-17
Engel, Georgia 1948- CTFT-2
Engel, Lehman 1910-1982 ....CTFT-2
Engel, Susan 1935- CTFT-3
  Earlier sketch in WWT-17
Engelbach, David CTFT-4
England, Paul 1893-1968 ....WWasWT
Englander, Ludwig 1853-1914 ....WWasWT
Engle, Debra 1953- CTFT-7
English Stage Company Ltd.,
  The ....WWasWT
Englund, Robert 1949- CTFT-8
Eno, Terry 1948- CTFT-2
Enriquez, Rene 1933-1990 ....CTFT-7
  Earlier sketch in CTFT-2
Enthoven, Gabrielle 1868-1950 ...WWasWT
Ephraim, Lee 1877-1953 ....WWasWT
Ephron, Nora 1941- CTFT-8
Epps, Sheldon 1952- CTFT-3
Epstein, Alvin 1925- CTFT-9
  Earlier sketch in WWT-17
Epstein, Pierre 1930- CTFT-4
  Earlier sketch in WWT-17
Erdman, Jean 1916- CTFT-4
Eric, Fred 1874-1935 ....WWasWT
Erickson, Mitchell 1927- CTFT-2
Erlanger, Abraham L.
  1860-1930 ....WWasWT
Erman, John 1935- CTFT-1
Erne, Vincent 1884-? ....WWasWT
Ernotte, Andre 1943- CTFT-1
Errol, Leon, 1881-1951 ....WWasWT
Erskine, Chester 1903-1986 ......WWasWT
Erskine, Howard (Weir) 1926- CTFT-1
Ervine, St. John Greer
  1883-1971 ....WWasWT
Esmond, Annie 1873-1945 ....WWasWT
Esmond, Carl 1905- ....WWasWT
Esmond, Henry V. 1869-1922 ....WWasWT
Esmond, Jill 1908-1990 ....WWasWT
Espinosa, Edouard 1872-1950 ....WWasWT
Essex, David 1947- CTFT-3
  Earlier sketch in WWT-17
Esslin, Martin 1918- WWT-17
Estabrook, Christine CTFT-6
Estabrook, Howard 1884-? ......WWasWT
Esterman, Laura CTFT-1
Estevez, Emilio CTFT-3
  Brief Entry in CTFT-2
Estrada, Erik 1949- CTFT-3
Eszterhas, Joe CTFT-7
Etherington, James 1902-1948 ....WWasWT
Etting, Ruth 1907-1978 ....WWasWT
Eustrel, Antony 1904- ....WWasWT
Evans, Caradoc 1878-1945 ......WWasWT
Evans, Clifford 1912- ....WWasWT
Evans, David
  See Evans, Dillon CTFT-6
Evans, Dillon 1921- CTFT-6
  Earlier sketch in WWT-17

Evans, Don 1938- CTFT-1
Evans, Edith 1888-1976 . . . . .WWT-16
Evans, Jessie 1918- WWT-17
Evans, Linda 1942- CTFT-3
Evans, Madge 1909-1981 . . . . .WWasWT
Evans, Maurice 1901-1989 . . . . .CTFT-7
  Earlier sketch in WWT-17
Evans, Michael 1922- . . . . .WWasWT
Evans, Michael Jonas 1949- CTFT-3
Evans, Nancy 1915- . . . . .WWasWT
Evans, Ray 1915- CTFT-1
Evans, Robert 1930- CTFT-6
Evans, Tenniel 1926- WWT-17
Evans, Will 1873-1931 . . . . .WWasWT
Evans, Winifred 1890- . . . . .WWasWT
Eve, Trevor 1951- CTFT-9
Eveling, (Harry) Stanley 1925- WWT-17
Evelyn, Clara 1886-? . . . . .WWasWT
Evelyn, Judith 1913-1967 . . . . .WWasWT
Evennett, Wallace 1888-? . . . . .WWasWT
Everest, Barbara 1890-1968 . . . . . .WWasWT
Everett, Chad 1937- CTFT-3
Everett, Rupert 1959- CTFT-8
Everhart, Rex 1920- WWT-17
Evett, Robert 1874-1949 . . . . .WWasWT
Evigan, Greg 1953- CTFT-7
Ewart, Stephen T. 1869-? . . . . . . .WWasWT
Ewell, Tom 1909- CTFT-4
  Earlier sketch in WWT-17
Eyen, Tom 1941- CTFT-3
  Earlier sketches in CTFT-1, WWT-17
Eyre, Laurence 1881-1959 . . . . . . .WWasWT
Eyre, Peter 1942- WWT-17
Eyre, Richard 1943- WWT-17
Eyre, Ronald 1929- CTFT-6
  Earlier sketch in WWT-17
Eysselinck, Walter 1931- WWT-17
Eythe, William 1918-1957 . . . . . . .WWasWT
Eyton, Frank 1894- . . . . .WWasWT

F

Fabares, Shelley 1944- CTFT-6
Faber, Beryl ?-1912 . . . . .WWasWT
Faber, Leslie 1879-1929 . . . . .WWasWT
Faber, Mrs. Leslie 1880-? . . . . . . .WWasWT
Faber, Ron 1933- CTFT-5
  Earlier sketch in WWT-17
Fabian, Madge 1880-? . . . . .WWasWT
Fabray, Nanette CTFT-4
  Earlier sketch in WWT-17
Fabre, Emile 1870-1955 . . . . .WWasWT
Fagan, James Bernard
  1873-1933 . . . . .WWasWT
Fagan, Myron C. . . . . .WWasWT
Fain, Sammy 1902-1989 . . . . .CTFT-9
Fair, Adrah 1897- . . . . .WWasWT
Fairbanks, Douglas 1883-1939 . . . .WWasWT
Fairbanks, Douglas Jr. 1909- CTFT-3
  Earlier sketch in WWT-17
Fairbrother, Sydney 1872-1941 . . .WWasWT
Fairchild, Morgan 1950- CTFT-5
  Earlier sketch in CTFT-2
Fairfax, Lance 1899- . . . . .WWasWT
Fairfax, Lettice 1876-1948 . . . . . . .WWasWT
Fairfax, Marion 1879-? . . . . .WWasWT
Fairman, Austin 1892-1964 . . . . . .WWasWT
Fairservis, Elfie 1957- CTFT-3
Fairweather, David C. 1899- WWT-17
Fairweather, Virginia 1922- WWT-17
Faison, Frankie CTFT-8
Faison, George 1947- CTFT-8

Faison, Matthew CTFT-8
Faison, Sandy CTFT-8
Faith, Rosemary CTFT-4
Faithfull, Marianne 1946- WWT-17
Faix, Anna 1930- CTFT-2
Falabella, John CTFT-6
Falck, Lionel 1889-1971 . . . . .WWasWT
Falconi, Armando . . . . .WWasWT
Falk, Peter 1927- CTFT-6
  Earlier sketch in CTFT-1
Fallon, Richard G. 1923- CTFT-1
Falls, Gregory A. 1922- CTFT-1
Fancourt, Darrell 1888-1953 . . . . .WWasWT
Faraday, Philip Michael
  1875-1969 . . . . .WWasWT
Farentino, James 1938- CTFT-7
  Earlier sketches in CTFT-2, WWT-17
Farer, Ronnie 1951- CTFT-7
Fargas, Antonio 1946- CTFT-8
  Earlier sketch in CTFT-1
Farjeon, Herbert 1887-1945 . . . . . .WWasWT
Farjeon, Joseph Jefferson
  1883-1955 . . . . .WWasWT
Farkoa, Maurice 1867-1916 . . . . . .WWasWT
Farleigh, Lynn 1942- CTFT-3
  Earlier sketch in WWT-17
Farley, Morgan 1898-1988 . . . . .CTFT-7
  Earlier sketch in WWasWT
Farnesworth, Richard CTFT-3
Farnum, Dustin 1874-1929 . . . . . . .WWasWT
Farnum, William 1876-1953 . . . . . .WWasWT
Farone, Felicia 1961- CTFT-7
Farquhar, Malcolm 1924- CTFT-5
  Earlier sketch in WWT-17
Farquharson, Robert 1877-1966 . .WWasWT
Farr, Derek 1912-1986 . . . . .CTFT-3
  Earlier sketch in WWT-17
Farr, Florence 1860-1917 . . . . .WWasWT
Farr, Jamie CTFT-1
Farrah 1926- CTFT-5
  Earlier sketch in WWT-17
Farrand, Jan 1925- WWT-17
Farrar, Gwen 1899-1944 . . . . .WWasWT
Farrell, Charles 1900(?)-1990 . . . . . .CTFT-9
  Earlier sketch in WWT-17
Farrell, Glenda 1904-1971 . . . . . . .WWasWT
Farrell, M. J. 1905- . . . . .WWasWT
Farrell, Mike 1939- CTFT-4
  Earlier sketch in CTFT-1
Farrell, Paul 1893- . . . . .WWasWT
Farrell, Shea 1957- CTFT-5
Farren, Babs 1904- . . . . .WWasWT
Farren, Fred ?-1956 . . . . .WWasWT
Farren, William 1853-1937 . . . . . .WWasWT
Farrer, Ann 1916- . . . . .WWasWT
Farrow, Mia 1945- CTFT-7
  Earlier sketches in CTFT-1, WWT-17
Farwell, Jonathan 1932- CTFT-2
Fassbinder, Rainer Werner
  1946-1982 . . . . .CTFT-1
Fauchois, Rene 1882-1962 . . . . . . .WWasWT
Favart, Edmee ?-1941 . . . . .WWasWT
Faversham, William 1868-1940 . . .WWasWT
Favre, Gina . . . . .WWasWT
Fawcett, Charles S. 1855-1922 . . .WWasWT
Fawcett, Eric 1904- . . . . .WWasWT
Fawcett, Farrah 1947- CTFT-4
  Earlier sketch in CTFT-1
Fawcett, George 1860-1939 . . . . . .WWasWT
Fawcett, L'Estrange . . . . .WWasWT
Fawcett, Marion 1886-1957 . . . . . .WWasWT
Fawn, James 1850-1961 . . . . .WWasWT
Fay, William George 1872-1949 . . .WWasWT

Faye, Joey 1910- WWT-17
Fayne, Greta . . . . .WWasWT
Fayre, Eleanor 1910- . . . . .WWasWT
Fazan, Eleanor 1930- WWT-17
Fealy, Maude 1883-1971 . . . . .WWasWT
Fearl, Clifford CTFT-1
Fearnley, John 1914- CTFT-1
Fearon, George Edward 1901- . . .WWasWT
Feast, Michael 1946- CTFT-2
  Earlier sketch in WWT-17
Featherston, Vane 1864-1948 . . . .WWasWT
Feder, A. H. 1909- CTFT-7
  Earlier sketch in WWT-17
Feely, Terence 1928- CTFT-6
  Earlier sketch in WWT-17
Feiffer, Jules 1929- CTFT-1
  Earlier sketch in WWT-17
Feingold, Michael 1945- CTFT-3
  Earlier sketch in WWT-17
Feist, Gene 1930- CTFT-5
  Earlier sketch in WWT-17
Feldman, Corey 1971- CTFT-8
Feldman, Marty 1934-1982 . . . . .CTFT-1
Feldon, Barbara 1941- CTFT-6
Feldshuh, Tovah CTFT-1
  Earlier sketch in WWT-17
Felgate, Peter 1919- . . . . .WWasWT
Felix, Hugo 1866-1934 . . . . .WWasWT
Fell, Norman 1924- CTFT-3
Fellini, Federico 1920- CTFT-7
  Earlier sketch in CTFT-1
Fellowes-Robinson, Dora
  ?-1946 . . . . .WWasWT
Fenn, Frederick 1868-1924 . . . . . .WWasWT
Fenton, George CTFT-9
Fenwick, Irene 1887-1936 . . . . . . .WWasWT
Feraudy, Jacques de . . . . .WWasWT
Feraudy, Maurice de 1859- . . . . . .WWasWT
Ferber, Edna 1887-1968 . . . . .WWasWT
Ferguson, Catherine 1895- . . . . . . .WWasWT
Ferguson, Elsie 1885-1961 . . . . . . .WWasWT
Fern, Sable 1876-? . . . . .WWasWT
Fernald, Chester Bailey
  1869-1938 . . . . .WWasWT
Fernald, John 1905- WWT-17
Fernandez, Bijou 1877-1961 . . . . . .WWasWT
Fernandez, James 1835-1915 . . . . .WWasWT
Ferrar, Beatrice ?-1958 . . . . .WWasWT
Ferrell, Conchata 1943- CTFT-8
Ferrer, Jose 1912- CTFT-2
  Earlier sketch in WWT-17
Ferrer, Mel 1917- CTFT-6
Ferrer, Miguel CTFT-9
Ferrers, Helen ?-1943 . . . . .WWasWT
Ferrier, Noel 1930- WWT-17
Ferrigno, Lou 1952- CTFT-8
Ferris, Barbara 1943- CTFT-5
  Earlier sketch in WWT-17
Ferris, Monk
  See Sharkey, Jack CTFT-1
Feuer, Cy WWT-17
Feuillere, Edwige 1907- . . . . .WWasWT
Ffolkes, David 1912- . . . . .WWasWT
Ffolliott, Gladys ?-1928 . . . . .WWasWT
Ffrangcon-Davies, Gwen 1896- WWT-17
Fiander, Lewis 1938- CTFT-4
  Earlier sketch in WWT-17
Fibich, Felix 1917- CTFT-4
Fichandler, Zelda 1924- WWT-17
Fiedler, John 1925- CTFT-7
  Earlier sketch in CTFT-1
Field, Alexander 1892-1939 . . . . . .WWasWT
Field, Barbara 1935- CTFT-1

Field, Betty 1918-1973 . . . . WWT-16
Field, Crystal 1940- CTFT-1
Field, Edward Salisbury
   1878-1936 . . . . .WWasWT
Field, Fern 1934- CTFT-4
Field, Jonathan 1912- . . . . .WWasWT
Field, Jules 1919- CTFT-5
Field, Leonard S. 1908- CTFT-4
Field, Ron ?-1989 . . . . .CTFT-5
   Earlier sketch in WWT-17
Field, Sally 1946- CTFT-3
Field, Sid 1904-1950 . . . . .WWasWT
Field, Sylvia 1902- . . . . .WWasWT
Field, Virginia 1917- . . . . .WWasWT
Fielding, Fenella 1934- CTFT-6
   Earlier sketch in WWT-17
Fielding, Harold WWT-17
Fielding, Marjorie 1892-1956 . . . .WWasWT
Fields, Dorothy 1905-1974 . . . . . .WWasWT
Fields, Freddie 1923- CTFT-5
Fields, Gracie 1898-1979 . . . . .WWasWT
Fields, Herbert 1897-1958 . . . . . . .WWasWT
Fields, Joseph 1895-1966 . . . . .WWasWT
Fields, Judy CTFT-2
Fields, Lew 1867-1941 . . . . .WWasWT
Fields, W. C. 1879-1946 . . . . .WWasWT
Fierstein, Harvey 1954- CTFT-6
   Earlier sketch in CTFT-1
Fifield, Elaine 1930- . . . . .WWasWT
Figman, Max 1868-1952 . . . . .WWasWT
Filippi, Rosina 1866-1930 . . . . . . .WWasWT
Filkins, Grace ?-1962 . . . . .WWasWT
Filmer, A. E. . . . . .WWasWT
Finch, Peter 1916-1977 . . . . .WWasWT
Finck, Herman 1872-? . . . . .WWasWT
Findon, B. W. 1859-1943 . . . . .WWasWT
Fingerhut, Arden CTFT-6
Finlay, Frank 1926- CTFT-5
   Earlier sketch in WWT-17
Finn, Arthur . . . . .WWasWT
Finnegan, Bill 1928- CTFT-1
Finney, Albert 1936- CTFT-5
   Earlier sketches in CTFT-1, WWT-17
Firth, Anne 1918- . . . . .WWasWT
Firth, Colin 1960- CTFT-9
Firth, David 1945- CTFT-4
   Earlier sketches in CTFT-3, WWT-17
Firth, Elizabeth 1884-? . . . . .WWasWT
Firth, Peter 1953- CTFT-7
Firth, Tazeena 1935- WWT-17
Fischer, Alice 1869-1947 . . . . .WWasWT
Fishburne, Larry CTFT-7
Fisher, Carrie 1956- CTFT-7
   Earlier sketch in CTFT-2
Fisher, Dan CTFT-6
Fisher, Douglas 1934- CTFT-1
Fisher, Frances CTFT-8
Fisher, Jules 1937- CTFT-4
   Earlier sketch in WWT-17
Fisher, Linda 1943- CTFT-9
   Earlier sketch in CTFT-1
Fisher, Lola 1896-1926 . . . . .WWasWT
Fisher, Robert CTFT-4
Fisk, Jack 1934- CTFT-8
Fiske, Harrison Grey 1861-1942 . .WWasWT
Fiske, Minnie Maddern
   1865-1932 . . . . .WWasWT
Fiske, Stephen 1840-1916 . . . . .WWasWT
Fitelson, William H. 1905- CTFT-5
Fitz, Paddy
   See McGoohan, Patrick CTFT-5
Fitzgerald, Aubrey Whitestone
   1876-? .WWasWT

Fitzgerald, Barry 1888-1961 . . . . .WWasWT
Fitzgerald, Edward 1876-? . . . . . . .WWasWT
Fitzgerald, Geraldine 1914- CTFT-8
   Earlier sketches in CTFT-1, WWT-17
Fitzgerald, Neil 1893- WWT-17
Fitzgerald, Percy Hetherington
   1834-1925 . . . . .WWasWT
Fitzgerald, S. J. Adair
   1859-1925 . . . . .WWasWT
Fitzgerald, Walter 1896- . . . . .WWasWT
Fitzsimmons, Maureen
   See O'Hara, Maureen CTFT-8
Fjelde, Rolf 1926- CTFT-1
Flagg, Fannie 1944- CTFT-1
Flaherty, Lanny 1942- CTFT-3
Flanagan, Bud 1896-1968 . . . . . . .WWasWT
Flanagan, Fionnula 1941- CTFT-8
Flanagan, Hallie 1890-1969 . . . . . .WWasWT
Flanagan, Pauline 1925- CTFT-1
Flanagan, Richard ?-1917 . . . . . . .WWasWT
Flanders, Ed 1934- CTFT-6
Flanders, Michael 1922-1975 . . . . .WWasWT
Flannery, Peter 1951- CTFT-5
   Earlier sketch in WWT-17
Flatt, Ernest O. 1918- CTFT-2
Flavin, Martin 1883-1967 . . . . . . .WWasWT
Fleetwood, Susan 1944- CTFT-6
   Earlier sketch in WWT-17
Fleischer, Charles 1950- CTFT-9
Fleischer, Richard CTFT-1
Fleming, Brandon 1889-? . . . . .WWasWT
Fleming, George 1858-1938 . . . . . .WWasWT
Fleming, Ian 1888-1969 . . . . .WWasWT
Fleming, Lucy 1947- CTFT-5
   Earlier sketch in WWT-17
Fleming, Tom 1927- WWT-17
Flemming, Claude 1884-1952 . . . .WWasWT
Flemyng, Robert 1912- WWT-17
Flers, P. L. 1867-? . . . . .WWasWT
Flers, Robert de 1872-1932 . . . . . .WWasWT
Fletcher, Allen 1922- WWT-17
Fletcher, Bramwell 1904-1988 . . . . . .CTFT-7
   Earlier sketch in WWT-17
Fletcher, Duane 1953- CTFT-4
Fletcher, Louise 1936- CTFT-6
   Earler sketch in CTFT-2
Fletcher, Percy 1879-1932 . . . . . . .WWasWT
Fletcher, Robert 1923- WWT-17
Flexner, Anne Crawford
   1874-1955 . . . . .WWasWT
Flicker, Ted 1930- CTFT-1
Flint-Shipman, Veronica 1931- WWT-17
Flood, Ann CTFT-3
Flory, Regine 1894-1926 . . . . .WWasWT
Flowers, Wayland 1939-1988 . . . . . .CTFT-5
Floyd, Gwendolen ?-1950 . . . . . . .WWasWT
Fluellen, Joel 1908-1990 . . . . .CTFT-9
Flynn, Barbara CTFT-9
Flynn, Don 1928- CTFT-1
Fo, Dario 1926- CTFT-7
Foan, John
   See Bava, Mario CTFT-8
Foch, Nina 1924- CTFT-4
   Earlier sketch in WWT-17
Fodor, Ladislaus (Lazlo) 1898- . . .WWasWT
Fogarty, Jack 1923- CTFT-3
Fogerty, Elsie 1866-1945 . . . . .WWasWT
Fokine, Michel 1880-1942 . . . . . . .WWasWT
Foley, Ellen 1951- CTFT-7
Follows, Megan 1968- CTFT-7
Folsey, George Jr. 1939- CTFT-7
   Earlier sketch in CTFT-1
Fonda, Bridget CTFT-8

Fonda, Henry 1905-1982 . . . . .CTFT-1
   Earlier sketch in WWT-17
Fonda, Jane 1937- CTFT-7
   Earlier sketches in CTFT-1, WWT-17
Fonda, Peter 1940- CTFT-2
Fontana, Tom 1951- CTFT-2
Fontanne, Lynn 1892-1983 . . . . . . .WWT-16
Fonteyn, Margo 1919- . . . . .WWasWT
Foote, Hallie CTFT-7
Foote, Horton CTFT-4
   Earlier sketch in WWT-17
Foray, June CTFT-8
Forbes, Brenda 1909- WWT-17
Forbes, Bryan WWT-14
Forbes, Freddie 1895-1952 . . . . . . .WWasWT
Forbes, James 1871-1938 . . . . .WWasWT
Forbes, Mary 1880-1964 . . . . .WWasWT
Forbes, Meriel 1913- WWT-17
Forbes, Norman 1858-1932 . . . . . . .WWasWT
Forbes, Ralph 1905-1951 . . . . .WWasWT
Forbes-Robertson, Beatrice
   1883-1967 . . . . .WWasWT
Forbes-Robertson, Frank
   1885-1947 . . . . .WWasWT
Forbes-Robertson, Jean
   1905-1962 . . . . .WWasWT
Forbes-Robertson, Johnstone
   1853-1937 . . . . .WWasWT
Ford, Audrey . . . . .WWasWT
Ford, Constance CTFT-1
Ford, Ed E. . . . . .WWasWT
Ford, Frances 1939- CTFT-1
Ford, Glenn 1916- CTFT-3
Ford, Harriet 1868-1949 . . . . .WWasWT
Ford, Harrison 1942- CTFT-8
Ford, Harry 1877-? . . . . .WWasWT
Ford, Helen . . . . .WWasWT
Ford, Nancy 1935- CTFT-1
Ford, Paul 1901-1976 . . . . .WWT-16
Ford, Ruth 1915- CTFT-7
   Earlier sketch in WWT-17
Ford, Wallace 1898-1966 . . . . .WWasWT
Ford Davies, Oliver CTFT-9
Forde, Florrie 1876-1940 . . . . .WWasWT
Fordin, Hugh 1935- CTFT-1
Foreman, Carl 1914-1984 . . . . .CTFT-2
Foreman, John CTFT-5
Foreman, Richard 1937- CTFT-6
Forlow, Ted 1931- CTFT-6
   Earlier sketch in CTFT-2
Forman, Milos 1932- CTFT-4
   Earlier sketch in CTFT-1
Formby, George 1904-1961 . . . . . .WWasWT
Fornes, Maria Irene 1930- CTFT-1
Forrest, Anne 1897- . . . . .WWasWT
Forrest, Frederic 1936- CTFT-7
Forrest, Sam 1870-1944 . . . . .WWasWT
Forrest, Steve 1925- CTFT-7
Forster, Robert 1941- CTFT-2
Forster, Wilfred 1872-1924 . . . . . .WWasWT
Forster-Bovill, W. B. 1871-? . . . . .WWasWT
Forsyth, Bill 1948- CTFT-6
Forsyth, Bruce 1928- CTFT-6
   Earlier sketch in WWT-17
Forsyth, Matthew 1896-1954 . . . . .WWasWT
Forsyth, Neil 1866-1915 . . . . .WWasWT
Forsythe, Charles CTFT-1
Forsythe, Colin 1961- CTFT-4
Forsythe, Henderson 1917- CTFT-4
   Earlier sketch in WWT-17
Forsythe, John 1918- CTFT-7
   Earlier sketch in CTFT-1
Fortescus, Miss 1862-1950 . . . . . . .WWasWT

Foss, George R. 1859-1938 ...... WWasWT
Fosse, Bob 1927-1987 .... CTFT-5
    Earlier sketches in CTFT-1, WWT-17
Fossey, Brigitte 1946- CTFT-8
Foster, Basil S. 1882-1959 .... WWasWT
Foster, Barry WWT-17
Foster, Claiborne 1896- .... WWasWT
Foster, David 1929- CTFT-5
Foster, Edward 1876-1927 .... WWasWT
Foster, Frances 1924- CTFT-6
    Earlier sketch in WWT-17
Foster, Gloria 1936- CTFT-8
    Earlier sketch in WWT-17
Foster, Jodie 1962- CTFT-7
    Earlier sketch in CTFT-2
Foster, Julia 1942- CTFT-4
    Earlier sketch in WWT-17
Foster, Meg 1948- CTFT-7
Foster, Norman 1900-1976 ...... WWasWT
Foster, Paul 1931- WWT-17
Foster, Phoebe 1896- .... WWasWT
Fowlds, Derek 1937- CTFT-9
Fowler, Beth 1940- CTFT-8
Fowler, Clement 1924- CTFT-1
Fowler, Keith 1939- CTFT-4
Fox, Bernard CTFT-8
Fox, Della 1871-1913 .... WWasWT
Fox, Edward 1937- CTFT-7
Fox, Frederick 1910- .... WWasWT
Fox, James 1939- CTFT-8
Fox, Michael J. 1961- CTFT-5
    Brief Entry in CTFT-2
Fox, Robin 1913-1971 .... WWasWT
Fox, Sidney 1910-1942 .... WWasWT
Fox, Terry Curtis 1948- CTFT-1
Fox, Will H. 1858-? .... WWasWT
Fox, William 1911- WWT-17
Fox, William
    See Fox, James CTFT-8
Foxworth, Robert 1941- CTFT-4
    Earlier sketch in CTFT-1
Foxx, Redd 1922- CTFT-2
Foy, Eddie 1854-1928 .... WWasWT
Fraker, Bill
    See Fraker, William A. CTFT-9
Fraker, William
    See Fraker, William A. CTFT-9
Fraker, William A. 1923- CTFT-9
France, Alexis 1906- .... WWasWT
France, Anatole 1868-1949 ...... WWasWT
France, Richard 1938- CTFT-4
France-Ellys .... WWasWT
Francine, Anne 1917- CTFT-4
Franciosa, Anthony 1928- CTFT-3
Francis, Alfred 1909-1985 .... WWT-17
Francis, Arlene 1908- CTFT-5
    Earlier sketch in WWT-17
Francis, Clive 1946- WWT-17
Francis, Doris 1903- .... WWasWT
Francis, Freddie 1917- CTFT-8
Francis, Ivor 1917-1986 .... CTFT-4
Francis, Kay 1905-1968 .... WWasWT
Francis, M. E. 1855-1930 .... WWasWT
Franciscus, James 1934- CTFT-3
Frank, Bruno 1887-1945 .... WWasWT
Frank, Judy 1936- CTFT-7
Frank, Mary K. ?-1988 .... CTFT-1
Frank, Richard 1953- CTFT-8
Frankau, Ronald 1894-1951 ..... WWasWT
Frankel, Gene 1923- CTFT-5
    Earlier sketch in WWT-17
Frankel, Kenneth 1941- CTFT-9
    Earlier sketch in CTFT-1

Franken, Rose 1895-1988 .... WWasWT
Frankenheimer, John 1930- CTFT-5
Frankiss, Betty 1912- .... WWasWT
Franklin, Bonnie 1944- CTFT-7
    Earlier sketch in CTFT-1
Franklin, Harold B. 1890-1941 ... WWasWT
Franklin, Irene 1876-1941 ...... WWasWT
Franklin, Pamela 1950- CTFT-8
Franklyn, Leo 1897-1975 .... WWasWT
Franks, Laurie 1929- CTFT-1
Frann, Mary CTFT-4
Franz, Dennis 1944- CTFT-7
Franz, Eduard 1902-1983 .... WWT-16
Franz, Elizabeth 1941- CTFT-6
Franz, Joy 1945- CTFT-1
Fraser, Agnes .... WWasWT
Fraser, Alec 1884-? .... WWasWT
Fraser, Alison 1955- CTFT-5
Fraser, Bill 1908-1987 .... CTFT-5
    Earlier sketch in WWT-17
Fraser, John 1931- WWT-17
Fraser, Lovat 1903- .... WWasWT
Fraser, Moyra 1923- WWT-17
Fraser, Shelagh WWT-17
Fraser, Winifred 1872-? .... WWasWT
Fraser-Simon, Harold
    1878-1944 .... WWasWT
Fratti, Mario 1927- CTFT-2
Frayn, Michael 1933- CTFT-6
    Earlier sketch in WWT-17
Frazee, Harry Herbert
    1880-1929 .... WWasWT
Frazer, Rupert 1947- CTFT-2
Frazier, Ronald 1942- CTFT-1
Frears, Stephen 1941- CTFT-6
Frederick, Pauline 1885-1938 .... WWasWT
Fredrick, Burry 1925- WWT-17
Freear, Louie 1871-1939 .... WWasWT
Freedley, George 1904-1967 ..... WWasWT
Freedley, Vinton 1891-1969 ...... WWasWT
Freedman, Bill 1929- WWT-17
Freedman, Gerald 1927- CTFT-6
    Earlier sketch in WWT-17
Freek, George 1945- CTFT-1
Freeman, Al Jr. 1934- CTFT-7
    Earlier sketch in WWT-17
Freeman, Arny 1908- WWT-17
Freeman, Frank 1892-1962 ...... WWasWT
Freeman, Harry .... WWasWT
Freeman, Morgan 1937- CTFT-6
    Earlier sketch in WWT-17
Freeman, Stella 1910-1936 ...... WWasWT
Frees, Paul 1919-1986 .... CTFT-4
Freleng, Friz 1906- CTFT-8
Freleng, I.
    See Freleng, Friz CTFT-8
Frelich, Phyllis 1944- CTFT-2
French, Elise .... WWasWT
French, Elizabeth .... WWasWT
French, Harold 1900- WWT-17
French, Hermene 1924- .... WWasWT
French, Hugh 1910- .... WWasWT
French, Leslie 1904- WWT-17
French, Stanley J. 1908-1964 ..... WWasWT
French, Valerie 1932- CTFT-4
    Earlier sketch in WWT-17
French, Victor 1934-1989 .... CTFT-6
Fresnay, Pierre 1897-1973 .... WWasWT
Freudenberger, Daniel 1945- WWT-17
Frewer, Matt 1958- CTFT-8
Frey, Leonard 1938-1988 .... WWT-17
Frey, Nathaniel 1913-1970 ...... WWasWT
Fridell, Squire 1943- CTFT-1

Fried, Martin 1937- WWT-17
Friedkin, William 1939- CTFT-5
Friedlander, W. B. ?-1968 .... WWasWT
Friedman, Bruce Jay 1930- CTFT-3
    Earlier sketches in CTFT-1, WWT-17
Friedman, Jake 1867-? .... WWasWT
Friedman, Lewis 1948- CTFT-4
Friedman, Phil 1921-1988 .... CTFT-1
Friedman, Stephen 1937- CTFT-4
Friel, Brian 1929- WWT-17
Friels, Colin CTFT-8
Friendly, Ed 1922- CTFT-8
Friendly, Fred 1915- CTFT-6
Frierson, Monte L. 1930- CTFT-4
Fries, Charles CTFT-2
Friesen, Rick 1943- CTFT-1
Friganzi, Trixie 1870-1955 ...... WWasWT
Friml, Charles Rudolf
    1881-1972 .... WWasWT
Frisby, Terence 1932- WWT-17
Frisch, Max 1911- WWT-17
Frith, J. Leslie 1889-1961 .... WWasWT
Frohman, Charles 1860-1915 ..... WWasWT
Frohman, Daniel 1851-1940 ..... WWasWT
Frost, David 1939- CTFT-3
Froyez, Maurice .... WWasWT
Fruchtman, Milton Allen CTFT-1
Fry, Christopher 1907- WWT-17
Fryer, Robert 1920- CTFT-2
    Earlier sketch in WWT-17
Fugard, Athol 1932- CTFT-3
    Earlier sketches in CTFT-1, WWT-17
Fuller, Benjamin John 1875-? .... WWasWT
Fuller, Charles 1939- CTFT-7
Fuller, Frances 1908- .... WWasWT
Fuller, Janice 1942- CTFT-2
Fuller, John G. 1913- CTFT-1
Fuller, Loie 1862-1928 .... WWasWT
Fuller, Rosalinde WWT-17
Fuller, Samuel 1911- CTFT-8
Fullerton, Fiona 1956- CTFT-8
Fulton, Charles J. 1857-1938 ..... WWasWT
Fulton, Maude 1881-1950 .... WWasWT
Funt, Allen 1914- CTFT-9
Furber, Douglas 1885-1961 ...... WWasWT
Furguson, Wesley
    See Link, William CTFT-6
Furniss, Grace Livingston
    1864-1938 .... WWasWT
Furse, Judith 1912- .... WWasWT
Furse, Roger 1903-1972 .... WWasWT
Furst, Anton CTFT-8
Furst, Stephen 1955- CTFT-4
Furth, George 1932- CTFT-3
    Earlier sketch in WWT-17
Fyfe, H. Hamilton 1869-1951 .... WWasWT

G

Gabel, Martin 1912-1986 .... CTFT-4
    Earlier sketch in WWT-17
Gable, Clark 1901-1960 .... WWasWT
Gable, June CTFT-1
Gabor, Eva CTFT-1
Gabor, Zsa Zsa 1919- CTFT-3
Gabriel, Gilbert W. 1890-1952 ... WWasWT
Gadd, Renee 1908- .... WWasWT
Gaffney, Liam 1911- .... WWasWT
Gagliano, Frank CTFT-4
    Earlier sketch in WWT-17
Gahagan, Helen 1900- .... WWasWT
Gaige, Crosby 1882-1949 .... WWasWT

Gail, Max 1943- CTFT-2
Gail, Zoe ....WWasWT
Gaines, Boyd 1953- CTFT-8
Gaines, Charles L. 1942- CTFT-3
Galarno, Bill 1938- CTFT-7
Gale, Bob 1952- CTFT-7
Gale, John 1929- CTFT-3
　Earlier sketch in WWT-17
Gale, Zona 1874-1938 ....WWasWT
Galipaux, Felix 1860-1931 ....WWasWT
Gallacher, Tom 1934- CTFT-5
　Earlier sketch in WWT-17
Gallagher, Helen 1926- CTFT-5
　Earlier sketch in WWT-17
Gallagher, Mary 1947- CTFT-1
Gallagher, Megan CTFT-7
Gallagher, Peter 1955- CTFT-9
　Brief Entry in CTFT-3
Gallagher, Richard 1900-1955 ....WWasWT
Galland, Bertha 1876-1932 ......WWasWT
Gallimore, Florrie 1867-? ....WWasWT
Gallo, Paul CTFT-7
Galloway, Don 1937- CTFT-2
Galloway, Jane 1950- CTFT-1
Galsworthy, John 1867-1933 .....WWasWT
Galvina, Dino 1890-1960 ....WWasWT
Gam, Rita 1928- CTFT-1
Gamble, Tom 1898- ....WWasWT
Gambon, Michael 1940- CTFT-5
　Earlier sketch in WWT-17
Gammon, James 1940- CTFT-3
Gance, Abel 1889-1981 ....CTFT-2
Ganz, Bruno 1941- CTFT-8
Ganz, Tony CTFT-9
Garber, Victor 1949- CTFT-9
Garbo, Greta 1905-1990 ....CTFT-9
Garcia, Andy 1956- CTFT-8
Garde, Betty 1905-1989 ....CTFT-9
　Earlier sketch in WWT-17
Garden, E. M. 1845-1939 ....WWasWT
Garden, Graeme 1943- CTFT-6
　Earlier sketch in WWT-17
Gardenia, Vincent 1922- CTFT-7
　Earlier sketches in CTFT-2, WWT-17
Gardiner, Cyril 1897- ....WWasWT
Gardiner, Reginald 1903-1980 ....WWasWT
Gardner, Ava 1922-1990 ....CTFT-9
　Earlier sketch in CTFT-3
Gardner, Herb 1934- CTFT-6
Gardner, Shayle 1890-1945 ......WWasWT
Gardner, Will 1879-? ....WWasWT
Garfein, Jack 1930- CTFT-5
Garfield, John 1913-1952 ....WWasWT
Garfield, Julie CTFT-1
Gargan, William (Dennis)
　1905-1979 ....WWasWT
Garland, Beverly CTFT-1
Garland, Geoff 1926- CTFT-1
Garland, Patrick WWT-17
Garland, Robert 1895-1955 ......WWasWT
Garner, James 1928- CTFT-9
　Earlier sketch in CTFT-3
Garnett, Edward 1868-1937 ......WWasWT
Garnett, Gale CTFT-1
Garr, Teri CTFT-3
Garrett, Arthur 1869-1941 ......WWasWT
Garrett, Betty 1919- CTFT-4
　Earlier sketch in WWT-17
Garrett, Joy CTFT-1
Garrick, Gus ....WWasWT
Garrick, John 1902- ....WWasWT
Garrison, David 1952- CTFT-4
Garside, John 1887-1958 ....WWasWT

Garson, Barbara 1941- CTFT-1
Garson, Greer 1908- CTFT-8
　Earlier sketch in WWasWT
Gary, Lorraine CTFT-7
Gascoigne, Bamber 1935- WWT-17
Gascon, Jean 1921-1988 ....WWT-17
Gaskill, William 1930- CTFT-3
　Earlier sketch in WWT-17
Gaspard, Ray
　See Gaspard, Raymond L. CTFT-9
Gaspard, Raymond L. 1949- CTFT-9
　Earlier sketch in CTFT-1
Gassman, Vittorio 1922- CTFT-8
Gassner, John 1903-1967 ....WWasWT
Gates, Eleanor 1875-1951 ....WWasWT
Gates, Larry 1915- WWT-17
Gateson, Marjorie 1897-1977 .....WWasWT
Gatti, John M. 1872-1929 ....WWasWT
Gaudet, Christie 1957- CTFT-4
Gaul, George 1885-1939 ....WWasWT
Gaunt, William 1937- WWT-17
Gavault, Paul 1867-? ....WWasWT
Gavin, John 1932- CTFT-2
Gawthorne, Peter A. 1884-1962 ..WWasWT
Gaxton, William 1893-1963 ......WWasWT
Gay, John 1924- CTFT-9
Gay, Maisie 1883-1945 ....WWasWT
Gay, Noel 1898-1954 ....WWasWT
Gaye, Freda 1907-1986 ....CTFT-4
　Earlier sketch in WWasWT
Gaynes, George 1917- CTFT-8
　Earlier sketch in WWT-17
Gaythorne, Pamela 1882-? ....WWasWT
Gazzara, Ben 1930- CTFT-3
　Earlier sketch in WWT-17
Gazzo, Michael V. 1923- CTFT-8
　Earlier sketch in CTFT-1
Gear, Luella 1899- ....WWasWT
Geary, Anthony 1947- CTFT-6
　Brief Entry in CTFT-2
Gedrick, Jason CTFT-7
Gee, George 1895-1959 ....WWasWT
Geer, Ellen 1941- CTFT-1
Geer, Will 1902-1978 ....WWT-16
Geeson, Judy 1948- CTFT-8
Geffen, David 1943- CTFT-5
Gelb, Arthur 1924- CTFT-1
Gelb, Barbara CTFT-1
Gelbart, Larry 1923- CTFT-3
　Earlier sketches in CTFT-1, WWT-17
Gelber, Jack 1932- CTFT-5
　Earlier sketch in WWT-17
Geller, Marc 1959- CTFT-1
Gellner, Julius 1899- WWT-17
Gemier, Firmin 1865-1933 ....WWasWT
Gemmell, Don 1903- WWT-17
Gems, Pam 1925- CTFT-6
　Earlier sketch in WWT-17
Genee, Dame Adeline
　1878-1970 ....WWasWT
Genet, Jean 1910-1986 ....CTFT-3
　Earlier sketch in WWT-17
Geniat, Marchell ?-1959 ....WWasWT
Genn, Leo 1905-1978 ....WWT-16
Gennaro, Peter 1919- CTFT-4
George, A. E. 1869-1920 ....WWasWT
George, Colin 1929- CTFT-2
　Earlier sketch in WWT-17
George, Gladys 1904-1954 ....WWasWT
George, Grace 1879-1961 ....WWasWT
George, Lynda Day 1946- CTFT-8
George, Marie 1879-1955 ....WWasWT
George, Muriel 1883-1965 ....WWasWT

Gerald, Ara 1900-1957 ....WWasWT
Geraldy, Paul 1885-? ....WWasWT
Gerard, Gil 1943- CTFT-6
Gerard, Teddie 1892-1942 ......WWasWT
Geray, Steve 1904-1973 ....WWasWT
Gerber, Ella 1916- CTFT-1
Gerdes, George 1948- CTFT-4
Gere, Richard 1949- CTFT-6
　Earlier sketch in CTFT-2
German, Edward 1862-1936 .....WWasWT
Gerrard Gene 1892-1971 ....WWasWT
Gerringer, Robert 1926-1989 .....CTFT-2
Gerrity, Dan 1958- CTFT-7
Gerroll, Daniel 1951- CTFT-5
　Earlier sketch in CTFT-1
Gershwin, George 1898-1937 ....WWasWT
Gershwin, Ira 1896-1983 ....WWasWT
Gerstad, John 1924- WWT-17
Gersten, Bernard 1923- CTFT-5
　Earlier sketch in WWT-17
Gertz, Jami 1965- CTFT-7
Gerussi, Bruno ....WWasWT
Gest, Morris 1881-1942 ....WWasWT
Getty, Estelle 1923- CTFT-6
Geva, Tamara 1907- ....WWasWT
Gheusi, Pierre B. 1867-? ....WWasWT
Ghostley, Alice 1926- CTFT-2
　Earlier sketch in WWT-17
Giagni, D. J. 1950- CTFT-4
Giannini, Giancarlo 1942- CTFT-7
Giannini, Olga ....WWasWT
Gibb, Lee
　See Waterhouse, Keith Spencer ..CTFT-5
Gibbons, Arthur 1871-1935 ......WWasWT
Gibbs, Marla 1931- CTFT-3
Gibbs, Nancy ?-1956 ....WWasWT
Gibbs, Timothy 1967- CTFT-5
Gibson, Brenda 1870-? ....WWasWT
Gibson, Chloe 1899- ....WWasWT
Gibson, Henry 1935- CTFT-3
Gibson, Mel 1956- CTFT-6
Gibson, Michael 1944- CTFT-5
Gibson, William 1914- CTFT-2
　Earlier sketch in WWT-17
Gibson, Wynne 1905-1987 ....WWasWT
Giddens, George 1845-1920 ......WWasWT
Gideon, Melville J. 1884-1933 ....WWasWT
Gielgud, John 1904- CTFT-7
　Earlier sketches in CTFT-1, WWT-17
Gielgud, Val 1900-1981 ....WWasWT
Gignoux, Regis 1878-? ....WWasWT
Gilbert, Bruce 1947- CTFT-9
　Earlier sketch in CTFT-1
Gilbert, Jean 1879-1943 ....WWasWT
Gilbert, Lewis 1920- CTFT-9
Gilbert, Lou 1909-1978 ....WWT-17
Gilbert, Melissa 1964- CTFT-5
　Brief Entry in CTFT-2
Gilbert, Olive WWT-17
Gilbert, Ronnie 1926- CTFT-2
Gilder, Rosamond de Kay
　1891-1986 ....CTFT-4
　Earlier sketch in WWT-17
Gilford, Jack 1909-1990 ....CTFT-2
　Earlier sketch in WWT-17
Gilhooley, Jack 1940- CTFT-1
Gill, Basil 1877-1955 ....WWasWT
Gill, Brendan 1914- WWT-17
Gill, Paul ?-1934 ....WWasWT
Gill, Peter 1939- CTFT-2
　Earlier sketch in WWT-17
Gill, Tom 1916-1971 ....WWT-16

Gillespie, Dana 1949- CTFT-5
Earlier sketch in WWT-17
Gillespie, Richard 1878-1952.....WWasWT
Gillespie, Robert 1933- CTFT-6
Earlier sketch in WWT-17
Gillett, Eric 1893-...............WWasWT
Gillette, Anita 1936-..............CTFT-4
Earlier sketch in WWT-17
Gillette, William 1855-1937 ......WWasWT
Gilliam, Terry 1940- CTFT-5
Gillian, Jerry
See Gilliam, Terry CTFT-5
Gilliatt, Penelope Ann
Douglass CTFT-1
Gillie, Jean 1915-1949 ....WWasWT
Gilliland, Helen 1897-1942 ....WWasWT
Gillman, Mabelle 1880-? ....WWasWT
Gillmore, Frank 1867-1943 ......WWasWT
Gillmore, Margalo 1897-1986 ....WWasWT
Gilmore, Janette 1905-..........WWasWT
Gilmore, Peter 1931- WWT-17
Gilmore, Virginia 1919-1986 .....WWasWT
Gilmore, W. H. ....WWasWT
Gilmour, Brian 1894-1954 ....WWasWT
Gilpin, Charles 1878-1930 ......WWasWT
Gilpin, Jack 1951- CTFT-1
Gilroy, Frank D. 1925- CTFT-3
Earlier sketch in WWT-17
Gingold, Hermione 1897-1987 .....CTFT-5
Earlier sketches in CTFT-2, WWT-17
Ginisty, Paul 1858-1932 ....WWasWT
Ginner, Ruby 1886-? ....WWasWT
Ginsbury, Norman 1903-........WWT-17
Ginty, Robert 1948- CTFT-2
Giordano, Tony 1939- CTFT-5
Giovanni, Paul 1940-1990 ....CTFT-9
Giraudeau, Philippe 1955- CTFT-4
Giraudoux, Jean 1882-1944 ......WWasWT
Gish, Dorothy 1898-1968 ....WWasWT
Gish, Lillian 1893- CTFT-4
Earlier sketch in WWT-17
Gisondi, John 1949- CTFT-4
Gitana, Gertie 1887-1957 ....WWasWT
Glaser, Lulu 1874-1958 ....WWasWT
Glaser, Paul Michael CTFT-3
Glaspell, Susan 1882-1948 ......WWasWT
Glass, Dudley 1899-..........WWasWT
Glass, Joanna McClelland
1936- CTFT-1
Glass, Montague 1877-1934 ......WWasWT
Glass, Ned 1906-1984 ....CTFT-2
Glass, Philip 1937- CTFT-6
Glass, Ron CTFT-3
Glassco, Bill 1935- CTFT-5
Earlier sketch in WWT-17
Glassford, David 1866-1935 .....WWasWT
Glaze, Susan 1956-..............CTFT-4
Gleason, Jackie 1916-1987 ....CTFT-5
Gleason, James 1886-1959 ....WWasWT
Gleason, Joanna 1950- CTFT-6
Gleason, John 1941-..............CTFT-5
Earlier sketch in WWT-17
Gleason, Paul 1944- CTFT-7
Glendinning, Ernest 1884-1936 ...WWasWT
Glendinning, Ethel 1910- ....WWasWT
Glendinning, John 1857-1916 ....WWasWT
Glenister, Frank 1860-1945 ......WWasWT
Glenn, Scott 1942- CTFT-4
Glennie, Brian 1912- ....WWasWT
Glenny, Charles H. 1857-1922 ...WWasWT
Glenville, Peter 1913-...........WWT-17
Glenville, Shaun 1884-1968 ......WWasWT
Gless, Sharon 1943-..............CTFT-6

Glines, John 1933- CTFT-1
Globus, Yoram CTFT-6
Glossop-Harris, Florence
See Harris, Florence Glossop ..WWasWT
Glover, Crispin CTFT-6
Glover, Danny 1947- CTFT-5
Glover, Halcott 1877-1949 ....WWasWT
Glover, James Mackey 1861-? ....WWasWT
Glover, John 1944- CTFT-4
Earlier sketch in WWT-17
Glover, Julian 1935- CTFT-4
Earlier sketch in WWT-17
Glover, William 1911- CTFT-3
Gluckman, Leon 1922-1978 ....WWT-16
Glynn, Carlin 1940- CTFT-1
Glynne, Angela 1933- ....WWasWT
Glynne, Mary 1898-1954 ....WWasWT
Gobel, George 1919-..............CTFT-7
Godard, Jean-Luc 1930- CTFT-7
Goddard, Charles W.
1879-1951 ....WWasWT
Goddard, Paulette 1911(?)-1990 ...CTFT-9
Goddard, Willoughby 1926- WWT-17
Godden, Jimmy 1879-1955 ....WWasWT
Godfrey, Derek 1924- WWT-17
Godfrey, Lynnie CTFT-5
Godfrey, Peter 1899-1970 ....WWasWT
Godfrey-Turner, L. ....WWasWT
Godunov, Alexander 1949-........CTFT-4
Goetz, Peter Michael 1941-........CTFT-2
Goetz, Ruth Goodman 1912- WWT-17
Goffin, Cora 1902-..............WWasWT
Goffin, Peter 1906-..............WWasWT
Goggin, Dan 1943-..............CTFT-3
Going, John 1936- CTFT-9
Earlier sketch in CTFT-1
Golan, Menahem 1931-...........CTFT-6
Goldberg, Leonard 1934- CTFT-3
Goldberg, Whoopi 1949- CTFT-6
Brief Entry in CTFT-3
Goldblum, Jeff 1952- CTFT-6
Goldemberg, Rose Leiman CTFT-1
Golden, Annie 1951- CTFT-7
Golden, John 1874-1955 ....WWasWT
Golden, Michael 1913-...........WWT-17
Goldie, F. Wyndham 1897-1957 ..WWasWT
Goldie, Hugh 1919- WWT-17
Goldin, Horace ....WWasWT
Goldman, Bo 1932- CTFT-8
Goldman, James 1927-............CTFT-8
Earlier sketch in WWT-17
Goldman, William 1931- CTFT-7
Goldner, Charles 1900-1955 .....WWasWT
Goldsmith, Jerry 1929- CTFT-3
Goldsmith, Merwin 1937- CTFT-4
Goldstone, James 1931-...........CTFT-9
Earlier sketch in CTFT-1
Goldthwait, Bob 1962-...........CTFT-6
Goldthwait, Bobcat
See Goldthwait, Bob CTFT-6
Goldwyn, Samuel Jr. 1926- CTFT-8
Gombell, Minna 1893-1973 ......WWasWT
Gooch, Steve 1945-..............CTFT-5
Earlier sketch in WWT-17
Goodall, Edyth 1886-1929 ....WWasWT
Gooden, Jack Kelly 1949-.........CTFT-6
Goodliffe, Michael 1914-1976 .....WWT-16
Goodman, Dody CTFT-4
Earlier sketch in WWT-17
Goodman, John 1952- CTFT-9
Goodman, Jules Eckert
1876-1962 ....WWasWT
Goodman, Philip ?-1940 ....WWasWT

Goodner, Carol 1904- ....WWasWT
Goodrich, Arthur 1878-1941 .....WWasWT
Goodrich, Edna 1883-1974 ....WWasWT
Goodrich, Louis 1865-1945 ......WWasWT
Goodson, Mark 1915- CTFT-3
Goodwin, J. Cheever 1850-1912 ..WWasWT
Goodwin, John 1921- WWT-17
Goodwin, Nat C. 1857-1920 .....WWasWT
Goolden, Richard 1895-..........WWT-17
Gopal, Ram 1917- ....WWasWT
Gorcey, Elizabeth 1965-..........CTFT-5
Gordon, Burt I. 1922- CTFT-8
Gordon, Charles Kilbourn
1888-? ....WWasWT
Gordon, Colin 1911-1972 ....WWasWT
Gordon, Douglas 1871-1935 .....WWasWT
Gordon, Gale 1906-..............CTFT-9
Earlier sketch in CTFT-3
Gordon, Gavin 1901-1970 ....WWasWT
Gordon, Hannah 1941- CTFT-1
Gordon, Hayes 1920- WWT-17
Gordon, Keith 1961- CTFT-7
Gordon, Kitty 1878-1974 ....WWasWT
Gordon, Leon 1884-1960 ....WWasWT
Gordon, Marjorie 1893- ....WWasWT
Gordon, Max 1892-1978 ....WWasWT
Gordon, Michael 1909-..........CTFT-1
Gordon, Noele 1923- ....WWasWT
Gordon, Ruth 1895-1985 ....CTFT-1
Earlier sketch in WWT-17
Gordon, Serena 1963- CTFT-9
Gordon-Lee, Kathleen ....WWasWT
Gordon-Lennox, Cosmo
1869-1921 ....WWasWT
Gordone, Charles Edward
1927- WWT-17
Gordy, Berry Jr. 1929-...........CTFT-5
Gore-Browne, Robert 1893- .....WWasWT
Gorelik, Mordecai 1899-1990 ......CTFT-9
Earlier sketch in WWT-17
Goring, Marius 1912-...........WWT-17
Gorman, Cliff CTFT-7
Earlier sketches in CTFT-2, WWT-17
Gorney, Karen Lynn CTFT-1
Gorshin, Frank 1934-............CTFT-1
Gorsse, Henry de 1868-? ....WWasWT
Gosling, Harold 1897-...........WWasWT
Goss, Bick 1942-................CTFT-4
Gossett, Louis Jr. 1936- CTFT-6
Gotlieb, Ben 1954- CTFT-1
Gott, Barbara ?-1944 ....WWasWT
Gottfried, Martin 1933- WWT-17
Gottlieb, Carl 1938-..............CTFT-6
Earlier sketch in CTFT-1
Gottlieb, Morton 1921- CTFT-5
Earlier sketch in WWT-17
Gottschalk, Ferdinand
1858-1944 ....WWasWT
Gough, Michael 1916-............CTFT-6
Earlier sketch in WWT-17
Gould, Diana 1913-.............WWasWT
Gould, Elliott 1938- CTFT-6
Earlier sketches in CTFT-2, WWT-17
Gould, Harold 1923- CTFT-8
Earlier sketch in CTFT-1
Gould, John 1940- CTFT-5
Earlier sketch in WWT-17
Gould, Morton 1913-............CTFT-1
Goulding, Edmund 1891-1959 ....WWasWT
Goulet, Robert 1933-.............CTFT-4
Earlier sketch in WWT-17
Gow, James 1907-1952...........WWasWT
Gow, Ronald 1897-.............WWT-17

Grable, Betty 1916-1973 . . . . WWasWT
Grace, Nickolas 1949- CTFT-6
Earlier sketch in WWT-17
Grade, Lew 1906- CTFT-6
Earlier sketch in WWT-17
Grady, Don 1944- CTFT-2
Graff, Ilene CTFT-9
Graff, Randy 1955- CTFT-9
Graff, Todd CTFT-7
Graham, Charlotte Akwyoe
1959- CTFT-4
Graham, Harry 1874-1936 . . . . . . .WWasWT
Graham, Martha 1902- . . . . .WWasWT
Graham, Morland 1891-1949 . . . .WWasWT
Graham, Ronny 1919- CTFT-7
Earlier sketch in WWT-17
Graham, Violet 1890-1967 . . . . . . .WWasWT
Graham-Browne, W.
See Browne, W. Graham . . . . . .WWasWT
Grahame, Margot 1911- . . . . .WWasWT
Grainer, Ron 1922- WWT-17
Grainger, Gawn 1937- CTFT-5
Earlier sketch in WWT-17
Gramatica, Emma 1874-1965 . . . .WWasWT
Gramatica, Irma 1873-1962 . . . . . .WWasWT
Grammer, Kelsey CTFT-7
Granger, Farley 1925- CTFT-3
Granger, Percy 1945- CTFT-4
Earlier sketch in CTFT-1
Granger, Stewart 1913- CTFT-8
Earlier sketch in WWasWT
Granier, Jeanne ?-1939 . . . . .WWasWT
Granick, Harry 1898- CTFT-4
Grant, Bob 1932- WWT-17
Grant, Cary 1904-1986 . . . . .CTFT-4
Earlier sketch in CTFT-3
Grant, David CTFT-3
Grant, Hugh CTFT-8
Grant, Joyce 1924- CTFT-2
Earlier sketch in WWT-17
Grant, Lee 1931- CTFT-8
Earlier sketch in CTFT-1
Grant, Micki WWT-17
Grant, Neil 1882-? . . . . .WWasWT
Grant, Pauline WWT-17
Grant, Richard E. 1957- CTFT-6
Grantham, Wilfrid 1898- . . . . .WWasWT
Granville, Bernard 1886-1936 . . . .WWasWT
Granville, Charlotte 1863-1942 . . .WWasWT
Granville, Sydney ?-1959 . . . . .WWasWT
Granville-Barker, Harley
1877-1946 . . . . .WWasWT
Granville-Barker, Helen ?-1950 . . .WWasWT
Grassle, Karen CTFT-3
Grasso, Giovanni 1875-1930 . . . . .WWasWT
Grattan, Harry 1867-1951 . . . . . . .WWasWT
Gratton, Fred 1894-1966 . . . . .WWasWT
Graves, Clotilde Inez Mary
1863-1932 . . . . .WWasWT
Graves, George 1876-1949 . . . . . . .WWasWT
Graves, Peter 1911- CTFT-2
Earlier sketch in WWT-17
Graves, Peter 1926- CTFT-1
Graves, Rupert 1963- CTFT-8
Gray, Amlin 1946- CTFT-1
Gray, Barry 1916- CTFT-2
Gray, Charles 1928- CTFT-8
Earlier sketch in WWT-17
Gray, Dolores 1924- CTFT-4
Earlier sketch in WWT-17
Gray, Dulcie 1919- CTFT-5
Earlier sketch in WWT-17
Gray, Elspet 1929- WWT-17

Gray, Eve 1904- . . . . .WWasWT
Gray, Jennifer 1916-1962 . . . . .WWasWT
Gray, Linda 1910- WWT-17
Gray, Linda CTFT-2
Gray, Nicholas Stuart 1919- WWT-17
Gray, Oliver
See Gray, Charles CTFT-8
Gray, Richard 1896- . . . . .WWasWT
Gray, Sam 1923- CTFT-1
Gray, Simon 1936- CTFT-6
Earlier sketches in CTFT-2, WWT-17
Gray, Spalding 1941- CTFT-7
Gray, Terence 1895- . . . . .WWasWT
Graydon, J. L. 1844-? . . . . .WWasWT
Grayson, Kathryn 1924- CTFT-1
Grayson, Richard 1925- CTFT-4
Greaza, Walter N. 1900-1973 . . . .WWasWT
Green, Abel 1900-1973 . . . . .WWasWT
Green, Adolph 1915- CTFT-2
Green, Dorothy 1886-1961 . . . . . .WWasWT
Green, Guy CTFT-1
Green, Harry 1892-1958 . . . . .WWasWT
Green, Hilton 1929- CTFT-1
Green, Janet 1914- . . . . .WWasWT
Green, Joann 1955- CTFT-1
Green, Johnny 1908-1989 . . . . .CTFT-3
Green, Mabel 1890- . . . . .WWasWT
Green, Marion 1890-1956 . . . . . . .WWasWT
Green, Martyn 1899-1975 . . . . . . .WWT-16
Green, Mitzi 1920-1968 . . . . .WWasWT
Green, Paul 1894-1981 . . . . .WWT-17
Green, Stanley 1923 . . . . .CTFT-1
Green, William 1926- CTFT-1
Greenbaum, Hyam 1910- . . . . .WWasWT
Greenberg, Edward M. 1924- CTFT-9
Earlier sketch in CTFT-1
Greenblatt, William R. 1944- CTFT-7
Greene, Clay M. 1850-1933 . . . . . .WWasWT
Greene, David 1921- CTFT-1
Greene, Ellen CTFT-4
Greene, Evie 1876-1917 . . . . .WWasWT
Greene, Graham 1904- WWT-17
Greene, James 1926- CTFT-9
Earlier sketch in CTFT-1
Greene, Lorne 1915-1987 . . . . .CTFT-5
Earlier sketch in CTFT-3
Greene, Lyn 1954- CTFT-2
Greene, Richard 1946- CTFT-1
Greener, Dorothy 1917-1971 . . . . .WWasWT
Greenfeld, Josh 1928- CTFT-2
Greenhut, Robert CTFT-8
Greenstreet, Sydney 1879-1954 . . .WWasWT
Greenwald, Joseph ?-1938 . . . . . . .WWasWT
Greenwald, Robert Mark 1943- CTFT-6
Earlier sketch in CTFT-1
Greenwood, Bruce CTFT-9
Greenwood, Charlotte
1893-1978 . . . . .WWasWT
Greenwood, Jane 1934- CTFT-4
Earlier sketch in WWT-17
Greenwood, Joan 1921-1987 . . . . . .CTFT-4
Earlier sketch in WWT-17
Greenwood, Walter 1903-1974 . . .WWasWT
Greer, Bettejane
See Greer, Jane CTFT-8
Greer, Dabbs 1917- CTFT-8
Greer, Jane 1924- CTFT-8
Greet, Clare 1871-1939 . . . . .WWasWT
Greet, Philip (Ben) 1857-1936 . . . .WWasWT
Gregg, Everley 1903-1959 . . . . . . .WWasWT
Gregg, Hubert 1916- WWT-17
Gregg, Virginia 1916-1986 . . . . .CTFT-2
Gregori, Mercia 1901- . . . . .WWasWT

Gregory, Andre CTFT-6
Earlier sketches in CTFT-2, WWT-17
Gregory, Don 1934- CTFT-3
Gregory, Dora 1872-1954 . . . . . . .WWasWT
Gregory, Frank 1884-? . . . . .WWasWT
Gregory, James 1911- CTFT-3
Gregory, Lady 1859-1932 . . . . . . .WWasWT
Gregory, Sara 1921- . . . . .WWasWT
Gregson, James R. 1889- . . . . .WWasWT
Grein, J. T. 1862-1935 . . . . .WWasWT
Grein, Mrs. J. T.
See Orme, Michael . . . . .WWasWT
Greist, Kim CTFT-5
Grenfell, Joyce 1910-1979 . . . . . . .WWT-16
Grenier, Zach 1959- CTFT-5
Gresac, Madame Fred . . . . .WWasWT
Greth, Roma 1935- CTFT-1
Grew, Mary 1902-1971 . . . . .WWasWT
Grey, Anne 1907- . . . . .WWasWT
Grey, Beryl 1927- . . . . .WWasWT
Grey, Clifford 1887-1941 . . . . .WWasWT
Grey, Eve .WWasWT
Grey, Jane 1883-1944 . . . . .WWasWT
Grey, Jennifer CTFT-7
Grey, Joel 1932- CTFT-4
Earlier sketch in WWT-17
Grey, Katherine 1873-1950 . . . . . .WWasWT
Grey, Mary . . . . .WWasWT
Gribble, George Dunning
1882-1956 . . . . .WWasWT
Gribble, Harry Wagstaff
1896-1981 . . . . .WWasWT
Gribov, Alexel Nikolaevich
1902- . . . . .WWasWT
Grifasi, Joe 1944- CTFT-1
Griffies, Ethel 1878-1975 . . . . .WWasWT
Griffin, Lynne CTFT-7
Griffin, Hayden 1943- WWT-17
Griffin, Merv 1925- CTFT-3
Griffin, Norman 1887-? . . . . .WWasWT
Griffin, Tom 1946- CTFT-1
Griffith, Andy 1926- CTFT-3
Griffith, David Wark 1880-1948 . . .WWasWT
Griffith, Hubert 1896-1953 . . . . . .WWasWT
Griffith, Hugh 1912-1980 . . . . .WWT-17
Griffith, Melanie 1957- CTFT-6
Griffiths, Derek 1946- WWT-17
Griffiths, Jane 1930-1975 . . . . .WWasWT
Griffiths, Trevor 1935- CTFT-6
Earlier sketch in WWT-17
Grimaldi, Alberto 1927- CTFT-8
Grimaldi, Marion 1926- WWT-17
Grimes, Stephen 1927-1988 . . . . . . .CTFT-7
Grimes, Tammy 1934- CTFT-9
Earlier sketches in CTFT-1, WWT-17
Grimston, Dorothy May . . . . .WWasWT
Grimwood, Herbert 1875-1929 . . .WWasWT
Grisman, Sam H. . . . . .WWasWT
Grismer, Joseph Rhode
1849-1922 . . . . .WWasWT
Griswold, Grace ?-1927 . . . . .WWasWT
Grizzard, George 1928- CTFT-6
Earlier sketch in WWT-17
Grodin, Charles 1935- CTFT-9
Earlier sketches in CTFT-3, WWT-17
Groenendaal, Cris 1948- CTFT-1
Groener, Harry 1951- CTFT-8
Grogg, Sam CTFT-5
Groh, David 1941- CTFT-3
Groody, Louise 1897-1961 . . . . . . .WWasWT
Gropper, Milton Herbert
1896-1955 . . . . .WWasWT

Grosbard, Ulu 1929- CTFT-2
  Earlier sketch in WWT-17
Gross, Ayre CTFT-8
Gross, Michael 1947- CTFT-6
Gross, Shelley 1921- CTFT-4
  Earlier sketch in WWT-17
Grossmith, Ena 1896-1944 ......WWasWT
Grossmith, George 1874-1912 ....WWasWT
Grossmith, Lawrence
  1877-1944 ....WWasWT
Grossmith, Weedon 1852-1919 ...WWasWT
Grossvogel, David I. 1925- CTFT-1
Grout, James 1927- CTFT-6
  Earlier sketch in WWT-17
Grout, Philip 1930- WWT-17
Grove, Barry 1951-..............CTFT-4
Grove, Fred 1851-1927 ....WWasWT
Groves, Charles 1875-1955 ......WWasWT
Groves, Fred 1880-1955 ....WWasWT
Gruenwald, Thomas 1935- CTFT-1
Grun, Bernard 1901-1972 ....WWasWT
Grundy, Lily ....WWasWT
Grundy, Sydney 1848-1914 ......WWasWT
Guardino, Harry 1925- CTFT-9
Guare, John 1938- CTFT-8
  Earlier sketches in CTFT-1, WWT-17
Guber, Lee 1920-1988 ....CTFT-6
  Earlier sketches in CTFT-4, WWT-17
Guber, Peter 1942- CTFT-2
Gudegast, Hans
  See Braeden, Eric CTFT-8
Guerra, Castulo 1945- CTFT-5
Guerra, Tonio 1920- CTFT-8
Guerrero, (Maria) 1868-1928 ....WWasWT
Guest, Christopher 1948-.........CTFT-7
Guest, Jean H. 1941- CTFT-5
Guetary, Georges 1915- CTFT-2
  Earlier sketch in WWasWT
Guettel, Henry A. 1928- CTFT-1
Guiches, Gustave 1860-? ....WWasWT
Guilbert, Yvette 1868-1944 ......WWasWT
Guillaume, Robert 1937- CTFT-9
  Earlier sketch in CTFT-3
Guillemaud, Marcel 1867-? ......WWasWT
Guimera, Angel 1845-1924 ......WWasWT
Guinness, Alec 1914- CTFT-8
  Earlier sketches in CTFT-1, WWT-17
Guinness, Matthew 1942- CTFT-8
Guinon, Albert 1863-1923 ......WWasWT
Guitry, Lucien 1860-1925 ......WWasWT
Guitry, Sacha 1885-1957 ....WWasWT
Gulager, Clu 1928- CTFT-7
Gullan, Campbell ?-1939 ....WWasWT
Gulliver, Charles 1882-1961 ....WWasWT
Gunn, Bill 1934-1989 ....CTFT-8
Gunn, Haidee 1882-1961 ....WWasWT
Gunn, Judy 1914-...............WWasWT
Gunn, Moses 1929- CTFT-4
  Earlier sketch in WWT-17
Gunning, Louise 1879-1960 ......WWasWT
Gunter, John 1938- CTFT-4
  Earlier sketch in WWT-17
Gunton, Bob 1945-..............CTFT-6
  Earlier sketch in CTFT-1
Gurney, A.R. Jr. 1930- CTFT-4
  Earlier sketch in WWT-17
Gurney, Claud 1897-1946 ....WWasWT
Gurney, Rachel CTFT-5
  Earlier sketch in WWT-17
Gussow, Mel 1933-..............WWT-17
Gustafson, Carol 1925- CTFT-1
Gustafson, Karin 1959- CTFT-3
Guthrie, Tyrone 1900-1971 ......WWasWT

Gutierrez, Gerald 1950- CTFT-4
  Earlier sketch in CTFT-1
Guttenberg, Steve 1958- CTFT-6
  Earlier sketch in CTFT-2
Guy, Jasmine 1964(?)- CTFT-9
Guzman, Claudio 1927-...........CTFT-9
Gwenn, Edmund 1877-1959 .....WWasWT
Gwilym, Mike 1949- CTFT-6
  Earlier sketch in WWT-17
Gwynn, Michael 1916-1976 ......WWT-16
Gwynne, Fred 1926-.............CTFT-8
  Earlier sketches in CTFT-2, WWT-17
Gwyther, Geoffrey Matheson
  1890-1944 ....WWasWT
Gynt, Greta 1916- ....WWasWT

H

Haas, Charlie 1952- CTFT-2
Haas, Lukas 1976- CTFT-8
Hack, Keith 1948- WWT-17
Hack, Shelley 1952- CTFT-7
Hackett, Buddy 1924- CTFT-8
Hackett, James K. 1869-1926 ....WWasWT
Hackett, Joan 1942-1983 ....CTFT-1
Hackett, Norman Honore
  1874-? ....WWasWT
Hackett, Raymond 1902-1958 ....WWasWT
Hackett, Walter 1876-1944 ......WWasWT
Hackford, Taylor 1944- CTFT-3
Hackman, Gene 1930- CTFT-5
  Earlier sketch in CTFT-1
Hackney, Mabel ?-1914 ....WWasWT
Haddon, Archibald 1871-1942 ...WWasWT
Haddon, Peter 1898-1962 ....WWasWT
Haddrick, Ron 1929- CTFT-2
  Earlier sketch in WWT-17
Hading, Jane 1859-1933 ....WWasWT
Hagen, Uta 1919- CTFT-2
  Earlier sketch in WWT-17
Haggard, Stephen 1911-1943 .....WWasWT
Hagerty, Julie 1955- CTFT-6
Haggerty, Dan 1941- CTFT-3
Hagman, Larry 1931-............CTFT-3
Hague, Albert 1920- CTFT-4
  Earlier sketch in WWT-17
Haid, Charles 1943- CTFT-7
Haig, Emma 1898-1939 ....WWasWT
Haigh, Kenneth 1931- CTFT-2
  Earlier sketch in WWT-17
Haight, George 1905-...........WWasWT
Hailey, Arthur 1920- CTFT-6
Hailey, Oliver 1932- CTFT-5
  Earlier sketch in WWT-17
Haim, Corey 1972-..............CTFT-8
Haines, Herbert E. 1880-1923 ....WWasWT
Haines, Larry CTFT-1
Haines, Robert Terrel
  1870-1943 ....WWasWT
Haire, Wilson John 1932- CTFT-6
  Earlier sketch in WWT-17
Hairston, William Jr. 1928- CTFT-1
Hajos, Mitzi 1891- ....WWasWT
Hakansson, Julia Mathilda
  1853-? ....WWasWT
Hale, Alan, Jr. 1918-1990 ....CTFT-9
Hale, Barbara 1922-.............CTFT-7
Hale, Binnie 1899-..............WWasWT
Hale, Fiona 1926-...............CTFT-1
Hale, Georgina 1943-............CTFT-2
  Earlier sketch in WWT-17
Hale, J. Robert 1874-1940 ....WWasWT

Hale, John 1926-................CTFT-6
  Earlier sketch in WWT-17
Hale, Lionel 1909-1977 ....WWT-16
Hale, Louise Closser 1872-1933 ..WWasWT
Hale, S. T. 1899-...............WWasWT
Hale, Sonnie 1902-1959 ....WWasWT
Hales, Jonathan 1937- CTFT-5
  Earlier sketch in WWT-17
Haley, Jack 1902-1979 ....WWasWT
Haley, Jack Jr. 1933-............CTFT-2
Halfpenny, Tony 1913- ....WWasWT
Hall, Adrian 1927- CTFT-5
  Earlier sketch in WWT-17
Hall, Anmer 1863-1953 ....WWasWT
Hall, Anthony Michael 1968- CTFT-7
Hall, Arsenio 1957- CTFT-7
Hall, Bettina 1906-.............WWasWT
Hall, David 1929-1953 ....WWasWT
Hall, Davis 1946-...............CTFT-1
Hall, Delores CTFT-1
Hall, Ed 1931- CTFT-2
Hall, Grayson WWT-17
Hall, J. W. ....WWasWT
Hall, Laura Nelson 1876-? ....WWasWT
Hall, Lois 1926-................CTFT-4
Hall, Monte 1924-...............CTFT-4
Hall, Natalie 1904-.............WWasWT
Hall, Pauline 1860-1919 ....WWasWT
Hall, Peter 1930- CTFT-3
  Earlier sketch in WWT-17
Hall, Phil 1952-................CTFT-2
Hall, Thurston 1882-1958 ....WWasWT
Hall, Willis 1929-..............CTFT-6
  Earlier sketch in WWT-17
Hallam, Basil 1889-1916 ....WWasWT
Hallard, Charles Maitland
  1865-1942 ....WWasWT
Hallatt, Henry 1888-1952 ....WWasWT
Hallett, Jack 1948-.............CTFT-4
Halliday, John 1880-1947 ....WWasWT
Halliday, Lena ?-1937 ....WWasWT
Halliday, Lynne 1958- CTFT-6
Halliday, Robert 1893-..........WWasWT
Halliwell, David 1936- CTFT-5
  Earlier sketch in WWT-17
Halstan, Margaret 1879-? ....WWasWT
Halston, Julie 1954-............CTFT-8
Hambleton, T. Edward 1911- WWT-17
Hambling, Arthur 1888-1952 ....WWasWT
Hamel, Veronica 1945- CTFT-7
Hamer, Joseph 1932- CTFT-7
Hamill, Mark 1951- CTFT-5
  Earlier sketch in CTFT-2
Hamilton, Carrie 1963- CTFT-6
Hamilton, Cicely 1872-1952 .....WWasWT
Hamilton, Clayton 1881-1946 ....WWasWT
Hamilton, Cosmo 1872?-1942 ....WWasWT
Hamilton, Diana 1898-1951 ......WWasWT
Hamilton, Dorothy 1897- ....WWasWT
Hamilton, George 1939- CTFT-3
Hamilton, Guy 1922- CTFT-8
Hamilton, Hale 1880-1942 ......WWasWT
Hamilton, Henry ?-1911 ....WWasWT
Hamilton, Joe 1929- CTFT-8
Hamilton, Kelly 1945- CTFT-1
Hamilton, Linda CTFT-7
Hamilton, Lindisfarne 1910- .....WWasWT
Hamilton, Lynn 1930-............CTFT-1
Hamilton, Margaret 1902-1985 ...CTFT-2
  Earlier sketch in WWT-17
Hamilton, Neil 1899-1984 ....CTFT-2
  Earlier sketch in WWasWT
Hamilton, Patrick 1904-1962 .....WWasWT

Hamilton, Rose 1874-1955 . . . . . . .WWasWT
Hamlett, Dilys 1928- CTFT-2
    Earlier sketch in WWT-17
Hamlin, Harry 1951- CTFT-6
Hamlisch, Marvin 1944- CTFT-4
    Earlier sketch in WWT-17
Hammer, Ben CTFT-4
Hammerstein, Arthur
    1876-1955 . . . . .WWasWT
Hammerstein, James 1931- WWT-17
Hammerstein, Oscar 1847-1919 . . .WWasWT
Hammerstein, Oscar II
    1895-1960 . . . . .WWasWT
Hammond, Aubrey 1893-1940 . . .WWasWT
Hammond, Bert E. 1880-? . . . . . .WWasWT
Hammond, David 1948- CTFT-1
Hammond, Dorothy ?-1950 . . . . . .WWasWT
Hammond, Kay 1909- . . . . .WWasWT
Hammond, Nicholas CTFT-8
Hammond, Percy 1873-1936 . . . . .WWasWT
Hammond, Peter 1923- . . . . .WWasWT
Hamner, Earl 1923- CTFT-6
Hampden, Walter 1879-1955 . . . . .WWasWT
Hampshire, Susan 1942- CTFT-2
    Earlier sketch in WWT-17
Hampton, Christopher 1946- CTFT-7
    Earlier sketch in WWT-17
Hampton, James 1936- CTFT-7
Hampton, Louise 1881-1954 . . . . .WWasWT
Hanado, Ohta 1882-? . . . . .WWasWT
Hancock, Christopher 1928- WWT-17
Hancock, Herbie 1940- CTFT-8
Hancock, John 1939- CTFT-1
Hancock, Sheila 1933- CTFT-2
    Earlier sketch in WWT-17
Hancox, Daisy 1898- . . . . .WWasWT
Handl, Irene 1901-1987 . . . . .CTFT-6
    Earlier sketch in WWT-17
Handler, Evan 1961- CTFT-1
Handman, Wynn 1922- CTFT-4
    Earlier sketch in WWT-17
Hands, Terry 1941- CTFT-5
    Earlier sketch in WWT-17
Hanket, Arthur 1954- CTFT-2
Hanks, Tom 1956- CTFT-5
    Brief Entry in CTFT-2
Hanley, William 1931- CTFT-2
    Earlier sketch in WWT-17
Hann, Walter 1838-1922 . . . . .WWasWT
Hanna, William 1910- CTFT-8
Hannafin, Daniel 1933- CTFT-5
Hannah, Daryl 1961- CTFT-6
Hannen, Hermione 1913- . . . . .WWasWT
Hannen, Nicholas James
    1881-1972 . . . . .WWasWT
Hanning, Geraldine 1923- CTFT-1
Hanray, Lawrence 1874-1947 . . . .WWasWT
Hansen, Nina CTFT-4
Hanson, Curtis 1945- CTFT-1
Hanson, Gladys 1887-1973 . . . . . .WWasWT
Hanson, Harry 1895- . . . . .WWasWT
Hanson, John 1922- WWT-17
Hansson, Sigrid Valborg 1874-? . .WWasWT
Harbach, Otto 1873-1963 . . . . . . .WWasWT
Harben, Hubert 1878-1941 . . . . . .WWasWT
Harben, Joan 1909-1953 . . . . .WWasWT
Harbord, Carl . . . . .WWasWT
Harbord, Gordon 1901- . . . . .WWasWT
Harbottle, G. Laurence 1924- WWT-17
Harburg, Edgar Y. 1898-1981 . . . . .WWT-17
Harcourt, Cyril ?-1924 . . . . .WWasWT
Harcourt, James 1873-1951 . . . . . .WWasWT
Harcourt, Leslie 1890- . . . . .WWasWT

Hardacred, John Pitt 1855-1933 . .WWasWT
Hardie, Russell 1906-1973 . . . . . . .WWasWT
Hardiman, Terrence 1937- CTFT-5
    Earlier sketch in WWT-17
Harding, Ann 1902-1981 . . . . .WWasWT
Harding, D. Lyn 1867-1952 . . . . . .WWasWT
Harding, John 1948- CTFT-6
    Earlier sketch in WWT-17
Harding, Rudge . . . . .WWasWT
Hardinge, H. C. M. . . . . .WWasWT
Hards, Ira 1872-1938 . . . . .WWasWT
Hardwick, Paul 1918- WWT-17
Hardwicke, Cedric 1893-1964 . . . .WWasWT
Hardwicke, Clarice 1900- . . . . .WWasWT
Hardwicke, Edward 1932- CTFT-8
    Earlier sketch in WWT-17
Hardy, Arthur F. 1870-? . . . . .WWasWT
Hardy, Betty 1904- . . . . .WWasWT
Hardy, Joseph 1929-1990 . . . . .WWT-17
Hardy, Robert 1925- WWT-17
Hare, Betty 1900- . . . . .WWasWT
Hare, David 1947- CTFT-4
    Earlier sketch in WWT-17
Hare, Doris 1905- WWT-17
Hare, Ernest Dudley 1900- WWT-17
Hare, J. Robertson 1891-1979 . . . . .WWT-16
Hare, John 1844-1921 . . . . .WWasWT
Hare, (John) Gilbert 1869-1951 . .WWasWT
Hare, Will 1919- WWT-17
Hare, Winifred 1875-? . . . . .WWasWT
Harewood, Dorian 1950- CTFT-7
Harford, W. . . . . .WWasWT
Hargrave, Roy 1908- . . . . .WWasWT
Harker, Gordon 1885-1967 . . . . . .WWasWT
Harker, Joseph C. 1855-1927 . . . .WWasWT
Harlan, Otis 1865-1940 . . . . .WWasWT
Harman, Barry 1950- CTFT-6
Harmon, Charlotte CTFT-1
Harmon, Lewis 1911- CTFT-1
Harmon, Mark 1951- CTFT-7
Harned, Virginia 1872-1946 . . . . . .WWasWT
Harnick, Sheldon 1924- CTFT-1
Harper, Gerald 1929- WWT-17
Harper, Jessica 1954- CTFT-6
Harper, Tess 1950- CTFT-7
Harper, Valerie 1940- CTFT-5
Harrell, Gordon Lowry 1940- CTFT-1
Harrigan, Nedda
    See Logan, Nedda Harrigan CTFT-8
Harrigan, William 1894-1966 . . . .WWasWT
Harrington, J. P. 1865-? . . . . .WWasWT
Harrington, Pat Jr. 1929- CTFT-3
Harris, Audrey Sophia
    1901-1966 . . . . .WWasWT
Harris, Barbara 1937- CTFT-4
    Earlier sketch in WWT-17
Harris, Clare ?-1949 . . . . .WWasWT
Harris, Cynthia CTFT-5
Harris, Ed 1950- CTFT-6
    Earlier sketch in CTFT-2
Harris, Elmer Blaney ?-1966 . . . . .WWasWT
Harris, Florence Glossop
    1883-1931 . . . . .WWasWT
Harris, Henry B. 1866-1912 . . . . . .WWasWT
Harris, Jed 1900-1979 . . . . .WWasWT
Harris, Julie 1925- CTFT-8
    Earlier sketches in CTFT-2, WWT-17
Harris, Margaret F. 1904- WWT-17
Harris, Richard 1933(?)- CTFT-9
    Earlier sketch in WWasWT
Harris, Robert 1900- WWT-17
Harris, Rosemary CTFT-3
    Earlier sketch in WWT-17

Harris, Sam H. 1872-1941 . . . . . . .WWasWT
Harris, William 1884-1946 . . . . . . .WWasWT
Harrison, Austin 1873-1928 . . . . . .WWasWT
Harrison, Frederick ?-1926 . . . . . .WWasWT
Harrison, George 1943- CTFT-8
Harrison, Gregory 1950- CTFT-3
Harrison, John 1924- CTFT-2
    Earlier sketch in WWT-17
Harrison, Kathleen 1898- WWT-17
Harrison, Mona ?-1957 . . . . .WWasWT
Harrison, Rex 1908-1990 . . . . .CTFT-9
    Earlier sketches in CTFT-4, WWT-17
Harrold, Kathryn 1950- CTFT-7
Harrow, Lisa CTFT-8
Harry, Deborah 1945- CTFT-8
Harry, Jackee CTFT-5
Harryhausen, Ray 1920- CTFT-8
Hart, Bernard 1911-1964 . . . . .WWasWT
Hart, Charles 1961- CTFT-4
Hart, Diane 1926- WWT-17
Hart, Harvey 1928-1989 . . . . .CTFT-1
Hart, Lorenz 1895-1945 . . . . .WWasWT
Hart, Moss 1904-1961 . . . . .WWasWT
Hart, Teddy 1897-1971 . . . . .WWasWT
Hart, Vivian . . . . .WWasWT
Hart, William S. 1870-1946 . . . . . .WWasWT
Hartley, Mariette 1940- CTFT-4
    Earlier sketch in CTFT-1
Hartley-Milburn, Julie
    1904-1949 . . . . .WWasWT
Hartman, David 1935- CTFT-3
Hartman, Jan 1938- CTFT-3
Hartman, Lisa 1956- CTFT-9
    Brief Entry in CTFT-3
Hartman, Phil 1948- CTFT-7
Hartnell, William 1908-1975 . . . . .WWasWT
Harvey, Anthony 1931- CTFT-9
    Earlier sketch in CTFT-1
Harvey, Frank 1885-1965 . . . . .WWasWT
Harvey, Frank 1912- WWT-17
Harvey, John Martin 1863-1944 . .WWasWT
Harvey, Laurence 1928-1973 . . . . .WWasWT
Harvey, Morris 1877-1944 . . . . . . .WWasWT
Harvey, Peter 1933- CTFT-5
    Earlier sketch in WWT-17
Harvey, Rupert 1887-1954 . . . . . . .WWasWT
Harwood, H. M. 1874-1959 . . . . . .WWasWT
Harwood, John 1876-1944 . . . . . . .WWasWT
Harwood, Ronald 1934- CTFT-8
    Earlier sketch in WWT-17
Haskell, Peter 1934- CTFT-1
Hassall, Christopher 1912-1963 . . .WWasWT
Hasselhoff, David 1952- CTFT-7
Hasselquist, Jenny . . . . .WWasWT
Hasso, Signe 1918- WWT-17
Hastings, Basil Macdonald
    1881-1928 . . . . .WWasWT
Hastings, Edward 1931- CTFT-3
Hastings, Fred . . . . .WWasWT
Hastings, Hugh 1917- CTFT-3
    Earlier sketch in WWT-17
Hastings, Michael 1938- CTFT-2
    Earlier sketch in WWT-17
Hastings, Patrick 1880-1952 . . . . .WWasWT
Haswell, Percy 1871-1945 . . . . . . .WWasWT
Hatherton, Arthur ?-1924 . . . . .WWasWT
Hatton, Fanny 1870-1939 . . . . . . .WWasWT
Hatton, Frederick 1879-1946 . . . . .WWasWT
Hauer, Rutger 1944- CTFT-7
Hauptman, William 1942- CTFT-4
Hauptmann, Gerhart 1862-1946 . .WWasWT
Hauser, Frank 1922- WWT-17
Hauser, Wings CTFT-8

Havard, Lezley 1944- CTFT-3
Havel, Vaclav 1936- CTFT-9
Havergal, Giles 1938- WWT-17
Havers, Nigel 1949- CTFT-6
Haviland, William 1860-1917 ....WWasWT
Havoc, June 1916- WWT-17
Hawk, Jeremy 1918-..............WWT-17
Hawkesworth, John 1920- CTFT-8
Hawkins, Iris 1893- ....WWasWT
Hawkins, Jack 1910-1973 ....WWasWT
Hawkins, Stockwell 1874-1927 ...WWasWT
Hawkins, Trish 1945- CTFT-1
Hawn, Goldie 1945- CTFT-5
    Earlier sketch in CTFT-1
Hawthorne, David ?-1942 ....WWasWT
Hawthorne, Lil ....WWasWT
Hawthorne, Nigel 1929- CTFT-2
    Earlier sketch in WWT-17
Hawtrey, Anthony 1909-1954 ....WWasWT
Hawtrey, Charles 1858-1923 .....WWasWT
Hawtrey, Charles 1914-1988 .....WWasWT
Hawtrey, Marjory 1900-1952 .....WWasWT
Hay, Ian 1876-1952 ....WWasWT
Hay, Joan 1894- ....WWasWT
Hay, Mary 1901-1957 ....WWasWT
Hay, Valerie 1910- ....WWasWT
Hayden, Larry 1950- CTFT-5
Hayden, Sophie CTFT-5
Hayden, Terese 1921-............WWT-17
Haydon, Ethel 1878-1954 ....WWasWT
Haydon, Florence ?-1918 ....WWasWT
Haydon, Julie 1910- CTFT-1
    Earlier sketch in WWasWT
Haydu, Peter 1948- CTFT-4
Haye, Helen 1874-1957 ....WWasWT
Hayers, Sidney 1922- CTFT-1
Hayes, Catherine Anne 1958- CTFT-4
Hayes, George 1888-1967 ....WWasWT
Hayes, Helen 1900- WWT-17
Hayes, J. Milton 1884-1940 .....WWasWT
Hayes, Joseph 1918- CTFT-1
Hayes, Patricia 1909- CTFT-1
    Earlier sketch in WWasWT
Hayes, Peter Lind 1915- CTFT-1
Hayman, Al ?-1917 ....WWasWT
Hayman, Lillian 1922- WWT-17
Hayman, Ronald 1932- WWT-17
Haymer, John
    See Haymer, Johnny............CTFT-9
Haymer, Johnny 1920-1989 ....CTFT-9
Haynes, Tiger 1914- WWT-17
Hays, Bill 1938- WWT-17
Hays, David 1930- WWT-17
Hays, Robert 1947- CTFT-6
Hayter, James 1907- WWT-17
Haythorne, Joan 1915- WWT-17
Hayward, Leland 1902-1971 .....WWasWT
Hazell, Hy 1922-1970 ....WWasWT
Hazzard, John E. 1881-1935 .....WWasWT
Headly, Glenne 1955-.............CTFT-8
Heal, Joan 1922- WWT-17
Heald, Anthony 1944- CTFT-8
Healy, Mary 1920- CTFT-1
Heap, Douglas 1934- CTFT-9
    Earlier sketch in WWT-17
Heard, John 1947- CTFT-5
Hearn, George 1934- CTFT-6
Hearn, Lew 1882-? ....WWasWT
Hearne, Richard 1909-...........WWasWT
Heath, Eira 1940- WWT-16
Heatherley, Clifford 1888-1937 ...WWasWT
Hecht, Ben 1894-1964 ....WWasWT

Hecht, Paul 1941- CTFT-8
    Earlier sketch in CTFT-1
Heckart, Eileen 1919- CTFT-4
    Earlier sketch in WWT-17
Heckerling, Amy 1954- CTFT-6
    Brief Entry in CTFT-2
Hedison, Al
    See Hedison, David CTFT-8
Hedison, David 1928- CTFT-8
Hedley, H. B. ?-1931 ....WWasWT
Hedley, Philip 1938-..............CTFT-2
    Earlier sketch in WWT-17
Hedman, Martha 1888-? ....WWasWT
Hedren, Tippi 1935- CTFT-7
Heeley, Desmond WWT-17
Heffernan, John 1934- CTFT-4
    Earlier sketch in WWT-17
Heflin, Frances 1924- CTFT-1
    Earlier sketch in WWasWT
Heggie, O. P. 1879-1936 ....WWasWT
Heifner, Jack 1946- CTFT-1
Heijermans, Herman 1864-1924 ..WWasWT
Heikin, Nancy 1948- CTFT-2
Heilbronn, William 1879-? ....WWasWT
Hein, Silvio 1879-1928 ....WWasWT
Heinsohn, Elisa 1962-.............CTFT-6
Heinz, Gerard 1904-1972 ....WWasWT
Helburn, Theresa 1887-1959 .....WWasWT
Held, Anna 1873-1918 ....WWasWT
Held, Dan 1948- CTFT-3
Heller, Buck CTFT-2
Heller, Paul 1927- CTFT-9
    Earlier sketch in CTFT-1
Heller, Paul M.
    See Heller, Paul CTFT-9
Hellman, Lillian 1905-1984 ....WWT-17
Helm, Levon 1943- CTFT-7
Helmond, Katherine 1934- CTFT-3
Helmore, Arthur 1859-1941 ......WWasWT
Helmsley, Charles Thomas
    Hunt 1865-1940 ....WWasWT
Helper, Stephen Lloyd 1957-.......CTFT-2
Helpmann, Robert 1909-1986 .....WWT-17
Heming, Percy 1885- ....WWasWT
Heming, Violet 1895- ....WWasWT
Hemingway, Alan 1951- CTFT-4
Hemingway, Marie 1893-1939 ....WWasWT
Hemingway, Mariel 1961- CTFT-3
    Brief Entry in CTFT-2
Hemion, Dwight 1926-.............CTFT-8
Hemmerde, Edward George
    1871-1948 ....WWasWT
Hemming, Lindy 1948- CTFT-9
Hemmings, David 1941- CTFT-7
Hemsley, Harry May 1877-1951 ..WWasWT
Hemsley, Sherman 1938-...........CTFT-3
Hemsley, W. T. 1850-1918 ......WWasWT
Henderson, Alex F. 1866-1933 ...WWasWT
Henderson, Dickie 1922- WWT-17
Henderson, Elvira 1903- ....WWasWT
Henderson, Florence 1934- CTFT-2
    Earlier sketch in WWT-17
Henderson, May 1884-..........WWasWT
Henderson, Ray 1896-1970 ......WWasWT
Henderson, Robert 1904-.........WWT-17
Henderson, Roy WWT-11
Hendrie, Ernest 1859-1929 ....WWasWT
Heneker, David 1906-...........WWT-17
Henig, Andi CTFT-2
Henley, Beth 1952- CTFT-1
Henley, Herbert James
    1882-1937 ....WWasWT
Henley, Joan 1904- ....WWasWT

Hennequin, Maurice ?-1926 ......WWasWT
Henner, Marilu 1952- CTFT-7
    Earlier sketch in CTFT-2
Hennessy, Roland Burke
    1870-1939 ....WWasWT
Henniger, Rolf 1925- ....WWasWT
Henning, Linda Kaye 1944- CTFT-3
Hennings, Betty 1850-1939 ......WWasWT
Henriksen, Lance CTFT-8
Henritze, Bette CTFT-2
    Earlier sketch in WWT-17
Henry, (Alexander) Victor
    1943- ....WWasWT
Henry, Buck 1930- CTFT-9
    Earlier sketch in CTFT-1
Henry, Charles 1890-1968 ....WWasWT
Henry, Martin 1872-1942 ....WWasWT
Henson, Gladys 1897-...........WWT-16
Henson, Jim 1936- CTFT-1
Henson, Leslie 1891-1957 ....WWasWT
Henson, Nicky 1945- CTFT-5
    Earlier sketch in WWT-17
Hentschel, Irene 1891- ....WWasWT
Hepburn, Audrey 1929- CTFT-7
Hepburn, Katharine 1909-.........CTFT-5
    Earlier sketches in CTFT-1, WWT-17
Hepple, Jeanne 1936- WWT-17
Hepple, Peter 1927- CTFT-5
    Earlier sketch in WWT-17
Heppner, Rosa ?-1979 ....WWT-16
Hepton, Bernard 1925-...........WWT-17
Herbert, Alan Patrick
    1890-1971 ....WWasWT
Herbert, Evelyn 1898- ....WWasWT
Herbert, F. Hugh 1897-1958 .....WWasWT
Herbert, Henry 1879-1947 ....WWasWT
Herbert, Jocelyn 1917-............CTFT-6
    Earlier sketch in WWT-17
Herbert, Rich 1956-.............CTFT-3
Herbert, Victor 1859-1924 ....WWasWT
Herlie, Eileen 1920- WWT-17
Herlihy, James Leo 1927-.........CTFT-1
Herman, Danny 1960- CTFT-2
Herman, Jerry 1933- CTFT-3
    Earlier sketches in CTFT-1, WWT-17
Herman, Pee-Wee 1952- CTFT-9
Hermant, Abel 1862-1950 ....WWasWT
Herndon, Richard G. ?-1958 .....WWasWT
Herne, (Katherine) Chrystal
    1883-1950 ....WWasWT
Heron, Joyce 1916-1980 ....WWT-17
Heros, Eugene ....WWasWT
Herrera, Anthony 1944-...........CTFT-5
Herrmann, Edward 1943- CTFT-6
    Earlier sketch in CTFT-1
Herrmann, Keith 1952- CTFT-1
Hersey, David 1939-.............CTFT-3
    Earlier sketch in WWT-17
Hershey, Barbara 1948- CTFT-3
Hertz, Carl 1859- ....WWasWT
Hervey, Grizelda 1901- ....WWasWT
Hervey, Jason 1972- CTFT-8
Hervieu, Paul 1857-1915 ....WWasWT
Herz, Ralph C. 1878-1921 ....WWasWT
Herzog, Werner 1942- CTFT-7
Heslewood, Tom 1868-1959 ......WWasWT
Heslop, Charles 1883-1966 ......WWasWT
Hesseman, Howard 1940- CTFT-3
Heston, Charlton 1922- CTFT-3
    Earlier sketches in CTFT-1, WWT-17
Hestor, George 1877-1925 ....WWasWT
Heuer, John Michael 1941- CTFT-6
Hewes, Henry 1917-.............WWT-17

Hewett, Christopher CTFT-6
  Earlier sketch in WWT-17
Hewett, Dorothy 1923- WWT-17
Hewitt, Agnes ?-1924 ....WWasWT
Hewitt, Alan 1915-1986 ....CTFT-4
  Earlier sketches in CTFT-1, WWT-17
Hewitt, Henry 1885-1968 ....WWasWT
Hewlett, Maurice 1861-1923 ....WWasWT
Hexum, Jon-Eric 1957-1984 ....CTFT-2
Heydt, Louis Jean 1905-1960 ....WWasWT
Heyman, Barton 1937- CTFT-1
Heyward, Dorothy 1890-1961 ...WWasWT
Heyward, Du Bose 1885-1940 ....WWasWT
Hibbard, Edna 1895?-1942 ......WWasWT
Hibbert, Henry George
  1862-1924 ....WWasWT
Hichens, Robert Smythe
  1864-1950 ....WWasWT
Hickey, William 1928- CTFT-7
Hicklin, Margery 1904- ....WWasWT
Hickman, Charles WWT-17
Hickman, Darryl 1933- CTFT-5
Hicks, Barbara CTFT-9
Hicks, Betty Seymour 1905- .....WWasWT
Hicks, Catherine 1951- CTFT-7
Hicks, (Edward) Seymour
  1871-1949 ....WWasWT
Hicks, Julian 1858-1941 ....WWasWT
Hickson, Joan 1906- WWT-17
Higgins, Anthony CTFT-7
Higgins, Clare CTFT-8
Higgins, Colin 1941-1988 ....CTFT-5
  Earlier sketch in CTFT-1
Higgins, James 1932- CTFT-1
Higgins, Michael 1925- CTFT-6
  Earlier sketch in CTFT-1
Higgins, Norman 1898- ....WWasWT
Highley, Reginald 1884-? ....WWasWT
Hightower, Marilyn 1923- ....WWasWT
Hignell, Rose 1896- ....WWasWT
Hignett, H. R. 1870-1959 ....WWasWT
Hiken, Gerald 1927- CTFT-7
  Earlier sketch in WWT-17
Hilary, Jennifer 1942- CTFT-5
  Earlier sketch in WWT-17
Hilferty, Susan CTFT-9
Hill, Ann Stahlman 1921- CTFT-4
Hill, Arthur 1922- WWT-17
Hill, Benny 1925- CTFT-5
Hill, Billie ....WWasWT
Hill, Dana 1964- CTFT-7
Hill, Debra CTFT-5
Hill, George Roy 1922- CTFT-6
  Earlier sketches in CTFT-1, WWT-17
Hill, Ken 1937- CTFT-5
  Earlier sketch in WWT-17
Hill, Leonard F. 1947- CTFT-1
Hill, Lucienne WWT-17
Hill, Mars Andrew III 1927- CTFT-1
Hill, Peter Murray 1908- ....WWasWT
Hill, Ronnie 1911- WWT-17
Hill, Rose 1914- WWT-17
Hill, Sinclair 1896-1945 ....WWasWT
Hill, Steven 1922- CTFT-8
Hill, Walter 1942- CTFT-5
Hillary, Ann 1930- CTFT-4
Hiller, Arthur 1923- CTFT-8
  Earlier sketch in CTFT-1
Hiller, Wendy 1912- CTFT-6
  Earler sketches in WWT-17
Hillerman, John 1932- CTFT-8
  Earlier sketch in CTFT-3

Hilliard, Harriet
  See Nelson, Harriet CTFT-3
Hilliard, Kathlyn 1896-1933 .....WWasWT
Hilliard, Patricia 1916- ....WWasWT
Hilliard, Robert C. 1857-1927 ....WWasWT
Hillman, Michael 1902-1941 .....WWasWT
Hindman, Earl CTFT-8
Hines, Elizabeth 1899-1971 ......WWasWT
Hines, Gregory 1946- CTFT-3
Hines, Patrick 1930- WWT-17
Hingle, Pat 1923- CTFT-8
  Earlier sketches in CTFT-2, WWT-17
Hinkle, Vernon 1935- CTFT-1
Hinton, Mary 1896- ....WWasWT
Hird, Thora 1913- WWT-17
Hirsch, Charles Henry 1870-? ....WWasWT
Hirsch, John Stephan
  1930-1989 ....CTFT-6
  Earlier sketch in WWT-17
Hirsch, Judd 1935- CTFT-4
  Earlier sketches in CTFT-1, WWT-17
Hirsch, Louis Achille
  1881-1924 ....WWasWT
Hirschfeld, Al 1903- CTFT-1
Hirschhorn, Clive 1940- WWT-17
Hirschmann, Henri 1872-? ....WWasWT
Hislop, Joseph 1887-? ....WWasWT
Hitchcock, Alfred 1899-1980 .....CTFT-1
Hitchcock, Raymond 1865-1929 ..WWasWT
Hoare, Douglas 1875-? ....WWasWT
Hobart, George V. 1867-1926 ....WWasWT
Hobart, Rose 1906- ....WWasWT
Hobbes, Herbert Halliwell
  1877-1962 ....WWasWT
Hobbs, Carleton 1898- ....WWasWT
Hobbs, Frederick 1880-1942 .....WWasWT
Hobbs, Jack 1893-1968 ....WWasWT
Hobbs, William 1939- WWT-17
Hobgood, Burnet M. 1922- WWT-17
Hobson, Harold 1904- WWT-17
Hobson, May 1889-? ....WWasWT
Hochhuth, Rolf 1931- WWT-17
Hochman, Larry 1953- CTFT-6
Hochwaelder, Fritz 1911-1986 .....CTFT-4
Hockridge, Edmund 1919- ....WWasWT
Hoctor, Harriet 1907-1977 ....WWasWT
Hodge, Merton 1904-1958 ....WWasWT
Hodge, Patricia 1946- CTFT-8
Hodge, William T. 1874-1932 ....WWasWT
Hodgeman, Edwin 1935- WWT-17
Hodges, Horace 1865-1951 ......WWasWT
Hodges, Patricia CTFT-8
Hoey, Dennis 1893-1960 ....WWasWT
Hoey, Iris 1885-? ....WWasWT
Hoffe, Barbara ....WWasWT
Hoffe, Monckton 1880-1951 .....WWasWT
Hoffman, Aaron 1880-1924 ......WWasWT
Hoffman, Basil 1938- CTFT-5
Hoffman, Dustin 1937- CTFT-7
  Earlier sketches in CTFT-1, WWT-17
Hoffman, Jane 1911- CTFT-4
  Earlier sketch in WWT-17
Hoffman, Maud ....WWasWT
Hoffman, William M. 1939- CTFT-4
  Earlier sketch in WWT-17
Hofsiss, Jack 1950- WWT-17
Hogan, Michael 1898- ....WWasWT
Hogan, Paul 1942- CTFT-7
Hogg, Ian 1937- WWT-17
Holbrook, Hal 1925- CTFT-7
  Earlier sketches in CTFT-1, WWT-17
Holbrook, Louise ....WWasWT

Hold, John
  See Bava, Mario CTFT-8
Holden, Jan 1931- WWT-17
Holder, Geoffrey 1930- WWT-17
Holder, Owen 1921- WWT-17
Holdgrive, David 1958- CTFT-4
Holdridge, Lee 1944- CTFT-8
Hole, John 1939- WWT-17
Holgate, Ron 1937- WWT-17
Holland, Anthony 1912-1988 .....WWT-17
Holland, Edmund Milton
  1848-1913 ....WWasWT
Holland, Jeffrey 1946- CTFT-8
Holland, Mildred 1869-1944 .....WWasWT
Holland, Tom 1943- CTFT-4
Holles, Antony 1901-1950 ....WWasWT
Holles, William 1867-1947 ......WWasWT
Holliday, Jennifer 1960- CTFT-6
Holliday, Judy 1923-1965 ....WWasWT
Holliday, Polly 1937- CTFT-7
Holliman, Earl 1928- CTFT-3
Hollis, Stephen 1941- WWT-17
Holloway, Baliol 1883-1967 ......WWasWT
Holloway, Julian 1944- WWT-17
Holloway, Stanley 1890-1982 ....WWT-17
Holloway, Sterling 1904- CTFT-5
Holloway, W. E. 1885-1952 ......WWasWT
Holm, Celeste 1919- CTFT-1
  Earlier sketch in WWT-17
Holm, Hanya WWT-17
Holm, Ian 1931- CTFT-9
  Earlier sketches in CTFT-2, WWT-17
Holm, John Cecil 1904-1981 .....WWT-17
Holman, Libby 1906-1971 ....WWasWT
Holme, Stanford 1904- ....WWasWT
Holme, Thea 1907- WWT-17
Holmes, Helen ?-1950 ....WWasWT
Holmes, Robert 1899-1945 ......WWasWT
Holmes, Taylor 1878-1959 ....WWasWT
Holmes-Gore, Dorothy
  1896-1915 ....WWasWT
Holt, Fritz 1940-1987 ....CTFT-5
  Earlier sketch in CTFT-1
Holt, Thelma 1933- WWT-17
Holt, Will 1929- WWT-17
Holtz, Lou 1898- ....WWasWT
Holzer, Adela WWT-17
Homan, David 1907- ....WWasWT
Home, William Douglas 1912- WWT-17
Homeier, Skip 1930- CTFT-8
Homfrey, Gladys ?-1932 ....WWasWT
Homolka, Oscar 1898-1978 ......WWasWT
Hone, Mary 1904- ....WWasWT
Honer, Mary 1914- ....WWasWT
Hong, James 1929(?)- CTFT-9
Hong, Wilson S. 1934- CTFT-5
Honri, Percy 1874-1953 ....WWasWT
Hood, Basil 1864-1917 ....WWasWT
Hood, Morag 1942- CTFT-2
  Earlier sketch in WWT-17
Hooks, Kevin 1958- CTFT-9
Hooks, Robert 1937- CTFT-5
  Earlier sketch in WWT-17
Hool, Lance CTFT-6
Hooper, Ewan 1935- WWT-17
Hooper, Tobe CTFT-7
Hope, Anthony 1863-1933 ....WWasWT
Hope, Bob 1903- CTFT-3
  Earlier sketch in WWasWT
Hope, Evelyn ?-1966 ....WWasWT
Hope, Maidie 1881-1937 ....WWasWT
Hope, Vida 1918-1963 ....WWasWT

Hope-Wallace, Philip A.
 1911-1979 ....WWT-16
Hopkins, Anthony 1937- CTFT-8
 Earlier sketches in CTFT-1, WWT-17
Hopkins, Arthur 1878-1950 ......WWasWT
Hopkins, Bo CTFT-3
Hopkins, Charles 1884-1953 .....WWasWT
Hopkins, Joan 1915-............WWasWT
Hopkins, John 1931- WWT-17
Hopkins, Miriam 1902-1972 .....WWasWT
Hopkins, Telma 1948- CTFT-6
Hopper, Dennis 1936- CTFT-4
Hopper, De Wolf 1858-1935 .....WWasWT
Hopper, Edna Wallace
 1864-1959 ....WWasWT
Hopper, Victoria 1909- ....WWasWT
Hopwood, Avery 1882-1928 .....WWasWT
Horan, Edward 1898-...........WWasWT
Hordern, Michael 1911-...........CTFT-6
 Earlier sketch in WWT-17
Horn, Mary 1916- ....WWasWT
Horne, A. P. ....WWasWT
Horne, David 1893-1970 ....WWasWT
Horne, Kenneth 1900- ....WWasWT
Horne, Lena 1917- CTFT-6
Horner, Richard 1920-..........CTFT-3
 Earlier sketch in WWT-17
Horniman, Annie Elizabeth
 Fredericka 1860-1937 ....WWasWT
Horniman, Roy 1872-1930 ......WWasWT
Hornsby, Nancy 1910-1958 ......WWasWT
Horovitch, David 1945-...........CTFT-6
 Earlier sketch in WWT-17
Horovitz, Israel 1939- CTFT-3
 Earlier sketch in WWT-17
Horsford, Anna Maria CTFT-1
Horsley, Lee CTFT-3
Horsnell, Horace 1883-1949 .....WWasWT
Horton, Edward Everett
 1886-1970 ....WWasWT
Horton, Peter CTFT-8
Horton, Robert 1870-? ....WWasWT
Horwitz, Murray 1949- CTFT-3
Hoskins, Bob 1942- CTFT-3
 Earlier sketch in WWT-17
Hotchkis, Joan 1927- CTFT-7
Houdini, Harry 1873-1926 ....WWasWT
Hough, John 1941-................CTFT-2
Houghton, Katharine CTFT-1
Houghton, Norris 1909-..........WWT-17
House, Eric WWT-17
Houseman, John 1902-1988 ....CTFT-7
 Earlier sketches in CTFT-2, WWT-17
Housman, Laurence 1865-1959 ...WWasWT
Houston, Donald 1923- WWT-17
Houston, Jane ....WWasWT
Houston, Josephine 1911- ....WWasWT
Houston, Renee 1902-1980 ....WWT-17
Howard, Alan 1937-..............CTFT-6
 Earlier sketch in WWT-17
Howard, Andree 1910-1968 ......WWasWT
Howard, Bart 1915- CTFT-3
Howard, Clint 1959- CTFT-7
Howard, Eugene 1880-1965 ......WWasWT
Howard, J. Bannister 1867-1946 ..WWasWT
Howard, Keble 1875-1928 ....WWasWT
Howard, Ken 1944- CTFT-4
 Earlier sketch in WWT-17
Howard, Leslie 1893-1943 ....WWasWT
Howard, Norah 1901-1968 ....WWasWT
Howard, Pamela 1939-...........CTFT-6
 Earlier sketch in WWT-17
Howard, Roger 1938-............WWT-17

Howard, Ron 1954- CTFT-4
 Earlier sketch in CTFT-1
Howard, Sidney 1891-1939 ......WWasWT
Howard, Sydney 1885-1946 ......WWasWT
Howard, Trevor 1916-1988 ....CTFT-4
 Earlier sketch in WWT-17
Howard, Walter 1866-1922 ......WWasWT
Howard, Willie 1883-1949 ....WWasWT
Howarth, Donald 1931- WWT-17
Howe, George 1900-.............WWT-17
Howe, Tina 1937-...............CTFT-7
Howell, C. Thomas 1966- CTFT-8
Howell, Jane WWT-17
Howell, John 1888-1928 ....WWasWT
Howell, Tom
 See Howell, C. Thomas CTFT-8
Howells, Ursula 1922- CTFT-9
 Earlier sketch in WWT-17
Howerd, Frankie 1921- CTFT-2
 Earlier sketch in WWT-17
Howes, Basil 1901-.............WWasWT
Howes, Bobby 1895-1972 ....WWasWT
Howes, Sally Ann CTFT-5
 Earlier sketch in WWT-17
Howland, Beth CTFT-3
Howland, Jobyna 1880-1936 .....WWasWT
Howlett, Noel 1901-1984 ....WWT-17
Hsiung, Shih I. 1902- ....WWasWT
Huban, Eileen 1895-1935 ....WWasWT
Hubbard, Lorna 1910-1954 ......WWasWT
Hubbell, Raymond 1879-1954 ....WWasWT
Huber, Gusti 1914-.............WWasWT
Huber, Kathleen 1947-............CTFT-7
Hubert, Janet CTFT-2
Hubley, Season CTFT-4
Huby, Roberta ....WWasWT
Hudd, Roy 1936- WWT-17
Hudd, Walter 1898-1963 ....WWasWT
Huddleston, David 1930-..........CTFT-7
Hudis, Norman 1922-.............CTFT-4
Hudson, Bill 1949-..............CTFT-8
Hudson, Ernie CTFT-8
Hudson, Jeffery
 See Crichton, Michael CTFT-5
Hudson, Rock 1925-1985 ....CTFT-2
Hudson, Verity 1923-1988 ....WWT-17
Huffman, Felicity CTFT-7
Hughes, Annie 1869-1954 ....WWasWT
Hughes, Barnard 1915- CTFT-7
 Earlier sketches in CTFT-1, WWT-17
Hughes, Del 1909-1985 ....CTFT-1
Hughes, Dusty 1947- WWT-17
Hughes, Hatcher 1883-1945 .....WWasWT
Hughes, Hazel 1913-............WWasWT
Hughes, John CTFT-5
Hughes, Laura 1959-.............CTFT-1
Hughes, Mick 1938-.............WWT-17
Hughes, Roddy 1891-............WWasWT
Hughes, Rupert 1872-1956 ......WWasWT
Hughes, Tom E. ....WWasWT
Hughes, Wendy CTFT-7
Hugo, Laurence 1927- CTFT-1
Huguenet, Felix 1858-1926 ......WWasWT
Hulbert, Claude 1900-1964 ......WWasWT
Hulbert, Jack 1892-1978 ....WWT-16
Hulce, Thomas 1953-.............CTFT-9
 Brief Entry in CTFT-3
Hulce, Tom
 See Hulce, Thomas CTFT-9
Hull, Henry 1890-1977 ....WWasWT
Hull, Josephine 1886-1957 ....WWasWT
Hume, Benita 1906-1968 ....WWasWT
Humphrey, Cavada WWT-17

Humphreys, Cecil 1883-1947 .....WWasWT
Humphries, Barry 1934- WWT-17
Humphries, John 1895-1927 .....WWasWT
Humphris, Gordon 1921-........WWasWT
Hunkins, Lee 1930- CTFT-1
Hunt, Charles W. 1943-1989 ....CTFT-5
Hunt, Hugh 1911- WWT-17
Hunt, Helen 1963- CTFT-8
Hunt, Linda 1945- CTFT-9
 Earlier sketch in CTFT-3
Hunt, Marsha 1917- CTFT-9
 Earlier sketch in WWasWT
Hunt, Marsha A.
 See Hunt, Marsha CTFT-9
Hunt, Martita 1900-1969 ....WWasWT
Hunt, Peter 1938-.................CTFT-1
 Earlier sketch in WWT-17
Hunter, George W. 1851-? ....WWasWT
Hunter, Glenn 1896-1945 ....WWasWT
Hunter, Holly 1958-.............CTFT-6
Hunter, Ian 1900-1975 ....WWasWT
Hunter, Kenneth 1882-? ....WWasWT
Hunter, Kim 1922-................CTFT-3
 Earlier sketch in WWT-17
Hunter, Marian 1944- CTFT-5
Hunter, Norman C. 1908-1971 ...WWasWT
Hunter, Victor William 1910- WWT-17
Huntley, G. P. 1868-1927 ....WWasWT
Huntley, G. P. 1904- ....WWasWT
Huntley, Raymond 1904-.........WWT-17
Huntley, Tim 1904- ....WWasWT
Huntley-Wright, Betty 1911- .....WWasWT
Huntley-Wright, Jose 1918- ......WWasWT
Huppert, Isabelle 1955- CTFT-7
Hurd, Gale Anne 1955-...........CTFT-9
Hurgon, Austen A. ?-1942 ....WWasWT
Hurlbut, W. J. 1883-? ....WWasWT
Hurley, Kathy 1947-.............CTFT-1
Hurndall, Richard 1910- WWT-17
Hurok, Sol 1888-1974 ....WWasWT
Hurran, Dick 1911- WWT-17
Hurry, Leslie 1909-1978 ....WWT-16
Hursey, Sherry CTFT-3
Hurst, Fannie 1889-1968 ....WWasWT
Hurst, Gregory S. 1947-..........CTFT-2
Hurt, John 1940- CTFT-3
 Earlier sketches in CTFT-1, WWT-17
Hurt, Mary Beth CTFT-4
 Earlier sketches in CTFT-1, WWT-17
Hurt, William 1950-..............CTFT-5
 Earlier sketch in CTFT-1
Husain, Jory CTFT-4
Husmann, Ron 1937- WWT-17
Hussey, Jimmy 1891-1930 ....WWasWT
Hussey, Olivia 1951- CTFT-7
Hussey, Ruth 1914- ....WWasWT
Huston, Anjelica 1951- CTFT-4
Huston, John 1909-1987 ....CTFT-5
 Earlier sketch in CTFT-2
Huston, Walter 1884-1950 ......WWasWT
Hutcheson, David 1905-1976......WWT-16
Hutchinson, Harry 1892-1980 .....WWT-16
Hutchinson, Josephine 1904- .....WWasWT
Hutchinson Scott, Jay 1924- .....WWasWT
Hutchison, Emma ?-1965 ....WWasWT
Hutchison, Muriel 1915-1975 ....WWasWT
Hutchison, Percy 1875-1945 .....WWasWT
Huth, Harold 1892-1967 ....WWasWT
Hutt, William 1920- WWT-17
Hutton, Geoffrey 1909- WWT-17
Hutton, Lauren 1944- CTFT-3
Hutton, Robert 1920-..........CTFT-9

Hutton, Timothy 1960- CTFT-6
  Earlier sketch in CTFT-2
Hwang, David Henry 1957-........CTFT-5
Hyams, Peter 1943- CTFT-5
Hyde-White, Alex 1959- CTFT-5
Hyde-White, Wilfrid 1903- WWT-17
Hyem, Constance Ethel ?-1928 ...WWasWT
Hyland, Frances 1927- WWT-17
Hylton, Jack 1892-1965 ....WWasWT
Hylton, Millie 1868-1920 ....WWasWT
Hylton, Richard 1920-1962 ......WWasWT
Hyman, Earle 1926- CTFT-3
  Earlier sketch in WWT-17
Hyman, Joseph M. 1901-1977 ....WWasWT
Hyman, Prudence ....WWasWT
Hymer, John B. ?-1953 ....WWasWT
Hyson, Dorothy 1915- ....WWasWT
Hytner, Nicholas 1956- CTFT-9

I

Ibbetson, Arthur 1922- CTFT-9
Ide, Patrick 1916- WWT-17
Iden, Rosalind 1911- ....WWasWT
Idle, Eric 1943-.................CTFT-5
Idzikowski, Stanislas ?-1977 .....WWasWT
Illing, Peter 1905-1966 ....WWasWT
Illington, Margaret 1881-1934 ....WWasWT
Illington, Marie ?-1927 ....WWasWT
Imi, Tony 1937- CTFT-9
Immerman, William J. 1937-.......CTFT-1
Imperato, Carlo 1963- CTFT-4
Inescort, Elaine ?-1964 ....WWasWT
Inescort, Frieda 1901-1976 ......WWasWT
Inge, William 1913-1973 ....WWasWT
Ingels, Marty 1936- CTFT-5
Ingham, Barrie CTFT-5
  Earlier sketch in WWT-17
Ingham, Robert E. 1934-..........CTFT-1
Inglesby, Mona 1918-............WWasWT
Ingram, Rex 1895-1969 ....WWasWT
Innaurato, Albert 1948- CTFT-4
  Earlier sketch in WWT-17
Innocent, Harold 1935- CTFT-6
  Earlier sketch in WWT-17
Ionesco, Eugene 1912- CTFT-4
  Earlier sketch in WWT-17
Ireland, Anthony 1902-1957 .....WWasWT
Ireland, Jill 1941-1990 ....CTFT-9
  Earlier sketch in CTFT-6
Ireland, John 1916- CTFT-8
  Earlier sketch in CTFT-1
Ireland, Kenneth 1920- CTFT-5
  Earlier sketch in WWT-17
Irish, Annie 1865-1947 ....WWasWT
Irons, Jeremy 1948- CTFT-7
  Earlier sketch in CTFT-2
Ironside, Michael 1950- CTFT-7
Irvin, John 1940- CTFT-8
Irvine, Robin 1901-1933 ....WWasWT
Irving, Amy 1953- CTFT-4
  Earlier sketch in CTFT-1
Irving, Daisy ?-1938 ....WWasWT
Irving, Elizabeth 1904-..........WWasWT
Irving, Ellis 1902-..............WWT-16
Irving, Ethel 1869-1963 ....WWasWT
Irving, George S. 1922- CTFT-4
  Earlier sketch in WWT-17
Irving, H. B. 1870-1919 ....WWasWT
Irving, Isabel 1871-1944 ....WWasWT
Irving, Jules 1925- WWT-17
Irving, K. Ernest 1878-1953 .....WWasWT

Irving, Laurence Henry Forster
  1897-1914 ....WWasWT
Irving, Laurence Sidney
  1871-1914 ....WWasWT
Irwin, Bill 1950- CTFT-7
Irwin, Edward 1867-1937 ....WWasWT
Irwin, May 1862-1938 ....WWasWT
Isaacs, Edith J. R. 1878-1956 ....WWasWT
Isham, Gyles (Bart) 1903-1976 ...WWasWT
Isham, Mark 1951-...............CTFT-4
Isherwood, Christopher
  1904-1986 ....WWasWT
Israel, Neal 1945(?)- CTFT-9
Italiano, Anne
  See Bancroft, Anne CTFT-7
Ito, Robert 1931- CTFT-7
Ivanek, Zeljko 1957-............CTFT-5
  Brief Entry in CTFT-2
Ives, Burl 1909- CTFT-3
  Earlier sketch in WWT-17
Ivey, Dana CTFT-5
  Earlier sketch in CTFT-2
Ivey, Judith 1951-...............CTFT-8
  Earlier sketch in CTFT-1
Ivor, Frances ....WWasWT
Ivory, James 1928-..............CTFT-6
  Earlier sketch in CTFT-1
Izenour, George C. 1912- WWT-17

J

Jablonski, Carl 1937- CTFT-3
Jack and Evelyn 1886-?, 1888-? ...WWasWT
Jacker, Corinne 1933- WWT-17
Jackness, Andrew 1952-..........CTFT-4
Jackson, Anne 1926- CTFT-7
  Earlier sketches in CTFT-1, WWT-17
Jackson, Barry Vincent
  1879-1961 ....WWasWT
Jackson, Ethel 1877-1957 ....WWasWT
Jackson, Freda 1909- WWT-17
Jackson, Frederic 1886-1953 .....WWasWT
Jackson, Glenda 1936- CTFT-4
  Earlier sketch in WWT-17
Jackson, Gordon 1923-1990 ......CTFT-9
  Earlier sketches in CTFT-5, WWT-17
Jackson, Kate 1949- CTFT-3
Jackson, Nagle 1936- CTFT-9
  Earlier sketch in CTFT-1
Jackson, Nelson 1870-? ....WWasWT
Jackson, Sherry 1942- CTFT-8
Jacob, Abe J. 1944- CTFT-6
  Earlier sketch in CTFT-2
Jacob, Naomi 1889-1964 ....WWasWT
Jacobi, Derek 1938- CTFT-7
  Earlier sketches in CTFT-1, WWT-17
Jacobi, Lou 1913- CTFT-7
  Earlier sketch in WWT-17
Jacobs, Jim 1942-...............CTFT-1
Jacobs, Rusty 1967- CTFT-1
Jacobs, Sally 1932- CTFT-5
  Earlier sketch in WWT-17
Jacobs, William Wymark
  1863-1943 ....WWasWT
Jacques, Hattie 1924-1980 ....WWT-17
Jaeckel, Richard 1926-...........CTFT-5
Jaffe, Herb CTFT-5
Jaffe, Michael 1945- CTFT-4
Jaffe, Sam 1893-1984 ....CTFT-1
  Earlier sketch in WWT-17
Jaffrey, Saeed 1929- CTFT-8
Jagger, Dean 1904-.............WWasWT

Jaglom, Henry 1943- CTFT-1
Jago, Raphael Bryan 1931- WWT-17
Jalland, Henry 1861-1928 ....WWasWT
James, Brian 1920- WWT-17
James, Clifton 1925-............CTFT-3
  Earlier sketch in CTFT-1
James, Daisy ....WWasWT
James, Dorothy Dorian 1930- CTFT-7
James, Emrys 1930-1989 ....CTFT-5
  Earlier sketch in WWT-17
James, Francis 1907- ....WWasWT
James, Gerald 1917-.............WWT-17
James, Geraldine 1950- CTFT-8
James, Jessica 1931(?)-1990 .....CTFT-9
  Earlier sketch in CTFT-2
James, John 1956-...............CTFT-8
James, Julia 1890-1964 ....WWasWT
James, Peter 1940-..............CTFT-5
  Earlier sketch in WWT-17
James, Polly 1941- CTFT-5
  Earlier sketch in WWT-17
James, Roderick
  See Coen, Ethan and Joel CTFT-7
James, Wilson 1872-? ....WWasWT
Jameson, Pauline 1920-..........WWT-17
Jampolis, Neil Peter 1943-.......CTFT-5
  Earlier sketch in WWT-17
Janis, Conrad 1928- CTFT-4
  Earlier sketch in WWT-17
Janis, Elsie (Bierbower)
  1889-1956 ....WWasWT
Janney, Russell 1884-1963 ......WWasWT
Jardine, Betty ?-1945 ....WWasWT
Jarman, Derek 1942-............CTFT-9
Jarman, Herbert 1871-1919 ......WWasWT
Jarmusch, Jim 1953-.............CTFT-9
  Brief Entry in CTFT-3
Jarre, Maurice 1924-............CTFT-5
Jarrott, Charles 1927-...........CTFT-2
Jarvis, Graham 1930-............CTFT-1
Jarvis, Martin 1941-............CTFT-4
  Earlier sketch in WWT-17
Jason, David 1940- CTFT-1
Jay, Dorothy 1897-.............WWasWT
Jay, Ernest 1893-1957 ....WWasWT
Jay, Harriett 1863-1932 ....WWasWT
Jay, Isabel 1879-1927 ....WWasWT
Jay, John Herbert 1871-1942 .....WWasWT
Jayston, Michael 1936-...........CTFT-5
  Earlier sketch in WWT-17
Jeakins, Dorothy 1914- CTFT-1
Jeans, Isabel 1891-.............WWT-17
Jeans, Michael CTFT-4
Jeans, Ronald 1887-? ....WWasWT
Jeans, Ursula 1906- ....WWasWT
Jeayes, Allan 1885-1963 ....WWasWT
Jecko, Timothy 1938-............CTFT-4
Jecks, Clara ?-1951 ....WWasWT
Jefferies, Douglas 1884-1959 .....WWasWT
Jefford, Barbara 1930- CTFT-6
  Earlier sketch in WWT-17
Jeffrey, Carl
  See Jablonski, Carl CTFT-3
Jeffrey, Peter 1929-.............CTFT-6
  Earlier sketch in WWT-17
Jeffreys, Anne 1923- WWT-17
Jeffreys, Ellis 1872-1943 ....WWasWT
Jeffries, Lionel 1926-............CTFT-9
Jeffries, Maud 1869-1946 ....WWasWT
Jellicoe, Ann 1927-.............CTFT-2
  Earlier sketch in WWT-17
Jenkins, David 1937- CTFT-9
  Earlier sketch in WWT-17

Jenkins, George WWT-17
Jenkins, Hugh 1908- WWT-17
Jenkins, Megs 1917- WWT-17
Jenkins, R. Claud 1878-1967 .....WWasWT
Jenkins, Warren WWT-17
Jenn, Myvanwy 1928- WWT-17
Jenner, Caryl 1917- ....WWasWT
Jennings, Gertrude E.
    1877?-1958 ....WWasWT
Jennings, Ken CTFT-1
Jennings, Peter 1938- CTFT-6
Jenoure, Aida ....WWasWT
Jenrette, Rita CTFT-4
Jens, Salome 1935- CTFT-5
    Earlier sketch in WWT-17
Jensen, John 1933- CTFT-1
Jerome, Daisy 1881-? ....WWasWT
Jerome, Helen 1883-? ....WWasWT
Jerome, Jerome Klapka
    1859-1927 ....WWasWT
Jerome, Rowena 1890- ....WWasWT
Jerome, Sadie 1876-1950 ....WWasWT
Jerrold, Mary 1877-1955 ....WWasWT
Jesse, F. Tennyson 1889-1958 ....WWasWT
Jesse, Stella 1897- ....WWasWT
Jessel, George 1898-1981 ....WWT-17
Jessel, Patricia 1920-1968 ......WWasWT
Jett, Joan CTFT-4
Jetton, Lisbeth 1962- CTFT-4
Jewel, Jimmy 1912- WWT-17
Jewell, Izetta 1883-? ....WWasWT
Jewison, Norman 1926- CTFT-6
    Earlier sketch in CTFT-1
Jhabvala, Ruth Prawer 1927- CTFT-6
    Earlier sketch in CTFT-1
Jillian, Ann 1951- CTFT-4
    Earlier sketch in CTFT-1
Job, Thomas 1900-1947 ....WWasWT
Joel, Clara 1890- ....WWasWT
Joffe, Charles H. 1929- CTFT-9
Joffe, Roland 1945- CTFT-5
Johann, Zita 1904- ....WWasWT
Johansen, Aud 1930- ....WWasWT
John, Evan 1901-1953 ....WWasWT
John, Graham 1887-? ....WWasWT
John, Rosamund 1913- ....WWasWT
Johns, Andrew 1935- CTFT-2
Johns, Eric 1907- ....WWasWT
Johns, Glynis 1923- CTFT-5
    Earlier sketch in WWT-17
Johns, Mervyn 1899- WWT-17
Johns, Stratford 1925- CTFT-6
    Earlier sketch in CTFT-1
Johnson, Alan CTFT-9
Johnson, Arte 1934- CTFT-3
Johnson, Ben 1918- CTFT-3
Johnson, Bill 1918-1957 ....WWasWT
Johnson, Bjorn 1957- CTFT-6
Johnson, Celia 1908-1982 ....WWT-17
Johnson, Chas. Floyd CTFT-8
Johnson, Chic 1891-1962 ....WWasWT
Johnson, Don 1950- CTFT-6
Johnson, Janet 1915- ....WWasWT
Johnson, Kay 1904-1975 ....WWasWT
Johnson, Linda Lee CTFT-1
Johnson, Mary Lea 1926-1990 .....CTFT-1
Johnson, Mike
    See Sharkey, Jack CTFT-1
Johnson, Molly 1903- ....WWasWT
Johnson, Orrin 1865-1943 ....WWasWT
Johnson, Philip 1900- ....WWasWT
Johnson, Richard 1927- CTFT-5
    Earlier sketch in WWT-17

Johnson, Van 1917- CTFT-4
    Earlier sketch in WWT-17
Johnston, Denis 1901-1984 ....WWT-17
    Earlier sketch in WWasWT
Johnston, Justine CTFT-1
Johnston, Margaret 1918- WWT-17
Johnston, Moffat 1886-1935 .....WWasWT
Johnstone, Anna Hill 1913- CTFT-1
Johnstone, Justine 1899- ....WWasWT
Jolivet, Rita 1894- ....WWasWT
Jolly, Peter 1951- CTFT-1
Jolson, Al 1886-1950 ....WWasWT
Jones, Allan 1907- CTFT-6
Jones, Barry 1893- ....WWasWT
Jones, Brooks 1934- CTFT-1
Jones, Chuck 1912- CTFT-6
Jones, David 1934- CTFT-5
    Earlier sketch in WWT-17
Jones, Davy 1946- CTFT-9
Jones, Dean 1933- CTFT-3
Jones, Disley 1926- WWT-17
Jones, Dudley 1914- WWT-17
Jones, Eddie CTFT-7
Jones, Edward ?-1917 ....WWasWT
Jones, Emrys 1915-1972 ....WWasWT
Jones, Freddie 1927- CTFT-7
Jones, Gemma 1942- WWT-17
Jones, Grace 1952- CTFT-7
Jones, Griffith 1910- WWT-17
Jones, Hazel 1896-1974 ....WWasWT
Jones, Henry 1912- CTFT-6
Jones, Henry Arthur 1851-1929 ..WWasWT
Jones, James Earl 1931- CTFT-4
    Earlier sketch in WWT-17
Jones, Jeffrey 1947- CTFT-8
    Earlier sketch in CTFT-2
Jones, John 1917- CTFT-2
Jones, L. Q. 1927- CTFT-1
Jones, Leslie Julian 1910- ....WWasWT
Jones, Margo 1913-1955 ....WWasWT
Jones, Mary WWT-17
Jones, Paul 1942- CTFT-5
    Earlier sketch in WWT-17
Jones, Peter 1920- WWT-17
Jones, Quincy 1933- CTFT-8
Jones, Robert Edmond
    1887-1954 ....WWasWT
Jones, Sam 1954- CTFT-7
Jones, Samuel Major ?-1952 .....WWasWT
Jones, Shirley 1934- CTFT-6
Jones, Sidney 1869-1946 ....WWasWT
Jones, Terry 1942- CTFT-7
Jones, Tom 1928- CTFT-6
    Earlier sketch in WWT-17
Jones, Tommy Lee 1946- CTFT-6
    Earlier sketch in CTFT-1
Jones, Trefor 1902-1965 ....WWasWT
Jones, Whitworth 1873-? ....WWasWT
Jongejans, George
    See Gaynes, George CTFT-8
Jooss, Kurt 1901-1979 ....WWasWT
Jordan, Dorothy 1908- ....WWasWT
Jordan, Glenn 1936- CTFT-9
    Earlier sketch in CTFT-2
Jordan, Neil 1950- CTFT-6
Jordan, Richard 1938- CTFT-6
Jorgensen, Robert 1903- ....WWasWT
Jory, Victor 1902-1982 ....CTFT-2
    Earlier sketch in WWT-17
Joselovitz, Ernest A. 1942- CTFT-1
Josephs, Wilfred 1927- CTFT-8
Josephson, Erland 1923- CTFT-8
Joslyn, Allyn 1905-1981 ....WWasWT

Joslyn, Betsy 1954- CTFT-1
Jourdan, Louis 1920- CTFT-6
Jourdry, Patricia 1921- CTFT-2
Jouvet, Louis 1887-1951 ....WWasWT
Joy, Nicholas 1889-1964 ....WWasWT
Joy, Robert 1951- CTFT-3
Joyce, Kiya Ann 1956- CTFT-6
Joyce, Stephen 1931- CTFT-5
    Earlier sketch in WWT-17
Julia, Raul 1940- CTFT-3
    Earlier sketches in CTFT-1, WWT-17
Julian, Pat 1947- CTFT-5
Jullien, Jean 1854-1919 ....WWasWT
Jump, Gordon CTFT-3
June 1901- ....WWasWT
Jurasas, Jonas R. 1936- CTFT-2
Justin, John 1917- WWT-17

K

Kaczmarek, Jane CTFT-7
Kael, Pauline 1919- CTFT-3
Kaelred, Katharine 1882-? ....WWasWT
Kagan, Diane CTFT-3
Kahn, Florence 1878-1951 ....WWasWT
Kahn, Madeline 1942- CTFT-8
    Earlier sketch in CTFT-3
Kahn, Michael CTFT-2
    Earlier sketch in WWT-17
Kaikkonen, Gus 1951- CTFT-1
Kain, Amber 1975- CTFT-7
Kaiser, Georg 1878-1945 ....WWasWT
Kalcheim, Lee 1938- CTFT-1
Kalember, Patricia CTFT-4
Kalfin, Robert 1933- CTFT-5
    Earlier sketch in WWT-17
Kalich, Bertha 1874-1939 ....WWasWT
Kalman, Emmerich 1882-1953 ...WWasWT
Kalmar, Bert 1884-1947 ....WWasWT
Kaminska, Ida 1899-1980 ....WWT-16
Kanaly, Steve 1946- CTFT-3
Kander, John 1927- CTFT-5
    Earlier sketch in WWT-17
Kane, Carol 1952- CTFT-6
    Earlier sketch in CTFT-2
Kane, Gail 1887-1966 ....WWasWT
Kane, Richard 1938- CTFT-6
    Earlier sketch in WWT-17
Kane, Whitford 1881-1956 ....WWasWT
Kanin, Fay CTFT-4
Kanin, Garson 1912- CTFT-2
    Earlier sketch in WWT-17
Kanin, Michael 1910- CTFT-9
    Earlier sketch in CTFT-1
Kann, Lilly 1898- ....WWasWT
Kanner, Alexis 1942- WWT-17
Kanter, Hal 1918- CTFT-2
Kanter, Marin 1960- CTFT-5
Kaplan, Gabe 1945- CTFT-3
Kaplan, Jonathan 1947- CTFT-5
Kapoor, Shashi 1938- CTFT-7
Karen, James 1923- CTFT-8
Karina, Anna 1940- CTFT-8
Karlen, John 1933- CTFT-9
Karlin, Fred 1936- CTFT-9
Karlin, Miriam 1925- WWT-17
Karloff, Boris 1887-1969 ....WWasWT
Karlweis, Oscar 1859-1956 ......WWasWT
Karnilova, Maria 1920- WWT-17
Karno, Fred 1866-1941 ....WWasWT
Karpf, Merrill H. 1940- CTFT-4

Karras, Alex 1935- CTFT-6
　Earlier sketch in CTFT-1
Karsavina, Tamara 1885-1978 ....WWasWT
Kasarda, John 1943- CTFT-3
Kasdan, Lawrence 1949- CTFT-5
Kasem, Casey 1933- CTFT-6
Kasha, Lawrence N. 1933- CTFT-4
　Earlier sketch in WWT-17
Kass, Jerome 1937- CTFT-1
Kassin, Michael B. 1947- CTFT-1
Kasznar, Kurt S. 1913-1979 ......WWT-17
Katselas, Milton 1933- WWT-17
Katt, William 1951- CTFT-3
Katzka, Grabriel 1931-1990 ......CTFT-9
Kaufman, Andy 1949-1984 ....CTFT-2
Kaufman, George S. 1889-1961 ..WWasWT
Kaufman, Lloyd 1945- CTFT-7
Kaufman, Philip 1936- CTFT-6
Kaufman, Victor 1943- CTFT-8
Kavner, Julie 1951- CTFT-5
　Brief Entry in CTFT-2
Kawalek, Nancy CTFT-4
Kay, Beatrice 1907-1986 ....CTFT-4
Kay, Charles 1930- CTFT-5
　Earlier sketch in WWT-17
Kay, Richard 1937- WWT-17
Kayden, William 1929-1987 ....CTFT-1
Kaye, Albert Patrick 1878-1946 ..WWasWT
Kaye, Danny 1913-1987 ....CTFT-3
　Earlier sketch in WWT-17
Kaye, Frederick ....WWasWT
Kaye, Judy 1948- CTFT-9
　Earlier sketch in CTFT-1
Kaye, Stubby 1918- WWT-17
Kazan, Elia 1909- CTFT-3
　Earlier sketch in WWasWT
Kazan, Lainie 1942- CTFT-4
Kazurinsky, Tim 1950- CTFT-6
Keach, James CTFT-6
Keach, Stacy 1941- CTFT-4
　Earlier sketch in WWT-17
Keagy, Grace CTFT-1
Keal, Anita CTFT-3
Kealy, Thomas J. 1874-1949 .....WWasWT
Kean, Jane 1928- CTFT-1
Kean, Marie 1922- CTFT-6
　Earlier sketch in WWT-17
Kean, Norman 1934-1988 ....CTFT-6
　Earlier sketch in WWT-17
Keane, Doris 1881-1945 ....WWasWT
Keane, John B. 1928- WWT-17
Keane, Robert Emmett 1883-? ...WWasWT
Kearns, Allen 1893-1956 ....WWasWT
Keating, Charles 1941- CTFT-5
　Earlier sketch in WWT-17
Keaton, Diane 1946- CTFT-6
　Earlier sketch in CTFT-1
Keaton, Michael 1951- CTFT-6
　Brief Entry in CTFT-2
Keats, Viola 1911- WWT-17
Keck, Michael 1946- CTFT-8
Keegan, Donna CTFT-4
Keel, Howard 1919- WWT-17
Keeler, Ruby 1909- WWT-17
Keen, Geoffrey 1916- WWT-17
Keen, Malcolm 1887-1970 ....WWasWT
Keenan, Frank 1858-1929 ....WWasWT
Keeshan, Robert J. 1927- CTFT-4
Keiber, Robert John 1946- CTFT-6
Keightley, Cyril 1875-1929 ......WWasWT
Keim, Adelaide 1880-? ....WWasWT
Keitel, Harvey 1941- CTFT-5

Keith, Brian 1921- CTFT-9
　Earlier sketches in CTFT-2, WWT-17
Keith, David 1954- CTFT-4
Keith, Ian 1899-1960 ....WWasWT
Keith, Paul 1944- CTFT-1
Keith, Penelope CTFT-3
　Earlier sketch in WWT-17
Keith, Robert 1898-1966 ....WWasWT
Keith-Johnston, Colin 1896- .....WWasWT
Kelcey, Herbert 1856-1917 ......WWasWT
Kelham, Avice 1892- ....WWasWT
Keller, Marthe 1946- CTFT-6
Keller, Max A. 1943- CTFT-2
Keller, Micheline 1948- CTFT-2
Kellerman, Sally 1936- CTFT-5
Kellermann, Annette 1888-1975 ..WWasWT
Kelley, DeForest 1920- CTFT-8
　Earlier sketch in CTFT-3
Kelley, William 1929- CTFT-7
Kellin, Mike 1922- WWT-17
Kellman, Barnet 1947- CTFT-2
Kellogg, Shirley 1888-? ....WWasWT
Kelly, Brian 1956- CTFT-1
Kelly, E. H. ....WWasWT
Kelly, Eva 1880-1948 ....WWasWT
Kelly, Gene 1912- CTFT-3
　Earlier sketch in WWasWT
Kelly, George 1890-1974 ....WWasWT
Kelly, Judy 1913- ....WWasWT
Kelly, Kevin 1934- CTFT-1
Kelly, Marguerite 1959- CTFT-7
Kelly, Nancy 1921- WWT-17
Kelly, Patsy 1910-1981 ....WWT-17
Kelly, Paul 1899-1956 ....WWasWT
Kelly, Renee 1888-1965 ....WWasWT
Kelly, Tim 1937- CTFT-1
Kelly, Vivian 1922- CTFT-4
Kelly, W. W. 1853-1933 ....WWasWT
Kelly, Walter C. 1873-1939 ......WWasWT
Kelsey, Linda 1946- CTFT-7
Kelso, Vernon 1893- ....WWasWT
Kemp, Elizabeth 1957- CTFT-8
Kemp, Jeremy 1935- CTFT-8
　Earlier sketches in CTFT-2, WWT-17
Kemp, T. C. 1891-1955 ....WWasWT
Kemper, Collin 1870-1955 ....WWasWT
Kemper, Victor J. 1927- CTFT-4
Kempson, Rachel 1910- CTFT-7
　Earlier sketch in WWT-17
Kemp-Welch, Joan WWT-17
Kendal, Doris ....WWasWT
Kendal, Felicity 1946- CTFT-3
　Earlier sketch in WWT-17
Kendal, Madge (Margaret)
　1848-1935 ....WWasWT
Kendal, William Hunter
　1843-1917 ....WWasWT
Kendall, Henry 1897-1962 ....WWasWT
Kendall, John 1869-? ....WWasWT
Kendall, William 1903- WWT-16
Kendrick, Alfred 1869-? ....WWasWT
Kennedy, Arthur 1914-1990 ......CTFT-3
　Earlier sketch in WWT-17
Kennedy, Burt 1922- CTFT-6
Kennedy, Charles Rann
　1871-1950 ....WWasWT
Kennedy, Cheryl 1947- CTFT-5
　Earlier sketch in WWT-17
Kennedy, Edmund 1873-? ....WWasWT
Kennedy, George 1926- CTFT-6
　Earlier sketch in CTFT-1
Kennedy, Harold J. 1914-1988 .....CTFT-6
　Earlier sketch in WWT-17

Kennedy, Joyce 1898-1943 ......WWasWT
Kennedy, Kathleen CTFT-5
Kennedy, Laurie CTFT-1
Kennedy, Madge 1892-1987 .....WWasWT
Kennedy, Margaret 1896-1967 ...WWasWT
Kennedy, Mary 1908- ....WWasWT
Kennedy, Mimi 1948- CTFT-8
Kennedy, Patrica 1917- WWT-17
Kenney, James 1930- WWT-16
Kenny, Jack 1958- CTFT-7
Kenny, Sean 1932-1973 ....WWasWT
Kensit, Patsy 1968- CTFT-9
Kent, Barry 1932- WWT-17
Kent, Jean 1921- WWT-17
Kent, John B. 1939- CTFT-5
Kent, Keneth 1892-1963 ....WWasWT
Kent, William 1886-1945 ....WWasWT
Kentish, Agatha 1897- ....WWasWT
Kenton, Godfrey 1902- WWT-17
Kenton, Maxwell
　See Southern, Terry CTFT-7
Kenwright, Bill 1945- WWT-17
Kenyon, Charles 1878-1961 .....WWasWT
Kenyon, Doris 1897- ....WWasWT
Kenyon, Neil ?-1946 ....WWasWT
Keown, Eric 1904-1963 ....WWasWT
Kepros, Nicholas 1932- CTFT-1
Kerbosch, Roeland 1940- CTFT-3
Kercheval, Ken 1935- CTFT-1
Kerin, Nora 1883-? ....WWasWT
Kerker, Gustave Adolph
　1857-1923 ....WWasWT
Kerman, Sheppard 1928- CTFT-4
Kern, Jerome David 1885-1945 ...WWasWT
Kernan, David 1939- WWT-17
Kerns, Joanna 1953- CTFT-8
Kerr, Bill WWT-17
Kerr, Deborah 1921- CTFT-4
　Earlier sketch in WWT-17
Kerr, E. Katherine 1942- CTFT-6
　Earlier sketch in CTFT-1
Kerr, Elaine
　See Kerr, E. Katherine CTFT-6
Kerr, Frederick 1858-1933 ......WWasWT
Kerr, Geoffrey 1895- ....WWasWT
Kerr, Jean 1923- CTFT-1
　Earlier sketch in WWT-17
Kerr, Molly 1904- ....WWasWT
Kerr, Walter 1913- CTFT-4
　Earlier sketch in WWT-17
Kerridge, Mary 1914- WWT-17
Kerrigan, J. M. 1885-1964 ....WWasWT
Kerry, Anne 1958- CTFT-1
Kershaw, Willette 1890-1960 .....WWasWT
Kert, Larry 1930- CTFT-4
　Earlier sketch in WWT-17
Kerwin, Brian 1949- CTFT-8
Kesdekian, Mesrop 1920- CTFT-2
Kesselring, Joseph O.
　1902-1967 ....WWasWT
Kestelman, Sara 1944- CTFT-5
　Earlier sketch in WWT-17
Kester, Paul 1870-1933 ....WWasWT
Ketron, Larry 1947- CTFT-4
　Earlier sketch in CTFT-1
Keyloun, Mark Anthony 1960- CTFT-1
Keys, Nelson 1886-1939 ....WWasWT
Keysar, Franklin 1939- CTFT-3
Kheel, Lee 1918- CTFT-4
Kidd, Michael 1919- WWT-17
Kidd, Robert 1943-1980 ....WWT-17
Kidder, Kathryn 1867-1939 ......WWasWT

Kidder, Margot 1948- CTFT-6
  Earlier sketch in CTFT-1
Kiel, Richard 1939- CTFT-9
Kiepura, Jan 1902-1966 ....WWasWT
Kiley, Richard 1922- CTFT-6
  Earlier sketches in CTFT-1, WWT-17
Killeen, Sheelagh 1940- WWT-17
Killick, C. Egerton 1891-1967 ....WWasWT
Kilmer, Val CTFT-7
Kilty, Jerome 1922- CTFT-3
  Earlier sketch in WWT-17
Kim, Willa CTFT-9
Kimball, Grace 1870-? ....WWasWT
Kimball, Louis 1889-1936 ....WWasWT
Kimmins, Anthony 1901-1964 ...WWasWT
Kimmins, Kenneth 1941- CTFT-5
Kinberg, Judy 1948- CTFT-7
Kindley, Jeffrey 1945- CTFT-1
King, Ada ?-1940 ....WWasWT
King, Alan 1927- CTFT-3
King, Cecil ?-1958 ....WWasWT
King, Charles 1889-1944 ....WWasWT
King, Claude 1876-1941 ....WWasWT
King, Dennis 1897-1971 ....WWasWT
King, Edith 1896- ....WWasWT
King, John Michael 1926- WWT-17
King, Mabel CTFT-9
King, Perry 1948- CTFT-9
  Earlier sketch in CTFT-2
King, Philip 1904-1979 ....WWT-16
King, Stephen 1947- CTFT-8
King, Walter Woolf 1899- ....WWasWT
King, Woodie Jr. 1937- CTFT-8
  Earlier sketch in WWT-17
King-Hall, Stephen 1893-1966 ....WWasWT
Kingsley, Ben 1943- CTFT-4
  Earlier sketches in CTFT-1, WWT-17
Kingsley, Sidney 1906- WWT-17
Kingston, Gertrude 1866-1937 ...WWasWT
Kingston, Mark 1934- WWT-17
Kinnear, Roy 1934-1988 ....CTFT-7
  Earlier sketch in WWT-17
Kinney, Terry 1954- CTFT-5
Kinski, Klaus 1928- CTFT-5
Kinski, Nastassja 1960- CTFT-6
  Earlier sketch in CTFT-1
Kinzer, Craig 1953- CTFT-3
Kipness, Joseph WWT-17
Kippax, H. G. 1920- WWT-17
Kipphardt, Heinar 1922- WWT-17
Kirby, B. Jr.
  See Kirby, Bruno CTFT-6
Kirby, Bruce Jr.
  See Kirby, Bruno CTFT-6
Kirby, Bruno CTFT-6
Kirby, John 1894- ....WWasWT
Kirchenbauer, Bill 1953- CTFT-8
Kirk, Lisa WWT-17
Kirkland, Alexander ....WWasWT
Kirkland, Jack 1902-1969 ....WWasWT
Kirkland, James R. III 1947- CTFT-1
Kirkland, Muriel 1903-1971 .....WWasWT
Kirkland, Patricia 1925- ....WWasWT
Kirkland, Sally 1944- CTFT-7
  Earlier sketch in WWT-17
Kirkwood, James 1930-1989 ......CTFT-5
  Earlier sketch in WWT-17
Kirkwood, Pat 1921- WWT-17
Kirtland, Lousie 1910- WWT-17
Kirwan, Patrick ?-1929 ....WWasWT
Kistemaeckers, Henry
  1872-1938 ....WWasWT
Kitchen, Michael 1948- CTFT-8

Kitchin, Laurence 1913- WWT-17
Kitt, Eartha 1928- CTFT-3
  Earlier sketch in WWT-17
Klar, Gary 1947- CTFT-1
Klaris, Harvey J. 1939- CTFT-1
Klauber, Adolph 1879-1933 .....WWasWT
Klaw, Marc 1858-1936..........WWasWT
Klein, Charles 1867-1915 ....WWasWT
Klein, Robert 1942- CTFT-3
  Earlier sketch in WWT-17
Kleiner, Harry 1916- CTFT-4
Kleiser, Randal CTFT-1
Klemperer, Werner 1920- CTFT-6
Kliban, Ken 1943- CTFT-1
Kliewer, Warren 1931- CTFT-1
Kline, Kevin 1947- CTFT-3
  Earlier sketches in CTFT-1, WWT-17
Klotz, Florence CTFT-2
  Earlier sketch in WWT-17
Klugman, Jack 1922- CTFT-3
  Earlier sketches in CTFT-1, WWT-17
Klunis, Tom 1930- CTFT-1
Kmeck, George 1949- CTFT-2
Knapp, Eleanore CTFT-1
Kneale, Nigel 1922- CTFT-9
Kneale, Patricia 1925- WWT-17
Knight, David 1927- WWT-17
Knight, Esmond 1906-1987 ......WWT-17
Knight, Joan 1924- WWT-17
Knight, Julius 1863-1941 ....WWasWT
Knight, June 1911-1987 ....WWasWT
Knight, Shirley 1936- CTFT-3
  Earlier sketch in WWT-17
Knight, Ted 1923-1986 ....CTFT-1
Knobeloch, Jim 1950- CTFT-1
Knoblock, Edward 1874-1945 ....WWasWT
Knopfler, Mark 1949- CTFT-8
Knott, Frederick 1916- CTFT-1
Knott, Roselle 1870-1948 ....WWasWT
Knotts, Don 1924- CTFT-3
Knowles, Alex 1850-1917 ....WWasWT
Knox, Alexander 1907- WWT-17
Knox, Terence CTFT-7
Kobart, Ruth 1924- WWT-17
Koch, Howard W. 1916- CTFT-1
Koch, Howard W. Jr. 1945- CTFT-1
Koenig, Walter 1936- CTFT-5
Kohler, Estelle WWT-17
Kolb, Therese 1856-1935 ....WWasWT
Kolber, Lynne
  See Halliday, Lynne CTFT-6
Kolker, Henry 1874-1947 ....WWasWT
Kollmar, Richard 1910-1971 .....WWasWT
Koltai, Ralph 1924- WWT-17
Komack, James 1930- CTFT-7
Komarov, Shelley 1949- CTFT-4
Komisarjevsky, Theodore
  1882-1954 ....WWasWT
Konchalovsky, Andrei 1937- CTFT-8
Kondazian, Karen CTFT-4
Konigsberg, Frank 1933- CTFT-2
Konstam, Anna 1914- ....WWasWT
Konstam, Phyllis 1907- ....WWasWT
Kopache, Tom 1945- CTFT-2
Kopit, Arthur 1937- CTFT-4
  Earlier sketch in WWT-17
Koppell, Bernie 1933- CTFT-6
Kops, Bernard 1926- WWT-17
Kopyc, Frank 1948- CTFT-1
Korman, Harvey 1927- CTFT-3
Kornfeld, Robert 1919- CTFT-4
Kornman, Cam 1949- CTFT-5
Korty, John Van Cleave 1936- CTFT-1

Korvin, Charles 1907- CTFT-3
Kosinski, Jerzy 1933- CTFT-1
Kossoff, David 1919- WWT-17
Kosta, Tessa 1893- ....WWasWT
Kotlowitz, Dan 1957- CTFT-3
Kotto, Yaphet 1944- CTFT-5
Koun, Karolos 1908-1987 ....WWasWT
Kovacs, Laszlo 1933- CTFT-3
Kove, Kenneth 1893- ....WWasWT
Kove, Martin CTFT-3
Kovens, Ed 1934- CTFT-2
Krabbe, Jeroen 1944- CTFT-4
Kramer, Bert CTFT-4
Kramer, Larry 1935- CTFT-5
Kramer, Marsha CTFT-4
Kramer, Stanley E. 1913- CTFT-4
  Earlier sketch in CTFT-1
Kramm, Joseph 1907- WWT-16
Kraselchik, R.
  See Dyer, Charles CTFT-6
Krasna, Norman 1909-1984......WWT-17
Krasner, Milton 1904-1988 ....CTFT-7
Krauss, Marvin A. 1928- CTFT-1
Krauss, Werner 1884-1959 ......WWasWT
Kremer, Theodore 1873-? ....WWasWT
Kretzmer, Herbert 1925- WWT-17
Krige, Alice 1954- CTFT-7
Kristel, Sylvia 1952- CTFT-8
Kristofferson, Kris 1936- CTFT-5
Kroeger, Gary 1957- CTFT-5
Kronenberger, Louis 1904-1980 ...WWT-16
Kruger, Alma 1871-1960 ....WWasWT
Kruger, Otto 1885-1974 ....WWasWT
Krupska, Danya 1923- WWT-17
Kruschen, Jack 1922- CTFT-6
Krutch, Joseph Wood
  1893-1970 ....WWasWT
Kubik, Alex CTFT-4
Kubrick, Stanley 1928- CTFT-7
  Earlier sketch in CTFT-1
Kulp, Nancy 1921- CTFT-3
Kulukundis, Eddie 1932- WWT-17
Kumchachi, Madame 1843-? .....WWasWT
Kummer, Clare 1888-1958.......WWasWT
Kummer, Frederic Arnold
  1873-1943 ....WWasWT
Kun, Magda 1912-1945 ....WWasWT
Kunneke, Eduard 1885-1953 ....WWasWT
Kuralt, Charles 1934- CTFT-5
Kureishi, Hanif CTFT-5
Kurnitz, Julie 1942- CTFT-4
Kurosawa, Akira 1910- CTFT-6
Kurth, Juliette 1960- CTFT-4
Kurton, Peggy ....WWasWT
Kurty, Hella ?-1954 ....WWasWT
Kurtz, Gary 1940- CTFT-6
Kurtz, Swoosie CTFT-4
  Earlier sketch in CTFT-1
Kurys, Diane 1949- CTFT-8
Kustow, Michael 1939- CTFT-6
  Earlier sketch in WWT-17
Kwan, Nancy 1939- CTFT-7
Kyasht, Lydia 1886-? ....WWasWT
Kyle, Barry 1947- CTFT-5
  Earlier sketch in WWT-17

L

Lablache, Luigi ?-1914 ....WWasWT
Lacey, Catherine 1904-1979.......WWT-16
Lacey, William J. 1931- CTFT-2
Lachman, Morton 1918- CTFT-1

Lack, Simon 1917- WWT-17
Lackaye, Wilton 1862-1932 ......WWasWT
Lacy, Frank 1867-1937 ....WWasWT
Lacy, George 1904- ....WWasWT
Lacy-Thompson, Charles
　　Robert 1922- WWT-17
Ladd, Cheryl 1951- CTFT-6
　　Earlier sketch in CTFT-2
Ladd, David Alan 1947- CTFT-2
Ladd, Diane 1939- CTFT-7
　　Earlier sketch in CTFT-1
Laffan, Patricia 1919- ....WWasWT
Laffran, Kevin Barry 1922- WWT-17
Lagerfelt, Caroline CTFT-2
Lahr, Bert 1895-1967 ....WWasWT
Lahr, John 1941- WWT-17
Lahti, Christine 1950- CTFT-4
　　Earlier sketch in CTFT-1
Lai, Francis 1932- CTFT-2
Laidler, Francis 1870-1955 ......WWasWT
Laine, Cleo 1927- CTFT-3
Laing, Peggie 1899- ....WWasWT
Laird, Jack 1923- CTFT-1
Laird, Jenny 1917- WWT-17
Lake, Harriette
　　See Sothern, Ann CTFT-8
Lake, Lew ?-1939 ....WWasWT
Lake, Ricki 1969(?)- CTFT-9
Lally, Gwen ?-1963 ....WWasWT
LaLoggia, Frank CTFT-4
Lalor, Frank 1869-1932 ....WWasWT
Lamas, Lorenzo 1958- CTFT-5
Lamb, Beatrice 1866-? ....WWasWT
Lambelet, Napoleon 1864-1932 ...WWasWT
Lambert, Christopher 1957- CTFT-3
Lambert, Constant 1905-1951 ....WWasWT
Lambert, J. W. 1917- WWT-17
Lambert, Jack 1899-1976 ....WWT-16
Lambert, Lawson 1870-1944 .....WWasWT
La Milo ....WWasWT
Lamos, Mark 1946- CTFT-9
　　Earlier sketch in CTFT-1
Lampert, Zohra 1937- CTFT-4
　　Earlier sketch in CTFT-1
Lampkin, Charles 1913-1989 ....CTFT-8
Lan, David 1952- CTFT-5
　　Earlier sketch in WWT-17
Lancaster, Burt 1913- CTFT-6
　　Earlier sketch in CTFT-1
Lancaster, Nora 1882-? ....WWasWT
Lanchester, Elsa 1902-1986 ....CTFT-4
　　Earlier sketches in CTFT-3, WWasWT
Lanchester, Robert 1941- CTFT-2
Land, David 1920- WWT-17
Landau, David 1878-1935 ....WWasWT
Landau, Martin CTFT-7
　　Earlier sketch in CTFT-1
Landau, Vivien CTFT-3
Landeau, Cecil 1906- ....WWasWT
Landeck, Ben 1864-1928 ....WWasWT
Landen, Dinsdale 1932- CTFT-5
　　Earlier sketch in WWT-17
Landers, Audrey CTFT-4
Landers, Harry 1921- CTFT-9
Landers, Judy CTFT-4
Landes, William-Alan 1945- CTFT-2
Landesberg, Steve CTFT-3
Landesman, Heidi CTFT-9
Landi, Elisa 1904-1948 ....WWasWT
Landis, Jessie Royce 1904-1972 ..WWasWT
Landis, John 1950- CTFT-7
　　Earlier sketch in CTFT-1
Landis, William 1921- CTFT-3

Landon, Avice 1908-1976 ....WWT-16
Landon, Michael 1936- CTFT-7
Landsburg, Valerie 1958- CTFT-4
Landstone, Charles 1891- ....WWasWT
Lane, Burton 1912- WWT-17
Lane, Charles 1905- CTFT-9
Lane, Diane 1963- CTFT-5
　　Brief Entry in CTFT-2
Lane, Dorothy 1890- ....WWasWT
Lane, Genette 1940- CTFT-4
Lane, Grace 1876-1956 ....WWasWT
Lane, Horace 1880-? ....WWasWT
Lane, Lupino 1892-1959 ....WWasWT
Lane, Stewart F. 1951- CTFT-3
Laneuville, Eric 1952- CTFT-6
Lang, Andre 1893-1986 ....CTFT-4
Lang, Belinda 1953- CTFT-8
Lang, Charles 1902- CTFT-9
Lang, Charles, Jr.
　　See Lang, Charles CTFT-9
Lang, Charles B.
　　See Lang, Charles CTFT-9
Lang, Charles B., Jr.
　　See Lang, Charles CTFT-9
Lang, Charley 1955- CTFT-1
Lang, Harold WWT-17
Lang, Howard 1876-1941 ....WWasWT
Lang, Matheson 1879-1948 ......WWasWT
Lang, Pearl 1922- CTFT-1
Lang, Philip J. 1911-1986 ....CTFT-1
Lang, Robert 1934- CTFT-5
　　Earlier sketch in WWT-17
Lang, Stephen 1952- CTFT-5
Langdon, Sue Ann 1936- CTFT-6
Lange, Hope 1933- CTFT-5
Lange, Jessica 1949- CTFT-6
　　Earlier sketch in CTFT-2
Lange, John
　　See Crichton, Michael CTFT-5
Lange, Ted CTFT-3
Langella, Frank 1940- CTFT-9
　　Earlier sketches in CTFT-1, WWT-17
Langham, Michael 1919- CTFT-6
　　Earlier sketch in WWT-17
Langley, Noel 1911- ....WWasWT
Langner, Lawrence 1890-1962 ....WWasWT
Langner, Philip 1926- WWT-17
Langton, Basil 1912- CTFT-2
　　Earlier sketch in WWasWT
Langtry, Lillie 1852-1929 ....WWasWT
Langtry, Lillie 1877-? ....WWasWT
Lansbury, Angela 1925- CTFT-7
　　Earlier sketches in CTFT-1, WWT-17
Lansbury, Edgar 1930- WWT-17
Lansing, Robert 1928- CTFT-3
Lansing, Sherry 1944- CTFT-1
Lantz, Robert 1914- CTFT-1
Laparcerie, Cora ....WWasWT
Lapine, James 1949- CTFT-7
Lapis, Peter CTFT-4
La Plante, Laura 1904- ....WWasWT
Lapotaire, Jane 1944- CTFT-3
　　Earlier sketch in WWT-17
Lara, Madame 1876-? ....WWasWT
Lardner, Ring Jr. 1915- CTFT-5
Larimore, Earle 1899-1974 ......WWasWT
Larkin, Peter 1926- WWT-17
Larra, Mariano ....WWasWT
Larrimore, Francine 1898-1975 ...WWasWT
Larroquette, John 1947- CTFT-3
Larson, Glen A. CTFT-7
Larson, Jack 1933- CTFT-9
La Rue, Danny CTFT-2

La Rue, Grace 1882-1956 ....WWasWT
LaRusso, Louis II 1935- WWT-17
Lashwood, George ?-1942 ....WWasWT
Lasser, Louise 1941- CTFT-3
Lassick, Sydney 1922- CTFT-1
Laszlo, Andrew 1926- CTFT-1
Latham, Frederick G. ?-1943 ....WWasWT
Lathan, Bobbi Jo 1951- CTFT-8
Lathan, Stanley 1945- CTFT-6
Lathbury, Stanley 1873-? ....WWasWT
Lathom, Earl of
　　See Wilbraham, Edward ....WWasWT
Latimer, Edyth ....WWasWT
Latimer, Hugh 1913- WWT-17
Latimer, Sally 1910- ....WWasWT
Latona, Jen 1881-? ....WWasWT
La Trobe, Charles 1879-1967 ....WWasWT
Lauchlan, Agnes 1905- WWT-17
Lauder, Harry 1870-1950 ....WWasWT
Laughlin, Sharon 1949- CTFT-1
Laughlin, Tom 1938- CTFT-5
Laughton, Charles 1899-1962 ....WWasWT
Laurance, Matthew CTFT-8
Laurence, Paula WWT-17
Laurents, Arthur 1918- CTFT-9
　　Earlier sketches in CTFT-2, WWT-17
Lauria, Dan 1947- CTFT-7
Laurie, John 1897-1980 ....WWT-17
Laurie, Piper 1932- CTFT-3
Laurier, Jay 1879-1969 ....WWasWT
Laurillard, Edward 1870-1936 ....WWasWT
Lauro, Shirley 1933- CTFT-1
Lauter, Ed 1940- CTFT-5
Lavalliere, Eve 1866-1929 ....WWasWT
Lavedan, Henri 1859-1940 ....WWasWT
Laver, James 1899-1975 ....WWasWT
Laverick, Beryl 1919- ....WWasWT
La Verne, Lucille 1872-1945 .....WWasWT
Lavin, Linda 1937- CTFT-3
　　Earlier sketch in WWT-17
Law, Arthur 1844-1913 ....WWasWT
Law, John Philip 1937- CTFT-7
Law, Mary 1891- ....WWasWT
Law, Moulon 1922- CTFT-2
Lawford, Betty 1910-1960 ....WWasWT
Lawford, Ernest ?-1940 ....WWasWT
Lawford, Peter 1923-1984 ....CTFT-2
Lawlor, Mary ....WWasWT
Lawrence, Boyle 1869-1951 ......WWasWT
Lawrence, Carol 1935- CTFT-4
　　Earlier sketch in WWT-17
Lawrence, Charles 1896- ....WWasWT
Lawrence, D. H. 1885-1930 ......WWasWT
Lawrence, Darrie CTFT-4
Lawrence, Eddie 1921- CTFT-1
Lawrence, Gerald 1873-1957 .....WWasWT
Lawrence, Gertrude 1898-1952 ...WWasWT
Lawrence, Jerome 1915- CTFT-5
　　Earlier sketch in WWT-17
Lawrence, Lawrence Shubert
　　Jr. 1916- CTFT-4
Lawrence, Marc 1910- CTFT-9
Lawrence, Margaret 1889-1929 ...WWasWT
Lawrence, Vicki 1949- CTFT-1
Lawrence, Vincent 1896- ....WWasWT
Lawrence, Vincent S. 1890-1946 ..WWasWT
Lawrence, William John
　　1862-1940 ....WWasWT
Lawson, Denis 1947- CTFT-9
Lawson, John 1865-1920 ....WWasWT
Lawson, John Howard
　　1895-1977 ....WWasWT
Lawson, Leigh 1943- CTFT-9

Lawson, Mary 1910-1941 . . . . WWasWT
Lawson, Richard CTFT-9
Lawson, Wilfrid 1900-1966 . . . . . . WWasWT
Lawson, Winifred 1894-1961 . . . . . WWasWT
Lawton, Frank 1904-1969 . . . . . . WWasWT
Lawton, Leslie 1942- WWT-17
Lawton, Thais 1881-1956 . . . . WWasWT
Laye, Dilys 1934- WWT-17
Laye, Evelyn 1900- WWT-17
Layton, Joe 1931- CTFT-5
  Earlier sketch in WWT-17
Lazaridis, Stefanos 1944- CTFT-4
Lazarus, Paul 1954- CTFT-4
Lazenby, George 1939- CTFT-2
Leabo, Loi 1935- CTFT-3
Leach, Robin 1941- CTFT-5
Leach, Rosemary 1935- CTFT-8
Leach, Wilford 1929-1988 . . . . CTFT-6
Leachman, Cloris 1930- CTFT-4
  Earlier sketch in CTFT-1
Leadlay, Edward O. ?-1951 . . . . . . WWasWT
Leahy, Eugene 1883-1967 . . . . WWasWT
Leamore, Tom 1865-1939 . . . . WWasWT
Lean, Cecil 1878-1935 . . . . WWasWT
Lean, David 1908- CTFT-6
Lear, Norman 1922- CTFT-8
  Earlier sketch in CTFT-1
Learned, Michael 1939- CTFT-6
  Earlier sketch in CTFT-1
Leary, David 1939- CTFT-3
Leaver, Philip 1904- . . . . WWasWT
Le Bargy, Charles Gustave
  Auguste 1858-1936 . . . . WWasWT
Le Baron, William 1883-1958 . . . WWasWT
Leblanc, Georgette 1876-1941 . . . WWasWT
Lebowsky, Stanley 1926-1986 . . . . . . CTFT-4
Le Breton, Flora 1898- . . . . WWasWT
Leconte, Marie . . . . WWasWT
Lederer, Francis 1899- CTFT-1
Lederer, George W. 1861-1938 . . . WWasWT
Lee, Anna 1913- CTFT-1
Lee, Auriol 1880-1941 . . . . WWasWT
Lee, Bernard 1908-1981 . . . . WWT-17
Lee, Bert 1880-1946 . . . . WWasWT
Lee, Canada 1907-1952 . . . . WWasWT
Lee, Christopher 1922- CTFT-6
Lee, Eugene 1939- CTFT-5
  Earlier sketch in WWT-17
Lee, Fran 1910- CTFT-5
Lee, Franne 1941- CTFT-5
  Earlier sketch in WWT-17
Lee, Gypsy Rose 1913-1970 . . . . . WWasWT
Lee, Irving Allen 1948- CTFT-3
Lee, Jack 1929- CTFT-1
Lee, Jennie ?-1930 . . . . WWasWT
Lee, Lance 1942- CTFT-1
Lee, Michele 1942- CTFT-1
Lee, Ming Cho 1930- CTFT-4
  Earlier sketch in WWT-17
Lee, Robert E. 1918- CTFT-4
  Earlier sketch in WWT-17
Lee, Spike 1956- CTFT-6
Lee, Vanessa 1920- WWT-17
Leech, Richard 1922- CTFT-6
  Earlier sketch in WWT-17
Leeds, Phil CTFT-9
Lefeaux, Charles 1909- . . . . WWasWT
Le Feuvre, Guy 1883-1950 . . . . . . WWasWT
LeFevre, Adam 1950- CTFT-1
Lefevre, Maurice . . . . WWasWT
LeFrak, Francine 1950- CTFT-4
  Earlier sketch in WWT-17
Le Fre, Albert 1870-? . . . . WWasWT

Leftwich, Alexander 1884-1947 . . . WWasWT
Le Gallienne, Eva 1899- CTFT-1
  Earlier sketch in WWT-17
Legarde, Millie . . . . WWasWT
LeGault, Lance CTFT-7
Leggatt, Alison (Joy) 1904-1990 . . . WWT-17
Legrand, Michel 1932- CTFT-9
Le Grand, Phyllis . . . . WWasWT
Lehar, Franz 1870-1948 . . . . WWasWT
Le Hay, Daisy 1883-? . . . . WWasWT
Le Hay, John 1854-1926 . . . . WWasWT
Lehmann, Beatrix 1903-1979 . . . . . . WWT-17
Lehmann, Carla 1917- . . . . WWasWT
Leiber, Fritz 1883-1949 . . . . WWasWT
Leibman, Ron 1937- CTFT-7
  Earlier sketches in CTFT-2, WWT-17
Leicester, Ernest 1866-1939 . . . . . . WWasWT
Leider, Jerry 1931- CTFT-9
  Earlier sketch in CTFT-1
Leigh, Andrew George
  1887-1957 . . . . WWasWT
Leigh, Charlotte 1907- . . . . WWasWT
Leigh, Dorma 1893- . . . . WWasWT
Leigh, Gracie ?-1950 . . . . WWasWT
Leigh, Janet 1927- CTFT-3
Leigh, Jennifer Jason 1958- CTFT-8
Leigh, Mary 1904-1943 . . . . WWasWT
Leigh, Mike 1943- CTFT-6
  Earlier sketch in WWT-17
Leigh, Mitch 1928- CTFT-1
Leigh, Rowland 1902-1963 . . . . . . WWasWT
Leigh, Vivien 1913-1967 . . . . WWasWT
Leigh, Walter 1905- . . . . WWasWT
Leigheb, Claudio 1848-? . . . . WWasWT
Leigh-Hunt, Barbara 1935- WWT-17
Leighton, Frank 1908-1962 . . . . . . WWasWT
Leighton, Margaret 1922-1976 . . . . WWT-16
Leighton, Queenie 1872-1943 . . . . WWasWT
Leister, Frederick 1885-1970 . . . . . WWasWT
Leisure, David CTFT-7
Lelouch, Claude 1937- CTFT-8
Lely, Madeline . . . . WWasWT
Lemaitre, Jules 1853-1914 . . . . WWasWT
Le Massena, William 1916- WWT-17
Le Mat, Paul CTFT-7
Lemay, Harding 1922- CTFT-1
Lemmon, Chris 1954- CTFT-7
Lemmon, Jack 1925- CTFT-7
  Earlier sketch in CTFT-2
Le Moyne, Sarah Cowell
  1859-1915 . . . . WWasWT
Lena, Lily 1879-? . . . . WWasWT
Lenard, Mark 1927- CTFT-9
Lender, Marcelle . . . . WWasWT
Lenihan, Winifred 1898-1964 . . . . WWasWT
Lennard, Arthur 1867-1954 . . . . . . WWasWT
Lennox, Vera 1904- . . . . WWasWT
Leno, Jay 1950- CTFT-6
Le Noire, Rosetta 1911- WWT-17
Lenormand, Henri-Rene
  1882-1951 . . . . WWasWT
Lenthall, Franklyn 1919- CTFT-1
Lenya, Lotte 1900-1981 . . . . WWT-17
Lenz, Kay 1953- CTFT-5
Leo, Frank 1874-? . . . . WWasWT
Leon, Anne 1925- . . . . WWasWT
Leonard, Billy 1892- . . . . WWasWT
Leonard, Hugh 1926- CTFT-6
  Earlier sketch in WWT-17
Leonard, Lu 1932- CTFT-1
Leonard, Patricia 1916- . . . . WWasWT
Leonard, Robert ?-1948 . . . . WWasWT
Leonard, Robert Sean 1969- CTFT-5

Leonard, Sheldon 1907- CTFT-3
Leonard-Boyne, Eva 1885-1960 . . . WWasWT
Leone, Sergio 1929-1989 . . . . CTFT-5
Leontovich, Eugenie 1900- WWT-17
Lerner, Alan Jay 1918-1986 . . . . CTFT-3
  Earlier sketch in WWT-17
Le Roux, Hugues 1860-? . . . . WWasWT
Le Roy, Servais . . . . WWasWT
Le Sage, Stanley 1880-1932 . . . . . . WWasWT
Leslie, Don 1948- CTFT-1
Leslie, Enid 1888-? . . . . WWasWT
Leslie, Fred 1881-1945 . . . . WWasWT
Leslie, Joan 1925- CTFT-5
Leslie, Lew 1886-1963 . . . . WWasWT
Leslie, Marguerite 1884-1958 . . . . WWasWT
Leslie, Sylvia 1900- . . . . WWasWT
Leslie-Stuart, May . . . . WWasWT
Lessing, Madge . . . . WWasWT
Lester, Alfred 1874-1925 . . . . WWasWT
Lester, Mark 1876-? . . . . WWasWT
Lester, Mark L. 1946- CTFT-1
Lester, Richard 1932- CTFT-3
Lester, Terry CTFT-4
Lestocq, William ?-1920 . . . . WWasWT
L'Estrange, Julian 1878-1918 . . . . WWasWT
Lethbridge, J. W. . . . . WWasWT
Letterman, David 1947- CTFT-7
Letts, Pauline 1917- WWT-17
Leveaux, Montagu V. 1875-? . . . . . WWasWT
Leven, Boris 1908-1986 . . . . CTFT-4
  Earlier sketch in CTFT-2
Levene, Sam 1905-1980 . . . . WWT-17
Leventon, Annabel 1942- CTFT-5
  Earlier sketch in WWT-17
Leverick, Beryl WWT-9
Levey, Adele . . . . WWasWT
Levey, Carlotta . . . . WWasWT
Levey, Ethel 1881-1955 . . . . WWasWT
Le Vien, Jack 1918- CTFT-1
Levin, Herman 1907- WWT-17
Levin, Ira 1929- CTFT-3
  Earlier sketches in CTFT-2, WWT-17
Levin, Peter CTFT-3
LeVine, David 1933- CTFT-5
Levine, Joseph E. 1905-1987 . . . . . . CTFT-5
Levine, Michael 1952- CTFT-4
Levinson, Barry 1932- CTFT-6
Levinson, Richard 1934-1987 . . . . . . CTFT-5
Levison, Charles
  See Lane, Charles CTFT-9
Levit, Ben 1949- CTFT-4
Leviton, Stewart 1939- WWT-17
Levy, Benn W. 1900-1973 . . . . WWasWT
Levy, David 1913- CTFT-6
  Earlier sketch in CTFT-3
Levy, Eugene 1946- CTFT-7
Levy, Jacques 1935- WWT-17
Levy, Jonathan 1935- CTFT-7
  Earlier sketch in CTFT-3
Levy, Jose G. 1884-1936 . . . . WWasWT
Lewenstein, Oscar 1917- WWT-17
Lewes, Miriam . . . . WWasWT
Lewey, Todd 1958- CTFT-2
Lewine, Richard 1910- CTFT-1
Lewis, Ada 1875-1925 . . . . WWasWT
Lewis, Al 1923- CTFT-8
Lewis, Arthur 1916- WWT-17
Lewis, Arthur 1846-1930 . . . . WWasWT
Lewis, Bertha 1887-1931 . . . . WWasWT
Lewis, Curigwen . . . . WWasWT
Lewis, Daniel E. 1944- CTFT-3
Lewis, Edmund 1959- CTFT-8
Lewis, Emmanuel 1971- CTFT-7

Lewis, Eric 1855-1935 ....WWasWT
Lewis, Fred 1850-1927 ....WWasWT
Lewis, Frederick G. 1873-1946 ...WWasWT
Lewis, Geoffrey 1940- CTFT-2
Lewis, Jenny 1976- CTFT-4
Lewis, Jerry 1926- CTFT-5
Lewis, Mabel Terry-
  See Terry-Lewis, Mabel ......WWasWT
Lewis, Marcia 1938- CTFT-5
  Earlier sketch in CTFT-1
Lewis, Martin 1888-1970 ....WWasWT
Lewis, Mary Rio 1922- CTFT-4
Lewis, Robert 1909- WWT-17
Lewis, Shari 1934- CTFT-3
Lewisohn, Victor Max
  1897-1934 ....WWasWT
Lewman, Lance 1960- CTFT-2
Lexy, Edward 1897- .... WWasWT
Leyden, Leo 1929- CTFT-4
Leyel, Carl F. 1875-1925 ....WWasWT
Leyton, George 1864-? ....WWasWT
Liberace 1919-1987 ....CTFT-3
Liberatore, Lou 1959- CTFT-5
Libertini, Richard CTFT-6
Libin, Paul 1930- CTFT-2
  Earlier sketch in WWT-17
Lichine, David 1909-1972 ....WWasWT
Licht, Jeremy 1971- CTFT-8
Lichterman, Victoria 1940- CTFT-4
Liebman, Marvin 1923- WWT-16
Lieven, Albert 1906-1971 ....WWasWT
Lieven, Tatiana 1910- ....WWasWT
Lifar, Serge 1905-1986 ....CTFT-4
  Earlier sketch in WWasWT
Light, Judith CTFT-3
Lightner, Winnie 1901-1971 .....WWasWT
Lillie, Beatrice 1898-1989 ....WWT-16
Lillies, Leonard 1860-1923 ......WWasWT
Lim, Paul Stephen 1944- CTFT-1
Limbert, Roy 1893-1954 ....WWasWT
Limerick, Mona ....WWasWT
Limpus, Alban Brownlow
  1878-1941 ....WWasWT
Linares-Rivas, Manuel
  1867-1938 ....WWasWT
Lincoln, Geoffrey
  See Mortimer, John CTFT-9
Lind, Gillian 1904- WWT-16
Lind, Letty 1862-1923 ....WWasWT
Lindberg, August 1846-1916 .....WWasWT
Linden, Eric 1909- ....WWasWT
Linden, Hal 1931- CTFT-3
  Earlier sketch in WWT-17
Linden, Marie 1862-? ....WWasWT
Lindfors, Viveca 1920- CTFT-1
  Earlier sketch in WWT-17
Lindley, Audra 1918- CTFT-3
  Earlier sketch in WWasWT
Lindo, Olga 1898-1968 ....WWasWT
Lindon, Millie 1878-? ....WWasWT
Lindsay, Howard 1889-1968 .....WWasWT
Lindsay, James 1869-1928 ....WWasWT
Lindsay, Robert CTFT-5
Lindsay, Vera 1911- ....WWasWT
Lindsay-Hogg, Michael 1940- CTFT-2
Link, Peter 1944- CTFT-5
  Earlier sketch in WWT-17
Link, Ron 1944- CTFT-6
Link, William 1933- CTFT-6
Linkletter, Art 1912- CTFT-3
Linley, Betty 1890-1951 ....WWasWT
Linn, Bambi 1926- CTFT-1
  Earlier sketch in WWasWT

Linn-Baker, Mark CTFT-5
  Brief Entry in CTFT-2
Linnea
  See Quigley, Linnea CTFT-8
Linnet & Dunfree Ltd. WWT-16
Linney, Romulus 1930- WWT-17
Linnit, S. E. ?-1956 ....WWasWT
Linville, Joanne CTFT-8
Linville, Larry 1939- CTFT-3
Lion, John 1944- CTFT-2
Lion, Leon M. 1879-1947 ....WWasWT
Liotta, Ray CTFT-7
Lipman, Clara 1869-1952 ....WWasWT
Lipman, Maureen 1946- CTFT-5
  Earlier sketch in WWT-17
Lipps, Roslyn 1925- CTFT-2
Lipscomb, Dennis 1942- CTFT-9
Lipscomb, William Percy
  1887-1958 ....WWasWT
Lipton, Celia 1923- ....WWasWT
Lipton, Peggy 1947(?)- CTFT-9
Lisle, Lucille ....WWasWT
Lister, Eve 1918- ....WWasWT
Lister, Francis 1899-1951 ....WWasWT
Lister, Frank 1868-1917 ....WWasWT
Lister, Lance 1901- ....WWasWT
Lister, Laurier 1907- WWT-17
Lister, Moira 1923- WWT-17
Lithgow, John 1945- CTFT-4
  Earlier sketch in CTFT-1
Littell, Robert 1896-1963 ....WWasWT
Little, Cleavon 1939- CTFT-4
  Earlier sketch in WWT-17
Little, Rich 1938- CTFT-5
  Earlier sketch in CTFT-3
Little, Stuart W. 1921- CTFT-4
Littlefield, Catherine 1904-1951 ..WWasWT
Littler, Blanche 1899- ....WWasWT
Littler, Emile 1903- WWT-17
Littler, Prince 1901- ....WWasWT
Littlewood, Joan CTFT-4
  Earlier sketch in WWT-17
Littlewood, Samuel Robinson
  1875-1963 ....WWasWT
Liveright, Horace B. 1886-1933 ..WWasWT
Livesay, Roger 1906-1976 ....WWT-16
Livesey, Barrie 1904- ....WWasWT
Livesey, E. Carter ....WWasWT
Livesey, Jack 1901-1961 ....WWasWT
Livesey, Sam 1873-1936 ....WWasWT
Livings, Henry 1929- WWT-17
Livingston, Harold 1924- CTFT-1
Livingston, Jay 1915- CTFT-1
Livingston, Robert H. 1934- CTFT-2
Livingston, Ruth 1927- CTFT-4
Llewellyn, Fewlass 1866-1941 ....WWasWT
Lloyd, Alice 1873-1949 ....WWasWT
Lloyd, Christopher 1938- CTFT-4
  Earlier sketch in CTFT-1
Lloyd, Doris 1900-1968 ....WWasWT
Lloyd, Emily CTFT-7
Lloyd, Florence 1876-? ....WWasWT
Lloyd, Frederick William
  1880-1949 ....WWasWT
Lloyd, Marie 1870-1922 ....WWasWT
Lloyd, Norman 1914- CTFT-6
Lloyd, Rosie 1879-1944 ....WWasWT
Lloyd, Sharon CTFT-4
Lloyd, Violet 1879-? ....WWasWT
Lloyd Pack, Roger 1944- CTFT-4
Lloyd Webber, Andrew 1948- CTFT-6
  Earlier sketches in CTFT-1, WWT-17
Loader, A. Mcleod 1869-? ....WWasWT

Loader, Rosa ....WWasWT
Lobel, Adrianne CTFT-1
Lo Bianco, Tony 1936- CTFT-3
Locke, Edward 1869-1945 ....WWasWT
Locke, Katherine 1910- ....WWasWT
Locke, Philip 1928- CTFT-6
  Earlier sketch in WWT-17
Locke, Sam 1917- CTFT-2
Locke, Sondra 1947- CTFT-5
Locke, William John 1863-1930 ..WWasWT
Lockhart, Gene 1891-1957 ....WWasWT
Lockhart, June 1925- CTFT-9
  Earlier sketch in CTFT-1
Locklear, Heather 1961- CTFT-6
  Brief Entry in CTFT-2
Lockridge, Richard 1898-1982 ...WWasWT
Lockton, Joan 1901- ....WWasWT
Lockwood, Gary 1937- CTFT-7
Lockwood, Margaret 1916-1990 ...WWT-17
Loder, Basil 1885-? ....,WWasWT
Loeb, Philip 1894-1955 ....WWasWT
Loesser, Frank 1910-1969 ....WWasWT
Loewe, Frederick 1901-1988 ......CTFT-6
  Earlier sketch in WWT-17
Loewenstern, Tara CTFT-1
Luft, Lorna 1952- CTFT-9
Loftus, Kitty 1867-1927 ....WWasWT
Loftus, Marie 1857-1940 ....WWasWT
Loftus, (Marie) Cecilia
  1876-1943 ....WWasWT
Logan, Ella 1910-1969 ....WWasWT
Logan, Joshua 1908-1988 ....CTFT-4
  Earlier sketch in WWT-17
Logan, Nedda Harrigan
  1900-1989 ....CTFT-8
Logan, Stanley 1885-1953 ....WWasWT
Loggia, Robert 1930- CTFT-4
  Earlier sketch in CTFT-1
Lohr, Marie 1890-1975 ....WWasWT
Lollobrigida, Gina CTFT-5
Lom, Herbert 1917- CTFT-8
  Earlier sketch in WWasWT
Lomas, Herbert 1887-1961 ......WWasWT
London, Chuck 1946- CTFT-4
London, Jerry 1937- CTFT-2
London, Roy 1943- CTFT-1
Lone, John 1952- CTFT-6
Loney, Glenn 1928- CTFT-1
Long, Avon 1910-1984 ....WWT-17
Long, Jodi CTFT-1
Long, John Luther 1861-1927 ....WWasWT
Long, Shelley 1949- CTFT-5
Long, William Ivey CTFT-8
Longbaugh, Harry
  See Goldman, William CTFT-7
Longden, John 1900- ....WWasWT
Longdon, Terence 1922- WWT-17
Longenecker, John 1947- CTFT-1
Longford, Earl of (Edward
  Arthur Henry Pakenham)
  1902-1961 ....WWasWT
Lonnen, Jessie 1886-? ....WWasWT
Lonnen, Nellie 1887-? ....WWasWT
Lonnon, Alice 1872-? ....WWasWT
Lonsdale, Frederick 1881-1954 ...WWasWT
Lonsdale, Michael
  See Lonsdale, Michel CTFT-8
Lonsdale, Michel 1931- CTFT-8
Loonin, Larry 1941- CTFT-2
Loos, Anita 1893-1981 ....WWT-17
Lopez, Priscilla 1948- CTFT-3
Lopokova, Lydia 1892-1981 .....WWasWT

Loquasto, Santo CTFT-6
  Earlier sketch in WWT-17
Loraine, Robert 1876-1935 . . . . . .WWasWT
Loraine, Violet 1886-1956 . . . . . . .WWasWT
Lord, Basil 1913-1979 . . . . .WWT-17
Lord, Jack 1930- CTFT-1
Lord, Pauline 1890-1950 . . . . .WWasWT
Lord, Robert 1945- CTFT-4
Lorde, Andre de 1871-? . . . . .WWasWT
Loren, Bernice 1951- CTFT-1
Loren, Sophia 1934- CTFT-3
Lorenzo, Tina di 1872-1930 . . . . . .WWasWT
Lorimer, Jack 1883-? . . . . .WWasWT
Loring, Gloria 1946- CTFT-3
Loring, Norman 1888-1967 . . . . . .WWasWT
Lorne, Constance 1914- WWT-16
Lorne, Marion 1888-1968 . . . . . . .WWasWT
Lorraine, Irma 1885-? . . . . .WWasWT
Lorraine, Lilian 1892-1955 . . . . . .WWasWT
Lortel, Lucille 1905- CTFT-5
  Earlier sketch in WWT-17
Losch, Tilly 1907-1975 . . . . .WWasWT
Lotinga, Ernest 1876-1951 . . . . . . .WWasWT
Lotta 1847-1924 . . . . .WWasWT
Loudon, Dorothy 1933- CTFT-4
  Earlier sketches in CTFT-1, WWT-17
Loughlin, Lori CTFT-8
Louis, Barbara CTFT-4
Louis, Tobi .CTFT-3
Louise, Tina 1938- CTFT-3
Lou-Tellegen 1881-1934 . . . . .WWasWT
Lovat, Nancie 1900-1946 . . . . .WWasWT
Love, Bessie ?-1986 . . . . .WWT-17
Love, Edward CTFT-6
Love, Mabel 1874-1953 . . . . .WWasWT
Love, Montagu 1877-1943 . . . . . . .WWasWT
Lovejoy, Robin 1923- WWT-17
Lovell, Dyson 1940- CTFT-2
Lovell, Raymond 1900-1953 . . . . .WWasWT
Lovell, W. T. 1884-? . . . . .WWasWT
Lovitz, Jon 1957- CTFT-7
Lowe, Arthur 1915- WWT-17
Lowe, Chad 1968- CTFT-7
Lowe, Douglas 1882-? . . . . .WWasWT
Lowe, Edmund 1892-1971 . . . . . . .WWasWT
Lowe, Enid 1908- . . . . .WWasWT
Lowe, Rachel 1876-? . . . . .WWasWT
Lowe, Rob 1964- CTFT-6
  Brief Entry in CTFT-2
Lowell, Helen 1866-1937 . . . . .WWasWT
Lowell, Mollie . . . . .WWasWT
Lowne, Charles Macready
  ?-1941 . . . . .WWasWT
Lowry, Jane 1937- CTFT-1
Lowry, W(ilson) McNeil 1913- CTFT-1
Loxley, Violet 1914- . . . . .WWasWT
Loy, Myrna 1905- CTFT-3
Lubliner, Sheldon R. 1950- CTFT-2
Lucas, George 1944- CTFT-4
  Earlier sketch in CTFT-1
Lucas, Hans
  See Godard, Jean-Luc CTFT-7
Lucas, J. Frank 1920- CTFT-7
Lucas, Jonathan 1936- CTFT-2
Lucci, Susan 1950- CTFT-7
Luce, Clare Boothe 1903-1987 . . . .WWT-17
Luce, Polly 1905- . . . . .WWasWT
Luckham, Cyril 1907-1989 . . . . . . .CTFT-8
  Earlier sketch in WWT-17
Luckinbill, Laurence 1934- CTFT-8
  Earlier sketches in CTFT-1, WWT-17
Luders, Gustav 1866-1913 . . . . . . .WWasWT

Ludlam, Charles 1943-1987 . . . . . . .CTFT-5
  Earlier sketches in CTFT-3, WWT-17
Ludlow, Patrick 1903- WWT-17
Ludwig, Salem 1915- WWT-17
Luedtke, Kurt 1939- CTFT-5
Luft, Lorna 1952- CTFT-9
Lugg, Alfred 1889- . . . . .WWasWT
Lugg, William 1852-1940 . . . . .WWasWT
Lugne-Poe, A. E. 1870-1940 . . . . .WWasWT
Lugosi, Bela 1888-1956 . . . . .WWasWT
Luguet, Andre 1892- . . . . .WWasWT
Lukas, Paul 1895-1971 . . . . .WWasWT
Luke, Keye 1904- CTFT-8
Luke, Peter 1919- WWT-17
Lukyanov, Sergei Vladimirovich
  1910- . . . . .WWasWT
Lumbly, Carl CTFT-7
Lumet, Sidney 1924- CTFT-6
  Earlier sketch in CTFT-1
Lund, Art 1920- WWT-17
Lundel, Kert Fritjof 1936- WWT-17
Lundgren, Dolph 1959- CTFT-9
Lunghi, Cherie 1953- CTFT-8
Lunt, Alfred 1892-1977 . . . . .WWT-16
Lupino, Stanley 1894-1942 . . . . . . .WWasWT
Lupino, Wallace 1897-1961 . . . . . .WWasWT
Lu Pone, Patti 1949- CTFT-5
  Earlier sketches in CTFT-1, WWT-17
Lu Pone, Robert 1946- CTFT-7
Lupus, Peter 1943- CTFT-1
Luscombe, Tim 1960- CTFT-8
Lyel, Viola 1900-1972 . . . . .WWasWT
Lyle, Lyston ?-1920 . . . . .WWasWT
Lyman, Dorothy 1947- CTFT-9
  Earlier sketch in CTFT-1
Lyman, Will 1948- CTFT-7
Lynch, Brian 1954- CTFT-4
Lynch, David 1947- CTFT-5
Lynch, Richard 1936- CTFT-5
Lynd, Rosa 1884-1922 . . . . .WWasWT
Lynde, Paul 1926-1982 . . . . .CTFT-2
Lyndeck, Edmund CTFT-1
Lyndon, Barre 1896- . . . . .WWasWT
Lyne, Adrian CTFT-7
Lynley, Carol 1942- CTFT-5
Lynn, Jonathan 1943- CTFT-5
  Earlier sketch in WWT-17
Lynn, Ralph 1882-1962 . . . . .WWasWT
Lynne, Carole 1918- . . . . .WWasWT
Lynne, Gillian 1926- CTFT-7
  Earlier sketches in CTFT-4, WWT-17
Lynton, Mayne 1885-? . . . . .WWasWT
Lyon, Ben 1901-1979 . . . . .WWasWT
Lyon, Milton 1923- CTFT-2
Lyon, Wanda 1897- . . . . .WWasWT
Lyons, A. Neil 1880-1940 . . . . .WWasWT
Lyons, Stuart 1928- CTFT-5
Lytell, Bert 1885-1954 . . . . .WWasWT
Lyttelton, Edith 1870-1948 . . . . . . .WWasWT
Lytton, Doris 1893-1953 . . . . .WWasWT
Lytton, Henry 1904-1965 . . . . .WWasWT
Lytton, Henry A. 1867-1936 . . . . . .WWasWT
Lytton, Ruth . . . . .WWasWT

M

Mabley, Edward 1906- CTFT-1
MacAdam, Will 1943- CTFT-2
MacArthur, Charles 1895-1956 . . .WWasWT
MacArthur, James 1937- CTFT-3
Macaulay, Joseph ?-1967 . . . . .WWasWT
Macaulay, Pauline CTFT-4

Macbeth, Helen . . . . .WWasWT
MacBridge, Aeneas
  See Mackay, Fulton CTFT-5
MacCaffrey, George 1870-1939 . . .WWasWT
MacCarthy, Desmond
  1877-1952 . . . . .WWasWT
Macchio, Ralph CTFT-3
MacCorkindale, Simon 1952- CTFT-4
MacDermot, Galt WWT-17
MacDermot, Robert 1910-1964 . . .WWasWT
Macdermott, Norman 1889-? . . . .WWasWT
MacDevitt, Brian 1956- CTFT-5
Macdona, Charles ?-1946 . . . . .WWasWT
Macdonald, Donald 1898-1959 . . .WWasWT
MacDonald, Jeanette 1907-1965 . .WWasWT
MacDonald, Murray 1899- WWT-17
MacDonell, Kathlene 1890-? . . . . .WWasWT
Macdonnell, Leslie A. 1903- . . . . .WWasWT
Macdonough, Glen 1870-1924 . . . .WWasWT
MacDougall, Roger 1910- WWT-17
MacDowell, Andie 1958(?)- CTFT-9
Macfarlane, Bruce 1910-1967 . . . . .WWasWT
Macfarlane, Elsa 1899- . . . . .WWasWT
MacGill, Moyna 1895-1975 . . . . . .WWasWT
MacGinnis, Niall 1913- . . . . .WWasWT
Macgowan, Kenneth 1888-1963 . . .WWasWT
MacGowran, Jack 1918-1973 . . . . .WWasWT
MacGrath, Leueen 1914- WWT-17
MacGraw, Ali 1939- CTFT-5
Machiz, Herbert 1923-1976 . . . . . . .WWT-16
MacHugh, Augustin 1887-1928 . . .WWasWT
MacIntosh, Joan 1945- CTFT-8
Mack, Andrew 1863-1931 . . . . . . .WWasWT
Mack, Carol K. CTFT-1
Mack, Willard 1878-1934 . . . . .WWasWT
Mackay, Barry 1906- . . . . .WWasWT
Mackay, Elsie 1894- . . . . .WWasWT
Mackay, Fulton 1922-1987 . . . . . . .CTFT-5
  Earlier sketch in WWT-17
Mackay, J. L. 1867-? . . . . .WWasWT
Mackay, John 1924- CTFT-5
Mackay, Lizbeth 1951- CTFT-6
  Earlier sketch in CTFT-1
Mackay, Ruth . . . . .WWasWT
Mackaye, Percy 1875-1956 . . . . . .WWasWT
Mackeller, Helen 1895- . . . . .WWasWT
Mackenna, Kenneth 1899-1962 . . .WWasWT
Mackenzie, Mary 1922-1966 . . . . .WWasWT
MacKenzie, Philip Charles CTFT-8
Mackinder, Lionel ?-1915 . . . . . . .WWasWT
Mackinlay, Jean Sterling
  1882-1958 . . . . .WWasWT
Mackintosh, Cameron 1946- CTFT-9
  Earlier sketch in CTFT-1
Mackintosh, William 1855-1929 . .WWasWT
Macklin, Albert 1958- CTFT-1
MacLachlan, Kyle 1959(?)- CTFT-9
MacLaine, Shirley 1934- CTFT-4
  Earlier sketch in CTFT-1
Maclaren, Ian 1879-? . . . . .WWasWT
MacLean, R. D. 1859-1948 . . . . . .WWasWT
MacLeish, Archibald 1892-1982 . . .WWT-17
Macleod, Gavin 1931- CTFT-1
Macleod, W. Angus 1874-1962 . . .WWasWT
Macliammoir, Michael
  1899-1978 . . . . .WWT-16
MacMahon, Aline 1899- WWT-17
MacManus, Clive ?-1953 . . . . .WWasWT
MacMurray, Fred 1903- CTFT-3
MacNaughton, Alan 1920- WWT-17
Macnee, Patrick 1922- CTFT-7
  Earlier sketch in CTFT-1
MacNichol, Peter 1954- CTFT-7

MacOwan, Michael 1906- WWT-17
MacOwan, Norman 1877-1961 ...WWasWT
Macqueen-Pope, W. J.
　1888-1960 ....WWasWT
Macquoid, Percy 1852-1925 .....WWasWT
Macrae, Arthur 1908-1962 ......WWasWT
Macrae, Duncan 1905-1967 ......WWasWT
MacRae, Gordon 1921-1986 ....CTFT-3
Macy, Bill 1922- CTFT-4
　Earlier sketch in CTFT-1
Madden, Cecil (Charles)
　1902-1987 ....WWasWT
Madden, Ciaran 1945- CTFT-5
　Earlier sketch in WWT-17
Madden, Donald 1933- WWT-17
Madeira, Marcia 1945- CTFT-1
Madigan, Amy CTFT-5
Madonna 1958(?)- CTFT-9
　Brief Entry in CTFT-3
Madsen, Virginia 1961- CTFT-7
Maeterlinck, Maurice
　1862-1949 ....WWasWT
Maffett, Debbie CTFT-3
Magee, Patrick ?-1982 ....WWT-17
Maggart, Brandon CTFT-8
Magnier, Pierre 1869-? ....WWasWT
Magnuson, Ann 1956- CTFT-7
Mahaffey, Valerie CTFT-1
Maher, Joseph 1933- CTFT-8
　Earlier sketch in CTFT-1
Mahoney, John 1940- CTFT-6
Mahoney, Will 1896-1967 ....WWasWT
Mainwaring, Ernest 1876-1941 ...WWasWT
Mair, George Herbert
　1887-1926 ....WWasWT
Mais, Stuart Petre Brodie
　1885-? ....WWasWT
Maitland, Lauderdale ?-1929 .....WWasWT
Maitland, Ruth 1880-1961 ....WWasWT
Major, Bessie ....WWasWT
Majors, Lee 1940- CTFT-5
Makarova, Natalia 1940- CTFT-9
Makavejev, Dusan 1932- CTFT-8
Makeham, Eliot 1882-1956 ....WWasWT
Makepeace, Chris 1964- CTFT-4
Mako 1932- CTFT-8
Malahide, Patrick 1945- CTFT-4
Malden, Herbert John
　1882-1966 ....WWasWT
Malden, Karl 1914- CTFT-6
　Earlier sketch in CTFT-1
Malick, Terrence 1943- CTFT-6
　Earlier sketch in CTFT-1
Malik, Art 1952- CTFT-7
Malina, Judith 1926- WWT-17
Malkovich, John 1953- CTFT-5
Mallalieu, Aubrey 1873-1948 .....WWasWT
Malle, Louis 1932- CTFT-6
　Earlier sketch in CTFT-1
Malleson, Miles 1888-1969 ......WWasWT
Malm, Mia 1962- CTFT-4
Malmuth, Bruce 1934- CTFT-2
Malo, Gina 1909-1963 ....WWasWT
Malone, Dorothy 1925- CTFT-5
Malone, J. A. E. ?-1929 ....WWasWT
Malone, Patricia 1899- ....WWasWT
Maloney, Peter CTFT-8
Maltby, Henry Francis
　1880-1963 ....WWasWT
Maltby, Richard Jr. 1937- CTFT-4
　Earlier sketch in WWT-17
Maltz, Albert 1908-1985 ....CTFT-1

Mamet, David 1947- CTFT-8
　Earlier sketches in CTFT-2, WWT-17
Mamoulian, Rouben 1897-1987 .....CTFT-6
　Earlier sketch in WWasWT
Manchester, Joe 1932- CTFT-3
Mancini, Henry 1924- CTFT-1
Mancuso, Nick 1956- CTFT-7
Mandel, Frank 1884-1958 ....WWasWT
Mandel, Howie 1955- CTFT-9
　Brief Entry in CTFT-3
Mandelker, Philip ?-1984 ....CTFT-1
Mander, Raymond Josiah Gale
　1917- WWT-17
Manfredi, Nino 1921- CTFT-8
Mangano, Silvana 1930-1989 ....CTFT-5
Mankiewicz, Don 1922- CTFT-4
Mankiewicz, Joseph L. 1909- CTFT-5
Mankiewicz, Tom 1942- CTFT-5
Mankofsky, Isidore 1931- CTFT-3
Mankowitz, Wolf 1924- WWT-17
Mann, Abby 1927- CTFT-5
Mann, Charlton 1876-1958 ....WWasWT
Mann, Christopher 1903- ....WWasWT
Mann, Delbert 1920- CTFT-1
Mann, Emily 1952- CTFT-1
Mann, Louis 1865-1931 ....WWasWT
Mann, Michael CTFT-5
Mann, Terrence CTFT-6
Mann, Theodore 1924- CTFT-2
　Earlier sketch in WWT-17
Mannering, Dore Lewin
　1879-1932 ....,.WWasWT
Mannering, Mary 1876-1953 .....WWasWT
Mannering, Moya 1888-? ....WWasWT
Manners, David 1905- ....WWasWT
Manners, John Hartley
　1870-1928 ....WWasWT
Mannheim, Lucie 1905- ....WWasWT
Manning, Ambrose ?-1940 ....WWasWT
Manning, Hugh Gardner 1920- WWT-17
Manning, Irene 1917- ....WWasWT
Mannock, Patrick L. 1887-? .....WWasWT
Manoff, Dinah CTFT-3
Mansfield, Alice ?-1938 ....WWasWT
Mantegna, Joe 1947- CTFT-3
Mantell, Robert Bruce
　1854-1928 ....WWasWT
Mantle, Burns 1873-1948 ....WWasWT
Manulis, John Bard 1956- CTFT-1
Manulis, Martin 1915- CTFT-1
Manus, Willard 1930- CTFT-1
Mapes, Victor 1870-1943 ....WWasWT
Marasco, Robert 1936- WWT-17
Maravan, Lila ?-1950 ....WWasWT
March, Elspeth CTFT-6
　Earlier sketch in WWT-17
March, Frederic 1897-1975 ......WWasWT
March, Nadine 1898-1944 ....WWasWT
Marchand, Nancy 1928- CTFT-7
　Earlier sketch in CTFT-1, WWT-17
Marcin, Max 1879-1948 ....WWasWT
Marcovicci, Andrea 1948- CTFT-6
　Brief Entry in CTFT-2
Marcum, Kevin 1955- CTFT-2
Marcus, Donald 1946- CTFT-2
Marcus, Frank 1928- WWT-17
Marcus, Jeffrey 1960- CTFT-2
Marcus, Lawrence 1925- CTFT-4
Marcus, Louis 1936- CTFT-5
Margetson, Arthur 1897-1951 ....WWasWT
Margo 1918- ....WWasWT
Margolin, Janet 1943- CTFT-5
Margolin, Stuart 1940- CTFT-6

Margolis, Mark 1939- CTFT-1
Margolyes, Miriam 1941- CTFT-6
Margueritte, Victor 1866-1942 ...WWasWT
Margulies, David 1937- CTFT-1
Margulies, Stan 1920- CTFT-7
Mariani-Zampieri, Terseina
　1871-? ....WWasWT
Marin, Cheech 1946- CTFT-6
　Brief Entry in CTFT-2
Marinaro, Ed 1951- CTFT-7
Marinoff, Fania 1890-1971 ....WWasWT
Mario, Emilio ....WWasWT
Marion, George Jr. ?-1968 ....WWasWT
Marion, Joan 1908-1945 ....WWasWT
Mark, Judy CTFT-4
Markey, Enid WWT-16
Markham, Daisy WWT-5
Markham, David 1913- WWT-17
Markham, Monte 1935- CTFT-7
　Earlier sketch in CTFT-1
Markinson, Martin 1931- CTFT-1
Markle, Christopher J. 1954- CTFT-2
Markoe, Gerald Jay 1941- CTFT-2
Markova, Alicia 1910- ....WWasWT
Marks, Alfred 1921- WWT-17
Marks, Arthur 1927- CTFT-7
Marks, Jack R. 1935- CTFT-3
Marley, John ?-1984 ....CTFT-1
Marlowe, Anthony 1913- WWT-16
Marlowe, Charles
　See Jay, Harriet ....WWasWT
Marlowe, Hugh 1911-1982 ....WWT-17
Marlowe, Joan 1920- CTFT-1
Marlowe, Julia 1866-1950 ....WWasWT
Marlowe, Theresa 1957- CTFT-8
Marmont, Percy 1883-? ....WWasWT
Marnac, Jane ....WWasWT
Marot, Gaston ?-1916 ....WWasWT
Marowitz, Charles 1934- CTFT-5
　Earlier sketch in WWT-17
Marquand, Richard 1937-1987 .....CTFT-2
Marquet, Mary 1895- ....WWasWT
Marquis, Don 1878-1937 ....WWasWT
Marr, Paula ....WWasWT
Marre, Albert 1925- WWT-17
Marriott, Anthony 1931- CTFT-1
Marriott, B. Rodney 1938-1990 ....CTFT-1
Marriott, Raymond Bowler
　1911- WWT-17
Marriott-Watson, Nan 1899- .....WWasWT
Mars, Kenneth 1936- CTFT-7
Mars, Marjorie 1903-1915 ....WWasWT
Marsden, Betty 1919- WWT-17
Marsden, Les 1957- CTFT-4
Marsden, Roy 1941- CTFT-7
Marsh, Garry 1902- ....WWasWT
Marsh, Jean 1934- CTFT-3
Marshall, Alan Peter 1938- CTFT-5
Marshall, Armina 1900- WWT-17
Marshall, E. G. 1910- CTFT-3
　Earlier sketch in WWT-17
Marshall, Everett 1901- ....WWasWT
Marshall, Frank CTFT-7
Marshall, Garry 1934- CTFT-6
　Earlier sketch in CTFT-1
Marshall, Herbert 1890-1966 .....WWasWT
Marshall, Norman 1901- WWT-17
Marshall, Penny 1943- CTFT-6
　Earlier sketch in CTFT-1
Marshall, Tully 1864-1943 ....WWasWT
Marshall, William 1924- CTFT-8
Marson, Aileen, 1912-1939 ......WWasWT
Martell, Gillian 1936- WWT-17

Marthold, Jules de 1842-1927 .... WWasWT
Martin, Andrea 1947- CTFT-7
Martin, Christopher 1942- CTFT-5
  Earlier sketch in WWT-17
Martin, Dean 1917- CTFT-8
Martin, Edie 1880-1964 .... WWasWT
Martin, Elliot 1924- CTFT-2
  Earlier sketch in WWT-17
Martin, Ernest H. 1919- WWT-17
Martin, George 1926- CTFT-8
Martin, Helen CTFT-8
Martin, Kiel 1945- CTFT-7
Martin, Mary 1913- WWT-17
Martin, Millicent 1934- CTFT-7
  Earlier sketch in WWT-17
Martin, Pamela Sue 1953- CTFT-6
  Brief Entry in CTFT-2
Martin, Quinn 1922-1987 .... CTFT-5
Martin, Steve 1945- CTFT-5
Martin, Vivian 1893-1987 .... WWasWT
Martin, Vivienne 1936-1987 ..... WWT-17
Martin, William 1937- CTFT-4
Martin-Harvey, John
  See Harvey, John Martin- ..... WWasWT
Martin-Harvey, Muriel
  1891-1988 .... WWasWT
Martinetti, Paul 1851-? .... WWasWT
Martinez, A CTFT-6
Martinot, Sadie 1861-1923 .... WWasWT
Martlew, Mary 1919- .... WWasWT
Marvenga, Ilse .... WWasWT
Marvin, Lee 1924-1987 .... CTFT-5
  Earlier sketch in CTFT-3
Marvin, Mel 1941- CTFT-4
Marx, Arthur 1921- CTFT-1
Mary, Jules 1851-1922 .... WWasWT
Maryan, Charles 1934- CTFT-2
Masak, Ron 1936- CTFT-1
Maschwitz, Eric 1901-1969 ..... WWasWT
Masefield, John 1878-1967 ...... WWasWT
Masina, Giulietta 1921- CTFT-8
Maskelyne, John Nevil 1839-? .... WWasWT
Mason, Alfred Edward
  Woodley 1865-1948 .... WWasWT
Mason, Beryl 1921- WWT-17
Mason, Brewster 1922-1987 ...... CTFT-5
  Earlier sketch in WWT-17
Mason, Elliot C. 1897-1949 ...... WWasWT
Mason, Ethelmae CTFT-3
Mason, Gladys 1886-? .... WWasWT
Mason, Herbert 1891-1960 ...... WWasWT
Mason, Jackie 1931- CTFT-6
Mason, James 1909-1984 .... CTFT-1
  Earlier sketch in WWasWT
Mason, John B. 1857-1919 ...... WWasWT
Mason, Kitty 1882-? .... WWasWT
Mason, Marsha 1942- CTFT-7
  Earlier sketch in CTFT-2
Mason, Marshall 1940- CTFT-3
  Earlier sketches in CTFT-1, WWT-17
Mason, Pamela 1918- CTFT-1
Mason, Reginald 1882-1962 ..... WWasWT
Massary, Fritzi 1882-1969 .... WWasWT
Massey, Anna 1937- CTFT-4
  Earlier sketch in WWT-17
Massey, Daniel 1933- CTFT-6
  Earlier sketch in WWT-17
Massey, Raymond 1896-1983 ..... WWT-17
Massi, Bernice WWT-17
Massine, Leonide 1896-1979 .... WWasWT
Massingham, Dorothy
  1889-1933 .... WWasWT
Masters, Ben 1947- CTFT-9

Masterson, Mary Stuart 1967- CTFT-7
Masterson, Peter 1934- CTFT-1
Mastrantonio, Mary Elizabeth
  1958- CTFT-4
  Earlier sketch in CTFT-1
Mastroianni, Marcello 1924- CTFT-5
Mastrosimone, William 1947- CTFT-8
Masur, Richard 1948- CTFT-6
Matalon, Vivian 1929- WWT-17
Mather, Aubrey 1885-1958 ...... WWasWT
Mather, Donald 1900- .... WWasWT
Mathers, Jerry 1948- CTFT-9
Matheson, Murray 1912-1985 ..... CTFT-1
Matheson, Richard 1926- CTFT-6
  Earlier sketch in CTFT-1
Matheson, Tim 1949- CTFT-3
Mathews, Carmen 1914- WWT-17
Mathews, Frances Aymar
  1865?-1925 .... WWasWT
Mathews, George 1911- WWT-16
Mathews, James W. ?-1920 ...... WWasWT
Matlin, Marlee 1965- CTFT-9
  Brief Entry in CTFT-6
Matsusaka, Tom CTFT-2
Matteson, Ruth 1909-1975 ...... WWasWT
Matthau, Walter 1920- CTFT-7
  Earlier sketch in WWT-17
Matthews, A. E. 1869-1960 ...... WWasWT
Matthews, Adelaide 1886-1948 ... WWasWT
Matthews, Brander 1852-1929 .... WWasWT
Matthews, Ethel 1870-? .... WWasWT
Matthews, Francis 1927- CTFT-1
Matthews, Jessie 1907-1981 ...... WWT-17
Matthews, Lester 1900-1975 ..... WWasWT
Matthison, Edith Wynne
  1875-1955 .... WWasWT
Matura, Mustapha 1939- WWT-17
Maturin, Eric 1883-1957 .... WWasWT
Mauceri, John 1945- CTFT-3
Maude, Charles Raymond
  ?-1943 .... WWasWT
Maude, Cyril 1862-1951 .... WWasWT
Maude, Elizabeth (Betty) 1912- .. WWasWT
Maude, Gillian .... WWasWT
Maude, Joan 1908- .... WWasWT
Maude, Margery 1889-1979 ...... WWT-16
Maude-Roxbury, Roddy 1930- WWT-17
Maugham, W. Somerset
  1874-1965 .... WWasWT
Maule, Annabel 1922- WWT-17
Maule, Donovan 1899- WWT-16
Maule, Robin 1924-1942 .... WWasWT
Maurey, Max ?-1947 .... WWasWT
Maurice, Edmund ?-1928 .... WWasWT
Max, Edouard Alexandre de
  1869-1925 .... WWasWT
Maxfield, James 1939- CTFT-8
Maxwell, Gerald 1862-1930 ...... WWasWT
Maxwell, Lois 1927- CTFT-8
Maxwell, Ronald F. 1947- CTFT-1
Maxwell, Walter 1877-? .... WWasWT
Maxwell, Wayne F. Jr. CTFT-3
May, Ada 1900- .... WWasWT
May, Akerman 1869-1933 .... WWasWT
May, Beverly 1927- CTFT-1
May, Edna 1878-1948 .... WWasWT
May, Elaine 1932- CTFT-5
  Earlier sketch in WWT-17
May, Hans 1891-1959 .... WWasWT
May, Jack 1922- WWT-17
May, Jane .... WWasWT
May, Pamela 1917- .... WWasWT
May, Val 1927- WWT-17

May, Winston 1937- CTFT-4
Mayer, Daniel 1856-1928 .... WWasWT
Mayer, Edwin Justus 1896-1960 .. WWasWT
Mayer, Gaston 1869-1923 .... WWasWT
Mayer, Henry ?-1941 .... WWasWT
Mayer, Renee 1900- .... WWasWT
Mayerl, Billy 1902-1959 .... WWasWT
Mayeur, E. F. 1866-? .... WWasWT
Mayfield, Cleo 1897-1954 .... WWasWT
Mayhew, Charles 1908- .... WWasWT
Mayne, Ernie .... WWasWT
Mayne, Ferdy 1920- WWT-17
Mayo, Margaret 1882-1951 ...... WWasWT
Mayo, Sam 1881-1938 .... WWasWT
Mayo, Virginia 1920- CTFT-1
Mayron, Melanie 1952- CTFT-1
Maysles, David 1933-1987 .... CTFT-4
Mazurki, Mike 1909- CTFT-9
Mazursky, Paul 1930- CTFT-6
  Earlier sketch in CTFT-1
Mazzola, John W. 1928- CTFT-1
McAnally, Ray 1926-1989 .... CTFT-7
  Earlier sketch in WWT-17
McAnuff, Des CTFT-6
McArdle, Andrea 1963- CTFT-6
McArdle, J. F. .... WWasWT
McArthur, Molly 1900- .... WWasWT
McAssey, Michael 1955- CTFT-2
McBain, Diane 1941- CTFT-1
McBride, Jim 1941- CTFT-8
McCall, Kathleen CTFT-4
McCall, Nancy 1948- CTFT-1
McCallin, Clement 1913-1977 ..... WWT-17
McCallum, David 1933- CTFT-7
  Earlier sketch in CTFT-1
McCallum, Joanna CTFT-8
McCallum, John 1918- CTFT-8
  Earlier sketch in WWT-17
McCambridge, Mercedes 1918- CTFT-5
McCann, Donal CTFT-7
McCarthy, Andrew 1963- CTFT-6
McCarthy, Daniel 1869-? .... WWasWT
McCarthy, Frank 1912-1986 ...... CTFT-4
McCarthy, Justin Huntly
  1860-1936 .... WWasWT
McCarthy, Kevin 1914- CTFT-4
  Earlier sketch in WWT-17
McCarthy, Lillah 1875-1960 ..... WWasWT
McCarthy, Mary 1910-1989 .... CTFT-1
McCarty, Mary 1923-1980 .... WWT-17
McClanahan, Rue CTFT-4
  Earlier sketch in WWT-17
McClelland, Allan 1917-1989 ...... CTFT-8
  Earlier sketch in WWT-17
McClintic, Guthrie 1893-1961 .... WWasWT
McClory, Sean 1924- CTFT-4
McClure, Doug 1935- CTFT-5
McClure, Michael 1932- CTFT-1
McClurg, Edie CTFT-8
McComas, Carroll 1891-1962 .... WWasWT
McCook, John CTFT-5
McCord, Nancy .... WWasWT
McCormack, Patty 1945- CTFT-8
McCormick, Arthur Langdon
  ?-1954 .... WWasWT
McCormick, Myron 1907-1962 ... WWasWT
McCowen, Alec 1925- CTFT-8
  Earlier sketch in CTFT-2
McCracken, Esther (Helen)
  1902- .... WWasWT
McCracken, Jeff CTFT-6
  Earlier sketch in CTFT-1
McCracken, Joan 1922-1961 ..... WWasWT

McCrane, Paul 1961- CTFT-4
  Earlier sketch in CTFT-1
McCullough, Paul 1883-1936 ....WWasWT
McCutcheon, Bill CTFT-7
McDermott, Hugh (Patrick)
  1908-1972 ....WWasWT
McDermott, Keith 1953- CTFT-4
McDermott, Tom 1912- CTFT-2
McDevitt, Ruth 1895-1976 ....WWT-16
McDiarmid, Ian CTFT-9
McDonald, Christie 1875-1962 ...WWasWT
McDonald, Tanny 1940- CTFT-1
McDonnell, Mary 1953(?)- CTFT-9
McDonough, Jerome 1946- CTFT-1
McDormand, Frances 1958- CTFT-7
McDougall, Gordon 1941-.........CTFT-5
  Earlier sketch in WWT-17
McDowall, Roddy 1928- CTFT-8
  Earlier sketches in CTFT-2, WWT-17
McDowell, Malcolm 1943- CTFT-5
McEnery, Peter 1940- CTFT-5
  Earlier sketch in WWT-17
McEvoy, Charles 1879-1929 .....WWasWT
McEvoy, J. P. 1897-1958 ....WWasWT
McEwan, Geraldine 1932- CTFT-6
  Earlier sketch in WWT-17
McFadden, Cheryl
  See McFadden, Gates CTFT-8
McFadden, Gates CTFT-8
McFarland, Robert 1931- CTFT-2
McGavin, Darren 1922- CTFT-5
McGill, Bruce 1950-..............CTFT-7
McGill, Everett Charles III
  1945- CTFT-1
McGillin, Howard 1953- CTFT-6
McGillis, Kelly 1958- CTFT-9
  Brief Entry in CTFT-3
McGinnis, Scott 1958- CTFT-7
McGiver, John 1913-1975 ....WWT-16
McGlynn, Frank 1866-1951 .....WWasWT
McGoohan, Patrick 1928- CTFT-5
  Earlier sketch in WWasWT
McGovern, Elizabeth 1961-........CTFT-6
  Earlier sketch in CTFT-3
  Brief Entry in CTFT-2
McGovern, Maureen 1949- CTFT-6
McGowan, John W. ....WWasWT
McGrath, John 1935-............WWT-17
McGrath, Paul 1904-1978 ....WWT-16
McGuane, Thomas 1939-.........CTFT-8
McGuire, Biff 1926- WWT-17
McGuire, Dorothy 1918- CTFT-3
  Earlier sketch in WWT-17
McGuire, Mitch 1936- CTFT-1
McGuire, William Anthony
  1885-1940 ....WWasWT
McHale, Rosemary 1944- CTFT-5
  Earlier sketch in WWT-17
McHattie, Stephen CTFT-6
McHenry, Don 1908- CTFT-1
McHugh, Florence 1906- ....WWasWT
McHugh, Therese ....WWasWT
McInerney, Bernie 1936- CTFT-1
McIntosh, Madge 1875-1950 .....WWasWT
McIntosh, Marcia CTFT-4
McIntyre, Dennis 1943(?)-1990 .....CTFT-9
McIntyre, Frank 1879-1949 ......WWasWT
McIntyre, Marilyn CTFT-2
McKay, Scott 1915-1987 ....WWT-17
McKayle, Donald 1930-...........CTFT-1
McKean, Michael CTFT-3
McKechnie, Donna 1940- CTFT-7
  Earlier sketch in WWT-17

McKee, Clive R. 1883-? ....WWasWT
McKee, Lonette 1954- CTFT-6
McKellen, Ian 1939- CTFT-4
  Earlier sketches in CTFT-1, WWT-17
McKenna, David, 1949-...........CTFT-4
McKenna, Siobhan 1923-1986 ......CTFT-4
  Earlier sketch in WWT-17
McKenna, T. P. 1929-...........WWT-17
McKenna, Virginia 1931- CTFT-6
  Earlier sketch in WWT-17
McKenzie, James B. 1926- WWT-17
McKenzie, Julia CTFT-1
McKeon, Doug 1966-.............CTFT-4
McKeon, Nancy 1966- CTFT-8
McKern, Leo 1920- CTFT-8
  Earlier sketches in CTFT-2, WWT-17
McKinnel, Norman 1870-1932 ...WWasWT
McKinney, Bill CTFT-8
McLain, John CTFT-2
McLaughlin, Emily CTFT-3
McLellan, C. M. S. 1865-1916 ...WWasWT
McLerie, Allyn Ann 1926- CTFT-5
  Earlier sketch in WWT-17
McMahon, Ed 1923- CTFT-1
McMartin, John CTFT-4
  Earlier sketch in WWT-17
McMaster, Anew 1894-1962 .....WWasWT
McMillan, Kenneth 1932-1989 .....CTFT-6
  Earlier sketch in CTFT-1
McMillan, Roddy 1923-1979 .....WWT-16
McMurray, Sam 1952-...........CTFT-7
McNabb, Barry 1960- CTFT-6
McNally, Terrence 1939-.........CTFT-4
  Earlier sketches in CTFT-1, WWT-17
McNamara, Brooks 1937- WWT-17
McNamara, Dermot 1925- CTFT-4
McNaughton, Gus 1884-1969 ....WWasWT
McNaughton, Stephen CTFT-1
McNaughton, Tom 1867-1923 ....WWasWT
McNaughtons, The ....WWasWT
McNeil, Claudia 1917- WWT-17
McNichol, James CTFT-3
McNichol, Kristy 1962- CTFT-3
McPherson, Mervyn 1892- ....WWasWT
McQueen, Butterfly 1911- WWT-17
McQueen, Steve 1930-1980 ....CTFT-1
McQuiggan, John A. 1935- CTFT-4
McRae, Bruce 1867-1927 ....WWasWT
McRae, Ellen
  See Burstyn, Ellen CTFT-6
McRae, Glory CTFT-4
McRaney, Gerald 1948-...........CTFT-8
McRobbie, Peter 1943- CTFT-4
McShane, Ian 1942- CTFT-2
  Earlier sketch in WWT-17
McTeer, Janet 1961-.............CTFT-9
McWade, Robert 1882-1938 .....WWasWT
McWhinnie, Donald 1920-1987 ....WWT-17
Meacham, Anne 1925- CTFT-3
  Earlier sketch in WWT-17
Meacham, Paul 1939-............CTFT-1
Meade, Julia CTFT-3
Meader, George 1888-1963 ....WWasWT
Meadow, Lynne 1946- CTFT-4
  Earlier sketch in WWT-17
Meadows, Audrey CTFT-2
Meaney, Colm CTFT-8
Meara, Anne CTFT-1
Measor, Adela 1860-1933 ....WWasWT
Measor, Beryl 1908-1965 ....WWasWT
Medak, Peter 1937- CTFT-2
Medford, Kay 1920-1980 ....WWT-17

Medoff, Mark 1940- CTFT-4
  Earlier sketch in WWT-17
Meek, Barbara CTFT-5
Meek, Donald 1880-1946 ....WWasWT
Meeker, Ralph 1920-1988 ....CTFT-7
  Earlier sketch in WWT-17
Megard, Andree 1869-? ....WWasWT
Megrue, Roi Cooper 1883-1927 ..WWasWT
Meighan, Thomas 1879-1936 .....WWasWT
Meiser, Edith 1898- WWT-17
Meister, Brian 1948-.............CTFT-2
Mekka, Eddie 1952- CTFT-2
Melendez, Bill CTFT-6
Melfi, Leonard 1935- WWT-17
Melford, Austin 1884-? ....WWasWT
Melford, Jack 1899- ....WWasWT
Melford, Jill 1934- WWT-17
Melia, Joe WWT-17
Mellish, Fuller 1865-1936 ....WWasWT
Melly, Andree 1932-.............WWT-17
Melnick, Daniel 1932- CTFT-3
Melnotte, Violet 1852-1935 ......WWasWT
Meltzer, Charles Henry
  1852-1936 ....WWasWT
Melville, Alan 1910-1984 ....WWT-17
Melville, Andrew 1912- ....WWasWT
Melville, Frederick 1876-1938 ....WWasWT
Melville, June 1915-1970 ....WWasWT
Melville, Rose 1873-1946 ....WWasWT
Melville, Walter 1875-1937 ......WWasWT
Melville, Winnie ?-1937 ....WWasWT
Melvin, Duncan 1913- ....WWasWT
Melvin, Murray CTFT-6
  Earlier sketch in WWT-17
Mendel ....WWasWT
Mendillo, Stephen W. 1943- CTFT-1
Menges, Chris 1941-.............CTFT-7
Menges, Herbert 1902-1972 .....WWasWT
Menken, Helen 1901-1966 ....WWasWT
Menzies, Archie 1904- ....WWasWT
Meppen, Adrian Joseph 1940-......CTFT-3
Merande, Doro 1935- ....WWasWT
Mercer, Beryl 1882-1939 ....WWasWT
Mercer, David 1928-1980 ....WWT-17
Mercer, Johnny 1909-1976 ......WWT-16
Mercer, Marian 1935- CTFT-7
  Earlier sketch in WWT-17
Merchant, Ismail 1936- CTFT-6
  Earlier sketch in CTFT-1
Merchant, Vivien 1929-1982 ......WWT-17
Mercouri, Melina 1925- CTFT-5
Mere, Charles 1883-? ....WWasWT
Meredith, Burgess 1909- CTFT-4
  Earlier sketch in WWT-17
Meredith, Don 1938- CTFT-1
Merivale 1882-1939 ....WWasWT
Merivale, Philip 1886-1946 ......WWasWT
Meriwether, Lee 1935- CTFT-2
Merkel, Una 1903-1986 ....WWasWT
Merman, Ethel 1909-1984 ....CTFT-1
  Earlier sketch in WWT-17
Merrall, Mary 1890-1973 ....WWasWT
Merriam, Eve 1916- CTFT-1
Merrick, David 1912-.............CTFT-6
  Earlier sketch in WWT-17
Merrick, Leonard 1864-1939 .....WWasWT
Merrill, Beth ....WWasWT
Merrill, Bob 1920- WWT-17
Merrill, Dina 1925- CTFT-8
  Earlier sketch in CTFT-1
Merrill, Gary 1915-1990 ....CTFT-1
Merritt, Grace 1881-? ....WWasWT
Merritt, Theresa 1922- CTFT-8

Merson, Billy 1881-1947 .... WWasWT
Mery, Andree .... WWasWT
Messager, Andre 1853-1929 ..... WWasWT
Messick, Don 1926- CTFT-9
   Earlier sketch in CTFT-3
Metaxa, Georges 1899-1950 ..... WWasWT
Metcalf, Laurie 1955- CTFT-7
Metcalf, Mark CTFT-8
Metcalfe, James Stetson
   1858-1927 .... WWasWT
Metcalfe, Stephen 1953- CTFT-7
Metenier, Oscar 1859-1913 ...... WWasWT
Metrano, Art 1937- CTFT-5
Meyer, Bertie Alexander
   1877-1967 .... WWasWT
Meyer, Louis 1871-1915 .... WWasWT
Meyer, Nicholas 1945- CTFT-1
Meyers, Ari 1969- CTFT-4
Meyers, Timothy 1945-1989 ....CTFT-1
Meynell, Clyde 1867-1934 ...... WWasWT
Michael, Gertrude 1910-1965 .... WWasWT
Michael, Kathleen 1917- WWT-17
Michael, Ralph 1907- WWT-17
Michaelis, Robert 1884-1965 ..... WWasWT
Michaels, Lorne 1944- CTFT-9
   Earlier sketch in CTFT-2
Michaels, Marilyn 1943- CTFT-8
Michaels, Richard 1936- CTFT-1
Michaelson, Knut 1846- .... WWasWT
Michell, Keith 1928- CTFT-8
   Earlier sketches in CTFT-2, WWT-17
Middlemass, Frank 1919- CTFT-8
Middleton, Edgar 1894-1939 ..... WWasWT
Middleton, George 1880-1967 .... WWasWT
Middleton, Guy 1907-1973 ...... WWasWT
Middleton, Josephine 1883-1971 .. WWasWT
Middleton, Ray 1907-1984 .... WWT-17
Midgley, Robin 1934- WWT-17
Midler, Bette 1945- CTFT-4
   Earlier sketch in WWT-17
Mifune, Toshiro 1920- CTFT-5
Mignot, Flore .... WWasWT
Milano, Alyssa 1972- CTFT-4
Miles, Bernard 1907- WWT-17
Miles, Joanna 1940- CTFT-1
Miles, Julia CTFT-1
Miles, Sarah 1941- CTFT-3
   Earlier sketch in WWT-17
Miles, Sylvia 1932- CTFT-7
   Earlier sketch in CTFT-1
Miles, Vera 1930- CTFT-5
Milgrim, Lynn 1940- CTFT-1
Militello, Anne E. 1957- CTFT-3
Milius, John 1944- CTFT-8
Milkis, Edward Kenneth 1931- CTFT-3
Milland, Ray 1905-1986 ....CTFT-3
Millar, Douglas 1875-1943 ...... WWasWT
Millar, Gertie 1879-1952 .... WWasWT
Millar, Mary WWT-17
Millar, Robins 1889-1968 .... WWasWT
Millar, Ronald 1919- WWT-17
Millard, Evelyn 1869-1941 ...... WWasWT
Millard, Ursula 1901- .... WWasWT
Miller, Agnes .... WWasWT
Miller, Ann 1919- CTFT-4
   Earlier sketch in WWT-17
Miller, Arthur 1915- CTFT-1
   Earlier sketch in WWT-17
Miller, Barry 1958- CTFT-2
Miller, Buzz 1923- CTFT-1
Miller, David 1871-1933 .... WWasWT
Miller, David 1909- CTFT-2
Miller, Dick 1928- CTFT-8

Miller, George CTFT-7
Miller, George 1945- CTFT-7
Miller, Gilbert Heron
   1884-1969 .... WWasWT
Miller, Harry M. 1934- WWT-17
Miller, Henry 1860-1926 .... WWasWT
Miller, Hugh (Lorimer) 1889-? ... WWasWT
Miller, J.P. 1919- CTFT-7
Miller, Jason 1939- CTFT-4
   Earlier sketch in WWT-17
Miller, Joan 1910-1988 ....CTFT-7
   Earlier sketch in WWT-17
Miller, Jonathan 1934- CTFT-5
   Earlier sketch in WWT-17
Miller, June 1934- CTFT-4
Miller, Marilynn 1898-1936 ...... WWasWT
Miller, Martin (Rudolf)
   1899-1969 .... WWasWT
Miller, Nolan 1935- CTFT-8
Miller, Penelope Ann 1964- CTFT-2
Miller, Richard 1930- CTFT-3
Miller, Ruby 1889-1976 .... WWasWT
Miller, Susan 1944- CTFT-1
Miller, Thomas L. 1940- CTFT-3
Millett, Maude 1867-1920 .... WWasWT
Millett, Tim 1954- CTFT-2
Millian, Andra CTFT-5
Millican, Jane 1902- .... WWasWT
Milliet, Paul 1858-? .... WWasWT
Milligan, Spike 1918- CTFT-6
   Earlier sketch in WWT-17
Milligan, Tuck CTFT-1
Millington, Rodney 1905-1990 ....WWT-17
Mills, A. J. 1872-? .... WWasWT
Mills, Mrs. Clifford ?-1933 ...... WWasWT
Mills, Donna CTFT-3
Mills, Florence 1901- .... WWasWT
Mills, Frank 1870-1921 .... WWasWT
Mills, Hayley 1946- CTFT-3
   Earlier sketch in WWT-17
Mills, Horace 1864-1941 .... WWasWT
Mills, John 1908- WWT-17
Mills, Juliet 1941- CTFT-3
   Earlier sketch in WWT-17
Millward 1861-1932 .... WWasWT
Milne, Alan Alexander
   1882-1956 .... WWasWT
Milner, Martin 1931- CTFT-7
Milstead, Harris Glenn
   See Divine CTFT-7
Miltern, John E. 1870-1937 ...... WWasWT
Milton, Billy 1905-1989 .... WWasWT
Milton, David Scott 1934- CTFT-1
Milton, Ernest 1890-1974 .... WWasWT
Milton, Harry 1900-1965 .... WWasWT
Milton, Maud 1859-1945 .... WWasWT
Milton, Robert ?-1956 .... WWasWT
Milward, Dawson 1870-1926 ..... WWasWT
Milward, Kristin CTFT-5
Mimieux, Yvette 1944- CTFT-5
Miner, Jan 1917- CTFT-4
   Earlier sketch in WWT-17
Miner, Stephen
   See Miner, Steve CTFT-9
Miner, Steve 1951- CTFT-9
Miner, Worthington C.
   1900-1982 .... WWasWT
Minetti, Maria .... WWasWT
Minkus, Barbara 1943- CTFT-1
Mineo, John 1942- CTFT-2
Mineo, Sal 1939-1976 ....CTFT-2
Minil, Renee du 1868-? .... WWasWT

Minnelli, Liza 1946- CTFT-8
   Earlier sketches in CTFT-1, WWT-17
Minnelli, Vincente 1903-1986 ......CTFT-1
Minney, Rubeigh James 1895- ....WWasWT
Minster, Jack 1901-1966 .... WWasWT
Minter, Mary Miles 1902- ....WWasWT
Minto, Dorothy 1891- ....WWasWT
Miou-Miou 1950- CTFT-8
Miramova, Elena ....WWasWT
Mirande, Yves..................WWasWT
Mirbeau, Octave 1848-1917 ...... WWasWT
Mirisch, Walter 1921- CTFT-8
Mirren, Helen 1946- CTFT-2
   Earlier sketch in WWT-17
Mischer, Don CTFT-1
Mr. T. 1952- CTFT-5
Mistinguett 1875-1956 .... WWasWT
Mitchelhill, J. P. 1879-1966 ...... WWasWT
Mitchell, Cameron 1918- CTFT-5
Mitchell, David 1932- CTFT-4
   Earlier sketch in WWT-17
Mitchell, Dodson 1868-1939 ..... WWasWT
Mitchell, Grant 1874-1957 ...... WWasWT
Mitchell, Gregory 1951- CTFT-8
Mitchell, James 1920- CTFT-1
Mitchell, John H. 1918-1988 .....CTFT-4
Mitchell, Julian 1935- CTFT-1
Mitchell, Julien 1888-1954 ...... WWasWT
Mitchell, Langdon Elwyn
   1862-1935 .... WWasWT
Mitchell, Lauren 1957- CTFT-1
Mitchell, Ruth 1919- WWT-17
Mitchell, Stephen 1907- WWT-17
Mitchell, Thomas 1895-1962 ..... WWasWT
Mitchell, Warren 1926- CTFT-2
   Earlier sketch in WWT-17
Mitchell, Yvonne 1925-1979 ..... WWT-16
Mitchenson, Joe WWT-17
Mitchum, Robert 1917- CTFT-3
Mitzi-Dalty, Mdlle. ....WWasWT
Miyori, Kim CTFT-8
Mobley, Mary Ann 1937- CTFT-3
Modine, Matthew 1959- CTFT-6
   Brief Entry in CTFT-2
Moeller, Philip 1880-1958 .... WWasWT
Moffat, Donald 1930- CTFT-4
   Earlier sketch in WWT-17
Moffat, Graham 1866-1951 ...... WWasWT
Moffat, Mrs. Graham
   1873-1943 .... WWasWT
Moffat, Kate ....WWasWT
Moffat, Margaret 1882-1942 ..... WWasWT
Moffat, Winifred 1899- .... WWasWT
Moffatt, Alice 1890- .... WWasWT
Moffatt, John 1922- CTFT-6
   Earlier sketch in WWT-17
Moffet, Harold 1892-1938 .... WWasWT
Mohyeddin, Zia 1933- WWT-17
Moiseiwitsch, Tanya 1914- WWT-17
Mokae, Zakes 1935- CTFT-7
   Earlier sketch in CTFT-2
Molesworth, Ida ?-1951 .... WWasWT
Molina, Alfred CTFT-8
Molinaro, Al 1919- CTFT-8
Molinaro, Edouard 1928- CTFT-8
Moll, Richard 1943- CTFT-4
Mollison, Clifford 1897-1986 .....WWT-17
Mollison, Henry 1905- .... WWasWT
Mollison, William 1893-1955 ..... WWasWT
Molnar, Ferencz 1878-1952 ...... WWasWT
Molnar, Robert 1927- CTFT-1
Molyneux, Eileen 1893-1962 ..... WWasWT
Monash, Paul CTFT-5

Monck, Nugent 1877-1958 ......WWasWT
Monckton, Lionel 1862-1924 .....WWasWT
Moncrieff, Gladys 1893- ....WWasWT
Monk, Isabell 1952- CTFT-2
Monk, Meredith 1942- CTFT-3
Monkhouse, Allan 1858-1936 ....WWasWT
Monkman, Phyllis 1892- ....WWasWT
Monna-Delza, Mdlle. ?-1921 .....WWasWT
Montagu, Elizabeth 1909- ....WWasWT
Montague, Bertram 1892- ....WWasWT
Montague, Charles Edward
   1867-1928 ....WWasWT
Montague, Harold 1874-? ....WWasWT
Montague, Lee 1927- CTFT-7
   Earlier sketch in WWT-17
Montalban, Ricardo 1920- CTFT-3
Montand, Yves 1921- CTFT-6
Montefiore, David 1944- CTFT-3
Montefiore, Eade 1866-1944 .....WWasWT
Montgomery, Douglass
   1909-1966 ....WWasWT
Montgomery, Earl 1921-1987 ....WWT-17
Montgomery, Elizabeth 1902- WWT-17
Montgomery, Elizabeth 1933- CTFT-3
Montgomery, James 1882-1966 ...WWasWT
Montgomery, Robert 1903-1981 ..WWasWT
Montgomery, Robert 1946- CTFT-1
Montgommery, David Craig
   1870-1917 ....WWasWT
Monticello, Roberto 1954- CTFT-5
Montrose, Muriel ....WWasWT
Moody, Ron 1924- CTFT-8
   Earlier sketches in CTFT-2, WWT-17
Moonblood, Q.
   See Stallone, Sylvester CTFT-8
Mooney, Debra CTFT-4
Mooney, William 1936- CTFT-1
Moor, Bill 1931- CTFT-1
Moore, A. P. 1906- ....WWasWT
Moore, Alvy 1925- CTFT-9
Moore, Carrie 1883-1956 ....WWasWT
Moore, Cherie
   See Ladd, Cheryl CTFT-6
Moore, Christopher 1952- CTFT-1
Moore, Decima 1871-1964 ....WWasWT
Moore, Demi CTFT-3
   Brief Entry in CTFT-2
Moore, Dudley 1935- CTFT-8
   Earlier sketches in CTFT-1, WWT-17
Moore, Eva 1870-1955 ....WWasWT
Moore, Florence 1886-1935 ......WWasWT
Moore, George 1852-1933 ....WWasWT
Moore, Grace 1901-1947 ....WWasWT
Moore, Hilda ?-1926 ....WWasWT
Moore, Judith 1944- CTFT-1
Moore, Kim 1956- CTFT-2
Moore, Mary 1861-1931 ....WWasWT
Moore, Mary Tyler 1937- CTFT-6
   Earlier sketch in CTFT-2
Moore, Maureen 1952- CTFT-1
Moore, Melba 1945- CTFT-4
Moore, Robert 1927-1984 ....CTFT-2
   Earlier sketch in WWT-17
Moore, Roger 1927- CTFT-5
Moore, Sonia 1902- CTFT-2
Moore, Stephen 1937- CTFT-6
   Earlier sketch in WWT-17
Moore, Tom 1943- CTFT-1
Moore, Victor Frederick
   1876-1962 ....WWasWT
Moorehead, Agnes 1906-1974 .....WWT-16
Morahan, Christopher 1929- CTFT-6
   Earlier sketches in CTFT-2, WWT-17

Morales, Esai CTFT-5
Moran, Lois 1907-1990 ....WWasWT
Morand, Eugene 1855-1930 ......WWasWT
Morand, Marcellue Raymond
   1860-1922 ....WWasWT
Moranis, Rick CTFT-7
More, Julian 1928- CTFT-6
More, Kenneth 1914-1982 ....WWT-17
More, Unity 1894- ....WWasWT
Moreau, Emile 1852-? ....WWasWT
Moreau, Jeanne 1928- CTFT-8
Morehouse, Ward 1899-1966 .....WWasWT
Morell, Andre 1909-1978 ....WWT-16
Moreno, Rita 1931- CTFT-3
   Earlier sketches in CTFT-1, WWT-17
Moreton, Ursula 1903- ....WWasWT
Morey, Charles 1947- CTFT-1
Morgan, Charles Langbridge
   1894-1958 ....WWasWT
Morgan, Claudia 1912-1974 ......WWasWT
Morgan, Diana 1910- WWT-17
Morgan, Frank 1890-1949 ....WWasWT
Morgan, Gareth 1940- CTFT-5
   Earlier sketch in WWT-17
Morgan, Harry 1915- CTFT-3
Morgan, Helen 1900-1941 ....WWasWT
Morgan, Joan 1905- WWT-17
Morgan, Ralph 1888-1956 ....WWasWT
Morgan, Roger 1938- WWT-17
Morgan, Sydney 1885-1931 ......WWasWT
Morgenstern, S.
   See Goldman, William CTFT-7
Morgenstern, Susan 1954- CTFT-5
Moriarty, Michael 1941- CTFT-4
   Earlier sketches in CTFT-1, WWT-17
Morison, Patricia 1915- ....WWasWT
Morita, Noriyuki "Pat" CTFT-3
Moriyasu, Atsushi 1956- CTFT-1
Morlay, Gaby 1896-1964 ....WWasWT
Morley, Christopher CTFT-5
   Earlier sketch in WWT-17
Morley, Malcolm 1890-1966 .....WWasWT
Morley, Robert 1908- CTFT-7
   Earlier sketch in WWT-17
Morley, Sheridan 1941- WWT-17
Mornel, Ted 1936- CTFT-2
Morosco, Oliver 1876-1945 ......WWasWT
Morricone, Ennio 1928- CTFT-7
Morris, Aldyth 1901- CTFT-1
Morris, Anita CTFT-8
Morris, Chester 1901-1970 ......WWasWT
Morris, Clara 1846-1925 ....WWasWT
Morris, Edmund 1912- CTFT-1
Morris, Garrett 1944- CTFT-8
Morris, Joan 1943- CTFT-1
Morris, John 1926- CTFT-1
Morris, Margaret 1891- ....WWasWT
Morris, Mary 1895-1970 ....WWasWT
Morris, Mary 1915-1988 ....CTFT-8
   Earlier sketch WWT-17
Morris, McKay 1891-1955 ....WWasWT
Morris, Phyllis 1894- WWT-17
Morris, William 1861-1936 ......WWasWT
Morrison, Ann 1956- CTFT-2
Morrison, George E. 1860-1938 ..WWasWT
Morrison, Hobe 1904- WWT-17
Morrison, Jack 1887-1948 ....WWasWT
Morrison, Jack 1912- WWT-17
Morrissey, Paul 1939- CTFT-8
Morritt, Charles 1860-? ....WWasWT
Morrow, Doretta 1928-1968 .....WWasWT
Morrow, Vic 1931-1982 ....CTFT-2
Morse, Barry 1919- ....WWasWT

Morse, David 1953- CTFT-7
Morse, Robert 1931- CTFT-7
   Earlier sketch in WWT-17
Mortimer, Charles 1885-1964 ....WWasWT
Mortimer, John 1923- CTFT-9
   Earlier sketch in WWT-17
Mortlock, Charles Bernard
   1888-1967 ....WWasWT
Morton, Arthur 1908- CTFT-5
Morton, Clive 1904-1975 ....WWasWT
Morton, Edward ?-1922 ....WWasWT
Morton, Hugh
   See McLellan, C. M. S. ....WWasWT
Morton, Joe 1947- CTFT-7
Morton, Leon 1912- ....WWasWT
Morton, Martha 1870-1925 ......WWasWT
Morton, Michael ?-1931 ....WWasWT
Moscovitch, Maurice 1871-1940 ..WWasWT
Moses, Charles Alexander
   1923- CTFT-3
Moses, Gilbert 1942- CTFT-5
   Earlier sketch in WWT-17
Moses, Montrose J. 1878-1934 ...WWasWT
Mosheim, Grete 1907- ....WWasWT
Mosher, Gregory 1949- CTFT-1
Moss, Arnold 1910-1989 ....WWT-17
Moss, (Horace) Edward 1854-? ...WWasWT
Moss, Jeffrey B. 1945- CTFT-4
Moss, W. Keith 1892-1935 ....WWasWT
Mosse, Spencer 1945- CTFT-1
Mossetti, Carlotta 1890-? ....WWasWT
Most, Donald 1953- CTFT-7
Mostel, Joshua 1946 ....CTFT-8
   Earlier sketch in CTFT-1
Mostel, Zero 1915-1977 ....WWT-17
Motley WWT-17
Motta, Bess CTFT-4
Mouezy-Eon, Andre 1880-? ......WWasWT
Mouillot, Gertrude ?-1961 ....WWasWT
Moulan, Frank 1875-1939 ....WWasWT
Mould, Raymond Wesley 1905- ..WWasWT
Moulton, Robert 1922- CTFT-1
Mounet, Jean Paul 1847-1922 ....WWasWT
Mounet-Sully, Jean 1841-1916 ....WWasWT
Mount, Peggy 1916- WWT-17
Moya, Natalie 1900- ....WWasWT
Moyers, Bill 1934- CTFT-7
Mozart, George 1864-1947 ....WWasWT
Mrozek, Slawomir 1930- WWT-17
Mudd, Roger 1928- CTFT-5
Mudie, Leonard 1884-1965 ......WWasWT
Muellerleile, Marianne 1948- CTFT-7
Muir, Jean 1911- ....WWasWT
Mulcaster, G. H. 1891-1964 ......WWasWT
Muldaur, Diana 1938- CTFT-8
Muldoon, Roland 1941- WWT-17
Mulgrew, Kate 1955- CTFT-1
Mulhern, Matt 1960- CTFT-2
Mulholland, J. B. 1858-1925 .....WWasWT
Mull, Martin 1943- CTFT-3
Mullavey, Greg 1939- CTFT-7
Mullen, Barbara 1914-1979 ....WWT-17
Mulligan, Richard 1932- CTFT-4
   Earlier sketch in WWT-17
Mumy, Bill 1954- CTFT-8
Mundin, Herbert 1898-1939 .....WWasWT
Mundy, Meg CTFT-1
   Earlier sketch in WWasWT
Muni, Paul 1895-1967 ....WWasWT
Munro, C. K. 1889- ....WWasWT
Munro, Nan 1905- WWT-17
Munson, Ona 1906-1955 ....WWasWT
Murcell, George 1925- WWT-17

Murch, Walter CTFT-9
Murdoch, Richard 1907- CTFT-8
    Earlier sketch in WWT-17
Murdoch, Rupert 1931- CTFT-5
Murdock, Ann 1890- ....WWasWT
Murfin, Jane ?-1955 ....WWasWT
Murin, David CTFT-2
Murphy, Ben 1942- CTFT-3
Murphy, Donn B. 1930- CTFT-4
Murphy, Eddie 1961- CTFT-6
    Earlier sketch in CTFT-2
Murphy, Michael 1938- CTFT-7
    Earlier sketch in CTFT-1
Murphy, Rosemary 1927- CTFT-7
    Earlier sketch in WWT-17
Murray, Alma 1854-1945 ....WWasWT
Murray, Barbara 1929- WWT-17
Murray, Bill 1950- CTFT-6
    Earlier sketch in CTFT-1
Murray, Braham 1943- WWT-17
Murray, Brian 1937- CTFT-4
    Earlier sketch in WWT-17
Murray, Don 1929- CTFT-1
Murray, Douglas ?-1936 ....WWasWT
Murray, George Gilbert Aime
    1866-1957 ....WWasWT
Murray, J. Harold 1891-1940 ....WWasWT
Murray, Mary Gordon 1953- CTFT-1
Murray, Paul 1885-1949 ....WWasWT
Murray, Peg WWT-17
Murray, Peter 1925- ....WWasWT
Murray, Sharon CTFT-2
Murray, Stephen 1912- WWT-17
Murray, T. C. 1973-1959 ....WWasWT
Musante, Tony 1936- CTFT-7
    Earlier sketch in CTFT-1
Musgrove, Gertrude 1912- ....WWasWT
Music, Lorenzo 1937- CTFT-8
Musky, Jane 1954- CTFT-4
Musser, Tharon 1925- CTFT-2
    Earlier sketch in WWT-17
"My Fancy" ....WWasWT
Myers, Paul 1917- WWT-17
Myers, Peter 1923-1978 ....WWT-16
Myers, Richard 1901- ....WWasWT
Myles, Lynda CTFT-1
Myrtil, Odette 1898-1978 ....WWasWT

N

Nabors, Jim 1933- CTFT-3
Nadel, Norman 1915- WWT-17
Nadell, Carol L. 1944- CTFT-1
Nader, Michael 1945- CTFT-8
Nagel, Conrad 1897-1970 ....WWasWT
Nainby, Robert 1869-1948 ....WWasWT
Naish, Archie 1878-? ....WWasWT
Naismith, Laurence 1908- WWT-17
Nallon, Steve 1960- CTFT-4
Namath, Joe 1943- CTFT-3
Nance, Jack CTFT-9
Napier, Alan 1903-1988 ....CTFT-7
    Earlier sketch in WWasWT
Napier, Charles CTFT-6
Napier, John 1944- CTFT-5
    Earlier sketch in WWT-17
Napierkowska, Stanislawa
    (Stasia) ....WWasWT
Napoli, Tony 1948- CTFT-2
Nardino, Gary 1935- CTFT-3
Nares, Geoffrey 1917-1942 ......WWasWT
Nares, Owen 1888-1943 ....WWasWT

Nash, Florence 1888-1950 ....WWasWT
Nash, George Frederick
    1873-1944 ....WWasWT
Nash, Mary 1885-? ....WWasWT
Nash, N. Richard 1913- WWT-17
Nassau, Paul 1930- CTFT-4
Nassivera, John 1950- CTFT-4
Nathan, Ben 1857-1965 ....WWasWT
Nathan, George Jean 1882-1958 ..WWasWT
Nathan, Vivian 1921- CTFT-2
Nation, W. H. C. 1843-1914 .....WWasWT
National Theatre Company,
    The ....WWasWT
Natwick, Mildred 1908- CTFT-7
    Earlier sketch in WWT-17
Naughton, Bill 1910- WWT-17
Naughton, David 1951- CTFT-6
    Brief Entry in CTFT-2
Naughton, James 1945- CTFT-5
    Earlier sketch in CTFT-1
Naylor, Robert 1899- ....WWasWT
Nazimova, Alla 1879-1945 ....WWasWT
Neagle, Anna 1904-1986 ....CTFT-4
    Earlier sketch in WWT-17
Neal, Patricia 1926- CTFT-3
    Earlier sketch in WWasWT
Neame, Christopher 1942- CTFT-7
Neame, Ronald 1911- CTFT-6
Near, Holly 1949- CTFT-6
Near, Timothy 1945- CTFT-9
Nedell, Bernard 1899-1972 ......WWasWT
Nederlander, James 1922- CTFT-2
    Earlier sketch in WWT-17
Needham, Hal 1931- CTFT-6
Neeson, Liam CTFT-7
Negro, Mary-Joan CTFT-1
Neil, Julian 1952- CTFT-3
Neill, Jeffrey K. 1938- CTFT-2
Neill, Sam 1948- CTFT-6
Neilson, Francis 1867-1961 .....WWasWT
Neilson, Harold V. 1874-1956 ...WWasWT
Neilson, Julia 1868-1957 ....WWasWT
Neilson, Perlita 1933- CTFT-5
    Earlier sketch in WWT-17
Neilson-Terry, Dennis
    1895-1932 ....WWasWT
Neilson-Terry, Phyllis 1892- ...WWasWT
Neiman, John M. 1935- ....WWasWT
Neipris, Wille Janet 1936- CTFT-4
Nelligan, Kate 1951- CTFT-7
    Earlier sketches in CTFT-1, WWT-17
Nelson, Barry 1925- CTFT-5
    Earlier sketch in WWT-17
Nelson, Craig T. CTFT-3
Nelson, David 1936- CTFT-5
Nelson, Gene 1920- CTFT-7
    Earlier sketch in WWT-17
Nelson, Harriet 1914- CTFT-3
Nelson, Judd 1959- CTFT-9
    Brief Entry in CTFT-4
Nelson, Kenneth 1930- WWT-17
Nelson, Novella 1938- CTFT-1
Nelson, Ralph 1916-1987 ....CTFT-1
Nelson, Richard CTFT-7
Nelson, Richard 1950- CTFT-8
Nelson, Rick 1940-1985 ....CTFT-3
Nelson, Ruth 1905- WWT-17
Nelson, Tracy CTFT-3
Nelson, Willie 1933- CTFT-5
Nemchinova, Vera ....WWasWT
Nero, Franco 1941- CTFT-6
Nesbitt, Cathleen 1888-1982 ....WWT-17

Nesbitt, Miriam Anne
    1879-1954 ....WWasWT
Nesbitt, Robert 1906- WWT-17
Nesmith, Michael 1942- CTFT-5
Nesmith, Ottola 1893-1972 ......WWasWT
Nethersole, Olga Isabel
    1866-1951 ....WWasWT
Nettlefold, Archibald 1870-1944 ..WWasWT
Nettlefold, Frederick John
    1867-1949 ....WWasWT
Nettleton, John 1929- CTFT-5
    Earlier sketch in WWT-17
Nettleton, Lois CTFT-4
    Earlier sketch in WWT-17
Neuberger, Jan 1953- CTFT-5
Neufeld, Mace 1928- CTFT-9
    Earlier sketch in CTFT-1
Neufeld, Peter 1936- CTFT-1
Neufeld, Sigmund Jr. 1931- CTFT-1
Neuman, Joan 1926- CTFT-1
Neville, John 1925- CTFT-4
    Earlier sketch in WWT-17
Nevins, Claudette CTFT-1
New, Babette 1913- CTFT-4
Newall, Guy 1885-1937 ....WWasWT
Neway, Patricia 1919- WWT-17
Newberry, Barbara 1910- ....WWasWT
Newcomb, Mary 1897-1966 ....WWasWT
Newell, Patrick CTFT-8
Newell, Raymond 1894- ....WWasWT
Newhart, Bob 1929- CTFT-9
    Earlier sketch in CTFT-2
Newland, Mary WWT-8
Newley, Anthony 1931- CTFT-5
    Earlier sketch in WWT-17
Newman, Barry 1938- CTFT-3
Newman, Claude 1903- ....WWasWT
Newman, David 1937- CTFT-5
Newman, Edwin 1919- CTFT-5
Newman, Emil ?-1984 ....CTFT-2
Newman, Greatrex 1892- ....WWasWT
Newman, Laraine 1952- CTFT-6
Newman, Lionel 1916-1989
Newman, Paul 1925- CTFT-3
    Earlier sketches in CTFT-1, WWasWT
Newman, Phyllis 1933- CTFT-2
    Earlier sketch in WWT-17
Newman, Randy 1943- CTFT-9
Newmar, Julie 1933- CTFT-1
Newnham-Davis, Nathaniel
    1854-1917 ....WWasWT
Newton, Henry Chance
    1854-1931 ....WWasWT
Newton, John 1925- CTFT-1
Newton, Robert 1905-1956 ....WWasWT
Newton-John, Olivia 1948- CTFT-5
Ney, Marie 1895- ....WWasWT
Ngema, Mbongeni 1955- CTFT-9
Nicander, Edwin 1876-1951 ......WWasWT
Nicastro, Michelle 1960- CTFT-2
Nicholas, Anna CTFT-4
Nicholas, Denise 1945- CTFT-6
Nicholas, Paul 1945- CTFT-2
Nicholls, Anthony 1907-1977 ....WWT-16
Nicholls, Harry 1852-1926 ......WWasWT
Nichols, Anne 1891-1966 ....WWasWT
Nichols, Beverly 1898-1983 .....WWasWT
Nichols, Leo
    See Morricone, Ennio CTFT-7
Nichols, Lewis 1903- ....WWasWT
Nichols, Mike 1931- CTFT-8
    Earlier sketches in CTFT-1, WWT-17
Nichols, Nichelle 1936- CTFT-8

Nichols, Peter 1927- CTFT-4
  Earlier sketch in WWT-17
Nichols, Robert 1924- CTFT-4
Nicholson, H. O. 1868-? ....WWasWT
Nicholson, Jack 1937- CTFT-3
  Earlier sketch in CTFT-1
Nicholson, Kenyon 1894- ......WWasWT
Nicholson, Nora 1889-1973 ......WWasWT
Nichtern, Claire CTFT-2
Nicodemi, Dario ?-1934 ....WWasWT
Nicoll, Allardyce 1894-1976 ......WWT-16
Nielsen, Alice 1876-1943 ....WWasWT
Nielsen, Leslie 1926- CTFT-3
Niesen, Gertrude 1910- ....WWasWT
Nightingale, Joe ....WWasWT
Nijinska, Bronislava 1891-1972 ...WWasWT
Nijinsky, Vaslav 1890-1950 ......WWasWT
Nikitna, Alice ....WWasWT
Nillson, Carlotta 1878?-1951 .....WWasWT
Nimmo, Derek 1932- WWT-17
Nimoy, Leonard 1931- CTFT-7
  Earlier sketch in CTFT-1
Nissen, Brian 1917- ....WWasWT
Nissen, Greta 1906-1988 ....WWasWT
Nitzsche, Jack CTFT-8
Niven, David 1910-1983 ....CTFT-1
Nixon, Agnes 1927- CTFT-6
Nixon, Cynthia 1966-............CTFT-7
Noble, Dennis 1898-1966 ....WWasWT
Noble, James 1922- CTFT-7
Noiret, Philippe 1931- CTFT-6
Nolan, Doris 1916-..............WWasWT
Nolan, Lloyd 1902-1985 ....CTFT-1
  Earlier sketch in WWasWT
Nolte, Nick 1942- CTFT-6
  Earlier sketch in CTFT-1
Noonan, Tom 1951- CTFT-8
Norden, Christine 1924-1988 ....CTFT-6
Nordstrom, Frances ....WWasWT
Norfolk, Edgar 1893-............WWasWT
Norgate, Matthew 1901- WWT-17
Norman, Maidie 1912- CTFT-2
Norman, Marsha 1947- CTFT-1
Norman, Norman J. 1870-1941 ...WWasWT
Norman, Norman V. 1864-1943 .WWasWT
Norman, Thyrza 1884-? ....WWasWT
Normington, John 1937-..........CTFT-5
  Earlier sketch in WWT-17
Norris, Chuck 1939-.............CTFT-6
Norris, William 1872-1929 ......WWasWT
North, Alex 1910- CTFT-2
North, Edmund H. 1911-1990.....CTFT-1
North, Sheree 1933-.............CTFT-6
Northcott, Richard 1871-1931 ....WWasWT
Northen, Michael 1921-..........WWT-17
Norton, Elliot 1903-............WWT-17
Norton, Frederic ?-1946.........WWasWT
Norton-Taylor, Judy CTFT-3
Norwood, Eille 1861-1948 ....WWasWT
Norworth, Jack 1879-1959 ....WWasWT
Noto, Lore CTFT-1
Nouri, Michael 1945- CTFT-7
  Earlier sketch in CTFT-1
Novak, Kim 1933- CTFT-7
  Earlier sketch in CTFT-2
Novello, Don 1943- CTFT-3
Novello, Ivor 1893-1951 ....WWasWT
Noyes, Thomas 1922-1989 ....CTFT-8
Noziere, Fernand 1874-1931 .....WWasWT
Nugent, Elliott 1899-1980 ....WWasWT
Nugent, John Charles
  1878-1947 ....WWasWT
Nugent, Moya 1901-1954 ....WWasWT

Nugent, Nelle 1939- CTFT-1
Nunn, Trevor 1940- CTFT-3
  Earlier sketch in WWT-17
Nureyev, Rudolf 1938-...........CTFT-5
Nuyen, France 1939- CTFT-1
Nuytten, Bruno 1945- CTFT-9
Nye, Carrie CTFT-5
  Earlier sketch in WWT-17
Nye, Pat 1908- WWT-17
Nykvist, Sven 1922-.............CTFT-5
Nype, Russell 1924- WWT-17

O

Oaker, Jane 1880-? ....WWasWT
Oakland, Simon 1922-1983 ......CTFT-1
Oates, Warren 1928-1982.........CTFT-1
O'Bannon, Dan 1946- CTFT-8
Ober, Philip 1902-1982 ....WWasWT
Obey, Andre 1892-1975 ....WWasWT
Obraztsov, Sergei
  Vladimirovich 1901- ....WWasWT
O'Brian, Hugh 1930- CTFT-2
  Earlier sketch in WWT-17
O'Brien, Barry 1893-1961 ....WWasWT
O'Brien, David 1930- ....WWasWT
O'Brien, Edmond 1915-1985 ......CTFT-2
O'Brien, Jack 1939- CTFT-8
  Earlier sketch in CTFT-1
O'Brien, Kate 1897-1974 ....WWasWT
O'Brien, Margaret 1937 ....CTFT-3
O'Brien, Maureen 1943-..........CTFT-5
  Earlier sketch in WWT-17
O'Brien, Terence 1887-1970 .....WWasWT
O'Brien, Timothy 1929-..........CTFT-2
  Earlier sketch in WWT-17
O'Brien, Virginia 1896-1987 .....WWasWT
O'Brien-Moore, Erin 1908-1979 ..WWasWT
O'Bryen, W. J. 1898-...........WWasWT
O'Callaghan, Richard 1940- CTFT-4
  Earlier sketch in WWT-17
O'Casey, Sean 1880-1964 ....WWasWT
O'Connell, Arthur 1908-1981 .....WWT-17
O'Connell, Hugh 1898-1943 .....WWasWT
O'Connor, Bill 1919-............WWasWT
O'Connor, Carroll 1924- CTFT-9
  Earlier sketch in CTFT-1
O'Connor, Charles Wm.
  1878-1955 ....WWasWT
O'Connor, Donald 1925- CTFT-3
O'Connor, Glynnis 1955-.........CTFT-6
O'Connor, John J. 1933- ....WWasWT
O'Connor, Kevin 1938-...........CTFT-4
  Earlier sketch in WWT-17
O'Connor, Pat CTFT-7
O'Connor, Una 1893-1959 ....WWasWT
O'Conor, Joseph 1916-...........WWT-17
O'Dea, Denis 1905- ....WWasWT
Odell, George C. D. 1866-1949 ...WWasWT
Odets, Clifford 1906-1963 ....WWasWT
Odette, Mary 1901- ....WWasWT
Oditz, Carl 1946- CTFT-2
O'Doherty, Eileen 1891- ....WWasWT
O'Doherty, Mignon 1890-1961 ...WWasWT
O'Donnell, Mark 1954- CTFT-1
O'Donnell, Mary Eileen 1948- CTFT-5
O'Donoghue, Michael CTFT-4
O'Donovan, Desmond 1933- CTFT-5
  Earlier sketch in WWT-17
O'Donovan, Fred 1889-1952 .....WWasWT
Oenslager, Donald 1902-1975 ....WWasWT
O'Farrell, Mary 1892-1968 ......WWasWT

Ogilvie, George 1931-............WWT-17
Ogilvie, Glencairn Stuart
  1858-1932 ....WWasWT
O'Hara, Catherine CTFT-7
O'Hara, David 1965- CTFT-4
O'Hara, Jenny CTFT-8
O'Hara, Maureen 1921- CTFT-8
O'Hearn, Robert 1921-...........CTFT-5
O'Herlihy, Dan 1919-............CTFT-6
O'Higgins, Harvey J. 1876-1929 ..WWasWT
Ohlmeyer, Don Jr. 1945- CTFT-6
Ohnet, Georges 1848-1918 ....WWasWT
O'Horgan, Tom 1926-............WWT-17
O'Keefe, Michael 1955- CTFT-6
  Brief Entry in CTFT-2
O'Keefe, Miles CTFT-7
Okhlopkov, Nikolai Pavlovich
  1900-1967 ....WWasWT
Olaf, Pierre 1928- WWT-17
Oland, Warner 1880-1938 ....WWasWT
Olcott, Chauncey 1860-1932 .....WWasWT
Old, John M.
  See Bava, Mario CTFT-8
Oldham, Derek 1892-1968 ....WWasWT
Oldland, Lillian 1905- ....WWasWT
Oldman, Gary 1958- CTFT-9
O'Leary, William CTFT-4
Oliansky, Joel 1935- CTFT-1
Oliffe, Geraldine ....WWasWT
Olim, Dorothy 1934- CTFT-1
Olin, Ken 1954- CTFT-9
Oliphant, Jack 1895-............WWasWT
Olive, Edyth ?-1956 ....WWasWT
Oliver, Anthony 1923- WWT-17
Oliver, Barrie 1900- ....WWasWT
Oliver, Edith 1912-.............WWT-17
Oliver, Edna May 1885-1942 .....WWasWT
Oliver, Rochelle 1937- CTFT-2
Oliver, Vic ?-1964 ....WWasWT
Olivier, Laurence 1907-1989 .....CTFT-8
  Earlier sketches in CTFT-1, WWT-17
Olkewicz, Walter CTFT-6
Olmi, Ermanno 1931-............CTFT-8
Olmos, Edward James CTFT-6
O'Loughlin, Gerald S. 1921- CTFT-7
Olsen, Merlin 1940- CTFT-8
Olsen, Ole 1892-1963 ....WWasWT
Olson, Glen 1945-..............CTFT-4
Olson, James 1930-.............CTFT-1
Olson, Nancy 1928- CTFT-7
O'Malley, Ellen ?-1961 ....WWasWT
O'Malley, Rex 1901- ....WWasWT
Oman, Julia Terelyan 1930-.......WWT-17
O'Mara, Kate 1939- CTFT-2
  Earlier sketch in WWT-17
O'Morrison, Kevin CTFT-1
O'Neal, Frederick 1905-..........WWT-17
O'Neal, Patrick 1927-............CTFT-4
  Earlier sketch in WWT-17
O'Neal, Ron 1937-..............CTFT-6
O'Neal, Ryan 1941- CTFT-6
  Earlier sketch in CTFT-1
O'Neal, Tatum 1963- CTFT-3
O'Neal, Zelma 1907- ....WWasWT
O'Neil, Colette CTFT-5
  Earlier sketch in WWT-17
O'Neil, Nancy 1911- ....WWasWT
O'Neil, Peggy 1898-1960 ....WWasWT
O'Neill, Dick 1928- CTFT-6
O'Neill, Edward 1946- CTFT-5
O'Neill, Eugene Gladstone
  1888-1953 ....WWasWT
O'Neill, Frank B. 1869-1959 .....WWasWT

O'Neill, Henry 1891-1961 .... WWasWT
O'Neill, James 1849-1920 .... WWasWT
O'Neill, Jennifer 1949- CTFT-6
O'Neill, Marie 1887-1952 .... WWasWT
O'Neill, Nance 1874-1965 .... WWasWT
O'Neill, Norman 1875-1934 ..... WWasWT
O'Neill, Sheila 1930- CTFT-5
    Earlier sketch in WWT-17
Ontkean, Michael 1950- CTFT-3
Opatoshu, David 1918- CTFT-7
    Earlier sketch in WWT-17
Openshaw, Charles Elton .... WWasWT
Ophuls, Marcel 1927- CTFT-8
Opp, Julie 1871-1921 .... WWasWT
Oppenheimer, Alan 1930- CTFT-7
Oppenheimer, Jess 1913-1988 ...... CTFT-8
O'Ramey, Georgia 1886-1928 .... WWasWT
Orbach, Jerry 1935- CTFT-7
    Earlier sketches in CTFT-1, WWT-17
Orchard, Julian 1930-1979 .... WWT-16
Orczy, Emmuska 1865-1947 ..... WWasWT
Ord, Robert .... WWasWT
Ord, Simon 1874-1944 .... WWasWT
Ordonneau, Maurice 1854-1916 .. WWasWT
Ordway, Sally CTFT-1
O'Regan, Kathleen 1903- .... WWasWT
Orlando, Tony 1944- CTFT-6
Orme, Denise 1884-1960 .... WWasWT
Orme, Michael 1894-1944 .... WWasWT
Ornbo, Robert 1931- CTFT-5
    Earlier sketch in WWT-17
O'Rorke, Brefni 1889-1946 ...... WWasWT
O'Rourke, Robert 1947- CTFT-1
Orr, Mary 1918- WWT-17
Osborn, E. W. 1860-1930 .... WWasWT
Osborn, Paul 1901-1988 .... CTFT-7
    Earlier sketch in WWasWT
Osborne, John 1929- CTFT-5
    Earlier sketch in WWT-17
Osborne, Kipp 1944- CTFT-4
    Earlier sketch in WWT-17
Osborne, Vivienne 1905- .... WWasWT
Oscar, Henry 1891-1969 .... WWasWT
O'Shea, Milo 1926- CTFT-6
Osmond, Cliff CTFT-6
Osmond, Marie 1959- CTFT-6
Osmun, Betsy 1954- CTFT-4
O'Steen, Michael 1962- CTFT-8
Osterhage, Jeffrey 1953- CTFT-5
Osterman, Lester 1914- CTFT-4
    Earlier sketch in WWT-17
Osterwald, Bibi 1920- CTFT-6
    Earlier sketch in WWT-17
Ostrow, Stuart 1931- WWT-17
O'Sullivan, Maureen 1911- CTFT-3
    Earlier sketch in WWT-17
Osuna, Jess 1928- CTFT-1
Oswald, Genevieve 1923- CTFT-2
O'Toole, Annette 1953- CTFT-6
O'Toole, Peter 1932- CTFT-4
    Earlier sketch in WWT-17
Ottaway, James 1908- WWT-17
Oughton, Winifred 1890-1964 .... WWasWT
Ould, Hermon 1885-1951 .... WWasWT
Oulton, Brian 1908- WWT-17
Ouspenskaya, Maria 1876-1949 ... WWasWT
Overend, Dorothy .... WWasWT
Overman, Lynne 1887-1943 ..... WWasWT
Overmyer, Eric 1951- CTFT-5
Overton, Rick CTFT-3
Owen, Alun 1925- CTFT-6
    Earlier sketch in WWT-17
Owen, Bill WWT-17

Owen, Catherine Dale
    1900-1965 .... WWasWT
Owen, Harold 1872-1930 .... WWasWT
Owen, Harrison 1890- .... WWasWT
Owen, Reginald 1887-1972 ...... WWasWT
Owens, Gary CTFT-2
Owens, Rochelle 1936- CTFT-5
    Earlier sketch in WWT-17
Oxenberg, Catherine 1961- CTFT-7
Oyra, Jan 1888-? .... WWasWT
Oz, Frank 1944- CTFT-7

P

Paar, Jack 1918- CTFT-6
Pacey, Steven 1957- CTFT-8
Pacino, Al 1940- CTFT-6
    Earlier sketches in CTFT-1, WWT-17
Packer, David CTFT-7
Pagano, Giulia 1949- CTFT-1
Page, Anthony 1935- CTFT-2
    Earlier sketch in WWT-17
Page, Austin .... WWasWT
Page, Geraldine 1924-1987 ...... CTFT-5
    Earlier sketches in CTFT-4, CTFT-1,
    WWT-17
Page, Harrison CTFT-7
Page, Norman ?-1935 .... WWasWT
Page, Philip P. 1889- .... WWasWT
Page, Rita 1906-1954 .... WWasWT
Page, Tilsa 1926- .... WWasWT
Paget, Cecil ?-1955 .... WWasWT
Paget-Bowman, Cicely 1910- WWT-17
Pagett, Nicola 1945- CTFT-5
    Earlier sketch in WWT-17
Pagnol, Marcel 1895-1974 .... WWasWT
Paige, Elaine CTFT-6
Paige, Janis CTFT-2
    Earlier sketch in WWT-17
Painter, Eleanor 1890-1947 ...... WWasWT
Paisner, Dina CTFT-2
Pakula, Alan J. 1928- CTFT-6
    Earlier sketch in CTFT-1
Paladini, Ettore 1849-? .... WWasWT
Paladini-Ando, Celestina .... WWasWT
Palance, Jack 1920- CTFT-5
Palerme, Gina .... WWasWT
Paley, William S. 1901-1990 ..... CTFT-5
Palfrey, May Lever 1867-1929 ... WWasWT
Palin, Michael 1951- CTFT-5
Palma, Loretta 1946- CTFT-2
Palmer, Barbara 1911- .... WWasWT
Palmer, Betsy 1929- CTFT-2
    Earlier sketch in WWT-17
Palmer, Charles 1869-1920 ...... WWasWT
Palmer, Geoffrey 1927- CTFT-8
    Earlier sketch in CTFT-2
Palmer, Gregg 1927- CTFT-7
Palmer, John 1885-1944 .... WWasWT
Palmer, Lilli 1914-1986 .... CTFT-3
    Earlier sketch in WWT-17
Palmer, Minnie 1857-1936 .... WWasWT
Palmieri, Joe 1939- CTFT-1
Paltrow, Bruce 1943- CTFT-9
Pan, Hermes 1910(?)-1990 .... CTFT-9
Pankin, Stuart 1946- CTFT-7
Pankow, John CTFT-8
Panter, Joan 1909- .... WWasWT
Pantoliano, Joe 1951- CTFT-5
Papas, Irene 1926- CTFT-8
    Earlier sketch in CTFT-2
Pape, Joan CTFT-1

Papp, Joseph 1921- CTFT-1
    Earlier sketch in WWT-17
Paragon, John CTFT-8
Pare, Michael 1959- CTFT-5
Parent, Gail 1940- CTFT-8
Parfitt, Judy CTFT-2
    Earlier sketch in WWT-17
Parichy, Dennis CTFT-8
Paris, Jerry 1925-1986 .... CTFT-3
Parish, James .... WWasWT
Parisys, Marcelle .... WWasWT
Parker, Alan 1944- CTFT-5
Parker, Anthony 1912- .... WWasWT
Parker, Cecil 1897-1971 .... WWasWT
Parker, Corey 1965- CTFT-8
Parker, Eleanor 1922- CTFT-5
Parker, Ellen 1949- CTFT-6
Parker, Frank 1864-1926 .... WWasWT
Parker, Jameson 1947- CTFT-6
Parker, John 1875-1952 .... WWasWT
Parker, Joy 1924- .... WWasWT
Parker, Lew 1906-1972 .... WWasWT
Parker, Lottie Blair 1858?-1937 .. WWasWT
Parker, Louis Napoleon
    1852-1944 .... WWasWT
Parker, Sarah Jessica 1965- CTFT-7
Parker, Thane 1907- .... WWasWT
Parkinson, Dian CTFT-4
Parks, Bert 1914- CTFT-5
Parks, Gordon 1912- CTFT-6
Parks, Hildy 1926- CTFT-5
    Earlier sketch in CTFT-1
Parks, Larry 1914-1975 .... WWasWT
Parks, Michael 1938- CTFT-7
Parlakian, Nishan 1925- CTFT-4
Parnell, Peter 1953- CTFT-1
Parnell, Val 1894- .... WWasWT
Parriott, James D. 1950- CTFT-2
Parry, Chris 1952- CTFT-5
Parry, Edward Abbott
    1863-1943 .... WWasWT
Parsons, Alan 1888-1933 .... WWasWT
Parsons, Donovan 1888-? .... WWasWT
Parsons, Estelle 1927- CTFT-3
    Earlier sketch in WWT-17
Parsons, Nancie 1904- .... WWasWT
Parsons, Percy 1878-1944 .... WWasWT
Parton, Dolly 1946- CTFT-5
Pasco, Richard 1926- CTFT-6
    Earlier sketch in WWT-17
Pasdar, Adrian CTFT-9
Pasekoff, Marilyn 1949- CTFT-2
Passer, Ivan 1933- CTFT-8
Passeur, Steve 1899-1966 .... WWasWT
Passmore, Walter 1867-1946 ..... WWasWT
Paston, George ?-1936 .... WWasWT
Patacano, Martino
    See Chacksfield, Frank CTFT-2
Pataki, Michael 1938- CTFT-9
Pataki, Mike
    See Pataki, Michael CTFT-9
Patch, Wally 1888-1970 .... WWasWT
Pateman, Robert 1840-1924 ...... WWasWT
Patinkin, Mandy 1952- CTFT-3
Patrice, Teryn 1956- CTFT-4
Patrick, John 1907- WWT-17
Patrick, Nigel 1913- WWT-17
Patrick, Q.
    See Wheeler, Hugh CTFT-5
Patrick, Robert 1937- WWT-17
Patricola, Tom 1891-1950 .... WWasWT
Patterson, Dick 1929- CTFT-8
Patterson, Jay 1954- CTFT-2

Patterson, Neva 1922- .... WWasWT
Patterson, Raymond 1955- CTFT-1
Patterson, Richard
    See Patterson, Dick CTFT-8
Patterson, Tom 1920- WWT-17
Patton, Will 1954- CTFT-7
Paul, Betty 1921- .... WWasWT
Paul, Kent 1936- CTFT-3
Paul, Steven 1958- CTFT-3
Pauley, Jane 1950- CTFT-5
Pauline, Princess 1873-? .... WWasWT
Paull, Harry Major 1854-1934 ... WWasWT
Paulsen, Albert 1929- CTFT-6
Paulsen, Pat 1927- CTFT-3
Paulton, Harry 1842-1917 .... WWasWT
Paumier, Alfred 1870-1951 ...... WWasWT
Pavlova, Anna 1885-1931 .... WWasWT
Pavlow, Muriel 1921- WWT-17
Pawle, J. Lennox 1872-1936 ..... WWasWT
Pawley, Nancy 1901- .... WWasWT
Pawson, Hargrave 1902-1945 .... WWasWT
Paxinou, Katina 1900-1974 ...... WWasWT
Paxton, Bill 1955- CTFT-5
Paxton, Sydney 1860-1930 .... WWasWT
Paymer, David CTFT-3
Payn, Grahm 1918- WWT-17
Payne, Ben Iden 1888-1976 ...... WWasWT
Payne, Edmund 1865-1914 .... WWasWT
Payne, John 1912-1989 .... CTFT-8
Payne, Laurence 1919- .... WWasWT
Payne, Millie .... WWasWT
Payne, Walter ?-1949 .... WWasWT
Payne-Jennings, Victor
    1900-1962 .... WWasWT
Pays, Amanda 1959- CTFT-7
Payton-Wright, Pamela 1941- CTFT-5
    Earlier sketch in WWT-17
Peacock, Kim 1901-1966 .... WWasWT
Peacock, Trevor 1931- CTFT-5
    Earlier sketch in WWT-17
Pearce, Alice 1917-1966 .... WWasWT
Pearce, Richard 1943- CTFT-8
Pearce, Vera 1896-1966 .... WWasWT
Pearl, Jack 1895-1982 .... WWasWT
Pearlman, Stephen 1935- CTFT-7
Pearson, Beatrice 1920- .... WWasWT
Pearson, Lloyd 1897-1966 .... WWasWT
Pearson, Molly 1876-1959 .... WWasWT
Pearson, Richard 1918- WWT-17
Pearson, Sybille 1937- CTFT-3
Peaslee, Richard 1930- CTFT-1
Peck, Bob 1945- CTFT-9
Peck, Gregory 1916- CTFT-6
    Earlier sketches in CTFT-1, WWasWT
Peckinpah, Sam 1925-1984 ...... CTFT-1
Pedgrift, Frederic Henchman ... WWasWT
Pedrick, Gale 1905-1970 .... WWasWT
Peek, Brent CTFT-4
Peel, David 1920- .... WWasWT
Peel, Eileen WWT-16
Peerce, Larry 1935(?)- CTFT-9
Peile, Frederick 1862-1934 ...... WWasWT
Peisley, Frederick 1904-1976 ..... WWT-16
Pelikan, Lisa CTFT-3
Pelissier, Harry Gabriel
    1874-1913 .... WWasWT
Peluce, Meeno 1970- CTFT-5
Pember, Ron 1934- CTFT-4
    Earlier sketch in WWT-17
Pemberton, Brock 1885-1950 ..... WWasWT
Pemberton, John Wyndham
    1883-1947 .... WWasWT
Pemberton, Max 1863-1950 ...... WWasWT

Pemberton, Reece 1914-1977 ..... WWT-16
Pemberton-Billing, Robin 1929- ... WWT-17
Pena, Elizabeth CTFT-5
Pendleton, Austin 1940- CTFT-4
    Earlier sketch in WWT-17
Pendleton, Wyman 1916- WWT-17
Penghlis, Thaao CTFT-8
Penley, Arthur 1881-1954 .... WWasWT
Penley, W. S. 1851-1912 .... WWasWT
Penn, Arthur 1922- CTFT-2
    Earlier sketch in WWT-17
Penn, Bill 1931- .... WWasWT
Penn, Christopher CTFT-7
Penn, Sean 1960- CTFT-3
    Brief Entry in CTFT-2
Pennington, Ann 1892-1971 ...... WWasWT
Pennington, Janice CTFT-4
Penny, Joe 1956- CTFT-7
Penrose, John 1917- .... WWasWT
Penzner, Seymour 1915- CTFT-2
Peple, Edward H. 1867-1924 .... WWasWT
Peppard, George 1928- CTFT-3
Perceval-Clark, Perceval
    1881-1938 .... WWasWT
Percy, Edward 1891-1968 .... WWasWT
Percy, S. Esme 1887-1957 .... WWasWT
Percy, William Stratford
    1872-1946 .... WWasWT
Percyval, T. Wigney 1865-? ...... WWasWT
Perez, Lazaro 1945- CTFT-5
Perkins, Anthony 1932- CTFT-6
    Earlier sketches in CTFT-2, WWT-17
Perkins, Don 1928- CTFT-2
Perkins, Elizabeth 1960- CTFT-7
Perkins, Osgood 1892-1937 ...... WWasWT
Perlman, Rhea 1948- CTFT-6
Perlman, Ron 1950- CTFT-8
Perloff, Carey CTFT-7
Perrey, Mireille .... WWasWT
Perrin, Vic
    See Perrin, Victor CTFT-9
Perrin, Victor 1916-1989 .... CTFT-9
Perrine, Valerie 1943- CTFT-3
Perrins, Leslie 1902-1962 .... WWasWT
Perry, Antoinette 1888-1946 ..... WWasWT
Perry, (Arthur) John 1906- ...... WWasWT
Perry, Elizabeth 1933- CTFT-2
Perry, Felton CTFT-7
Perry, Frank 1930- CTFT-9
Perry, Keith 1931- CTFT-8
Perry, Margaret 1913- .... WWasWT
Perry, Roger 1933- CTFT-1
Perryman, Dwayne B. III 1963- ... CTFT-8
Perryman, Jill 1933- CTFT-5
    Earlier sketch in WWT-17
Persky, Lester 1927- CTFT-7
    Earlier sketch in CTFT-1
Persky, Lisa Jane CTFT-4
Persoff, Nehemiah 1920- CTFT-7
    Earlier sketch in WWT-17
Pertwee, Jon 1919- WWT-17
Pertwee, Michael 1916- WWT-17
Pertwee, Roland 1885-1963 ...... WWasWT
Pesci, Joe 1943- CTFT-8
Pescow, Donna CTFT-3
Pesola, Robert 1949- CTFT-2
Peters, Bernadette 1948- CTFT-3
    Earlier sketches in CTFT-1, WWT-17
Peters, Brock 1927- CTFT-6
Peters, Jon 1947- CTFT-3
Peters, Roberta 1930- CTFT-4
Peters, Rollo 1892-1967 .... WWasWT
Peters, William 1921- CTFT-2

Petersen, Erika 1949- CTFT-4
Petersen, William L. CTFT-3
Peterson, Cassandra 1951- CTFT-9
Peterson, Lenka 1925- CTFT-5
    Earlier sketch in CTFT-1
Peterson, Roger 1928- CTFT-5
Peterson, Wolfgang 1941- CTFT-8
Petherbridge, Edward 1936- CTFT-7
    Earlier sketch in WWT-17
Petit, Roland 1924- .... WWasWT
Petley, Frank E. 1872-1945 ...... WWasWT
Petrass, Sari 1890-1930 .... WWasWT
Petrides, Avra CTFT-2
Petrie, Daniel 1920- CTFT-9
    Earlier sketch in CTFT-1
Petrie, David Hay 1895-1948 .... WWasWT
Petrie, George O. CTFT-9
Petrova, Olga 1886-1977 .... WWasWT
Pettet, Joanna 1944- CTFT-7
Pettingell, Frank 1891-1968 ...... WWasWT
Peyser, Penny CTFT-7
Pezzullo, Ralph 1951- CTFT-2
Pfeiffer, Michelle 1957- CTFT-8
    Brief Entry in CTFT-3
Phethean, David 1918- WWT-17
Philips, F. C. 1849-1921 .... WWasWT
Philips, Mary 1901- .... WWasWT
Phillips, Arlene 1943- CTFT-4
Phillips, Bob 1953- CTFT-4
Phillips, Cyril L. 1894- .... WWasWT
Phillips, Kate 1856-1931 .... WWasWT
Phillips, Leslie 1924- CTFT-6
    Earlier sketch in WWT-17
Phillips, Lou Diamond CTFT-7
Phillips, Lloyd CTFT-8
Phillips, Mackenzie 1959- CTFT-7
Phillips, Margaret 1923-1984 ..... WWT-17
Phillips, Michael 1943- CTFT-7
Phillips, Michelle 1944- CTFT-5
Phillips, Peter 1949- CTFT-2
Phillips, Robin 1942- CTFT-5
    Earlier sketch in WWT-17
Phillips, Sian 1934- CTFT-8
    Earlier sketches in CTFT-2, WWT-17
Phillips, Stephen 1866-1915 ...... WWasWT
Phillpotts, Adelaide 1896- .... WWasWT
Phillpotts, Ambrosine 1912- WWT-17
Phillpotts, Eden 1862-1960 ...... WWasWT
Phipps, Nicholas 1913-1980 ...... WWT-16
Phoenix, River 1970- CTFT-9
    Brief Entry in CTFT-6
Pialat, Maurice 1925- CTFT-8
Piazza, Ben 1934- CTFT-5
    Earlier sketch in WWT-17
Picard, Andre 1874-1926 .... WWasWT
Pickard, Helena 1900-1959 ...... WWasWT
Pickard, Margery 1911- .... WWasWT
Pickens, Slim 1919-1983 .... CTFT-2
Pickering, Edward A. 1871-? ..... WWasWT
Pickering, Edward W. WWT-17
Pickett, Cindy 1947- CTFT-7
Pickford, Mary 1893-1979 .... WWasWT
Pickles, Christina CTFT-3
Pickrell, Piper 1950- CTFT-4
Pickup, Ronald 1940- CTFT-6
    Earlier sketch in WWT-17
Picon, Molly 1898- WWT-17
Piddock, Jim 1956- CTFT-2
Pidgeon, Walter 1897-1984 .... CTFT-2
    Earlier sketch in WWT-17
Pielmeier, John 1949- CTFT-1
Pierat, Marie Therese ?-1934 ..... WWasWT
Pierce, Paula Kay 1942- CTFT-3

Pierson, Geoffrey 1949- CTFT-4
Pifer, Drury CTFT-6
Piffard, Frederic 1902- ....WWasWT
Pigott, A. S. ....WWasWT
Pigott-Smith, Tim 1946- CTFT-6
Pilbeam, Nova 1919- ....WWasWT
Pilbrow, Richard 1933- WWT-17
Pilcer, Harry 1885-1961 ....WWasWT
Pimlott, Steven CTFT-9
Pinchot, Bronson 1959- CTFT-9
  Brief Entry in CTFT-5
Pine, Robert 1928- CTFT-4
Pinero, Arthur Wing 1855-1934 ..WWasWT
Pink, Wal ?-1922 ....WWasWT
Pino, Rosario ?-1933 ....WWasWT
Pintauro, Joseph T. 1930- CTFT-1
Pinter, Harold 1930- CTFT-2
  Earlier sketch in WWT-17
Piper, Franco ....WWasWT
Pippin, Donald 1931- CTFT-1
Pirandello, Luigi 1867-1936 ......WWasWT
Piscopo, Joe 1951- CTFT-3
Pisier, Marie-France 1944- CTFT-8
Pithey, Wensley 1914- WWT-17
Pitkin, William 1925- WWT-17
Pitoeff, Georges 1886-1939 ......WWasWT
Pitoeff, Ludmilla 1896-1951 ......WWasWT
Pitoniak, Anne 1922- CTFT-1
Pitou, Augustus 1843-1915 ......WWasWT
Pitt, Archie 1885-1924 ....WWasWT
Pitts, ZaSu 1900-1963 ....WWasWT
Pixley, Frank 1867-1919 ....WWasWT
Place, Mary Kay 1947- CTFT-3
Plachy, William J. 1948- CTFT-2
Plana, Tony 1953- CTFT-9
Planchon, Roger 1931- ....WWasWT
Plater, Alan 1935- WWT-17
Platt, Agnes ....WWasWT
Platt, Livingston 1885-1968 ......WWasWT
Playfair, Arthur 1869-1918 ......WWasWT
Playfair, Nigel 1874-1934 ....WWasWT
Playten, Alice 1947- CTFT-8
Pleasants, Jack 1874-? ....WWasWT
Pleasence, Angela CTFT-5
  Earlier sketch in WWT-17
Pleasence, Donald 1919- CTFT-7
  Earlier sketches in CTFT-2, WWT-17
Pleshette, John 1942- CTFT-8
Pleshette, Suzanne CTFT-7
  Earlier sketch in CTFT-1
Pleydell, George 1868-? ....WWasWT
Plimpton, Martha 1970- CTFT-4
Plinge, Walter ....WWasWT
Plouviez, Peter 1931- WWT-17
Plowright, Joan 1929- CTFT-4
  Earlier sketch in WWT-17
Plumb, Eve CTFT-2
Plumley, Don 1934- CTFT-1
Plummer, Amanda 1957- CTFT-6
  Brief Entry in CTFT-2
Plummer, Christopher 1927- CTFT-4
  Earlier sketch in WWT-17
Plunkett, Patricia 1926- ....WWasWT
Plymale, Trip 1949- CTFT-2
Plymptom, Eben 1853-1915 ......WWasWT
Poel, William 1852-1934 ....WWasWT
Poggi, Gregory 1946- CTFT-1
Poggi, Jack 1928- CTFT-4
Pointer, Priscilla 1924- CTFT-2
Poiret, Jean 1926- CTFT-1
Poitier, Sidney 1927- CTFT-7
  Earlier sketch in CTFT-2
Polaire, Mdlle. 1879-1939 ....WWasWT

Polan, Lou 1904-1976 ....WWT-16
Poland, Albert 1941- CTFT-4
Polanski, Roman 1933- CTFT-6
  Earlier sketch in CTFT-1
Poliakoff, Stephen 1952- CTFT-5
  Earlier sketch in WWT-17
Poliakoff, Vera
  See Lindsay, Vera ....WWasWT
Polic, Henry CTFT-7
Polini, Marie ?-1960 ....WWasWT
Pollack, Sydney 1934- CTFT-7
  Earlier sketch in CTFT-2
Pollan, Tracy CTFT-7
Pollard, Daphne 1890- ....WWasWT
Pollard, Michael J. 1939- CTFT-7
Pollock, Arthur 1886-? ....WWasWT
Pollock, Channing 1880-1946 ....WWasWT
Pollock, Elizabeth 1898-1970 ....WWasWT
Pollock, Ellen 1903- WWT-17
Pollock, John 1878-1963 ....WWasWT
Pollock, Nancy R. 1905-1979 .....WWT-16
Pollock, William 1881-1944 ......WWasWT
Poluskis, The ....WWasWT
Pomeroy, Jay 1895-1955 ....WWasWT
Pompian, Paul 1944- CTFT-1
Pond, Helen 1924- CTFT-2
  Earlier sketch in WWT-17
Ponicsan, Darryl 1942- CTFT-2
Ponti, Carlo 1913- CTFT-3
Poole, Roy 1924-1986 ....CTFT-1
Pooley, Olaf ....WWasWT
Pope, Muriel ....WWasWT
Pope, Peter 1955- CTFT-1
Poppenger, Carol 1937- CTFT-4
Popplewell, Jack 1911- WWT-17
Porel, Paul 1843-1917 ....WWasWT
Porteous, Gilbert 1868-1928 .....WWasWT
Porter, Caleb 1867-1940 ....WWasWT
Porter, Cole 1893-1964 ....WWasWT
Porter, Don 1912- WWT-17
Porter, Eric 1928- CTFT-3
  Earlier sketch in WWT-17
Porter, Neil 1895-1944 ....WWasWT
Porter, Stephen 1925- CTFT-4
  Earlier sketch in WWT-17
Porterfield, Robert (Huffard)
  1905-1971 ....WWasWT
Portman, Eric 1903-1969 ....WWasWT
Porto-Riche, Georges de
  1849-1930 ....WWasWT
Posford, George 1906- ....WWasWT
Possart, Ernst Ritter von
  1841-1921 ....WWasWT
Post, Guy Bates 1875-1968 ......WWasWT
Post, Markie 1950- CTFT-9
Post, Mike CTFT-6
Poster, Steven CTFT-7
Poston, Tom 1921- CTFT-4
  Earlier sketch in WWT-17
Potter, Cora 1857-1936 ....WWasWT
Potter, Dennis 1935- CTFT-3
  Earlier sketch in WWT-17
Potter, H. C. 1904-1977 ....WWasWT
Potter, Paul 1853-1921 ....WWasWT
Potts, Annie CTFT-7
Potts, David 1949- CTFT-1
Potts, Nancy CTFT-3
  Earlier sketch in WWT-17
Poul, Alan Mark 1954- CTFT-3
Poulton, A. G. 1867-? ....WWasWT
Pounder, C.C.H. 1952- CTFT-8
Pounds, Charles Courtice
  1862-1927 ....WWasWT

Pounds, Louie ....WWasWT
Povah, Phyllis 1920- ....WWasWT
Powell, Addison 1921- CTFT-6
Powell, Eleanor 1912-1982 ......WWasWT
Powell, Jane 1929- CTFT-7
Powell, Peter 1908- ....WWasWT
Powell, Robert 1944- CTFT-5
  Earlier sketch in WWT-17
Powell, William 1892-1984 ......WWasWT
Power, Hartley 1894-1966 ....WWasWT
Power, Tyrone 1869-1931 ....WWasWT
Power, Tyrone 1914-1958 ....WWasWT
Powers, Eugene 1872-? ....WWasWT
Powers, James T. 1862-1942 .....WWasWT
Powers, John 1935- WWT-17
Powers, Leona 1898-1967 ....WWasWT
Powers, Stephanie 1942- CTFT-6
  Earlier sketch in CTFT-2
Powers, Tom 1890-1955 ....WWasWT
Powys, Stephen 1907- ....WWasWT
Praga, Marco 1862-1929 ....WWasWT
Pratt, Muriel ?-1945 ....WWasWT
Preece, Tim 1938- WWT-17
Preedy, George R. 1888-1952 ....WWasWT
Preminger, Otto 1906-1986 ....CTFT-3
Prentice, Charles W. 1898- ......WWasWT
Prentice, Herbert M. 1890- ......WWasWT
Prentiss, Paula 1939- CTFT-7
Presbrey, Eugene Wyley
  1853-1931 ....WWasWT
Prescott, Ken 1948- CTFT-3
Presley, Priscilla 1946- CTFT-8
Presnell, Harve 1933- CTFT-8
Pressburger, Emeric 1902-1988 .....CTFT-7
Pressman, Edward R. 1943- CTFT-9
Pressman, Lawrence 1939- CTFT-5
Pressman, Michael 1950- CTFT-6
  Earlier sketch in CTFT-1
Preston, Kelly CTFT-8
Preston, Robert 1918-1987 ....CTFT-5
  Earlier sketches in CTFT-2, WWT-17
Preston, William 1921- CTFT-2
Prevost, Marcel 1862-1941 ......WWasWT
Price, Dennis 1915-1973 ....WWasWT
Price, Don 1933- CTFT-2
Price, Evadne 1896- ....WWasWT
Price, Lonny 1959- CTFT-4
  Earlier sketch in CTFT-1
Price, Michael P. 1938- CTFT-1
Price, Nancy 1880-1970 ....WWasWT
Price, Vincent 1911- CTFT-4
  Earlier sketch in WWT-17
Pride, Malcolm 1930- WWT-17
Priestley, J. B. 1894-1984 ....WWT-17
Primrose, Dorothy 1916- WWT-17
Primus, Barry 1938- CTFT-2
Prince, Adelaide 1866-1941 ......WWasWT
Prince, Arthur 1881-? ....WWasWT
Prince, Elsie 1902- ....WWasWT
Prince, Faith CTFT-8
Prince, Hal
  See Prince, Harold CTFT-8
Prince, Harold 1928- CTFT-8
  Earlier sketches in CTFT-2, WWT-17
Prince, Jonathan 1958- CTFT-3
Prince, William 1913- CTFT-7
  Earlier sketch in WWT-17
Principal, Victoria 1945- CTFT-5
Prine, Andrew 1936- CTFT-6
Prinsep, Anthony Leyland
  1888-1942 ....WWasWT
Printemps, Yvonne 1895-1977 ....WWasWT
Prinz, Rosemary CTFT-1

Prior, Allan ....WWasWT
Prochnow, Jurgen 1941- CTFT-7
Proett, Daniel 1953- CTFT-2
Prosky, Robert 1930- CTFT-3
Provost, Jeanne ....WWasWT
Prowse, Juliet 1936- CTFT-9
Prussing, Louise 1897- ....WWasWT
Pryce, Jonathan 1947- CTFT-7
Pryce, Richard 1864-1942 ......WWasWT
Pryde, Peggy 1869-? ....WWasWT
Pryor, Nicholas 1935- CTFT-5
Pryor, Richard 1940- CTFT-3
Pryor, Roger 1901-1974 ....WWasWT
Pryse, Hugh 1910-1955 ....WWasWT
Psacharopoulos, Nikos
    1928-1989 ....CTFT-8
    Earlier sketch in WWT-17
Pudenz, Steve 1947- CTFT-2
Pullman, Bill CTFT-7
Purcell, Charles 1883-1962 ......WWasWT
Purcell, Harold 1907- ....WWasWT
Purcell, Irene 1903-1972 ....WWasWT
Purcell, Lee 1953- CTFT-4
Purdell, Reginald 1896-1953 .....WWasWT
Purdham, David 1951- CTFT-1
Purdom, C.B. 1883-1965 ....WWasWT
Purl, Linda CTFT-5
Purnell, Louise 1942- CTFT-5
    Earlier sketch in WWT-17
Pusey, Arthur ....WWasWT
Pyant, Paul 1953- CTFT-8
Pyle, Denver 1920- CTFT-9

Q

Quaid, Dennis 1954- CTFT-6
    Brief Entry in CTFT-2
Quaid, Randy 1950- CTFT-6
    Brief Entry in CTFT-2
Quarry, Robert 1924- CTFT-7
Quartermaine, Charles
    1877-1958 ....WWasWT
Quartermaine, Leon 1876-1967 ...WWasWT
Quartermass, Martin
    See Carpenter, John CTFT-8
Quayle, Anna 1937- CTFT-4
    Earlier sketch in WWT-17
Quayle, Anthony 1913-1989 ....CTFT-5
    Earlier sketch in WWT-17
Quentin, Patrick
    See Wheeler, Hugh CTFT-5
Quesenbery, Whitney 1954- CTFT-3
Questel, Mae 1908- CTFT-1
Quick, Diana 1946- CTFT-8
Quigley, Linnea CTFT-8
Quigley, William J. 1951- CTFT-9
Quillan, Eddie 1907-1990 ....CTFT-9
Quilley, Denis 1927- CTFT-5
    Earlier sketch in WWT-17
Quine, Richard 1920-1989 ....CTFT-8
Quinlan, Gertrude 1875-1963 ....WWasWT
Quinlan, Kathleen 1954- CTFT-5
Quinn, Aidan 1959- CTFT-6
    Brief Entry in CTFT-2
Quinn, Anthony 1915- CTFT-7
    Earlier sketches in CTFT-1, WWT-17
Quinn, Henry J. 1928- CTFT-2
Quinn, J.C. CTFT-8
Quinn, Patrick 1950- CTFT-6
    Earlier sketch in CTFT-1
Quinn, Tony 1899-1967 ....WWasWT

Quintero, Jose 1924- CTFT-8
    Earlier sketches in CTFT-2, WWT-17
Quinteros, Joaquin 1873-1944 ....WWasWT
Quinteros, Serafin 1871-1938 .....WWasWT

R

Rabb, Ellis 1930- CTFT-4
    Earlier sketch in WWT-17
Rabe, David 1940- CTFT-3
    Earlier sketches in CTFT-1, WWT-17
Rachins, Alan CTFT-7
Rademakers, Fons 1920- CTFT-8
Radford, Basil 1897-1952 ....WWasWT
Radner, Gilda 1946-1989 ....CTFT-8
    Earlier sketch in CTFT-3
Radnitz, Robert B. CTFT-1
Radosh, Stephen 1951- CTFT-2
Rae, Charlotte 1926- CTFT-2
    Earlier sketch in WWT-17
Rae, Eric 1899- ....WWasWT
Rae, Kenneth 1901- ....WWasWT
Raeburn, Henzie 1900-1973 ....WWasWT
Raedler, Dorothy 1917- WWT-17
Raevsky, Iosif Moiseevich 1900- ..WWasWT
Rafelson, Bob 1933- CTFT-6
Rafferty, Pat 1861-1952 ....WWasWT
Raffin, Deborah 1953- CTFT-5
Rafkin, Alan 1928- CTFT-3
Raglan, James 1901-1961 ....WWasWT
Ragno, Joseph CTFT-2
Railsback, Steve CTFT-6
Raimu, M. 1883-1946 ....WWasWT
Rain, Douglas CTFT-5
    Earlier sketch in WWT-17
Rainbow, Frank 1913- WWT-17
Raine, Jack 1897- ....WWasWT
Rainer, Luise 1912- ....WWasWT
Rainey, Ford 1918- CTFT-2
Rains, Claude 1889-1967 ....WWasWT
Raitt, John 1917- CTFT-5
    Earlier sketch in WWT-17
Rakoff, Alvin 1927- CTFT-8
Raleigh, Cecil 1856-1914 ....WWasWT
Raleigh, Mrs. Saba ?-1923 ....WWasWT
Ralph, Sheryl Lee CTFT-6
Ramage, Cecil B. 1895- ....WWasWT
Rambeau, Marjorie 1889-1970 ...WWasWT
Rambert, Marie ....WWasWT
Rambo, Dack CTFT-5
Ramin, Sid 1924- CTFT-8
Ramis, Harold 1944- CTFT-2
Ramont, Mark S. 1956- CTFT-8
Rampling, Charlotte 1946- CTFT-6
    Earlier sketch in CTFT-1
Ramsay, Remak 1937- CTFT-7
    Earlier sketch in WWT-17
Ramsden, Dennis 1918- WWT-17
Ramsey, Alicia ?-1933 ....WWasWT
Ranalow, Frederick Baring
    1873-1953 ....WWasWT
Randall, Carl ?-1965 ....WWasWT
Randall, Harry 1860-1932 ....WWasWT
Randall, Leslie 1924- WWT-17
    Earlier sketch in WWasWT
Randall, Tony 1920- CTFT-7
    Earlier sketches in CTFT-1, WWT-17
Randel, Melissa CTFT-2
Randell, Ron 1923- WWT-17
Randolph, Elsie 1904- WWT-17
Randolph, John 1915- CTFT-8
    Earlier sketch in CTFT-2

Randolph, Robert 1926- CTFT-2
    Earlier sketch in WWT-17
Ranevsky, Boris 1891- ....WWasWT
Ranft, Albert Adam 1858-? ......WWasWT
Rankin, Arthur McKee
    1841-1914 ....WWasWT
Rankin, Molly ....WWasWT
Rankin, Phyllis 1874-1934 ....WWasWT
Ransley, Peter 1931- CTFT-5
Ranson, Herbert 1889- ....WWasWT
Rapf, Matthew 1920- CTFT-5
Raphael, Frederic M. 1931- CTFT-2
Raphael, Gerriane 1939- CTFT-5
Raphael, John N. 1868-1917 .....WWasWT
Raphael, William 1858-? ....WWasWT
Raphaelson, Samson 1896-1983 ..WWasWT
Rappaport, David 1951-1990 ......CTFT-9
    Earlier sketch in CTFT-7
Rappoport, David Steven 1957- CTFT-4
Rasch, Albertina 1891-1967 ......WWasWT
Rascoe, Burton 1892-1957 ....WWasWT
Rashad, Phylicia 1948- CTFT-6
Rashovich, Gordana CTFT-2
Rasulala, Thalmus 1939- CTFT-8
Rathbone, Basil 1892-1967 ......WWasWT
Rathbone, Guy B. 1884-1916 ....WWasWT
Rather, Dan 1931- CTFT-5
Ratoff, Gregory 1893-1960 ......WWasWT
Rattigan, Terence 1911-1977 ......WWT-17
Ratzenberger, John CTFT-3
Raucher, Herman 1928- CTFT-1
Ravin, Linda 1956- CTFT-2
Rawlings, Margaret 1906- WWT-17
Rawlins, Adrian CTFT-9
Rawlins, Lester 1924-1988 ....CTFT-7
    Earlier sketch in WWT-17
Rawlinson, A. R. (Arthur
    Richard) 1894- ....WWasWT
Rawls, Eugenia 1916- CTFT-4
    Earlier sketch in WWT-17
Rawson, Graham 1890-1955 .....WWasWT
Rawson, Tristan 1888-? ....WWasWT
Ray, Aldo 1926-1991 ....CTFT-9
    Earlier sketches in CTFT-8, CTFT-1
Ray, Gabrielle 1883-? ....WWasWT
Ray, James 1932- CTFT-5
    Earlier sketch in WWT-17
Ray, Phil 1872-? ....WWasWT
Ray, Rene ....WWasWT
Rayburn, Gene 1917- CTFT-3
Raye, Carol 1923- ....WWasWT
Raye, Martha 1916- CTFT-4
    Earlier sketch in WWT-17
Raymond, Cyril 1897?-1973 .....WWasWT
Raymond, Gene 1908- CTFT-7
    Earlier sketch in WWT-17
Raymond, Helen 1885?-1965 .....WWasWT
Raymond, Paul WWT-17
Raynal, Paul 1885?-1971 ....WWasWT
Rayne, Leonard 1869-1925 ....WWasWT
Rayner, Minnie 1869-1941 ....WWasWT
Rea, Alec L. 1878-1953 ....WWasWT
Rea, William J. 1884-1932 ....WWasWT
Read, James 1952- CTFT-8
Reade, Hamish
    See Gray, Simon CTFT-6
Reader, Ralph 1903- WWT-17
Reams, Lee Roy CTFT-2
Reardon, Dennis J. 1944- CTFT-1
Reardon, John ?-1988 ....CTFT-2
Reasoner, Harry 1923- CTFT-6
Reaves-Phillips, Sandra CTFT-9
Recht, Ray 1947- CTFT-2

Reddy, Helen 1942- CTFT-5
Redeker, Quinn K. 1936- CTFT-1
Redfield, Adam 1959- CTFT-2
Redfield, William 1926-1976 ......WWT-16
Redford, Robert 1937- CTFT-3
    Earlier sketch in CTFT-1
Redgrave, Corin 1939- CTFT-5
    Earlier sketch in WWT-17
Redgrave, Lynn 1943- CTFT-7
    Earlier sketches in CTFT-1, WWT-17
Redgrave, Michael 1908-1985 .....WWT-17
Redgrave, Vanessa 1937- CTFT-7
    Earlier sketches in CTFT-1, WWT-17
Redington, Michael 1927- CTFT-7
    Earlier sketch in CTFT-1
Redman, Joyce 1918- CTFT-5
    Earlier sketch in WWT-17
Redmond, Liam 1913- WWT-17
Redmond, Moira WWT-17
Reece, Brian 1913-1962 ....WWasWT
Reed, Carol 1906-1976 ....WWasWT
Reed, Donna 1921-1986 ....CTFT-3
Reed, Florence 1883-1967 ....WWasWT
Reed, Joseph Verner Sr.
    1902-1973 ....WWasWT
Reed, Mark 1893- ....WWasWT
Reed, Oliver 1938- CTFT-3
Reed, Pamela 1949- CTFT-7
Reed, Rex 1938- CTFT-8
Reed, Robert 1932- CTFT-6
Reed, Sheila CTFT-7
Reedy, Pat 1940- CTFT-5
Rees, Angharad 1949- CTFT-8
Rees, Llewellyn 1901- WWT-17
Rees, Roger 1944- CTFT-4
    Earlier sketches in CTFT-1, WWT-17
Reeve, Ada 1874-1966 ....WWasWT
Reeve, Christopher 1952- CTFT-6
    Earlier sketches in CTFT-1, CTFT-3
Reeves, Geoffrey 1939- WWT-17
Reeves, Keanu 1965- CTFT-9
Reeves, (Philip) Kynaston
    1893-1971 ....WWasWT
Reeves-Smith, H. 1862-1938 .....WWasWT
Regalbuto, Joe CTFT-8
Regan, Sylvia 1908- CTFT-2
Regina, Paul 1956- CTFT-3
Regnier, Marthe 1880-? ....WWasWT
Rehan, Ada 1860-1916 ....WWasWT
Reich, John 1906-1988 ....CTFT-2
Reich, Richard CTFT-4
Reicher, Frank 1875-1965 ....WWasWT
Reid, Beryl 1920- CTFT-6
    Earlier sketch in WWT-17
Reid, Frances 1918- CTFT-4
    Earlier sketch in WWasWT
Reid, Hal ?-1920 ....WWasWT
Reid, Kate 1930- CTFT-5
    Earlier sketches in CTFT-1, WWT-17
Reid, Tim 1944- CTFT-7
    Earlier sketch in CTFT-1
Reid, Wallace 1891-1923 ....WWasWT
Reidy, Kitty 1902- ....WWasWT
Reilly, Charles Nelson 1931- CTFT-3
    Earlier sketch in WWT-17
Reinach, Enrico 1850-? ....WWasWT
Reinglas, Fred CTFT-4
Reiner, Carl 1922- CTFT-5
Reiner, Rob 1945- CTFT-5
Reinhardt, Max 1873-1943 ......WWasWT
Reinhold, Judge CTFT-5
Reinking, Ann 1949- CTFT-4
    Earlier sketch in WWT-17

Reiser, Paul CTFT-5
Reisman, Jane CTFT-5
Reisner, Allen CTFT-1
Reiss, Alvin H. 1930- CTFT-5
Reiss, Stuart 1921- CTFT-5
Reisz, Karel 1926- CTFT-5
Reiter, Virginia ....WWasWT
Reitman, Ivan 1946- CTFT-7
Rejane, Gabrielle 1857-1920 .....WWasWT
Relph, George 1888-1960 ....WWasWT
Relph, Michael 1815-? ....WWasWT
Relph, Phyllis 1888-? ....WWasWT
Remar, James 1953- CTFT-8
Remick, Lee 1935- CTFT-7
    Earlier sketch in CTFT-2
Remme, John 1935- CTFT-8
    Earlier sketch in CTFT-2
Renaud, Madeleine ....WWasWT
Rendle, Thomas McDonald
    1856-1926 ....WWasWT
Rene, Ida ....WWasWT
Rennie, James 1890-1965 ....WWasWT
Renouardt, Jeanne ....WWasWT
Repole, Charles CTFT-1
Resnais, Alain 1922- CTFT-5
Resnick, Patricia 1953- CTFT-1
Retford, Ella ?-1962 ....WWasWT
Rettura, Joseph 1953- CTFT-2
Reubens, Paul
    See Herman, Pee-Wee CTFT-9
Revelle, Arthur Hamilton
    1872-1958 ....WWasWT
Revere, Anne 1906-1972 ....WWasWT
Revill, Clive (Selsby) 1930- WWT-17
Rey, Antonia 1927- CTFT-2
Rey, Fernando 1917- CTFT-8
Reynolds, Alfred 1884-1969 .....WWasWT
Reynolds, Burt 1936- CTFT-6
    Earlier sketch in CTFT-1
Reynolds, Debbie 1932- CTFT-3
Reynolds, Dorothy 1913-1977 .....WWT-16
Reynolds, E. Vivian 1866-1952 ...WWasWT
Reynolds, Gene 1925- CTFT-3
Reynolds, George Francis
    1880-? ....WWasWT
Reynolds, Jonathan 1942- CTFT-3
Reynolds, Thomas ?-1947 ....WWasWT
Reynolds, Tom 1866-1942 ....WWasWT
Rho, Stella 1886-? ....WWasWT
Rhoades, Barbara 1947- CTFT-8
Rhodes, Harrison 1871-1929 .....WWasWT
Rhodes, Leah 1902-1986 ....CTFT-4
Rhodes, Marjorie 1903-1979 .....WWT-16
Rhodes, Nancy 1946- CTFT-3
Rhodes, Raymond Crompton
    1887-1935 ....WWasWT
Rhue, Madlyn 1934- CTFT-8
Rhys-Davies, John 1944- CTFT-7
Riabouchinska, Tatiana 1916- ....WWasWT
Ribeiro, Alfonso 1971- CTFT-4
Ribman, Ronald 1932- WWT-17
Rice, Edward Everett
    1848-1924 ....WWasWT
Rice, Elmer 1892-1967 ....WWasWT
Rice, Peter 1928- CTFT-3
    Earlier sketch in WWT-17
Rice, Roy 1909- ....WWasWT
Rice, Tim 1944- CTFT-2
    Earlier sketch in WWT-17
Rich, Frank 1949- CTFT-6
Rich, John 1925- CTFT-4
Rich, Lee CTFT-6
Richard, Cliff 1940- CTFT-5

Richards, Angela 1944- CTFT-5
    Earlier sketch in WWT-17
Richards, Beah CTFT-7
Richards, Cicely ?-1933 ....WWasWT
Richards, Evan CTFT-3
Richards, Jess 1943- CTFT-4
Richards, Lloyd CTFT-1
Richards, Martin 1932- CTFT-1
Richards, Paul David 1934- CTFT-2
Richards, Susan 1898- ....WWasWT
Richardson, Claibe 1929- CTFT-1
Richardson, Frank 1871-1917 ....WWasWT
Richardson, Ian 1934- CTFT-3
    Earlier sketch in WWT-17
Richardson, Leander 1856-1918 ..WWasWT
Richardson, Lee 1926- CTFT-7
Richardson, Miranda CTFT-7
Richardson, Myrtle ....WWasWT
Richardson, Natasha 1963- CTFT-6
Richardson, Patricia 1951- CTFT-3
Richardson, Ralph 1902-1983 ....WWT-17
Richardson, Ron 1952- CTFT-2
Richardson, Tony 1928- CTFT-3
    Earlier sketch in WWT-17
Riche, Robert 1925- CTFT-4
Richepin, Jacques 1880-1946 .....WWasWT
Richepin, Jean 1849-1926 ....WWasWT
Richman, Arthur 1886-1944 .....WWasWT
Richman, Charles J. 1870-1940 ...WWasWT
Richman, Harry 1895-1972 ......WWasWT
Richman, Mark
    See Richman, Peter Mark CTFT-8
Richman, Peter Mark 1927- CTFT-8
Richmond, John Peter
    See Carradine, John CTFT-7
Richmond, Peter
    See Carradine, John CTFT-7
Richmond, Susan 1894-1959 .....WWasWT
Richter, Deborah CTFT-7
Rickaby, J. W. ....WWasWT
Ricketts, Charles 1866-1931 .....WWasWT
Rickles, Don 1926- CTFT-2
Rickman, Alan CTFT-8
Riddle, Nelson 1921-1985 ....CTFT-5
Ridgeway, Philip 1891-1954 .....WWasWT
Ridgeway, Philip 1920- ....WWasWT
Ridley, Arnold 1896- WWT-17
Riegert, Peter 1947- CTFT-6
    Brief Entry in CTFT-2
Riehle, Richard 1948- CTFT-3
Rietti, Victor 1888-1963 ....WWasWT
Rietty, Robert 1923- WWT-17
Rifkin, Harmon "Bud" 1942- CTFT-5
Rigby, Arthur 1870-1944 ....WWasWT
Rigby, Arthur 1900-1971 ....WWT-16
Rigby, Edward 1879-1951 ....WWasWT
Rigby, Harry 1925- WWT-17
Rigdon, Kevin 1956- CTFT-1
Rigg, Diana 1938- CTFT-3
    Earlier sketch in WWT-17
Riggs, Lynn 1899-1954 ....WWasWT
Rignold, George ?-1912 ....WWasWT
Rignold, Lionel ?-1919 ....WWasWT
Riker, William 1923- CTFT-3
Riley, Jack 1935- CTFT-3
Riley, Larry CTFT-3
Rinaldo ....WWasWT
Rinehart, Elaine 1952- CTFT-5
Rinehart, Mary 1876-1958 ......WWasWT
Rinehimer, John 1951- CTFT-4
Ring, Blanche 1877-1961 ....WWasWT
Ring, Frances 1882-1951 ....WWasWT

Ringwald, Molly 1968- CTFT-6
  Brief Entry in CTFT-2
Rinker, Kenneth 1945-............CTFT-6
  Earlier sketch in CTFT-2
Rip, Georges ?-1941 ....WWasWT
Ripley, Patricia T. 1924- CTFT-2
Riscoe, Arthur 1896-1954 ....WWasWT
Risdon, Elizabeth 1887-1958 .....WWasWT
Ritchard, Cyril 1897-1977 ....WWT-16
Ritchie, Adele 1874-1930 ....WWasWT
Ritchie, June CTFT-5
  Earlier sketch in WWT-17
Ritchie, Michael 1938- CTFT-6
Ritman, William ?-1984 ....WWT-17
Ritt, Martin 1914-1990 ....CTFT-9
  Earlier sketch in CTFT-6
Ritter, John 1948-................CTFT-2
Rivera, Chita 1933- CTFT-8
  Earlier sketches in CTFT-1, WWT-17
Rivera, Geraldo 1943- CTFT-6
Rivers, Joan 1937- CTFT-1
Rix, Brian 1924- CTFT-6
  Earlier sketch in WWT-17
Roache, Viola 1885-1931 ....WWasWT
Robards, Jason 1922-..............CTFT-7
  Earlier sketches in CTFT-1, WWT-17
Robards, Sam 1962(?)- CTFT-9
Robb, David 1947- CTFT-7
Robb, R. D. 1972- CTFT-5
Robbe, Scott D. 1955- CTFT-4
Robbe-Grillet, Alain 1922- CTFT-8
Robbins, Carrie Fishbein 1943- , ,...CTFT-5
  Earlier sketch in WWT-17
Robbins, Jana CTFT-1
Robbins, Jane Marla 1949- CTFT-2
Robbins, Jerome 1918- CTFT-4
  Earlier sketch in WWT-17
Robbins, Matthew CTFT-6
Robbins, Rex 1935- CTFT-2
Robbins, Tim CTFT-7
Robert, Eugene 1877-? ....WWasWT
Roberti, Lyda 1909-1938 ....WWasWT
Roberts, Arthur 1852-1933 ......WWasWT
Roberts, Christian 1944- CTFT-8
Roberts, Doris 1930- CTFT-4
  Earlier sketches in CTFT-2, WWT-17
Roberts, Eric 1956- CTFT-7
  Brief Entry in CTFT-2
Roberts, Evelyn 1886-1962 ......WWasWT
Roberts, Ewan 1914- WWT-17
Roberts, Florence 1871-1927 .....WWasWT
Roberts, J. H. 1884-1961 ....WWasWT
Roberts, Joan 1918- ....WWasWT
Roberts, John 1916-1972 ....WWT-16
Roberts, Julia 1967- CTFT-9
Roberts, Julie 1966- CTFT-4
Roberts, Lance 1959- CTFT-2
Roberts, Marilyn CTFT-3
Roberts, Pernell CTFT-3
Roberts, R. A. 1870-? ....WWasWT
Roberts, Rachel 1927-1980 ......WWT-17
Roberts, Ralph ?-1944 ....WWasWT
Roberts, Tanya 1955-.............CTFT-7
Roberts, Theodore 1861-1928 ....WWasWT
Roberts, Tony 1939-...............CTFT-7
  Earlier sketches in CTFT-2, WWT-17
Robertshaw, Jerrold 1866-1941 ...WWasWT
Robertson, Beatrice Forbes-
  See Forbes-Robertson, Beatrice . WWasWT
Robertson, Cliff 1925- CTFT-3
Robertson, Dale 1923- CTFT-5
Robertson, Guy 1892- ....WWasWT
Robertson, Ian 1858-1936 ....WWasWT

Robertson, Joel 1950- CTFT-3
Robertson, Johnston Forbes-
  See Forbes-Robertson, Johnston WWasWT
Robertson, Lanie CTFT-7
Robertson, Malcolm 1933- WWT-17
Robertson, Scott 1954-.............CTFT-4
Robertson, Toby 1928-.............CTFT-9
  Earlier sketches in CTFT-4, WWT-17
Robertson, W. Graham
  1867-1948 ....WWasWT
Robeson, Paul 1898-1976 ....WWasWT
Robey, George 1869-1954 ....WWasWT
Robins, Edward H. 1880-1955 ...WWasWT
Robins, Elizabeth 1865-1952 .....WWasWT
Robins, Gertrude L. ?-1917 .....WWasWT
Robins, Laila 1959- CTFT-3
Robinson, Andrew 1942- CTFT-7
Robinson, Bill 1878-1949 ....WWasWT
Robinson, Dar 1948-1986 ....CTFT-4
Robinson, Edward G.
  1893-1972 ....WWasWT
Robinson, John 1908-1979 ....WWT-16
Robinson, Kathleen 1909- ....WWasWT
Robinson, Lennox 1886-1958 .....WWasWT
Robinson, Madeleine 1908- ....WWasWT
Robinson, Martin P. 1954- CTFT-1
Robinson, Norah 1901- ....WWasWT
Robinson, Patrick 1963-............CTFT-4
Robinson, Percy 1889-1967 ....WWasWT
Robson, E. M. 1855-1932 ....WWasWT
Robson, Eleanor Elise 1879-? ....WWasWT
Robson, Flora 1902-1984 ....WWT-17
Robson, Mary 1893-............WWasWT
Robson, May 1865-1942 ....WWasWT
Rocco, Alex 1936- CTFT-9
Roch, Madeleine ?-1930 ....WWasWT
Roche, Eugene 1928- CTFT-7
Rocher, Rene 1890- ....WWasWT
Rock, Charles 1866-1919 ....WWasWT
Rodd, Marcia 1940- CTFT-5
  Earlier sketch in WWT-17
Roddam, Franc 1946- CTFT-7
Roddenberry, Gene 1921- CTFT-3
Rodgers, Anton 1933- CTFT-6
  Earlier sketch in WWT-17
Rodgers, Mark CTFT-7
Rodgers, Mary 1931- WWT-17
Rodgers, Richard 1902-1979 .....WWT-17
Rodriguez, Paul CTFT-7
Rodway, Norman 1929-...........WWT-17
Roe, Bassett 1860-1934 ....WWasWT
Roebling, Paul 1934- WWT-17
Roeg, Nicolas 1928- CTFT-6
Roerick, William 1912- WWT-17
Rogan, Josh
  See Matheson, Richard CTFT-6
Rogers, Anne 1933- WWT-17
Rogers, Fred 1928-...............CTFT-6
Rogers, Gil 1934- CTFT-1
Rogers, Ginger 1911- CTFT-3
  Earlier sketch in WWT-17
Rogers, Kenny 1938- CTFT-8
Rogers, Max ?-1932 ....WWasWT
Rogers, Melody CTFT-4
Rogers, Mimi CTFT-7
Rogers, Paul 1917-...............CTFT-6
  Earlier sketch in WWT-17
Rogers, Wayne 1933-.............CTFT-3
Rogers, Will 1879-1935 ....WWasWT
Rohmer, Sax 1886-1959 ....WWasWT
Roker, Roxie 1929- CTFT-8
Rolf, Frederick 1926-..............CTFT-2
Rolin, Judi 1946- ...:............CTFT-5

Rolle, Esther CTFT-3
  Earlier sketch in WWT-17
Rolle, Georges ?-1916 ....WWasWT
Rollins, Howard E. Jr. 1950-.......CTFT-6
  Brief Entry in CTFT-2
Rollins, Jack CTFT-5
Rolly, Jeanne ?-1929 ....WWasWT
Rolston, Mark 1956- CTFT-5
Rolyat, Dan 1872-1927 ....WWasWT
Romaine, Claire 1873-1964 ......WWasWT
Roman, Arlene 1959-..............CTFT-5
Roman, Lawrence CTFT-1
Roman, Ruth 1924- CTFT-5
Romano, John 1948- CTFT-4
Romberg, Sigmund 1887-1951 ...WWasWT
Rome, Fred 1874-? ....WWasWT
Romero, Cesar 1907- CTFT-1
Romero, George A. 1940- CTFT-6
Romney, Edana 1919- ....WWasWT
Ronald, Landon 1873-1938 ......WWasWT
Ronstadt, Linda 1946- CTFT-9
Rooke, Irene 1878-1958 ....WWasWT
Rooke, Valentine 1912- ....WWasWT
Rooker, Michael 1955(?)- CTFT-9
Rooney, Andy 1920- CTFT-5
Rooney, Mickey 1922- CTFT-3
Roos, Fred 1934- CTFT-7
Roos, Joanna 1901-1989 ....WWasWT
Roose, Olwen 1900- ....WWasWT
Roose-Evans, James 1927-........WWT-17
Rorie, Yvonne 1907-1959 ....WWasWT
Rorke, Hayden 1910-1987- CTFT-5
Rorke, Kate 1866-1945 ....WWasWT
Rorke, Mary 1858-1938 ....WWasWT
Rosay, Françoise 1891-1974 . .WWasWT
Rose, Alex CTFT-3
Rose, Billy 1899-1966 ....WWasWT
Rose, Clarkson 1890-1968 ....WWasWT
Rose, Edward Everett
  1862-1939 ....WWasWT
Rose, George 1920-1988 ....CTFT-4
  Earlier sketch in WWT-17
Rose, Jack 1911-.................CTFT-7
Rose, L. Arthur 1887-1958 ......WWasWT
Rose, Maxine B. 1928-............CTFT-4
Rose, Philip 1921- WWT-17
Rosebery, Lilian ....WWasWT
Rosemont, Norman 1924- CTFT-7
Rosenblum, M. Edgar 1932- CTFT-8
Rosenfeld, Sydney 1855-1931 ....WWasWT
Rosenfield, Stephen 1946- CTFT-6
  Earlier sketch in CTFT-2
Rosenman, Leonard 1924- CTFT-9
Rosenthal, Rick 1949- CTFT-1
Rosenwald, Richard S. 1943- CTFT-1
Rosmer, Milton 1882-1971 ......WWasWT
Rosoff, Barbara 1946-............CTFT-2
Ross, Adrian 1859-1933 ....WWasWT
Ross, Annie 1930- WWT-17
Ross, Anthony 1906-1955 ....WWasWT
Ross, Charles Cowper
  1929-1985 ....WWT-17
Ross, Diana 1944- CTFT-5
Ross, Frank 1904-1990 ....CTFT-9
Ross, Frederick 1879-1957 ....WWasWT
Ross, George I. 1907-...........WWT-17
Ross, Harry 1913- ....WWasWT
Ross, Hector 1915- ....WWasWT
Ross, Herbert 1865-1934 ....WWasWT
Ross, Herbert 1927- CTFT-6
Ross, Justin 1954- CTFT-1
Ross, Katharine 1943- CTFT-3
Ross, Marion CTFT-3

Ross, Michael CTFT-2
Ross, Oriel 1907- ....WWasWT
Ross, Stuart 1950- CTFT-4
Ross, Thomas W. 1875-1959 .....WWasWT
Ross-Clarke, Betty ....WWasWT
Rossellini, Isabella 1952- CTFT-7
Rossen, Howard 1951- CTFT-6
Rossiter, Leonard 1926-1984 ....CTFT-2
Earlier sketch in WWT-17
Rossovich, Rick 1957- CTFT-7
Rostand, Edmond 1868-1918 ....WWasWT
Roth, Ann CTFT-4
Earlier sketch in WWT-17
Roth, Joe CTFT-7
Roth, Lillian 1910-1980 ....WWT-17
Roth, Michael S. 1954- CTFT-4
Rotha, Wanda WWT-17
Rothenstein, Albert Daniel
1883-? ....WWasWT
Rothman, John 1949-............CTFT-4
Rothschild, Ami 1959-............CTFT-3
Rotunno, Giuseppe 1923- CTFT-8
Roughwood, Owen 1876-1947 ....WWasWT
Roundtree, Richard 1942- CTFT-3
Rounseville, Robert 1914-1974 ....WWT-16
Rourke, Mickey 1956- CTFT-5
Rous, Helen ?-1934 ....WWasWT
Roussel, Pamela CTFT-5
Routledge, Patricia 1929-..........CTFT-6
Earlier sketch in WWT-17
Roven, Glen 1958- CTFT-4
Rovetta, Girolamo 1850-1910 ....WWasWT
Rowe, Dee Etta 1953- CTFT-4
Rowe, Fanny 1913-1988 ....WWasWT
Rowe, Hansford 1924- CTFT-4
Rowland, Margery 1910-1945 ....WWasWT
Rowland, Toby 1916-............WWT-17
Rowlands, Gena 1936-............CTFT-5
Rowlands, Patsy 1935-............WWT-17
Rowles, Polly 1914- CTFT-2
Earlier sketch in WWT-17
Rowley, J. W. ?-1925 ....WWasWT
Royaards, Wilhem ?-1929 ....WWasWT
Royal Shakespeare Company,
The ....WWasWT
Royce, Edward 1870-1964 ....WWasWT
Royce, Edward William
1841-1926 ....WWasWT
Royce, Julian 1870-1946 ....WWasWT
Royde, Frank 1882-? ....WWasWT
Royde-Smith, Naomi ?-1964 ....WWasWT
Royle, Edwin Milton 1862-1942 ..WWasWT
Royle, Josephine ....WWasWT
Royle, Selena 1904-1955 ....WWasWT
Royston, Roy 1899- ....WWasWT
Rozakis, Gregory 1913-1989 ....CTFT-4
Roze, Raymond 1875-1920 ......WWasWT
Rozenberg, Lucien ....WWasWT
Rozsa, Miklos 1907-.............CTFT-8
Ruben, Jose 1888-1969 ....WWasWT
Ruben, Joseph 1951- CTFT-9
Rubens, Paul 1876-1917 ....WWasWT
Rubin, John Gould 1951- CTFT-6
Rubin, Mann 1927- CTFT-3
Rubinstein, Harold F. 1891- .....WWasWT
Rubinstein, Ida ?-1960 ....WWasWT
Rubinstein, John 1946-...........CTFT-1
Ruby, Harry 1895-1974 ....WWasWT
Ruby, Thelma 1925-.............WWT-17
Rudd, Enid 1934- CTFT-1
Rudd, Paul 1940-...............CTFT-5
Earlier sketch in WWT-17
Ruddock, John 1897-............WWT-17

Ruddy, Albert S. 1934- CTFT-9
Rudkin, David 1936- CTFT-6
Earlier sketch in WWT-17
Rudman, Michael 1939-..........WWT-17
Rudnicki, Stefan 1945- CTFT-6
Rudolph, Alan 1948- CTFT-5
Rudolph, Louis 1942-.............CTFT-1
Rudrud, Kristin CTFT-2
Ruehl, Mercedes CTFT-9
Ruffelle, Frances 1966-............CTFT-9
Ruggles, Charles 1890-1970 ......WWasWT
Rule, Janice 1931- WWT-17
Runyon, Jennifer CTFT-7
Rupnik, Kevin 1956- CTFT-2
Rush, Barbara 1950- CTFT-5
Rush, Philip
See Lardner, Ring Jr. CTFT-5
Rush, Richard 1931- CTFT-6
Rusler, Robert 1965- CTFT-5
Russ, William 1951(?)-............CTFT-9
Russell, Annie 1864-1936 ....WWasWT
Russell, Edward Richard
1834-1920 ....WWasWT
Russell, Fred 1862-1957 ....WWasWT
Russell, H. Scott 1868-1949 ......WWasWT
Russell, Irene 1901- ....WWasWT
Russell, Iris 1922-...............WWT-17
Russell, Jane 1921- CTFT-9
Russell, Ken 1927- CTFT-5
Russell, Kurt 1951- CTFT-3
Russell, Lillian 1861-1922 ....WWasWT
Russell, Mabel 1887-1951 ....WWasWT
Russell, Nipsey 1924- CTFT-6
Russell, Rosiland 1912-1976 ......WWT-16
Russell, Theresa 1957- CTFT-4
Russell, Willy 1947- CTFT-9
Rutherford, Margaret
1892-1972 ....WWasWT
Rutherford, Mary 1945-...........CTFT-5
Earlier sketch in WWT-17
Rutherston, Albert Daniel
1883-1953 ....WWasWT
Ruttan, Susan CTFT-7
Ryan, Fran CTFT-9
Ryan, John P. 1938-.............CTFT-8
Ryan, Madge 1919- WWT-17
Ryan, Mary 1885-1948.........WWasWT
Ryan, Meg 1963- CTFT-9
Brief Entry in CTFT-6
Ryan, Mitchell 1928-............CTFT-7
Ryan, Robert 1913-1973 ....WWasWT
Rydell, Chris
See Rydell, Christopher CTFT-9
Rydell, Christopher CTFT-9
Rydell, Mark 1934- CTFT-3
Ryder, Winona 1971-............CTFT-8
Ryder, Alfred 1919- WWT-17
Rye, Daphne 1916-.............WWasWT
Ryland, Cliff 1856-? ....WWasWT
Rylands, George 1902-...........WWT-17
Ryley, Madeleine Lucette
1865-1934 ....WWasWT
Ryskind, Morrie 1895-1985 ......WWasWT

S

Sabatini, Rafael 1875-1950 ....WWasWT
Sabella, Ernie CTFT-8
Sabin, David 1937- CTFT-1
Sabine, Martin 1876-? ....WWasWT
Sabinson, Lee 1911- ....WWasWT

Sachs, Andrew 1930- CTFT-9
Earlier sketch in CTFT-1
Sachs, Leonard 1909-............WWT-17
Sacks, Joseph Leopold
1881-1952 ....WWasWT
Sadanji, Ichi Kawa 1881-1940 ....WWasWT
Saddler, Donald 1920-...........CTFT-8
Earlier sketches in CTFT-2, WWT-17
Sadler, Bill 1950- CTFT-7
Safan, Craig 1948- CTFT-8
Sagal, Katey CTFT-5
Sagan, Leontine 1889-1974 ......WWasWT
Saget, Bob 1956-................CTFT-7
Sahagen, Nikki CTFT-4
Sahl, Mort 1927-...............CTFT-7
Saint, Eva Marie 1924-...........CTFT-5
Earlier sketch in CTFT-3
St. Clair, F. V. 1860-? ....WWasWT
St. Denis, Teddie 1909- ....WWasWT
St. Helier, Ivy ?-1971 ....WWasWT
St. Jacques, Raymond
1930-1990 ....CTFT-9
Saint James, Susan 1946- CTFT-8
Earlier sketch in CTFT-2
St. John, Christopher Marie
?-1960 ....WWasWT
St. John, Florence 1854-1912 ....WWasWT
St. John, Howard 1905-1974 .....WWasWT
St. John, Jill 1940-..............CTFT-3
St. John, Lily 1895-.............WWasWT
Saint Johns, Richard R. 1929-.....CTFT-1
Saint-Denis, Michel 1897-1971 ...WWasWT
Saintsbury, H. A. 1869-1939 .....WWasWT
Saint-Subber, Arnold 1918- WWT-17
Saire, Rebecca 1963- CTFT-9
Saker, Annie 1882-1932 ....WWasWT
Saker, Mrs. Edward 1847-1912 ...WWasWT
Saks, Gene 1921-...............CTFT-9
Earlier sketches in CTFT-2, WWT-17
Salacrou, Armand 1899-1989 ....WWasWT
Salberg, Derek S. 1912- WWT-17
Salinger, Matt 1960-.............CTFT-7
Salisbury, Frank 1930-...........CTFT-4
Salkind, Alexander CTFT-6
Salle, Charles (Chic) 1885-1936 ..WWasWT
Sallis, Peter 1921-..............CTFT-8
Earlier sketch in WWT-17
Salmi, Albert 1928-1990..........CTFT-5
Salt, Jennifer 1944-.............CTFT-7
Salt, Waldo 1914-1987 ....CTFT-6
Saltz, Amy 1946-...............CTFT-6
Earlier sketch in CTFT-1
Salvini, Tomasso 1829-1915 .....WWasWT
Samms, Emma 1960- CTFT-4
Samples, M. David CTFT-4
Samson, Ivan 1894-1963 ....WWasWT
Sand, Paul CTFT-4
Earlier sketch in WWT-17
Sanda, Dominique 1951- CTFT-1
Sanders, Richard 1940-...........CTFT-2
Sanderson, Julia 1887-1975 ......WWasWT
Sandford, Marjorie 1910-.........WWasWT
Sandino, Enrique 1951- CTFT-5
Sandison, Gordon 1913-1958 .....WWasWT
Sandrich, Jay 1932- CTFT-4
Earlier sketch in CTFT-1
Sands, Diana 1934- ....WWasWT
Sands, Dorothy 1893-1980 ....WWT-17
Sands, Leslie 1921- WWT-17
Sands, Julian 1958-..............CTFT-8
Sandy, Gary 1946-..............CTFT-6
Sanford, Isabel 1917- CTFT-2
Sanger, Jonathan 1944- CTFT-1

Sangster, Alfred 1880-? ....WWasWT
Santley, Frederic 1887-1953 ......WWasWT
Santley, Joseph 1889-1971 ....WWasWT
Santley, Kate ?-1923 ....WWasWT
Santoni, Reni CTFT-4
  Earlier sketch in CTFT-1
Santos, Joe 1931- CTFT-7
Saphier, Peter 1940- CTFT-1
Sara, Mia 1968- CTFT-9
Sarandon, Chris 1942- CTFT-4
  Earlier sketch in WWT-17
Sarandon, Susan 1946- CTFT-3
Sargent, Frederic 1879-? ....WWasWT
Sargent, Herbert C. 1873-? ......WWasWT
Sargent, Joseph 1925- CTFT-6
Sarment, Jean 1897-1976 ....WWasWT
Sarner, Alexander 1892-1948 .....WWasWT
Sarony, Leslie 1897- WWT-17
  Earlier sketch in WWasWT
Saroyan, William 1908-1981 ......WWT-17
Sarrazin, Michael 1940- CTFT-5
Sartre, Jean-Paul 1905-1980 .....WWT-17
Sass, Edward ?-1916 ....WWasWT
Sass, Enid 1889-1959 ....WWasWT
Sato, Isao 1949-1990 ....CTFT-9
  Earlier sketch in CTFT-1
Saucier, Claude-Albert 1953- CTFT-2
Saunders, Florence ?-1926 ....WWasWT
Saunders, James 1925- CTFT-6
  Earlier sketch in WWT-17
Saunders, Madge 1894-1967 .... WWasWT
Saunders, Nicholas 1914- CTFT-6
  Earlier sketch in CTFT-1
Saunders, Peter 1911- CTFT-1
  Earlier sketch in WWT-17
Savage, Fred 1976- CTFT-8
Savage, Henry Wilson
  1859-1927 ....WWasWT
Savage, John 1950- CTFT-5
Savalas, Telly 1923- CTFT-7
  Earlier sketch in CTFT-2
Savant, Doug CTFT-4
Savini, Tom CTFT-7
Saviola, Camille CTFT-3
Savo, Jimmy 1895-1960 ....WWasWT
Savory, Gerald 1909- WWT-17
Sawyer, Dorie 1897- ....WWasWT
Sawyer, Ivy 1896- ....WWasWT
Saxon, John 1936- CTFT-6
  Earlier sketch in CTFT-1
Sayers, Dorothy L. 1893-1957 ....WWasWT
Sayle, Alexei 1952- CTFT-8
Sayler, Oliver Martin 1887-1958 ..WWasWT
Sayles, John 1950- CTFT-6
  Earlier sketch in CTFT-1
Sayre, Theodore Burt
  1874-1954 ....WWasWT
Sbarge, Raphael 1964- CTFT-8
Scacchi, Greta CTFT-7
Scaife, Gillian ....WWasWT
Scales, Prunella CTFT-6
  Earlier sketch in WWT-17
Scalia, Jack 1951- CTFT-7
Scarborough, George 1875-? .....WWasWT
Scarfe, Alan 1946- CTFT-4
Scarwid, Diana CTFT-6
Schaal, Richard 1928- CTFT-2
Schachter, Felice 1963- CTFT-4
Schaefer, George 1920- CTFT-8
  Earlier sketches in CTFT-2, WWT-17
Schafer, Natalie CTFT-1
  Earlier sketch in WWasWT
Schaffel, Robert 1944- CTFT-1

Schaffner, Franklin J.
  1920-1989 ....CTFT-7
Schallert, William 1922- CTFT-3
Schapiro, Seth L. 1931- CTFT-4
Schary, Dore 1905-1980 ....WWT-17
Schatzberg, Jerry 1927- CTFT-4
Schechner, Richard 1934- WWT-17
Scheeder, Louis W. 1946- CTFT-5
  Earlier sketch in WWT-17
Scheff, Fritzi 1879-1954 ....WWasWT
Scheherazade CTFT-2
Scheider, Roy 1935- CTFT-5
Schell, Maria 1926- CTFT-6
Schell, Maximilian 1930- CTFT-5
Schellow, Erich 1915- ....WWasWT
Schenkkan, Robert 1953- CTFT-4
Schepisi, Fred 1939- CTFT-5
Scherick, Edgar J. 1924- CTFT-6
Schevill, James 1920- CTFT-4
Schiavelli, Vincent CTFT-6
Schiffer, Michael 1948- CTFT-6
Schifrin, Lalo 1932- CTFT-5
Schildkraut, Joseph 1896-1964 ...WWasWT
Schiller, Bob 1918- CTFT-2
Schiller, Lawrence 1936- CTFT-2
Schimmel, William 1946- CTFT-4
Schisgal, Murray 1926- CTFT-5
  Earlier sketch in WWT-17
Schlarth, Sharon CTFT-4
  Earlier sketch in CTFT-3
Schlatter, George CTFT-7
Schlesinger, John 1926- CTFT-6
  Earlier sketch in WWT-17
Schloendorff, Volker 1939- CTFT-8
Schmidt, Douglas W. 1942- CTFT-2
  Earlier sketch in WWT-17
Schmidt, Harvey 1929- WWT-17
Schmidt, Marlene CTFT-4
  Earlier sketch in CTFT-1
Schmoeller, David L. 1947- CTFT-1
Schnabel, Stefan 1912- CTFT-4
  Earlier sketch in WWT-17
Schnee, Thelma ....WWasWT
Schneider, Alan 1917-1984 ....CTFT-1
  Earlier sketch in WWT-17
Schneider, Helen CTFT-7
Schneider, John CTFT-5
Schneider, Romy 1938-1982 ....CTFT-2
Schoenbaum, Donald 1926- CTFT-1
Schoenfeld, Gerald 1924- CTFT-6
Schoonmaker, Thelma 1945- CTFT-9
Schottenfeld, Barbara CTFT-1
Schrader, Frederick Franklin
  1859-1943 ....WWasWT
Schrader, Paul 1946- CTFT-4
Schreiber, Avery 1935- CTFT-7
Schrieber, Terry 1937- CTFT-4
Schroder, Ricky 1970- CTFT-3
  Brief Entry in CTFT-2
Schroeder, Barbet 1941- CTFT-9
Schuck, John 1940- CTFT-7
Schulberg, Budd 1914- CTFT-6
Schull, Rebecca CTFT-3
Schultz, Dwight CTFT-9
Schultz, Michael A. 1938- WWT-17
Schumacher, Joel 1939- CTFT-6
Schwab, Laurence 1893-1956 .....WWasWT
Schwab, Sophie
  See Hayden, Sophie CTFT-5
Schwartz, Archibald
  See McGoohan, Patrick CTFT-5
Schwartz, Arthur 1900-1984 ......WWT-17
Schwartz, Jean 1878-1956 ....WWasWT

Schwartz, Maurice 1890-1960 ....WWasWT
Schwartz, Stephen 1948- CTFT-5
  Earlier sketch in WWT-17
Schwarzenegger, Arnold 1947- CTFT-4
  Brief Entry in CTFT-2
Scofield, Paul 1922- CTFT-4
  Earlier sketch in WWT-17
Scola, Ettore 1931- CTFT-8
Scolari, Peter 1954- CTFT-6
Scorsese, Martin 1942- CTFT-5
  Earlier sketch in CTFT-1
Scotland, J. H. 1873-? ....WWasWT
Scott, Bennett 1875-? ....WWasWT
Scott, Campbell CTFT-9
Scott, Cyril 1866-1945 ....WWasWT
Scott, George C. 1927- CTFT-7
  Earlier sketches in CTFT-1, WWT-17
Scott, Gertrude ?-1951 ....WWasWT
Scott, Harold 1891-1964 ....WWasWT
Scott, Jay Hutchinson
  1924-1977 ....WWT-17
Scott, Joan Clement-
  See Clement-Scott, Joan ....WWasWT
Scott, John 1937- CTFT-1
Scott, Maidie ....WWasWT
Scott, Malcolm 1872-1929 ....WWasWT
Scott, Margaret Clement ....WWasWT
Scott, Margaretta 1912- WWT-17
Scott, Martha WWT-17
Scott, Noel 1889-1956 ....WWasWT
Scott, Peter 1932- ....WWasWT
Scott, Ridley 1939- CTFT-9
  Brief Entry in CTFT-5
Scott, Rosemary 1914- ....WWasWT
Scott, Timothy ?-1988 ....CTFT-2
Scott, Tony 1944- CTFT-5
Scott, Walter M. 1906-1989 ....CTFT-8
Scott-Gatty, Alexander
  1876-1937 ....WWasWT
Scotti, Vito 1918- CTFT-7
Scourby, Alexander 1913-1985 ....WWT-17
Scudamore, Margaret
  1884-1958 ....WWasWT
Scully, Anthony 1942- CTFT-1
Scully, Joe 1926- CTFT-4
  Earlier sketch in CTFT-1
Seabrooke, Thomas Q.
  1860-1913 ....WWasWT
Seacombe, Dorothy 1905- ....WWasWT
Seagram, Wilfrid 1884-1938 .....WWasWT
Seagrove, Jenny CTFT-7
Seal, Elizabeth 1933- CTFT-5
  Earlier sketch in WWT-17
Sealby, Mabel 1885-? ....WWasWT
Seale, Douglas 1913- WWT-17
Seale, Kenneth 1916- WWT-17
Seale, Petie Trigg 1930- CTFT-5
Seaman, Owen 1861-1936 ....WWasWT
Seamon, Edward 1932- CTFT-8
  Earlier sketch in CTFT-1
Sears, Austin 1947- CTFT-5
Sears, Heather 1935- WWT-17
Sears, Joe 1949- CTFT-1
Sears, Zelda 1873-1935 ....WWasWT
Seawell, Donald R. WWT-17
Secombe, Harry 1921- WWT-17
Secrest, James ?-1987 ....CTFT-1
Secretan, Lance 1939- ....WWasWT
See, Edmond 1875-1959 ....WWasWT
Seff, Richard 1927- CTFT-1
Segal, Erich 1937- CTFT-1
Segal, George 1934- CTFT-3
Segal, Vivienne 1897- ....WWasWT

Segond-Weber,
    Eugenie-Caroline 1867-? . . . . . . WWasWT
Seidelman, Arthur Allan CTFT-4
Seidelman, Susan 1952- CTFT-3
Seidl, Lea 1902-1987 . . . . WWasWT
Selby, David CTFT-5
Selby, Nicholas 1925- CTFT-3
    Earlier sketch in WWT-17
Selby, Percival M. 1886-1955 . . . . WWasWT
Selby, Tony 1938- CTFT-7
    Earlier sketch in WWT-17
Seldes, Marian 1928- CTFT-2
    Earlier sketch in WWT-17
Sell, Janie 1941- CTFT-5
    Earlier sketch in WWT-17
Sellars, Elizabeth 1923- WWT-17
Sellecca, Connie 1955- CTFT-6
Selleck, Tom 1945- CTFT-3
    Earlier sketch in CTFT-1
Sellers, Peter 1925-1980 . . . . CTFT-1
Selten, Morton 1860-1939 . . . . WWasWT
Seltzer, David 1920(?)- CTFT-9
Selwart, Tonio 1896- . . . . WWasWT
Selwyn, Archibald ?-1959 . . . . WWasWT
Selwyn, Edgar 1875-1944 . . . . WWasWT
Selzer, Julie CTFT-3
Selznick, Daniel 1936- CTFT-1
Semple, Lorenzo Jr. CTFT-5
Seneca, Joe CTFT-8
Senicourt, Roger
    See Chacksfield, Frank CTFT-2
Senn, Herbert 1924- CTFT-2
    Earlier sketch in WWT-17
Seppe, Christopher 1955- CTFT-2
Serban, Andrei 1943- CTFT-8
    Earlier sketches in CTFT-2, WWT-17
Serf, Joseph
    See McGoohan, Patrick CTFT-5
Sergine, Vera . . . . WWasWT
Serjeantson, Kate ?-1918 . . . . WWasWT
Serlin, Oscar 1901-1971 . . . . WWasWT
Serra, Raymond 1936- CTFT-4
Serrano, Vincent 1870-1935 . . . . . . WWasWT
Servoss, Mary 1908-1968 . . . . WWasWT
Setrakian, Ed 1928- CTFT-2
Seven, Johnny 1926- CTFT-4
Seven, Marilyn CTFT-4
Sevening, Dora 1883-? . . . . WWasWT
Sevening, Nina . . . . WWasWT
Seyler, Athene 1889-1990 . . . . WWT-16
Seymour, Alan 1927- WWT-17
Seymour, Anne 1909-1988 . . . . CTFT-1
Seymour, Jane 1951- CTFT-6
    Earlier sketch in CTFT-1
Seymour, Madeline 1891- . . . . WWasWT
Seymour, William 1855-1933 . . . . . WWasWT
Shackelford, Ted 1946- CTFT-8
Shaffer, Anthony 1926- CTFT-6
    Earlier sketch in WWT-17
Shaffer, Paul 1949- CTFT-7
Shaffer, Peter 1926- CTFT-4
    Earlier sketch in WWT-17
Shagan, Steve 1927- CTFT-5
Shairp, Alexander Mordaunt
    1887-1939 . . . . WWasWT
Shale, T. A. 1867-1953 . . . . WWasWT
Shallard, Michael 1951- CTFT-8
Shallo, Karen CTFT-2
Shand, Ernest 1868-? . . . . WWasWT
Shand, John 1901-1955 . . . . WWasWT
Shand, Phyllis 1894- . . . . WWasWT
Shandling, Garry 1949- CTFT-9

Shange, Ntozake 1948- CTFT-5
    Earlier sketch in WWT-17
Shangold, Joan CTFT-2
Shank, Theodore 1929- CTFT-5
Shanks, Alec WWT-17
Shanley, John Patrick 1950- CTFT-9
Shannon, Effie 1867-1954 . . . . WWasWT
Shannon, Frank 1875-1959 . . . . . . WWasWT
Shannon, Peggy 1909-1941 . . . . . . WWasWT
Shapiro, Debbie 1954- CTFT-8
Shapiro, Esther 1934- CTFT-8
Shapiro, Ken 1943- CTFT-5
Shapiro, Richard 1934- CTFT-8
Sharaff, Irene WWT-17
Sharif, Omar 1932- CTFT-5
Sharkey, Jack 1931- CTFT-1
Sharkey, Ray 1952- CTFT-5
Sharland, Reginald 1886-1944 . . . . WWasWT
Sharp, Anthony 1915- WWT-17
Sharp, Eileen 1900- . . . . WWasWT
Sharp, F. B. J. 1874-? . . . . WWasWT
Sharp, Margery 1905- . . . . WWasWT
Sharpe, Cornelia 1943- CTFT-5
Sharpe, Edith 1894- . . . . WWasWT
Shatner, William 1931- CTFT-3
    Earlier sketch in CTFT-1
Shattuck, Truly 1876-1954 . . . . . . WWasWT
Shavelson, Melville 1917- CTFT-1
Shaver, Helen 1952- CTFT-7
Shaw, Anthony 1897- . . . . WWasWT
Shaw, Fiona CTFT-9
Shaw, George Bernard
    1856-1950 . . . . WWasWT
Shaw, Glen Byam 1904-1986 . . . . . . WWT-17
Shaw, Irwin 1913-1984 . . . . WWT-17
Shaw, Lewis 1910- . . . . WWasWT
Shaw, Mary 1854-1929 . . . . WWasWT
Shaw, Oscar 1899-1967 . . . . WWasWT
Shaw, Robert 1927-1978 . . . . WWT-16
Shaw, Run Run 1907- CTFT-8
Shaw, Sebastian 1905- WWT-17
Shawn, Dick 1923-1987 . . . . CTFT-5
    Earlier sketch in WWT-17
Shawn, Wallace 1943- CTFT-6
    Earlier sketch in CTFT-1
Shaye, Robert 1939- CTFT-3
Shea, John CTFT-5
Shean, Al 1868-1949 . . . . WWasWT
Shearer, Harry 1943- CTFT-8
Sheedy, Ally 1962- CTFT-6
    Brief Entry in CTFT-2
Sheehan, Douglas 1949- CTFT-8
Sheely, Nelson 1942- CTFT-4
Sheen, Charlie CTFT-4
Sheen, Martin 1940- CTFT-6
    Earlier sketches in CTFT-2, WWT-17
Sheffer, Craig 1960- CTFT-7
Sheffield, Flora 1902- . . . . WWasWT
Sheffield, Leo 1873-1951 . . . . WWasWT
Sheffield, Reginald 1901-1957 . . . . WWasWT
Sheiness, Marsha 1940- CTFT-1
Sheldon, Edward 1886-1946 . . . . . WWasWT
Sheldon, H. Sophus ?-1940 . . . . . . WWasWT
Sheldon, Suzanne 1875-1924 . . . . . WWasWT
Shelley, Carole 1939- CTFT-4
    Earlier sketch in WWT-17
Shelton, George 1852-1932 . . . . . . WWasWT
Shelton, Reid 1924- CTFT-1
Shelton, Ron 1945- CTFT-9
Shelton, Sloane 1934- CTFT-1
Shelving, Paul ?-1968 . . . . WWasWT
Shena, Lewis 1948- CTFT-3
Shenar, Paul 1936-1989 . . . . CTFT-8

Shenburn, Archibald A.
    1905-1954 . . . . WWasWT
Shepard, Jewel CTFT-4
Shepard, Sam 1942- CTFT-6
    Earlier sketches in CTFT-1, WWT-17
Shepeard, Jean 1904- . . . . WWasWT
Shephard, Firth 1891-1949 . . . . . . WWasWT
Shepherd, Cybill 1950- CTFT-7
    Earlier sketch in CTFT-2
Shepherd, Jack 1940- WWT-17
Shepherd, Leonard 1872-? . . . . WWasWT
Shepley, Michael 1907-1961 . . . . . WWasWT
Shepley, Ruth 1892-1951 . . . . WWasWT
Sherbrooke, Michael 1874-1957 . . WWasWT
Sherek, Henry 1900-1967 . . . . WWasWT
Sheridan, Dinah 1920- CTFT-6
    Earlier sketch in WWT-17
Sheridan, Jamey 1951- CTFT-2
Sheridan, Jim 1949- CTFT-9
Sheridan, Mark ?-1917 . . . . WWasWT
Sheridan, Mary 1903- . . . . WWasWT
Sherin, Edwin 1930- CTFT-2
    Earlier sketch in WWT-17
Sheringham 1885-1937 . . . . WWasWT
Sherman, Guy 1958- CTFT-2
Sherman, Hiram 1908-1989 . . . . . . CTFT-8
    Earlier sketch in WWT-17
Sherman, Lowell J. 1885-1934 . . . . WWasWT
Sherman, Martin CTFT-2
Sherohman, Tom 1945- CTFT-1
Sherriff, Robert Cedric
    1896-1975 . . . . WWasWT
Sherrin, Ned 1931- WWT-17
Sherwin, Jeannette ?-1936 . . . . WWasWT
Sherwin, Manning 1903-1974 . . . . WWasWT
Sherwin, Mimi CTFT-4
Sherwood, Garrison P.
    1902-1963 . . . . WWasWT
Sherwood, Henry 1931- WWT-17
Sherwood, James Peter 1894- . . . . WWasWT
Sherwood, Lydia 1906-1989 . . . . . WWasWT
Sherwood, Madeleine 1922- CTFT-1
    Earlier sketch in WWT-17
Sherwood, Michael
    See Weathers, Philip CTFT-4
Sherwood, Robert Emmet
    1896-1955 . . . . WWasWT
Shevelove, Burt 1915- WWT-17
Shields, Arthur 1900-1970 . . . . WWasWT
Shields, Brooke 1965- CTFT-9
    Brief Entry in CTFT-3
Shields, Ella 1879-1952 . . . . WWasWT
Shields, Sammy 1874-? . . . . WWasWT
Shiels, George 1886-1949 . . . . WWasWT
Shigeta, James 1933- CTFT-8
Shilling, Ivy . . . . WWasWT
Shimono, Sab 1943- CTFT-6
Shine, Bill 1911- WWT-17
Shine, John L. 1854-1930 . . . . WWasWT
Shine, Wilfred E. 1864-1939 . . . . . WWasWT
Shiner, Ronald 1903-1966 . . . . WWasWT
Shingler, Helen 1919- . . . . WWasWT
Shipley, Joseph T. 1893-1988 . . . . WWT-17
Shipley, Sandra 1947- CTFT-4
Shipman, Ernest 1871-? . . . . WWasWT
Shipman, Louis Evan
    1869-1933 . . . . WWasWT
Shipman, Samuel 1883-1937 . . . . . WWasWT
Shire, David 1937- CTFT-5
Shire, Talia 1946- CTFT-4
    Earlier sketch in CTFT-1
Shirley, Arthur 1853-1925 . . . . WWasWT
Shirvell, James 1902- . . . . WWasWT

Shockley, Ed 1957- CTFT-4
Shoemaker, Ann 1891-1978 ....WWT-16
Shore, Dinah 1917- CTFT-3
Shores, Del 1957- CTFT-8
Short, Hassard 1877-1956 ....WWasWT
Short, Martin CTFT-5
Short, Sylvia 1927- CTFT-2
Shotter, Winifred 1904- ....WWasWT
Showalter, Max 1917- CTFT-8
Shrader, Frederick Franklin
  1859-? ....WWasWT
Shubert, Jacob J. 1880-1963 .....WWasWT
Shubert, Lee 1875-1953 ....WWasWT
Shue, Larry 1946-1985 ....CTFT-3
Shukat, Scott 1937- CTFT-5
Shull, Leo 1913- WWT-17
Shull, Richard B. 1929- CTFT-7
  Earlier sketch in CTFT-1
Shulman, Milton 1913- WWT-17
Shultz, Tony 1947-...............CTFT-1
Shumlin, Herman E. 1898-1979 ...WWT-17
Shust, William CTFT-4
Shuster, Rosie 1950-.............CTFT-4
Shutta, Ethel 1896-1976 ....WWasWT
Shyer, Charles 1941- CTFT-8
Shyre, Paul 1929-1989 ....CTFT-6
  Earlier sketch in WWT-17
Sidney, Sylvia 1910- CTFT-9
  Earlier sketch in WWT-17
Siebert, Charles 1938- CTFT-2
Siegel, Arthur 1923-.............CTFT-1
Siegel, Don 1912- CTFT-6
Sierra, Gregory CTFT-7
Sieveking, Margot ....WWasWT
Siff, Ira 1946- CTFT-4
Signoret, Gabriel 1878-1937 .....WWasWT
Signoret, Simone 1921-1985 ....CTFT-3
Sikking, James B. 1934- CTFT-6
Silber, Chic CTFT-4
Silliman, Maureen 1949- CTFT-2
Silliphant, Stirling CTFT-3
Sillman, Leonard 1908-1982 ......WWT-17
Sills, Paul CTFT-5
  Earlier sketch in WWT-17
Silva, Henry 1928- CTFT-8
Silva, Trinidad 1950-1988 ....CTFT-7
Silvain, Eugene 1851-1930 ......WWasWT
Silver, Christine 1884-1960 ......WWasWT
Silver, Joan Micklin 1935- CTFT-4
Silver, Joe 1922-1989 ....CTFT-8
  Earlier sketch in WWT-17
Silver, Joel 1939- CTFT-9
Silver, Ron 1946-.................CTFT-4
  Earlier sketch in CTFT-1
Silverman, Fred 1937- CTFT-7
Silvers, Cathy 1961- CTFT-3
Silvers, Phil 1911-1985 ....WWT-17
Silverstein, Elliot 1927- CTFT-1
Silvestri, Alan CTFT-7
Sim, Alastair 1900-1976 ....WWT-16
Sim, Millie 1895- ....WWasWT
Sim, Sheila 1922- ....WWasWT
Simmons, Gene 1949-..............CTFT-8
Simmons, Jean 1929- CTFT-3
Simmons, Jonathan 1955-..........CTFT-5
Simms, Hilda 1920- WWT-17
Simon, John 1925-...............WWT-17
Simon, Louis M. 1906-...........WWT-17
Simon, Neil 1927-................CTFT-6
  Earlier sketches in CTFT-1, WWT-17
Simone, Madame 1880-? ....WWasWT
Simonson, Lee 1888-1967 ....WWasWT
Simpson, Don 1945- CTFT-5

Simpson, Harold ....WWasWT
Simpson, N. F. 1919- WWT-17
Simpson, O. J. 1947- CTFT-7
Simpson, Peggy ....WWasWT
Simpson, Ronald 1896-1957 .....WWasWT
Sims, George Robert 1847-1922 ..WWasWT
Sims, Joan 1930-.................WWT-17
Sinatra, Frank 1915- CTFT-9
Sinclair, Arthur 1883-1951 ......WWasWT
Sinclair, Barry 1911-............WWT-17
Sinclair, Hugh 1903-1962 ....WWasWT
Sinclair, Madge CTFT-4
Sinden, Donald 1923-..............CTFT-7
  Earlier sketch in WWT-17
Sinden, Jeremy 1950- CTFT-9
Sinden, Topsy 1878-? ....WWasWT
Singer, Campbell 1909-1976 ......WWT-16
Singer, Lori CTFT-2
Singer, Marc CTFT-6
Singer, Marla 1957- CTFT-4
Sinise, Gary CTFT-9
Sinkys, Albert 1940-..............CTFT-4
Sirola, Joe 1929- CTFT-8
Sisto, Rocco 1953-................CTFT-4
Sitgreaves, Beverley 1867-1943 ...WWasWT
Skala, Lilia WWT-17
Skelly, Hal 1891-1934 ....WWasWT
Skelton, Red 1913- CTFT-8
Skelton, Thomas CTFT-4
  Earlier sketch in WWT-17
Skerritt, Tom 1933- CTFT-6
Skillan, George 1893-..........WWasWT
Skinner, Cornelia Otis
  1901-1979 ....WWT-16
Skinner, Otis 1858-1942 ....WWasWT
Skipworth, Alison 1863-1952 ....WWasWT
Skulnik, Menasha 1894-1970 .....WWasWT
Skye, Ione 1971- CTFT-9
Slade, Bernard 1930- CTFT-1
Slade, Julian 1930- CTFT-3
  Earlier sketch in WWT-17
Slater, Christian 1969- CTFT-9
Slater, Daphne 1928- ....WWasWT
Slater, Helen 1963-...............CTFT-7
Slater, John 1916-...............WWasWT
Slaughter, Bessie 1879-? ....WWasWT
Slaughter, N. Carter (Tod)
  1885-1956 ....WWasWT
Sleath, Herbert 1870-1921 ......WWasWT
Sleeper, Martha 1911- ....WWasWT
Slezak, Erika 1946-...............CTFT-4
Slezak, Walter 1902-1983 ....WWT-17
Sloane, Alfred Baldwin
  1872-1925 ....WWasWT
Sloane, Michael 1946- CTFT-5
Sloane, Olive 1896-1963 ....WWasWT
Sloyan, James CTFT-8
Small, Neva CTFT-2
Small, Robert Grahm 1949- CTFT-2
Smart, Jean 1951(?)-.............CTFT-9
Smiar, Brian 1937- CTFT-7
Sminkey, Tom CTFT-7
Smith, Alexis 1921- CTFT-3
  Earlier sketch in WWT-17
Smith, Anna Deavere 1950-........CTFT-2
Smith, Aubrey 1863-1948 ....WWasWT
Smith, Bubba 1945-...............CTFT-7
Smith, Charles Martin 1955-.....CTFT-6
Smith, Clay 1885-? ....WWasWT
Smith, Cotter 1949-...............CTFT-7
  Earlier sketch in CTFT-1
Smith, Cyril 1892-1963 ....WWasWT

Smith, Derek 1927- CTFT-7
  Earlier sketch in WWT-17
Smith, Derek David 1959-.........CTFT-8
  Earlier sketch in CTFT-2
Smith, Dick 1922- CTFT-6
Smith, Dodie WWT-17
Smith, Edgar McPhail
  1857-1938 ....WWasWT
Smith, H. Reeves-
  See Reeves-Smith, H. ....WWasWT
Smith, Harry Bache 1860-1936 ...WWasWT
Smith, Howard I. 1894-1968 .....WWasWT
Smith, J. Sebastian 1869-1948 ....WWasWT
Smith, Jaclyn 1947- CTFT-7
  Earlier sketch in CTFT-2
Smith, Kent 1907-1985 ....WWT-17
Smith, Kurtwood CTFT-8
Smith, Lane CTFT-7
Smith, Liz 1925- CTFT-9
Smith, Lois CTFT-8
  Earlier sketch in WWT-17
Smith, Loring 1895- ....WWasWT
Smith, Maggie 1934- CTFT-4
  Earlier sketches in CTFT-1, WWT-17
Smith, Martha CTFT-7
Smith, Oliver 1918- WWT-17
Smith, Paul Girard ....WWasWT
Smith, Queenie 1902- ....WWasWT
Smith, Rex 1956- CTFT-7
Smith, Robert B. 1875-1951 .....WWasWT
Smith, Sheila 1933-...............CTFT-1
Smith, Sidney 1877-1935 ....WWasWT
Smith, Sukie 1964-................CTFT-4
Smith, Surrey
  See Dinner, William CTFT-4
Smith, Winchell 1872-1933 ......WWasWT
Smithers, Florence ....WWasWT
Smithers, Jan 1949-..............CTFT-7
Smithers, William 1927-..........CTFT-8
  Earlier sketch in CTFT-2
Smithson, Florence 1884-1936 ....WWasWT
Smithson, Laura 1885-1963 ......WWasWT
Smitrovich, Bill CTFT-8
Smits, Jimmy 1955- CTFT-6
Smothers, Dick 1939-.............CTFT-3
Smothers, Tom 1937-..............CTFT-3
Smuin, Michael 1938- CTFT-9
Snodgress, Carrie 1946- CTFT-5
Snow, Donna CTFT-3
Snow, Mark 1946- CTFT-6
Sobel, Bernard 1887-1964 ....WWasWT
Sobieski, Carol 1939-1990 ....CTFT-9
  Earlier sketch in CTFT-1
Soboloff, Arnold 1930-1979 ......WWT-17
Sofaer, Abraham 1896-1988 ....CTFT-7
  Earlier sketch in WWT-17
Sohlke, Gus 1865-1924 ....WWasWT
Sohmers, Barbara CTFT-1
Sokol, Marilyn CTFT-1
Sokolova, Natasha 1917- ....WWasWT
Sokolow, Anna 1910-..............CTFT-1
Soler, Antonio Ruiz 1927- ....WWasWT
Solodovnikov, Alexandr
  Vasilievich 1904-.............WWasWT
Soman, Claude 1897-1960 ....WWasWT
Somers, Suzanne CTFT-3
Somerset, C. W. 1847-1929 ......WWasWT
Somerset, Patrick 1897-1974 .....WWasWT
Somerville, John Baxter
  1907-1963 ....WWasWT
Somes, Michael (George) 1917-...WWasWT
Somkin, Steven 1941- CTFT-4
Sommars, Julie CTFT-8

Sommer, Elke 1941- CTFT-3
Sommer, Josef 1934- CTFT-1
Somner, Pearl 1923- CTFT-2
Sonal, Marc 1858-? . . . . .WWasWT
Sondergaard, Gale 1901-1985 . . . . .WWT-17
Sondheim, Stephen 1930- CTFT-1
    Earlier sketch in WWT-17
Sorel, Cecil 1873-1966 . . . . .WWasWT
Sorel, Theodore 1936- CTFT-2
Soria, Madeleine . . . . .WWasWT
Sorvino, Paul 1939- CTFT-4
    Earlier sketch in WWT-17
Sothern, Ann 1909- CTFT-8
    Earlier sketch in WWasWT
Sothern, Edward H. 1859-1933 . . .WWasWT
Sothern, Janet Evelyn . . . . .WWasWT
Sothern, Sam 1870-1920 . . . . .WWasWT
Soto, Rosana
    See DeSoto, Rosana CTFT-7
Souchet, H. A. du . . . . .WWasWT
Soul, David 1943- CTFT-3
Soule, Olan 1909- CTFT-9
Sousa, John Philip 1854-1932 . . . .WWasWT
Soutar, J. Farren 1870-1962 . . . . .WWasWT
Southern, John 1893- . . . . .WWasWT
Southern, Terry 1927- CTFT-7
Southgate, Elsie 1890- . . . . .WWasWT
Sovey, Raymond 1897-1966 . . . . . .WWasWT
Sowerby, Katherine Githa . . . . . . .WWasWT
Soyinka, Wole 1934- CTFT-6
Spacek, Sissy 1950- CTFT-3
    Earlier sketch in CTFT-1
Spacey, Kevin 1959- CTFT-9
Spackman, Tom 1950- CTFT-4
Spader, James 1961- CTFT-9
Spain, Elsie . . . . .WWasWT
Spano, Joe 1946- CTFT-5
Spano, Vincent 1962- CTFT-6
Sparer, Paul CTFT-5
    Earlier sketch in WWT-17
Speaight, Robert 1904-1976 . . . . . .WWT-16
Spear, David 1953- CTFT-2
Speechley, Billy 1911- . . . . .WWasWT
Spelling, Aaron 1928- CTFT-3
    Earlier sketch in CTFT-1
Spelvin, George Jr.
    See Douglas, Kirk CTFT-7
Spence, Edward F. 1860-1932 . . . .WWasWT
Spencer, Helen 1903- . . . . .WWasWT
Spencer, Jessica 1919- . . . . .WWasWT
Spencer, Marian 1905- WWT-17
Spewack, Bella 1899-1990 . . . . . . .WWasWT
Spewack, Samuel 1899-1971 . . . . .WWasWT
Spielberg, David 1939- CTFT-5
    Earlier sketch in CTFT-1
Spielberg, Steven 1947- CTFT-1
Spigelgass, Leonard 1908-1985 . . . .WWT-17
Spiller, Tom 1949- CTFT-2
Spindell, Ahvi CTFT-4
Spinell, Joe ?-1989 . . . . .CTFT-8
Spinelli, Andree 1891- . . . . .WWasWT
Spiner, Brent CTFT-9
Spinetti, Victor 1933- CTFT-2
    Earlier sketch in WWT-17
Spong, Hilda 1875-1955 . . . . .WWasWT
Spooner, Cecil . . . . .WWasWT
Spooner, Edna May ?-1953 . . . . . .WWasWT
Spota, George 1917- CTFT-1
Spriggs, Elizabeth WWT-17
Springer, Ashton Jr. 1930- CTFT-1
Springett, Freddie 1915- . . . . .WWasWT
Springfield, Rick CTFT-2
Squibb, June 1935- CTFT-2

Squire, Katherine 1903- WWT-17
Squire, Ronald 1886-1958 . . . . . . .WWasWT
Squire, William 1920-1989 . . . . .CTFT-6
    Earlier sketch in WWT-17
Stack, Robert 1919- CTFT-3
Stack, William 1882-? . . . . .WWasWT
Stacy, James 1936- CTFT-6
Stadlen, Lewis J. 1947- WWT-17
Stafford-Clark, Max 1941- CTFT-4
    Earlier sketch in WWT-17
Stagge, Jonathan
    See Wheeler, Hugh CTFT-5
Stahl, Richard 1932- CTFT-6
Stahl, Rose 1870-1955 . . . . .WWasWT
Stainton, Philip 1908-1961 . . . . . . .WWasWT
Stallings, Laurence 1894-1968 . . . .WWasWT
Stallone, Sylvester 1946- CTFT-8
    Earlier sketch in CTFT-1
Stamos, John CTFT-4
    Brief Entry in CTFT-3
Stamp Taylor, Enid
    See Taylor, Enid Stamp . . . . . . .WWasWT
Stamp, Terence 1938- CTFT-6
Stamper, Dave 1883-1963 . . . . . . .WWasWT
Stamper, F. Pope 1880-1950 . . . . .WWasWT
Stander, Lionel 1908- CTFT-5
Standing, Charles Wyndham
    1880-? . . . . .WWasWT
Standing, Guy 1873-1937 . . . . .WWasWT
Standing, Herbert 1846-1923 . . . . .WWasWT
Standing, John 1934- CTFT-7
    Earlier sketch in WWT-17
Standish, Pamela 1920- . . . . .WWasWT
Stanford, Henry 1872-1921 . . . . . .WWasWT
Stang, Arnold 1925- CTFT-2
Stange, Stanislaus ?-1917 . . . . . . .WWasWT
Stanislawski, Constantine
    1863-1938 . . . . .WWasWT
Stanley, Adelaide 1906- . . . . .WWasWT
Stanley, Alma 1854-1931 . . . . .WWasWT
Stanley, Erie 1884-? . . . . .WWasWT
Stanley, Florence CTFT-7
    Earlier sketch in WWT-17
Stanley, Gordon 1951- CTFT-7
    Earlier sketch in CTFT-1
Stanley, Kim 1921- CTFT-3
    Earlier sketch in WWT-17
Stanley, Martha 1879-? . . . . .WWasWT
Stanley, Pamela 1909- . . . . .WWasWT
Stanley, Phyllis 1914- . . . . .WWasWT
Stanley, S. Victor 1892-1939 . . . . .WWasWT
Stanmore, Frank 1878-1943 . . . . . .WWasWT
Stannard, Heather 1928- . . . . .WWasWT
Stanton, Harry Dean 1926- CTFT-5
Stanton, Robert 1963- CTFT-8
Stanwyck, Barbara 1907-1990 . . . . .CTFT-8
    Earlier sketches in CTFT-3, WWasWT
Stapleton, Jean 1923- CTFT-7
    Earlier sketches in CTFT-1, WWT-17
Stapleton, Maureen 1925- CTFT-4
    Earlier sketch in WWT-17
Stark, Ray CTFT-6
Starkie, Martin 1925- WWT-17
Starling, Lynn 1891-1955 . . . . .WWasWT
Starr, Frances Grant 1886-1973 . .WWasWT
Starr, Muriel 1888-1950 . . . . .WWasWT
Starr, Ringo 1940- CTFT-7
Stattel, Robert 1932- CTFT-1
Stayton, Frank 1874-1951 . . . . . . .WWasWT
Steadman, Alison 1946- CTFT-5
    Earlier sketch in WWT-17
Steafel, Sheila 1935- CTFT-8
Steel, Vernon 1882-1955 . . . . .WWasWT

Steele, Dawn 1946- CTFT-5
Steele, Lezley 1944- CTFT-4
Steele, Tommy 1936- CTFT-3
    Earlier sketch in WWT-17
Steenburgen, Mary 1953- CTFT-7
Steiger, Rod 1925- CTFT-3
Stein, Joseph CTFT-4
    Earlier sketch in WWT-17
Stein, Ronald 1930-1988 . . . . .CTFT-5
Steinbeck, John (Ernst)
    1902-1968 . . . . .WWasWT
Steinberg, David 1942- CTFT-7
Steinberg, Norman 1939- CTFT-1
Steinberg, Roy 1951- CTFT-2
Steiner, Sherry 1948- CTFT-1
Stenborg, Helen 1925- CTFT-1
Stepanek, Karel 1899- . . . . .WWasWT
Stephens, Frances 1906- . . . . .WWasWT
Stephens, Robert 1931- CTFT-6
    Earlier sketch in WWT-17
Stephens, Stephanie 1900- . . . . . . .WWasWT
Stephens, Yorke 1862-1937 . . . . . .WWasWT
Stephenson, Henry 1874-1956 . . . .WWasWT
Sterling, Clark 1956- CTFT-2
Sterling, Jan 1923- CTFT-7
    Earlier sketch in WWT-17
Sterling, Jane
    See Sterling, Jan CTFT-7
Sterling, Richard 1880-1959 . . . . .WWasWT
Stern, Daniel 1957- CTFT-7
    Brief Entry in CTFT-2
Stern, Ernest 1876-1954 . . . . .WWasWT
Stern, G. B. 1890-1973 . . . . .WWasWT
Stern, Sam 1883-? . . . . .WWasWT
Sterndale-Bennett, T. C.
    1882-1942 . . . . .WWasWT
Sternhagen, Frances 1930- CTFT-8
    Earlier sketches in CTFT-2, WWT-17
Sternroyd, Vincent 1857-1948 . . . .WWasWT
Stevens, Andrew 1955- CTFT-3
Stevens, Ashton 1872-1951 . . . . . .WWasWT
Stevens, Connie 1938- CTFT-3
Stevens, Craig 1918- CTFT-7
Stevens, Edwin 1860-1923 . . . . . . .WWasWT
Stevens, Emily 1882-1928 . . . . . . .WWasWT
Stevens, Emily Favella CTFT-3
Stevens, George, Jr. 1932- CTFT-4
Stevens, H.C.G. 1892-1967 . . . . . .WWasWT
Stevens, K.T. 1919- CTFT-2
    Earlier sketch in WWasWT
Stevens, Leslie 1964- CTFT-2
Stevens, Onslow 1906-1977 . . . . . .WWasWT
Stevens, Roger L. 1910- WWT-17
Stevens, Ronnie 1925- WWT-17
Stevens, Scooter 1973- CTFT-8
Stevens, Stella 1938- CTFT-7
Stevens, Tony 1948- CTFT-4
Stevenson, Margot 1914- WWT-17
Stevenson, McLean 1929- CTFT-6
Stevenson, Parker 1953- CTFT-6
Stewart, Alexandra 1939- CTFT-8
Stewart, Athole 1879-1940 . . . . . . .WWasWT
Stewart, Catherine Mary CTFT-7
Stewart, Donald Ogden
    1894-1980 . . . . .WWasWT
Stewart, Ellen CTFT-5
    Earlier sketch in WWT-17
Stewart, Fred 1906-1970 . . . . .WWasWT
Stewart, James 1908- CTFT-4
    Earlier sketch in WWT-17
Stewart, James
    See Granger, Stewart CTFT-8
Stewart, Larry J. 1951- CTFT-2

Stewart, Michael 1929-1987 . . . . .CTFT-5
  Earlier sketches in CTFT-1, WWT-17
Stewart, Nancye 1893- . . . . .WWasWT
Stewart, Nellie 1860-1931 . . . . . . .WWasWT
Stewart, Patrick 1940- CTFT-7
  Earlier sketch in WWT-17
Stewart, Sophie 1908-1977 . . . . .WWT-16
Stickney, Dorothy 1900- WWT-17
Stiers, David Ogden 1942- CTFT-6
Stigwood, Robert 1934- CTFT-5
Stiles, Leslie 1876-? . . . . .WWasWT
Stiller, Jerry CTFT-1
Stilwell, Diane CTFT-6
Sting 1951- CTFT-7
  Brief Entry in CTFT-2
Stinton, Colin 1947- CTFT-1
Stirling, W. Edward 1891-1948 . . .WWasWT
Stitt, Don 1956- CTFT-5
Stock, Nigel 1919-1986 . . . . .CTFT-4
  Earlier sketch in WWT-17
Stockfield, Betty 1905-1966 . . . . . .WWasWT
Stockwell, Dean 1936- CTFT-5
Stockwell, John 1961- CTFT-7
Stoddard, Haila 1913- WWT-17
Stoker, Hew Gordon Dacre
  1885-1966 . . . . .WWasWT
Stoker, Willard 1905-1978 . . . . . . .WWT-16
Stokes, Sewell 1902- . . . . .WWasWT
Stoler, Shirley 1929- CTFT-8
Stoll, Oswald 1866-1942 . . . . .WWasWT
Stoltz, Eric CTFT-4
Stolz, Robert 1886-1975 . . . . .WWasWT
Stone, Alix WWT-17
Stone, Carol 1915- . . . . .WWasWT
Stone, Charles . . . . .WWasWT
Stone, Dee Wallace CTFT-6
Stone, Dorothy 1905-1974 . . . . . . .WWasWT
Stone, Ezra 1917- CTFT-1
Stone, Fred Andrew 1873-1959 . . .WWasWT
Stone, Lewis 1878-1953 . . . . .WWasWT
Stone, Oliver 1946- CTFT-6
  Earlier sketch in CTFT-1
Stone, Paddy 1924- WWT-17
Stone, Paula 1916- WWT-17
Stone, Peter H. 1930- CTFT-6
  Earlier sketch in WWT-17
Stone, Sharon CTFT-7
Stoppard, Tom 1937- CTFT-4
  Earlier sketches in CTFT-1, WWT-17
Stoppelmoor, Cheryl
  See Ladd, Cheryl CTFT-6
Stoppelmoor, Cherly Jean
  See Ladd, Cheryl CTFT-6
Storaro, Vittorio 1940- CTFT-8
Storch, Arthur 1925- CTFT-2
  Earlier sketch in WWT-17
Storch, Larry 1923- CTFT-6
Storey, David 1933- WWT-17
Storey, Fred 1861-1917 . . . . .WWasWT
Storm, Lesley 1903-1975 . . . . .WWasWT
Stothart, Herbert P. 1885-1949 . . .WWasWT
Stott, Judith 1929- . . . . .WWasWT
Stout, Paul 1972- CTFT-4
Strachan, Alan 1946- WWT-17
Strachey, Jack 1894- . . . . .WWasWT
Stradling, Harry Jr. 1925- CTFT-8
Straiges, Tony CTFT-9
Straight, Beatrice 1918- CTFT-7
  Earlier sketch in WWT-17
Strange, Robert 1882-1952 . . . . . . .WWasWT
Strangis, Greg 1951- CTFT-1
Strasberg, Lee 1901-1982 . . . . .WWT-17
Strasberg, Susan 1938- CTFT-1

Strassman, Marcia 1948- CTFT-7
Strathairn, David CTFT-8
Stratton, Eugene 1861-1918 . . . . . .WWasWT
Stratton, John 1925- WWT-17
Straus, Oscar 1870-1954 . . . . .WWasWT
Strauss, Peter 1947- CTFT-5
Streep, Meryl 1949- CTFT-8
  Earlier sketches in CTFT-1, WWT-17
Street, George Slythe 1867-1936 . .WWasWT
Streisand, Barbra 1942- CTFT-7
  Earlier sketches in CTFT-1, WWT-17
Stretton, Charles
  See Dyer, Charles CTFT-6
Strick, Joseph 1923- CTFT-1
Strickler, Dan 1949- CTFT-4
Strickler, Jerry 1939- CTFT-2
Stride, John 1936- CTFT-6
  Earlier sketch in WWT-17
Stritch, Elaine 1926- CTFT-7
  Earlier sketch in WWT-17
Strode, Warren Chetham 1897- . . .WWasWT
Strong, Austin 1881-1952 . . . . .WWasWT
Stroud, Don 1943- CTFT-2
Stroud, Gregory 1892- . . . . .WWasWT
Strouse, Charles 1928- CTFT-1
  Earlier sketch in WWT-17
Strozzi, Kay . . . . .WWasWT
Strudwick, Shepperd 1907-1983 . . .WWT-17
Struthers, Sally 1948- CTFT-7
  Earlier sketch in CTFT-2
Stuart, Aimee . . . . .WWasWT
Stuart, C. Douglas 1864-? . . . . . . .WWasWT
Stuart, Cosmo 1869-? . . . . .WWasWT
Stuart, Jeanne 1908- . . . . .WWasWT
Stuart, John 1898-1979 . . . . .WWT-16
Stuart, Leslie 1864-1928 . . . . .WWasWT
Stuart, Lynne 1930- CTFT-3
Stuart, Madge 1897- . . . . .WWasWT
Stuart, Otho 1865-1930 . . . . .WWasWT
Stuart, Philip 1887-1936 . . . . .WWasWT
Stuart, Tom 1878-? . . . . .WWasWT
Stubbs, Una 1937- WWT-17
Stuckey, Phyllis . . . . .WWasWT
Studholme, Marie 1875-1930 . . . . .WWasWT
Sturges, Preston 1898-1959 . . . . . .WWasWT
Styles, Edwin 1899-1960 . . . . .WWasWT
Styne, Jule 1905- CTFT-4
  Earlier sketch in WWT-17
Su, Louis
  See Kaufman, Lloyd CTFT-7
Suchet, David 1946- CTFT-7
Sugarman, Burt CTFT-8
Sugden, Charles 1850-1921 . . . . . .WWasWT
Sugden, Mrs. Charles . . . . .WWasWT
Sulka, Elaine CTFT-1
Sullavan, Margaret 1911-1960 . . . .WWasWT
Sullivan, Francis L. 1903-1956 . . .WWasWT
Sullivan, James E. 1864-1931 . . . .WWasWT
Sullivan, Susan CTFT-2
Sullivan, Tom 1947- CTFT-2
Sully, Mariette 1878-? . . . . .WWasWT
Summerfield, Eleanor 1921- . . . . . .WWasWT
Summerhays, Jane CTFT-9
Summers, Montague 1880-1948 . . .WWasWT
Sumner, Geoffrey 1908-1989 . . . . . .CTFT-9
  Earlier sketch in WWT-17
Sumner, Gordon Matthew
  See Sting CTFT-2
Sumner, John 1924- CTFT-6
  Earlier sketch in WWT-17
Sumner, Mary 1888-1956 . . . . .WWasWT
Sunde, Karen 1942- CTFT-2
Sunderland, Scott 1883-? . . . . .WWasWT

Surovy, Nicholas 1946- CTFT-1
Surtees, Bruce CTFT-8
Susman, Todd 1947- CTFT-6
Susskind, David 1920-1987 . . . . . . .CTFT-5
Sussman, Peter 1958- CTFT-8
Sutherland, Annie 1867-1942 . . . .WWasWT
Sutherland, Donald 1935- CTFT-6
  Earlier sketch in CTFT-1
Sutherland, Kiefer 1966(?)- CTFT-9
  Brief Entry in CTFT-5
Sutro, Alfred 1863-1933 . . . . .WWasWT
Sutton-Vane, Vane 1888-1963 . . . .WWasWT
Suzman, Janet 1939- CTFT-4
  Earlier sketches in CTFT-1, WWT-17
Svennberg, Tore 1852-? . . . . .WWasWT
Svenson, Bo 1941- CTFT-7
  Earlier sketch in CTFT-3
Svoboda, Josef 1920- WWT-17
Swados, Elizabeth A. 1951- CTFT-1
  Earlier sketch in WWT-17
Swaffer, Hannen 1879-1962 . . . . . .WWasWT
Swaim, Bob 1943- CTFT-8
Swain, Elizabeth 1941- CTFT-1
Swallow, Margaret 1896-1932 . . . .WWasWT
Swan, Mark Elbert 1871-1942 . . . .WWasWT
Swan, William 1928- CTFT-4
Swann, Donald 1923- WWT-17
Swansen, Larry 1932- CTFT-6
  Earlier sketch in CTFT-1
Swanson, Gloria 1899-1983 . . . . . .WWT-17
Swanson, Logan
  See Matheson, Richard CTFT-6
Swarm, Sally Ann CTFT-6
Swash, Bob 1929- WWT-17
Swayze, Pat
  See Swayze, Patrick CTFT-9
Swayze, Patrick 1954(?)- CTFT-9
  Brief Entry in CTFT-3
Sweet, Dolph 1920-1985 . . . . .CTFT-1
Swenson, Inga 1934- CTFT-7
  Earlier sketch in WWT-17
Swenson, Swen 1932- WWT-17
Swerling, Jo Jr. 1931- CTFT-7
Swete, E. Lyall 1865-1930 . . . . . . .WWasWT
Swift, Allen 1924- CTFT-3
Swift, Clive 1936- CTFT-7
  Earlier sketch in WWT-17
Swinburne, Mercia 1900- . . . . .WWasWT
Swinburne, Nora 1902- WWT-17
Swindells, John 1931- CTFT-1
Swinley, Ion 1891-1937 . . . . .WWasWT
Swinstead, Joan 1903- . . . . .WWasWT
Swit, Loretta 1937- CTFT-3
Swope, Tracy Brooks CTFT-3
Sydney, Basil 1894-1968 . . . . .WWasWT
Sydow, Jack 1921- CTFT-2
Sykes, Brenda 1949- CTFT-6
Sykes, Eric 1924- CTFT-5
Sylbert, Anthea 1939- CTFT-9
Sylbert, Dick
  See Sylbert, Richard CTFT-9
Sylbert, Paul 1928- CTFT-9
Sylbert, Richard 1928- CTFT-9
Sylva, Ilena 1916- . . . . .WWasWT
Sylva, Vesta 1907- . . . . .WWasWT
Sylvaine, Vernon 1897-1957 . . . . . .WWasWT
Sylvane, Andre 1850-? . . . . .WWasWT
Sylvester, Harold CTFT-8
Sylvester, William 1922- . . . . .WWasWT
Sylvie, Louise 1885-? . . . . .WWasWT
Symonds, Robert 1926- CTFT-5
  Earlier sketch in WWT-17
Sympson, Tony 1906- WWT-17

Syms, Sylvia 1934- CTFT-3
Szabo, Istvan 1938- CTFT-8
Szwarc, Jeannot 1939- CTFT-9

T

Tabbert, William 1921- ....WWasWT
Tabor, Susan 1939-..................CTFT-5
Tabori, George 1914- WWT-17
Tabori, Kristoffer CTFT-1
   Earlier sketch in WWT-17
Tagg, Alan 1928- CTFT-5
   Earlier sketch in WWT-17
Taggart, Rita.....................CTFT-8
Taikeff, Stanley 1940- CTFT-4
Takei, George CTFT-5
Talbot, Howard 1865-1928 ......WWasWT
Talbot, Lyle 1902- CTFT-7
Talbot, Nita CTFT-8
Talbott, Michael 1955-............CTFT-6
Taliaferro, Edith 1893-1958 ......WWasWT
Taliaferro, Mabel 1889-1979 .....WWasWT
Tallchief, Maria 1925- ....WWasWT
Talli, Virgilio 1857-1928 ....WWasWT
Tallis, George 1867-1948 ....WWasWT
Tally, Ted 1952- CTFT-1
Talma, Mdlle. ....WWasWT
Tamara 1907-1943 ....WWasWT
Tamblyn, Russ 1935- CTFT-9
Tambor, Jeffrey CTFT-6
Tamiris, Helen 1905-1966 ....WWasWT
Tandy, Jessica 1909-..............CTFT-7
   Earlier sketches in CTFT-1, WWT-17
Tandy, Valerie 1921-1965 ....WWasWT
Tanguay, Eva 1878-1947 ....WWasWT
Tanner, Alain 1929-...............CTFT-8
Tanner, James T. ?-1951 ....WWasWT
Tanner, Tony 1932- CTFT-6
   Earlier sketch in WWT-17
Tapping, Mrs. A. B. 1852-1926 ...WWasWT
Tapping, Alfred B. ?-1928 ....WWasWT
Tarasova, Alla Konstantinovna
   1898-1973 ....WWasWT
Tariol-Bauge, Anna 1872-? ......WWasWT
Tarkington, Booth 1862-1946 ....WWasWT
Tarride, Abel 1867-?............WWasWT
Tarses, Jay 1939- CTFT-6
Tartikoff, Brandon CTFT-5
Tasca, Jules 1938-................CTFT-3
Tashman, Lilyan 1899-1934 ......WWasWT
Tate, Beth 1890-? ....WWasWT
Tate, Harry 1872-1940 ....WWasWT
Tate, James W. 1875-1922 ....WWasWT
Tate, Reginald 1896-1955 ....WWasWT
Tatum, Bill 1947- CTFT-4
Tauber, Richard 1891-1948 ......WWasWT
Taubman, Howard 1907- ....WWasWT
Tavel, Ronald 1941-...............CTFT-5
   Earlier sketch in WWT-17
Tavernier, Bertrand 1941- CTFT-7
Tawde, George 1883-? ....WWasWT
Tayback, Vic 1930(?)-1990.........CTFT-9
   Earlier sketch in CTFT-3
Taylor, Cecil P. 1929-1981 ....WWT-17
Taylor, Clarice 1927-.............CTFT-7
   Earlier sketch in WWT-17
Taylor, Deems 1885-1966 ....WWasWT
Taylor, Don CTFT-5
Taylor, Elizabeth 1932- CTFT-7
   Earlier sketch in CTFT-1
Taylor, Enid Stamp 1904-1946 ...WWasWT

Taylor, Harry
   See Granick, Harry CTFT-4
Taylor, Hiram 1952- CTFT-3
Taylor, Holland 1943- CTFT-7
Taylor, John Russell 1935- CTFT-5
   Earlier sketch in WWT-17
Taylor, Laurette 1884-1946 ......WWasWT
Taylor, Meshach CTFT-8
Taylor, Nellie 1894-1932 ....WWasWT
Taylor, Noel 1917- WWT-17
Taylor, Pat 1918- ....WWasWT
Taylor, Renee CTFT-3
Taylor, Rip CTFT-3
Taylor, Rod 1930- CTFT-6
Taylor, Samuel 1912- WWT-17
Taylor, Valerie 1902-1988 ....CTFT-8
   Earlier sketch in WWT-17
Taylor, William Buchanan
   1877-? ....WWasWT
Taylor-Young, Leigh 1945- CTFT-6
Taymor, Julie 1952- CTFT-1
Teague, Lewis 1941-...............CTFT-7
Tearle, Conway 1878-1938 ......WWasWT
Tearle, Godfrey 1884-?..........WWasWT
Teasdale, Verree 1906-1987 ......WWasWT
Tedrow, Irene 1910-...............CTFT-2
Teed, John 1911-1921 ....WWasWT
Teer, Barbara Ann 1937-..........CTFT-1
Teichmann, Howard Miles
   1916-1987 ....CTFT-1
Teitel, Carol ?-1986 ....WWT-17
Teitel, Nathan 1910-..............CTFT-6
Teixeira de Mattos, Alexander
   Louis 1865-1921 ....WWasWT
Tell, Alma 1892-1937 ....WWasWT
Tell, Olive 1894-1951 ....WWasWT
Tellegen, Lou-
   See Lou-Tellegen ....WWasWT
Temperley, Stephen 1949- CTFT-4
Tempest, Marie 1864-1942 ......WWasWT
Tempest, Francis Adolphus
Vane-
   See Vane-Tempest ....WWasWT
Temple, Helen 1894- ....WWasWT
Temple, Joan ?-1965 ....WWasWT
Temple, Madge ?-1943 ....WWasWT
Temple, Richard 1847-? ....WWasWT
Templeton, Fay 1865-1939 ....WWasWT
Templeton, W. P. 1913-..........WWasWT
Tennant, Victoria 1950- CTFT-3
Tennent, Henry M. 1879-1941 ...WWasWT
Tennent Ltd., H. M. WWT-17
Ter-Arutunian, Rouben 1920- CTFT-7
   Earlier sketch in WWT-17
Terris, Norma 1904-1989 ....WWasWT
Terriss, Ellaline 1871-1971 ....WWasWT
Terriss, Tom 1874-1964 ....WWasWT
Terry, Beatrice ....WWasWT
Terry, Edward O'Connor
   1844-1912 ....WWasWT
Terry, Ellen Alice 1847-1928 .....WWasWT
Terry, Ethelind 1900- ....WWasWT
Terry, Fred 1863-1933 ....WWasWT
Terry, Hazel 1918-1974 ....WWasWT
Terry, J. E. Harold 1885-1939 ...WWasWT
Terry, Kate 1844-1924 ....WWasWT
Terry, Marlon 1856-1930 ....WWasWT
Terry, Megan 1932- CTFT-5
   Earlier sketch in WWT-17
Terry, Minnie 1882-1964 ....WWasWT
Terry, Nigel 1945- CTFT-8
Terry, Olive 1884-1957 ....WWasWT
Terson, Peter 1932- WWT-17

Tesich, Steve 1942- CTFT-5
Tester, Desmond 1919- ....WWasWT
Tetley, Dorothy ....WWasWT
Tetzel, Joan 1921-1977 ....WWT-16
Tewes, Lauren 1953- CTFT-1
Tewkesbury, Joan 1936-...........CTFT-7
Tewson, Josephine CTFT-5
Teyte, Maggie 1889-1976 ....WWasWT
Thacker, David 1950-..............CTFT-5
Thane, Elswyth ....WWasWT
Thatcher, Heather ?-1987 ....WWasWT
Thatcher, Torin 1905- ....WWasWT
Thaw, John 1942-.................CTFT-9
   Earlier sketch in WWT-17
Thaxter, Phyllis 1920- WWT-17
Theilade, Nini 1915-.............WWasWT
Theiss, Bill
   See Theiss, William Ware CTFT-9
Theiss, William
   See Theiss, William Ware CTFT-9
Theiss, William Ware CTFT-9
Thelen, Jodi 1962- CTFT-8
Thesiger, Ernest 1879-1961 ......WWasWT
Theus, B. J. 1947-................CTFT-3
Thibeau, Jack CTFT-7
Thicke, Alan 1947- CTFT-6
Thigpen, Lynne CTFT-8
Thimm, Daisy ....WWasWT
Thinnes, Roy 1936- CTFT-6
Thomas, A. E. 1872-1947 ....WWasWT
Thomas, Agnes ....WWasWT
Thomas, Augustus 1857-1934 ...WWasWT
Thomas, Basil 1912-1957 ....WWasWT
Thomas, Betty 1948- CTFT-7
Thomas, Brandon 1856-1914 .....WWasWT
Thomas, Danny 1914- CTFT-3
Thomas, Dave 1949- CTFT-6
Thomas, Dorothy 1882-? ....WWasWT
Thomas, Evan 1891-.............WWasWT
Thomas, Gerald 1920- CTFT-5
Thomas, Gwyn 1913- WWT-17
Thomas, Heather 1957- CTFT-7
Thomas, Henry 1972-.............CTFT-6
Thomas, Herbert 1868-?........WWasWT
Thomas, Marlo 1943- CTFT-3
Thomas, Philip Michael 1949- CTFT-6
Thomas, Phyllis 1904- ....WWasWT
Thomas, Richard 1951- CTFT-7
   Earlier sketch in CTFT-1
Thomas, Thom 1941- CTFT-4
Thomassin, Jeanne ....WWasWT
Thomerson, Tim CTFT-8
Thompson, Alexander M.
   1861-1948 ....WWasWT
Thompson, Brian CTFT-7
Thompson, Eric 1929- CTFT-6
   Earlier sketch in WWT-17
Thompson, Evan 1931- CTFT-5
Thompson, Frank 1920-1977 .....WWT-16
Thompson, Fred 1884-1949 ......WWasWT
Thompson, Frederick W.
   1872-1919 ....WWasWT
Thompson, Gerald Marr
   1856-1938 ....WWasWT
Thompson, J. Lee 1914-..........WWasWT
Thompson, Jack 1940- CTFT-7
Thompson, Lea 1961-.............CTFT-9
Thompson, Robert 1937- CTFT-7
   Earlier sketch in CTFT-1
Thompson, Sada 1929-.............CTFT-4
   Earlier sketch in WWT-17
Thompson, W. H. 1852-1923 ....WWasWT
Thomson, Beatrix 1900-1986 .....WWasWT

Thomson, Gordon 1951- CTFT-8
Thorburn, H. M. 1884-1924 .....WWasWT
Thorndike, (Arthur) Russell
    1885-1972 ....WWasWT
Thorndike, Eileen 1891-1954 .....WWasWT
Thorndike, Sybil 1882-1976 ....WWT-16
Thorne, Angela 1939-.............CTFT-3
Thorne, Raymond 1933- CTFT-5
Thorne, Thomas 1841-1918 ......WWasWT
Thornton, Frank 1921-...........CTFT-8
    Earlier sketch in WWT-17
Thornton, John 1944-............CTFT-4
Thornton, Molly
    See Norden, Christine CTFT-6
Thorp, Joseph Peter 1873-1962 ...WWasWT
Thorpe, George 1891-1961 ......WWasWT
Thorpe-Bates, Peggy 1914-1989 ....CTFT-9
    Earlier sketch in WWT-17
Thorson, Linda 1947- CTFT-9
Threlfall, David 1953-...........CTFT-9
Throckmorton, Cleon
    1897-1965 ....WWasWT
Throne, Malachi CTFT-8
Thuillier, Emilio ....WWasWT
Thulin, Ingrid 1929-...........CTFT-9
Thun, Nancy 1952-............CTFT-4
Thurburn, Gwynneth 1899-.......WWT-16
Thurm, Joel CTFT-2
Thurston, Ernest Temple
    1879-1933 ....WWasWT
Thurston, Todd 1956- CTFT-3
Tibbett, Lawrence 1896-1960 ....WWasWT
Tich, Little 1868-? ....WWasWT
Tickle, Frank 1893-1955 ....WWasWT
Tidmarsh, Vivian 1896-1941 .....WWasWT
Tiercelin, Louis 1849-? ....WWasWT
Tierney, Harry 1894-1965 ....WWasWT
Tierney, Larry 1919- CTFT-6
Tigar, Kenneth 1942-...........CTFT-8
Tighe, Kevin 1944-.............CTFT-7
Tilbury, Zeffie 1863-1950 ....WWasWT
Tilley, Vesta 1864-1952 ....WWasWT
Tillinger, John 1939- CTFT-5
Tilly, Meg CTFT-7
    Brief Entry in CTFT-2
Tilton, Charlene 1958- CTFT-8
Tilton, James F. 1937- CTFT-2
    Earlier sketch in WWT-17
Timothy, Christopher 1940- CTFT-4
    Earlier sketch in CTFT-1
Tinker, Grant 1926- CTFT-5
Tinker, Jack 1938- WWT-17
Tinney, Frank 1878-1940 ....WWasWT
Tipton, Jennifer 1937- CTFT-9
Tisch, Lawrence 1923- CTFT-5
Tisch, Steve CTFT-3
Titheradge 1889-1934 ....WWasWT
Ththeradge, George S.
    1848-1916 ....WWasWT
Titheradge, Madge 1887-1961 ....WWasWT
Titmus, Phyllis 1900-1946 ....WWasWT
Titterton, William Richard
    1876-1963 ....WWasWT
Toback, James 1944- CTFT-7
Tobin, Genevieve 1902- ....WWasWT
Tobin, Vivian 1904- ....WWasWT
Todd, Ann WWT-17
Todd, Beverly 1946-............CTFT-8
Todd, J. Garrett ....WWasWT
Todd, Michael 1907-1958 ....WWasWT
Todd, Richard 1919- CTFT-3
    Earlier sketch in WWT-17

Toguri, David CTFT-7
    Earlier sketch in WWT-17
Tolan, Michael 1925- CTFT-1
Toler, Sidney 1874-1947 ....WWasWT
Tolkan, James 1931-............CTFT-8
Toller, Ernst 1893-1939 ....WWasWT
Toller, Rosalie 1885-? ....WWasWT
Tom, Lauren 1959-............CTFT-2
Tomlin, Blanche 1889-? ....WWasWT
Tomlin, Lily 1939- CTFT-6
    Earlier sketch in CTFT-2
Tomlinson, David 1917- WWT-17
Tompkins, Angel CTFT-8
Toms, Carl 1927- CTFT-6
    Earlier sketch in WWT-17
Tone, Franchot 1906-1968 ....WWasWT
Toner, Thomas 1928-...........CTFT-4
Tong, Jacqueline 1950-..........CTFT-7
Tonge, Philip 1892-1959 ....WWasWT
Toone, Geoffrey 1910- WWT-17
Topol 1935-................CTFT-9
Toporkov, Vasily Osipovich
    1889-? ....WWasWT
Torn, Rip 1931- CTFT-4
    Earlier sketch in WWT-17
Torrence, David 1870-? ....WWasWT
Torrence, Ernest 1878-1933 ......WWasWT
Toser, David CTFT-1
Totheroh, Dan 1894- ....WWasWT
Toumanova, Tamara 1917- ....WWasWT
Tours, Frank E. 1877-1963 ....WWasWT
Toutain, Blanche ?-1932 ....WWasWT
Towb, Harry 1925-.............WWT-17
Towers, Constance 1933- CTFT-3
    Earlier sketch in WWT-17
Towers, Harry P. 1873-? ....WWasWT
Towne, Robert 1936- CTFT-8
Townsend, Robert 1957- CTFT-3
Toye, Geoffrey Edward
    1889-1942 ....WWasWT
Toye, Wendy 1917- WWT-17
Toyne, Gabriel 1905-1963 ....WWasWT
Tracy, John 1938-.............CTFT-7
Tracy, Lee 1898-1968 ....WWasWT
Tracy, Spencer 1900-1967 ....WWasWT
Tracy, Steve 1952-1986 ....CTFT-4
Traill, Peter 1896-1968 ....WWasWT
Trarieux, Gabriel 1870-? ....WWasWT
Traube, Shepard 1907-1983 ......WWT-17
Traux, Sarah WWT-6
Travanti, Daniel John CTFT-3
Travers, Ben 1886-1980 ....WWT-17
Travers, Henry 1874-1965 ....WWasWT
Travers, Linden 1913- ....WWasWT
Travolta, John 1954-...........CTFT-2
Treat, Martin 1950-............CTFT-4
Treble, Sepha ....WWasWT
Treckman, Emma 1909-..........WWasWT
Tree, David 1915-............WWasWT
Tree, Herbert Beerbohm
    1853-1917 ....WWasWT
Tree, Lady 1863-1937 ....WWasWT
Tree, Viola 1884-1938 ....WWasWT
Trench, Herbert 1865-1923 ......WWasWT
Trenholme, Helen 1911-1962 .....WWasWT
Trent, Bruce WWT-16
Trentini, Emma 1885?-1959 ......WWasWT
Tresahar, John ?-1936 ....WWasWT
Tresmand, Ivy 1898- ....WWasWT
Trevelyan, Hilda 1880-1959 ......WWasWT
Treville, Roger 1903- ....WWasWT
Trevor, Ann 1918-1970 ....WWasWT
Trevor, Austin 1897- ....WWasWT

Trevor, Claire 1909- CTFT-9
    Earlier sketch in WWasWT
Trevor, Leo ?-1927 ....WWasWT
Trevor, Norman 1877-1945 ......WWasWT
Trewin, John Courtenay
    1908-1990 ....WWT-17
Treyz, Russell 1940-...........CTFT-1
Trilling, Ossia 1913-...........WWT-17
Trinder, Tommy 1909-..........WWT-17
Trintignant, Jean-Louis 1930- CTFT-9
Tripp, Paul 1916-.............CTFT-2
Troell, Jan 1931-.............CTFT-8
Troll, Kitty 1950-.............CTFT-4
Troobnick, Eugene 1926-.........CTFT-5
    Earlier sketch in WWT-17
Trott, Karen CTFT-6
Trouncer, Cecil 1898-1953 ....WWasWT
Troutman, Ivy 1883-1979 ....WWasWT
Troy, Louise WWT-17
Truax, Sarah 1877-? ....WWasWT
Trudeau, Garry 1948-...........CTFT-7
Trueman, Paula 1907- WWT-17
Truex, Ernest 1889-1973 ....WWasWT
Truffaut, Francois 1932-1984 ......CTFT-2
Truffier, Jules 1856-? ....WWasWT
Trussell, Fred 1858-1923 ....WWasWT
Trussler, Simon 1942- CTFT-5
    Earlier sketch in WWT-17
Tryon, Thomas 1926-...........CTFT-5
Tubau, Maria ....WWasWT
Tucci, Maria CTFT-1
    Earlier sketch in WWT-17
Tucci, Michael 1950- CTFT-7
Tucker, Forrest 1919-1986 ....CTFT-4
    Earlier sketch in CTFT-3
Tucker, Lael
    See Wertenbaker, Timberlake CTFT-9
Tucker, Michael 1944-...........CTFT-6
Tucker, Sophie 1884-1966 ....WWasWT
Tudor, Anthony 1909-1987 ......WWasWT
Tudor, Valerie 1910- ....WWasWT
Tuggle, Richard 1948- CTFT-4
Tulean, Ingrid
    See Thulin, Ingrid CTFT-9
Tull, Patrick 1941- CTFT-8
    Earlier sketch in CTFT-2
Tully, George F. 1876-1930 ......WWasWT
Tully, Richard Walton
    1877-1945 ....WWasWT
Tumarin, Boris 1910-1979 ....WWT-17
Tunbridge, Joseph A.
    1886-1961 ....WWasWT
Tune, Tommy 1939-...........CTFT-7
    Earlier sketches in CTFT-1, WWT-17
Tupou, Manu CTFT-5
    Earlier sketch in WWT-17
Turell, Saul 1920-1986 ....CTFT-3
Turleigh, Veronica 1903-1971 ....WWasWT
Turman, Lawrence 1926-.........CTFT-1
Turnbull, John 1880-1956 ....WWasWT
Turnbull, Stanley ?-1924 ....WWasWT
Turner, Alfred 1870-1941 ....WWasWT
Turner, Bridget 1939-...........CTFT-5
    Earlier sketch in WWT-17
Turner, David 1927-...........WWT-17
Turner, Dorothy 1895-1969 ......WWasWT
Turner, Douglas
    See Ward, Douglas Turner CTFT-4
Turner, L. Godfrey-
    See Godfrey-Turner, L. ....WWasWT
Turner, Harold 1909-1962 ....WWasWT
Turner, John Hastings
    1892-1956 ....WWasWT

Turner, Kathleen 1954- CTFT-5
Turner, Michael 1921- WWT-17
Turner, Ted 1938- CTFT-5
Turturro, John 1957- CTFT-9
Tushingham, Rita 1942- CTFT-7
  Earlier sketch in WWT-17
Tutin, Dorothy 1930- CTFT-5
  Earlier sketch in WWT-17
Twain, Norman 1930- CTFT-1
Twiggy 1949- CTFT-3
Tyars, Frank 1848-1918 . . . . .WWasWT
Tyler, George Crouse
  1867-1946 . . . . .WWasWT
Tyler, Odette 1869-1936 . . . . .WWasWT
Tynan, Brandon 1879-1967 . . . . . .WWasWT
Tynan, Kenneth 1927-1980 . . . . . . .WWT-17
Tyner, Charles 1925- CTFT-8
Tyrrell, Susan 1946- CTFT-6
Tyson, Cicely 1933- CTFT-1
  Earlier sketch in WWT-17
Tyzack, Margaret WWT-17

U

Uggams, Leslie 1943- CTFT-6
Ullman, Tracey 1959(?)- CTFT-9
  Brief Entry in CTFT-4
Ullmann, Liv 1939- CTFT-3
  Earlier sketch in CTFT-1
Ullrick, Sharon 1947- CTFT-2
Ulmar, Geraldine 1862-1932 . . . . .WWasWT
Ulric, Lenore 1892-1970 . . . . .WWasWT
Underwood, Blair CTFT-9
Unger, Deborah 1953- CTFT-3
Unger, Gladys B. 1885-1940 . . . . .WWasWT
Upbin, Shari 1941- CTFT-3
Upton, Leonard 1901- . . . . .WWasWT
Ure, Mary 1933-1975 . . . . .WWasWT
Urich, Robert 1946- CTFT-3
Urquhart, Molly . . . . .WWasWT
Urquhart, Robert 1922- CTFT-9
Ustinov, Peter 1921- CTFT-8
  Earlier sketches in CTFT-1, WWT-17

V

Vaccaro, Brenda 1939- CTFT-7
  Earlier sketches in CTFT-2, WWT-17
Vachell, Horace Annesley
  1861-1955 . . . . .WWasWT
Vadim, Roger 1928- CTFT-5
Vail, Lester 1900-1959 . . . . .WWasWT
Vajda, Ernest 1887-1954 . . . . .WWasWT
Valabregue, Albin . . . . .WWasWT
Valaida . . . . .WWasWT
Valdez, Luis 1940- CTFT-5
  Earlier sketch in WWT-17
Valentine 1876-? . . . . .WWasWT
Valentine, Grace 1884-1964 . . . . . .WWasWT
Valentine, James 1930- CTFT-1
Valentine, Karen 1947- CTFT-3
Valentine, Scott 1958- CTFT-5
Valentine, Sydney 1865-1919 . . . . .WWasWT
Valk, Frederick 1901-1956 . . . . . . .WWasWT
Valli, Valli 1882-1927 . . . . .WWasWT
Vallone, Raf 1916- CTFT-1
Valverde, Balbina . . . . .WWasWT
Van, Billy B. 1870-1950 . . . . .WWasWT
Van, Bobby 1930-1980 . . . . .WWT-17
Van Ark, Joan 1948- CTFT-7
Van Beers, Stanley 1911-1961 . . . .WWasWT

Van Biene, Auguste 1850-1913 . . .WWasWT
Vanbrugh, Irene 1872-1949 . . . . . .WWasWT
Vanbrugh, Prudence 1902- . . . . . . .WWasWT
Vanbrugh, Violet 1867-1942 . . . . .WWasWT
Van Buskirk, June 1882-? . . . . . . .WWasWT
Vance, Charles 1929- CTFT-5
  Earlier sketch in WWT-17
Vance, Courtney 1960- CTFT-8
Vance, Nina ?-1980 . . . . .WWT-17
Van Cleef, Lee 1925-1989 . . . . .CTFT-8
Van Devere, Trish 1943- CTFT-3
Van Druten, John 1901-1957 . . . . .WWasWT
Van Dyke, Dick 1925- CTFT-3
Vane-Tempest, Francis
  Adolphus 1863-1932 . . . . .WWasWT
Van Fleet, Jo 1922- CTFT-5
  Earlier sketch in WWT-17
Van Gelder, Holtropp . . . . .WWasWT
Van Griethuysen, Ted 1934- CTFT-5
  Earlier sketch in WWT-17
Van Gyseghem, Andre
  1906-1979 . . . . .WWT-17
Van Heusen, James 1913-1990 . . . .WWT-17
Van Itallie, Jean-Claude 1936- CTFT-3
  Earlier sketch in WWT-17
Van Kamp Merete 1961- CTFT-4
Vanloo, Albert ?-1920 . . . . .WWasWT
Vanne, Marda ?-1970 . . . . .WWasWT
Van Patten, Dick 1928- CTFT-1
Van Patten, Joyce 1934- CTFT-4
  Earlier sketch in WWT-17
Van Peebles, Mario CTFT-6
Van Peebles, Melvin 1932- CTFT-7
  Earlier sketch in WWT-17
Vansittart, Robert G.
  1881-1957 . . . . .WWasWT
Van Studdiford, Grace
  1873-1927 . . . . .WWasWT
Van Thal, Dennis 1909- . . . . .WWasWT
Van Volkenburg, Ellen . . . . .WWasWT
Varda, Agnes 1928- CTFT-8
Varden, Evelyn 1895-1958 . . . . . . .WWasWT
Varesi, Gilda 1887-? . . . . .WWasWT
Varnel, Marcel 1894-1947 . . . . . . .WWasWT
Vaucaire, Maurice 1865-1918 . . . . .WWasWT
Vaughan, Hilda 1898-1957 . . . . . . .WWasWT
Vaughan, Stuart 1925- CTFT-5
  Earlier sketch in WWT-17
Vaughan, Susie 1853-1950 . . . . . . .WWasWT
Vaughn, Robert 1932- CTFT-5
  Earlier sketch in CTFT-3
Vaz Dias, Selma 1911- . . . . .WWasWT
Vazak, P.H.
  See Towne, Robert CTFT-8
Veber, Pierre 1869-1942 . . . . .WWasWT
Vedrenne, John E. 1867-1930 . . . .WWasWT
Vega, Jose 1920- CTFT-1
Veiller, Bayard 1869-1943 . . . . . . .WWasWT
Velez, Eddie 1958- CTFT-5
Velez, Lupe 1909-1944 . . . . .WWasWT
VelJohnson, Reggie
  See VelJohnson, Reginald CTFT-9
VelJohnson, Reginald 1952- CTFT-9
Venables, Clare 1943- CTFT-6
Venne, Lottie 1852-1928 . . . . .WWasWT
Vennema, John C. 1948- CTFT-2
Vennera, Chick CTFT-7
Venning, Una 1893- . . . . .WWasWT
Venora, Diane 1952- CTFT-6
Venuta, Benay 1911- WWT-17
Verchinina, Nina . . . . .WWasWT
Verdon, Gwen 1925- CTFT-3
  Earlier sketch in WWT-17

Vereen, Ben 1946- CTFT-8
  Earlier sketches in CTFT-2, WWT-17
Verga, Giovanni 1840-1922 . . . . . .WWasWT
Verheyen, Mariann 1950- CTFT-1
Verhoeven, Paul 1940- CTFT-8
Verlaque, Robert 1955- CTFT-8
Vermilyea, Harold 1889-1958 . . . .WWasWT
Vernacchio, Dorian 1953- CTFT-2
Verneuil, Louis 1893-1952 . . . . . . .WWasWT
Verno, Jerry 1895- . . . . .WWasWT
Vernon, Anne 1924- CTFT-1
Vernon, David 1959- CTFT-2
Vernon, Frank 1875-1940 . . . . .WWasWT
Vernon, Harriet ?-1923 . . . . .WWasWT
Vernon, Harry M. 1878-? . . . . .WWasWT
Vernon, John 1932- CTFT-7
Vernon, Richard 1925- CTFT-5
  Earlier sketch in WWT-17
Vernon, Virginia 1894- . . . . .WWasWT
Verona, Stephen CTFT-4
Vezin, Arthur 1878-? . . . . .WWasWT
Vibart, Henry 1863-1939 . . . . .WWasWT
Vickery, John 1951- CTFT-7
Victor, Charles 1896-1965 . . . . . . .WWasWT
Victor, Josephine 1885-? . . . . .WWasWT
Victoria, Vesta 1873-1951 . . . . . . .WWasWT
Vidal, Gore 1925- CTFT-3
  Earlier sketch in WWT-17
Viertel, Thomas 1941- CTFT-7
Vigoda, Abe 1921- CTFT-3
Vilar, Jean 1912-1971 . . . . .WWasWT
Villard, Tom 1953- CTFT-5
Villechaize, Herve 1943- CTFT-5
Villiers, James 1933- CTFT-5
  Earlier sketch in WWT-17
Vincent, Jan-Michael 1944- CTFT-5
Vincent, Madge 1884-? . . . . .WWasWT
Vincent, Michael
  See Vincent, Jan-Michael CTFT-5
Vincent, Ruth 1877-1955 . . . . .WWasWT
Vines, Margaret 1910- . . . . .WWasWT
Vinovich, Steve 1945- CTFT-8
Vinson, Helen 1907- . . . . .WWasWT
Vivian, Anthony Crespigny
  Claud 1906- . . . . .WWasWT
Vivian-Rees, Joan . . . . .WWasWT
Voelpel, Fred WWT-17
Vogel, Paula A. 1951- CTFT-2
Voight, Jon 1938- CTFT-7
  Earlier sketches in CTFT-2, WWT-17
Voigts, Richard 1934- CTFT-4
Volage, Charlotte CTFT-2
Voland, Herb CTFT-6
Vollmer, Lula 1898-1955 . . . . .WWasWT
Volpe, Frederick 1865-1932 . . . . . .WWasWT
Volz, Nedra CTFT-8
Von Dohlen, Lenny 1959- CTFT-2
Von Furstenberg, Betsy 1931- CTFT-5
  Earlier sketch in WWT-17
Von Mayrhauser, Jennifer 1948- CTFT-4
Vonnegut, Kurt, Jr. 1922- CTFT-6
Von Scherler, Sasha 1939- CTFT-6
  Earlier sketch in WWT-17
Von Sydow, Max 1929- CTFT-5
Von Zerneck, Frank 1940- CTFT-1
Voskovic, George 1905-1981 . . . . . .WWT-17
Vosper, Frank 1899-1937 . . . . .WWasWT
Voss, Stephanie 1936- WWT-17

W

Waddington, Patrick 1901-1987 . . .WWT-17

Wade, Adam 1935- CTFT-1
Wade, Allan 1881-1955 ....WWasWT
Wagenhals, Lincoln A.
 1869-1931 ....WWasWT
Wager, Michael 1925- CTFT-5
 Earlier sketch in WWT-17
Waggoner, Lyle 1935- CTFT-7
Wagner, Charles L. ?-1956 ......WWasWT
Wagner, Jane 1935- CTFT-6
Wagner, Lindsay 1949- CTFT-3
Wagner, Robert 1930- CTFT-3
Wagner, Robin 1933- CTFT-3
 Earlier sketch in WWT-17
Wahl, Ken 1957- CTFT-7
Wain, Edward
 See Towne, Robert CTFT-8
Wainwright, Marie 1853-1923 ....WWasWT
Waissman, Kenneth 1940- CTFT-5
 Earlier sketch in WWT-17
Waite, Ralph 1928- CTFT-8
 Earlier sketch in CTFT-1
Waits, Tom 1949- CTFT-6
Wajda, Andrzej 1927- CTFT-8
 Earlier sketch in CTFT-2
Wakefield, Douglas 1899-1951 ...WWasWT
Wakefield, Gilbert Edward
 1892-1963 ....WWasWT
Wakefield, Hugh 1888-1971 .....WWasWT
Wakeman, Keith 1866-1933 .....WWasWT
Walbrook, Anton 1900-1966 .....WWasWT
Walbrook, Henry Mackinnon
 1863-1941 ....WWasWT
Walcott, Derek 1930- CTFT-6
Waldegrave, Lilias ....WWasWT
Walden, Stanley 1932- CTFT-2
Waldo, Janet 1930- CTFT-9
Waldron, Charles D. 1874-1946 ..WWasWT
Wales, William
 See Ambrose, David CTFT-5
Walford, Ann 1928- ....WWasWT
Walken, Christopher 1943- CTFT-3
 Earlier sketch in WWT-17
Walker, Charlotte 1878-1958 .....WWasWT
Walker, Jimmie 1947- CTFT-7
Walker, June 1904-1966 ....WWasWT
Walker, Kathryn CTFT-7
Walker, Martin 1901-1955 ....WWasWT
Walker, Nancy 1921- CTFT-3
 Earlier sketch in WWT-17
Walker, Polly 1908- ....WWasWT
Walker, Stuart 1888-1941 ....WWasWT
Walker, Syd 1886-1945 ....WWasWT
Walker, Sydney 1921- WWT-17
Walker, Zena 1934- CTFT-5
 Earlier sketch in WWT-17
Walkley, Arthur Bingham
 1855-1926 ....WWasWT
Wall, Harry 1886-1966 ....WWasWT
Wall, Max 1908-1990 ....WWT-17
Wallace, Dee
 See Stone, Dee Wallace CTFT-6
Wallace, Edgar 1875-1932 ....WWasWT
Wallace, George D. 1917- CTFT-1
Wallace, Hazel Vincent 1919- WWT-17
Wallace, Lee 1930-1989 ....CTFT-7
 Earlier sketch in CTFT-1
Wallace, Marcia 1942- CTFT-8
Wallace, Nellie 1882-1948 ....WWasWT
Wallace, Ray 1881-? ....WWasWT
Wallace, Tommy Lee CTFT-1
Wallach, Eli 1915- CTFT-7
 Earlier sketches in CTFT-1, WWT-17

Waller, David 1920- CTFT-6
 Earlier sketch in WWT-17
Waller, Edmund Lewis 1884-? ...WWasWT
Waller, Jack 1885-1957 ....WWasWT
Waller, Lewis 1860-1915 ....WWasWT
Waller, Mrs. Lewis 1862-1912 ....WWasWT
Wallis, Bertram 1874-1952 ......WWasWT
Wallis, Ellen Lancaster
 1856-1940 ....WWasWT
Wallis, Hal 1889-1986 ....CTFT-4
Wallis, Shani 1933- ....WWasWT
Walls, Tom 1883-1949 ....WWasWT
Walmer, Cassie 1888-? ....WWasWT
Walpole, Hugh 1884-1941 ....WWasWT
Walsh, Blanche 1873-1915 ....WWasWT
Walsh, Dermot 1924- CTFT-1
Walsh, J. T. CTFT-9
Walsh, James 1937- CTFT-1
Walsh, M. Emmet 1935- CTFT-7
Walsh, Sam 1877-1920 ....WWasWT
Walston, Ray 1924- CTFT-3
 Earlier sketch in WWT-17
Walter, Eugene 1874-1941 ....WWasWT
Walter, Jessica 1944- CTFT-7
 Earlier sketch in CTFT-1
Walter, Olive 1898- ....WWasWT
Walter, Wilfrid 1882-1958 ....WWasWT
Walter-Ellis, Desmond 1914- WWT-17
Walters, Barbara 1931- CTFT-6
Walters, Ewart James 1950- CTFT-8
Walters, Julie 1950- CTFT-7
Walters, Polly 1910- ....WWasWT
Walters, Thorley 1913- WWT-17
Walthers, Gretchen 1938- CTFT-5
Walton, Tony 1934- CTFT-4
 Earlier sketch in WWT-17
Walz, Ken 1942- CTFT-4
Wanamaker, Sam 1919- CTFT-3
 Earlier sketch in WWT-17
Wang, Peter CTFT-5
Wang, Wayne 1949- CTFT-5
Wanshel, Jeff 1947- CTFT-2
Waram, Percy 1881-1961 ....WWasWT
Ward, Betty ....WWasWT
Ward, David S. 1945- CTFT-1
Ward, Dorothy 1890-1987 ....WWasWT
Ward, Douglas Turner 1930- CTFT-4
 Earlier sketch in WWT-17
Ward, Fannie 1872-1952 ....WWasWT
Ward, Fred 1943- CTFT-9
 Brief Entry in CTFT-3
Ward, Genevieve 1837-1922 .....WWasWT
Ward, Hugh J. 1871-1941 ....WWasWT
Ward, Jay 1920-1989 ....CTFT-8
Ward, Jonathan 1970- CTFT-4
Ward, Mackenzie 1903- ....WWasWT
Ward, Penelope Dudley 1914- ....WWasWT
Ward, Polly 1909- ....WWasWT
Ward, Rachel 1957- CTFT-6
Ward, Ronald 1901- ....WWasWT
Ward, Simon 1941- CTFT-5
 Earlier sketch in WWT-17
Warde, Frederick B. 1851-1935 ...WWasWT
Warde, Willie 1857-1943 ....WWasWT
Warden, Jack 1920- CTFT-8
 Earlier sketch in CTFT-1
Wardle, (John) Irving 1929- WWT-17
Wardwell, Geoffrey 1900-1955 ...WWasWT
Ware, Helen 1877-1939 ....WWasWT
Ware, John
 See Mabley, Edward CTFT-1
Wareing, Alfred 1876-1942 ......WWasWT
Wareing, Lesley 1913- ....WWasWT

Warfield, David 1866-1951 ......WWasWT
Warfield, Joe 1937- CTFT-4
Warfield, Marsha 1955- CTFT-7
Waring, Barbara 1912- ....WWasWT
Waring, Dorothy May Graham
 1895- ....WWasWT
Waring, Herbert 1857-1932 ......WWasWT
Waring, Richard 1912- WWT-16
Warmington, Stanley J.
 1884-1941 ....WWasWT
Warner, David 1941- CTFT-5
 Earlier sketch in WWT-17
Warner, Grace 1873-1925 ....WWasWT
Warner, Henry Byron
 1876-1958 ....WWasWT
Warner, Malcolm-Jamal CTFT-5
Warre, Michael 1922- CTFT-6
 Earlier sketch in WWT-17
Warren, Betty 1905- ....WWasWT
Warren, C. Denier 1889-1971 ....WWasWT
Warren, Jeff 1921- WWT-17
Warren, Jennifer CTFT-5
Warren, Jennifer Leigh CTFT-2
Warren, Kenneth J. 1929-1973 ....WWT-16
Warren, Lesley Ann 1946- CTFT-6
 Earlier sketch in CTFT-1
Warren, Michael 1946- CTFT-7
Warrender, Harold 1903-1953 ....WWasWT
Warrick, Ruth 1916- CTFT-3
 Earlier sketch in WWT-17
Warrilow, David 1934- CTFT-2
Warriner, Frederic 1916- WWT-17
Warwick, Ethel 1882-1951 ....WWasWT
Warwick, Robert 1878-1964 .....WWasWT
Washbourne, Mona 1903-1988 ....CTFT-8
 Earlier sketch in WWT-17
Washington, Denzel 1954- CTFT-9
 Brief Entry in CTFT-3
Wass, Ted 1952- CTFT-7
Wasser, Jane 1957- CTFT-7
Wasserman, Dale 1917- CTFT-5
Wasserstein, Wendy 1950- CTFT-8
 Earlier sketch in CTFT-1
Wasson, Craig 1954- CTFT-8
Wasson, Susanne CTFT-2
Watanabe, Gedde CTFT-5
Waterhouse, Keith Spencer
 1929- CTFT-5
 Earlier sketch in WWT-17
Waterlow, Marjorie 1888-1921 ...WWasWT
Waterman, Dennis 1948- CTFT-6
 Earlier sketch in WWT-17
Waters, Ethel 1900-1977 ....WWT-16
Waters, James ?-1923 ....WWasWT
Waters, Jan 1937- CTFT-5
 Earlier sketch in WWT-17
Waters, John CTFT-5
Waterston, Samuel A. 1940- CTFT-3
 Earlier sketch in WWT-17
Watford, Gwen 1927- CTFT-6
 Earlier sketch in WWT-17
Watkin, David 1925- CTFT-7
 Earlier sketch in CTFT-1
Watkins, Linda 1908- ....WWasWT
Watkins, Peter 1935- CTFT-8
Watkyn, Arthur 1907-1965 ......WWasWT
Watling, Dilys 1946- WWT-17
Watling, Jack 1923- WWT-17
Watson, Betty Jane 1926 ....WWasWT
Watson, Douglass 1921-1989 ......CTFT-8
 Earlier sketch in WWT-17
Watson, Elizabeth ?-1931 ....WWasWT
Watson, Henrietta 1873-1964 ....WWasWT

Watson, Horace 1867-1934 ...... WWasWT
Watson, Lucile 1879-1962 ...... WWasWT
Watson, Malcolm 1853-1929 ..... WWasWT
Watson, Margaret ?-1940 .... WWasWT
Watson, Minor 1889-1965 .... WWasWT
Watson, Moray 1928- CTFT-6
  Earlier sketch in CTFT-1
Watson, Vernon 1885-1949 ...... WWasWT
Watson, Wylie 1889-1966 .... WWasWT
Watt, Douglas 1914- CTFT-1
Wattis, Richard 1912- .... WWasWT
Watts, Dodo 1910- .... WWasWT
Watts, Richard, Jr. 1898- WWT-17
Watts, Robert 1938- CTFT-1
Watts, Stephen 1910- WWT-17
Watts-Phillips, John Edward
  1894-1960 .... WWasWT
Waxman, Al 1934- CTFT-3
Wayburn, Ned 1874-1942 .... WWasWT
Wayne, David 1914- CTFT-7
  Earlier sketch in WWT-17
Wayne, Naunton 1901-1970 ..... WWasWT
Wayne, Patrick 1939- CTFT-3
Wayne, Rollo 1899-1954 .... WWasWT
Weakland, Kevin L. 1963- CTFT-4
Weathers, Carl CTFT-7
Weathers, Philip 1908- CTFT-4
Weaver, Dennis 1924- CTFT-3
Weaver, Fritz 1926- CTFT-8
  Earlier sketches in CTFT-2, WWT-17
Weaver, Lee 1930- CTFT-6
Weaver, Sigourney 1949- CTFT-3
Weaver, William 1917- CTFT-1
Webb, Alan 1906- WWT-17
Webb, Chloe CTFT-8
Webb, Clifton 1893-1966 .... WWasWT
Webb, Jack 1920-1982 .... CTFT-1
Webb, Lizbeth 1926- .... WWasWT
Webb, Lucy CTFT-4
Webber, Robert 1924-1989 .... CTFT-7
Weber, Carl 1925- CTFT-3
Weber, Joseph 1867-1942 .... WWasWT
Weber, L. Lawrence ?-1940 ...... WWasWT
Webster, Ben 1864-1947 .... WWasWT
Webster, Margaret 1905-1972 ..... WWT-16
Webster-Gleason, Lucile
  1888-1947 .... WWasWT
Wedgeworth, Ann 1935- CTFT-7
Weeden, Evelyn ?-1961 .... WWasWT
Weege, Reinhold CTFT-6
Weguelin, Thomas N. 1885-? .... WWasWT
Wehlen, Emmy 1887-? .... WWasWT
Weidman, Jerome 1913- CTFT-6
  Earlier sketch in WWT-17
Weidner, Paul 1934- CTFT-5
  Earlier sketch in WWT-17
Weigel, Helene 1900-1971 .... WWasWT
Weight, Michael 1906- .... WWasWT
Weil, Samuel
  See Kaufman, Lloyd CTFT-7
Weill, Claudia CTFT-1
Weill, Kurt 1900-1950 .... WWasWT
Weinberg, Gus 1866-1952 .... WWasWT
Weiner, Robert ?-1989 .... CTFT-1
Weiner, Zane 1953- CTFT-2
Weintraub, Fred 1928- CTFT-8
  Earlier sketch in CTFT-1
Weintraub, Jerry 1937- CTFT-7
Weir, Peter 1944- CTFT-6
  Earlier sketch in CTFT-1
Weis, Don 1922- CTFT-7
Weisbarth, Michael L. CTFT-4
Weiskopf, Bob CTFT-2

Weiss, Joel 1953- CTFT-2
Weiss, Marc B. CTFT-2
  Earlier sketch in WWT-17
Weiss, Peter 1916-1982 .... WWT-17
Weissmuller, Donald 1922- CTFT-6
Weitz, Bruce 1943- CTFT-7
Weitzenhoffer, Max 1939- CTFT-3
Welch, Elisabeth 1909- WWT-17
Welch, James 1865-1917 .... WWasWT
Welch, Raquel 1940- CTFT-3
Welchman, Harry 1886-1966 ..... WWasWT
Weld, Tuesday 1943- CTFT-3
Welden, Ben 1901- .... WWasWT
Weldon, Duncan Clark 1941- CTFT-5
  Earlier sketch in WWT-17
Weldon, Harry 1882-? .... WWasWT
Welford, Dallas 1874-1946 ...... WWasWT
Welland, Colin 1934- CTFT-7
Weller, Bernard 1870-1943 ...... WWasWT
Weller, Michael 1942- CTFT-2
  Earlier sketch in WWT-17
Weller, Peter 1947- CTFT-7
Welles, Orson 1915-1985 .... CTFT-3
  Earlier sketch in WWasWT
Wellesley, Arthur 1890- .... WWasWT
Welling, Sylvia 1901- .... WWasWT
Wellman, Wendell 1944- CTFT-2
Wells, Deering 1896-1961 .... WWasWT
Welsh, Jane 1905- .... WWasWT
Welsh, Kenneth CTFT-7
Wenders, Wim 1945- CTFT-5
Wendkos, Paul 1922- CTFT-8
Wendt, George 1948- CTFT-7
Wenham, Jane CTFT-6
  Earlier sketch in WWT-17
Wenman, Henry N. 1875-1953 ... WWasWT
Wertenbaker, L. T.
  See Wertenbaker, Timberlake CTFT-9
Wertenbaker, Lael
  See Wertenbaker, Timberlake CTFT-9
Wertenbaker, Lael Tucker
  See Wertenbaker, Timberlake CTFT-9
Wertenbaker, Timberlake 1909- CTFT-9
Wertmuller, Lina 1928- CTFT-6
  Earlier sketch in CTFT-1
Wesker, Arnold 1932- CTFT-7
  Earlier sketch in WWT-17
Wesley, Richard 1945- CTFT-5
  Earlier sketch in WWT-17
West, Adam 1928- CTFT-8
West, Algernon 1886-? .... WWasWT
West, Caryn CTFT-8
West, Con 1891- .... WWasWT
West, Henry St. Barbe
  1880-1935 .... WWasWT
West, Joan 1936- CTFT-4
West, Lockwood 1905-1989 ...... CTFT-8
  Earlier sketch in WWT-17
West, Mae 1892-1980 .... CTFT-1
  Earlier sketch in WWT-17
West, Thomas E. 1954- CTFT-2
West, Timothy 1934- CTFT-4
  Earlier sketch in WWT-17
West, Will 1867-1922 .... WWasWT
Westbrook, John 1922- WWT-17
Westcott, Netta ?-1953 .... WWasWT
Westenberg, Robert 1953- CTFT-7
Westley, Helen 1879-1942 .... WWasWT
Westman, Nydia 1907-1970 ...... WWasWT
Westmore, Michael
  See Westmore, Michael G. CTFT-9
Westmore, Michael G. 1938- CTFT-9

Westmore, Mike
  See Westmore, Michael G. CTFT-9
Weston, Jack 1915- CTFT-8
  Earlier sketches in CTFT-2, WWT-17
Weston, Robert P. 1878-1936 .... WWasWT
Weston, Ruth 1911- .... WWasWT
Wetherall, Frances ?-1923 .... WWasWT
Wetmore, Joan 1911-1989 .... WWasWT
Wettig, Patricia 1951- CTFT-9
Wexler, Haskell 1926- CTFT-6
Wexler, Peter 1936- CTFT-6
  Earlier sketch in WWT-17
Wexley, John 1902- .... WWasWT
Weyand, Ron 1929- CTFT-4
Whale, James 1896-1957 .... WWasWT
Whalley, Joanne
  See Whalley-Kilmer, Joanne CTFT-9
Whalley, Norma ?-1943 .... WWasWT
Whalley-Kilmer, Joanne 1964- CTFT-9
Wharton, Anthony P.
  1877-1943 .... WWasWT
Whatmore, A. R. 1889-1960 ..... WWasWT
Wheatley, Alan 1907- WWT-17
Wheatley, Jane 1881-1935 .... WWasWT
Wheaton, Wil CTFT-5
Wheeler, Hugh 1912-1987 .... CTFT-5
  Earlier sketch in WWT-17
Wheeler, Ira 1920- CTFT-7
Wheeler, Lois 1922- .... WWasWT
Whelan, Albert 1875-1961 .... WWasWT
Whelchel, Lisa CTFT-3
Whelen, Frederick 1867-? .... WWasWT
Whiffin, Blanche 1845-1936 ...... WWasWT
Whiley, Manning 1915- .... WWasWT
Whipple, Sidney Beaumont
  1888-1975 .... WWasWT
Whistler, Rex 1905-1944 .... WWasWT
Whitaker, Forest 1961- CTFT-8
Whitby, Arthur 1869-1922 .... WWasWT
Whitby, Gwynne 1903- WWT-17
White, Betty 1924- CTFT-3
White, George 1890-1968 .... WWasWT
White, George C. 1935- CTFT-1
White, J. Fisher 1865-1945 ...... WWasWT
White, James ?-1927 .... WWasWT
White, Jane 1922- WWT-17
White, Jesse 1919- CTFT-6
White, Joan 1909- WWT-17
White, Lee 1886-1927 .... WWasWT
White, Michael 1936- CTFT-5
  Earlier sketch in WWT-17
White, Miles 1914- WWT-17
White, Onna WWT-17
White, Valerie 1915-1975 .... WWT-16
White, Wilfrid Hyde 1903- ...... WWasWT
Whiteford, Jock .... WWasWT
Whitehead, Paxton 1937- CTFT-4
  Earlier sketches in CTFT-1, WWT-17
Whitehead, Robert 1916- CTFT-2
  Earlier sketch in WWT-17
Whitehead, Ted (E. A.) 1933- WWT-17
Whitelaw, Arthur 1940- CTFT-6
  Earlier sketch in WWT-17
Whitelaw, Billie CTFT-2
  Earlier sketch in WWT-17
Whitemore, Hugh 1936- CTFT-7
Whiteside, Walker 1869-1942 .... WWasWT
Whitford, Bradley CTFT-7
Whiting, Jack 1901-1961 .... WWasWT
Whiting, John 1917-1963 .... WWasWT
Whitley, Clifford 1894- .... WWasWT
Whitling, Townsend 1869-1952 ... WWasWT
Whitman, Stuart 1928- CTFT-9

Whitmore, James 1921- CTFT-7
Earlier sketches in CTFT-2, WWT-17
Whitney, David
See Malick, Terrence CTFT-6
Whitney, Fred C. ?-1930 ....WWasWT
Whitrow, Benjamin 1937- WWT-17
Whittaker, Herbert 1911-.........WWT-17
Whittle, Charles R. ?-1947 ......WWasWT
Whitton, Margaret CTFT-2
Whitty, May 1865-1948 ....WWasWT
Whitworth, Geoffrey 1883-1951 ..WWasWT
Whorf, Richard 1906-1966 ......WWasWT
Whytal, Russ 1860-1930 ....WWasWT
Whytal, Mrs. Russ ....WWasWT
Whyte, Robert 1874-1916 ....WWasWT
Whyte, Ron ?-1989 ....CTFT-6
Earlier sketch in CTFT-1
Wickes, Mary 1916- CTFT-7
Earlier sketches in CTFT-2, WWasWT
Wickham, Glynne 1922- WWT-17
Wickham, Tony 1922-1948 ......WWasWT
Wickwire, Nancy 1925-1975 ......WWT-16
Widdoes, James 1953- CTFT-3
Widdoes, Kathleen 1939-.........CTFT-5
Earlier sketch in WWT-17
Widmark, Richard 1914-.........CTFT-3
Wied, Gustav 1858-1914 ....WWasWT
Wiehe, Dagmar ....WWasWT
Wiemer, Robert 1938- CTFT-3
Wiener, Sally Dixon 1926-.........CTFT-1
Wiest, Dianne 1948-............CTFT-5
Wilbraham, Edward 1895-1930 ...WWasWT
Wilbur, Crane 1889-1973 ....WWasWT
Wilbur, Richard 1921- CTFT-3
Earlier sketch in WWT-17
Wilby, James 1958- CTFT-8
Wilcox, Barbara 1906-..........WWasWT
Wilcox, Larry 1947-............CTFT-8
Wilcoxon, Henry 1905- ....WWasWT
Wildberg, John J. 1902-1959 .....WWasWT
Wilde, Cornel 1915-1989 ....CTFT-8
Wilder, Billy 1906- CTFT-4
Earlier sketch in CTFT-1
Wilder, Clinton 1920-1986.......WWT-17
Wilder, Gene 1935-.............CTFT-7
Earlier sketch in CTFT-2
Wilder, Thornton N. 1897-1975 ..WWasWT
Wilding, Michael 1912- ....WWasWT
Wilford, Isabel ....WWasWT
Wilhelm, C. 1858-1925..........WWasWT
Wilkie, Allan 1878-1970 ....WWasWT
Wilkinson, Henry Spenser
1853-? ....WWasWT
Wilkinson, Marc 1929-..........WWT-17
Wilkinson, Norman 1882-1934 ...WWasWT
Wilkof, Lee 1951-..............CTFT-1
Willard, Catherine ?-1954 ....WWasWT
Willard, Edmund 1884-1956 .....WWasWT
Willard, Edward Smith
1853-1915 ....WWasWT
Willard, Fred 1939-.............CTFT-7
Willard, John 1885-1942 ....WWasWT
William, David 1926-...........WWT-17
William, Warren 1895-1948 ......WWasWT
Williams, Ann 1935- CTFT-2
Williams, Anson 1949-...........CTFT-9
Williams, Arthur 1844-1915 .....WWasWT
Williams, Barry 1954-...........CTFT-8
Williams, Billy Dee 1937- CTFT-8
Earlier sketches in CTFT-2, WWT-17
Williams, Bradford Cody 1951-.....CTFT-1
Williams, Bransby 1870-1961 ....WWasWT
Williams, Campbell 1906- ....WWasWT

Williams, Cara CTFT-3
Williams, Cindy 1947- CTFT-3
Williams, Clarence III 1939- CTFT-7
Earlier sketch in WWT-17
Williams, Clifford 1926-...........CTFT-5
Earlier sketch in WWT-17
Williams, Dennis 1944-..........CTFT-4
Williams, Derek 1910-..........WWasWT
Williams, Dick Anthony 1938- CTFT-5
Earlier sketch in WWT-17
Williams, Elmo 1913-.............CTFT-1
Williams, Emlyn 1905-1987 ....CTFT-5
Earlier sketch in WWT-17
Williams, Florence 1912- ....WWasWT
Williams, Frances 1903-1959 ....WWasWT
Williams, Fritz 1865-1930 ....WWasWT
Williams, Hal 1938- CTFT-6
Williams, Harcourt 1880-1957 ...WWasWT
Williams, Hattie 1872-1942 ......WWasWT
Williams, Hope 1901-...........WWasWT
Williams, Hugh 1904-1969 ......WWasWT
Williams, Hugh Steadman
1935- CTFT-4
Williams, Jessie Lynch
1871-1929 ....WWasWT
Williams, Jobeth CTFT-6
Earlier sketch in CTFT-1
Williams, John 1903- WWT-16
Williams, John D. ?-1941 ....WWasWT
Williams, John T. 1932-..........CTFT-3
Williams, Kenneth 1926-1988 ....CTFT-7
Earlier sketch in WWT-17
Williams, Michael 1935- CTFT-5
Earlier sketch in WWT-17
Williams, Paul 1940- CTFT-4
Earlier sketch in CTFT-3
Williams, Rhys 1897-1969 ....WWasWT
Williams, Robin 1952-...........CTFT-3
Williams, Samm
See Williams, Samm-Art CTFT-8
Williams, Samm-Art 1946- CTFT-8
Williams, Sonia 1926-..........WWasWT
Williams, Stephen 1900-1957 ....WWasWT
Williams, Steven CTFT-7
Williams, Tennessee 1911-1983 .....CTFT-1
Earlier sketch in WWT-17
Williams, Treat 1951-............CTFT-8
Earlier sketch in CTFT-2
Williams, Walter 1887-1940 .....WWasWT
Williamson, David 1942- WWT-17
Williamson, Fred 1937- CTFT-7
Williamson, Hugh Ross 1901-....WWasWT
Williamson, James Cassius
1845-1913 ....WWasWT
Williamson, Nicol 1938- CTFT-8
Earlier sketches in CTFT-2, WWT-17
Willis, Bruce 1955-..............CTFT-9
Brief Entry in CTFT-3
Willis, Gordon 1931-.............CTFT-7
Willis, Ted 1918-..............CTFT-7
Earlier sketch in WWT-17
Willison, Walter 1947-...........CTFT-1
Willman, Noel 1918-1988 ....CTFT-8
Earlier sketch in WWT-17
Willoughby, Hugh 1891- ....WWasWT
Wills, Brember ?-1948 ....WWasWT
Wills, Drusilla 1884-1951 ....WWasWT
Willson, Osmund 1896-..........WWasWT
Willy, M. 1859-1931 ....WWasWT
Wilmer, Douglas 1920- WWT-17
Wilshin, Sunday 1905- ....WWasWT
Wilson, Albert Edward
1885-1960 ....WWasWT

Wilson, August 1945-............CTFT-5
Wilson, Beatrice ?-1943 ....WWasWT
Wilson, Diana 1897-1937 ....WWasWT
Wilson, Edith ....WWasWT
Wilson, Elizabeth 1921- CTFT-8
Earlier sketches in CTFT-2, WWT-17
Wilson, Flip 1933- CTFT-3
Wilson, Francis 1854-1935.......WWasWT
Wilson, Frank 1891-1956 ....WWasWT
Wilson, Grace 1903-............WWasWT
Wilson, Harry Leon 1867-1939 ...WWasWT
Wilson, Hugh 1943- CTFT-7
Wilson, John C. 1899-1961 ......WWasWT
Wilson, Joseph 1858-1940 ....WWasWT
Wilson, Julie 1924(?)-.............CTFT-9
Wilson, Katherine 1904-........WWasWT
Wilson, Lambert CTFT-7
Wilson, Lanford 1937- CTFT-3
Earlier sketches in CTFT-1, WWT-17
Wilson, Lucy....................6
Wilson, Mary 1944-.............CTFT-4
Wilson, Perry 1916-............WWasWT
Wilson, Robert 1941-............CTFT-5
Earlier sketch in WWT-17
Wilson, Sandy 1924-............WWT-17
Wilson, Scott 1942-.............CTFT-7
Wilson, Snoo 1948-..............CTFT-7
Earlier sketch in WWT-17
Wilson, Trey 1948-1989 ....CTFT-8
Wilson, W. Cronin ?-1934 ....WWasWT
Wilson, William J. ?-1936 ....WWasWT
Wilstach, Paul 1870-1952 ....WWasWT
Wilton, Penelope 1946- CTFT-9
Wiltse, David 1940- CTFT-6
Wiman, Anna Deere 1924-1963 ..WWasWT
Wiman, Dwight Deere
1895-1951 ....WWasWT
Wimperis, Arthur 1874-1953 .....WWasWT
Winant, Forrest 1888-1928 ......WWasWT
Wincer, Simon CTFT-9
Winchell, Paul 1922- CTFT-9
Winchell, Walter 1897-1972 .....WWasWT
Windeatt, George (Alan)
1901-1959 ....WWasWT
Windermere, Charles 1872-1955 ..WWasWT
Windom, William 1923-...........CTFT-7
Earlier sketch in CTFT-2
Windsor, Barbara 1937- WWT-17
Windsor, Marie 1921- CTFT-1
Windust, Bretaigne 1906-1960 ....WWasWT
Windust, Penelope CTFT-6
Winfield, Paul 1941-.............CTFT-6
Winfrey, Oprah 1954-............CTFT-9
Brief Entry in CTFT-3
Winger, Debra 1955- CTFT-6
Brief Entry in CTFT-2
Winkler, Henry 1945- CTFT-2
Winkler, Irwin 1931- CTFT-3
Winn, Anona ....WWasWT
Winn, Godfrey 1906-1971 ....WWasWT
Winn, Kitty 1944- CTFT-8
Winner, Michael R. 1935- CTFT-2
Winninger, Charles 1884-1969 ...WWasWT
Winningham, Mare CTFT-6
Brief Entry in CTFT-2
Winslow, Michael CTFT-7
Winston, C. Bruce 1879-1946 ....WWasWT
Winter, Edward 1937-............CTFT-7
Winter, Jessie ....WWasWT
Winter, Keith 1906- ....WWasWT
Winter, William 1836-1917 ......WWasWT
Winters, Deborah CTFT-7
Winters, Jonathan 1925- CTFT-5

Winters, Marian 1924- WWT-17
Winters, Shelley 1922- CTFT-4
   Earlier sketch in WWT-17
Winters, Time 1956- CTFT-5
Winters, Warrington 1909- CTFT-1
Winwood, Estelle 1883-? . . . . .WWasWT
Wisberg, Aubrey 1909(?)-1990 . . . . .CTFT-9
Wisdom, Norman 1925- WWT-17
Wise, Herbert 1924- WWT-17
Wise, Robert E. 1914- CTFT-2
Wise, Thomas A. 1865-1928 . . . . .WWasWT
Wiseman, Frederick 1930- CTFT-8
Wiseman, Joseph 1918- CTFT-9
   Earlier sketch in WWT-17
Witcover, Walt 1924- CTFT-4
Withers, Googie 1917- CTFT-9
   Earlier sketch in WWT-17
Withers, Iva 1917- WWT-16
Witherspoon, Cora 1890-1957 . . . .WWasWT
Witt, Paul Junger 1941- CTFT-3
Wittop, Freddy WWT-17
Wittstein, Ed 1929- CTFT-6
   Earlier sketch in WWT-17
Wodehouse, Pelham Granville
   1881-1975 . . . . .WWasWT
Wohl, David 1953- CTFT-7
Woizikovsky, Leon 1897-1922 . . . .WWasWT
Wojtasik, George 1935- CTFT-2
Woldin, Judd 1925- CTFT-3
Wolf, Dick 1946- CTFT-4
Wolfe, Ian 1896- CTFT-9
Wolff, Pierre 1863-1944 . . . . .WWasWT
Wolff, Ruth 1932- CTFT-2
Wolfit, Donald 1902-1968 . . . . . . .WWasWT
Wollheim, Eric 1879-1948 . . . . . . .WWasWT
Wolper, David 1928- CTFT-4
   Earlier sketch in CTFT-2
Wolsk, Eugene V. 1928- WWT-17
Wolston, Henry 1877-? . . . . .WWasWT
Wolveridge, Carol 1940- . . . . .WWasWT
Wong, Anna May 1907-1961 . . . . .WWasWT
Wong, B. D. CTFT-7
Wonsek, Paul 1948- CTFT-2
Wontner, Arthur 1875-1960 . . . . .WWasWT
Wood, Arthur 1875-1953 . . . . .WWasWT
Wood, Charles 1932- WWT-17
Wood, Daisy 1877-? . . . . .WWasWT
Wood, David 1944- WWT-17
Wood, Edna 1918- . . . . .WWasWT
Wood, Florence . . . . .WWasWT
Wood, G. 1919- CTFT-9
Wood, Haydn 1882-1959 . . . . .WWasWT
Wood, Jane 1886-? . . . . .WWasWT
Wood, John CTFT-5
   Earlier sketch in WWT-17
Wood, Mrs. John 1833-1915 . . . . .WWasWT
Wood, Metcalfe . . . . .WWasWT
Wood, Natalie 1938-1982 . . . . .CTFT-1
Wood, Peggy 1892-1978 . . . . .WWT-16
Wood, Peter 1927- WWT-17
Wood, Wee Georgie 1897- . . . . . . .WWasWT
Woodard, Alfre 1953- CTFT-9
   Brief Entry in CTFT-5
Woodbridge, George 1907- . . . . . .WWasWT
Woodbridge, Patricia 1946- CTFT-2
Woodburn, James 1888-1948 . . . . .WWasWT
Woodhouse, Vernon 1874-1936 . . .WWasWT
Woodman, William 1932- CTFT-6
   Earlier sketch in WWT-17
Woodruff, Henry 1870-1916 . . . . .WWasWT
Woods, Albert Herman
   1870-1951 . . . . .WWasWT
Woods, James 1947- CTFT-5

Woods, Richard CTFT-2
Woodthorpe, Peter 1931- WWT-17
Woodvine, John 1929- CTFT-9
   Earlier sketch in WWT-17
Woodward, Charles Jr. CTFT-5
   Earlier sketch in WWT-17
Woodward, Edward 1930- CTFT-6
   Earlier sketch in WWT-17
Woodward, Joanne 1930- CTFT-3
   Earlier sketch in WWT-17
Wooland, Norman 1905-1989 . . . . . .CTFT-8
   Earlier sketch in WWT-17
Wooldridge, Susan CTFT-8
Woolf, Edgar Allan ?-1943 . . . . . .WWasWT
Woolf, Walter
   See King, Walter Woolf . . . . . . .WWasWT
Woolfenden, Guy Anthony
   1937- WWT-17
Woollcott, Alexander
   1887-1943 . . . . .WWasWT
Woolley, Monty 1888-1963 . . . . . .WWasWT
Woolsey, Robert 1889-1938 . . . . . .WWasWT
Wootwell, Tom 1865-? . . . . .WWasWT
Wopat, Tom 1951- CTFT-7
Wordsworth, Richard 1915- WWT-17
Wordsworth, William Derrick
   1912-1988 . . . . .WWasWT
Workman, C. Herbert
   1873-1923 . . . . .WWasWT
Worley, Jo Anne 1939- CTFT-2
Worlock, Frederic G.
   1886-1973 . . . . .WWasWT
Worms, Jean 1884-? . . . . .WWasWT
Woronov, Mary 1946- CTFT-8
Worrall, Lechmere 1875-? . . . . . . .WWasWT
Worsley, Bruce 1899- . . . . .WWasWT
Worster, Howett 1882-? . . . . .WWasWT
Worth, Irene 1916- CTFT-3
   Earlier sketch in WWT-17
Wouk, Herman 1915- CTFT-1
Wray, Fay 1907- CTFT-8
Wray, John 1888-1940 . . . . .WWasWT
Wray, Maxwell 1898- . . . . .WWasWT
Wright, Amy 1950- CTFT-9
Wright, Cowley 1889-1923 . . . . . . .WWasWT
Wright, David 1941- WWT-17
Wright, Fred 1871-1928 . . . . .WWasWT
Wright, Garland CTFT-7
Wright, Haidee 1868-1943 . . . . . . .WWasWT
Wright, Hugh E. 1879-1940 . . . . . .WWasWT
Wright, Huntley 1869-1943 . . . . . .WWasWT
Wright, Max 1943- CTFT-8
Wright, Nicholas 1940- WWT-17
Wright, Steven 1955- CTFT-9
Wright, Teresa 1918- CTFT-3
   Earlier sketch in WWT-17
Wright, Mrs. Theodore ?-1922 . . .WWasWT
Wuhl, Robert CTFT-9
Wurtzel, Stuart 1940- CTFT-5
Wyatt, Frank Gunning
   1851-1926 . . . . .WWasWT
Wyatt, Jane 1912- CTFT-3
   Earlier sketch in WWasWT
Wycherly, Margaret 1884-1956 . . .WWasWT
Wyckham, John 1926- CTFT-6
   Earlier sketch in WWT-17
Wyckoff, Evelyn 1917- . . . . .WWasWT
Wyler, Gretchen 1932- CTFT-6
   Earlier sketch in CTFT-1
Wylie, John 1925- CTFT-7
Wylie, Julian 1878-1934 . . . . .WWasWT
Wylie, Lauri 1880-? . . . . .WWasWT
Wyman, Jane 1914- CTFT-3

Wymark, Patrick 1926-1970 . . . . .WWasWT
Wyn, Marjery 1909- . . . . .WWasWT
Wyndham, Charles 1837-1919 . . . .WWasWT
Wyndham, Dennis 1887-? . . . . . . .WWasWT
Wyndham, Gwen . . . . .WWasWT
Wyndham, Howard 1865-1947 . . .WWasWT
Wyndham, Olive 1886-? . . . . .WWasWT
Wyner, George CTFT-7
Wyngarde, Peter WWT-17
Wynn, Ed 1886-1966 . . . . .WWasWT
Wynn, Keenan 1916-1986 . . . . .CTFT-4
Wynn, Tracy Keenan 1945- CTFT-8
   Earlier sketch in CTFT-1
Wynne, Wish 1882-1931 . . . . .WWasWT
Wynter, Dana 1930- CTFT-7
Wynyard, Diana 1906-1964 . . . . . .WWasWT
Wynyard, John 1915- WWT-16
Wyse, John 1904- WWT-16

X

Xanrof, Leon 1867-1953 . . . . .WWasWT

Y

Yablans, Frank 1935- CTFT-8
   Earlier sketch in CTFT-1
Yablans, Irwin 1934- CTFT-8
   Earlier sketch in CTFT-1
Yakko, Sada ?-1946 . . . . .WWasWT
Yale, Kathleen Betsko 1939- CTFT-2
Yalman, Tunc 1925- CTFT-2
Yanez, Michael CTFT-3
Yang, Ginny CTFT-4
Yankowitz, Susan 1941- CTFT-1
Yannis, Michael 1922- . . . . .WWasWT
Yapp, Cecil .CTFT-8
Yarde, Margaret 1878-1944 . . . . . .WWasWT
Yarrow, Duncan 1884-? . . . . .WWasWT
Yates, Peter 1929- CTFT-6
   Earlier sketch in CTFT-1
Yavorska, Lydia 1874-1921 . . . . . .WWasWT
Yeamans, Annie 1835-1912 . . . . . .WWasWT
Yearsley, Claude Blakesley
   1885-1961 . . . . .WWasWT
Yeats, William Butler
   1865-1939 . . . . .WWasWT
Yellen, Linda 1949- CTFT-3
Yeston, Maury 1945- CTFT-1
Yniguez, Richard CTFT-6
Yohe, May 1869-1938 . . . . .WWasWT
Yokel, Alexander 1887-1947 . . . . .WWasWT
York, Michael 1942- CTFT-6
   Earlier sketch in CTFT-1
York, Susannah 1941- CTFT-5
Yorke, Augustus ?-1939 . . . . .WWasWT
Yorke, Oswald ?-1943 . . . . .WWasWT
Yorkin, Bud 1926- CTFT-1
Youmans, Vincent 1898-1946 . . . .WWasWT
Young, Arthur 1898-1959 . . . . . . .WWasWT
Young, Bertram Alfred 1912- WWT-17
Young, Burt 1940- CTFT-5
Young, Chris 1971- CTFT-8
Young, David 1928- CTFT-4
Young, Dawn CTFT-4
Young, Gig 1917-1978 . . . . .WWT-16
Young, Howard Irving 1893- . . . . .WWasWT
Young, Howard L. 1911- . . . . .WWasWT
Young, Joan 1903-1984 . . . . .WWT-17
Young, Karen CTFT-8
Young, Loretta 1913- CTFT-8

Young, Rida Johnson
  1875-1926 . . . . .WWasWT
Young, Robert 1907- CTFT-7
Young, Robert M. 1924- CTFT-9
Young, Robert Malcolm
  See Young, Robert M. CTFT-9
Young, Roger 1942- CTFT-3
Young, Roland 1887-1953 . . . . . . .WWasWT
Young, Sean 1959- CTFT-7
Young, Stark 1881-1963 . . . . .WWasWT
Young, Terence 1915- CTFT-7
Youngs, Jim CTFT-7
Yulin, Harris 1937- CTFT-7
Yurka, Blanche 1887-1974 . . . . . . .WWasWT

Z

Zabelle, Flora 1880-1968 . . . . .WWasWT
Zabka, William CTFT-7
Zabriskie, Grace CTFT-8
Zacconi, Ermete 1857-1948 . . . . . .WWasWT
Zadan, Craig CTFT-1
Zadora, Pia 1956- CTFT-9

Zaentz, Saul .CTFT-9
Zaks, Jerry 1946- CTFT-6
  Earlier sketch in CTFT-1
Zal, Roxana 1969- CTFT-4
Zaloom, Paul 1951- CTFT-1
Zamacois, Miguel 1866-1939 . . . . .WWasWT
Zampieri, Vittorio 1862-? . . . . . . .WWasWT
Zangwill, Israel 1864-1926 . . . . . . .WWasWT
Zanuck, Richard D. 1934- CTFT-7
Zanussi, Krzysztof 1939- CTFT-8
Zapata, Carmen 1927- CTFT-9
Zeffirelli, Franco 1923- CTFT-4
  Earlier sketch in WWT-17
Zeman, Jacklyn CTFT-5
Zemeckis, Robert 1952- CTFT-7
Zerbe, Anthony CTFT-6
Zetterling, Mai 1925- . . . . .WWasWT
Ziegfeld, Florenz 1867-1932 . . . . .WWasWT
Ziegler, Anne 1910- . . . . .WWasWT
Ziemba, Karen 1957- CTFT-3
Zien, Chip 1947- CTFT-6
Ziff, Irwin 1929- CTFT-4
Zimbalist, Efrem Jr. 1923- CTFT-3
Zimbalist, Stephanie CTFT-6
Zimmerman, Mark 1952- CTFT-2
Zimmerman, Paul 1938- CTFT-2

Zindel, Paul 1936- CTFT-3
  Earlier sketch in WWT-17
Zinkeisen, Doris Clare . . . . .WWasWT
Zinneman, Fred 1907- CTFT-7
  Earlier sketch in CTFT-1
Zipprodt, Patricia 1925- CTFT-7
  Earlier sketches in CTFT-2, WWT-17
Zmed, Adrian 1954- CTFT-8
Zola, Fred .WWasWT
Zollo, Frederick M. 1950- CTFT-1
Zorich, Louis 1924- CTFT-2
Zorina, Vera 1917- WWT-17
Zsigmond, Vilmos 1930- CTFT-8
  Earlier sketch in CTFT-2
Zsigmond, William
  See Zsigmond, Vilmos CTFT-8
Zucco, George 1886-1960 . . . . . . .WWasWT
Zucker, David 1947- CTFT-9
  Earlier sketch in CTFT-1
Zucker, Jerry 1950- CTFT-8
Zuckmayer, Carl 1896-1977 . . . . . . .WWT-16
Zuniga, Daphne CTFT-8
Zwar, Charles 1914-1989 . . . . .WWT-17
Zwerdling, Allen 1922- CTFT-4
Zwick, Edward 1952- CTFT-3
Zwick, Joel 1942- CTFT-9

Cumulative Index